# Math & Science

## For Young Children

### SIXTH EDITION

# Math & Science

## For Young Children

### SIXTH EDITION

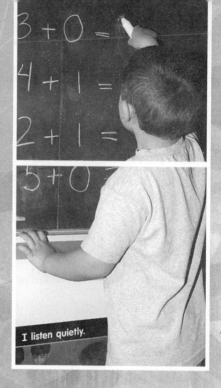

**Rosalind Charlesworth**

Weber State University, Emerita

**Karen K. Lind**

Illinois State University

**WADSWORTH**
CENGAGE Learning

Australia • Canada • Mexico • Singapore • Spain • United Kingdom • United States

**WADSWORTH**
CENGAGE Learning™

**Math and Science for Young Children, Sixth Edition**

**Rosalind Charlesworth and Karen K. Lind**

Education Editor: **Christopher Shortt**

Development Editor: **Tangelique Williams**

Assistant Editor: **Caitlin Cox**

Editorial Assistant: **Janice Bockelman**

Technology Project Manager: **Ashley Cronin**

Marketing Manager: **Kara Kindstrom**

Marketing Assistant: **Andy Yap**

Marketing Communications Manager: **Martha Pheiffer**

Project Manager, Editorial Production: **Tanya Nigh**

Creative Director: **Rob Hugel**

Art Director: **Maria Epes**

Print Buyer: **Rebecca Cross**

Permissions Editor: **Mardell Glinski Schultz**

Production Service: **Newgen**

Designer: **Lee Anne Dollison**

Copy Editor: **Matt Darnell**

Cover Designer: **Lee Anne Dollison**

Compositor: **Newgen**

For product information and technology assistance, contact us at
**Cengage Learning Customer & Sales Support, 1-800-354-9706.**
For permission to use material from this text or product,
submit all requests online at **www.cengage.com/permissions.**
Further permissions questions can be e-mailed to
**permissionrequest@cengage.com.**

Library of Congress Control Number:

ISBN-13: 978-1-4283-7586-4
ISBN-10: 1-4283-7586-4

**Wadsworth/Cengage Learning**
10 Davis Drive
Belmont, CA 94002-3098
USA

Cengage Learning is a leading provider of customized learning solutions with office locations around the globe, including Singapore, the United Kingdom, Australia, Mexico, Brazil, and Japan. Locate your local office at **www.cengage.com/international.**

Cengage Learning products are represented in Canada by Nelson Education, Ltd.

To learn more about Wadsworth, visit **www.cengage.com/wadsworth.**

Purchase any of our products at your local college store or at our preferred online store **www.ichapters.com.**

**Notice to the Reader**

Publisher does not warrant or guarantee any of the products described herein or perform any independent analysis in connection with any of the product information contained herein. Publisher does not assume, and expressly disclaims, any obligation to obtain and include information other than that provided to it by the manufacturer. The reader is expressly warned to consider and adopt all safety precautions that might be indicated by the activities described herein and to avoid all potential hazards. By following the instructions contained herein, the reader willingly assumes all risks in connection with such instructions. The publisher makes no representations or warranties of any kind, including but not limited to, the warranties of fitness for particular purpose or merchantability, nor are any such representations implied with respect to the material set forth herein, and the publisher takes no responsibility with respect to such material. The publisher shall not be liable for any special, consequential, or exemplary damages resulting, in whole or part, from the readers' use of, or reliance upon, this material.

Printed in the United States of America
1  2  3  4  5  6  7  12  11  10  09  08

# Contents

# Preface

*Math & Science for Young Children,* Sixth Edition, is designed to be used by students in training and by teachers in service in early childhood education. To the student, it introduces the excitement and extensiveness of math and science experiences in programs for young children. For teachers in the field, it presents an organized, sequential approach to creating a developmentally appropriate math and science curriculum for preschool and primary school children. Further, it is designed in line with the guidelines and standards of the major professional organizations: NAEYC, NCTM, NSTA, AAAS, and NRC.

## DEVELOPMENT OF THE TEXT

The text was developed and directed by the concept that the fundamental concepts and skills that form the foundation for mathematics and science are identical. Each edition has focused on these commonalities. As changes have emerged in each area, the text has been updated. Acquaintance with child development from birth through age 8 would be a helpful prerequisite.

## ORGANIZATION OF THE TEXT

Activities are presented in a developmental sequence designed to support young children's construction of the concepts and skills essential to a basic understanding of mathematics and science. A developmentally appropriate approach to assessment is stressed in order to have an individualized program in which each child is presented at each level with tasks that can be accomplished successfully before moving on to the next level.

A further emphasis is placed on three types of learning: naturalistic, informal, and structured. Much learning can take place through the child's natural exploratory activities if the environment is designed to promote such activity. The adult can reinforce and enrich this naturalistic learning by careful introduction of information and structured experiences.

The test-driven practices that are currently re-emerging have produced a widespread use of inappropriate instructional practices with young children. Mathematics for preschoolers has been taught as "pre-math," apparently under the assumption that math learning begins only with addition and subtraction in the primary grades. It also has been taught in both preschool and primary school as rote memory material using abstract paper and pencil activities. This text emphasizes the recognition by the National Council of Teachers of Mathematics of the inclusion of the pre-K level in its revised mathematics principles and standards (NCTM, 2000). Science, on the other hand, has been largely ignored—with the excuse that teaching the basics precluded allowing time for science. This text is designed to counteract these developments and to bring to the attention of early childhood educators the interrelatedness of math and science and the necessity of providing young children with opportunities to explore concretely these domains of early concept learning. Further integration is stressed with language arts, social studies, art, and music; the goal is to provide a totally integrated program.

Section 1 sets the theoretical and conceptual foundation. Section 2 provides units on fundamental concepts: one-to-one correspondence, number sense and counting, logic and classifying, comparing, shape, spatial sense, parts and wholes, language, and application of these concepts to science. Each mathematics unit is introduced with the relevant NCTM content standard—and curriculum focal points (NCTM, 2007)—followed by assessment; naturalistic, informal, and structured activities; evaluation, and summary. Every unit includes references, further reading and resources, suggested activities (with a list of software), and review questions. Most of the units in Sections 3, 4, and 5 follow the same format. Unit 15 (in Section 2) sums up the application of process skills and important vocabulary. Unit 22 (which concludes Section 3) provides basic ideas for integrating math and science through dramatic play and thematic units and projects. Section 6 focuses on science investigations in the primary grades. Section 7 has three units: materials and resources, math and science in action, and math and science in the home. The appendices contain additional assessment tasks; lists of books, periodicals, and technology publishers; and the National Research Council's *National Science Education Standards* (NRC, 1996). A glossary and index are also included.

## NEW FEATURES

Specific features of the sixth edition include the following:

- Inclusion of the NCTM curriculum focal points, which highlight the important concepts children should learn at each early childhood age/grade level from pre-K through grade 3.

- Inclusion of the National Science Education Standards in Appendix C, with correlations to the appropriate units given in Appendix D.

- Additional material on teaching children with disabilities, multicultural education, and English Language Learners.

- Expanded technology information, including design technology.

- Updated references and further readings.

- Expanded and updated software lists.

- New books have been added to Appendix B.

- Photos are included within units, and many have been updated.

# ROAD MAP

The text is set up in a logical progression, and students should follow the text in sequence. Applying the assessment tasks and teaching one (or more) of the sample lessons will provide the student with hands-on experience relevant to each concept and each standard. The reviews provide a checkup for the student's self-examination of learning. Selection of activities will provide further applications of the content.

# SUPPLEMENT PACKAGE

## Instructor's Manual

The instructor's manual provides suggestions for course organization, introductory activities, and answers to Unit Reviews.

## e-Resource

The e-Resource component is geared to provide instructors with all the tools they need on one convenient CD-ROM. Instructors will find that this resource provides them with a turnkey solution to help them teach by making available PowerPoint slides for each book unit, the Computerized Test Bank, an electronic version of the Instructor's Manual, and other text-specific resources.

## Online Companion

The Online Companion™ and Professional Enhancement Text have been updated. The Online Companion that accompanies *Math and Science for Young Children* contains many features to help the student focus his or her understanding of teaching mathematics and science to young children. For each unit, the student will find:

- Web links and activities
- Critical thinking sections
- Quizzes

## Professional Enhancement Text

The Professional Enhancement Text (PET) is a new accompaniment to many of Cengage Learning's Early Childhood Education core textbooks. The supplement contains:

- Lesson plans specific to math and science
- Resources
- Observation information
- Case studies
- Issues and more

The PET is intended for use by students in their first classrooms; it is fully customizable, and there is ample space for users to make notes of their own experiences, successes, and suggestions for future lessons. The editors at Cengage Learning encourage and appreciate any feedback on this new venture. Go to www.earlychilded.delmar.com and click on the "Professional Enhancement series feedback" link to let us know what you think.

## REFERENCES

National Council of Teachers of Mathematics (NCTM). (2000). *Principles and standards for school mathematics*. Reston, VA: Author.

National Council of Teachers of Mathematics (NCTM). (2007). *Curriculum focal points*. Reston, VA: Author.

National Research Council (NRC). (1996). *National science education standards*. Washington, DC: National Academy Press.

The authors and Cengage Learning make every effort to ensure that all Internet resources are accurate at the time of printing. However, the fluid nature of the Internet precludes any guarantee that all URLs will remain current throughout the life of this edition.

# Acknowledgments

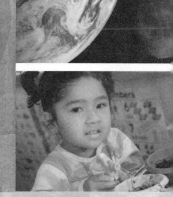

The authors wish to express their appreciation to the following individuals and Early Childhood and Development Centers.

- Dee Radeloff, for her collaboration in the writing of *Experiences in Math for Young Children*, which served as the starting point for this book.

- Dr. Mark Malone of the University of Colorado at Colorado Springs, who contributed to the planning of this text. Dr. Malone also demonstrated great patience while introducing Dr. Charlesworth to the mysteries of word processing on a personal computer.

- Artist Bonita S. Carter, for the care and accuracy taken in her original art.

- Kate Charlesworth, for her tolerance of her mother's writing endeavors.

- Gaile Clement, for sharing her knowledge and expertise in the area of portfolio assessment with Dr. Charlesworth.

- The 30 East Baton Rouge Parish (Louisiana) K–3 teachers who participated in a six-week summer Mathematics/Child Development in-service workshop and to the other workshop faculty— Thelamese Porter, Robert Perlis, and Colonel Johnson—all of whom provided enrichment to Dr. Charlesworth's view of mathematics for young children.

- To Shirley A. Leali, professor of teacher education at Weber State University, for many helpful math conversations.

- Thank you to my family: Paul and Marian Anglund Kalbfleisch, my sister Pamela J. Kalbfleisch, and all of my dear Anglund and Kalbfleisch family members for their encouragement during the writing process—especially the advice of two beloved aunts: author and illustrator Joan Walsh Anglund, for her advice to "work with love," even when I did not feel like it; and of my well-traveled aunt Beulah Kalbfleisch Archer, who climbed Mt. Hood as a college student in 1928 and is a role model for "never giving up," even when I felt like it.

- The following teachers, who provided a place for observation and/or cooperated with our efforts to obtain photographs:

  Lois Rector, Kathy Tonore, Lynn Morrison, and Nancy Crom (LSU Laboratory Elementary School); Joan Benedict (LSU Laboratory Preschool); Nancy Miller and Candy Jones (East Baton Rouge Parish Public Schools) and 30 East Baton Rouge Parish School System K–3 teachers and their students; and Krista Robinson (Greatho Shryock), Maureen Awbrey (Anchorage Schools), Elizabeth Beam (Zachary Taylor), and Dr. Anna Smythe (Cochran, Jefferson County Public Schools).

- Jill Hislop Gibson and her students at Polk Elementary School, who welcomed Dr. Charlesworth into their kindergarten.

- Anchorage Schools computer teacher Sharon Campbell and Rutherford Elementary computer teacher Phyllis E. Ferrell, who provided recommendations for using computers with young children.

- University of Louisville graduate students Shawnita Adams, Kate Clavijo, Phyllis E. Ferrell, Christy D. McGee, and Stephanie Gray, who provided assistance in researching and compiling information for earlier editions of the text.

- Special thanks to Illinois State University's CeMaST Technical Editor, Amanda Fain, for her careful attention to detail and effort in the compiling of the sixth edition of this text. Thanks also to the many supportive new colleagues at Illinois State University, especially the CeMaST associate directors for mathematics (Jeffrey Barrett), technology (Christopher Merrill), science education (Marilyn Morey), and chemistry (Willy Hunter), and the indispensable CeMaST Office staff for all of their support.

- Phyllis Marcuccio, retired editor of *Science and Children* and director of publications for the National Science Teachers Association, for generously facilitating the use of articles appearing in *Science and Children* and other NSTA publications.

- The staff of Cengage Learning for their patience and understanding throughout this project.

- The following reviewers, who provided many valuable ideas:

**Susan M. Baxter,**
*El Camino Community College*

**Nancy H. Beaver,**
*Eastfield College*

**Denise Collins,**
*Eastfield Community College*

**Jorja Davis,**
*Blinn College*

**Linda Estes,**
*Saint Charles Community College*

**Eugene Geist,**
*Ohio University*

**Arlene Harrison,**
*Towson University*

**Kathy Head,**
*Lorain County Community College*

**Sammie Holloway,**
*Atlanta Technical College*

**Amy Huffman,**
*Guilford Technical Community College*

**Jennifer Johnson,**
*Vance-Granville Community College*

**Debra L. Kimble,**
*Clark State Community College*

**Linda Lowman,**
*San Antonio College*

**Leanna Manna,**
*Villa Maria College*

**Paul Narguizian,**
*California State University, Los Angeles*

**Paula Packer,**
*Lock Haven University*

**Christine Pegorraro Schull,**
*Northern Virginia Community College*

**Dorothy J. Sluss,**
*James Madison University*

**Lisa Starnes,**
*The University of Texas at Tyler*

**Rose Weiss,**
*Palm Beach Community College*

# About the Authors

**Rosalind Charlesworth** is professor emerita and retired department chair in the Department of Child and Family Studies at Weber State University in Ogden, Utah. During her tenure at Weber State University, she worked with the faculty of the Department of Teacher Education to develop continuity from preprimary to primary school in the program for students in the early childhood education licensure program. She continues to contribute to the Elementary Mathematics Methods class.

Dr. Charlesworth's career in early childhood education has included experiences with both typical and atypical young children in laboratory schools, public schools, and day care and through research in social and cognitive development and behavior. She is also known for her contributions to research on early childhood teachers' beliefs and practices. She taught courses in early education and child development at other universities before joining the faculty at Weber State University. In 1995 she was named the Outstanding Graduate of the University of Toledo College of Education and Allied Professions. In 1999, she was the co-recipient of the NAECTE/Allyn & Bacon Outstanding Early Childhood Teacher Education award. She is the author of the popular Delmar text *Understanding Child Development,* has published many articles in professional journals, and gives presentations regularly at major professional meetings. Dr. Charlesworth has provided service to the field through active involvement in professional organizations. She has been a member of the NAEYC Early Childhood Teacher Education Panel, a consulting editor for *Early Childhood Research Quarterly,* and a member of the NAECTE (National Association of Early Childhood Teacher Educators) Public Policy and Long-Range Planning Committees. She served two terms on the NAECTE board as regional representative and one as vice-president for membership. She was twice elected treasurer and most recently was elected as newsletter editor of the Early Childhood/Child Development Special Interest Group of the American Educational Research Association (AERA), is past president of the Louisiana Early Childhood Association, and was a member of the editorial board of the Southern Early Childhood Association journal *Dimensions.* She is currently on the editorial board of the *Early Childhood Education Journal.*

**Dr. Karen K. Lind** is the Director of the Center for Mathematics, Science, and Technology (CeMaST) at Illinois State University (Normal, Illinois), where she holds a joint appointment as Professor of Curriculum & Instruction and Professor of Biological Sciences. Dr. Lind is a Professor Emerita in the Department of Teaching and Learning at the University of Louisville in Kentucky, where she is the Recipient of the Distinguished Teaching Professor award from the university. Dr. Lind was elected as National Science Teachers Association (NSTA) Teacher Education Director and served as Chair of the NSTA Science Teacher Education Committee. Dr. Lind's career in education has included teaching young children of differing socioeconomic backgrounds in a variety of settings.

Dr. Lind has served the field while at the National Science Foundation, where she was a program director in the Directorate of Education and Human Resources—working primarily with programs in Teacher Enhancement, Instructional Materials Development, and Informal Education. Dr. Lind served a member of the board of examiners for the National Council for Accreditation of Teacher Education (NCATE) and as a member of the NCATE New Professional Teacher Standards drafting committee. Dr. Lind is past president of the Council for Elementary Science International (CESI) and has served as CESI Business/Foundation liaison and as publication director for the organization. She served as the early childhood column editor of *Science and Children,* a publication of the National Science Teachers Association (NSTA), for ten years and as a member of the NSTA Preschool–Elementary Committee. She served two terms on the board of directors for NSTA and co-chaired the NSTA/Monsanto Company–funded invitational conference, *A Strategy for Change in Elementary School Science.* Her research publications and in-service programs focus on integrating science into preschool and primary classroom settings and on the identification of teaching and learning strategies that encourage inquiry.

# SECTION 1

## Concept Development in Mathematics and Science

# Unit 1

# How Concepts Develop

## OBJECTIVES

After reading this unit, you should be able to:

- Define concept development.
- Identify the concepts children are developing.
- Describe the commonalities between math and science.
- Explain the purpose of the principles for school mathematics.
- Understand the importance of professional standards for mathematics and science.
- Describe the purpose of focal points.
- Label examples of Piaget's developmental stages of thought.
- Compare Piaget's and Vygotsky's theories of mental development.
- Identify conserving and nonconserving behavior, and state why conservation is an important developmental task.
- Explain how young children acquire knowledge.

Early childhood is a period when children actively engage in acquiring fundamental concepts and learning fundamental process skills. **Concepts** are the building blocks of knowledge; they allow people to organize and categorize information. Concepts can be applied to the solution of new problems that are met in everyday experience. As we watch children in their everyday activities, we can observe concepts being constructed and used. For example:

- *One-to-one correspondence.* Passing apples, one to each child at a table; putting pegs in pegboard holes; putting a car in each garage built from blocks.

- *Counting.* Counting the pennies from a penny bank, the number of straws needed for the children at a table, or the number of rocks in a rock collection.

- *Classifying.* Placing square shapes in one pile and round shapes in another; putting cars in one garage and trucks in another.

- *Measuring.* Pouring sand, water, rice, or other materials from one container to another.

As you proceed through this text, you will see that young children begin to construct many concepts during the **preprimary** period (the years before children enter first grade). They also develop processes that enable them to apply their newly acquired concepts and to enlarge current concepts and develop new ones.

During the preprimary period, children learn and begin to apply concepts basic to both mathematics and science. As children enter the **primary** period (grades 1–3), they apply these early basic concepts to explore more abstract inquiries in science and to help them understand the use of standard units of measurement as well as such mathematical concepts as addition, subtraction, multiplication, and division.

As young children grow and develop physically, socially, and mentally, their concepts also grow and develop. **Development** refers to changes that take place as a result of growth and experience. Development follows an individual timetable for each child; it is a series or sequence of steps that each child reaches one at a time. Different children of the same age may be weeks, months, or even a year or two apart in reaching certain stages and still be within the normal range of development. This text examines concept development in math and science from birth through the primary grades. For an overview of this development sequence, see Figure 1–1.

Concept growth and development begins in infancy. Babies explore the world with their **senses**. They look, touch, smell, hear, and taste. Children are born curious. They want to know all about their environment. Babies begin to learn ideas of size, weight, shape, time, and space. As they look about, they sense their relative smallness. They grasp things and find that some fit in their tiny hands and others do not. Infants learn about weight when items of the same size cannot always be

| Period | Concepts and Skills: Beginning Points for Understanding | | | |
| | Section II Fundamental | Section III Applied | Section IV Higher Level | Section V Primary |
| --- | --- | --- | --- | --- |
| Sensorimotor (Birth to age 2) | Observation<br>Problem solving<br>One-to-one correspondence<br>Number<br>Shape<br>Spatial sense | | | |
| Preoperational (2 to 7 years) | Sets and classifying<br>Comparing<br>Counting<br>Parts and wholes<br>Language | Ordering, seriation, patterning<br>Informal measurement:<br>　Weight<br>　Length<br>　Temperature<br>　Volume<br>　Time<br>　Sequence | Number symbols<br>Sets and symbols | |
| Transitional (5 to 7 years) | | Graphing | Concrete addition and subtraction | |
| Concrete operations (7 to 11 years) | | | | Whole number operations<br>Fractions<br>Number facts<br>Place value<br>Geometry<br>Measurement with standard units |

Figure 1–1 The development of math and science concepts and process skills.

lifted. They learn about shape. Some things stay where they put them, whereas others roll away. Children learn time sequence. When they wake up, they feel wet and hungry. They cry. The caretaker comes. They are changed and then fed. Next they play, get tired, and go to bed to sleep. As infants begin to move, they develop spatial sense. They are placed in a crib, in a playpen, or on the floor in the center of the living room. As babies first look and then move, they discover space. Some spaces are big. Some spaces are small.

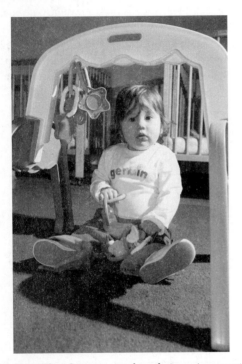

As infants crawl and creep to explore their environment, they develop a concept of space.

As children learn to crawl, stand, and walk, they are free to discover more on their own and learn to think for themselves. They hold and examine more things. They go over, under, and inside large objects and discover their size relative to them. Toddlers sort things. They put them in piles—of the same color, the same size, the same shape, or with the same use. Young children pour sand and water into containers of different sizes. They pile blocks into tall structures and see them fall and become small parts again. They buy food at a play store and pay with play money. As children cook imaginary food, they measure imaginary flour, salt, and milk. They set the table in their play kitchen, putting one of everything at each place just as is done at home. The free exploring and experimentation of the first two years are the opportunity for the development of muscle coordination and the senses of taste, smell, sight, and hearing. Children need these skills as a basis for future learning.

As young children leave toddlerhood and enter the preschool and kindergarten levels of the preprimary period, exploration continues to be the first step in dealing with new situations; at this time, however, they also begin to apply basic concepts to collecting and organizing data to answer a question. Collecting data requires skills in observation, counting, recording, and organizing. For example, for a science investigation, kindergartners might be interested in the process of plant growth. Supplied with lima bean seeds, wet paper towels, and glass jars, the children place the seeds so they are held against the sides of the jars with wet paper towels. Each day they add water as needed and observe what is happening to the seeds. They dictate their observations to their teacher, who records them on a chart. Each child also plants some beans in dirt in a small container, such as a paper or plastic cup. The teacher supplies each child with a chart for his or her bean garden. The children check off each day on their charts until they see a sprout (Figure 1–2). Then they count how many days it took for a sprout to appear; they compare this number with those of the other class members and also with the time it takes for the seeds in the glass jars to sprout. Thus, the children have used the concepts of number and counting, one-to-one correspondence, time, and comparison of the number of items in two groups. Primary children might attack the same problem but can operate more independently and record more information, use standard measuring tools (i.e., rulers), and do background reading on their own. References that provide development guidelines charts for mathematics instruction include Clements and Sarama (2003), Clements and Sarama (2004), Geist (2001), and "Learning PATHS" (2003).

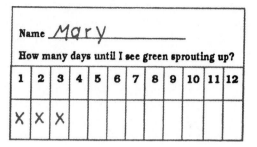

Figure 1–2 Mary records each day that passes until her bean seed sprouts.

Children learn through hands-on experience.

## COMMONALITIES IN MATH AND SCIENCE IN EARLY CHILDHOOD

The same fundamental concepts, developed in early childhood, underlie a young child's understanding of math and science. Much of our understanding of how and when this development takes place comes from research based on Jean Piaget's and Lev Vygotsky's theories of concept development. These theories are briefly described in the next part of the unit. First, the commonalities that tie math and science together are examined.

Math and science are interrelated; fundamental mathematics concepts such as comparing, classifying, and measuring are simply called **process skills** when applied to science problems. (See Unit 5 for a more in-depth explanation.) That is, fundamental math concepts are needed to solve problems in science. The other science process skills (observing, communicating, inferring, hypothesizing, and **defining and controlling variables**) are equally important for solving problems in both science and mathematics. For example, consider the principle of the ramp, a basic concept in physics. Suppose a 2-foot-wide plywood board is leaned against a large block so that it becomes a ramp. The children are given a number of balls of different sizes and weights to roll down the ramp. Once they have the idea of the game through free exploration, the teacher might pose some questions: "What do you think would happen if two balls started to roll at exactly the same time from the top of the ramp?" "What would happen if you changed the height of the ramp or had two ramps of different heights, or of different lengths?" The students could guess, explore what actually happens when using ramps of varying steepness and length and balls of various types, communicate their observations, and describe commonalities and differences. They might observe differences in speed and distance traveled contingent on the size or weight of the ball, the height and length of the ramp, or other variables. In this example, children could use math concepts of speed, distance, height, length, and counting (how many blocks are propping each ramp?) while engaged in scientific observation.

Block building also provides a setting for the integration of math and science (Chalufour, Hoisington, Moriarty, Winokur, & Worth, 2004). Chalufour and colleagues identify the overlapping processes of questioning, problem solving, analyzing, reasoning, communicating, connecting, representing, and investigating as well as the common concepts of shape, pattern, measurement, and spatial relationships. For another example, suppose the teacher brings several pieces of fruit to class: one red apple, one green apple, two oranges, two grapefruit, and two bananas. The children examine the fruit to discover as much about it as possible. They observe size, shape, color, texture, taste, and composition (juicy or dry, segmented or whole, seeds or seedless, etc.). Observations may be recorded using counting and classification skills (How many of each fruit type? Of each color? How many are spheres? How many are juicy?). The fruit can be weighed and measured, prepared for eating, and divided equally among the students.

As with these examples, it will be seen throughout the text that math and science concepts and skills can be acquired as children engage in traditional early childhood activities—such as playing with blocks, water, sand, and manipulative materials—and also during dramatic play, cooking, literacy, and outdoor activities.

## PRINCIPLES AND STANDARDS FOR SCHOOL MATHEMATICS AND SCIENCE

In 1987, the National Association for the Education of Young Children (NAEYC) published *Developmentally Appropriate Practice in Early Childhood Programs Serving Children from Birth through Age Eight* (Bredekamp, 1987) as a guide for early childhood instruction. In 1997, a revised set of guidelines was published (Bredekamp & Copple, 1997) by NAEYC. In 1989, the National Council of Teachers of Mathematics (NCTM) published standards for kindergarten through grade 12 mathematics curriculum, evaluation, and teaching. This publication was followed by two others, *Professional Standards for Teaching Mathematics* (1991) and *Assessment Standards for School Mathematics* (1995). In 2000, based on an evaluation and review of the previous standards' publications, NCTM published *Principles and Standards for School Mathematics*. A major change in the age and grade category levels is the inclusion of preschool. The first level is now prekindergarten through grade 2. It is important to recognize that preschoolers have an informal knowledge of mathematics that can be built on and reinforced, but one must keep in mind that, as with older children, not all preschoolers will enter school with equivalent knowledge and capabilities. During the preschool years, young children's natural curiosity and eagerness to learn can be exploited to develop a joy and excitement in learning and applying mathematics concepts and skills. As in the previous standards, the recommendations in the current publication are based on the belief that "students learn important mathematical skills and processes with **understanding**" (NCTM, 2000, p. ix). That is, rather than simply memorizing, children should acquire a true knowledge of concepts

and processes. Understanding is not present when children learn mathematics as isolated skills and procedures. Understanding develops through interaction with materials, peers, and supportive adults in settings where students have opportunities to construct their own relationships when they first meet a new topic. Exactly how this takes place will be explained further in the text.

In 2002, the NAEYC and NCTM issued a joint position statement on early childhood mathematics (NCTM & NAEYC, 2002). This statement focuses on math for 3–6-year-olds, elaborating on the NCTM (2000) pre-K–2 standards. The highlights for instruction are summarized in "Math Experiences That Count!" (2002).

### Principles of School Mathematics

The Principles of School Mathematics are statements reflecting basic rules that guide high-quality mathematics education. The following six **principles** describe the overarching themes of mathematics instruction (NCTM, 2000, p. 11).

*Equity*: High expectations and strong support for all students.

*Curriculum*: More than a collection of activities; must be coherent, focused on important mathematics, and well articulated across the grades.

*Teaching*: Effective mathematics teaching requires understanding of what students know and need to learn and then challenging and supporting them to learn it well.

*Learning*: Students must learn mathematics with understanding, actively building new knowledge from experience and prior knowledge.

*Assessment*: Assessment should support the learning of important mathematics and furnish useful information to both teachers and students.

*Technology*: Technology is essential in teaching and learning mathematics; it influences the mathematics that is taught and enhances student learning. (See Appendix B for a list of suggested software for children and software resources.)

These principles should be used as a guide to instruction in all subjects, not just mathematics.

## Standards for School Mathematics

**Standards** provide guidance as to what children should know and be able to do at different ages and stages. Ten standards are described for prekindergarten through

grade 2, with examples of the expectations outlined for each standard (Figure 1–3). The first five standards are content goals for operations, algebra, geometry, measurement, and data analysis and probability. The next five standards include the processes of problem solving,

| Number and operations standard | |
| --- | --- |
| *Instructional programs from prekindergarten through grade 12 should enable all students to—* | **Expectations for grades pre-K–2**<br>*In prekindergarten through grade 2 all students should—* |
| Understand numbers, ways of representing numbers, relationships among numbers, and number systems | ■ count with understanding and recognize "how many" in sets of objects<br>■ use multiple models to develop initial understandings of place value and the base-ten number system<br>■ develop understanding of the relative position and magnitude of whole numbers and of ordinal and cardinal numbers and their connections<br>■ develop a sense of whole numbers and represent and use them in flexible ways, including relating, composing, and decomposing numbers<br>■ connect number words and numerals to the quantities they represent, using various physical models and representations<br>■ understand and represent commonly used fractions, such as ¼, ⅓, and ½ |
| Understand meanings of operations and how they relate to one another | ■ understand various meanings of addition and subtraction of whole numbers and the relationship between the two operations<br>■ understand the effects of adding and subtracting whole numbers<br>■ understand situations that entail multiplication and division, such as equal groupings of objects and sharing equally |
| Compute fluently and make reasonable estimates | ■ develop and use strategies for whole-number computations, with a focus on addition and subtraction<br>■ develop fluency with basic number combinations for addition and subtraction<br>■ use a variety of methods and tools to compute, including objects, mental computation, estimation, paper and pencil, and calculators |

**Figure 1–3** Expectations for prekindergarten through second grade. From "Standards for Grades Pre-K–2," *Principles and Standards for School Mathematics* (pp. 392, 394, 396, 398, 400) by the National Council of Teachers of Mathematics, 2000, Reston, VA: Author. Reprinted with permission. Standards are listed with the permission of the National Council of Teachers of Mathematics (NCTM). NCTM does not endorse the content or validity of these alignments.

## Patterns, functions, and algebra standard

| *Instructional programs from prekindergarten through grade 12 should enable all students to—* | **Expectations for grades pre-K–2**<br>*In prekindergarten through grade 2 all students should—* |
|---|---|
| Understand patterns, relations, and functions | ■ sort, classify, and order objects by size, number, and other properties<br>■ recognize, describe, and extend patterns such as sequences of sounds and shapes or simple numeric patterns and translate from one representation to another<br>■ analyze how both repeating and growing patterns are generated |
| Represent and analyze mathematical situations and structures using algebraic symbols | ■ illustrate general principles and properties of operations, such as commutativity, using specific numbers<br>■ use concrete, pictorial, and verbal representations to develop an understanding of invented and conventional symbolic notations |
| Use mathematical models to represent and understand quantitative relationships | ■ model situations that involve the addition and subtraction of whole numbers, using objects, pictures, and symbols |
| Analyze change in various contexts | ■ describe qualitative change, such as a student's growing taller; describe quantitative change, such as a student's growing two inches in one year |

## Geometry standard

| *Instructional programs from prekindergarten through grade 12 should enable all students to—* | **Expectations for grades pre-K–2**<br>*In prekindergarten through grade 2 all students should—* |
|---|---|
| Analyze characteristics and properties of two- and three-dimensional geometric shapes and develop mathematical arguments about geometric relationships | ■ recognize, name, build, draw, compare, and sort two- and three-dimensional shapes<br>■ describe attributes and parts of two- and three-dimensional shapes<br>■ investigate and predict the results of putting together and taking apart two- and three-dimensional shapes |

**Figure 1–3** *Continued*

| Specify locations and describe spatial relationships using coordinate geometry and other representational systems | ▪ describe, name, and interpret relative positions in space and apply ideas about relative position<br>▪ describe, name, and interpret direction and distance in navigating space and apply ideas about direction and distance<br>▪ find and name locations with simple relationships such as "near to" and in coordinate systems such as maps |
|---|---|
| Apply transformations and use symmetry to analyze mathematical situations | ▪ recognize and apply slides, flips, and turns<br>▪ recognize and create shapes that have symmetry |
| Use visualization, spatial reasoning, and geometric modeling to solve problems | ▪ create mental images of geometric shapes using spatial memory and spatial visualization<br>▪ recognize and represent shapes from different perspectives<br>▪ relate ideas in geometry to ideas in number and measurement<br>▪ recognize geometric shapes and structures in the environment and specify their location |

## Measurement standard

| Instructional programs from prekindergarten through grade 12 should enable all students to— | Expectations for grades pre-K–2<br>In prekindergarten through grade 2 all students should— |
|---|---|
| Understand measurable attributes of objects and the units, systems, and processes of measurement | ▪ recognize the attributes of length, volume, weight, area, and time<br>▪ compare and order objects according to these attributes<br>▪ understand how to measure using nonstandard and standard units<br>▪ select an appropriate unit and tool for the attribute being measured |
| Apply appropriate techniques, tools, and formulas to determine measurements | ▪ measure with multiple copies of units of the same size, such as paper clips laid end to end<br>▪ use repetition of a single unit to measure something larger than the unit, for instance, measuring the length of a room with a single meterstick<br>▪ use tools to measure<br>▪ develop common referents for measures to make comparisons and estimates |

**Figure 1–3** *Continued*

## Data analysis and probability standard

| Instructional programs from prekindergarten through grade 12 should enable all students to— | **Expectations for grades pre-K–2**<br>*In prekindergarten through grade 2 all students should—* |
| --- | --- |
| Formulate questions that can be addressed with data and collect, organize, and display relevant data to answer them | ■ pose questions and gather data about themselves and their surroundings<br>■ sort and classify objects according to their attributes and organize data about the objects<br>■ represent data using concrete objects, pictures, and graphs |
| Select and use appropriate statistical methods to analyze data | ■ describe parts of the data and the set of data as a whole to determine what the data show |
| Develop and evaluate inferences and predictions that are based on data | ■ discuss events related to students' experiences as likely or unlikely |
| Understand and apply basic concepts of probability | |

## Problem solving standard

| Instructional programs from prekindergarten through grade 12 should enable all students to— | |
| --- | --- |
| | ■ Build new mathematical knowledge through problem solving<br>■ Solve problems that arise in mathematics and in other contexts<br>■ Apply and adapt a variety of appropriate strategies to solve problems<br>■ Monitor and reflect on the process of mathematical problem solving |

## Reasoning and proof standard

| Instructional programs from prekindergarten through grade 12 should enable all students to— | |
| --- | --- |
| | ■ Recognize reasoning and proof as fundamental aspects of mathematics<br>■ Make and investigate mathematical conjectures<br>■ Develop and evaluate mathematical arguments and proofs<br>■ Select and use various types of reasoning and methods of proof |

**Figure 1–3** *Continued*

## Connections standard

| *Instructional programs from prekindergarten through grade 12 should enable all students to—* | ■ Recognize and use connections among mathematical ideas<br>■ Understand how mathematical ideas interconnect and build on one another to produce a coherent whole<br>■ Recognize and apply mathematics in contexts outside of mathematics |
| --- | --- |

## Communication standard

| *Instructional programs from prekindergarten through grade 12 should enable all students to—* | ■ Organize and consolidate their mathematical thinking through communication<br>■ Communicate their mathematical thinking coherently and clearly to peers, teachers, and others<br>■ Analyze and evaluate the mathematical thinking and strategies of others<br>■ Use the language of mathematics to express mathematical ideas precisely |
| --- | --- |

## Representation standard

| *Instructional programs from prekindergarten through grade 12 should enable all students to—* | ■ Create and use representations to organize, record, and communicate mathematical ideas<br>■ Select, apply, and translate among mathematical representations to solve problems<br>■ Use representations to model and interpret physical, social, and mathematical phenomena |
| --- | --- |

Figure 1–3 *Continued*

reasoning and proof, connections, communication, and representation. These two sets of standards are linked together as the process standards are applied to learning the content. The standards and principles are integrated within the units that follow.

In 2006, NCTM published *Curriculum Focal Points*. The **focal points** break the standards areas down by grade levels. Table 1–1 outlines the focal points for prekindergarten (pre-K) through grade 3. Note that there are three focal points at each level with suggested con-

nections to the NCTM Standards in other curriculum areas. The focal points will be discussed further in each relevant unit.

## Standards for Science Education

In 1996 the National Academies of Sciences's National Research Council (NRC) published the *National Science Education Standards*, which present a vision of a scientifically literate populace. These standards outline what

**Table 1–1**

**Curriculum Focal Points by Age/Grade**

| Age/Grade | Focal Points | Connections | Units |
|---|---|---|---|
| Prekindergarten | ■ Number and operations<br>■ Geometry<br>■ Measurement | ■ Data analysis<br>■ Number and operations<br>■ Algebra | Focal points: 8, 9, 11, 12, 13, 18, 19<br>Connections: 3, 10, 17, 20 |
| Kindergarten | ■ Number and operations<br>■ Geometry<br>■ Measurement | ■ Data analysis<br>■ Geometry<br>■ Algebra | Focal points: 8, 9, 12, 13, 20, 23, 24<br>Connections: 3, 12, 13, 17, 18, 20, 25 |
| First Grade | ■ Number and operations and algebra<br>■ Number and operations<br>■ Geometry | ■ Number and operations and algebra<br>■ Measurement and data analysis<br>■ Algebra | Focal points: 3, 27, 31<br>Connections: 30, 31, 32 |
| Second Grade | ■ Number and operations<br>■ Number and operations and algebra<br>■ Measurement | ■ Number and operations<br>■ Geometry and measurement<br>■ Algebra | Focal points: 3, 30, 32<br>Connections: 28, 30, 31 |
| Third Grade | ■ Number and operations<br>■ Number and operations and algebra<br>■ Geometry | ■ Algebra<br>■ Measurement<br>■ Data analysis<br>■ Number and operations | Focal points: 3, 27, 29, 31<br>Connections: 27, 31, 32 |

a student should know and be able to do in order to be considered scientifically literate at different grade levels.

A prominent feature of the NRC standards is a focus on *inquiry*. This term refers to the abilities students should develop in designing and conducting scientific investigations as well as the understanding they should gain about the nature of scientific inquiry. Students who use inquiry to learn science engage in many of the same activities and thinking processes as scientists who are seeking to expand human knowledge. In order to better understand the use of inquiry, the NRC (2000) produced a research-based report, *Inquiry and the National Science Education Standards: A Guide for Teaching and Learning*, that outlines the case for inquiry with practical examples of engaging students in the process. Addendums to the *National Science Education Standards* include *Classroom Assessment and the National Science Education Standards* (2001) and *Selecting Instructional Materials: A Guide for K–12* (1999). These will be discussed later in the text.

A national consensus has evolved around what constitutes effective science education. This consensus is reflected in two major national reform efforts in science education that affect teaching and learning for young children: the NRC's *National Science Education Standards* (1996) and the American Association for the Advancement of Science's (AAAS) Project 2061, which has produced *Science for All Americans* (1989) and *Benchmarks for Science Literacy* (1993). With regard to philosophy, intent, and expectations, these two efforts share a commitment to the essentials of good science teaching and have many commonalities, especially regarding how children learn and what science content students should know and be able to understand within grade ranges and levels of difficulty. Although they take different approaches, both the AAAS and NRC efforts align with the 1997 NAEYC guidelines for developmentally appropriate practice and the 2000 NCTM standards for the teaching of mathematics.

These national science reform documents are based on the idea that active, hands-on conceptual learning that leads to understanding—along with the acquisition of basic skills—provides meaningful and relevant learning experiences. The reform documents also emphasize and reinforce Oakes's (1990) observation that all students, especially underrepresented groups, need to learn scientific skills (such as observation and analysis) that have been embedded in a "less-is-more" curriculum that starts when children are very young.

The 1996 *National Science Education Standards* were coordinated by the NRC and were developed in association with the major professional organizations in science and with individuals having expertise germane to the process of producing such standards. The document presents and discusses the standards, which provide qualitative criteria to be used by educators and others making decisions and judgments, in six major components: (1) science teaching standards, (2) standards for the professional development of teachers, (3) assessment in science education, (4) science content standards, (5) science education program standards, and (6) science education system standards.

The *National Science Education Standards* are directed to all who have interests, concerns, or investments in improving science education and ultimately achieving higher levels of scientific literacy for all students. The standards intend to provide support for the integrity of science in science programs by presenting and discussing criteria for the improvement of science education.

The AAAS Project 2061 initiative constitutes a long-term plan to strengthen student literacy in science, mathematics, and technology. Using a "less is more" approach to teaching, the first Project 2061 report recommends that educators use five major themes

that occur repeatedly in science to weave together the science curriculum: models and scale, evolution, patterns of change, stability, and systems and interactions. Although aspects of all or many of these themes can be found in most teaching units, *models and scale, patterns of change,* and *systems and interactions* are the themes considered most appropriate for younger children.

The second AAAS Project 2061 report, *Benchmarks for Science Literacy,* categorizes the science knowledge that students need to know at all grade levels. The report is not in itself a science curriculum, but it is a useful resource for those who are developing one.

One of the AAAS's recent efforts to clarify linkages and understandings is the *Atlas of Science Literacy* (2001). This AAAS Project 2061 publication graphically depicts connections among the learning goals established in *Benchmarks for Science Literacy* and *Science for All Americans.* The *Atlas* is a collection of 50 linked maps that show how students from kindergarten through grade 12 can expand their understanding and skills toward specific science literacy goals. The maps also outline the connections across different areas of mathematics, technology, and science. Of particular interest is the emphasis that the maps put on the prerequisites needed for learning a particular concept at each grade.

The NAEYC guidelines for mathematics and science (Bredekamp, 1987; Bredekamp & Copple, 1997) state that mathematics begins with exploration of materials such as building blocks, sand, and water for 3-year-olds and extends on to cooking, observation of environmental changes, working with tools, classifying objects with a purpose, and exploring animals, plants, machines, and so on for 4- and 5-year-olds. For children ages 5–8, exploration, discovery, and problem solving are appropriate. Mathematics and science are integrated with other content areas such as social studies, the arts, music, and language arts. These current standards for mathematics and science curriculum and instruction take a constructivist view based on the theories of Jean Piaget and Lev Vygotsky (described in the next section).

A consensus report entitled *Taking Science to School: Learning and Teaching Science in Grades K-8*, published in 2007 by the NRC, brings together literature from cognitive and developmental psychology, science education, and the history and philosophy of science to synthesize what is known about how children in the early grades learn the ideas and practice of science. Findings from this research synthesis suggest that educators are underestimating the capabilities of young children as students of science. The report makes the following conclusions.

## What Children Know and How They Learn

- We know that children entering school already have substantial, mostly implicit knowledge of the natural world.

- What children are capable of at a particular age results from the complex interplay of maturation, experience, and instruction. What is developmentally appropriate is not a simple function of age or grade but instead is largely contingent on children's prior learning opportunities.

- Students' knowledge and experience play a critical role in their science learning, influencing all strands of science understanding.

- Race and ethnicity, language, culture, gender, and socioeconomic status are among the factors that influence the knowledge and experience children bring to the classroom.

- Students learn science by actively engaging in the practices of science.

- A range of instructional approaches is necessary as part of a full development of science proficiency.

## PIAGETIAN PERIODS OF CONCEPT DEVELOPMENT AND THOUGHT

Jean Piaget contributed enormously to understanding the development of children's thought. Piaget identified four periods of cognitive, or mental, growth and development. Early childhood educators are concerned with the first two periods and the first half of the third.

The first period identified by Piaget, called the **sensorimotor period** (from birth to about age 2), is de-scribed in the first part of this unit. It is the time when children begin to learn about the world. They use all their sensory abilities—touch, taste, sight, hearing, smell, and muscular. They also use growing motor abilities to grasp, crawl, stand, and eventually walk. Children in this first period are explorers, and they need opportunities to use their sensory and motor abilities to learn basic skills and concepts. Through these activities, the young child *assimilates* (takes into the mind and comprehends) a great deal of information. By the end of this period, children have developed the concept of **object permanence**. That is, they realize that objects exist even when they are out of sight. They also develop the ability of **object recognition**, learning to identify objects using the information they have acquired about features such as color, shape, and size. As children near the end of the sensorimotor period, they reach a stage where they can engage in **representational thought**; that is, instead of acting impetuously, they can think through a solution before attacking a problem. They also enter into a time of rapid language development.

The second period, called the **preoperational period**, extends from about ages 2–7. During this period, children begin to develop concepts that are more like those of adults, but these are still incomplete in comparison to what they will be like at maturity. These concepts are often referred to as **preconcepts**. During the early part of the preoperational period, language continues to undergo rapid growth and speech is used increasingly to express concept knowledge. Children begin to use concept terms such as *big and small* (size), *light and heavy* (weight), *square and round* (shape), *late and early* (time), *long and short* (length), and so on. This ability to use language is one of the **symbolic behaviors** that emerges during this period. Children also use symbolic behavior in their representational play, where they may use sand to represent food, a stick to represent a spoon, or another child to represent father, mother, or baby. Play is a major arena in which children develop an understanding of the symbolic functions that underlie later understanding of abstract symbols such as numerals, letters, and written words.

An important characteristic of preoperational children is **centration**. When materials are changed in form or arrangement in space, children may see them as changed in amount as well. This is because preoperational children tend to *center* on the most obvious aspects of what is seen. For instance, if the same amount of liquid is put in both a tall, thin glass and a short, fat glass, preoperational children say there is more in the tall glass "because it is taller." If clay is changed in shape from a ball to a snake, they say there is less clay "because it is thinner." If a pile of coins is placed close together, preoperational children say there are fewer coins than they would say if the coins were spread out. When the physical arrangement of material is changed, preoperational children seem unable to hold the original picture of its shape in mind. They lack **reversibility**; that is, they cannot reverse the process of change mentally. The ability to hold or save the original picture in the mind and reverse physical change mentally is referred to as **conservation**, and the inability to conserve is a critical characteristic of preoperational children. During the preoperational period, children work with the precursors of conservation such as counting, one-to-one correspondence, shape, space, and comparing. They also work on **seriation** (putting items in a logical sequence, such as fat to thin or dark to light) and **classification** (putting things in logical groups according to some common criteria such as color, shape, size, or use).

During the third period, called **concrete operations** (usually from ages 7–11), children are becoming *conservers*. That is, they are becoming more and more skilled at retaining the original picture in mind and making a mental reversal when appearances are changed. The time between ages 5 and 7 is one of transition to concrete operations. Each child's thought processes are changing at his or her own rate and so, during this time of transition, a normal expectation is that some children are already conservers and others are not. This is a critical consideration for kindergarten and primary teachers because the ability to conserve number (the pennies problem) is a good indication that children are ready to deal with **abstract symbolic activities**. That is, they will be able to mentally manipulate groups that are presented by number symbols with a real understanding of what the mathematical operations mean. Section 2 of this text covers the basic concepts that children must understand and integrate

in order to conserve. (See Figure 1–4 for examples of conservation problems.)

Piaget's final period is called **formal operations** (ages 11 through adulthood). During this period, children can learn to use the scientific method independently; that is, they learn to solve problems in a logical and systematic manner. They begin to understand abstract concepts and to attack abstract problems. They can imagine solutions before trying them out. For example, suppose a person who has reached the formal operations level is given samples of several colorless liquids and is told that some combination of these liquids will result in a yellow liquid. A person at the formal operations level would plan out how to systematically test to find the solution; a person still at the concrete operational level might start to combine the liquids without considering a logical approach to the problem, such as labeling each liquid and keeping a record of which combinations have been tried. Note that this period may be reached as early as age 11; however, it may not be reached at all by many adults.

## PIAGET'S VIEW OF HOW CHILDREN ACQUIRE KNOWLEDGE

According to Piaget's view, children acquire knowledge by constructing it through their interaction with the environment. Children do not wait to be instructed to do this; they are continually trying to make sense out of everything they encounter. Piaget divides knowledge into three areas.

- **Physical knowledge** is the type that includes learning about objects in the environment and their characteristics (color, weight, size, texture, and other features that can be determined through observation and are physically within the object).

- **Logico-mathematical knowledge** is the type that includes the relationships (same and different, more and less, number, classification, etc.) that each individual constructs to make sense out of the world and to organize information.

| Original | Physical Change | Question | Nonconserving Answer | Conserving Answer |
|---|---|---|---|---|
| Same amount of drink | | Is there still the same amount of drink? | No, there is more in the tall glass. | Yes, you just put the drink in different size glasses. |
| Same amount of clay | | Is there still the same amount of clay? | No, there is more clay in the snake because it is longer. | Yes, you just rolled it out into a different shape. |
| Same amount of pennies | | Are there still the same number of pennies? | No, there are more in the bottom row because it is longer. | Yes, you just moved the pennies closer together (points to top row). |

**Figure 1–4**  Physical changes in conservation tasks.

■ **Social** (or conventional) **knowledge** is the type that is created by people (such as rules for behavior in various social situations).

Physical and logico-mathematical knowledge depend on each other and are learned simultaneously. That is, as the physical characteristics of objects are learned, logico-mathematical categories are constructed to organize information. In the popular story *Goldilocks and the Three Bears*, for example, papa bear is big, mama bear is middle sized, and baby bear is the smallest (seriation), but all three (number) are bears because they are covered with fur and have a certain body shape with a certain combination of features common only to bears (classification).

Constance Kamii, a student of Piaget's, has actively translated Piaget's theory into practical applications for the instruction of young children. Kamii emphasizes that, according to Piaget, **autonomy** (independence) is the aim of education. Intellectual autonomy develops in an atmosphere where children feel se-

cure in their relationships with adults; where they have an opportunity to share their ideas with other children; and where they are encouraged to be alert and curious, to come up with interesting ideas, problems and questions, to use initiative in finding the answers to problems, to have confidence in their abilities to figure out things for themselves, and to speak their minds. Young children need to be presented with problems that can be solved through games and other activities that challenge their minds. They must work with concrete materials and real problems such as the examples provided earlier in this unit.

In line with the NCTM focus on math for understanding, Duckworth (2006) explains how Piaget's view of understanding focuses on the adult attending to the child's point of view. That is, we should not view "understanding" from our own perspective but should rather try to find out what the child is thinking. When the child provides a response that seems illogical from an adult point of view, the adult should consider and explore the child's logic. For example, if a child (when presented with a conservation problem) says there are more objects in a spread-out row of ten objects than in a tightly packed row of ten objects, it is important to ask the child for a reason.

## VYGOTSKY'S VIEW OF HOW CHILDREN LEARN AND DEVELOP

Like Piaget, Lev Vygotsky was also a cognitive development theorist. He was a contemporary of Piaget's, but Vygotsky died at the age of 38 before his work was fully completed. Vygotsky contributed a view of cognitive development that recognizes both developmental and environmental forces. Vygotsky believed that—just as people developed tools such as knives, spears, shovels, and tractors to aid their mastery of the environment— they also developed mental tools. People develop ways of cooperating and communicating as well as new capacities to plan and to think ahead. These mental tools help people to master their own behavior, mental tools that Vygotsky referred to as **signs**. He believed that *speech* was the most important sign system because it freed us from distractions and allowed us to work on problems in our minds. Speech both enables the child to interact socially and facilitates thinking. In Vygotsky's view, *writing and numbering* were also important sign systems.

Piaget looked at development as if it came mainly from the child alone, from the child's inner maturation and spontaneous discoveries, but Vygotsky believed this was true only until about the age of 2. At that point, culture and the cultural signs become necessary to expand thought. He believed that these internal and external factors interacted to produce new thoughts and an expanded menu of signs. Thus, Vygotsky put more emphasis than Piaget on the role of the adult (or a more mature peer) as an influence on children's mental development.

Whereas Piaget placed an emphasis on children as intellectual explorers making their own discoveries and *constructing* knowledge independently, Vygotsky developed an alternative concept known as the **zone of proximal development (ZPD)**. The ZPD is the area between where the child is now operating independently in mental development and where she might go with assistance from an adult or more mature child. Cultural knowledge is acquired with the assistance or **scaffolding** provided by more mature learners. According to Vygotsky, good teaching involves presenting material that is a little ahead of development. Children might not fully understand it at first, but in time they can understand it given appropriate scaffolding. Rather than pressuring development, instruction should support development as it moves ahead. Concepts constructed independently and spontaneously by children lay the foundation for the more scientific concepts that are part of the culture. Teachers must identify each student's ZPD and provide developmentally appropriate instruction. Teachers will know when they have hit upon the right zone because children will respond with enthusiasm, curiosity, and active involvement.

Piagetian constructivists tend to be concerned about the tradition of pressuring children and not allowing them freedom to construct knowledge independently. Vygotskian constructivists are concerned with children being challenged to reach their full potential. Today, many educators find that a combination of Piaget's and Vygotsky's views provides a foundation for instruction that follows the child's interests and enthusiasms while providing an intellectual challenge. The *learning cycle* view provides such a framework.

## THE LEARNING CYCLE

The authors of the Science Curriculum Improvement Study (SCIS) materials designed a Piagetian-based learning cycle approach based on the assumption expressed by Albert Einstein and other scientists that "science is a quest for knowledge" (Renner & Marek, 1988). The scientists believed that, in the teaching of science, students must interact with materials, collect data, and make some order out of that data. The order that students make out of that data is (or leads to) a conceptual invention.

The **learning cycle** is viewed as a way to take students on a quest that leads to the construction of knowledge. It is used both as a curriculum development procedure and as a teaching strategy. Developers must organize student activities around phases, and teachers must modify their role and strategies during the progressive phases. The phases of the learning cycle are sometimes assigned different labels and are sometimes split into segments. However, the essential thrust of each of the phases remains: exploration, concept development, and concept application (Barman, 1989; Renner & Marek, 1988).

During the *exploration phase*, the teacher remains in the background, observing and occasionally inserting a comment or question (see Unit 2 on naturalistic and informal learning). The students actively manipulate materials and interact with each other. The teacher's knowledge of child development guides the selection of materials and how they are placed in the environment so as to provide a developmentally appropriate setting in which young children can explore and construct concepts.

For example, in the exploration phase of a lesson about shapes, students examine a variety of wooden or cardboard objects (squares, rectangles, circles) and make observations about the objects. The teachers may ask them to describe how they are similar and how they are different.

During the *concept introduction phase*, the teacher provides direct instruction; this begins with a discussion of the information the students have discovered. The teacher helps the children record their information. During this phase the teacher clarifies and adds to what the children have found out for themselves by using explanations, print materials, films, guest speakers, and other available resources (see Unit 2 on structured learning experiences). For example, in this phase of the lesson, the children exploring shapes may take the shapes and classify them into groups.

The third phase of the cycle, the *application phase*, provides children with the opportunity to integrate and organize new ideas with old ideas and relate them to still other ideas. The teacher or the children themselves suggest a new problem to which the information learned in the first two phases can be applied. In the lesson about shape, the teacher might introduce differently shaped household objects and wooden blocks. The children are asked to classify these items as squares, rectangles, and circles. Again, the children are actively involved in concrete activities and exploration.

The three major phases of the learning cycle can be applied to the ramp-and-ball example described earlier in this unit. During the first phase, the ramp and the balls are available to be examined. The teacher offers some suggestions and questions as the children work with the materials. In the second phase, the teacher communicates with the children regarding what they have observed. The teacher might also provide explanations, label the items being used, and otherwise assist the children in organizing their information; at this point, books and/or films about simple machines could be provided. For the third phase, the teacher poses a new problem and challenges the children to apply their concept of the ramp and how it works to the new problem. For example, some toy vehicles might be provided to use with the ramp(s).

Charles Barman (1989) describes three types of learning cycle lessons in *An Expanded View of the Learning Cycle: New Ideas about an Effective Teaching Strategy*. The lessons vary in accordance with the way data are collected by students and with the type of reasoning the students engage in. Most young children will be involved in **descriptive lessons** in which they mainly observe, interact, and describe their observations. Although young children may begin to generate guesses regarding the reasons for what they have observed, serious hypothesis generation requires concrete operational thinking (*empirical-inductive lesson*). In the third type of lesson, students observe, generate hypotheses, and design experiments to test their hypotheses (*hypothetical-deductive lesson*). This type of lesson requires formal operational thought. However, this does not mean that preoperational and concrete operational children should be discouraged from generating ideas on how to find out if their guesses will prove to be true. Quite the contrary: They should be encouraged to take this step. Often they will propose an alternative solution even though they may not yet have reached the level of mental maturation necessary to understand the underlying physical or logico-mathematical explanation.

## ADAPTING THE LEARNING CYCLE TO EARLY CHILDHOOD

Bredekamp and Rosegrant (1992) have adapted the learning cycle to early childhood education (Figure 1–5). The learning cycle for young children encompasses four repeating processes, as follows.

### CYCLE OF LEARNING AND TEACHING

| | WHAT CHILDREN DO | WHAT TEACHERS DO |
|---|---|---|
| **Awareness** | Experience | Create the environment |
| | Acquire an interest | Provide opportunities by introducing new objects, events, people |
| | Recognize broad parameters | Invite interest by posing problem or question |
| | Attend | Respond to child's interest or shared experience |
| | Perceive | Show interest, enthusiasm |
| **Exploration** | Observe | Facilitate |
| | Explore materials | Support and enhance exploration |
| | Collect information | Provide opportunities for active exploration |
| | Discover | Extend play |
| | Create | Describe child's activity |
| | Figure out components | Ask open-ended questions—"What else could you do?" |
| | Construct own understanding | Respect child's thinking and rule systems |
| | Apply own rules | Allow for constructive error |
| | Create personal meaning | |
| | Represent own meaning | |
| **Inquiry** | Examine | Help children refine understanding |
| | Investigate | Guide children, focus attention |
| | Propose explanations | Ask more focused questions—"What else works like this?" "What |
| | Focus | happens if ___?" |
| | Compare own thinking with that of others | Provide information when requested—"How do you spell ___?" |
| | Generalize | Help children make connections |
| | Relate to prior learning | |
| | Adjust to conventional rule systems | |
| **Utilization** | Use the learning in many ways; learning becomes functional | Create vehicles for application in real world |
| | Represent learning in various ways | Help children apply learning to new situations |
| | Apply learning to new situations | Provide meaningful situations in which to use learning |
| | Formulate new hypotheses and repeat cycle | |

**Figure 1–5** Cycle of learning and teaching. From *Reaching Potentials: Appropriate Curriculum and Assessment for Young Children* (Vol. 1, p. 33), by S. Bredekamp and T. Rosegrant (Eds.), 1992, Washington, DC: National Association for the Education of Young Children. Reprinted with permission.

■ **Awareness**: a broad recognition of objects, people, events, or concepts that develops from experience.

■ **Exploration**: the construction of personal meaning through sensory experiences with objects, people, events, or concepts.

■ **Inquiry**: learners compare their constructions with those of the culture, commonalities are recognized, and generalizations are made that are more like those of adults.

■ **Utilization**: at this point in the cycle, learners can apply and use their understandings in new settings and situations.

Each time a new situation is encountered, learning begins with awareness and moves on through the other levels. The cycle also relates to development. For example, infants and toddlers will be at the awareness level, gradually moving into exploration. Children who are 3, 4, or 5 years old may move up to inquiry, whereas 6-, 7-, and 8-year-olds can move through all four levels when meeting new situations or concepts. Bredekamp and Rosegrant (1992) provide an example in the area of measurement:

- 3- and 4-year-olds are aware of and explore comparative sizes;
- 4-, 5-, and 6-year-olds explore with nonstandard units, such as how many of their own feet wide is the rug;
- 7- and 8-year-olds begin to understand standard units of measurement and use rulers, thermometers, and other standard measuring tools.

The authors caution that the cycle is not hierarchical; that is, utilization is not necessarily more valued than awareness or exploration. Young children may be aware of concepts that they cannot fully utilize in the technical sense. For example, they may be aware that rain falls from the sky without understanding the intricacies of meteorology. Using the learning cycle as a framework for curriculum and instruction has an important aspect: The cycle reminds us that children may not have had experiences that provide for awareness and exploration. To be truly individually appropriate in planning, we need to provide for these experiences in school.

The learning cycle fits nicely with the theories of Piaget and Vygotsky. For both, learning begins with awareness and exploration. Both value inquiry and application. The format for each concept provided in the text is from naturalistic to informal to structured learning experiences. These experiences are consistent with providing opportunities for children to move through the learning cycle as they meet new objects, people, events, or concepts.

## TRADITIONAL VERSUS REFORM INSTRUCTION

A current thrust in mathematics and science instruction is the reform of classroom instruction, changing from the traditional approach of drill and practice mem-

orization to adoption of the constructivist approach. A great deal of tension exists between the traditional and reform approaches. *Telling* has been the traditional method of ensuring that student learning takes place. When a teacher's role changes to that of guide and facilitator, the teacher may feel a lack of control. Current research demonstrates that students in reform classrooms learn as well or better than those in traditional classrooms. In this text we have tried to achieve a balance between the traditional and reform approaches by providing a guide to ensuring students have the opportunity to explore and construct their own knowledge while also providing examples of developmentally appropriate direct instruction.

## ORGANIZATION OF THE TEXT

This text is divided into seven sections. The sequence is both integrative and developmental. Section 1 is an integrative section that sets the stage for instruction. We describe development, acquisition, and promotion of math and science concepts, and we provide a plan for assessing developmental levels. Finally, the basic concepts of science and their application are described.

Sections 2, 3, and 4 encompass the developmental mathematics and science program for sensorimotor-level and preoperational-level children. Section 2 includes descriptions of the fundamental concepts that are basic to both math and science along with suggestions for instruction and materials. Section 3 focuses on applying these fundamental concepts, attitudes, and skills at a more advanced level. Section 4 deals with higher-level concepts and activities.

Sections 5 and 6 encompass the acquisition of concepts and skills for children at the concrete operations level. At this point, the two subject areas conventionally become more discrete in terms of instruction. However, they should continue to be integrated because science explorations can enrich children's math skills and concepts through concrete applications and also because mathematics is used to organize and interpret the data collected through observation.

Section 7 provides suggestions of materials and resources—and descriptions of math and science in action—in the classroom and in the home. Finally, the

| Standard | Units |
|---|---|
| Number and operations | 8, 9, 14, 23, 24, 25, 27, 29, 30 |
| Patterns, functions, and algebra | 10, 17, 25, 28, 31 |
| Geometry | 12, 13, 25, 31 |
| Measurement | 11, 18, 19, 32 |
| Data analysis and probability | 20, 25, 31 |
| Problem solving | 3, 22 |
| Reasoning | 15, 22 |
| Connections | 15, 22 |
| Communication | 15, 22 |
| Representation | 15, 22 |

This chart shows the text units that focus most directly on the mathematics standards, although the process standards apply to all the content goal areas.

| Standard | Units |
|---|---|
| Unifying Concepts and Processes | Throughout all units |
| Science as Inquiry | Throughout all units |
| Life Science | 16, 21, 26, 33, and 34 |
| Physical Science | 21, 26, 33, 35, 37, and 40 |
| Earth and Space Science | 16, 21, 33, and 36 |
| Science and Technology | 12, 13, 16, 21, 22, 23, 24, 33, 37, 38, and 40 |
| Science in Personal and Social Perspectives | 33, 34, 37, 38, 40, and 41 |
| History and Nature of Science | Throughout all units |

This chart shows the text units that focus most directly on the *National Science Education Standards* (National Research Council, 1996), although the process standards apply to all the content areas.

appendices include concept assessment tasks, lists of children's books that contain math and science concepts, and the *National Science Education Standards*.

As Figure 1–1 illustrates, concepts are not acquired in a series of quick, short-term lessons; development begins in infancy and continues throughout early childhood and beyond. As you read each unit, keep referring back to Figure 1–1; it can help you relate each section to periods of development.

## SUMMARY

Concept development begins in infancy and grows through four periods throughout a lifetime. The explor- atory activities of the infant and toddler during the sensorimotor period are the basis of later success. As they use their senses and muscles, children learn about the world. During the preoperational period, concepts grow rapidly and children develop the basic concepts and skills of science and mathematics, moving toward intellectual autonomy through independent activity, which serves as a vehicle for the construction of knowledge. Between the ages of 5 and 7, children enter the concrete operations period and learn to apply abstract ideas and activities to their concrete knowledge of the physical and mathematical world. The learning cycle lesson is an example of a developmentally inspired teaching strategy. Both mathematics and science instruction should be guided by principles and standards developed by the major professional organizations in each content area. Mathematics is also guided by curriculum focal points. The text presents the major concepts, skills, processes, and attitudes that are fundamental to mathematics and science for young children as their learning is guided in light of these principles and standards.

## KEY TERMS

abstract symbolic activities
autonomy
awareness
centration
classification
concepts
concrete operations
conservation
defining and controlling
   variables
descriptive lessons
development
exploration
focal points

formal operations
inquiry
learning cycle
logico-mathematical
   knowledge
object permanence
object recognition
physical knowledge
preconcepts
preoperational period
preprimary
primary
principles
process skills

representational thought
reversibility
scaffolding
senses
sensorimotor period
seriation
signs
social knowledge
standards
symbolic behaviors
understanding
utilization
zone of proximal
   development (ZPD)

## SUGGESTED ACTIVITIES

1. Using the descriptions in this unit, prepare a list of behaviors that would indicate that a young child at each of Piaget's first three periods of development is engaged in behavior exemplifying the acquisition of math and science concepts. Using your list, observe four young children at home or at school. One child should be 6–18 months old, one 18 months to 2½ years old, one of age 3–5, and one of age 6–7. Record everything each child does that is on your list. Note any similarities and differences observed among the four children.

2. Interview three mothers of children ages 2–8. Using your list from Activity 1 as a guide, ask them which of the activities each of their children does. Ask the mothers if they realize that these activities are basic to the construction of math and science concepts, and note their responses. Did you find that they appreciate the value of their children's play activities in math and science concept development?

3. Observe science and/or math instruction in a prekindergarten, kindergarten, or primary classroom. Describe the teacher's approach to instruction, and compare the approach with Vygotsky's guidelines.

4. Interview two or three young children. Present the conservation of number problem illustrated in Figure 1–4 (see Appendix A for detailed instructions). Audio tape or videotape their responses. Listen to the tape and describe what you learn. Describe the similarities and differences in the children's responses.

5. Look carefully at the standards and expectations outlined in Figure 1–3. Decide which expectations would most likely be appropriate for students at the preschool, kindergarten, and primary levels. Discuss your selections with a small group in class. Each group should appoint a scribe to list your selections (and your reasons for those selections) and to report the group decisions to the class.

**6.** You should begin to record, on 5½" × 8" file cards, each math and science activity that you learn about. Buy a package of cards, some dividers, and a file box. Label your dividers with the titles of Units 8 through 40. Figure 1–6 illustrates how your file should look.

**Figure 1–6** Start a math/science Activity File now so you can keep it up to date.

## REVIEW

**A.** Define the term *concept development*.

**B.** Describe the commonalities between math and science.

**C.** Explain the importance of Piaget's and Vygotsky's theories of cognitive development.

**D.** Decide which of the following describes a child in the sensorimotor (SM), preoperational (P), or concrete operational (CO) Piagetian stages.

   1. Mary watches as her teacher makes two balls of clay of the same size. The teacher then rolls one ball into a snake shape and asks, "Mary, do both balls still have the same amount, or does one ball have more clay?" Mary laughs, "They are still the same amount. You just rolled that one out into a snake."

   2. Michael shakes his rattle and then puts it in his mouth and tries to suck on it.

   3. John's mother shows him two groups of pennies. One group is spread out, and one group is stacked up. Each group contains 10 pennies. "Which bunch of pennies would you like to have, John?" John looks carefully and then says as he picks up the pennies that are spread out, "I'll take these because there are more."

**E.** In review question D, which child (Mary or John) is a conserver? How do you know? Why is it important to know whether or not a child is a conserver?

**F.** Explain how young children acquire knowledge. Include the place of the learning cycle in knowledge acquisition. Provide examples from your observations.

**G.** Explain the purpose and value of having principles and standards for mathematics and science instruction.

**H.** Describe the purpose of focal points.

## REFERENCES

American Association for the Advancement of Science. (1989). *Science for all Americans: A Project 2061 report on literacy goals in science, mathematics and technology.* Washington, DC: Author.

American Association for the Advancement of Science. (1993). *Benchmarks in science literacy.* Washington, DC: Author.

American Association for the Advancement of Science. (2001). *Atlas of science literacy.* Washington, DC: Author.

Barman, C. R. (1989). *An expanded view of the learning cycle: New ideas about an effective teaching strategy* (Council of Elementary Science International Monograph No. 4). Indianapolis, IN: Indiana University Press.

Bredekamp, S. (Ed.). (1987). *Developmentally appropriate practice in early childhood programs serving children from birth through age eight.* Washington, DC: National Association for the Education of Young Children.

Bredekamp, S., & Copple, C. (Eds.). (1997). *Developmentally appropriate practice in early childhood programs* (Rev. ed.). Washington, DC: National Association for the Education of Young Children.

Bredekamp, S., & Rosegrant, T. (1992). *Reaching potentials: Appropriate curriculum and assessment for young children* (Vol. 1). Washington, DC: National Association for the Education of Young Children.

Chalufour, I., Hoisington, C., Moriarty, R., Winokur, J., & Worth, K. (2004). The science and mathematics of building structures. *Science and Children, 41*(4), 31–34.

Clements, D. H., & Sarama, J. (2003, January/February). Creative pathways to math. *Early Childhood Education Today,* 37–45.

Clements, D. H., & Sarama, J. (2004, March). Building abstract thinking through math. *Early Childhood Education Today,* 34–41.

Committee on Science Learning, Kindergarten through Eighth Grade. Board on Science Education, Center for Education. (2007). *Taking science to school: Learning and teaching science in grades K–8.* Washington, DC: National Academies Press.

*Curriculum focal points for prekindergarten through grade 8 mathematics.* (2006). Retrieved May 24, 2007, from http://www.nctm.org

Duckworth, E. (2006). *The having of wonderful ideas* (3rd ed.). New York: Teachers College Press.

Geist, E. (2001). Children are born mathematicians: Promoting the construction of early mathematical concepts in children under five. *Young Children, 56*(4), 12–19.

Learning PATHS and teaching STRATEGIES in early mathematics. (2003). In D. Koralek (Ed.), *Spotlight on young children and math* (pp. 29–31). Washington

DC: National Association for the Education of Young Children.

Math experiences that count! (2002). *Young Children, 57*(4), 60–61.

National Council of Teachers of Mathematics. (1989). *Curriculum and evaluation standards for school mathematics.* Reston, VA: Author.

National Council of Teachers of Mathematics. (1991). *Professional standards for teaching mathematics.* Reston, VA: Author.

National Council of Teachers of Mathematics. (1995). *Assessment standards for school mathematics.* Reston, VA: Author.

National Council of Teachers of Mathematics. (2000). *Principles and standards for school mathematics.* Reston, VA: Author.

National Council of Teachers of Mathematics & National Association for the Education of Young Children. (2002). NCTM position statement: Early childhood mathematics: Promoting good beginnings. *Teaching Children Mathematics, 9*(1), 24.

National Research Council. (1996). *National science education standards.* Washington, DC: National Academies Press.

National Research Council. (1999). *Selecting instructional materials: A guide for K–12.* Washington, DC: National Academies Press.

National Research Council. (2000). *Inquiry and the national science education standards: A guide for teaching and learning.* Washington, DC: National Academies Press.

National Research Council. (2001). *Classroom assessment and the national science education standards.* Washington, DC: National Academies Press.

Oakes, J. (1990). *Lost talent: The underparticipation of women, minorities, and disabled persons in science.* Santa Monica, CA: Rand.

Renner, R. W., & Marek, E. A. (1988). *The learning cycle and elementary school science teaching.* Portsmouth, NH: Heinemann.

## FURTHER READING AND RESOURCES

Adams, L. A. (2000). Helping children learn mathematics through multiple intelligences and standards for school mathematics. *Childhood Education, 77,* 86–92.

Aubrey, C. (2001). Early mathematics. In T. David (Ed.), *Promoting evidenced-based practice in early childhood education: Research and its implications* (Vol. 1, pp. 185–210). Amsterdam: Elsevier Science.

Baroody, A. J. (2000). Research in review. Does mathematics instruction for three- to five-year-olds really make sense? *Young Children*, 55, 61–67.

Berk, L. E., & Winsler, A. (1995). *Scaffolding children's learning: Vygotsky and early childhood education.* Washington, DC: National Association for the Education of Young Children.

Bodrova, E., & Leong, D. J. (2007). *Tools of the mind: The Vygotskian approach to early childhood education* (2nd ed.). Upper Saddle River, NJ: Pearson-Merrill/Prentice-Hall.

Bowe, F. G. (2007). *Early childhood special education: Birth to eight* (4th ed.). Clifton Park, NY: Thomson Delmar Learning.

Charlesworth, R. (2003). *Understanding child development* (6th ed.). Clifton Park, NY: Thomson Delmar Learning.

Charlesworth, R. (2005). Prekindergarten math: Connecting with national standards. *Early Childhood Education Journal*, 32(4), 229–236.

Children as mathematicians [Focus issue]. (2000). *Teaching Children Mathematics*, 6.

Clements, D. H. (2001). Mathematics in the preschool. *Teaching Children Mathematics*, 7, 270–275.

Clements, D. H., & Sarama, J. (2000). The earliest geometry. *Teaching Children Mathematics*, 7, 82–86.

Clements, D. H., & Sarama, J. (2000). Standards for preschoolers. *Teaching Children Mathematics*, 7, 38–41.

Copley, J. V. (Ed.). (1999). *Mathematics in the early years.* Washington, DC: National Association for the Education of Young Children.

Copley, J. V. (2000). *The young child and mathematics.* Washington, DC: National Association for the Education of Young Children.

Coulter, B. (2000). What's it like where you live? Meeting the standards through technology-enhanced inquiry. *Science and Children*, 37(4), 36–50.

Decker, K. A. (1999). Meeting state standards through integration. *Science and Children*, 36(6), 28–32, 69.

de Melendez, W. R., & Beck, V. (2007). *Teaching young children in multicultural classrooms* (2nd ed.). Clifton Park, NY: Thomson Delmar Learning.

Demers, C. (2000). Analyzing the standards. *Science and Children*, 37(4), 22–25.

Epstein, A. S. (2007). *The intentional teacher.* Washington, DC: National Association for the Education of Young Children.

Furner, J. M., & Berman, B. T. (2003). Math anxiety: Overcoming a major obstacle to the improvement of student math performance. *Childhood Education*, 79(3), 170–174.

Golbeck, S. L., & Ginsburg, H. P. (Eds.). (2004). Early learning in mathematics and science [Special Issue]. *Early Childhood Research Quarterly*, 19.

Gullo, D. F. (Ed.). (2006). *Kindergarten today.* Washington, DC: National Association for the Education of Young Children.

Inhelder, B., & Piaget, J. (1969). *The early growth of logic in the child.* New York: Norton.

Kamii, C. K., & Housman, L. B. (1999). *Young children reinvent arithmetic: Implications of Piaget's theory* (2nd ed.). New York: Teachers College Press.

Karplus, R., & Thier, H. D. (1967). *A new look at elementary school science—Science curriculum improvement study.* Chicago: Rand McNally.

Kilpatrick, J., Martin, W. G., & Schifter, D. (2003). *A research companion to principles and standards for school mathematics.* Reston, VA: National Council of Teachers of Mathematics.

Kline, K. (2000). Early childhood teachers discuss the *Standards. Teaching Children Mathematics*, 6, 568–571.

Lawson, A. E., & Renner, J. W. (1975). Piagetian theory and biology teaching. *American Biology Teacher*, 37(6), 336–343.

Mathematics education [Special section]. (2007). *Phi Delta Kappan*, 88(9), 664–697.

National Research Council, Committee on Early Childhood Pedagogy. (2001). *Eager to learn: Educating our preschoolers* (B. Bowman, S. Donovan, & M. Burns, Eds.). Washington, DC: National Academies Press.

National Research Council. (2002). *Investigating the influence of standards: A framework for research in mathematics, science, and technology education.* Washington, DC: National Academies Press.

National Research Council. (2005). *How students learn: History, mathematics, and science in the classroom.* Committee on How People Learn, a targeted report for teachers (M. S. Donovan & J. D. Bransford, Eds.). Washington, DC: National Academies Press.

National Research Council. (2005). *Mathematical and scientific development in early childhood: A workshop summary.* Washington, DC: National Academies Press.

National Science Teachers Association. (1994). An NSTA position statement: Elementary school science. In *NSTA handbook*. Washington, DC: National Science Teachers Association.

Piaget, J. (1965). *The child's conception of number.* New York: Norton.

Richardson, K. (2000, October). Mathematics standards for pre-kindergarten through grade 2. *ERIC Digest* [EDO-PS-00-11].

Silverman, H. J. (2006). Explorations and discovery: A mathematics curriculum for toddlers. *ACEI Focus on Infants and Toddlers, 19*(2), 1–3, 6–7.

# Unit 2

## How Concepts Are Acquired

## OBJECTIVES

After reading this unit, you should be able to:

- List and define the three types of learning experiences described in the unit.
- Recognize examples of each of the three types of learning experiences.
- State possible responses to specific opportunities for the child to learn concepts.
- Be aware of variations in individual and cultural learning styles and capabilities and the need for curriculum integration.
- Know that children learn through interaction with peers as well as adults.
- Recognize the value of technology for young children's math and science learning.

Children learn with understanding when the learning takes place in meaningful and familiar situations. As children explore their familiar environments, they encounter experiences through which they actively construct knowledge and discover new relationships. The adult's role is to build upon this knowledge and support children as they move to higher levels of understanding. These initial child-controlled learning experiences can be characterized as **naturalistic learning**. Two other types of experiences are those characterized as **informal learning** and those that are **structured learning**.

*Naturalistic experiences* are those in which the child controls choice and action; *informal* is where the child chooses the activity and action, but with adult intervention at some point; and *structured* is where the adult chooses the experience for the child and gives some direction to the child's action (Figure 2–1).

Naturalistic experiences relate closely to the Piagetian view, and the informal and structured relate to the Vygotskian view.

Referring back to the learning cycle as described in Unit 1, it can be seen that these three types of experiences fit into the cycle. The learning cycle is basically a way to structure lessons so that all three ways of learning are experienced. Naturalistic experiences are encouraged at the awareness and the exploration levels. Informal experiences are added at the exploration, inquiry, and utilization levels. Structured experiences are more likely to appear at the inquiry and utilization levels.

In providing settings for learning and types of instruction, keep in mind that there are variations in learning styles among groups of children and among different cultural and ethnic groups. Some of these types of variations will be described later in the unit.

| TYPES OF ACTIVITY | INTERACTION EMPHASIZED |
|---|---|
| Naturalistic | Child/Environment |
| Informal | Child/Environment/Adult |
| Structured | Adult/Child/Environment |

**Figure 2–1** Concepts are learned through three types of activity.

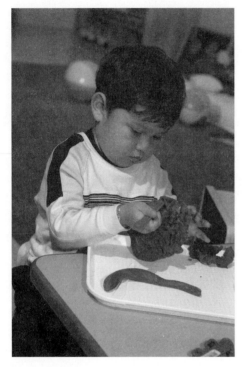

Children's naturalistic learning experiences involve the exploration of the environment.

## NATURALISTIC EXPERIENCES

Naturalistic experiences are those initiated spontaneously by children as they go about their daily activities. These experiences are the major mode of learning for children during the sensorimotor period. Naturalistic experiences can also be a valuable mode of learning for older children.

The adult's role is to provide an interesting and rich environment. That is, there should be many things for the child to look at, touch, taste, smell, and hear. The adult should observe the child's activity, note how it is progressing, and then respond with a glance, a nod, a smile, a verbal description of the child's actions or elaboration of the child's comments, or a word of praise to encourage the child. The child needs to know when he is doing the appropriate thing.

Some examples of naturalistic experiences include the following.

- Kurt hands Dad two pennies saying, "Here's your two dollars!"
- Isabel takes a spoon from the drawer—"This is big." Mom says, "Yes, that is a big spoon."
- Tito is eating orange segments. "I got three." (Holds up three fingers.)
- Nancy says, "Big girls are up to here," as she stands straight and points to her chin.
- Aika (age 4) sits on the rug and sorts colored rings into plastic cups.
- Tanya and Javier (both age 4) are having a tea party. Javier says, "The tea is hot."
- Sam (age 5) is painting. He makes a dab of yellow and then dabs some blue on top. "Hey! I've got green now."
- Trang Fung (age 6) is cutting her clay into many small pieces. Then she squashes it together into one big piece.
- Pilar (age 6) is restless during the after-lunch rest period. As she sits quietly with her head on her desk, her eyes rove around the room. Each day she notices the clock. One day she realizes that, when the teacher says, "One-fifteen, time to get up," the short hand is always on the 1 and the long hand is always on the 3. After that, Pilar knows how to watch the clock for the end of rest time.
- Theresa (age 7) is drawing with markers. They are in a container that has a hole to hold each one. Theresa notices that there is one extra hole. "There must be a lost marker," she comments.
- Mei (age 8) is experimenting with cup measures and containers. She notices that each cup measure holds the same amount even though each is a different shape. She also notices that you cannot always predict how many cups of liquid a container holds just by looking at it; the shape can fool you.

Informal learning experiences involve an adult or more advanced peer who provides comments or asks questions.

## INFORMAL LEARNING EXPERIENCES

Informal learning experiences are initiated by the adult as the child is engaged in a naturalistic experience. These experiences are not preplanned for a specific time. They occur when the adult's experience and/or intuition indicates it is time to scaffold. This might happen for various reasons—for example, the child might need help or is on the right track in solving a problem but needs a cue or encouragement. It might also happen because the adult has in mind some concepts that should be reinforced and takes advantage of a **teachable moment**. Informal learning experiences occur when an opportunity for instruction presents itself by chance. Some examples follow.

- "I'm six years old," says 3-year-old Kate while holding up three fingers. Dad says, "Let's count those fingers. One, two, three fingers. How old are you?"

- José (age 4) is setting the table. He gets frustrated because he does not seem to have enough cups. "Let's check," says his teacher. "There is one place mat for each chair. Let's see if there is one cup on each mat." They move around the table checking. They come to a mat with two cups. "Two cups," says José. "Hurrah!" says his teacher.

- With arms outstretched at various distances, Tim (age 4) asks, "Is this big? Is this big?" Mr. Brown says, "What do you think? What is 'this' big?" Tim looks at the distance between his hands with his arms stretched to the fullest. "This is a big person." He puts his hands about 18 inches apart. "This is a baby." He places his thumb and index finger about half of an inch apart. "This is a blackberry." Mr. Brown watches with a big smile on his face.

- Juanita (age 4) has a bag of cookies. Mrs. Ramirez asks, "Do you have enough for everyone?" Juanita replies, "I don't know." Mrs. R. asks, "How can you find out?" Juanita says, "I don't know." Mrs. R. suggests, "How about if we count the cookies?"

- Kindergartners Jorge and Sam are playing with some small rubber figures called Stackrobats. Jorge links some together horizontally, while Sam joins his vertically. The boys are competing to see who can make the longest line. When Jorge's line reaches across the diameter of the table, he encounters a problem. Miss Jones suggests that he might be able to figure out another way to link the figures together. He looks at Sam's line of figures and then at his. He realizes that if he links his figures vertically he can continue with the competition.

- Dean, a first grader, runs into Mrs. Red Fox's classroom on a spring day after a heavy rainstorm. He says, "Mrs. Red Fox! I have a whole bunch of worms." Mrs. Red Fox asks Dean where he found the worms and why there are so many out this morning. She suggests he put the worms on the science table where everyone can see them. Dean follows through and places a sign next to the can: "Wrms fnd by Dean."

- Second grader Liu Pei is working with blocks. She shows her teacher, Mr. Wang, that she has made three stacks of four blocks. She asks, "When I have three stacks of four, is that like when my big brother says 'three times four'?" "Yes," responds Mr. Wang. "When you have three stacks of four, that is three times four." Liu Pei has discovered some initial ideas about multiplication.

- Third grader Jason notices that each time he feeds Fuzzy the hamster, Fuzzy runs to the food pan before Jason opens the cage. He tells his teacher, who uses the opportunity to discuss anticipatory responses, why they develop, and their

Structured learning experiences are preplanned by an adult in order to meet specific learning objectives.

significance in training animals. He asks Jason to consider why this might happen so consistently and to think about other times he has noticed this type of response in other animals or humans. Several other children join the discussion. They decide to keep individual records of any anticipatory responses they observe for a week, compare observations, and note trends.

## STRUCTURED LEARNING EXPERIENCES

Structured experiences are preplanned lessons or activities. They can be done with individuals or small or large groups at a special time or an opportune time. They may follow the learning cycle sequence or consist of more focused direct instruction. The following are examples of some of these structured activities.

- *With an individual at a specific time with a specific focus.* Cindy is 4 years old. Her teacher decides that she needs some practice counting. She says, "Cindy, I have some blocks here for you to count. How many are in this pile?"
- *A learning cycle example.* Mrs. Red Fox sets up a new activity center in her room. There is a large tub filled with balls of several different sizes, colors, and textures. The children all have had some experience with balls and are aware of

them in the environment. Mrs. Red Fox points out the tub of balls to the students and tells them that they can explore the balls, looking at what is the same and different. She provides paper and markers that can be used to record what they learn. Each day the students gather for group reports about their daily activities. Those who have explored the balls report on their findings and share what they have recorded. Mrs. Red Fox asks questions and encourages the students to insert comments and questions. Finally, they discuss other things they might try to find out about the balls and other investigations they might make concerning the balls.

- *With an individual at an opportune time with a specific focus.* Mrs. Flores knows that Tanya needs help with the concept of shape. Tanya is looking for a game to play. Mrs. Flores says, "Try this shape-matching game, Tanya. There are squares, circles, and triangles on the big card. You find the little cards with the shapes that match."
- *With a group at an opportune time.* Mrs. Raymond has been working with the children on the concepts of light and heavy. They ask her to bring out some planks to make ramps to attach to the packing boxes and the sawhorses. She brings out the planks and explains to the group, "These are the heavy planks. These are the light planks. Which are stronger? Where should they go?"
- *With a large group at a specific time.* The students have had an opportunity to explore a collection of bones that they brought from home. Ms. Hebert realizes classification is an important concept that should be applied throughout the primary grades, since it is extremely important in organizing science data. Ms. Hebert puts out three large sheets of construction paper and has the students explore the different ways bones can be classified (such as chicken, turkey, duck, cow, pig, deer) or placed in subcategories (such as grouping chicken bones into wings, backs, legs, and so on).

Observe that, throughout the examples in this unit, the adults ask a variety of questions and provide different types of directions for using the materials. It is extremely important to ask many different types of questions. Questions vary as to whether they are *divergent* or *convergent*, and they also vary as to how difficult they are. **Divergent questions and directions** do not have one right answer but provide an opportunity for creativity, guessing, and experimenting. Questions that begin "Tell me about _____," "What do you think _____?," "What have you found out _____?," "What can we do with _____?," "Can you find a way to _____?," "What would happen if _____?," "Why do you think _____?," and directions such as "You can examine these _____" or "You may play with these _____" are divergent.

**Convergent questions and directions** ask for a specific response or activity. There is a specific piece of information called for, such as "How many _____?," "Tell me the names of the parts of a plant," "Find a ball smaller than this one," and so on. Adults often ask only convergent questions and give convergent directions. Remember that children need time to construct their ideas. Divergent questions and directions encourage them to think and act for themselves. Convergent questions and directions can provide the adult with specific information regarding what the child knows, but too many of these questions tend to make the child think that there might be only one right answer to all problems. This can squelch creativity and the willingness to guess and experiment.

By varying the difficulty of the questions asked, the teacher can reach children of different ability levels. For example, in the office supply store center, pencils are 2¢ and paper is 1¢ per sheet. An easy question might be, "If you want to buy one pencil and two sheets of paper, then how many pennies will you need?" A harder question would be, "If you have 10¢, how many pencils and how much paper could you buy?"

## ◼ LEARNING STYLES

In planning learning experiences for children, it is essential to consider individual and culturally determined styles of learning. Learning styles may relate to modalities such as auditory, visual, kinesthetic, or multisensory preferences. They may relate to temperamental characteristics such as the easygoing, serious student or the easily frustrated student. They also may relate

to strengths in particular areas such as those identified by Howard Gardner in his theory of **multiple intelligences** (Gardner, 1999). Gardner originally identified seven intelligences: *linguistic, logical-mathematical, bodily-kinesthetic, interpersonal, intrapersonal, musical,* and *spatial*. More recently he added two additional intelligences: *naturalist* and *existential*. Gardner conceptualizes these nine intelligences as combined biological and psychological potentials to process information that can be used in a culture to solve problems or create products that are valuable to the culture. It is important to provide children with opportunities to solve problems using their strongest modalities and areas of intelligence. Too often, conventional learning experiences focus on the linguistic (language) and logical-mathematical intelligences while ignoring the other areas. Children who may have strength in learning through active movement and concrete activities (bodily-kinesthetic learners) or those who learn best through interacting with peers (interpersonal learners) or via one of the other modalities may lose out on being able to develop concepts and skills to the fullest. Incorporating peer tutoring and offering opportunities for group projects expands on the chances for success.

The variety of learning styles can be accommodated by integrating the various curriculum areas rather than teaching each particular area (mathematics, science, social studies, language arts, visual arts, musical arts, etc.) separately. More and more attention is now being paid to integrated approaches to instruction (see Unit 22). In this text we focus on mathematics and science as the major focus with other content areas integrated. However, any one of the content areas can be the hub at different times with different purposes. The section on Further Reading and Resources includes some resources for curriculum integration. Integration is frequently pictured in a weblike structure similar to that constructed by spiders (Figure 2–2). The focus or theme of study is placed in the center, and the other content areas and/or major concepts are attached by the radials.

In planning and instruction, it is important to consider not only diversity in modality-related learning styles but also diversity in race, ethnicity, social class, gender, out-of-school experiences, and special needs. Whereas reform mathematics appears to have positive

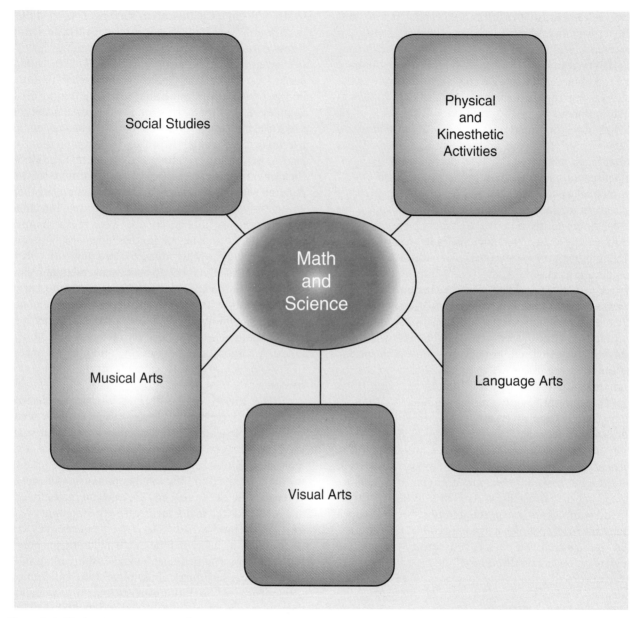

**Figure 2–2** The basic content area web pattern.

effects on achievement, research has not looked closely at how reform mathematics affects different groups. The reform classroom itself is a culture different from the traditional classroom. The reform movement is progressing from a linear, formal view of the teacher passing out knowledge to passive students to a setting where mathematics is constructed, discussed, and questioned by active students. The reform mathematics and science classroom is an active, productive culture. Unfortunately, developing this type of classroom is not easy because it requires the teacher to be tuned into each student's learning style and abilities. Reform mathematics is increasingly being criticized as "fuzzy math" (Lewin, 2006), and there is a movement toward again emphasizing basic drills and memorization. Yet there is a need to provide balanced instruction that provides for memorization *and* understanding.

Many fundamental concepts in mathematics and science are learned before the child enters school. Mathematics learned outside of school is referred to as **ethnomathematics** (Nunes, 1992). This type of mathematics is embedded in the out-of-school cultural activities whose primary purpose is not mathematics but rather to accomplish a culturally relevant task. Examples would be activities such as counting out equal shares, setting the table, calculating a recipe, exchanging money, or measuring one's height or weight. Each culture has its own way of doing these tasks. The problem teachers face is how to capitalize on what children learn outside of school while considering that some of these tasks may apply mathematics differently than it is used in the classroom. Teachers must learn about the everyday lives of their students and how mathematics concepts may be applied on a day-to-day basis. To connect out-of-school to in-school experiences, mathematics and science in school should be introduced by providing students with problems based on everyday experiences. Teachers can then observe as students construct solutions based on their out-of-school life experiences. Once students have developed their own strategies, the conventional strategies or algorithms and formulas can be introduced as an alternative means of solving problems.

Teachers need to be responsive to the diverse cultural values and experiences of their students in order to identify each individual's zone of proximal development and build from where the children are operating independently to where their capabilities can take them with appropriate scaffolding. Multicultural education is not a topic to be presented in one week or one month and then forgotten; it should permeate the whole curriculum. Practice should be both developmentally and culturally appropriate (de Melendez & Beck, 2007). Across cultures, children develop in the same sequence physically, socially, and intellectually but experience varied cultural experiences within their environments. Child-rearing practices and environmental variation provide the content of children's knowledge and views of the world. Behavior that is considered normal within a particular culture may be viewed as unacceptable by a teacher from another culture. Teachers need to study the cultures of their students before making any behavioral decisions. Claudia Zaslavsky (1996) emphasizes the incorporation of math games from many cultures as a means for promoting multiculturalism in the mathematics curriculum.

Equity also needs to be considered in relation to socioeconomic status (Clements & Sarama, 2002a). Research indicates that children from lower socioeconomic status (SES) homes lack important mathematics concepts. For example, counting might be limited to small groups and may not be accurate. Low-SES children who have had very little number experience at home might not be able to tell if one amount is more than another. However, several researchers have developed early childhood instructional programs that improve lower-SES children's mathematics understanding.

## Children with Special Needs

A great deal of research has documented the quantitative development of typical young children—information that can guide our instruction (Mix, Huttenlocher, & Levine, 2002)—but it is also important to consider the mathematical development and instruction of children with special needs. Wilmot and Thornton (1989) describe the importance of identifying appropriate mathematics instruction for special learners: those who are gifted and those with learning disabilities. Gifted students can be provided with enrichment experiences that go beyond numeracy and into probability, problem solving, geometry, and measurement. Children with disabilities may have any one or a combination of problems in memory, visual or auditory perception, discrimination deficits, abstract reasoning difficulties, or other difficulties that intrude on learning. Different approaches must be taken with each type of learner. Cooperative learning groups can be effective. Clements and Sarama (2002b) cite studies indicating that computer activities can help to increase all young children's mathematics skills and understanding. Providing positive experiences for young students with special needs can promote confidence as they move through school.

Geary (1996) describes how math anxiety and math disabilities can impede progress. Math anxiety results from a fear of mathematics, but it is hoped that a positive math experience in early childhood will prevent the development of math anxiety. About 6% of school-age children may have a **mathematics learning disorder (MLD)**. Some children cannot remember basic facts. Others cannot carry out basic procedures like solving a simple addition problem. Math disabilities may also result from brain injury. In his research, Geary found that about half of the students identified with MLD had no perceptual or neurological problem but more likely lacked experience, had poor motivation, or suffered from anxiety. Procedural problems are usually related to slow cognitive development and usually clear up by the middle elementary grades. The fact retrieval problem tends to continue. Some children have problems in reading and writing numbers and may also have problems in reading and writing words and letters. However, these problems usually are developmental and eventually disappear. Some children may have spatial relations problems, which show up when they misalign numbers in columns or reverse numbers. Geary concludes that early experiences that make necessary neural connections in the brain can lessen the chances of MLD.

Geary (1996, p. 285) suggests several ways to help children who have MLD.

- ■ *Memory problems.* Don't expect the child to memorize the basic facts. Provide alternative methods.
- ■ *Procedural problems.* Make sure the child understands the fundamental concepts. For example, be sure that they understand counting before being taught to count on. Then have the child practice the procedures.
- ■ *Visuospatial problems.* Provide prompts or cues that will help the child organize numbers so they are lined up correctly.
- ■ *Problem-solving difficulties.* First help the child with any basic skill difficulties. Have the child identify different types of word problems and help identify the steps needed to solve the problem.

Young children need to be carefully assessed and provided with extra practice and direct instruction if they don't seem to be developing and acquiring the fundamental concepts. Wright, Martland, Stafford, and Stanger (2002) provide a sequenced assessment and instruction method for teaching numbers to young children. Karp and Howell (2004) emphasize the importance of individualized approaches for children with learning disabilities. They describe four components of individualization.

- ■ *Remove specific barriers.* For example, if a child has motor difficulties that make writing difficult, let him give his explanations orally and put his responses on tape.
- ■ *Structure the environment.* Children with learning disabilities need a simple environment that is not overstimulating. They also require transitions that are carefully planned and clearly set up.
- ■ *Incorporate more time and practice.* Practice should be for frequent short periods, avoiding "drill and kill."
- ■ *Provide clarity.* Present problems clearly by using modeling, questioning, and presenting activities in small steps.

Ritz (2007) provides suggestions for supporting children with special needs in doing science. For example, many children have allergies or asthma. If a nonallergenic alternative material is not available for a science investigation, children might be supplied with protective gloves. A nature walk might be planned for a time of year when there is the least pollen and mold. Classroom accommodations for children with physical challenges should include the provision of easily accessible tables and areas. Teachers need to be responsive to each student's special needs and make appropriate accommodations.

## TECHNOLOGY

Technology is providing us with an ever-increasing array of learning tools. For example, young children can use interactive websites and software. Teachers can create their own websites. Teacher websites may provide a look into their classrooms, lists of favorite websites, and descriptions of student projects. The Internet provides many opportunities for learning.

Besides collecting information from the Internet, children can enjoy a variety of educational software. More and more preschools and elementary schools are including computers in the classrooms. Douglas H. Clements is a major researcher on the effective use of computers with young children (Clements, 1999, 2001; Clements & Sarama, 2002b). Computer activities can help children bridge the gap from concrete to abstract. Children can learn math and science concepts from software that presents a task, asks for a response, and provides feedback. However, software should go beyond drill and practice and provide for expressions of the child's creativity. Creating new shapes from other shapes or using turtles to draw shapes provides children with opportunities for exploration and discovery. Computers also provide social opportunities because children enjoy working together. One or more computers can serve as centers in the classroom. As children explore, the adult can provide suggestions or ask questions. Most importantly, the adult can observe and learn something about how children think and solve problems. Virtual manipulatives are now available online and in CD-ROM format (http://www.mattimath.com).

Calculators also can provide a tool for learning. In Unit 27 we describe some simple activities that young children can explore with calculators. An area for some concern centers on video games and whether children can learn through them (Sherman, 2007). Video games designed to teach basic concepts to young children are now on the market, and more are being designed.

## Assistive Technology

Assistive technology supports the learning of children with disabilities (Mulligan, 2003). Technology is available that can help children with developmental challenges "express ideas, play with a toy, or demonstrate understanding of developmental concepts" (Mulligan, 2003, p. 50). There are high-tech tools such as voice synthesizers, Braille readers, switch-activated toys, and computers. There are also low-tech tools that can expand the experiences of children with special needs. Special handles can be put on pans and paintbrushes. Pillows and bolsters can help a child have a place in circle time activities. A board with photos can be used as a means for a child to make choices. Selection of technology must consider the children served and their abilities, the environment, and the cost. Further information can be obtained from the Division of Early Childhood (DEC) of the Council for Exceptional Children. You may access the Online Companion™ to find a link to their website.

## SUMMARY

We have described and defined three types of learning experiences. Through practice, the teacher and parent learn how to make the best use of naturalistic, informal, and structured experiences so that the child has a balance of free exploration and specific planned activities. When planning activities, the children's learning styles and areas of strength should be considered. Culture, socioeconomic status, special needs, and previous experience are all important factors. Technology—in the form of computers and calculators—provides valuable tools for learning math and science concepts.

## KEY TERMS

| | | |
|---|---|---|
| convergent questions and directions | ethnomathematics | multiple intelligences |
| divergent questions and directions | informal learning | naturalistic learning |
| | mathematics learning disorder (MLD) | structured learning |
| | | teachable moment |

## SUGGESTED ACTIVITIES

1. Observe a prekindergarten, kindergarten, and primary classroom. Keep a record of concept learning experiences that are naturalistic, informal, and structured. Compare the differences in the numbers of each type of experience observed in each of the classrooms.

2. During your observations, also note any times you think opportunities for naturalistic or informal learning experiences were missed.

3. Note whether or not the various types of diversity (learning styles, ethnic, gender, and so on) appear to be considered in the instructional program.

4. Visit a teacher-developed website. Write a report describing the ways students use the Internet and contribute to the site.

5. Douglas Clements (1999) describes the software listed below. See if you can find a classroom that has any of these items available and observe children using it. Write a description of the children's thinking and problem solving you observe.

   - *Shapes* (Lebanon, IN: Dale Seymour Publications)

   - *Turtle Geometry* program (Highgate Springs, VT: LCSI)

   - *LEGO-Logo* (Enfield, CT: Lego Systems, Inc.)

   - *Millie's Math House* (San Francisco: Riverdeep-Edmark)

   - *Kid Pix Deluxe 3* (San Francisco: Broderbund)

   Try out one of the software evaluation tools found on the Internet. Examples can be found in the Online Companion at http://www.Early ChildEd.delmar.com.

6. Explore the National Library of Virtual Manipulatives materials online at http://nlvm.usu .edu. Evaluate their usefulness. What are the strengths and weakness? Have a child try an activity at his or her developmental level.

7. Evaluate a website that provides mathematics and/or science information and activities for children. Suggested sites can be found in the Online Companion at http://www .EarlyChildEd.delmar.com. Write an analysis using the following suggestions from Maria Timmerman (2004).

   - Briefly describe the website.

   - Describe the interactive features of the site.

   - Describe the concept understanding promoted by the site.

   - Describe how one manipulative might be paired with a concept included in the site.

   - Describe a feature of the site that motivates children to continue.

   - Explain how you would assess student learning (such as by journal writing, a recording sheet, observation, or an interview).

## REVIEW

A. Write a description of each of the three types of learning experiences described in this unit.

B. Decide if each of the following examples is naturalistic, informal, or structured:

   1. "Mother, I'll cut this apple in two parts so you can have some." "Yes, then I can have half of the apple."

   2. John (age 19 months) is lining up small blocks and placing a toy person on each one.

   3. A teacher and six children are sitting at a table. Each child has a pile of Unifix Cubes. "Make a train with the pattern A-B-A-B."

4. "I think I gave everyone two cookies," says Zang He. "Show me how you can check to be sure," says Mr. Brown.

5. Four children are pouring sand in the sandbox. They have a variety of containers of assorted sizes and shapes. "I need a bigger cup, please," says one child to another.

6. The children are learning about recycling. "Everyone sort your trash collection into a pile of things that can be used again and a pile of things that will have to be discarded."

7. Trang Fung brings her pet mouse to school. Each child observes the mouse and asks Trang Fung questions about its habits. Several children draw pictures and write stories about the mouse.

8. Mrs. Red Fox introduces her class to LOGO through structured floor games. The children take turns pretending to be a turtle and try to follow commands given by the teacher and the other students.

C. Read each of the following situations and explain how you would react:

1. George and Dina are setting the table in the home living center. They are placing one complete place setting in front of each chair.

2. Samantha says, "I have more crayons than you do, Hillary." "No, you don't." "Yes, I do!"

3. The children in Mr. Wang's class are discussing the show they must put on for the students in the spring. Some children want to do a show with singing and dancing; others do not. Brent suggests that they vote. The others agree. Derrick and Theresa count the votes. They agree that there are 17 in favor of a musical show and 10 against.

D. Explain why it is important to consider individual and cultural learning styles when planning instruction for young children.

E. Match the math learning problem on the left with the correct definition on the right.

1. Memory problem

2. Procedural problem

3. Visuospatial problem

4. Difficulty solving problems involving basic number facts

a. Child needs help in basic problem solving and fundamental skills

b. May be evidenced by misaligning numbers

c. Evidenced by student continuing to do finger counting well into the primary grades when engaged with math problems

d. Usually related to slow cognitive development and clears up by the middle elementary grades

F. Decide which of the following statements are true about technology.

1. Computers and calculators are not appropriate tools for young children to use.

2. Kindergartners can learn to use the Internet to gain information.

3. The value of computers as learning tools depends on the developmental appropriateness and quality of the software selected.

4. Drill and practice computer software is the most appropriate for young children.

5. Assistive technology is available to enhance the learning experiences of children with disabilities.

## REFERENCES

Clements, D. H. (1999). The effective use of computers with young children. In J. V. Copely (Ed.), *Mathematics in the early years* (pp. 119–128). Washington, DC: National Association for the Education of Young Children, and Reston, VA: National Council of Teachers of Mathematics.

Clements, D. H. (2001). Mathematics in the preschool. *Teaching Children Mathematics, 7*(5), 270–275.

Clements, D. H., & Sarama, J. (2002a). Mathematics curricula in early childhood. *Teaching Children Mathematics, 9*(3), 163–166.

Clements, D. H., & Sarama, J. (2002b). The role of technology in early childhood learning. *Teaching Children Mathematics, 8*(6), 340–343.

de Melendez, W. R., & Beck, V. (2007). *Teaching young children in multicultural classrooms* (2nd ed.). Albany, NY: Thomson Delmar Learning.

Gardner, H. (1999). *Intelligence reframed*. New York: Basic Books.

Geary, D. C. (1996). *Children's mathematical development*. Washington, DC: American Psychological Association.

Karp, K., & Howell, P. (2004). Building responsibility for learning in students with special needs. *Teaching Children Mathematics, 11*(3), 118–126.

Lewin, T. (2006, November 14). As Math Scores Lag, a New Push for the Basics. *New York Times*. Retrieved November 20, 2006, from http://www.newyorktimes.com

Mix, K. S., Huttenlocher, J., & Levine, S. C. (2002). *Quantitative development in infancy and early childhood*. New York: Oxford University Press.

Mulligan, S. A. (2003). Assistive technology: Supporting the participation of children with disabilities. *Young Children, 58*(6), 50–51.

Nunes, T. (1992). Ethnomathematics and everyday cognition. In D. A. Grouws (Ed.), *Handbook of research on mathematics teaching and learning* (pp. 557–574). New York: Macmillan.

Ritz, W. C. (Ed.). (2007). *Head start on science*. Arlington, VA: National Science Teachers Association.

Sherman, D. (2007, March 16). *More video games, fewer books at schools?* Retrieved May 25, 2007, from http://uk.reuters.com

Timmerman, M. (2004). Using the Internet: Are prospective elementary teachers prepared to teach with technology? *Teaching Children Mathematics, 10*(8), 410–415.

Wilmot, B., & Thornton, C. A. (1989). Mathematics teaching and learning: Meeting the needs of special learners. In P. R. Trafton & A. P. Shulte (Eds.), *New directions for elementary school mathematics* (pp. 212–222). Reston, VA: National Council of Teachers of Mathematics.

Wright, R. J., Martland, J., Stafford, A. K., & Stanger, G. (2002). *Teaching number: Advancing children's skills and strategies*. Thousand Oaks, CA: Chapman.

Zaslavsky, C. (1996). *The multicultural math classroom*. Portsmouth, NH: Heinemann.

## FURTHER READING AND RESOURCES

Adams, T. L. (2000/2001). Helping children learn mathematics through multiple intelligences and standards for school mathematics. *Childhood Education, 77*(2), 86–92.

Baker, A., Schirner, K., & Hoffman, J. (2006). Multiage mathematics: Scaffolding young children's mathematical learning. *Teaching Children Mathematics, 13*(1), 19–21.

Balfanz, R., Ginsburg, H. P., & Greenes, C. (2003). The *Big Math for Little Kids* early childhood mathematics program. *Teaching Children Mathematics, 9*(5), 264–268.

Baroody, A. J. (2000). Does mathematics instruction for three- to five-year-olds really make sense? *Young Children, 55*(4), 61–67.

Buckleitner, W. (2007, April). Helping young children find and use information. *Scholastic Early Childhood Today*, 33–38.

Charlesworth, R. (2003). *Understanding child development* (6th ed.). Clifton Park, NY: Thomson Delmar Learning.

Clements, D. H., & Sarama, J. (2002). The role of technology in early childhood learning. *Teaching Children Mathematics, 8*(6), 340–343.

Clements, D. H., & Sarama, J. (2003, January/ February). Creative pathways to math. *Early Childhood Today*, 37–45.

Copely, J. V. (Ed.). (1999). *Mathematics in the early years*. Washington, DC: National Association for the Education of Young Children, and Reston, VA: National Council of Teachers of Mathematics.

Creative integration [Focus section]. (2007). *Science and Children*, 44(6).

Donovan, M. S., & Bransford, J. D. (Eds.). (2005). *How students learn: History, mathematics, and science in the classroom*. Washington, DC: National Academies Press.

Epstein, A. (2007). *The intentional teacher*. Washington, DC: National Association for the Education of Young Children.

Geist, E. (2001). Children are born mathematicians: Promoting the construction of early mathematical concepts in children under five. *Young Children*, 56(4), 12–17.

Ginsburg, H. P., Inoue, N., & Seo, K. (1999). Young children doing mathematics. In J. V. Copely (Ed.), *Mathematics in the early years* (pp. 88–91). Washington, DC: National Association for the Education of Young Children, and Reston, VA: National Council of Teachers of Mathematics.

Helm, J. H., & Katz, L. G. (2001). *Young investigators: The project approach in the early years*. New York: Teachers College Press.

Henderson, A., & Miles, E. (2001). *Basic topics in mathematics for dyslexics*. Florence, KY: Whurr/ Taylor & Francis.

Kamii, C. (with Housman, L. B.). (2000). *Young children reinvent arithmetic: Implications of Piaget's theory* (2nd ed.). New York: Teachers College Press.

Kerrigan, J. (2002). Powerful software to enhance the elementary school mathematics program. *Teaching Children Mathematics*, 8(6), 364–370.

Leonard, J., & Guha, S. (2002). Creating cultural relevance in teaching and learning mathematics. *Teaching Children Mathematics*, 9(2), 114–118.

Mathematics and culture [Focus issue]. (2001). *Teaching Children Mathematics*, 7(6).

Moyer, P. S., Bolyard, J. J., & Spikell, M. A. (2002). What are virtual manipulatives? *Teaching Children Mathematics*, 8(6), 372–377.

National Research Council. (1996). *National science education standards*. Washington, DC: National Academies Press.

Sarama, J., & Clements, D. H. (2003). Building blocks of early childhood mathematics. *Teaching Children Mathematics*, 9(8), 480–484.

Sarama, J., & Clements, D. H. (2006). Mathematics in kindergarten. In D. F. Gullo (Ed.), *Teaching and learning in the kindergarten year* (pp. 85–115). Washington, DC: National Association for the Education of Young Children.

Silverman, H. J. (2006). Explorations and discovery to a mathematics curriculum for toddlers. *ACEI Focus on Infants & Toddlers*, 19(2), 1–3, 6–7.

Stavy, R., & Tirosh, D. (2000). *How students (mis)understand science and mathematics: Intuitive rules*. New York: Teachers College Press.

Yoon, J., & Onchwari, J. A. (2006). Teaching young children science: Three key points. *Early Childhood Education Journal*, 33(6), 419–423.

Zaslavsky, C. (1998). *Math games and activities from around the world*. Chicago: Chicago Review Press.

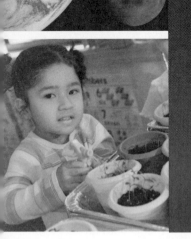

# Unit 3

# Promoting Young Children's Concept Development through Problem Solving

## OBJECTIVES

After reading this unit, you should be able to:

■ List and describe the six steps in instruction suggested in this unit.

■ Identify examples of each of the six steps in instruction.

■ Describe the advantages of using the six steps in instruction.

■ Evaluate a teacher's instructional approach relative to the six steps.

■ Recognize routine and nonroutine problems.

■ Explain the term *heuristic* and its significance for mathematics problem solving.

■ List the five NCTM process standards.

■ Understand the value of estimation techniques.

■ Implement developmentally appropriate problem-solving assessment and instruction.

The focus of instruction in science and mathematics should be **problem solving** and **inquiry**. Not only should teacher-developed problems and investigations be worked on, but child-generated problems and investigations also should be important elements in instruction. A problem-solving/inquiry focus emphasizes children working independently and in groups while the teacher serves as a facilitator and a guide. For the program to succeed, the teacher must know the students well so that she can support them in reaching their full capacities within the zone of proximal development. This unit outlines the basic instructional process and then describes the problem-solving inquiry approach to instruction as it applies to mathematics. In later units,

science investigations serve as examples of problem solving and inquiry in science.

The steps involved in planning concept experiences are the same as those used for any subject area. Six questions must be answered (Figure 3–1).

■ **Assess**: Where is the child now?

■ **Choose objectives**: What should she learn next?

■ **Plan experiences**: What should the child do to accomplish these objectives?

■ **Select materials**: Which materials should be used to carry through the plan?

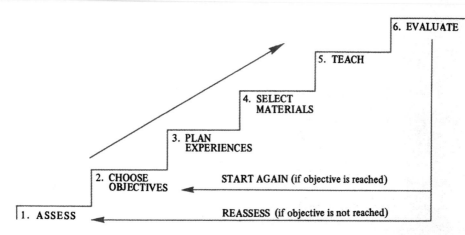

**Figure 3–1** What should be taught and how?—FOLLOW THE STEPS.

■ **Teach**: (do the planned experiences with the child): Do the plan and the materials fit?

■ **Evaluate**: Has the child learned what was taught (reached objectives)?

## ASSESSING

Each child should be individually *assessed*. Two methods for this are used most frequently. Children can be interviewed individually using specific tasks, and they can be observed during their regular activities. The purpose of assessment is to find out what children know and what they can do before instruction is planned. The topic of assessment is covered in detail in Unit 4.

### Specific Task Assessment

The following are examples of some specific tasks that can be given to a child.

■ Present the child with a pile of 10 counters (buttons, coins, poker chips, or other small things) and say, "Count these for me."

■ Show the child two groups of chips: a group of three and a group of six. Ask, "Which group has more chips?"

■ Show the child five cardboard dolls, each one a half inch taller than the next. Say: "Which is the tallest?" "Which is the smallest?" "Line them up from the smallest to the tallest."

■ Provide a 6-year-old with an assortment of toy cars. Say: "Pretend you have a used car business. A customer wants to buy all your red cars and all your blue cars. Figure out how many of each he would be buying and how many he would be buying altogether. See how many ways you can solve this problem using the toy cars. You may also want to draw a picture or write about what you did."

■ Provide a 7-year-old with a container of at least 100 counting chips. Say: "The zoo has a collection of 17 birds. They buy 12 more birds. Five birds get out of the aviary and fly away. How many birds do they have now? You can use the counters to figure it out. Then draw a picture and even write about what you did."

■ Place a pile of 30 counting chips in front of an 8-year-old. Say: "Find out how many different sets of two, three, five, and six you can make from this pile of chips." Record your findings.

### Assessment by Observation

The following are examples of observations that can be made as children play and/or work.

■ Does the 1-year-old show an interest in experimenting by pouring things in and out of containers of different sizes?

Assessment can be done through observation of children using math materials.

■ Does the 2-year-old spend time sorting objects and lining them up in rows?

■ Does the 3-year-old show an interest in understanding size, age, and time by asking how big he is, how old he is, and "when will _____" questions?

■ Does the 4-year-old set the table correctly? Does he ask for help to write numerals, and does he use numbers in his play activities?

■ Can the 5-year-old divide a bag of candy so that each of his friends receives an equal share?

■ If there are five children and three chairs, can a 6-year-old figure out how many more chairs are needed so that everyone will have one?

■ If a 7-year-old is supposed to feed the hamster two tablespoons of pellets each day, can she decide how much food should be left for the weekend?

■ Four 8-year-olds are making booklets. Each booklet requires four pieces of paper. Can the children figure out how many pieces of paper will be needed to make the four booklets?

Through observation, the teacher can find out if the child can apply concepts to real-life problems and activities. By keeping a record of these observations, the teacher builds up a more complete picture of the child's strengths and weaknesses. The current trend involves collecting samples of student work, photographs, audio tapes, and videotapes to construct a portfolio that represents student accomplishments over time. Assessment will be discussed in more detail in Unit 4.

## CHOOSING OBJECTIVES

Once the child's level of knowledge is identified, *objectives can be selected*. That is, a decision can be made as to what the child should be able to learn next. For instance, look at the first task example in the previous section. Suppose a 5-year-old child counts 50 objects correctly. The objective for this child would be different from the one for another 5-year-old who can count only seven objects accurately. The first child does not need any special help with object counting. A child who counts objects at this level at age 5 can probably figure out how to go beyond 50 alone. The second child might need some help and specific activities with counting objects beyond groups of seven.

Suppose a teacher observes that a 2-year-old spends very little time sorting objects and lining them up in rows. The teacher knows that this is an important activity for a child of this age, one that most 2-year-olds engage in naturally without any special instruction. The objective selected might be that the child would choose to spend five minutes each day sorting and organizing objects. Once the objective is selected, the teacher then decides how to go about helping the child reach it.

## PLANNING EXPERIENCES

Remember that young children construct concepts through naturalistic activities as they explore the environment. As they grow and develop, they feel the need to organize and understand the world around them. Children have a need to label their experiences and the things they observe. They notice how older children and adults count, use color words, label time, and so on. An instinctive knowledge of math and science concepts develops before an abstract understanding. When planning, it is important for adults to keep the following in mind.

- Naturalistic experiences should be emphasized until the child is into the preoperational period.
- Informal instruction is introduced during the sensorimotor period and increases in frequency during the preoperational period.
- Structured experiences are used sparingly during the sensorimotor and early preoperational periods and are brief and sharply focused.
- Follow the learning cycle format.

Abstract experiences can be introduced gradually during the preoperational and transitional periods and increased in frequency as the child reaches concrete exploratory operations, but they should always be preceded by concrete experiences. Keep these factors in mind when planning for young children. These points are covered in detail in the following section on selecting materials. In any case, the major focus for instructional planning is the promotion of individual and group problem solving and inquiry.

Planning involves deciding the best way for each child to accomplish the selected objectives. Will naturalistic, informal, and/or structured experiences be best? Will the child acquire the concept best on her own? With a group of children? One-to-one with an adult? In a small group directed by an adult? Once these questions have been answered, the materials can be chosen. Sections 2 through 6 tell how to plan these experiences for the concepts and skills that are acquired during the early years.

## SELECTING MATERIALS

Three things must be considered when selecting science and math materials. First, there are some general characteristics of good materials. They should be sturdy, well made, and constructed so that they are safe for children to use independently. They should also be useful for more than one kind of activity and for teaching more than one concept.

Second, the materials must be designed for acquisition of the selected concepts. In other words, they must fit the objective(s).

Third, the materials must fit the children's levels of development; that is, they must be developmentally appropriate. As stated, acquiring a concept begins with concrete experiences with real things. For each concept included in the curriculum, materials should be sequenced from concrete to abstract and from three-dimensional (real objects), to two-dimensional (cutouts), to pictorial, to paper and pencil. Too often, however, the first steps are skipped and children are immersed in paper-and-pencil activities without the prerequisite concrete experiences and before they have developed the perceptual and motor skills necessary to handle a writing implement with ease. Five steps to be followed from concrete materials to paper and pencil are described as follows. Note that Step 1 is the first and last step during the sensorimotor period; during the preoperational period, the children move from Step 1 through Step 4; and during the transition and concrete operations periods, they move into Step 5.

- *Step 1*. Real objects are used for this first step. Children are given time to explore and manipulate many types of objects such as blocks, chips, stones, and sticks as well as materials such as sand, water, mud, clay, and Play-Doh. Whether instruction is naturalistic, informal, or structured, concrete materials are used.
- *Step 2*. Real objects are used along with pictorial representations. For example, blocks can be matched with printed or drawn patterns. When cooking, each implement to be used (measuring spoons and cups, bowls, mixing spoons, etc.) can be depicted on a pictorial sequenced recipe chart. Children can draw pictures each day showing the height of their bean sprouts.
- *Step 3*. Cutouts that can be manipulated by hand are introduced. For example, cardboard cutouts of different sizes, colors, and shapes can be sorted. Cutout dogs can be matched with

cutout doghouses. Cutout human body parts can be put together to make a whole body. Although the materials have moved into two dimensions, they can still be manipulated. By manipulating the materials, the child can try a variety of solutions to the problem by trial and error and can engage in self-correction.

■ *Step 4*. Pictures are next. Commercially available pictorial materials, teacher-created or magazine pictures, and cut-up workbook pages can be used to make card games as well as sequencing, sorting, and matching activities. For example, pictures of people in various occupations might be matched with pictures of their work tools. Pictures of a person at different ages can be sequenced from baby to old age. Groups of objects drawn on a card can be counted and matched with the appropriate numeral.

## Stop Here If the Children Have Not Yet Reached the Transition Stage

■ *Step 5*. At this level, paper-and-pencil activities are introduced. When the teacher observes that the children understand the concept with materials at the first four levels, it is time for Step 5. If the materials are available, children usually start experimenting when they feel ready. Now they can draw and write about mathematics.

An example of sequencing materials using the five steps follows. Suppose one of the objectives for children in kindergarten is to compare differences in dimensions. One of the dimensions to be compared is length. Materials can be sequenced as follows:

■ *Step 1: Real objects*. Children explore the properties of Unifix Cubes and Cuisinaire Rods. They fit Unifix Cubes together into groups of various lengths. They compare the lengths of the Cuisinaire Rods. They do measurement activities such as comparing how many Unifix Cubes fit across the short side of the table versus the long side of the table.

■ *Step 2: Real objects with pictures*. The Unifix Cubes are used to construct rows that match pictured

patterns of various lengths. Sticks are used to measure pictured distances from one place to another.

■ *Step 3: Cutouts*. Unifix and Cuisinaire cutouts are used to make rows of various lengths. Cutouts of snakes, fences, and so on are compared.

■ *Step 4: Pictures*. Cards with pictures of pencils of different lengths are sorted and matched. A picture is searched for the long and the short path, the dog with long ears, the dog with short ears, the long hose, the short hose, and so on.

## Stop Here If the Children Have Not Yet Reached the Transition Stage

■ *Step 5: Paper and pencil activities*. For example, students might draw long and short things.

At the early steps, children might be able to make comparisons of materials with real objects or even with cutouts and picture cards, but they might fail if given just paper-and-pencil activities. In this case it would be falsely assumed that they do not understand the concept when, in fact, it is the materials that are inappropriate. Calculators and computers can be used at every step. Virtual manipulatives can be supportive of learning.

The chart in Figure 3–2 depicts the relationship between the cognitive developmental periods—naturalistic, informal, and structured ways of acquiring concepts—and the five levels of materials. Each unit of this text has examples of various types of materials. Section 7 contains lists and descriptions of many that are excellent teaching aids.

## TEACHING

Once the decision has been made as to what the child should be able to learn next and in what context the concept acquisition will take place, the next stage in the instructional process is teaching. *Teaching* occurs when the planned experiences using the selected materials are put into operation. If the first four questions have been answered with care, the experience should go smoothly. A child will be interested and will learn from

| PERIODS OF DEVELOPMENT | HOW CONCEPTS ARE ACQUIRED | | |
|---|---|---|---|
| | Naturalistic | Informal | Structured |
| Sensorimotor | Real objects<br>Objects and pictures<br>Pictures | Real objects<br>Objects and pictures<br>Pictures | |
| Preoperational | Real objects<br>Objects and pictures<br>Cutouts<br>Pictures | Real objects<br>Objects and pictures<br>Cutouts<br>Pictures<br>Calculators and computers | Real objects<br>Objects and pictures<br>Cutouts<br>Pictures<br>Calculators and computers |
| Transitional | Real objects<br>Objects and pictures<br>Cutouts<br>Pictures | Real objects<br>Objects and pictures<br>Cutouts<br>Pictures<br>Paper and pencil<br>Calculators and computers | Real objects<br>Objects and pictures<br>Cutouts<br>Pictures<br>Calculators and computers |
| Concrete Operations | Real objects<br>Objects and pictures<br>Cutouts<br>Pictures | Real objects<br>Objects and pictures<br>Cutouts<br>Pictures<br>Paper and pencil<br>Calculators and computers | Real objects<br>Objects and pictures<br>Cutouts<br>Pictures<br>Paper and pencil<br>Calculators and computers |

Figure 3–2 Two dimensions of early childhood concept instruction with levels of materials used.

the activities because they match his level of development and style of learning. The child might even acquire a new concept or skill or extend and expand one already learned.

The time involved in the teaching stage might be a few minutes or several weeks, months, or even years, depending on the particular concept being acquired and the age and ability of the child. For instance, time sequence is initially learned through naturalistic activity. From infancy, children learn that there is a sequence in their daily routines: sleeping; waking up wet and hungry; crying; being picked up, cleaned, fed, and played with; and sleeping again. In preschool, children learn a daily routine such as coming in, greeting the teacher, hanging up coats, eating breakfast, playing indoors, having a group activity time, snacking, playing outdoors, having a quiet activity, lunch, playing outdoors, napping, having a small group activity time, and going home. Time words are acquired informally as children

hear terms such as *yesterday, today, tomorrow, o'clock, next, after,* and so on. In kindergarten, special events and times are noted on a calendar. Children learn to name the days of the week and months of the year and to sequence the numerals for each of the days. In first grade, they might be given a blank calendar page to fill in the name of the month, the days of the week, and the number for each day. Acquiring the concept of time is a complex experience and involves many prerequisite concepts that build over several years. Some children will learn at a fast rate, others at a slow pace. One child might learn that there are seven days in a week the first time this idea is introduced; another child might take all year to acquire this information. Some children need a great deal of structured repetition; others learn from naturalistic and informal experiences. Teaching developmentally involves flexible and individualized instruction.

Even with careful planning and preparation, an activity might not work well the first time. When this happens, analyze the situation by asking the following questions.

- ■ Was the child interested?
- ■ Was the task too easy or too hard?
- ■ Did the child understand what she was asked to do?
- ■ Were the materials right for the task?
- ■ Were the materials interesting?
- ■ Is further assessment needed?
- ■ Was the teacher enthusiastic?
- ■ Was it just a "bad day" for the child?

You might try the activity again using the same method and the same materials or with a change in the method and/or materials. In some cases, the child might have to be reassessed in order to ensure that the activity is appropriate for her developmental level.

## EVALUATING

The sixth question concerns *evaluation*. What has the child learned? What does he know and what can he do after the concept experiences have been presented? The assessment questions are asked again. If the child has reached the objective, a new one can be chosen. The stages of planning, choosing materials, teaching, and evaluating are repeated. If the child has not reached the objective, the same activities can be continued or a new method may be tried. For example, a teacher wants a 5-year-old to count out the correct number of objects for each of the number symbols from 0 to 10. She tries many kinds of objects for the child to count and many kinds of containers in which to place the things he counts, but the child is just not interested. Finally she gives him small banks made from baby food jars and real pennies. The child finds these materials exciting and goes on to learn the task quickly and with enthusiasm.

Evaluation may be done using formal, structured questions as well as tasks and specific observations (see Unit 4). Informal questions and observations of naturalistic experiences can also be used for evaluation. For example, when a child sets the table in the wrong way, it can be seen without formal questioning that he has not learned from instruction. He needs some help. Maybe organizing and placing a whole table setting is more than he can do now. Can he place one item at each place? Does he need to go back to working with a smaller number (such as a table for two or three)? Does he need to work with simpler materials that have more structure (such as pegs in a pegboard)? To look at these more specific skills, the teacher would then return to the assessment step. At this point she would assess not only the child but also the types of experiences and materials that she has been using. Sometimes assessment leads the teacher to the right objective, but the experience and/or materials chosen are not (as in the example given) the ones that fit the child.

Frequent and careful evaluation helps both teacher and child avoid frustration. An adult must never take it for granted that any one plan or any one material is the best choice for a specific child. The adult must keep checking to be sure the child is learning what the experience was planned to teach him.

## PROBLEM SOLVING AND THE PROCESS STANDARDS

In Unit 1 we outlined the process standards for school mathematics (NCTM, 2000). These five standards include problem solving, reasoning and proof, communication, connections, and representation. *Problem solving* involves application of the other four standards. Although preoperational children's *reasoning* is different from that of older children and adults, it is logical from their own point of view. Pattern recognition and classification skills provide the focus for much of young children's reasoning. Adults should encourage children to make guesses and to explain their reasoning. Language is a critical element in mathematics (see Unit 15). Children can explain how they approach problem solving by *communication* with language. Even the youngest students can talk about mathematics and, as they grow older, can write and draw about it. The important *connections* for young mathematicians are those made between informal mathematics and the formal mathematics of the school curriculum. The transition can be made with the use of concrete objects and by connecting to everyday activities such as table setting, finding out how many children are present in the class, and recognizing that when they surround a parachute they are forming a circle. Young children use several kinds of *representations* to explain their ideas: oral language, written language using invented and conventional symbols, physical gestures, and drawings.

Skinner (1990, p. 1) provides the following definition of a problem: "A problem is a question which engages someone in searching for a solution." This means a problem is some question that is important to the student and thus focuses her attention and enthusiasm on the search for a solution. Problem solving is not a special topic; it should be a major focus for every concept and skill in the mathematics and science programs. Problem solving becomes a type of lesson where the teacher sets up a situation for children to learn through inquiry.

Problems should relate to and include the children's own experiences. From birth onward, children want to learn and naturally seek out problems to solve. Problem solving in school should build on the informal methods learned out of school. Problem solving through the prekindergarten years focuses on naturalistic and informal learning, which promotes exploration and discovery. In kindergarten and primary classes, a more structured approach can be instituted. Every new topic should be introduced with a problem designed to afford children the opportunity to construct their own problem-solving strategies. For an overall look at implementing a problem-solving approach for kindergarten and primary students, read Skinner's book, *What's Your Problem?* (1990). Also refer to the resources listed at the end of this unit.

# PROBLEM SOLVING IN SCIENCE

The driving force behind problem solving is curiosity—an interest in finding out. Problem solving is not as much teaching strategy as it is a student behavior. The challenge for the teacher is to create an environment in which problem solving can occur. Encouragement of problem-solving behavior in a primary classroom can be seen in the following examples.

■ After his class has studied the movement and structure of the human body, Mr. Brown adds a final challenge to the unit. He has the children work with partners and poses the following situation, asking each pair to come up with a solution to the problem: "You like to play video games, but your family is worried because your wrists seem to be hurting from the motion you use to play the games. Plan a solution to the problem and role-play the family discussion that might take place."

■ Mr. Wang's class is studying the habitats of animals that live in water and the impact of humans on the environment. One of the problems he poses to the students is to decide what they will do in the following situation: "You are looking forward to an afternoon of fishing at the lake near your home. When you get there you see a sign that was never there before. It says 'No Fishing.' What do you do?"

The asking and answering of questions is what problem solving is all about. When the situations and problems that the students wonder about are perceived as real, their curiosity is stimulated and they want to find an answer.

Research indicates that working with concrete materials and drawing and/or writing explanations of solutions for problems are the best support for improving problem-solving skills. It is important to keep in mind that the process skills discussed in Unit 5 are essential to thinking and acting on a problem.

## Four Steps in Problem Solving

Although people disagree about the exact number of steps it takes for a learner to solve a problem, there seem to be four basic steps that are essential to the process.

1. *Identifying a problem and communicating it in a way that is understood.* This might involve assessing the situation and deciding exactly what is being asked or what is needed.

2. *Determining what the outcome of solving the problem might be.* This step involves the students

in organizing a plan that will achieve their problem-solving goal(s).

3. *Exploring possible solutions and applying them to the problem*. In this step, the plan is executed using appropriate strategies and materials. Children must learn that their first approach to solving a problem might be erroneous but that a solution will materialize if they keep trying. It is essential that children have the opportunity to explain their solutions to others; this will help clarify the problem and help them be better able to explain the problem to themselves.

4. *Explain the possible solutions and revised solution* if they do not seem to work as well as hoped. Because there is no one correct answer or way to arrive at an answer, there will be a variety of results. There may, in fact, be no answer to the problem.

Whether the lesson is part of the learning cycle, a culminating activity, or an unstructured experience, keep in mind that, first and foremost, student curiosity must be stimulated with problems that engage, intrigue, and motivate before problem solving can occur. As students understand and learn how to apply the basic steps of the problem-solving process, they will be able to make connections with their past experiences while keeping an open mind. The teacher's role is that of a facilitator, using instructional strategies to create a classroom rich with opportunities and where students are enthusiastic about learning and developing problem-solving skills that will last a lifetime.

## OVERVIEW OF PROBLEM SOLVING IN MATHEMATICS

Problem solving is a major focus in the mathematics program today. As students enter the transition into concrete operations, they can engage in more structured problem-solving activities. These activities promote children's abilities to develop their own problems and translate them into a symbolic format (writing and/or drawing). This sequence begins with the teacher providing problems and then gradually pulling back as students develop their own problems.

There are two major types of problems: **routine** and **nonroutine**. Consider the following descriptions of students working on problems.

■ Brent and the other children in his class have been given the following problem by their teacher, Mr. Wang. "Derrick has 10 pennies. John has 16 pennies. How many pennies do they have altogether?" Brent notes the key words "How many altogether?" and decides that this is an addition problem. He adds $10 + 16$ and finds the answer: 26 pennies.

■ Mr. Wang has also given them the following problem to solve. "Juanita and Lai want to buy a candy bar that costs 35¢. Juanita has 15 pennies and Lai has 16 pennies. Altogether, do they have enough pennies to buy the candy bar?" Brent's attention is caught by the word "altogether," and again he adds $15 + 16$. He writes down his answer: 31 pennies.

■ Brent has five sheets of $8\frac{1}{2}" \times 11"$ construction paper. He needs to provide paper for himself and six other students. If he gives everyone a whole sheet, two people will be left with no paper. Brent draws a picture of the five sheets of paper, and then he draws a line down the middle of each. If he cuts each sheet in half, there will be ten pieces of paper. Since there are seven children, this would leave three extra pieces. What will he do with the extras? He decides that it would be a good idea to have the three sheets in reserve in case someone makes a mistake.

The first problem is a *routine problem*. It follows a predictable pattern and can be solved correctly without actually reading the whole question carefully. The second is called a *nonroutine problem*. There is more than one step, and the problem must be read carefully. Brent has focused on the word "altogether" and stopped with the addition of the two girls' pennies. He misses the question asked, which is: "Once you know there are 31 pennies, is that enough money to buy a 35¢ candy bar?" The current focus in mathematics problem solving is on providing more opportunities for solving nonroutine problems, including those that occur in naturalistic situations such as the problem in the third example. Note that the third problem is multistepped: subtract five from seven, draw a picture, draw a line down the middle of each sheet, count the halves, decide if there are enough, subtract seven from 10, and decide what to do with the three extras. This last problem really has no single correct answer. For example, Brent could have left two of the children out, or he could have given three children whole sheets and four children halves. Real problem-solving skills go beyond simple one-step problems.

Note that, when dealing with each of the problems, the children went through a process of self-generated questions. This process is referred to as **heuristics**. There are three common types of self-generated questions:

- Consider a similar but simpler problem as a model.
- Use symbols or representations (build concrete representations; draw a picture or a diagram; make a chart or a graph).
- Use means–ends analysis such as identifying the knowns and the unknowns, working backward, and setting up intermediate goals.

We often provide children with a learned idea or heuristic such as a series of problem-solving steps. Unfortunately, if the rules are too specific then they will not transfer (note Brent's focus on the key word). Yet if the rules are too general, how will you know if the idea has been mastered? It is important to recognize that applying a heuristic—such as developing the relevant charts, graphs, diagrams, or pictures or performing needed operations—requires a strong grounding in such basics as counting, whole number operations, geometry, and the like.

Researchers have investigated not only whether heuristics can be taught but also what it is that successful problem solvers do that leads to their success. It has been found that general heuristics cannot be taught. When content is taught with heuristics, content knowledge improves but not problem-solving ability. The study of successful problem solvers has shown that they know the content and organize it in special ways. Therefore, content and problem solving should be taught together, not first one and then the other. Good problem solvers think in ways that are qualitatively different from poor problem solvers. Children must learn how to think about their thinking and manage it in an organized fashion. Heuristics is this type of learning; it is not simply learning a list of strategies that might not always work. Children need to learn to apply consciously the following steps.

1. Assess the situation and decide exactly what is being asked.
2. Organize a plan that is directed toward answering the question.
3. Execute the plan using appropriate strategies.
4. Verify the results—that is, evaluate the outcome of a plan.

It is important that children deal with real problems that might not have clearly designated unknowns, that might contain too much or too little information, that can be solved using more than one method, that have no one right answer (or even no answer), that combine processes, that have multiple steps necessitating some trial and error, and that take considerable time to solve. Unfortunately, most textbook problems are of the routine variety: the unknown is obvious, only the necessary information is provided, the solution procedure is obvious, there is only one correct answer, and the solution can be arrived at quickly. It is essential that students have the opportunity to share possible solutions with their peers. If children have the opportunity to explain solutions to others, they will clarify the problem and be better able to explain problems to themselves.

Formal problem solving can be introduced using **contrived problems**—that is, problems devised or selected by teachers. This procedure provides an opportunity for the teacher to model problem-solving behavior by posing the problem and then acting out the solution. The children can then be asked to think of some variations.

Skinner (1990) presented the first problems to her 5-year-olds in book form to integrate mathematics and reading/language arts. The tiny books were on sturdy cardboard with an illustration and one sentence on a page. They were held together with spiral binding. Skinner encouraged students to use manipulatives such as Unifix Cubes to aid in solving problems or to act out their solutions. Eventually, the students moved into dictating problems and then into writing. By age 7, they were creating most of their own problems. Research indicates that working with concrete materials and drawing and/or writing explanations of solutions for problems are the best experiences for improving problem-solving skills.

## Assessment

Assessment of children's problem-solving expertise is not an easy task. It demands that teachers be creative and flexible. Development of problem-solving skills is a long-term activity; it is not learned in one lesson. It must be focused on the process of problem solving, not solely on the answers. Therefore, you must provide children with problem-solving situations and observe how they meet them, interview students, have small groups of children describe how they solved problems, and have students help each other solve problems.

Observe the following as students work on problems:

■ Do they attack the problem in an organized fashion; that is, do they appear to have a logical strategy?

■ If one strategy does not work, do they try another?

■ Are they persistent in sticking with the problem until they arrive at what they believe is a satisfactory solution?

■ How well do they concentrate on the problem-solving task?

■ Do they use aids such as manipulatives and drawings?

■ Do their facial expressions indicate interest, involvement, frustration, or puzzlement?

Behaviors noted can be recorded with anecdotal records or on checklists.

Interviews will be emphasized as a format for assessment throughout the text. The interview is also an excellent way to look at problem-solving behavior. Present the child with a problem or have the child invent a problem and let the child find a solution, describing what she is thinking as she works. Make a tape recording or take notes.

## Instruction

Researchers agree that children should experience a variety of problem-solving strategies so that they do not approach every problem in the same stereotyped way. They should be given problems that are at their developmental level. Natural and informal methods of instruction should begin the exploration of problem solving. For example, ask how many children are in the classroom today, how many glasses of juice we will need at Kate's table, and so on.

To be effective problem solvers, children need time to mull over problems, to make mistakes, to try various strategies, and to discuss problems with their friends. When teaching in the kindergarten and primary grades, if you must use a textbook then check the problems carefully. If you find that most of the problems are routine, you will have to obtain some nonroutine problems or devise some yourself. You may use the following criteria.

■ Devise problems that contain extra information or that lack necessary information.

1. George paid 10¢ a bag for two bags of cookies with six cookies in each bag. How many cookies did George buy? (Price is extra information.)

2. John's big brother is 6 feet tall. How much will John have to grow to be as big as his brother? (We don't know John's height.)

■ Devise problems that involve estimation or that do not have clearly right or wrong answers.

1. Vanessa has $1. She would like to buy a pen that costs 49¢ and a notebook that costs 39¢. Does she have enough money? (Yes/no rather than numerical answer)

2. How many times can you ride your bike around the block in 10 minutes? In one hour? In a week? In a month? (Estimation)

■ Devise problems that apply mathematics in practical situations such as shopping, cooking, or building.

■ Base problems on things children are interested in, or make up problems that are about students in the class (giving them a personal flavor).

- Devise problems that require more than one step and provide opportunities for application of logic, reasoning, and testing out of ideas.
- Ask questions that will require the children to make up a problem.
- Design problems whose solutions will provide data for decision making.
  1. There are 25 students in the third-grade class. The students are planning a party to celebrate the end of the school year. They need to decide on a menu, estimate the cost, and calculate how much money each of them will have to contribute.

Collect resources that children can use for problem solving. Gather statistics that children can work with (such as the weather information from the daily newspaper). Use children's spontaneous questions (How far is it to the zoo?). Provide children with problems such as those described by Marilyn Burns (1998). Literature (see Unit 15) provides a wealth of information for problem solving. Have children write problems that other children can try to solve. Calculators can be helpful tools for problem solving: Children can try out more strategies because of time saved that might otherwise be spent in tedious hand calculations.

Computers can also be used for problem solving. LOGO programming is a problem-solving activity in itself. Remember, have children work in pairs or small groups. Software is described and referred to in each of the units on mathematics and science content.

The conventional problem-solving strategies taught (Reys, Lindquist, Lambdin, Smith, & Suydam, 2001) have been as follows:

- Understand the problem.
- Devise a plan for solving it.
- Carry out your plan.
- Look back to examine the solution obtained.

However, start by letting children develop their own solutions. They will gradually become more direct in their approaches. Through modeling, new strategies can be introduced. Reys and colleagues (2001) suggest several such strategies.

1. Act out the problem. That is, use real objects or representations to set up the problem and go through the steps of finding a solution. This is the type of activity used to introduce whole number operations.

2. Make a drawing or a diagram. The pictures must be extremely simple and should include only the important elements. For example:

George wants to build a building with his blocks that is triangular shaped with seven blocks in the bottom row. How many blocks will he need?

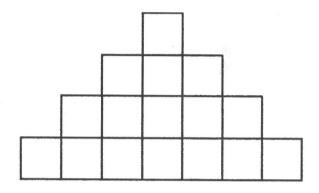

Theresa's mother's van has three rows of seats. One row holds three passengers, the next row holds two, and the back row holds four. Can ten passengers and the driver ride comfortably?

The van holds eight passengers and the driver. Ten passengers and the driver would be crowded.

3. Look for a pattern. (See Unit 28.)
4. Construct a table. (See Unit 31.)

5. Account systematically for all possibilities. In other words, as different strategies are tried or different calculations are made, keep track of what has been used.

   Below is a map showing all the roads from Jonesville to Clinton. Find as many different ways as you can to get from Jonesville to Clinton without ever backtracking.

**Jonesville**

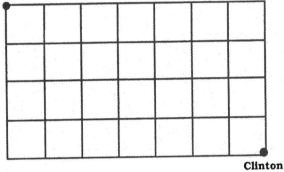

**Clinton**

6. Guess and check. Make an educated guess based on attention to details of the problem and past experience. Some problems demand trial and error and a "best guess" to solve.

   Using only the numbers 1 through 9, fill the squares so that the sum in every row and column is 15.

7. Work backward. In some problems, the endpoint is given and the problem solver must work backward to find out how the endpoint was reached. A maze is a concrete example of this type of problem.

   Chan's mother bought some apples. She put half of them in her refrigerator and gave two to each of three neighbors. How many apples did she buy?

8. Identify wanted, given, and needed information. Rather than plunging right into calculations or formulating conclusions, the problem solver should sort out the important and necessary information from the extraneous factors and may need to collect additional data. Taking a poll is a common way of collecting data to make a decision.

   Trang Fung says that most of the girls would like to have pepperoni pizza at the slumber party. Sara claims that most of the girls prefer hamburger. To know how much of each to order, they set up a chart, question their friends, and tally their choices.

9. Turn a word problem into an equation or "number sentence."

   Mary gives Johnny half of her allowance. With the rest of her money, she uses half to buy an ice cream cone for two dollars. How much allowance did Mary receive? Number sentence: $2 \times \$2 = \$4 \times 2 = \$8$ allowance.

   This process is not easy for students, but too frequently it is the only strategy included in a textbook.

10. Solve a simpler or similar problem. Sometimes large numbers or other complications get in the way of seeing how to solve a problem, so making a similar problem may help the child discover the solution. For example, in the following problem, the amounts could be changed to "Derrick has $4 and Brent has $6."

    If Derrick has saved $4.59 and Brent has saved $6.37, how much more money has Brent saved?

    Sometimes problems have to be broken down into smaller parts. Also, a strategy may be clarified if a problem is put into the child's own words.

11. Change your point of view. Is the strategy being used based on incorrect assumptions? Stop and ask, "What is really being said in this problem?"

All these strategies will not be learned right away. They will be introduced gradually and acquired throughout the elementary grades. Prekindergarten through fourth

Estimation is a challenge for young children.

grade play a crucial role in providing the foundations for problem solving.

## ESTIMATION

*Estimation* is arriving at an approximation of the answer to a problem. Estimation should be taught as a unique strategy. Estimation is mental and should not be checked to see how accurate it is. Later on, children can apply estimation after computation to help decide if a computed answer is a reasonable one. First, however, the concept must be developed. At the primary level, the most common problems for applying estimation involve length or numerosity and are solved through visual

perception. Children might guess how wide the rug is or how many objects are in a container. Computational estimation is usually introduced near the end of the primary period (i.e., in the third grade).

There are a number of strategies that can be used for estimation. At the introductory levels, students work with concrete situations. For example, they might explore by estimating how many trucks could be parked in their classroom or how many shoes will fit in the closet. Children can select some benchmarks for measurement such as a body part; that is, they could estimate how many hands wide the hallway is. Another example would be estimating how many beans would fill a jar using a one-cup measure that holds 100 beans as the benchmark. Keeping the same jar and changing the size or type of objects placed in it will help children build on their prior knowledge and increase their estimation skills.

Two strategies might be used for more advanced estimation. The *front-end* strategy is one that young children can use. This strategy focuses on the first number on the left when developing an estimate. For example:

$$\begin{array}{r} 37 \\ 43 \\ +24 \\ \hline \end{array}$$

To estimate the sum, focus on the left column first. Note that there are nine 10s, which would be 90. Then look at the right column. Obviously, the answer is more than 90, and noting that the right column adds up to more than 10, an estimate of $90 + 10 = 100$ is reached.

Another strategy is called *clustering*. Clustering can be used when numbers are close in value. For example, estimate the total attendance in class for the week.

**Class attendance**

| Monday | 27 |
| --- | --- |
| Tuesday | 29 |
| Wednesday | 31 |
| Thursday | 32 |
| Friday | 30 |

1. There were about 30 students each day.

2. $5 \times 30 = 150$, the estimated total for the week.

*Rounding* is a strategy that is helpful for mental computation. Suppose you wondered how many primary grade children had eaten lunch at school this week. You found out that there were 43 first graders, 38 second graders, and 52 third graders.

| Number of Primary Students Eating Lunch | | Round | Add |
|---|---|---|---|
| First graders | 43 | 40 | 40 |
| Second graders | 38 | 40 | 40 |
| Third graders | 52 | 50 | 50 |
| | | | 130 |
| | | | (estimate) |

There are two additional strategies that are much more complex and would be used by more advanced students beyond the elementary grades. *Compatible numbers* strategy involves more complex rounding. *Special numbers* strategy is one that overlaps several strategies. For the most part, primary grade children will be using only the noncomputational and the front-end strategies. The important point is that children begin early to realize that mathematics is not just finding the one right answer but can also involve making good guesses or estimates.

## MULTICULTURAL PROBLEM SOLVING

Claudia Zaslavsky (1996) suggests games from many cultures as fun ways to teach mathematics while learning about other cultures. Games offer challenges to children. Problem-solving skills are developed as students think through strategies, think ahead, and evaluate their selections of moves. Older children can teach the games to younger children, and games can be related to the customs of cultures. Games can be played by men or by women, by children or adults, on special occasions or at any time. Young children like to change the rules of the game, which changes the strategies to be used.

## MEETING SPECIAL NEEDS

As with other children, instruction for children with special needs must be individualized and related to how children best learn (Bowe, 2007). Children with special needs tend to lose ground and get farther behind in each year of school. Meeting their unique needs and teaching them the required academic skills and knowledge presents an enormous problem. Each type of disability provides a different instructional challenge. Planning is required to be individualized for each child and documented in an **IFSP** (Individualized Family Service Plan) for infants and toddlers and an **IEP** (Individualized Educational Plan) for older children. Children with disabilities require much more individualized instruction than do other children. Approaches to instruction in **ECSE** (Early Childhood Special Education) tend to be behaviorist based, in contrast to the constructivist-based approaches used in regular **ECE** (Early Childhood Education). However, there is no evidence that suggests all ECSE students do best with behaviorist instructional approaches. Special education requirements for the youngest children focus on learning in the family and other natural environments that include outdoor activities, experiences with animals, experiences with art materials, and other opportunities recommended for all children. Instruction is embedded in the activities through verbal descriptions, questions, and descriptive statements. Children with disabilities may need ancillary services such as physical therapy, occupational therapy, and/or speech-language therapy. Children with disabilities learn math and science through the same types of activities as described in this textbook for other children but with adaptations and accommodations as needed. Teaching needs to be from the concrete to the abstract as described in this unit.

The needs of English Language Learners (**ELL**) can also be addressed by special instructional approaches. It is important for teachers to maintain a close relationship with the ELL students' families and to learn as much as possible about the students' home countries, language, and customs. Pair language with visual communication using objects, pictures, and gestures. Be sure these students are situated where they can see and hear everything. Vocabulary is critical in both math and science. Bilingual vocabulary, both visual and oral, can be very helpful.

## SUMMARY

This unit has described six steps that provide a guide for what to teach and how to teach it. Following these steps can minimize guesswork. The steps are (1) assess,

(2) choose objectives, (3) plan experiences, (4) select materials, (5) teach, and (6) evaluate.

Problem solving and inquiry are processes that underlie all instruction in mathematics and science. Problem solving is first on the list of mathematics processes as developed by the National Council of Teachers of Mathematics, and inquiry is the focus promoted by the National Science Teachers Association. Problem solving and inquiry emphasize the process rather than the final product (or correct answer). The important factor is that, during the early childhood years, children gradually learn a variety of problem-solving strategies as well as when and where to apply them. For young children, problems develop out of their everyday naturalistic activities. It is critical that children have opportunities to solve many nonroutine math problems—that is, problems that are not just simple and straightforward with obvious answers but those that will stretch their minds. It is also important that children are afforded the opportunity to investigate science problems in areas of interest. Assessment and evaluation should each focus on the process rather than the answers. Observation and interview techniques may both be used.

Problem-solving instruction for young children begins with their natural explorations in the environment. It requires time and careful guidance as teachers move from teacher-initiated to child-initiated problems.

Games can provide a multicultural problem-solving experience. Children with disabilities need more individualized instruction than do other children. English Language Learners need work with objects, pictures and gestures.

## KEY TERMS

| | | |
|---|---|---|
| assess | evaluate | plan experiences |
| choose objectives | heuristics | problem solving |
| contrived problems | IEP | routine problems |
| ECE | IFSP | select materials |
| ECSE | inquiry | teach |
| ELL | nonroutine problems | |

## SUGGESTED ACTIVITIES

1. Interview two teachers who teach prekindergarten, kindergarten, and/or primary students. Ask them to describe their mathematics and science programs. Find out how they address each of the instructional steps described in this unit.

2. Observe a prekindergarten, kindergarten, or primary classroom. Write a description of the math and science activities/experiences that you see. Could you fit what you observed into the steps described in the text? How?

3. Start a section on problem solving in your Activity File. As you progress through the text, look through the units that involve problem solving. If you find some routine problems, rewrite them as nonroutine problems. Look through other resources for additional problem ideas. Write some problems of your own. Look through your favorite science and social studies texts and develop some problems that fit the unit themes in those books.

4. Look through the problem-solving activities in a kindergarten, first-, second-, or third-grade mathematics textbook. Categorize the problems as *routine* or *nonroutine*. Report your findings to the class.

5. Select or create three nonroutine math problems. Have the students in the class try to solve them. Ask them to write a description of the steps they take and the strategies they use. Have them compare their strategies with those described in the unit and with each other.

6. Try some estimation activities with children of ages 4–8.

7. Review some problem-solving software such as listed below. Use one of the review procedures suggested in Activity 5 of Unit 2.

   ■ *I SPY Fantasy* (ages 6–10; Scholastic), Windows and MAC

   ■ *Math Missions: The Race to Spectacle City Arcade* (ages 5–8; Scholastic), Windows and MAC

   ■ *The Little Raven & Friends* (ages 3–7; Tivola), Windows and MAC

   ■ *Ollo and the Sunny Valley Fair* (ages 3–5; Hulabee Entertainment), Windows and MAC

   ■ *The Magic School Bus Explores the Ocean* (ages 6–10; Microsoft Corp.), Windows and MAC

   ■ *Kidspiration* (ages 5–9; Inspiration Software, Inc.), Windows and MAC

   ■ *The Magic School Bus Explores the World of Animals* (ages 6+; Microsoft Corp.), Windows CD-ROM

   ■ *The Magic School Bus Explores the Rainforest* (ages 6+; Microsoft Corp.), Windows CD-ROM

   ■ *Theme Weaver: Nature* and *Theme Weaver: Animals* (ages 4–8; Riverdeep-Edmark), MAC and Windows CD-ROM

## REVIEW

A. List in order the six steps for instruction described in this unit.

B. Define each of the steps listed in A.

C. Read each of the following descriptions and label them with the correct step name.

   1. From her Activity File, the teacher selects two cards from the Classification section.

   2. Mrs. Brown has just interviewed Joey and discovered that he can count accurately through 12. He then continues, "15, 14, 19, 20." She thinks about what the next step in instruction should be for Joey.

   3. The teacher is seated at a table with Fwang. "Fwang, you put three red teddy bears and two blue teddy bears together in one group. Then you wrote 3 + 2 = 5. Explain to me how you figured out how to solve the problem."

   4. During the first month of school, Mrs. Garcia interviews each of her students individually to find out which concepts they know and what skills they have.

   5. Mr. Black has set up a sand table, and the children are pouring and measuring sand using standard measuring cups to learn the relationship between the different size cups.

   6. Katherine needs to work on A-B-A-B type patterns. Her teacher pulls out three cards from the Pattern section of her Activity File.

   7. Mr. Wang looks through the library of computer software for programs that require logical thinking strategies.

D. Describe the advantages of following the instructional steps suggested in this unit.

E. Read the description of Miss Conway's method of selecting objectives and activities. Analyze and evaluate her approach.

   Miss Conway believes that all her students are at about the same level in their mathematics and science capabilities and knowledge. She has a math and science program that she has used for 15 years and that she believes is satisfactory. She assumes that all students enter her class at the same level and leave knowing everything she has taught.

F. Write an *R* for routine problems and an *N* for nonroutine problems.

___1. Larry has four pennies, and his dad gave him five more pennies. How many pennies does Larry have now?

___2. Nancy's mother has five cookies. She wants to give Nancy and her friend Jody the same number of cookies. How many cookies will each girl receive?

___3. Larry has four small racing cars. He gives one to his friend Fred. How many does he have left?

___4. Nancy has three dolls and Jody has six. How many more dolls does Jody have?

___5. Tom and Tasha each get part of a candy bar. Does one child get more candy? If so, which one?

**G.** Explain what a *heuristic* is.

**H.** Put an *X* by the statements that are correct.

___1. If children have mastered the heuristics, then mastery of the content is not important.

___2. Good and poor problem solvers have about the same heuristic skills.

___3. Expert problem solvers are skilled at thinking about thinking. They can assess the situation, decide what is being asked, organize a plan, carry out the plan, and verify the results in an organized fashion.

___4. Most textbooks today include plenty of nonroutine problems to solve.

___5. Having children work in small groups to solve problems is the most productive instructional approach.

___6. Explaining a problem to someone else will help a child clarify the problem for himself.

**I.** List three techniques that can be used to assess children's problem-solving skills.

**J.** Critique the following instructional situation:

"We are going to do some more math problems today. I will pass out the problems to you, and you will have 15 minutes to complete them. Do not talk to your neighbors. Follow the steps on the board." The following steps are listed on the board:

1. Understand    3. Follow the plan
2. Plan          4. Check

There are no manipulatives in evidence, and there is no room on the paper for drawing pictures or diagrams.

**K.** List the five processes that are included in the NCTM mathematics process standards.

**L.** In the third-grade math center there are two glass jars filled with marbles. One jar is tall and thin; the other jar is short and fat. There are some 3" × 5" cards and a shoebox next to the jars. There is a sign that reads

---

**TODAY'S ESTIMATION EXERCISE**

Remember, don't count!

How many marbles are in the TALL jar?

How many marbles are in the SHORT jar?

Does one jar have more, or do they both have the same amount?

On a card write:

1. Your name
2. Number of marbles in the TALL jar
3. Number of marbles in the SHORT jar
4. Put your card in the shoebox.

---

Evaluate this activity. How would you follow up on the information collected?

**M.** Why are games good for helping children learn math and science?

**N.** Explain how children with special needs and disabilities can learn math and science skills and concepts.

## REFERENCES

Bowe, F. G. (2007). *Early childhood special education: Birth to eight*. Albany, NY: Thomson Delmar Learning.

Burns, M. (1998, January/February). Math in action. Raccoon math: A story for numerical reasoning. *Instructor*, 86–88.

National Council of Teachers of Mathematics. (2000). *Principles and standards for school mathematics*. Reston, VA: Author.

Reys, R. E., Lindquist, M. M., Lambdin, D. V., Smith, N. L., & Suydam, M. N. (2001). *Helping children learn mathematics*. New York: Wiley.

Skinner, P. (1990). *What's your problem?* Portsmouth, NH: Heinemann.

Zaslavsky, C. (1996). *The multicultural math classroom*. Portsmouth, NH: Heinemann.

## FURTHER READING AND RESOURCES

Andrews, A. G. (2004). Adapting manipulatives to foster the thinking of young children. *Teaching Children Mathematics, 11*(1), 15–17.

Baker, A., & Baker, J. (1991). *Counting on a small planet*. Portsmouth, NH: Heinemann.

Baroody, A. J., & Dowker, A. (Eds.). (2003). *The development of arithmetic concepts and skills*. Mahwah, NJ: Erlbaum.

Blake, S., Hurley, S., & Arenz, B. (1995). Mathematical problem solving and young children. *Early Childhood Education Journal, 23*(2), 81–84.

Buschman, L. (2002). Becoming a problem solver. *Teaching Children Mathematics, 9*(2), 98–103.

Buschman, L. (2003). Children who enjoy problem solving. *Teaching Children Mathematics, 9*(9), 539–544.

Buschman, L. (2004). Teaching problem solving in mathematics. *Teaching Children Mathematics, 10*(6), 302–309.

Buyea, R. W. (2007). Problem solving in a structured mathematics program. *Teaching Children Mathematics, 13*(6), 300–307.

Clarke, D. M., & Clarke, B. A. (2003). Encouraging perseverance in elementary mathematics: A tale of two problems. *Teaching Children Mathematics, 10*(4), 204–209.

Clements, D. H., Sarama, J., & DiBiase, A. (Eds.). (2004). *Engaging young children in mathematics*. Mahwah, NJ: Erlbaum.

Committee on Science Learning, Kindergarten through Eighth Grade. Board on Science Education, Center for Education. (2007). *Taking science to school: Learning and teaching science in grades K–8*. Washington, DC: National Academies Press.

Dougherty, B. J., & Venenciano, L. C. H. (2007). Measure up for understanding. *Teaching Children Mathematics, 13*(9), 452–456.

Fernandez, C., & Yoshida, M. (2004). *Lesson study: A Japanese approach to improving mathematics teaching and learning*. Mahwah, NJ: Erlbaum.

Findell, C. R., Cavanagh, M., Dacey, L., Greenes, C. E., Sheffield, L. J., & Small, M. (2004). *Navigating through problem solving and reasoning in grade 1*. Reston, VA: National Council of Teachers of Mathematics.

Fiori, N. (2007). Four practices that math classrooms could do without. *Phi Delta Kappan, 88*(9), 695–696.

Forrest, K., Schnabel, D., & Williams, M. E. (2006). Math by the month: Earth day. *Teaching Children Mathematics, 12*(8), 408.

Forrest, K., Schnabel, D., & Williams, M. E. (2007). Math by the month: Birds of a feather stick . . . with math. *Teaching Children Mathematics, 13*(6), 320.

Forrest, K., Schnabel, D., & Williams, M. E. (2007). Math by the month: How does your garden grow? *Teaching Children Mathematics, 13*(8), 424.

Ginsburg, H. P., Inoue, N., & Seo, K. (1999). Young children doing mathematics. In J. V. Copley (Ed.), *Mathematics in the early years* (pp. 88–99). Reston, VA: National Council of Teachers of Mathematics, and Washington, DC: National Association for the Education of Young Children.

Green, D. A. (2002). Last one standing: Cooperative problem solving. *Teaching Children Mathematics, 9*(3), 134–139.

Greenes, C. E., Dacey, L., Cavanagh, M., Findell, C. R., Sheffield, L. J., & Small, M. (2003). *Navigating through problem solving and reasoning in prekindergarten–kindergarten.* Reston, VA: National Council of Teachers of Mathematics.

Hartweg, K. (2003). Responses to the bike trike problem. *Teaching Children Mathematics, 9*(8), 457–460.

Hartweg, K. (2004). Responses to the Farmer MacDonald problem. *Teaching Children Mathematics, 10*(9), 446–449.

Hartweg, K., & Heisler, M. (2007). No tears here! Third-grade problem solvers. *Teaching Children Mathematics, 13*(7), 362–368.

Hoosain, E., & Chance, R. H. (2004). Problem-solving strategies of first graders. *Teaching Children Mathematics, 10*(9), 474–479.

Kamii, C., & Houseman, L. B. (1999). *Children reinvent arithmetic* (2nd ed.). New York: Teachers College Press.

Leitze, A. R., & Stump, S. (2007). Sharing cookies. *Teaching Children Mathematics, 13*(7), 378–379.

Lind, K. K. (1999). Science in early childhood: Developing and acquiring fundamental concepts and skills. In *Dialogue on early childhood sciences, mathematics, and technology education.* Washington, DC: American Association for the Advancement of Science.

Mann, R., & Miller, N. (2003). Responses to the marble mayhem problem: A solution evolution. *Teaching Children Mathematics, 9*(9), 516–520.

Methany, D. (2001). Consumer investigations: What is the "best" chip? *Teaching Children Mathematics, 7*(8), 418–420.

National Research Council. (1996). *National science education standards.* Washington, DC: National Academies Press.

Richardson, K. M. (2004). Designing math trails for the elementary school. *Teaching Children Mathematics, 11*(1), 8–14.

Rigelman, N. R. (2007). Fostering mathematical thinking and problem solving: The teacher's role. *Teaching Children Mathematics, 13*(6), 308–319.

Rivkin, M. S. (2005, April). Building teamwork through science. *Scholastic Early Childhood Today,* 36–42.

Small, M., Sheffield, L. J., Cavanagh, M., Dacey, L., Findell, C. R., & Greenes, C. E. (2004). *Navigating through problem solving and reasoning in grade 2.* Reston, VA: National Council of Teachers of Mathematics.

Stofac, V. J., & Wesley, A. (1987). *Logic problems for primary people* (Books 1–3). Sunnyvale, CA: Creative Publications.

Warfield, J. (2001). Teaching kindergarten children to solve word problems. *Early Childhood Education Journal, 28,* 161–167.

Whitin, D. J. (2006). Problem posing in the elementary classroom. *Teaching Children Mathematics, 13*(1), 14–18.

Whitin, P., & Whitin, D. J. (2006). Making connections through math-related book pairs. *Teaching Children Mathematics, 13*(4), 196–202.

Williams, C. V., & Kamii, C. (1986). How do children learn by handling objects? *Young Children, 42*(1), 23–26.

Young, E., & Marroquin, C. L. (2006). Posing problems from children's literature. *Teaching Children Mathematics, 12*(7), 362–366.

Zaslavsky, C. (1998). *Math games and activities from around the world.* Chicago: Chicago Review Press.

Ziemba, E. (2005/2006). Sorting and patterning in kindergarten: From activities to assessment. *Teaching Children Mathematics, 12*(5), 236–241.

# Unit 4

# Assessing the Child's Developmental Level

## OBJECTIVES

After reading this unit, you should be able to:

- Explain the National Council of Teachers of Mathematics' basic assessment standards.
- Explain the National Research Council's basic assessment standards for science.
- Explain how to find the child's level of concept development.
- Explain the value of commercial assessment instruments for concept assessment.
- Make a developmental assessment task file.
- Be able to assess the concept development level of young children.
- Understand how to record, report, and evaluate using naturalistic/performance-based assessment.
- Explain the advantages of portfolio assessment.
- Plan how to maintain equity when assessing children's progress.

Children's levels of concept development are determined by seeing which concept tasks they are able to perform independently. The first question in teaching is "Where is the child now?" To find the answer to this question, the teacher assesses. The purpose of *assessment* is to gather information and evidence about student knowledge, skills, and attitudes (or dispositions) regarding mathematics and science. This evidence is then used to *plan* a program of instruction for each child and to *evaluate* each child's progress and the effectiveness of instruction. Assessment may be done through observation, through questioning as the child works on a problem or investigation, and/or through interviews in which the child is given a specific task to perform. This information is used to guide the next steps in teaching. The long-term objective for young children is to be sure

that they have a strong foundation in basic concepts that will take them through the transition into the concrete operational stage, when they begin to deal seriously with abstract symbols in math and independent investigations in science. Following the methods and sequence in this text helps reach this goal and at the same time achieves some further objectives:

- Builds a positive feeling in the child toward math and science.
- Builds confidence in the child that he can do math and science activities.
- Builds a questioning attitude in response to children's curiosity regarding math and science problems.

The National Council of Teachers of Mathematics (NCTM) assessment principle (2000, p. 22) states that "**assessment** should support the learning of important mathematics and furnish useful information to both teachers and students." It should be an integral part of instruction, not just something administered at the end of instruction. Assessment should include the following elements.

■ It should enhance children's learning by being a part of everyday instruction.

■ Assessment tasks that are similar or identical to instructional tasks can indicate to students exactly what they should be able to know and do.

■ Student communication skills can be enhanced when assessment involves observations, conversations, interviews, oral reports, and journals.

■ Evaluation guides (or *rubrics*) can clarify for the students exactly what their strengths and weaknesses are and so enable their self-assessment.

Assessment should be integrated into everyday activities so that it is not an interruption but rather a part of the instructional routine. Assessment should provide both teacher and student with valuable information. There should not be overreliance on formal paper-and-pencil tests; instead, information should be gathered from a variety of sources. "Many assessment techniques can be used by mathematics teachers, including open-ended questions, constructed-response tasks, selected response items, performance tasks, observations, conversations, journals and portfolios" (NCTM, 2000, p. 23). In this text the focus is on observations, interviews, and portfolios of children's work, which may include problem solutions, journal entries, results of conversations, photos, and other documentation. It is also important to take heed of the equity principle and diversify assessment approaches to meet the needs of diverse learners such as English language learners, gifted students, and students with learning disabilities.

The NCTM (1995) also advocates decreased attention to a number of traditional assessment elements:

■ Assessing what students do not know, comparing them with other students, and/or using assessments to track students relative to apparent capability.

■ Simply counting correct answers on tests for the sole purpose of assigning grades.

■ Focusing on assessment of students' knowledge of only specific facts and isolated skills.

■ Using exercises or word problems requiring only one or two skills.

■ Excluding calculators, computers, and manipulatives from the assessment process.

■ Evaluating teacher success only on the basis of test scores.

The NCTM (1989) has this to say about the assessment of young children: "methods should consider the characteristics of the students themselves. . . . At this stage, when children's understanding is often closely tied to the use of physical materials, assessment tasks that allow them to use such materials are better indicators of learning" (p. 202).

The National Research Council created standards for assessment in science education (NRC, 1996). According to the NRC, assessment is primarily a way to obtain feedback. For young children, the feedback tells how well students are meeting the expectations of teachers and parents and tells teachers how effective their instruction is. Through assessment, data are collected for use in planning teaching and guiding learning. The important areas for data collection focus on students' achievement and attitudes (dispositions). For young children, the important assessment methods in science are much the same as in mathematics: performance testing, interviews, portfolios, performances, and observations. A variety of methods should be used to get an accurate assessment picture. Furthermore, methods should be *authentic*—that is, they should match the intended science outcomes and be situations that match how scientists actually work. There are five assessment standards designed for K–12; the following are modified to meet pre-K–3.

■ *Assessment Standard A*: The consistency of assessments with the decisions they are designed to inform. There should be a clear purpose that assesses specific knowledge, skills, and attitudes. Decisions are made on the basis of the assessment data.

■ *Assessment Standard B*: Achievement in science must be assessed. Assessments and instruction should be guided by the science content standards. Assessment should provide information on the students' ability to inquire; to know and understand facts, concepts, and principles; to reason scientifically; and to communicate about science.

■ *Assessment Standard C*: The technical quality of the data collected is well matched to the decisions and actions taken on the basis of their interpretation. Assessments actually measure what they say they are measuring, tasks are authentic, an individual student's performance is similar on at least two tasks designed to measure the same concept(s), and students have adequate opportunity to demonstrate their achievements.

■ *Assessment Standard D*: Assessment practices must be fair. Tasks must be modified to accommodate the needs of students with physical disabilities, learning disabilities, or limited English proficiency. Assessment tasks must be set in a variety of contexts, be engaging to students with different interests and experiences, and must not assume the perspective or experience of a particular gender, racial, or ethnic group.

■ *Assessment Standard E*: The inferences made from assessments about student achievement must be

sound. In other words, decisions should be made in an objective manner.

Following these standards will enable teachers to collect information for improving classroom practice, planning curricula, developing self-directed learners, and reporting student progress.

The 1996 *National Science Education Standards* (the NSES *Standards*) were developed over the course of four years and involved tens of thousands of educators and scientists in extensive comment and review. The resultant standards offered a vision of effective science education for all students. However, more guidance was needed in some areas to sufficiently develop the deep understanding of key topics that is needed for classroom implementation. Groups of experts were convened with an appropriate balance of viewpoints, experience, and expertise in the research to develop addendums to the NSES *Standards* in the identified areas. As a result of this effort, the report *Classroom Assessment and the National Science Education Standards* (NRC, 2001) was developed. This document takes a closer look at the ongoing assessment that occurs each day in classrooms between teachers and students and provides vignettes of classroom activity wherein students and teachers are engaged in assessment. Highlights of these findings are integrated into Units 5 and 7 and throughout the units of this book that address science content.

## ASSESSMENT METHODS

Observation and interview are assessment methods that teachers use to determine a child's level of development. Examples of both of these methods were included in

---

*The National Science Education Standards envision the following changes in emphases:*

| **Less emphasis on assessing** | **More emphasis on assessing** |
| --- | --- |
| ■ what is easily measured | ■ what is most highly valued |
| ■ discrete knowledge | ■ rich, well-structured knowledge |
| ■ scientific knowledge | ■ scientific understanding and reasoning |
| ■ to learn what students do not know | ■ to learn what students do understand |

Unit 3, and more are provided in this unit. Assessment is most appropriately done through conversations, observation, and interviews using teacher-developed assessment tasks (Glanfield, Bush, & Stenmark, 2003). Commercial instruments used for initial screening may also supply useful information, but their scope is too limited for the everyday assessment needed for planning. Initial screening instruments usually cover a broad range of areas and provide a profile that indicates overall strengths and weaknesses. These strengths and weaknesses can be looked at in more depth by the classroom teacher to glean information needed for making normal instructional decisions or by a diagnostic specialist (i.e., a school psychologist or speech and language therapist) when an initial screening indicates some serious developmental problem. Individually administered screening instruments should be the only type used with young children. Child responses should require the use of concrete materials and/or pictures, verbal answers, or motoric responses such as pointing or rearranging some objects. Paper and pencil should be used only for assessment of perceptual motor development (i.e., tasks such as name writing, drawing a person, or copying shapes). Booklet-type paper-and-pencil tests administered to groups or individuals are inappropriate until children are well into concrete operations, can deal with abstract symbols, and have well-developed perceptual motor skills.

Assessment information can be obtained through observations of children working with materials to solve problems and inquire into questions.

## Observational Assessment

Observation is used to find out how children use concepts during their daily activities. Observation can occur during naturalistic, informal, and structured activities. The teacher has in mind the concepts the children should be using. Whenever she sees a concept reflected in a child's activity, she writes down the incident and places it in the child's record folder. This helps her plan future experiences.

Throughout this book, suggestions are made for behaviors that should be observed. The following are examples of behaviors as the teacher would write them down for the child's folder.

■ Brad (18 months old) dumped all the shape blocks on the rug. He picked out all the circles and stacked them up. Shows he can sort and organize.

■ Rosa (4 years old) carefully set the table for lunch all by herself. She remembered everything. Rosa understands one-to-one correspondence.

■ Chris (3 years old) and Kai (5 years old) stood back to back and asked Rosa to check who was taller. Good cooperation—it is the first time Chris has shown an interest in comparing heights.

■ Mary (5 years old), working on her own, put the right number of sticks in juice cans marked with the number symbols 0 through 20. She is ready for something more challenging.

■ Last week I set out a tub of water and a variety of containers of different sizes in the mathematics and science center. The children spent the week exploring the materials. Trang Fung and Sara seemed especially interested in comparing the amount of liquid that could be held by each container. I gave each of them a standard one-cup measure and asked them to estimate how many cups of water would fill each container. Then I left it up to them to measure and record the actual amounts. They did a beautiful job of setting up a recording sheet and working together to measure the number of cups of water each container would hold. They then lined up the containers from largest to smallest volume, which demonstrated their understanding of ordering or seriation.

■ Today I read Chin's (second grader) math journal. Yesterday's entry included a chart showing the names and amounts of each type of baseball card in his collection. He also wrote his conclusions about which players and teams were his favorites as evidenced by the number of cards. Chin is skilled at organizing data and drawing conclusions, and he understands the concepts of more and less.

■ Ann and Jason (8-year-olds) argue about which materials will float and sink. They asked their teacher if they could test their theories. They got the water, collected some objects, and set up a chart to record their predictions and then the names of the items that sink and those that float. This demonstrates understanding of how to develop an investigation to solve a problem.

Observational information may also be recorded on a **checklist**. For example, concepts can be listed and then, each time the child is observed demonstrating one of the behaviors, the date can be put next to that behavior. Soon there will be a profile of the concepts the child demonstrates spontaneously (Figure 4–1).

## Assessment through Informal Conversations

As children explore materials, the teacher can informally make comments and ask them questions about their activity in order to gain insight into their thinking. Glanfield and colleagues (2003, p. 56) suggest several types of questions that can prompt students to share their thinking.

■ Tell me more about that.
■ Can you show me another way?
■ Help me understand.
■ Why did you . . . ?
■ How did you know what to do next?
■ What else do you know about . . . ?
■ What were you thinking when you . . . ?

## Interview Assessment

The individual interview is used to find out specific information in a direct way. The teacher can present a task to the child and observe and record the way the child works on the task as well as the solution she arrives at for the problem presented by the task. The accuracy of the answers is not as important as how the child arrives at the answers. Often a child starts out on the right track but gets off somewhere in the middle of the problem. For example, Kate (age 3) is asked to match four saucers with four cups. This is an example of one-to-one correspondence. She does this task easily. Next she is asked to match five cups with six saucers: "Here are some cups and saucers. Find out if there is a cup for every saucer." She puts a cup on each saucer. Left with an extra saucer, she places it under one of the pairs. She smiles happily. By observing the whole task, the teacher can see that Kate does not feel comfortable with the concept of "one more than." This is normal for a preoperational 3-year-old. She finds a way to "solve" the problem by putting two saucers under one cup. She understands the idea of matching one to one but cannot have things out of balance. Only by observing the whole task can the teacher see the reason for what appears to be a "wrong" answer to the task.

Another example: Tim, age 6, has been given 20 Unifix Cubes®, 10 red and 10 blue. His teacher asks him to count the red cubes and then the blue cubes, which he does with care and accuracy. Next, she asks him to see how many combinations of 10 he can make using the red cubes and the blue cubes. To demonstrate she counts out nine blue cubes and adds one red cube to her group to make 10. She tells him to write and/or draw each combination that he finds. His teacher watches as he counts out eight blue cubes and two red cubes. He then draws on his paper eight blue squares and two red squares.

Finally, in the second-grade class, Theresa's teacher notices that she is not very accurate in her work. The class is working on two-digit addition and subtraction with no regrouping, and the teacher is concerned that Theresa will be totally lost when they move on to regrouping. He decides to assess her process skills by having her show him with Unifix Cubes how she perceives the problems. For $22 + 31$ she takes 22 cubes and 31 cubes and makes a pile of 53. For $45 - 24$ she takes a pile of 45 and adds 24 more cubes. Her teacher

## CONCEPT ACTIVITY OBSERVATION CHECKLIST

Child's Name _____ Birth Date _____

School Year _____ Grade/Group _____

| **Concept Activities**<br>*(Concepts and activities*<br>*are described in the text)* | **Dates Observed** |
|---|---|
| Selects math center | |
| Selects science center | |
| Selects cooking center | |
| Selects math concept book | |
| Selects science book | |
| Selects sand or water | |
| Sets the table correctly | |
| Counts spontaneously | |
| Sorts play materials into logical groups | |
| Uses comparison words (i.e., *bigger, fatter,* etc.) | |
| Builds with blocks | |
| Works with part/whole materials | |
| Demonstrates an understanding of order and sequence | |
| Points out number symbols in the environment | |
| Demonstrates curiosity by asking questions, exploring the environment, and making observations | |
| Uses concept words | |

**Figure 4–1** Concept observation checklist.

An individual interview can help the teacher understand a child's thinking about math.

An individual interview can provide insight into a child's thinking about science.

realizes that Theresa is not attentive to the signs for plus and minus. He also decides she needs to work on place value and grouping by 10s and 1s.

If Kate's, Tim's, and Theresa's answers were observed only at the endpoint and recorded as right or wrong, the crux of their problems would be missed. Only the individual interview offers the opportunity to observe a child solving a problem from start to finish without distractions or interruptions.

An important factor in the one-to-one interview is that it must be done in an accepting manner by the adult. The teacher must value and accept the child's answers regardless of whether they are right or wrong from the adult point of view. If possible, the interview should be done in a quiet place where nothing else might take the child's attention off the task. The adult should be warm, pleasant, and calm. Let the child know that he is doing well with smiles, gestures (nods of approval, a pat on the shoulder), and specific praise ("You are very careful when you count the cubes"; "I can see you know how to match shapes"; "You work hard until you find an answer"; etc.).

If someone other than a teacher does the assessment interview, the teacher should be sure that the assessor spends time with the children before the interviews. Advise a person doing an interview to sit on a low chair or on the floor next to where the children are playing. Children are usually curious when they see a new person. One may ask, "Who are you? Why are you here?" The children can be told, "I am Ms. X. Someday I am going to give each of you a turn to do some special work with me. It will be a surprise. Today I want to see what you do in school and learn your names." If the interviewer pays attention to the children and shows an interest in them and their activities, they will feel comfortable and free to do their best when the day comes for their assessment interviews.

If the teacher does the assessment herself, she also should stress the special nature of the activity for her and each child: "I'm going to spend some time today doing some special work with each of you. Everyone will get a turn."

## ASSESSMENT TASK FILE

Each child and each group of children is different. The teacher needs to have on hand questions to fit each age and stage she might meet in individual young children. She also needs to add new tasks as she discovers more about children and their development. A card file or loose-leaf notebook of assessment tasks should be set up. Such a file or notebook has three advantages.

■ The teacher has a personal involvement in creating her own assessment tasks and is more likely to use them, understand them, and value them.

■ The file card or loose-leaf notebook format makes it easy to add new tasks and to revise or remove old ones.

■ There is room for the teacher to use her own creativity by adding new questions and making materials.

Use the tasks in each unit and in Appendix A to begin the file. Other tasks can be developed as students proceed through the units in this book and during the teacher's future career with young children. Directions for each task can be put on five-by-eight-inch plain white file cards. Most of the tasks will require the use of concrete materials and/or pictures. Concrete materials can be items found around the home and center. Pictures can be purchased or cut from magazines and readiness-type workbooks and glued on cards.

The basic materials needed are a five-by-eight-inch file card box, 5" × 8" unlined file cards, 5" × 8" file dividers or a loose-leaf notebook with dividers, a black pen, a set of colored markers, a ruler, scissors, glue, clear Contac or laminating material, and preschool/kindergarten readiness workbooks with artwork.

In Appendix A, each assessment task is set up as it would be on a 5" × 8" card. Observe that, on each card, what the adult says to the child is always printed in CAPITAL LETTERS so that the instructions can be found and read easily. The tasks are set up developmentally from the sensorimotor level (birth to age 2) to the preoperational level (ages 2–7) to early concrete operations (ages 6–8). The ages are flexible relative to the stages and are given only to serve as a guide for selecting the first tasks to present to each child.

Each child is at his or her own level. If the first tasks are too hard, the interviewer should go to a lower level. If the first tasks are quite easy for the child, the interviewer should go to a higher level. Figure 4–2 is a sample recording sheet format that could be used to keep track of each child's progress. Some teachers prefer an individual sheet for each child; others prefer a master sheet for the whole class. The names and numbers of the tasks to be assessed are entered in the first column. Several columns are provided for entering the date and the level of progress (+, accomplished; √, needs some help; −, needs a lot of help) for children who need repeated periods of instruction. The column on the right is for comments on the process used by the child that might give some clues as to specific instructional needs.

## ASSESSMENT TASKS

The assessment tasks included in each content unit and in Appendix A address the concepts that must be acquired by young children from birth through the primary grades. Most of the tasks require an individual interview with the child. Some tasks are observational and require recording of activities during playtime or class time. The infant tasks and observations assess the development of the child's growing sensory and motor skills. As discussed in Unit 1, these sensory and motor skills are basic to all later learning.

The assessment tasks are divided into nine developmental levels. *Levels 1 and 2* are tasks for the child in the sensorimotor stage. *Levels 3–5* include tasks of increasing difficulty for the prekindergarten child. The *Level-6* tasks are those things that most children can do upon entering kindergarten between the ages of 5 and 6; this is the level that children are growing toward during the prekindergarten years. Some children will be able to accomplish all these tasks by age 5; others, not until 6 or over. *Level 7* summarizes the math words that are usually a part of the child's natural speech by age six. *Level 8* is included as an assessment for advanced prekindergartners and for children enrolled in a kindergarten program. The child about to enter first grade should be able to accomplish the tasks at levels 6 and 8 and should also be using most of the concept words (level 7) correctly. *Level 9* includes tasks to be accomplished during the primary grades.

## EXAMPLE OF AN INDIVIDUAL INTERVIEW

Table 4–1 recounts part of the level-5 assessment interview as given to Bob (4½ years old). A corner of the storage room has been made into an assessment center. Mrs. Ramirez comes in with Bob. "You sit there, and I'll sit here, Bob. We have some important things to do." They both sit down at a low table, and Mrs. Ramirez begins the interview.

## DEVELOPMENTAL TASKS RECORDING SHEET

Child's Name ——————————————————— Birth Date ——————————

School Year ——————————— School ——————————— Teacher ———————————

Grade/Group ——————————— Person Doing Assessment ———————————

Levels: +, accomplishes; √, partial; −, cannot do task

| Task | Levels | | | Comments |
|------|--------|--------|--------|----------|
|      | Date   | Date   | Date   |          |
|      |        |        |        |          |
|      |        |        |        |          |
|      |        |        |        |          |
|      |        |        |        |          |
|      |        |        |        |          |
|      |        |        |        |          |
|      |        |        |        |          |

**Comments:**

**Figure 4–2** Recording sheet for developmental tasks.

An interview need not include any special number of tasks. For the preoperational child, the teacher can begin with matching and proceed through the ideas and skills one at a time, so each interview can be quite short if necessary.

If the interviewer has the time for longer sessions and the children are able to work for a longer period of time, the following can serve as suggested maximum amounts of time.

- 15 to 20 minutes for 2-year-olds
- 30 minutes for 3-year-olds
- 45 minutes for 4-year-olds
- Up to an hour for 5-year-olds and older

## Table 4–1

### Assessment Interview

| Mrs. Ramirez: | Bob's Response: |
|---|---|
| HOW OLD ARE YOU? | "I'm four." (He holds up four fingers.) |
| COUNT TO 10 FOR ME, BOB. (Mrs. Ramirez nods her head up and down.) | "One, two, three, four, five, six, seven, eight, nine, ten . . . I can go some more. Eleven, twelve, thirteen, twenty!" |
| HERE ARE SOME BLOCKS. HOW MANY ARE THERE? (She puts out 10 blocks.) | (He points, saying) "One, two, three, four, five, six, seven, eight, nine, ten, eleven, twelve." (He points to some more than once.) |
| GOOD, YOU COUNTED ALL THE BLOCKS, BOB. NOW COUNT THESE. (She puts out 5 blocks.) | (He counts, pushing each one he counts to the left.) "One, two, three, four, five." |
| (She puts the blocks out of sight and brings up five plastic horses and riders.) FIND OUT IF EACH RIDER HAS A HORSE. | (Bob looks over the horses and riders. He lines up the horses in a row and then puts a rider on each.) "Yes, there are enough." |
| FINE, YOU FOUND A RIDER FOR EACH HORSE, BOB. (She puts the riders and horses away. She takes out some inch cube blocks. She puts out two piles of blocks: five yellow and two orange.) | |
| DOES ONE GROUP HAVE MORE? | "Yes." (He points to the yellow.) |
| OKAY. (She puts out four blue and three green.) | |
| DOES ONE GROUP HAVE LESS? | (He points to the green blocks.) |
| GOOD THINKING. | |
| (She takes out five cutouts of bears of five different sizes.) FIND THE BIGGEST BEAR. | "Here it is." (He picks the biggest.) |
| FIND THE SMALLEST BEAR. | (He points to the smallest.) |
| PUT ALL THE BEARS IN A ROW FROM BIGGEST TO SMALLEST. | (Bob works slowly and carefully.) "All done." (Two of the middle bears are reversed.) |
| (Mrs. Ramirez smiles.) | |
| GOOD FOR YOU, BOB. YOU'RE A HARD WORKER. | |

## RECORD KEEPING AND REPORTING

The records of each child's progress and activities are kept in a **record folder** and a **portfolio**. The record folder contains anecdotal records and checklists, as already described. The portfolio is a purposeful collection of student work that tells the story of the student's efforts, progress, and achievements. It is a systematic collection of material designed to provide evidence of understanding and to monitor growth. Portfolios provide a vehicle for "authentic" assessment—that is, examples of student work done in many real-world contexts. Students and teacher work together to gather work, reflect on it, and evaluate it.

The physical setup for portfolios is important. A box or file with hanging folders is a convenient place to begin. As work accumulates, it can be placed in the hanging folders. At regular intervals, teacher and child go through the hanging files and select work to place in the portfolio. An expanding legal-size file pocket makes a convenient portfolio container. It is critical that each piece of work be dated so that growth can be tracked.

Sticky notes or self-stick mailing labels can be used to write notations on each piece of work. Labels should include the date, the type of activity, and the reason for selecting each sample.

An essential attribute of a portfolio is that items are *selected* through regularly scheduled student/teacher conferences. Teachers have always kept folders of student work, but portfolios are more focused and contain specially selected work that can be used for assessment. A portfolio offers a fuller picture than does traditional assessment because the former provides a vehicle for student reflection and self-evaluation.

Here are some examples of items that might be included in a portfolio:

■ written or dictated descriptions of the results of investigations

■ pictures—drawings, paintings, photographs of the child engaged in a significant activity; teacher or student sketches of products made with manipulatives or construction materials such as unit blocks, Unifix Cubes, buttons, and so on

■ dictated (from younger children) or written (from older children) reports of activities, investigations, experiences, ideas, and plans

■ diagrams, graphs, or other recorded data

■ excerpts from students' math, science, and/or social studies journals

■ samples of problem solutions, explanations of solutions, problems created, and the like

■ videotapes and/or audiotapes

■ journal entries

This material is invaluable for evaluation and for reporting progress to parents. When beginning portfolio

---

## SAMPLE PORTFOLIO RUBRIC

|  | Strong, Well Established | Beginning to Appear | Not Yet Observed |
|---|---|---|---|
| 1. Can organize and record data | | | |
| 2. Explores, analyzes, looks for patterns | | | |
| 3. Uses concrete materials or drawings to aid in solving problems | | | |
| 4. Investigations and activities help develop concepts | | | |
| 5. Persistent, flexible, self-directed | | | |
| 6. Works cooperatively | | | |
| 7. Enjoys math and science | | | |

Figure 4–3  General format for a rubric.

---

## PORTFOLIO SUMMARY ANALYSIS

---

CHILD'S NAME _____ DATE _____

OVERALL EVALUATION




STRENGTHS AND WEAKNESSES




FURTHER RECOMMENDATIONS




---

**Figure 4–4** Format for portfolio summary analysis.

assessment, it is wise to start small. Pick one focus such as mathematics or science, or focus on one particular area (e.g., problem solving, data from thematic investigations, artwork, writing, etc.). Beginning with a scope that is too broad can make the task overwhelming.

Evaluating a portfolio involves several steps. First, a **rubric** should be developed. A rubric is a list of general statements that define the attributes of the portfolio that should be evaluated, that is, a list of the qualities you believe are important. Rubrics should be developed based on what you are looking for in your class—not on isolated skills but rather on broad criteria that reflect understanding. The statements will vary with the content focus of the portfolio. Figure 4–3 provides a general format and sample statements. Next, a summary providing an overview should be written (Figure 4–4). If grades must be assigned, then there is a final step: the **holistic evaluation** (Figure 4–5). For a holistic evaluation, the portfolios are grouped into piles such as

| | |
|---|---|
| **4** | Strong on all the characteristics listed in the rubric. |
| **3** | Consistent evidence of the presence of most of the characteristics. |
| **2** | Some presence of the characteristics but incomplete communication or presence of ideas, concepts, and/or behaviors. |
| **1** | Little or no presence of desired characteristics. |

**Figure 4–5** Sample of a holistic scoring format.

strong, average, and weak (or very strong, strong, high average, low average, somewhat weak, and very weak) based on the rubric and the summary. This comparative analysis can then guide grading. See the reference list for publications that offer additional ideas regarding the development of portfolio assessment practices. Glanfield and colleagues (2003) suggest rubrics for evaluation of K–2 work samples.

## MAINTAINING EQUITY

As already mentioned, it is extremely important to maintain equity in assessment. Assessment must be done in an appropriate manner relative to culture, gender, language, and disabilities. It is important to gather information from multiple sources (de Melendez & Beck, 2007). Observations by teachers and family members as well as specialists should be documented. Anecdotal records, photos, videos and audiotapes can be extremely valuable. Conversations with children and parents, home visits, and interviews with family members and with other professionals can provide important information. Portfolios of work products and information from checklists can be compiled. Formal testing, if used at all, should be just one source of information and should never constitute the sole criteria for making high-stakes decisions. De Melendez and Beck underscore the importance of making modifications and adaptations for children with special needs or with cultural and linguistic differences. Ideally, assessments are done in the child's primary language. Authentic assessment tools such as portfolios are recommended for equitable assessment.

For young children with special needs, assessment should be "multidisciplinary, multidimensional, multimethod, multicontext, proactive and should involve ongoing information exchange" (Gargiulo & Kilgo, 2005, p. 103). Assessment of young children with disabilities is done by a team of professionals and family members. However, day-to-day assessment is the responsibility of the individual teacher. As with other children, the assessment must be authentic. Teachers and parents need to know when to request assessments by specialists such as the physical therapist or the speech-language therapist. Equity requires that appropriate materials are used for instruction to allow for fair assessment. In addition, adequate time must be allowed for students with disabilities to complete tasks. Gargiulo and Kilgo emphasize the importance of regular and systematic collection of assessment information. The goals included in the IFSP or IEP must be checked for progress.

## SUMMARY

The focus of assessment in mathematics and science is on assessment integrated with instruction during naturalistic classroom activities and during activities that involve performance of concrete, hands-on problem solving and child-directed investigations. The major ways to assess the developmental levels of young children are informal conversation and questioning, observation, interview, and the collection of materials in a portfolio. Observation is most useful when looking at how children use concepts in their everyday activities. The interview with one child at a time gives the teacher an opportunity to look at specific ideas and skills.

We have given guidelines for conducting an interview and a summary of the nine levels of developmental tasks, which are included in Appendix A. A sample of part of an interview showed how the exchange between interviewer and child might progress.

We described a system for record keeping, reporting, and evaluation using a record folder and a portfolio. A holistic approach to evaluation is recommended, and we have emphasized the importance of equitable systems and methods of assessment.

### KEY TERMS

| | | |
|---|---|---|
| assessment | holistic evaluation | record folder |
| checklist | portfolio | rubric |

### SUGGESTED ACTIVITIES

1. Find out what the expectations are for mathematics concept development for students entering kindergarten and/or first grade in your local school system. Compare the school system list with the tasks suggested at levels 6 and 7 in the text and in Appendix A. What are the similarities and differences?

2. Secure permission to assess the concept development level of two children at different age levels (between 4 and 8). Make assessment cards and obtain materials needed to administer two or three of the tasks to each child. Compare your results and reactions with those of other students in the class. Make a class list of improvements and suggestions.

3. Find a prekindergarten, kindergarten, or first-grade teacher who has an established portfolio assessment system. Invite the teacher to be a guest speaker in your class.

4. Obtain permission to help a child develop a math portfolio.

5. Find three articles in professional journals that discuss assessment and evaluation of young children. What are the main ideas presented? Explain how you might apply these ideas in the future.

## REVIEW

A. Explain why it is important to make assessment the first step in teaching.

B. Describe the NCTM and NRC guidelines for assessment.

C. Describe the advantages of portfolio assessment.

D. Read incidents 1 and 2, which follow. What is being done in each situation? What should be done?

   1. Ms. Collins is interviewing a child in the school hallway. Other teachers and students are continuously passing by. The child frequently looks away from the materials to watch the people passing by.

   2. Mr. Garcia is interviewing Johnny. Mr. Garcia places five rectangle shapes on the table. Each is the same length, but they vary in width.

**Mr. Garcia:**

WATCH WHAT I DO. (Mr. Garcia lines up the rectangles from widest to thinnest.) NOW I'LL MIX THEM UP. YOU PUT THEM IN A ROW FROM FATTEST TO THINNEST. (Mr. Garcia is looking ahead at the next set of instructions. He glances at Johnny with a rather serious expression.)

**Johnny's response:**

(Johnny picks out the fattest and thinnest rectangles. He places them next to each other. Then he examines the other three rectangles and lines them up in sequence next to the first two. He looks up at Mr. Garcia.)

**Mr. Garcia:**

ARE YOU FINISHED?

Johnny's response:

(Johnny nods his head yes.)

Mr. Garcia:

TOO BAD, YOU MIXED THEM UP.

E. Explain how you would plan for math and science assessment that meets the standards of equity for all types of students.

## REFERENCES

de Melendez, W. R., & Beck, V. (2007). *Teaching young children in multicultural classrooms* (2nd ed.). Albany, NY: Thomson Delmar Learning.

Gargiulo, R., & Kilgo, J. (2005). *Young children with special needs* (2nd ed.). Albany, NY: Thomson Delmar Learning.

Glanfield, F., Bush, W. S., & Stenmark, J. K. (Eds.). (2003). *Mathematics assessment: A practical handbook for grades K–2.* Reston, VA: National Council of Teachers of Mathematics.

National Council of Teachers of Mathematics. (1989). *Curriculum and evaluation standards for school mathematics.* Reston, VA: Author.

National Council of Teachers of Mathematics. (1995). *Assessment standards for school mathematics.* Reston, VA: Author.

National Council of Teachers of Mathematics. (2000). *Principles and standards for school mathematics.* Reston, VA: Author.

National Research Council. (1996). *National science education standards.* Washington, DC: National Academies Press.

National Research Council. (2001). *Classroom assessment and the national science education standards.* Washington, DC: National Academies Press.

## FURTHER READING AND RESOURCES

Alternative assessments [Focus issue]. (2003). *Science and Children, 40*(8).

Assessment tools and strategies [Focus issue]. (2004). *Science and Children, 42*(1).

Atkin, J. M., & Coffey, J. E. (2003). *Everyday assessment in the science classroom.* Arlington, VA: NSTA Press.

Buschman, L. (2001). Using student interviews to guide classroom instruction: An action research project. *Teaching Children Mathematics, 8*(4), 222–227.

Charlesworth, R., Fleege, P. O., & Weitman, C. (1994). Research on the effects of standardized testing on instruction: New directions for policy. *Early Education and Child Development, 5,* 195–212.

Committee on Science Learning, Kindergarten through Eighth Grade. Board on Science Education, Center for Education. (2007). *Taking science to school: Learning and teaching science in grades K–8.* Washington, DC: National Academies Press.

Cooney, T. J., Mewborn, D. S., Sanchez, W. B., & Leatham, K. (2002). *Open-ended assessment in math: Grades 2–12.* Westport, CT: Heinemann.

Copley, J. V. (1999). Assessing the mathematical understanding of the young child. In J. V. Copley (Ed.), *Mathematics in the early years* (pp. 182–188). Reston, VA: National Council of Teachers of Mathematics, and Washington, DC: National Association for the Education of Young Children.

Dios, B., & Gist, N. (2006). *Math assessment tasks.* Monterey, CA: Evan-Moor.

Guha, S., & Doran, R. (1999). Playful activities for young children: Assessment tasks with low reading and writing demands for young children. *Science and Children, 37*(2), 36–40.

Huniker, D. (Ed.). (2006). *Pre-K–grade 2 mathematics assessment sampler.* Reston, VA: National Council of Teachers of Mathematics.

Jacobs, V. R., Ambrose, R. C., Clement, L., & Brown, D. (2006). Using teacher-produced videotapes of student interviews as discussion catalysts. *Teaching Children Mathematics, 12*(6), 276–281.

Kamii, C. (Ed.). (1990). *Achievement testing in the early grades: The games grown-ups play.* Washington, DC: National Association for the Education of Young Children.

Kamii, C., & Lewis, B. A. (1991). Achievement tests in primary mathematics: Perpetuating lower order thinking. *Arithmetic Teacher, 38*(9), 4–9.

Kohn, A. (2000). *The case against standardized testing: Raising the scores, ruining the schools.* Portsmouth, NH: Heinemann.

Kohn, A. (2001). Fighting the tests: Turning frustration into action. *Young Children, 56*(2), 19–24.

Leatham, K. R., Lawrence, K., & Mewborn, D. S. (2005). Getting started with open-ended assessment. *Teaching Children Mathematics, 11*(8), 413–419.

Mindes, G. (2007). *Assessing young children* (3rd ed.). Upper Saddle River, NJ: Pearson-Merrill/Prentice-Hall.

Shores, E. F., & Grace, C. (1998). *The portfolio book.* Beltsville, MD: Gryphon House.

St. Clair, J. (1993). Assessing mathematical understanding in a bilingual kindergarten. In N. L. Webb & A. F. Coxford (Eds.), *Assessment in the mathematics classroom, 1993 yearbook* (pp. 65–73). Reston, VA: National Council of Teachers of Mathematics.

Wesson, K. A. (2001). The "Volvo effect"—Questioning standardized tests. *Young Children, 56*(2), 16–18.

# Unit 5
## The Basics of Science

## OBJECTIVES

After reading this unit, you should be able to:

- Define the relative importance of science content, processes, and attitudes in teaching young children.
- Explain why science should be taught to young children.
- Identify the major areas of science instruction.
- List the science attitudes and process skills appropriate to preschool and primary grades.
- Select appropriate science topics for teaching science to young children.
- Select appropriate science content topics from the *National Science Education Standards*.

## SCIENCE AND WHY WE TEACH IT TO YOUNG CHILDREN

When people think of science, they generally think first of the content of science. Science is often viewed as an encyclopedia of discoveries and technological achievements. Formal training in science classes often promotes this view by requiring the memorization of seemingly endless science concepts. Science has been compiling literally millions of discoveries, facts, and data over thousands of years. We are now living in an age that has been described as the "knowledge explosion." Consider that the amount of scientific information amassed between 1900 and 1950 equals that which was learned from the beginning of recorded history until the year 1900. Since 1950, the rate of newly discovered scientific information has increased even further. Some scientists estimate that the total amount of scientific information produced now doubles every 2–5 years.

If you tried to teach all that has been learned in science—starting in preschool and continuing daily straight through high school—you could make only a small dent in the body of knowledge. It is simply impossible to learn everything. Yet despite this, far too many teachers approach the task of teaching children science as if it were a body of information that anyone can memorize. In fact, it is nearly impossible to predict what specific information taught to preschool and primary grade students today will be of use to them as they pursue a career through the twenty-first century.

It is entirely possible that today's body of science knowledge will change before a child graduates from high school. Scientists are constantly looking at data in different ways and arriving at new conclusions. Thus, it cannot be predicted with any certainty which facts will be the most important for students to learn for life in the years to come. What *is* known is that individuals will always be facing new problems that they will attempt to solve. Life, in a sense, is a series of problems. Those who are most successful in future decades will be the ones who are best equipped to solve the problems they encounter.

This discussion is intended to put the nature of science in perspective. Science in preschool through college should be viewed more as a verb than a noun. It is not so much a body of knowledge as it is a way of thinking and acting. Science is a way of trying to discover the nature of things. The attitudes and thinking skills that have moved science forward through the centuries are the same attitudes and skills that enable individuals to solve the problems they encounter in everyday life.

An approach to science teaching that emphasizes the development of thinking and the open-minded attitudes of science would seem to be most appropriate for the instruction of young children. It is also important for the exploration of science topics to be enjoyable. This supports a lifelong learning of science. This unit covers science processes, attitudes, content, and the importance of science in language arts and reading. In 1996, the National Research Council published the ***National Science Education Standards***, which were designed to support the development of a scientific literate society. The content standards help identify what children at different ages and stages should know and be able to do in the area of science. The standards describe appropriate content for children in kindergarten through the fourth grade. They also identify the processes, skills, and attitudes needed to successfully understand science (Figure 5–1).

| Content Standards, Grades K–4 | | | |
|---|---|---|---|
| **Unifying Concepts and Processes** | **Science as Inquiry** | **Physical Science** | **Life Science** |
| Systems, order, and organization | Abilities necessary to do scientific inquiry | Properties of objects and materials | Characteristics of organisms |
| Evidence, models, and explanation | Understandings about scientific inquiry | Position and motion of objects | Life cycles of organisms |
| Change, constancy, and measurement | | Light, heat, electricity, and magnetism | Organisms and environments |
| Evolution and equilibrium | | | |
| Form and function | | | |
| **Earth and Space Science** | **Science and Technology** | **Science in Personal and Social Perspectives** | **History and Nature of Science** |
| Properties of earth materials | Abilities of technological design | Personal health | Science as a human endeavor |
| Objects in the sky | Understandings about science and technology | Characteristics and changes in populations | |
| Changes in earth and sky | Abilities to distinguish between natural objects and objects made by humans | Types of resources | |
| | | Changes in environments | |
| | | Science and technology in local challenges | |

**Figure 5–1** Content standards, grades K–4, from the *National Science Education Standards* (National Research Council, 1996).

# SCIENCE AS INQUIRY

The *National Science Education Standards* emphasize science as inquiry, which is divided into abilities children need for sound scientific inquiry and understandings they should have about scientific inquiry. Inquiry is presented as a step beyond such process learning skills as observing, inferring, and predicting. These skills are required for inquiry, but students must combine these skills with scientific knowledge as they use scientific reasoning and critical thinking to develop understanding. According to the standards, engaging students in inquiry serves five essential functions:

- Assists in the development of understanding of scientific concepts.
- Helps students "know how we know" in science.
- Develops an understanding of the nature of science.
- Develops the skills necessary to become independent inquirers about the natural world.
- Develops the dispositions to use the skills, abilities, and habits of mind associated with science.

Inquiry-oriented instruction, often contrasted with expository methods, reflects the constructivist model of learning and is often referred to as *active learning*. Osborne and Freyberg (1985) describe the constructivist model of learning as the result of ongoing changes in our mental frameworks as we attempt to make meaning out of our experiences. In order to develop scientific inquiry skills, kindergarten and primary grade children need the following skills.

- Plan and conduct a simple investigation.
- Employ simple equipment and tools to gather data.
- Use data to construct reasonable explanations.
- Communicate the results of the investigations and give explanations.

Additional strategies that encourage students in the active search for knowledge are discussed in Unit 6.

# TEACHING THE PROCESSES OF INQUIRY

The *National Science Education Standards* emphasize that, as a result of science investigations in the primary grades, all students should begin to develop the abilities necessary to do more advanced scientific inquiry in later years. Children discover the content of science by using the processes of science inquiry. This can be done through science investigations, class discussions, reading and writing, and a variety of other teaching strategies. These are the thinking skills and processes necessary to learn science.

Science **process skills** are those that allow students to process new information through concrete experiences (Figure 5–2). They are also progressive, each building on and overlapping one another. The skills most appropriate for preschool and primary students are the basic skills of **observing**, **comparing**, **classifying**, **measuring**, and **communicating**. Sharpening these skills is essential for coping with daily life as well as for future study in science and mathematics. As students move through the primary grades, mastery of these skills will enable them to perform intermediate process skills that include gathering and organizing information, **inferring**, and **predicting**. If students have a strong base of primary and intermediate process skills, they will be prepared by the time they reach the intermediate grades to apply those skills to the more sophisticated and abstract skills, such as forming **hypotheses** and separating **variables**, that are required in experimentation.

Grade-level suggestions for introducing specific science process skills are given as a general guide for their appropriate use. Because students vary greatly in experience and intellectual development, you may find that your early childhood students are ready to explore higher-level process skills sooner. In such cases you should feel free to stretch their abilities by encouraging them to work with more advanced science process skills. For example, 4- and 5-year-olds can begin with simple versions of intermediate process skills, such as making a reasonable guess about a physical change (What will happen when the butter is heated?) as a first step toward predicting. They can gather and organize simple data (such as counting the days until the chicks hatch) and

---

Basic Process Skills

1. *Observing.* Using the senses to gather information about objects or events.
2. *Comparing.* Looking at similarities and differences in real objects. In the primary grades, students begin to compare and contrast ideas, concepts, and objects.
3. *Classifying.* Grouping and sorting according to properties such as size, shape, color, use, and so on.
4. *Measuring.* Quantitative descriptions made by an observer either directly through observation or indirectly with a unit of measure.
5. *Communicating.* Communicating ideas, directions, and descriptions orally or in written form such as pictures, maps, graphs, or journals so others can understand what you mean.

Intermediate Process Skills

6. *Inferring.* Based on observations but suggests more meaning about a situation than can be directly observed. When children infer, they recognize patterns and expect these patterns to recur under similar circumstances.
7. *Predicting.* Making reasonable guesses or estimations based on observations and prior knowledge and experiences.

Advanced Process Skills

8. *Hypothesizing.* Devising a statement, based on observations, that can be tested by experiment. A typical form for a hypothesis is, "*If* water is put in the freezer overnight, *then* it freezes."
9. *Defining and controlling variables.* Determining which variables in an investigation should be studied or should be controlled to conduct a controlled experiment. For example, when we find out if a plant grows in the dark, we must also grow a plant in the light.

---

**Figure 5–2** Science process skills.

make simple graphs like those described in Unit 20. Giving preoperational children the opportunity to engage in inferring and predicting allows them to refine these skills. Teachers understand that young children need repeated experiences before they can become proficient.

## SCIENCE PROCESS SKILLS USED IN INQUIRY

Knowledge and concepts are developed through the use of the processes used in inquiry. It is with these processes and skills that individuals think through and study problems and begin to develop an understanding about scientific inquiry.

## Observing

The most fundamental of the scientific thinking process skills is observation. It is only through this process that we are able to receive information about the world around us. The senses of sight, smell, sound, touch, and taste are the means by which our brains receive information and give us the ability to describe something. As young children use their senses in a firsthand exploratory way, they are using the same skills that scientists extend to construct meaning and knowledge in the world.

Sometimes we *see* but do not properly *observe*. Teaching strategies that reinforce observation skills require children to observe carefully to note specific phenomena that they might ordinarily overlook. For example, when Mr. Wang's class observes an aquarium, he guides them by asking, "Which fish seems to spend the most time on the bottom of the tank? In what way do the fish seem to react to things like light or shadow or an object in their swimming path?"

Observation is the first step in gathering information to solve a problem. Students will need opportunities to observe size, shape, color, texture, and other observable properties in objects. Teacher statements and questions facilitate the use of this process: "Tell me what you see." "What do you hear?" "What does this feel like?" "How would you describe the object?"

## Comparing

As children develop skills in observation, they will naturally begin to compare and contrast and to identify similarities and differences. The comparing process, which sharpens their observation skills, is the first step toward classifying.

Teachers can encourage children to find likenesses and differences throughout the school day. A good example of this strategy can be seen when, after a walk through a field, Mrs. Red Fox asks her first graders, "Which seeds are sticking to your clothes?" and "How are these seeds alike?"

The comparing process builds upon the process of observing. In addition to observing the characteristics of an object such as a leaf, children learn more about the leaf by comparing it to other leaves. For example, a child finds a leaf and brings it to class to compare with other leaves in the leaf collection. Statements and questions that facilitate the comparing process include: "How are these alike?" "How are these different?" "Which of these is bigger?" "Compare similarities and differences between these two animals." Begin by having children tell you about the characteristics of the objects. Next, have the children compare objects and discuss how and why they feel the objects are similar or different.

## Classifying

*Classifying* begins when children group and sort real objects. The grouping and sorting are done based on the observations they make about the objects' characteristics. To *group*, children need to compare objects and develop subsets. A **subset** is a group that shares a common characteristic unique to that group. For example, the jar may be full of buttons, but children are likely to begin grouping by sorting the buttons into subsets of red buttons, yellow buttons, blue buttons, and other colors.

Mrs. Jones has her kindergarten children collect many kinds of leaves. They place individual leaves between two squares of wax paper. Mrs. Jones covers the wax paper squares with a piece of smooth cloth and presses the cloth firmly with a warm steam iron. The leaf is now sealed in and will remain preserved for the rest of the year.

Once the leaves are prepared, the children choose a leaf to examine, draw, and describe. They carefully observe and compare leaves to discover each leaf's unique characteristics. Then, the children classify the leaves into subsets of common characteristics. Once the children have completed their classifications, have them explain how they made their decisions. The discussion generated will give the teacher insight into a child's thinking.

Children initially group by one property, such as sorting a collection of leaves by color, size, shape, and so on. As children grow older and advance in the classification process, objects or ideas are put together on the basis of two or more characteristics that are inherent in the items. For example, brown-colored animals with four legs can be grouped with all brown-colored animals (regardless of the number of legs) or with four-legged animals (regardless of color). Scientists from all disciplines use organization processes to group and classify their work, whether that work involves leaves, flowers, animals, rocks, liquids, or rockets. Statements and questions that facilitate this process include: "Put together all of the animals that belong together." "Can you group them in another way?" "How are these animals organized?" "Identify several ways that you used to classify these animals."

## Measuring

*Measuring* is the skill of quantifying observations. This can involve numbers, distances, time, volumes, and temperature, which may or may not be quantified with standard units. Nonstandard units are involved when children say that they have used two "shakes" of salt while cooking or a "handful" of rice and a "couple" of beans when creating their collage.

Children can also invent units of measure. For example, when given beans to measure objects, Vanessa may state that the book is "12 beans long" while Ann finds that the same book is "11 beans long." Activities such as this help children see a need for a standard unit of measure. Questions that facilitate the measuring process include: "How might you measure this object?" "Which object do you think is heavier?" "How could you find out?"

## Communicating

All humans communicate in some way. Gestures, body postures and positions, facial expressions, vocal sounds, words, and pictures are some of the ways we communicate with each other and express feelings. It is through communication that scientists share their findings with the rest of the world.

In early childhood science explorations, communicating refers to the skill of describing a phenomenon. A child communicates ideas, directions, and descriptions orally or in written form, such as in pictures, dioramas, maps, graphs, journals, and reports. Communication requires that information be collected, arranged, and presented in a way that helps others understand your meaning.

Teachers encourage communication when they ask children to keep logs, draw diagrams or graphs, or otherwise record an experience they have observed. Children respond well to tasks such as recording daily weather by writing down the date, time of day, and drawing pictures of the weather that day. They will enjoy answering questions about their observations, such as: "What was the temperature on Tuesday?" "Was the sun out on Wednesday?" "What did you see?" "Draw a picture of what you see."

## Inferring

When children *infer*, they make a series of observations, categorize them, and then try to give them some meaning. An inference is arrived at indirectly (not directly, as with simple observations). For example: You look out the window, see the leaves moving on the trees, and infer that the wind is blowing. You have not experienced the wind directly but—based on your observations and prior knowledge and experience—you know that the wind is blowing. In this case, your inference can be tested simply by walking outside.

The process skill of inferring requires a reasonable assumption of prior knowledge. It requires children to infer something that they have not yet seen—either because it has not happened or because it cannot be observed directly. For this reason, the inferring process is most appropriate for middle-level grades and the science content associated with those grades. However, science content and inferences associated with past experiences can be appropriate for older primary grade children. For instance, younger children can make inferences about what animals made a set of tracks, the loss of water from plants, and the vapor in air.

In another example, a teacher prepares four film canisters by filling them with different substances such as sand, chalk, stones, marbles, and paper clips. As the students observe the closed canisters, the teacher asks: "What do you think is inside of these canisters?" "What did you observe that makes you think that?" "Could there be anything else in the canister?" "How could you find out?"

## Predicting

When you predict, you are making a statement about what you expect to happen in the future. You make a reasonable guess or estimation based on observations of data. Keep in mind that this process is more than a simple guess. Children should have the prior knowledge necessary to make a reasonable prediction. Children enjoy simple prediction questions.

After reading Seymour Simon's *Science in a Vacant Lot* (1970), children can count the number of seeds in a seed package and then predict how many of the seeds will grow into plants. As they prepare to keep a record of how two plants grow (one has been planted in topsoil; the other in subsoil), they are asked: "Which plant do you think will grow better?"

The ability and willingness to take a risk and form a prediction (e.g., "If you race the metal car with the wooden car, the metal car will go faster") is of great importance in developing an awareness and understanding of cause and effect. This awareness can be developed and refined in many situations into the related skill of perceiving a pattern emerging and predicting accurately how it will continue. For example, if children are investigating changes in the shape of a piece of clay as more weight is added, they can be encouraged to look for patterns in their results, which can be recorded by drawing or measuring, and to predict what each succeeding result will be. The more predictions children are able to make, the more accurate they become. Always ask children to explain how they arrived at their prediction. By listening to their reasoning you may find that children know more than you think.

## Hypothesizing and Controlling Variables = Investigation

To be called an *experiment*, an investigation must contain a hypothesis and control variables. A *hypothesis* is a more formal operation than the investigative questions that young children explore in the preschool and primary grades. A hypothesis is a statement of a relationship that might exist between two variables. A typical form of a hypothesis is: if _____, then _____. With young children, a hypothesis can take the form of a question such as, "What happens if the magnet drops?"

In a formal experiment, variables are defined and controlled. Although experiments can be attempted with primary grade children, experimental investigations are most appropriate in the middle and upper grades.

The question of "What is a hypothesis?" has probably caused more confusion than the other science processes. Hypotheses can be described as simply the tentative answers or untried solutions to the questions, puzzles, or problems that scientists are investigating. The major types of hypotheses are varied in character, but they correspond to the types of knowledge or understanding that the investigation aims to develop. Strategies for creating an environment that encourages investigation can be found in Unit 6.

## DEVELOPING SCIENTIFIC ATTITUDES USED IN INQUIRY

In some ways, attitudes toward a subject or activity can be as important as the subject itself. Examples include individuals who continue to smoke even though they know it could kill them and people who don't wear seat belts even though they know that doing so would greatly improve their chances of surviving an automobile accident. The same is true with scientific attitudes.

The scientific attitudes of **curiosity**, **skepticism**, positive self-image, and positive approach to failure are listed together with other relevant attitudes in Figure 5–3.

### Curiosity

Preschool and primary students are obviously not mentally developed to a point where they can think

| | |
|---|---|
| Curiosity | Checking evidence |
| Withholding judgment | Positive approach to failure |
| Skepticism | Positive self-image |
| Objectivity | Willingness to change |
| Open-mindedness | Positive attitude toward change |
| Avoiding dogmatism | Avoiding superstitions |
| Avoiding gullibility | Integrity |
| Observing carefully | Humility |
| Making careful conclusions | |

**Figure 5–3** Scientific attitudes.

consciously about forming attitudes for systematically pursuing problems, but they can practice behaviors that will create lifelong habits that reflect scientific attitudes.

Curiosity is thought to be one of the most valuable attitudes that can be possessed by anyone. It takes a curious individual to look at something from a new perspective, question something long believed to be true, or look more carefully at an exception to the rule. This approach, which is basic to science, is natural to young children. They use all their senses and energies to find out about the world around them. Often this valuable characteristic is squelched by years of formalized school experiences that allow little time for exploration and questioning. Educational experiences that incorporate firsthand inquiry experiences, as characterized by the learning cycle described in Unit 6, exploit a child's natural curiosity instead of suppressing it.

### Skepticism

Do you hesitate to believe everything that you see? Are you skeptical about some things that you hear? Good! This attitude reflects the healthy skepticism required by both science and the child's environment. Children need to be encouraged to question, wonder, ask "why," and be cautious about accepting things at face value. Experiences designed to incorporate direct observation of phenomena and the gathering of data naturally encourage children to explore new situations in an objective and open-minded fashion. This type of experience can do much toward developing confidence and a healthy skepticism.

### Positive Approach to Failure and Self-Image

A positive approach to failure and a positive self-image are closely related attitudes. Students need the opportunity to ask their own questions and seek their own solutions to problems. At times this may mean that they will pursue dead ends, but often much more is learned in the pursuit than in the correct answer. Children who are conditioned to expect adult authority figures to identify and solve problems will have a difficult time approaching new problems—both as students and as adults.

For the last 20 years, some educators have believed that children should not be allowed to experience failure. Educational situations were structured so that every child could be successful nearly all the time. It was reasoned that the experience of failure would discourage students from future study. In the field of science, however, it is as important to find out what does not work as it is to find out what does. In fact, real advances in science tend to occur when solutions do not fit the predictions. Although students should not be constantly confronted with frustrating learning situations, a positive attitude toward failure may better serve them in developing problem-solving skills. After all, in much of science inquiry, there are no "right" or "wrong" answers.

The remaining science attitudes, *willingness to change, positive attitude toward change, withholding judgment, avoiding superstitions, integrity,* and *humility* are important both for science and for functioning as a successful adult. These attitudes can be encouraged in science teaching by the teacher's exhibiting them and acknowledging students who demonstrate them. All of these attitudes that support the enterprise of science are also valuable tools for young students in approaching life's inevitable problems.

## SCIENCE CONTENT KNOWLEDGE AND LEARNING AND THE DEVELOPMENT OF LITERACY

An often-heard question is, "Why bother teaching science to young children?" Many teachers believe that they have too much to do in a day and that they cannot afford to take the time to teach science. The answer to why science should be taught is: "You cannot afford *not* to teach science." Piaget's theory leaves no question as to the importance of learning through activity. The Council for Basic Education reports that there is impressive evidence that hands-on science programs aid in the development of language and reading skills. Some evidence indicates that achievement scores increase as a result of such programs. This statement is supported by many researchers. The following are possible explanations for this improvement:

In its early stages, literacy can be supported by giving children an opportunity to manipulate familiar and unfamiliar objects. During science experiences, children use the thinking skills of science to match, discriminate, sequence, describe, and classify objects. These perceptual skills are among those needed for reading and writing (Figure 5–4). A child who is able to make fine discriminations between objects will be better prepared to discriminate between letters and words of the alphabet. As children develop conventional reading and writing skills, they can apply their knowledge to facilitate their explorations in science by reading background material and recording hypotheses, observations, and interactions.

What better way to allow for children to develop communication skills than to participate in the "action plus talk" of science! Depending on the age level, children may want to communicate what they are doing to the teacher and other students. They may even start talking about themselves. Communication by talking, drawing, painting, modeling, constructing, drama,

| THINKING SKILLS USED DURING SCIENCE EXPERIENCES | THINKING SKILLS NEEDED FOR READING AND WRITING |
| --- | --- |
| Matching similar and logical characteristics | Comparing information and events |
| Discriminating physical observations and data | Discriminating letters and sounds |
| Sequencing procedures | Arranging ideas and following sequential events |
| Describing observations | Communicating ideas |
| Classifying objects | Distinguishing concepts |

**Figure 5–4** Science and reading connection.

puppets, and writing should be encouraged. These are natural communication outcomes of hands-on science.

Reading and listening to stories about the world is difficult when you do not have a base of experience. If story time features a book about a hamster named Charlie, it might be difficult to understand what is happening if you have not seen a hamster. However, the communication gap is bridged if children have knowledge about small animals. Once a child has contact with the object represented by the written word, meaning can be developed. Words do not make a lot of sense when you do not have the background experience to understand what you read.

The relationship of language developed in the context of the direct experiences of science is explored in Unit 7. Ideas for working with experience charts, tactile sensations, listening, writing, and introducing words are included in curriculum integration.

Science also provides various opportunities to determine cause-and-effect relationships. A sense of self-esteem and control over their lives develops when children discover cause-and-effect relationships and when they learn to influence the outcome of events. For example, a child can experience a causal relationship by deciding whether to add plant cover to an aquarium. Predicting the most probable outcome of actions gives children a sense of control, which is identified by Mary Budd Rowe as "fate control." She found that problem-solving behaviors seem to differ according to how people rate on measures of fate control: Children scoring high on these measures performed better at solving problems.

Keep in mind that the child who is academically advanced in math and reading is not always the first to solve a problem or assemble the most interesting collection. If sufficient time to work with materials is provided, children with poor language development may exhibit good reasoning. It is a mistake to correlate language skills with mental ability.

## APPROPRIATE SCIENCE CONTENT

The science content for preschool and primary education is not greatly different from that of any other elementary grade level in the following sense: The depth and complexity of the science content and process skills are determined by the developmental level of the child. As previously mentioned, the way that science is taught is probably far more important than the science content itself. The four main areas of science emphasis that are common in the primary grades are life science, health science, physical science, and earth and environmental science. Ideally, each of the four main areas should be given a balanced coverage. Appropriate science concepts for the early childhood years can be found throughout the text and specifically in the units dealing with science content.

## LIFE SCIENCE, PHYSICAL SCIENCE, AND EARTH AND SPACE SCIENCE STANDARDS

The *National Science Education Standards* (1996) content standards for life science, physical science, and earth and space science (Figure 5–5) describe the changing emphasis in subject matter of science using the widely accepted divisions of the domains of science. All of these content areas focus on the science facts, concepts, principles, theories, and models that are important for all students to know, understand, and use.

### Life Science

In life science, children in kindergarten through grade four are expected to develop an understanding of the characteristics of organisms, the life cycles of organisms, and organisms and environments. The observations and skills needed to gain an understanding of life science in the primary grades and beyond begin with the observations and investigative explorations of prekindergarten children.

Science teaching at this level is traditionally dominated by life science experiences. This is not because it is most appropriate but rather because of tradition. Teaching at early elementary grades has its roots in the nature study and garden school movements of the first half of the twentieth century. Many programs and materials for young children concentrate much time on life science to the exclusion of other science content. This can be attributed to teachers seeking to take advantage of children's interest in what makes up their world. Children are natural observers and enjoy finding

CHANGING EMPHASES IN THE NATIONAL SCIENCE EDUCATION STANDARDS

The National Science Education Standards envision change throughout the system. The science content standards encompass the following changes in emphases:

| LESS EMPHASIS ON | MORE EMPHASIS ON |
|---|---|
| Knowing scientific facts and information | Understanding scientific concepts and developing abilities of inquiry |
| Studying subject matter disciplines (physical, life, earth science) for their own sake | Learning subject matter disciplines in the context of inquiry, technology, science in personal and social perspectives, and history and nature of science |
| Separating science knowledge and science processes | Integrating all aspects of science content |
| Covering many science topics | Studying a few fundamental science concepts |
| Implementing inquiry as a set of processes | Implementing inquiry as instructional strategies, abilities, and ideas to be learned |

**Figure 5–5** Changing emphases in the *National Science Education Standards* (National Research Council, 1996).

out about the living world around them. Still, although life science is an important part of the curriculum for young children, it should not be the entire curriculum.

Life science investigations lend themselves quite readily to simple observations, explorations, and classifications. As with all science content at this level, hands-on experiences are essential to development of relevant concepts, skills, and attitudes. The areas of content typically covered with young children are plants, animals, and ecology. These experiences should build a foundation for students' understanding of environmental problems and solutions in higher grade levels and in adult life. Intelligent decision making regarding the interaction of science, technology, and the environment may well be a critical factor for survival in the twenty-first century. Examples of strategies for teaching appropriate life science content are found in Units 33, 34, 39, and 40.

## Physical Science

In physical science, children in kindergarten through grade four are expected to develop an understanding of the properties of objects and materials; position and motion of objects; and light, heat, electricity, and mag-

netism. Although prekindergarten children are not able to learn the science concepts at this level, they are able to learn the basic concepts and skills as they become familiar with the materials needed to prepare them for higher-level thinking.

Young children enjoy pushing on levers, making bulbs light, working with magnets, using a string-and-can telephone, and changing the form of matter. This is the study of physical science—forces, motion, energy, and machines. Teachers will enjoy watching a child assemble an assortment of blocks, wheels, and axles into a vehicle that really works. Physical science activities are guaranteed to make a child's face light up and ask, "How did you do that?" It may take years for children to fully understand systems and levers, but children of all ages recognize that gears must make physical contact with each other in order to form a working system.

Sometimes the content of this area is overlooked, which is unfortunate because physical science lends itself quite well to the needs of young children. One advantage of physical science activities is that they are more foolproof than many other activities. For example, if a young child is investigating the growth of plants, many things can go wrong that will destroy the investigation. Plants can die, get moldy, or take so long to give the desired effect that the children lose interest. Physical science usually "happens" more quickly. If something damages the investigation, it can always be repeated in a matter of minutes. Repeatability of activities is a significant advantage in developing a process orientation to science.

Keep in mind that children are growing up in a technological world. They interact daily with technology. It is likely that future lifestyles and job opportunities may depend on skills related to the realm of physical science.

## Earth and Space Science

In earth and space science, students in kindergarten through grade 4 gain an understanding of properties of earth materials, objects in the sky, and changes in the earth and sky.

The study of earth science also allows many opportunities to help children develop process skills. Children are eager to learn about weather and how soil is formed. Air, land, water, and rocks as well as the sun, moon, and stars are all a part of earth science. Although these topics are attention grabbers, to be effective the teacher of young children must be certain to make the phenomena concrete for them. Hands-on experiences need not be difficult. Try making fossil cookies, weather and temperature charts, parachutes, and rock and cloud observations to teach a concept. Unit 36 gives a number of examples of how the earth sciences can be made appropriate for young children. Refer to Units 33, 34, 37, 39, and 40 for environmental education ideas.

## SCIENCE IN PERSONAL AND SOCIAL PERSPECTIVES

### Health Science and Nutrition

In the *National Science Education Standards* content standard for science in personal and social perspectives, children are expected to develop an understanding of personal health, characteristics and changes in populations, types of resources, changes in environments,

and science and technology in local challenges. Refer to Units 36, 37, 38, 40, and 41 for additional strategies.

The study of health and the human body is receiving increased emphasis in elementary education. Recent concerns about problems of drug abuse, communicable diseases, and the relationship of nutrition and health have given rise to education in both factual information and refusal skills like "saying no." Such education will help children take action to prevent the spread of disease, maintain a healthy body, and ask the types of questions that will ensure informed decisions.

Young children are curious about their bodies and are eager to learn more about themselves. They will enjoy exploring body parts and their relationships, body systems, foods, and nutrition. Misconceptions and worries that children have can be clarified by learning "all about me" in a variety of hands-on experiences.

## Science and Technology Education

The content standard for science and technology focuses on establishing connections between the natural and designed worlds and providing opportunities for children to develop their decision-making skills. By the fourth grade, a child is expected to be able to distinguish between natural objects and objects made by humans (technological design) and to exhibit a basic understanding of science and technology. Strategies for using science and technology education are integrated throughout the text but are emphasized in Units 26, 36, 37, 38, and 40.

## History and Nature of Science

In the *National Science Education Standards* content standard for history and nature of science, students are expected to develop an understanding of science as a human endeavor. When children are at an early age, teachers should begin to encourage their questions and investigations and, when appropriate, offer experiences that involve investigating and thinking about explanations.

Fundamental concepts and principles that underlie this standard have been practiced by people for a long time and extend over all of the units.

## SCIENCE AS INQUIRY STANDARDS

**LEVELS K-4**
Abilities necessary to do scientific inquiry

Understanding about scientific inquiry

**LEVELS 5-8**
Abilities necessary to do scientific inquiry

Understanding about scientific inquiry

**LEVELS 9-12**
Abilities necessary to do scientific inquiry

Understanding about scientific inquiry

## PHYSICAL SCIENCE STANDARDS

**LEVELS K-4**
Properties of objects and materials

Position and motion of objects

Light, heat, electricity, and magnetism

**LEVELS 5-8**
Properties and changes of properties in matter

Motions and forces

Transfers of energy

**LEVELS 9-12**
Structure of atoms

Structure and properties of matter

Chemical reactions
Motions and forces
Conservation of energy and increase in disorder
Interactions of energy and matter

## LIFE SCIENCE STANDARDS

**LEVELS K-4**
Characteristics of organisms

Life cycles of organisms
Organisms and environments

**LEVELS 5-8**
Structure and function in living systems

Reproduction and heredity
Regulation and behavior
Populations and ecosystems
Diversity and adaptations of organisms

**LEVELS 9-12**
The cell

Molecular basis of heredity
Biological evolution
Interdependence of organisms
Matter, energy, and organizations in living systems
Behavior of organisms

## EARTH AND SPACE SCIENCE STANDARDS

**LEVELS K-4**
Properties of earth materials
Objects in the sky
Changes in the earth and sky

**LEVELS 5-8**
Structure of the earth system
Earth's history
Earth in the solar system

**LEVELS 9-12**
Energy in the earth system
Geochemical cycles
Origin and evolution of the earth system
Origin and evolution of the universe

**Figure 5–6** The *National Science Education Standards* (National Research Council, 1996).

| SCIENCE AND TECHNOLOGY SCIENCE STANDARDS | | |
|---|---|---|
| **LEVELS K-4**<br>Abilities to distinguish between natural objects and objects made by humans<br><br>Abilities of technological design<br><br>Understanding about science and technology | **LEVELS 5-8**<br>Abilities of technological design<br><br><br><br>Understanding about science and technology | **LEVELS 9-12**<br>Abilities of technological design<br><br><br><br>Understanding about science and technology |
| SCIENCE IN PERSONAL AND SOCIAL PERSPECTIVES | | |
| **LEVELS K-4**<br>Personal health<br>Characteristics and changes in populations<br>Types of resources<br>Changes in environments<br>Science and technology in local challenges | **LEVELS 5-8**<br>Personal health<br>Populations, resources, and environments<br>Natural hazards<br>Risks and benefits<br>Science and technology in society | **LEVELS 9-12**<br>Personal and community health<br>Population growth<br>Natural resources<br>Environmental quality<br>Natural and human-induced hazards<br>Science and technology in local, national, and global challenges |
| HISTORY AND NATURE OF SCIENCE STANDARDS | | |
| **LEVELS K-4**<br>Science as a human endeavor | **LEVELS 5-8**<br>Science as a human endeavor<br>Nature of science<br>History of science | **LEVELS 9-12**<br>Science as a human endeavor<br>Nature of scientific knowledge<br>Historical perspectives |

**Figure 5–6** *Continued*

- Men and women have made a variety of contributions throughout the history of science and technology.
- Although men and women using scientific inquiry have learned much about the objects, events, and phenomena in nature, much more remains to be understood. Science will never be "finished."
- Many people choose science as a career and devote their entire lives to studying it. Many people derive great pleasure from doing science.

The units in this book look at developmental levels from birth through the primary grades. The science content standards also begin with the young child and build over the years. It is important to understand that knowledge in science and mathematics begins with an early understanding and that future understandings build on that initial learning. An overview of the *National Science Education Standards* is included in Figure 5–6 to illustrate the way that science content builds over time.

Refer to Appendix C for an overview of the *National Science Education Standards* that include *Science Teaching Standards, Standards for Professional Development for Teachers of Science, Assessment in Science Education, Science Content Standards, Science Education Program Standards,* and *Science Education System Standards.* The development of the *National Science Education Standards* is premised on the conviction that *all* students deserve and must have the opportunity to become scientifically literate. The *Standards* look toward a future in which all Americans, through their familiarity with basic scientific ideas and processes, can lead fuller and more productive lives.

*Taking Science to School* (Committee on Science Learning, 2007) highlights four themes that cut across all discussions of knowledge growth after preschool. These themes will be elaborated in Unit 6.

1. Primary grade children are building on the products of preschool knowledge growth. It is clear that an individual's cognitive achievements while an infant and toddler will provide the foundation for further understanding in later years.

2. A great deal of developmental science learning in elementary school involves learning about more detailed aspects of mechanisms and facts that were explored in earlier years. Whether it is gear action or notions of digestion, primary grade children use concrete thinking to explore the details learned in preschool and infancy.

3. As children develop more concrete models of thinking, they will form many misconceptions—some of them dramatic. However, this is not necessarily a step backward. Moving through a series of misconceptions may be the only way to progress toward developing more accurate notions.

4. Keep in mind that the primary and elementary years include further periods of conceptual change for children. New insights can change the way a concept is understood, and there is a growing awareness of both the similarities and differences between children's and scientists' concept development.

## SUMMARY

Our major goal in science education is to develop scientifically literate people who can think critically. To teach science to tomorrow's citizens, process skills and attitudes must be established as major components of any science content lesson. Facts alone will not be sufficient for children who are born into a technological world. Children interact daily with science. Their toasters pop; their can openers whir; and televisions, recording devices, and computers are commonplace. Preparation to live as productive individuals in a changing world should begin early in a child's life.

The manipulation of science materials, whether initiated by the child or the teacher, creates opportunities for language and literacy development. Hands-on experiences that emphasize the process skills of science are essential if the child is to receive the maximum benefits from science instruction. The aim of this book is to suggest ways of planning and teaching these kinds of experiences for young children.

## KEY TERMS

| | | |
|---|---|---|
| classifying | inferring | predicting |
| communicating | measuring | process skills |
| comparing | *National Science Education* | skepticism |
| curiosity | *Standards* | subset |
| hypotheses | observing | variables |

## SUGGESTED ACTIVITIES

1. The results of science are everywhere. Make a list of all of the science examples that you encountered on your way to class.

2. Recall a typical primary school day from your past. What type of science activities were introduced? How were they introduced? Com-

pare your experience with that of a child in a classroom you have observed. What are the similarities and differences? Do technological advancements make a difference?

3. Examine the teacher's edition of a recent elementary science textbook at the primary grade level. What science attitudes are claimed to be taught in the text? Decide if there is evidence of these attitudes being taught in either the student or teacher edition of the text.

4. Interview teachers of preschool and primary grade children to find out what types of science activities they introduce to students. Is the science content balanced? Which activities include the exploration of materials? Record your observations for class discussion.

5. If you were to teach science to urban children, what type of activities would you provide? Apply the question to rural and suburban environments. Would you teach science differently? Why or why not?

6. Pick one of your favorite science topics. Plan how you would include process, attitude, and content.

7. Compare copies of the *National Science Education Standards* with state and local written expectations. What are the similarities and differences?

## REVIEW

A. Discuss how the traditional view of science as a body of knowledge differs from the contemporary view of science as a process of inquiry.

B. How does the knowledge explosion affect the science that is taught to young children?

C. List process skills that should be introduced to all preschool and primary grade students.

D. What is meant by the term *healthy skepticism*?

E. What are the four major areas of science content appropriate for early childhood education?

F. Why has health education received increased attention in early childhood education?

## REFERENCES

Committee on Science Learning, Kindergarten through Eighth Grade. Board on Science Education, Center for Education. (2007). *Taking science to school: Learning and teaching science in grades K–8.* Washington, DC: National Academies Press.

National Research Council. (1996). *National science education standards.* Washington, DC: National Academies Press.

Osborne, M., & Freyberg, P. (1985). *Learning science: Implications of children's knowledge.* Portsmouth, NH: Heinemann.

Simon, S. (1970). *Science in a vacant lot.* New York: Viking Press.

## FURTHER READING AND RESOURCES

Carter, G. S., & Simpson, R. D. (1989). Science and reading: A basic duo. *Science Teacher, 45*(3), 19–21.

Enger, S. K., & Yager, R. E. (2001). *Assessing student understanding in science.* Thousand Oaks, CA: Corwin Press.

Forman, G. E., & Hill, F. (1984). *Constructive play: Applying Piaget in the classroom.* Menlo Park, CA: Addison-Wesley.

Forman, G. E., & Kuschner, D. S. (1983). *The child's construction of knowledge.* Washington, DC: National Association for the Education of Young Children.

Harlan, J., & Rivkin, M. (2007). *Science experiences for the early childhood years: An integrated affective approach* (9th ed.). Upper Saddle River, NJ: Merrill/Prentice-Hall.

Harlan, W. (1995). *Teaching and learning primary science* (3rd ed.). London: Chapman.

Howe, A. C. (2002). *Engaging children in science* (3rd ed.). Upper Saddle River, NJ: Prentice-Hall.

Howe, A. C., & Nichols, S. E. (2001). *Case studies in elementary science: Learning from teachers.* Upper Saddle River, NJ: Prentice-Hall.

International Technology Education Association. (2000). *Standards for technological literacy: Content for the study of technology.* Reston, VA: Author.

Kamii, C., & Devries, R. (1993). *Physical knowledge in the classroom: Implications of Piaget's theory* (Rev. ed.). Englewood Cliffs, NJ: Prentice-Hall.

Kamii, C., & Lee-Katz, L. (1979). Physics in preschool education: A Piagetian approach. *Young Children, 34,* 4–9.

Lind, K. K. (1991). Science process skills: Preparing for the future. In *Professional handbook: The best of everything.* Morristown, NJ: Silver Burdett & Ginn.

Lind, K. K., & Milburn, M. J. (1988). Mechanized childhood. *Science and Children, 25*(5), 32–33.

Lowery, L. F. (1997). *NSTA pathways to the science standards.* Arlington, VA: National Science Teachers Association.

Mechling, K. R., & Oliver, D. L. (1983). *Science teaches basic skills.* Washington, DC: National Science Teachers Association.

National Academy of Engineering and National Research Council. (2002). *Technically speaking: Why all Americans need to know more about technology.* Washington, DC: National Academies Press.

National Research Council. (2002). *Investigating the influence of standards: A framework for research in mathematics, science, and technology education.* Washington, DC: National Academies Press.

National Research Council. (2005). *How students learn: History, mathematics, and science in the classroom.* Committee on How People Learn, a targeted report for teachers (M. S. Donovan & J. D. Bransford, Eds.). Washington, DC: National Academies Press.

National Research Council. (2005). *Mathematical and scientific development in early childhood: A workshop summary.* Washington, DC: National Academies Press.

National Science Resources Center. (1997). *Science for all children: A guide for improving elementary science education in your school district.* Washington, DC: National Academies Press.

Rowe, M. B. (1973). *Teaching science as continuous inquiry.* New York: McGraw-Hill.

Sunal, C. S. (1982). Philosophical bases for science and mathematics in early childhood education. *School, Science and Mathematics, 82*(1), 2–10.

Tipps, S. (1982). Making better guesses: A goal in early childhood science. *School Science and Mathematics, 82*(1), 29–37.

Wenham, M. (1995). *Understanding primary science.* London: Chapman.

Zubrowski, B. (1979). *Bubbles.* Boston: Little, Brown.

# Unit 6

# How Young Scientists Use Concepts

## OBJECTIVES

After reading this unit, you should be able to:

■ Develop lessons using a variety of science process skills such as observing, comparing, measuring, classifying, and predicting.

■ Apply problem-solving strategies to lessons designed for young students.

■ Use data collecting and analysis as a basis for designing and teaching science lessons.

■ Design experiences for young children that enrich their experience at the preoperational level and prepare them for the concrete operational level.

■ Describe the process of self-regulation.

■ Describe the proper use of a discrepant event in teaching science.

## CONCEPT FORMATION IN YOUNG CHILDREN

Young children try very hard to explain the world around them. Do any of the following statements sound familiar?

"Thunder is the sound of the angels bowling."

"Chickens lay eggs, and pigs lay bacon."

"Electricity comes from a switch on the wall."

"The sun follows me when I take a walk."

These are the magical statements of intuitive thinkers. Children use their senses or intuition to make judgments. Their logic is unpredictable, and they frequently prefer to use "magical explanations" to account for what is happening in their world. Clouds become the

"smoke of angels," and rain falls because "it wants to help the farmers." These comments are typical of the self-centered view of intuitive children. They think that the sun rises in the morning just to shine on them. It never occurs to them that there may be another explanation. They also have a difficult time remembering more than one thing at a time.

Statements and abilities such as these inspired Jean Piaget's curiosity about young children's beliefs. His search for answers about how children think and learn has contributed to our understanding that learning is an internal process. In other words, it is the child who brings meaning to the world and not vice versa. A child's misconceptions are normal. This is what the child believes; thus, this is what is real to the child (Figure 6–1).

The temptation is to try to move children out of their magical stage of development. This is a mistake.

"*The sun follows me!*"

**Figure 6–1** Children have misconceptions.

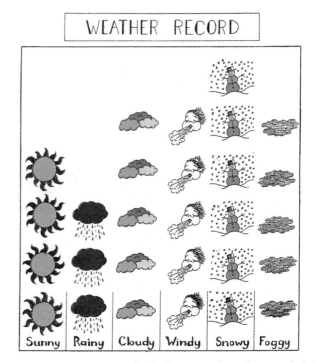

**Figure 6–2** "How many cloudy days were there this month?"

Although some misconceptions can be corrected, others must wait for more advanced thinking to develop. Students cannot be pushed, pulled, or dragged through developmental stages. Instead, the goal is to support the development of young children at their present level of operation. In this way, they have the richness of experiences to take with them when the next level of development naturally occurs.

## Enhancing Awareness

When teaching concepts that are too abstract for children to fully understand, try to focus on aspects of the concept that can be understood. This type of awareness can be enhanced by the use of *visual depictions, observing, drawing,* and *discussion.*

Although some aspects of weather might remain a mystery, understanding can be developed by recording the types of weather that occur in a month. Construct a large calendar and put it on the wall. Every day, have a student draw a picture that represents the weather for the day. When the month is completed, cut the calendar into individual days. Then, glue the days that show similar weather in columns to create a bar graph. Ask the children to form conclusions about the month's weather from the graph. In this way, children can relate to weather patterns and visualize that these patterns change from day to day (Figure 6–2).

In a similar way, children will be better prepared for later studies of nutrition if they have some understanding of their own food intake. Graphing favorite foods is a way for children to visually compare and organize what they eat. On poster board, make five columns and mount pictures from the basic food groups at the bottom of each column. Discuss to which food group each child's favorite food belongs. Have the children write their initials or attach a picture of themselves in the appropriate food column or draw a picture of their favorite food. Ask, "What do most of us like to eat?" Discuss healthy foods, and make a new chart at the end of the week. Is there a difference in choices? (Figure 6–3)

To enhance awareness and to be effective, observations should be done in 10 minutes or less, conducted with a purpose, and brought together by discussions. Unconnected observations do not aid in concept formation. For example, if a purpose is not given for observing

## FAVORITE FOODS

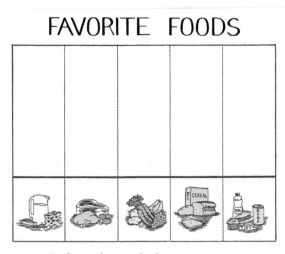

**Figure 6–3** Find your favorite foods.

**Figure 6–4** Children notice that the candles are not the same size.

two flickering, different-sized candles, then children will lose interest within minutes. Instead of telling children to "go look" at two burning candles, ask them to look and to find the difference between the candles. Children will become excited with the discovery that the candles are not the same size (Figure 6–4).

Discussions that follow observations heighten a child's awareness of that observation. A group of children observing a fish tank to see where the fish spends most of its time will be prepared to share what they saw in the tank. However, there may not be agreement.

Differences of opinion about observations stimulate interest and promote discussion. The children are likely to return to the tank to see for themselves what others say they saw. This would probably not happen without the focusing effect of discussion.

Drawing can provide excellent opportunities for observation and discussion. An effective use of drawing to enhance concept development would be to have children draw a tiger from memory before going to the zoo. Strategies like this usually reveal that more information is needed to construct an accurate picture. After visiting the zoo, have the children draw a tiger and compare it with the one drawn before the field trip. Discussion should focus on the similarities and differences between the two drawings. Children will be eager to observe details that they might not otherwise notice about the tigers in the zoo (Figure 6–5).

**Figure 6–5** Robin's drawing of a tiger after a visit to the zoo.

## Teacher Magic and Misconceptions

Children need time to reflect and absorb ideas before they fully understand a concept. Misconceptions can occur at any stage. Be sure to give them plenty of time to manipulate and explore. For example, when a teacher mixes yellow and blue paints to create green, children might think the result is teacher magic. However, if given the paints and the opportunity to discover green, they might remember that yellow and blue mixed together make green. Because children cannot carry out most operations mentally, they need to manipulate materials in order to develop concepts. Teachers can enhance a child's understanding by making comments or asking questions that draw attention to a particular event. Using the previous color example, a teacher might ask, "Why do you think that happened?" or "How did you do that?"

Misconceptions can occur at any stage of development. Some children in the primary grades may be in a transitional stage or have moved into the concrete operation stage of development. Although these students will be able to do much logical thinking, the concepts they work with must still be tied to concrete objects that they can manipulate. Firsthand experiences with materials continue to be essential for learning.

The child in this developmental stage no longer looks at the world through "magical eyes." Explanations for natural events are influenced by other natural objects and events. For example, a child may now say, "The rain comes from the sky" rather than "It rains to help farmers." This linking of physical objects will first appear in the early concrete development stages. Do not be misled by an apparent new awareness. The major factor in concept development is still contingent upon children's need to manipulate, observe, discuss, and visually depict things to understand what is new and different about them. This is true in all of the Piagetian developmental stages discussed in this book.

## SELF-REGULATION AND CONCEPT ATTAINMENT

Have you ever seen someone plunge a turkey skewer through a balloon? Did you expect the balloon to burst? What was your reaction when it stayed intact? Your curiosity was probably piqued—you wanted to know why the balloon did not burst. Actually, you had just witnessed a **discrepant event** and entered the process of **self-regulation**. This is when your brain responds to interactions between you and your environment. Gallagher and Reid (1981) describe *self-regulation* as the active mental process of forming concepts. Knowing a

little bit about how the brain functions in concept development will help to explain this process. Visualize the human mind as thousands of concepts stored in various sections of the brain—much like a complex system of mental pigeonholes, a postal sorting system, or a filing cabinet filled with individual file folders. As children move through the world and encounter new objects and phenomena, they assimilate and accommodate new information and store it in the correctly labeled mental category in their minds.

Lind (2005) describes the brain as functioning like a postal worker, naturally classifying and storing information in the appropriate pigeonholes (Figure 6–6). New information is always stored close to all of the related information that has been previously stored. This grouping of closely related facts and phenomena that is related to a particular concept is known as a **cognitive structure** or schema. In other words, all we know about the color red is stored in the same area of the brain. Our cognitive structure of red is developed further each time we have a color-related experience. The word *red* becomes a symbol for what we understand and perceive as the color red.

**Figure 6–6** The brain functions like a postal worker.

Our understanding of the world is imperfect because, sooner or later, there is some point at which true understanding ends and misconceptions exist but go unquestioned. This is because incorrect interpretations of the world are stored alongside correct ones.

Continuing the postal worker analogy: If the information doesn't quite fit into an existing pigeonhole, then another pigeonhole must be made.

A point can also be reached where new information conflicts with older information stored in a given cognitive structure. When children realize that they do not understand something they previously thought they understood, they are said to be in what Piaget calls a state of **disequilibrium**. This is where you were when the balloon did not burst: The balloon did not behave as you expected, and things no longer fit neatly together.

This is the *teachable moment*. When children are perplexed, their minds will not rest until they can find some way to make the new information fit. Because existing structures are inadequate to accommodate all of the existing information, they must continually modify or replace it with new cognitive structures. When in this state, children actively seek out additional information to create the new structure. They ask probing questions, observe closely, and inquire independently about the materials at hand. In this state, they are highly motivated and receptive to learning. When children have gathered enough information to satisfy their curiosity and to create a new cognitive structure that explains most or all of the facts, they return to a state of **equilibrium**, where everything appears to fit together. As children move from disequilibrium to equilibrium, two mental activities take place. When confronted with something they do not understand, children fit it into a scheme, something they already know. If this does not work for them, they modify the scheme or make a new one. This is called **accommodation**. **Assimilation** and accommodation work together to help students learn concepts (Figure 6–7).

To make use of the process of self-regulation in your classroom, find out at what point your students misunderstand or are unfamiliar with the topic you are teaching. Finding out what children know can be done in a number of ways. In addition to referring to the assessment units in this book, listen to children's responses to a lesson or question, or simply ask them to describe their understanding of a concept. For example, before teaching a lesson on animals, ask, "What does an animal look like?" You'd be surprised at the number of young children who think that a life-form must have legs to be considered an animal.

Using this process will allow you to present information contrary to or beyond your students' existing cognitive structure and thus put them in a state of disequilibrium, where learning occurs.

## DISCREPANT EVENTS

A *discrepant event* puts students in disequilibrium and prepares them for learning. They are curious and want to find out what is happening. It is recommended that you take advantage of the natural learning process to teach children what you want them to understand. The following scenes might give you some ideas for discrepant events that might improve lessons you plan to teach.

- Mr. Wang's second-grade class is studying the senses. His students are aware of the function of the five senses, but they may not know that the sense of smell plays as large a role in appreciating food as does the sense of taste. His students work in pairs with one child blindfolded. The blindfolded students are asked to pinch their noses shut and taste several foods such as bread, raw potatoes, or apples to see if they can identify them.

- Students switch roles and try the same investigation with various juices such as apple, orange, tomato, and so on. Most students cannot identify juices. Having experienced this discrepant event, the students will be more interested in finding out about the structures of the nose related to smell. They may be more motivated to conduct an investigation about how the appearance of food affects its taste.

- Mrs. Fox fills two jars with water while her first-grade class watches. She fills one jar to the rim and leaves about an inch of space in the other

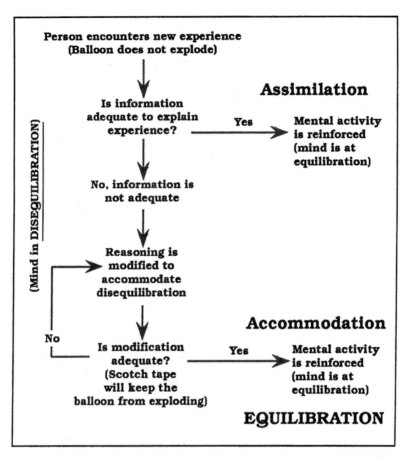

**Figure 6–7** The self-regulation process. (Courtesy of the Council for Elementary Science International.)

jar. She puts a lid on each jar and places it on a tray in the school yard on a cold winter day. Her students return later in the day and find that both have frozen but that the completely filled jar has burst. Students are eager to find out why.

■ Kindergarten students Ann and Vanessa have been instructed to place two ice cubes in a glass and then fill it to the brim with water. The ice cubes float on the water and extend about half an inch above the edge of the glass. Ms. Hebert asks them what will happen when the ice cubes melt. Vanessa thinks the water will overflow because there will be more water. Ann thinks the water level will drop because

**Figure 6–8** Ann and Vanessa check their predictions.

the ice cubes will contract when they melt. They watch in puzzlement as they realize that the water level stays the same as the cubes melt (Figure 6–8).

## USING THE LEARNING CYCLE TO BUILD CONCEPTS

You can assist your students in creating new cognitive structures by designing learning experiences in a manner congruent with how children learn naturally. One popular approach is the application of the learning cycle. The learning cycle, described in Unit 1, is based upon the cycle of equilibration originally described by Piaget. The learning cycle, which is used extensively in elementary science education, combines aspects of naturalistic, informal, and structured activity methods—suggested elsewhere in this book—into a method of presenting a lesson.

As you have learned, the discrepant event is an effective device for motivating students and placing them in disequilibrium. The learning cycle can be a useful approach to learning for many of the same reasons. Learning begins with a period of free exploration. During the **exploration phase**, the children's prior knowledge can be assessed. Teachers can assess inquiry skills and gain clues to what the children know about a science concept as they explore the materials. Refer to the "Strategies That Encourage Inquiry" section in this unit for more information on assessing inquiry. Additionally, any misconceptions the children may have are often revealed during this phase. Exploration can be as simple as giving students the materials to be used in a day's activity at the beginning of a lesson so they can play with them for a few minutes. Minimal or no instructions should be given other than those related to safety, breaking the materials, or logistics in getting the materials. By letting students manipulate the materials, they will explore and very likely discover either something they did not know before or something other than what they expected. The following example, "Making the Bulb Light," utilizes all three steps of the learning cycle.

## Making the Bulb Light

*Exploration Phase*

Mr. Wang placed a wire, a flashlight bulb, and a size-D battery on a tray. Each group of three students was given a tray of materials and told to try to figure out a way to make the bulb light. As each group successfully lit the bulb, he asked them if they could find another arrangement of materials that would make the bulbs light. After about 10 minutes, most groups had found at least one other way to light the bulb.

*Concept Introduction Phase*

After playing with the wires, batteries, and bulbs, Mr. Wang had the students bring their trays and form a circle on the floor. He asked the students if they had found out anything interesting about the materials. Jason showed the class one arrangement that worked to light the bulb. To introduce the class to the terms *open, closed,* and *short circuit,* Mr. Wang explained to the class that an arrangement that lights is called a closed circuit. Ann showed the class an arrangement that she thought would work but did not. Mr. Wang explained that this is an open circuit. Chad showed the class an arrangement that did not light the bulb but made the wire and battery very warm. Mr. Wang said this was a short circuit. Then he drew an example of each of the three types of circuit on the board and labeled them.

*Concept Application Phase*

Next, Mr. Wang showed the class a worksheet with drawings of various arrangements of batteries and bulbs. He asked the children to predict which arrangements would not light and form an open circuit; which would form a closed circuit by lighting; and which would heat up the battery and wire, forming a short circuit. After recording their predictions independently, the children returned to their small groups to test each

*(continued)*

of the arrangements. They recorded the actual answers beside their predictions (Figure 6–9).

After the students completed the task, Mr. Wang called them together. They discussed the results of their investigation, sharing which arrangements of batteries, wire, and bulbs they predicted correctly and incorrectly. Then Mr. Wang reviewed the terms learned during the lesson and asked the students to read a short section of their science text that talked about fire and electrical safety. The reading discussed the dangers of putting metal objects in wall sockets or fingers in light sockets and suggested precautions when flying kites near power lines.

After reading the section aloud, Mr. Wang asked the class if they could see any relationship between the reading and the day's activity. Chad responded that flying a kite into an electrical power line or sticking a dinner fork in a wall socket were similar to what he did when he created a short circuit with the battery and wire. Other students found similar relationships between the reading activity and their lives.

**Figure 6–9** Battery prediction sheet.

In the preceding activity, you have seen a functioning model of Piaget's theory of cognitive development implemented in the classroom. The exploration phase invites assimilation and disequilibrium; the concept development phase provides for accommodation; the **concept application phase** expands the concept; and strategies for retaining the new concept are provided.

## USING PART OF THE LEARNING CYCLE TO BUILD CONCEPTS

Although a formal investigation using the learning cycle is an excellent way to present lessons to children, teaching all lessons in this manner is not desirable. At times, exploration and observation might be the full lesson. Giving students an opportunity to practice their skills of observation is often sufficient for them to learn a great deal about unfamiliar objects or phenomena. In

the following scenarios, teachers made use of exploration observations to create lessons.

■ Mr. Brown constructed a small bird feeder and placed it outside the window of his prekindergarten room. One cold winter day his efforts were rewarded. Students noticed and called attention to the fact that there were several kinds of birds at the feeder. Brad said that they all looked the same to him. Leroy pointed out different characteristics of the birds to Brad. Diana and Cindy noticed that the blue jay constantly chased other birds away from the feeder and that a big cardinal moved away from the feeder as soon as any other bird approached. Students wondered why the blue jay seemed to scare all the other birds and why the cardinal seemed to be afraid of even the small birds. They spent several minutes discussing the possibilities.

■ On Richard's birthday, his preschool teacher, Miss Collins, decided that the class should make a microwave cake to celebrate the occasion. The students helped Miss Collins mix the ingredients and commented on the sequence of events as the cake cooked for seven minutes in the microwave. Richard was the first to observe how bubbles started to form in small patches. Then George commented that the whole cake was bubbling and getting bigger. After removing the cake from the microwave, many children noticed how the cake shrank, got glossy, then lost its gloss as it cooled.

Some lessons can be improved by having children do more than just observing and exploring. These exploration lessons include **data collection** as an instructional focus. Data collection and interpretation are important to real science and real problem solving. Although firsthand observation will always be important, most breakthroughs in science are made by analyzing carefully collected data. Scientists usually spend much more time searching through stacks of data than peering down the barrel of a microscope or through a telescope.

Data collection for young children is somewhat more abstract than firsthand observation. Therefore, it is important that students have sufficient practice in making predictions, speculations, and guesses with firsthand observations before they begin to collect and interpret data. Nevertheless, young students can benefit from early experience in data collection and interpretation. Initial data collections are usually pictorial in form. Long-term patterns and changes that children cannot easily observe in one setting are excellent beginnings for data collection.

■ Weather records such as those discussed previously can expose children to patterns during any time of the year. After charting the weather with drawings or attaching pictures that represent changing conditions, have children decide which clothing is most appropriate for a particular kind of weather. Drawing clouds, sun, rain, lightning, snow, and so on that correspond to the daily weather and relating that information to what is worn can give students a sense of why data collection is useful.

■ Growing plants provides excellent opportunities for early data collection. Mrs. Fox's first-grade class charted the progress of bean plants growing in paper cups on the classroom windowsill. Each day students cut a strip of paper the same length as the height of their plant and glued the strips to a large sheet of newsprint. Over a period of weeks, students could see how their plants grew continuously even though they noticed few differences by just watching them. After pondering the plant data, Dean asked Mrs. Fox if the students could measure themselves with a strip of paper and chart their growth for the rest of the year. Thereafter, Mrs. Fox measured each student once a month. Her students were amazed to see how much they had grown during the year.

Another technique for designing science lessons is to allow students to have input into the process of problem solving and designing investigations. This might be called a *concept introduction lesson* because it utilizes the **concept introduction phase** of the learning cycle as the basis for a lesson. Although initial investigation and problem-solving experiences may be designed by the teacher, students eventually will be able to contribute to planning their own investigations. Most students probably will not be able to choose a topic and plan the entire investigation independently until they reach the intermediate grades, but their input into the process of planning gives them some ownership of the lesson and increases their confidence to explore ideas more fully. When solving real problems, identifying the problem is often more critical than the skills of attacking it. Students need practice in both aspects of problem solving.

The following examples depict students giving input into the problem to be solved and then helping to design how the problem should be approached.

■ Mr. Wang's second-grade class had some previous experience in charting the growth of plants. He told his class, "I'd like us to design an investigation about how fast plants grow. What things do you think could affect how fast a plant grows?" Mr. Wang used the chalkboard to list his students' suggestions, which included such factors as the amount of water, fertilizer, sunshine, and temperature as well as the type of seed, how much the plants are talked to, whether they are stepped on, and so forth. Students came up with possibilities that had never occurred to Mr. Wang. Next, he divided the class into small groups and told each group that it could have several paper cups, seeds, and some potting soil. Each group was asked to choose a factor from the list that it would like to investigate. Then, Mr. Wang helped each group plan its investigation.

■ Derrick and Brent decided to study the effect of light on their plant. Mr. Wang asked them how they would control the amount of light their plants receive. Brent suggested that they bring a light bulb to place near the plants so that they could leave the light on all day. Derrick said that he would put the plants in a cardboard box for the hours they were not supposed to receive light. Mr. Wang asked them to think about how many plants they should use. They decided to use three: one plant would receive light all day, one plant would receive no light, and one plant would receive only six hours of light.

## STRATEGIES THAT ENCOURAGE INQUIRY

The fundamental abilities and concepts that underlie the "science as inquiry" content standard of the *National Science Education Standards* establish a groundwork for developing and integrating strategies that encourage inquiry. Young children should experience science in a form that engages them in the active construction of ideas and explanations and that enhances their opportunities to develop the skills of doing science. In the early years, when children investigate materials and properties of common objects, they can focus on the process of doing investigations and develop the ability to ask questions. The *National Science Education Standards* suggest the following strategies to engage students in the active search for knowledge.

■ *Ask a question about objects, organisms, and events in the environment.* Children should be encouraged to answer their questions by seeking information from their own observations and investigations and from reliable sources of information. When possible, children's answers can be compared with what scientists already know about the world.

■ *Plan and conduct a simple investigation.* When children are in their earliest years, investigations are based on systematic observation. As children develop, they may design and conduct simple investigations to answer questions. (However, the fair tests necessary for experimentation may not be possible until the fourth grade.) Types of investigations that are appropriate for younger children include describing objects, events, and organisms; classifying them; and sharing what they know with others.

■ *Employ simple equipment and tools to gather data and extend the senses.* Simple skills such as how to observe, measure, cut, connect, switch, turn on/off, pour, hold, and hook—together with simple instruments such as rulers, thermometers, magnifiers, and microscopes—should be used in the early years. Children can use simple equipment and can gather data by, for example, observing and recording attributes of the daily weather. They can also develop skills in the use of computers and calculators.

■ *Use data to construct a reasonable explanation.* In inquiry, students' thinking is emphasized as they use data to formulate explanations. Even at the earliest grade levels, students can learn what counts as evidence and can judge the merits of the data and explanations.

■ *Communicate investigations and explanations.* Students should begin developing the abilities to communicate, critique, and analyze their work and the work of other students. This communication could be spoken or drawn as well as written.

The natural inquiry of young children can be seen as they observe, group, sort, and order objects. By incorporating familiar teaching strategies, such as providing a variety of objects for children to manipulate and talking to children as they go about what they are doing with objects, teachers can help children to learn more about their world. Children also can learn about their world through observations and discussions about those observations. When opportunities are provided for children to work individually at constructing their own knowledge, they will gain experiences in organizing data and understanding processes. A variety of activities that let children use all of their senses should be offered. In this way, children may explore at their own pace and self-regulate their experiences.

## Assessing Inquiry Learning

Observation is vital for the teacher as she assesses children's progress. It is essential that the teacher watch carefully as the children group and order materials. Are the materials ordered in a certain way? Do the objects in the group have similar attributes? Are the children creating a random design, or are they making a pattern? Clues to children's thinking can be gained by watching what children do and having them explain what they are doing to each other or to you. In the following ex-

ample, the teacher assesses the students' abilities to do scientific inquiry by making use of an activity that invites children to manipulate objects.

Mrs. Raymond's classroom contains a variety of objects with a number of characteristics (size, color, texture, and shape) for children to group and sort. She has enough sets of keys, buttons, beans, nuts and bolts, fabric swatches, and wooden shapes for each child to work alone. To expose children to science content, she also has sets of leaves, nuts, bark, twigs, seeds, and other objects related to the science content that she wants to emphasize. As the children group and sort the objects, either by a single characteristic or in some other way, Mrs. Raymond observes them carefully and asks them to tell her about the ways they are organizing the objects. The teacher moves around and listens to the individual children as they make decisions. She makes notes in the anecdotal records she is keeping and talks with the children: "Can you put the ones that go together in a pile?" "How did you decide to put this leaf in the pile?"

### CHANGING EMPHASES TO PROMOTE INQUIRY

| LESS EMPHASIS ON | MORE EMPHASIS ON |
|---|---|
| Activities that demonstrate and verify science content | Activities that investigate and analyze science questions |
| Investigations confined to one class period | Investigations over extended periods of time |
| Process skills out of context | Process skills in context |
| Emphasis on individual process skills such as observation | Using multiple process skills—manipulation, cognitive, procedural |
| Getting an answer | Using evidence and strategies for developing or revising an explanation |
| Science as exploration and experiment | Science as argument and explanation |
| Providing answers to questions about science content | Communicating science explorations |
| Individuals and groups of students analyzing and synthesizing data without defending a conclusion | Groups of students analyzing and synthesizing data after defending conclusions |
| Doing few investigations in order to leave time to cover large amounts of content | Doing more investigations in order to develop understanding, ability, values of inquiry, and knowledge of science content |
| Concluding inquiries with the result of the experiment | Applying the results of the experiment to scientific arguments and explanations |
| Management of materials and equipment | Management of ideas and information |
| Private communication of student ideas and conclusions to teacher | Public communication of student ideas and work to classmates |

**Figure 6–10** Changing emphases to promote inquiry from the *National Science Education Standards* (National Research Council, 1996).

Figure 6–10 illustrates the NRC's 1996 *National Science Education Standards* recommendations for changing emphases to promote inquiry.

## SUMMARY

For all the preschool and primary grade developmental stages described by Piaget, keep in mind that children's views of the world and concepts are not the same as yours. Their perception of phenomena is from their own perspective and experiences. Misconceptions arise, so help them explore the world to expand thinking and always be ready for the next developmental stage. Teach children to observe with all of their senses and to classify, predict, and communicate so they can discover other viewpoints.

There are many possible ways to design science instruction for young children. The learning cycle is an application of the theory of cognitive development described by Piaget. The learning cycle can incorporate a number of techniques into a single lesson, or each of the components of the learning cycle can be used independently to develop lessons. Other effective methods for designing lessons include discrepant events, data collection and analysis, problem solving, and cooperative planning of investigations. All of these methods emphasize science process skills that are important to the development of concepts in young children.

## KEY TERMS

| | | |
|---|---|---|
| accommodation | concept introduction phase | equilibrium |
| assimilation | data collection | exploration phase |
| cognitive structure | discrepant event | self-regulation |
| concept application phase | disequilibrium | |

## SUGGESTED ACTIVITIES

1. Interview children to determine their understanding of cause-and-effect relationships. Their answers to your questions will provide insight into the perceptions and misconceptions of young children. Compare the responses of different children.

2. Brainstorm at least three strategies for preparing children to understand such topics as rain, lightning, clouds, mountains, and night. Pick a topic and prepare a learning experience that will prepare children for future concept development.

3. Pretend you are presenting two lessons about seeds that grow into plants for a class of first graders. What types of learning experiences will you design for these students? How will you apply Piaget's theory of development to this topic? In what way would you adapt the planned experiences for a different developmental level?

4. Present a discrepant event to your students. After discovering how the event was achieved, analyze the process of equilibration that the class went through. Design a discrepant event that focuses on senses and that would be effective for children in kindergarten.

5. The learning cycle has been presented as an effective way to build concepts in young children. What is your concept of the learning cycle, and how will you use it with children? Select a concept, and prepare a learning cycle to teach it.

6. Reflect on your own primary grade science experiences. What types of learning strategies did you encounter? Were they effective? Why or why not?

# REVIEW

A. Describe what is meant by a *discrepant event*.

B. Why are discrepant events used in science education?

C. List the three major parts of the learning cycle.

D. Describe how cognitive structures change over time.

E. Why is data collection important for young children?

F. Create an example of a discrepant event that you might use with young children.

G. Describe strategies you will use to encourage inquiry.

H. Describe six changes in the emphases on promoting inquiry in the *National Science Education Standards*.

# REFERENCES

Gallagher, J. M., & Reid, D. K. (1981). *The learning theory of Piaget and Inhelder*. Monterey, CA: Brooks/Cole.

Lind, K. K. (2005). *Exploring science in early childhood education* (4th ed.). Clifton Park, NY: Thomson Delmar Learning.

National Research Council. (1996). *National science education standards*. Washington, DC: National Academies Press.

# FURTHER READING AND RESOURCES

Abruscato, J. (2004). *Teaching children science: A discovery approach* (6th ed.). Boston: Allyn & Bacon.

Barman, C. (1990). *New ideas about an effective teaching strategy*. Council for Elementary Science International. Indianapolis: Indiana University Press.

Benham, N. B., Hosticka, A., Payne, J. D., &Yeotis, C. (1982). Making concepts in science and mathematics visible and viable in the early childhood curriculum. *School Science and Mathematics, 82*(1), 45–64.

Bowman, B. T., Donovan, M. S., & Burns, M. S. (Eds.). (2000). *Eager to learn: Educating our preschoolers.* Washington, DC: National Research Council.

Bredekamp, S., & Rosegrant, T. (1992). *Reaching potentials: Appropriate curriculum and assessment for young children* (Vol. 1). Washington, DC: National Association for the Education of Young Children.

Bredekamp, S., & Rosegrant, T. (1995). *Reaching potentials: Transforming early childhood curriculum and assessment* (Vol. 2). Washington, DC: National Association for the Education of Young Children.

Charlesworth, R. (2003). *Understanding child development* (6th ed.). Clifton Park, NY: Thomson Delmar Learning.

Confrey, J. (1990). A review of research on student conceptions in mathematics, science, and programming. In C. Cazden (Ed.), *Review of research in education*. Washington, DC: American Educational Research Association.

Gill, A. J. (1993). Multiple strategies: Product of reasoning and communication. *Arithmetic Teacher, 40*(7), 380–386.

Harlen, W. (Ed.). (1996). *Primary science, taking the plunge: How to teach primary science more effectively.* Portsmouth, NH: Heinemann.

Lederman, N. G., Lederman, J. S., & Bell, R. L. (2005). *Constructing science in elementary classrooms.* Boston: Allyn & Bacon.

Price, G. G. (1982). Cognitive learning in early childhood education: Mathematics, science, and social studies. In *Handbook of research in early childhood education.* New York: Free Press.

Renner, J. W., & Marek, E. A. (1988). *The learning cycle.* Portsmouth, NH: Heinemann.

Shaw, J. M., & Owen, L. L. (1987). Weather—Beyond observation. *Science and Children, 25*(3), 27–29.

Sprung, B., Froschl, M., & Campbell, P. B. (1985). *What will happen if . . .?* New York: Educational Equity Concepts.

Tipps, S. (1982). Making better guesses: A goal in early childhood science. *School Science and Mathematics, 82*(1), 29–37.

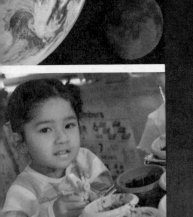

# Unit 7
# Planning for Science

## OBJECTIVES

After reading this unit, you should be able to:

■ Develop science concepts with subject area integrations.

■ Explain and use the strategy of webbing in unit planning.

■ Identify and develop science concepts in a lesson and design lesson plans for teaching science to children.

■ Construct evaluation strategies.

## INTEGRATING SCIENCE INTO THE CURRICULUM

Concepts will more likely be retained by children if presented in a variety of ways and extended over a period of time. For example, after a trip to the zoo, extend the collective experience by having children dictate a story about their trip or have the children build their own zoo and demonstrate the care and feeding of the animals. The children can also depict the occupations found at the zoo. Other activities can focus on following up on pre-visit discussions that directed children to observe specifics at the zoo, such as differences in animal noses. Children might enjoy comparing zoo animal noses with those of their pets by matching pictures of similar noses on a bulletin board. In this way, concepts can continue to be applied and related to past experiences as the year progresses.

Additional integrations might include drawing favorite animal noses, creating plays about animals with specific types of noses, writing about an animal and its

nose, and creating "smelling activities." You might even want to introduce reasons an animal has a particular type of nose. One popular idea is to purchase plastic animal noses, distribute them to children, and play a "Mother may I"-like game. Say, "If you have four legs and roar, take two steps back. If you have two legs and quack, take three steps forward" (Figure 7–1).

Think of how much more science can be learned if we make connections to other subjects. This requires preparing planned activities and taking advantage of every teachable moment that occurs in your class to introduce children to science.

Opportunities abound for teaching science in early childhood. Consider actively involving children with art, blocks, dramatic play, woodworking, language arts, math, and creative movement. Learning centers are one way to provide excellent integration and provide opportunities for assessment. (Centers are discussed in Unit 39.) The following are ideas meant to encourage your thinking about possible learning centers.

**Figure 7–1** "If you have two legs and quack, take three steps forward."

- *Painting.* Finger painting helps children learn to perceive with their fingertips and demonstrates the concept of color diffusion as they clean their hands. Shapes can be recognized by painting with fruit and familiar objects.

- *Water center.* Concepts such as volume and conservation begin to be grasped when children measure with water and sand. Buoyancy can be explored with boats and with sinking and floating objects.

- *Blocks.* Blocks are an excellent way to introduce children to friction, gravity, and simple machines. Leverage and efficiency can be reinforced with *woodworking.*

- *Books.* Many books introduce scientific concepts while *telling a story.* Books with pictures give views of unfamiliar things as well as an opportunity to explore detail and to infer and discuss.

- *Music and rhythmic activities.* These let children experience the movement of air against their bodies. Air resistance can also be demonstrated by dancing with a scarf.

- *Manipulative center.* Children's natural capacities for inquiry can be seen when they observe, group, sort, and order objects during periods of play. Children can pair objects, such as animals, and use fundamental skills, such as one-to-one correspondence.

- *Creative play.* Dressing, moving, and eating like an animal will provide children with opportunities for expressing themselves. Drama and poetry are a natural integration with learning about living things.

- *Playground.* The playground can provide an opportunity to predict weather, practice balancing, and experience friction. Children's natural curiosity will lead them to many new ideas and explorations.

- *Literacy.* The concrete world of science integrates especially well with reading and writing. Basic words, object guessing, experience charts, writing stories, and working with tactile sensations all encourage early literacy development.

## Children Learn in Different Ways

It is important to provide children with a variety of ways to learn science. Even very young children have developed definite patterns in the way they learn. Observe a group of children engaged in free play: Some prefer to work alone quietly; others do well in groups. Personal learning style also extends to a preference for visual or auditory learning. The teacher in the following scenario keeps these individual differences in mind when planning science experiences.

Ms. Hebert knows that the children in her kindergarten class exhibit a wide range of learning styles and behaviors. For example, Ann wakes up slowly. She hesitates to jump in and explore, and she prefers to work alone. On the other hand, Vanessa is social, verbal, and ready to go first thing in the morning. As Ms. Hebert plans activities to reinforce the observations of flamingos that her class made at the zoo, she includes experiences that involve both group discussion and individual work. Some of the visual, auditory, and small- and large-group activities include flamingo number puzzles, drawing and painting flamingos, and acting out how flamingos eat, rest, walk, and honk. In this way, Ms. Hebert meets the diverse needs of the class and integrates concepts

**Figure 7–2**  A flamingo lacing card.

about flamingos into the entire week (Figure 7–2). Organizing science lessons with subject matter correlations in mind ensures integration. The following section outlines ways to plan science lessons and units.

# ORGANIZING FOR TEACHING SCIENCE

To teach effectively, teachers must organize what they plan to teach. How they organize depends largely on their teaching situation. Some school districts require that a textbook series or curriculum guide be used when teaching science. Some have a fully developed program to follow, and others have no established guidelines. Regardless of state or district directives, the strategies discussed in this chapter can be adapted to a variety of teaching situations.

## Planning for Developing Science Concepts

After assessing what your students know and want to know about a science topic, the first questions to ask when organizing for teaching are "What is the appropriate science content that the children need to know?" and "What is the best way to organize learning experiences?" You might have a general topic in mind, such as air, but do not know where to go from there. One technique that might help organize your thoughts is **webbing**, a strategy borrowed from literature. A web depicts a variety of possible concepts and curricular experiences that you might use to develop concepts. By visually depicting your ideas, you will be able to tell at a glance the concepts covered in your unit. As the web emerges, projected activities can be balanced by subject area (e.g., social studies, movement, art, drama, and math) and by a variety of naturalistic, informal, or structured activities.

Start your planning by selecting what you want children to know about a topic. For example, the topic *air* contains many science concepts. Four concepts about air that are commonly taught to first graders begin the web depicted in Figure 7–3 and are as follows:

1. Air is all around us.
2. Air takes up space.
3. Air can make noise.
4. Air can be hot or cold.

After selecting the concepts you plan to develop, begin adding appropriate activities to achieve your goal. Look back at Unit 6 and think of some of these strategies that will best help you teach about air. Remember that "messing around" time and direct experience are both vital for learning.

The developed web in Figure 7–4 shows at a glance the main concepts and activities that will be included in

**Figure 7–3**  Begin by making a web for each science concept you want to teach.

**Figure 7–4** Example of a webbed unit.

this unit. You may not want to teach all of these activities, but you will have the advantage of flexibility when you make decisions.

Next, turn your attention to how you will evaluate children's learning. Preschool and primary grade children will not be able to verbalize their true understanding of a concept. They simply have not advanced to the formal stages of thinking. Instead, have students show their knowledge in ways that can be observed. Have them explain, predict, tell, draw, describe, construct, and so on (Figure 7–5). These are the verbs that indicate an action of some kind. For example, as students explain to you why they have grouped buttons together in a certain way, be assured that the facts are there and so are the concepts; one day, they will come together in a fully developed concept statement. Concept development takes time and cannot be rushed.

The webbed unit that you have developed is a long-term plan for organizing science experiences around a specific topic. Formal units usually contain

**ACTION VERBS**

Simple Action Words

| | | |
|---|---|---|
| arrange | design | match |
| attempt | distinguish | measure |
| chart | explain | name |
| circle | formulate | order |
| classify | gather | organize |
| collect | graph | place |
| compare | identify | point |
| compile | include | report |
| complete | indicate | select |
| contrast | label | sort |
| count | list | state |
| define | locate | tell |
| describe | map | |

**Figure 7–5** Verbs that indicate action.

overall goals and objectives, a series of lessons, and an evaluation plan. **Goals** are the broad statements that indicate where you are heading with the topic or outcomes you would like to achieve. **Objectives** state how you plan to achieve your goals. Practical teaching direction is provided by daily lesson plans. An evaluation plan is necessary to assess student learning and your own teaching. There are a variety of ways these components can be organized, but Figure 7–6 outlines the essential ingredients. Refer to the "Assessment Strategies" section of this unit for suggestions on how to build on children's existing knowledge when designing learning experiences.

## Lesson Planning

The **lesson plan** is a necessary component of the unit. It helps you plan the experiences that will aid in concept development. The following lesson plan is adaptable and focuses on developing a science concept, manipulating materials, and extending and reinforcing the concept with additional activities and subject area integrations. Refer to Figure 7–7 and Figure 7–8, the bubble machine, for an example of this lesson plan format.

## Basic Science Lesson Plan Components

*Concept.* Concepts are usually the most difficult part of a lesson plan. The temptation is to write an objective or topic title. However, to really focus your teaching on the major concept to be developed, you must find the science in what you intend to teach. For example, ask yourself, "What do I want the children to learn about air?"

*Objective.* Then ask, for example, "What do I want the children *to do* in order to help them understand that air takes up space?" When you have decided on the basic experience, be sure to identify the process skills that children will use. In this way, you will be aware of both content and process.

Define the teaching process in behavioral terms. State what behavior you want the children to exhibit. This will make evaluation easier because you have stated what you expect the children to accomplish. Although many educators state behavioral objectives with conditions, most teachers find that beginning a statement with "the child should be able to" followed by an action verb is an effective way to state objectives. Some examples follow:

The child should be able to describe the parts of a flower.

The child should be able to construct a diorama of the habitat of a tiger.

The child should be able to draw a picture that shows different types of animal noses.

*Materials.* If children are to manipulate materials, you must decide which materials should be organized in advance of the lesson. Ask, "What materials will I need to teach this lesson?"

*Advanced preparation.* These are the tasks that the teacher needs to complete prior to implementing the plan with the children. Teachers should ask themselves, "What do I need to have prepared to teach this lesson?"

*Procedure.* The procedure section of a lesson plan provides the step-by-step directions for completing the activity with the children. When planning the lesson, try the procedure yourself and ask: "How will this experience be conducted?" You must decide how you will initiate the lesson with children, present the learning experience, and relate the concept to the children's past experiences. Questions that encourage learning should be considered and included in the lesson plan.

It is recommended that an initiating experience begin the lesson. This experience could be the "messing

| COMPONENTS IN A UNIT PLAN | |
|---|---|
| TOPIC/CONCEPT | What is the topic or concept? |
| GOAL | Where are you heading? |
| OBJECTIVE | How do you plan to achieve your goals? |
| ADVANCED PREPARATION | What do you need to have prepared to teach this lesson? |
| MATERIALS | What will you need? |
| LESSONS | What will you teach? |
| EVALUATION | Did the students learn what you wanted them to learn? |

**Figure 7–6** Components in unit planning.

CONCEPT: "Air takes up space. Bubbles have air inside of them."

OBJECTIVE: Construct a bubble-making machine by manipulating materials and air to produce bubbles. Observe and describe the bubbles.

MATERIALS: Bubble solution of eight tablespoons liquid detergent and one quart water (expensive detergent makes stronger bubbles), straws, four-ounce plastic cups.

ADVANCED PREPARATION:

1. Collect materials.
2. Cut straws into small sections.
3. Mix bubble solution.

PROCEDURE:

*Initiating Activity*: Demonstrate an assembled bubble machine. Have children observe the machine and tell what they think is happening.

*How to do it*: Help children assemble bubble machines. Insert straw into the side of the cup. Pour the bubble mixture to just below the hole in the side of the cup. Give children five minutes to explore blowing bubbles with the bubble machine. Then ask children to see how many bubbles they can blow. Ask: "What do your bubbles look like? Describe your bubbles." Add food coloring for more colorful bubbles.

"What happens to your bubbles? Do they burst? How can you make them last longer?"

"What do you think is in the bubbles? How can you tell? What did you blow into the bubble? Can you think of something else that you blow air into to make larger?" (balloon)

**Figure 7–8** Laticia makes a bubble machine.

EVALUATION:

1. Were the children able to blow bubbles?
2. Did they experiment with blowing differing amounts of air?
3. Did the children say things like, "Look what happens when I blow real hard?"

EXTENSION:

1. Have students tell a story about the bubble machine as you record it on chart paper.
2. Encourage children to make bubble books with drawings that depict their bubbles, bubble machines, and the exciting time they had blowing bubbles. Encourage the children to write or pretend to write about their pictures. Threes and fours enjoy pretending to write; by five or six, children begin to experiment with inventing their own spellings. Be sure to accept whatever they produce. Have children read their books to the class. Place them in the library center for browsing.
3. Make a bubbles bulletin board. Draw a cluster of bubbles and have students add descriptive words about bubbles.
4. Challenge students to invent other bubble machines. (Unit 35 of this book contains activities that teach additional concepts of air and bubbles.)

**Figure 7–7** The bubble machine lesson.

around with materials" stage of the learning cycle, a demonstration or discrepant event, or a question sequence that bridges what you intend to teach with a previous lesson or experience. The idea is that you want to stimulate and interest the children about what they are going to do in the lesson.

*Extension.* To ensure maximum learning of the concept, plan ways to keep the idea going. This can be done by extending the concept and building on students' interest with additional learning activities, integrating the concept into other subject areas, preparing learning centers, and so on.

## Assessment Strategies

You cannot teach a lesson or unit effectively if you do not plan for assessment. There is no point in continuing with another lesson before you know what students understand from the current lesson. Engaging in ongoing assessment of your own teaching and of student progress is essential to improving teaching and learning. Bear in mind that your major role is to help students build concepts, use process skills, and reject incorrect ideas. To do this, students should be engaged in meaningful experiences and should have the time and tools needed to learn. Recall that assessment of students' progress and the guidance of students toward self-assessment is at the heart of good teaching.

The *National Science Education Standards* emphasize that the content and form of an assessment task must be congruent with what is supposed to be measured. The task of establishing the complexity of the science content while addressing the importance of collecting data on all aspects of student science achievement can be challenging.

A variety of assessment formats have been suggested that will help to determine what students understand and are able to do with their knowledge and how they will apply these learnings. Examples of effective strategies include the use of *teacher recorded observations*, which describe what the students are able to do and the areas that need improvement. *Interviews* or *asking questions* and *interacting* with the children are effective assessment strategies. *Portfolios* are examples of individual student work that indicate progress, improvement, and accomplishments, and *science journal writing* cap-

tures yet another dimension of student understanding. **Performance-based assessment** involves assigning one or more students a task that will reveal the extent of their thinking skills and level of understanding of science concepts. Regardless of the assessment strategy used, enough information needs to be provided so that both the student and teacher know what needs to happen for improvement to take place. Additional strategies are discussed in Units 4 and 6 and throughout the text.

Assessment that takes place before teaching is diagnostic in nature and occurs when you assess the children's experiences and ideas about a science concept. For example, when you ask children where they think rain comes from, you are assessing what is known about rain and discovering any misconceptions that might exist.

One effective strategy for science learning is to build upon children's existing knowledge and to challenge students' preconceptions and misconceptions. It is important to find out what your students already know, or think they know, about a science topic before you begin teaching. A popular method for finding out what students already know is the *K-W-L strategy*, described by Ogle (1986) for literacy and adapted for use in science, in which children are asked what they *know*, what they *want* to know, and what they *learned*. Most teachers begin by recording the children's brainstormed responses to the first two questions on a large piece of paper that has been divided into three columns, each headed by one of the K-W-L questions. As the responses are recorded, some difference of opinion is bound to occur. Such disagreement is positive and can provide a springboard for student inquiry. At this point, potential investigations, projects, or inquiry topics can be added to the curriculum plan. The scenario on the following page describes the K-W-L strategy in a primary classroom.

As teachers assess student progress during teaching, changes in teaching strategies are decided. If one strategy is not working, try something else.

As children work on projects, you will find yourself interacting with them on an informal basis. Listen carefully to children's comments, and watch them manipulate materials. You cannot help but assess how things are going. You might even want to keep a record

Ms. Collins is preparing to teach a unit on pond life. She wants to find out what her students already know about life in ponds, so she gathers the class together and asks, "What do you think lives in a pond?" Students are excited to answer. Richard says that ducks live in a pond. Ms. Collins asks how he knows this, and he tells her he saw one at the lake last summer. On the large piece of chart paper mounted on the board, Ms. Collins writes "ducks" under the heading "What We Know about What Lives in Ponds." Cindy says, "You saw a duck in a lake, but is a pond the same as a lake?" Ms. Collins takes the opportunity to write this question under the heading "What We Want to Know about What Lives in Ponds." Kate wants to know, "Do ducks live in ponds, or do they just swim there sometimes?" Ms. Collins continues to write the questions down, as well as other animals that are suggested. When the process is complete, she asks the students, "How can we find out the answers to your questions?" Richard says they should go to a pond. Cindy responds that she has a book about ponds that she can bring to school to share. Lai reminds the class that there is something about ponds on their computer. Kate says maybe they could ask someone who knows about ponds. Ms. Collins writes the students' suggestions: ask someone, read about it, use the computer, and investigate. Ms. Collins has assessed what her students already know. Now she can make further plans for her unit, including lessons that will address the students' questions.

**RECORDED OBSERVATIONS**

Things to record when observing, discussing, or keeping anecdotal records

Cognitive:

How well do the children handle the materials?

Do the children cite out-of-school examples of the science concept?

Is the basic concept being studied referred to as the children go about their day?

Attitude and skill:

Do the children express like or dislike of the topic?

Are there any comments that suggest prejudice?

Do children evidence self-evaluation?

Are ideas freely expressed in the group?

Are there any specific behaviors that need to be observed each time science is taught?

Figure 7–9 Keeping anecdotal records.

of your observations or create a chart that reflects areas of concern to you, such as the attitudes of or the interactions between students. When observations are written down in an organized way, they are called *anecdotal records* (Figure 7–9).

If you decide to use anecdotal records, be sure to write down dates and names and to tell students you are keeping track of things that happen. A review of your records will be valuable when you complete the unit.

Recording observations can become a habit and provides an additional tool for assessing children's learning and your teaching strategies. Anecdotes are also invaluable resources for parent conferences. Refer to Units 4 and 6 for an example of assessing prior knowledge and keeping anecdotal notes.

Responses to oral questions can be helpful in evaluating while teaching. Facial expressions are especially telling. Everyone has observed the blank look that usually indicates a lack of understanding. This look may be because the question asked was too difficult. So, ask an easier question or present your question in a different manner for improved results.

One way to assess teaching is to ask questions about the activity in a lesson review. Some teachers write main idea questions on the chalkboard. Then, they put a chart next to the questions and label it "What We Found Out." As the lesson progresses, the chart is filled in by the class as a way of showing progress and reviewing the lesson or unit.

**Figure 7–10** The golden rule.

Another strategy is to observe children applying the concept. For example, as the *Three Billy Goats Gruff* (Rounds, 1993) is being read, Joyce comments, "The little billy goat walks just like the goat that we saw at the zoo." You know from this statement that Joyce has some idea of how goats move. (Refer to Units 3 and 4.)

Sometimes students have difficulty learning because an activity just doesn't work. One basic rule when teaching science is: "Always do the activity yourself first." This includes noting questions or possible problems you may encounter. If you have trouble, then students will too (Figure 7–10).

## Evaluating the Unit Plan

How well did you design your unit? Reflect and **evaluate** your unit plan before you begin teaching the unit and ask yourself some questions, such as the following, to help evaluate your work. These questions pull together the major points of this unit.

1. Have you related the unit to the children's prior knowledge and past experiences?

2. Are a variety of science process skills used in the lessons?

3. Is the science content developmentally appropriate for the children? How will you know?

4. Have you integrated other subject areas with the science content of the unit?

5. When you use reading and writing activities, do they align with the science content and relate to hands-on learning?

6. Do you allow for naturalistic, informal, and directed activities?

7. Have you included a variety of strategies to engage students in the active search for knowledge? (Refer to Unit 6.)

8. What opportunities are included for investigation and problem solving?

9. Are both open-ended and narrow questions included?

10. Will the assessment strategies provide a way to determine if children can apply what they have learned?

11. What local resources are included in the unit?

When publishers design a unit, they usually field-test it with a population of teachers. In this case, *you* are field-testing the unit as you teach your students. It is important that you keep notes and records on what worked well and what needs to be modified when the lesson is taught again. After teaching the unit you have designed, the *National Science Education Standards* suggest that you take time to reflect on the experience and use assessment data that you have gathered to guide in making judgments about the effectiveness of your teaching. Consider the following categories when making judgments about curricula:

- development appropriateness of the science content
- student interest in the content
- effectiveness of activities in producing the desired learning outcomes
- effectiveness of the selected examples
- understanding and abilities students must have to benefit from the selected activities and examples

## Three Basic Types of Units

Some teachers like to develop *resource units*. The resource unit is an extensive collection of activities and suggestions focusing on a single science topic. The advantage of a resource unit is the wide range of appropriate strategies available to meet the needs, interests, and abilities of the children. As the unit is taught, additional strategies and integrations are usually added. For example, Mrs. Jones knows that she is going to teach a unit on seeds in her kindergarten class. She collects all of the activities and teaching strategies that she can find.

When she is ready to teach the seed unit, she selects the activities that she believes are most appropriate.

Teachers who design a *teaching unit* plan to develop a science concept, objectives, materials, activities, and evaluation procedures for a specific group of children. This unit is less extensive than a resource unit and contains exactly what will be taught, a timeline, and the order of activities. Usually, general initiating experiences begin the unit and culminating experiences end the unit. The specific teaching unit has value and may be used again with other classes after appropriate adaptations have been made. For example, Mr. Wang has planned a two-week unit on batteries and bulbs. He has decided on activities and planned each lesson period of the two weeks.

Extending the textbook in a *textbook unit* is another possibility. The most obvious limitation of this approach is that the school district might change textbooks. A textbook unit is designed by outlining the science concepts for the unit and checking the textbook for those already covered in the book or teacher's manual. Additional learning activities are added for concepts not included in the text or sometimes to replace those in the text. Initiating activities to spark students' interest in the topic might be needed. One advantage of this type of unit is using the textbook to better advantage. For example, after doing animal activities, use the text as a resource to confirm or extend knowledge.

## Open-Ended and Narrow Questions

Asking questions can be likened to driving a car with a stick shift. When teaching the whole class, start in low gear with a narrow question that can be answered yes or no or with a question that has an obvious answer. This usually puts students at ease. They are happy; they know something. Then, try an open-ended question that has many answers. Open-ended questions stimulate discussion and offer opportunities for thinking. However, if the open-ended question is asked before the class has background information, the children might just stare at you, duck their heads, or exhibit undesirable behavior. Do not panic; quickly shift gears and ask a narrow question. Then, work your way back to what you want to find out.

Teachers who are adept at shifting between narrow and open-ended questions are probably excellent discussion leaders and have little trouble with classroom management during these periods.

Open-ended questions are excellent interest builders when used effectively. For example, consider Ms. Hebert's initiating activity for a lesson about buoyancy.

Ms. Hebert holds a rock over a pan of water and asks a narrow, yes-or-no question: "Will this rock sink when dropped in water?" Then she asks an open-ended question, "How can we keep the rock from sinking into the water?" The children answer: "Tie string around it." "Put a spoon under it." "Grab it."

As the discussion progresses, the open-ended question leads the children into a discussion about how they can find out if their ideas will work. The teacher provides materials such as plastic containers, clay, and other items for them to use in designing a device that will float the rock.

Good questions excite and motivate children. When questions are posed that are open-ended and do not depend on yes-or-no answers, children will begin to expand their own capacity for problem solving and inquiry learning.

## SUMMARY

Children are more likely to retain science concepts that are integrated with other subject areas. Making connections between science and other aspects of a child's school day requires that opportunities for learning be well planned and readily available to children. Learning science in a variety of ways encourages personal learning styles and ensures subject integration.

The key to effective teaching is organization. Unit and lesson planning provides a way to plan what and how you want children to learn. A planning web is a useful technique for depicting ideas, outlining concepts, and integrating content.

The three basic types of planning units are resource units, teaching units, and textbook units. Teachers utilize whichever unit best suits their classroom needs. By asking open-ended and narrow questions, teachers develop science concepts and encourage higher-order thinking skills in their students.

## KEY TERMS

evaluate
goals
lesson plan
objectives

performance-based
assessment
webbing

## SUGGESTED ACTIVITIES

1. Select an appropriate science concept and work in teams to construct a planning web of the major concepts that are important to know. Add the activities that you plan to use to teach these concepts and suggest appropriate assessment strategies.

2. Select a lesson from a primary level textbook or from a local science curriculum. Compare the book's presentation of the concept with what you know about how children learn science.

3. Interview a teacher to determine his or her approach to planning—for example, whether a textbook series or curriculum guide is used, how flexibility is maintained, and what assessment techniques are found to be most effective. Ask teachers to describe how they plan units and lessons and to compare the strategies used during their first year of teaching with those they use now. Discuss responses to your questions in a group.

4. Reflect on your past experiences in science classes. Which were the most exciting units? Which were the most boring? Do you remember what made a unit exciting or dull? Or do you primarily remember a specific activity?

5. Observe a primary grade science lesson and write down all of the assessment strategies used during the lesson. Analyze the strategies in terms of what you have learned about assessment.

6. Can you integrate a concept in life science with concepts in language arts? After integrating science and language arts, add mathematics, social studies, art, music, and drama.

7. Design a question-asking strategy that will help you assess children's understanding of the sense of taste.

8. Develop an assessment strategy for the bubble machine lesson in Figure 7–7. Your assessment should include questioning strategies and a checklist of behaviors and responses that would guide your anecdotal record keeping.

## REVIEW

A. What is webbing, and how can it be applied in designing a science unit?

B. Which process skills are involved in the bubble machine lesson, including extensions?

C. Identify learning cycle components in the bubble machine lesson.

D. What strategies could you use to integrate subject areas into science? Give an example.

E. List the major components of a lesson plan for science and describe the importance of each component.

F. Identify three strategies for determining student progress. In what way will these strategies be used in student assessment?

G. What is a unit? List three basic types of units and describe how they are used.

H. Explain the difference between narrow and open-ended questions and how each is used. What are the strengths and weaknesses of each type?

## REFERENCES

Ogle, D. M. (1986). K-W-L: A teaching model that develops active reading of expository text. *The Reading Teacher, 39*(6), 564–570.

Rounds, G. (1993). *Three billy goats gruff.* New York: Holiday House.

## FURTHER READING AND RESOURCES

Carin, A. A., Bass, J. E., & Contant, T. L. (2005). *Teaching science as inquiry* (10th ed.). Upper Saddle River, NJ: Prentice-Hall.

Ferrell, F. (1997). Ponds and technology. *Science and Children, 34*(4), 37–39.

Harlan, J., & Rivkin, M. (2007). *Science experiences for the early childhood years* (9th ed.). New York: Macmillan.

Jacobson, W. J., & Bergman, A. B. (1990). *Science for children: A book for teachers.* Englewood Cliffs, NJ: Prentice-Hall.

Lederman, N. G., Lederman, J. S., & Bell, R. L. (2005). *Constructing science in elementary classrooms.* Boston: Allyn & Bacon.

Lind, K. K. (1993). Concept mapping: Making learning meaningful. In *Teacher's desk reference: A professional guide for science educators.* Englewood Cliffs, NJ: Prentice-Hall.

McAfee, O., Leong, D., & Bodrova, E. (2004). *Basics of assessment: A primer for early childhood educators.* Washington, DC: National Association for the Education of Young Children.

National Research Council. (1996). *National science education standards.* Washington, DC: National Academies Press.

National Research Council. (1999). *Selecting instructional materials: A guide for K–12.* Washington, DC: National Academies Press.

National Research Council. (2002). *Investigating the influence of standards: A framework for research in mathematics, science, and technology education.* Washington, DC: National Academies Press.

National Research Council. (2005). *Mathematical and scientific development in early childhood: A workshop summary.* Washington, DC: National Academies Press.

Peters, J. M., & Gega, P. C. (2002). *Science in elementary education* (9th ed.). Upper Saddle River, NJ: Prentice-Hall.

Rice, K. (1986). Soap films and bubbles. *Science and Children, 23*(8), 4–9.

Schwartz, J. I. (1991). *Literacy begins at home: Helping your child grow up reading and writing.* Springfield, IL: Thomas.

Shavelson, R. J. (1991). Performance assessment in science. *Applied Measurement in Education, 4*(4), 347–362.

Townsend, J., & Schiller, P. (1984). *More than a magnet, less than a dollar.* Houston, TX: Evergreen.

Victor, E., & Kellough, R. D. (2007). *Science K–8: An integrated approach* (11th ed.). Upper Saddle River, NJ: Prentice-Hall.

Wassermann, S., & Ivany, J. W. G. (1990). *Teaching elementary science.* New York: Harper Collins.

# SECTION 2

## Fundamental Concepts and Skills

# Unit **8**

# One-to-One Correspondence

## OBJECTIVES

After reading this unit, you should be able to:

■ Explain the NCTM expectations for one-to-one correspondence.

■ Define one-to-one correspondence.

■ Identify naturalistic, informal, and structured one-to-one correspondence activities.

■ Describe five ways to vary one-to-one correspondence activities.

■ Assess and evaluate children's one-to-one correspondence skills.

The National Council of Teachers of Mathematics (NCTM, 2000) expectations for **one-to-one correspondence** relate to **rational counting** (attaching a number name to each object counted) as described in Unit 9. We believe that placing items in one-to-one correspondence as described in this unit is a supportive concept and skill for rational counting. One-to-one-correspondence is a focal point for number and operations at the prekindergarten level (NCTM, 2007). It is used in connection with solving such problems as having enough (cups, dolls, cars, etc.) of a whole group.

One-to-one correspondence is the most fundamental component of the concept of number. It is the understanding that one group has the same number of things as another. For example, each child has a cookie, each foot has a shoe, each person wears a hat. It is preliminary to counting and basic to the understanding of equivalence and to the concept of conservation of number described in Unit 1. As with other mathematics concepts, it can be integrated across the curriculum (Figure 8–1).

## ASSESSMENT

To obtain information of an informal nature, note the children's behavior during their work, play, and routine activities. Look for one-to-one correspondence that happens naturally. For example, when the child plays train, he may line up a row of chairs so there is one for each child passenger. When he puts his mittens on, he shows that he knows there should be one for each hand; when painting, he checks to be sure he has each paintbrush in the matching color of paint. Tasks for formal assessment are given on page 120 and in Appendix A.

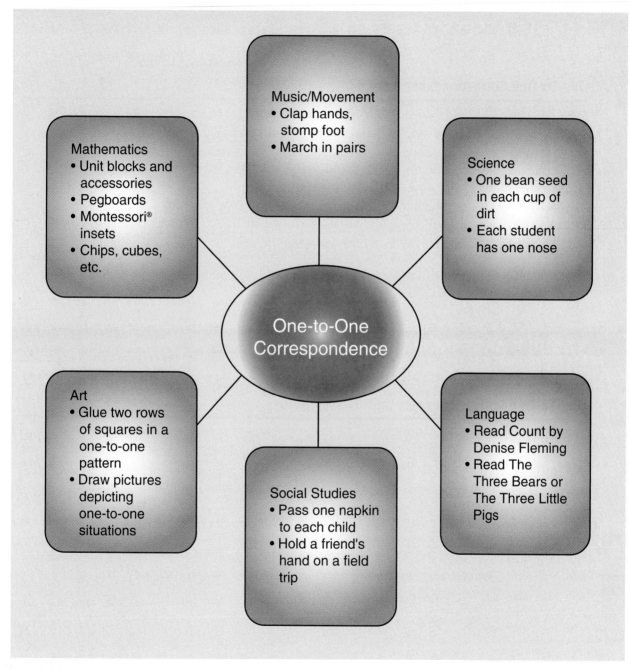

**Figure 8–1** Integrating one-to-one correspondence across the curriculum.

## SAMPLE ASSESSMENT TASK

**3A**                                          **Preoperational Ages 2–3**

### One-To-One Correspondence: Unit 8

**METHOD:**        Observation, individuals or groups.

**SKILL:**         Child demonstrates one-to-one correspondence during play activities.

**MATERIALS:**     Play materials that lend themselves to one-to-one activities, such as small blocks
                   and animals, dishes and eating utensils, paint containers and paintbrushes, pegs
                   and pegboards, sticks and stones, etc.

**PROCEDURE:**     Provide the materials and encourage the children to use them.

**EVALUATION:**    Note if the children match items one to one, such as putting small peg dolls in each
                   of several margarine containers or on top of each of several blocks that have been
                   lined up in a row. Record on checklist, with anecdote and/or photo or video.

**INSTRUCTIONAL RESOURCE:** Charlesworth, R., and Lind, K. K. (2010). *Math and science for young
children* (6th ed.). Clifton Park, NY: Cengage Learning.

## SAMPLE ASSESSMENT TASK

**6A**                                          **Preoperational Ages 5–6**

### One-To-One Correspondence: Unit 8

**METHOD:**        Interview.

**SKILL:**         The child can place two groups of ten items each in one-to-one correspondence.

**MATERIALS:**     Two groups of objects of different shapes and/or color (such as pennies and cube blocks
                   or red chips and white chips). Have at least ten of each type of object.

**PROCEDURE:**     Place two groups of ten objects in front of the child. FIND OUT IF THERE IS THE SAME
                   AMOUNT (NUMBER) IN EACH GROUP (BUNCH, PILE). If the child cannot do the task,
                   try it with two groups of five objects.

**EVALUATION:**    The children should arrange each group so as to match the objects one-to-one, or they
                   might count each group to determine equality. Record on checklist.

**INSTRUCTIONAL RESOURCE:** Charlesworth, R., and Lind, K. K. (2010). *Math and science for young
children* (6th ed.). Clifton Park, NY: Cengage Learning.

## NATURALISTIC ACTIVITIES

One-to-one correspondence activities develop from the infant's early sensorimotor activity. She finds out that she can hold one thing in each hand but can put only one object at a time in her mouth. As a toddler she discovers that five peg dolls will fit one each in the five holes of her toy bus. Quickly she learns that one person fits on each chair, one shoe goes on each foot, and so on. The 2-year-old spends a great deal of his playtime

Checking on whether everyone has accomplished a task or has what she needs is another chance for informal one-to-one correspondence. Does everyone have a chair to sit on? Does everyone have on two boots or two mittens? Does each person have on his coat? Does each person have a cup of milk or a sandwich? A child can check by matching: "Larry, find out if everyone has a pair of scissors, please."

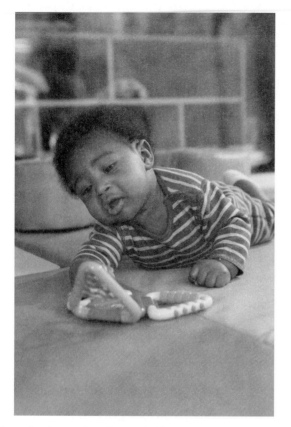

The infant learns that she can hold one object in each hand.

in one-to-one correspondence activities. He lines up containers such as margarine cups, dishes, or boxes and puts a small toy animal in each one. He pretends to set the table for lunch. First he sets one place for himself and one for his bear, with a plate for each. Then he gives each place a spoon and a small cup and saucer. He plays with his large plastic shapes and discovers there is a rod that will fit through the hole in each shape.

## INFORMAL ACTIVITIES

There are many daily opportunities for informal one-to-one correspondence activities. Oftentimes things must be passed out to a group: food items, scissors, crayons, paper, napkins, paper towels, or notes to go home. Each child should do as many of these things as possible.

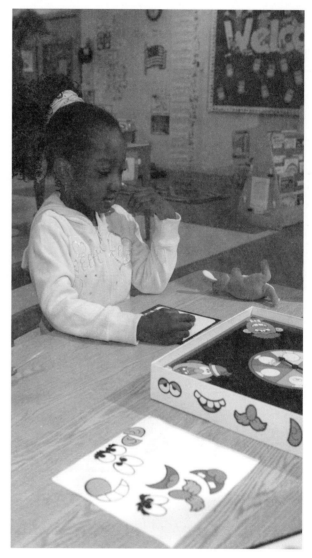

Young children need many opportunities to practice one-to-one matching.

One-to-one correspondence helps to solve difficulties. For instance, the children are washing rubber dolls in soap suds. Jeanie is crying: "Petey has two dolls and I don't have any." Mrs. Carter comes over. "Petey, more children want to play here now so each one can have only one baby to wash." One-to-one correspondence is often the basis for rules such as, "Only one person on each swing at a time" or "Only one piece of cake for each child today."

Other informal activities occur when children pick out materials made available during free play. These kinds of materials include pegboards, felt shapes on a flannelboard, bead and inch-cube block patterns, shape sorters, formboards, lotto games, and other commercial materials. Materials can also be made by the teacher to serve the same purposes. Most of the materials described in the next section can be made available

for informal exploration both before and after they have been used in structured activities.

## STRUCTURED ACTIVITIES

The extent and variety of materials that can be used for one-to-one correspondence activities is almost endless. Referring to Unit 3, remember the six steps from concrete to abstract materials. These steps are especially relevant when selecting one-to-one correspondence materials. Five characteristics must be considered when selecting materials:

- perceptual characteristics
- number of items to be matched
- concreteness

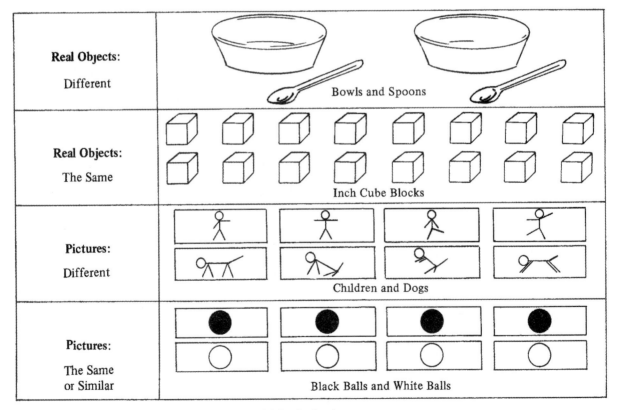

**Figure 8–2** Examples of groups with different perceptual difficulty levels.

■ physically joined or not physically joined

■ groups of the same or not the same number

The teacher can vary or change one or more of the five characteristics and can use different materials. In this way, more difficult tasks can be designed (Figure 8–2).

Perceptual qualities are critical in matching activities. The way the materials to be matched look is important in determining how hard it will be for the child to match them. Materials can vary a great deal with regard to how much the same or how much different they look. Materials are easier to match if the groups are different. To match animals with cages or to find a spoon for each bowl is easier than making a match between two groups of blue chips. In choosing objects, the task can be made more difficult by picking out objects that look more the same.

The number of objects to be matched is important. The more objects in each group, the more difficult it is to match. Groups with fewer than five things are much easier than groups with five or more. In planning activities, start with small groups (fewer than five), and work up step by step to groups of nine. A child who is able to place groups of ten in one-to-one correspondence has a well-developed sense of the concept.

**Concreteness** refers to the extent to which materials are real (Figure 8–3). Remember from Unit 3 that instruction should always begin with concrete real objects. The easiest and first one-to-one correspondence activities should involve the use of real things such as small toys and other familiar objects. Next, objects that are less familiar and more similar (e.g., cube blocks, chips, popsicle sticks) can be used. The next level would be cutout shapes such as circles and squares, cowboys and horses, or dogs and doghouses, to be followed by pictures of real objects and pictures of shapes. Real objects and pictures could also be employed. Computer software can be used by young children who need practice in one-to-one correspondence. The following software programs serve this purpose.

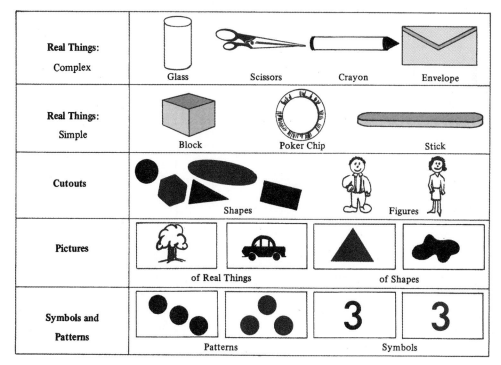

**Figure 8–3** Concreteness: How close to real?

- *Coco's Math Project 1* (Singapore: Times Learning Systems Pte. Ltd.)

- *Learning with Leeper* (Coarsegold, CA: Sierra On-Line, Inc.)

- Match-ups for toddlers can be found online at http://www.lil-fingers.com

Learning to hit the computer keys one at a time with one finger is a one-to-one experience in both the kinesthetic and perceptual-motor domains.

When using objects or pictures of objects, it is easier to tell if there is one-to-one correspondence if the objects are joined than if they are not joined. For example, it is easier to tell if there are enough chairs for each child if the children are sitting in them than if the chairs are on one side of the room and the children on the other. In beginning activities, the objects can be hooked together with a line or a string so that the children can more clearly see whether or not there is a match. In Figure 8–4, each foot is joined to a shoe and each animal to a bowl; neither the hands and mittens nor the balls and boxes are joined.

Placing unequal groups in one-to-one correspondence is harder than placing equal groups. When the groups have the same number, the child can check to be sure he has used all the items. When one group has more, he does not have this clue (Figure 8–5).

The sample lessons presented in Figures 8–6 through 8–11 illustrate some basic types of one-to-one correspondence activities. Note that they also show an increase in difficulty by varying the characteristics just described. Each activity begins by presenting the students with a problem to solve. The lessons are shown as they would be put on cards for the Idea File.

## IDEAS FOR CHILDREN WITH SPECIAL LEARNING NEEDS

One-to-one correspondence games with objects or picture cards can support the learning of perceptual-motor skills and vocabulary. For the child with a language disability or the child who is an English Language Learner, one-to-one correspondence experiences can

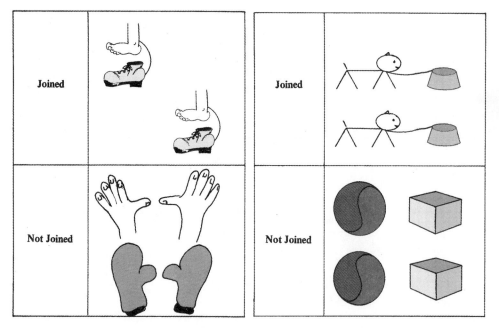

**Figure 8–4** Joined groups and groups that are not joined.

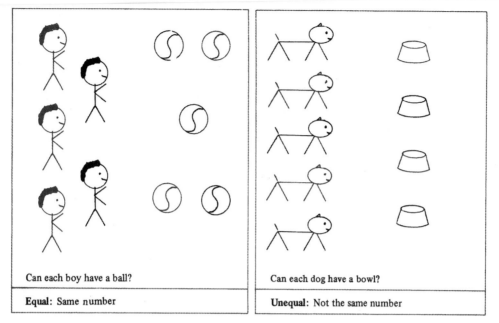

| | |
|---|---|
| Can each boy have a ball? | Can each dog have a bowl? |
| **Equal**: Same number | **Unequal**: Not the same number |

**Figure 8–5** Matching equal and unequal groups.

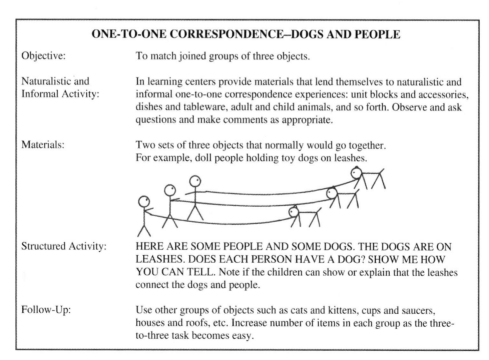

**ONE-TO-ONE CORRESPONDENCE—DOGS AND PEOPLE**

| | |
|---|---|
| Objective: | To match joined groups of three objects. |
| Naturalistic and Informal Activity: | In learning centers provide materials that lend themselves to naturalistic and informal one-to-one correspondence experiences: unit blocks and accessories, dishes and tableware, adult and child animals, and so forth. Observe and ask questions and make comments as appropriate. |
| Materials: | Two sets of three objects that normally would go together. For example, doll people holding toy dogs on leashes. |
| Structured Activity: | HERE ARE SOME PEOPLE AND SOME DOGS. THE DOGS ARE ON LEASHES. DOES EACH PERSON HAVE A DOG? SHOW ME HOW YOU CAN TELL. Note if the children can show or explain that the leashes connect the dogs and people. |
| Follow-Up: | Use other groups of objects such as cats and kittens, cups and saucers, houses and roofs, etc. Increase number of items in each group as the three-to-three task becomes easy. |

**Figure 8–6** One-to-one correspondence activity card—Dogs and people: Matching objects that are perceptually different.

**ONE-TO-ONE CORRESPONDENCE—THE THREE PIGS**

Objective:  To match joined groups of three items.

Naturalistic and  Read the story "The Three Little Pigs." In the literacy center place the three
Informal Activity:  pigs, wolf, houses, straw, sticks, and bricks. These might be flannelboard
figures or puppets. Observe how the children use the materials. Do they play
out the story matching each pig with the appropriate house building material and house? Ask questions or make comments as appropriate.

Materials:  Two sets of cutouts for the bulletin board. Three pieces of yarn. Make three
pig cutouts and three house cutouts: straw, sticks, and bricks. Put them on
bulletin board and connect each pig to his house with thick yarn:

Structured Activity:  WHO ARE THESE FELLOWS? (Children answer) YES, THE THREE
LITTLE PIGS. IS THERE A HOUSE FOR EACH PIG? Have one of the
children show you how he knows there is by tracing from each pig to his
house along the yarn "path." Leave the display up for use by the children
during free playtime.

Follow-Up:  Make a set of pigs, houses, and a wolf for the flannelboard. Both teachers
and children can use these for storytelling.

**Figure 8–7** One-to-one correspondence activity card—Matching the three little pigs to cutouts that are perceptually different.

**ONE-TO-ONE CORRESPONDENCE—PENNIES FOR TOYS**

Objective:  To match groups of two and more objects.

Naturalistic and  Set up a store center such as toys, groceries, or clothing. Provide play
Informal Activity:  money pennies. Put a price of 1¢ on each item. Discuss with the students
what they might do in the store. Observe and note if they exchange one
penny for each item. Make comments and ask questions as appropriate.

Materials:  Ten pennies and 10 small toys (for example, a ball, a car, a truck, three animals, three peg people, a crayon).

Structured Activity:  LET'S PRETEND WE ARE PLAYING STORE. HERE ARE SOME PEN-
NIES AND SOME TOYS. Show the child(ren) two toys. Place two pennies
near the toys. DO I HAVE ENOUGH PENNIES TO BUY THESE TOYS
IF EACH ONE COSTS ONE PENNY? SHOW ME HOW YOU CAN
FIND OUT.

Follow-Up:  Use more toys and more pennies as the children can match larger and larger
groups.

**Figure 8–8** One-to-one correspondence activity card—Pennies for toys: Matching real objects.

**ONE-TO-ONE CORRESPONDENCE—PICTURE MATCHING**

| | |
|---|---|
| Objective: | To match groups of pictured things, animals, or people. |
| Naturalistic and Informal Activity: | Place card sets as described below on a table in one of the classroom learning centers. Observe what the students do with the picture card sets. Do they sort them, match them, and so on? Make comments and ask questions as appropriate. |
| Materials: | Make or purchase picture cards that show items familiar to young children. Each set should have two groups of 10. Pictures from catalogs, magazines, or readiness workbooks can be cut out, glued on cards, and covered with clear Contac® or laminated. For example, pictures of 10 children should be put on 10 different cards. Pictures of 10 toys could be put on 10 other cards. |
| Structured Activity: | Present two people and two toys. DOES EACH CHILD HAVE A TOY? SHOW ME HOW YOU CAN FIND OUT. Increase the number of items in each group. |
| | Make some more card sets. Fit them to current science or social studies units. For example, if the class is studying jobs, have pilot with plane, driver with bus, etc. |

**Figure 8–9** One-to-one correspondence activity card—Picture matching.

**ONE-TO-ONE CORRESPONDENCE—SIMILAR OR IDENTICAL OBJECTS**

| | |
|---|---|
| Objective: | To match 2 to 10 similar and/or identical objects. |
| Naturalistic and Informal Activity: | Each day in the math center provide opportunity to explore manipulatives such as inch cube blocks, Unifix®Cubes, Lego®, and so on. Observe what the students do with the materials. Note if they do any one-to-one correspondence as they explore. Make comments and ask questions as appropriate. |
| Materials: | Twenty objects such as poker chips, inch cube blocks, coins, cardboard circles, etc. There may be 10 of one color and 10 of another or 20 of the same color (more difficult perceptually). |
| Structured Activity: | Begin with two groups of two and increase the size of the groups as the children are able to match the small groups. HERE ARE TWO GROUPS (BUNCHES, SETS) OF CHIPS (BLOCKS, STICKS, PENNIES, ETC.). DO THEY HAVE THE SAME NUMBER, OR DOES ONE GROUP HAVE MORE? SHOW ME HOW YOU KNOW. Have the children take turns using different sizes of groups and different objects. |
| Follow-Up: | Glue some objects to a piece of heavy cardboard or plywood. Set out a container of the same kinds of objects. Have this available for matching during center time. Also, baggies with groups of objects of varied amounts can be placed in the math center where students can select pairs of objects for matching. |

**Figure 8–10** One-to-one correspondence activity card—Similar or identical objects.

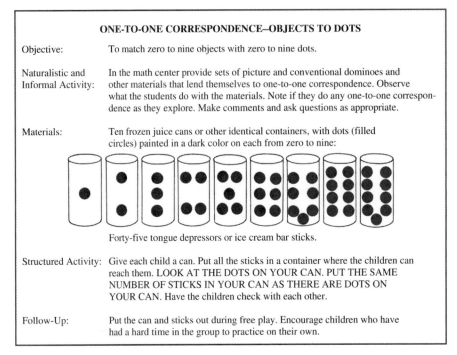

**Figure 8–11** One-to-one correspondence activity card—Matching number of objects to number of dots.

provide vocabulary support. When playing a matching game the adult can label the examples. For example, when matching toy animals: "THIS IS A CAT, FIND ANOTHER CAT." When passing out materials: "GIVE EACH FRIEND SOME PLAY-DOH." When using a pegboard: "PUT A PEG IN EACH HOLE. YOU PUT A RED PEG IN THE HOLE." Or ask questions that encourage speech: "WHAT SHOULD YOU LOOK FOR TO MATCH THIS PICTURE?"

Finger plays can promote one-to-one correspondence. For example, "Where is thumbkin?" requires the recognition of one finger at a time. ELL students whose primary language is Spanish can learn popular Latin American fingerplays in Spanish and English (Orozco & Kleven, 1997).

## EVALUATION

Informal evaluation can be accomplished by noticing each child's response during structured activities. Also observe each child during free play to see whether he or she can pass out toys or food to other children, giving one at a time. On the shelves in the housekeeping area, paper shapes of each item (dishes, cups, tableware, purses, etc.) may be placed on the shelf where the item belongs. Hang pots and pans on a pegboard with the shapes of each pot drawn on the board. Do the same for blocks and other materials. Notice which children can put materials away by making the right match.

Using the same procedures as in the assessment tasks, a more formal check can be made regarding what the children have learned. Once children can do one-to-one with 10 objects, try more—see how far they can go.

## SUMMARY

The most basic number skill is one-to-one correspondence. Starting in infancy, children learn about one-to-one relationships. Sensorimotor and early pre-operational children spend much of their playtime in one-to-one correspondence activities.

Many opportunities for informal one-to-one correspondence activities are available during play and daily routines. Materials used for structured activities with individuals and/or small groups should also be made available for free exploration.

Materials and activities can be varied in many ways to make one-to-one correspondence fun and interesting. They can also be designed to serve children with special learning needs. Once children have a basic understanding of the one-to-one concept, they can apply the concept to higher-level activities involving equivalence and the concept of *conservation of number*.

The World Wide Web contains a multitude of resources for teaching strategies in mathematics and other content areas. See the Online Companion for examples.

## KEY TERMS

concreteness       one-to-one correspondence       rational counting

## SUGGESTED ACTIVITIES

1. Present a toddler (18 months to 2 years old) with a plastic container and some small (but safe) objects, such as empty wooden thread spools or plastic lids. Observe how he uses the materials. Note whether anything the child does might indicate the development of the concept of one-to-one correspondence.

2. Collect the materials for one or more of the structured activities described in this unit. Try the activities with two or more children of ages 4 or 5. Describe to the class what the children do.

3. Develop your own one-to-one correspondence game. Play the game with a young child. Share the game with the class. Are there any improvements you would make?

4. Make copies of the structured activities, and add them to your Idea File. Add one or two more activities that you create or find suggested in another resource.

5. Discuss with the class what you might do if a 5-year-old seemed not to have the concept of one-to-one correspondence beyond two groups of three.

6. If possible, observe a young child interacting with one of the software items listed in this unit. See if the activity appears to support the child's ability to engage in one-to-one correspondence.

7. Select a one-to-one correspondence activity from the Internet. Assemble any materials needed and use the activity with a small group of pre-K or kindergarten students.

## REVIEW

A. Explain how you would define one-to-one correspondence when talking with a parent.

B. Determine which of the following one-to-one correspondence activities is naturalistic, informal, or structured. Give a reason for your decision.

    1. Mr. Conklin has six cat pictures and six mouse pictures. "Patty, does each cat have a mouse to chase?"

    2. Rosa lines up five red blocks in a row. Then she places a smaller yellow block on each red block.

    3. Candy puts one bootie on each of her baby doll's feet.

    4. Aisha passes one glass of juice to each child at her table.

    5. Mrs. Garcia shows 5-year-old José two groups of ten pennies. "Find out if both

groups of pennies have the same amount, or if one group has more."

**C.** Give examples of several ways that one-to-one correspondence activities may be varied.

**D.** Look at the following pairs of groups of items. Decide which one in each pair would be more difficult to place in one-to-one correspondence.

    1.  (a) five red chips and five yellow chips

          (b) twelve white chips and twelve orange chips

2.  (a) four feet and four shoes

     (b) four circles and four squares

3.  (a) two groups of seven

     (b) a group of seven and a group of eight

4.  (a) cards with pictures of knives and forks

     (b) real knives and forks

## REFERENCES

National Council of Teachers of Mathematics. (2000). *Principles and standards for school mathematics.* Reston, VA: Author.

National Council of Teachers of Mathematics. (2007). *Curriculum focal points for prekindergarten through grade 8 mathematics.* Retrieved May 24, 2007, from http://www.nctm.org

Orozco, J., & Kleven, E. (1997). *Diez deditos* [Ten little fingers]. New York: Scholastic Books.

## FURTHER READING AND RESOURCES

American Association for the Advancement of Science (AAAS). (2007). *Atlas of science literacy: Project 2061* (Vol. 2). Washington, DC: Author.

Baratta-Lorton, M. (1972). *Workjobs.* Menlo Park, CA: Addison-Wesley.

Burk, D., Snider, A., & Symonds, P. (1988). *Box it or bag it mathematics: Kindergarten teachers resource guide.* Portland, OR: Math Learning Center.

Clements, D. H., & Sarama, J. (2004). Mathematics everywhere, every time. *Teaching Children Mathematics, 10*(8), 421–426.

Copley, J. V. (Ed.). (1999). *Mathematics in the early years.* Washington, DC: National Association for the Education of Young Children.

Copley, J. V. (2000). *The young child and mathematics.* Washington, DC: National Association for the Education of Young Children.

Copley, J. V. (2004). The sharing game. In J. V. Copley (Ed.), *Showcasing mathematics for the young child.* Reston, VA: National Council of Teachers of Mathematics.

Copley, J. V., Jones, C., & Dighe, J. (2007). *Mathematics: The creative curriculum approach.* Washington, DC: Teaching Strategies.

Epstein, A. S. (2007). *The intentional teacher.* Washington, DC: National Association for the Education of Young Children.

National Research Council. (1996). *National science education standards.* Washington, DC: National Academies Press.

Newberger, A., & Vaughn, E. (2006). *Teaching numeracy, language, and literacy with blocks.* St. Paul, MN: Redleaf Press.

Richardson, K. (1984). *Developing number concepts using Unifix Cubes.* Menlo Park, CA: Addison-Wesley.

Richardson, K. (1999). *Developing number concepts: Planning guide.* Parsippany, NJ: Seymour.

Zaslavsky, C. (1996). *The multicultural classroom.* Portsmouth, NH: Heinneman.

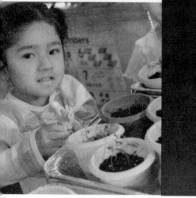

# Unit 9

# Number Sense and Counting

## OBJECTIVES

After reading this unit, you should be able to:

- Explain the NCTM expectations for number.
- Describe the concept of number sense and its relationship to counting.
- Define rote and rational counting and explain their relationship.
- Identify examples of rote and rational counting.
- Teach counting using naturalistic, informal, and structured activities appropriate to each child's age and level of maturity.

The NCTM (2000) expectations for number focus on the ability of children in prekindergarten through second grade to count with understanding and to recognize "how many?" in sets of objects. The children are also expected to develop understanding of the relative position and size of whole numbers, ordinal and cardinal numbers, and their connections to each other. Finally, they are expected to develop a sense of whole numbers and be able to represent and use them in many ways. These expectations should be achieved through real-world experiences and through using physical materials.

Included in the NCTM standards is the standard that children should develop whole number skills that enable them to "construct number meanings through real-world experiences and the use of physical materials; understand our number system by relating, counting, grouping, and (eventually) place-value concepts; and develop number sense." Number sense and counting can be integrated into other content areas (Figure 9–1).

A major focal point for prekindergarten within number and operations is the development of an understanding of whole numbers (NCTM, 2007). Prekindergartners need to learn to recognize objects in small groups by counting and without counting. They need to understand that numbers refer to quantities. They begin to use number to solve everyday problems like how many spoons they will need for a group or how many sides there are in a rectangle. They need to be prepared to relate numerals and groups when they enter kindergarten (Units 23 and 24).

The concept of number or understanding number is referred to as **number sense**. *Number sense* makes the connection between quantities and counting. Number sense underlies the understanding of more and less, of relative amounts, of the relationship between space and quantity (i.e., number conservation), and parts and wholes of quantities. Number sense enables children to understand important benchmarks such as 5 and 10 as

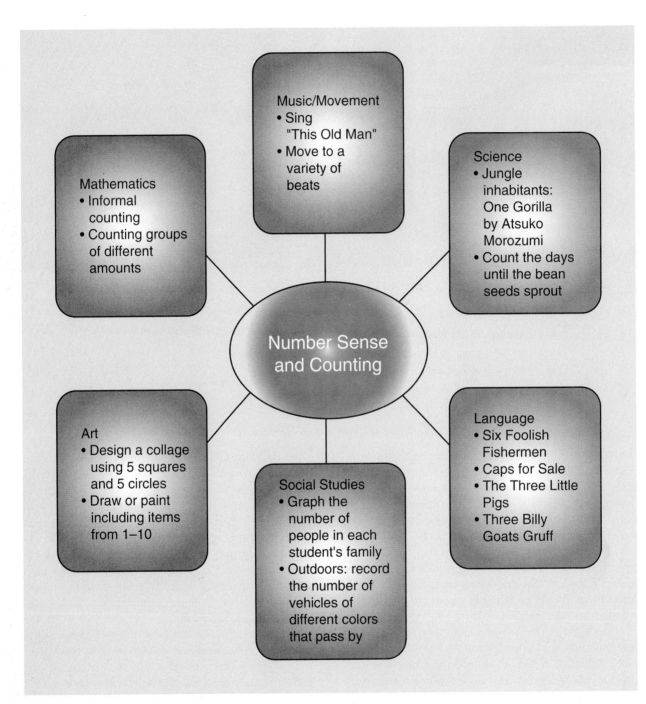

**Figure 9–1** Integrating number sense and counting across the curriculum.

they relate to other quantities. Number sense also helps children estimate quantities and measurements. Counting assists children in the process of understanding quantity. Understanding that the last number named is the quantity in the group is a critical fundamental concept. It is the understanding of the "oneness" of one, the "twoness" of two, and so on.

When shown a group, seeing "how many" instantly is called **subitizing**. There are two types of subitizing: perceptual and conceptual. **Perceptual subitizing** is when one can state how many items are in a group without actually counting them. Young children usually learn to subitize up to four items perceptually. That is, when shown a group of four items, they can tell you "four" without counting. **Conceptual subitizing** involves seeing number patterns within a group, such as the larger dot patterns on a domino. The viewer may break the eight-dot pattern down into two groups of four, which makes up the whole. Perceptual subitizing is thought to be the basis for counting and **cardinality** (understanding the last number named is the amount in a group). Conceptual subitizing develops from counting and patterning and helps develop number sense and arithmetic skills. Preschoolers can subitize perceptually. Conceptual subitizing for small quantities usually begins in first grade. Clements (1999) suggests some games for kindergarten play that can bridge into conceptual subitizing.

Quantities from one to four or five are the first to be recognized. Infants can perceive the difference between these small quantities, and children as young as 2½ or 3 years may recognize these small amounts so easily that they seem to do so without counting. The concept of number is constructed bit by bit from infancy through the preschool years and gradually becomes a tool that can be used in problem solving.

Number's partner, counting, includes two operations: **rote counting** and **rational counting**. *Rote counting* involves reciting the names of the numerals in order from memory. That is, the child who says "One, two, three, four, five, six, seven, eight, nine, ten" has correctly counted in a rote manner from 1 to 10. *Rational counting* involves matching each numeral name in order to an object in a group. It builds on children's understanding of one-to-one correspondence. Reys, Lindquist, Lambdin, Smith, and Suydam (2001) identify four principles of rational counting.

1. Only one number name may be assigned to each of the objects to be counted.

2. There is a correct order in which the number names may be assigned (i.e., one, two, three, etc.).

3. Counting can start with any of the items in the group.

4. The *cardinality rule* states that the last number name used is the number of objects in the group.

As an example, Maria has some pennies in her hand. She takes them out of her hand one at a time and places them on the table. Each time she places one on the table she says the next number name in sequence: "one," places first penny; "two," places another penny; "three," places another penny. She has successfully done rational counting of three objects. Rational counting is a higher level of one-to-one correspondence.

A basic understanding of accurate rote counting and one-to-one correspondence is the foundation of rational counting. The ability of rational counting assists children in understanding the concept of number by enabling them to check their labeling of quantities as being a specific amount. It also helps them to compare equal quantities of different things—such as two apples, two children, and two chairs—and to realize that the quantity two is *two*, regardless of what makes up a group. Number, counting, and one-to-one correspondence all serve as the basis for developing the concept of number conservation, which is usually mastered by age 6 or 7. Too often, the preprimary mathematics program centers on counting with repeated teacher-directed drill and practice. Children need repeated and frequent practice to develop counting skills, but this practice should be of short duration and should center on naturalistic and informal instruction. Structured activities should include many applications, such as the examples of data collection that follow.

■ How many children in the class have brothers? Sisters? Neither?

■ How many days will it be until the first seed sprouts? Let's make some guesses, and then we'll keep track and see who comes close.

■ How many days did we mark off before the first egg hatched?

- How many carrots do we need so that each rabbit will get one?
- How many of the small blocks will balance the big block on the balance scale?

It is a normal expectation that rote counting develops ahead of rational counting. For example, a 2- or 3-year-old who has a good memory might rote count to 10 but only be able to rational count one or two or three objects accurately. When given a group of more than three to count, a young child might perform as described in the following example: Six blocks are placed in front of a 2½-year-old, who is asked, "How many blocks do you have?" Using her pointer finger, she "counts" and points.

- "One, two, three, four, five, six, seven, eight" (pointing at some blocks more than once and some not at all).
- "One, two, four, six, three, ten" (pointing to each block only once but losing track of the correct order).

Rational counting is a fairly complex task. To count objects accurately, the child must know the number names in the correct order and be able to coordinate eyes, hands, speech, and memory. This is difficult for the 2- or 3-year-old because she is still in a period of rapid growth in coordination. She is also limited in her ability to stick to a task. The teacher should not push a child to count more things than he can count easily and with success. Most rational counting experiences should be naturalistic and informal.

By age 4 or 5, the rate of physical growth is slowing. Coordination of eyes, hands, and memory is maturing. Rational counting skills should begin to catch up with rote counting skills. Structured activities can be introduced. At the same time, naturalistic and informal activities should continue.

During the kindergarten year, children usually become skilled at rote and rational counting. Many kindergartners are ready to play more complex games with quantities such as counting backward and counting on from a given quantity. Counting backward and counting on lay the foundation for the whole number operations of addition and subtraction. Estimation activities can begin with prekindergartners playing simple games such as "Guess how many beans are in a small jar" or "How

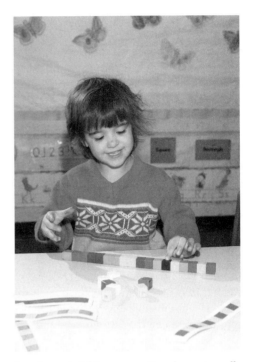

By age 3 or 4, most children can rational count small groups.

many paper clips wide is the table?"—followed by checking their guesses by counting the beans and paper clips.

In *Number in Preschool and Kindergarten* (Kamii, 1982), the author particularly emphasizes that it is necessary to be aware of the coordination of one-to-one correspondence and counting in the development of the concept of number. Four levels of development in counting have been identified by asking children to put out the same number of items as an adult put out in groups of sizes four to eight.

1. Children cannot understand what they are supposed to do.
2. They do a rough visual estimation or copy (that is, they attempt to make their group look like the model).
3. They do a methodical one-to-one correspondence. Childen seldom reach this stage before age 5½.
4. They count. That is, the child counts the items in the model and then counts out another group with the same amount. Children usually reach this stage at about age 7.

To develop the coordination of the two concepts, it is essential that children count and do one-to-one correspondence using movable objects. It becomes obvious that, among other weaknesses, the use of workbook pages precludes moving the objects to be counted and/ or matched. In addition, opportunities should be provided for children to work together so they can discuss and compare ideas. As the children work individually and/or with others, watch closely and note the thinking process that seems to take place as they solve problems using counting and one-to-one correspondence.

## ASSESSMENT

The adult should note the child's regular activity. Does she recognize groups of zero to four without counting? "Mary has no cookies," "I have two cookies," "John has four cookies." Does she use rational counting correctly when needed? "Here, Mr. Black, six blocks for you." (Mr. Black has seen her count them out on her own.) For formal assessment, see the tasks on pages 135–136

and those in Appendix A. Be sure to record naturalistic and informal events.

## NATURALISTIC ACTIVITIES

Number sense and the skill of counting are used a great deal by young children in their everyday activities. Once these are in the child's thoughts and activity, he will be observed often in number and counting activities. He practices rote counting often. He may run up to the teacher or parent saying, "I can count—one, two, three." He may be watching a TV program and hear "one, two, three, four . . .," after which he may repeat "one, two, . . . ."At first he may play with the number names, saying "one, two, five, four, eight, . . ." to himself in no special order. Listen carefully and note that gradually he gets more of the names in the right order.

Number appears often in the child's activities once she has the idea in mind. A child is eating crackers and says, "Look at all my crackers. I have two crackers." One and two are usually the first amounts used by children

---

### SAMPLE ASSESSMENT TASK

**4G**                                                      **Preoperational Ages 3–6**

**Rote Counting: Unit 9**

**METHOD:**      Interview, individual.

**SKILL:**      Demonstrates the ability to rote count.

**MATERIALS:**   None.

**PROCEDURE:**  COUNT FOR ME. COUNT AS FAR AS YOU CAN. If the child hesitates or looks puzzled, ask again. If the child still doesn't respond, say, ONE, TWO, WHAT'S NEXT?

**EVALUATION:** Note how far the child counts and the accuracy of the counting. Young children often lose track (i.e., "One, two, three, four, five, six, ten, seven, . . ." ) or miss a number name. Children ages 2 and 3 may only be able to count their ages, whereas 4-year-olds usually can count accurately to ten and might try the teens and even beyond. By age 5 or 6, children will usually begin to understand the commonalities in the 20s and beyond and move on toward counting to 100. Young children vary a great deal at each age level, so it is important to find where each individual is and move along from there.

**INSTRUCTIONAL RESOURCE:** Charlesworth, R., and Lind, K. K. (2010). *Math and science for young children* (6th ed.). Clifton Park, NY: Cengage Learning.

## SAMPLE ASSESSMENT TASK

**4H**                                                            **Preoperational Ages 3–6**

**Rational Counting: Unit 9**

**METHOD:**   Interview, individual or small group.

**SKILL:**   Child demonstrates ability to rational count.

**MATERIALS:**   30 or more objects such as cube blocks, chips, or Unifix Cubes.

**PROCEDURE:**   Place a pile of objects in front of the child (about 10 for a 3-year-old, 20 for a 4-year-old, 30 for a 5-year-old, and as many as 100 for older children). COUNT THESE FOR ME. HOW MANY CAN YOU COUNT?

**EVALUATION:**   Note how accurately the child counts and how many objects are attempted. In observing the process, note the following.
  1. Does the child use just his eyes, or does he actually touch each object as he counts?
  2. Is some organizational system used, such as lining the objects up in rows or moving the ones counted to the side?
  3. Compare accuracy on rational counting with the child's rote counting ability.

**INSTRUCTIONAL RESOURCE:**  Charlesworth, R., and Lind, K. K. (2010). *Math and science for young children* (6th ed.). Clifton Park, NY: Cengage Learning.

2 and 3 years old. They may use one and two for quite a while before they go on to larger groups. Number names are used for an early form of division. For example, a child has three cookies, which he divides equally with his friends: "One for you, one for you, and one for me." Looking at a picture book, the child says, "There is one daddy and two babies." The child wants another toy: "I want one more little car, Dad."

## INFORMAL ACTIVITIES

The alert adult can find a multitude of ways to take advantage of opportunities for informal instruction. For example, the child is watching a children's television program and the teacher is sitting next to her. A voice from the TV rote counts by singing, "One, two, three, four, five, six." The teacher says to the child, "That's fun, let's count too." They then sing together: "One, two, three, four, five, six." Or, the teacher and children are waiting for the school bus to arrive. "Let's count as far as we can while we wait. One, two, three . . . ." Because rote counting is learned through frequent but

short periods of practice, informal activities should be used most for teaching.

Everyday activities offer many opportunities for informal rational counting and number activities. For instance, the teacher is helping a child get dressed after his nap. "Find your shoes and socks. How many shoes do you have? How many socks? How many feet?" Some children are meeting at the door. The teacher says, "We are going to the store. There should be five of us. Let's count and be sure we are all here."

Table setting offers many chances for rational counting. "Put six place mats on each table." "How many more forks do we need?" "Count out four napkins." Play activities also offer times for rational counting. "Mary, please give Tommy two trucks." A child is looking at his hands, which are covered with finger paint: "How many red hands do you have, Joey?"

A more challenging problem can be presented by asking an open-ended question. For instance: "Get enough napkins for everyone at your table" or "Be sure everyone has the same number of carrot sticks." In these situations, children aren't given a clue to help them decide how many they need or how many each person should get; they must figure out how to solve the problem on their own. Often children will forget to count themselves. This presents an excellent opportunity for group discussion to try to figure out what went wrong. The teacher could follow up such an incident by reading the book *Six Foolish Fishermen* (Elkin, 1968/1971; see Appendix B), in which the fishermen make the same mistake.

## STRUCTURED ACTIVITIES

Rote counting is learned mostly through naturalistic and informal activities. However, there are short, fun things that can be used to help children learn the number names in the right order. There are many rhymes, songs, and finger plays. Songs include those such as "This Old Man," "Johnny Works with One Hammer," and "Five Little Ducks."

A favorite old rhyme is as follows:

One, two, buckle your shoe.
Three, four, shut the door.
Five, six, pick up sticks.
Seven, eight, shut the gate.
Nine, ten, a big fat hen.

A finger play can be used, as follows.

### "Five Little Birdies"
(Hold up five fingers. As each bird leaves, "fly" your hand away and come back with one less finger standing up.)
Five little birdies sitting by the door,
One flew away and then there were four.

Four little birdies sitting in a tree,
One flew away and then there were three.
Three little birdies sitting just like you,
One flew away and then there were two.
Two little birdies having fun,
One flew away and then there was one.
One little birdie sitting all alone,
He flew away and then there were none.

More direct ways of practicing rote counting are also good. Clapping and counting at the same time teaches number order and gives practice in rhythm and coordination. With a group, everyone can count at the same time, "Let's count together. One, two, three . . . ." Individual children can be asked, "Count as far as you can."

Groups that have zero to four items are special in the development of rational counting skills. The number of items in groups this size can be perceived without counting. For this reason, these groups are easy for children to understand. They should have many experiences and activities with groups of size zero to four before they work with groups of five and more. With structured activities it is wise to start with groups of size two because, as mentioned before, there are so many that occur naturally. For example, the child has two eyes, two hands, two arms, and two legs. Two pieces of bread are used to make a sandwich, and riding a bike with two wheels is a sign of being big. For this reason, activities using two are presented first in the following examples. The activities are set up so that they can be copied onto activity cards for the file.

## ACTIVITIES

### Number: Groups of Two

**OBJECTIVE:** To learn the idea of two.

**MATERIALS:** The children's bodies, the environment, a flannelboard and/or a magnetic board, pairs of objects, pictures of pairs of objects.

**NATURALISTIC AND INFORMAL ACTIVITIES:** As children play with materials in the classroom, note any occasions when they identify two objects. Ask questions such as, "How many shoes do you need for your dress-up outfit?" "Can two cups of sand fill the bowl?"

*(continued)*

**STRUCTURED ACTIVITIES:**
1. Put several pairs of felt pieces (e.g., hearts, triangles, or bunnies) on the flannelboard (or magnets on the magnet board). Point to each group in turn: WHAT ARE THESE? HOW MANY ARE THERE?
2. Have the children check their bodies and the other children's bodies for groups of two.
3. Have the children, one at a time, find groups of two in the room.
4. Using rummy cards, other purchased picture cards, or cards you have made, make up sets of cards with identical pairs. Give each child a pack with several pairs mixed up. Have them sort the pack and find the groups of two.
5. Fill a container with many objects. Have the children sort out as many groups of two as they can find.

**FOLLOW-UP:** Have the materials available during center time.

## Number: Groups of Three

**OBJECTIVE:** To learn the idea of three.

**MATERIALS:** Flannelboard and/or magnet board, objects, picture cards.

**NATURALISTIC AND INFORMAL ACTIVITIES:** As children play with materials in the classroom, note any occasions when they identify three objects. Ask leading questions: if three children are playing house, "How many cups do you need for your party?" "Can three cups of sand fill the bowl?" To a 3-year-old, "How many candles were on your birthday cake?"

**STRUCTURED ACTIVITIES:** Do the same types of activities as before, now using groups of three instead of two. Emphasize that three is one more than two.

**FOLLOW-UP:** Have the materials available during center time.

## Number: Groups of One

**OBJECTIVE:** To learn the idea that one is a group.

**MATERIALS:** Flannelboard and/or magnet board, objects, picture cards.

**NATURALISTIC AND INFORMAL ACTIVITIES:** As children play with materials in the classroom note any occasions when they identify a single object. Ask such questions as "How many cups does each person need for the party?" "How many glasses does each person get for milk at lunch?"

**STRUCTURED ACTIVITIES:** Do the same types of activities using groups of one as were done for groups of two and three.

**FOLLOW-UP:** Have the materials available during center time.

## Number: Zero

**OBJECTIVE:** To understand the idea that a group with nothing in it is called *zero*.

**NATURALISTIC AND INFORMAL ACTIVITIES:** Note if children use the term *none* or *zero* during their play activities. Ask questions such as, "If all the sand falls on the floor, how much will be left in the sandbox?" "If you eat all of your beans, then you will have how many?"

**MATERIALS:** Flannelboard, magnet board, and objects.

**STRUCTURED ACTIVITIES:**
1. Show the children groups of things on the flannelboard, magnet board, and/or groups of objects. SEE ALL THESE THINGS? Give them a chance to look and respond. NOW I TAKE THEM AWAY. WHAT DO I HAVE NOW? They should respond with "nothing," "all gone," and/or "no more."
2. Put out a group (of flannel pieces, magnet shapes, or objects) of a size the children all know (such as one, two, three, or four). Keep taking one away. HOW MANY NOW? When none are left, say: THIS AMOUNT IS CALLED ZERO. Repeat until they can answer "zero" on their own.
3. Play a silly game. Ask HOW MANY REAL LIVE TIGERS DO WE HAVE IN OUR ROOM? (Continue with other things that obviously are not in the room.)

**FOLLOW-UP:** Work on the concept informally. Ask questions: HOW MANY CHILDREN ARE HERE AFTER EVERYONE GOES HOME? After snack, if all the food has been eaten: HOW MANY COOKIES (CRACKERS, PRETZELS, etc.) DO YOU HAVE NOW?

After the children have grasped the ideas of groups of zero, one, two, and three, then go on to four. Use the same kinds of activities. Once they have four in mind, go on to activities using groups of all five amounts. Emphasize the idea of *one more than* as you move to each larger group.

## Number: Using Sets Zero Through Four

**OBJECTIVE:** To understand groups of zero through four.

**MATERIALS:** Flannelboard, magnet board, and/or objects.

1. Show the children several groups of objects of different amounts. Ask them to point to sets of one, two, three, and four.
2. Give the children a container of many objects. Have them find sets of one, two, three, and four.
3. Show the children containers of objects (pennies, buttons, etc.). Ask them to find the ones with groups of zero, one, two, three, and four.
4. Give each child four objects. Ask each one to make as many different groups as she can.
5. Ask the children to find out HOW MANY _____ ARE IN THE ROOM? (Suggest things for which there are fewer than five.)

When the children have the idea of groups from zero to four, they can then go on to groups larger than four. Some children are able to perceive five without counting, just as they perceive zero through four without actually counting. Having learned the groups of four and fewer, children can be taught five by adding one to groups of four. Once the children understand five as "four with one more" and six as "five with one more," then more advanced rational counting can begin. That is, children can work with groups of objects where they can find the number only by actually counting each ob-ject. Before working with a child on counting groups of six or more, the adult must be sure the child can do the following activities.

■ Recognize groups of zero to four without counting.

■ Rote count to six or more correctly and quickly.

■ Recognize that a group of five is a group of four with one more added.

The following are activities for learning about groups larger than four.

## Number/Rational Counting: Introducing Five

**OBJECTIVE:** To understand that five is four with one more item added.

**MATERIALS:** Flannelboard, magnet board, and/or objects.

**NATURALISTIC AND INFORMAL ACTIVITIES:** Have a variety of manipulatives in the math center. Note how children group the materials and whether they mention "how many"; for example, "I have five red cubes." "I need three green cubes." Ask questions such as "How many white cubes have you hooked together?"

**STRUCTURED ACTIVITIES:** 1. Show the children a group of four. HOW MANY IN THIS GROUP? Show the children a group of five. HOW MANY IN THIS GROUP? Note how many children already have the idea of five. Tell them YES, THIS IS A GROUP OF FIVE. Have them make other groups with the same amount by using the first group as a model.

2. Give each child five objects. Ask them to identify how many objects they have.

3. Give each child seven or eight objects. Ask them to make a group of five.

**FOLLOW-UP:** Have containers of easily counted and perceived objects always available for the children to explore. These would be items such as buttons, poker chips, Unifix Cubes, and inch cubes. Use books that focus on five, such as *Five Little Ducks* (Raffi: Songs to Read Series, Crown) and *Five Little Monkeys Sitting in a Tree* (Christfellow, Clarion).

## Number/Rational Counting: Groups Larger than Five

**OBJECTIVE:** To be able to count groups of amounts greater than five.

**MATERIALS:** Flannelboard and/or magnet board, objects for counting, pictures of groups on cards, items in the environment.

**NATURALISTIC AND INFORMAL ACTIVITIES:** Have a variety of manipulatives in the math center. Note how children group the materials and whether they mention "how many," such as "I have seven red cubes." "I need six green cubes." Ask questions such as "How many white cubes have you hooked together?" "If you hooked one more cube to your line, how many would you have?"

**STRUCTURED ACTIVITIES:**
1. One step at a time, present groups on the flannelboard and magnet board or groups made up of objects such as buttons, chips, inch-cube blocks, etc. Have the children take turns counting them—together and individually.
2. Present cards with groups of six or more, showing cats, dogs, houses, or similar figures. Ask the children as a group or individually to tell how many items are pictured on each card.
3. Give the children small containers with items to count.
4. Count things in the room. HOW MANY TABLES (CHAIRS, WINDOWS, DOORS, CHILDREN, TEACHERS)? Have the children count all at the same time and individually.

**FOLLOW-UP:** Have the materials available for use during center time. Watch for opportunities for informal activities.

## Number/Rational Counting: Follow-Up with Stories

**OBJECTIVE:** To be able to apply rational counting to fantasy situations.

**MATERIALS:** Stories that will reinforce the ideas of groups of numbers and rational counting skills. Some examples are *The Three Little Pigs, The Three Bears, Three Billy Goats Gruff, Snow White and the Seven Dwarfs, Six Foolish Fishermen*.

**ACTIVITIES:** As these stories are read to the younger children, take time to count the number of characters who are the same animal or same kind of person. Use felt cutouts of the characters for counting activities and for one-to-one matching (as suggested in Unit 8). Have older children dramatize the stories. Get them going with questions such as HOW MANY PEOPLE WILL WE NEED TO BE BEARS? HOW MANY PORRIDGE BOWLS (SPOONS, CHAIRS, BEDS) DO WE NEED? JOHN, YOU GET THE BOWLS AND SPOONS.

**FOLLOW-UP:** Have the books and other materials available for children to use during center time.

## Number/Rational Counting: Follow-Up with Counting Books

**OBJECTIVE:** To strengthen rational counting skills.

**MATERIALS:** Counting books (see list in Appendix B).

**ACTIVITIES:** Go through the books with one child or small group of children. Discuss the pictures as a language development activity, and count the items pictured on each page.

## Rational Counting: Follow-Up with One-to-One Correspondence

**OBJECTIVE:** To combine one-to-one correspondence and counting.

**MATERIALS:** Flannelboard and/or magnet board and counting objects.

**ACTIVITIES:** As the children work with the counting activities, have them check their sets that they say are the same number by using one-to-one correspondence. See activities for Unit 8.

**FOLLOW-UP:** Have materials available during center time.

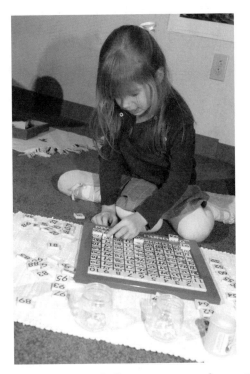

A 100s board provides a challenging way to apply counting skills and explore number sequence.

| Student | Score |
|---------|-------|
| Derrick | ////// |
| Liu Pei | //////// |
| Brent | //// |
| Theresa | /////// |

**Figure 9–2** By age 6 or 7, children can keep a cumulative score using tick marks.

Children of ages 4 to 6 can play simple group games that require them to apply their counting skills. For example, a bowling game requires them to count the number of pins they knock down. A game in which they try to drop clothespins into a container requires them to count the number of clothespins that land in the container. They can compare the number of pins knocked down or the number of clothespins dropped into the containers by each child. By age 6 or 7, children can keep a cumulative score using tick marks (lines) (see Figure 9–2). Not only can they count, they can compare amounts to find out who has the most and if any of them have the same amount. Older children (see Units 23 and 24) will be interested in writing numerals and might realize that, instead of tick marks, they can write down the numeral that represents the amount to be recorded.

Students who are skilled at counting enjoy sorting small objects such as colored macaroni, beads, miniature animals, or buttons. At first they might be given a small amount such as ten items with which to work. They can compare the amounts in each of the groups that they construct as well as compare the amounts in their groups with a partner's. Eventually they can move on to larger groups of objects and to more complex activities such as recording data with number symbols and constructing graphs (see Unit 20). As a special treat, this type of activity can be done with small edibles such as m&m's, Trix, Teddy Grahams, or Gummy Bears; m&m® activities can be introduced with *The m&m's Counting Book* by Barbara McGrath (1994).

Another activity that builds number concepts is the hundred days celebration. Starting the first day of school, the class uses concrete materials to record how many days of school have gone by. Attach two large, clear plastic cups to the bulletin board. Use a supply of drinking straws or tongue depressors as recording devices. Each day, count in unison the number of days of school, and add a straw to the cup on the right. Whenever 10 straws are collected, bundle them with a rubber band, and place them in the left-hand cup. Explain that when there are 10 bundles, it will be the 100th day. Ten is used as an informal benchmark. On the 100th day, each child brings a plastic zip-top bag containing 100 items. It is exciting to see what they bring: pieces of dry macaroni, dry beans, pennies, candy, hairpins, and so on. Working in pairs, they can check their collections by counting out groups of 10 and counting how many groups they have. To aid their organization, large mats with 10 circles on each or 10 clear plastic glasses can be supplied. Late 4-year-olds as well as kindergarten and primary grade students enjoy this activity.

Kindergartners can work with simple problem-solving challenges. Schulman and Eston (1998) described a type of problem that kindergartners find intriguing. The children were in the second half of kindergarten and had previously worked in small groups. The basic situation was demonstrated as the "carrot and raisin" problem.

> Jackie had carrots and raisins on her plate. She had seven items in all. What did Jackie have on her plate?

The children selected orange rods and small stones to represent carrots and raisins, respectively. They were given paper plates to use as work mats. When they had a solution that worked, they recorded it by drawing a picture. As they worked and shared ideas, they realized that many different groupings were surfacing. They recorded all the solutions. Of course, what they were discovering were the facts that compose seven. This same context led to other problems of varying degrees of difficulty (sea stars and hermit crabs in a tide pool, pineapples and pears in a fruit basket, seeds that germinated and seeds that didn't). Some children continued with random strategies while others discovered organized strategies.

Other kinds of problem-solving activities can provide challenges for children learning to count. The activities in "Bears in the House and in the Park" provide simple word problems for pre-K–2 students (Greenes et al., 2003). Using teddy-bear counters or chips, children model problems such as the following.

*Story Problem 1*

There are two bears in the kitchen.

There are three bears in the living room.

How many bears are downstairs? (Five) (p. 11)

Copley (2004) includes activities such as "Hanny Learns to Count from the Prairie Dogs," "Benny's Pennies," and "How Many Are Hiding?"

Quite a bit of computer software has been designed to reinforce counting skills and the number concept. Five-year-old George sits at the computer, deeply involved with *Stickybear Numbers*. Each time he presses the space bar, a group with one fewer appears on the screen. Each time he presses a number, a group with that amount appears. His friend Kate joins him and comments on the pictures. They both count the figures in each group and compare the results. Activity 7 includes a list of software the reader might wish to review.

## IDEAS FOR CHILDREN WITH SPECIAL NEEDS

Most young children learn to count and develop number sense through informal everyday experiences and through books and rhymes, but others need additional teacher-directed experiences. Some children will need extra verbalization through finger plays and rhymes. Others will need more multisensory experiences using their motor, tactual, auditory and visual senses. Examples include:

- Jumping up and down on a trampoline saying "one, one, one . . ." to get an understanding of the unit.
- Doing other exercises counting the number of movements.
- Connect with nursery rhymes, such as by seeing how many times they can jump over a candle stick after reciting "Jack Be Nimble."

Rational counting follows a prescribed sequence that should take on a rhythmical pattern. Children can be helped to achieve this goal through the following types of activities.

- Counting objects while putting them into containers provides an auditory, tactile, and verbal experience. Various types of containers can be used. Cube blocks or large beads can be dropped and counted. Children who have difficulty with motor control may need to take a break between dropping each block or have the adult hand the blocks over one at a time.
- Self-correcting form boards or peg-boards as well as Montessori cylinder boards and pegboards can be used to help develop counting and number sense.

Some children have difficulty organizing their work. They may count a group in a random manner. They may need to be taught to methodically pick up each object for counting and put each in a new place. Start with straight lines and then move to irregular patterns. Gradually move toward asking the child to count out a specific number of objects. Count each object with the child.

Most young children enjoy learning a new language. As ELL students learn to count in English, English-speaking students can learn to count in a second language.

## EVALUATION

Informal evaluation can be done by noting the answers given by children during direct instruction sessions. The teacher should also observe the children during center time and notice whether they apply what they have learned. When children choose to explore materials used in the structured lessons during center time, questions can be asked. For instance, Kate is at the flannelboard arranging the felt shapes in rows. As her teacher goes by, he stops and asks "How many bunnies do you have in that row?" If four children are playing house, the teacher can ask, "How many children in this family?" Formal evaluation can be done with one child by using tasks such as those in Appendix A.

"Hundreds" collections and graphs can be placed in portfolios. Photos of children working with materials might also be included. Anecdotes and checklists can be used to record milestones in number concept growth and development.

Kathy Richardson (1999, p. 7) provides questions to guide evaluation of counting and number sense. Some key questions for counting include:

■ To what amount can children work with (i.e., five, ten, twelve, etc.)?

■ What kinds of errors do the children make? Are they consistent or random?

■ Do they stick with the idea of one-to-one correspondence as they count?

■ Are they accurate? Do they check their results?

■ Do they remember the number they counted to and realize that is the amount in the group (cardinal number)?

Key questions to consider when evaluating number sense include:

■ Can the children subitize perceptually—that is, recognize small groups of four or five without counting?

■ Knowing the amount in one group, can they use that information to figure out how many are in another group?

■ Can children make reasonable estimates of the amount in a group and revise their estimate after counting some items?

■ When items are added to a group that they have already counted, do children count on or start over?

The answers to these questions will help you evaluate whether the children understand the concepts of number and number sense.

## SUMMARY

Number sense or the number concept connects counting with quantity. Counting, one-to-one correspondence, arranging and rearranging groups, and comparing quantities (see Unit 11) help to develop number sense, which underlies all mathematical operations. The number concept involves an understanding of *oneness*, *twoness*, and so on. Perceptual subitizing or recognizing groups of less than four or five without counting usually develops during the preschool/kindergarten period. Counting includes two types of skills: rote counting and rational counting. Rote counting is saying from memory the names of the numbers in order. Rational counting consists of using number sense to attach the number names in order to items in a group to find out how many items are in the group. There are four principles of rational counting: (1) saying the number names in the correct order; (2) achieving one-to-one correspondence between number name and object; (3) understanding that counting can begin with any object; and (4) understanding that the last number named is the total.

Rote counting is mastered before rational counting. Rational counting begins to catch up with rote counting after age 4 or 5. The number concept is learned simultaneously. Quantities greater than four are not identified until the child learns to rational count beyond four. Counting is learned for the most part through naturalistic and informal activities supported by structured lessons. However, some children may need additional multisensory experiences to reinforce their counting skills and understanding of number.

## KEY TERMS

cardinality
conceptual subitizing
number sense

perceptual subitizing
rational counting

rote counting
subitizing

## SUGGESTED ACTIVITIES

1. Try the sample assessment tasks included in this unit with three or four children of different ages (between 2½ and 6½ years). Record the results, and compare the answers received at each age level.

2. Go to the children's section of the library or a local bookstore. Find three number books (such as those listed in Appendix B). Write a review of each one, giving a brief description and explaining why and how you would use each book.

3. With one or more young children, try some of the counting activities suggested in this unit. Evaluate the success of the activity.

4. Add rote counting and rational counting activity cards to your Idea File or Idea Notebook.

5. Make a counting kit by putting together a collection of objects such as shells, buttons, coins, or poker chips.

6. Visit one or more preschool or kindergarten classrooms. Record any counting and/or number concept activities or events observed. Decide if each recorded incident should be identified as naturalistic, informal, or structured. Give a reason for each decision.

7. Try to obtain some of the computer software and/or CDs listed below. Using the criteria suggested in Unit 2, review and evaluate the software.

   ■ *Learn About Numbers and Counting.* Includes counting and other concepts and skills. (Elgin, IL: Sunburst Technologies)

   ■ *Reader Rabbit's Math Ages 4–6.* Counting and other concepts and skills. (San Francisco: Broderbund at Riverdeep)

   ■ *Destination Math* (San Francisco: Riverdeep)

   ■ *Tenth Planet Number Bundle* (Elgin, IL: Sunburst Technologies).

   ■ *Math Blaster Ages 4-6* (Elgin, IL: Sunburst Technologies)

   ■ *Arthur's Math Games* (http://www.kidsclick.com)

   ■ *Caillou Counting* (http://www.kidsclick.com)

   ■ *How Many Bugs in a Box* (http://www.kidsclick.com)

   ■ *The Counts Countdown* (http://www.shop.com), CD

   ■ *Numbers* (Sesame Street) (http://www.shop.com), CD

8. Using some manipulatives, show 3-, 4-, and 5-year-olds some groups of two, three, four, and five. Observe whether they can tell you "how many" in each group without counting.

9. Search the Web for number and number sense activities, and find some similar to those suggested in the unit. Try out one of your selections with one or more 3–5-year-old children.

## REVIEW

**A.** Discuss the relationships between number sense, counting, and the understanding of quantities and subitizing.

**B.** Explain the relationship between rote and rational counting.

**C.** Describe two examples of rote counting and two examples of rational counting.

**D.** How should the adult respond in each of the following situations?

    1. Rudy (age 3½) looks up at his teacher and proudly recites: "One, two, three, five, seven, ten."

2. Tony, age 2, says, "I have two eyes, you have two eyes."

3. Jada has been asked to get six spoons for the children at her lunch table. She returns with seven spoons.

4. Lan is 4½ years old. He counts a stack of six Unifix Cubes: "One, two, three, four, five, seven—seven cubes."

5. An adult is sitting with some 4- and 5-year-olds who are waiting for the school bus. She decides to do some informal counting activities.

## REFERENCES

Clements, D. H. (1999). Subitizing: What is it? Why teach it? *Teaching Children Mathematics, 5*(7), 400–405.

Copley, J. V. (Ed.). (2004). *Showcasing mathematics for the young child.* Reston, VA: National Council of Teachers of Mathematics.

Elkin, B. (1968/1971). *Six foolish fishermen.* New York: Scholastic Books.

Greenes, C. E., Dacey, L., Cavanagh, M., Findell, C. R., Sheffield, L. J., & Small, M. (2003). *Navigating through problem solving and reasoning in prekindergarten–kindergarten.* Reston, VA: National Council of Teachers of Mathematics.

Kamii, C. (1982). *Number in preschool and kindergarten.* Washington, DC: National Association for the Education of Young Children.

McGrath, B. B. (1994). *The m&m's counting book.* Watertown, MA: Charlesbridge.

National Council of Teachers of Mathematics. (2000). *Principles and standards for school mathematics.* Reston, VA: Author.

National Council of Teachers of Mathematics. (2007). *Curriculum focal points for prekindergarten through grade 8 mathematics.* Retrieved May 24, 2007, from http://www.nctm.org

Reys, R. E., Lindquist, M. M., Lambdin, D. V., Smith, N. L., & Suydam, M. N. (2001). *Helping children learn mathematics.* New York: Wiley.

Richardson, K. (1999). *Developing number concepts: Planning guide.* Parsippany, NJ: Seymour.

Schulman, L., & Eston, R. (1998). A problem worth revisiting. *Teaching Children Mathematics, 5*(2), 73–77.

## FURTHER READING AND RESOURCES

Baratta-Lorton, M. (1976). *Math their way.* Menlo Park, CA: Addison-Wesley.

Burk, D., Snider, A., & Symonds, P. (1988). *Box it or bag it mathematics: Kindergarten teachers resource guide.* Salem, OR: Math Leaning Center.

Clements, D. H., & Sarama, J. (2004). Mathematics everywhere, every time. *Teaching Children Mathematics, 10*(8), 421–426.

Copley, J. V. (Ed.). (1999). *Mathematics in the early years.* Washington, DC: National Association for the Education of Young Children.

Copley, J. V. (2000). *The young child and mathematics.* Washington, DC: National Association for the Education of Young Children.

Copley, J. V., Jones, C., & Dighe, J. (2007). *Mathematics: The creative curriculum approach.* Washington, DC: Teaching Strategies.

Epstein, A., & Gainsley, S. (2005). *Math in the preschool classroom.* Ypsilanti, MI: High/Scope.

Fuson, K. C., Grandau, L., & Sugiyama, P. A. (2001). Achievable numerical understandings for all young children. *Teaching Children Mathematics, 7*(9), 522–526.

Griffin, S. (2003). Laying the foundation for computational fluency in early childhood. *Teaching Children Mathematics, 9*(6), 306–309.

*Hands-on standards.* (2007). Vernon Hill, IL: Learning Resources.

Hoover, H. M. (2003). The dollar game: A tool for promoting number sense among kindergartners. *Teaching Children Mathematics, 10*(1), 23–25.

Kilderry, A., Yelland, N., Lazaeidis, V., & Dragicevic, S. (2003). ICT and numeracy in the knowledge era: Creating contexts for new understandings. *Childhood Education, 79*(5), 293–298.

McDonald, J. (2007). Selecting counting books: Mathematical perspectives. *Young Children, 62*(3), 38–42.

Mix, K. S., Huttenlocher, J., & Levine, S. C. (2002). *Quantitative development in infancy and early childhood.* New York: Oxford University Press.

Pagani, L. S., Jalbert, J., & Girard, A. (2006). Does preschool enrichment of precursors to arithmetic influence intuitive knowledge of number in low-income children? *Early Childhood Education Journal, 34*(2), 133–146.

Richardson, K. (1984). *Developing number concepts using Unifix Cubes.* Menlo Park, CA: Addison-Wesley.

Richardson, K. (1999). *Developing number concepts: Counting, comparing, and pattern.* Parsippany, NJ: Seymour.

Sztajn, P. (2002). Celebrating 100 with number sense. *Teaching Children Mathematics, 9*(4), 212–217.

Varol, F., & Farran, D. C. (2006). Early mathematical growth: How to support young children's mathematical development. *Early Childhood Education Journal, 33*(6), 381–388.

Wright, R. J., Martland, J., Stafford, A. K., & Stanger, G. (2002). *Teaching number: Advanced skills and strategies.* London: Chapman.

# Unit 10

# Logic and Classifying

## OBJECTIVES

After reading this unit, you should be able to:

- Explain the NCTM expectations for logic and classifying.
- Describe features of groups.
- Describe the activity of classifying.
- Identify five types of criteria that children can use when classifying.
- Assess, plan, and teach classification activities appropriate for young children.

The NCTM (2000) expectations for logic and classifying include being able to sort, classify, and order objects by size, number, and other properties (see also Units 11 and 17), to sort and classify objects according to their attributes, and to organize data about the objects (see also Unit 20).

The focal points for prekindergarten and kindergarten number and operations connect with sorting. By kindergarten, children should be able to use sorting and grouping to solve logical problems. For example, they can collect data to answer such questions as what kinds of pets class members have or how birth dates are distributed over the year. They can also sort and group collections of objects in a variety of ways.

In mathematics and science, an understanding of **logical grouping** and **classifying** is essential. The NCTM standards identify the importance of connecting counting to grouping. Constructing logical groups provides children with valuable logical thinking ex-

periences. As children construct logical groups, they organize materials by classifying them according to some common criteria. A group may contain from zero (an empty group) to an endless number of things. The youngest children may group by criteria that are not apparent to adults but make sense to them. As children develop, they gradually begin constructing groups for which the criteria are apparent to adults. Children also note common groupings that they observe in their environment: dishes that are alike in pattern go together; and cars have four tires plus a spare, making a total of five in the group. Logical thinking and classification skills are fundamental concepts that apply across the curriculum (Figure 10–1).

To **add** is to put together or join groups. The four tires on the wheels plus the spare in the trunk equals five tires. To **subtract** is to separate a group into smaller groups. For example, one tire goes flat and is taken off. It is left for repairs, and the spare is put on. A group of one

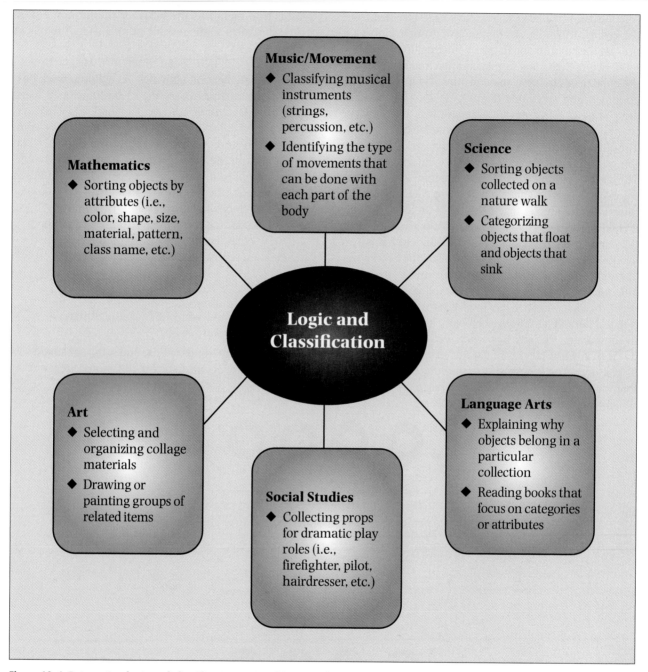

**Figure 10–1** Integrating logic and classification across the curriculum.

(the flat tire) has been taken away or subtracted from the group of five. There are now two groups: four good tires on the car and one flat tire being repaired.

Before doing any formal addition and subtraction, the child needs to learn about groups and how they can be joined and separated (Figure 10–2). That is, children must practice **sorting** (separating) and **grouping** (joining). This type of activity is called *classification*. The child performs tasks where he separates and groups things because they belong together for some reason. Things may belong together because they are the same color or the same shape, do the same work, are the same size, are always together, and so on. For example, a child may have a box of wooden blocks and a box of toy cars (wood, metal, and plastic). The child has two groups: blocks and cars. He then takes the blocks out of the box and separates them by grouping them into four piles: blue blocks, red blocks, yellow blocks, and green blocks. He now has four groups of blocks. He builds a garage with the red blocks. He puts some cars in the garage. He now has a new group of toys. If he has put only red cars in the garage, he now has a group of red toys. The blocks and toys could be grouped in many other ways by using shape and material (wood,

plastic, and metal) as the basis for the groups. Figure 10–3 illustrates some possible groups using the blocks and cars.

Young children spend much of their playtime in just such classification activities. As children work busily at these sorting tasks, they simultaneously learn words that label their activity. This happens when another person tells them the names and makes comments: "You have made a big pile of red things." "You have a pile of blue blocks, a pile of green blocks, . . . ." "Those are plastic, and those are wood." As children learn to speak, the adult questions them: "What color are these? Which ones are plastic?" "How many _____?" In order to count, a specific group must be identified.

The child learns that things may be grouped together using several kinds of common features.

- **Color**: Things can go together that are the same color.
- **Shape**: Things may all be round, square, triangular, and so on.
- **Size**: Some things are big and some are small; some are fat and some are thin; some are short and some are tall.

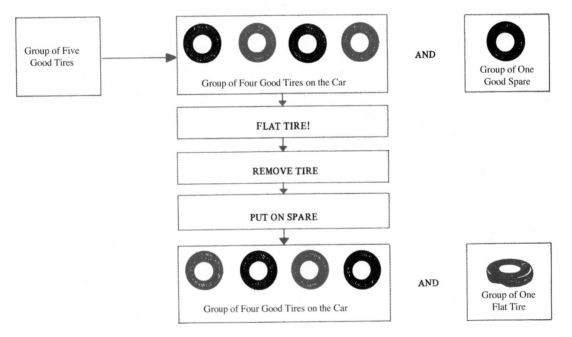

**Figure 10–2** Groups can be joined and separated.

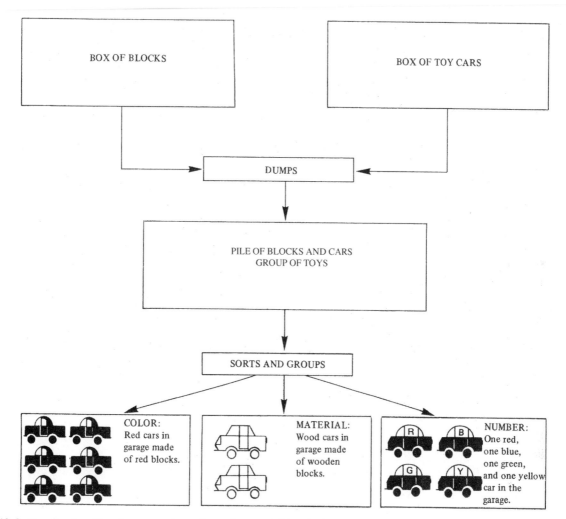

**Figure 10–3** Classification (forming groups) may be evident in children's play—as with this child, who sorts blocks and cars into several logical groupings.

- **Material**: Things are made out of different materials such as wood, plastic, glass, paper, cloth, or metal.
- **Pattern**: Things have different visual patterns—such as stripes, dots, or flowers—or they may be plain (no design).
- **Texture**: Things feel different from each other (smooth, rough, soft, hard, wet, dry).
- **Function**: Some items do the same thing or are used for the same thing (e.g., all in a group are for eating, writing, or playing music).

- **Association**: Some things do a job together (candle and match, milk and glass, shoe and foot), come from the same place (bought at the store or seen at the zoo), or belong to a special person (the hose, truck, and hat belong to the firefighter).
- **Class name**: There are names that may belong to several things (people, animals, food, vehicles, weapons, clothing, homes).
- **Common features**: All have handles or windows or doors or legs or wheels, for example.

■ **Number**: All are groups of specific amounts (see Unit 6) such as pairs and groups of three, four, five, and so forth.

Which criteria children select or exactly how they group is not as important as the process of logical thinking that they exercise as they sort and group.

## ASSESSMENT

The adult should note and record the child's play activities. Does she sort and group her play materials? For example, she might play with a pegboard and put each color peg in its own row, or build two garages with big cars in one and small cars in another. When offered several kinds of crackers for snack, she might pick out only triangle shapes. She might say, "Only boys can be daddies—girls are mothers."

More formal assessment can be made using the tasks in Appendix A. Two examples are shown here.

## NATURALISTIC ACTIVITIES

Sorting and grouping are some of the most basic and natural activities for the young child. Much of his play is organizing and reorganizing the things in his world. The infant learns the group of people who take care of him most of the time (child-care provider, mother, father, and/or relatives and friends), and others are put in the set of "strangers." He learns that some objects when pressed on his gums reduce the pain of growing teeth. These are his set of teething things.

As soon as the child is able to sit up, he finds great fun in putting things in containers and dumping them

## SAMPLE ASSESSMENT TASK

**5J**                                                                      **Preoperational Ages 4–6**

### Logic and Classifying, Clue Sort: Unit 10

**METHOD:** Interview.

**SKILL:** Child is able to classify and form sets using verbal and/or object clues.

**MATERIALS:** 20 to 25 objects (or pictures of objects or cutouts) that can be grouped into several possible sets by criteria such as color, shape, size, or category (i.e., animals, plants, furniture, clothing, or toys).

**PROCEDURE:** Set all the objects in front of the child in a random arrangement. Try the following types of clues.
1. FIND SOME THINGS THAT ARE _____ (name a specific color, shape, size, material, pattern, function, or class).
2. Hold up one object, picture, or cutout; say, FIND SOME THINGS THAT BELONG WITH THIS. After the choices are made, ask, WHY DO THESE THINGS BELONG TOGETHER?

**EVALUATION:** Note whether the child makes a conventional logical group and provides a conventional logical reason such as "because they are cars," "they are all green," "you can eat with them," or a "creative" reason that is logical to the child if not to the adult; for example: "My mother would like them," "they all have points," "I like these colors, I don't like those."

**INSTRUCTIONAL RESOURCE:** Charlesworth, R., and Lind, K. K. (2010). *Math and science for young children* (6th ed.). Clifton Park, NY: Cengage Learning.

## SAMPLE ASSESSMENT TASK

**5K**                                                    **Preoperational Ages 4–6**

### Logic and Classifying, Free Sort: Unit 10

**METHOD:**        Interview.

**SKILL:**         Child is able to classify and form sets in a free sort.

**MATERIALS:**     20 to 25 objects (or pictures of objects or cutouts) that can be grouped into several possible sets by criteria such as color, shape, size, or category (i.e., animals, plants, furniture, clothing, or toys).

**PROCEDURE:**     Set all the objects in front of the child in a random arrangement. Say, PUT THE THINGS TOGETHER THAT BELONG TOGETHER. If the child looks puzzled, backtrack to the previous task, hold up one item, and say, FIND SOME THINGS THAT BELONG WITH THIS. When a group is completed, say, NOW FIND SOME OTHER THINGS THAT BELONG TOGETHER. Keep on until all the items are grouped. Then point to each group and ask, WHY DO THESE BELONG TOGETHER?

**EVALUATION:**  Note the criteria that the child uses, as listed in task 5J.

**INSTRUCTIONAL RESOURCE:** Charlesworth, R., and Lind, K. K. (2010). *Math and science for young children* (6th ed.). Clifton Park, NY: Cengage Learning.

---

out. He can never have too many boxes, plastic dishes, and coffee cans along with such items as large plastic beads, table tennis balls, and teething toys (just be sure the items are too large to swallow). With this type of activity, children have their first experiences making groups.

By age 3, the child sorts and groups to help organize his play activities. He sorts out from his things those that he needs for what he wants to do. He may pick out wild animal toys for his zoo, people dolls for his family play, big blocks for his house, blue paper circles to paste on paper, girls for friends, and so on.

The adult provides the free time, the materials (recycled material is fine as long as it is safe), and the space. The child does the rest.

## INFORMAL ACTIVITIES

Adults can let children know that sorting and grouping activities are of value in informal ways by showing that they approve of what the children are doing. This can be done with a look, smile, nod, or comment.

Adults can also build children's classification vocabulary in informal ways. They can label the child's product and ask questions about what the child has done: "You have used all blue confetti in your picture." "You've used all the square blocks." "You have the pigs in this barn and the cows in that barn." "You painted green and purple stripes today." "Can you put the wild animals here and the farm animals here?" "Separate the spoons from the forks." "See if any of the cleaning rags are dry." "Put the crayons in the can and the pencils in the box." "Show me which things will roll down the ramp." "Which seeds are from your apple? Which are from your orange?" "Put the hamsters in the silver cage and the mice in the brown cage." As the children's vocabularies increase, they will be able to label and describe how and why they are sorting and grouping. In addition, words give them shortcuts for labeling groups.

## STRUCTURED ACTIVITIES

Sorting and grouping, which form the basis of classifying sets of things, lend themselves to many activities

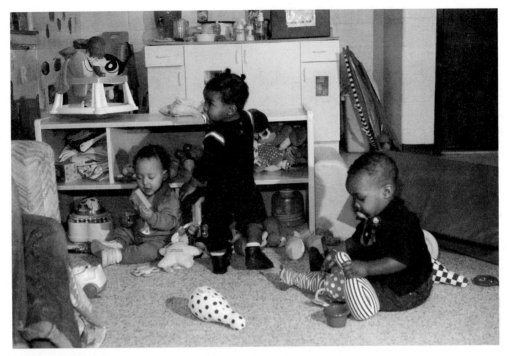

Naturalistic classifying and sorting take place during young children's daily play activities.

Informal instruction takes place when an adult provides comments or questions as the children explore objects.

with many materials. As discussed in Unit 3, real objects are used first and then representations of objects (e.g., cutouts, pictures). One-to-one correspondence skills go hand in hand with sorting and grouping. For example, given three houses and three pigs, the child may give each pig a house (three groups) or place the pigs in one group and the houses in another (two groups).

The following activities help children develop the process of constructing groups.

## ACTIVITIES

### Logic and Classification: Color

**OBJECTIVE:** To sort and group by color.

**MATERIALS:** Several different objects that are the same color and four objects each of a different color. For example: a red toy car, a red block, a red bead, a red ribbon, a red sock; and one yellow car, one green ribbon, one blue ball, and one orange piece of paper.

**NATURALISTIC AND INFORMAL ACTIVITIES:** Provide students with many opportunities to experiment with color. Provide objects and art materials such as crayons, paint, colored paper, etc. Label the colors: "You have lots of *green* in your picture." "You've used all *red* LEGO blocks." Note when the children label the colors, "Please pass me a piece of *yellow* paper." "I can't find my *orange* crayon." Ask questions: "Which colors will you use for your penguins?"

**STRUCTURED ACTIVITIES:** 1. Hold up one red object, FIND THE THINGS THAT ARE THE SAME COLOR AS THIS. After all the red things have been found: THESE THINGS ARE ALL THE SAME COLOR. TELL ME THE NAME OF THE COLOR. If there is no correct answer: THE THINGS YOU PICKED OUT ARE ALL RED THINGS. Ask, WHAT COLOR ARE THE THINGS THAT YOU PICKED OUT?

2. Put all the things together again: FIND THE THINGS THAT ARE *NOT* RED.

**FOLLOW-UP:** Repeat this activity with different colors and different materials. During center time, put out a container of brightly colored materials. Observe whether the children put them into groups by color. If they do, ask, WHY DID YOU PUT THOSE TOGETHER? Accept any answer they give, but note whether they give a color answer.

### Logic and Classification: Association

**OBJECTIVE:** To form sets of things that go together by association.

**MATERIALS:** Picture card sets may be bought or made. Each set can have a theme such as one of the following.

1. Pictures of people in various jobs and pictures of things that go with their job:

| Worker | Things that go with the worker's job |
|---|---|
| letter carrier | letter, mailbox, stamps, hat, mailbag, mail truck |
| airplane pilot | airplane, hat, wings |

*(continued)*

| | |
|---|---|
| doctor | stethoscope, thermometer, bandages |
| trash collector | trash can, trash truck |
| police officer | handcuffs, pistol, hat, badge, police car |
| firefighter | hat, hose, truck, boots and coat, hydrant, house on fire |
| grocer | various kinds of foods, bags, shopping cart, cash register |

Start with about three groups, and keep adding more.

2.  Things that go together for use:

| Item | Goes with |
|---|---|
| glass tumbler | carton of milk, pitcher of juice, can of soda pop |
| cup and saucer | coffeepot, teapot, steaming teakettle |
| match | candle, campfire |
| paper | pencil, crayon, pen |
| money | purse, wallet, bank |
| table | four chairs |

Start with three groups, and keep adding more.

3.  Things that are related, such as animals and their babies.

**NATURALISTIC AND INFORMAL ACTIVITIES:** During center time, provide groups of items that go together such as those just described. Provide both objects and picture sets. Note what the children do with the items. Do they group related items for play? Ask questions such as "Which things belong together?" "What do you need to eat your cereal?"

**STRUCTURED ACTIVITIES:**
1.  One at a time, show the pictures of people or things that are the main clue (the workers, for example) and ask, WHO (WHAT) IS THIS? When they have all been named, show the "go with" pictures one at a time: WHO (WHAT) DOES THIS BELONG TO?
2.  Give each child a clue picture. Hold each "go with" picture up in turn: WHO HAS THE PERSON (or THING) THIS BELONGS WITH? WHAT DO YOU CALL THIS?
3.  Give a group of pictures to one child: SORT THESE OUT. FIND ALL THE WORKERS AND PUT THE THINGS WITH THEM THAT THEY USE. Or: HERE IS A GLASS, A CUP AND SAUCER, AND SOME MONEY. LOOK THROUGH THESE PICTURES, AND FIND THE ONES THAT GO WITH THEM.

**FOLLOW-UP:** Have groups of pictures available for children to use during center time. Note whether they use them individually or make up group games to play. Keep introducing more groups.

## Logic and Classification: Simple Sorting

**OBJECTIVE:** To practice the act of sorting.

**MATERIALS:** Small containers, such as plastic margarine dishes, filled with small objects: buttons of various sizes, colors, and shapes; or dried beans, peas, corn. Another container with smaller divisions in it (such as an egg carton).

**NATURALISTIC AND INFORMAL ACTIVITIES:** Notice whether children sort as they play. Do they use pretend food when pretending to cook and eat a meal? Do the children playing adult select adult clothing to wear? When provided with animal figures, do children demonstrate preferences? During center time, place materials such as those just described on a table. Observe how the children sort.

**STRUCTURED ACTIVITIES:** 1. Have the sections of the larger container marked with a model, such as each kind of button or dried bean. The children match each thing from their container with the model until everything is sorted into new groups in the egg carton (or other large container with small sections).

2. Use the same materials but do not mark the sections of the sorting container. See how the children sort on their own.

**FOLLOW-UP:** Have these materials available during center time. Make up more groups using different kinds of things for sorting.

## Logic and Classification: Class Names, Discussion

**OBJECTIVE:** To discuss groups of things that can be put in the same class and decide on the class name.

**MATERIALS:** Things that can be put in the same group on the basis of class name, such as:
1. animals—several toy animals;
2. vehicles—toy cars, trucks, motorcycles;
3. clothing—a shoe, a shirt, a belt;
4. things to write with—pen, pencil, marker, crayon, chalk.

**NATURALISTIC AND INFORMAL ACTIVITIES:** During center time, note whether children use class names during their play. Give examples of labeling classes: "You like to play with the *horses* when you select from the *animal* collection." Ask questions such as "Which is your favorite *vehicle*?"

**STRUCTURED ACTIVITIES:** The same plan can be followed for any group of things.
1. Bring the things out one at a time until three have been discussed. Ask about each

   a. WHAT CAN YOU TELL ME ABOUT THIS?

   b. Five specific questions:

   WHAT DO YOU CALL THIS? (WHAT IS ITS NAME?)

   WHAT COLOR IS IT?

   WHAT DO YOU DO WITH IT? or WHAT DOES IT DO? or WHO USES THIS?

   WHAT IS IT MADE OUT OF?

   WHERE DO YOU GET ONE?

   c. Show the three things discussed: WHAT DO YOU CALL THINGS LIKE THIS? THESE ARE ALL (ANIMALS, VEHICLES, CLOTHING, THINGS TO WRITE WITH).

2. Put two or more groups of things together that have already been discussed. Ask the children to sort them into new groups and to give the class name for each group.

**FOLLOW-UP:** Put together groups (in the manner described here) that include things from science and social studies.

Classification is one of the most important fundamental skills in science. The following are examples of how classification might be used during science activities.

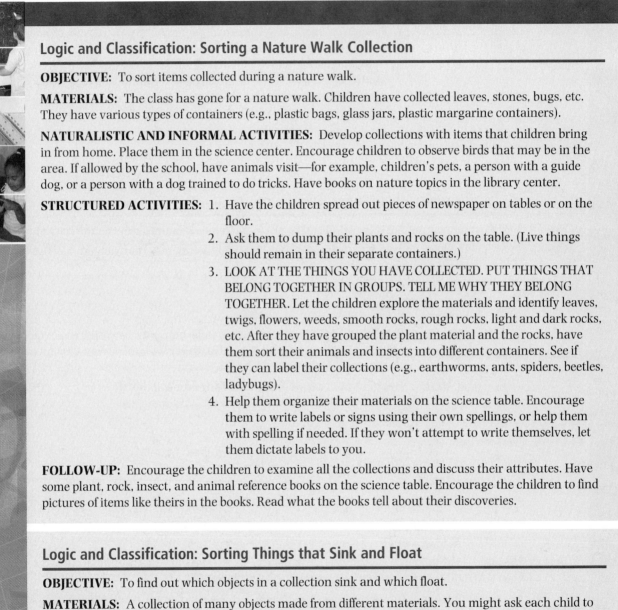

## Logic and Classification: Sorting a Nature Walk Collection

**OBJECTIVE:** To sort items collected during a nature walk.

**MATERIALS:** The class has gone for a nature walk. Children have collected leaves, stones, bugs, etc. They have various types of containers (e.g., plastic bags, glass jars, plastic margarine containers).

**NATURALISTIC AND INFORMAL ACTIVITIES:** Develop collections with items that children bring in from home. Place them in the science center. Encourage children to observe birds that may be in the area. If allowed by the school, have animals visit—for example, children's pets, a person with a guide dog, or a person with a dog trained to do tricks. Have books on nature topics in the library center.

**STRUCTURED ACTIVITIES:**
1. Have the children spread out pieces of newspaper on tables or on the floor.
2. Ask them to dump their plants and rocks on the table. (Live things should remain in their separate containers.)
3. LOOK AT THE THINGS YOU HAVE COLLECTED. PUT THINGS THAT BELONG TOGETHER IN GROUPS. TELL ME WHY THEY BELONG TOGETHER. Let the children explore the materials and identify leaves, twigs, flowers, weeds, smooth rocks, rough rocks, light and dark rocks, etc. After they have grouped the plant material and the rocks, have them sort their animals and insects into different containers. See if they can label their collections (e.g., earthworms, ants, spiders, beetles, ladybugs).
4. Help them organize their materials on the science table. Encourage them to write labels or signs using their own spellings, or help them with spelling if needed. If they won't attempt to write themselves, let them dictate labels to you.

**FOLLOW-UP:** Encourage the children to examine all the collections and discuss their attributes. Have some plant, rock, insect, and animal reference books on the science table. Encourage the children to find pictures of items like theirs in the books. Read what the books tell about their discoveries.

## Logic and Classification: Sorting Things that Sink and Float

**OBJECTIVE:** To find out which objects in a collection sink and which float.

**MATERIALS:** A collection of many objects made from different materials. You might ask each child to bring one thing from home and then add some items from the classroom. Have a large container of water and two empty containers labeled *sink* and *float*. Make a large chart with a picture/name of each item where the results of the explorations can be recorded (Figure 10–4).

**NATURALISTIC AND INFORMAL ACTIVITIES:** Provide many opportunities for water play. Include items that float and sink. Note the children's comments as they play with the objects. Make comments such as "Those rocks seem to stay on the bottom while the boat stays on top of the water." Ask questions: "What do you think will happen if you put a rock in a boat?"

**STRUCTURED ACTIVITIES:**
1. Place the materials on the science table, and explain to everyone what the activity is for.
2. During center time, let individuals and/or groups of two or three experiment by placing the objects in the water and then in the appropriate container after they float or sink.
3. When the objects are sorted, the children can record the objects' names at the top of the next vacant column on the chart and check off which items sank and which floated.
4. After the items have been sorted several times, have the students compare their lists. Do the items float and/or sink consistently? Why?

**FOLLOW-UP:** The activity can continue until everyone has had an opportunity to explore it. New items can be added. Some children might like to make a boat in the carpentry center.

**Figure 10–4** The students can record the results of their exploration of the floating and sinking properties of various objects.

Sam and Mary are sitting at the computer using the program *Gertrude's Secrets*. This is a game designed to aid in basic classification skills of matching by specific common criteria. Mary hits a key that is the correct response, and both children clap their hands as a tune plays and Gertrude appears on the screen in recognition of their success. A list of software that helps the development of classification is included in Activity 5.

The teacher provides a structured classification experience when she asks, "Which group does this belong with?"

# IDEAS FOR CHILDREN WITH SPECIAL NEEDS

Copley, Jones, and Dighe (2007) suggest methods of meeting the needs of English language learners, advanced learners, and children with disabilities. It is suggested that language should be kept simple for ELL students and that rhymes and chants should be repeated. Classification activities provide many opportunities for building English vocabulary. It is important to include culturally relevant materials and to use the children's primary language if possible. Advanced learners may become bored unless they are offered more challenging experiences. Some prekindergartners may be ready to use number symbols, create charts and graphs, or use more advanced computer programs. Children with disabilities can benefit from accommodations that meet their needs and provide support to their strengths while working with their problem areas. As described in Unit 9, children with disabilities may need more multisensory experiences, may need to have concepts broken down for them into smaller parts, and may benefit from special technology or other accommodations. In Units 39 and 40 there will be more discussion of these factors.

# EVALUATION

As the children play, note whether each one sorts and groups as part of his or her play activities. There should be an increase in such behavior as children grow and have more experiences with sorting and classification activities. Children should use more names of features when they speak during work and play. They should use color, shape, size, material, pattern, texture, function, association words, and class names.

1. Enrique has a handful of colored candies. "First I'll eat the orange ones." He carefully picks out the orange candies and eats them one at a time. "Now, the reds." He goes on in the same way until all the candies are gone.

2. Diana plays with some small wooden animals. "These farm animals go here in the barn. Richard, you build a cage for the wild animals."

3. Mr. Flores tells Bob to pick out, from a box of toys, some plastic ones to use in the water table.

4. Yolanda asks the cook if she can help sort the clean tableware and put it away.

5. George and Sam build with blocks. George tells Sam: "Put the big blocks here, the middle-sized ones here, and the small blocks here."

6. Tito and Ako take turns reaching into a box that contains items that are smooth or rough. When they touch an item, they say whether it is smooth or rough, guess what it is, and then remove it and place it on the table in the smooth or the rough pile.

7. Jin-sody is working with some containers that contain substances with either pleasant, unpleasant, or neutral odors. On the table are three pictures: a happy face, a sad face, and a neutral face. She puts each of the containers on one of the three faces according to her feelings about each odor.

For more structured evaluation, the sample assessment tasks and the tasks in Appendix A may be used.

# SUMMARY

By sorting objects and pictures into groups based on one or more common criteria, children exercise and build on their logical thinking capabilities. The act of putting things into groups by sorting out things that have one or more common features is called *classification*.

Classifying is a part of children's normal play. They build a sense of logic that will form the basis of their understanding that mathematics makes sense and is not contrived. Children learn that mathematics is natural and flows from their intrinsic curiosity and play. Classifying also adds to their store of ideas and words, and they learn to identify more attributes that can be used as criteria for sorting and grouping.

Naturalistic, informal, and structured classification activities can be done following the sequence of materials described in Unit 3. The sequence progresses from objects to objects combined with pictures to cutouts to picture cards. Books are another excellent pictorial mode for learning class names and members. Computer games that reinforce classification skills and concepts are also available. Logical grouping and classification are essential math and science components. Accommodations need to be made for children with special needs.

## KEY TERMS

| | | |
|---|---|---|
| add | function | shape |
| association | grouping | size |
| classifying | logical grouping | sorting |
| class name | material | subtract |
| color | number | texture |
| common features | pattern | |

## SUGGESTED ACTIVITIES

1. Assemble a collection of objects of various sizes, shapes, colors, classes, textures, and uses. Put them in an open container (such as a small plastic dishpan). Present the collection to children of different ages from 18 months through age 8. Tell the children that they may play with the objects, and observe and record what each child does with them. Particularly note any classifying and sorting as well as the criteria used.

2. Find some sorting and classifying activities to include in your Activity File.

3. Devise a sorting and classifying game, and ask one or more children to play the game. Explain the game to the class, and describe what happened when you tried it out with a child (or children). Ask the class for any suggestions for modifying the game.

4. Visit a prekindergarten, kindergarten, and/or primary grade classroom. Make a list of all the materials that could be used for sorting and classifying. Write a description of any sorting and/or classifying activities that you observe while in the classroom. Ask the teacher how he or she includes sorting and classifying in the instructional program.

5. Using the evaluation suggestions in Activity 5 of Unit 2, review any of the software listed below to which you have access.

■ *Arthur's Math Games*. Counting and other concepts and skills. (San Francisco: Broderbund at Riverdeep)

■ *Coco's Math Project 1*. Logical thinking problems. (Singapore: Times Information Systems Ptd. Ltd.)

■ *Millie's Math House*. Problem solving in a variety of math areas. (San Francisco: Riverdeep-Edmark)

■ *Thinkin' Things 1*. Logical thinking activities. (San Francisco: Riverdeep-Edmark)

■ *Baby Einstein Videos* (Glendale, CA: Baby Einstein Company)

• *Baby MacDonald: A Day on the Farm.* Farm animals.

• *Baby Van Gogh.* The world of color.

• *Neighborhood Animals.* Animals that live in and around the home.

• *World Animals.* Animals that live in the jungle, savannah, or ocean.

6. Surf the Web for logic and classification activities. Locate some like the ones listed in this unit or find some others. Try out an activity with some young children.

## REVIEW

A. Explain what is meant by the terms *logical group* and *classification*. Relate your definitions to the NCTM expectations.

B. Decide which features, as described in this unit, are being used in each of the following incidents.

1. "Find all the things that are rough."
2. "Pour the milk into Johnny's glass."
3. "Put on warm clothes today."
4. Tina says, "There are leaves on all of the trees. Some are green, some are brown, some are orange, and some are yellow."

5. "Find all the things that you can use to write and draw."

6. Carlos makes a train using only the red cube blocks.

7. Tony is putting the clean silverware away. He carefully places the knives, spoons, and forks in the appropriate sections of the silverware container.

8. Fong makes a design using square parquetry blocks.

9. "Please get me six paper napkins."

10. "I'll use the long blocks, and you use the short blocks."

11. Mrs. Smith notices that Tom is wearing a striped shirt and checked pants.

## REFERENCES

Copley, J. V., Jones, C., & Dighe, J. (2007). *Mathematics: The creative curriculum approach*. Washington, DC: Teaching Strategies.

National Council of Teachers of Mathematics. (2000). *Principles and standards for school mathematics*. Reston, VA: Author.

## FURTHER READING AND RESOURCES

American Association for the Advancement of Science (AAAS). (2007). *Atlas of science literacy: Project 2061* (Vol. 2). Washington, DC: Author.

Ashbrook, P. (2006). The early years. Rocks tell a story. *Science & Children, 44*(4), 18–19.

Baratta-Lorton, M. (1976). *Math their way*. Menlo Park, CA: Addison-Wesley.

Baratta-Lorton, M. (1979). *Workjobs II*. Menlo Park, CA: Addison-Wesley.

Burk, D., Snider, A., & Symonds, P. (1988). *Box it or bag it mathematics: Kindergarten teachers resource guide*. Salem, OR: Math Learning Center.

Copley, J. V. (Ed.). (1999). *Mathematics in the early years*. Washington, DC: National Association for the Education of Young Children.

Copley, J. V. (2000). *The young child and mathematics*. Washington, DC: National Association for the Education of Young Children.

Epstein, A. S., & Gainsley, S. (2005). *Math in the preschool classroom*. Ypsilanti, MI: High/Scope.

Gallenstein, N. L. (2004). Creative discovery through classification. *Teaching Children Mathematics, 11*(2), 103–108.

*Hands-on standards*. (2007). Vernon Hills, IL: Learning Resources.

Mangianti, E. S. (2006). Geosciences for preschoolers. *Science & Children, 44*(4), 30–39.

National Research Council. (1996). *National science education standards*. Washington, DC: National Academies Press.

Richardson, K. (1999). *Developing number concepts: Planning guide*. Parsippany, NJ: Seymour.

Schwerdtfeger, J. K., & Chan, A. (2007). Counting collections. *Teaching Children Mathematics, 3*(7), 356–361.

Shreero, B., Sullivan, C., & Urbano, A. (2002). Math by the month: Pets. *Teaching Children Mathematics, 9*(3), 172.

Young, S. L. (1998). *What to wear?* (Harry's Math Books Series). Thousand Oaks, CA: Outside the Box.

Ziemba, E. J., & Hoffman J. (2006). Sorting and patterning in kindergarten: From activities to assessment. *Teaching Children Mathematics, 12*(5), 236–241.

# Unit 11
## Comparing

## OBJECTIVES

After reading this unit, you should be able to:

- Explain the NCTM expectations for comparison.
- List and define comparison terms.
- Identify the concepts learned from comparing.
- Do informal measurement and quantity activities with children.
- Do structured measurement and quantity comparing activities with children.

The NCTM (2000) expectations include relating physical materials and pictures to mathematical ideas; understanding the attributes of length, capacity, weight, area, volume, time, and temperature; and developing the process of measurement. Development of measurement relationships begins with simple comparisons of physical materials and pictures. The expectation is that students will be able to describe qualitative change, such as "Mary is taller than Jenny." Figure 11–1 shows how comparing might be integrated across the content areas.

Comparing is a focal point for measurement in prekindergarten and kindergarten. Prekindergartners identify and compare measurable attributes such as height, weight, and temperature. Kindergartners move into comparing three or more cases by sequencing measurable attributes, as described in Unit 17. Connections are made to data analysis as children compare attributes (such as distribution of hair color in the class) and amounts (such as the number of children with birthdays in each month).

When **comparing**, the child finds a relationship between two things or groups of things on the basis of some specific characteristic or attribute. One type of attribute is an **informal measurement** such as size, length, height, weight, or speed. A second type of attribute involves **quantity comparison**. To compare quantities, the child looks at two groups of objects and decides if they have the same number of items or if one group has more. Comparing is the basis of ordering (see Unit 17) and measurement (see Units 18 and 19).

Some examples of measurement comparisons are:

- John is taller than Maria.
- This snake is long; that worm is short.
- Father bear is bigger than baby bear.

Examples of number comparisons:

- Does everyone have two gloves?
- I have more cookies than you have.
- We each have two dolls—that's the same.

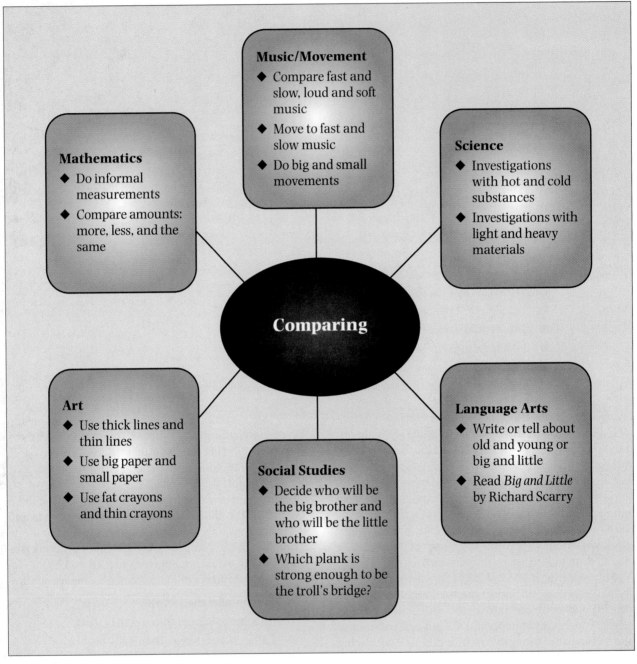

Figure 11–1 Integration of comparing across the curriculum.

# THE BASIC COMPARISONS

To make comparisons and understand them, the child learns the following basic comparisons.

■ Informal Measurement

| | |
|---|---|
| large | small |
| big | little |
| long | short |
| tall | short |
| fat | skinny |
| heavy | light |
| fast | slow |
| cold | hot |
| thick | thin |
| wide | narrow |
| near | far |
| later | sooner (earlier) |
| older | younger (newer) |
| higher | lower |
| loud | soft (sound) |

■ Number

| | |
|---|---|
| more | less/fewer |

The child also finds that sometimes there is no difference when the comparison is made. For instance, the compared items might be the same size or the same age. With regard to quantity, they may discover that there is the same amount (or number) of things in two groups that are compared. The concept of one-to-one correspondence and the skills of counting and classifying assist the child in comparing quantities.

# ASSESSMENT

During the child's play, the teacher should note any of the child's activities that might show she is comparing. For example, when a bed is needed for a doll and two shoe boxes are available, does she look the boxes over carefully and try different combinations to find the right size box for each doll? If she has two trucks, one large and one small, does she build a bigger garage for the larger truck? The adult should also note whether children use the words given in the preceding list of basic comparisons.

In individual interview tasks, the child is asked questions to see if he understands and uses the basic comparison words. The child is presented with some objects or pictures of things that differ or are the same regarding some attribute(s) or number and then is asked to tell if they are the same or different. Two sample tasks are given here; see also Appendix A.

## SAMPLE ASSESSMENT TASK

**5D**                                    **Preoperational Ages 4–5**

**Comparing, Informal Measurement: Unit 11**

**SKILL:** The child will be able to point to big (large) and small objects.

**MATERIALS:** A big block and a small block (a big truck and a small truck, a big shell and a small shell, etc.).

**PROCEDURE:** Present two related objects at a time and say, FIND (POINT TO) THE BIG BLOCK. FIND (POINT TO) THE SMALL BLOCK. Continue with the rest of the object pairs.

**EVALUATION:** Note whether the child is able to identify big and small for each pair.

**INSTRUCTIONAL RESOURCE:** Charlesworth, R., and Lind, K. K. (2010). *Math and science for young children* (6th ed.). Clifton Park, NY: Cengage Learning.

## SAMPLE ASSESSMENT TASK

**4D**                                                                   **Preoperational Ages 3–4**

**Comparing, Number: Unit 11**

**SKILL:** The child will compare groups and identify which group has more or less (fewer).

**MATERIALS:** Two dolls (toy animals or cutout figures) and ten cutout poster board cookies.

**PROCEDURE:** Place the two dolls (toy animals or cutout figures) in front of the child. Say, WATCH, I'M GOING TO GIVE EACH DOLL SOME COOKIES. Put two cookies in front of one doll and six in front of the other. Say, SHOW ME THE DOLL THAT HAS MORE COOKIES. Now pick up the cookies and put one cookie in front of one doll and three in front of the other. Say, SHOW ME THE DOLL THAT HAS FEWER COOKIES. Repeat with different amounts.

**EVALUATION:** Note whether the child consistently picks the correct amounts. Some children might understand *more* but not *fewer*. Some might be able to discriminate if there is a large difference between groups, such as two versus six, but not small differences, such as four versus five.

**INSTRUCTIONAL RESOURCE:** Charlesworth, R., and Lind, K. K. (2010). *Math and science for young children* (6th ed.). Clifton Park, NY: Cengage Learning.

---

Before giving the number comparison tasks, the teacher should be sure the child has begun to match, count, and classify.

## NATURALISTIC ACTIVITIES

The young child has many contacts with comparisons in his daily life. At home mother says, "Get up, it's *late*. Mary was up *early*. Eat *fast*. If you eat slowly, we will have to leave before you are finished. Use a *big* bowl for your cereal; that one is too *small*." At school, the teacher might say: "I'll pick up this *heavy* box; you pick up the *light* one." "Sit on the *small* chair, that one is too *big*." "Remember, the father bear's porridge was too *hot*, and the mother bear's porridge was too *cold*."

As the child uses materials, he notices that things are different. The infant finds that some things can be grabbed and held because they are *small* and *light*, whereas others cannot be held because they are *big* and *heavy*. As he crawls about, he finds he cannot go behind the couch because the space is too *narrow*. He can go behind the chair because there is a *wide* space between the chair and the wall. The young child begins to build with blocks and finds that he has *more small* blocks than *large* ones. He notices that there are people in his environment who are big and people who are small in relation to him. One of the questions most often asked is "Am I a big boy?" (or "Am I a big girl?").

## INFORMAL ACTIVITIES

Small children are very concerned about size and number, especially in relation to themselves. They want to be bigger, taller, faster, and older. They want to be sure they have more—not fewer—things than other children have. These needs of young children bring about

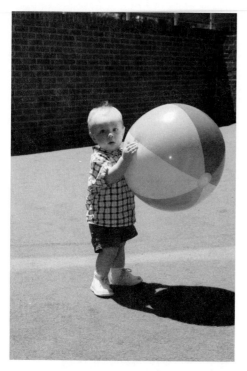

The toddler learns about "big" through a naturalistic experience.

many situations where the adult can help in an informal way to aid the child in learning the skills and ideas of comparing.

Informal measurements are made in a concrete way. That is, the things to be compared are looked at, felt, lifted, listened to, and so on, and the attribute is labeled.

■ Kato (18 months old) tries to lift a large box of toy cars. Mr. Brown squats down next to him, holding out a smaller box of cars. "Here, Kato, that box is too big for your short arms. Take this small box."

■ Kate and Chris (3-year-olds) run up to Mrs. Raymond, "We can run fast. Watch us. We can run faster than you. Watch us." Off they go across the yard while Mrs. Raymond watches and smiles.

■ Sam and George (5-year-olds) stand back to back. "Check us, Mr. Flores. Who is taller?" Mr. Flores says, "Stand by the mirror, and check yourselves." The boys stand by the mirror, back to back. "We are the same," they shout. "You are taller than both of us," they tell their teacher.

■ After a fresh spring rain, the children are on the playground looking at worms. Various comments are heard: "This worm is longer than that one." "This worm is fatter." Miss Collins comes up. "Show me your worms. It sounds like they are different sizes." "I think this small, skinny one is the baby worm," says Badru.

Comparative numbers are also developed in a concrete way. When comparing sets of things, just a look may be enough if the difference in number is large.

■ "Teacher! Juanita has all the spoons and won't give me one!" cries Tanya.

If the difference is small then the child will have to use his matching skill (one-to-one correspondence). Depending on his level of development, the child may physically match each time or he may count.

■ "Teacher! Juanita has more baby dolls than I do." "Let's check," says Mr. Brown. "I already checked," replies Tanya; "She has four, and I have three." Mr. Brown notes that each girl has four dolls. "Better check again," says Mr. Brown. "Here, let's see. Tanya, put each one of your dolls next to one of Juanita's." Tanya matches them up. "I was wrong. We have the same."

A child at a higher level of development could have been asked to count in this situation.

To promote informal learning, the teacher must put out materials that can be used by the child to learn comparisons on his own. The teacher must also be ready to step in and support the child's discovery by using comparison words and giving needed help with comparison problems that the child meets in his play and other activities.

## STRUCTURED ACTIVITIES

Most children learn the idea of comparison through naturalistic and informal activities. For those who do not, more formal experiences can be planned. There are many commercial materials available individually and in kits that are designed for teaching comparison skills and words. Also, the environment is full of things that can be used. The following are some basic types of activities that can be repeated with different materials.

A preschooler learns how fast his vehicle will move as he experiments with ramps at different angles.

## ACTIVITIES

### Comparisons: Informal Measurements

**OBJECTIVES:** To gain skill in observing differences in size, speed, temperature, age, and loudness; to learn the words associated with these differences.

**MATERIALS:** Use real objects first. Once the child can do the tasks with real things, then introduce pictures and chalkboard drawings.

| Comparison | Things to Use |
| --- | --- |
| large–small and big–little | buttons, dolls, cups, plates, chairs, books, records, spools, toy animals, trees, boats, cars, houses, jars, boxes, people, pots and pans |
| long–short | string, ribbon, pencils, ruler, snakes, worms, lines, paper strips |
| tall–short | people, ladders, brooms, blocks, trees, bookcases, flagpoles, buildings |
| fat–skinny | people, trees, crayons, animals, pencils, books |

| heavy–light | containers of the same size but different weight (e.g., shoe boxes or coffee cans filled with items of different weights and taped shut) |
| fast–slow | toy cars or other vehicles for demonstration, the children themselves and their own movements, cars on the street, music, talking |
| hot–cold | containers of water, food, ice cubes, boiling water, chocolate milk and hot chocolate, weather |
| thick–thin | paper, cardboard, books, pieces of wood, slices of food (bologna, cucumber, carrot), cookie dough |
| wide–narrow | streets, ribbons, paper strips, lines (chalk, crayon, paint), doorways, windows |
| near–far | children and fixed points in the room, places in the neighborhood, map |
| later–sooner (earlier) | arrival at school or home, two events |
| older–younger (newer) | babies, younger and older children, adults of different ages: any items brought in that were not in the environment before |
| higher–lower | swings, slides, jungle gyms, birds in trees, airplanes flying, windows, stairs, elevators, balconies, shelves |
| loud–soft | voices singing and talking, claps, piano, drums, records, doors slamming |

**NATURALISTIC AND INFORMAL ACTIVITIES:** Observe children as they use a variety of classroom materials. Take note of their vocabulary—do they use any of the terms listed above? Observe whether they make any informal measurements or comparisons as they interact with materials. Comment on their activities: "You built a *tall* building and a *short* building." "You can pour the *small* cup of water into the *big* bowl." Ask questions such as "Which clay snake is *fat* and which is *skinny?*" "Who is *taller*, you or your sister?"

**STRUCTURED ACTIVITIES:** The basic activity involves the presentation of two items to be compared using opposite terms. The items can be real objects, cutouts, or pictures—whatever is most appropriate. Then ask the comparison question. For example:

- The teacher places two pieces of paper in front of the children. Each piece is 1 inch wide. One is 6 inches long, and the other is 12 inches long. LOOK CAREFULLY AT THESE STRIPS OF PAPER. TELL ME WHAT IS DIFFERENT ABOUT THEM. If there is no response, ARE THEY THE SAME LENGTH OR ARE THEY DIFFERENT LENGTHS? If no one responds with long(er) or short(er), SHOW ME WHICH ONE IS LONGER (SHORTER). From a variety of objects, ask the children to select two and to tell which is longer and which is shorter.

- The teacher places two identical coffee cans on the table. One is filled with sand; the other is empty. They are both taped closed so the children cannot see inside. PICK UP EACH CAN. TELL ME WHAT IS DIFFERENT ABOUT THEM. If there is no response or an incorrect response, hold each can out in turn to the child. HOLD THIS CAN IN ONE HAND AND THIS ONE IN THE OTHER. (point) THIS CAN IS HEAVY; THIS CAN IS LIGHT. NOW, YOU SHOW ME THE HEAVY CAN; THE LIGHT CAN. Children who have a problem with this should do more activities that involve the concept.

There is an almost endless variety of experience that can be offered with many things that give the child practice exploring comparisons.

*(continued)*

**FOLLOW-UP:** On a table, set up two empty containers (so that one is tall, and one is short; one is fat, and one is thin; or one is big, and one is little) and a third container filled with potentially comparable items such as tall and short dolls, large and small balls, fat and thin cats, long and short snakes, big and little pieces of wood, and so on. Have the children sort the objects into the correct empty containers.

## Comparisons: Number

**OBJECTIVE:**

- To enable the child to compare groups that are different in number.
- To enable the child to use the terms *more, less, fewer*, and *same number*.

**MATERIALS:** Any of the objects and things used for matching, counting, and classifying.

**NATURALISTIC AND INFORMAL ACTIVITIES:** Notice whether children use any of the comparison vocabulary during their daily activities, "He has *more* red Unifix Cubes than I do." "I have *fewer* jelly beans than Mark." Ask questions: "Does everyone have the *same number* of cookies?" Make comments such as "I think you need *one more* dress for your dolls."

**STRUCTURED ACTIVITIES:** The following basic activities can be done using many different kinds of materials.

1. Set up a flannelboard with many felt shapes or a magnet board with many magnet shapes. Put up two groups of shapes: ARE THERE AS MANY CIRCLES AS SQUARES? (RED CIRCLES AS BLUE CIRCLES? BUNNIES AS CHICKENS?) WHICH GROUP HAS MORE? HOW MANY CIRCLES ARE THERE? HOW MANY SQUARES? The children can point, tell with words, and/or move the pieces around to show that they understand the idea.

2. Have cups, spoons, napkins, or food for snack or lunch. LET'S FIND OUT IF WE HAVE ENOUGH _____ FOR EVERYONE. Wait for the children to find out. If they have trouble, suggest they match or count.

3. Set up any kind of matching problems where one group has more things than the other group: cars and garages, firefighters and fire trucks, cups and saucers, fathers and sons, hats and heads, cats and kittens, animals and cages, and so on.

**FOLLOW-UP:** Put out groups of materials that the children can use on their own. Go on to cards with pictures of different numbers of things that the children can sort and match. Watch for chances to present informal experiences.

- Are there more boys or girls here today?
- Do you have more thin crayons or more fat crayons?
- Do we have the same number of cupcakes as we have people?

Mr. Flores introduced his class of 4- and 5-year-olds to the concept of comparisons that involve opposites by using books, games, and other materials. To support their understanding of the opposed concepts, he has shown the students how to use the computer software *Stickybear Opposites Deluxe* (English and Spanish, http://www.stickybear.com). This program is controlled by two keys, making it a natural for two children working

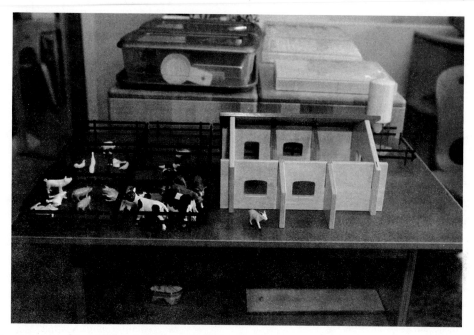

A structured lesson is prepared for children to figure out which corral has more animals.

together cooperatively. Jorge and Cindy can be observed making the seesaw go *up* and *down*, watching the plant grow from *short* to *tall*, and comparing the eight (*many*) bouncing balls with the three (*few*) bouncing balls.

## IDEAS FOR CHILDREN WITH SPECIAL NEEDS

Comparing sets begins with concrete objects and one-to-one correspondence comparisons. The comparison of pictorial representations is a more advanced step that may require extra time and practice for some children. Begin with card sets that show groups in a variety of configurations (e.g., several groups of three or four). Make up matching lotto games such as those depicted in Unit 24. Have the children compare all kinds of visual configurations such as stripes, shapes, animals, and so forth. Have children count out loud to experience auditory stimulation. Tactile stimulation can be provided by sandpaper shapes or sand glued on card drawings. Use terms such as "the same as," "less than," and "more." Auditory comparisons can also be made with

sounds—for instance, one drumbeat compared with three drumbeats.

## EVALUATION

The teacher should note whether the child can use more comparing skills during her play and routine activities. Without disrupting her activity, the adult asks questions as the child plays and works.

■ Do you have more cows or more chickens in your barn?

■ (The child has made two clay snakes.) Which snake is longer? Which is fatter?

■ (The child is sorting blue chips and red chips into bowls.) Do you have more blue chips or more red chips?

■ (The child is talking about her family.) Who is older, you or your brother? Who is taller?

The assessment tasks in Appendix A may be used for formal evaluation interviews.

# SUMMARY

Comparing involves finding the relationship between two things or two groups of things. An informal measurement may be made by comparing two things. Comparing two groups of things incorporates the use of one-to-one correspondence, counting, and classifying skills to find out which sets have more, less/fewer, or the same quantities. Naturalistic, informal, and structured experiences support the learning of these concepts.

## KEY TERMS

| comparing | informal measurement | quantity comparison |
|---|---|---|

## SUGGESTED ACTIVITIES

1. Prepare the materials needed for the assessment tasks in this unit and then interview two or more children. Based on their responses, plan comparison activities that fit their level of development. Do the activities with the children. Record their responses and report the results in class.

2. Find some comparison activities to include in your Activity File or Activity Notebook.

3. Observe some 3–5-year-olds during play activities. Record any instances where they use comparison words and/or make comparisons.

4. Using the guidelines suggested in Activity 5 of Unit 2, evaluate some of the following software.

   ■ *Coco's Math Project 1* (Singapore: Times Information Systems Ptd. Ltd.)
   ■ *Millie's Math House.* Includes comparing and matching sizes. (San Francisco: Riverdeep-Edmark)
   ■ *Learning about Number Meanings and Counting* (Sunburst, 1-800-321-7511)
   ■ *Destination Math* (Riverdeep, http://www.riverdeep.net)

5. On the Web, find an activity like one suggested in this unit or another activity that provides comparison experiences. Try it out with one or more young children.

## REVIEW

A. Explain with examples the two aspects of comparing: informal measurement and number/quantity comparisons. Relate your examples to the NCTM expectations for comparison.

B. Decide which type of comparison (number, speed, weight, length, height, or size) is being made in the examples that follow:
   1. This block is longer than your block.
   2. My racing car is faster than your racing car.
   3. My doll is bigger than Janie's doll.
   4. Mother gave you one more apple slice than she gave me.
   5. I'll take the heavy box and you take the light box.
   6. My mom is taller than your mom.

C. Give two examples of naturalistic, informal, and structured comparison activities.

## REFERENCE

National Council of Teachers of Mathematics. (2000). *Principles and standards for school mathematics.* Reston, VA: Author.

# FURTHER READING AND RESOURCES

AIMS Educational Products. AIMS Education Foundation, P.O. Box 8120, Fresno, CA 93747-8120.

American Association for the Advancement of Science (AAAS). (2007). *Atlas of science literacy: Project 2061* (Vol. 2). Washington, DC: Author.

Baratta-Lorton, M. (1972). *Workjobs.* Menlo Park, CA: Addison-Wesley.

Baratta-Lorton, M. (1976). *Mathematics their way* Menlo Park, CA: Addison-Wesley.

Burk, D., Snider, A., & Symonds, P. (1988). *Box it or bag it mathematics: Kindergarten teachers resource guide.* Salem, OR: Math Learning Center.

Copley, J. V. (Ed.). (1999). *Mathematics in the early years.* Washington, DC: National Association for the Education of Young Children.

Copley, J. V. (2000). *The young child and mathematics.* Washington, DC: National Association for the Education of Young Children.

Copley, J. V. (Ed.). (2004). *Showcasing mathematics for the young child* (chap. 5, Measurement). Reston, VA: National Council of Teachers of Mathematics.

Copley, J. V., Jones, C., & Dighe, J. (2007). *Mathematics: The creative curriculum approach.* Washington, DC: Teaching Strategies.

Epstein, A., & Gainsley, S. (2005). *Math in the preschool classroom.* Ypsilanti, MI: High/Scope.

Gallenstein, N. L. (2004). *Creative construction of mathematics and science concepts in early childhood.* Olney, MD: Association for Childhood Education International.

Learning Resources. (2007). *Hands-on standards.* Vernon Hills, IL: Author.

National Council of Teachers of Mathematics. (2007). *Curriculum focal points.* Reston, VA: Author.

National Research Council. (1996). *National science education standards.* Washington, DC: National Academies Press.

Porter, J. (1995). Balancing acts: K–2. *Teaching Children Mathematics, 1*(7), 430.

Richardson, K. (1999). *Developing number concepts: Counting, comparing, and pattern.* Parsippany, NJ: Seymour.

Richardson, K. (1999). *Developing number concepts: Planning guide.* Parsippany, NJ: Seymour.

Yusawa, M., Bart, W. M., Yuzawa, M., & Junko, I. (2005). Young children's knowledge and strategies for comparing sizes. *Early Childhood Research Quarterly, 20*(2), 239–253.

# Unit 12

## Early Geometry: Shape

### OBJECTIVES

After reading this unit, you should be able to:

- Explain the NCTM expectations for shape as the foundation of beginning geometry.
- Describe naturalistic, informal, and structured shape activities for young children.
- Assess and evaluate a child's knowledge of shape.
- Help children learn shape through haptic, visual, and visual-motor experiences.

During the preprimary years, children should be able to reach the first expectation for geometry (NCTM, 2000): recognize, name, build, draw, compare, and sort two- and three-dimensional shapes. This beginning knowledge of geometry can be integrated with other content areas as illustrated in Figure 12–1. Geometry for young children is more than naming shapes; it is understanding the attributes of shape and applying them to problem solving. Geometry also includes spatial sense, which is the focus of Unit 13.

Identifying shapes and describing spatial relationships is a focal point for prekindergarten. This unit examines identification of shapes, and Unit 13 examines spatial relations. The focal point for kindergarten focuses on further shape identification, including three-dimensional shapes and verbalization of shape characteristics.

Each object in the environment has its own shape. Much of the play and activity of the infant during the sensorimotor stage centers on learning about shape.

The infant learns through looking and through feeling with hands and mouth. Babies learn that some shapes are easier to hold than others. They learn that things of one type of shape will roll. They learn that some things have the same shape as others. Young children see and feel shape differences long before they can describe these differences in words. In the late sensorimotor and early preoperational stages, the child spends a lot of time matching and classifying things. Shape is often used as the basis for these activities.

Children also enjoy experimenting with creating shapes. Three-dimensional shapes grow out of their exploration of malleable substances such as Play-Doh and clay. When they draw and paint, children create many kinds of two-dimensional shapes from the stage of controlled scribbles to representational drawing and painting. Their first representative drawings usually consist of circles and lines. Young children enjoy drawing blob shapes, cutting them out, and gluing them onto another piece of paper.

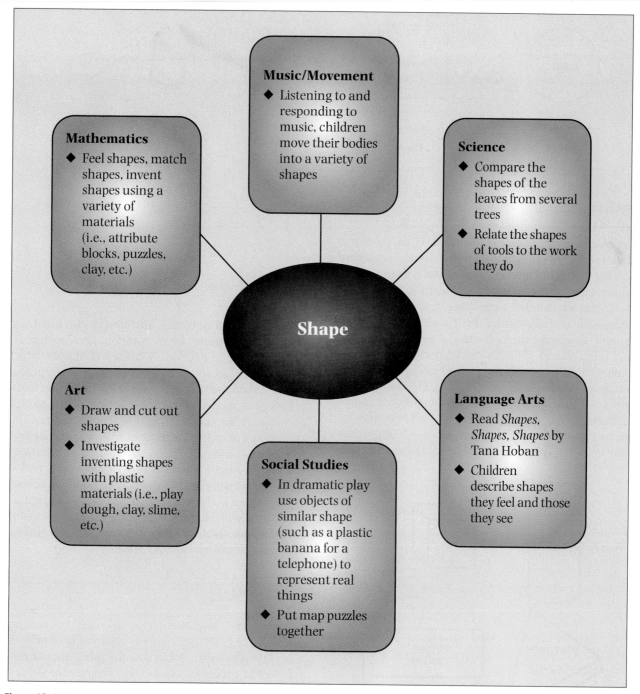

**Figure 12–1** Integrating shape across the curriculum.

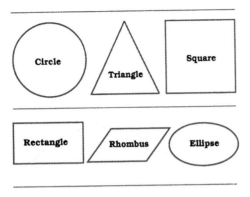

**Figure 12–2** Geometric shapes.

As children move into the middle of the preoperational period, they begin to learn that some shapes have specific names such as **circle**, **triangle**, **square**, **cylinder**, and **sphere**. Children first learn to describe the basic characteristics of each shape in their own words, such as "four straight sides" or "curved line" or "it has points." Gradually, the conventional geometry vocabulary is introduced. Children need opportunities to freely explore both two- and three-dimensional shapes. Examples of two-dimensional shapes are illustrated in Figure 12–2, and examples of three-dimensional shapes (cylinder, sphere, **triangular prism**, and **rectangular prism**) are illustrated in Figure 12–3. Children need time to freely explore the properties of shapes. Manipu-

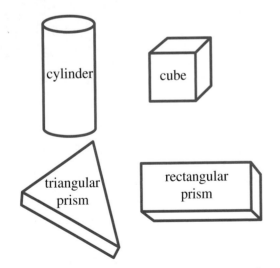

**Figure 12–3** Examples of three-dimensional geometric figures.

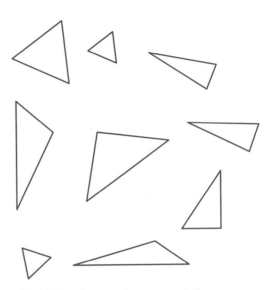

**Figure 12–4** Triangles come in many varieties.

latives such as unit blocks, attribute blocks, and LEGO provide opportunities for exploration. Preschoolers are just beginning to develop definitions of shapes, which probably are not solidified until after age 6 (Hannibal, 1999). When working with shapes it is important to use a variety of models of each category of shape so children generalize and perceive that there is not just one definition. For example, triangles with three equal sides are the most common models so children frequently do not perceive right triangles, isosceles triangles, and so forth as real triangles (Figure 12–4). Many preschoolers do not see that squares are a type of rectangle. After experience with many shape examples and discussion of attributes, children begin to see beyond the obvious and can generalize to related shapes.

## ASSESSMENT

Observational assessment can be done by noticing whether the child uses shape to organize his world. As the child plays with materials, the adult should note whether he groups things together because the shape is the same or similar. For example, a child plays with a set of plastic shape blocks. There are triangles, squares, and circles that are red, blue, green, yellow, or orange. Sometimes he groups them by color, sometimes by shape. A child is playing with pop beads of different colors and shapes. Sometimes he makes strings of the same shape and sometimes of the same color. The child may use certain shape names in everyday conversation.

The individual interview tasks for shape will center on discrimination, labeling, matching, and sorting. *Discrimination* tasks assess whether the child can see that one form has a different shape from another form.

*Labeling* tasks assess whether the child can find a shape when the name is given and whether he can name a shape when a picture is shown to him. At a higher level, he finds shapes in pictures and in his environment. *Matching* would require the child to find a shape like one shown to him. A *sorting* task would be one in which the child must separate a mixed group of shapes into groups (see Unit 10). Two sample tasks follow.

---

## SAMPLE ASSESSMENT TASK

**4E**                                                                 **Preoperational Ages 3–4**

**Shape, Identification: Unit 12**

| | |
|---|---|
| **METHOD:** | Interview. |
| **SKILL:** | When provided with shapes of varying types, size, and colors, the child will be able to label and describe them using his or her current knowledge. |
| **MATERIALS:** | A variety of shapes, both two- and three-dimensional. Select items from small unit blocks, cube block sets, tangrams, and/or attribute blocks; you can also make cardboard cutouts or cover cylindrical containers and small boxes with Contac paper. Have 15 to 20 different objects. |
| **PROCEDURE:** | Lay out the materials in front of the child. TELL ME ABOUT THESE SHAPES. DO YOU HAVE ANY NAMES FOR ANY OF THESE SHAPES? WHAT MAKES THE SHAPE A (name of shape)? ARE ANY OF THE SHAPES THE SAME IN ANY WAY? HAVE YOU SEEN ANYTHING ELSE WITH THIS SHAPE? (Either one the child selected or one you selected.) AT SCHOOL? OUTSIDE? AT HOME? WHAT KIND OF A PICTURE CAN YOU MAKE WITH THESE SHAPES? |
| **EVALUATION:** | Note if the child has labels for any of the shapes, if she makes any connections to familiar items in the environment, if she can make a picture with them that is logical, and, in general, if she appears to have noticed the attributes of shape in the environment. Whether or not she uses conventional labels at this point is not important. |

**INSTRUCTIONAL RESOURCE:** Charlesworth, R., and Lind, K. K. (2010). *Math and science for young children* (6th ed.). Clifton Park, NY: Cengage Learning.

---

## SAMPLE ASSESSMENT TASK

**5E**                                                                 **Preoperational Ages 5–6**

**Shape, Geometric Shape Recognition: Unit 12**

| | |
|---|---|
| **METHOD:** | Interview. |
| **SKILL:** | The child can identify shapes in the environment. |

*(continued)*

**MATERIALS:** The natural environment.

**PROCEDURE:** Once a child has had experience with a variety of two- and three-dimensional shapes, the following question can be used to assess his ability to recognize and generalize. LOOK AROUND THE ROOM. FIND AS MANY SHAPES AS YOU CAN. CAN YOU FIND A (square, triangle, rectangle, cylinder, sphere, circle, rectangular prism)?

**EVALUATION:** Note how observant the child is. Does he note the obvious shapes such as windows, doors, and tables? Does he look beyond the obvious? How many shapes and which shapes is the child able to find?

**INSTRUCTIONAL RESOURCE:** Charlesworth, R., and Lind, K. K. (2010). *Math and science for young children* (6th ed.). Clifton Park, NY: Cengage Learning.

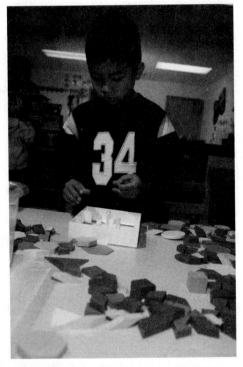

Children learn about shape as they sort and match pattern blocks in their naturalistic play.

**Figure 12–5** Blob shapes: You can make up your own.

## NATURALISTIC ACTIVITIES

Naturalistic activities are most important in the learning of shape. The child perceives the idea of shape through sight and touch. The infant needs objects to look at, to grasp, and to touch and taste. The toddler needs different things of many shapes to use as she sorts and matches. She needs many containers (bowls, boxes, coffee cans) and many objects (e.g., pop beads, table tennis balls, poker chips, empty thread spools). She needs time to fill containers with these objects of different shapes and to dump the objects out and begin again. As she holds each thing, she examines it with her eyes, hands, and mouth.

The older preoperational child enjoys a junk box filled with things such as buttons, checkers, bottle caps, pegs, small boxes, and plastic bottles that she can explore. The teacher can also put out a box of *attribute blocks* (wood or plastic blocks in geometric shapes). Geometric shapes and other shapes can also be cut from paper and/or cardboard and placed out for the child to use. Figure 12–5 shows some blob shapes that can be put into a box of shapes to sort.

In dramatic play, the child can put to use his ideas about shape. The preoperational child's play is representational. He uses things to represent something else that he does not have at the time. He finds something that is "close to" and thus can represent the real thing. Shape is one of the main characteristics used when the child picks a representational object.

- A stick or a long piece of wood is used for a gun.
- A piece of rope or old garden hose is used to put out a pretend fire.
- The magnet board shapes are pretend candy.
- A square yellow block is a piece of cheese.
- A shoe box is a crib, a bed, or a house—as needed.
- Some rectangular pieces of green paper are dollars, and some round pieces of paper are coins.
- A paper towel roll is a telescope for looking at the moon.
- A blob of Play-Doh is a hamburger or a cookie.

## INFORMAL ACTIVITIES

The teacher can let the child know that he notices her use of shape ideas in activities through comments and attention. He can also supply her with ideas and objects that will fit her needs. He can suggest or give the child a box to be used for a bed or a house, some blocks or other small objects for her pretend food, or green rectangles and gray and brown circles for play money.

Labels can be used during normal activities. The child's knowledge of shape can be used, too.

- "The forks have sharp points; the spoons are round and smooth."
- "Put square place mats on the square tables and rectangular place mats on the rectangular tables."

- "Today we'll have some crackers that are shaped like triangles."
- As a child works on a hard puzzle, the teacher takes her hand and has her feel the empty space with her index finger, "Feel this shape and look at it. Now find the puzzle piece that fits here."
- As the children use clay or Play-Doh, the teacher remarks: "You are making lots of shapes. Kate has made a ball, which is a sphere shape; Jose, a snake, which is a cylinder shape; and Kaho, a pancake, which is a circle shape."
- During cleanup time, the teacher says, "Put the square rectangular prism blocks here and the other rectangular prism blocks over there."

The teacher should respond when the child calls attention to shapes in the environment. The following examples show that children can generalize; they can use what they know about shape in new situations.

- "Ms. Moore, the door is shaped like a rectangle." Ms. Moore smiles and looks over at George. "Yes, it is. How many rectangles can you find on the door?" "There are big wide rectangles on the sides and thin rectangles on the ends and the top and bottom."
- "The plate and the hamburger look round like circles." "They do, don't they?" agrees Mr. Brown.
- "Where I put the purple paint, it looks like a butterfly." Mr. Flores looks over and nods.
- "The roof is shaped like a witch's hat." Miss Conn smiles.
- Watching a variety show on TV, the child asks: "What are those things that are shaped like bananas?" (Some curtains over the stage are yellow and do look just like big bananas!) Dad comments laughingly, "That is funny. Those curtains look like bananas."

## STRUCTURED ACTIVITIES

Structured activities are designed to help children see the attributes that are critical to each type of shape. These activities should provide more than learning the

Puzzles provide informal shape experiences.

names of a limited number of models. Models should vary. For example, not every figure should have a horizontal base. Some examples should be rotated, as in Figure 12–4. Some nonexamples should be provided for comparison. Preoperational children need to learn that orientation, color, and size are irrelevant to the identification of shape. Clements and Sarama (2000, p. 487) suggest that children can be helped to learn what is relevant and what is irrelevant through the following kinds of activities:

■ identifying shapes in the classroom, school, and community;

■ sorting shapes and describing why they believe a shape belongs to a group;

■ copying and building with shapes using a wide range of materials.

Children need both haptic and visual experiences to learn discrimination and labeling. These experiences can be described as follows.

■ *Haptic activities* use the sense of touch to match and identify shapes. These activities involve experiences where the child cannot see to solve a problem but must use only his sense of touch. The items to be touched are hidden from view. The things may be put in a bag or a box or wrapped in cloth or paper. Sometimes a clue is given. The child can feel one thing and then find another that is the same shape. The child can be shown a shape and then asked to find one that is the same. Finally, the child can be given just a name (or label) as a clue.

■ *Visual activities* use the sense of sight. The child may be given a visual or a verbal clue and asked to choose, from several things, the one that is the same shape. Real objects or pictures may be used.

■ *Visual-motor activities* use the sense of sight and motor coordination at the same time. This type of experience includes the use of puzzles, formboards, attribute blocks, flannelboards, magnet boards, Colorforms, and paper cutouts, all of which the child can manipulate by herself. She may sort the things into sets or arrange them into a pattern or picture. Sorting was described in Unit 10; examples of making patterns or pictures are shown in Figure 12–6.

The National Library of Virtual Manipulatives (2007) includes a variety of shape activities. For example, the selection includes activities with attribute blocks, triangles, geoboards, pattern blocks, and tangrams.

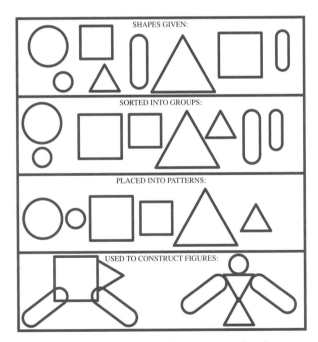

**Figure 12–6** Shapes can be sorted into groups, placed into a pattern, or made into figures.

As the child engages in haptic, visual, and visual-motor activities, the teacher can provide labels (words such as *round, circle, square, triangle, rectangle, shape, corners, points, cone, cylinder, rectangular prism*). The following activities are some examples of basic types of shape experiences for the young child.

## ACTIVITIES

### Shape: Feeling Box

**OBJECTIVE:** To provide children with experiences that will enable them to use their sense of touch to label and discriminate shapes.

**MATERIALS:** A medium-sized cardboard box with a hole cut in the top that is big enough for the child to put his hand in but small enough that he cannot see inside; some familiar objects, such as a toy car, a small wooden block, a spoon, a small coin purse, a baby shoe, a pencil, and a rock.

**NATURALISTIC AND INFORMAL ACTIVITIES:** During daily center time, the children should have opportunities to become acquainted with the objects just listed during their play activities. During their play, the teacher should comment on the objects and supply the appropriate names: "You have used the *rectangular square prism blocks* to build a garage for your *car.*"

**STRUCTURED ACTIVITIES:**
1. Show the children each of the objects. Be sure they know the name of each one. Have them pick up each object and name it.
2. Out of their sight, put the objects in the box.
3. Then do the following:

   - Have another set of identical objects. Hold them up one at a time: PUT YOUR HAND IN THE BOX. FIND ONE LIKE THIS.

   - Have yet another set of identical objects. Put each one in its own bag: FEEL WHAT IS IN HERE. FIND ONE JUST LIKE IT IN THE BIG BOX.

   - Use just a verbal clue: PUT YOUR HAND IN THE BOX. FIND THE ROCK (CAR, BLOCK).

   - PUT YOUR HAND IN THE BOX. TELL ME THE NAME OF WHAT YOU FEEL. BRING IT OUT, AND WE'LL SEE IF YOU GUESSED IT.

**FOLLOW-UP:** Once the children understand the idea of the "feeling box," a "mystery box" can be introduced. In this case, familiar objects are placed in the box but the children do not know what they are: They must feel them and guess. Children can take turns. Before a child takes the object out, encourage her to describe it (smooth, rough, round, straight, bumpy, it has wheels, and so on). After the child learns about geometric shapes, the box can be filled with cardboard cutouts, attribute blocks, or three-dimensional models.

### Shape: Discrimination of Geometric Shapes

**OBJECTIVE:** To see that geometric shapes may be the same or different from each other.

**MATERIALS:** Any or all of the following may be used:
- Magnet board with magnet shapes of various types, sizes, and colors
- Flannelboard with felt shapes of various types, shapes, and colors

*(continued)*

- Attribute blocks (blocks of various shapes, sizes, and colors)
- Cards with pictures of various geometric shapes in several sizes (they can be all outlines or solids of the same or different colors)
- Three-dimensional models

**NATURALISTIC AND INFORMAL ACTIVITIES:** During the daily center time, provide opportunities for the children to explore the materials. Observe whether they use any shape words, sort the shapes, match the shapes, make patterns, or make constructions. Ask them to describe what they have done. Comment, using shape words.

**STRUCTURED ACTIVITIES:** The activities are matching, classifying, and labeling.

- *Matching.* Put out several different shapes. Show the child one shape: FIND ALL THE SHAPES LIKE THIS ONE. TELL ME WHY THOSE BELONG TOGETHER.
- *Classifying.* Put out several different kinds of shapes: PUT ALL THE SHAPES THAT ARE THE SAME KIND TOGETHER. TELL ME HOW YOU KNOW THOSE SHAPES ARE ALL THE SAME KIND.
- *Labeling.* Put out several kinds of shapes: FIND ALL THE TRIANGLES (SQUARES, CIRCLES) or TELL ME THE NAME OF THIS SHAPE (point to one at random).

**FOLLOW-UP:** Do individual and small group activities. Do the same basic activities with different materials.

## Shape: Discrimination and Matching Game

**OBJECTIVE:** To practice matching and discrimination skills (for the child who has already had experience with the various shapes).

**MATERIALS:** Cut out some shapes from cardboard. The game can be made harder by increasing the number of shapes used and/or by varying the size of the shapes and the number of colors. Make six bingo-type cards (each one should be different) as well as a spinner card that includes all the shapes used.

**ACTIVITIES:** 1. Give each child a bingo card.
2. Have the children take turns spinning the spinner. Anyone whose card has the shape that the spinner points to can cover the shape with a paper square or put a marker on it.

**FOLLOW-UP:** Once the rules of the game are learned, the children can play it on their own.

## Shape: Environmental Geometry

**OBJECTIVE:** To see that there are geometric shapes all around in the environment.

**MATERIALS:** The classroom, the school building, the playground, the home, and the neighborhood.

**ACTIVITIES:**  1. Look for shapes on the floor, the ceiling, doors, windows, materials, clothing, trees, flowers, vehicles, walls, fences, sidewalks, etc.
2. Make a shape table. Cover the top, and divide it into sections. Mark each section with a sample shape. Have the children bring things from home and put them on the place on the table that matches the shape of what they brought.
3. Make "Find the Shape" posters (see Figure 12–7).

**Figure 12–7** "Find the shapes."

## IDEAS FOR CHILDREN WITH SPECIAL NEEDS

### Addressing Perceptual-Motor Challenges

Children who are challenged by perceptual-motor tasks can learn to identify shapes by practicing their perceptual-motor skills with shape templates. Large shape templates can be used on the chalkboard or whiteboard. Students should start with a circle and then try repro-ducing the square, the triangle, the rectangle, and the diamond. After completing the large templates, they can work with desktop templates on paper. Once they have mastered drawing with the templates, they can move on to tracing and then to free drawing.

### Bilingual Geometry

Alfinio Flores (1995) provides an approach to geometry for bilingual students in grades K–3. Geometry was taught in Spanish in order to develop higher-order thinking skills in the children's primary language. Kindergartners did five activities. The students used five templates: one square, one equilateral triangle, and four right triangles. They were given problems that required them to compare the template shapes with shapes on paper in different positions.

## Multicultural Geometry

Zaslavsky (1996) presents a focus on comparing the shapes of homes in a variety of cultures. When asked to draw a floor plan, most children in Western culture start with a rectangle. They can then move on to study the shapes of homes in other cultures. Some Native Americans believed that the circle had great power and thus built their tepees on a circular base. The Kamba people in Africa also built on a circular base. The Yoruba of Nigeria and the Egyptians built rectangular homes. Students can learn how cultural beliefs and lifestyles influence the shapes of houses. Zaslavsky describes how art is a reflection of shape. Art is evident in items such as decorative pieces, household items, architecture, clothing, and religious artifacts. Art may have symbolic meaning, and art patterns are frequently based on geometric shapes. In Unit 13 we will see how art can reflect spatial concepts.

## EVALUATION

Through observing during center time and during structured experiences, the teacher can see whether the child shows advances in ideas regarding shape. She observes whether the child uses the word *shape* and other shape words as he goes about his daily activities. When he sorts and groups materials, the teacher notices whether he sometimes uses shape as the basis for organizing. The adult gives the child informal tasks such as "Put the box on the square table," "Fold the napkins so they are rectangle shapes," "Find two boxes that are the same shape," "Look carefully at the shapes of your puzzle pieces," and "Make a design with these different shaped tiles."

After a period of instruction, the teacher may use interview tasks such as those described in Appendix A.

## SUMMARY

Each thing the child meets in the environment has shape. The child explores his world and learns in a naturalistic way about the shape of each object in it. Adults help by giving the child things to view, hold, and feel. Adults also teach the child words that describe shapes and the names of geometric shapes: square, circle, triangle, cylinder, triangular prism, and so on. It is through exploration of shapes and spatial relations (see Unit 13) that the foundation of geometry is laid. Concepts of shape can be applied to developing perceptual-motor integration, bilingual lessons, and comparisons of the meaning of shape across cultures.

## KEY TERMS

| | | |
|---|---|---|
| circle | sphere | triangle |
| cylinder | square | triangular prism |
| rectangular prism | | |

## SUGGESTED ACTIVITIES

1. Perform an assessment of a child's concept of shape. Plan and do some activities with the child that will enhance her shape understanding. Report on your evaluation of the results.

2. Make or assemble some materials for a haptic activity. Have the class use the materials and give you feedback. Make any needed changes, and add the activity to your file or notebook.

3.  Maria Montessori created some haptic activities. Research her method in the library and by visiting a Montessori school. Write an evaluation of her materials.

4.  In a preprimary classroom, place some shape materials out where the children can explore them informally. Record what the children do, and share the results with the class.

5.  Using one of the guidelines suggested in Activity 5 of Unit 2, evaluate one or more of the following computer programs designed to reinforce shape concepts.

    ■ *Little Raven and Friends.* Includes application of many problem-solving skills including shape recognition. (New York: Tivola)

    ■ *Arthur's Math Games.* Children use many math skills including geom-etry. (San Francisco: Broderbund at Riverdeep)

    ■ *Millie's Math House.* Includes exploration of shapes. (San Francisco: Riverdeep-Edmark)

    ■ *Geometry Bundle* (Tenth Planet). This bundle includes: Spatial Relationships, Combining Shapes, Introduction to Patterns, Creating Patterns from Shapes, Mirror Symmetry, and Shapes within Shapes. (Hazelton, PA: K–12 Software)

    ■ *Shape up!* A variety of shape activities. (Hazelton, PA: K–12 Software)

    ■ *Baby Einstein Discovering Shapes* (http://www.disneyshopping.go.com), DVD

## REVIEW

A.  What follows is a description of 4-year-old Maria's activities on a school day. Identify the shape activities she experiences and decide whether each is naturalistic, informal, or structured.

Maria's mother wakes her up at 7:00 a.m. "Time to get up." Maria snuggles her teddy bear, Beady. His soft body feels very comforting. Mom comes in and gets her up and into the bathroom to wash her face and brush her teeth. "What kind of cereal do you want this morning?" Maria responds, "Those round ones, Cheerios." Maria rubs her hands over the slippery surface of the soap before she rubs it on her face.

Maria goes into the kitchen, where she eats her cereal out of a round bowl. Occasionally, she looks out the window through its square panes. After breakfast, Maria gets dressed, and then she and her mother drive to school. Along the way, Maria notices a stop sign, a railroad crossing sign, a school zone sign, buildings with many windows, and other cars and buses.

At the child development center, Maria is greeted by her teacher. She hangs her coat in her cubby and runs over to where several of her friends are building with unit blocks. Maria builds, using combinations of long blocks, short blocks, rectangular blocks, square blocks, and curved blocks. She makes a rectangular enclosure and places some miniature animals in it.

Next, Maria goes to the art center. She cuts out a large and a small circle as well as four rectangles. She glues them on a larger sheet of paper. "Look," she says to her teacher, "I made a little person."

The children gather around Miss Collins for a group activity. "Today we will see what kinds of shapes we can make with our bodies." Individually and in small groups, the children form a variety of shapes with their bodies.

For snack, the children have cheese cut into cubes and elliptical crackers. Following snack, Maria goes to a table of puzzles and formboards and selects a geometric shape formboard. After successfully completing the formboard, Maria selects the shape blocks. She sorts and stacks them according to shape. "Look, I made a stack of triangles and a stack of squares."

B. Give an example of shape discrimination, shape labeling, shape matching, and shape sorting.

C. Decide whether each of the following is an example of discrimination, labeling, matching, or sorting.

1. The child is shown an ellipse. "Tell me the name of this kind of shape."

2. The children are told to see how many rectangular prisms they can find in the classroom.

3. The teacher passes around a bag with an unknown object inside. Each child feels the bag and makes a guess about what is inside.

4. The teacher holds up a cylinder block and tells the children to find some things that are the same shape.

5. A child is fitting shapes into a shape matrix board.

6. A small group of children is playing shape lotto.

## REFERENCES

Clements, D. H., & Sarama, J. (2000). Young children's ideas about geometric shapes. *Teaching Children Mathematics, 6*(8), 482–488.

Flores, A. (1995). Bilingual lessons in early grades geometry. *Teaching Children Mathematics, 1,* 420–424.

Hannibal, M. A. (1999). Young children's developing understanding of geometric shapes. *Teaching Children Mathematics, 5*(6), 353–357.

National Council of Teachers of Mathematics. (2000). *Principles and standards for school mathematics.* Reston, VA: Author.

National Library of Virtual Manipulatives. (2007). *Geometry (grades pre-K–2)*. Retrieved July 27, 2007, from http://nlvm.usu.edu

Zaslavsky, C. (1996). *The multicultural math classroom.* Portsmouth, NH: Heinemann.

## FURTHER READING AND RESOURCES

Burk, D., Snider, A., & Symonds, P. (1988). *Box it or bag it mathematics: Kindergarten teachers resource guide.* Salem, OR: Math Learning Center.

Copley, J. V. (Ed.). (1999). *Mathematics in the early years.* Washington, DC: National Association for the Education of Young Children.

Copley, J. V. (2000). *The young child and mathematics.* Washington, DC: National Association for the Education of Young Children.

Copley, J. V. (Ed.). (2004). *Showcasing mathematics for the young child* (chap. 3, Geometry). Reston, VA: National Council of Teachers of Mathematics.

Copley, J. V., Jones, C., & Dighe, J. (2007). *Mathematics: The creative curriculum approach.* Washington, DC: Teaching Strategies.

Del Grande, J. (1993). *Curriculum and evaluation standards for school mathematics: Geometry and spatial sense.* Reston, VA: National Council of Teachers of Mathematics.

Dobbs, J., Doctoroff, G. L., & Fisher, P. H. (2003). The "Math Is Everywhere" preschool mathematics curriculum. *Teaching Children Mathematics, 10*(1), 20–22.

Epstein, A. S., & Gainsley, S. (2005). *Math in the preschool classroom.* Ypsilanti, MI: High/Scope.

Gallenstein, N. L. (2003). *Creative construction of mathematics and science concepts in early childhood.* Olney, MD: Association for Childhood Education International.

Geometry and geometric thinking [Focus issue]. (1999). *Teaching Children Mathematics, 5*(6).

Greenes, C. E., & House, P. A. (Eds.). (2001). *Navigating through geometry in prekindergarten–grade 2.* Reston, VA: National Council of Teachers of Mathematics.

Greenes, C. E., & House, P. A. (Eds.). (2003). *Navigating through problem solving and reasoning in prekindergarten–kindergarten.* Reston, VA: National Council of Teachers of Mathematics.

Learning Resources. (2007). *Hands-on standards.* Vernon Hills, IL: Author.

Marsh, J., Loesing, J., & Soucie, M. (2004). Math by the month: Gee-whiz geometry. *Teaching Children Mathematics, 11*(4), 208.

National Council of Teachers of Mathematics. (2007). *Curriculum focal points.* Reston, VA: Author.

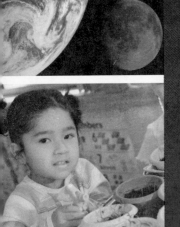

# Unit 13

# Early Geometry: Spatial Sense

## OBJECTIVES

After reading this unit, you should be able to:

■ Explain the NCTM expectations regarding spatial sense for prekindergarten through grade two.

■ Define the five spatial sense concepts and tell how each answers specific questions.

■ Assess and evaluate a child's spatial concepts.

■ Do informal and structured spatial activities with young children.

The NCTM (2000) lists several expectations concerning young children's understanding and application of spatial relationships as one of the foundations of early geometry. Young children are expected to (1) describe, name, and interpret relative positions in space and apply ideas about relative position; (2) describe, name, and interpret direction and distance in navigating space and apply ideas about direction and distance; and (3) find and name locations with simple relationships such as "near to" and "in." A sense of spatial relationships along with an understanding of shape (Unit 12) is fundamental to "interpreting, understanding, and appreciating our inherently geometric world" (NCTM, 1989, p. 48). Spatial sense experiences can integrate across content areas (Figure 13–1).

A focal point for prekindergarten and kindergarten is describing spatial relations and space. Children build with blocks and other construction materials. They construct collages in two and three dimensions. They learn to verbally label directions and positions in

space. They connect geometry, measurement, and number (e.g., "move three steps to the left").

Math, science, and technology are integrated in the area of engineering known as **design technology** (Dunn & Larson, 1990). Young children apply their knowledge of spatial relations to building and construction projects. They are natural engineers who continuously engage in problem-solving activities. Their activities as engineers are primitive but are the basis for what adult engineers do. An engineer can be playful and imaginative, just like a young child. According to Petroski (2003), the professional engineer's fundamental activity is design. "Design is rooted in imagination and choice—and play" (Petroski, 2003, pp. 4–5).

According to Dunn and Larson (1990, p. 5):

Design technology is a natural, intellectually and physically interactive process of design, realization, and reflection. Through consideration of ideas, aesthetics, implications,

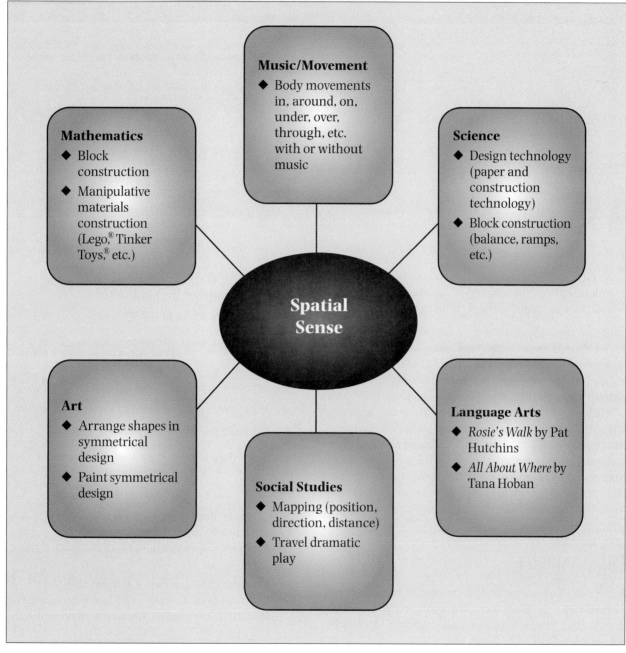

**Figure 13–1** Integrating spatial sense across the curriculum.

| Space Concept | Question | Answers |
|---|---|---|
| **Position** | Where (am I, are you, is he)? | on, off; on top of, over, under; in, out; into, out of; top, bottom; above, below; in front of, in back of, behind; beside, by, next to; between |
| **Direction** | Which way? | up, down; forward, backward; around, through; to, from; toward, away from; sideways; across |
| **Distance** | What is the relative distance? | near, far; close to, far from |
| **Organization and pattern** | How can things be arranged so they fit in a space? | arrange things in the space until they fit, or until they please the eye |
| **Construction** | How is space made? How do things fit into the space? | arrange things in the space until they fit; change the size and shape of the space so things will fit |

and available resources, children become imaginative engineers, exploring alternative solutions to contextualized challenges.

Children naturally assemble materials and construct things that fit their needs. They place a blanket over a card table to make a tent or a cave, and an empty box covered with wallpaper scraps is transformed into a doll bed. Building on their own ideas and solving their own problems, children can create their own curriculum. They build with blocks and other construction toys. At the preoperational level, children need construction materials to explore. At the elementary level as they emerge into concrete operations, design engineering takes on a more formalized structure, which will be discussed later in this text.

## ASSESSMENT

A great deal about the child's concept of space can be learned through observation. The adult notes the child's use of space words. Does he respond with an appropriate act when he is told the following?

- Put the book *on* the table.
- Please *take off* your hat.
- You'll find the soap *under* the sink.
- Stand *behind* the gate.

- Sit *between* Kate and Chris.
- Move *away from* the hot stove.
- It's on the table *near* the window.

Does she answer space questions using space words?

- Where is the cat? *On* the bed.
- Where is the cake? *In* the oven.
- Which way did John go? He went *up* the ladder.
- Where is your house? *Near* the corner.

The adult should note the child's use of organization and pattern arrangement during his play activities.

- When he does artwork, such as a collage, does he take time to place the materials on the paper in a careful way? Does he seem to have a design in mind?
- Does the child's drawing and painting show balance? Does he seem to get everything into the space that he wants to have it in, or does he run out of space?
- As he plays with objects, does he place them in straight rows, circle shapes, square shapes, and so on?

The teacher should note the child's use of construction materials such as blocks and containers.

- Does the child use small blocks to make structures into which toys (such as cars and animals) can be placed?

- Does she use larger blocks to make buildings into which large toys and children will fit?

- Can she usually find the right size of container to hold things (e.g., a shoe box that makes an appropriately sized bed for her toy bear)?

The teacher should also note the child's use of his own body in space.

- When he needs a cozy place to play, does he choose one that fits his size or does he often get stuck in tight spots?

- Does he manage to move his body without too many bumps and falls?

The individual interview tasks for space will center on relationships and use of space. The following are examples of interview tasks.

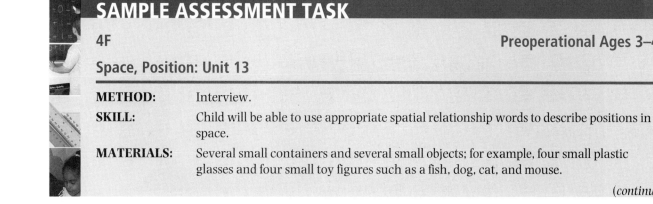

## SAMPLE ASSESSMENT TASK

**3G**                                                       **Preoperational Ages 2–3**

**Space, Position: Unit 13**

| | |
|---|---|
| **METHOD:** | Interview. |
| **SKILL:** | Given a spatial relationship word, the child is able to place objects relative to other objects on the basis of that word. |
| **MATERIALS:** | A small container such as a box, cup, or bowl; an object such as a coin, checker, or chip. |
| **PROCEDURE:** | PUT THE COIN (CHECKER, CHIP) IN THE CONTAINER. Repeat using other space words: ON, OFF OF, OUT OF, IN FRONT OF, NEXT TO, UNDER, OVER. |
| **EVALUATION:** | **Observe** whether the child is able to follow the instructions and place the object correctly relative to the space word used. |

**INSTRUCTIONAL RESOURCE:** Charlesworth, R., and Lind, K. K. (2010). *Math and science for young children* (6th ed.). Clifton Park, NY: Cengage Learning.

## SAMPLE ASSESSMENT TASK

**4F**                                                       **Preoperational Ages 3–4**

**Space, Position: Unit 13**

| | |
|---|---|
| **METHOD:** | Interview. |
| **SKILL:** | Child will be able to use appropriate spatial relationship words to describe positions in space. |
| **MATERIALS:** | Several small containers and several small objects; for example, four small plastic glasses and four small toy figures such as a fish, dog, cat, and mouse. |

*(continued)*

**PROCEDURE:**    Ask the child to name each of the objects (so you can use his name for them if it differs from yours). Line up the glasses in a row. Place the animals so that one is *in*, one *on*, one *under*, and one *between* the glasses. Then say, TELL ME WHERE THE FISH IS. Then, TELL ME WHERE THE DOG IS. Then, TELL ME WHERE THE CAT IS. Finally, TELL ME WHERE THE MOUSE IS. Frequently, children will insist on pointing. Say, DO IT WITHOUT POINTING. TELL ME WITH WORDS.

**EVALUATION:**    Note whether the child responds with position words and whether or not the words used are correct.

**INSTRUCTIONAL RESOURCE:**  Charlesworth, R., and Lind, K. K. (2010). *Math and science for young children* (6th ed.). Clifton Park, NY: Cengage Learning.

## NATURALISTIC ACTIVITIES

It is through everyday motor activities that the child first learns about space. As she moves her body in space, she learns position, direction, and distance relationships and also learns about the use of the space. Children in the sensorimotor and preoperational stages need equipment that lets them place their own bodies on, off, under, over, in, out, through, above, below, and so on. They need places to go up and down, around and through, and sideways and across. They need things that they can put in, on, and under other things. They need things that they can place near and far from other things. They need containers of many sizes to fill; blocks with which to build; and paint, collage materials, wood, clay, cutouts, and such that can be made into patterns

Young children naturally engage in spatial activities.

and organized in space. Thus, when the child is matching, classifying, and comparing, she is learning about space at the same time.

The child who crawls and creeps often goes under furniture. At first she sometimes gets stuck when she has not judged correctly the clearance under which she will fit. As she begins to pull herself up, she tries to climb on things. This activity is important not only for her motor development but for her spatial learning. However, many pieces of furniture are not safe or are too high. An empty beverage bottle box with the dividers still in it may be taped closed and covered with some colorful Contac paper. This makes a safe and inexpensive place to climb. The adults can make several, and the child will have a set of large construction blocks.

Each time the child handles an object, she may learn more than one skill or idea. For instance, Juanita builds a house with some small blocks. The blocks are different colors and shapes. First Juanita picks out all the blue rectangular prisms and piles them three high in a row. Next she picks all the red rectangular prisms and piles them in another direction in a row. Next she piles orange rectangular prisms to make a third side to her structure. Finally, she lines up some yellow cylinders to make a fourth side. She places two pigs, a cow, and a horse in the enclosure. Juanita has sorted by color and shape. She has made a structure with space for her farm animals (a class) and has put the animals *in* the enclosure.

With the availability of information on outer space flight in movies and on television, children might demonstrate the concept during their dramatic play activities. For example, they might build a space vehicle with large blocks and fly off to a distant planet or become astronauts on a trip to the moon.

Children begin to integrate position, direction, distance, organization, pattern, and construction through mapping activities. Early mapping activities involve developing more complex spaces such as building houses and laying out roads in the sand or laying out roads and buildings with unit blocks. Another activity is playing with commercial toys that include a village printed on plastic along with houses, people, animals, and vehicles that can be placed on the village. When provided with such materials, children naturally make these types of constructions, which are the concrete beginnings of understanding maps.

Block construction supports the development of spatial concepts.

## INFORMAL ACTIVITIES

Spatial sense involves many words to be learned and attached to actions. The teacher should use spatial words (as listed earlier in the unit) as they fit into the daily activities. She should give spatial directions, ask spatial questions, and make spatial comments. Examples of directions and questions are in the assessment section of this unit. Examples of spatial comments include the following.

■ Carlos is at the *top* of the ladder.

■ Cindy is *close* to the door.

■ You have the dog *behind* the mother in the car.

- Tanya can move the handle *backward* and *forward*.
- You children made a house big enough for all of you. (construction)
- You pasted all the square shapes on your paper. (organization and pattern)

Jungle gyms, packing crates, ladders, ramps, and other equipment designed for large muscle activity give the child experiences with space. They climb *up, down,* and *across.* They climb *up* a ladder and crawl or slide *down* a ramp. On the jungle gym they go *in* and *out, up* and *down, through, above, below,* and *around.* They get *in* and *out* of packing crates. On swings they go *up* and *down* and *backward* and *forward* and see the world *down below.*

With large blocks, boxes, and boards, children make structures that they can get *in* themselves. Chairs and tables may be added to make a house, train, airplane, bus, or ship. Props such as a steering wheel, firefighter or police hats, ropes, hoses, discarded radios, and the like inspire children to build structures on which to play. With small blocks, children make houses, airports, farms, grocery stores, castles, and trains. They then place their toy animals, people, and other objects in spatial arrangements, patterns, and positions. They learn to fit their structures into the space available: say, on the floor or on a large or small table. They might also build space vehicles and develop concrete mapping representations in the sand or with blocks. The teacher can ask questions about their space trip or their geographic construction: "How far is it to the moon?" "Show me the roads you would use to drive from Richard's house to Kate's house."

As the child works with art materials, he chooses what to glue or paste on his paper. A large selection of collage materials such as scrap paper, cloth, feathers,

A compass provides experience finding directions.

plastic bits, yarn, wire, gummed paper, cotton balls, bottle caps, and ribbon offer children a choice of things to organize within the available space. As he gets past the first stages of experimentation, the child plans his painting. He may paint blobs, geometric shapes, stripes, or realistic figures. He enjoys printing with sponges or potatoes. All these experiences add to his ideas about space.

## STRUCTURED ACTIVITIES

Structured activities of many kinds can be done to help the child with her ideas about space and her skills in the use of space. We next describe basic activities for the three kinds of space relations (position, direction, and distance) and the two ways of using space (organization/pattern and construction through design technology).

## ACTIVITIES

### Space: Relationships, Physical Self

**OBJECTIVE:** To help the child relate his position in space to the positions of other people and things.

**MATERIALS:** The child's own body, other people, and things in the environment.

**NATURALISTIC AND INFORMAL ACTIVITIES:** Children should be encouraged to use their bodies in gross motor activity such as running, climbing, jumping, lifting, pulling, and so on. They should be assisted in motor control behaviors such as defining their own space and keeping a safe distance from others.

**STRUCTURED ACTIVITIES:** 1. Set up an obstacle course using boxes, boards, ladders, tables, chairs, and similar items. Set it up so that, by following the course, children can physically experience position, direction, and distance. This can be done indoors or outdoors. As the child proceeds along the course, use space words to label his movement: "Leroy is going *up* the ladder, *through* the tunnel, *across* the bridge, *down* the slide, and *under* the table. Now he is *close to* the end."

2. Find Your Friend

Place children in different places: sitting or standing on chairs or blocks or boxes, under tables, sitting three in a row on chairs facing different directions, and so on. Have each child take a turn to find a friend.

FIND A FRIEND WHO IS ON A CHAIR (A BOX, A LADDER).

FIND A FRIEND WHO IS UNDER (ON, NEXT TO) A TABLE.

FIND A FRIEND WHO IS BETWEEN TWO FRIENDS (BEHIND A FRIEND, NEXT TO A FRIEND).

FIND A FRIEND WHO IS SITTING BACKWARDS (FORWARDS, SIDEWAYS).

FIND A FRIEND WHO IS ABOVE (BELOW) ANOTHER FRIEND.

Have the children think of different places they can place themselves. When they know the game, let the children take turns making the FIND statements.

3. Put Yourself Where I Say

One at a time, give the children instructions for placing themselves in a position.

CLIMB UP THE LADDER.

WALK BETWEEN THE CHAIRS.

STAND BEHIND TANYA.

GET ON TOP OF THE BOX.

GO CLOSE TO (FAR FROM) THE DOOR.

Once the children learn the game, they can give the instructions.

4. Where Is Your Friend?

As in Activity 2, "Find Your Friend," place the children in different places. This time ask WHERE questions. The child must answer in words. For example: WHERE IS YOUR FRIEND? The child answers: "Tim is under the table" or "Mary is on top of the playhouse."

**FOLLOW-UP:** Set up indoor and outdoor obstacle courses for the children to use during playtime.

## Space, Relationships, Objects

**OBJECTIVE:** To be able to relate the position of objects in space to other objects.

**MATERIALS:** Have several identical containers (cups, glasses, or boxes) and some small objects such as blocks, pegs, buttons, sticks, and toy animals.

*(continued)*

**NATURALISTIC AND INFORMAL ACTIVITIES:** Observe how children play with objects during center time. Do they stack their blocks? Do they put dolls in beds? Do they place vehicles in structures? Comment on their placements: "The red block is *on* two green blocks." "The doll is *in* the bed." Give instructions: "Sit *next to* Mary." "Put the place mat *under* the dishes." "Put this brush *in* the red paint." Note whether the children are able to comply.

**STRUCTURED ACTIVITIES:** 1. Point To
Place objects in various spatial relationships such as shown in the diagram.

POINT TO THE THING THAT IS IN (ON, UNDER, BETWEEN, BEHIND) A BOX.
2. Put The
Set some containers out and place some objects to the side. Tell the child, PUT THE (object name) IN (ON, THROUGH, ACROSS, UNDER, NEAR) THE CONTAINER.
3. Where Is?
Place objects as in activity 1 and/or around the room. Ask, WHERE IS (object name)? TELL ME WHERE THE (object name) IS. Child should reply using a space word.

**FOLLOW-UP:** Repeat the activity using different objects and containers. Leave the materials out for the children to use during center time.

## Space, Use, Construction—Design Technology

**OBJECTIVE:** To organize materials in space in three dimensions through construction.

**MATERIALS:** Wood chips, polythene, cardboard, wire, bottle caps, small empty boxes (e.g., tea, face cream, toothpaste, frozen foods) and other waste materials that can be recycled for construction projects, glue, cardboard, and/or plywood scraps.

**NATURALISTIC AND INFORMAL ACTIVITIES:** Provide children with the opportunity to build using construction toys (unit blocks, LEGO, Unifix Cubes, etc.) during center time. Also provide opportunities to make a variety of collages, which provide the children with experience in organizing materials and using glue.

**STRUCTURED ACTIVITY:** Give the child a bottle of glue, a roll of masking tape, and a piece of cardboard or plywood for a base. Let her choose, from the scrap materials, things that can be used to build a structure on the base. Encourage her to take her time, to plan, and to choose carefully which items to use and where to put them.

**FOLLOW-UP:** Keep plenty of waste materials on hand so that children can make structures when they are in the mood.

## Space, Use, Construction—Design Technology

**OBJECTIVE:** To organize materials in three-dimensional space through construction.

**MATERIALS:** Many kinds of construction materials can be purchased that help the child to understand space and also improve hand–eye coordination and small muscle skills. For example:

1. LEGO: jumbo for the younger child, regular for the older child or one with good motor skills
2. Tinker Toys
3. Bolt-It
4. Snap-N-Play blocks
5. Rig-A-Jig
6. Octons, Play Squares (and other things with parts that fit together)

**NATURALISTIC AND INFORMAL ACTIVITIES:** Once the child understands how the toys can be used, he can be left alone with the materials and his imagination.

**STRUCTURED ACTIVITY:** Structure can be added by having the children think first about what they might like to construct. Older children can draw a sketch of their plan. Next, they can make their project. After they are finished, ask them to reflect on the result. Is it what they had planned? Is it different? In what ways? Do they need to make any changes? When they are satisfied with their construction they can draw a sketch or (if a camera is available) take a photo to place in their portfolio.

**FOLLOW-UP:** Encourage the students to engage in further design technology projects.

## Space: Mapping

**OBJECTIVE:** To integrate basic space concepts through simple mapping activities.

**MATERIALS:** Make a simple treasure map on a large piece of poster board. Draw a floor plan of the classroom, indicating major landmarks (learning centers, doors, windows, etc.) with simple drawings. Draw in some paths going from place to place. Make a brightly colored treasure chest from a shoe box. Make a matching two-dimensional movable treasure chest that can be placed anywhere on the floor plan.

**NATURALISTIC AND INFORMAL ACTIVITIES:** Children should have opportunities for sand play and unit block play with a variety of vehicles. Note if they construct roads, bridges, tunnels, and so on. Ask, "Where does your road go?" They should have a miniature house with miniature furniture to arrange. Ask, "How do you decide where to place the furniture?" Include maps as a dramatic play prop. Observe whether children find a way to use the maps in their play. How do they use them? Does their activity reflect an understanding of what a map is for?

**STRUCTURED ACTIVITY:** Hide the treasure chest somewhere in the room. Place the small treasure chest on the floor plan. Have the children discuss the best route to get from where they are to the treasure using only the paths on the floor plan. Have them try out their routes to see if they can discover the treasure.

**FOLLOW-UP:** Let class members hide the treasure and see if they are able to place the treasure chest correctly on the floor plan. Let them use trial and error when hiding the treasure, marking the spot on the plan, and finding the treasure. Make up some other games using the same basic format. Try this activity outdoors. Supply some adult maps for dramatic play and observe how children use them.

## IDEAS FOR CHILDREN WITH SPECIAL NEEDS

Much of young children's knowledge and understanding of spatial relations comes through their outdoor experiences of running, jumping, and climbing. Children with physical disabilities often miss out on these experiences. There is a movement across the country to construct Boundless Playgrounds (*Boundless Playgrounds*, 2008; *Shane's Inspiration*, 2007). These playgrounds are designed to enable physically challenged children to play alongside their more able-bodied peers. Children with perceptual-motor disabilities can work at a chalkboard, whiteboard, or flannel board putting chalk marks or markers above (below, on, etc.) lines or drawings of objects.

Children of all cultures need opportunities for play (de Melendez & Beck, 2007). Music and movement provide opportunities for learning about space and spatial relations. Movement can be inspired by playing instruments from a variety of cultures. Children of all cultures can construct spatial arrangements through their art projects (Zaslavsky, 1996).

## EVALUATION

Informal evaluation can be done through observation. The teacher should note the following as the children proceed through the day.

- Does the child respond to space words in a way that shows understanding?
- Does she answer space questions and use the correct space words?
- Do her artwork and block building show an increase in organization and use of pattern?
- Does the child handle her body well in space?
- Does her use of geoboards, parquetry blocks, inch cubes, and/or pegboards show an increase in organization and patterning?

After children have completed several space activities, the teacher can assess their progress using the interview tasks described in Appendix A.

## SUMMARY

Spatial sense is an important part of geometry. The child needs to understand the spatial relationship between his body and other things. He must also understand the spatial relationship among things around him. Things are related through position, direction, and distance.

Children must also be able to use space in a logical way. They learn to fit things into the space available and to make constructions in space. Playground and art experiences help build spatial concepts.

### KEY TERMS

| | | |
|---|---|---|
| construction | direction | **organization and pattern** |
| design technology | distance | position |

### SUGGESTED ACTIVITIES

1. Observe some young children on the playground using large motor equipment such as the jungle gym, slides, or tricycles. Note instances that reflect children's concepts of space as listed in the chart at the beginning of this unit and in the assessment tasks.

2. Observe some young children in their classroom playing with blocks and other construc-

tion materials. Note instances that reflect children's concepts of space as listed in the chart at the beginning of this unit and in the assessment tasks.

3. Design a piece of equipment (i.e., jungle gym or slide) for large motor skills that offers children a variety of spatial experiences. Explain where and how these experiences might take place.

4. Pretend you have a budget of $500, and select from a catalog the construction toys you would purchase. Provide a rationale for each selection.

5. Add two or more space activities to your file or notebook.

6. Review one of the following computer programs using the guidelines suggested in Activity 5 of Unit 2.

   ■ *Geometry Bundle* (Tenth Planet). This bundle includes: Spatial Relationships, Combining Shapes, Introduction to Patterns, Creating Patterns from Shapes, Mirror Symmetry, and Shapes within Shapes. (Hazelton, PA: K–12 Software)

   ■ *My Make Believe Castle.* Each room offers a different challenging activity. The woods are a maze, which provides the child with an opportunity to apply spatial relations skills. (Highgate Springs, VT: LCSI)

   ■ *MicroWorlds JR.* Focus is on problem solving, project building, design, and construction. (Highgate Springs, VT: LCSI)

   ■ *James Discovers Math.* Includes spatial visualization. (Hazelton, PA: K–12 Software)

   ■ *Arthur's Math Games.* Includes geometry. (San Francisco: Broderbund at Riverdeep)

   ■ Try geometry activities from the National Library of Virtual Manipulatives (http://nlvm.usu.edu/).

## REVIEW

A. Describe how a teacher can assess children's concepts of space by observing their play.

B. Decide which of items 1–15 below are examples of:

   a. Position
   b. Direction
   c. Distance
   d. Organization
   e. Construction
   f. Mapping

   1. Several children are building with blocks. "Is Carl's building closer to Kate's or to Bob's?"
   2. LEGO construction materials.
   3. "How can we get all these trucks into this garage?"
   4. Mario works with the trucks until he manages to park them all in the garage he has built.
   5. Mary is next to Carlo and behind Jon.
   6. "Are we closer to the cafeteria or to the playground? Let's measure on our school floor plan."
   7. Parquetry blocks.
   8. "Let's play 'London Bridge.'"
   9. "Where am I?" is the central question.
   10. "Which way?" is the focus question.
   11. Geoboards are useful in the development of which spatial concept?
   12. "We don't have enough room for everyone who wants to play house. What can we change?"

13. "Let's act out *The Three Billy Goats Gruff*."
14. The children are building tunnels and roads in the sandbox.
15. As Angelena swings, she chants: "Up and down, up and down."

C. Explain how the NCTM expectations for spatial sense relate to each of the examples in question B.

## REFERENCES

*Boundless Playgrounds*. Retrieved July 2, 2008, from http://www.boundlessplaygrounds.org (This site has links to 100 boundless playground sites.)

de Melendez, W. R., & Beck, V. (2007). *Teaching young children in multicultural classrooms*. Albany, NY: Thomson Delmar Learning.

Dunn, S., & Larson, R. (1990). *Design technology: Children's engineering*. Bristol, PA: Falmer, Taylor & Francis.

National Council of Teachers of Mathematics. (1989). *Curriculum and evaluation standards for school mathematics*. Reston, VA: Author.

National Council of Teachers of Mathematics. (2000). *Principles and standards for school mathematics*. Reston, VA: Author.

Petroski, H. (2003, January 24). *Early education*. Presentation at the Children's Engineering Convention (Williamsburg, VA). Retrieved November 20, 2004, from http://www.vtea.org

*Shane's Inspiration*. Retrieved August 1, 2007, from http://www.shanesinspiration.org

Zaslavsky, C. (1996). *The multicultural math classroom*. Portsmouth, NH: Heinemann.

## FURTHER READING AND RESOURCES

Andrews, A. G. (2004). Adapting manipulatives to foster the thinking of young children. *Teaching Children Mathematics, 11*(1), 15–17.

Casey, B., & Bobb, B. (2003). The power of block building. *Teaching Children Mathematics, 10*(2), 98–102.

Chalufour, I., Hoisington, C., Moriarty, R., Winokur, J., & Worth, K. (2004). The science and mathematics of building structures. *Science and Children, 41*(4), 30–34.

Children's engineering [Focus issue]. (2002). *Children's Engineering Journal, 1*(1). Retrieved November 20, 2004, from http://www.vtea.org

Children's engineering: Achieving excellence in education [Focus issue]. (2006). *Children's Engineering Journal, 4*(1). Retrieved August 1, 2007, from http://www.vtea.org

Copley, J. V. (Ed.). (1999). *Mathematics in the early years*. Washington, DC: National Association for the Education of Young Children.

Copley, J. V. (2000). *The young child and mathematics*. Washington, DC: National Association for the Education of Young Children.

Copley, J. V. (Ed.). (2004). *Showcasing mathematics for the young child* (chap. 3, Geometry). Reston, VA: National Council of Teachers of Mathematics.

Epstein, A. S., & Gainsley, S. (2005). *Math in the preschool classroom*. Ypsilanti, MI: High/Scope.

Geometry and geometric thinking [Focus issue]. (1999). *Teaching Children Mathematics, 5*(6).

Golbeck, S. L. (2005). Research in review: Building foundations for spatial literacy in early childhood. *Young Children, 60*(6), 72–83.

Greenes, C. E., & House, P. A. (Eds.). (2001). *Navigating through geometry in prekindergarten–grade 2*. Reston, VA: National Council of Teachers of Mathematics.

Hewitt, K. (2001). Blocks as a tool for learning: A historical and contemporary perspective. *Young Children, 56*(1), 6–12.

Hynes, M. E., Dixon, J. K., & Adams, T. L. (2002). Investigations: Rubber-band rockets. *Teaching Children Mathematics, 8*(7), 390–393.

Learning Resources. (2007). *Hands-on standards.* Vernon Hills, IL: Author.

Lindquist, M. M., & Clements, D. H. (2001). Principles and standards. Geometry must be vital. *Teaching Children Mathematics, 7*(7), 409–415.

Marsh, J., Loesing, J., & Soucie, M. (2004). Math by the month: Martian frontiers. *Teaching Children Mathematics, 11*(2), 80.

National Council of Teachers of Mathematics. (2007). *Curriculum focal points.* Reston, VA: Author. Retrieved May 24, 2007, from http://www.nctm.org

Newburger, A., & Vaughn, E. (2006). *Teaching numeracy, language and literacy with blocks.* St. Paul, MN: Redleaf Press.

Richardson, K. (2004). Designing math trails for the elementary school. *Teaching Children Mathematics, 11*(1), 8–14.

Sarow, G. A. (2001). Miniature sleds, Go go go! *Science and Children, 39*(3), 16–21.

Tickle, L. (1990). *Design technology in primary classrooms.* London: Falmer.

# Unit 14
## Parts and Wholes

## OBJECTIVES

After reading this unit, you should be able to:

- Explain and apply the NCTM expectations for part–whole relationships.
- Describe the three types of part–whole relationships.
- Assess and evaluate a child's knowledge of parts and wholes.
- Do informal and structured part–whole activities with young children.

Young children have a natural understanding and interest in **parts** and **wholes** that can be used later as a bridge to understanding **fractions**, which are a third-grade focal point (see Unit 29). NCTM (2000) expectations include that young children will develop a sense of whole numbers and represent them in many ways by breaking groups down into smaller parts. They will also understand and represent commonly used fractions such as one-quarter, one-third, and one-half. They should learn that objects and their own bodies are made up of special (unique) parts, that sets of things can be divided into parts, and that whole things can be divided into smaller parts.

### Parts of Wholes

- Bodies have parts (arms, legs, head).
- A car has parts (engine, doors, steering wheel, seats).
- A house has parts (kitchen, bathroom, bedroom, living room).
- A chair has parts (seat, legs, back).

### Division of Groups into Parts

- They pass out cookies for snack.
- They deal cards for a game of picture rummy.
- They give each friend one of their toys with which to play.
- They divide their blocks so that each child may build a house.

### Division of Whole Things into Parts

- One cookie is broken in half.
- An orange is divided into several segments.
- A carrot or banana is sliced into parts.
- The contents of a bottle of soda pop are put into two or more cups.
- A large piece of paper is cut into smaller pieces.

The young child focuses on the number of things he sees. Two-year-old Pablo breaks up his graham cracker into small pieces. "I have more than you," he says to Mukki, who has one whole graham cracker also. Pablo does not see that—although he has more *pieces* of cracker—he does not have more cracker. Ms. Moore shows Chris a whole apple. "How many apples do I have?" "One," says Chris. "Now watch," says Ms. Moore as she cuts the apple into two pieces. "How many apples do I have now?" "Two!" answers Chris. As the child enters concrete op-

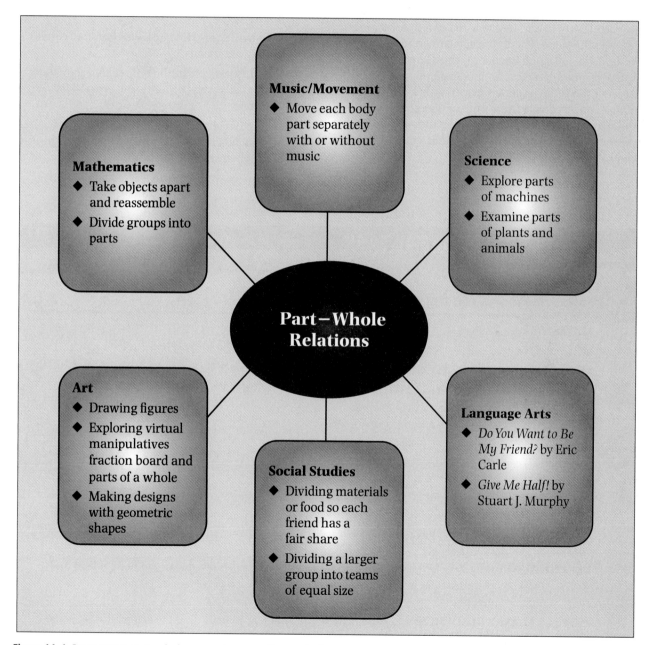

**Figure 14–1** Integrating part–whole concepts across the curriculum.

erations, he will see that a single apple is always a single apple even though it may be cut into parts.

Gradually the child is able to see that a whole is made up of parts. He also begins to see that parts may be the same (equal) in size and amount or different (unequal) in size and amount. He compares number and size (see Unit 11) and develops the concepts of more, less, and the same. These concepts are prerequisites to the understanding of fractions, which are introduced in the primary grades. An understanding of more, less, and the same underlies learning that objects and groups can be divided into two or more equal parts while still remaining the same amount. Part–whole concepts can be integrated into other content areas (Figure 14–1).

## ASSESSMENT

The teacher should observe, as the child works and plays, whether she uses the words *part* and *whole* and whether she uses them correctly. The teacher should note her actions.

■ Does she try to divide items to be shared equally among her friends?

■ Will she think of cutting or breaking something into smaller parts if there is not enough for everyone?

■ Does she realize when a part of something is missing (such as the wheel of a toy truck, the arm of a doll, the handle of a cup)?

Interview questions would be of the following form.

---

## SAMPLE ASSESSMENT TASK

**3H**                                                                **Preoperational Ages 2–3**

**Parts and Wholes, Missing Parts: Unit 14**

| | |
|---|---|
| **METHOD:** | Interview. |
| **SKILL:** | Child is able to tell which part(s) of objects and/or pictures of objects are missing. |
| **MATERIALS:** | Several objects and/or pictures of objects and/or people with parts missing. |
| **Objects:** | A doll with a leg or an arm missing |
| | A car with a wheel missing |
| | A cup with a handle broken off |
| | A chair with a leg gone |
| | A face with only one eye |
| | A house with no door |
| **Pictures:** | Mount pictures of common things on poster board. Parts can be cut off before mounting. |
| **PROCEDURE:** | Show the child each object or picture. LOOK CAREFULLY. WHICH PART IS MISSING FROM THIS? |
| **EVALUATION:** | Observe whether the child is able to tell which parts are missing in both objects and pictures. Does he have the language label for each part? Can he perceive what is missing? |

**INSTRUCTIONAL RESOURCE:** Charlesworth, R., and Lind, K. K. (2010). *Math and science for young children* (6th ed.). Clifton Park, NY: Cengage Learning.

## SAMPLE ASSESSMENT TASK

**5F** Preoperational Ages 4–5

### Parts and Wholes, Parts of a Whole: Unit 14

| | |
|---|---|
| **METHOD:** | Interview. |
| **SKILL:** | The child can recognize that a whole divided into parts is still the same amount. |
| **MATERIALS:** | Apple and knife. |
| **PROCEDURE:** | Show the child the apple. HOW MANY APPLES DO I HAVE? After you are certain the child understands that there is one apple, cut the apple into two equal halves. HOW MANY APPLES DO I HAVE NOW? HOW DO YOU KNOW? If the child says "Two," press the halves together and ask, HOW MANY APPLES DO I HAVE NOW? Then cut the apple into fourths and eighths, following the same procedure. |
| **EVALUATION:** | If the child can tell you that there is still one apple when it is cut into parts, she is able to mentally reverse the cutting process and may be leaving the preoperational period. |

**INSTRUCTIONAL RESOURCE:** Charlesworth, R., and Lind, K. K. (2010). *Math and science for young children* (6th ed.). Clifton Park, NY: Cengage Learning.

## SAMPLE ASSESSMENT TASK

**6D** Preoperational Ages 5–6

### Parts and Wholes, Parts of Sets: Unit 14

| | |
|---|---|
| **METHOD:** | Interview. |
| **SKILL:** | The child can divide a group of objects into smaller groups. |
| **MATERIALS:** | Three small dolls (or paper cutouts) and a box of pennies or other small objects. |
| **PROCEDURE:** | Have the three dolls arranged in a row. I WANT TO GIVE EACH DOLL SOME PENNIES. SHOW ME HOW TO DO IT SO EACH DOLL WILL HAVE THE SAME AMOUNT. |
| **EVALUATION:** | Note how the child approaches the problem. Does he give each doll one penny at a time in sequence? Does he count out pennies until there are three groups with the same amount? Does he divide the pennies in a random fashion? Does he have a method for finding out if each has the same amount? |

**INSTRUCTIONAL RESOURCE:** Charlesworth, R., and Lind, K. K. (2010). *Math and science for young children* (6th ed.). Clifton Park, NY: Cengage Learning.

## NATURALISTIC ACTIVITIES

The newborn infant is not aware that all her body parts are part of her. Her early explorations lead her to find out that her hand is connected via an arm to her shoulder and that those toes she sees at a distance are connected to her legs. As she explores objects, she learns that they also have different parts. As she begins to sort and move objects around, she learns about parts and wholes of groups.

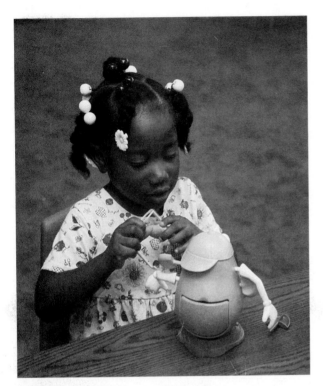

This child is engaged in naturalistic experiences that provide opportunities for activities involving parts and wholes.

The following are some examples of the young child's use of the part–whole idea.

■ Two-year-old Pablo has a hotdog on his plate. The hotdog is cut into six pieces. He gives two pieces to his father, gives two to his mother, and keeps two for himself.

■ Three-year-old Han is playing with some toy milk bottles. He says to Ms. Brown, "You take two like me."

■ Three-year-old Kate is sitting on a stool in the kitchen. She sees three eggs boiling in a pan on the stove. She points as she looks at her mother. "One for you, one for me, and one for Dad."

■ Tanya is slicing a carrot. "Look, I have a whole bunch of carrots now."

■ Juanita is lying on her cot at the beginning of nap time. She holds up her leg. "Mrs. Raymond, is this part of a woman?"

■ Ayi runs up to Mr. Brown. "Look! I have a whole tangerine."

## INFORMAL ACTIVITIES

There are many times during the day when a teacher can help children develop their understanding of parts and wholes. The teacher can use the words *part, whole*, **divide**, and **half**.

■ "Today, everyone gets *half* of an apple and *half* of a sandwich."

■ "Too bad; *part* of this game is missing."

■ "Take this basket of crackers, and *divide* them up so everyone gets some."

■ "No, we won't cut the carrots up. Each child gets a *whole* carrot."

■ "Give John *half* the blocks so he can build, too."

■ "We have only one apple left. Let's *divide* it up."

■ "Point to the *part* of the body when I say the name."

Adults take the opportunity to provide an informal lesson. "Good, you gave everyone at our picnic a drink."

Children can be given tasks that require them to learn about parts and wholes. When children are asked to pass something, to cut up vegetables or fruit, or to share materials, they learn about parts and wholes.

## STRUCTURED ACTIVITIES

The child can be given structured experiences in all three types of part–whole relationships. Activities can be done that help the child become aware of special parts of people, animals, and things. Other groups of activities involve dividing groups into smaller groups. The third type of activity gives the child experiences in dividing wholes into parts.

These children are engaged in a structured activity with their teacher. After he asks them to separate and play their instruments individually, he will then have them all play together again as a whole group.

## ACTIVITIES

### Parts and Wholes: Parts of Things

**OBJECTIVE:** To learn the meaning of the term *part* as it refers to parts of objects, people, and animals.

**MATERIALS:** Objects or pictures of objects with parts missing.

**NATURALISTIC AND INFORMAL ACTIVITIES:** Provide students time to play with a wide variety of toys and other objects. Label the parts—such as doll body parts or parts of vehicles or furniture—as fits naturally occurring situations. For example: "You put a shoe on each of the doll's feet." "There are four wheels on the truck." "You found all the pieces of the puzzle." Ask questions such as "Which toys have wheels?" "Which toys have arms and legs?" Comment on sharing: "That is really nice that you gave your friend some of your blocks." Note the examples given earlier in this unit.

**STRUCTURED ACTIVITIES:**  1.  The Broken Toys
Show the child some broken toys or pictures of broken toys. WHAT'S MISSING FROM THESE TOYS? After the child tells what is missing from each toy, bring out the missing parts (or pictures of missing parts). FIND THE MISSING PART THAT GOES WITH EACH TOY.

2.  Who (or What) Is Hiding?
The basic game is to hide someone or something behind a screen so that only a part is showing. The child then guesses who or what is hidden. Here are some variations.

a.  Two or more children hide behind a divider screen, a door, or a chair. Only a foot or a hand of one is shown. The other children guess whose body part can be seen.

*(continued)*

b. The children are shown several objects. The objects are then placed behind a screen, and a part of one object is shown. The child must guess which thing the part belongs to. (To make the task harder, the parts can be shown without the children knowing first what the choices will be.)

c. Repeat the activity using pictures.

- Cut out magazine pictures (or draw your own) and mount them on cardboard. Cut a piece of construction paper to use for screening most of the picture. Say, LOOK AT THE PART THAT IS SHOWING. WHAT IS HIDDEN BEHIND THE PAPER?

- Mount magazine pictures on construction paper. Cut out a hole in another piece of construction paper of the same size. Staple the piece of paper onto the one with the picture on it so that a part of the picture can be seen. Say, LOOK THROUGH THE HOLE. GUESS WHAT IS IN THE PICTURE UNDER THE COVER.

**FOLLOW-UP:** Play the "What's Missing" lotto game (Childcraft) or games from "What's Missing? Parts & Wholes, Young Learners' Puzzles" (Teaching Resources) (company addresses are given in Unit 39). Read and discuss books such as *Tail Toes Eyes Ears Nose* by Marilee Robin Burton and those listed in the Figure 14–1 web.

## Parts and Wholes: Dividing Groups

**OBJECTIVE:**  To give the child practice in dividing groups into parts (smaller groups).

**MATERIALS:**  Two or more small containers and some small objects such as pennies, dry beans, or buttons.

**NATURALISTIC AND INFORMAL ACTIVITIES:**  Provide the children with opportunities to explore small objects and containers. Observe how they use the materials. Do they put materials together that are the same or similar? (See Unit 10.) Do they count items? Do they compare groups? Do they put some similar items in different containers? Note the examples given earlier in this unit.

**STRUCTURED ACTIVITIES:**  Set out the containers (start with two and increase the number as the child is able to handle more). Put the pennies or other objects in a bowl next to the containers. DIVIDE THESE UP SO EACH CONTAINER HAS SOME. Note whether the child goes about the task in an organized way and whether he tries to put the same number in each container. Encourage the children to talk about what they have done. DO THEY ALL HAVE THE SAME AMOUNT? DOES ONE HAVE MORE? HOW DO YOU KNOW? IF YOU PUT ALL THE PENNIES BACK IN THE SAME CONTAINER, WOULD YOU STILL HAVE THE SAME AMOUNT? LET'S DO IT AND CHECK THE AMOUNT. Note whether the children realize that the total amount does not change when the objects in the group are separated. In other words, can they conserve number?

**FOLLOW-UP:**  Increase the number of smaller groups to be made. Use different types of containers and different objects.

## Parts and Wholes

**OBJECTIVE:** To divide whole things into two or more parts.

**MATERIALS:** Real things or pictures of things that can be divided into parts by cutting, tearing, breaking, or pouring.

**NATURALISTIC AND INFORMAL ACTIVITIES:** Children should have plenty of opportunities to explore puzzles, construction toys, easily divisible fruits (such as oranges), etc. Talk about the parts and wholes as in the examples given earlier in this unit.

**STRUCTURED ACTIVITIES:**
1. Have the children cut up fruits and vegetables for snack or lunch. They have a sharp knife so that the job is not frustrating, but be sure they are shown how to cut properly so as not to hurt themselves. Children with poor coordination can tear lettuce, break off orange slices, and cut the easier things such as string beans or bananas.
2. Give the child a piece of paper. Have her cut (or tear) it and then fit the pieces back together. Ask her to count how many parts she made.
3. Give the child a piece of Play-Doh or clay. Have her cut it with a dull knife or tear it into pieces. How many parts did she make?
4. Use a set of plastic measuring cups and a larger container of water. Have the children guess how many of each of the smaller cups full of water will fill the one-cup measure. Let each child try the one-fourth, one-third, and one-half cups, and ask them to count how many of each of these cups will fill the one cup.

**FOLLOW-UP:** Make or purchase* some structured part–whole materials. Examples include the following.

1. Fraction pies—circular shapes available in rubber and magnetic versions.
2. Materials that picture two halves of a whole.
   Halves to Wholes (DLM)
   Match-ups (Childcraft and Playskool)
3. Puzzles that have a sequence of difficulty with the same picture cut into two, three, and more parts.
   Basic Cut Puzzles (DLM)
   Fruit and Animal Puzzles (Teaching Resources)
4. Dowley Doos take-apart transportation toys (Lauri)

*Addresses are given in Unit 39.

## IDEAS FOR CHILDREN WITH SPECIAL NEEDS

Preprimary grade children learn about parts and wholes as an aspect of both their social skills and their mathematics concept development. Children with behavior problems may have difficulty sharing materials but should be provided with many opportunities to do so—for example, passing out materials to a group or giving part of what he or she is using to another child.

## EVALUATION

The adult should observe and note if the child shows increased use of part–whole words and more skills in his daily activities.

- ■ Can he divide groups of things into smaller groups?
- ■ Can he divide wholes into parts?
- ■ Does he realize that objects, people, and animals have parts that are unique to each?
- ■ Can he share equally with others?

## SUMMARY

Young children have a natural interest in parts and wholes. This interest and the ideas learned are the foundations of learning about fractions.

The child learns that things, people, and animals have parts. She learns that sets can be divided into parts (sets with smaller numbers of things). She learns that whole things can be divided into smaller parts or pieces.

Experiences in working with parts and wholes help the young child move from the preoperational level to the concrete view and to understanding that the whole is no more than the sum of all its parts. Such experiences can also teach some essential social skills.

## KEY TERMS

| divide | half | wholes |
|--------|------|--------|
| fractions | parts | |

## SUGGESTED ACTIVITIES

1. Observe in a Montessori classroom. Write a description of all the materials that are designed to teach the concept of part–whole.
2. Assess the part–whole concept as exhibited by one or more young children. Based on the results, plan some part–whole activities. Do the activities with the children and evaluate the results.
3. Add part–whole activities to your file or notebook.
4. If the school budget allocated $300 for part–whole materials, how would you spend it?
5. Using guidelines from Activity 5 of Unit 2, evaluate one or more of the following software programs that are designed to reinforce the concept of parts and wholes.
   - ■ *Math Express: Fractions* (preschool–grade 6). A variety of fraction activities. (Hazelton, PA: K–12 Software)

- ■ *Richard Scarry's Busytown* (preschool–grade 1). Many construction activities. (http://www.childrenssoftwareonline.com)
- ■ *Richard Scarry's Best Activity Center Ever* (ages 3–7). Put Mr. Fumble's billboard back together. (http://www.childrenssoftwareonline.com)
- ■ *Encyclopedia Britannica Math Club* (preschool–grade 1). A magical journey through the Fairy Tale Forest helps children acquire many math concepts. (http://www.TRLstore.com)
- ■ The National Library of Virtual Manipulatives (http://nlvm.usu.edu/) includes activities entitled "fraction bars" and "parts of a whole."

## REVIEW

**A.** Into which of the following categories do the eight listed items fit? (a) Things, people, and animals have parts. (b) Sets can be divided into parts. (c) Whole things can be divided into smaller parts or pieces.

1. Chris shares his doughnut.
2. Pieces of a cat puzzle.
3. Tina gives Fong some of her crayons.
4. Larry tears a piece of paper.
5. Pete takes half of the clay.
6. Kate puts the yellow blocks in one pile and the orange blocks in another pile.
7. A teddy bear's leg.
8. Juanita takes the fork from the place setting of utensils.

**B.** Describe the types of experiences and activities that support a child's development of the concept of parts and wholes.

**C.** Explain how a child's knowledge of parts and wholes can be assessed through observation and interview.

**D.** Decide which of the NCTM expectations for parts and wholes match the examples in question A.

## REFERENCES

Burton, M. R. (1992). *Tail, toes, eyes, ears, nose*. New York: Harper Trophy. (Children's book that teaches parts of eight animals.)

National Council of Teachers of Mathematics. (2000). *Principles and standards for school mathematics*. Reston, VA: Author.

## FURTHER READING AND RESOURCES

Axworhy, A. (1998). *Guess what I am*. Cambridge, MA: Candlewick Press. (Children's peephole book; they can guess to whom body parts belong.)

Colomb, J., & Kennedy, K. (2005). Your better half. *Teaching Children Mathematics, 12*(4), 180–190.

Copley, J. V. (Ed.). (1999). *Mathematics in the early years*. Washington, DC: National Association for the Education of Young Children.

Copley, J. V. (2000). *The young child and mathematics*. Washington, DC: National Association for the Education of Young Children.

Giles, R. M., Parmer, L., & Byrd, K. (2003). Putting the pieces together: Developing early concepts of fractions. *Dimensions, 31*(1), 3–8.

Kosbob, S., & Moyer, P. S. (2004). Picnicking with fractions. *Teaching Children Mathematics, 10*(7), 375–381.

Lietze, A. R., & Stump, S. (2007). Sharing cookies. *Teaching Children Mathematics, 13*(7), 378–379.

Luciana, B., & Tharlet, E. (2000). *How will we get to the beach?* New York: North-South. (Children's book that illustrates part–whole of a group.)

National Council of Teachers of Mathematics. (2007). *Curriculum focal points*. Reston, VA: Author. Retrieved May 24, 2007, from http://www.nctm.org

Powell, C. A., & Hunting, R. P. (2003). Fractions in the early-years curriculum. *Teaching Children Mathematics, 10*(1), 6–7.

Richardson, K. (1999). *Developing number concepts: Planning guide*. Parsippany, NJ: Seymour.

Riddle, M., & Rodzwell, B. (2000). Fractions: What happens between kindergarten and the army? *Teaching Children Mathematics, 7*(4), 202–206.

# Unit 15

## Language and Concept Formation

### OBJECTIVES

After reading this unit, you should be able to:

- Explain the importance of language to the NCTM process expectations.
- Explain two ways to describe a child's understanding of concept words.
- Describe the philosophy of literacy instruction as it applies to mathematics and science.
- Use literature, writing, drawing, and speaking to support the development of mathematics and science language.

The NCTM (2000) standards include expectations in five process areas: **problem solving**, **reasoning**, **communications**, **connections**, and **representation**. *Problem solving* was discussed in Unit 3 as the major process focus in mathematics. For the youngest mathematicians, problem solving is the most important means of building mathematical knowledge. Problems usually arise from daily routines, play activities and materials, and stories. As children work with the materials and activities already described, they figure things out using the processes of reasoning, communications, connections, and representation. Logical *reasoning* develops in the early years and is especially important in working with classification and with patterns. Reasoning enables students to draw logical conclusions, apply logical classification skills, explain their thinking, justify their problem solutions and processes, apply patterns and relationships to arrive at solutions, and make sense out of mathematics and science. *Communication* via oral, written, and pictorial language provides the means for explaining problem-solving and reasoning processes. Children need to provide a description of what they do, why they do it, and what they have accomplished. They need to use the language of mathematics in their explanations. The important *connections* for young mathematicians are the ones between the naturalistic and informal mathematics they learn first and the formal mathematics they learn later in school. Concrete objects can serve as the bridge between informal and formal mathematics. Young children can "*represent* their thoughts about, and understanding of, mathematical ideas through oral and written language, physical gestures, drawings, and invented and conventional symbols" (NCTM, 2000, p. 136).

What the child does—and what the child says—tells the teacher what the child knows about math and science. The older the child gets, the more important concepts become. The language the child uses and how she uses it provide clues to the teacher regarding the child's conceptual development. However, children may imitate adult use of words before the concept is highly developed. The child's language system is usually well developed by age 4; by this age, children's sentences are much the same as an adult's. Children are at a point where their vocabulary is growing rapidly.

The adult observes what the child does from infancy through age 2 and looks for the first understanding and the use of words. Between the ages of 2 and 4, the child starts to put more words together into longer sentences. She also learns more words and what they mean.

Questions are used to assess the young child's concept development. Which is the big ball? Which is the circle? The child's understanding of words is checked by having her respond with an appropriate action.

- "Point to the big ball."
- "Find two chips."
- "Show me the picture in which the boy is on the chair."

These tasks do not require the child to say any words. She need only point, touch, or pick up something. Once the child demonstrates her understanding of math words by using gestures or other nonverbal answers, she can move on to questions she must answer with one or more words. The child can be asked the same questions as before in a way that requires a verbal response.

- (The child is shown two balls, one big and one small.) "Tell me, what is different about these balls?"
- (The child is shown a group of objects.) "Tell me, how many are there in this group?"
- (The child is shown a picture of a boy sitting on a chair.) "Tell me, where is the boy?"

The child learns many concept words as she goes about her daily activities. It has been found that, by the time a child starts kindergarten, she uses many concept words that have been learned in a naturalistic way. Examples have been included in each of Units 8 through 14. The child uses both comments and questions. Comments might be as follows:

- "Mom, I want two *pieces* of cheese."
- "I have a *bunch* of birdseed."

- "Mr. Brown, this chair is *small*."
- "*Yesterday* we went to the zoo."
- "The string is *long*."
- "This is the *same* as this."
- "The foot fits *in* the shoe."
- "This cracker is a *square* shape."
- "Look, some of the worms are *long* and some are *short*, some are *fat* and some are *thin*."
- "The *first* bean seed I planted is *taller* than the *second* one."
- "Outer space is *far* away."

Questions could be like these:

- "How *old* is he?"
- "*When* is Christmas?"
- "*When* will I grow as *big* as you?"
- "*How many* are coming for dinner?"
- "Who has *more*?"
- "What *time* is my TV program?"
- "Is this a school *day*, or is it *Saturday*?"
- "What makes the bubbles when the water gets *hot*?"
- "Why does this roller always go *down* its ramp *faster* than that roller goes *down* its ramp?"
- "Why are the leaves turning *brown* and *red* and *gold* and falling *down on* the ground?"

The answers that the child gets to these questions can help increase the number of concept words she knows and can use.

The teacher needs to be aware of using concept words during center time, lunch, and other times when a structured concept lesson is not being done. She should also note which words the child uses during free times.

The teacher should encourage the child to use concept words even though they may not be used in an accurate, adult way. For example:

- "I can count—one, two, three, five, ten."
- "Aunt Helen is coming after my last nap." (indicates future time)

- "I will measure my paper." (holds ruler against the edge of the paper)
- "Last night Grandpa was here." (actually several days ago)
- "I'm six years old." (really 2 years old)
- "I have a million dollars." (has a handful of play money)

Adults should accept the child's use of the words but use the words correctly themselves. Soon the child will develop a higher-level use of words as she is able to grasp higher-level ideas. For the 2- or 3-year-old, any group of more than two or three things may be called a *bunch*. Instead of using *big* and *little*, the child may use family words: "This is the mommy block" and "This is the baby block." Time (see Unit 19) is one concept that takes a long time to grasp. A young child may use the same word to mean different time periods. The following examples were said by a three-year-old.

- "*Last night* we went to the beach." (meaning last summer)
- "*Last night* I played with Chris." (meaning yesterday)
- "*Last night* I went to Kenny's house." (meaning three weeks ago)

For this child, *last night* means any time in the past. One by one he will learn that there are words that refer to times past such as last summer, yesterday, and three weeks ago.

Computer activities can also add to vocabulary. The teacher uses concept words when explaining how to use the programs. Children enjoy working at the computer with friends and will use the concept words to communicate with each other as they work cooperatively to solve the problems presented on the screen.

We have already introduced many concept words, and more will appear in the units to come. The pre-kindergarten child continually learns words. The next section presents the concept words that most children can use and understand by the time they complete kindergarten. However, caution must be taken in assessing children's actual understanding of the concept words they use. The use of a concept word does not in

We'll have a party *tomorrow*.

itself indicate an understanding of the concept. Children imitate behavior they hear and see. Real understanding can be determined through an assessment interview.

## CONCEPT WORDS

The words that follow have appeared in Units 8 through 14.

- *One-to-one correspondence*: one, pair, more, each, some, group, bunch, amount
- *Number and counting*: zero, one, two, three, four, five, six, seven, eight, nine, ten; how many, count, group, one more than, next, number
- *Logic and classifying*: groups; descriptive words for color, shape, size, materials, pattern, texture, function, association, class names, and common features; belong with; goes with; is used with; put with; the same
- *Comparing*: more, less, big, small, large, little, long, short, fat, skinny, heavy, light, fast, slow, cold, hot, thick, thin, wide, narrow, near, far, later, sooner, earlier, older, younger, newer, higher, lower, loud, soft (sound)
- *Geometry (shape)*: circle, square, triangle, rectangle, ellipse, rhombus, shape, round,

point, square prism (cube), rectangular prism, triangular prism, cylinder, pyramid

- *Geometry (spatial sense): where* (on, off, on top of, over, under, in, out, into, out of, top, bottom, above, below, in front of, in back of, behind, beside, by, next to, between); *which way* (up, down, forward, backward, around, through, to, from, toward, away from, sideways, across); *distance* (near, far, close to, far from); map, floor plan
- *Parts and wholes*: part, whole, divide, share, pieces, some, half, one-quarter, one-third

Words that will be introduced later include:

- *Ordering*: first, second, third; big, bigger, biggest; few, fewer, fewest; large, larger, largest; little, littler, littlest; many, more, most; thick, thicker, thickest; thin, thinner, thinnest; last, next, then
- *Measurement of volume, length, weight, and temperature*: little, big, medium, tiny, large, size, tall, short, long, far, farther, closer, near, high, higher, thin, wide, deep, cup, pint, quart, gallon, ounces, foot, inch, mile, narrow, measure, hot, cold, warm, cool, thermometer, temperature, pounds
- *Measurement of time and sequence*: morning, afternoon, evening, night, day, soon, week, tomorrow, yesterday, early, late, a long time ago, once upon a time, minute, second, hour, new, old, already, Easter, Kwanza, Christmas, Passover, Hanukkah, June 10th, Pioneer Days, Cinco de Mayo, birthday, now, year, weekend, clock, calendar, watch, when, time, date, sometimes, then, before, present, soon, while, never, once, sometime, next, always, fast, slow, speed, Monday (and other days of the week), January (and other months of the year), winter, spring, summer, fall
- *Practical*: money, cash register, penny, dollar, buy, pay, change, cost, check, free, store, map, recipe, measure, cup, tablespoon, teaspoon, boil, simmer, bake, degrees, time, hours, minutes, freeze, chill, refrigerate, pour, mix, separate, add, combine, ingredients

Words can be used before they are presented in a formal structured activity. The child who speaks can become familiar with words and even say them before he understands the concepts they stand for. As children between ages 5 and 7 shift into concrete operations they gain a conceptual understanding of more math vocabulary, some of which they have already used and applied in their preoperational way.

- *Primary-level words*: addition, subtraction, number facts, plus, add, minus, take away, total, sum, equal, difference, amount, altogether, in all, are left, number line, place value, rename, patterns, 1s, 10s, 100s, digit, multiplication, division, equation, times, divide, product, even, odd, fractions, halves, fourths, thirds, wholes, numerator, denominator, hours, minutes, seconds, measure, inches, feet, yards, miles, centimeter, meter, kilometer

## MATHEMATICS, SCIENCE, AND LITERACY

Written language learning is also critical during the preschool, kindergarten, and primary years. Children's literature is an important element in the curriculum. Preschoolers need to engage in pre-reading and pre-writing experiences through exploration of quality children's literature, story dictation, and story retelling (Morrow & Gambrell, 2004). By first grade, children are expected to be in the beginning stages of becoming readers. How they should be taught has been a subject of controversy. Wren (2003) summarized the situation as follows: Some educators believe reading should begin with instruction in the rules of printed text (letters, sounds, etc.), whereas others believe reading should develop naturally through experiences with good literature. These two views are referred to as **phonics** versus **whole language**. The **balanced reading** approach, whereby phonics and whole language are used in a balanced fashion, is an attempt to settle the question. However, according to Wren (2003), there is no agreement on what constitutes a balanced reading program. Wren suggests that a truly balanced program should include both phonics and whole language approaches but should be refocused on the needs of children.

The focus needs to shift to the student and the individual learning needs that can be revealed through ongoing, diagnostic assessment. Only when all teachers learn to diagnose student reading skills and respond with focused, deliberate instruction will literacy be available to all children. (p. 8)

Literacy instruction has turned away from a strictly whole language philosophy, yet that approach may still be valuable for placing mathematics and sci-

Literature experiences can provide a basis for problem solving and concept development.

ence concepts and skills in meaningful contexts given the emphasis in those disciplines on communication, reasoning, and making connections. Children can listen to good literature that is relevant to mathematics and science and then experiment with writing. They can explain and discuss, record data, and write about their mathematics and science explorations. Through these activities, children develop their spoken and written language vocabulary in a meaningful context. Refer to Unit 3 for applications to problem solving.

## LITERATURE AND MATHEMATICS AND SCIENCE

There has been a tremendous growth in the use of children's literature as a springboard to curriculum integration in mathematics and science instruction. There have long been many books that include mathematics and science concepts (see Appendix B), but there has recently been an increasing number of major journal articles that describe literature-centered activities, books that present thematic activities centered on pieces of literature, and books featuring annotated lists of children's books related to mathematics and science. Examples of such literature have been included in previous units, and more can be found in subsequent units. The "Further Reading and Resources" section of this unit includes references to articles describing mathematics and science studies that focus on children's literature.

An example of a book used as a focus for mathematics, science, and writing is described by Charlesworth and Lind (1995). In Claudia Wangsgaard's firstgrade classroom in Kaysville, Utah, the students kept math journals in which they wrote about their solutions to math problems. For example, one day's math activities centered on the book *One Gorilla* by Atsuko Morozumi. The narrative starts with one gorilla who wanders through each page; the book includes scenes in the jungle as well as in other locations. Jungle and nonjungle inhabitants are introduced in groups in numerical order up to ten: two butterflies and one gorilla among the flowers, three budgies and one gorilla in the house, four squirrels and one gorilla in the woods, and so on. The students discussed each illustration, locating the gorilla and counting the other creatures.

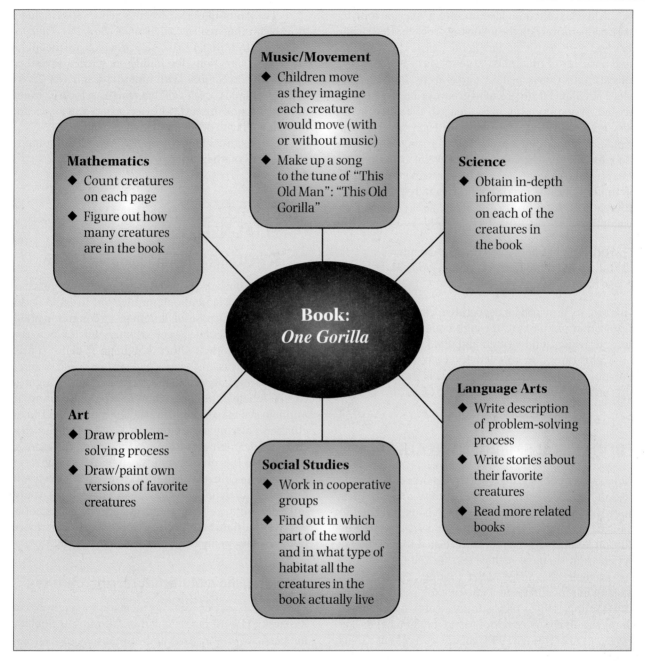

**Music/Movement**

◆ Children move as they imagine each creature would move (with or without music)

◆ Make up a song to the tune of "This Old Man": "This Old Gorilla"

**Mathematics**

◆ Count creatures on each page

◆ Figure out how many creatures are in the book

**Science**

◆ Obtain in-depth information on each of the creatures in the book

**Book:**
*One Gorilla*

**Art**

◆ Draw problem-solving process

◆ Draw/paint own versions of favorite creatures

**Social Studies**

◆ Work in cooperative groups

◆ Find out in which part of the world and in what type of habitat all the creatures in the book actually live

**Language Arts**

◆ Write description of problem-solving process

◆ Write stories about their favorite creatures

◆ Read more related books

**Figure 15–1** An integration across the curriculum with literature as the focus.

The class then divided up into groups of four to work cooperatively on the following problem: *How many creatures were there altogether in this story?* The students used a variety of materials: large sheets of blank paper, tubs of Unifix Cubes, pencils, and crayons. Mrs. Wangsgaard circulated from group to group, providing help as needed. When everyone was finished, the class members reassembled. A reporter from each small group explained the group results, summarizing what was recorded on the group's poster. Several communication procedures were used, such as drawing the number of Unifix Cubes or making marks to tally the number of creatures. Each group also wrote its procedure. For example:

> We did unafick cubes and then we did tally Marcks and there were 56. *Jason, Caitlin, Malorie, and Kady* (p. 171)

This activity provided for cooperative learning and communication of thinking through concrete representations, drawings, and written and oral language. Figure 15–1 illustrates how this activity might be included in a planning web for an extended study of jungle inhabitants using the book *One Gorilla* as the focus.

## BOOKS FOR EMERGENT READERS

Zaner-Bloser publishes sets of easy readers that provide beginning readers with the opportunity to apply their math and science process skills. Each book is related to the NCTM standards. *Harry's Math Books*, authored by Sharon Young, present problems related to real-life experiences in simple repetitive text for the early reader. For example, *The Shape Maker* (Young, 1997) relates making cutout shapes to a kite-making project. *At The Park* (Young, 1998) moves from identifying circles in the environment to a circle of friends holding hands. *Six Pieces of Cake* (Young, 1998) relates a whole cake to its parts as pieces are distributed one by one. Other books in the series include concepts such as numeracy and counting skills, skip-counting forward and backward, using fractions, using ordinal numbers, comparing and ordering, sorting and classifying, and performing early operations. The teacher guide suggests extension activities based on each book.

The Zaner-Bloser emergent science series includes little beginning readers such as *A Bird Has Feathers*, *Seeds*, and *How Many Legs?* Also provided are meaningful stories, directions for hands-on science investigations, and correlations with national standards. Topics include animals, cycles of life, earth, self-care, water, light and sound, insects, weather, space, and forces and motion—all with accompanying teacher guides.

As resources increase on the Web, ideas for literature-related mathematics are increasing.

## IDEAS FOR CHILDREN WITH SPECIAL NEEDS

### Speech, Language, and Communication

Allen and Cowdery (2005) describe the importance of speech, language, and communication in child development. The purpose of language is communication, and clearly articulated speech makes for the best verbal communication. Other language systems consist of facial expressions, signs, and gestures. For children with hearing disabilities, American Sign Language can be a helpful augmentation for communicating. In an inclusive classroom, the teacher must attend to all children's attempts to communicate. Math and science can provide many opportunities for communication, as indicated in this unit. Teachers can be alert for children who may need extra help in the areas of speech and language. Allen and Cowdrey point out that, for young English Language Learners, drill and practice is not as effective as naturally occurring language experience. Books can be an important language mediator.

### Maintaining a Multicultural Approach to Language with Books

Zaslavsky (1996) points out that literature is a means for participating in lives and cultures, both past and present, of people all over the world. Many picture books are available in translations from English to other languages and vice versa. A simple counting book is *¿Cuantos animals hay?* by Brian Wildsmith (1997). For Spanish speakers, this book supports their first language; for English speakers, there is the joy of learning another language. *We All Went on a Safari*, by Laurie Krebs and

Julia Cairns (2003), takes the reader on a counting journey through Tanzania. Children of African heritage see the respect given to their culture, and all children learn some Tanzanian vocabulary, customs, and geography. As can be found from the resources listed at the end of this unit, there are any math and science literacy resources that support a multicultural approach to instruction.

## SUMMARY

As children learn math and science concepts and skills, they also add many words to their vocabularies. Math and science have a language that is basic to their content and activities. Language is learned through naturalistic, informal, and structured activities. Computer activities are excellent for promoting communication among children. Books are a rich source of conceptual language that matches a child's growing understanding. They can also support a multicultural approach to instruction. The whole language philosophy of literacy learning fits well with the emphasis in mathematics and science on processes of problem solving, representation, communication, reasoning, and making connections. The current focus of reading instruction is a balanced whole language–phonics approach. For young children, books open the door to reading.

## KEY TERMS

| balanced reading | phonics | representation |
| communications | problem solving | whole language |
| connections | reasoning | |

## SUGGESTED ACTIVITIES

1. Visit a prekindergarten, a kindergarten, and a primary classroom. Observe for at least 30 minutes in each room. Write down every child and adult math and science word used. Compare the three age groups and teachers for number and variety of words used.

2. Make the concept language assessment materials described in Appendix A. Administer the tasks to 4-, 5-, and 6-year-old children. Make a list of the concept words recorded in each classroom, and count the number of times each word was used. Compare the number of different words and the total number of words heard in each classroom.

3. In the library, research the area of whole language and its relationship to mathematics and science instruction. Write a report summarizing what you learn.

4. Observe some young children engaged in concept development computer activities. Record their conversations and note how many concept words they use.

5. Select one of the concept books mentioned in this unit or from the list in Appendix B. Familiarize yourself with the content. Read the book with one or more young children. Question them to find out how many of the concept words they can use.

## REVIEW

A. Explain how language learning relates to science and mathematics concept learning.

B. Describe how a whole language approach to instruction might increase the concept vocabulary of young children.

C. Describe how the five mathematics process expectations relate to young children's learning.

## REFERENCES

Allen, K. E., & Cowdery, G. E. (2005). *The exceptional child: Inclusion in early childhood education* (5th ed.). Albany, NY: Thomson Delmar Learning.

Charlesworth, R., & Lind, K. K. (1995). Whole language and primary grades mathematics and science: Keeping up with national standards. In S. Raines (Ed.), *Whole language across the curriculum: Grades 1, 2, 3* (pp. 146–178). New York: Teachers College Press.

Krebs, L., & Cairns, J. (2003). *We all went on a safari: A counting journey through Tanzania*. Cambridge, MA: Barefoot Books.

Morrow, L. M., & Gambrell, L. B. (2004). *Using children's literature in preschool*. Newark, DE: International Reading Association.

National Council of Teachers of Mathematics. (2000). *Principles and standards for school mathematics*. Reston, VA: Author.

Wildsmith, B. (1997). *¿Cuantos animals hay?* New York: Star Bright Books.

Wren, S. (2003). *What does a "balanced approach" to reading instruction mean?* Retrieved November 26, 2004, from http://www.balancedreading.com

Young, S. (1997). *The shape maker*. Columbus, OH: Zaner-Bloser.

Young, S. (1998). *At the park*. Columbus, OH: Zaner-Bloser.

Young, S. (1998). *Six pieces of cake*. Columbus, OH: Zaner-Bloser.

Zaslavsky, C. (1996). *The multicultural math classroom*. Portsmouth, NH: Heinemann.

## FURTHER READING AND RESOURCES

Ameis, J. A. (2002). Stories invite children to solve mathematical problems. *Teaching Children Mathematics, 8*(5), 260–264.

American Association for the Advancement of Science (AAAS). (2007). *Atlas of science literacy: Project 2061* (Vol. 2). Washington, DC: Author.

Aram, R. J., Whitson, S., & Dieckhoff, R. (2001). Habitat sweet habitat. *Science and Children, 38*(4), 23–27.

Borden, J., & Geskus, E. (2001). Links to literature. The most magnificent strawberry shortcake. *Teaching Children Mathematics, 7*(9), 538–541.

Butterworth, S., & Cicero, A. M. L. (2001). Storytelling: Building a mathematics curriculum from the culture of the child. *Teaching Children Mathematics, 7*(7), 396–399.

Chapman, S. A. (2000). The M.O.O.K. Book: Students author a book about mathematics. *Teaching Children Mathematics, 6*(6), 388–390.

Cherry, L. (2006). Trade books for learning: An author's view. *Science & Children, 44*(3), 44–47.

Clements, C. H., & Sarama, J. (2006). Math all around the room! *Early Childhood Today, 21*(2), 24–30.

Dobler, C. P., & Klein, J. M. (2002). Links to literature. First graders, flies, and Frenchman's fascination: Introducing the cartesian coordinate system. *Teaching Children Mathematics, 8*(9), 540–545.

Ducolon, C. K. (2000). Quality literature as a springboard to problem solving. *Teaching Children Mathematics, 6*(7), 442–446.

Ellis, B. F. (2001). The cottonwood. *Science and Children, 38*(4), 42–46.

Farland, D. (2006). Trade books and the human endeavor of science. *Science & Children, 44*(3), 35–37.

Fleege, P. O., & Thompson, D. R. (2000). From habits to legs: Using science-themed counting books to foster connections. *Teaching Children Mathematics, 7*(2), 74–78.

Fleener, C. E., & Bucher, K. T. (2003/2004). Linking reading, science, and fiction books. *Childhood Education, 80*(2), 76–83.

Forbringer, L. L. (2004). The thirteen days of Halloween: Using children's literature to differentiate instruction in the mathematics classroom. *Teaching Children Mathematics, 11*(2), 82–90.

Forrest, K., Schnabel, D., & Williams, M. E. (2005). Math by the book. *Teaching Children Mathematics, 12*(4), 200.

Forrest, K., Schnabel, D., & Williams, M. E. (2006). Mathematics and literature, anyone? *Teaching Children Mathematics, 13*(4), 216.

Ginsburg, H. P., & Seo, K. (2000). Preschoolers' mathematical reading. *Teaching Children Mathematics, 7*(4), 226–229.

Gomez-Zwiep, S., & Straits, W. (2006). Analyzing anthropomorphisms. *Science & Children, 44*(3), 26–29.

Harms, J. M., & Lettow, L. J. (2000). Poetry and environment. *Science and Children, 37*(6), 30–33.

Hellwig, S. J., Monroe, E. E., & Jacobs, J. S. (2000). Making informed choices: Selecting children's trade books for mathematics instruction. *Teaching Children Mathematics, 7*(3), 138–143.

Henry, K. E. (2004). Links to literature. Math rules in the animal kingdom. *Teaching Children Mathematics, 10*(9), 456–463.

Hesse, P., & Lane, F. (2003). Media literacy starts young: An integrated curriculum approach. *Young Children, 58*(6), 20–26.

Keenan, S. (2004). Teaching English Language Learners. *Science and Children, 42*(2), 49–51.

Krech, B. (2003). Picture-book math. *Instructor, 112*(7), 42–43.

Kulczewski, P. (2004/2005). Vygotsky and the three bears. *Teaching Children Mathematics, 11*(5), 246–248.

Lowe, J. L., & Matthew, K. I. (2000). Puppets and prose. *Science and Children, 37*(8), 41–45.

Martinez, J. G. R., & Martinez, N. C. (2000, January). Teaching math with stories. *Teaching Pre-K–8*, 54–56.

Mathematics and literature: Celebrating children's book week, November 15–21, 2004. *Teaching Children Mathematics, 11*(4), 237–240.

McDuffie, A. M. R., & Young, T. A. (2003). Promoting mathematical discourse through children's literature. *Teaching Children Mathematics, 9*(7), 385–389.

Monhardt, L., & Monhardt, R. (2006). Creating a context for the learning of science process skills through picture books. *Early Childhood Education Journal, 34*(1), 67–72.

Monroe, E. E., Orme, M. P., & Erickson, L. B. (2002). Links to literature. *Working Cotton*: Toward an understanding of time. *Teaching Children Mathematics, 8*(8), 475–479.

National Research Council. (1996). *National science education standards*. Washington, DC: National Academies Press.

Orozco, J., & Kleven, E. (1997). *Diez deditos* [Ten little fingers]. New York: Scholastic Books.

Outstanding science trade books for children—2000. (2000). *Science and Children, 37*(6), 19–25.

Outstanding science trade books for children—2001. (2001). *Science and Children, 38*(6), 27–34.

Outstanding science trade books for students K–12—2001. (2002). *Science and Children, 39*(6), 31–38.

Outstanding science trade books for students K–12—2002. (2003). *Science and Children, 40*(6), 31–38.

Outstanding science trade books for students K–12—2003. (2004). *Science and Children, 41*(6), 35–38.

Plummer, D. M., MacShara, J., & Brown, S. K. (2003). The tree of life. *Science and Children, 40*(6), 18–21.

Ponce, G. A., & Garrison, L. (2004/2005). Overcoming the "walls" surrounding word problems. *Teaching Children Mathematics, 11*(5), 256–262.

Rice, D. C., Dudley, A. P., & Williams, C. S. (2001). How do you choose science trade books? *Science and Children, 38*(6), 18–22.

Robinson, L. (2003). Technology as a scaffold for emergent literacy: Interactive storybooks for toddlers. *Young Children, 58*(6), 42–48.

Royce, C. A. (2003). Teaching through trade books. It's pumpkin time! *Science and Children, 41*(2), 14–16.

Royce, C. A. (2004). Teaching through trade books: Fascinating fossil finds. *Science and Children, 42*(2), 22–24.

Rozanski, K. D., Beckmann, C. E., & Thompson, D. R. (2003). Exploring size with *The Grouchy Lady Bug. Teaching Children Mathematics, 10*(2), 84–89.

Rubenstein, R. N., & Thompson, D. R. (2002). Understanding and supporting children's mathematical vocabulary development. *Teaching Children Mathematics, 9*(2), 107–111.

Sarama, J., & Clements, D. H. (2006). Early math: Connecting math and literacy. *Early Childhood Today, 21*(1), 17.

Sarama, J., & Clements, D. H. (2006). Picture books that build math skills. *Early Childhood Today, 21*(3), 20.

Schon, I. (2000). Libros de ciencias en Español. *Science and Children, 37*(6), 26–29.

Schon, I. (2001). Libros de ciencias en Español. *Science and Children, 38*(6), 23–26.

Schon, I. (2002). Libros de ciencias en Español. *Science and Children, 39*(6), 22–25.

Schon, I. (2003). Libros de ciencias en Español. *Science and Children, 40*(6), 39–43.

Schon, I. (2004). Libros de ciencias en Español. *Science and Children, 41*(6), 43–47.

Shih, J. C., & Giorgis, C. (2004). Building the mathematics and literature connection through children's responses. *Teaching Children Mathematics, 10*(6), 328–333.

Taylor, G. M. (1999). Reading, writing, arithmetic—Making connections. *Teaching Children Mathematics, 6*(3), 190–197.

Texley, J. (2004). Summertime and the reading is easy. *Science and Children, 41*(9), 38–49.

Thatcher, D. (2001). Reading in the math class: Selecting and using picture books for math investigations. *Young Children, 56*(4), 20–26.

Thiessen, D. (Ed.). (2004). *Exploring mathematics through literature.* Reston, VA: National Council of Teachers of Mathematics.

Thiessen, D., Matthias, M., & Smith, J. (1998). *The wonderful world of mathematics: A critically annotated list of children's books in mathematics* (2nd ed.). Reston, VA: National Council of Teachers of Mathematics.

Torres-Velasquez, D., & Lobo, G. (2004/2005). Culturally responsive mathematics teaching and English Language Learners. *Teaching Children Mathematics, 11*(5), 249–254.

Welchman-Tischler, R. (1992). *How to use children's literature to teach mathematics.* Reston, VA: National Council of Teachers of Mathematics.

West, S., & Cox, A. (2004). *Literacy play.* Beltsville, MD: Gryphon House.

Whitin, D. J. (2002). The potentials and pitfalls of integrating literature into the mathematics program. *Teaching Children Mathematics, 8*(9), 503–504.

Whitin, D. J., & Whitin, P. (2004). *New visions for linking literature and mathematics.* Urbana, IL: National Council of Teachers of English, and Reston, VA: National Council of Teachers of Mathematics.

Worth, K., Moriarty, R., & Winokur, J. (2004). Capitalizing on literacy connections. *Science and Children, 41*(5), 35–39.

Writing to learn science [Focus issue]. (2004). *Science and Children, 42*(3).

Yopp, H. K., & Yopp, R. H. (2006). Primary students and informational texts. *Science and Children, 44*(3), 22–29.

Journals such as *Teaching Children Mathematics, Childhood Education, Dimensions, Science and Children* and *Young Children* have book review columns in each issue; many of the books reviewed apply to math and science concepts.

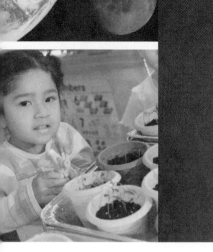

# Unit 16

## Fundamental Concepts in Science

### OBJECTIVES

After reading this unit, you should be able to:

- Design lessons that integrate fundamental science and math concepts.
- Develop naturalistic, informal, and structured activities that utilize science and math concepts.

The *National Science Education Standards* emphasize that, for children, the essence of learning lies not in memorizing fact but in carrying out the processes of inquiry—asking questions; making observations; and gathering, organizing, and analyzing data. The concepts and skills that children construct during the preprimary period are essential to investigating science problems.

The fundamental concepts and skills of one-to-one correspondence, number sense and counting, sets and classifying, comparing, shape, space, and parts and wholes are basic to developing the abilities needed for scientific inquiry. This unit shows how the concepts presented in Units 8 through 14 can be explored and used in science with children in the sensorimotor and preoperational period of development. Recommendations can be found in Unit 4, and individual assessments are detailed in Appendix A.

## ONE-TO-ONE CORRESPONDENCE

When engaged in one-to-one correspondence, children are pairing and learning basic concepts about how things are alike or different. At an early age, the pairings are made on the basis of single attributes inherent in objects (e.g., shape or color), and objects are arranged in various piles or in a chained linear sequence. This skill must be developed before grouping, sorting, and classifying can take place.

Science topics such as animals and their homes lend themselves well to matching activities. Not only are children emphasizing one-to-one correspondence by matching one animal to a particular home, they are also increasing their awareness of animals and their habitats. The questions that teachers ask will further reinforce the process skills and science content contained in the activities. The following science-related activities work well with young children.

1. Create a bulletin board background of trees (one tree should have a cavity), a cave, a plant containing a spiderweb, and a hole in the ground. Hang a beehive from a branch, and place a nest on another branch. Ask the children to tell you where each of the following animals might live: owl, bird, bee, mouse, spider, and bear. Place the animal by the appropriate home. Then, make backgrounds and animals for each

Figure 16–1 "Find a home for the bear."

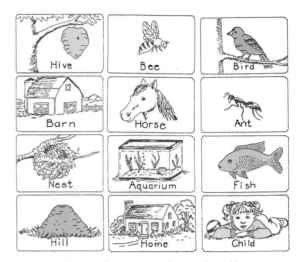

Figure 16–2 Cut out the pictures of animals and homes. Mount them on cardboard for the children to match.

child, and let the children paste the animal where it might live (Figure 16–1). Ask, "Do you think a plant is a good place for a spider to spin a web?" "Why do you think so?" (Outdoor insects can land in the web.) Have the children describe the advantages of living in the different homes.

2. Another popular animal matching activity involves the preparation of six animals and six homes. These animals and homes may be used as a cut-and-paste activity or put in a poster-and-folder game format that can be used repeatedly in learning centers. In the matching activity, the children must cut out a home and paste it in the box next to the animal that lives there. For example, a bee lives in a beehive, a horse in a barn, an ant in an anthill, a bird in a nest, a fish in an aquarium, and a child in a human home (Figure 16–2). Ask, "Why would an ant live in the ground?" Emphasize that animals try to live in places that offer them the best protection or

source of food. Discuss how each animal is suited to its home.

3. Counters are effective in reinforcing the fundamental concept of one-to-one correspondence. For example, when children study about bears, make and use bear counters that can be put into little bear caves. As the children match each bear to its cave, they understand that there are the same number of bears as there are caves. Lead the children in speculating why bears might take shelter in caves (convenient, will not be disturbed, hard to find, good place for baby bears to be born, etc.).

4. Children enjoy working with felt shapes. Cut out different-sized felt ducks, bears, ponds, and caves for children to match on a flannelboard. If children have the materials available, they will be likely to play animal matching games on their own, such as "match the baby and adult animals" or "line up all of the ducks, and find a pond for each one." Have children compare the baby ducks with the adult ducks by asking: "In what ways do the babies look like their parents?" "How are they alike?" "Can you find any differences?" Emphasize camouflage as the primary reason that baby animals usually

blend in with their surroundings. The number of animals and homes can be increased as the children progress in ability.

5.  After telling the story *Goldilocks and the Three Bears*, draw three bears of different sizes without noses. Cut out noses that will match the blank spaces, and have the children match the nose to the bear (Figure 16–3). You might want to do this first as a group and then have the materials available for the children to work with individually. Point out that larger bears have bigger noses.

One-to-one correspondence and the other skills presented in this unit cannot be developed in isolation of content. Emphasize the science concepts and process skills when you utilize animals as a means of developing fundamental skills. Further animal matching and sorting activities can be created by putting pictures into categories of living and nonliving things, **invertebrates**, **reptiles**, **amphibians**, birds, and fish.

When comparing major groups of animals—reptiles, for example—try to include as many representatives of the group as possible. Children can study pictures of turtles (land turtles are called **tortoises**, and some freshwater turtles are called **terrapins**), snakes,

**Figure 16–3** "Which nose belongs to Baby Bear?"

lizards, alligators, and crocodiles and then match them to their respective homes. The characteristics of each reptile can be compared and contrasted. The possibilities for matching, counting, comparing, and classifying animals are limitless and make for a natural integration of math and science.

## NUMBER SENSE AND COUNTING

Emphasizing science content while learning number concepts enables children to relate these subjects to their everyday lives and to familiar, concrete instances. The following example shows a kindergarten class using concrete experiences to reinforce counting and the concept that apples grow on trees.

When Mrs. Jones teaches an apple unit in the fall, she sorts apples of different sizes and colors. Then she has the children count the apples before they cook them to make applesauce and apple pies. Children can also taste different types of apples, graph their choices, and count to see which apple the class likes best.

For additional number concept extensions, she uses a felt board game that requires the children to pick apples from trees. For this activity, she creates two rows of apple trees with four felt trees in each row. The trees are filled with one to nine apples, and the corresponding numerals are shown at the bottom of each row. As the children play with the game, Mrs. Jones asks, "How many apples can you pick from each tree?" As Sam picks apples off a tree, he counts aloud: "one, two, three, four, five—I picked five apples from the apple tree." He smiles and points to the numeral five (Figure 16–4).

When presenting science activities, do not miss opportunities to count. The following activities emphasize counting.

1.  If bugs have been captured for study, have your children count the number of bugs in the bug keeper. Keep in mind that insects can be observed for a couple of days but should then be released to the area in which they were originally found.

2.  Take advantage of the eight tentacles of an octopus to make an octopus counting board. Enlarge a picture of an octopus on a piece of poster board, and attach a curtain hook to

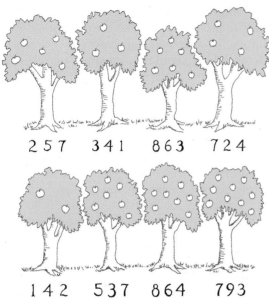

**Figure 16–4** "How many apples can you pick?"

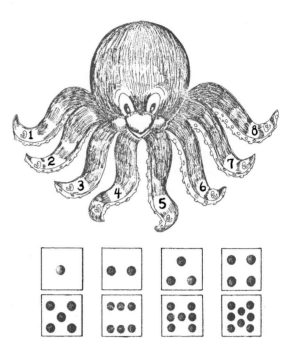

**Figure 16–5** "Count the dots and hang the square on the correct tentacle."

each tentacle above a number. Make circles with dots (one to eight) to hang on hooks. Ask children to count the number of tentacles that the octopus has. Explain that all octopuses have eight tentacles. Discuss how an octopus uses its armlike tentacles. Then, have children count the dots on the squares and put the squares on the hook over the correct number (Figure 16–5).

3. A fish-tank bulletin board display emphasizes counting and prepares children for future activities in addition. Prepare construction-paper fish, a treasure chest, rocks, and plants, and attach them to a 12" × 20" rectangle made from light blue poster board. Glue some of the fish, the treasure chest, rocks, and plants to the blue background. Then, using thumbtacks, attach a 13" × 21" clear plastic rectangle to the top of the light blue oak tag to create a fish-tank bulletin board. Before the students arrive the next day, put more fish in the tank. Then ask, "How many fish are swimming in the tank?" Each day, add more fish and ask the class: "How many fish are swimming in the tank today?" "How many were swimming in the tank yesterday?" "Are there more fish swimming in the tank today, or were

there more yesterday?" Use as many fish as are appropriate for your students (Figure 16–6).

4. Read Ruth Brown's *Ten Seeds* (2001). Count the seeds and animals on each page as you read with the children. Then ask, "What happened to the seeds that the child planted?" Next, reread the story while having the children watch for a change in either the seed or plant.

Children love to count. They count informally and with direction from the teacher. Counting cannot be removed from a context—you have to count *some*thing. As children count, emphasize the science in which they are counting. If children are counting the number of baby ducks following an adult duck, lead the children in speculating where the ducks might be going and what they might be doing.

## Sequencing and Ordinal Position

Science offers many opportunities for reinforcing sequencing and ordinal position. Observing the life cycle

Figure 16–6 "Create a fish-tank bulletin board for counting fish."

Figure 16–7 "Move your arms like a bird."

of a butterfly is a good way to learn about the life of an insect. Like all insects, butterflies go through four distinct life stages: (1) egg, (2) **larva** (the caterpillar that constantly eats), (3) **pupa** (the caterpillar slowly changes inside of a **chrysalis**), and (4) adult (the butterfly emerges from the chrysalis). Pictures of each of these stages can be mounted on index cards, matched with numerals, and put in sequence. Children will enjoy predicting which stage they think will happen next and comparing this to what actually happens.

## Animal Movement

Children can be encouraged to learn how different animals move as they learn one-to-one correspondence and practice the counting sequence.

Arrange the children in a line. Have them stamp their feet as they count, raising their arms in the air to emphasize the last number in the sequence. A bird might move this way, raising its wings in the air in a threatening manner or in a courtship dance (Figure 16–7). Have children change directions without losing the beat by counting "one" as they turn. For example, "One, two, three, four (up go the arms, turn); one, two, three, four (up go the arms, turn); one, two, three, four," and so on.

Now have the children move to different parts of the room. Arm movements can be left out and the children can tiptoe, lumber, or sway to imitate the ways various animals move. A bear has a side-to-side motion; a monkey might swing its arms and an elephant its trunk. This activity is also a good preparation strategy for the circle game described in the next section.

## A Circle Game

Practice in counting, sequencing, one-to-one correspondence, looking for patterns, and the process skills of predicting are all involved in the following circle game, which focuses attention on the prediction skills necessary in many science activities. Rather than be the source of the "right" answer, Mrs. Jones allows the results of the game to reveal this. For maximum success, refer to the move-like-an-animal activity in the previous section.

Mrs. Jones asks six children to stand in a circle with their chairs behind them. The child designated as the "starter," Mary, wears a hat and initiates the counting. Mary counts one and then each child counts off in sequence: two, three, and so on. The child who says the last number in the sequence (six) sits down. The next child begins with one and again the last sits down. The children go around and around the circle, skipping over those sitting down, until only one child is left standing.

Mrs. Jones repeats the activity exactly, starting with the same child and going in the same direction and in the same sequence, neither adding nor removing any children. She asks the children to predict who they think will be the last one standing. Mrs. Jones accepts all guesses equally, asking "Who has a different idea?" until everyone who wishes has guessed. She repeats the activity so children can check their predictions. Then the activity is repeated, but this time Mrs. Jones says, "Whisper in my ear who you think will be the last child standing." The kindergarten teacher plans to repeat this game until every child can predict correctly who will be the one left standing.

The game can be played with any number of players and with any length number sequence. Rather than evaluate the children's predictions, Mrs. Jones uses the predictions as a good indication of children's development. Try this game; you will be surprised by children's unexpected predictions.

## Sets and Classifying

A *set* is a group of things with common features that are put together by the process of classifying. Children classify when they sort (separate) and group (join) things that belong together for some reason. Although classification requires grouping by more than one characteristic and usually takes place when children are older, in young children the simple grouping process is usually called classification. The following classification activities develop analytical thinking and encourage clear expression of thought in a variety of settings.

1. One way to encourage informal classifying is to keep a button box. Children will sort buttons into sets on their own. Ask, "How do these go together?" Let the children explain.

2. Kindergartners can classify animals into **mammals**, reptiles, and amphibians by their body coverings. Provide them with pictures, plastic animals, or materials that simulate the body coverings of the animals.

3. Children can classify colors with color-coordinated snacks. As children bring in snacks, help them classify the foods by color. For example:

*Green*—lettuce, beans, peas
*Yellow*—bananas, lemonade, corn, cake
*Orange*—carrots, oranges, cheese
*White*—milk, cottage cheese, bread
*Red*—ketchup, cherry-flavored drinks, apples, jams, tomatoes
*Brown*—peanut butter, whole wheat bread, chocolate

4. Display a collection of plant parts such as stems, leaves, flowers, fruit, and nuts. Have the children sort all of the stems into one pile, all of the leaves into another, and so on. Ask a child to explain what was done. Stress that things that are alike in some way are put together to form a group. Then, have the children re-sort the plant parts into groups by properties such as size (small, medium, and large).

5. Children might enjoy playing a sorting game with objects or pictures of objects. One child begins sorting a collection of objects. Once he is halfway through, the next child must complete the activity by identifying the properties the first child used and then continuing to sort using the same system.

## Using Charts and Lists in Classification

The following example shows a first-grade teacher using classification activities to help make her class aware of the technological world around them.

First, Mrs. Red Fox has the children look around the classroom and name all the **machines** that they can see. She asks, "Is a chair a machine?" Dean answers, "No, it does not move." Mrs. Red Fox follows up with an open question, "Do you know what is alike about machines?" Mary and Judy have had experience in the machine center and say, "Machines have to have a moving part." This seems to jog Dean's memory, and he says, "And I think they have to do a job." (A *machine* is the term for a device that, by applying and transferring forces, enables people to do something they cannot do unaided; most hand tools—such as screwdrivers, levers, and hammers—are examples of simple machines and, whenever possible, should be investigated by actually working with them.) Mrs. Red Fox writes down all of the suggestions on a list titled "Machines in Our Classroom." The children add the pencil sharpener, a door hinge, a light switch, a water faucet, a record player, and an aquarium to the list. Mrs. Red Fox then asks the children to describe what the machines do and how they make work easier. After discussing the machines found in the classroom, the students talk about the machines that are in their homes.

The next day the children brainstorm, make a list called "Machines in Our Home," and hang it next to the classroom machine list. When the lists are completed, Mrs. Red Fox asks the children, "Do you see any similarities between the machines found at home and the machines found in our classroom?" Trang Fung answers, "There is a clock in our classroom, and we have one in the kitchen, too." Other children notice that both places have faucets and sinks. The teacher asks, "What differences do you see between the machines found at home and at school?" Dean notices that there isn't a telephone or a bicycle at school, and Sara did not find a pencil sharpener in her home.

Mrs. Red Fox extends the activity by giving the children old magazines and directing them to cut out pictures of machines to make a machine book. The class also decides to make a large machine collage for the bulletin board.

# COMPARING

When young children compare, they look at similarities and differences with each of their senses. Children are able to detect small points of difference and, because of this, enjoy spotting mistakes and finding differences between objects. Activities such as observing appearances and sizes, graphing, and dressing figures give experience in comparing.

1. Compare appearances by discussing likeness between relatives, dolls, or favorite animals. Then, make a block graph (see Unit 20) to show the different hair colors in the room or any other characteristics that interest your students.

2. Size comparisons seem to fascinate young children. They want to know who is the biggest, tallest, and shortest. Compare the lengths of hand spans and arm spans and lengths of paces and limbs. Have a few facts ready. Children will want to know which animals are the biggest, smallest, run the fastest, and so on. They might even decide to test which paper towel is the strongest or which potato chip is the saltiest.

3. Clothes can be compared and matched to paper dolls according to size, weather conditions, occupations, and activities such as swimming, playing outdoors, or going to a birthday party. This comparison activity could be a regular part of a daily weather chart activity.

## Comparing and Collecting

What did you collect as a child? Did you collect baseball cards, leaves, small cereal box prizes, shells, or pictures of famous people? Chances are you collected something. This is because young children are natural scientists; they are doing what comes naturally. They collect and organize their environment in a way that makes sense to them. Even as adults, we still retain the natural tendency to organize and collect.

Consider for a moment: Do you keep your coats, dresses, shoes, slacks, and jewelry in separate places? Do the spoons, knives, forks, plates, and cups have their own space in your house? In all likelihood, you have a preferred spot for each item. Where do you keep your soup? The cans are probably lined up together. Do you have a special place just for junk? Some people call such a place a junk drawer. Take a look at your house or room as evidence that you have a tendency to think like scientists by trying to bring the observable world into some sort of structure.

In fact, when you collect, you may be at your most scientific. As you collect, you combine the processes of observation, comparison, classification, and measurement, and you think like a scientist thinks. For example, when you add a leaf to your collection, you observe it and compare it with the other leaves in your collection. Then, you ask yourself, "Does this leaf measure up to my standards?" "Is it too big, small, old, drab?" "Have insects eaten its primary characteristics?" You make a decision based on comparisons between the leaf and the criteria you have set.

## ACTIVITIES

### Collecting and Comparing Fall Leaves

**OBJECTIVE:** Exploring the sizes and shapes of fall leaves.

**MATERIALS:** Leaves of different sizes and shapes. Check to be sure that there are not any harmful plants such as poison ivy or poison oak.

**NATURALISTIC AND INFORMAL ACTIVITIES:** Take children on a walk to collect leaves. As the children explore the leaves, encourage them to notice and talk about similarities and differences between the leaves.

**STRUCTURED ACTIVITIES:** As the children inspect the leaves that they have collected, help them to observe closely by asking, WHAT OTHER LEAVES ARE LIKE THIS ONE? Then ask HOW ARE THE LEAVES DIFFERENT? Give the children construction paper to arrange groups of similar leaves, and encourage discussion of the similarities and differences. Some children will enjoy creating a picture with the leaves and others will wonder if the leaves will grow into a tree.

**FOLLOW-UP:** Children will enjoy drying and pressing leaves between newspaper and cardboard. The children can write their names beside the leaves they collect. When the leaves are pressed and dry, they can be made into holiday cards, or the dry leaves can be pressed for display in the classroom or at home. Place the leaves between waxed paper squares, with the waxed side toward the leaves; then cover with a cloth and press with a warm iron. See *Crinkleroot's Guide to Knowing the Trees* by Jim Arnosky (1992).

## Similarities and Differences

Finding similarities, concepts, or characteristics that link things together may be even more difficult than identifying differences in objects. For example, dogs, cats, bears, lizards, and mice are all animals. But in order to gain an understanding of these concepts, children need to develop the idea that some similarities are more important than others. Even though the lizard has four legs and is an animal, the dog, cat, bear, and mouse are more alike because they are mammals. Unit 34 shows ways of teaching differences in animals.

In addition to quantitative questions (e.g., "How long?" or "How many?"), qualitative questions are necessary to bring about keener observations of similarities and differences. Observe the contrast in Chris's responses to his teacher in the following scenario.

Mrs. Raymond asks Chris, "How many seeds do you have on your desk?" Chris counts the seeds, says "eight," and goes back to arranging the seeds. Mrs. Ray-mond then asks Chris, "Tell me how many ways your seeds are alike and how they are different." Chris reports his observations as he closely observes the seeds for additional differences and similarities. "Some seeds are small, some seeds are big, some have cracks, and some feel rough." Chris's answers began to include descriptions of shape, size, color, texture, structure, markings, and so on. He is beginning to find order in his observations.

## Everyday Comparisons

Comparisons can help young children become more aware of their environment. Here are some examples.

1. Go for a walk, and have the children observe different trees. Ask them to compare the general shape of the trees and the leaves. Let them feel the bark and describe the differences between rough or smooth, peeling, and thin or thick bark.

As the children compare the trees, discuss the ways that trees help people and animals (home, shelter, food, shade, etc.).

2. Activities that use sound to make comparisons utilize an important way that young children learn. Try comparing winter sounds with summer sounds. Go for a walk in the winter or summer and listen for sounds. For example, the students in Mrs. Hebert's class heard their boots crunching in snow, the wind whistling, and a little rain splashing; a few even noticed a lack of sound on their winter walk. Johnny commented that he did not hear any birds. This initiated a discussion of where the birds might be and what the class could do to help the birds that remained in the area all winter.

3. The sense walk can be extended by separating the children into three groups and asking each of the groups to focus on a different sense: one group focuses on the *sounds* of spring, another on the *smells* of spring, and the other on the *sights* of spring. As the teacher records children's responses on the "spring sense walk experience chart," she will be able to assess the children's observation and comparison skills.

4. Insect investigations are natural opportunities for comparison questions and observation. Take advantage of the young children's curiosity by letting them collect four or five different insects for observation. Mr. Wang's class collected insects on a field trip. Theresa found four different kinds of insects. She put them carefully in a jar with leaves and twigs from the area in which she found them and punched holes in the jar lid (Figure 16–8). Mr. Wang helped her observe differences, such as size and winged or wingless, and also similarities, such as six legs, three body parts, and two antennae. All insects have these latter characteristics. If your captive animal does not have these, it is not an insect; it is something else.

5. Snack time is a good time to compare the changes in the color and texture of vegetables before and after they are cooked. Ask, "How do they look different?" When you make butter, ask the

**Figure 16–8** A bug collector.

children what changes they see in the cream. Make your own lemonade with fresh lemons and ask, "What happens to the lemons?" Then let the children taste the lemonade before and after sugar is added. "How does sugar change the taste of the lemonade?"

## SHAPE

Learning activities relating to shape are essential in *describing the physical environment*, which is a part of any aspect of science. These descriptions are not possible without an understanding of spatial relationships, which include the study of shapes, symmetry, time, and motion.

Most things have a shape, and children can identify and classify objects by their shapes. Basic two-dimensional geometric shapes include the circle, triangle, square, and rectangle. Each of these shapes is constructed from a straight line. The following scenario is a fundamental kindergarten lesson that introduces shapes and applies them to how children learn.

Mrs. Jones arranges children in groups and gives each child a different sponge shape. After the children have had time to explore the outer edges of their sponge shape, she picks up one of the shapes and asks, "How many sides does this shape have?" Mary and Lai answer, "Three." Mrs. Jones says, "Hold your shape up if it is just like my shape." She makes sure that each child gets a chance to examine each shape. If the shape has sides, the children count the sides of the shape aloud. Then she asks all children who have circles to hold them up and pass them to other members of the group for examination. Yarn is passed out and the children begin to duplicate the shapes on the tabletop.

The next day, Mrs. Jones asks George to pick up a shape from the table. He selects a circle. Mrs. Jones asks George if he can find a shape in the room that matches the circle (clock, button, table, pan, record). Sam and Mary take turns finding triangle shapes (sailboat sails, diagonally cut sandwiches), and Lai finds square shapes (floor tiles, crackers, cheese slices, napkins, paper towels, bulletin boards, books, tables). Then, each child stands next to the shape and identifies its name. Mrs. Jones leads the group in shape matching until everyone has found and reported objects of each shape.

To extend the activity, Mrs. Jones has the children use their sponge shapes to paint pictures. She prepares the paint by placing a wet paper towel in a pie tin and coating the towel with tempera paint. The towel and paint work like a stamp pad in which to dip damp sponge shapes. After the children complete their pictures, she asks: "Which shapes have you used in your picture?"

## More Shape Activities

The following activities integrate shape with other subject areas.

1. Construction-paper shapes can be used to create fantasy animal shapes, such as "the shape from outer space" or "the strangest insect shape ever seen." Have the children design an appropriate habitat and tell the background for their imaginary shape creature.

2. Take students on a shape walk to see how many shapes they can find in the objects they see. Keep a record. When you return to your classroom, make a bar graph. Ask the children to determine which shape was seen most often.

3. Shape books are an effective way of reinforcing the shape that an animal has. For example, after viewing the polar bears, make a book in the shape of a polar bear. Children can paste pictures in the book, create drawings of what they saw, and dictate or write stories about bears. Shape books can be covered with Contac paper or decorated in the way that the animal appears.

## Shape and the Sense of Touch

Young children are ardent touchers; they love to finger and stroke different materials. The following activities are a few ways that touch can be used to classify and identify shapes.

1. A classic touch bag gives children a chance to recognize and match shapes with their sense of touch. Some children might not want to put their hands into a bag or box, so be sure to use bright colors and cheerful themes when decorating a touch bag or box. A touching apron with several pockets is an alternative. The teacher wears the apron, and students try to identify what is in the pockets.

2. Extend this activity by making pairs of tactile cards with a number of rough- and smooth-textured shapes. Have the children close their eyes and match the cards with partners. Ask: "Can you find the cards that match?" "How do you know they match?" You can also play "mystery shapes" by cutting different shapes out of sandpaper and mounting them on cards. Ask the children to close their eyes, feel the shape, and guess what it is.

3. Students will enjoy identifying shapes with their feet, so you can make a foot feely box. Students will probably realize that they can feel things better with their fingertips than with their toes. A barefoot trail of fluffy rugs, a beach towel, ceramic tiles, bubble packing wrap, a pillow, and a window screen would be a good warm-up activity for identifying shapes with feet. Students

**Figure 16–9** Taking a tactile walk.

should describe what they feel as they walk over each section of the trail (Figure 16–9).

## SPACE

Although young children are not yet ready for the abstract level of formal thinking, they can begin thinking about space and shape relationships. The following science board game being played in a primary classroom is a good example.

"Put the starfish on top of the big rock."

"Which rock do you mean?"

"The big gray one next to the sunken treasure chest."

This is the conversation of two children playing a game with identical boards and pieces. One child gives directions and follows them, placing the piece in the correct position on a hidden game board. Another child, after making sure she understands the directions, chooses a piece and places it on the board. Then the first child continues with another set of directions: "Put the clam under that other rock."

The children are having fun, but there's more to their game than might first appear. A great deal about the child's concept of space can be learned by observing responses to directions such as up–down, on–off, on top of, over–under, in front of, behind, and so on. Is the child being careful when placing the objects on the paper?

## Bird's-Eye View

Children sometimes have difficulty with concepts involved in reading and making maps. One reason for this is that maps demand that they look at things from an unusual perspective: a bird's-eye view of spatial relations. To help children gain experience with this perspective, try the following strategy.

Ask children to imagine what it's like to look down on something from high above. Say, "When a bird looks down as it flies over a house, what do you think it sees?" You will need to ask some directed questions for young children to appreciate that objects will look different. "What would a picnic table look like to a bird?" "Does your house look the same to the bird in the air as it does to you when you're standing on the street?" Next have the children stand on a stepladder and describe a toy that is on the ground.

Then tell the children to stand and look down at their shoes. Ask them to describe what they can see from this perspective. Then ask them to draw their bird's-eye view. Some children will be able to draw a faithful representation of their shoes; others may be able only to scribble what they see. Give them time to experiment with perspective; if they are having difficulty getting started, have them trace the outlines of their shoes on a piece of drawing paper. Ask: "Do you need to fill in shoelaces or fasteners?" "What else do you see?" Put the children's drawings on their desks for open house. Have parents locate their child's desk by identifying the correct shoes.

This lesson lends itself to a simple exercise that reinforces a new way of looking and gives parents a chance to share what is going on at school. Ask children to look at some familiar objects at home (television, kitchen table, or even the family pet) from their new bird's-eye perspective and draw one or two of their favorites (Figure 16–10). When they bring their drawings to school, other children can try to identify the objects depicted.

## On the Playground

Playground distance can be a good place to start to get children thinking about space. Use a stopwatch to time them as they run from the corner of the building to the

**Figure 16–10** Katie's cat from a bird's-eye view.

**Figure 16–11** A bear has symmetry.

fence. Ask, "How long did it take?" Then, have the children walk the same route. Ask, "Did it take the same amount of time?" Discuss the differences in walking and running and moving faster or slower over the same space.

## PARTS AND WHOLES

After students are accustomed to identifying shapes, introduce the concept of balanced proportions known as *symmetry*. **Bilateral symmetry** is frequently found in nature and means that a dividing line can be drawn through the middle of the shape to create two matching parts. Each of the shapes that students have worked with so far can be divided into two matching halves (Figure 16–11). Point out these divisions on a square, circle, and equilateral triangle. Provide lots of pictures of animals, objects, and other living things. Have the children show where a line could be drawn through each picture. Ask, "How might your own body be divided like this?" Provide pictures for the children to practice folding and drawing lines.

Food activities commonly found in early childhood classrooms provide many opportunities for demonstrating parts and wholes. For example, when working with apples, divide them into halves or fourths. Ask, "How many apples will we need for everyone to receive a piece?" When you cut open the apples, let the children count the number of seeds inside. If you are making applesauce, be sure the children notice the difference between a whole cup and a half cup of apples (or sugar). A pizza lends itself well to discussions about dividing into parts. Ask: "Can you eat the whole pizza?" "Would you like a part of the pizza?"

During snack time, ask the students to notice how their sandwiches have been cut. Ask: "What shape was your sandwich before it was cut?" "What shape are the two halves?" "Can you think of a different way to cut your sandwich?" Discuss the whole sandwich and parts of a sandwich.

## Instructional Technology

There are several computer programs that teachers can use as an additional tool for teaching fundamental concepts. Although not a substitute for manipulating materials, using the computer can reinforce concepts that have already been introduced, especially as children become familiar with the use of a computer as a tool.

Teachers can create all sorts of computerized activities to reinforce fundamental concepts and skills in science. Teachers can use the *ClarisWorks* program to create an activity in which the child must place objects in some correct order, match objects, or follow some directions requiring spatial skills. This is done by creating a "stationary file," which becomes an untitled document that is renamed and saved. Each child can open the same file, do the activity, and save the com-

pleted activity in her own name; the teacher's original *ClarisWorks* file is not affected. Children can share each other's work by bringing up the file. In the *ClarisWorks* file example in Figure 16–12, the child must click on the baby animal and drag it over to the corresponding mother animal. *ClarisWorks 4.0* comes with a clip-art "library" for this purpose.

*Sammy's Science House* is a software program that features a section called "The Workshop," where children choose the pieces that will make whatever object is displayed. Another section of *Sammy's Science House* is called "The Sorting Station," where children sort items (plants vs. animals) into the correct category. *ThemeWeavers: Animals* (pre-K–2) is another software package that uses beginning math concepts and skills to explore science.

Figure 16–12 "Can you match the baby animals to the mother animals?"

## ACTIVITIES

### Fabric Pictures: Using the Sense of Touch

**OBJECTIVE:** Identifying and exploring various materials with the sense of touch.

**MATERIALS:** Cardboard cut into squares of any size, nontoxic glue, swatches of various fabrics, a variety of different textures such as sandpaper, wallpaper, cotton, silk, velvet, etc.

**NATURALISTIC AND INFORMAL ACTIVITIES:** Place all of the fabrics on the activity table for the children to touch, pick up, and examine. Provide time for the children to explore the textures. Then, encourage discussion about the fabrics the children are touching. DOES ANYONE ELSE HAVE A PIECE OF FABRIC THAT FEELS THE SAME AS YOURS? HOW DOES YOUR FABRIC FEEL ON YOUR FINGERS?

**STRUCTURED ACTIVITIES:** Give the children the cardboard squares and demonstrate how to use one or two drops of glue to affix each piece of fabric on their cardboard square. Ask the children to create a touching board by selecting fabric pieces and arranging them on their cardboard. Older children may want to create a picture using the fabrics. Display the touching pictures and ask the children to find their fabric picture. HOW DID YOU KNOW THAT WAS YOUR FABRIC PICTURE?

**FOLLOW-UP:** You may want to stick to fabrics and paper initially. Once the children are comfortable with the activity, add three-dimensional objects such as sticks, string, yarn, and other objects to the fabric pictures.

## SUMMARY

One-to-one correspondence is the most basic number skill. Children can increase their awareness of this skill and science concept as they complete science-related matching activities such as putting animals with their homes and imitating animal movement.

Animal and plant life cycles offer many opportunities to reinforce sequencing and ordinal position, and number concepts can be emphasized with familiar concrete examples of counting.

Sets are composed of items put together in a group based on one or more common criteria. When children put objects into groups by sorting out items that share some feature, they are classifying. Comparing requires that children look for similarities and differences with each of their senses. Activities requiring observation, measuring, graphing, and classifying encourage comparisons.

Adults help children learn shape when they give them things to view, hold, and feel. Each thing that the child meets in the environment has a shape. The child also needs to use space in a logical way. Things must fit into the space available. As children make constructions in space, they begin to understand the spatial relationship between themselves and the things around them.

The idea of parts and wholes is basic to objects, people, and animals. Sets and wholes can be divided into smaller parts or pieces. The concept of bilateral symmetry is introduced when children draw a line through the middle of a shape and divide it into two halves.

Naturalistic, informal, and structured experiences support the learning of these basic science and math skills. A variety of evaluation techniques should be used. Informal evaluation can be done simply by observing the progress and choices of the child. Formal assessment tasks are available in Appendix A.

## KEY TERMS

| | | |
|---|---|---|
| amphibians | larva | reptiles |
| bilateral symmetry | machine | terrapins |
| chrysalis | mammals | tortoises |
| invertebrates | pupa | |

## SUGGESTED ACTIVITIES

1. How will you evaluate children's learning? How will you assess whether or not children are developing science and math concepts and skills?

2. Select a science topic, such as *air*, and identify possible ways the science and math concepts in this unit can be integrated with the curriculum.

3. Choose one or more of the fundamental concepts discussed in this unit that you can teach to a student or a small group of students. Align the concepts and skills with the science content being emphasized in the class. Videotape the lesson and assess the extent to which the student(s) understand the concepts.

4. Describe your childhood collection to the class. Discuss the basis for your interest and where you kept your collection. Do you continue to add to this collection?

5. Begin a nature collection. Mount and label your collection, and discuss ways that children might collect objects in a formal way. Refer to Unit 33 of this book for nature collection suggestions.

6. Observe a group of students engaged in a science activity. Record the informal math and science discoveries they make.

7. Design a questioning strategy that will facilitate the development of classification skills and encourage student discussion. Try the strategy with children. Develop questioning strategies for two more of the concepts and skills presented in this unit.

8. Gain access to a computer with *ClarisWorks* and create a "stationary file" that teaches or reinforces one of the fundamental concepts and skills discussed in this unit and/or previous units. Once your work is saved on the stationary file, open it and see that it has a name and is not an "untitled" document. Try your activity with a child, asking her to save her work with her name as the document title. Save the student work to a diskette and share the work with classmates. Discuss ways these files can be useful with children.

9. Using the evaluation criteria found in Activity 5, Unit 2, review any of the following software to which you have access.

   ■ *Sammy's Science House* (pre-K–2; Redmond, WA: Edmark)

   ■ *ClarisWorks* (all ages; Santa Clara, CA: Claris)

   ■ *ClarisWorks for Kids* (ages 5 and 6; Santa Clara, CA: Claris)

10. Develop a science activity, and have a partner identify science and math concepts the children would learn.

## REVIEW

A. Match each term to an activity that emphasizes the concept.

____ Using the sense of touch to match similar objects

____ Looking down on things from a bird's-eye view

____ Matching animals to their homes

a. One-to-one correspondence

b. Counting

c. Sets and classifying

_____ Figuring out how many fish are swimming in the tank

_____ Classifying animals into groups of mammals and reptiles

_____ Duplicating yarn triangles and circles

_____ Drawing an imaginary line through the middle of a sandwich

d. Comparing

e. Shape

f. Space

g. Parts and whole

**B.** Describe how children use math concepts and skills to learn about science.

## REFERENCES

Arnosky, J. (1992). *Crinkleroot's guide to knowing the trees*. New York: Bradbury.

Brown, R. (2001). *Ten seeds*. New York: Knopf.

*ClarisWorks*. Santa Clara, CA: Claris.

*ClarisWorks for kids*. Santa Clara, CA: Claris.

*Goldilocks and the three bears*. Bedford, MA: Applewood.

*Sammy's science house*. (1995). Redmond, WA: Edmark.

*Themeweavers: Animals*. Redmond, WA: Edmark.

## FURTHER READING AND RESOURCES

Abruscato, J. (2004). *Teaching children science: Discovery activities and demonstrations for the elementary and middle grades* (2nd ed.). Boston: Allyn & Bacon.

Benenson, G., & Neujahr, J. L. (2002). *Designed environments: Places, practices, and plans*. Portsmouth, NH: Heinemann.

Benenson, G., & Neujahr, J. L. (2002). *Mapping*. Portsmouth, NH: Heinemann.

Chalufour, I., & Worth, K. (2003). *Discovering nature with young children*. St. Paul, MN: Redleaf Press.

Day, B. (1988). *Early childhood education*. New York: Macmillan.

Grollman, S., & Worth, K. (2003). *Worms, shadows, and whirlpools: Science in the early childhood classroom*. Portsmouth, NH: Heinemann.

Harlan, J., & Rivkin, M. (2003). *Science experiences for the early childhood years: An integrated affective approach*. Upper Saddle River, NJ: Pearson-Merrill/Prentice-Hall.

Harlan, W. (Ed.). (1995). *Primary science, taking the plunge: How to teach primary science more effectively*. Portsmouth, NH: Heinemann.

Hunder-Grundin, E. (1979). *Literacy: A systematic experience*. New York: Harper & Row.

Kamii, C. (1982). *Number in preschool and kindergarten*. Washington, DC: National Association for the Education of Young Children.

Koppel, S., & Lind, K. K. (1985). Follow my lead: A science board game. *Science and Children, 23*(1), 48–50.

Lind, K. K. (1984). A bird's-eye view: Mapping readiness. *Science and Children, 22*(3), 39–40.

Lind, K. K., & Milburn, M. J. (1988). Mechanized childhood. *Science and Children, 25*(5), 39–40.

Markle, S. (1988). *Hands-on science*. Cleveland, OH: Instructor Publications.

National Research Council. (1996). *National science education standards*. Washington, DC: National Academies Press.

Pugh, A. F., & Dukes-Bevans, L. (1987). Planting seeds in young minds. *Science and Children, 25*(3), 19–21.

Richards, R., Collis, M., & Kincaid, D. (1987). *An early start to science*. London: MacDonald Educational.

Sprung, B., Foschl, M., & Campbell, P. B. (1985). *What will happen if . . .?* New York: Educational Equity Concepts.

Warren, J. (1984). *Science time*. Palo Alto, CA: Monday Morning Books.

# SECTION 3

## Applying Fundamental Concepts, Attitudes, and Skills

# Unit 17

## Ordering, Seriation, and Patterning

### OBJECTIVES

After reading this unit, you should be able to:

■ Define ordering, seriation, and patterning.

■ List and describe four basic types of ordering activities.

■ Provide for naturalistic ordering, seriation, and patterning experiences.

■ Do informal and structured ordering, seriation, and patterning activities with young children.

■ Assess and evaluate a child's ability to order, seriate, and pattern.

■ Relate ordering, seriation, and patterning to the NCTM standard for prekindergarten through grade-2 algebra.

The NCTM (2000, p. 90) standard for prekindergarten through grade-2 algebra includes the expectations that students will order objects by size, number, and other properties; recognize and extend patterns; and analyze how patterns are developed. Very young children learn repetitive rhymes and songs and hear stories with predictive language. They develop patterns with objects and eventually with numbers. They recognize change, as in the seasons or in their height as they grow.

National Council of Teachers of Mathematics (NCTM) Standard 13 provides that students "recognize, extend, and create a wide variety of patterns" (p. 60). Underlying the concept of patterning are the concepts of comparing, ordering, and seriation. A focal point connection for algebra at the prekindergarten level is that children recognize and duplicate simple pattern sequences of the A-B model. At the kindergarten level,

children identify, duplicate and extend patterns made with objects or shapes.

**Ordering** is a higher level of comparing (Unit 11). Ordering involves comparing more than two things or more than two groups. It also involves placing things in a sequence from first to last. In Piaget's terms, ordering is called **seriation**. **Patterning** is related to ordering in that children need a basic understanding of ordering before they can do patterning. Patterning involves making or discovering auditory, visual, and motor regularities. Patterning includes (1) simple patterns such as placing Unifix Cubes in a sequence by color and/or number, (2) number patterns such as days of the week and patterns on the 100s chart, (3) patterns in nature such as spiderwebs and designs on shells, (4) quilt patterns, and (5) graphs. Movement can also be used to develop pattern and sequence through clapping, marching, standing, sitting, jumping, and the like.

Ordering and seriation start to develop in the sensorimotor stage. Before the age of 2, the child likes to work with nesting toys. *Nesting toys* are items of the same shape but of varying sizes so that each one fits into the larger ones. If put into each other in order by size, they will all fit in one stack. Ordering and seriation involve seeing a pattern that follows continuously in equal increments. Other types of patterns involve repeated sequences that follow a preset rule. Daily routine is an example of a pattern that is learned early; that is, infants become cued into night and day and to the daily sequence of diaper changing, eating, playing, and sleeping. As they experiment with rattles, they might use a regular pattern of movement that involves motor, auditory, and visual sequences repeated over and over. As the sensorimotor period progresses, toddlers can

be observed lining up blocks: placing a large one, then a small one, large, small or perhaps red, green, yellow, red, green, yellow.

An early way of ordering is to place a pattern in one-to-one correspondence with a model, as in Figure 17–1. This gives the child the idea of ordering. Next, he learns to place things in ordered rows on the basis of length, width, height, and size. At first the child can think of only two things at one time. When ordering by length, he places sticks in a sequence such as shown in Figure 17–1(C). As he develops and practices, he will be able to use the whole sequence at once and place the sticks as in Figure 17–1(D). As the child develops further, he becomes able to order by other characteristics, such as color shades (dark to light), texture (rough to smooth), and sound (loud to soft).

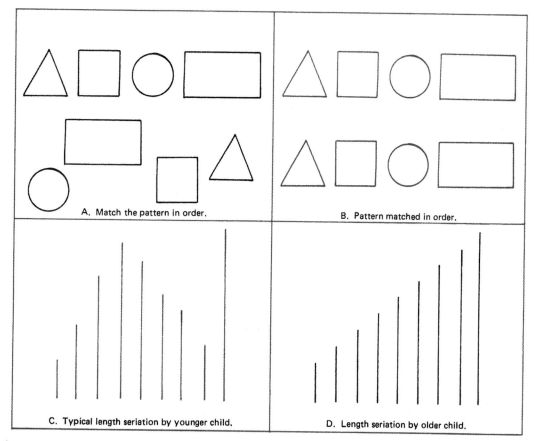

A. Match the pattern in order.

B. Pattern matched in order.

C. Typical length seriation by younger child.

D. Length seriation by older child.

**Figure 17–1** Ordering by pattern and seriating by size.

**Figure 17–2** Ordering sets.

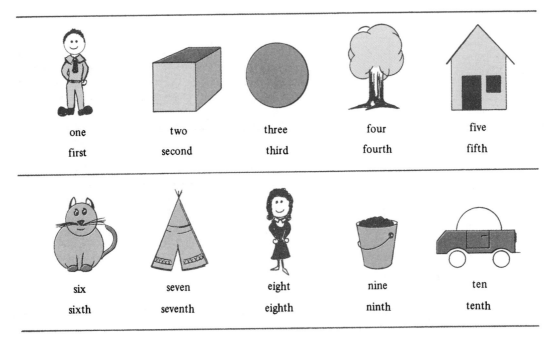

| one | two | three | four | five |
|-----|-----|-------|------|------|
| first | second | third | fourth | fifth |

| six | seven | eight | nine | ten |
|-----|-------|-------|------|-----|
| sixth | seventh | eighth | ninth | tenth |

**Figure 17–3** Counting numbers and ordinal numbers.

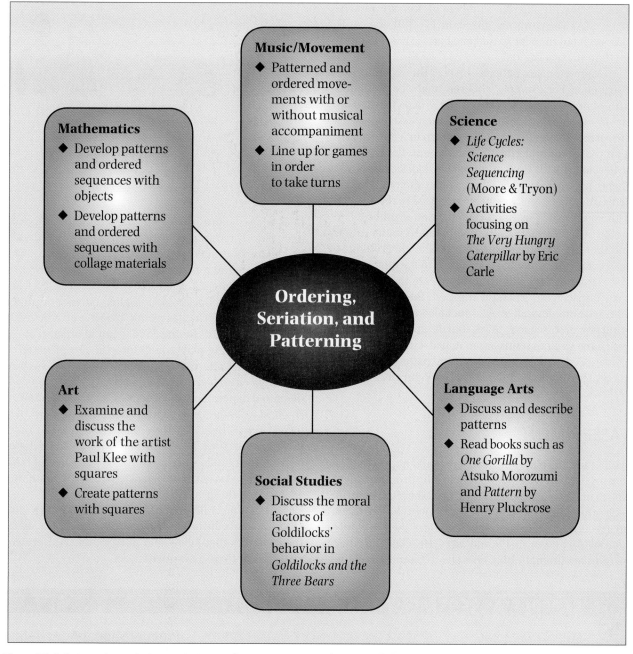

**Figure 17–4** Integrating ordering, seriation, and patterning across the curriculum.

Once the child can place one set of things in order, he can go on to double seriation. For double seriation he must put two groups of things in order. This is a use of matching, or one-to-one correspondence (Unit 8).

Groups of things can also be put in order by the number of things in each group. By ordering groups, each with one more thing than the others, the child learns the concept of **one more than**. In Figure 17–2, some cards with different numbers of dots are shown. In 17–2(A), the cards are mixed; in 17–2(B), the cards have been put in order so that each group has one more dot than the one before.

More complex patterns involve the repetition of a sequence. For example, children might be presented with a pile of shapes such as those depicted in Figure 17–1, shown the pattern, and then asked to select the correct shapes to repeat the pattern in a line (rather than matching underneath, one to one). Patterns can be developed with Unifix Cubes, cube blocks, beads, alphabet letters, numerals, sticks, coins, and many other items. Auditory patterns can be developed by the teacher with sounds such as hand clapping and drumbeats or motor activities such as the command to jump, jump, and then sit. To solve a pattern problem, children must be able to figure out what comes next in a sequence.

Ordering and patterning words are those such as next, last, biggest, smallest, thinnest, fattest, shortest, tallest, before, and after. Also included are the ordinal numbers: first, second, third, fourth, and so on to the last thing. Ordinal terms are matched with counting in Figure 17–3. Ordering, seriation, and patterning can be integrated into the content areas (see Figure 17–4).

## ASSESSMENT

While the child plays, the teacher should note activities that might show that the child is learning to order things. Notice how she uses nesting toys. Does she place them in each other so she has only one stack? Does she line them up in rows from largest to smallest? Does she use words such as *first* ("I'm first") and *last* ("He's last") on her own? In her dramatic play, does she go on train or plane

**Figure 17–5** A young child draws his family in order by size.

rides where chairs are lined up for seats and each child has a place (first, second, last)? Seriation may be reflected in children's drawings. For example, in Figure 17–5 a child has drawn a picture of his family members in order of their height. Paint chips can be seriated from light to dark, such as from light pink to dark burgundy. Sequence stories (such as a child blowing up a balloon) can be put on cards for the child to put in order.

Also during play, watch for evidence of patterning behavior. Patterns might appear in artwork such as paintings or collages; in motor activity such as movement and dance; in musical activity such as chants and rhymes; in language activities such as acting out patterned stories (e.g., *The Three Billy Goats Gruff* or *Goldilocks and the Three Bears*); or with manipulative materials such as Unifix Cubes, Teddy Bear Counters, LEGO, building blocks, attribute blocks, beads for stringing, geoboards, and so on.

Ask the child to order different numbers and kinds of items during individual interview tasks, as in the examples that follow and in Appendix A. Here are examples of three assessment tasks.

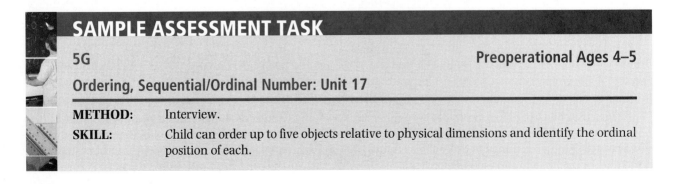

## SAMPLE ASSESSMENT TASK

**5G**                                                                      **Preoperational Ages 4–5**

**Ordering, Sequential/Ordinal Number: Unit 17**

**METHOD:** Interview.

**SKILL:** Child can order up to five objects relative to physical dimensions and identify the ordinal position of each.

**MATERIALS:** Five objects or cutouts that vary in equal increments of height, width, length, or overall size dimensions.

**PROCEDURE:** Start with five objects or cutouts. If this proves to be difficult, remove the objects or cutouts; then put out three and ask the same questions. FIND THE (TALLEST, BIGGEST, FATTEST or SHORTEST, SMALLEST, THINNEST). PUT THEM ALL IN A ROW FROM TALLEST TO SHORTEST (BIGGEST TO SMALLEST, FATTEST TO THINNEST). If the child accomplishes the task, ask, WHICH IS FIRST? WHICH IS LAST? WHICH IS SECOND? WHICH IS THIRD? WHICH IS FOURTH?

**EVALUATION:** Note whether the children find the extremes but mix up the three objects or cutouts that belong in the middle. This is a common approach for preoperational children. Note if children take an organized approach to solving the problem or if they seem to approach it in a disorganized, unplanned way.

**INSTRUCTIONAL RESOURCE:** Charlesworth, R., and Lind, K. K. (2010). *Math and science for young children* (6th ed.). Clifton Park, NY: Cengage Learning.

## SAMPLE ASSESSMENT TASK

**6H**                                                            **Transitional Ages 5–7**

**Ordering, Double Seriation: Unit 17**

**METHOD:** Interview.

**SKILL:** Child will place two sets of 10 items in double seriation.

**MATERIALS:** Two sets of 10 objects, cutouts, or pictures of objects that vary in one or more dimensions in equal increments such that one item in each set is the correct size to go with an item in the other set. The sets could be children and baseball bats, children and pets, chairs and tables, bowls and spoons, cars and garages, hats and heads, etc.

**PROCEDURE:** Suppose you have decided to use hats and heads. First, place the heads in front of the child in random order. Instruct the child to line the heads up in order from smallest to largest. Help can be given, such as: FIND THE SMALLEST. GOOD, NOW WHICH ONE COMES NEXT? AND NEXT? If the child is able to line up the heads correctly, then put out the hats in a random arrangement. Tell the child, FIND THE HAT THAT FITS EACH HEAD, AND PUT IT ON THE HEAD.

**EVALUATION:** Note how the children approach the problem—in an organized or haphazard fashion. Note whether their solution is entirely or only partially correct. If they get a close approximation, go through the procedure again with 7 items or 5 to see if they grasp the concept when fewer items are used. A child going into concrete operations should be able to accomplish the task with two groups of 10. Transitional children may be able to perform the task correctly with fewer items in each group.

**INSTRUCTIONAL RESOURCE:** Charlesworth, R., and Lind, K. K. (2010). *Math and science for young children* (6th ed.). Clifton Park, NY: Cengage Learning.

# SAMPLE ASSESSMENT TASK

**6I**                                                                    **Transitional Period Ages 5–7**

## Ordering, Patterning: Unit 17

**METHOD:**        Interview.

**SKILL:**           Child can copy, extend, and describe patterns made with concrete objects.

**MATERIALS:**    Color cubes, Unifix Cubes, Teddy Bear Counters, attribute blocks, small toys, or other objects that can be placed in a sequence to develop a pattern.

**PROCEDURE:**   1. *Copy patterns.* One at a time, make patterns of various levels of complexity (each letter stands for one type of item such as one color of a color cube, one shape of an attribute block, or one type of toy). For example, A-B-A-B could be red block–green block–red block–green block or big triangle–small triangle–big triangle–small triangle. Using the following series of patterns, tell the child to MAKE A PATTERN JUST LIKE THIS ONE. (If the child hesitates, point to the first item and say, START WITH ONE LIKE THIS.)

   a. A-B-A-B
   b. A-A-B-A-A-B
   c. A-B-C-A-B-C
   d. A-A-B-B-C-C-A-A-B-B-C-C

2. *Extend patterns.* Make patterns as in item 1, but this time say: THIS PATTERN ISN'T FINISHED. MAKE IT LONGER. SHOW ME WHAT COMES NEXT.

3. *Describe patterns.* Make patterns as in items 1 and 2. Say: TELL ME ABOUT THESE PATTERNS. (WHAT COMES FIRST? NEXT? NEXT?) IF YOU WANTED TO CONTINUE THE PATTERN, WHAT WOULD COME NEXT? NEXT?

4. If the foregoing tasks are easily accomplished, then try some more difficult patterns such as

   a. A-B-A-C-A-D-A-B-A-C-A-D
   b. A-B-B-C-D-A-B-B-C-D
   c. A-A-B-A-A-C-A-A-D

**EVALUATION:**  Note which types of patterns are easiest for the children. Are they more successful with the easier patterns? With copying? With extending? With describing?

**INSTRUCTIONAL RESOURCE:** Charlesworth, R., and Lind, K. K. (2010). *Math and science for young children* (6th ed.). Clifton Park, NY: Cengage Learning.

## NATURALISTIC ACTIVITIES

Just as children's natural development guides them to sort things, it also guides them to put things in order and to place things in patterns. As children sort, they often put the items in rows or arrange them in patterns. For example, Kate picks out blocks that are all of one size, shape, and color and lines them up in a row. She then adds to the row by lining up another group of blocks of the same size, shape, and

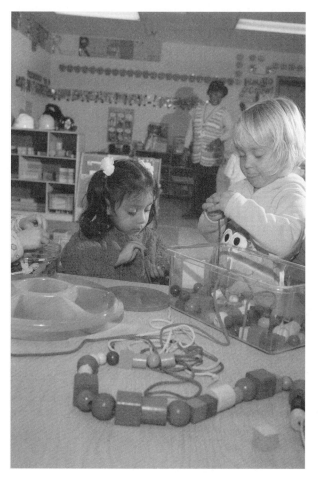

Children construct concepts of ordering, seriation, and patterning as they explore materials during play.

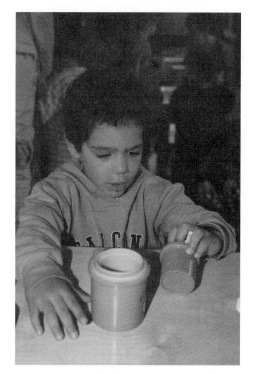

Nesting cups provide for exploration of ordering by size.

## INFORMAL ACTIVITIES

Informal teaching can go on quite often during the child's daily play and routine activities. The following are some examples.

■ Eighteen-month-old Brad has a set of mixing bowls and measuring cups to play with on the kitchen floor. He puts the biggest bowl on his head. His mother smiles and says, "The *biggest* bowl fits on your head." He tries the smaller bowls, but they do not fit. Mom says, "The *middle-sized* bowl and the *smallest* bowl don't fit, do they?" She sits down with him and picks up a measuring cup. "Look, here is the cup that is the *biggest*. These are *smaller*." She lines them up by size. "Can you find the *smallest* cup?" Brad proceeds to put the cups one in the other until they are in a single stack. His mother smiles, "You have them all in *order*."

color. She picks out blue blocks and yellow blocks and lines them up, alternating colors. Pete is observed examining his mother's measuring cups and spoons. He lines them up from largest to smallest. Then he makes a pattern: cup-spoon-cup-spoon-cup-spoon-cup-spoon.

As speech ability increases, the child uses order words. "I want to be *first*." "This is the *last* one." "Daddy Bear has the *biggest* bowl." "I'll sit in the *middle*." As he starts to draw pictures, he often draws mothers, fathers, and children and places them in a row from smallest to largest.

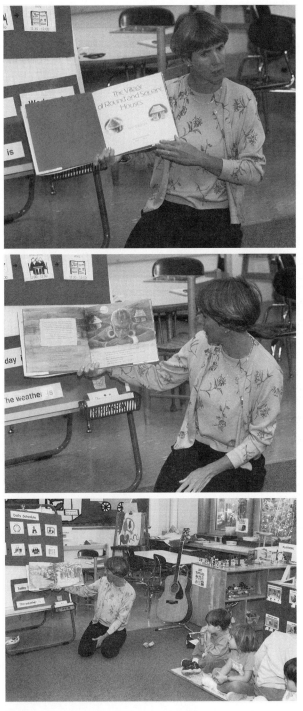

Children's literature provides structured pattern and sequence experiences.

■ 5-year-old Enrique, 4-year-old Chin, and 3-year-old Jim come running across the yard to Mr. Brown. "You are all fast runners." "I was *first*," shouts Enrique. "I was *second*," says Chin. "I was *third*," says Jim. Enrique shouts, "You were *last*, Jim, 'cause you are the *littlest*." Jim looks mad. Mr. Brown says, "Jim was both *third* and *last*. It is true Jim is the *littlest* and the *youngest*. Enrique is the *oldest*. Is he the *biggest?*" "No!" says Jim, "He's *middle size*."

■ Mary has some small candies she is sharing with some friends and her teacher. "Mr. Brown, you and I get five because we are the *biggest*. Diana gets four because she's the *next* size. Pete gets three. Leroy gets two, and Brad gets one. Michael doesn't get any 'cause he is a baby." "I see," says Mr. Brown, "you are dividing them so the *smallest* people get the least and the *biggest* get the most."

■ Mrs. Red Fox tells her first graders that she would like them to line up boy-boy-girl-girl.

■ Second grader Liu Pei decides to draw a picture each day of her bean sprout that is the same height as it is that day. Soon she has a long row of bean-sprout pictures, each a little taller than the one before. Mr. Wang comments on how nice it is to have a record of the bean sprout's growth from the day it sprouted.

■ Miss Collins tells the children, "You have to take turns on the swing. Tanya is *first* today."

These examples show how comments can be made that help the child see her own use of order words and activities. Many times in the course of the day, opportunities come up where children must take turns. These times can be used to the fullest for teaching order and ordinal number. Many kinds of materials can be put out for children that help them practice ordering. Some of these materials are self-correcting, such as the Montessori cylinders (see Figure 39–2): Each cylinder fits in only one place.

## STRUCTURED ACTIVITY

Structured experiences with ordering and patterning can be done with many kinds of materials. These materials can be purchased or they can be made by the teacher. Things of different sizes are easy to find at home or school. Measuring cups and spoons, mixing bowls, pots and pans, shoes, gloves, and other items of clothing are easy to get in several different sizes. Paper and cardboard can be cut into different sizes and shapes. Paper-towel rolls can be made into cylinders of graduated sizes. The artistic teacher can draw pictures of the same item in graduated sizes. Already drawn materials such as Richardson's (1999) Unifix Cube train patterns, counting boards, or working-space papers can be used for patterning. The following are basic activities that can be done with many different kinds of objects, cutouts, and pictures.

Jorge, a kindergartner, enjoys exploring patterns with Virtual Manipulatives online (http://nlvm.usu.edu): *color pattern* challenges Jorge to arrange colors to complete a pattern; *pattern blocks* provides opportunities to build patterns with virtual pattern blocks.

## ACTIVITIES

### Ordering and Patterning: The Basic Concept

**OBJECTIVE:**  To help the child understand the idea of order and sequence.

**MATERIALS:**  Large colored beads with a string for the teacher and each child.

**NATURALISTIC AND INFORMAL ACTIVITIES:**  Have the container of beads available during center time. As the children explore the beads, note if they develop patterns based on color. Comment such as, "First you lined up the blue beads and then the red beads"; "You lined up two yellow, two red, and two blue beads."

**STRUCTURED ACTIVITIES:**  The beads are in a box or bowl where they can be reached by each child. Say, WATCH ME. I'M GOING TO MAKE A STRING OF BEADS. Start with three beads. Add more as each child learns to do each amount. Lay the string of three beads down where each child can see it: NOW YOU MAKE ONE LIKE MINE. WHICH KIND OF BEAD SHOULD YOU TAKE FIRST? When the first bead is on: WHICH ONE IS NEXT? When two are on: WHICH ONE IS NEXT?

Use patterns of varying degrees of complexity.
1. A-B-A-B
2. A-B-C-A-B-C
3. A-A-B-A-A-C-A-A-D
4. Make up your own patterns.

**FOLLOW-UP:**  1. Make a string of beads. Pull it through a paper-towel roll so that none of the beads can be seen. Say, I'M GOING TO HIDE THE BEADS IN THE TUNNEL. NOW I'M GOING TO PULL THEM OUT. WHICH ONE WILL COME OUT FIRST? NEXT? NEXT? and so on. Then pull the beads through and have the children check as each bead comes out.
2. Dye some macaroni with food coloring. Set up a pattern for a necklace. The children can string the macaroni to make their own necklaces in the same pattern.

### Ordering/Seriation: Different Sizes, Same Shape

**OBJECTIVE:**  To make comparisons of three or more items of the same shape and different sizes.

**MATERIALS:**  Four to 10 squares cut with sides 1 inch, 1¼ inch, 1½ inch, and so on.

(*continued*)

**NATURALISTIC AND INFORMAL ACTIVITIES:** Have a container of the squares and other shapes in a sequence of sizes available during center time. Note how the children use the shapes. Do they sequence them by size? Comment, such as: "You put the biggest square first"; "You put all the same sizes in their own piles."

**STRUCTURED ACTIVITY:** Lay out the shapes. HERE ARE SOME SQUARES. STACK THEM UP SO THE BIGGEST IS ON THE BOTTOM. Mix the squares up again. NOW, PUT THEM IN A ROW STARTING WITH THE SMALLEST.

**FOLLOW-UP:** Do the same thing with other shapes and materials.

## Ordering/Seriation: Length

**OBJECTIVE:** To make comparisons of three or more things of the same width but different lengths.

**MATERIALS:** Sticks, strips of paper, yarn, string, Cuisinaire Rods, drinking straws, or anything similar cut in different lengths and such that each item is the same difference in length from the next one.

**NATURALISTIC AND INFORMAL ACTIVITIES:** Have containers of each type of material available during center time. Some of the items could be placed in the art center to be used for collages. Note how the children explore the materials. Do they line them up in sequence? Comment, such as: "You put the largest (smallest) first"; "Tell me about what you made."

**STRUCTURED ACTIVITY:** Put the sticks out in a mixed order. LINE THESE UP FROM SHORTEST TO LONGEST (LONGEST TO SHORTEST). Help if needed. WHICH ONE COMES NEXT? WHICH ONE OF THESE IS LONGEST? IS THIS THE NEXT ONE?

**FOLLOW-UP:** Do this activity with many different kinds of materials.

## Ordering/Seriation: Double Seriation

**OBJECTIVE:** To match, one-to-one, two or more ordered sets of the same number of items.

**MATERIALS:** *Three Bears* flannelboard figures or cutouts made by hand: mother bear, father bear, baby bear, Goldilocks, three bowls, three spoons, three chairs, and three beds.

**NATURALISTIC AND INFORMAL ACTIVITIES:** Have the flannelboard and story pieces available during center time. Note how the children use the material. Do they tell the story? Do they line up the pieces in sequence? Comment if they hesitate; "What comes next in the story?" Note if they sequence and/or match the materials by size; "You matched up each bear with its chair, bowl, bed."

**STRUCTURED ACTIVITY:** Tell the story. Use all the order words biggest, middle-sized, smallest, next. Follow up with questions: WHICH IS THE BIGGEST BEAR? FIND THE BIGGEST BEAR'S BOWL (CHAIR, BED, SPOON). Use the same sequence with each character.

**FOLLOW-UP:** Let the children act out the story with the felt pieces or cutouts. Note if they use the order words; if they change their voices; and if they match each bear to the correct bowl, spoon, chair, and bed.

## Ordering: Sets

**OBJECTIVE:** To order groups of one to five objects.

**MATERIALS:** Glue buttons or draw dots on five cards.

**NATURALISTIC AND INFORMAL ACTIVITIES:** Have the cards available during center time. Note if the children sequence them from one to five items. Comment, such as: "Tell me how many buttons (dots) there are on each card"; "Which cards have more than one?"

**STRUCTURED ACTIVITY:** Lay out the cards. Put the card with one button in front of the child. HOW MANY BUTTONS ON THIS CARD? Child answers. Say, YES, THERE IS ONE BUTTON. FIND THE CARD WITH ONE MORE BUTTON. If child picks out the card with two, say, YOU FOUND ONE MORE. NOW FIND THE CARD WITH ONE MORE BUTTON. Keep on until all five are in line. Mix the cards up. Give the stack to the child. LINE THEM ALL UP BY YOURSELF. START WITH THE SMALLEST GROUP.

**FOLLOW-UP:** Repeat with other materials. Increase the number of groups as each child learns to recognize and count larger groups. Use loose buttons (chips, sticks, or coins), and have the child count out her own groups. Each set can be put in a small container or on a small piece of paper.

## Order: Ordinal Numbers

**OBJECTIVE:** To learn the ordinal numbers *first, second, third*, and *fourth*. (The child should be able to count easily to four before doing this activity.)

**MATERIALS:** Four balls or beanbags, four common objects, four chairs.

**NATURALISTIC AND INFORMAL ACTIVITIES:** Have the materials available during center time or gym time as appropriate. Note how the children use them. Note if they figure out that they must take turns. Comment such as, "You are doing a good job taking turns. Mary is first, José is second, Larry is third, and Jai Li is fourth."

**STRUCTURED ACTIVITIES:** 1. Games requiring that turns be taken can be used. Just keep in mind that young children cannot wait very long. Limit the group to four children, and keep the game moving fast. For example, give each of the four children one beanbag or one ball. Say: HOW MANY BAGS ARE THERE? LET'S COUNT. ONE, TWO, THREE, FOUR. CAN I CATCH THEM ALL AT THE SAME TIME? NO, I CAN'T. YOU WILL HAVE TO TAKE TURNS: YOU ARE FIRST, YOU ARE SECOND, YOU ARE THIRD, AND YOU ARE FOURTH. Have each child say his number, "I am (first, second, third, and fourth)." OKAY, FIRST, THROW YOURS. (Throw it back.) SECOND, THROW YOURS. (Throw it back.) After each has had his turn, have them all do it again. This time have them tell you their ordinal number name.

2. Line up four objects. Say, THIS ONE IS FIRST, THIS ONE IS SECOND, THIS ONE IS THIRD, THIS ONE IS FOURTH. Ask the children: POINT TO THE (FOURTH, FIRST, THIRD, SECOND).

*(continued)*

3. Line up four chairs. WE ARE GOING TO PLAY BUS (PLANE, TRAIN). Name a child, _____ YOU GET IN THE THIRD SEAT. Fill the seats. Go on a pretend trip. NOW WE WILL GET OFF. SECOND SEAT GET OFF. FIRST SEAT GET OFF. FOURTH SEAT GET OFF. THIRD SEAT GET OFF.

**FOLLOW-UP:** Make up some games that use the same basic ideas. As each child knows first through fourth, add fifth, then sixth, and so on.

## Patterning: Auditory

**OBJECTIVE:** To copy and extend auditory patterns.

**MATERIALS:** None needed.

**NATURALISTIC AND INFORMAL ACTIVITIES:** Note if the children engage in spontaneous chants and rhymes. Encourage them by joining in their rhythmic activities.

**STRUCTURED ACTIVITIES:** Start a hand-clapping pattern. Ask the children to join you. LISTEN TO ME CLAP. Clap, clap, (pause), clap (repeat several times). YOU CLAP ALONG WITH ME. Keep on clapping for 60 to 90 seconds so everyone has a chance to join in. Say, LISTEN. WHEN I STOP, YOU FINISH THE PATTERN. Do three repetitions, then stop. Say, YOU DO THE NEXT ONE. Try some other patterns such as "Clap, clap, slap the elbow" or "Clap, stamp the foot, slap the leg."

**FOLLOW-UP:** Help the children develop their own patterns. Have them use rhythm instruments (e.g., drums, jingle bells, or sound cans) to develop patterns.

## Patterning: Objects

**OBJECTIVE:** To copy and extend object patterns.

**MATERIALS:** Several small plastic toys such as vehicles, animals, or peg people; manipulatives such as Unifix Cubes, inch cubes, or attribute blocks; or any other small objects such as coins, bottle caps, eating utensils, or cups.

**NATURALISTIC AND INFORMAL ACTIVITIES:** Provide opportunities to explore many kinds of materials such as those listed above. After the children have had some structured pattern activities, note if they develop patterns during their independent activity periods. Do they call your attention to their pattern constructions? Can they describe their constructions when you ask them to?

**STRUCTURED ACTIVITIES:** Have the children explore ways to make patterns with the objects. Have them see how many different kinds of patterns they can make.

**FOLLOW-UP:** Find additional ideas for pattern activities in this unit's Further Reading and Resources listing.

## Patterning: Exploring Patterns in Space

**OBJECTIVE:**  To organize materials in space in a pattern.

**MATERIALS:**  Many kinds of materials are available that will give the child experiences with making patterns in space.

1. *Geoboards* are square boards with attached pegs. Rubber bands of different colors can be stretched between the pegs to form patterns and shapes.
2. *Parquetry* and *pattern blocks* are blocks of various shapes and colors that can be organized into patterns.
3. *Pegboards* are boards with holes evenly spaced. Individual pegs can be placed in the holes to form patterns.
4. *Color inch cubes* are cubes with 1-inch sides. They come in sets with red, yellow, blue, green, orange, and purple cubes.

**NATURALISTIC AND INFORMAL ACTIVITIES:**  Provide time for exploration of materials during center time. Note the patterns the children construct. Do they call your attention to their pattern constructions? Can they describe their constructions when you ask them to?

**STRUCTURED ACTIVITIES:**  1. The children can experiment freely with the materials and create their own patterns.

2. Patterns can be purchased or made for the children to copy.

**FOLLOW-UP:**  After the children have been shown how to use them, the materials can be left out during center time.

## Patterning: Organizing Patterns in Space

**OBJECTIVE:**  To organize materials in space in a pattern.

**MATERIALS:**  Construction paper, scissors, and glue.

**NATURALISTIC AND INFORMAL ACTIVITIES:**  Children should already have been involved with many activities (naturalistic as well as informal and structured) and have had many opportunities to work in small groups before being assigned the following activity.

**STRUCTURED ACTIVITY:**  Provide a poster-size piece of construction paper. Provide an assortment of precut construction paper shapes (e.g., squares, triangles, circles). Suggest that the children, working in small groups, create as many different patterns as they can and glue them on the big piece of paper.

**FOLLOW-UP:**  Offer the activity several times. Use different colors for the shapes, use different sizes, and change the choice of shapes.

# IDEAS FOR CHILDREN WITH SPECIAL NEEDS

An understanding of patterns and ordering provides a foundation for understanding algebraic relationships. A multisensory approach to instruction can be used to meet the needs of all children. The art of many cultures includes special patterns (Zaslavsky, 1996). Children can make stamped repeated patterns with sponges and other materials. Stencils can also be used for creating patterns. Pattern blocks can be explored. Children can be introduced to the patterns common to a variety of cultures. They might bring materials from home that include patterns.

Children with perceptual-motor challenges may benefit from extra time using large colored beads. Beads usually come in six colors and three shapes. For the first step the children can select 5 or six beads of any color or shape to practice stringing. Once the children feel comfortable with stringing they can begin to string patterns. They can begin with the simplest patterns such as all cubes or all spheres or all cylinders in one color and gradually move to A-B and more complex patterns in small steps. Sequence terms can be applied to instructions—for example, "First blue, second yellow."

For auditory learners, more opportunities for auditory patterns can support their understanding of pattern and ordering. Rhymes with repeated patterns work well with these children. Kinesthetic learners do well with patterned movement activities such as two steps, two jumps. Movement can also be used to work with sequence; for example, children can line up "first, second, third," and so forth to do patterned movement or take turns doing patterns.

## EVALUATION

Note whether children's use of ordering and patterning words—and their involvement in ordering and patterning activities—has increased during play and routine activities. Without disrupting the children's activities, ask questions or make comments and suggestions.

- ■ Who is the biggest? (The smallest?)
- ■ (As the children put their shoes on after their nap) Who has the longest shoes? (The shortest shoes?)
- ■ Who came in the door first today?
- ■ Run fast. See who can get to the other side of the gym first.

- ■ (The children are playing train) Well, who is in the last seat? She must be the caboose. Who is in the first seat? She must be the engineer.
- ■ Everyone can't get a drink at the same time. Line up with the shortest person first.
- ■ Great, you found a new pattern to make with the Unifix Cubes!
- ■ Sam made some patterns with the ink pad and stamps.

Richardson (1999, pp. 78–79) suggests noting whether children can

- ■ copy patterns
- ■ extend patterns
- ■ create patterns
- ■ analyze a given pattern

The assessment tasks in Appendix A can be used for individual evaluation interviews.

## SUMMARY

When more than two things are compared, the process is called ordering or seriation. There are four basic types of ordering activities. The first is to put things in sequence by size. The second is to make a one-to-one match between two sets of related things. The third is to place sets of different numbers of things in order from the least to the most. The last is ordinal numbers (first, second, third, etc.). Some children may need extra ordering and sequencing experiences.

Patterning is related to ordering and includes auditory, visual, and physical motor sequences that are repeated. Patterns may be copied, extended, or verbally described. Children can learn about patterns common to a variety of cultures.

## KEY TERMS

| | | |
|---|---|---|
| one more than | patterning | seriation |
| ordering | | |

## SUGGESTED ACTIVITIES

1. Observe children at school. Note those activities that show the children are learning order and patterning. Share your observations with the class.

2. Add ordering and patterning activities to your Activity File.

3. Assemble the materials needed to do the ordering and patterning assessment tasks in this unit. Try out the tasks with several young children. What did the children do? Share the results with the class.

4. Plan and do one or more ordering and/or patterning activities with a small group of preschool and/or kindergarten students.

5. Look through two or three educational materials catalogs. Pick out 10 materials you think would be best to use for ordering and/or patterning activities.

6. Using one of the evaluation systems suggested in Activity 5, Unit 2, evaluate one or more of the following software programs in terms of each program's value for learning about ordering and/or patterning.

   ■ *Math Blaster* (ages 4–6; Hazelton, PA: K–12 Software). Includes pattern completion activities.

   ■ *James Discovers Math* (http://www.smart kidssoftware.com). Includes pattern matching.

   ■ *Introduction to Patterns* (http://store .sunburst.com). Exploration of linear and geometric patterns and creation of patterns.

   ■ *MicroWorlds JR* (Highgate Springs, VT: LCSI). Includes pattern exploration.

   ■ *Millie's Math House* (San Francisco: Riverdeep-Edmark). Compare and match sizes and see and hear patterns.

## REVIEW

A. List at least seven of the major characteristics of ordering/seriation.

B. Describe the major characteristics of patterning.

C. Decide whether the descriptions below are examples of the following ordering and patterning behaviors: (a) size sequence, (b) one-to-one comparison, (c) ordering groups, (d) using ordinal words or numbers, (e) basic concept of ordering, (f) using double seriation, (g) patterning.

   1. Child arranges tokens in groups: one in the first group, two in the second, three in the third, and so on.

   2. Pablo says, "I'm last."

   3. Maria lines up sticks of various lengths from shortest to longest.

   4. Kate is trying to place all the nesting cups inside each other in order by size.

   5. Child chants, "Ho, ho, ho. Ha, ha, ha. Ho, ho, ho. Ha, ha, ha."

   6. Jim strings blue beads in this manner: large-small-large-small-large-small.

   7. Fong places a white chip on each red chip.

   8. Nancy places the smallest flower in the smallest flowerpot, the middle-sized flower in the middle-sized flowerpot, and the largest flower in the largest flowerpot.

   9. Mr. Mendez says, "Today we will line up with the shortest child first."

   10. Child parks cars: yellow car, blue car, yellow car, blue car.

   11. Tanja tells Josie, "I'm first this time."

   12. In the Montessori class, the pink tower is constructed with the largest cube at the bottom, the next smaller cube second, and so on until all the cubes are used.

D. Summarize the NCTM expectations for algebra that are described in this unit.

## REFERENCES

National Council of Teachers of Mathematics. (2000). *Principles and standards for school mathematics.* Reston, VA: Author.

Richardson, K. (1999). *Developing number concepts: Counting, comparing, and pattern (Book 1).* Parsippany, NJ: Seymour.

Zaslavsky, C. (1996). *The multicultural math classroom.* Portsmouth, NH: Heinemann.

## FURTHER READING AND RESOURCES

AIMS Educational Products. AIMS Education Foundation, P.O. Box 8120, Fresno, CA 93747-8120.

American Association for the Advancement of Science (AAAS). (2007). *Atlas of science literacy: Project 2061* (Vol. 2). Washington, DC: Author.

Baratta-Lorton, M. (1976). *Math their way.* Menlo Park, CA: Addison-Wesley.

Copley, J. V. (Ed.). (1999). *Mathematics in the early years.* Washington, DC: National Association for the Education of Young Children.

Copley, J. V. (2000). *The young child and mathematics.* Washington, DC: National Association for the Education of Young Children.

Copley, J. V. (Ed.). (2004). *Showcasing mathematics for the young child* (chap. 4, Algebra). Reston, VA: National Council of Teachers of Mathematics.

Copley, J. V., Jones, C., & Dighe, J. (2007). *Mathematics: The creative curriculum approach.* Washington, DC: Teaching Strategies.

Danisa, D., Gentile, J., McNamara, K., Pinney, M., Ross, S., & Rule, A. C. (2006). Geoscience for preschoolers. *Science & Children, 44*(4), 30–33.

Epstein, A. S., & Gainsley, S. (2005). *Math in the preschool classroom.* Ypsilanti, MI: High/Scope.

Greenes, C. E., Cavanagh, M., Dacey, L., Findell, C. R., & Small, M. (2001). *Navigating through algebra in prekindergarten–kindergarten.* Reston, VA: National Council of Teachers of Mathematics.

Greenes, C. E., Dacey, L., Cavanagh, M., Findell, C. R., Sheffield, L. J., & Small, M. (2003). *Navigating through problem solving and reasoning in prekindergarten–kindergarten.* Reston, VA: National Council of Teachers of Mathematics.

Learning Resources. (2007). *Hands-on standards.* Vernon Hills, IL: Author.

Moore, J. E., & Tryon, L. (1986). *Life cycles. Science sequencing* (2nd ed.). Monterey, CA: Evan Moor.

National Council of Teachers of Mathematics. (2007). *Curriculum focal points.* Reston, VA: Author.

National Research Council. (1996). *National science education standards.* Washington, DC: National Academies Press.

Richardson, K. (1984). *Developing number concepts using Unifix Cubes.* Menlo Park, CA: Addison-Wesley.

Richardson, K. (1999). *Developing number concepts: Planning guide.* Parsippany, NJ: Seymour.

Ziemba, E. J., & Hoffman, J. (2005/2006). Sorting and patterning in kindergarten: From activities to assessment. *Teaching Children Mathematics, 12*(5), 236–241.

# Unit 18

# Measurement: Volume, Weight, Length, and Temperature

## OBJECTIVES

After reading this unit, you should be able to:

■ Explain how measurement develops in five stages.

■ Assess and evaluate the measurement skills of a young child.

■ Do informal and structured measurement with young children.

■ Provide for naturalistic measurement experiences.

■ Explain the NCTM standard for measurement as it applies to preschool/kindergarten children.

The NCTM (2000, p. 102) expectations for children in the beginning stages of **measurement** include recognizing the attributes of **length**, **volume**, **weight**, and time as well as comparing and ordering objects according to these attributes. Time is addressed in Unit 19. Also included in this unit are the attributes of **temperature**. By the time they reach kindergarten, young children are expected to understand measurement with nonstandard units such as multiple copies of objects of the same size (e.g., paper clips). Measurement connects geometry and number and builds on children's experiences with comparisons (Unit 11). Length is the major focus for younger children, but experiences with volume, weight, and temperature are also important. Estimation is an important measurement tool in the early stages. The curriculum focal point (NCTM, 2007) for measurement in prekindergarten is identifying measurable attributes and comparing objects using these attributes; for kindergarten, the focal point in measure-

ment is ordering objects by measurable attributes such as length and weight. Two objects might be compared with a third.

Measurement is one of the most useful math skills. *Measurement* involves assigning a number to things so they can be compared on the same attributes. Numbers can be assigned to attributes such as volume, weight, length, and temperature. For example, the child drinks *one cup* of milk. Numbers can also be given to time measurement. However, time is not an attribute of things and so is presented separately (Unit 19). **Standard units** such as pints, quarts, liters, yards, meters, pounds, grams, and degrees tell us exactly how much (*volume*); how heavy (*weight*); how long, wide, or deep (*length*); and how hot or cold (*temperature*). A number is put with a standard unit to let a comparison be made. Two quarts contain more than one quart, two pounds weigh less than three pounds, one meter is shorter than four meters, and 30° is colder than 80°.

## STAGES OF DEVELOPMENT

The concept of measurement develops through five stages, as outlined in Figure 18–1. The first stage is a **play stage**. The child imitates older children and adults. She plays at measuring with rulers, measuring cups, measuring spoons, and scales as she sees others do. She pours sand, water, rice, beans, and peas from one container to another as she explores the properties of volume. She lifts and moves things as she learns about weight. She notes that those who are bigger than she can do many more activities and has her first concept of length (height). She finds that her short arms cannot always reach what she wants them to reach (length). She finds that she has a preference for cold or hot food and cold or hot bathwater. She begins to learn about temperature. This first stage begins at birth and continues through the sensorimotor period into the preoperational period.

The second stage in the development of the concept of measurement is the one of making **comparisons** (Unit 11). This is well underway by the preoperational stage. The child is always comparing: bigger-smaller, heavier-lighter, longer-shorter, and hotter-colder.

The third stage, which comes at the end of the preoperational period and at the beginning of concrete operations, is one in which the child learns to use what are called **arbitrary units**; that is, anything the child has can be used as a unit of measure. She will try to find out how many coffee cups of sand will fill a quart milk carton. The volume of the coffee cup is the arbitrary unit. She will find out how many toothpicks long her foot is. The length of the toothpick is the arbitrary unit. As she goes through the stage of using arbitrary units, she learns concepts that she will need in order to understand standard units.

When the child enters the period of concrete operations, she can begin to see the need for standard units. She can see that to communicate with someone else in a way the other person will understand, she must use the same units the other person uses. For example, the child says that her paper is nine thumbs wide. Another person cannot find another piece of the same width unless the child and the thumb are there to measure it. But if she says her paper is eight and one-half inches wide, another person will known exactly the width of the paper. In this case, the thumb is an arbitrary unit and the inch is a *standard unit*. The same is true for other units. Standard measuring cups and spoons must be used when cooking in order for the recipe to turn out correctly. If any coffee cup or teacup and just any spoon are used when following a recipe, the measurement will be arbitrary and inexact, and the chances of a successful outcome will be poor. The same can be said of building a house. If nonstandard measuring tools are used, the house will not come out as it appears in the plans, and one carpenter will not be communicating clearly with another.

The last stage in the development of the concept of measurement begins in the concrete operations period. In this last stage, the child begins to use and understand the standard units of measurement such as inches, meters, pints, liters, grams, and degrees.

Obviously, prekindergartners and most kindergartners are still exploring the concept of measurement. Prekindergartners are usually in stages one (play and imitation) and two (making comparisons). The kindergartners begin in stage two and move into stage three (arbitrary units). During the primary grades, students begin to see the need for standard units (stage four) and move into using standard units (stage five). Measurement can be integrated into the other content areas (see Figure 18–2).

| Piagetian Stage | Age | Measurement Stage |
|---|---|---|
| Sensorimotor and Preoperational | 0–7 | 1. Plays and imitates |
| | | 2. Makes comparisons |
| Transitional: Preoperational to Concrete Operations | 5–7 | 3. Uses arbitrary units |
| Concrete Operations | 6+ | 4. Sees need for standard units |
| | | 5. Uses standard units |

Figure 18–1 Stages in the development of the concept of measurement.

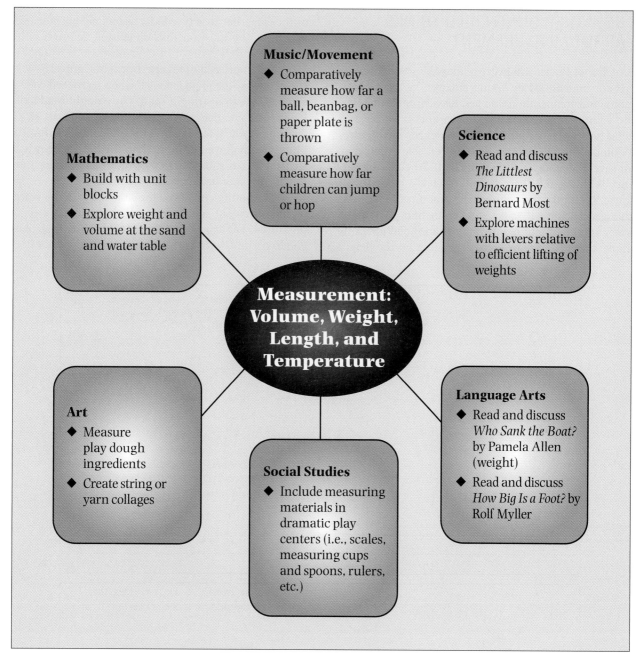

**Figure 18–2** Integrating measurement across the curriculum.

## HOW THE YOUNG CHILD THINKS ABOUT MEASUREMENT

A review of Piaget will help explain why standard units are not understood by young children in the sensori-motor and preoperational stages. Recall from Unit 1 that the young child is fooled by appearances. He believes what he sees before him. He does not keep old pictures in mind as he will do later. He is not yet able to conserve (or save) the first way something looks when its appearance is changed. When the ball of clay is made into a snake, he thinks the volume (the amount of clay) has changed because it looks smaller to him. When the water is poured into a differently shaped container, he thinks there is more or less—depending on the height of the glass. Because he can focus on only one attribute at a time, the most obvious dimension determines his response.

Two more examples are shown in Figure 18–3. In the first task, the child is fooled when a crooked road is compared with a straight road. The straight road looks longer (*conservation of length*). In the second task, size is dominant over material, and the child guesses that the Ping-Pong ball weighs more than the hard rubber ball. He thinks that since the table tennis ball is larger than the hard rubber ball, it must be heavier.

The young child becomes familiar with the words of measurement and learns which attributes can be measured. He learns mainly through observing older children and adults as they measure. He does not need

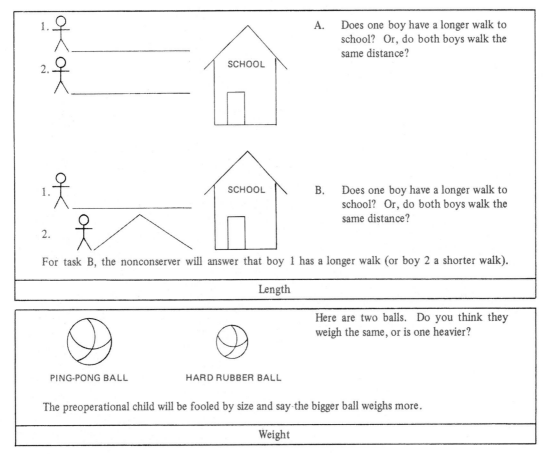

A. Does one boy have a longer walk to school? Or, do both boys walk the same distance?

B. Does one boy have a longer walk to school? Or, do both boys walk the same distance?

For task B, the nonconserver will answer that boy 1 has a longer walk (or boy 2 a shorter walk).

Length

Here are two balls. Do you think they weigh the same, or is one heavier?

PING-PONG BALL     HARD RUBBER BALL

The preoperational child will be fooled by size and say the bigger ball weighs more.

Weight

Figure 18–3 Conservation of length and weight.

to be taught the standard units of measurement in a formal way. The young child needs to gain a feeling that things differ on the basis of "more" and "less" of some attributes. He gains this feeling mostly through his own observations and firsthand experimental experiences.

## ASSESSMENT

To assess measurement skills in the young child, the teacher observes. He notes whether the child uses the term *measure* in the adult way. He notes whether she uses adult measuring tools in her play as she sees adults use them. He looks for the following kinds of incidents.

■ Mary is playing in the sandbox. She pours sand from an old bent measuring cup into a bucket and stirs it with a sand shovel. "I'm measuring the flour for my cake. I need three cups of flour and two cups of sugar."

■ Juanita is seated on a small chair. Kate kneels in front of her. Juanita has her right shoe off. Kate puts Juanita's foot on a ruler. "I am measuring your foot for your new shoes."

■ The children have a play grocery store. Jorge puts some plastic fruit on the toy scale. "Ten pounds here."

■ Azam is the doctor, and Bob is his patient. Azam takes an imaginary thermometer from Bob's mouth. "You have a hot fever."

Individual interviews for the preoperational child may be found in Unit 11. For the child who is near concrete operations (past age 5), the conservation tasks in Appendix A and in Unit 1 may be used to determine if children are conservers and thus probably ready to use standard units of measurement.

## NATURALISTIC ACTIVITIES

Young children's concepts of measurement come, for the most part, from their natural everyday experiences exploring the environment, discovering its properties,

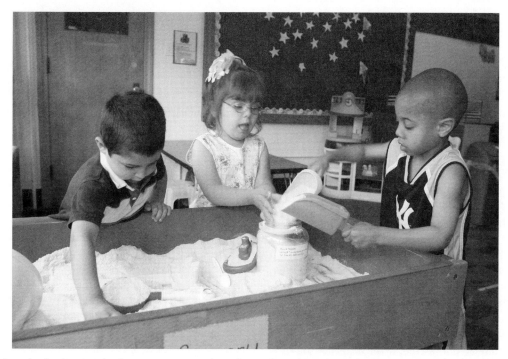

Children explore the fundamentals of measurement as they play at the sand and water table.

and so constructing their own knowledge. The examples in the assessment section of this unit demonstrate how children's play activities reflect their concepts of measurement. Mary has seen and may have helped someone make a cake. Kate has been to the shoe store and knows the clerk must measure the feet before he brings out a pair of shoes to try on the customer. Jorge has seen the grocer weigh fruit. Azam knows that a thermometer tells how "hot" a fever is. The observant young child picks up these ideas on his own without being told specifically that they are important.

The child uses his play activities to practice what he has seen adults do. He also uses play materials to learn ideas through experimentation and trial and error. Water, sand, dirt, mud, rice, and beans teach the child about volume. As he pours these substances from one container to another, he learns about *how much*, or amount. The child can use containers of many sizes and shapes: buckets, cups, plastic bottles, dishes, bowls, and coffee cans. Shovels, spoons, strainers, and funnels can also be used with these materials. When playing with water, the child can also learn about weight if he has some small objects—like sponges, rocks, corks, small pieces of wood, and marbles—that may float or sink. Any time a child tries to put something in a box, envelope, glass, or any other container, he learns something about volume.

The child can begin to learn the idea of linear measure (length, width, height) and area in his play. The unit blocks that are usually found in the early childhood classroom help the child learn the idea of units. He will soon learn that each block is a unit of another block. Two, four, or eight of the small blocks are the same length when placed end to end as one of the longest blocks. As he builds enclosures (houses, garages, farmyards, and so on), he is forced to pick his blocks so that each side is the same length as the one across from it.

The child learns about weight and balance on the teeter-totter. He soon learns that it takes two to go up and down. He also learns that it works best when the two are near the same weight and are the same distance from the middle.

The child makes many contacts with temperature. He learns that his soup is hot, warm, and then, as it sits out, cold. He likes cold milk and hot cocoa. He learns that the air may be hot or cold. If the air is hot, he may wear shorts or just a bathing suit. If the air is cold, he will need a coat, hat, and mittens.

Adult scaffolding helps children construct measurement concepts.

## INFORMAL ACTIVITIES

The young child learns about measurement through the kinds of experiences just described. During these activities there are many opportunities for informal teaching. One job for the adult as the child plays is to help her by pointing out properties of materials that the child may not be able to find on her own. For instance, if a child says she must have all the long blocks to make her house large enough, the teacher can show her how several small blocks can do the job. She can show the child how to measure how much string will fit around a box before she cuts off a piece to use.

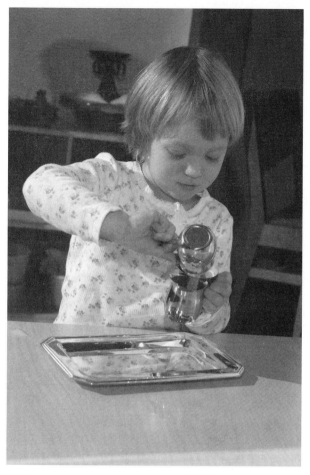

Kindergartners can carry out nonstandard measurement activities.

The teacher can also take these opportunities to use measurement words such as the names of units of measurement and the words listed in Unit 15. She can also pose problems for the child.

■ How can we find out if we have enough apple juice for everyone?

■ How can we find out how many paper cups of milk can be poured from a gallon container?

■ How can we find out if someone has a high fever?

■ How can we find out without going outside if we need to wear a sweater or coat?

■ How can we find out who is the tallest boy in the class? The child who weighs the most?

■ How many of these place mats will fit around the table?

■ Who lives the longest distance from school?

It is the teacher's responsibility to provide environmental opportunities for the exploration and discovery of measurement concepts.

## STRUCTURED ACTIVITIES

The young child learns most of his basic measurement ideas through his play and home activities that come through the natural routines of the day. He gains a feeling for the need for measurement and learns the language of measurement. Structured activities must be chosen with care. They should make use of the child's senses. They should be related to what is familiar to the child and expand what he already knows. They should pose problems that will show him the need for measurement. They should give the child a chance to use measurement words to explain his solution to the problem. The following activities are examples of these kinds of experiences and the naturalistic and informal experiences that serve as their foundation.

## ACTIVITIES

### Measurement: Volume

**OBJECTIVES:** ■ To learn the characteristics of volume
■ To see that volume can be measured
■ To learn measurement words used to tell about volume (more, less, too big, too little, the same)

*(continued)*

**MATERIALS:**
■ Sandbox (indoors and/or out), water table (or sink or plastic dishpans)
■ Many containers of different sizes: bottles, cups, bowls, milk cartons, cans (with smooth edges), boxes (for dry materials)
■ Spoons, scoops, funnels, strainers, beaters
■ Water, sand, rice,* beans,* peas,* seeds, or anything else that can be poured

**NATURALISTIC AND INFORMAL ACTIVITIES:** Allow plenty of time for experimenting with the materials listed above during center time. Observe if children are into the pretend play measurement stage, are making comparisons, or if they mention any standard units. Ask questions or make comments, such as: "How many of the blue cups of sand will fill up the purple bowl?"; "Which bottle will hold more water?"; "You filled that milk carton up to the top."

**STRUCTURED ACTIVITIES:**
1. Have several containers of different kinds and sizes. Fill one with water (or sand or rice or peas or beans). Pick out another container. Ask the children: IF I POUR THIS WATER FROM THIS BOTTLE INTO THIS OTHER BOTTLE, WILL THE SECOND BOTTLE HOLD ALL THE WATER? After each child has made her prediction, pour the water into the second container. Ask a child to tell what she saw happen. Continue with several containers. Have the children line them up from the one that holds the most to the one that holds the least.

2. Pick out one standard container (coffee cup, paper cup, measuring cup, tin can). Have one or more larger containers. Say, IF I WANT TO FILL THE BIG BOWL WITH SAND AND USE THIS PAPER CUP, HOW MANY TIMES WILL I HAVE TO FILL THE PAPER CUP AND POUR SAND INTO THE BOWL? Write down the children's predictions. Let each child have a turn to fill the cup and pour sand into the bowl. Record by making slash marks how many cups of sand are poured. Have the children count the number of marks when the bowl is full. Compare this amount with what the children thought the amount would be.

**FOLLOW-UP:** Do the same types of activities using different sizes of containers and common objects. For example, have a doll and three different-sized boxes. Have the children decide which box the doll will fit into.

*Some educators feel it is inappropriate to use food for play—be cautious.

## Measurement: Weight

**OBJECTIVES:**
■ To learn firsthand the characteristics of weight
■ To learn that weight and size are different attributes (big things may have less weight than small things)
■ To learn that light and heavy are relative terms

**MATERIALS:**
■ Things in the classroom or brought from home, e.g., manipulatives, paper clips, buttons, crayons, pencils, small toys
■ A teeter-totter, a board and a block, a simple pan balance

- Sand, sugar, salt, flour, sawdust, peas, beans, rice
- A ball collection with balls of different sizes and materials: ball bearings, table tennis, golf, solid rubber, foam rubber, Styrofoam, balsa wood, cotton, balloons

**NATURALISTIC AND INFORMAL ACTIVITIES:** During center time, provide opportunities for the children to experiment with a simple pan balance using a variety of materials. Note if they use any weight vocabulary (such as heavy or light). Ask them to explain their actions. Outdoors or in the gym, provide a teeter-totter. Note how they find ways to balance. Ask them what happens when children of different weights or different numbers of children sit on each end.

**STRUCTURED ACTIVITIES:**

1. Have the child name things in the room that he can lift and things he cannot lift. Which things can he not lift because of size? Which because of weight? Compare things such as a stapler (small and heavy) and a large paper bag (large and light). Have the children line up things from heaviest to lightest.

2. Have the children experiment with the teeter-totter. How many children does it take to balance the teacher? Make a balance with a block and a board. Have the child experiment with different things to see which will make the board balance.

3. A fixed-position pan balance can be used for firsthand experiences with all types of things.

   a. The child can try balancing small objects such as paper clips, hair clips, bobby pins, coins, toothpicks, cotton balls, and so on in the pans.

   b. Take the collection of balls and pick out a pair. Have the child predict which is heavier (lighter). Let him put one in each pan to check his prediction.

   c. Put one substance such as salt in one pan. Have the child fill the other pan with flour until the pans balance. IS THE AMOUNT (VOLUME) OF FLOUR AND SALT THE SAME?

   d. Have equal amounts of two different substances such as sand and sawdust in the balance pans. DO THE PANS BALANCE?

**FOLLOW-UP:** Make some play dough with the children. Have them measure out one part flour and one part salt. Mix in some powder tempera. Add water until the mixture is pliable but not too sticky. See Unit 22 for cooking ideas. Read *Who Sank the Boat?* by Pamela Allen.

## Measurement: Length and Height

**OBJECTIVES:**
- To learn firsthand the concepts of length and height
- To help the child learn the use of arbitrary units

**MATERIALS:**
- The children's bodies
- Things in the room that can be measured, e.g., tables, chairs, doors, windows, shelves, books
- Balls of string and yarn, scissors, construction paper, markers, beans, chips, pennies, other small counters, pencils, toothpicks, ice-cream-bar sticks, unit blocks

*(continued)*

**NATURALISTIC AND INFORMAL ACTIVITIES:** During center time, note if the children engage in any comparison or play length measurement activities. Unit blocks are especially good for naturalistic and informal measurement explorations. For example, observe whether children—when using unit blocks—appear to use trial and error to make their blocks fit as they wish. Comment, "You matched the blocks so your house has all the sides the same length."

**STRUCTURED ACTIVITIES:**

1. Present the child with problems where she must pick out something of a certain length. For example, a dog must be tied to a post. Have a picture of the dog and the post. Have several lengths of string. Have the child find out which string is the right length. Say, WHICH ROPE WILL REACH FROM THE RING TO THE DOG'S COLLAR?

2. LOOK AROUND THE ROOM. WHICH THINGS ARE CLOSE? WHICH THINGS ARE FAR AWAY?

3. Have several children line up. Have a child point out which is the tallest, the shortest. Have the children line up from tallest to shortest. The child can draw pictures of friends and family in a row from shortest to tallest.

4. Draw lines on construction paper. HOW MANY BEANS (CHIPS, TOOTHPICKS, or OTHER SMALL THINGS) WILL FIT ON EACH LINE? WHICH LINE HAS MORE BEANS? WHICH LINE IS LONGEST? Gradually use paper with more than two lines.

5. Put a piece of construction paper on the wall from the floor up to about 5 feet. Have each child stand next to the paper. Mark their heights and label the marks with their names. Check each child's height each month. Note how much each child grows over the year.

6. Create an arbitrary unit such as a pencil, a toothpick, a stick, a long block, or a piece of yarn or string. Have the child measure things in the room to see how many units long, wide, or tall the things are.

**FOLLOW-UP:** Keep the height chart out so the children can look at it and talk about their heights. Read *The Littlest Dinosaurs* by Bernard Most and *How Big Is a Foot?* by Rolf Myller.

## Measurement: Temperature

**OBJECTIVES:**
■ To give the child firsthand experiences that will help him learn that temperature is the relative measure of heat
■ To learn that the thermometer is used to measure temperature
■ To experience hot, warm, and cold as related to things, to weather, and to the seasons of the year

**MATERIALS:** Ice cubes, hot plate, teakettle or pan, pictures of the four seasons, poster board, markers, scissors, glue, construction paper, old magazines with pictures, real thermometers (body, indoors, and outdoors).

**NATURALISTIC AND INFORMAL ACTIVITIES:** Note children's talk regarding temperature. Make comments, such as: "Be careful, the soup is very hot"; "It's cold today, you must button up your coat." Ask questions such as, "Do we need to wear mittens or gloves today?"

**STRUCTURED ACTIVITIES:**

1. Have the children decide whether selected things in the environment are hot, cold, or warm—for example, ice and boiling water, the hot and cold water taps, the radiators, the glass in the windows, their skin.

2. Show pictures of summer, fall, winter, and spring. Discuss the usual temperatures in each season. What is the usual weather? What kinds of clothes are worn? Make a cardboard thermometer. At the bottom put a child in heavy winter clothes, above put a child in a light coat or jacket, then a child in a sweater, then one in short sleeves, then one in a bathing suit.

3. Each day discuss the outside temperature relative to what was worn to school.

4. Give the children scissors and old magazines. Have them find and cut out pictures of hot things and cold things. Have them glue the hot things on one piece of poster board and the cold things on another.

5. Show the children three thermometers: one for body temperature, one for room temperature, and one for outdoor use. Discuss when and where each is used.

**FOLLOW-UP:**  Each day the outside temperature can be discussed and recorded in some way (as in activity 3 or on a graph as discussed in Unit 20).

## IDEAS FOR CHILDREN WITH SPECIAL NEEDS

Measurement lends itself very well to the first cooperative learning activities. Two children can form a buddy group. They can work together with the younger children comparing attributes (such as grouping objects into long and short) and with the kindergartners measuring with nonstandard units. Children of different cultures and children of different abilities can be put into buddy pairs. Each child can be assigned a responsibility: for example, one could handle the measuring tool and the other could record the measurements.

## EVALUATION

The adult should note the children's responses to the activities given them. She should observe them as they try out the materials and note their comments. She must also observe whether they are able to solve everyday problems that come up by using informal measurements such as comparisons. Use the individual interviews in Unit 11 and in Appendix A.

## SUMMARY

The concept of measurement develops through five stages. Preoperational children are in the early stages: play, imitation, and comparing. They learn about measurement mainly through naturalistic and informal experiences that encourage them to explore and discover. Transitional children move into the stage of experimenting with arbitrary units. During the concrete operations period, children learn to use standard units of measurement. Measurement activities lend themselves to cooperative learning groups with two members.

## KEY TERMS

| | | |
|---|---|---|
| arbitrary units | measurement | temperature |
| comparisons | play stage | volume |
| length | standard units | weight |

## SUGGESTED ACTIVITIES

1. Watch young children during group play. Note and record any measurement activities that you observe. Identify the stage of measurement understanding that is represented by each activity.

2. In class, discuss ways in which children can be encouraged at home and at school to develop concepts of measurement.

3. Plan two or three measurement activities. Assemble the necessary materials, and use the activities with a group of young children.

4. Look through an early childhood school supply catalog. Make a list of the measurement materials that you would purchase if you had $400 to spend.

5. Add several measurement activities to your file/notebook.

6. Use the evaluation scheme in Activity 5, Unit 2, to evaluate any of the following software programs.

■ *Key Skills Math Shapes, Numbers, and Measurement* (http://www.campus tech.com). Measures of time and temperature; coin values up to $2.00.

■ *Numbers Undercover* (Sunburst: 1-800-321-7511; fax, 1-888-800-3028). Measurement, time, and money.

■ *Ani's Rocket Ride* (Evanston, IL: APTE). Includes exploration of a balancing scale.

■ *Light Weights/Heavy Weights* (NASA explores, http://media.nasaexplores .com). Activities for comparing relative weights of common objects.

■ *James Discovers Math* (http://www .smartkidssoftware.com). Includes measurement.

■ *One Hen* (http://www.onehen.org). Money.

## REVIEW

A. List, in order, the five stages of measurement.

B. Describe each of the five stages of measurement.

C. Identify the level of measurement described in each of the following incidents.

1. Johnny says, "My block building is bigger than yours."

2. Linda checks the thermometer. "It's 32 degrees today—very cold!"

3. Cindy, Juanita, and Li pour dry beans in and out of an assortment of containers.

4. "I weigh 60 pounds. How much do you weigh?"

5. "Dad, it would take two of my shoes to make one as long as yours."

D. Explain how a young child's measurement skills can be assessed.

E. Describe the NCTM (2000, 2007) expectations for measurement for preschool/kindergarten children.

## REFERENCES

Allen, P. (1982). *Who sank the boat?* New York: Sandcastle Books.

Most, B. (1989). *The littlest dinosaurs.* San Diego, CA: Harcourt Brace.

Myller, R. (1972). *How big is a foot?* New York: Atheneum.

National Council of Teachers of Mathematics. (2000). *Principles and standards for school mathematics.* Reston, VA: Author.

National Council of Teachers of Mathematics. (2007). *Curriculum focal points.* Reston, VA: Author.

## FURTHER READING AND RESOURCES

Cline, L. J. (2001). Investigations: Bubble-mania. *Teaching Children Mathematics, 8*(1), 20–22.

Copley, J. V. (2000). *The young child and mathematics.* Washington, DC: National Association for the Education of Young Children.

Copley, J. V. (Ed.). (2004). *Showcasing mathematics for the young child* (chap. 5, Measurement). Reston, VA: National Council of Teachers of Mathematics.

Copley, J. V., Glass, K., Nix, L., Faseler, A., DeJesus, M., & Tanksley, S. (2004). Early childhood corner: Measuring experiences for young children. *Teaching Children Mathematics, 10*(6), 314–319.

Dacey, L., Cavanagh, M., Findell, C. R., Greenes, C. E., Sheffield, L. J., & Small, M. (2003). *Navigating through measurement in prekindergarten–grade 2.* Reston, VA: National Council of Teachers of Mathematics.

Dougherty, B. J., & Venenciano, L. C. H. (2007). Measure up for understanding. *Teaching Children Mathematics, 13*(9), 452–456.

Kribs-Zaleta, C. M., & Bradshaw, D. (2003). A case of units. *Teaching Children Mathematics, 9*(7), 397–399.

Lubinski, C. A., & Thiessen, D. (1996). Exploring measurement through literature. *Teaching Children Mathematics, 2*, 260–263.

Mailley, E., & Moyer, P. S. (2004). Investigations: The mathematical candy store: Weight matters. *Teaching Children Mathematics, 10*(8), 388–391.

McGregor, J. (1996). Math by the month: How do you measure up?: K–2. *Teaching Children Mathematics, 3*, 84.

Measurement [Focus Issue]. (2006). *Science & Children, 44*(2).

Newburger, A., & Vaughan, E. (2006). *Teaching numeracy, language, and literacy with blocks.* St. Paul, MN: Redleaf Press.

Teaching and learning measurement [Focus Issue]. (2006). *Teaching Children Mathematics, 13*(3).

West, S., & Cox, A. (2001). *Sand and water play.* Beltsville, MD: Gryphon House.

Young, S., & O'Leary, R. (2002). Creating numerical scales for measuring tools. *Teaching Children Mathematics, 8*(7), 400–405.

# Unit 19

# Measurement: Time

## OBJECTIVES

After reading this unit, you should be able to:

■ Describe what is meant by time sequence.

■ Describe what is meant by time duration.

■ Explain the three kinds of time.

■ Do informal and structured time measurement activities with young children.

■ Explain the NCTM (2000) expectations for preschool and kindergarten students' understanding of time.

The NCTM standards (2000) for measurement include expectations for the understanding of time. Preschool and kindergarten children are learning the attributes of time such as **sequence** and **duration**. *Sequence* of time concerns the order of events. It is related to the ideas about ordering presented in Unit 17. While the child learns to sequence things in patterns, he also learns to sequence events. He learns that small, middle-sized, and large beads go in order for a pattern sequence. He gets up, washes his face, brushes his teeth, dresses, and eats breakfast for a time sequence. *Duration* of time has to do with how long an event takes (seconds, minutes, hours, days, a short time, a long time).

## KINDS OF TIME

There are three kinds of time a child has to learn. Time is a hard measure to learn. The child cannot see it and feel it as she can weight, volume, length, and temperature.

There are fewer clues to help the child. The young child relates time to three things: **personal experience**, **social activity**, and culture.

In her *personal experience*, the child has her own past, present, and future. The past is often referred to as "When I was a baby." "Last night" may mean any time before right now. The future may be "After my night nap" or "When I am big." The young child has difficulty with the idea that there was a time when mother and dad were little and she was not yet born.

Time in terms of *social activity* is a little easier to learn and makes more sense to the young child. The young child tends to be a slave to order and routine. A change of schedule can be very upsetting. This is because time for her is a sequence of predictable events. She can count on her morning activities being the same each day when she wakes up. Once she gets to school, she learns that there is order there, too: first she takes off her coat and hangs it up, next she is greeted by her teacher, then she goes to the big playroom to play, and so on through the day.

A third kind of time is **cultural time**. It is the time that is fixed by clocks and calendars. Everyone learns this kind of time. It is a kind of time that the child probably does not really understand until she is in the concrete operations period. She can, however, learn the language (seconds, minutes, days, months, and so on) and the names of the timekeepers (clock, watch, calendar). She can also learn to recognize a timekeeper when she sees one.

## LANGUAGE OF TIME

Learning time depends on language no less than learning any part of math. Time and sequence words are listed in Unit 15 and are listed again here for easy reference.

- **General words**: time, age
- **Specific words**: morning, afternoon, evening, night, day, noon
- **Relational words**: soon, tomorrow, yesterday, early, late, a long time ago, once upon a time, new, old, now, when, sometimes, then, before, present, while, never, once, next, always, fast, slow, speed, first, second, third, and so on
- **Duration words**: clock and watch (minutes, seconds, hours); calendar (date, days of the week names, names of the month, names of seasons, year)
- **Special days**: birthday, Passover, Juneteenth, Cinco de Mayo, Kwanza, Ramadan, Easter, Christmas, Thanksgiving, vacation, holiday, school day, weekend

Time concept experiences can be integrated into the other content areas (see Figure 19–1).

## ASSESSMENT

The teacher should observe the child's use of time language. She should note if he makes an attempt to place himself and events in time. Does he remember the sequence of activities at school and at home? Is he able to wait for one thing to finish before going on to the next? Is he able to order things (Unit 17) in a sequence?

The following are examples of the kinds of interview tasks that are included in Appendix A.

## SAMPLE ASSESSMENT TASK

**5H**                                                                    **Preoperational Ages 4–5**

**Time, Labeling and Sequence: Unit 19**

**METHOD:** Interview.

**SKILL:** Shown pictures of daily events, the child can use time words to describe the action in each picture and place the pictures in a logical time sequence.

**MATERIALS:** Pictures of daily activities such as meals, nap, bath, playtime, bedtime.

**PROCEDURE:** Show the child each picture. Say, TELL ME ABOUT THIS PICTURE. WHAT'S HAPPENING? After the child has described each picture, place all the pictures in front of him, and tell the child, PICK OUT (SHOW ME) THE PICTURE OF WHAT HAPPENS FIRST EACH DAY. After a picture is selected, ask WHAT HAPPENS NEXT? Continue until all the pictures are lined up.

**EVALUATION:** When describing the pictures, note whether the child uses time words such as breakfast time, lunchtime, playtime, morning, night, etc. Note whether a logical sequence is used in placing the pictures in order.

**INSTRUCTIONAL RESOURCE:** Charlesworth, R., and Lind, K. K. (2010). *Math and science for young children* (6th ed.). Clifton Park, NY: Cengage Learning.

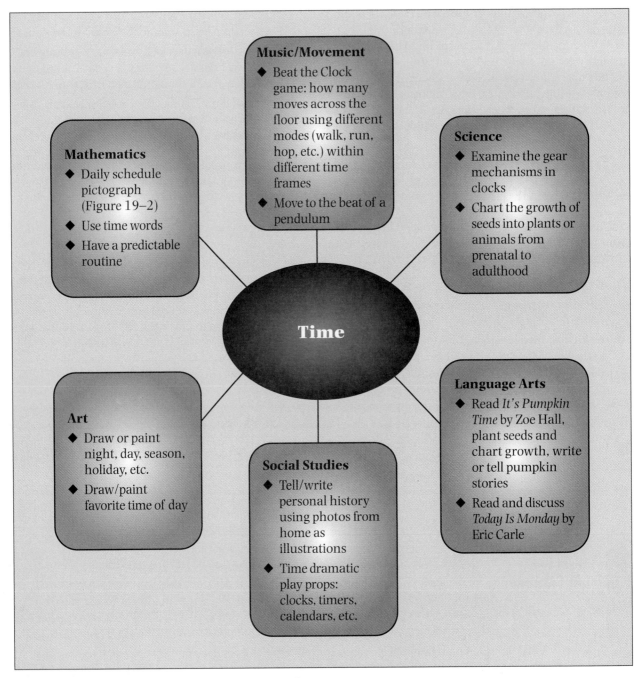

**Figure 19–1** Integrating time experiences across the curriculum.

## SAMPLE ASSESSMENT TASK

| | |
|---|---|
| **4I** | **Preoperational Ages 3–6** |

**Time, Identify Clock or Watch: Unit 19**

**METHOD:** Interview.

**SKILL:** The child can identify a clock and/or watch and describe its function.

**MATERIALS:** One or more of the following timepieces: conventional clock and watch, digital clock and watch. Preferably at least one conventional and one digital should be included. If real timepieces are not available, use pictures.

**PROCEDURE:** Show the child the timepieces or pictures of timepieces. Ask, WHAT IS THIS? WHAT DOES IT TELL US? WHAT IS IT FOR? WHAT ARE THE PARTS, AND WHAT ARE THEY FOR?

**EVALUATION:** Note whether the child can label watch(es) and clock(s), how much she is able to describe about the functions of the parts (long and short hands, second hands, alarms set, time changer, numerals). Note also if the child tries to tell time. Compare knowledge of conventional and digital timepieces.

**INSTRUCTIONAL RESOURCE:** Charlesworth, R., and Lind, K. K. (2010). *Math and science for young children* (6th ed.). Clifton Park, NY: Cengage Learning.

## NATURALISTIC ACTIVITIES

From birth on, children are capable of learning time and sequence. In an organized, nurturing environment, infants learn quickly that when they wake up from sleep, they are held and comforted, their diapers are changed, and then they are fed. The first sense of time duration comes from how long it takes for each of these events. Infants soon have a sense of how long they will be held and comforted, how long it takes for a diaper change, and how long it takes to eat. Time for the infant is a sense of sequence and of duration of events.

The toddler shows his understanding of time words through his actions. When he is told "It's lunchtime," he runs to his high chair. When he is told it is time for a nap, he may run the other way. He will notice cues that mean it is time to do something new: toys are being picked up, the table is set, or Dad appears at the door. He begins to look for these events that tell him that one piece of time ends and a new piece of time is about to start.

As spoken language develops, the child will use time words. He will make an effort to place events and himself in time. It is important for adults to listen and respond to what he has to say. The following are some examples.

■ Carlos (18 months old) tugs at Mr. Flores's pants leg; "Cookie, cookie." "Not yet Carlos. We'll have lunch first. Cookies are after lunch."

■ Kai (age 20 months) finishes her lunch and gets up. "No nap today. Play with dollies." Ms. Moore picks her up; "Nap first. You can play with the dolls later."

■ "Time to put the toys away, Kate." Kate (age 30 months) answers, "Not now. I'll do it a big later on."

■ Chris (3 years old) sits with Mrs. Raymond. Chris says, "Last night we stayed at the beach house." "Oh yes," answers Mrs. Raymond, "You were at the beach last summer, weren't you?" (For Chris, anything in the past happened "last night.")

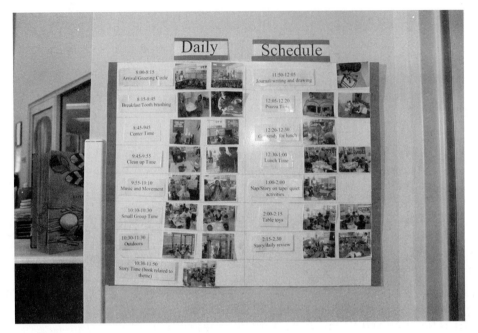

A consistent routine is the basis of the young child's understanding of time.

■ Mr. Flores is showing the group a book with pictures of the zoo. Richard (4 years old) comments, "I want to go there yesterday." Mr. Flores says, "We'll be going to the zoo on Friday."

■ Rosa (6 years old) says, "One time, when I was real small, like three or something, _____." Her teacher listens as Rosa relates her experience.

It is important for the young child to have a predictable and regular routine. It is through this routine that the child gains his sense of time duration and time sequence. It is also important for him to hear time words and to be listened to when he tries to use his time ideas. It is especially important that his own time words be accepted. For instance Kate's "a big later on" and Chris's "last night" should be accepted. Kate shows an understanding of the future and Chris of the past even though they are not as precise as an adult would be.

## INFORMAL ACTIVITIES

The adult needs to capitalize on the child's efforts to gain a sense of time and time sequence. Reread the situations described in the previous section. In each, the adults do some informal instruction. Mr. Flores reminds Brad of the coming sequence. So does Ms. Moore, and so does the adult with Kate. Mrs. Raymond accepts what Chris says but also uses the correct time words "last summer." It is important that adults listen to and expand on what children say.

The adult serves as a model for time-related behavior. The teacher checks the clock and the calendar for times and dates. The teacher uses the time words listed in the Language of Time section. She makes statements and asks questions.

■ "*Good morning*, Tom."

■ "*Goodnight*, Mary. See you *tomorrow*."

■ "What did you do over the *weekend?*"

■ "Who will be our guest for lunch *tomorrow?*"

■ "*Next week* on *Tuesday* we will go to the park for a picnic."

■ "Let me check the *time*. No wonder you are hungry. It's almost *noon*."

■ "You are the *first* one here *today*."

Children will observe and imitate what the teacher says and does even before they understand the ideas completely.

An excellent tool for informal classroom time instruction is a daily picture/word schedule placed in a prominent place. Figure 19–2 is an example of such a schedule. Children frequently ask, "When do we _____?"

"What happens after this?" and so on. Teachers can take them to the pictorial schedule and help them find the answer for themselves. "What are we doing now?" "Find (activity) on the schedule." "What comes next?" Eventually, children will just have to be reminded to "Look at the schedule" and they will answer their own questions.

**DAILY SCHEDULE**

8:00 A.M.–8:30 A.M.
**Breakfast**

8:30 A.M.–9:00 A.M.
**Playtime**
**Outdoors or in Gym**

9:00 A.M.–9:15 A.M.
**Group Meeting**

9:15 A.M.–10:30 A.M.
**Center Activities**

10:30 A.M.–10:45 A.M.
**Snack**

10:45 A.M.–11:15 A.M.
**Playtime**
**Outdoors or in Gym**

**Figure 19–2** A picture/word daily schedule supports the development of the concept of time sequence.

**11:15–11:45 A.M.**
**Story and Language**
**Development Group Activities**

**11:45–12:00 A.M.**
**Wash Hands, Go to**
**Lunch**

**12:00–12:30**
**Lunch**

**12:30–1:00 P.M.**
**Playtime**
**Outdoors or in Gym**

**1:00–2:00 P.M.**
**Rest**

**2:00–3:00 P.M.**
**Art, Music, Writing,**
**Reading**

**3:00–3:30 P.M.**
**Clean-Up**
**Prepare to Leave or**
**Go to Extended Day**

**Figure 19–2** *Continued*

## STRUCTURED ACTIVITIES

Structured time and sequence activities include sequence patterns with beads, blocks, and other objects; sequence stories; work centering around the calendar; and work centering around clocks. Experiences with pattern sequence and story sequence can begin at an early age. The infant enjoys looking at picture books, and the toddler can listen to short stories and begin to use beads and clocks to make her own sequences. The more structured pattern, story, calendar, clock, and other time activities described next are for children older than 4½ years.

# ACTIVITIES

## Time: Sequence Patterns

**OBJECTIVE:** To be able to understand and use the sequence idea of *next*.

**MATERIALS:** Any real things that can be easily sequenced by category, color, shape, size, etc. For example:

- Wooden beads and strings
- Plastic eating utensils
- Poker chips or buttons or coins
- Shapes cut from cardboard
- Small toy animals or people

**NATURALISTIC AND INFORMAL ACTIVITIES:** If they've had opportunities to explore the materials, the children should be familiar with the names of all the items and be able to identify their colors. For example, a child selects all the horses from a container of animals: "You have all the horses: brown ones (teacher points), black (teacher points), and white (teacher points)."

**STRUCTURED ACTIVITIES:** This activity uses plastic eating utensils. There are knives (K), forks (F), and spoons (S) in three colors (C1, C2, and C3). The teacher sets up a pattern to present to the child. Many kinds of patterns can be presented, including any of the following.

- *Color:* C1-C2-C1-C2 . . .
         C2-C3-C3-C2-C3-C3 . . .
- *Identity:* K-F-S-K-F-S . . .
          K-S-S-K-S-S . . .

   Say to the child: THIS PATTERN IS KNIFE-FORK-SPOON (or whatever pattern is set up). WHAT COMES NEXT? Once the child has the idea of pattern, set up the pattern and say, THIS IS A PATTERN. LOOK IT OVER. WHAT COMES NEXT?

**FOLLOW-UP:** Do the same activity with some of the other materials suggested. Also try it with the magnet board, flannelboard, and chalkboard.

## Time: Sequence Stories

**OBJECTIVE:** To learn sequences of events through stories.

**MATERIALS:** Picture storybooks* that have clear and repetitive sequences of events, such as:

- *The Gingerbread Man*
- *The Three Little Pigs*
- *The Three Billy Goats Gruff*
- *Henny Penny*
- *Caps for Sale*
- *Brown Bear, Brown Bear*
- *Polar Bear, Polar Bear*

(continued)

**NATURALISTIC AND INFORMAL ACTIVITIES:** Place the books in the library center where children can make selections during center time, rest time, or book time. Note which children appear to be familiar with the stories as they turn the pages pretending to read to themselves, a friend, or a doll or stuffed animal.

**STRUCTURED ACTIVITIES:** Read the stories several times until the children are familiar with them. Begin by asking, WHAT HAPPENS NEXT? before going on to the next event. Have the children say some of the repeated phrases such as "Little pigs, little pigs, let me come in," "Not by the hair on my chinny-chin-chin," "Then I'll huff and I'll puff and I'll blow your house in." Have the children try to repeat the list of those who chase the gingerbread man. Have them recall the whole story sequence.

**FOLLOW-UP:** Obtain some sequence story cards, such as Life Cycles Puzzles and Stories from Insect Lore or Lakeshore's Logical Sequence Tiles and Classroom Sequencing Card Library. Encourage children to reenact and retell the stories and events that are read to them. Encourage them to pretend to read familiar storybooks. This kind of activity helps with comprehending the stories and the sequences of events in them.

*References are given in Appendix B.

## Time: Sequence Activity, Growing Seeds

**OBJECTIVE:** To experience the sequence of the planting of a seed and the growth of a plant.

**MATERIALS:** Radish or lima bean seeds, Styrofoam cups, a sharp pencil, a 6-inch paper plate, some rich soil, a tablespoon.

**NATURALISTIC AND INFORMAL ACTIVITIES:** During center time, provide dirt and small shovels, rakes, pots, and so on in the sand and water table. Talk with the children about what else they might need in order to grow something. Note if they talk about planting seeds.

**STRUCTURED ACTIVITIES:**
1. Give the child a Styrofoam cup. Have her make a drainage hole in the bottom with the sharp pencil.
2. Set the cup on the paper plate.
3. Have the child put dirt in the cup up to about an inch from the top.
4. Have the child poke three holes in the dirt with her pointer finger.
5. Have her put one seed in each hole and cover the seeds with dirt.
6. Have the child add 1 tablespoon of water.
7. Place the pots in a sunny place, and watch their sequence of growth.
8. Have the children water the plants each day. Ask them to record how many days go by before the first plant pops through the soil.

**FOLLOW-UP:** Plant other types of seeds. Make a chart, or obtain a chart that shows the sequence of growth of a seed. Discuss which steps take place before the plant breaks through the ground. In the fall, use the book *It's Pumpkin Time* by Zoe Hall to introduce a seed project and explain how we get the pumpkins we carve for Halloween.

## Time: The First Calendar

**OBJECTIVE:** To learn what a calendar is and how it can be used to keep track of time.

**MATERIALS:** A one-week calendar is cut from poster board with sections for each of the seven days, identified by name. In each section, tabs are cut with a razor blade to hold signs made to be slipped under the tabs to indicate special times and events or the daily weather. These signs may have pictures of birthday cakes, items seen on field trips, umbrellas to show rainy days, the sun to show fair days, and so on.

**NATURALISTIC AND INFORMAL ACTIVITIES:** In the writing center or in the dramatic play center, place a number of different types of calendars. Note if the children know what they are and if they use them in their pretend play activities. Ask them to explain how they are using the calendars. Where else have they seen them? Who uses them?

**STRUCTURED ACTIVITIES:** Each day the calendar can be discussed. Key questions may include:

- WHAT IS THE NAME OF TODAY?
- WHAT IS THE NAME OF YESTERDAY?
- WHAT IS THE NAME OF TOMORROW?
- WHAT DAY COMES AFTER_____?
- WHAT DID WE DO YESTERDAY?
- DO WE GO TO SCHOOL ON SATURDAY AND SUNDAY?
- HOW MANY DAYS UNTIL_____?
- HOW MANY DAYS OF THE WEEK DO WE GO TO SCHOOL?
- WHAT DAY OF THE WEEK IS THE FIRST DAY OF SCHOOL?
- WHAT DAY OF THE WEEK IS THE LAST DAY OF SCHOOL?

**CAUTION:** You do not have to ask every question every day. The calendar is still an abstract item for young children (see Schwartz, 1994).

**FOLLOW-UP:** Read *Today Is Monday* by Eric Carle. Discuss which foods the students like to eat on each day of the week. They could draw/dictate/write their own weekly menus.

## Time: The Use of the Clock

**OBJECTIVE:** To find out how the clock is used to tell us when it's time to change activity.

**MATERIALS:** School wall clock and a handmade or a purchased large clock face such as that made by the Judy Company.

**NATURALISTIC AND INFORMAL ACTIVITIES:** Place a large wooden toy clock in the dramatic play center. Note if the children use it as a dramatic play prop. Do they use time words? Do they make a connection to the clock on the classroom wall or to the daily schedule picture?

**STRUCTURED ACTIVITY:** Point out the wall clock to the children. Show them the clock face. Let them move the hands around. Explain how the clock face is made just like the real clock face. Show them how you can set the hands on the clock face so that they are the same as the ones on the real clock. Each day

*(continued)*

set the clock face for important times (e.g., cleanup, lunch, time to get up from the nap). Explain that when the real clock and the clock face have their hands in the same place, it will be time to (do whatever the next activity is).

**FOLLOW-UP:** Do this every day. Soon each child will begin to catch on and check the clocks. Instead of asking "When do we get up from our nap?" they will be able to check for themselves.

## Time: Beat the Clock Game

**OBJECTIVE:** To learn how time limits the amount of activity that can be done.

**MATERIALS:** Minute Minder or similar timer.

**NATURALISTIC AND INFORMAL ACTIVITIES:** Note how children react to time limit warnings (e.g., five minutes until cleanup). Use a signal (bell, buzzer, dim the lights, etc.) as a cue. Note if the children react with an understanding of time limits (five minutes to clean up the room).

**STRUCTURED ACTIVITIES:** Have the child see how much of some activity can be done in a set number of minutes—for example, in three, four, or five minutes.
1. How many pennies can be put in a penny bank one at a time?
2. How many times can he bounce a ball?
3. How many paper clips can he pick up one at a time with a magnet?
4. How many times can he move across the room: walking, crawling, running, going backward, sideways, etc. Set the timer between three and five minutes. When the bell rings the child must stop. Then count to find out how much was accomplished.

**FOLLOW-UP:** Try many different kinds of activities and different lengths of time. Have several children do the tasks at the same time. Who does the most in the time given?

## Time: Discussion Topics for Language

**OBJECTIVE:** To develop use of time words through discussion.

**MATERIALS:** Pictures collected or purchased. Pictures could show the following.

- Day and night
- Activities that take a long time and a short time
- Picture sequences that illustrate times of day, yesterday, today, and tomorrow
- Pictures that illustrate seasons of the year
- Pictures that show early and late

**NATURALISTIC AND INFORMAL ACTIVITIES:** During center time, place the time pictures on a table. Observe as the children examine the pictures. Note if they use any time words. Ask them to describe the pictures.

**STRUCTURED ACTIVITIES:** Discuss the pictures using the key time words.

**FOLLOW-UP:** Put pictures on the bulletin board that the children can look at and talk about during their center time.

# IDEAS FOR CHILDREN WITH SPECIAL NEEDS

Working with diverse families, time is an important factor to keep in mind, because different cultures vary in their view of time. It is important to respect these views and try to work with families that view time in different ways. Westerners, particularly Americans and Europeans, view scheduling and organization of time as critical in managing any organization—including schools and classrooms. Clocks, watches, and calendars run Western culture. Time is viewed as a commodity not to be wasted, and being late is considered rude. Yet other cultures have different views. For example, Latin Americans, Middle Easterners, and Native Americans view time as being more indefinite. The Chinese also are less concerned with time and schedules. When these two kinds of views meet, the result can be conflict and confusion. If we are socialized to depend on clock time, then promptness is valued. If we are geared to natural events such as the rising and setting of the sun or the time it takes to finish the job, then promptness is not so important. As it applies to schooling, being "on time" may not (at least initially) be valued by some families. The importance of not missing important instructional events can be explained, but children and parents shouldn't be punished; instead, they should be helped to see the importance of Western beliefs and uses of time to being successful in Western culture.

# EVALUATION

The teacher should note whether the child's use of time words increases. He should also note whether her sense of time and sequence develops to a more mature level: Does she remember the order of events? Can she wait until one thing is finished before she starts another? Does she talk about future and past events? How does she use the calendar? The clock? The sequence stories? The teacher may use the individual interview tasks in this unit and in Appendix A.

# SUMMARY

The young child can begin to learn that time has duration and that time is related to sequences of events. The child first relates time to his personal experience and to his daily sequence of activities. It is not until the child enters the concrete operations period that he can use units of time in the ways that adults use them.

For the most part, the young child learns his concept of time through naturalistic and informal experiences. When he is about the age of 4½ or 5, he can do structured activities as well. It is important to understand that some families from non-Western cultures may not view time as Westerners do.

## KEY TERMS

| | | |
|---|---|---|
| cultural time | personal experience | social activity |
| duration | relational (time) words | special days |
| duration (time) words | sequence | specific (time) words |
| general (time) words | | |

## SUGGESTED ACTIVITIES

1. Observe some young children engaged in group play. Record any examples of time measurement that take place. What stage of measurement did each incident represent?

2. In class, discuss some ways that time measurement skills can be developed through home and school activities.

3. Plan and gather materials for at least one time-sequence and one time-measurement activity. Do the activities with a small group of young children. Report the results in class.

4. Use the evaluation scheme in Activity 5, Unit 2, to evaluate one of the following selections.

   ■ *Trudy's Time and Place House* (San Francisco: Riverdeep-Edmark). Includes clocks and calendars.

   ■ *Shapes, Numbers, and Measurement* (http://www.campustech.com). Includes time and temperature activities.

   ■ *James Discovers Math* (http://www.smartkids.com). Includes telling time.

   ■ *Telling Time by the Hour Sheet* (Arlington, MA: Dositey Corporation)

   ■ *Destination Math* (http://www.riverdeep.net). Includes length, weight, clock and calendar time.

   ■ *Match-time CD-ROM* (http://www.k12software.com). Time concepts.

5. Add some time measurement activities to your file/notebook.

## REVIEW

A. Describe and compare time sequence and time duration.

B. Decide if the children's comments below reflect (a) time sequence, (b) time duration, or (c) neither sequence nor duration:

   1. A child playing with a ball says, "The ball went up high."
   2. Mario asks his dad, "Please read me a bear story at bedtime."
   3. Janie says, "I stayed with Grandma for three nights."
   4. Lindsey says, "I love to play with Daddy for hours and hours."
   5. Li says, "It's lunchtime, everybody."
   6. Donny says, "This box weighs a million tons."
   7. Tina sighs, "It took me a long time to draw the pictures in my dog book."

C. Explain the three kinds of time. Include an example of each type.

D. Decide which of the words in the list below are (a) general time words, (b) specific time words, (c) relational words, (d) duration words, or (e) special day words:

   1. yesterday
   2. three hours
   3. this afternoon
   4. Easter
   5. twice
   6. four years old
   7. birthday
   8. two minutes
   9. today

E. Explain the NCTM (2000) expectations for preschool/kindergarten time understanding.

## REFERENCES

Carle, E. (1993). *Today is Monday.* New York: Scholastic Books.

Hall, Z. (1999). *It's pumpkin time.* New York: Scholastic Books.

National Council of Teachers of Mathematics. (2000). *Principles and standards for school mathematics.* Reston, VA: Author.

Schwartz, S. (1994). Calendar reading: A tradition that begs remodeling. *Teaching Children Mathematics, 1*(2), 104–109.

# FURTHER READING AND RESOURCES

Barnes, M. K. (2006). "How many days 'til my birthday?" Helping kindergarten students understand calendar connections and concepts. *Teaching Children Mathematics, 12*(6), 290–295.

Church, E. B. (1997, January). "Is it time yet?" *Early Childhood Today,* 33–34.

Copley, J. V. (Ed.). (1999). *Mathematics in the early years.* Washington, DC: National Association for the Education of Young Children.

Copley, J. V. (2000). *The young child and mathematics.* Washington, DC: National Association for the Education of Young Children.

Copley, J. V. (Ed.). (2004). *Showcasing mathematics for the young child* (chap. 5, Measurement). Reston, VA: National Council of Teachers of Mathematics.

Dacey, L., Cavanagh, M., Findell, C. R., Greenes, C. E., Sheffield, L. J., & Small, M. (2003). *Navigating through measurement in prekindergarten–grade 2.* Reston, VA: National Council of Teachers of Mathematics.

Epstein, A.S., & Gansley, S. (2005). *Math in the preschool classroom* (chap. 6, Time). Ypsilanti, MI: High/Scope.

Friederitzer, F. J., & Berman, B. (1999). The language of time. *Teaching Children Mathematics, 6*(4), 254–259.

Harms, J. M., & Lettow, L. J. (2007). Nurturing children's concepts of time and chronology through literature. *Childhood Education, 83*(4), 211–218.

Moustafa, K. S., Bhagat, R. S., & Babakus, E. (2005). A cross-cultural investigation of polychronicity: A study of organizations in three countries. Retrieved August 9, 2007, from http://www.midwestacademy.org

Pliske, C. (2000). Natural cycles: Coming full circle. *Science and Children, 37*(6), 35–39, 60.

Shreero, B., Sullivan, C., & Urbano, A. (2002). Math by the month: Calendar math. *Teaching Children Mathematics, 9*(2), 96.

# Unit 20

## Interpreting Data Using Graphs

### OBJECTIVES

After reading this unit, you should be able to:

■ Explain the use of graphs.

■ Describe the three stages that young children go through in making graphs.

■ List materials to use for making graphs.

■ Describe the NCTM (2000) expectations for preschool/kindergarten level graphing activities and understanding.

The NCTM (2000, p. 108) expectations for data analysis for prekindergarten and kindergarten focus on children sorting and classifying objects according to their attributes, organizing data about the objects, and describing the data and what they show. "The main purpose of collecting data is to answer questions when the answers are not immediately obvious" (NCTM, 2000, p. 109). Children's questions should be the major source of data. The beginnings of data collection are included in the fundamental concepts learned and applied in classifying in a logical fashion (Unit 10).

Data collection activities can begin even before kindergarten, as students collect sets of data from their real-life experiences and depict the results of their data collection in simple graphs. Consider the following example from Ms. Moore's classroom:

Ms. Moore hears George and Sam talking in loud voices. She goes near them and hears the following discussion.

GEORGE: "More kids like green than blue."

SAM: "No! No! More like blue!"

GEORGE: "You are all wrong."

SAM: "I am not. You are wrong."

Ms. Moore goes over to the boys and asks, "What's the trouble, boys?" George replies, "We have to get paint to paint the house Mr. Brown helped us build. I say it should be green. Sam says it should be blue."

Sam insists, "More kids like blue than green."

Ms. Moore asks, "How can we find out? How do we decide on questions like who will be our next president?" George and Sam looked puzzled. Then George says, "I remember when Mom and Dad voted. We could have the class vote." Sam agreed that this would be a good idea. Ms. Moore then asked them how they might have all the students vote. They were afraid that if they asked for a show of hands their classmates might just copy whoever voted first. Ms. Moore then suggested that they put out a green box and a blue box and a bowl of green and blue cube blocks. George's eyes lit up. "I see then each person could vote by putting either a blue block in the blue box or a green block in the green box." Sam agreed.

After setting up the boxes and blocks, Sam and George go around the room. They explain the problem to each child. Each child comes over to the table. They each choose one block of the color they like better and place the block in the matching box. When the voting is completed, George and Sam empty the boxes and stack the blocks as shown in Figure 20–1.

Ms. Moore asks the boys what the vote shows. Sam says, "The green stack is higher. More children like the idea of painting the house green." "Good," answers Ms. Moore, "would you like me to write that down for you?" Sam and George chorus, "Yes!"

"I have an idea," says George, "Let's make a picture of this for the bulletin board so everyone will know. Will you help us, Ms. Moore?"

Ms. Moore shows them how to cut out squares of green and blue paper to match each of the blocks used. The boys write "green" and "blue" on a piece of white paper and then paste the green squares next to the word "green" and the blue squares next to the word "blue." Ms. Moore shows them how to write the title: "Choose the Color for the Playhouse." Then they glue the description of the results at the bottom. The results can be seen in Figure 20–2.

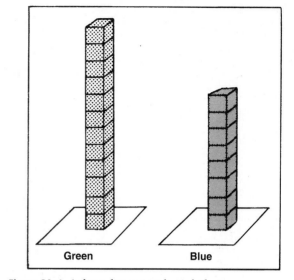

Figure 20–1 A three-dimensional graph that compares children's preferences for green or blue.

In the preceding example, the teacher helped the children solve their problem by helping them make two kinds of graphs. **Graphs** are used to show visually two or more comparisons in a clear way. When a child

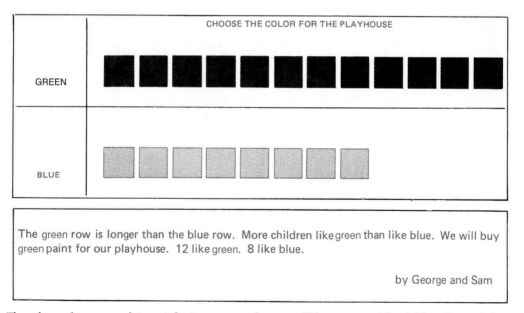

Figure 20–2 The color preference graph is copied using squares of green and blue paper, and the children dictate their interpretation.

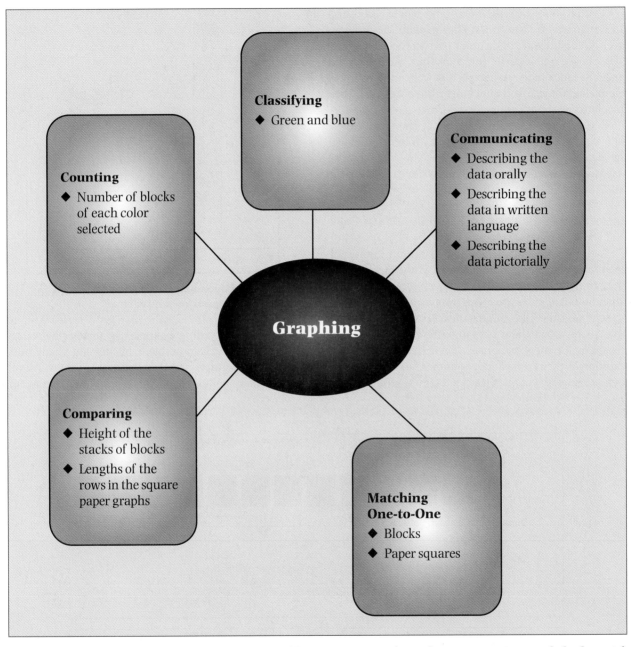

**Figure 20–3** Graphing can be used to describe data in any of the content areas and provides an opportunity to apply fundamental concepts and skills.

makes a graph, he uses basic skills such as classification, counting, comparing quantities, one-to-one matching, and communicating through describing data. By making a concrete structure or a picture that shows some type of information, they visualize a variety of different quantities. Graphing provides an opportunity to apply several fundamental concepts and skills, as illustrated in Figure 20–3.

## STAGES OF DEVELOPMENT FOR MAKING AND UNDERSTANDING GRAPHS

The types of graphs that young children can construct progress through five stages of development. The first three stages are described in this unit; the fourth is included in Unit 25, and the fifth in Unit 31. In **stage one, object graphs**, the child uses real objects to make her graph. Sam and George used cube blocks. At this stage only two things are compared. The main basis for comparison is one-to-one correspondence and visualization of length and height.

In **stage two, picture graphs**, more than two items are compared. In addition, a more permanent record is made—such as when Sam and George glued squares of colored paper on a chart for the bulletin board. An example of this type of graph is shown in Figure 20–4. The teacher has lined off 12 columns on poster board (or large construction paper). Each column stands for one month of the year. Each child is given a paper circle. Crayons, water markers, glue, and yarn scraps are available so each child can draw her own head and place it on the month for her birthday. When each child has put her "head" on the graph, the children can compare the months to see which month has the most birthdays.

In **stage three, square paper graphs**, the children progress through the use of more pictures to block charts. They no longer need to use real objects but can start right off with cutout squares of paper. Figure 20–5 shows this type of graph. In this stage, the children work more independently.

Figure 20–4 "When is your birthday?"

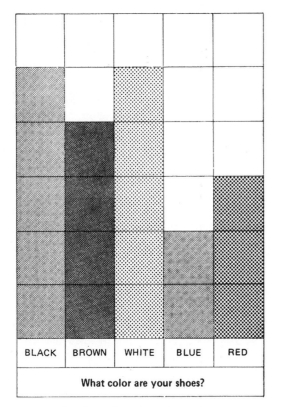

Figure 20–5  A block graph made with paper squares.

which cube blocks were used. Other materials can be used just as well.

At first it is best to use materials that can be kept in position without being knocked down or pushed apart by young children. Stands can be made from dowel rods. A washer or curtain ring is then placed on the dowel to represent each thing or person (Figure 20–6[A]). Strings and beads can be used. The strings can be hung from hooks or a rod; the lengths are then compared (Figure 20–6[B]). Unifix Cubes (Figure 20–6[C]) or pop beads (Figure 20–6[D]) can also be used.

Once the children have worked with the more stable materials, they can use the cube blocks and any other things that can be lined up. Poker chips, bottle caps, coins, spools, corks, and beans are good for this type of graph work (Figure 20–7).

At the second stage, graphs can be made with these same materials but with more comparisons made. Then the child can go on to more permanent recording by gluing down cutout pictures or markers of some kind (Figure 20–8).

At the third stage, the children can use paper squares. This prepares the way for the use of squared paper (see Unit 25).

Many interesting graphing materials are available on the Internet and in the form of software. Some of these materials are listed on the Online Companion that accompanies *Math and Science for Young Children*, which can be accessed at www.earlychilded.delmar.com.

## DISCUSSION OF A GRAPH

As the children talk about their graphs and dictate descriptions for them, they use concept words such as

| | |
|---|---|
| less than | the same as |
| more than | none |
| fewer than | all |
| longer, longest | some |
| shorter, shortest | a lot of |
| the most | higher |
| the least | taller |

## MATERIALS FOR MAKING GRAPHS

There are many kinds of materials that can be used for the first-stage graphs. An example has been shown in

## TOPICS FOR GRAPHS

Any type of student question can be researched and the information put into graphical form. For example, a group of kindergartners collected information about their school bus (Colburn & Tate, 1998), and another group of young children studied a tree that grows on their campus (El Harim, 1998).

Once children start making graphs, they often think of problems to solve on their own. The following are some comparisons that might be of interest:

■ number of brothers and sisters

■ hair color, eye color, clothing colors

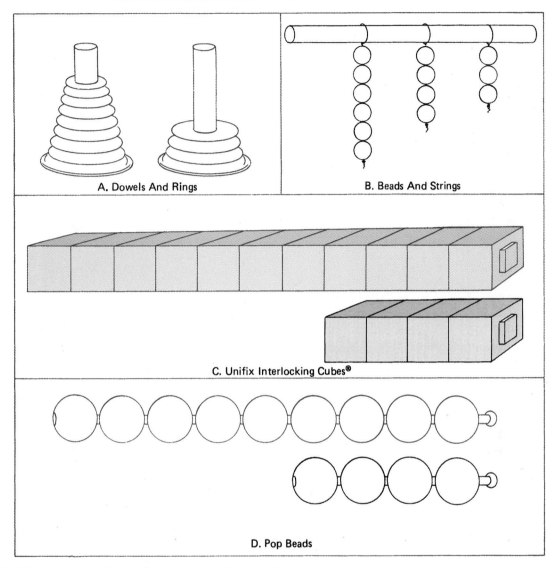

A. Dowels And Rings

B. Beads And Strings

C. Unifix Interlocking Cubes®

D. Pop Beads

**Figure 20–6**  Four examples of three-dimensional graph materials.

■  kinds of pets children have
■  heights of children in the class
■  number of children in class each day
■  sizes of shoes
■  favorite TV programs (or characters)
■  favorite foods
■  favorite colors

■  favorite storybooks
■  type of weather each day for a month
■  number of cups of water or sand that will fill different containers
■  time, in seconds, to run across the playground
■  number of baby hamsters class members predict that their female hamster will bear

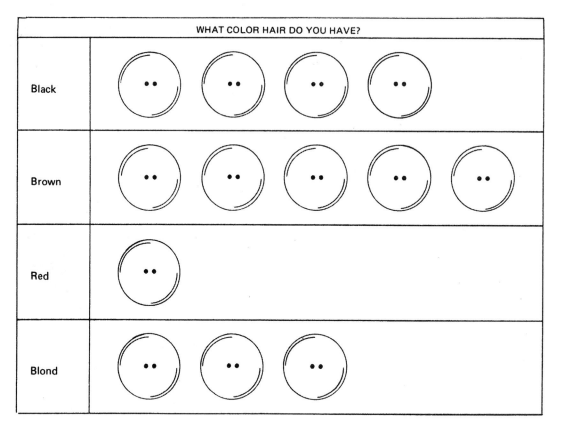

**Figure 20–7** Graph made with buttons glued to cardboard.

- number of days class members predict that it will take for their bean seeds to sprout
- data obtained regarding sinking and floating objects (Unit 10)
- comparison of the number of seeds found in an apple, an orange, a lemon, and a grapefruit
- students' predictions regarding which items will be attracted by magnets
- frequency with which different types of insects are found on the playground
- distance that rollers will roll when ramps of different degrees of steepness are used
- comparison of the number of different items that are placed in a balance pan to weigh the same as a standard weight

- frequency count of each color in a bag of m&m's, Skittles, or Trix
- frequency with which the various combinations of yellow and orange show up when the counters (orange on one side and yellow on the other) are shaken and then tossed out on the table

## SUMMARY

Making graphs provides an opportunity for using some basic math skills in a creative way. Children can put into "picture" form the results of classifying, comparing, counting, and measuring activities. Graphs also serve as a means of integrating mathematics with other content areas, such as science and social studies, by providing a vehicle for depicting and analyzing data.

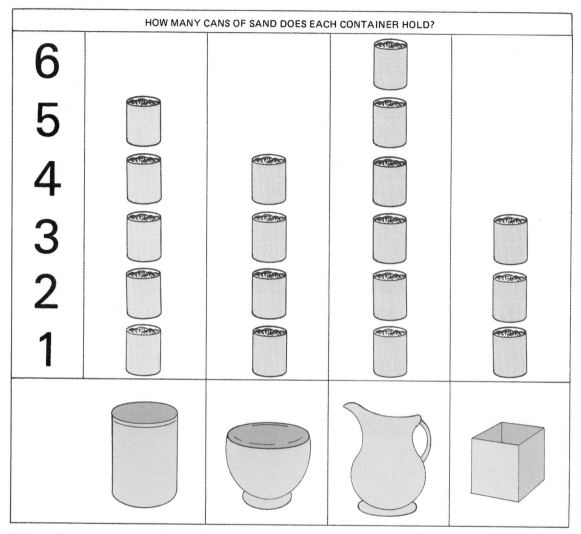

**Figure 20–8** Graph made with paper cutouts.

The first graphs are three-dimensional and are made with real objects. The next are made with pictures and the next with paper squares. Children can discuss the results of their graph projects and dictate a description of the graph's meaning to be put on the bulletin board alongside the graph.

## KEY TERMS

graphs
stage one, object graphs

stage two, picture graphs

stage three, square paper graphs

## SUGGESTED ACTIVITIES

1. Interview several prekindergarten and kindergarten teachers. Find out if and how they use graphs in their classrooms. Report your findings in class.

2. With a small group of 4–6-year-olds, discuss some topics that might be of interest for collecting information and making a graph. Then make the graph with the group. Bring the graph to class, and explain the process to the class.

3. Use one of the evaluation schemes suggested in Activity 5, Unit 2, to evaluate one of the following graphing software programs (all from Sunburst: 1-800-321-7511; fax, 1-888-800-3028).

■ *Numbers Recovered.* Includes creating and interpreting graphs.

■ *Graphers.* Manipulation and creation of a variety of graphs.

■ *Tabletop Jr.* Grouping, sorting, and classifying data; graphing and interpreting data; measurement.

■ *The Graph Club.* For creative projects and displays of data.

4. Add ideas for graphs to your Activity File/Notebook.

## REVIEW

A. Explain the importance and values of graph making.

B. There are three levels of making and understanding graphs that are appropriate for prekindergarten and kindergarten students. Name and describe each of these stages.

C. Sketch out three graphs that are representative of (respectively) each of the three beginning stages of graph making.

D. Describe the NCTM (2000) expectations for preschool and kindergarten students constructing and analyzing information displayed in graphs.

## REFERENCES

Colburn, K., & Tate, P. (1998). The big, yellow laboratory. *Science and Children, 36*(1), 22–25.

El Harim, J. L. (1998). A *tree*mendous learning experience. *Science and Children, 35*(8), 26–29.

National Council of Teachers of Mathematics. (2000). *Principles and standards for school mathematics.* Reston, VA: Author.

## FURTHER READING AND RESOURCES

Copley, J. V. (Ed.). (1999). *Mathematics in the early years.* Washington, DC: National Association for the Education of Young Children.

Copley, J. V. (2000). *The young child and mathematics.* Washington, DC: National Association for the Education of Young Children.

Copley, J. V. (Ed.). (2004). *Showcasing mathematics for the young child* (chap. 6, Data Analysis). Reston, VA: National Council of Teachers of Mathematics.

Curcio, F. R., & Folkson, S. (1996). Exploring data: Kindergarten children do it their way. *Teaching Children Mathematics, 2,* 382–385.

Greenes, C. E., Dacey, L., Cavanagh, M., Findell, C. R., Sheffield, L. J., & Small, M. (2003). *Navigating through problem solving and reasoning in prekindergarten–kindergarten.* Reston, VA: National Council of Teachers of Mathematics.

Lamphere, P. (1994). Classroom data. *Teaching Children Mathematics, 1,* 28–31.

Litton, N. (1995). Graphing from A to Z. *Teaching Children Mathematics, 2,* 220–223.

Pearlman, S., & Pericak-Spector, K. (1995). Graph that data! *Science and Children, 32*(4), 35–37.

Schwartz, S. L. (1995). Authentic mathematics in the classroom. *Teaching Children Mathematics, 1,* 580–584.

Sheffield, L. J., Cavanagh, M., Dacey, L., Findell, C. R., Greenes, C. E., & Small, M. (2002). *Navigating through data analysis and probability in prekindergarten–grade 2.* Reston, VA: National Council of Teachers of Mathematics.

Spurlin, Q. (1995). Put science in a bag. *Science and Children, 32*(4), 19–22.

Whitin, D. J., & Whitin, P. (2003). Talk counts: Discussing graphs with young children. *Teaching Children Mathematics, 10*(3), 142–149.

Young, S. L. (1990). Ideas: Dinosaur data. *Arithmetic Teacher, 38*(1), 23–33.

Young, S. L. (1990). Ideas: Popcorn data. *Arithmetic Teacher, 38*(2), 24–33.

Young, S. L. (1990). Ideas: Ball data. *Arithmetic Teacher, 38*(3), 23–32.

Young, S. L. (1991). Ideas: Pizza math. *Arithmetic Teacher, 38*(8), 26–33.

# Unit 21

## Applications of Fundamental Concepts in Preprimary Science

### OBJECTIVES

After reading this unit, you should be able to:

■ Apply the concepts and skills related to ordering and patterning, measuring, and graphing to science lessons and units at the preprimary level.

■ Design science lessons that include naturalistic, informal, and structured activities.

The *National Science Education Standards* (National Research Council, 1996) emphasize the inquiring nature of children and the responsibility of teachers to provide appropriate classroom settings for children to carry out inquiry investigations. This unit presents activities, lessons, and scenarios that focus on the fundamental concepts, attitudes, and skills of ordering and patterning, measuring, and graphing as they apply to experiences in preprimary science investigations.

## ORDERING AND PATTERNING

Underlying the concept of patterning are the concepts of **comparing** and **ordering**. Ordering is a higher level of comparing because ordering involves comparing more than two things or more than two sets. It also involves placing things in a sequence from first to last. In Piaget's terms, this ordering is called seriation. Children must have some understanding of seriation before they develop the more advanced skill of **patterning**.

Ordering and patterning build on the skills of comparing. If children have not had prior experience in com-

paring, they will not be ready to order and find patterns. The following activities involve using a science emphasis in shape, animals, color, and sound while making or discovering visual, auditory, and motor regularities.

1. *Sun, moon, and stars.* Use your flannelboard to help children recognize patterns in flannel figures of the moon, sun, and star shapes. Start the activity by discussing the shapes in the night sky. Then place the moon, sun, and star shapes in a pattern on the flannelboard. Make a game of placing a figure in the pattern and having the children decide which figure comes next. As the children go through the process of making a pattern with the flannel figures, they are also reinforcing the concept of shapes existing in the night sky (Figure 21–1).

   The natural patterns found in the night sky are an ideal observational activity for young children. When the sun goes down and the child can see the moon and stars, it is time to observe the night sky. Observing the changes in the sky from day to night reinforces the patterns that

Figure 21–1  Cindy creates a pattern.

Figure 21–2  Macaroni necklaces make a pattern.

children learn at a very young age. Children may also be aware of the changes in the shape of the moon and may want to draw those shapes.

2. *Animal patterns.* Make patterns for shapes that go together in some way such as zebra, tiger, and leopard (wild animals) or pig, duck, and cow (farm animals). After introducing children to the pattern game described in activity 1, have them manipulate tagboard animal shapes in the same way.

3. *Changing colors.* Create original patterns in necklaces by dyeing macaroni with food color. Children will be fascinated by the necklace and by the change in the appearance of the macaroni. Have children help prepare the macaroni: mix one tablespoon of alcohol, three drops of food coloring, and a cup of macaroni in a glass jar.

Screw the lid on tightly, and take turns shaking the jar. Then, lay the macaroni out on a piece of newspaper to dry overnight. Do this for each color you select. Have children compare the macaroni before and after dyeing; ask them to describe the similarities and differences.

4. *Stringing macaroni.* To help children string macaroni, tie one end through a piece of tagboard. Then, have students practice threading the macaroni with the string. When they are comfortable, let each invent a pattern of colors. The pattern is then repeated over and over until the necklace is completed. Have the children say aloud the patterns they are stringing, for example, "Red, blue, yellow; red, blue, yellow," until they complete the necklace. In this way, both the auditory and visual patterns are reinforced. To extend this activity, have children guess each other's patterns, tell patterns, and try to duplicate patterns. Children will enjoy wearing their creations when they dress up for a Thanksgiving feast (Figure 21–2). The following activity emphasizes ordering and comparing.

## ACTIVITIES

### Fabric Cards: Ordering and Comparing

**OBJECTIVE:**  Ordering and comparing fabrics by touch.

**MATERIALS:**  Cardboard cut into small squares (2–3 inches works well), nontoxic glue, swatches of various fabrics with different textures (rough, smooth, ridged, soft, etc.).

*(continued)*

**NATURALISTIC AND INFORMAL ACTIVITIES:** Give the children a variety of different cardboard squares, each covered with a different fabric on one side, and observe them as they explore and talk about the textures of these fabric cards. Ask, DOES ANYONE HAVE A FABRIC CARD THAT FEELS VERY SOFT? ARE THERE ANY ROUGH-FEELING FABRIC CARDS?

**STRUCTURED ACTIVITIES:** Ask the children to order their fabric cards from the smoothest to the roughest. The cards can be shuffled to play matching games or placed on a classroom board that displays what the children know about ordering and comparing with their sense of touch.

**FOLLOW-UP:** You may want to have a large classroom fabric card display that shows the students' skills in ordering and comparing fabrics. Smaller individual sets can be used by the children on their own or in pairs. Try using as many types of fabrics as possible.

## Sound Patterns

In the following scenario, Mrs. Jones introduces sound patterns to her kindergarten children.

Mrs. Jones brings out plastic bells. She selects three widely varied tones, rings them for the children, and asks: "Can you tell me what you hear?" Jane responds, "Bells, I hear bells!" The teacher asks, "Do any of the bells sound different?" "Yes," the children say. "In what way do they sound different?" Mrs. Jones asks. "Some sound like Tinkerbell, and some do not," George responds. After giving the children a chance to ring the bells, Mrs. Jones puts out a red, a yellow, and a blue construction-paper square on a table. She asks, "Will someone put the bell with the highest sound on the red card?" After Lai completes the task, Mrs. Jones asks the children to find the bell with the lowest sound and, finally, the one whose sound is between the highest and lowest. Each bell has its own color square.

Patterns can be found in the sounds that rubber bands make. Construct a rubber band banjo by placing three different widths of rubber bands around a cigar box, the open end of a coffee can, a milk carton, or a margarine tub. Have children experiment with the rubber band "strings" of varying length, and see if they notice differences in sound. Playing around with strings and homemade instruments helps prepare children for future concept development in sound.

Rhythmic patterns can be found in classic poems and songs such as "There Was a Little Turtle." Have children add actions as they sing the song.

There was a little turtle
He lived in a box
He swam in a puddle
He climbed on the rocks
He snapped at a mosquito
He snapped at a flea
He snapped at a minnow
And he snapped at me.
He caught the mosquito
He caught the flea
He caught the minnow
But he didn't catch me.

## Making Patterns with a Computer Software Resource

There are many computer software resources that allow children to draw. Most of these have "stamps" that children can use in their pictures. For example, a child might choose a "stamp" of a tree, a person, a heart, or a star. Children enjoy selecting stamps and colors for making patterns. Children can work in pairs to repeat each other's patterns or design new ones. *KidWare*, *KidWorks*, and *Kid Pix* are three programs that seem to be popular with children and adults.

## MEASUREMENT: VOLUME, WEIGHT, LENGTH, AND TEMPERATURE

The *National Science Education Standards* emphasize that the meaning of measurement and how to use measurement tools are a part of any investigation. These ideas are introduced frequently throughout the early years.

Measurement is basically a spatial activity that must include the manipulation of objects to be understood. If children are not actively involved with materials as they measure, they simply will not understand measurement. Water and sand are highly sensory science resources for young children. Both substances elicit a variety of responses to their physical properties, and they can be used in measurement activities. Keep in mind that, for sand and water to be effective as learning tools, long periods of "messing around" with the substances should be provided. For further information on the logistics of handling water and sand and a discussion of basic equipment needs, see Unit 39 of this book. The following activities and lessons use sand and water as a means of introducing measurement.

1. *Fill it up.* Put out containers and funnels of different sizes and shapes, and invite children to pour liquid from one to the other. Aspects of pouring can be investigated. Ask: "Is it easier to pour from a wide- or narrow-mouthed container?"; "Do you see anything that could help you pour liquid into a container?"; "Does the funnel take longer? Why?" Add plastic tubing to the water center. Ask, "Can a tube be used to fill up a container?" and "Which takes longer?" (Figure 21–3).

2. *Squeeze and blow.* Plastic squeeze bottles or turkey basters will encourage children to find another way to fill the containers. After the children have manipulated the baster and observed air bubbling out of it, set up the water table for a race. You will need table tennis balls, tape, and basters. The object is to move the ball across the water by squeezing the turkey baster. After allowing the children some practice time, place a piece of tape lengthwise down the center of the table and begin. Use a piece of string to measure how far the ball is moved. Compare the distances with the length of string. Ask, "How many squeezes does it take to cover the distance?"

3. *A cup is a cup.* Volume refers to how much space a solid, liquid, or gas takes up or occupies. For example, when a one-cup measure is full of water, the volume of water is one cup. Volume can be compared by having children fill small boxes or jars with sand or beans. Use sand in similar containers, and compare the way the sand feels. Compare the heft of a full container with an empty container. Use a balance scale to dramatize the difference. If you do not have a commercial balance, provide a homemade balance and hanging cups. Children will begin to weigh different levels of sand in the cups. Statements such as, "I wonder if sand weighs more if I fill the container even higher?" can be overheard. Let children check predictions and discuss what they have found (Figure 21–4).

**Figure 21–3** "Can a tube be used to fill a container?"

**Figure 21–4** Children explore volume by weighing sand.

**Figure 21–5** "Will it sink or float?"

**Figure 21–6** "Do you think the leaf will sink or float?"

4. *Sink or float.* Comparisons such as big-little and heavy-light are made when children discover that objects of different sizes sink and float. Make a chart to record observations. After discussing what the terms *sink* and *float* mean, give the children a variety of floating and nonfloating objects to manipulate. Ask, "What do you think will float? Big corks? Small marbles?" As children sort objects by size and shape and then test whether they sink or float, they are discovering science concepts and learning about measurement (Figure 21–5).

Ms. Moore has her class predict, "Will it sink or float?" Her materials include a leaf, nail, balloon, cork, wooden spoon, and metal spoon. She makes a chart with columns labeled *sink* and *float* and has the children place the leaf and so on where they think they will go.

Cindy excitedly floats the leaf. "It floats, it floats!" she says. Because Cindy correctly predicts that the leaf would float, the leaf stays in the *float* column on the chart. Diana predicts that the metal spoon will float. "Oh, it's not floating. The metal spoon is sinking." Diana moves the metal spoon from the *float* column to the *sink* column on the chart. In this way, children can predict and compare objects as they measure weight and buoyancy (Figure 21–6).

5. *Little snakes.* Many children in preschool and kindergarten are not yet conserving length.

For example, they still think that a flexible stick may vary in length if its shape is changed in some way. Therefore, use care in assessing your students' developmental stages. The child must be able to conserve in order for measurement activities to make sense. In the following scenario, a teacher of young children assesses the conservation of length while relating length to animals.

Mrs. Raymond reinforces the shape/space concept by giving each child in her class two pipe cleaners. She instructs them to place the pipe cleaners side by side and asks, "Which pipe cleaner is longer?" Then she tells the children to bend one of the pipe cleaners and asks, "Which is longer now?" She repeats this several times, having the children create different shapes.

Then the children make the pipe cleaners into little snakes by gluing small construction-paper heads on one end of each pipe cleaner. Mrs. Raymond shows the children pictures of a snake that is coiled and one that is moving on the ground (try to find pictures of the same kind of snake). She asks, "Is the coiled snake shorter?" "Yes," the children say. "Let's see if we can make our pipe cleaners into coiled snakes," instructs Mrs. Raymond. "Oh," says Jimmie, "this really looks like a coiled snake."

The teacher asks the students to lay out the other pipe cleaners to resemble a moving snake and asks, "Which is longer?" There are a variety of responses as the children manipulate the pipe cleaner snakes to help them understand that the coiled and moving snakes are the same lengths. Then, have the children glue a small black construction-paper end on each pipe cleaner. Let them practice coiling and uncoiling the "snakes" and discuss how snakes move. Ask, "Can you tell how long a snake is when it is coiled up?" and "Was your coiled-up snake longer than you thought?"

6. *A big and little hunt.* Height, size, and length can be compared in many ways. For example, Mrs. Jones takes her children on a big and little hunt.

After taking the children outside, Mrs. Jones has them sit in a circle and discuss the biggest and smallest things that they can see. Then she asks them, "Of all the things we have talked about, which is the smallest?" George and Mary are certain that the leaves are the smallest, but Sam and Lai do not agree. "The blades of grass are smaller," Sam observes. "Are they?" Mrs. Jones asks. "How can we tell which is smaller?" "Let's put them beside each other," Mary suggests. The children compare the length of each item and discuss which is longer and wider.

7. *Body part measures.* Children enjoy measuring with body parts, such as a hand or foot length. Ask, "How many feet is it to the door?" and let the children count the number of foot lengths they must take. Or ask, "How many hands high are you?"

Give children pieces of string and have them measure head sizes. Then take the string, and measure other parts of their bodies. Compare their findings.

8. *How long will it take to sink?* Let children play for five minutes with dishpans of water, a kitchen scale, a bucket of water, and an assortment of objects. Then, give the children plastic tubes to explore and measure. As one child drops a marble into a plastic tube filled with water, count in measured beats the amount of time that the marble takes to sink. Ask, "Will it sink faster in cold water or hot water?"

9. *Hot or not.* The following activities and questions correlate with science and, in many cases, integrate into the curriculum of a preschool or kindergarten.

■ Take an outdoor walk to feel the effects of temperature. "Is it warmer or colder outside?"

■ Visit a greenhouse. Predict what the temperature will be inside the greenhouse; discuss the reasons for these predictions.

■ Notice differences in temperature in different areas of the supermarket. Ask, "Are some areas colder?" and "Which is the warmest area of the supermarket?"

■ Melt crayons for dripping on bottles and painting pictures. Notice the effect of heat on the crayons. Ask, "Have you ever felt like a melted crayon?" and "Act out the changes in a melting crayon with your bodies."

■ Put some finger paints in the refrigerator. Have children compare how the refrigerated paints and room-temperature paints feel on their hands.

■ Ask, "What happens to whipped cream as we fingerpaint with it?" Have children observe the whipped cream as it warms up and melts.

■ Ask, "What happens to an ice cream cone as you eat it?" and "Why do you think this happens?"

# COMMUNICATING WITH GRAPHS

When children make graphs, they use the basic process skills of observing, classifying, comparing, and measuring visually communicated information. In fact, making a graph is in itself an act of communication. A graph is a way of displaying information so that predictions, inferences, and conclusions can be made. Refer to Unit 20 for helpful hints on introducing graphs to children and for problem-solving topics that result in graph making.

When using graphs, it is essential that the meaning of the completed graph be clear to the children. With questions and discussion, it is possible for a graph to answer a question, solve a problem, or show data so that something can be understood. In the following scenario, Mrs. Jones uses common kitchen sponges to provide children with an opportunity to manipulate and construct two types of graphs.

Mrs. Jones distributes sponges of different colors to her kindergarten class. After allowing children time to examine the sponges, she suggests that they stack the sponges by color. As the sponges are stacked, a bar graph is naturally created. Mrs. Jones lines up each stack of sponges and asks, "Which color sponge do we have the most of?" Lai says, "The blue stack is the tallest. There are more blue sponges." "Good," answers Mrs. Jones. "Can anyone tell me which stack of sponges is the smallest?" "The yellow ones," says Mary. The children count the number of sponges in each stack and duplicate the three-dimensional sponge graph by making a graph of colored poster board sponges. The children place pink, blue, yellow, and green oak tag sponges in columns of color that Mrs. Jones has prepared on a tagboard background. In this way, children learn in a concrete way the one-to-one correspondence that a bar graph represents.

Mrs. Jones follows up the graphing activity with other sponge activities. Sam says, "Sponges in my house are usually wet." "Yes," chorus the children. George says, "Our sponges feel heavier, too." The children's comments provide an opportunity to submerge a sponge in water and weigh it. The class weighs the wet and dry sponges, and an experience chart of observations is recorded. The next day, Sam brings in a sponge with bird seed on it. He says, "I am going to keep it damp and see what happens."

## Calendar Graph

Calendars are another way to reinforce graphing, the passage of time, and one-to-one correspondence. Mrs. Carter laminates small birthday cakes and then writes each child's name and birth date on the paper cake with a permanent marker. At the beginning of the year, she shows the children the chart and points out which cake belongs to them. At the beginning of each month, the children with birthdays move their cakes to the calendar. Various animals, trees, and birds can be substituted for cakes (Figure 21–7).

## Pets

Graphs can be used to compare pets and give early literacy experiences. Make a list of the pets that your children have. Divide a bristol board into columns to represent every pet named. Cover the board with clear laminate film. Make labels with pet categories such as dogs, cats, snakes, fish, lizards, turtles, and so on. Glue the labels to clothespins. Then, place a labeled clothespin at the top of each column. Have the children write their names in the appropriate column (Figure 21–8).

## Favorite Foods

Divide a poster board into columns and paste or draw a picture of each food group at the top of each column.

## MARCH

| SUNDAY | MONDAY | TUESDAY | WEDNESDAY | THURSDAY | FRIDAY | SATURDAY |
|--------|--------|---------|-----------|----------|--------|----------|
|  |  |  | 1 | 2 | 3 JAY | 4 |
| 5 | 6 | 7 AMY | 8 | 9 | 10 | 11 |
| 12 | 13 | 14 | 15 | 16 | 17 | 18 |
| 19 | 20 | 21 | 22 MIKE | 23 | 24 | 25 |
| 26 | 27 | 28 | 29 | 30 | 31 |  |

**Figure 21–7** Calendars reinforce graphing, time, and one-to-one correspondence.

**Figure 21–8** Graphing our pets.

Allow each child to draw a picture of their favorite food and paste it under the appropriate column. Velcro can also be used to attach the pictures, and the children can write their names under their choice.

## Graphing Attractions

Simple magnets can be fun to explore. A real object graph can be made with ruled bristol board. Rule the board into columns to equal the number of magnets. Trace the shape of a magnet at the top of each column. Attach a drapery hook below each picture and proceed as Mrs. Carter does in the following description.

After letting the children explore metal objects such as paper clips, Mrs. Carter places a pile of paper clips on the table along with different types of magnets. She invites Cindy to choose a magnet and see how many paper clips it will attract. Cindy selects a horseshoe-shaped magnet and hangs paper clips from the end, one at a time, until the magnet no longer attracts any clips. "Good," says Mrs. Carter. "Now, make a chain of the paper clips that your magnet attracts." After Cindy makes the paper-clip chain, Mrs. Carter directs her to hang it on the drapery hook under the drawing of the horseshoe-shaped magnet.

"I bet the magnet that looks like a bar will attract more paper clips," predicts Richard. He selects the rod magnet and begins to attract as many paper clips as he can. Then, he makes a chain and hangs it on the drapery hook under the rod magnet. The process is repeated until each child in the group has worked with a magnet. Mrs. Carter makes no attempt to teach the higher-level concepts involved in magnetic force; rather, her purpose is to increase the children's awareness and give them some idea of what magnets do.

In this scenario, children observe that magnets can be different shapes and sizes (horseshoe, rod, disk, the letter U, ring, and so on) and attract a different amount of paper clips. They also have a visual graphic reminder of what they have accomplished. When snack time arrives, Mrs. Carter prepares a plate of chocolate candy balls, each wrapped in metallic paper, and a jar of peanut butter. She gives each child two large pretzel sticks. The children dip the pretzels into the peanut butter and then try to "attract" the metallic-wrapped candy, imitating the way the magnets attracted the paper clips. The following activity demonstrates another way to communicate with magnets.

## ACTIVITIES

### Which is the Strongest?

**OBJECTIVE:** Observing, sequencing, and ordering; communicating with graphs.

**MATERIALS:** Ideally, a magnet of the same size for each child to begin magnet exploration, a variety of magnets sizes and strength to be introduced later, a variety of metallic and nonmetallic items available for testing—the larger, the better. If using metal magnets, be sure that they are clean and free of rust and/or sharp edges.

*(continued)*

**NATURALISTIC AND INFORMAL ACTIVITIES:** Give students a lot of time to explore the magnets and the effect they have on different objects. Have both metallic and nonmetallic objects available for the children to explore with magnets. Listen to the children's discussion about the magnets. Ask, WHAT DO YOU THINK WILL BE ATTRACTED TO YOUR MAGNETS?

**STRUCTURED ACTIVITIES:** Ask the children what they know about magnets. Then have them group the objects that are attracted to their magnets and those that are not attracted to the magnets and communicate their findings on charts labeled "Things Magnets Pick Up" and "Things Magnets Do Not Pick Up."

**FOLLOW-UP:** Depending on the children's interest, metal balls can be used with ramps and tubes to form the basis of a "magnet race." Or, objects can be pulled out of a jar containing a variety of objects. Challenge the students to find out which objects are pulled the fastest or the farthest.

## SUMMARY

When more than two things are ordered and placed in sequence, the process is called seriation. If children understand seriation, they will be able to develop the more advanced skills of patterning. Patterning involves repeating auditory, visual, or physical motor sequences.

Children begin to understand measurement by actively manipulating measurement materials. Water and sand are highly sensory and are effective resources for young children to develop concepts of volume, temperature, length, and weight. Time measurement is related to sequencing events. The use of measurement units will formalize and develop further when children enter the concrete operations period.

Graph making gives children an opportunity to classify, compare, count, measure, and visually communicate information. A graph is a way of displaying information so that predictions, inferences, and conclusions can be made.

## KEY TERMS

| comparing | ordering | patterning |
| --- | --- | --- |

## SUGGESTED ACTIVITIES

1. Interview a preprimary teacher about the kinds of problems and challenges encountered when teaching about ordering and patterning, measurement, and graphing. Ask the teacher to discuss ways that he has overcome or modified the challenges of applying fundamental concepts in preprimary science. Share the interview results with your classmates and compare strategies used by different teachers. Videotape or tape-record yourself in a similar teaching situation; this can help to clearly illustrate a problem.

2. To measure is to match things. Observe and record every comparison that one child makes in a day. Record all forms of measuring that you observe this child performing. Teachers will probably tell you that children are not very interested in measuring for its own sake, so find the measuring in the child's everyday school life.

3. Reflect on measurement in your own life. What did you measure this morning? In groups, brainstorm all of the measuring that you did on your way to class. Predict the types of measuring that you will do tonight. Then reflect on ordering, patterning, and graphing in the same way.

4. Design a lesson that emphasizes one of the concepts and skills discussed in this unit. Teach the lesson to a class, and note the reactions of the children to your teaching. Discuss these reactions in class. "Did you teach what you intended to teach?" "How do you know your lesson was effective?" "If not, why not, and how could the lesson be improved?"

5. Use the evaluation system in Activity 5, Unit 2, to evaluate the following software.
   - ■ *KidWare* (Redmond, WA: Edmark)
   - ■ *KidWorks* (pre-K–2; Torrance, CA: Davidson & Associates)
   - ■ *Kid Pix* (San Francisco: Broderbund at Riverdeep)

   Design a lesson that would integrate one of these computer programs into the classroom environment. Try teaching the lesson to a child who has experience manipulating objects in patterns and evaluate the results. What factors do you think need to be taken into account when using computers in this way?

## REVIEW

A. What is seriation? Why must children possess this skill before they are able to pattern objects?

B. Which activities might be used to evaluate a child's ability to compare and order?

C. How will you teach measurement to young children?

D. Explain how graphing assists in learning science concepts.

## REFERENCE

National Research Council. (1996). *National science education standards*. Washington, DC: National Academies Press.

## FURTHER READING AND RESOURCES

Baratta-Lorton, M. (1976). *Mathematics their way*. Menlo Park, CA: Addison-Wesley.

Baratta-Lorton, M. (1994). *Mathematics their way 20th anniversary edition*. Reading, MA: Addison-Wesley.

Benenson, G., & Neujahr, J. L. (2002). *Designed environments: Places, practices, and plans*. Portsmouth, NH: Heinemann.

Benenson, G., & Neujahr, J. L. (2002). *Mapping*. Portsmouth, NH: Heinemann.

Benenson, G., & Neujahr, J. L. (2002). *Mechanisms and other systems*. Portsmouth, NH: Heinemann.

Benenson, G., & Neujahr, J. L. (2002). *Packaging and other structures*. Portsmouth, NH: Heinemann.

Benenson, G., & Neujahr, J. L. (2002). *Signs, symbols, and codes*. Portsmouth, NH: Heinemann.

Burk, D., Snider, A., & Symonds, P. (1988). *Box it or bag it mathematics: Kindergarten teachers resource guide*. Portland, OR: Math Learning Center.

Chaille, C., & Britain, L. (2003). *Young child as scientist: A constructivist approach to early childhood science education*. Boston: Allyn & Bacon.

Chalufour, I., & Worth, K. (2005). *Exploring water with young children*. St. Paul, MN: Redleaf Press.

Council for Elementary Science International Sourcebook IV. (1986). *Science experiences for preschoolers*. Columbus, OH: SMEAC Information Reference Center.

Forman, G. E., & Kuschner, D. (1983). *Child's construction of knowledge*. Washington, DC: National Association for the Education of Young Children.

Fowlkes, M. A. (1985). Funnels and tunnels. *Science and Children, 22*(6), 28–29.

Grollman, S., & Worth, K. (2003). *Worms, shadows, and whirlpools: Science in the early childhood classroom*. Portsmouth, NH: Heinemann.

Hill, D. M. (1977). *Mud, sand and water*. Washington, DC: National Association for the Education of Young Children.

Howe, A. C. (2002). *Engaging children in science* (3rd ed.). Upper Saddle River, NJ: Prentice-Hall.

James, J. C., & Granovetter, R. F. (1987). *Water works*. Lewisville, NC: Kaplan Press.

McIntyre, M. (1984). *Early childhood and science*. Washington, DC: National Science Teachers Association.

Phillips, D. G. (1982). Measurement or mimicry? *Science and Children, 20*(3), 32–34.

Rockwell, R. E., Sherwood, E. A., & Williams, R. A. (1986). *Hug a tree*. Beltsville, MD: Gryphon House.

Shaw, E. L. (1987). Students and sponges—Soaking up science. *Science and Children, 25*(1), 21.

Warren, J. (1984). *Science time*. Palo Alto, CA: Monday Morning Books.

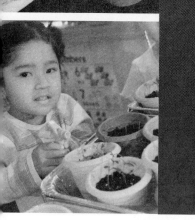

# Unit 22

# Integrating the Curriculum through Dramatic Play and Thematic Units and Projects

## OBJECTIVES

After reading this unit, you should be able to:

- Describe how children apply and extend concepts through dramatic play.
- Describe how children apply and extend concepts through thematic units and projects.
- Encourage dramatic role-playing that promotes concept acquisition.
- Recognize how dramatic role-playing and thematic units and projects promote interdisciplinary instruction and learning.
- Use dramatic play and thematic units and projects as settings for science investigations, mathematical problem solving, social learning, and language learning.
- Connect the math and science standards to integrated curriculum.

The standards for mathematics (NCTM, 2000) and science (National Research Council, 1996) focus on content areas skills, understandings, and processes that can be applied across the curriculum. Problem solving, reasoning, communication, connections, and hands-on learning can be applied and experienced through *dramatic play, thematic and project approaches*, and an **integrated curriculum**. **Play** is the major medium through which children learn (Unit 1). They experiment with grown-up roles, explore materials, and develop rules for their actions. Curriculum that meets the national standards can be implemented through the use of **thematic units and projects** that integrate mathematics, science, social studies, language arts, music, and movement. Themes may be selected by the teacher (Isbell, 1995) and/or the child (Helm & Katz, 2001; Katz & Chard, 1989). Integrated curriculum can also

support state standards (Akerson, 2001; Clark, 2000; Decker, 1999).

Integrated curriculum can easily include mathematics. Remember that mathematics is composed of fundamental concepts that are used for thinking in all the content areas (Whitin & Whitin, 2001). These concepts are used to investigate the world. According to the authors, authentic, real-world learning experiences can be provided to children through the use of two strategies: (1) having children make direct observations; and (2) posing questions or "wonders" based on these observations (Whitin & Whitin, 2001, p. 1). For example, a first-grade class went outside in February to look for insects. They wondered why they did not find any. This question led to the study of the life cycles of insects, which applied their knowledge of time. A month later there were insects in abundance. The students took measurements (length) to find out how far grasshoppers can jump. Their observations caused them to wonder why spiders made webs in corners (spatial relations). Eventually, the class made a map of the best places to find bugs. This type of activity exemplifies a student-selected project that applies mathematics to answer questions developed from observation (Whitin & Whitin, 2001).

The purpose of this unit is to demonstrate how dramatic play and thematic units can enrich children's acquisition of concepts and knowledge, not only in science and mathematics but also in the other content areas. Furthermore, these areas offer rich settings for social learning, science investigations, and mathematical problem solving. Unit 1 described the commonalities between math and science. Unit 7 provided a basic unit plan and examples of science units that incorporate math, social studies, language arts, fine arts, motor development, and dramatic play. Units 33 through 38 include integrated units and activities for the primary level. This unit emphasizes the natural play of young children as the basis for developing thematic units that highlight the potentials for an interdisciplinary curriculum for young children.

Concepts and skills are valuable to children only if they can be used in everyday life. Young children spend most of their waking hours involved in play. Play can be used as a vehicle for the application of concepts. Young children like to feel big and do "big person" things. They like to pretend they are grown up and want to do as many grown-up things as they can. Role-playing can be used as a means for children to apply what they know as they take on a multitude of grown-up roles.

**Dramatic role-playing** is an essential part of thematic units. For example, using food as the theme for a unit could afford opportunities not only for applying concepts and carrying out science investigations and mathematics problem solving but also for children to try out adult roles and do adult activities. Children can grow food and shop for groceries; plan and prepare meals, snacks, and parties; serve food; and enjoy sharing and eating the results of their efforts. Opportunities can be offered that provide experiences for social education as children learn more about adult tasks, have experiences in the community, and learn about their own and other cultures. Teachers can use these experiences to assess and evaluate through observation.

Butterworth and Lo Cicero (2001) described a project that grew from the interests of 4- and 5-year-old Latino children in a transitional kindergarten class. The teachers used the Reggio Emilia approach (Edwards, Gandini, & Forman, 1998) in developing the project. That is, they began with the children's culture. In this case they had the children tell stories about their trips to the supermarket, and these stories were transformed into math problems. The market provided a setting that led the children naturally to talk about quantity and money. After presenting their stories, the children re-enacted them through dramatic play. They pretended to buy fruit and take it home to eat. Setting the table naturally posed problems in rational counting and one-to-one correspondence. The project continued on into more complex problems and other types of child-selected dramatic play.

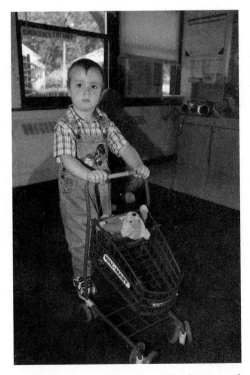

With his grocery cart and his "babies," this boy is ready to shop.

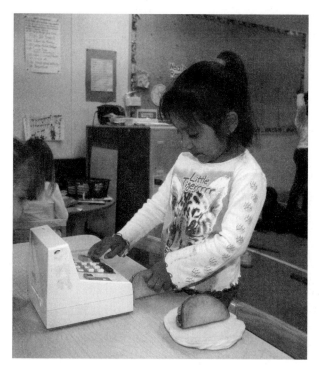

As their dramatic play experience increases, children can add more realistic props and personalities to a setting. This girl has learned that she needs a cash register to "ring out" a customer who is buying these tacos.

## DRAMATIC ROLE-PLAYING

When children are engaged in dramatic role-playing, they practice what it is like to be an adult. They begin with a simple imitation of what they have observed. Their first roles reflect what they have seen at home. They bathe, feed, and rock babies. They cook meals, set the table, and eat. One of their first outside experiences is to go shopping. This experience is soon reflected in dramatic play. They begin by carrying things in bags, purses, and other large containers. At first, they carry around anything that they can stuff in their containers. Gradually, they move into using more realistic props such as play money and empty food containers. Next, they might build a store with big blocks and planks. Eventually, they learn to play cooperatively with other children. One child might be the mother, another the father, another the child, and another the store clerk. As the children

move toward this stage, teachers can provide more props and background experiences that will expand the raw material children have for developing their role-playing. Problem-solving skills are refined as children figure out who will take which role, provide a location for the store and home, and develop the rules for the activity.

Children can learn about adult roles through field trips to businesses such as restaurants, banks, the post office, and stores both in the local neighborhood and in the extended community. Museums, construction sites, hospitals, fire stations, and other places offer experiences that can enrich children's knowledge of adult roles. Books, tapes, films, and classroom visitors can also provide valuable experiences for children. Following such experiences, props can be provided to support children's dramatic role-playing. Each type of business or service center can be set up in the classroom with appropriate props.

Some examples of dramatic play centers and props follow.

- A toy store could be set up by having the children bring old toys from home, which they could pretend to buy and sell.

- A grocery store can also be set up using items that might otherwise be discarded, such as empty food containers that the children could bring from home. The children could make food from play dough, clay, or papier-mâché. Plastic food replicas can be purchased.

- A clothing store can be organized into children's, ladies', and men's departments; children can bring discarded clothing and shoes from home.

- A jewelry store can be stocked with old and pretend jewelry (such as macaroni necklaces and cardboard watches).

- Services centers such as the post office, fire station, police station, automobile repair shop, hospital, beauty shop, and the like can be stocked with appropriate props.

- Transportation vehicles such as space vehicles, automobiles, trucks, and buses can be built with large blocks, with lined-up chairs, or with commercially made or teacher-made steering wheels and other controls.

■ A zoo, veterinarian's office, circus, farm, or pet shop could be set up. Have children bring stuffed animals from home to live in the zoo, visit the vet, act in the circus, live on the farm, or be sold in the pet shop. Classify the animals as to which belong in each setting. Children can predict which animals eat the most, are dangerous to humans, are the smartest, and so on. Provide play money to pay for goods and services.

■ Health and medical service centers can be organized. Provide props for medical play. Tie these in with discussions of good nutrition and other health practices. The children can "pay the bill" for the services.

■ Space science vehicles can be created. Provide props for space travel (e.g., a big refrigerator carton that can be made into a spaceship, paper bag space helmets, and so on). Provide materials for making mission control and for designing other planetary settings.

■ Water environments can be created. Provide toy boats, people, rocks for islands, and the like. Discuss floating and sinking. Outdoors, use water for firefighter play and for watering the garden. Have a container (bucket or large dishpan) that can be a fishing hole, and use waterproof fish with a safety pin or other metal object attached so they can be caught with a magnet fish bait. Investigate why the magnet/metal combination makes a good combination for pretend fishing. Count how many fish each child catches.

■ Simple machines can be set up. Vehicles, a packing box elevator, a milk carton elevator on a pulley, a plank on rollers, and so on, make interesting dramatic play props, and their construction and functioning provide challenging problems for investigation.

Concepts are applied in a multitude of play activities such as those just described. The following are some examples:

■ One-to-one correspondence can be practiced by exchanging play money for goods or services.

■ Sets and classifying are involved in organizing each dramatic play center in an orderly manner (e.g., placing all the items in the drugstore in the proper place).

■ Counting can be applied to figuring out how many items have been purchased and how much money must be exchanged.

■ Comparing and measuring can be used to decide if clothing fits, to determine the weight of fruits and vegetables purchased, to check a sick person's temperature, and to decide on which size box of cereal or carton of milk to purchase.

■ Spatial relations and volume concepts are applied as items purchased are placed in bags, boxes, and/or baskets and as children discover how many passengers will fit in the space shuttle or can ride on the bus.

■ Number symbols can be found throughout dramatic play props—for example, on price tags, play money, telephones, cash registers, scales, measuring cups and spoons, thermometers, rulers, and calculators.

Pocket calculators are excellent props for dramatic play. Children can pretend to add up their expenses, costs, and earnings. As they explore calculators, they will learn how to use them for basic mathematical operations. Methods for introducing calculators are described in Section 4. (See resources in Figure 22–1.)

## A THEMATIC UNIT EXAMPLE: FOOD

A thematic unit that focuses on food can involve many science, mathematics, social studies, language arts, art, music, and movement experiences. As scientists, children observe the growth of food, the physical changes that take place when food is prepared, and the effects of food on growth of humans and animals. They also compare the tastes of different foods and categorize them into those they like and those they dislike and into sweet and sour; liquid and solid; "junk" and healthful; and groups such as meat and dairy products, breads and cereals, and fruits and vegetables.

As mathematicians, children pour, measure, count, cut wholes into parts, and divide full pans or full

**Figure 22–1** Examples of resources for integrating mathematics and science across the curriculum.

These boys are dramatizing based on their cooking experiences.

bowls into equal servings. They count the strokes when mixing a cake, make sure the oven is on the correct temperature setting, and set the clock for the required baking time. At the store, they exchange money for food and weigh fruits and vegetables. They count the days until their beans sprout or the fruit ripens.

Through food experiences, children learn much about society and culture. They can make foods from different cultures. They learn where food is grown, how it is marketed, and how it must be purchased with money at the grocery store. They cooperate with each other and take turns when preparing food. Then they share what they make with others.

Children can sing about food and draw pictures of their food-related experiences. They can move like an eggbeater, like a stalk of wheat blowing in the wind, or like a farmer planting seeds. The following are some examples of dramatic play, mathematics, and science food experiences.

## Food and Dramatic Play

In the home living center at school, children purchase, cook, serve, and eat food as part of their role-playing.

It was suggested in Unit 18 that a simple measuring activity could be to make flour and salt dough. The dough can be made into pretend food to use as dramatic play props.

## Food and Math

Cooking activities are a rich source of mathematics experiences. Following a recipe provides a sequencing activity. Each ingredient must be measured exactly using a standard measuring tool. The correct number of cups, tablespoons, eggs, and so on must be counted out. Baked foods must be cooked at the correct temperature for the prescribed amount of time. Some foods are heated, while others are placed in the refrigerator or freezer. When the food is ready to eat, it must be divided into equal portions so that each person gets a fair share. A simple pictograph recipe can help children to be independent as they assemble ingredients (Figure 22–2).

Children who live in the country or who have a garden have additional opportunities to apply math concepts to real-life experiences. They can count the number of days from planting until the food is ready to be picked. They can measure the growth of the plants at regular intervals. The number of cucumbers harvested and the weight of the potatoes can be measured. If the child lives where livestock can be kept, the daily number of eggs gathered can be counted, the young calf can be weighed each week, and the amount of money collected for products sold can be counted.

Setting the table at the home living center or for a real meal is an opportunity for applying math skills. The number of people to be seated and served is calculated and matched with the amount of tableware and the number of chairs, napkins, and place mats needed. Putting utensils and dishes away is an experience in sorting things into sets. Pictographs can be used to provide clues about where each type of item should be placed.

## Food and Science

Each of the activities described under the Food and Math section also involves science. Children can be asked to predict what will happen when the wet ingre-

**Figure 22–2**  A pictograph for making a peanut butter and jelly sandwich.

dients (oil and milk) are mixed with the dry ingredients (flour, baking powder, and salt) when making the play dough biscuits. They can then make the mixture; observe and describe its texture, color, and density; and compare their results with their predictions. Next, they can predict what will happen when the dough is baked in the oven. When it is taken out, they can observe and describe the differences that take place during the baking process. They can be asked what would happen if the oven is too hot or if the biscuits are left in too long.

If the children have the opportunity to see eggs produced, this can lead to a discussion of where the eggs come from and what would happen if the eggs were fertilized. They could observe the growth from seed to edible food as vegetables are planted, cultivated, watered, and picked. Applesauce exemplifies several physical changes: from whole to parts, from solid chunks to soft lumps, and to smooth and thick as cutting, heating, and grinding each have an effect. Children can also note the change in taste before and after

the sugar is added. Stone soup offers an opportunity for discussion of the significance of the stone. What does the stone add to the soup? Does a stone have nutrients? What really makes the soup taste good and makes it nutritious?

## Food and Social Studies

Each of the activities described also involves social studies. City children might take a trip to the farm. For example, a trip to an orchard to get apples for applesauce is an enriching and enjoyable experience. They might also take a trip to the grocery store to purchase the ingredients needed in their recipes. Then they can take turns measuring, cutting, adding ingredients, or whatever else is required as the cooking process proceeds. Stone soup is an excellent group activity because everyone in the class can add an ingredient. Invite people from different cultures to bring foods to class and/or help the children make their special foods. Children can note similarities and differences across cultures.

## IDEAS FOR CHILDREN WITH SPECIAL NEEDS

The multicultural curriculum can include learning about the favorite foods of different cultures. Children can make a variety of ethnic dishes. They can construct graphs of their favorite foods and write their favorite recipes. Young children can come up with delightful recipes for a class cookbook. Projects can center on the study of ethnic groups, geographical area, and customs of different cultures. Parents can contribute to these projects. Costumes, dolls, musical instruments, and other diverse cultural artifacts can be included in the dramatic play center.

## SUMMARY

Dramatic play and thematic units and projects provide math, science, and social studies experiences that afford children an opportunity to apply concepts and skills. They can predict, observe, and investigate as they explore these areas. As children play home, store, and service roles, they match, count, classify, compare, measure, and use spatial relations concepts and number symbols. They also practice the exchange of money for goods and services. Through dramatic play they try out grown-up roles and activities.

Through thematic units and projects, mathematics and science can be integrated with other content areas. The thematic experiences provide real-life connections for abstract concepts. For teachers, these activities offer valuable opportunities for naturalistic and informal instruction as well as time to observe children and assess their ability to use concepts in everyday situations.

## KEY TERMS

dramatic role-playing
integrated curriculum

play

thematic units and projects

## SUGGESTED ACTIVITIES

1. Observe young children at play in school. Note if any concept experiences take place during dramatic role-playing or while doing thematic activities. Share what you observe with your class.
2. Add a section for dramatic play and thematic resources to your Activity File/Notebook.
3. Review several cookbooks (the ones suggested in this unit and/or others) and examine recipes recommended for young children. Explain to the class which recipe books you think are most appropriate for use with young children.
4. Use the evaluation system suggested in Activity 5, Unit 2, to evaluate any of the following software.

- *The Learn About Science Series* (K–2; http://store.sunburst.com). Animals, astronomy, dinosaurs, the human body, matter, measurement and mixtures, plants, the senses, simple machines, weather.
- *Carmen San Diego's Great Chase through Time* (ages 8–12; http://www.learning company.com)
- *Rainbow Fish* (ages 3–7; http://childrens softwareonline.com).
- *Sammy's Science House* (ages 3–7; http:// www.riverdeep.net)

- *Ani's Rocket Ride* (http://www.apte.com)
- *Coco's Math Project 2* (http://mathequity.terc.edu)
- *Math Missions* (Scholastic, http://www.kidsclick.com)
- *Richard Scarry's Busytown* (Simon & Schuster, http://www.childrenssoftwareonline.com)
- *Shopping Math* (http://www.dositey.com)

Devise a plan for using one of these programs to stimulate a thematic unit or project that includes dramatic play. Find out whether there is any other software that could be used to support a thematic unit or project.

5. Add to your Activity File five food experiences that enrich children's concepts and promote application of concepts.

## REVIEW

**A.** Briefly answer each of the following questions.
1. Why should dramatic role-playing be included as a math, science, and social studies concept experience for young children?
2. Why should food activities be included as math, science, and social studies concept experiences for young children?
3. How can teachers encourage dramatic role-playing that includes concept experiences?
4. Describe four food activities that can be used in the early childhood math, science, and social studies program.
5. Explain how thematic units promote an integrated curriculum.

**B.** Describe the props that might be included in three different dramatic play centers.

**C.** Describe the relationship between integrated curriculum and the math and science standards.

## REFERENCES

Akerson, V. L. (2001). Teaching science when your principal says "Teach language arts." *Science and Children, 38*(7), 42–47.

Butterworth, S., & Lo Cicero, A. M. (2001). Storytelling: Building a mathematics curriculum from the culture of the child. *Teaching Children Mathematics, 7*(7), 396–399.

Clark, A. M. (2000). Meeting state standards through the project approach. *Eric/EECE Newsletter, 12*(1), 1–2.

Decker, K. A. (1999). Meeting state standards through integration. *Science and Children 36*(6), 28–32, 69.

Edwards, C., Gandini, L., & Forman, G. (Eds.). (1998). *The hundred languages of children: The Reggio Emilia approach—Advanced reflections.* Greenwich, CT: Ablex.

Helm, J. H., & Katz, L. G. (2001). *Young investigators: The project approach in the early years.* New York: Teachers College Press.

Isbell, R. (1995). *The complete learning center book.* Beltsville, MD: Gryphon House.

Katz, L. G., & Chard, S. C. (1989). *Engaging children's minds: The project approach.* Norwood, NY: Ablex.

National Council of Teachers of Mathematics. (2000). *Principles and standards for school mathematics.* Reston, VA: Author.

National Research Council. (1996). *National science education standards.* Washington, DC: National Academies Press.

Whitin, D., & Whitin, P. (2001). Where is the mathematics in interdisciplinary studies? *Dialogues* [On-line serial]. Retrieved July 17, 2008, from http://www.nctm.org/resources/content.aspx?id=1684

## FURTHER READING AND RESOURCES

Guha, S. (2002). Integrating mathematics for young children through play. *Young Children, 57*(3), 90–92.

McCoy, M. K. (2003). Language, math, social studies, and . . . worms? Integrating the early childhood curriculum. *Dimensions of Early Childhood, 31*(2), 3–8.

Ohana, C., & Ryan, K. (2003). A blended neighborhood. *Science and Children, 40*(7), 32–37.

Percival, I. (2003). Time-travel days: Cross-curricular adventures in mathematics. *Teaching Children Mathematics, 9*(7), 374–380.

Phillips, S. K., Dufferin, M. W., & Geist, E. A. (2004). Be a food scientist. *Science and Children, 41*(4), 24–29.

Seefeldt, C. (2004). Teaching science through the visual arts and music. *Early Childhood Today, 18*(6), 28–34.

Ward, C. D., & Dias, M. J. (2004). Ladybugs across the curriculum. *Science and Children, 41*(7), 40–44.

Worsley, M., Beneke, S., & Helm, J. H. (2003). The pizza project: Planning and integrating math standards in project work. In D. Koralek (Ed.), *Spotlight on young children and math* (pp. 35–42). Washington, DC: National Association for the Education of Young Children.

### Theme, Project, and Integration

American Association for the Advancement of Science (AAAS). (2007). *Atlas of science literacy: Project 2061* (Vol. 2). Washington, DC: Author.

Clements, D. H., & Sarama, J. (2006). Math all around the room! *Early Childhood Today, 21*(2), 25–30.

Conezio, K., & French, L. (2002). Science in the preschool classroom: Capitalizing on children's fascination with the everyday world to foster language and literacy development. *Young Children, 57*(5), 12–18.

Cook, H., & Matthews, C. E. (1998). Lessons from a "living fossil." *Science and Children, 36*(3), 16–19.

Draznin, Z. (1995). *Writing math: A project-based approach.* Glenview, IL: Goodyear Books.

Edelson, R. J., & Johnson, G. (2003/2004). Music makes math meaningful. *Childhood Education, 80*(2), 65–70.

Fioranelli, D. (2000). Recycling into art: Integrating science and art. *Science and Children, 38*(2), 30–33.

Fogelman, Y. (2007). The early years: Water works. *Science and Children, 44*(9), 16–18.

Forrest, K., Schnabel, D., & Williams, M. (2006). Water wonders, K–2. *Teaching Children Mathematics, 12*(5), 248.

French, L. (2004). Science as the center of a coherent, integrated early childhood curriculum. *Early Childhood Research Quarterly, 19*(1), 138–149.

Hamm, M., & Adams, D. (1998). What research says. Reaching across disciplines. *Science and Children, 36*(1), 45–49.

Johnson, G. L., & Edelson, R. J. (2003). Integrating music and mathematics in the elementary classroom. *Teaching Children Mathematics, 9*(8), 474–479.

Krogh, S., & Morehouse, P. J. (2007). *The early childhood curriculum: Inquiry learning through integration.* New York: McGraw-Hill.

Owens, K. (2001). An integrated approach for young students. *Dialogues* [On-line serial]. Retrieved July 17, 2008, from http://www.nctm.org/resources/content.aspx?id=1680

Patton, M. M., & Kokoski, T. M. (1996). How good is your early childhood science, mathematics, and technology program? Strategies for extending your curriculum. *Young Children, 51*(5), 38–44.

Schnur-Laughlin, J. (1999). Pantry math. *Teaching Children Mathematics, 6*(4), 216–218.

Shreero, B., Sullivan, C., & Urbano, A. (2002). Math in art. *Teaching Children Mathematics, 9*(4), 218–220.

Smith, R. R. (2002). Cooperation and consumerism: Lessons learned at a kindergarten mini-mall. *Teaching Children Mathematics, 9*(3), 179–183.

Trepanier-Street, M. (2000). Multiple forms of representation in long-term projects: The garden project. *Childhood Education, 77*(1), 19–25.

Warner, L., & Morse, P. (2001). Studying pond life with primary-age children: The project approach in action. *Childhood Education, 77*(3), 139–143.

Yagi, S., & Olson, M. (2007). Supermarket math: K–2. *Teaching Children Mathematics, 13*(7), 376.

### Cooking and Food

Albyn, C. L., & Webb, L. S. (1993). *The multicultural cookbook for students.* Phoenix, AZ: Oryx.

*Better Homes and Gardens New Junior Cookbook* (7th ed.). (2004). Des Moines, IA: Meredith.

Christenberry, M. A., & Stevens, B. (1984). *Can Piaget cook?* Atlanta, GA: Humanics.

Cloke, G., Ewing, N., & Stevens, D. (2001). Food for thought. *Teaching Children Mathematics, 8*(3), 148–150.

Colker, L. J. (2005). *The cooking book.* Washington, DC: National Association for the Education of Young Children.

Cook, D. (2006). *Family fun cooking with kids.* Burbank/Glendale, CA: Disney.

*Cooking with Kids.* A parent helper. Retrieved July 17, 2008, from http://www.pbs.org/parents/parenthelpers/cooking.html

Dahl, K. (1998). Why cooking in the curriculum? *Young Children, 53*(1), 81–83.

Faggella, K., & Dixler, D. (1985). *Concept cookery.* Bridgeport, CT: First Teacher Press.

Howell, N. M. (1999). Cooking up a learning community with corn, beans and rice. *Young Children, 54*(5), 36–38.

Lowry, P. K., & McCrary, J. H. (2001). Someone's in the kitchen with science. *Science and Children, 39*(2), 22–27.

Metheny, D., & Hollowell, J. (1994). Food for thought. *Teaching Children Mathematics, 1,* 164.

Owen, S., & Fields, A. (1994). Eggs, eggs, eggs. *Teaching Children Mathematics, 1,* 92–93.

Partridge, E., Austin, S., Wadlington, E., & Bitner, J. (1996). Cooking up mathematics in the kindergarten. *Teaching Children Mathematics, 2,* 492–495.

Ray, R. (2004). Cooking rocks: *Rachael Ray 30 minute meals for kids.* New York: Lake Isle Press.

Richardson, M. V., Hoag, C. L., Miller, M. B., & Monroe, E. E. (2001). Children's literature and mathematics: Connections through cooking. *Focus on Elementary, 14*(2), 1–6.

Rothstein, G. L. (1994). *From soup to nuts: Multicultural cooking activities and recipes.* New York: Scholastic Books.

Taylor, S. I., & Dodd, A. T. (1999). We can cook! Snack preparation with toddlers and twos. *Early Childhood Education Journal, 27*(1), 29–33.

# SECTION 4

## Symbols and Higher-Level Activities

# Unit 23
## Symbols

**OBJECTIVES**

After reading this unit, you should be able to:

- List the six number symbol skills.
- Describe four basic types of self-correcting number symbol materials.
- Set up an environment that supports naturalistic and informal number symbol experiences.
- Do structured number symbol activities with children.

Number symbols are called **numerals**. Each numeral represents an amount and acts as a shorthand for recording *how many*. The young child sees numerals all around (Figure 23–1). He has some idea of what they are before he can understand and use them. He sees that there are numerals on his house, the phone, the clock, and the car license plate. He may have one or more counting books. He may watch a children's TV program where numeral recognition is taught. Sometime between the ages of 2 and 5, a child learns to name the numerals from 0 to 10. However, the child is usually 4 or older when he begins to understand that each numeral stands for a group of things of a certain amount that is always the same. He may be able to tell the name of the symbol "3" and count three objects, but he may not realize that the "3" can stand for the three objects or the **cardinal meaning** of three. This is illustrated in Figure 23–2.

It can be confusing to the child to spend time on drills with numerals before he has had many concrete experiences with basic math concepts. Most experiences with numerals should be naturalistic and informal.

## THE NUMBER SYMBOL SKILLS

There are six number symbol skills that young children acquire during the preoperational period.

- She learns to recognize and say the name of each numeral.
- She learns to place the numerals in order: 0-1-2-3-4-5-6-7-8-9-10.
- She learns to associate numerals with groups: "1" goes with one thing.
- She learns that each numeral in order stands for one more than the numeral that comes before it. (That is, 2 is one more than 1, 3 is one more than 2, and so on.)

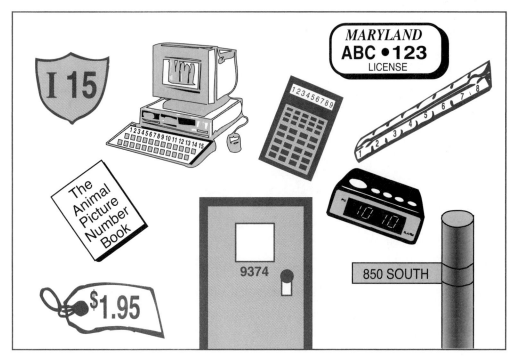

**Figure 23–1** Numerals are everywhere in the environment.

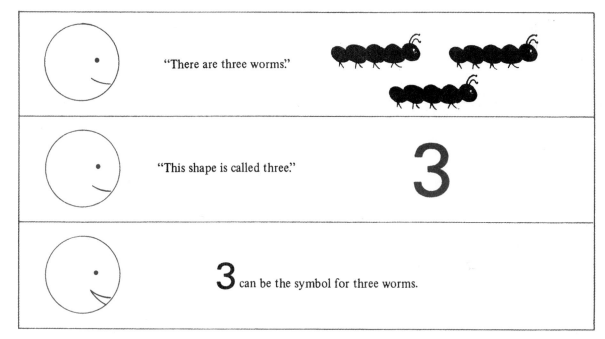

**Figure 23–2** The child counts the objects, learns the symbol, and realizes that the symbol can represent the group.

- She learns to match each numeral to any group of the size that the numeral stands for and to make groups that match numerals.
- She learns to reproduce (write) numerals.

The first four skills are included in this unit. The last two are the topics for Unit 24.

## Assessment

The teacher should observe whether the child shows an interest in numerals. Does he repeat the names he hears on television? Does he use self-correcting materials? (These are described in this unit's Informal Activities section.) What does he do when he uses these materials? Individual interviews would include the types of tasks that follow.

### SAMPLE ASSESSMENT TASK

**4J**                                                             **Preoperational Ages 3–6**

#### Symbols, Recognition: Unit 23

| | |
|---|---|
| **METHOD:** | Interview. |
| **SKILL:** | Child is able to recognize numerals 0 to 10 presented in sequence. |
| **MATERIALS:** | 5" × 8" cards with one numeral from 0 to 10 written on each. |
| **PROCEDURE:** | Starting with 0, show the child each card in numerical order from 0 to 10. WHAT IS THIS? TELL ME THE NAME OF THIS. |
| **EVALUATION:** | Note if the child uses numeral names (correct or not), indicating she knows the kinds of words associated with the symbols. Note which numerals she can label correctly. |

**INSTRUCTIONAL RESOURCE:**  Charlesworth, R., and Lind, K. K. (2010). *Math and science for young children* (6th ed.). Clifton Park, NY: Cengage Learning.

### SAMPLE ASSESSMENT TASK

**5L**                                                             **Preoperational Ages 4–6**

#### Symbols, Sequencing: Unit 23

| | |
|---|---|
| **METHOD:** | Interview. |
| **SKILL:** | Child is able to sequence numerals from 0 to 10. |
| **MATERIALS:** | 5" × 8" cards with one numeral from 0 to 10 written on each. |
| **PROCEDURE:** | Place all the cards in front of the child in random order. PUT THESE IN ORDER. WHICH COMES FIRST? NEXT? NEXT? |
| **EVALUATION:** | Note whether the child seems to understand that numerals belong in a fixed sequence. Note how many are placed in the correct order and which, if any, are labeled. |

**INSTRUCTIONAL RESOURCE:**  Charlesworth, R., and Lind, K. K. (2010). *Math and science for young children* (6th ed.). Clifton Park, NY: Cengage Learning.

## SAMPLE ASSESSMENT TASK

| 6J | Preoperational Ages 5 and Older |
|---|---|

### Symbols, One More Than: Unit 23

**METHOD:** Interview.

**SKILL:** Child is able to identify numerals that are "one more than."

**MATERIALS:** 5" × 8" cards with one numeral from 0 to 10 written on each.

**PROCEDURE:** Place the numeral cards in front of the child in order from 0 to 10. TELL ME WHICH NUMERAL MEANS ONE MORE THAN TWO. WHICH NUMERAL MEANS ONE MORE THAN SEVEN? WHICH NUMERAL MEANS ONE MORE THAN FOUR? (If the child answers these, then try LESS THAN.)

**EVALUATION:** Note whether the child is able to answer correctly.

**INSTRUCTIONAL RESOURCE:** Charlesworth, R., and Lind, K. K. (2010). *Math and science for young children* (6th ed.). Clifton Park, NY: Cengage Learning.

## NATURALISTIC ACTIVITIES

As the young child observes his environment, he sees numerals around him. He sees them on clocks, phones, houses, books, food containers, television programs, money, calendars, thermometers, rulers, measuring cups, license plates, and on many other objects in many places. He hears people say number names, as in the following examples:

- My phone number is 622-7732.
- My house number is 1423.
- My age is 6.
- I have a five-dollar bill.
- The temperature is 78 degrees.
- Get a five-pound bag of rabbit food.
- We had three inches of rain today.
- This pitcher holds eight cups of juice.

Usually children start using the names of the number symbols before they actually match them with the symbols.

- Tanya and Juanita are ready to take off in their spaceship. Juanita does the countdown, "Ten, nine, eight, three, one, blast off!"

- Tim asks Ms. Moore to write the number 7 on a sign for his race car.
- Ako notices that the thermometer has numbers written on it.
- Becca is playing house. She takes the toy phone and begins dialing, "One-six-two. Hello dear, will you please stop at the store and buy a loaf of bread?"
- "How old are you, Pete?" "I'm six," answers 2-year-old Pete.
- "One, two, three, I have three dolls."
- Tanya is playing house. She looks up at the clock. "Eight o'clock and time for bed," she tells her doll. (The clock actually says 9:30 a.m.)

Children begin to learn number symbols as they look and listen and then, in their play, imitate what they have seen and heard.

## INFORMAL ACTIVITIES

During the preoperational period, most school activities with numerals should be informal. Experimentation and practice in perception with sight and touch are most important. These experiences are made available by means of activities with self-correcting manipulative materials. **Self-correcting materials** are those the child can use by trial and error to solve a problem without adult assistance. The material is made in such a way that it can be used with success with very little help. **Manipulative materials** are things that have parts and pieces that can be picked up and moved by the child to solve the problem presented by the materials. The teacher observes the child as she works. He notes whether the child works in an organized way and whether she sticks with the material until she has finished the task.

There are four basic types of self-correcting manipulative math materials that can be used for informal activities. These materials can be bought, or they can be made. The four basic groups of materials are those that teach discrimination and matching, those that teach sequence (or order), those that give practice in association of symbols with groups, and those that combine association of symbols and groups with sequence. Examples of each type are illustrated in Figures 23–3 through 23–5.

The child can learn to discriminate one numeral from the other by sorting packs of numeral cards. She can also learn which numerals are the same as she matches. Another type of material that serves this purpose is a lotto-type game. The child has a large card divided equally into four or more parts. She must match individual numeral cards to each numeral on the big card. These materials are shown in Figure 23–3 (A and B). She can also experiment with felt, plastic, magnetic, wooden, rubber, and cardboard numerals.

There are many materials that teach sequence or order. These may be set up so that parts can only be put together in such a way that, when the child is done, she sees that the numerals are in order in front of her. An example is the Number Worm by Childcraft (Figure 23–4A). Sequence is also taught through the use of a number line or number stepping-stones. The Childcraft giant Walk-On Number Line lets the child walk from one numeral to the next in order (Figure 23–4B). The teacher can set out numerals on the floor (e.g., Stepping Stones from Childcraft) that the child must step on in order (Figure 23–4C). There are also number sequence wooden inset puzzles (such as Constructive Playthings' Giant Number Puzzle and Number Art Puzzle).

**Figure 23–3** Sorting and matching.

**Figure 23–4** Materials that help the child learn numeral sequence.

The hand calculator lends itself to informal exploration of numerals. First, show the students how to turn the calculator on and off. Tell them to watch the display window and then turn on the calculator. A 0 will appear. Explain that when they first turn on their calculators a 0 will always appear. Then tell them to turn on their calculators and tell you what they see in the window. Have them practice turning their calculators on and off until you are sure they all understand this operation. Next, tell them to press **1**. Ask them what they see in the window. Note if they tell you they see the same number. Next, have them press **2**. A 2 will appear in the window next to the 1. Show them that they just need to press the **C** key to erase. Then let them explore and discover on their own. Help them by answering their questions and posing questions to them such as, "What will happen if _____?"

Many materials can be purchased that help the child associate each numeral with the group that goes with it. Large cards that can be placed on the bulletin board (such as Childcraft Poster Cards) give a visual association (Figure 23–5A). Numerals can be seen and touched on textured cards, such as Didax Tactile Number Cards. Numeral cards can be made using sandpaper for the sets of dots and for the numerals (Figure 23–5B). Other materials require the child to use visual and motor coordination. She may have to match puzzlelike pieces (such as Math Plaques from Childcraft; Figure 23–5C). She may put pegs in holes (such as Peg Numerals from Childcraft, Figure 23–5D). Unifix inset pattern boards require the same type of activity. The teacher can make cards that have numerals and dots the size of buttons or other counters. The child could place a counter on each dot (Figure 23–5E).

Materials that give the child experience with sequence and association at the same time are also available. These are shown in Figure 23–6. The basis of these materials is that the numerals are in a fixed order and the child adds some sort of counter that can be placed only in the right amount. Unifix stairs are like the inset patterns but are stuck together (Figure 23–6A). Other materials illustrated are counters on rods (Figure 23–6B), pegs in holes (Number-Ite from Childcraft; Figure 23–6C), or 1–5 pegboard (Figure 23–6D).

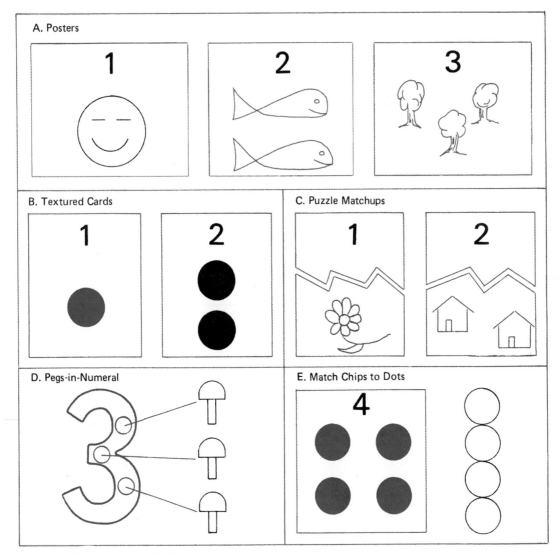

**Figure 23–5** Numeral and group association.

The teacher's role with these materials is to show the child how they can be used and then step back and watch. After the child has learned to use the materials independently, the teacher can make comments and ask questions.

■ How many pegs are on this one?

■ Can you tell me the name of each numeral?

■ You put in the four pegs that go with that numeral 4.

■ How many beads are there here? (point to stack of one) How many here? (stack of two, and so on)

■ Good, you separated all the numerals into piles. Here are all 1s, and here are all 2s.

Numerals can also be introduced informally as part of daily counting activities. For example, the class can keep track of the first 100 days of school (see Unit 9). Children can make a 100-number line around the room. They add the appropriate numeral each day to a

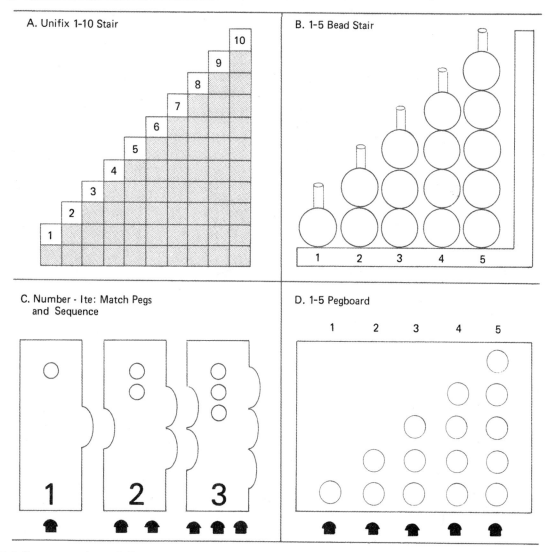

**Figure 23–6** Sequence and association.

number line strip after they have agreed on how many straws they have accumulated. The strip should be wide enough so that large-sized numerals (that the students can easily see) can be glued or written on it.

The children can draw special symbols representing special days, such as birthdays, Halloween, Thanksgiving, and so on, below the appropriate numeral on the line. The number line then serves as a timeline recording the class history. A weekly or monthly calendar may

also be placed on the bulletin board next to the 100-days display. Calendars were introduced in Unit 19.

Most children will learn through this informal use of materials to recognize and say the name of each numeral, to place the numerals in order, to see that each numeral stands for one more than the one before

| Numeral | Amount in Group |
|---------|-----------------|
| 0 | |
| 1 | X |
| 2 | XX |
| 3 | XXX |
| 4 | XXXX |
| 5 | XXXXX |
| 6 | XXXXXX |
| 7 | XXXXXXX |
| 8 | XXXXXXXX |
| 9 | XXXXXXXXX |
| 10 | XXXXXXXXXX |

it, and to associate numerals with amounts. However, some children will need the structured activities described next.

## STRUCTURED ACTIVITIES

By the time young children finish kindergarten, they should be able to do the following activities.

■ Recognize the numerals from 0 to 10

■ Place the numerals from 0 to 10 in order

■ Know that each numeral represents a group one larger than the numeral before (and one less than the one that comes next)

■ Know that each numeral represents a group of things

They may not always match the right numeral to the correct amount, but they will know that there is such a relationship. The 5-year-old child who cannot do one or more of the tasks listed needs some structured help.

## ACTIVITIES

### Numerals: Recognition

**OBJECTIVE:** To learn the names of the number symbols.

**MATERIALS:** Write the numerals from 0 to 10 on cards.

**NATURALISTIC AND INFORMAL ACTIVITIES:** Place the cards in the math center for exploration. Note if children label and/or sequence the numerals or in any way demonstrate a knowledge of the symbols and what they mean. Ask questions such as, "What are those?" "Do they have names?"

**STRUCTURED ACTIVITY:** This is an activity that a child who can name all the numbers can do with a child who needs help. Show the numerals one at a time in order. THIS NUMERAL IS CALLED _____. LET'S SAY IT TOGETHER: _____. Do this for each numeral. After 10, say, I'LL HOLD THE CARDS UP ONE AT A TIME. YOU NAME THE NUMERAL. Go through once. Five minutes at a time should be enough.

**FOLLOW-UP:** Give the child a set of cards to review on his own.

### Numerals: Sequence and One More Than

**OBJECTIVE:** To learn the sequence of numerals from 0 to 10.

**MATERIALS:** Flannelboard or magnet board, felt or magnet numerals, felt or magnet shapes (such as felt primary cutouts, or magnetic geometric shapes).

**NATURALISTIC AND INFORMAL ACTIVITIES:** Place the numerals and shapes in the math center for exploration. Note if the children make groups and place numerals next to the groups. Ask questions such as, "How many does this numeral mean?"; "Why does this numeral go next to this group?"; "Tell me about your groups."

**STRUCTURED ACTIVITY:** Put the 0 up first at the upper left-hand corner of the board. WHAT IS THIS NUMERAL CALLED? If the child cannot tell you, say: THIS IS CALLED 0. Put the 1 numeral up next to the right. WHAT IS THIS NUMERAL CALLED? If the child cannot tell you, say: THIS IS 1. SAY IT WITH ME. ONE. Continue to go across until the child does not know two numerals in a row. Then, go back to the beginning of the row. TELL ME THE NAME OF THIS NUMERAL. YES, 0. WHAT IS THE NAME OF THE NEXT ONE? YES, IT IS 1, SO I WILL PUT ONE RABBIT HERE. Put one rabbit under the 1. THE NEXT NUMERAL IS ONE MORE THAN 1. WHAT IS IT CALLED? After the child says "two" on his own or with your help, let him pick out two shapes to put on the board under the 2. Keep going across until you have done the same with each numeral he knows, plus two that he does not know.

**FOLLOW-UP:** Have the child set up the sequence. If he has trouble, ask: WHAT COMES NEXT? WHAT IS ONE MORE THAN _____? Leave the board and the numerals and shapes out during playtime. Encourage the children who know how to do this activity to work with a child who does not.

## Numerals: Recognition, Sequence, Association with Groups, One More Than

**OBJECTIVE:** To help the child to integrate the concepts of "association with groups" and "one more than" while learning the numeral names and sequence.

**MATERIALS:** Cards with numerals 0 to 10 and cards with numerals and groups 0 to 10.

**NATURALISTIC AND INFORMAL ACTIVITIES:** Place the cards in the math center for exploration. Note if the children make matches and/or sequences. Ask, "Can you tell me about what you are doing with the cards?"

**STRUCTURED ACTIVITIES:**
1. I'M GOING TO PUT DOWN SOME CARDS. EACH ONE HAS A NUMERAL ON IT. THEY GO UP TO 10. SAY THE NAMES WITH ME IF YOU KNOW THEM.
2. HERE IS ANOTHER SET OF CARDS WITH NUMERALS. Give the cards with numerals and groups to the child. MATCH THESE UP WITH THE OTHER CARDS. LET'S SAY THE NAMES AS YOU MATCH.

**FOLLOW-UP:** Let the child do this activity on his own. Encourage him to use the self-correcting materials also.

Most of the software programs described in Unit 9 include numeral recognition. See also Activity 6 in this unit for additional software recommendations. Number symbols can be incorporated in other content areas (Figure 23–7).

# IDEAS FOR CHILDREN WITH SPECIAL NEEDS

Cristina Gillanders (2007) examined the factors that enabled an English-speaking prekindergarten teacher to successfully teach Latino English Language Learners (ELLs). First and foremost were the teacher's efforts to develop a positive relationship with the students. The teacher took the time to learn some Spanish. Her use of Spanish, however meager, in the classroom gave the Latino children social status. They were then accepted by the English-speaking students as play partners. The teacher's experience as a second language learner gave her empathy for the Latino students' struggles with learning English. Providing one-to-one attention and a consistent routine helped the Latino children feel comfortable. The teacher spoke some Spanish in the classroom and included Spanish materials in her program. Some of the English-speaking children became

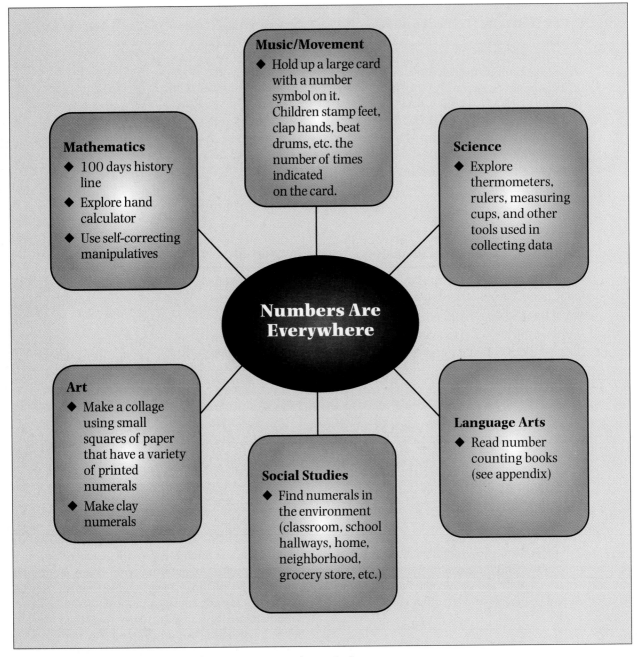

**Figure 23–7** Integrating number symbol experiences across the curriculum.

enthralled with the bilingual songs and videotapes included in the program. She also enlisted the help of the Latino children in translations. Spanish became valued in the classroom and supported cross-language cooperative play. How does this example relate to mathematics and science? In any classroom the quality of the social/emotional climate is important. In math and science, presenting some concepts using Spanish or other primary language vocabulary can make children feel more comfortable because their primary language and culture become a valued part of the classroom culture.

## EVALUATION

The teacher may question each child as she works with the self-correcting materials. He should note which numerals she can name and if she names them in sequence. He may interview her individually using the assessment questions in this unit and in Appendix A.

## SUMMARY

Numerals are the symbols used to represent amounts. The name of each numeral must be learned. The sequence, or order, must also be learned. The child needs to understand that each numeral represents a group that is one larger than the one before (and one less than the one that comes next).

Most children learn the properties and purposes of numerals through naturalistic and informal experiences. There are many excellent self-correcting materials that can be bought or made for informal activities. Any structured activities should be brief.

### KEY TERMS

cardinal meaning                    numerals                    self-correcting materials
manipulative materials

### SUGGESTED ACTIVITIES

1. Observe children to see how they use numerals. Share your experience with your class.

2. Interview preschool and kindergarten teachers to find out how they teach number symbols. Share your findings with the class.

3. Add numeral activities to your Activity File/Notebook.

4. Make a number symbol game. Try it out with 4- and 5-year-olds. Report to the class on the children's responses.

5. Go to a school supply or toy store, and evaluate the developmental appropriateness of the number symbol materials you find.

6. Use the evaluation system suggested in Activity 5, Unit 2, to review and evaluate one of the following software programs: See Unit 9 software also.

■ *James Discovers Math* (http://www.smart kidssoftware.com). Includes number recognition.

■ *Winnie the Pooh Ready for Math* (http://www.amazon.com). Includes number recognition.

■ *Arthur's Kindergarten* (http://www.smartkidssoftware.com). Activities in many areas including number.

■ *1, 2, 3 Count With Me* (http://store.sesameworkshop.org/product/show). Video starring Ernie.

■ *Learn About Numbers and Counting* (Elgin, IL: Sunburst). Includes counting and other concepts and skills.

## REVIEW

**A.** Respond to each of the following.

1. Explain what numerals are.

2. List and define the six number symbol skills.

3. Explain what is meant by self-correcting manipulative materials.

4. Describe and sketch examples of the four basic types of self-correcting number symbol manipulative materials.

5. Describe the teacher's role in the use of self-correcting number symbol materials.

**B.** What type of number symbol knowledge might children gain from each of the following numeral materials?

1. Magnet board, 0–5 numerals, and various magnetic animals

2. Matchmates (match plaques)

3. A set of 11 cards containing the number symbols 0 to 10

4. Lotto numeral game

5. Number Worm

6. Pegs-in-Numerals

7. Unifix 1–10 Stair

8. Walk on Line

9. Number-Ite

10. 1-2-3 Puzzle

11. Hand calculator

12. Personal computer

## REFERENCE

Gillanders, C. (2007). An English-speaking prekindergarten teacher of young Latino children: Implications of the teacher-child relationship on second language learning. *Early Childhood Education Journal, 35*(1), 47–54.

## FURTHER READING AND RESOURCES

American Association for the Advancement of Science (AAAS). (2007). *Atlas of science literacy: Project 2061* (Vol. 2). Washington, DC: Author.

Baratta-Lorton, M. (1972). *Workjobs*. Menlo Park, CA: Addison-Wesley.

Baratta-Lorton, M. (1976). *Mathematics their way*. Menlo Park, CA: Addison-Wesley.

*Box it or bag it mathematics (K–2)*. Portland, OR: Math Learning Center.

*Bridges in mathematics (K–2)*. Portland, OR: Math Learning Center.

Brizuela, B. M. (2004). *Mathematical development in young children: Exploring notations*. New York: Teachers College Press.

Copley, J. V. (Ed.). (1999). *Mathematics in the early years*. Washington, DC: National Association for the Education of Young Children.

Copley, J. V. (2000). *The young child and mathematics*. Washington, DC: National Association for the Education of Young Children.

Copley, J. V. (Ed.). (2004). *Showcasing mathematics for the young child* (chap. 2, Number and Operations). Reston, VA: National Council for Teachers of Mathematics.

Copley, J. V., Jones, C., & Dighe, J. (2007). *Mathematics: The creative curriculum approach*. Washington, DC: Teaching Strategies.

Epstein, A. S. (2007). *The intentional teacher*. Washington, DC: National Association for the Education of Young Children.

Gallenstein, N. L. (2003). *Creative construction of mathematics and science concepts in early childhood*. Olney, MD: Association for Childhood Education International.

Haylock, D., & Cockburn, A. (2003). *Understanding mathematics in the lower primary years: A guide for teachers of children 3–8* (2nd ed.). Thousand Oaks, CA: Chapman.

Mix, K. S., Huttenlocher, J., & Levine, S. C. (2002). *Quantitative development in infancy and early childhood.* New York: Oxford University Press.

National Council of Teachers of Mathematics. (2000). *Principles and standards for school mathematics.* Reston, VA: Author.

National Research Council. (1996). National science education standards. Washington, DC: National Academies Press.

Richardson, K. (1999). *Developing number concepts: Counting, comparing, and pattern* (Book 1). Parsippany, NJ: Seymour.

Wakefield, A. P. (1998). *Early childhood number games.* Boston: Allyn & Bacon.

# Unit 24

# Groups and Symbols

## OBJECTIVES

After reading this unit, you should be able to:

■ Describe the three higher-level tasks that children do with groups and symbols.

■ Set up an environment that provides for naturalistic and informal groups and symbols activities.

■ Plan and do structured groups and symbols activities with young children.

■ Assess and evaluate a child's ability to use math groups and symbols.

The activities in this unit build on many of the ideas and skills presented in earlier units: matching, numbers and counting, sets and classifying, comparing, ordering, and symbols. A curriculum focal point (NCTM, 2007) for kindergarten is the use of written numerals to represent quantities and solve simple quantitative problems.

The experiences in this unit will be most meaningful to the child who can already do the following activities:

■ match things one-to-one and match groups of things one-to-one

■ recognize groups of one to four without counting and count groups up to at least ten things accurately

■ divide large groups into smaller groups and compare groups of different amounts

■ place groups containing different amounts in order from least to most

■ name each of the numerals from 0 to 10

■ recognize each of the numerals from 0 to 10

■ be able to place each of the numerals in order from 0 to 10

■ understand that each numeral stands for a certain number of things

■ understand that each numeral stands for a group of things one more than the numeral before it and one less than the numeral after it

When the child has reached the objectives in the preceding list, she can then learn to do the following activities:

■ Match a symbol to a group; that is, if she is given a set of four items, she can pick out or write the numeral 4 as the one that goes with that group.

■ Match a group to a symbol; that is, if she is given the numeral 4 she can make or pick out a group of four things to go with it.

■ Reproduce symbols; that is, she can learn to write the numerals.

The movement from working with groups alone to working with groups and symbols and finally to symbols alone must be done carefully and sequentially. In *Workjobs II* (1979), Mary Baratta-Lorton describes three levels of increasing abstraction and increasing use of symbols: the concept level, connecting level, and symbolic level. These three levels can be pictured as follows:

| Concept level | △△△△ | Number sense—child has concept of amounts |
| Connecting level | △△△△4 | Child connects group amount with numeral |
| Symbolic level | 4 | Child understands numeral is the symbol for an amount |

Units 9, 10, and 11 worked at the concept level. In Unit 23, the connecting level was introduced informally. The major focus of this unit is the connecting level. In Unit 25, the symbolic level will be introduced.

## ASSESSMENT

If the children can do the assessment tasks in Units 8 through 14, 17, and 23, then they have the basic skills and knowledge necessary to connect groups and symbols. In fact, they may be observed doing some symbol and grouping activities on their own if materials are made available for exploration in the math center. The following are some individual interview tasks.

## SAMPLE ASSESSMENT TASK

**6M**                                         **Preoperational/Concrete Ages 5–7**

**Groups And Symbols, Match Symbols to Groups: Unit 24**

**METHOD:**  Interview.

**SKILL:**  Child will be able to match symbols to groups using numerals from 0 to 10 and groups of amounts 0 to 10.

**MATERIALS:**  5" × 8" cards with numerals 0 to 10, ten objects (e.g., chips, cube blocks, buttons).

**PROCEDURE:**  Lay out the cards in front of the child in numerical order. One at a time, show the child groups of each amount in this order: 2, 5, 3, 1, 4. PICK OUT THE NUMERAL THAT TELLS HOW MANY THINGS ARE IN THIS GROUP. If the child does these correctly, go on to 7, 9, 6, 10, 8, 0 using the same procedure.

*(continued)*

**EVALUATION:** Note which groups and symbols the child can match. The responses will indicate where instruction can begin.

**INSTRUCTIONAL RESOURCE:** Charlesworth, R., and Lind, K. K. (2010). *Math and science for young children* (6th ed.). Clifton Park, NY: Cengage Learning.

## SAMPLE ASSESSMENT TASK

**6L**                                                            **Preoperational/Concrete Ages 5–7**

**Groups and Symbols, Match Groups to Symbols: Unit 24**

**METHOD:**    Interview.

**SKILL:**    Child will be able to match groups to symbols using groups of amounts 0 to 10 and numerals from 0 to 10.

**MATERIALS:**    5" × 8" cards with numerals 0 to 10, 60 objects (e.g., chips, cube blocks, coins, buttons).

**PROCEDURE:**    Lay out the numeral cards in front of the child in a random arrangement. Place the container of objects within easy reach. MAKE A GROUP FOR EACH NUMERAL. Let the child decide how to organize the materials.

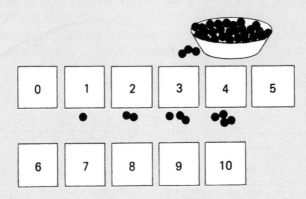

**EVALUATION:**    Note for which numerals the child is able to make groups. Note how the child goes about the task. For example, does he sequence the numerals from 0 to 10? Does he place the objects in an organized pattern by each numeral? Can he recognize some amounts without counting? When he counts does he do it carefully? His responses will indicate where instruction should begin.

**INSTRUCTIONAL RESOURCE:** Charlesworth, R., and Lind, K. K. (2010). *Math and science for young children* (6th ed.). Clifton Park, NY: Cengage Learning.

## SAMPLE ASSESSMENT TASK

**6K**                                               **Preoperational/Concrete Ages 5–7**

**Groups and Symbols, Write/Reproduce Numerals: Unit 24**

**METHOD:** Interview.

**SKILL:** Child can reproduce (write) numerals from 0 to 10.

**MATERIALS:** Pencil, pen, black marker, black crayon, white paper, numeral cards from 0 to 10.

**PROCEDURE:** HERE IS A PIECE OF PAPER. PICK OUT ONE OF THESE (point to writing tools) THAT YOU WOULD LIKE TO USE. NOW, WRITE AS MANY NUMBERS AS YOU CAN. If the child is unable to write from memory, show him the numeral cards. COPY ANY OF THESE THAT YOU CAN.

**EVALUATION:** Note how many numerals the child can write and if they are in sequence. If the child is not able to write the numerals with ease, then at this time writing is probably not an appropriate mode of response to problems; instead, have him do activities in which movable numerals or markers can be placed on the correct answers.

**INSTRUCTIONAL RESOURCE:** Charlesworth, R., and Lind, K. K. (2010). *Math and science for young children* (6th ed.). Clifton Park, NY: Cengage Learning.

## NATURALISTIC ACTIVITIES

As the child learns that groups and symbols go together, this will be reflected in her daily play activities.

- Mary and Dean have set up a grocery store. Dean has made price tags, and Mary has made play money from construction paper. They have written numerals on each price tag and piece of money. Sam comes up and picks out a box of breakfast cereal and a carton of milk. Dean takes the tags, "That will be four dollars." Sam counts out four play dollar bills. Dean takes a piece of paper from a note pad and writes a "receipt." "Here, Sam."

- Brent has drawn a picture of a birthday cake. There are six candles on the cake and a big numeral 6. "This is for my next birthday. I will be six."

- The flannelboard and a group of primary cutouts have been left out in a quiet corner. George sits deep in thought as he places the numerals in order and counts out a group of cutouts to go with each numeral.

Each child uses what she has already learned in ways that she has seen adults use these skills and concepts.

## INFORMAL ACTIVITIES

The child can work with groups and numerals best through informal experiences. Each child needs a different amount of practice. By making available many materials that the child can work with on his own, the teacher can help each child have the amount of practice he needs. Each child can choose to use the group of materials that he finds the most interesting.

*Workjobs* (Baratta-Lorton, 1972) and *Workjobs II* (Baratta-Lorton, 1979) are excellent resources for groups and symbols activities and materials. The basic activities for matching symbols to groups and groups to symbols require the following kinds of materials.

Games provide an enjoyable way for children to apply their knowledge of the relationships between groups and number symbols.

1. Materials where the numerals are "fixed" and counters are available for making the groups. These are called *counting trays* and may be made or purchased. They may be set up with the numerals all in one row or in two or more rows.

2. Materials where there are movable containers on which the numerals are written and counters of some kind. There might be pennies and banks, cups and buttons, cans and sticks, or similar items.

3. Individual numeral cards with a space for the child to make a group to match.

4. Groups of real things or pictures of things that must be matched to numerals written on cards.

Each child can be shown each new set of materials. He can then have a turn to work with them. If the teacher finds that a child is having a hard time, she can give him some help and make sure he takes part in some structured activities.

Informal experiences in which the child writes numerals come up when the child asks how to write his age, phone number, or address. Some children who are interested in writing may copy numerals that they see in the environment—on the clock and calendar or on the numeral cards used in matching and group-making activities. These children should be encouraged and helped if needed. The teacher can make or buy a group of sandpaper numerals. The child can trace these with his finger to get the feel of the shape and the movement needed to make the numeral. Formal writing lessons should not take place until the child's fine muscle coordination is well developed. For some children this might not be until they are 7 or 8 years of age.

## STRUCTURED ACTIVITIES

Structured activities with symbols and groups for the young child are done in the form of games. One type of game has the child match groups and numerals using a theme such as "Letters to the Post Office" or "Fish in the Fishbowl." A second is the basic board game. A third type of game is the lotto or bingo type. In each case, the teacher structures the game. However, once the children know the rules, two or more can play on their own. One example of each game is described. With a little imagination, the teacher can think of variations. The last three activities are for the child who can write numerals.

# ACTIVITIES

## Groups and Symbols: Fish in the Fishbowl

**OBJECTIVE:** To match groups and symbols for the numerals 0 through 10.

**MATERIALS:** Sketch 11 fishbowls about 7" × 10" on separate pieces of cardboard or poster board. On each bowl write one of the numerals from 0 to 10. Cut out 11 fish, one for each bowl. On each fish, put dots—from 0 on the first to 10 on the last.

**NATURALISTIC AND INFORMAL ACTIVITIES:** Place the fish and fishbowls in the math center for the children to explore. Note if they make any matches as they play with them. Do they notice the dots and numerals and attempt to make matches? If they make matches, ask them to tell you about them.

**STRUCTURED ACTIVITY:** Play with two or more children. Line up the fishbowls (on a chalk tray is a good place). One at a time, have each child choose a fish, sight unseen. Have her match her fish to its own bowl.

**FOLLOW-UP:** 1. Make fish with other kinds of sets such as stripes or stars.
2. Line up the fish, and have the children match the fishbowls to the right fish.

## Groups and Symbols: Basic Board Games

**OBJECTIVE:** To match groups and symbols.

**MATERIALS:** The basic materials can be purchased or can be made by the teacher. Basic materials would include:

- A piece of poster board (18" × 36") for the game board
- Clear Contac or laminating material
- Marking pens
- Spinner cards, plain 3" × 5" file cards, or a die
- Place markers (chips, buttons, or other counters)

Materials for three basic games are shown in Figure 24–1. The game boards can be set up with a theme for interest such as the race car game. Themes might be "Going to School," "The Road to Happy Land," or whatever the teacher's or children's imaginations can think of.

**NATURALISTIC AND INFORMAL ACTIVITIES:** Put the games out, one at a time, during center time. Note if any of the children are familiar with these types of games. Take note of what they do. Do they know about turn taking? Do they know how to use the spinners and count the jumps? Do they make up rules?

**STRUCTURED ACTIVITY:** The basic activity is the same for each game. Each child picks a marker and puts it on START. Then each in turn spins the spinner (or chooses a card or rolls the die) and moves to the square that matches.

**FOLLOW-UP:** 1. The children can learn to play the games on their own.
2. Make new games with new themes. Make games with more moves and using more numerals and larger groups to match.
3. Let the children make up their own rules.

*(continued)*

Figure 24–1 Materials for three basic board games.

## Groups and Symbols: Lotto and Bingo Games

**OBJECTIVE:** To match groups and symbols.

**MATERIALS:** For both games, there should be six basic game cards, each with six or more squares (the more squares, the longer and harder the game). For lotto, there is one card to match each square. For bingo, there must also be markers to put on the squares. For bingo, squares on the basic game cards are repeated; for lotto, they are not.

**NATURALISTIC AND INFORMAL ACTIVITIES:** Put the games out, one at a time, during center time. Note if any of the children are familiar with these types of games. Take note of what they do. Do they know about turn taking? Do they know how to use the materials and make matches? Do they recognize the numerals on the bingo cards? Do they make up rules?

**STRUCTURED ACTIVITIES:**  1.  *Lotto game.* Each child receives a basic game card. The matching cards are shuffled and held up one at a time. The child must call out if the card has her mark on it (dot, circle, triangle) and then match the numeral to the right group. The game can be played until one person fills her card or until everyone does.

2.  *Bingo game.* Each child receives a basic game card together with nine chips. The matching set cards are shuffled and are then held up, one at a time. The child puts a chip on the numeral that goes with the group on the card. When someone gets a row full in any direction, the game starts again.

**FOLLOW-UP:**  More games can be made using different picture groups and adding more squares to the basic game cards. Bingo cards must always have the same (odd) number of squares in both directions (i.e., grids that are three-by-three, five-by-five, or seven-by-seven).

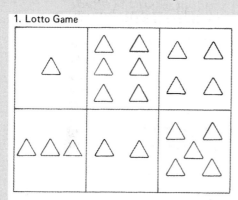

1. Lotto Game

Make six cards for six players.

Matching cards:
Make a set for each big card.

2. Bingo Game

| 1 | 2 | 3 |
|---|---|---|
| 8 | 0 | 4 |
| 7 | 6 | 5 |

| 2 | 5 | 3 |
|---|---|---|
| 7 | 0 | 9 |
| 4 | 6 | 1 |

| 6 | 1 | 5 |
|---|---|---|
| 9 | 0 | 4 |
| 7 | 10 | 8 |

| 10 | 2 | 6 |
|---|---|---|
| 3 | 0 | 4 |
| 8 | 1 | 7 |

| 10 | 6 | 1 |
|---|---|---|
| 9 | 0 | 7 |
| 8 | 3 | 2 |

| 7 | 3 | 9 |
|---|---|---|
| 2 | 0 | 8 |
| 1 | 6 | 5 |

| 4 | 5 | 9 |
|---|---|---|
| 8 | 0 | 1 |
| 10 | 3 | 2 |

| 10 | 3 | 8 |
|---|---|---|
| 1 | 0 | 2 |
| 6 | 4 | 5 |

Markers: ● ● ● (54 chips)

Matching cards:
11 cards with sets 0 to 10:

and so on.

## Groups and Symbols: My Own Number Book

**OBJECTIVE:**  To match groups and symbols.

**MATERIALS:**  Booklets made with construction paper covers and several pages made from newsprint or other plain paper, hole puncher and yarn or brads to hold book together, crayons, glue, scissors, and more paper or stickers.

*(continued)*

**NATURALISTIC AND INFORMAL ACTIVITIES:** The children should have had opportunities to make their own books in the writing center. They should also have had number books read to them and have explored them independently.

**STRUCTURED ACTIVITY:** The child writes (or asks the teacher to write) a numeral on each page of the book. The child then puts a group on each page. Groups can be made using

1. Stickers
2. Cutouts made by the child
3. Drawings done by the child

**FOLLOW-UP:** Have the children show their books to each other and then take the books home. Also read to the children some of the number books listed in Appendix B.

## Groups and Symbols: Writing Numerals to Match Groups

**OBJECTIVE:** To write the numeral that goes with a group.

**MATERIALS:** Objects and pictures of objects, chalk and chalkboard, crayons, pencils, and paper.

**NATURALISTIC AND INFORMAL ACTIVITIES:** Children should have explored many numerals and groups and numeral materials. Numeral models should be available in the writing center for the children to observe and copy.

**STRUCTURED ACTIVITY:** Show the child some objects or pictures of objects. WRITE THE NUMERAL THAT TELLS HOW MANY _____ THERE ARE. The child then writes the numeral on the chalkboard or on a piece of paper.

**FOLLOW-UP:** Get some clear acetate. Make some set pictures that can be placed in acetate folders for the child to use on her own. Acetate folders are made by taking a piece of cardboard and taping a piece of acetate of the same size on with some plastic tape. The child can write on the acetate with a nonpermanent marker and then erase her mark with a tissue or a soft cloth.

Counting books are another resource for connecting groups and symbols. In most counting books, the numerals are included with each group to be counted. Caution must be taken in selecting counting books. Ballenger, Benham, and Hosticka (1984) suggest the following criteria for selecting counting books.

1. Be sure the numerals always refer to how many and not to ordinal position or sequence.
2. The numeral names should also always refer to how many.
3. The narrative on the page should clearly identify the group of objects that the numeral is associated with.
4. The illustrations of objects to be counted and connected to the numeral on each page should be clear and distinct.
5. When ordinals are being used, the starting position (e.g., first) should be clearly identified.
6. When identifying ordinal positions, the correct terms should be used (e.g., first, second, third).
7. When numerals are used to indicate ordinal position, they should be written as 1st, 2nd, 3rd, and so on.
8. The numerals should be uniform in size (not small numerals for small groups and larger numerals for larger groups).

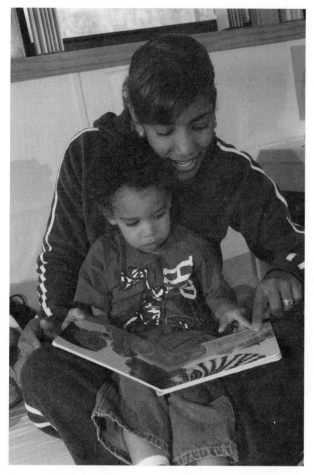

Counting books provide motivation for connecting groups and numerals.

9. The book should emphasize the concept of one-to-one correspondence.

10. When amounts above 10 and their associated numerals are illustrated, the amounts should be depicted as a group of 10 plus the additional items.

Computers and calculators can also be used for helping children acquire the groups and symbols connection. Most of the software listed in Units 9 and 23 as supportive of counting and symbol recognition also connects groups and symbols. These programs should also be evaluated with the same criteria suggested for books. Students could play games with their calculators such as closing their eyes, pressing a key, identifying the numeral, and then selecting or constructing a group that goes with the numeral. There are also many self-correcting computer/calculator-type toys available that children enjoy using.

Groups and symbol activities may be included in other content areas. See Figure 24–2 for examples.

## IDEAS FOR CHILDREN WITH SPECIAL NEEDS

Many materials can be purchased or made that provide experiences for children that support making the connection between symbols and the groups they represent. Verbal counting comes before the written symbol is introduced. Some children will take longer to learn the written number sequence before connecting with groups. The following are examples of materials and activities that can be used to support number recognition and sequence:

1. Make or buy cards with numbers (be sure there are several cards for each number). Children divide cards and then turn them over one at a time, identifying matches.

2. In kindergarten, learning one's street address and phone number provides a meaningful context for number identification. Each child can be provided with two sentence strips: one with address and one with phone number.

3. Numbers above nine may be difficult for children with poor concepts of spatial awareness. Color cueing can be used to indicate concepts of left and right. Teens can be especially difficult: whereas the "2" provides a clue in the twenties, the numeral "1" does not say "teen."

4. Number sequencing can be done individually, in small groups, or by the whole class. During a class meeting, several children can be given large-size number cards and asked to line up in sequence. Individual or pairs of children can work at a table with numbers on 3" × 5" cards.

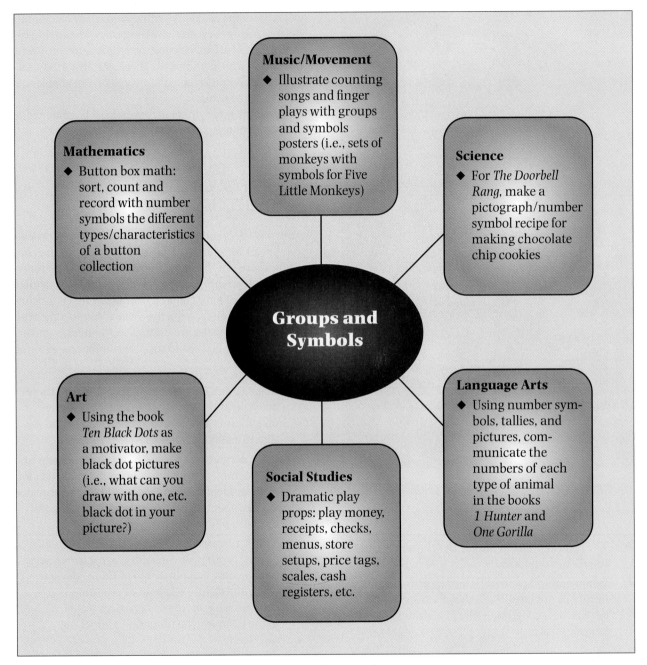

**Music/Movement**

◆ Illustrate counting songs and finger plays with groups and symbols posters (i.e., sets of monkeys with symbols for Five Little Monkeys)

**Mathematics**

◆ Button box math: sort, count and record with number symbols the different types/characteristics of a button collection

**Science**

◆ For *The Doorbell Rang,* make a pictograph/number symbol recipe for making chocolate chip cookies

**Groups and Symbols**

**Art**

◆ Using the book *Ten Black Dots* as a motivator, make black dot pictures (i.e., what can you draw with one, etc. black dot in your picture?)

**Social Studies**

◆ Dramatic play props: play money, receipts, checks, menus, store setups, price tags, scales, cash registers, etc.

**Language Arts**

◆ Using number symbols, tallies, and pictures, communicate the numbers of each type of animal in the books *1 Hunter* and *One Gorilla*

**Figure 24–2** Integrating groups and symbols experiences across the curriculum.

Technology provides a means for making symbol/group connections.

Felt boards can also be used. Calendars can be used for matching.

5. Two calendars of the same month can be used. One can be kept intact and mounted while the other is cut up for matching. Children can name each numeral as matched.

Once children can identify and name numerals in sequence, they can begin to associate the written number symbols with number concepts. A variety of activities have been described in this unit, and some additional ideas follow.

1. Make a hopscotch pattern on the ground. Write a number in each square. The child can jump or hop from square to square in order, stopping to clap the number in each square.

2. Child can trace around his hand and then number each finger.

3. Provide the child with random written number symbols and some counting objects. Have him count out the amount that goes with each symbol.

4. Provide the child with a sheet of paper with numbers written along the left side. Next to each number the child can:
   a. draw the correct number of objects;
   b. place the correct number of stickers; or
   c. place the correct number of objects.

## EVALUATION

With young children, most evaluation can be done by observing their use of the materials for informal activities. The adult can also notice how the children do when they play the structured games.

For children about to enter first grade, an individual interview should be done using the assessment interviews in this unit and in Appendix A.

## SUMMARY

When the child works with groups and symbols, he puts together the skills and ideas learned earlier. He must match, count, classify, compare, order, and associate written numerals with groups.

He learns to match groups to symbols and symbols to groups. He also learns to write each number symbol.

The child uses mostly materials that can be used informally on his own. He can also learn from more structured game kinds of activities, number books, computer games, and calculator activities.

## SUGGESTED ACTIVITIES

1. Observe prekindergarten, kindergarten, and first-grade students during work and play. Note instances where they match groups and symbols.

2. Add groups and symbols assessment tasks to your Assessment File/Notebook and activities to your Activity File/Notebook.

3. Make groups and symbols instructional materials. Use them with prekindergarten, kindergarten, and first-grade students. Share the results with the class.

4. Look through some early childhood materials catalogs for groups and symbols materials. If you had $400 to spend, what would you purchase?

5. Review one or more software programs listed on the Online Companion for Units 9 and 23. Use the procedure suggested in Activity 5, Unit 2, and the criteria suggested in this unit for children's counting books.

6. Go to a bookstore, the children's literature library, and/or your local public library. Identify three or more counting books and evaluate them using the criteria suggested by Ballenger and colleagues (1984).

## REVIEW

A. List and describe the skills a child should have before doing the activities suggested in this unit or in higher-level units.

B. Decide which of the following incidents are examples of (a) matching a symbol to a group, (b) reproducing symbols, or (c) matching a group to a symbol.
   1. Mario is writing down his phone number.
   2. Kate selects three Unifix Cubes to go with the numeral 3.
   3. Fong selects the magnetic numeral 6 to go with the six squares on the magnet board.

C. Describe three kinds of materials that are designed to be used for matching symbols to groups and groups to symbols.

D. If 4-year-old John tells you he wants to know how to write his phone number, what should you do?

E. Describe two structured groups and symbols activities.

F. List some materials that young children could use for reproducing symbols.

G. Describe two informal groups and symbols activities young children might be engaged in.

H. What criteria should be used when selecting books and software to use in helping children acquire the groups and symbols connection?

## REFERENCES

Ballenger, M., Benham, N. B., & Hosticka, A. (1984). Children's counting books. *Childhood Education*, *61*(1), 30–35.

Baratta-Lorton, M. (1972). *Workjobs.* Menlo Park, CA: Addison-Wesley.

Baratta-Lorton, M. (1979). *Workjobs II.* Menlo Park, CA: Addison-Wesley.

National Council of Teachers of Mathematics. (2007). *Curriculum focal points.* Reston, VA: Author.

## FURTHER READING AND RESOURCES

American Association for the Advancement of Science (AAAS). (2007). *Atlas of science literacy: Project 2061* (Vol. 2). Washington, DC: Author.

Baratta-Lorton, M. (1976). *Mathematics their way.* Menlo Park, CA: Addison-Wesley.

*Box it or bag it mathematics (K–2).* Portland, OR: The Math Learning Center.

*Bridges in mathematics (K–2).* Portland, OR: Math Learning Center.

Brizuela, B. M. (2004). *Mathematical development in young children: Exploring notations.* New York: Teachers College Press.

Copley, J. V. (Ed.). (1999). *Mathematics in the early years.* Washington, DC: National Association for the Education of Young Children.

Copley, J. V. (2000). *The young child and mathematics.* Washington, DC: National Association for the Education of Young Children.

Copley, J. V. (Ed.). (2004). *Showcasing mathematics for the young child* (chap. 2, Number and Operations). Reston, VA: National Council for Teachers of Mathematics.

Copley, J. V., Jones, C., & Dighe, J. (2007). *Mathematics: The creative curriculum approach.* Washington, DC: Teaching Strategies.

Cutler, K. M., Gilkerson, D., Parrott, S., & Bowne, M. T. (2003). Developing games based on children's literature. *Young Children, 58*(1), 22–27.

Gallenstein, N. L. (2003). *Creative construction of mathematics and science concepts in early childhood.*

Olney, MD: Association for Childhood Education International.

Haylock, D., & Cockburn, A. (2003). *Understanding mathematics in the lower primary years: A guide for teachers of children 3–8* (2nd ed.). Thousand Oaks, CA: Chapman.

Mix, K. S., Huttenlocher, J., & Levine, S. C. (2002). *Quantitative development in infancy and early childhood.* New York: Oxford University Press.

National Council of Teachers of Mathematics. (2000). *Principles and standards for school mathematics.* Reston, VA: Author.

National Research Council. (1996). *National science education standards.* Washington, DC: National Academies Press.

Richardson, K. (1984). *Developing number concepts using Unifix Cubes.* Menlo Park, CA: Addison-Wesley.

Richardson, K. (1999). *Developing number concepts: Counting, comparing, and pattern* (Book 1). Parsippany, NJ: Seymour.

Richardson, K. (1999). *Developing number concepts: Planning guide.* Parsippany, NJ: Seymour.

Wakefield, A. P. (1998). *Early childhood number games.* Boston: Allyn & Bacon.

Zaslavsky, C. (1996). *The multicultural math classroom.* Portsmouth, NH: Heinemann.

*See also* the games and materials resources suggested in Unit 23 and the books suggested in Appendix B.

# Unit 25

# Higher-Level Activities and Concepts

## OBJECTIVES

After reading this unit, you should be able to:

■ List the eight areas in which higher-level concept activities are described in the unit.

■ Describe the three higher levels of classification.

■ Plan higher-level activities for children who are near the stage of concrete operations.

The experiences in this unit include further applications of skills that children learned through the activities in the previous units. These experiences support more complex application of the processes of problem solving, reasoning, communication connections, and representation (NCTM, 2000; see also Unit 15). They are appropriate for preschool/kindergarten students who are developing at a fast rate and can do the higher-level assessment tasks with ease or for the older students who still need concrete experiences. The ten areas presented are **algebra**, **classification**, **shape**, **spatial relations**, **concrete whole number operations**, **graphs**, **symbolic level** activities, **quantities above ten**, **estimation**, and **design technology**.

## ASSESSMENT

Assessment determines where the children are in their zones of proximal development (ZPD; see Unit 1)—that is, where they can work independently and where they

can complete tasks with support from scaffolding by an adult or a more advanced peer.

The teacher looks at the child's level in each area. Then he makes a decision as to when to introduce these activities. When introduced to one child, any one activity could capture the interest of another child who might be at a lower developmental level. Therefore, it is not necessary to wait for all the children to be at the highest level to begin. Children at lower levels can participate in these activities as observers and as contributors. The higher-level child can serve as a model for the lower-level child. The lower-level child might be able to do part of the task following the leadership of the higher-level child. For example, if a floor plan of the classroom is being made, the more advanced child might design it while everyone draws a picture of a piece of furniture to put on the floor plan. The more advanced child might get help from the less advanced child when she makes a graph. The less advanced child can count and measure; the more advanced child records the results. Children can work in pairs to solve concrete addition, subtraction, multiplication, and division problems. They can move into higher levels of symbol use and work with numerals and quantities greater than ten. They can also work together exploring calculators and computer software.

By the end of kindergarten, children should have an understanding of number (Marshall, 2006). That is, number sense should be well established. Children should understand the idea of "twoness," "threeness," and so forth. They need to understand that the concept of number is independent of size, shape, and color. They need to find groups everywhere that are two, three, four, five, et cetera. They must understand that arrangement in space (conservation of number) is independent of amount. They need to examine and construct groups using different objects. The book *What comes in 2's, 3's, and 4's?* by Suzanne Aker demonstrates the concept of number in pictures. With number understood, students are ready to move on to more abstract ideas that are based on an understanding of number. *One Hundred Hungry Ants* by Pinczes demonstrates how 100 is still 100 when broken down into smaller groups, and *Miss Bindergarten Celebrates the 100th Day* by Slate shows how 100 is still 100 no matter how it is composed.

## ALGEBRAIC THINKING

Algebra is viewed by many people as a blockade to their progress in understanding mathematics. It is seen as the mindless abstract manipulation of symbols. The NCTM has promoted a new vision of algebra as "a way of thinking, a method of seeing and expressing relationships" (Moses, 1997). It is seen as a way of thinking that goes beyond numerical reasoning and that can begin in the elementary grades.

For preprimary-level children, algebraic thinking is reflected in their discovery of patterns as they sort and group objects, combine groups and count totals, build with blocks, and use objects as symbolic representations. As young children explore these materials, they construct generalizations that reflect an increasing understanding of patterns and relationships (Curcio & Schwartz, 1997).

Children figure out how to balance their block buildings. They discover that 10 groups of 10 is 100. Exploring with a pan balance, they find that if they put certain objects on each side, the pans will balance. They find that groups will break down into smaller sets and still be the same number. These discoveries are the outcome of the beginnings of algebraic thinking. As children move into higher-level activities, it is important to continue to provide them with opportunities for exploration and discovery. Algebraic reasoning is also supported by science inquiry activities.

## CLASSIFICATION

The higher levels of classification are called **multiple classification**, **class inclusion**, and **hierarchical classification**. Multiple classification requires the child to classify things in more than one way and to solve matrix problems. Figures 25–1 and 25–2 illustrate these two types of multiple classification. In Figure 25–1, the child is shown three shapes, each in three sizes and in three colors. He is asked to put the ones together that belong together. He is then asked to find another way to organize the shapes.

The preoperational child will not be able to do this. He centers on his first sort. Some games are suggested that will help the child move to concrete operations.

Matrix problems are illustrated in Figure 25–2. A simple two-by-two matrix is shown in Figure 25–2A. In this case, size and number must both be considered in order to complete the matrix. The problem can be made more difficult by making the matrix larger (there are always the same number of squares in each row, both across and up and down). Figure 25–2B shows a four-by-four matrix. The easiest problem is to fill in part of a matrix. The hardest problem is to fill in a whole blank matrix, as illustrated in Figure 25–2C.

The preoperational child cannot see that one class may be included within another (*class inclusion*). For example, the child is shown ten flowers: two roses and eight daisies. The child can divide the flowers into two groups: roses and daisies. He knows that they are all flowers. When asked if there are more flowers or more daisies, he will answer "More daisies." He is fooled by what he sees and centers on the greater number of daisies. He is not able to hold in his mind that daisies are also flowers. This problem is shown in Figure 25–3.

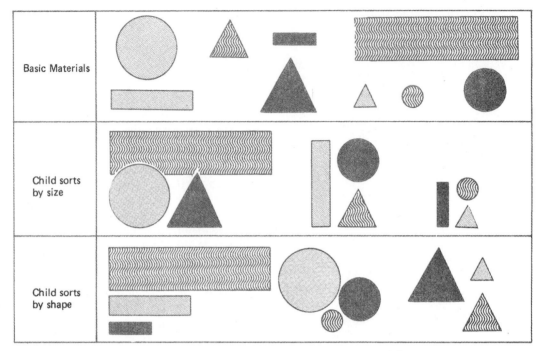

**Figure 25–1** *Multiple classification* involves sorting one way and then sorting again using different criteria.

**Figure 25–2** The matrix problem is another type of multiple classification.

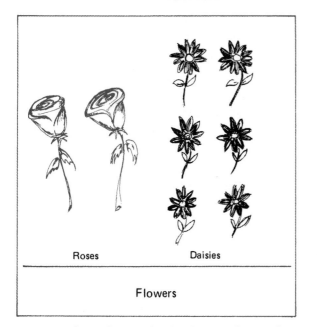

**Figure 25–3** *Class inclusion* is the idea that one class can be included in another.

Hierarchical classification involves classes within classes. For example, black kittens ⊂ kittens ⊂ house cats ⊂ cats ⊂ mammals (here "⊂" denotes "subgroup"

or "are contained within"). As can be seen in Figure 25–4, this forms a *hierarchy*, or a series of ever-larger classes. Basic-level concepts are usually learned first. This level includes categories such as dogs, monkeys, cats, cows, and elephants (see Figure 25–4). Superordinate-level concepts such as mammals, furniture, vehicles, and so on are learned next. Finally, children learn subordinate categories such as domestic cats and wildcats or types of chairs such as dining room, living room, rocking, kitchen, folding, and so on.

Another interesting aspect of young children's concept learning is their view of which characteristics the members of a class have in common. Although preoperational-level children tend to be perceptually bound when they attempt to solve many types of conceptual problems, they are able to classify based on category membership when shown things that are perceptually similar. For example, 4-year-olds were shown pictures of a blackbird; a bat, which looked much like the blackbird; and a flamingo. They were told that the flamingo gave its baby mashed-up food and the bat gave its baby milk. When asked what the blackbird fed its baby, they responded that it gave its baby mashed-up food. In this case the children looked beyond the most obvious physical attributes.

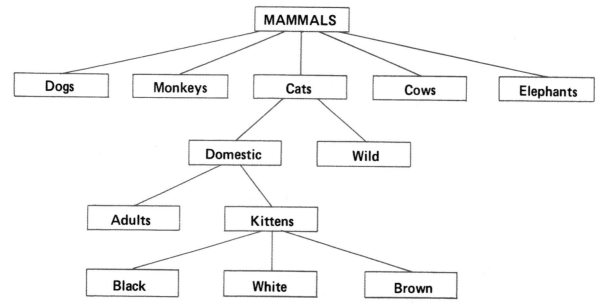

**Figure 25–4** In a *hierarchical classification*, all things in each lower class are included in the next higher class.

Another type of characteristic that is interesting to ask young children about is their view of what is inside members of a class. When young children are asked if members of a class all have the same "stuff" inside, preschoolers tend to say that yes, they have; that is, all dogs, people, chairs, and dolls are the same inside. Children are aware of more than just observable similarities. By second grade, they can discriminate between natural and synthetic items; that is, they realize that living things such as dogs, people, or apples are, for the most part, the same inside as other dogs, people, or apples, although the insides of different types of chairs, dolls, or other manufactured items are not necessarily the same. For younger children, category membership overwhelms other factors.

The following activities will help the transitional child (usually ages 5–7) to enter concrete operations.

## ACTIVITIES

### Higher-Level Classification: Multiple Classification, Reclassify

**OBJECTIVE:** To help the transitional child learn that groups of objects or pictures can sometimes be sorted in more than one way.

**MATERIALS:** Any group of objects or pictures of objects that can be classified in more than one way—for example, pictures or cardboard cutouts of dogs of different colors (brown and white), sizes (large and small), and hair lengths (long and short).

**ACTIVITY:** Place the dogs in front of the child. WHICH DOGS BELONG TOGETHER? or ARE THEY THE SAME? Note whether she groups by size, color, or hair length. NOW, WHAT IS ANOTHER WAY TO PUT THEM IN GROUPS? CAN THEY BE PUT LIKE (name another way)? Put them in one pile again if the child is puzzled. OKAY, NOW TRY TO SORT THE _____ FROM THE _____. Repeat using different criteria each time.

**FOLLOW-UP:** Make other groups of materials. Set them up in boxes where the child can get them out and use them during free playtime. Make some felt pieces to use on the flannelboard.

### Higher-Level Classification: Multiple Classification: Matrices

**OBJECTIVE:** To help the transitional child see that things may be related on more than one criterion.

**MATERIALS:** Purchase or make a matrix game. Start with a two-by-two matrix and gradually increase the size (three-by-three, four-by-four, etc.). Use any of the criteria from Unit 10 such as color, size, shape, material, pattern, texture, function, association, class name, common feature, or number. Make a game board from poster board or wood. Draw or paint permanent lines. Use a flannelboard, and make the lines for the matrix with lengths of yarn. An example of a three-by-three board is shown in Figure 25–5. Start with three-dimensional materials, then cutouts, then cards.

**ACTIVITIES:** Start with the matrix filled except for one space, and ask the child to choose from two items the one that goes in the empty space. WHICH ONE OF THESE GOES HERE? After the item is placed, say, WHY DOES IT BELONG THERE? Once the child understands the task, more spaces can be left empty until it is left for the child to fill in the whole matrix.

**FOLLOW-UP:** Add more games that use different categories and larger matrices.

Items to be placed:
1. Color and size: red, green, and yellow apples.

2. Position and class: dog, cat, bird; right side up, upside down, and sideways.

3. Number and shape: triangles, squares, circles; rows of one, two, and three.

**Figure 25–5** A matrix game.

## Higher-Level Classification: Class Inclusion

**OBJECTIVE:** To help the transitional child see that a smaller set may be included within a larger set.

**MATERIALS:** Seven animals. Two kinds should be included (such as horses and cows, pigs and chickens, dogs and cats). There should be four of one animal and three of the other. These can be cutouts or toy animals.

**ACTIVITY:** Place the animals within an enclosure (a yarn circle or a fence made of blocks). WHO IS INSIDE THE FENCE? Children will answer "horses," "cows," "animals." SHOW ME WHICH ONES ARE HORSES (COWS, ANIMALS). ARE THERE MORE HORSES OR MORE ANIMALS? HOW DO YOU KNOW? LET'S CHECK (use one-to-one correspondence).

**FOLLOW-UP:** Play the same game. Use other categories such as plants, types of material, size, and so on. Increase the size of the sets.

## Higher-Level Classification: Hierarchical

**OBJECTIVE:** To help the transitional child see that each thing may be part of a larger category (or set of things).

**MATERIALS:** Make some sets of sorting cards. Glue pictures from catalogs and/or workbooks onto file cards or poster board. For example:

■ One black cat, several house cats, cats of other colors, one tiger, one lion, one panther, one bobcat, one dog, one horse, one cow, one squirrel, one bear

(*continued*)

■ One duck, three swans, five other birds, five other animals

■ One teaspoon, two soupspoons, a serving spoon, two baby spoons, three forks, two knives

**ACTIVITIES:** Place the cards where they can all be seen. Give the following instructions.

1. FIND ALL THE ANIMALS. FIND ALL THE CATS. FIND ALL THE HOUSE CATS. FIND ALL THE BLACK CATS. Mix up the cards, and lay them out again. PUT THEM IN GROUPS THE WAY YOU THINK THEY SHOULD BE. When the child is done, WHY DID YOU PUT THEM THAT WAY? Mix them up, and lay them out. IF ALL THE ANIMALS WERE HUNGRY, WOULD THE BLACK CAT BE HUNGRY? IF THE BLACK CAT IS HUNGRY, ARE ALL THE ANIMALS HUNGRY?

2. FIND ALL THE ANIMALS. FIND ALL THE BIRDS. FIND THE WATERBIRDS. FIND THE DUCK. Mix up the cards, and lay them out again. PUT THEM IN GROUPS THE WAY YOU THINK THEY SHOULD BE. When the child is done, WHY DO THEY BELONG THAT WAY? Mix them up, and lay them out again. IF ALL THE BIRDS WERE COLD, WOULD THE DUCK BE COLD? IF THE DUCK WERE COLD, WOULD ALL THE WATERBIRDS BE COLD? IF ALL THE ANIMALS WERE COLD, WOULD THE WATERBIRDS BE COLD?

3. FIND ALL THE THINGS THAT WE EAT WITH. FIND ALL THE KNIVES. FIND ALL THE FORKS. FIND ALL THE SPOONS. Mix them up, and lay them out again. PUT THEM IN GROUPS THE WAY YOU THINK THEY BELONG. When the child is done, WHY DO THEY BELONG THAT WAY? Mix them up, and lay them out again. IF ALL THE SPOONS ARE DIRTY, WOULD THE TEASPOON BE DIRTY? IF ALL THE THINGS WE EAT WITH WERE DIRTY, WOULD THE BIG SPOON BE DIRTY? IF THE TEASPOON IS DIRTY, ARE ALL THE OTHER THINGS WE EAT WITH DIRTY TOO?

**FOLLOW-UP:** Make up other hierarchies. Leave the card sets out for the children to sort during play. Ask them some of the same kinds of questions informally.

## Higher-Level Classification: Multiple Classification

**OBJECTIVE:** To help the transitional child learn to group things in a variety of ways using logical reasoning.

**MATERIALS:** *What to Wear?* (1998), an emergent reader book by Sharon Young. The book depicts a boy who has two shirts, two pairs of shorts, and two caps, with each item a different color. The problem presented to the reader is figuring out how many different outfits the boy can put together.

**ACTIVITIES:** The *Teacher Guide for Harry's Math Books, Set B* (Young, 1998) suggests a number of activities that can be done to support the concepts in *What to Wear?* Here are some examples.

1. Have the children discuss ways clothes can be sorted, such as school clothes/play clothes/dress-up clothes or clean clothes/dirty clothes.

2. Use cutouts to see that although there are only two of each type of clothing in the book, more than two outfits can be constructed.

3. Make connections with other areas such as meal combinations with two main dishes, two vegetables, two potatoes, two desserts, and two drinks.

4. Have the students draw the eight different outfits that can be derived from the book.

**FOLLOW-UP:** Provide real clothing in the dramatic play center. Note how many combinations of outfits the students can put together.

## SHAPE

Once the child can match, sort, and name shapes, she can also reproduce shapes. This can be done informally. The following are some materials that can be used:

**Geoboards** can be purchased or made. A *geoboard* is a square board with headed screws or pegs sticking up at equal intervals. The child is given a supply of rubber bands and can experiment in making shapes by stretching the rubber bands around the pegs.

A container of pipe cleaners or straws can be put out. The children can be asked to make as many different shapes as they can. These can be glued onto construction paper. Strips of paper, toothpicks, string, and yarn can also be used to make shapes.

Pattern blocks are an important material for children to use in exploring shape (Wilson, 2001). For beginners, puzzle frames are usually provided that indicate the shapes to be used to fill the frame. For more advanced students, frames are provided where the pattern block shapes are partially indicated. Children who can select pieces to fill in the puzzle without trial and error may be provided puzzle frames with no hints as to which pattern block shapes will fill the frame. Children who master these advanced frames can be offered the challenge of filling the frames in more than one way.

## SPATIAL RELATIONS

After playing the treasure hunt game described in Unit 13, children can learn more about space by reproducing the space around them as a floor plan or a map. Start with the classroom for the first map. Then move to the whole building, the neighborhood, and the town or city. Be sure the children have maps among their dramatic play props.

## ACTIVITIES

### Higher-Level Activities: Spatial Relations, Floor Plans

**OBJECTIVE:** To relate position in space to symbols of position in space.

**MATERIALS:** Large piece of poster board or heavy paper, markers, pens, construction paper, glue, crayons, scissors, some simple sample floor plans.

**ACTIVITY:**  1.  Show the children some floor plans. WHAT ARE THESE? WHAT ARE THEY FOR? IF WE MAKE A FLOOR PLAN OF OUR ROOM, WHAT WOULD WE PUT ON IT? Make a list.
2.  Show the children a large piece of poster board or heavy paper. WE CAN MAKE A PLAN OF OUR ROOM ON HERE. EACH OF YOU CAN MAKE SOMETHING THAT IS IN THE ROOM, JUST LIKE ON OUR LIST. THEN YOU CAN GLUE IT IN THE RIGHT PLACE. I'VE MARKED IN THE DOORS AND WINDOWS FOR YOU. As each child draws and cuts out an item (a table, shelf, sink, chair) have her show you where it belongs on the plan and glue it on.

**FOLLOW-UP:** After the plan is done, it should be left up on the wall so the children can look at it and talk about it. They can also add more things to the plan. The same procedure can later be used to make a plan of the building. Teacher and children should walk around the whole place. They should talk about which rooms are next to each other and which rooms are across from each other. Sticks or straws can be used to lay out the plan.

*(continued)*

## Higher-Level Activities: Spatial Relations, Maps

**OBJECTIVE:** To relate position in space to symbols of position in space.

**MATERIALS:** Map of the city, large piece of poster board or heavy paper, marking pens, construction paper, glue, crayons, scissors.

**ACTIVITY:** Show the children the map of the city (or county in a rural area). Explain that this is a picture of where the streets would be if the children were looking down from a plane or a helicopter. Label each child's home on the map and mark where the school is. Talk about who lives closest and who lives farthest away. Each child's address can be printed on a card and reviewed with her each day. The teacher can help mark out the streets and roads. The children can then cut out and glue down strips of black paper for the streets (and/or roads). Each child can draw a picture of her home and glue it on the map. The map can be kept up on the wall for children to look at and talk about. As field trips are taken during the year, each place can be added to the map.

**FOLLOW-UP:** Encourage the children to look at and talk about the map. Help them add new points of interest. Help children who would like to make their own maps. Bring in maps of the state, the country, and the world. Try to purchase United States and world map puzzles.

## DESIGN TECHNOLOGY

In Unit 13, design technology was described as a natural component of children's play. The more advanced 5- and 6-year-olds may be challenged by more complex design technology problems. In these more advanced design technology projects, children go through several steps:

- A problem is identified.
- Ideas are generated for ways of investigating and solving the problem.
- A plan of action is devised.
- A product is designed.
- The product is made and tested.
- Students reflect on the results of their process and product.

Problems may be worked on by individuals or small groups.

The youngest children should start with simple projects that focus on one item, such as designing an airplane, building a house, or constructing a miniature piece of playground equipment. Supplied with small boxes and other recycled materials, tape, and glue, children's imaginations take off. The Virginia Children's En-

gineering Council website provides detailed instructions for design technology projects. For kindergarten, plans are provided for four designs: Building a Letter, Shapes All Around Us, Magnet Motion, and Old-Fashioned Paper Dolls (download the teacher resource guide via http://CTEresource.org).

Some samples of more complex long-term projects are provided by Children Designing and Engineering (n.d.). For example, a class decides to construct a safari park. They investigate the types of animals to be included and their size, habitats, and diets. The students then plan how to construct an appropriate habitat and proceed with construction. Next they identify the needs of the workers and visitors. Then they design and build an official safari vehicle. Finally, they plan an Opening Day event. At each step the students reflect on the results and offer constructive criticism.

Budding engineers can join the Kids Design Network (KDN). This website (http://www.dupagechildrens museum.org) is sponsored by the Dupage Children's Museum. Children are presented with design problems that encourage investigation, invention, problem solving, design, and the actual building of a product. Members can communicate with an engineer through text chat and an interactive whiteboard. There is no cost to belong.

# GRAPHS

The fourth level of graphs introduces the use of squared paper. The child may graph the same kind of things as discussed in Unit 20. He will now use squared paper with squares that can be colored in or filled with glued-in paper squares. These should be introduced only after the child has had many experiences of the kinds described in Unit 20. The squares should be large. A completed graph might look like the one shown in Figure 25–6.

# CONCRETE WHOLE NUMBER OPERATIONS

Once children have a basic understanding of one-to-one correspondence, number and counting, and comparing, they can sharpen their problem-solving skills with concrete whole number operations. That is, they can solve

**Figure 25–6** Square paper graphs can be made by the child who's had many experiences with simpler graphs.

simple addition, subtraction, division, and multiplication problems using concrete materials. You can devise some simple problems to use as models as described in Unit 3. Some examples are in the box that follows. Provide the children with 10 counters (pennies, chips, Unifix Cubes, and so on) or the real items or replicas of the real items described in the problems. The children will gradually catch on and begin devising their own problems, such as those described by Skinner (1990).

As children grow and develop and have more experiences with whole number operations, they learn more strategies for solving problems. They gradually stop using the less efficient strategies and retain the more efficient ones. For example, 4- and 5-year-olds usually begin addition with the *counting all* strategy. That is, for a problem such as "John has three cars and Kate gives him two more. How many does John have now?", the 4- or 5-year-old will count all the cars (one-two-three-four-five). Fives will gradually change to *counting on*; that is, considering that John has three cars, they then count on two more (four-five). Even older children who are using recall (3 + 2 = 5) will check with counting all and counting on. When observing children working with division, note whether or not they make use of their concept of one-to-one correspondence (e.g., when giving three people equal numbers of cookies, does the child pass out the cookies, one at a time, consecutively to each of the three recipients?).

*One More Child* by Sharon Young (1998) takes the emergent reader through the process of adding on one from one to four. This affords an opportunity to see the logic that when you add one more, the total is the next number in order. The students can use objects or a calculator to continue adding ones. Suggest they add several ones and discover how many they obtain. The book *Six Pieces of Cake* (Young, 1998) takes the emergent reader through the subtraction process in which, one by one, pieces of cake are taken off a plate.

# THE SYMBOLIC LEVEL

Children who can connect groups and symbols (Unit 24), identify numerals 0 to 9, and do concrete addition and subtraction problems can move to the next step, which is connecting groups and symbols in addition and subtraction.

As children continue to create their own problems and work on teacher-created problems, they can be encouraged to communicate their findings. Suggest that they draw, write, and use numerals to show their results. They can use cards with numerals written on them and gradually write the numerals themselves. Children can work in pairs on problems and trade problems with other students.

## Addition

■ If Mary has three pennies and her mother gives her one more penny, how many pennies will Mary have?

■ George wants two cookies for himself and two for Richard. How many cookies should he ask for?

## Subtraction

■ Mary has six pennies. She gives three pennies to her sister. How many does she have now?

■ George has six cookies. He gives Richard three. How many does he have left?

## Multiplication

■ Mary gives two pennies to her sister, two to her brother, and two to her friend Kate. How many pennies did she give away?

■ Tanya had three friends visiting. Mother said to give each one three cookies. How many cookies should Tanya get from the cookie jar?

## Division

■ Lai has three dolls. Two friends come to play. How many dolls should she give each friend so they will each have the same number?

■ Lai's mother gives her a plate with nine cookies. How many cookies should Lai and each of her two friends take so they each have the same number?

Problems can be devised with stories that fit thematic topics.

As the children work with these concrete symbol/set addition and subtraction problems, they will begin to store the basic facts in their memories and retrieve them without counting. They can then do problems without objects. Just have the objects on hand in case they are needed to check the answers.

Excellent resources for games and materials are *Workjobs II* (Baratta-Lorton, 1979), *Mathematics Their Way* (Baratta-Lorton, 1976), *The Young Child and Mathematics* (Copley, 2000), *Developing Number Concepts: Addition and Subtraction, Book 2* (Richardson, 1999), *Developing Number Concepts Using Unifix Cubes* (Richardson, 1984), *Navigating through Problem Solving and Reasoning in Prekindergarten–Kindergarten* (Greenes et al., 2003), *Showcasing Mathematics for the Young Child* (Copley, 2004), *Hands-on standards* (2007), and *A head-start on science* (Ritz, 2007). In *What's Your Problem?* (Skinner, 1990), a means is provided for encouraging children to develop their own problems. Unit 27 provides a more detailed description of the procedure for introducing the symbols needed for whole number operations.

Calculators are also useful as tools for experimentation. Children will learn to make connections between problem solving and the signs on the calculator (i.e., $+$, $-$, and $=$).

## QUANTITIES ABOVE TEN

Once children can count ten objects correctly, can identify the numerals 1 to 10, have a good grasp of one-to-one correspondence, and can accurately count by rote past ten, they are ready to move on to counting quantities above ten. They can acquire an understanding of quantities above ten through an exploration of the relationship of groups of ten with additional amounts. For example, they can count out ten Unifix Cubes and stick them together. Then they can pick one more Unifix Cube. Ask if they know which number comes after 10. If they cannot provide an answer, tell them that 11 comes after 10. Have them take another cube. Ask if they know what comes after 11. If they do not know the answer, tell them 12. Go as far as they can count by rote accurately. When they get to 20, have them put their cubes together, lay them next to the first 10, and compare the number of cubes in the two rows. See if they can tell you that there are two 10s. Give them numeral cards for 11 to 19. See if they can discover that the right-hand numeral matches up with how many more than 10 that numeral stands for.

Once the children understand through 19, they can move on to 20, 30, 40, and so on. By exploring the number of 10s and 1s represented by each numeral, they will discover the common pattern from 20 to 99; that is, that the 2 in 20 means two 10s, and no 1s, the 2 in 21 means two 10s and the 1 means one 1, and so on, and that the same pattern holds true through 99.

## ESTIMATION

*Estimation* for young children involves making a sensible and reasonable response to the problem of how many are in a quantity or how much of a measurement something is. It is the "process of thinking about a 'how many' or 'how much' problem and possible solutions" (Lang, 2001, p. 463). Children might estimate how many objects (e.g., candies, teddy bears, screws) are in a jar or how many shoes tall the bookcase is. In order to come up with a reasonable response, children must already have developed number, spatial, and measurement sense. Without these prerequisite concepts they will make wild guesses rather than reasonable estimates.

Lang (2001) suggests several ways to assist children so they can make reasonable estimates. A *referent* can be used such as, "If I know how tall John is, I can estimate how tall the bookcase is if he stands next to it." *Chunking* involves taking a known measurement and using it as a guide for estimating a larger measurement. For example, if the children know how long 10 Unifix Cubes are, they can use this information to estimate the length of the table in cubes. Unitizing is another type of chunking where, if one part is known, then the whole can be estimated. For example, if a cup of pennies fills a jar half full, then two cups will fill the whole jar. If the number of pennies in the cup is known, then the number to fill the jar can be estimated. It is important that children understand the language of comparison (Units 11 and 15) in order to give and receive communications regarding their estimates.

## IDEAS FOR CHILDREN WITH SPECIAL NEEDS

Unit 27 describes a progression suggested by Kathy Richardson for moving from concrete arithmetic to algorithms. For some children, a useful step for beginning arithmetic is to play a thinking game. Using numbers 2 to 9, the children are asked a series of questions. The children are asked "What number comes *after* 6?" Next, "What number comes *before* 6?" and finally "What is 6 and one more?" Patterns are also useful in helping children move into arithmetic. For example, when making a bead pattern the child must think, "How many more beads will I need to complete my pattern?"

## SUMMARY

This unit builds on the concepts and skills presented in the previous units. Areas are reviewed and children moved to higher levels that will shift them into concrete operations and primary grade arithmetic.

## KEY TERMS

| | | |
|---|---|---|
| algebra | design technology | multiple classification |
| class inclusion | estimation | quantities above ten |
| classification | geoboard | shape |
| concrete whole number operations | graphs | spatial relations |
| | hierarchical classification | symbolic level |

## SUGGESTED ACTIVITIES

1. Observe in a kindergarten classroom. Note any behaviors that suggest that any of the children are ready for higher-level concept activities. Share your observations with the class.

2. Interview one or more kindergarten teachers. Ask them to describe the concept activities available for students who are entering the concrete operations period.

3. In a kindergarten or first-grade class, identify one or more transitional-level students. Plan and prepare two higher-level activities to try with them. Share the results with the class.

4. Include higher-level concept activities in your Activity File/Notebook.

5. Select some software listed on the Online Companion for this unit or past units and evaluate whether it supports higher-level concepts and skills. Use the evaluation format suggested in Activity 5, Unit 2.

## REVIEW

A. Describe areas in this unit that provide higher-level concept activities.

B. Characterize the three higher levels of classification.

C. Which of the examples below can be identified as (a) multiple classification, (b) class inclusion, or (c) hierarchical classification?

　1. Basset hound, dog, animal.
　2. Matrix that varies horizontally by size and vertically by color.
　3. Two cars and three airplanes; are there more airplanes or more vehicles?
　4. Texture, weight, and material.
　5. Markers, pens, pencils, things you can write with.
　6. Three apples and one banana; are there more apples or more fruit?

D. Read the following descriptions carefully. Identify the higher-level activity the child seems to be engaged in, and suggest how the teacher should respond.

　1. Kate says, "Donny lives on the other side of the street from me."
　2. Liu takes the Unifix Cubes and places them in groups of three.
　3. Cindy takes some cube blocks and some toy cars and places them on the balance scale.
　4. Bret points to the orange in the picture book and says, "Look at that round orange."
　5. Liu says that chocolate ice cream is the best. Kate says vanilla is best. Kate insists that most children like vanilla ice cream better than chocolate.
　6. "John, give me two more blocks so that I will have six, too."
　7. Mrs. Jones notices that Sam is laboriously drawing four oranges and five apples.

Then he writes a numeral 4 by the oranges and the number 5 by the apples. Finally he writes in invented spelling, "thrs 9 froots."

8. Mrs. Carter notices that 5-year-old George can rote count to 99 accurately.

9. Tanya explains that all people have blood, bones, and fat inside, but all dolls are filled with cotton.

10. We counted out 20 jelly beans in this scoop. How can we use that information to estimate how many jelly beans this jar will hold when full?

E. Look back through all the ideas for children with special needs. Set up a plan for children with disabilities, ELL students, and for insuring your classroom meets the needs of culturally diverse students.

## REFERENCES

Aker, S. (1990). *What comes in 2's, 3's, and 4's.* New York: Aladdin.

Baratta-Lorton, M. (1976). *Mathematics their way.* Menlo Park, CA: Addison-Wesley.

Baratta-Lorton, M. (1979). *Workjobs II.* Menlo Park, CA: Addison-Wesley.

Children Designing and Engineering. (n.d.). *What is CD&E?* Retrieved November 20, 2004, from http://www.childrendesigning.org

Copley, J. V. (2000). *The young child and mathematics.* Washington, DC: National Association for the Education of Young Children.

Copley, J. V. (2004). *Showcasing mathematics for the young child.* Reston, VA: National Council of Teaches of Mathematics.

Curcio, F. R., & Schwartz, S. L. (1997). What does algebraic thinking look like with preprimary children? *Teaching Children Mathematics, 3*(6), 296–300.

Greenes, C. E., Dacey, L., Cavanagh, M., Findell, C. R., Sheffeld, L. J. & Small, M. (2003). *Navigating through problem solving and reasoning in prekindergarten–kindergarten.* Reston, VA: National Council of Teaches of Mathematics.

Lang, F. K. (2001). What is a "good guess" anyway? Estimation in early childhood. *Teaching Children Mathematics, 7*(8), 462–466.

Learning Resources. (2007). *Hands-on standards.* Vernon Hills, IL: Author.

Marshall, J. (2006). Math wars 2: It's the teaching, stupid! *Phi Delta Kappan, 87*(5), 356–363.

Moses, B. (1997). Algebra for a new century. *Teaching Children Mathematics, 3*(6), 264–265.

National Council of Teachers of Mathematics. (2000). *Principles and standards for school mathematics.* Reston, VA: Author.

Pinczes, E.J. (1993). *One hundred hungry ants.* New York: Scholastic Books.

Richardson, K. (1984). *Developing number concepts: Using Unifix Cubes.* Menlo Park, CA: Addison-Wesley.

Richardson, K. (1999). *Developing number concepts: Addition and subtraction* (Book 2). Parsippany, NJ: Seymour.

Ritz, W. C. (Ed.). (2007). *A head-start on science.* Arlington, VA: NSTA Press.

Skinner, P. (1990). *What's your problem?* Portsmouth, NH: Heinemann.

Slate, J. (1998). *Miss Bindergarten celebrates the 100th day.* New York: Puffin Books.

Virginia Children's Engineering Council. (n.d.). *Inspiring the next generation.* Retrieved November 20, 2004, from http://www.vtea.org

Wilson, D. C. (2001). Patterns of thinking in pattern block play. *Building Blocks News, 3,* 2.

Young, S. (1998). *Harry's Math Books, Set B, Teacher Guide.* Columbus, OH: Zaner-Bloser.

Young, S. (1998). *One more child.* Columbus, OH: Zaner-Bloser.

Young, S. (1998). *Six pieces of cake.* Columbus, OH: Zaner-Bloser.

Young, S. (1998). *What to wear?* Columbus, OH: Zaner-Bloser.

## FURTHER READING AND RESOURCES

*Box it or bag it mathematics (K–2)*. Portland, OR: Math Learning Center.

*Bridges in mathematics (K–2)*. Portland, OR: Math Learning Center.

Buschman, L. (2002). Becoming a problem solver. *Teaching Children Mathematics, 9*(2), 98–103.

*Children's Engineering Journal*, http://www.vtea.org

Clements, D. H., & Sarama, J. (2000). Predicting pattern blocks on and off the computer. *Teaching Children Mathematics, 6*(7), 458–461.

Clements, D. H., Swaminathan, S., Hannibal, M. A. Z., & Sarama, J. (1999). Young children's concepts of shape. *Journal for Research in Mathematics Education, 30*(2), 192–212.

Copley, J. V. (Ed.). (1999). *Mathematics in the early years*. Washington, DC: National Association for the Education of Young Children.

Dunn, S., & Larson, R. (1990). *Design technology: Children's Engineering*. Bristol, PA: Falmer, Taylor & Francis.

Falkner, K. P., Levi, L., & Carpenter, T. R. (1999). Children's understanding of equality: A foundation for algebra. *Teaching Children Mathematics, 6*(4), 232–236.

Fitzsimmons, P. F., & Goldhaber, J. (1997). Siphons, pumps, and missile launchers: Inquiry at the water tables. *Science and Children, 34*(4), 16–19.

Gallenstein, N. L. (2004). Creative discovery through classification. *Teaching Children Mathematics, 11*(2), 103–108.

Greenes, C. E., Cavanagh, M., Dacey, L., Findell, C. R., & Small, M. (2001). *Navigating through algebra in prekindergarten–kindergarten*. Reston, VA: National Council of Teachers of Mathematics.

Holly, K. A. (1997). Math by the month: Patterns and functions. *Teaching Children Mathematics, 3*(6), 312.

Outhred, L., & Sarelich, S. (2005). Problem solving by kindergartners, *Teaching Children Mathematics, 12*(3), 146–154.

Petroski, H. (2003, January 24). *Early education*. Presentation at the Children's Engineering Convention (Williamsburg, VA). Retrieved November 20, 2004, from http://www.vtea.org

Sheffield, L. J., Cavanagh, M., Dacey, L., Findell, C. R., Greenes, C. E., & Small, M. (2002). *Navigating through data analysis and probability in prekindergarten–grade 2*. Reston, VA: National Council of Teachers of Mathematics.

Shulman, L., & Eston, R. (1998). A problem worth revisiting. *Teaching Children Mathematics, 5*(2), 72–77.

Taylor-Cox, J. (2001). How many marbles in the jar? Estimation in the early grades. *Teaching Children Mathematics, 8*(4), 208–214.

# Unit 26

# Higher-Level Activities Used in Science Units and Activities

## OBJECTIVES

After reading this unit, you should be able to:

■ Plan and do structured lessons in sets and symbols, classification, and measurement.

■ Apply the concepts, skills, and attitudes found in math to lessons in science.

■ Design higher-level lessons that develop science concepts for children closer to the concrete level of development.

## SETS, SYMBOLS, AND CLASSIFICATION

Children in the transitional stage apply and develop fundamental concepts in sets and symbols, classification, shape, spatial relations, measurement, and graphs as they are exposed to higher-level experiences. As they near the concrete operational level of development, they will continue to develop these concepts. The higher-level experiences described in this unit offer opportunities to build on many of the ideas presented in Units 23 through 25 of this book.

### Vegetable Time

Although children will be asked to bring vegetables from home for this lesson, you will need to prepare a variety of vegetables for maximum learning. Seed and garden catalogs and magazine pictures can provide illustrations of how the vegetables grow. Three major categories of vegetables that work well with children are *leaf*

and *stem vegetables* (cabbage, lettuce, spinach, mustard, parsley), *root vegetables* (sweet potatoes, carrots, beets, turnips, onions), and *seed vegetables* (cucumbers, peas, beans, corn, soybeans). Mrs. Red Fox conducts the following activity in the fall with her first-grade class.

First, she invites the children to join her on a rug to examine the different vegetables. Then she asks her class to describe the vegetables in front of them. They answer, "Long, rough, smooth, peeling, hard, scratchy, lumpy, bumpy, crunchy, white, orange." Mrs. Red Fox holds up a potato and asks, "Can someone describe this potato?" "I can," Trang Fung says. "The potato is bumpy and brown." "Good," says Mrs. Red Fox. "Who can find another vegetable that is bumpy?" "A pea is a little bumpy," suggests Sara. Mrs. Red Fox writes the word *bumpy* on a card and groups the potato and pea together. Then she holds up a carrot and asks, "Is there another vegetable that looks like this one?" Dean studies the assortment of vegetables and says, "How about the pumpkin?" "Yes, the pumpkin and the carrot are both orange." Mrs. Red Fox writes the word *orange* on a card and places the carrot and pumpkin together with the card. The children continue to classify by characteristics until each vegetable is in a group. Mrs. Red Fox refrigerates the vegetables overnight and readies them for a series of activities that emphasize a variety of concepts.

1. *Where do they grow?* The class discusses how the different vegetables looked while they were growing. Consider that, for all most children know, potatoes come from produce sections of supermarkets and corn comes from a can. The children have fun matching the vegetable with pictures of the vegetable growing. Mrs. Red Fox makes a game of matching actual vegetables with how they look as they grow.

2. *Digging for potatoes.* After matching actual vegetables with pictures of growing vegetables, children practice digging for potatoes. Mrs. Red Fox fills the sandbox with rows of potatoes, and children take turns digging. Carrots, beets, and turnips are planted with their leafy tops above the soil, and children take turns gardening.

3. *What is inside?* Bowls of peas are set out to be opened and explored, and the idea of starting a garden begins to occur to children.

4. *Under, on, and above.* Mrs. Red Fox makes a bulletin board backdrop of a garden, and the children match cutout vegetables to where they grow. Onions are placed *under the ground*; peas, beans, and corn are shown *above the ground*; and lettuce, cabbage, and parsley are displayed *on the ground.*

5. *Patterns.* Children place the vegetables in patterns. Trang Fung made a pattern of potatoes, pumpkins, celery, and cucumbers. She said, "Bumpy, bumpy, bumpy, smooth. Look at my pattern. Dean, can you make a pattern?" Dean began his own pattern. "I am not going to tell you my pattern," said Dean. He laid out mustard, carrots, peas, cabbage, potato, and beans. Trang Fung smiled and continued the pattern. "On the ground, under the ground, and above the ground, spinach, onion, corn," she said.

6. *Vegetable prints.* As the week continued, some children wondered if the insides of the vegetables were alike and different, too. So, Mrs. Red Fox cut up several vegetables and let the children explore printing with vegetables. She poured tempera paint on sponges for a stamp pad. Then the children dipped the vegetable in paint and printed on construction paper. Mrs. Red Fox labeled some of the prints with vegetable words and hung them up for decoration. The prints were then classified by color and characteristics. Some children made patterns with their prints and asked others to guess the pattern and which vegetable made the pattern.

## Stone Soup

Children can also learn about vegetables through literature and cooking. After vegetables are identified as members of the vegetable and fruit food group, read the book *Stone Soup* (Paterson, 1981) and act out the story on the flannelboard.

Print the recipe on poster board (see Unit 22), add picture clues, and have the children wash vegetables for cooking. The children will quickly learn to use vegetable peelers and table knives as they cut the vegetables into small pieces. Then, act out the story once again. This time, really add the stone and vegetables to a crockpot to cook for the day. Bouillon cubes, salt, and pepper will spice up the soup. Do not be surprised if younger children think that the stone made all of the soup.

Prepare a set of cards with pictures of the ingredients, and have students put the cards in the correct sequence of the cooking activity (Figure 26–1). The children will want to make an experience chart of preparing the stone soup. They could even graph their favorite parts of the soup.

## Animal Sets

Stuffed animals are familiar to the children and can be grouped in many ways. One way is to group stuffed animals on a table by sets: a group of one, two, three, and so on. Ask the children to draw the set of animals at their table on a piece of white paper. After the children have drawn the animals, include early literacy experiences by having them dictate or write a story about the animals. Staple the drawings at each table into a book. The children at each table have made an animal book of

**Figure 26–1** "What did we add to the soup first? Then what did we add?"

ones, twos, and so on. Read each book with the children and make all books available for independent classroom reading.

## More First Mapping Experiences

The everyday experience of reading maps is abstract and takes practice to develop. The following mapping activities include the use of symbols and build on the early "bird's-eye view" mapping experiences in Unit 21 and the mapping experiences suggested in Units 13 and 25.

1. *Tangible mapping.* Children will not be able to deal with symbols on maps if they have not had experience with tangible mapping. Observe children as they create roads, valleys, and villages in clay or at the sand table. Keep in mind the perspective of *looking down* as children place objects on a huge base map. Such a map can be made from oilcloth and rolled up when not in use.

2. *Pictorial mapping.* Take children to the top of a hill or building, and ask them to draw what they see. This activity can emphasize spatial relations and relative locations. After you have returned from a field trip, discuss what was seen on the bus ride. Use crayons or paint to construct a mural of the trip.

3. *Semipictorial mapping.* Children will use more conventional symbols when they construct a semipictorial map. As they discover that pictures take up a lot of room, they search for symbols to represent objects. Colors become symbolic and can be used to indicate water and vegetation.

4. *Base map.* The base map contains the barest minimum detail filled in by the teacher, that is, outline, key streets, and buildings. This is a more abstract type of map; thus the area must be known to the child. Add tangible objects to the abstract base, that is, toy objects and pictures. A flannel base map is a variation.

5. *Caution.* Never use one map to do many things. If your mapping experience tries to do too much, children cannot rethink the actual experience and relationships. Each mapmaking experience must fulfill some specific purpose. Each map must represent something in particular that children look for and understand.

6. *Start small.* Begin with maps of the children's block constructions. Next, move to mapping a center in the classroom before moving to something larger. Gradually increase the size of the space you are planning to map. Remember to discuss directionality.

## Exploring Pumpkins: October Science

If you live where pumpkins grow, take a field trip to purchase some; if not, buy some at the grocery store. You will need a pumpkin for each child. Plan to organize the children in groups with an adult helper. The following activities use the senses to apply and integrate the skills and fundamental concepts used in measuring, counting, classifying, and graphing into the exploration of pumpkins.

## Time to Explore

Give children time to examine their pumpkins and their stems. Ask, "How does the pumpkin feel?" "How does it smell?" and "Do all pumpkins have stems?" Later, when the pumpkins are carved, encourage the children to describe the differences in texture between the inside and outside of their pumpkins.

Ask, "Which pumpkin is the heaviest?" "Who has the lightest pumpkin?" After the children decide, bring out a scale, and make an accurate measurement. The children probably cannot comprehend what the scale means or read the numbers, but they like to weigh things anyway. Tape the weight (mass) on the bottom of each pumpkin. Then, when jack-o'-lanterns are created, the children can compare the difference in mass.

Have children measure the circumference of a pumpkin with yarn. Ask, "Where shall we put the yarn on the pumpkin?" and "Why?" Instruct the children to wrap the yarn around the middle of the pumpkin. Then, help children cut the yarn and label it. Write the child's name on masking tape and attach it to the yarn length.

After the children have measured their pumpkins and labeled their yarn, have them thumbtack the yarn length to a bulletin board. Ask, "Which pumpkin is the smallest around the middle?" "Which is the largest?" "How can you tell?" Have the children refer to the yarn graph (Figure 26–2). Some kindergarten children might be ready to lay the yarn length along a measuring stick and draw horizontal bar graphs instead of yarn ones.

Children will want to measure height as well as circumference. The major problem to solve will probably be where to measure from—the top of the stem or the indentation where the stem was. This time, cut a piece of yarn that fits around the height of the pumpkin. Label the yarn, and attach it to pieces of masking tape. Order the yarn lengths from shortest to tallest. Ask, "Which yarn is the longest?" and "Can you tell me who has the tallest pumpkin?"

## Observing Pumpkins

Mrs. Jones has kindergarten children count the number of curved lines along the outside of the pumpkin. She asks, "How many lines are on your pumpkin?" She instructs the children to help each other. One child places a finger on the first line of the pumpkin and another child

**Figure 26–2** "How big is your pumpkin?"

counts the lines. Then Mrs. Jones asks, "Do all the pumpkins have the same number of lines?" "No," answers Mary. "My pumpkin has more lines than Lai's pumpkin." Some children even begin to link the number of lines with the size of the pumpkin as they compare findings.

Mrs. Jones asks, "How does your pumpkin feel?" George says his pumpkin is rough, but Sam insists that his is smooth. "Yes," Mrs. Jones observes. "Some pumpkins are rough, and some are smooth." "Are they the same color?" This question brings a buzz of activity as the children compare pumpkin color. Mrs. Jones attaches the name of each child to his or her pumpkin and asks the children to bring their pumpkins to the front table. She asks the children to group the pumpkins by color variations of yellow, orange, and so on. Some of the children are beginning to notice other differences in the pumpkins such as brown spots and differences in stem shapes.

The children gather around Mrs. Jones as she carves a class pumpkin. She carefully puts the seeds and pulp on separate plates and asks the children to compare the inside color of the pumpkin with the outside color. She asks, "What colors do you see?" and "What colors do you see inside of the pumpkin?" "I see a lighter color," Mary says. "Do all pumpkins have light insides?" George is more interested in the stringy fibers. "This looks like string dipped in pumpkin stuff." "I am glad you noticed, George," Mrs. Jones comments. "The stringy stuff is called fiber. It is part of the pumpkin." Students learn the word *pulp* and also compare the seeds for future activities.

Children will also notice that *pumpkins smell.* Ask them to describe the smell of their pumpkins. Have them turn their pumpkins over and smell all parts. Then ask them to compare the smell of the inside of their pumpkins with the outside rind and with the seeds, fiber, and pulp. "Does the pumpkin smell remind you of anything?" Record dictated descriptions and create an experience chart of pumpkin memories. Ask, "What do you think of when you smell pumpkins?"

As children make jack-o'-lantern faces, discuss the shapes they are using. Then, ask them to draw faces on the surfaces of their pumpkins using a felt-tip pen. Closely supervise children as they carve their pumpkins. Instruct them to cut away from their bodies. They will need help in holding the knife, and their partici-

pation might be limited to scooping out the pumpkin. Note: Apple corers work well for these experiences and are easier to use.

After the jack-o'-lanterns are cut and have been admired, Mrs. Jones begins a measurement activity. She asks, "How can we tell if the pumpkin is lighter than it was before it was carved?" "Lift it," say the children. "Yes," says Mrs. Jones, "that is one way to tell, but I want to know for sure." George suggests, "Let's use the scale again." But before the pumpkins are weighed, Mrs. Jones asks the children to whisper a prediction in her ear. She asks, "Do you think the pumpkin will weigh more or less after it has been carved and the seeds and pulp removed? Whisper 'More,' 'Less,' or 'The same.'" As the children respond, Mrs. Jones writes their responses on paper pumpkins and begins a more, less, and the same graph of predictions (Figure 26–3).

Figure 26–3 "Do you think the pumpkin will weigh more, less, or the same after the seeds are removed?"

Last but not least in a series of pumpkin activities is tasting. Pumpkin pulp can be made into pumpkin bread; or, for science and Halloween party time, make drop cookies with raisins for eyes, nose, and mouth. For a tasty snack, cut some of the pumpkin pulp into chunks for cooking. Once cooked, dot the pieces with butter, and add a dash of nutmeg.

Try roasting some pumpkin seeds. Have the children wash the seeds to remove the pulp and fiber. The seeds can be dried between layers of paper towels and then roasted in a single layer on a cookie sheet. Bake in a 350° oven for 30 to 40 minutes. The children can tell when the seeds are ready by their pale brown color. To make a comparison lesson, show them seeds that you have previously roasted, and invite them to tell you when the color of the roasting seeds matches yours. Cool the seeds, then have a snack. Before cooking the seeds have each child count the seeds found in his or her pumpkin and compare to see which pumpkin had the most and least. If the seeds are not being eaten they can be dried and used for counting and making sets.

# ACTIVITIES

## Sets, Symbols, and Ordering

**OBJECTIVE:** Identifying and Ordering Symbols

**MATERIALS:** A variety of magazines or picture cards, crayons, glue, and tape.

**NATURALISTIC AND INFORMAL ACTIVITIES:** As the children share their morning experiences, encourage them to name some of the things that they saw on the way to school. Ask, WHAT WAS THE FIRST THING YOU SAW ON YOUR WAY TO SCHOOL THIS MORNING? THEN WHAT DID YOU SEE? WHAT WAS THE LAST THING THAT YOU SAW BEFORE YOU WALKED INTO OUR CLASSROOM?

**STRUCTURED ACTIVITIES:** Draw a horizontal line across the chalkboard or on a large piece of paper. Give children numerous pictures cut from magazines and ask them to select five pictures of something that they saw on their way to school. Then, have them tape or paste the first picture of something that they saw at the beginning of the line. Children may want to work in pairs, especially if they are neighbors, to order their picture from the first to the last thing they saw. Ask, IS THERE ENOUGH ROOM ON OUR LINE TO HOLD ALL OF THE PICTURES? WHAT CAN WE DO TO MAKE THIS EASIER? Introduce the idea of making a classroom symbol that everyone could use to represent what they saw on their way to school.

**FOLLOW-UP:** Have each child cut out symbols (for a house, tree, dog, cat, etc.), so that each child has a set of pictographs or symbols of what they passed on their way to school. Take children on a walk around the school or around the block and ask them to work in pairs to order the symbols to show what they saw on their walk. Children may want to develop more symbols to better reflect what they saw.

# MEASURING THE WORLD AROUND US

Playgrounds, yards, and sidewalks provide many opportunities for measuring in science. The following activities emphasize the science and measurement in outdoor adventures.

1. *How far will it blow?* After talking about air and how it moves, take the children outside to determine how far the wind will blow dandelion seeds. Draw bull's-eye-like circles on the playground with chalk. Label the circles. Have a child stand in the middle of the circle and hold a mature dandelion up to the wind. Record which direction the wind blows the seeds and the circle in which most of them landed. This would be a good time to discuss wind as a way of dispersing seeds. If dandelions are not available,

then small pieces of tissue paper with seeds drawn on them can be used.

2. *Weed watch.* Place a stick next to a growing plant such as a dandelion or similar weed. Have the children mark the height of the weed on the stick. Check the weed each day for a week and see how tall it gets. (You might have to talk to the groundskeeper before trying this activity.) Children enjoy seeing the weeds grow. Discuss differences and possible factors in weed growth.

3. *How long does it take?* After students have had time to explore the water center, select some of the containers used in the center. Lead the children to an area that has pinecones, acorns, or other natural objects available. Recall the amount of time it took to fill the containers with water. Then, give a container to each group of children and instruct them to fill it with specific objects. Note the time that it takes to fill the containers. Vary the activity by assigning different groups of contrasting objects (i.e., small, big, rough, etc.) with which to fill the containers.

4. *Line them up.* Have children count the objects that they have collected in the containers. Ask each group to line up the objects. Compare the number of objects that it took to fill each container. If the objects collected were different, compare the number of each type of object that was needed to fill the container.

5. *How can we tell?* Children will probably find many ways to compare objects they have found. After they have examined and compared their objects visually, encourage them to weigh several of the objects. Ask, "Which container is the heaviest?" and "How can we tell?" A balance provides an objective measure. Balance the content of one container (acorns) against the content of another (walnuts). Have children predict which will be heavier. Some might want to draw a picture of what they think will happen.

## Popcorn Time

Children will sequence events as they act out a favorite snack. Have two or three children become popcorn by asking them to crouch down in the middle of a masking tape circle or hula hoop. As you pour imaginary oil on them, have the rest of the class make sizzling noises and wait for them to pop. When ready, each child should jump up, burst open like a popcorn kernel, and leap out of the popper circle. Children will want to take turns acting out the popcorn sequence.

Then, place a real popcorn popper on a sheet in the middle of the floor. Seat the children around the popper, remove the popcorn lid, and watch the popcorn fly. Before eating the popcorn, measure how far the popcorn popped with Unifix Cubes or string. (Be careful of the hot popper.) Ask, "Which popcorn flew the farthest?" and "Which flew the shortest?"

## SPATIAL RELATIONS

### Inside and Outside

Young children are curious about their bodies. They are familiar with outside body parts, which they can see and touch, but they are just beginning to notice that things happen inside their bodies. To increase this awareness and reinforce the concepts of inside and outside, Mrs. Jones has children look at, feel, and listen to what is going on inside of their bodies in the following scenario.

Mrs. Jones fills a garbage bag with an assortment of items—a wound-up alarm clock, rubber balls, a book, a few sticks, and a bunch of grapes in a small sandwich bag (Figure 26–4). She places the bag on a chair in the front of the room, allowing it to drape down to show the outlines of some of the objects inside. She asks, "What is on the chair?" George says, "A garbage bag." "Is anything on the chair besides the bag?" asks the teacher. "No," the children respond. Mrs. Jones invites the children to gather around the bag and feel it. She asks, "Do you hear or feel anything?" "Yes," Mary says. "I feel something sharp." "And squishy," adds Sam. George is certain that he hears a clock ticking, and Lai feels a round and firm object that moves.

After the children guess what might be in the bag, Mrs. Jones opens it and shows the children what was inside. "Did you guess correctly?" "I did," says George. "I heard something ticking." "Good," answers

**Figure 26–4** "Do you feel anything inside of the bag?"

Mrs. Jones. "How did you know that sticks were in the bag?" Mary says, "I could feel them poking through the plastic." "Yes," Sam adds, "the grapes must have been the squishy stuff."

After the children discuss the contents of the bag, Mrs. Jones takes the bag off the chair, asks the children to return to their places, and invites Mary to sit in the chair. She asks, "Now, what is on the chair?" The class choruses, "Mary." "Yes, Mary is on the chair," says Mrs. Jones. "How is Mary like the bag?" After a few responses, George says, "Mary has something inside of her, too." The children come up to look at Mary, but do not touch her. Mrs. Jones asks, "Do you see what's inside showing through the way it did with the bag?" The children notice bones, knuckles, the funny bone, kneecap, and some veins. Mrs. Jones asks Mary to flex her arm muscles so the children can see muscles moving beneath her skin.

Mrs. Jones encourages the children to discover other muscles and feel them working. She has them stretch out on mats on the floor, curl up tightly, then slowly uncurl. "What have your muscles done?" Then she has them stretch out like a cat and curl up into a ball. Facial muscles are fun for the children. Mrs. Jones asks them to find and use all the muscles that they can on their faces. They wiggle noses, flutter eyelids, tighten

jaws, and raise eyebrows. The teacher asks, "Does your tongue have muscles in it?" "How do you know?" Finally, the children move to music as they focus on what is happening inside their bodies. Mrs. Jones has them dancing like marionettes, stiffly with a few joints moving; then bending and curling the way rag dolls do; and finally, dancing like people, with muscles, joints, and bones controlling their movements.

The children are fascinated with the thought of something important inside of them. They make toy stethoscopes from funnels and rubber tubing and take turns finding and listening to their heartbeats. Some begin to count the beats; others enjoy tapping a finger in time with the sound of their hearts.

Mrs. Jones has the children simulate the way a heart works by folding their hands one over the other and squeezing and releasing them rhythmically. (This motion is somewhat like the way the heart muscles move to expand and contract the heart, pushing blood through.) She has them place their clasped hands close to their ears and asks, "What do you hear?" "Is this squeezing sound like the soft thumping you heard through the stethoscope?" "How is it different?"

## Assessment Tasks

If they can do the assessment tasks for Units 8 through 25, children will have the basic skills and knowledge necessary to connect sets and symbols and successfully complete higher-level learning activities. The following example is a strategy many teachers use when children have made differing progress in classification, shape, spatial relations, measurement, and graphing.

As different concepts and activities are introduced, children of differing developmental levels will express interest in the same material. This is not a problem, because children at lower levels can participate as observers and contributors. For example, lower-level children could do part of the task following the higher-level child's lead. Children can work in pairs to solve problems, to move into higher levels of symbol use and measurement, and to explore calculators and computer software together. Most activities in science promote working in teams as well as sharing roles and responsibilities. This makes science an especially appropriate way to address differing levels of development.

# TECHNOLOGY

Technology can be used to expand and supplement your science program. It can and should be used to enhance the understanding of beginning math and science concepts. The two main uses of technology in early childhood classes are software and the Internet. Software is usually used to support the acquisition and practice of concepts and skills. The Internet is often used to research topics of interest, connect with people in other locations, and illustrate concepts that children are unable to experience directly.

Appropriate software should reinforce what children are learning in the classroom. It should not be used as the sole method of instruction or take the place of actual hands-on experience. When choosing software, teachers should ask themselves the following questions.

1. Does the software ask children to engage in activities appropriate for their age?

2. Is the software interactive? The more interactive choices a child is able to make, the more appropriate the software will be.

3. Does the software come in multiple languages and utilize diverse populations in their graphics?

4. Does the software have a range of complexity that can be tailored to individual children?

Some examples of appropriate software are *Sammy's Science House* and *KidWare*.

The Internet is another form of technology that is often used in early childhood classrooms. Before accessing the Internet, be sure the computers in the classroom are equipped with filtering software so the children will not be exposed to undesirable websites. If the school or center is networked, one should always check to see if the server is protected with a firewall that will filter inappropriate websites.

Internet websites should be used to reinforce topics under study. For example, if the class is unable to visit a pumpkin patch, then do a virtual tour. If the class is studying weather, then the class can track the changes in weather by accessing the Online Companion for relevant links to websites.

# SUMMARY

Children in the transitional stage develop fundamental concepts in sets and symbols, classification, shape, spatial relations, measurement, and graphs as they are exposed to higher-level experiences. As children near the concrete operational level of development, they continue to need hands-on exploration.

Science activities at this level allow children to pull together skills and ideas learned earlier. Most children incorporate these skills through naturalistic and informal experiences. Structured activities are also appropriate but should be brief.

## SUGGESTED ACTIVITIES

1. Design a graphing experience for transitional children. Select an appropriate science topic, describe procedures, and develop a questioning strategy. Share the lessons in groups, and teach the lesson to a class.

2. Accompany a class on a field trip or walk around the block. Make a picture map of the field trip. Record the types of comments children make as they recall their trip. What types of objects made an impression on the children?

Are the comments in keeping with what you know about children and the way they think?

3. Select a software program for young children that emphasizes one of the concepts or skills discussed in this unit. Try the program yourself and develop a lesson that uses this program. What kinds of experiences will children need to have before they use this program? What science concepts or skills will be taught or reinforced? What kinds of follow-up

experiences will be needed? Here is a list of suggested software.

- *Computergarten* (pre-K–1; New York: Scholastic Books)
- *Greeting Card* option of Print Shop (San Francisco: Broderbund at Riverdeep)
- *KidWare* (Alexandria, VA: MOBIUS)
- *KidWorks Deluxe* (pre-K–2; Torrance, CA: Davidson & Associates)
- *Micros for Micros: Estimation* (K–2; Berkeley, CA: Lawrence Hall of Science)

- *Quicktake 150 or 200 Digital Camera* (all grades; Cupertino, CA: Apple Computer)
- *Sammy's Science House* (pre-K–2; San Francisco: Edmark)
- *ThemeWeavers: Animals* (San Francisco: Edmark)

Please refer to the software resources listed on the Online Companion for Units 33 through 39 for additional software recommendations.

## REVIEW

**A.** List areas discussed in this unit that have higher-level concept activities.

**B.** Name three types of mapping activities that can be used with young children. Why use these strategies with children?

**C.** Why is it essential that children have time to explore materials when learning a science concept?

**D.** Discuss things a teacher should keep in mind when choosing software.

## REFERENCE

Paterson, D. (1981). *Stone soup*. Mahwah, NJ: Troll Associates.

## FURTHER READING AND RESOURCES

American Association for the Advancement of Science (AAAS). (2007). *Atlas of science literacy: Project 2061* (Vol. 2). Washington, DC: Author.

Ashbrook, P. (2003). *Science is simple: Over 250 activities for preschoolers*. Beltsville, MD: Gryphon House.

Benenson, G., & Neujahr, J. L. (2002). *Designed environments: Places, practices, and plans*. Portsmouth, NH: Heinemann.

Benenson, G., & Neujahr, J. L. (2002). *Mapping*. Portsmouth, NH: Heinemann.

Benenson, G., & Neujahr, J. L. (2002). *Mechanisms and other systems*. Portsmouth, NH: Heinemann.

Benenson, G., & Neujahr, J. L. (2002). *Packaging and other structures*. Portsmouth, NH: Heinemann.

Benenson, G., & Neujahr, J. L. (2002). *Signs, symbols, and codes*. Portsmouth, NH: Heinemann.

Buckleitner, W. (1993). *Survey of early childhood software*. Ypsilanti, MI: High/Scope Press.

Burk, D., Snider, A., & Symonds, P. (1988). *Box it or bag it mathematics: Kindergarten teachers resource guide*. Portland, OR: Math Learning Center.

Carin, A. A., Bass, J. E., & Contant, T. L. (2005). *Teaching science as inquiry* (10th ed.). Upper Saddle River, NJ: Prentice-Hall.

Chalufour, I., & Worth, K. (2004). *Building structure with young children*. St. Paul, MN: Redleaf Press.

Davidson, J. I. (1989). *Children and computers together in the early childhood classroom*. Clifton Park, NY: Thomson Delmar Learning.

Harlan, J., & Rivkin, M. (2003). *Science experiences for the early childhood years: An integrated affective approach*. Upper Saddle River, NJ: Pearson-Merrill/ Prentice-Hall.

Haughland, S. W., & Wright, J. L. (1997). *Young children and technology: A world of discovery*. Boston: Allyn & Bacon.

Kamii, C., & Devries, R. (1993). *Physical knowledge in the classroom: Implications of Piaget's theory* (Rev. ed.). Englewood Cliffs, NJ: Prentice-Hall.

Lind, K. K. (1984). A bird's-eye view: Mapping readiness. *Science and Children, 22*(3), 39–40.

Lind, K. K. (1985). The inside story. *Science and Children, 22*(4), 122–123.

McIntyre, M. (1984). *Pumpkin science. Early childhood and science*. Washington, DC: National Science Teachers Association.

McNair, S. (Ed.). (2005). *Start Young! Early Childhood Science Activities*. Arlington, VA: NSTA Press Journals Collection.

National Research Council. (1996). *National science education standards*. Washington, DC: National Academies Press.

Rhoton, J. & Shane, P. (2005). *Teaching Science in the 21st Century*. Arlington, VA: NSTA Press and the National Science Education Leadership Association (NSELA).

Rockwell, R. E., Sherwood, E. A., & Williams, R. A. (1986). *Hug a tree*. Mt. Rainier, MD: Gryphon House.

Stronck, D. (Ed.). (1983). *Understanding the healthy body* (Council for Elementary Science International Sourcebook III). Columbus, OH: SMEAC Information Reference Center.

Ukens, L. (Ed.). (1985). *Science experiences for preschoolers* (Council for Elementary Science International Sourcebook IV). Columbus, OH: SMEAC Information Reference Center.

# Mathematics Concepts and Operations for the Primary Grades

# Unit 27

## Operations with Whole Numbers

### OBJECTIVES

After reading this unit, you should be able to:

- Define the whole number operations of addition, subtraction, multiplication, and division.
- Introduce the whole number operations to primary grade children.
- Administer whole number operations assessment tasks.
- Introduce whole number operations notation and number sentence format following a three-step process.
- Develop instructional activities and materials for whole number operations at the primary level.

This unit looks at arithmetic, which includes the areas that were conventionally the core of the elementary grades mathematics program; that is, the **whole number operations** of addition, subtraction, multiplication, and division (Charlesworth & Senger, 2001). Today, however, the term *mathematics* refers to all the related concepts and skills included in this text—algebra, geometry, number sense, data analysis, and so on. Mathematics is a much more inclusive content area than it used to be.

The NCTM (2000) standard on number and operations includes expectations for the understanding of operations and how they relate to each other and for fluent computation and making reasonable estimates (discussed in Unit 25). During the primary grades, students should reach an understanding of a variety of means for adding and subtracting and of the relationship between the two operations, of the effects of adding and subtracting whole numbers, and of situations where multiplication and division are used. Children should develop skill at whole number computation for addition and subtraction, should be able to use the basic addition and subtraction number combinations, and use many different computation tools such as "objects, mental computation, estimation, paper and pencil, and calculators" (p. 78).

The curriculum focal points (NCTM, 2007) for the primary level are organized by grades 1, 2, and 3. The focal points for grade 1 focus largely on number and operations:

- developing understandings of addition and subtraction strategies and addition and subtraction facts; and
- connecting with concepts of 10s and 1s and solving two-digit problems.

The focal points for grade 2 in number and operations focus on:

■ developing quick recall of addition and related subtraction facts;

■ developing fluency with multidigit addition and subtraction;

■ connecting with a beginning understanding of multiplication; and

■ connecting with applying their understanding of number to solving a variety of problems.

The focal points for grade 3 in number and operations focus on:

■ developing understandings of multiplication and division;

■ understanding and using basic multiplication and division facts;

■ connecting with algebra by developing an understanding of the patterns in multiplication and division; and

■ connecting with data analysis by using the whole number operations in collecting data and graphing.

Today, the most complex calculations are done with calculators and computers. However, children are encouraged to use estimation and mental computation. In order to reach an understanding of each operation, children must learn how to solve problems using conventional and/or invented **algorithms**, which are step-by-step procedures for solving problems (Warshauer & Warshauer, 2001, p. 23). Once this understanding is established, more can be accomplished by working on how to set up problems and then using technology to do the calculations. In this unit, methods are described for introducing children to whole number operations and whole number notation at a basic level. Once children understand the concepts, they can move on to more complex operations using calculators and computers to perform calculations.

Children naturally engage in the whole number operations of addition, subtraction, multiplication, and division prior to reaching the primary grades. In previous units (see Units 23, 24, and 25), the beginnings of the whole number operations are described as they grow out of naturalistic and informal experiences. Prior to entering first grade, young children also usually have an understanding of number symbols as they represent quantities. During the primary period (grades 1–3), children gradually learn the meaning of **action symbols** such as + (add), − (subtract), × (multiply), ÷ (divide), = (equals), < (less than), and > (greater than).

Teachers are expected to use state and locally developed lists of objectives and selected textbooks to provide a structure for planning instruction. Unfortunately, primary teachers tend to rely too heavily on textbooks, workbooks, and photocopied support materials. Conventionally, students are expected to be able to do paper-and-pencil arithmetic even though it might be developmentally inappropriate. Opportunities for the use of exploration as a route to the construction of concepts and operations are too seldom observed in the primary classroom. Students usually sit at individual desks with social interaction kept at a minimum (if allowed at all).

Constance Kamii is a major critic of the conventional approach to mathematics instruction in the primary grades. She presents her point of view in her books *Young Children Reinvent Arithmetic* (2000), *Young Children Continue to Reinvent Arithmetic, Second Grade* (2003), and *Young Children Reinvent Arithmetic, Third Grade* (1994). As a Piagetian, Kamii believes that—just as our ancestors did—children reinvent arithmetic through their own actions and needs rather than learning through what someone else tells them. Children need to reinvent arithmetic through naturalistic and informal exploration with naturally occurring problems and through group games. They should be encouraged to invent their own procedures and use their own thinking. Kamii explains that paper-and-pencil worksheet approaches remove the child from the logical thinking that is the heart of arithmetic. Kamii's emphasis on group games and social interaction as the basis for the understanding of arithmetic has its roots in Piaget's view that social interaction is essential as a stimulus for construction of knowledge. The following are examples of children solving problems through peer interaction.

■ Three nonconservers are going to drink juice. The server pours juice into glass A. Now he must pour equal amounts into glasses B and C, which are different in size and shape from each other and from glass A. The children discuss how to do this in a fair manner and arrive at a solution: Use glass A as a measuring cup to fill the other two glasses.

■ Derrick has written $7 + 4 = 10$, and Brent has written $7 + 4 = 12$. Their teacher has them explain to each other why they think that their respective answers are correct. Soon they discover that they are both wrong.

A danger in primary math instruction is that students will be pushed too fast before they have developed the cognitive capacity to understand the logical reasoning that underlies the operations. Keep in mind that children must be in the concrete operations period before they can successfully meet primary-level expectations. Beginning in kindergarten, standardized testing is performed each year, and teachers are pressured to teach the concepts and skills that are included in the tests. This pressure leads teachers to instruct arithmetic as a rote memory activity that has no logical meaning to the children. Children should be allowed to move at their own pace through primary math just as they did prior to entering first grade. They should also be allowed to invent their own procedures for solving problems. Herbert Ginsburg (1977) claims that young children naturally invent their own methods and should be able to use and experiment with them. For example, young children usually learn on their own to use counting methods for addition. When adding $2 + 2$, the child might say, "One, two, three, four" using fingers or objects. If left on their own, they will eventually stop counting because they've internalized $2 + 2 = 4$.

Carpenter, Carey, and Kouba (1990) point out that children enter first grade with informal concepts of the whole number operations. They also state the importance of observing the processes children use in solving problems. The authors believe that symbols should be introduced only to represent concepts that children already know. Instruction should begin with observations of naturalistic and informal activities.

Fuson, Grandau, and Sugiyama (2001) support the importance of informal teaching. "Such informal teaching can be done while children play, eat, get dressed, go up and down stairs, jump, and otherwise move through the day" (p. 522). During these activities, adults and more advanced peers can model mathematical concepts and skills, which children can then combine with understandings obtained during more structured mathematics activities.

In this text, a sequence of concept instruction is described with the caution to the teacher to bear in mind that children move at their own pace. As in previous units, naturalistic, informal, and structured activities are described. Structured activities emphasize the use of concrete materials, with paper and pencil introduced through children's natural interests when they are ready.

## BASIC COMBINATIONS (FACTS) AND ALGORITHMS

Isaacs and Carroll (1999) pose several questions about the value and purpose of learning the **basic facts** (or combinations) in the early grades. Will making first graders learn the addition facts interfere with their mathematical thinking? What kinds of instructional practices can build understanding and quick recall? Can children learn the facts through problem-solving activities, or is drill and practice needed? Isaacs and Carroll go on to provide answers to these questions. Knowing the facts is certainly essential to furthering mathematical understanding, but drill and practice and timed tests lead only to stress and anxiety. We should instead build on the knowledge children bring to school and support children in developing strategies for learning the basic facts. Children enter the primary grades with counting skills and an understanding that quantities can be broken down into parts. Facts can be learned through solving problems using their understanding of counting and parts and wholes. Building concrete models supports understanding and remembering. Having students share strategies will move them toward more efficient ones. Useful practice that is brief and nonstressful—such as games, computers, or even flash cards—can support the learning of basic facts.

Baroody (2006) contrasts the conventional drill and practice approach to instruction with the number sense approach to learning the facts with understanding. Children usually learn the facts in three phases (Baroody, 2006, p. 22) as follows.

- *Phase 1*. Uses object counting (blocks, fingers, tally marks) or verbal counting—for 5 + 2 the child says five and then counts on, using two fingers, to get 7 (typical first grader).

- *Phase 2*. Uses reasoning strategies to arrive at the answer to an unknown combination—for 5 + 4 the child thinks 4 + 4 = 8 and so one more would be 9 (typical second grader).

- *Phase 3*. Mastery is achieved as answers come quickly and accurately—"5 + 4 = 9" is responded without counting and reasoning (typical third grader).

The number sense view promotes learning the facts through discovering patterns and relationships that interconnect the basic combinations. Phases 1 and 2 serve this purpose by supporting the exploration and discovery that lead to seeing the patterns in each group of number facts. Adults should support children's use of informal strategies and focus on families of facts and their relationships. Children will gradually become more efficient. According to Baroody (2006), practice should be meaningful and should allow for flexible strategies.

Assessment should be process oriented in the primary grades; that is, children can use a number of strategies for solving problems. By the end of third grade and the beginning of fourth grade, children should be able to recall the addition and subtraction facts quickly and automatically.

*Algorithms* may be thought of as procedures, efficient methods, or rules for computation (Curcio & Schwartz, 1998). Several questions arise when it comes to instructional practice. Should algorithms be taught before, along with, or after children have had the opportunity to invent some of their own strategies? Curcio and Schwartz suggest that we begin with the children's own strategies and, through questioning, guide their reasoning toward more efficient and possibly conventional methods.

## COMPUTATIONAL FLUENCY

An important goal for the primary grades is the development of **computational fluency** with whole numbers (NCTM, 2000). Russell (2000) provides guidelines for developing computational fluency. Fluency involves three ideas: efficiency, accuracy, and flexibility. Efficiency means the student can proceed directly without being distracted from his goal. Accuracy depends on being careful and double-checking results. Flexibility means being able to try out more than one strategy for solving problems. Fluency goes beyond memorizing one procedure or algorithm. As they learn more basic facts, this knowledge can be applied to recording their methods of problem solving. Children in grades K–2 should be encouraged to invent computational methods as they invent strategies to solve problems (Reys & Reys, 1998). Children in the early grades should be encouraged to invent their own problem-solving procedures (Heuser, 2005).

## ACTION AND RELATIONAL SYMBOLS

At the primary level, children are usually introduced to the action and relational symbols. *Action symbols* show that some quantities have been or will be acted upon, or changed, in some way (+, −, ÷, ×); **relational symbols** show that quantities are in some way related (=, <, >). These symbols appear in **number sentences** that symbolize an operation, such as:

- 2 + 3 = 5 (two things put together in a group with three things is the same amount as five things).

- 5 > 2 (five is more than, or greater than, two).

Kamii (1994; 2003; Kamii & DeClark, 2000) and others have found that young children often learn to deal with these symbols without a genuine understanding of how they relate to real quantities. Children should work with operations mentally through concrete experiences before connecting these operations to symbols and using complete conventional written number sentences such as 1 + 5 = 6, 5 − 3 = 2, 6 > 2, and so on.

Kamii (2003; Kamii & DeClark, 2000) suggests that full number sentences (e.g., 4 + 2 = 6) should not be introduced until second grade. Children should be encouraged to devise their own notation systems and apply them as a bridge to formal notation. Children need experiences in joining and separating quantities

Children often need concrete help such as manipulatives or fingers when first doing written problems.

and verbalizing about their actions prior to really understanding what symbols represent. Just filling in blanks in a workbook or marking answers in a standardized test booklet does not indicate that children understand the deeper meaning of number sentences.

In summary, formal number sentences should be introduced gradually. First, children should have extensive exploratory experiences that provide opportunities to invent their own solutions to everyday problems. They should be encouraged to find their own systems of recording solutions using their own notation. Develop the language of number sentences through word problems that come from real-life experiences. Introduce formal number sentences when children have developed to the level where they can understand that number sentences are a shorthand representation for words. Introduce numeral notation first, then operational signs, and finally relational signs. Richardson's books (1984; 1999) are excellent resources for methods and materials that can be used for accomplishing these tasks. Some of these ideas for introducing formal symbolic notation will be described in the discussions that follow.

## INSTRUCTIONAL STRATEGIES

Fraivillig (2001) outlines instructional strategies for advancing children's mathematical thinking. Effective teaching includes three aspects: eliciting, supporting, and extending children's solution methods. This frame-

work is called advancing children's thinking (ACT). *Eliciting* (p. 456) involves supporting a variety of solutions for any problem by listening to children, encouraging elaboration, being accepting of errors, promoting collaborative problem solving, and being sure everyone has an opportunity to report. *Supporting* (p. 457) involves pointing out problems that are similar, providing background knowledge, supporting students as they review their strategies, putting symbolic representations of solutions on the board, and encouraging children to ask for help. *Extending* (p. 457) requires maintaining high standards and expectations for all children, encouraging the drawing of generalizations, listing all solutions on the board in order to promote reflection, encouraging children to try alternative solutions and more efficient solutions, and promoting enthusiasm for challenge. Overall, the learning must take place in a safe environment where all students feel comfortable and respected.

## Assessment

Observations and interviews can be used to assess children's progress in constructing operations with whole numbers. Assessment should be done through concrete activities with real-life or pretend situations. Assessment should be incorporated into instruction. Paper-and-pencil tests are not appropriate for primary students until they can read and comprehend story problems on their own. Assessment examples will be provided as each whole number operation is discussed.

To find out if children are ready to move on to whole number operations, use the assessment interviews in Appendix A, Concrete Operations: Level 8. These tasks include conservation of number; knowledge of symbols and sets; multiple classification; and class inclusion.

## ADDITION

Constructing the concept of addition involves an understanding that adding is putting together groups of objects to find out how many there are. It also involves learning the application of terms such as **total, sum,** and **equals,** as well as the operation signs (+ and =) that represent these terms, and connecting these amounts to symbols. Before children make these connections, they must understand quantity and what happens when quantities are combined.

## Assessment

Assessment of children's understanding of addition is more than finding out if they know the so-called number facts. It is important to observe the process each child goes through in dealing with quantities. Observing the process and questioning children regarding what they have done will reveal what they do and do not understand. Their mistakes are informative and can be used to help them develop a more accurate knowledge of arithmetic.

Observations can be made during naturalistic and informal activities. Dean figures out that if he has two dimes and his grandmother gives him four more, he will have six dimes. Liu Pei decides that if there are three children at one table, two at another, and four at a third, then she will need nine pieces of paper to pass out. Ann realizes that, instead of counting everyone to find out if there are enough pencils, she can record the number at each table, find the total, and compare it with the number of pencils in the box.

Observations can also be made during structured activities. Sara's teacher tells her to take groups of six cube blocks and place them in as many combinations of group sizes as she can. Does Sara realize that, however she arranges six objects (in groups of three and three; one and five; two, two, and two; two and four; or six and zero), there are still six altogether? The children are playing a card game called "Double War." Each player has two stacks of cards, which are turned over two cards at a time. The player with the higher sum gets the other player's two cards. The teacher can observe the children's strategies and whether they help each other. He can also suggest that they write and/or draw descriptions of their strategies.

As with the assessment of other math concepts, addition can also be measured using an interview approach. The following is a sample task.

## SAMPLE ASSESSMENT TASK

**9A**                            **Concrete Operations Ages 6–8**

**Addition, Combining Sets up to 10: Unit 27**

**METHOD:** Interview.

**SKILL:** Child is able to combine sets to form new sets up to ten.

**MATERIALS:** Twenty counters (cube blocks, Unifix Cubes, chips): ten of one color and ten of another.

**PROCEDURE:** Have the child select two groups of counters from each color so that the total is ten or less. Say, PUT THREE YELLOW CUBES OVER HERE AND FIVE BLUE CUBES OVER HERE. Child completes task. Say, NOW TELL ME, IF YOU PUT ALL THE CUBES IN ONE BUNCH, HOW MANY CUBES DO YOU HAVE ALTOGETHER? HOW DO YOU KNOW? Do this with combinations that add up to 1 through 10.

**EVALUATION:** Note if the child is able to make the requested groups with or without counting. Note the strategy used by the child to decide on the sum.
1. Does he begin with one and count all the blocks?
2. Does he count on? That is, in the example given, does he put his two small groups together and then say, "Three blocks, four, five, six, seven, eight. I have eight now"?
3. Does he just say, "Eight, because I know that three plus five is eight"?

**INSTRUCTIONAL RESOURCE:** Charlesworth, R., and Lind, K. K. (2010). *Math and science for young children* (6th ed.). Clifton Park, NY: Cengage Learning.

## Instruction

Instruction begins with naturalistic and informal experiences that familiarize children with quantities and how they relate to each other. Students can be guided toward constructing their own concepts if they are provided with games and word or story problems to solve and are encouraged to make up their own problems.

In *Young Children Reinvent Arithmetic* (2000), Constance Kamii and Georgia DeClark describe a number of types of games that can support the development of addition concepts. The following are examples of activities.

---

## ACTIVITIES

### Addition: Double War

**OBJECTIVE:** Constructing combinations of addends (i.e., 1 + 1, 1 + 2, etc.) up to four.

**MATERIALS:** Two decks of cards with different patterns on the back.

**PLAYING THE GAME:** Start using the cards with addends up to four (aces, twos, threes, and fours). Two children play together. To play the game, the children begin with half the cards in each of the two decks, which are stacked facedown next to each other in front of them. Without looking at the cards, they simultaneously turn over the top two cards from each deck. Each finds the total of her two cards. The child with the highest total keeps all four cards.

**FOLLOW-UP:** Add the cards with the next higher addends as the students become adept with the first four. If the game takes too long, remove some of the smaller addends as the larger ones are included. Have the students write and/or draw descriptions of their strategies.

### Addition: Board Games

**OBJECTIVE:** Constructing combinations of addends up to six.

**MATERIALS:** A pair of dice, a marker for each player (four), and a board game. Board games can be purchased or teacher made. Teacher-made games can be designed with themes that fit units in science and social studies. Some basic board-game patterns and the materials needed for construction are described in Unit 24. Board games at the primary level can be designed with more spaces than those in Unit 24 because older students may move farther on each turn and will have longer attention spans.

**PLAYING THE GAME:** Each player, in turn, rolls the dice, finds the sum of the roll, and moves the marker that many spaces.

**FOLLOW-UP:** Bring in new games as the students become skilled at playing the old ones. As the students become adept at playing board games, purchase or make some with pitfalls. That is, on some spaces the player might have to move backward or lose a turn (i.e., when a player lands on a red space, the dice are rolled again, and the player moves backward the sum of the dice; or, when a player lands on a certain space, a turn is lost).

---

The importance of problem solving was described in Unit 3. Placing operations in the context of real-life situations makes them come alive for the students so they can see the practical applications of mathematics. Richardson (1984, 1999) suggests that the children act out stories using real objects from around the room as props. For example, Derrick brings six books from the library center and Theresa brings four. "How many did they bring altogether?" Derrick and Theresa actually demonstrate by going to the library center and obtaining the number of books in the problem. Trang Fung joins Dean and Sara. "How many children were there to start with?" "How many are there now?" Again, the children act out the situation. Richardson (1999) provides resources for acting out story problems with Unifix Cubes and other objects.

Carpenter and colleagues (1990) identify four types of addition problems.

*Join, result unknown.* Kim has two cars. Mario gives her five more cars. How many does Kim have altogether?

*Separate, start unknown.* Kim has some cars and gives two to Mario. Now she has five cars. How many cars did Kim have to start with?

*Part-part-whole, whole unknown.* Kim has two yellow cars and five blue cars. How many cars does she have?

*Compare, compare quantity unknown.* Mario has two cars. Kim has five more cars than Mario. How many cars does Kim have?

The authors caution that textbooks often contain only join and separate problems even though all four types should be introduced. A further caution is that these types are not formulas to be memorized but just problem variations that children need to explore.

As children become more advanced, the numbers can be larger and more addends can be included. More complex, **nonroutine problems** should also be used (see Unit 3).

Once the children have had some experiences with teacher-made problems, they can create their own problems.

## ACTIVITIES

### Addition: Story Problems

**OBJECTIVE:** To construct the concept of addition by solving story problems.

**MATERIALS:** Twenty small toys that fit a current unit. For example:

- Miniature dinosaurs during a dinosaur unit
- Miniature dogs, cats, horses, etc., during a pet unit
- Miniature farm animals during a farm unit
- Miniature vehicles during a safety unit

**DEVELOPING THE PROBLEMS:** Let the students act out the problems as you tell the stories.

- FIND THREE PLANT-EATING DINOSAURS. FIND FOUR MEAT-EATING DINOSAURS. HOW MANY DINOSAURS DO YOU HAVE?
- MARY HAS SOME PUPPIES. SHE SELLS THREE PUPPIES. NOW SHE HAS TWO PUPPIES LEFT. HOW MANY DID SHE HAVE TO START WITH?
- OFFICER SMITH GAVE TICKETS TO THE DRIVERS OF TWO CARS FOR SPEEDING. OFFICER VARGAS GAVE THE DRIVERS OF THREE CARS TICKETS FOR GOING TOO SLOW ON THE INTERSTATE. HOW MANY TICKETS DID THE OFFICERS GIVE?
- FARMER SMITH HAS FIVE HORSES. FARMER VALDEZ HAS THREE MORE HORSES THAN FARMER SMITH. HOW MANY HORSES DOES FARMER VALDEZ HAVE?
- FOUR PUPPIES WENT OUT TO PLAY. TWO PUPPIES JUMPED IN A MUD PUDDLE. HOW MANY MUDDY FEET WERE THERE? HOW MANY DRY FEET?

**FOLLOW-UP:** Create problems to fit units and other activities and events.

*(continued)*

## Addition: Creating Problems Using Dice or a Fishbowl

**OBJECTIVE:** The children will create their own addition problems.

**MATERIALS:** A pair of dice or a container (fishbowl) full of numerals written on small pieces of cardboard cut into fish shapes, objects such as cube blocks, chips, or Unifix Cubes.

**PLAYING THE GAME:** Either by rolling the dice or picking two fish, each child obtains two addends. He counts out the amount for each addend and then tells how many objects or fish he has.

**FOLLOW-UP:** Once students are having an easy time making up problems using the dice or the written numerals as cues, suggest that they write or dictate their favorite problem, draw it, and write or dictate the solution. For example, Brent's dog is expecting pups. He writes, "I have one dog. I hope she has five pups." Then he draws his dog and the five pups. He writes, "Then I will have six dogs."

Using number symbols is referred to as **notation**. Gradually, number symbols can be connected to problems as you find that the children understand the process of addition and understand class inclusion. Although most first graders can fill in the blanks correctly on worksheets, this does not indicate a real understanding of what notation means. To find out if a child really understands notation, present a problem such as the following.

Show the child several (four, five, or six) counters. Then show how you add some (two, three, or four) more. Then say, "Write on your paper what I did." Even at the end of first grade you will find very few children who will write the correct notation (i.e., 5 + 3 = 8). It is very common for first graders to write the first and last numeral (5 8) or to write all three (5 3 8) and omit

the action symbols. They may also be unable to tell you what they did and why. It is important that the use of notation be an integral part of concrete problem-solving activities.

Richardson (1984, 1999) suggests that formal instruction in connecting symbols to the process of addition begin with modeling of the writing of equations. After acting out a problem such as described previously, write the problem on the chalkboard, explaining that this is another way to record the information. For example, "Another way to write three cows plus six cows makes nine cows is: 3 + 6 = 9 (three plus six equals nine)." Help the children learn what the plus sign means by playing games and doing activities that require the use of the plus sign with the equals sign. For example, try the following activity.

## ACTIVITIES

### Addition: Using Notation at the Connecting Level

**OBJECTIVE:** Children will connect symbols to problems using numerals and the plus operation symbol.

**MATERIALS:** Objects to count and one die.

**PLAYING THE GAME:** Children take turns rolling the die to find out how many to add. For example, a three is rolled. Each child counts out three counters, and the teacher writes 3 on the board. A five is rolled. The students count out groups of five to put with their groups of three, and the teacher writes 3 + 5.

**FOLLOW-UP:** After working in small groups with the teacher, students can work independently with problems written on cards: 2 + 3, 4 + 6, and so on. As you go by, observe what they do, and ask them to read the problems to you.

Children sometimes look upon the equals sign as indicating that the answer is coming next rather than understanding that it indicates there is the same amount on each side of the equation. This concept can be clarified using a balance scale to explore equality.

When the children are comfortable with connecting the symbols to the problems and using the plus symbol, they can begin to write the notation themselves. Start with problems in which you write the notation, and have the children copy what you do before they go on to independent work. For example, have everyone pick five groups of five counters each. Then tell them to separate each group of five counters as many ways as they can, and you write the results.

$$
\begin{array}{cccccccc}
1 + 4 = 5 & & 1 & 2 & 1 & 2 & 5 \\
2 + 3 = 5 & & +4 & +3 & 1 & 2 & +0 \\
1 + 1 + 3 = 5 & & 5 & 5 & +3 & +1 & 5 \\
2 + 2 + 1 = 5 & & & & 5 & 5 \\
5 + 0 = 5 & & & & &
\end{array}
$$

After you write each equation, have the children write it on a piece of paper and put it next to the counters they have counted out. Follow up by having the students work independently, finding out how many ways they can break the amounts up to six and write the equations. When they are doing well up to six, have them move on to seven and above.

## SUBTRACTION

To conceptualize subtraction is to develop an understanding that subtracting involves taking objects away to find out how many are left or comparing groups of objects to find out the difference between them. It also involves learning the application of terms such as minus, difference, and equal as well as the action signs ($-$ and $=$) that represent these terms. Subtraction also involves thinking about **more than (>)** and **less than (<)** and the symbols that stand for these relationships. It also includes connecting to symbols as a shorthand notation for concrete operations. As with addition, before children make the connections to and between symbols, they must understand quantity and what happens when something is taken away from a group or when two groups are compared.

## Assessment

Assessment of children's understanding of addition is more than finding out if they know the so-called number facts. It is important to observe the process each child goes through in dealing with quantities. Observing the process and questioning children regarding what they have done will reveal what they do and do not understand. Their mistakes are informative and can be used to help them develop a more accurate knowledge of arithmetic.

As with addition, assessment of children's understanding of subtraction should involve more than mere number facts. Observing and questioning children about their processes for dealing with quantities will indicate the level of their knowledge.

Observations can be made during naturalistic and informal activities. Chan figures out that, if there are ten more minutes until school is out and if Ms. Hebert says that they will start to get ready to leave in five minutes, then they will have five minutes to get ready. Jason has ten bean seeds. He decides that he can give Ann four because the six he will have left will be enough for his seed-sprouting experiment. Six children are allowed to work in the science center at one time. Brent notices that there are only four children there now. He suggests to Derrick that they hurry over while there is room for two more. Vanessa observes that there is room for eight children in the library center, whereas six at a time may work in the math center. Thus there is room for two more in the library center than in the math center.

Observations can be made during structured activities. Dean is trying to figure out how many different amounts he can take away from five. Mrs. Red Fox notes that Dean is well organized and systematic as he constructs one group of five after another and takes a different amount away until he has the combinations five minus zero, one, two, three, four, and five. Derrick and Liu Pei are playing "Double War." They have to subtract the amount that is smaller from the amount that is larger. Mr. Wang can note whether the children can figure out the correct differences and whether they help each other.

Subtraction can be assessed using an interview approach. The following is a sample task.

## SAMPLE ASSESSMENT TASK

**9B**                                                    **Concrete Operations Ages 6–8**

**Subtraction, Sets of Ten and Less: Unit 27**

**METHOD:**  Interview.

**SKILL:**  Child is able to subtract groups to make new groups using groups of ten and smaller.

**MATERIALS:**  Twenty counters (cube blocks, Unifix Cubes, chips): ten of one color and ten of another and a small box or other small container.

**PROCEDURE:**  Pick out a group of ten or fewer counters. Say, I HAVE SEVEN CUBES. I'M GOING TO HIDE SOME IN THE BOX. (Hide three in the box.) NOW HOW MANY DO I HAVE LEFT? HOW MANY DID I HIDE? If the child cannot answer, give him seven of the other color cubes and ask him to take three away and tell you how many are left. Do this with amounts of ten and less. For the less mature or younger child, start with five and less.

**EVALUATION:**  Note if the child is able to solve the problem and the process used. Note whether the child has to count or whether he just knows without counting.

**INSTRUCTIONAL RESOURCE:**  Charlesworth, R., and Lind, K. K. (2010). *Math and science for young children* (6th ed.). Clifton Park, NY: Cengage Learning.

## Instruction

Just as with addition, instruction should involve informal experiences that familiarize children with how quantities are related to each other. Again, providing students with games or story problems can help them to construct their own concepts and problems. Once the students evidence an understanding of addition, subtraction can be introduced. Children can work with both addition and subtraction problems so that they can learn the clues for deciding which operation to use.

The game "Double War" can be modified and played as a subtraction game by having the player with the largest difference between her pair of cards keep all four cards. As with addition, begin with numbers up to four and then gradually include higher numbers as the children become adept at the game. Board games can also be purchased or devised that use subtraction as the operation that indicates which way to move. A board game could be made where all the moves are backward. The theme might be running away from a wild animal or going home from a friend's house. Or dice could be thrown, and each move would be the difference between the two.

Of course, word or story problems are an essential ingredient in the instruction of subtraction, just as they are for addition. Problems should be set in real-life contexts and acted out. For example, suppose Derrick and Theresa have brought ten books from the library center. The activity could be continued by asking children to take different numbers of books back to the library center and finding out how many are left after each trip. Place children in groups of different sizes. If there are five children in this group and three in this group, which group has more? How many more? How will we find out?

There are a number of different basic patterns that can be used for subtraction story problems. Carpenter and colleagues (1990) identify seven types of subtraction problems, as follows.

*Join, change unknown.* Kim has three cars. How many more cars will she need to have eight altogether?

*Join, start unknown.* Kim has some cars, and Mario gives her three more cars. Now she has eight cars. How many cars did Kim have to start with?

*Separate, result unknown.* Kim had eight cars and she gave Mario three cars. How many cars does Kim have left?

*Separate, change unknown.* Kim had eight cars and gave some to Mario. Now she has five cars. How many did she give to Mario?

*Part-part-whole, part unknown.* Kim has eight cars. Five are yellow and the rest are green. How many are green?

*Compare, difference unknown.* Kim has eight cars and Mario has three cars. How many more cars does Kim have than Mario?

*Compare, referent unknown.* Kim has eight cars. She has five more cars than Mario. How many cars does Mario have?

As with addition, once the children have experiences with teacher-devised story problems, they can dictate or write their own. The dice/fishbowl game can be modified for subtraction. Children can also dictate or write original problems, draw them, and write or dictate the solutions.

Subtraction notation can be introduced gradually. Number symbols can be connected to problems as you find that the children have an understanding of the process of subtraction. To find out if a child really understands notation, the same type of procedure can be used as for addition. That is, show the child several counters (five, six, or seven). Have her tell you how many you have. Hide one or more of the counters, and ask the child to show you on paper what you did. Do not be surprised if very few late first graders and only some second graders will be able to write the correct equation.

Formal introduction of subtraction can begin with modeling. Act out a problem and then explain that there is another way to record the information. Write the number sentence for the problem on the chalkboard. For example, "Another way to write five rabbits take away three rabbits is $5 - 3 = 2$ (five minus three equals two)." Help the children learn what the minus sign means by playing games and doing activities that require its use with the equals sign. For example, try the following activity.

## ACTIVITIES

### Subtraction: Using Notation at the Connecting Level

**OBJECTIVE:** The children will connect symbols to problems using numerals and the minus action symbol.

**MATERIALS:** Objects to count and two dice.

**PLAYING THE GAME:** The children take turns rolling the dice to find out which numbers to subtract. First they identify the larger number and count out that amount of counters. The teacher writes [larger number −]. Then they remove the smaller number of counters, and the teacher continues [larger number − smaller number]. Then the children identify how many are left in the original pile, and the teacher completes the equation [larger number − smaller number = difference]. For example, they roll six and two. They make a group of six counters, and the teacher writes $6 -$. Then they remove two counters, and the teacher continues: $6 - 2$. Then they identify the difference (four). The teacher finishes the equation: $6 - 2 = 4$.

**FOLLOW-UP:** After working in small groups with the teacher, students can work independently with problems written on cards: $5 - 1$, $3 - 2$, etc. They can also make up problems using dice or pulling numbers out of a fishbowl. As you observe what the children are doing, stop and ask them to read the problems to you.

As with addition, when the students are comfortable with connecting the symbols to the problems and using the minus symbol, they can begin to write the notation themselves. Start with problems where you write the notation and the children copy you before they go on to independent work. For example, have everyone pick six counters. Have them see what kinds of problems appear as different amounts are taken away. After each problem, take a new group of six so the problems can be compared. You write the results of each takeaway on the chalkboard (e.g., $6 - 1 = 5$); have the children copy it on a piece of paper and put it next to the counters they have counted out. Follow up by having the students work independently, finding out how many subtraction problems they can discover starting with groups of different amounts up through six. When they are doing well up to six, have them move on to seven and above.

The notation for greater (more) than (>) and less than (<) is conventionally introduced in first grade along with subtraction but is usually not really understood until grade 3. For the most part, students in early primary grades work with *more* and *less* using concrete materials such as those described in Unit 11. As they begin to understand the concepts, the children can apply them to playing games. For example, lotto and bingo boards (see Unit 24) can be used. For bingo the players can roll a die and cover a square on their card containing a number or set that is more than or less than the number rolled. For lotto they would pick a numeral or set card and again cover a card on the board that was either more than or less than the numeral or set on the card. As students become familiar with the action symbols, cards could be used that indicate that they pick an amount or numeral that is > (more or greater than) or < (less than) one of those on the card. They could then move on to using cards that indicate an amount such as [__ > 2] or [__ < 5] and thus be required the use of addition or subtraction to arrive at a selection.

## MULTIPLICATION

Conceptualizing multiplication requires that the students understand what equal quantities are. Then they can proceed to learn that multiplication is a shorthand way of adding equal quantities. That is, $4 \times 3$ is the same as $3 + 3 + 3 + 3$. Multiplication also involves learning the application of terms such as **factors** (the two numbers that are operated on) and **product** (the result of the operation). Students also learn the action terms **times** and *equals* and connect them to the action signs ($\times$ and $=$). Multiplication with concrete objects was introduced prior to the primary level and continues at this level for most primary students. Notation and the more formal aspects may be introduced toward the end of the primary level, but students are not usually proficient at the most fundamental level until fourth grade.

## ASSESSMENT

Assessment of children's understanding of multiplication, as with the other whole number operations, is more than finding out if children know the number facts. It is important to observe the process each child goes through in dealing with quantities and to ask questions that will reveal the thoughts behind their actions.

Observations can be made during naturalistic and informal activities. Use the terms *rows, stacks,* and *groups* to refer to equal groups that will be added. There is no rush to use the term *times*. Many children learn to recite the times tables by heart without any understanding of what *times* really means. Children must first understand that, when they multiply, they are not counting individual objects but rather groups of objects. Watch for incidents when children work with equal groups. For example, Dean comments that every child at his table has three carrot sticks. Theresa makes sure that each of the six children working in the science center receives four bean seeds to plant. Chan tells Ms. Hebert that he has purchased three miniature dinosaurs for each of the five friends invited to his birthday party. She asks him if he can figure out how many he bought altogether.

Multiplication can also be assessed by using an interview approach. The following is a sample task.

## SAMPLE ASSESSMENT TASK

**9F**                                                                    **Concrete Operations Ages 7–8**

**Multiplication, Readiness: Unit 27**

| | |
|---|---|
| **METHOD:** | Interview. |
| **SKILL:** | Child is able to demonstrate readiness for multiplication by constructing equal groups of different sizes from groups of the same size. |
| **MATERIALS:** | Twenty counters (cube blocks, Unifix Cubes, chips). |
| **PROCEDURE:** | Make two groups of six counters each. Ask the child, MAKE THREE GROUPS OF TWO CHIPS (BLOCKS, CUBES) EACH WITH THIS BUNCH OF SIX CHIPS (BLOCKS, CUBES). When the child finishes (right or wrong), point to the other group of counters. NOW MAKE TWO GROUPS OF THREE WITH THESE CHIPS (BLOCKS, CUBES). |
| **EVALUATION:** | Note if the child is able to make the two different subgroups. Children who are not ready for multiplication will become confused and not see the difference between the two tasks. |

**INSTRUCTIONAL RESOURCE:** Charlesworth, R., and Lind, K. K. (2010). *Math and science for young children* (6th ed.). Clifton Park, NY: Cengage Learning.

## Instruction

Just as with addition and subtraction, instruction in multiplication begins with naturalistic and informal experiences that familiarize children with quantities and how they relate to each other. Students can be guided toward constructing their own concepts if they are provided with games and story problems to solve and are encouraged to make up their own problems. Richardson (1984, 1999) suggests that the children should first be asked to look for equal groups in the environment. How many tables have four chairs? How many girls have two barrettes in their hair? How many children have three cookies for dessert? How many parts of the body can they identify that come in groups of two? What parts do cars have that come in groups of four?

Of course, word or story problems are an essential ingredient in the instruction of multiplication, just as they are for subtraction and addition. Problems should be set in real-life contexts and acted out. Dean gives four children two crayons each. How many crayons did he pass out? Chan makes three stacks of books. He puts three books in each stack. How many books does he have? Ann gives each of the five people at her table four pieces of paper. How many pieces of paper did she pass out?

Build models of multiplication problems with the students. Counters can be stacked, put in rows, and placed in groups as illustrated in Figure 27–1. For example, working with inch cubes:

- Make three stacks of four cubes each.
- Make four rows of five cubes each.
- Make six groups of two cubes each.

Notation can be introduced gradually. Number symbols can be connected to problems as you find that the children have an understanding of the process of multiplication. Formal introduction of multiplication can begin with modeling. Act out a problem, and then explain that there is another way to record the information. Write the number sentence for the problem on the chalkboard. For example: "Another way to write 'Dean gave four children two crayons each' is [4 groups of 2 = 8].

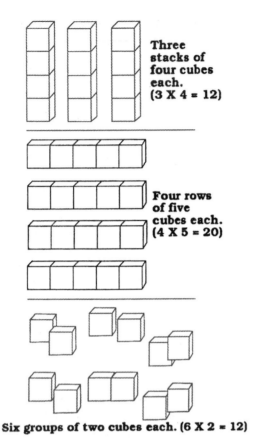

Three stacks of four cubes each. (3 X 4 = 12)

Four rows of five cubes each. (4 X 5 = 20)

Six groups of two cubes each. (6 X 2 = 12)

**Figure 27–1** Equal rows, stacks, and groups are the basis of multiplication.

Another way to write 'Chan has three stacks of three books' is [3 stacks of $3 = 9$]." Do several problems in this manner. Then introduce the multiplication sign. First model. Explain that there is an even shorter way to write problems. Erase "stacks of" or "groups of" and write $\times$ in its place. Then write problems on the board and have the children work them out with their counters. Next, have them work out problems and copy you as you write the whole equation, that is [$4 \times 2 = 8$]. Finally, have them make models and write the equations on their own.

The following is an example of an independent activity that can be done with multiplication using notation.

To find out if a child really understands notation, the same type of procedure can be used as was used for addition and subtraction. For example, show the child three or more equivalent groups and explain that you are going to put the groups together into one group. Ask him to write what you did. If you showed three groups of four, he should write [$3 \times 4 = 12$].

## DIVISION

Division is an activity that children engage in frequently during their natural everyday activities (see Unit 25). They are encouraged to share equally, and they are often asked to pass out items so that everyone has the

## ACTIVITIES

### Multiplication: Using Notation at the Connecting Level

**OBJECTIVE:** The children will connect symbols to problems using numerals and the times action symbol.

**MATERIALS:** Counters, a die, several small containers, and a sheet for recording the problems.

**ACTIVITY:** Children can work on their own writing equations. First they decide how many containers to use. They can roll the die or just pick a number. They line up the cups and then, starting with zero and one at a time, fill the cups and write the resulting equation. For example, if they pick four cups, they would first put zero blocks in each cup and write the equation, then one block in each, then two, three, and so on. Their work would look like that shown in Figure 27–2.

**FOLLOW-UP:** Develop some more independent activities using the resources suggested on the Online Companion for this unit.

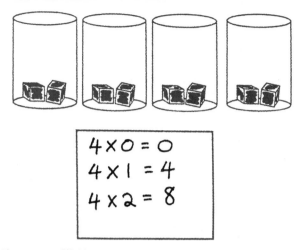

**Figure 27–2** Writing equations using counters and containers.

same amount. Formal instruction in division is usually introduced toward the end of the primary period during the third grade, but children are not expected to be proficient in doing division problems until the fifth grade. Division is used to solve two types of problems.

■ *Grouping* is the process used to find out how many subgroups of a particular size a larger group

contains. For example, George has 15 blocks. He wants to make towers that are five blocks high. How many can he make?

■ *Sharing* is the process of dividing a larger group into a particular number of groups to find out how many items will be included in that number of subgroups. Six children will work in the science center exploring the reaction of different types of items when they are touched by magnets. There are 32 items. How many will each child get? Are there any left over?

The children do not have to distinguish between these types of problems, which serve mainly as a guide for making up problems for them to explore. Eventually they will learn the terminology of division: **dividend ÷ divisor = quotient** and, if some are left over, **remainder**.

## Assessment

Assessment of children's understanding of division focuses on the processes they use to group and to share. The following task can be used to assess the child's understanding of grouping and sharing.

### SAMPLE ASSESSMENT TASK

**9I**                                                 **Concrete Operations Ages 7–8**

**Division, Basic Concept: Unit 27**

| | |
|---|---|
| **METHOD:** | Interview. |
| **SKILL:** | Child can demonstrate an understanding that division consists of grouping or sharing objects. |
| **MATERIALS:** | Thirty counters (cube blocks, Unifix Cubes, chips) and five small containers (such as clear plastic glasses). |
| **PROCEDURE:** | Put out eight chips and four containers. DIVIDE UP THE CHIPS SO THAT EACH CUP HAS THE SAME AMOUNT. When the chips are divided ask, HOW MANY CUBES DO YOU HAVE IN EACH CUP? The child should respond "Two in each cup" rather than "I have two, two, and two." Try the same procedure with more cups and larger amounts to divide. Then try it with uneven amounts. Note if the child becomes confused or can recognize that there are more cups than are needed. Also do some sharing problems; for |

(*continued*)

example, put out 16 chips. I WANT TO GIVE THREE FRIENDS THE SAME AMOUNT OF CHIPS. HOW MANY WILL EACH ONE RECEIVE? ARE THERE ANY LEFT OVER?

**EVALUATION:** Note how the children handle the problem. Do they proceed in an organized fashion? Can they deal with the remainders?

**INSTRUCTIONAL RESOURCE:** Charlesworth, R., and Lind, K. K. (2010) *Math and science for young children* (6th ed.). Clifton Park, NY: Cengage Learning.

Passing out things so that everyone gets an equal amount is the initial step in division.

## Instruction

Division also begins with naturalistic and informal experiences. Children can be given many tasks that give them division experiences. Passing out items, putting items into groups to be shared, and finding out if there is enough for everyone are opportunities to develop the division concept. Games and story problems can be used as guides in supporting the child's construction of the concept of division as she ventures into more formal activities.

As with the other whole number operations, begin formal instruction by doing concrete problems. As Richardson (1984) suggests, tell the children stories and have them act them out. Start with real objects from the classroom. Here are two examples.

■ Ann has 16 pieces of paper. Each child in her group needs four pieces. How many children can receive four pieces of paper?

■ Jason, Chan, and Vanessa want to feed the guinea pig. The guinea pig gets six pellets of food. How many pellets can each child give it?

Next, have the children act out similar stories, using counters to represent real objects. Have the children make many models by constructing rows and stacks and dividing them into groups.

## ACTIVITIES

### Division: Making Models

**OBJECTIVE:** The children will construct models of division.

**MATERIALS:** Counters (cube blocks, Unifix Cubes, chips) and several 16-ounce clear plastic cups.

**ACTIVITY:** Using different amounts initially and having the children divide them up into groups of different sizes and into different numbers of groups, have the students do many problems using the following patterns:

1. MAKE A ROW (TRAIN) WITH (number of) BLOCKS (CUBES, CHIPS). HOW MANY STACKS OF (number) CAN YOU MAKE? DIVIDE YOUR ROW (TRAIN) OF (number) INTO (number of) ROWS. HOW MANY CUBES (BLOCKS, CHIPS) ARE IN EACH ROW?

2. GET (number) CUPS. DIVIDE (number) CUBES INTO EACH CUP SO THAT THERE IS THE SAME AMOUNT OF CUBES IN EACH CUP. Continue with different numbers of cups and counters.

**FOLLOW-UP:** Develop some more independent activities using the resources suggested on the Online Companion for this unit.

Division notation can be introduced with modeling. Act out problems just as you did with the other whole number operations.

■ "John has twelve crackers." Write [12] on the board. "He has three friends. He wants to give himself and each friend the same number of crackers." Write [12 ÷ 4]. "Each child got three crackers." Write [12 ÷ 4 = 3].

■ "The children are going to explore how pendulums work. There are four pendulums and eight children. How many children will have to share each pendulum? Eight children (write 8), divided by four pendulums (write [8 ÷ 4]) equals two children must share each pendulum" (write [8 ÷ 4 = 2]).

After you have modeled several problems, the children can go to the next step by acting out the problems

and copying what you write. Next, you can give them problems that they can act out with counters and write the equations themselves. When the children have completed the equations, you can write them on the board and they can check theirs. Check each child's model and equation. Note whether there are any difficulties, and help children figure out how to act out and write the equation correctly. Move on to giving the children written problems (i.e., 10 ÷ 2), and ask them to act the problems out using counters. Finally, have them make up their own problems, act them out, draw them, and write them.

To find out if a child really understands notation, use the same procedure as suggested for the other whole number operations. Namely, act out division and then ask the children to write what you did. For example, count out fifteen counters and divide them into five groups of three. See whether the children can write

[15 ÷ 5 = 3] and tell you that fifteen divided into five groups makes three in each group.

## INTEGRATION WITH OTHER CONTENT AREAS

Whole number operations can be applied in the other major content areas, as depicted in Figure 27–3. With an art project, for example, students can create squared paper designs, count the number of each color used in their design, and add the total number of squares included. For science they can do environmental math such as graphing the contents of the trash can in the classroom and determining which type of trash is found in the largest amount. Social studies offers many opportunities, such as adding up the cost of a meal in a restaurant, dividing food into equal portions, or finding out how many of an item will be needed if each person in the group gets a fixed amount. Books, as previously described in Unit 15, offer many opportunities for solving whole number problems.

## TECHNOLOGY

Computers and hand calculators are useful tools for supporting the exploration of whole number operations and the properties of whole numbers. There are a multitude of software and Internet resources available for working with basic whole number operations. Most of these programs are designed to help children remember the basic addition, subtraction, multiplication, and division facts. Many have interesting graphics that catch the children's attention and make drill and practice fun. With the capability of letting the children know right away whether the response is correct, the programs give the children immediate feedback and allow them to move along at their own pace.

During preprimary activities, children have explored some of the basic calculator capabilities. During primary activities, the calculator can be used for further exploration, for checking and comparing with manual calculations, and for problem solutions. A basic activity with the calculator is the exploration of multiples.

Young children are fascinated with rhymes such as "Two, four, six, eight, who do we appreciate?" This type of counting is called **skip counting**. Skip counting in this example defines the multiples of two—that is, all the numbers that result when a series is multiplied by two ($2 \times 2 = 4$, $2 \times 3 = 6$, $2 \times 4 = 8$, etc.). Children can explore these properties with the calculator through calculator counting (Figure 27–4).

## IDEAS FOR CHILDREN WITH SPECIAL NEEDS

In the primary grades, children are expected to become proficient readers. This is a special challenge for ELL students, and the challenge is compounded when they are given written or oral math problems to solve. Garrison, Ponce, and Amarel (2007) explored how mathematics teachers can find ways to help ELL students understand both the language and the mathematical concepts. Garrison and colleagues studied the results of a problem-based approach featuring adaptations for English Language Learners compared with more traditional instruction—with no ELL adaptations—in two first-grade classrooms that included ELL students. "Our study found that students in the problem-based class were better and more persistent problem solvers than their peers in the traditional mathematics class" (Garrison et al., 2007, p. 13).

The teacher started the year with simple problems using familiar vocabulary. These first problems were in the present tense and any new words were discussed. Children first worked independently and then were put into pairs. A successful child was paired with a struggling child. Finally children shared their strategies with the whole class. Gradually the problems became more complex. By combining the teaching of English with mathematics, the class gained in both areas.

## EVALUATION

Evaluation, just as with assessment, should be done first with concrete tasks and should involve observing both the process and the product. The tasks in Appendix A and in this unit can be used for evaluation as well as

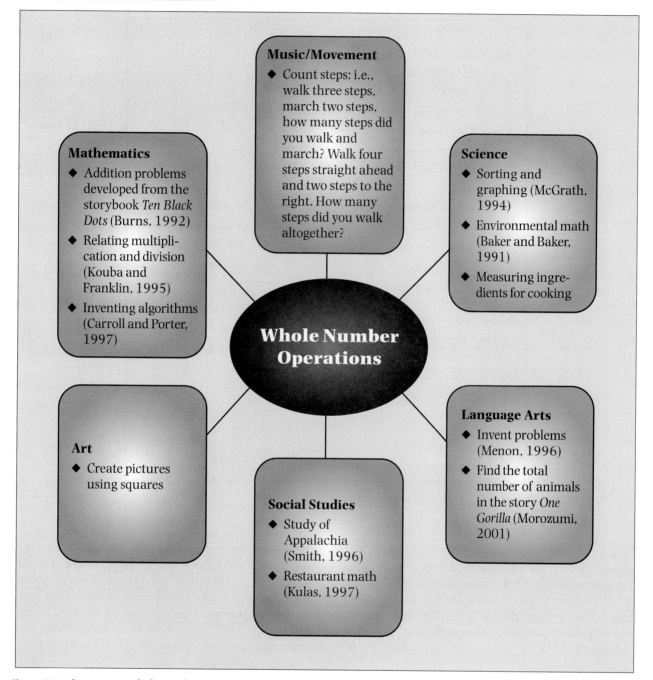

**Music/Movement**
- Count steps: i.e., walk three steps, march two steps, how many steps did you walk and march? Walk four steps straight ahead and two steps to the right. How many steps did you walk altogether?

**Mathematics**
- Addition problems developed from the storybook *Ten Black Dots* (Burns, 1992)
- Relating multiplication and division (Kouba and Franklin, 1995)
- Inventing algorithms (Carroll and Porter, 1997)

**Science**
- Sorting and graphing (McGrath, 1994)
- Environmental math (Baker and Baker, 1991)
- Measuring ingredients for cooking

**Whole Number Operations**

**Art**
- Create pictures using squares

**Social Studies**
- Study of Appalachia (Smith, 1996)
- Restaurant math (Kulas, 1997)

**Language Arts**
- Invent problems (Menon, 1996)
- Find the total number of animals in the story *One Gorilla* (Morozumi, 2001)

**Figure 27–3** Integrating whole number operations across the curriculum.

COUNT WITH YOUR CALCULATOR

Push Ⓒ ⓪ ⊕ ② ⊜

What do you see? _____

Push ⊜ again

What do you see? _____

What will the calculator show if you

push ⊜ again? _____

Do it. Were you correct? _____

Push ⊜ ⊜ ⊜ .

Guess what the calculator will show each time. _____ _____ _____

What happened? _____

Complete the following. Then use your calculator to see if you are correct.

Push Ⓒ ⓪ ⊕ ③ ⊜

The calculator will show _____

Push

⊜ _____

⊜ _____

⊜ _____

Push Ⓒ ⓪ ⊕ ④ ⊜

The calculator will show _____

Push

⊜ _____

⊜ _____

⊜ _____

Figure 27–4  The calculator can be used to count by equal multiples.

for initial assessment. Standardized achievement tests should not be administered until the students have the concepts internalized with concrete activities. For guidelines for testing young children, see the National Association for the Education of Young Children (NAEYC, 1991) position statement on standardized testing of children aged 3–8.

## SUMMARY

The whole number operations of addition, subtraction, multiplication, and division have begun to de-velop through naturalistic and informal experiences during the preprimary years. As children's cognitive development takes them into the concrete operational level, they are ready for the move into learning about action symbols and written notation. Problem solving with whole numbers involves the learning of basic facts and algorithms as well as developing computational fluency. Conventionally, children start with addition and subtraction in the beginning of the primary period (grade 1). They move on to more complex addition and subtraction, and are introduced to multiplication, in the second grade. Division is usually introduced in the third grade. Each operation begins with informal activities and acting out problems using concrete objects and then moves gradually into the use of formal notation and written problems. Story or word problems that put the operations into real-life contexts are the core around which the whole number operations are con-

structed in the young child's mind. English Language Learners can improve mathematical skill and increase their knowledge of English through a problem-solving approach to mathematics.

## KEY TERMS

action symbols
algorithms
basic facts
computational
    fluency
dividend
divisor
equals

factors
less than (<)
more than (>)
nonroutine problems
notation
number sentences
product
quotient

relational symbols
remainder
skip counting
sum
times
total
whole number
    operations

## SUGGESTED ACTIVITIES

1. Develop at least two of the independent activities suggested by Kathy Richardson and/or the group games described by Constance Kamii in their respective books. Add the instructions to your Activity File. If possible, try out the activities with one or more primary grade children. Report to the class regarding what you developed, whom you tried it with, what happened, and how well you believe it worked.

2. Do a comparison of concrete versus paper-and-pencil modes of math assessment. Select three whole number operations assessment tasks from this unit or Appendix A. Devise a paper-and-pencil test that includes the same kinds of problems. Use the interview tasks with two primary students. Return a week later and use the conventional paper-and-pencil test with the same two students. Take careful notes on the process used by the students to solve the problems. Write a report describing the two types of assessment tasks; the results, including the students' performance; and your comparison and evaluation of the two methods of assessment.

3. Observe in two or more primary classrooms during times when math activities are occurring. Your report to the class should include a description of what you observed, how the instruction compared with the methods described in this unit, and suggestions for any changes you would make if you were teaching in those classrooms.

4. Review some whole number operations software using the format described in Activity 5, Unit 2. You might try one of the following programs if available.

   ■ *Flash Action Software—Addition and Subtraction* (ages 6 and up; Grand Haven, MI: School Zone Publishing)

   ■ *Math Missions: The Race to Spectacle City Arcade* (ages 5 to 8; New York: Scholastic, http://www.kidsclick.com)

   ■ *Stickybear Math Town Bilingual* (ages 5 to 10; Hazelton, PA: K–12 Software). Addition, subtraction, multiplication, and division.

   ■ *Key Skills for Math: Addition and Subtraction* (grades 1–3; http://store.sunburst.com)

   ■ *Destination Math* (K–1; http://www.riverdeep.net)

■ *Mighty Math Zoo Zillions* (K–2; http://www.riverdeep.net)

■ *Mighty Math Carnival Countdown* (K–2; http://www.riverdeep.net)

■ *Math Express: Addition, Division, Multiplication, Subtraction* (pre-K–6; http://www.k12software.com)

## REVIEW

**A.** Explain why it is essential that children have the opportunity to construct their own whole number algorithms.

**B.** Match the action symbols in Column I with the words they stand for in Column II.

| Column I | Column II |
|----------|-----------|
| 1. + | a. multiply, times |
| 2. − | b. equals |
| 3. × | c. more than or greater than |
| 4. ÷ | d. add, plus |
| 5. = | e. less than |
| 6. < | f. divide |
| 7. > | g. subtract, minus |

**C.** Select the statements that are correct.

1. Constance Kamii believes that children learn arithmetic by being told about it.

2. Kamii believes that group games are excellent vehicles for supporting the construction of math concepts.

3. Paper-and-pencil worksheets are excellent for helping children develop the logic of arithmetic.

4. Kamii believes that children should always work alone at their desks when learning math.

**D.** Explain why standardized testing is a threat to the development of logical thinking.

**E.** When introducing whole number sentences (equations), a three-stage sequence should be followed. List the steps.

**F.** Explain briefly the instructional processes for addition, subtraction, multiplication, and division.

## REFERENCES

Baroody, A. J. (2006). Why children have difficulties mastering the basic number combinations and how to help them. *Teaching Children Mathematics, 13*(1), 22–31.

Carpenter, T., Carey, D., & Kouba, V. (1990). A problem-solving approach to the operations. In J. N. Payne (Ed.), *Mathematics for the young child* (pp. 111–131). Reston, VA: National Council of Teachers of Mathematics.

Charlesworth, R., & Senger, E. (2001). Arithmetic. In L. S. Grinstein & S. I. Lipsey (Eds.), *Encyclopedia of mathematics* (pp. 37–43). New York: RoutledgeFalmer.

Curcio, F. R., & Schwartz, S. L. (1998). There are no algorithms for teaching algorithms. *Teaching Children Mathematics, 5*(1), 26–30.

Fraivillig, J. (2001). Strategies for advancing children's mathematical thinking. *Teaching Children Mathematics, 7*(8), 454–459.

Fuson, K. C., Grandau, L., & Sugiyama, P. A. (2001). Achievable numerical understandings for all young children. *Teaching Children Mathematics, 7*(9), 522–526.

Garrison, L., Ponce, G. A., & Amaral, O. M. (2007). "Ninety percent of the game is half mental." *Teaching Children Mathematics, 14*(1), 12–17.

Ginsburg, H. (1977). *Children's arithmetic*. New York: Van Nostrand.

Heuser, D. (2005). Teaching without telling: Computational fluency and understanding through invention. *Teaching Children Mathematics, 11*(8), 404–412.

Isaacs, A. C., & Carroll, W. M. (1999). Strategies for basic-facts instruction. *Teaching Children Mathematics, 5*(9), 508–515.

Kamii, C. K. (1994). *Young children reinvent arithmetic, third grade.* New York: Teachers College Press.

Kamii, C. K. (2003). *Young children continue to reinvent arithmetic, second grade* (2nd ed.). New York: Teachers College Press.

Kamii, C. K., & DeClark, G. (2000). *Young children reinvent arithmetic.* New York: Teachers College Press.

National Association for the Education of Young Children (NAEYC) and National Association of Early Childhood Specialists in State Departments of Education (NAECSSDE). (1991). Guidelines for appropriate curriculum content and assessment in programs serving children ages 3 through 8: A position statement. *Young Children, 46*(3), 21–38.

National Council of Teachers of Mathematics. (2000). *Principles and standards for school mathematics.* Reston, VA: Author.

National Council of Teachers of Mathematics. (2007). *Curriculum focal points.* Reston, VA: Author.

Reys, B. J., & Reys, R. E. (1998). Computation in the elementary curriculum: Shifting the emphasis. *Teaching Children Mathematics, 5*(4), 236–241.

Richardson, K. (1984). *Developing number concepts using Unifix Cubes.* Menlo Park, CA: Addison-Wesley.

Richardson, K. (1999). *Developing number concepts: Book 2. Addition and subtraction.* Parsippany, NJ: Seymour.

Russell, S. J. (2000). Developing computational fluency with whole numbers. *Teaching Children Mathematics, 7*(3), 154–158.

Warshauer, H. K., & Warshauer, M. L. (2001). Algorithms. In L. S. Grinstein & S. I. Lipsey (Eds.), *Encyclopedia of mathematics* (pp. 23–24). New York: RoutledgeFalmer.

## FURTHER READING AND RESOURCES

Baker, A., & Baker, J. (1991). *Counting on a small planet.* Portsmouth, NH: Heinemann.

Barlow, A. T., & Gates, J. M. (2006/2007). The answer is 20 cookies. What is the question? *Teaching Children Mathematics, 13*(5), 252–255.

Behrend, J. L. (2003). Learning-disabled students make sense of mathematics. *Teaching Children Mathematics, 9*(5), 269–273.

Boerst, T. A., & Schielack, J. F. (2003). Toward understanding of "computational fluency." *Teaching Children Mathematics, 9*(6), 292–293.

*Box it or bag it mathematics. (K–2).* Portland, OR: Math Learning Center.

Bresser, R. (2003). Helping English-language learners develop computational fluency. *Teaching Children Mathematics, 9*(6), 294–299.

*Bridges in mathematics. (K–2).* Portland, OR: Math Learning Center.

Buchholz, L. (2004). Learning strategies for addition and subtraction facts: The road to fluency and the license to think. *Teaching Children Mathematics, 10*(7), 362–367.

Burns, M. (1992). *Math and literature: K–3.* Sausalito, CA: Math Solutions.

Burns, M., & Silbey, R. (2001, April). Math journals boost real learning. *Instructor,* 18–20.

Carroll, W. M., & Porter, D. (1997). Invented strategies can develop meaningful mathematical procedures. *Teaching Children Mathematics, 3*(7), 370, 374.

DeGroot, C., & Whalen, T. (2006). Investigations. Longing for division. *Teaching Children Mathematics, 12*(8), 410–418.

Findell, C. R., Cavanagh, M., Dacey, L., Greenes, C. E., Sheffield, L. J., & Small, M. (2004). *Navigating through problem solving and reasoning in grade 1.* Reston, VA: National Council of Teachers of Mathematics.

Fosnot, C. T., & Dolk, M. (2001). *Young mathematicians at work: Constructing number sense, addition, and subtraction.* Portsmouth, NH: Heinemann.

Ittigson, R. (2002). Helping students become mathematically powerful. *Teaching Children Mathematics, 9*(2), 91–95.

Kamii, C., & Anderson, C. (2003). Multiplication games: How we made and used them. *Teaching Children Mathematics, 10*(3), 135–141.

Kamii, C., & Lewis, B. A. (2003). Single-digit subtraction with fluency. *Teaching Children Mathematics, 10*(4), 230–236.

Kamii, C., Lewis, B. A., & Booker, B. M. (1998). Instead of teaching missing addends. *Teaching Children Mathematics, 4*(8), 458–461.

Kamii, C. K., Lewis, B. A., & Livingston, S. J. (1993). Primary arithmetic: Children inventing their own procedures. *Arithmetic Teacher, 41*(4), 200–203.

Kouba, V. L., & Franklin, K. (1995). Multiplication and division: Sense making and meaning. *Teaching Children Mathematics, 1*(9), 574–577.

Kulas, L. (1997). May I take your order? *Teaching Children Mathematics, 3*(5), 230–234.

Mann, R., & Miller, N. (2003). Responses to the marble mayhem problem: A solution evolution. *Teaching Children Mathematics, 9*(9), 516–520.

McGrath, B. B. (1994). *The m&m's brand counting book.* Watertown, MA: Charlesbridge.

Menon, R. (1996). Mathematical communication through student-constructed questions. *Teaching Children Mathematics, 2*(9), 530–532.

Morozumi, A. (2001). *One gorilla.* New York: Farrar, Strauss, & Giroux.

O'Connell, S. (2000). Introduction to problem solving: Strategies for the elementary math classroom. Portsmouth, NH: Heinemann.

Postlewait, K. B., Adams, M. R., & Shih, J. C. (2003). Promoting meaningful mastery of addition and subtraction. *Teaching Children Mathematics, 9*(6), 354–357.

Reys, B. J., & Arbaugh, F. (2001). Clearing up the confusion over calculator use in grades K–5. *Teaching Children Mathematics, 8*(2), 90–94.

Skinner, P. (1990). *What's your problem?* Portsmouth, NH: Heinemann.

Small, M., Sheffield, L. J., Cavanagh, M., Dacey, L., Findell, C. R., & Greenes, C. E. (2004). *Navigating through problem solving and reasoning in grade 2.* Reston, VA: National Council of Teachers of Mathematics.

Smith, J. J. (1996). Counting on company row. *Teaching Children Mathematics, 3,* 34–38.

Varol, F., & Farran, D. C. (2006). Early mathematical growth: How to support children's mathematical development. *Early Childhood Education Journal, 33*(6), 381–388.

Wakefield, A. P. (1998). *Early childhood number games.* Boston: Allyn & Bacon.

Wells, P. J., & Coffey, D. C. (2005). Are they wrong? Or did they just answer a different question? *Teaching Children Mathematics, 12*(4), 202–207.

Whitenack, J. W., Knipping, N., Novinger, S., & Underwood, G. (2001). Second graders circumvent addition and subtraction difficulties. *Teaching Children Mathematics, 8*(4), 228–233.

Whitin, D. J. (2006). Problem posing in the elementary classroom. *Teaching Children Mathematics, 13*(1), 14–18.

Zaslavsky, C. (1996). *The multicultural math classroom.* Portsmouth, NH: Heinemann.

Zaslavsky, C. (1998). *Math games and activities from around the world.* Chicago: Chicago Review Press.

*See also* the monthly issues of *Teaching Children Mathematics* for activities, materials, and reviews of software and websites.

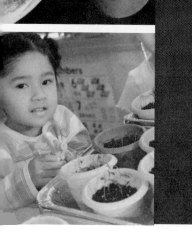

# Unit 28

# Patterns

## OBJECTIVES

After reading this unit, you should be able to:

- Describe patterning as it applies to primary age mathematics.
- Explain why the cognitive developmental level of primary children makes looking for patterns an especially interesting and appropriate activity.
- Assess primary grade children's understanding of patterning.
- Plan and teach patterning activities for primary grade children.

As described in Unit 17, the NCTM (2000, p. 90) standard for prekindergarten through grade 2 algebra includes the expectations that students will order objects by size, number, and other properties; recognize and extend patterns; and analyze how patterns are developed. Very young children learn repetitive rhymes and songs and hear stories with predictive language. They develop patterns with objects and eventually with numbers. They recognize change, such as in the seasons or in their height as they grow. During the primary grades children make a transition into more complex patterning activities such as comparing patterns, learning number patterns, extending complex patterns, and gaining an understanding of **equality** (that two quantities are the same amount).

The curriculum focal points (NCTM, 2007) continue to make connections with pre-algebra during the primary grades. During first grade, problem solving connects number and operations and algebra. Children also learn about number patterns such as

odd and even and those discovered in the 1–100 and 0–99 charts. At the second-grade level, children use number patterns to extend their understanding of number and operations. During grade 3, a part of pre-algebra readiness is the understanding of multiplication and the relationship between multiplication and division.

**Ordering**, or putting things into a sequence, is basic to patterning. **Patterning** is the process of discovering auditory, visual, and motor regularities. There are many regularities in the number system that children must understand. During the primary years, children work with more complex problems with concrete materials, connect concrete patterns to symbols, and learn to recognize some of the patterns and higher-level sequences in the number system.

This unit focuses on extending the concept of patterning to more complex patterns and connecting symbols and patterns. It also describes activities for looking at patterns in the environment.

## ASSESSMENT

Look back at Unit 17 for a description of naturalistic and informal patterning behaviors that can be observed during children's activities. By the primary grades, children should be able to copy and extend patterns with ease. During the primary grades they develop the ability to extend patterns further, make more complex patterns, become more adept at describing patterns with words, build their own patterns, and see patterns in numbers. See Unit 17 for a sample assessment task procedure for pattern copying, extending patterns, and describing patterns and more difficult extensions. The following are examples of higher-level assessment tasks.

---

### SAMPLE ASSESSMENT TASK

**9K**                                                   **Concrete Operations Ages 6–8**

**Patterns, Extension in Three Dimensions: Unit 28**

**METHOD:** Interview.

**SKILL:** The child can extend complex patterns in three dimensions by predicting what will come next.

**MATERIALS:** Inch or centimeter cubes, Unifix Cubes, or other counters that can be stacked.

**PROCEDURE:** Present the child with various patterns made of stacked counters. Ask the child to describe the pattern and to continue it as far as he can. Stack the blocks as follows one pattern at a time:

c.

For each pattern ask, TELL ME ABOUT THIS PATTERN. WHAT COMES NEXT? HOW DO YOU KNOW? CONTINUE THE PATTERN FOR ME.

**EVALUATION:** Note whether the child can continue each pattern and state his rationale. Note where the child might need further help and practice.

**INSTRUCTIONAL RESOURCE:** Charlesworth, R., and Lind, K. K. (2010). *Math and science for young children* (6th ed.). Clifton Park, NY: Cengage Learning.

## SAMPLE ASSESSMENT TASK

**9M**                                             **Concrete Operations Ages 7–9**

**Patterns, Multiple Numbers: Unit 28**

**METHOD:** Interview.

**SKILL:** The child can use a 1-to-100 chart to discover and predict number multiple patterns.

**MATERIALS:** Inch or centimeter cubes, Unifix Cubes, or other counters, and a 1-to-100 chart (Figure 28–1).

**PROCEDURE:** Start a pattern using multiples of two blocks. Tell the child, CIRCLE OR MARK THE AMOUNT IN MY GROUP ON THE CHART. If the child has a problem, show her the 2, and circle it for her if necessary. Next to the group of two blocks construct a group of four blocks. Use the same procedure as above. Continue up to 10. Then say, SHOW ME WHICH NUMBERS YOU WOULD CIRCLE IF I KEPT CONTINUING WITH THIS PATTERN. When children can predict accurately with multiples of two, try threes, fours, fives, and so on.

**EVALUATION:** Note whether the children can connect the numbers in the pattern to the numerals on the chart and whether they can predict what comes next. If they cannot accomplish these tasks, note where their errors are: Do they need more help with basic pattern construction? With counting? With connecting sets to symbols? With finding numbers on the chart?

**INSTRUCTIONAL RESOURCE:** Charlesworth, R., and Lind, K. K. (2010). *Math and science for young children* (6th ed.). Clifton Park, NY: Cengage Learning.

| 1 | 2 | 3 | 4 | 5 | 6 | 7 | 8 | 9 | 10 |
|---|---|---|---|---|---|---|---|---|---|
| 11 | 12 | 13 | 14 | 15 | 16 | 17 | 18 | 19 | 20 |
| 21 | 22 | 23 | 24 | 25 | 26 | 27 | 28 | 29 | 30 |
| 31 | 32 | 33 | 34 | 35 | 36 | 37 | 38 | 39 | 40 |
| 41 | 42 | 43 | 44 | 45 | 46 | 47 | 48 | 49 | 50 |
| 51 | 52 | 53 | 54 | 55 | 56 | 57 | 58 | 59 | 60 |
| 61 | 62 | 63 | 64 | 65 | 66 | 67 | 68 | 69 | 70 |
| 71 | 72 | 73 | 74 | 75 | 76 | 77 | 78 | 79 | 80 |
| 81 | 82 | 83 | 84 | 85 | 86 | 87 | 88 | 89 | 90 |
| 91 | 92 | 93 | 94 | 95 | 96 | 97 | 98 | 99 | 100 |

**Figure 28–1** 1-to-100 chart.

## ACTIVITIES

Children who have reached concrete operations are in a stage of cognitive development where they are naturally seeking out the rules and regularities in the world.

Creating patterns begins with concrete materials such as Unifix Cubes.

Patterning activities fit the natural inclinations and interests of children in this stage. While engaged in calendar and "100 days" activities, children are challenged to note number patterns and count by multiples (i.e., two, four, six, eight, . . .). They also enjoy arranging paper shapes into quilt patterns. The following examples are activities adapted from Richardson (1984, 1999) and Baratta-Lorton (1976). Patterning examples are also included in Greenes, Cavanagh, Dacey, Findell, and Small (2001).

## ACTIVITIES

### Patterning: Increasing Patterns

**OBJECTIVE:** To copy and extend patterns using objects.

**MATERIALS:** Counters such as chips, cube blocks, or Unifix Cubes; paper; and pencil.

**ACTIVITY:** The following are examples of patterns that can be developed. In each case, the teacher models the first three elements in the pattern; then the children are asked to predict what comes next and to extend the pattern as far as they can. The children may write down the pattern in numerals under each element and compare the patterns with both the objects and the numeral representations.

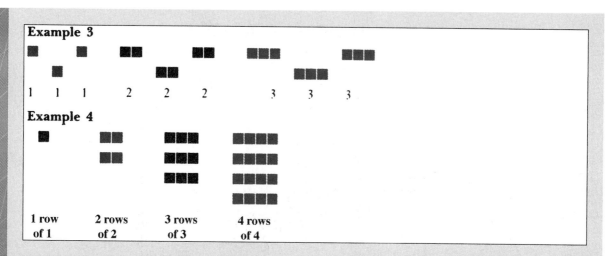

**Example 3**

1   1   1       2   2   2           3   3   3

**Example 4**

| 1 row of 1 | 2 rows of 2 | 3 rows of 3 | 4 rows of 4 |

**FOLLOW-UP:** Have children work with various types of patterns until you believe they have grasped the concept. Then present the higher-level pattern activities that follow.

## Patterning: Task Cards

**OBJECTIVE:** To copy and extend patterns using task cards.

**MATERIALS:** Counters such as chips, inch or centimeter cubes, or Unifix Cubes; task cards with the first three steps in a pattern; for example:

Task cards with the first step in a pattern.

(continued)

**ACTIVITY:** Provide the task cards and a good supply of counters. The children copy the models and then proceed to extend the patterns. With the three-step models, the pattern is set. With the one-step models, the children can create their own rules for extending the patterns. Always have them explain their pattern to you.

**FOLLOW-UP:** When the children have the concept of working from the abstract to the concrete with the task cards, have them create their own patterns, first with objects and then drawing them using the objects as models.

## Patterning: Activities with 1-To-100 Chart

**OBJECTIVE:** For children who have the concept of place value (see Unit 30) for the 1s and 10s place, activities using the 1-to-100 chart activities are appropriate. The objective is to perceive patterns on the chart in pictorial form.

**MATERIALS:** Copies of the 1-to-100 chart (see Figure 28–1) and counters.

**ACTIVITY:** On the chart, the children can color in or mark the amounts in their patterns. For example, they made the following pattern.

The children then mark off on the chart the amount in each part of the pattern: 5, 10, 15, 20, and so on.

**FOLLOW-UP:** The children can transfer to the charts from patterns you provide and then move on to patterns that they devise themselves.

## Patterning: Exploring Natural Materials

**OBJECTIVE:** To be able to observe and describe patterns in natural materials.

**MATERIALS:** Fruits and vegetables such as cabbage, onion, orange, lemon, grapefruit, and apple; magnifying glass; pencil and paper.

**ACTIVITY:** Let the children explore and examine the whole fruits and vegetables. Encourage them to describe what they see and feel. Suggest that they examine them with the magnifying glass and draw them if they wish. After a few days, ask them to predict what each item looks like inside. Then cut each one in half. Talk about what they discover. Compare what they see with what they predicted. Suggest that they draw the inside patterns.

**FOLLOW-UP:** Have each child use his or her pictures to make a "What's inside?" book. The children can write or dictate what they know about each item.

## Patterning: Multiples Graphs

**OBJECTIVE:** To collect data regarding natural patterns and depict the data on graphs.

**MATERIALS:** 1. Number line templates. These templates are made from heavy tagboard. The numbers are written across. A hole is cut or punched below each one so that the numbers can be copied.

2. Large sheets of manila paper, rulers, crayons, markers, and picture magazines.

**ACTIVITY:** With the children, discuss a question such as

- How many eyes do five people have among them?
- How many legs do three chairs have among them?

Have the children draw lines about 3 to 4 inches apart on a large piece of manila paper with their rulers. Have them copy their number line at the bottom of the paper using a template. Have them draw or cut out and paste pictures on their paper as shown in Figure 28–2. Then have them record the number of eyes (legs) down the right side of the paper and circle the corresponding numerals on the number line. Ask them to examine the number line and describe the pattern they have made.

**FOLLOW-UP:** Have the children think of other items that they could graph in multiples to create patterns.

## Patterning: Division

**OBJECTIVE:** To make division patterns.

**MATERIALS:** Large pieces of paper (11" × 18"), smaller pieces of paper (4¼" × 5½"), scissors, crayons or markers, and glue.

**ACTIVITY:** With the whole group, start with a large piece of paper. Have a child cut it in half and give one half to another child. Then have each child cut the paper in half and give one part away. Keep a record of the number of cuts and the number of children until everyone has a piece of paper. Next, give each child a large piece of paper and a small piece of paper. Have them glue the smaller piece at the top of the larger sheet (Figure 28–3). Have them take another small piece, cut it in half, and glue the two parts on the large paper below the first whole piece (Figure 28–3). Have them take another small piece, cut it in half, and then cut each half in half. Glue these four parts on the large sheet. Let them continue as long as they wish. Have them record the number of pieces in each row on the right-hand side of the chart.

**FOLLOW-UP:** Have the more advanced children cut three parts each time and see what kind of pattern they make.

**Figure 28–2** Multiples graph.

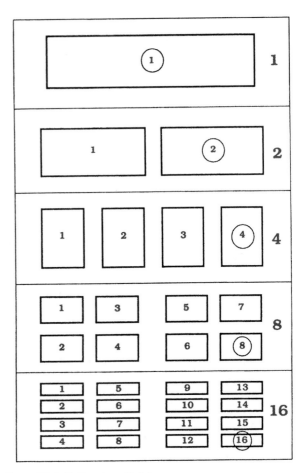

**Figure 28–3** Patterning: Division.

Other patterning activities can be developed using manipulatives such as pattern blocks. Pattern blocks come in a variety of sizes, thicknesses, and colors. There are many supplementary materials available such as tracing templates, stickers, rubber stamps, and puzzles (see the Creative Publications catalog, address in Unit 39). You can also make your own materials. Pattern blocks can be used to make quilt designs. Patterning activities can also be developed from children's literature (see Appendix B for book list). As with other concepts, patterning activities can be integrated across the curriculum (Figure 28–4).

As already described in Unit 27, calculator activities are interesting ways to look at number patterns. After some practice with patterns as suggested in Unit 27, have the children discover and extend patterns with their calculators; for example, make up some more patterns for the children to explore with calculators.

Clements and Sarama (2000) describe the "predict and cover" activity, which can be done both on and off the computer. First the children explore pattern blocks, developing their own designs. Then they are provided with specific shapes and asked to predict and select which pattern blocks will cover the shapes provided. Patterning activities can be found online at Virtual Manipulatives (http://nlvm.usu.edu) and at Illuminations (http://illuminations.nctm.org). Several advantages of doing the activity on the computer are: it gives children more flexibility, work can be saved and retrieved, children can design their own patterns,

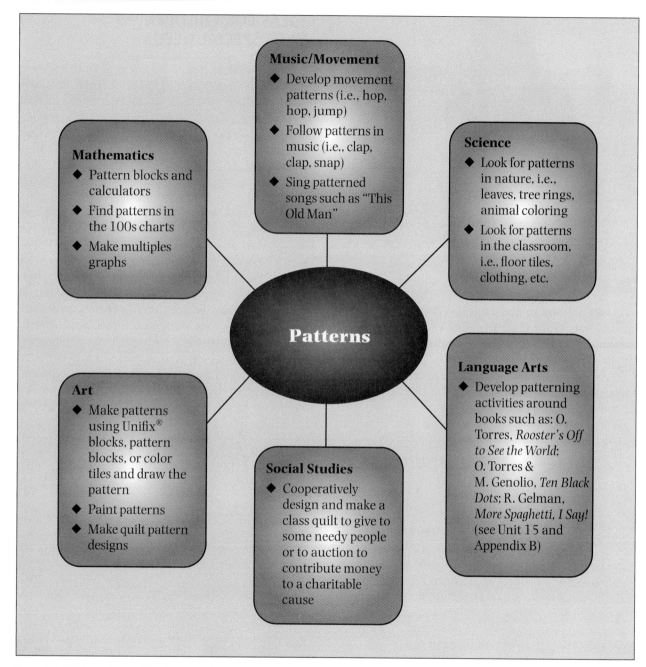

**Figure 28–4** Integrating patterning experiences across the curriculum.

Calculators can provide opportunities to explore number patterns.

and tasks are broken down in ways that clarify mathematical mental actions. You may access the Online Companion for relevant links to websites and online activities.

As with other math concepts, pattern software is available. See the activities at the end of this unit and at the end of Unit 17 for suggestions.

## IDEAS FOR CHILDREN WITH SPECIAL NEEDS

In this unit and each of those following in this section, the practical developmental implications of a different disability will be described. In this unit the focus is on the blind child (Lewis, 2003). When considering any disability it is important to avoid stereotypes. Every child is an individual. Children with visual disabilities must depend on their other senses for information. Rhymes and routines are essential for the visually impaired young child. The adult should talk during routines, describing what is happening. Give and take games can be very educational. Objects can be incorporated into routines and rhymes, because touch is an important element in their learning about the environment. Toys should be labeled and explained. Spatial relationships (such as putting a cup on the table or climbing on a chair) should be practiced. In the classroom, the blind child needs time to explore. A peer can be helpful as a mentor. Consistent routines are very important. During the primary grades, reading is a major focus and children who are blind learn Braille. The concrete materials used in mathematics instruction are extremely useful for the child who is blind. He may need

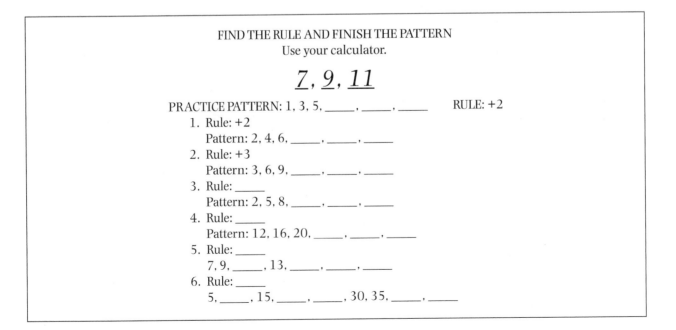

FIND THE RULE AND FINISH THE PATTERN
Use your calculator.

$$\underline{7}, \underline{9}, \underline{11}$$

PRACTICE PATTERN: 1, 3, 5, _____, _____, _____          RULE: +2

1. Rule: +2
   Pattern: 2, 4, 6, _____, _____, _____
2. Rule: +3
   Pattern: 3, 6, 9, _____, _____, _____
3. Rule: _____
   Pattern: 2, 5, 8, _____, _____, _____
4. Rule: _____
   Pattern: 12, 16, 20, _____, _____, _____
5. Rule: _____
   7, 9, _____, 13, _____, _____, _____
6. Rule: _____
   5, _____, 15, _____, _____, 30, 35, _____, _____

extra time in order to become familiar with materials and learn to organize them. Texture can be very helpful. For example, patterns using rough and smooth or pattern blocks of different shapes are appropriate adaptations.

## EVALUATION

Note how the children deal with the suggested pattern activities. Do they count each part out loud? Do they seem to be doing the patterning logically through application of their number sense concept (i.e., through subitizing)? When asked, can they explain the pattern? Use the assessment tasks in Appendix A for individual evaluation interviews.

## SUMMARY

Primary level children extend the work they did with patterning at earlier levels. Now they begin to identify and work with patterns in the number system as they connect numerals to patterns and develop number patterns using counting and calculators. Number patterns are the basis for multiplication and division.

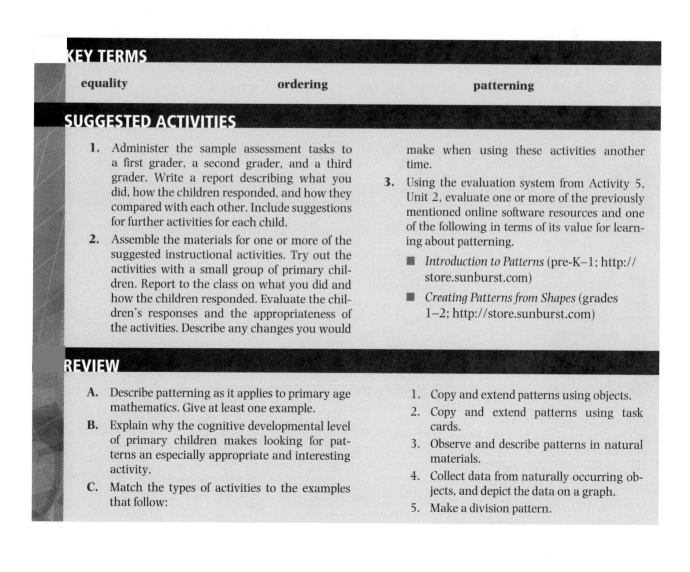

### KEY TERMS

| equality | ordering | patterning |
|----------|----------|------------|

### SUGGESTED ACTIVITIES

1. Administer the sample assessment tasks to a first grader, a second grader, and a third grader. Write a report describing what you did, how the children responded, and how they compared with each other. Include suggestions for further activities for each child.

2. Assemble the materials for one or more of the suggested instructional activities. Try out the activities with a small group of primary children. Report to the class on what you did and how the children responded. Evaluate the children's responses and the appropriateness of the activities. Describe any changes you would make when using these activities another time.

3. Using the evaluation system from Activity 5, Unit 2, evaluate one or more of the previously mentioned online software resources and one of the following in terms of its value for learning about patterning.
   ■ *Introduction to Patterns* (pre-K–1; http://store.sunburst.com)
   ■ *Creating Patterns from Shapes* (grades 1–2; http://store.sunburst.com)

### REVIEW

A. Describe patterning as it applies to primary age mathematics. Give at least one example.

B. Explain why the cognitive developmental level of primary children makes looking for patterns an especially appropriate and interesting activity.

C. Match the types of activities to the examples that follow:

1. Copy and extend patterns using objects.
2. Copy and extend patterns using task cards.
3. Observe and describe patterns in natural materials.
4. Collect data from naturally occurring objects, and depict the data on a graph.
5. Make a division pattern.

Examples:

a. Chan carefully draws the pattern that appears in half of an orange.

b. Sara examines three groups of blocks and proceeds to create the group she believes should come next.

c. Theresa draws lines across a large sheet of paper, copies her number line with a template, then looks through a magazine for animals with four legs.

d. Vanessa has a large sheet of paper and several smaller sheets. First she glues one small sheet at the top of the large sheet and writes the numeral 1 to the right.

e. Brent examines some patterns drawn on a card. Then he takes some Unifix Cubes, makes the same designs, and adds two more.

D. Describe how a 1-to-100 chart might be used to assist in illustrating multiple number patterns.

## REFERENCES

Baratta-Lorton, M. (1976). *Mathematics their way.* Menlo Park, CA: Addison-Wesley.

Clements, D. H., & Sarama, J. (2000). Predicting pattern blocks on and off the computer. *Teaching Children Mathematics, 6*(7), 458–462.

Greenes, C., Cavanagh, M., Dacey, L., Findell, C., & Small, M. (2001). *Navigating through algebra in prekindergarten–grade 2.* Reston, VA: National Council of Teachers of Mathematics.

Lewis, V. (2003). *Development and disability* (2nd ed.). Malden, MA: Blackwell.

National Council of Teachers of Mathematics. (2000). *Principles and standards for school mathematics.* Reston, VA: Author.

National Council of Teachers of Mathematics. (2007). *Curriculum focal points.* Reston, VA: Author.

Richardson, K. (1984). *Developing number concepts using Unifix Cubes.* Menlo Park, CA: Addison-Wesley.

Richardson, K. (1999). *Developing number concepts:* Book 1. *Counting, comparing and pattern.* Parsippany, NJ: Seymour.

## FURTHER READING AND RESOURCES

*Box it or bag it mathematics. (K–2).* Portland, OR: Math Learning Center.

Brahier, D. J. (2003). Patterns at your fingertips. *Teaching Children Mathematics, 9*(9), 521–528.

*Bridges in mathematics. (K–2).* Portland, OR: Math Learning Center.

Britton, B. (2006). Patterns galore! *Teaching Children Mathematics, 12*(6), 296–302.

Burris, A.C. (2005). *Understanding the math you teach.* Upper Saddle River, NJ: Pearson-Merrill/Prentice-Hall.

Chen, J., & McNamee, G. D. (2007). *Bridging: Teaching and learning in early childhood classrooms, pre-K–3.* Thousand Oaks, CA: Corwin.

Copley, J. V. (Ed.). (1999). *Mathematics in the early years.* Washington, DC: National Association for the Education of Young Children.

Copley, J. V. (2000). *The young child and mathematics.* Washington, DC: National Association for the Education of Young Children.

Copley, J. V. (Ed.). (2004). *Showcasing mathematics for the young child.* Reston, VA: National Council of Teachers of Mathematics.

Filliman, P. (1999). Patterns all around. *Teaching Children Mathematics, 5*(5), 282–283.

Findell, C. R., Cavanagh, M., Dacey, L., Greenes, C. E., Sheffield, L. J., & Small, M. (2004). *Navigating through problem solving and reasoning in grade 1.* Reston, VA: National Council of Teachers of Mathematics.

Greenes, C. E., Cavanagh, M., Dacey, L., Findell, C. R., Sheffield, L. J., & Small, M. (2003). *Navigating through problem solving and reasoning in prekindergarten–kindergarten.* Reston, VA: National Council of Teachers of Mathematics.

Greenes, C. E., Cavanagh, M., Dacey, L., Findell, C. R., & Small, M. (2001). *Navigating through algebra in prekindergarten–grade 2.* Reston, VA: National Council of Teachers of Mathematics.

Holly, K. A. (1997). Patterns and functions. *Teaching Children Mathematics, 3*, 312–313.

Lee, J. (2007). Context in mathematical learning. Problems and possibilities. *Teaching Children Mathematics, 14*(1), 40–44.

MacDonald, S. (2001). *Block play: The complete guide to learning and playing with blocks*. Beltsville, MD: Gryphon House.

Reynolds, A., Cassel, D., & Lillard, E. (2006). A mathematical exploration of grandpa's quilt. *Teaching Children Mathematics, 12*(7), 340–345.

Small, M., Sheffield, L. J., Cavanagh, M., Dacey, L., Findell, C. R., & Greenes, C. E. (2004). *Navigating through problem solving and reasoning in grade 2*. Reston, VA: National Council of Teachers of Mathematics.

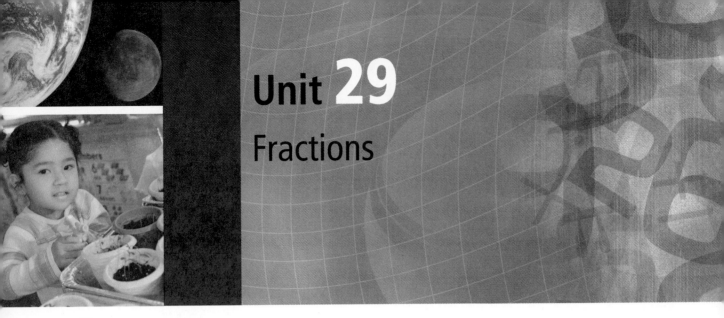

# Unit 29
# Fractions

## OBJECTIVES

After reading this unit, you should be able to:

- Explain how the concept of fractions is based on an understanding of part/whole relationships.
- Explain why primary children should not be rushed into using fraction notation.
- Assess primary children's understanding of the concept of fractions.
- Plan and teach fraction lessons appropriate for primary children.

In Unit 14, it was explained that young children have a natural understanding and interest in **parts** and **wholes** that can be used later as a bridge to understanding **fractions**. The NCTM (2000, p. 78) expectations include that young children will develop a sense of whole numbers and represent them in many ways by breaking groups down into smaller parts. By the end of second grade they should understand and be able to represent commonly used fractions such as ¼, ⅓, and ½.

Fractions become a focal point (NCTM, 2007) in number and operations during grade 3. During third grade, children develop an understanding of fractions and fraction equivalence. They understand how fractional parts relate to the whole and study a variety of models. They solve fraction problems.

As described in Unit 14, the fundamental concept of *parts* and *wholes* is the basis for the understanding of fractions. Through naturalistic, informal, and structured experiences, preprimary children become familiar with three aspects of the part/whole concept: things have special parts, a whole object can be divided into

parts, and groups of things can be divided into smaller groups. They also become familiar with the application of the terms *more, less,* and *same.* During the primary level, young children expand on the concrete activities that they engaged in during the preprimary level. It is important not to introduce notation and symbols too soon. Even 9-year-olds have difficulty with fractions at the symbolic level. This would indicate that, for most children, fraction symbols cannot safely be introduced until the end of the primary period (the latter part of grade 3) and may not be fully understood until well into the intermediate level (grade 4 or higher). Fraction problems cannot be solved by counting as can whole number problems. This factor makes them much more abstract and thus more difficult.

At the presymbolic level, work with fractions should be limited to **halves**, **thirds**, and **fourths**. These are the fractions we deal with most frequently in life, and once children develop an understanding of them, they should be able to transfer this knowledge to fractions in general. Children can learn fraction terminology relative to concrete experiences without being concerned with the corresponding symbols. Terms such as *one-half, one-third,* and *one-fourth* can be associated with parts of concrete objects and subgroups of large groups of concrete objects. During the primary period, children continue to work with fractions as part/whole relationships. They can work with volume, regions, length, and groups. Experiences with foods (such as cutting up a carrot) and cooking (measuring ingredients) involve volume. Regions are concrete and easy to work with. They involve working with shapes such as circles, rectangles, squares, and triangles. Lengths can also be divided into parts. Long, narrow pieces of paper, string, thread, and ribbon are useful for this type of activity. When working with groups, a whole group of objects serves as the unit to be divided into smaller subgroups.

Payne, Towsley, and Huinker (1990, pp. 175–200) sum up the sequence in the development of conceptual knowledge of fractions. As you have already seen, 3–5-year-old children work with the concept of parts and wholes; 5–8-year-olds work on equal parts and on oral (*not* written) names. That is, children learn to use terms such as *halves, thirds, fourths,* and the like. They also use terms such as *part,* **pieces,** *whole,* and **almost whole.**

## ASSESSMENT

In Unit 14, both observational and interview tasks for assessment of part/whole concepts were described. When children understand that a whole can be divided into parts, that when a quantity is divided its whole is conserved, and that the size of each part gets smaller as the number of equal divisions increases, then they are ready to understand fractions. If children evidence some of the behaviors described in Unit 14 as indicating an understanding of the part/whole concept and are able to respond successfully to the Unit 14 assessment tasks, then try the following kinds of higher-level assessment tasks.

## SAMPLE ASSESSMENT TASK

**9N**                                              **Concrete Operations Ages 6–8**

**Fractions, Equivalent Parts: Unit 29**

**METHOD:**       Interview.

**SKILL:**        The child can divide a rectangle into smaller equal parts.

**MATERIALS:**    A supply of paper rectangles of equal size (8½" × 2¾") in four different colors and a pair of scissors.

**PROCEDURE:**    Show the child a paper rectangle. THIS IS A RECTANGLE. Place two more rectangles (color #2) below the first one. HERE ARE TWO MORE RECTANGLES. ARE ALL THREE THE SAME SIZE? Be sure the child agrees. Let him compare them to be sure. NOW I'M GOING TO FOLD ONE OF THE RECTANGLES (color #2) SO BOTH PARTS ARE THE SAME. Fold the rectangle. NOW YOU FOLD THIS OTHER ONE (also color #2) JUST LIKE I DID. Offer assistance if necessary. The three rectangles should look like this:

Color #1

(continued)

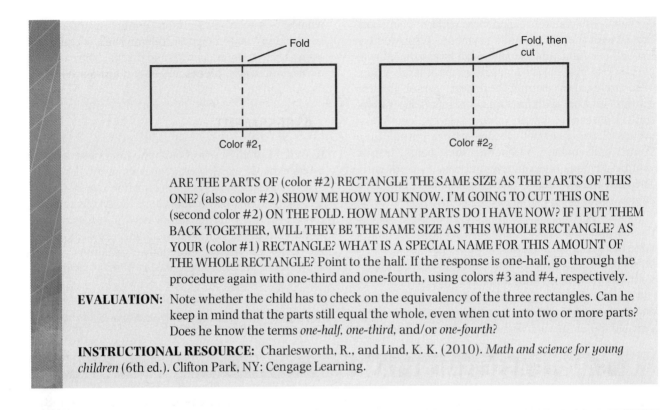

Color #2₁

Color #2₂

ARE THE PARTS OF (color #2) RECTANGLE THE SAME SIZE AS THE PARTS OF THIS ONE? (also color #2) SHOW ME HOW YOU KNOW. I'M GOING TO CUT THIS ONE (second color #2) ON THE FOLD. HOW MANY PARTS DO I HAVE NOW? IF I PUT THEM BACK TOGETHER, WILL THEY BE THE SAME SIZE AS THIS WHOLE RECTANGLE? AS YOUR (color #1) RECTANGLE? WHAT IS A SPECIAL NAME FOR THIS AMOUNT OF THE WHOLE RECTANGLE? Point to the half. If the response is one-half, go through the procedure again with one-third and one-fourth, using colors #3 and #4, respectively.

**EVALUATION:** Note whether the child has to check on the equivalency of the three rectangles. Can he keep in mind that the parts still equal the whole, even when cut into two or more parts? Does he know the terms *one-half, one-third,* and/or *one-fourth*?

**INSTRUCTIONAL RESOURCE:** Charlesworth, R., and Lind, K. K. (2010). *Math and science for young children* (6th ed.). Clifton Park, NY: Cengage Learning.

## SAMPLE ASSESSMENT TASK

**90**                                                                    **Concrete Operations Ages 6–8**

**Fractions, One-Half of a Group: Unit 29**

**METHOD:**        Interview.

**SKILL:**         The child can divide a set of objects into smaller groups when given directions using the term *one-half.*

**MATERIALS:**     Ten counters (cube blocks, chips, Unifix Cubes, or other concrete objects).

**PROCEDURE:**     Place the counters in front of the child. I HAVE SOME (name of counters). DIVIDE THESE SO THAT WE EACH HAVE ONE-HALF OF THE GROUP. If the child completes this task easily, go on to nine counters and ask her to divide the group into thirds. Then go on to eight counters and ask her to divide the group into fourths.

**EVALUATION:**    Note the method used by the child. Does she use counting, or does she pass the counters out: "One for you and one for me"? Does she really seem to understand the terms *one-half, one-fourth,* and *one-third*?

**INSTRUCTIONAL RESOURCE:** Charlesworth, R., and Lind, K. K. (2010). *Math and science for young children* (6th ed.). Clifton Park, NY: Cengage Learning.

## ACTIVITIES

In Unit 14, naturalistic and informal activities were emphasized as the foundation for structured experiences. These activities should be encouraged and continued. Primary children continue to need time to explore materials and construct their concept of parts and wholes through their own actions on the environment. There are many materials that children can explore independently in developing the foundations for the understanding of fractions. Any of the usual kinds of counting objects can be organized as a group, which can then be divided (or partitioned) into smaller groups. Some materials for dividing single objects or shapes into parts are illustrated in Figure 29–1. The examples include Fit-a-Fraction (Lakeshore), Fraction Circles and Skittles (Nienhuis-Montessori), and Fractional Wood Fruit Plate (ETA). Figure 29–2 illustrates materials that promote the construction and comparison of parts and wholes. These materials include Unit Blocks (Community Playthings), Cuisinaire Rods (Cuisinaire of America), puzzles (Lakeshore), and LEGO (Lakeshore).

Following are structured activities that can be used to develop fraction concepts.

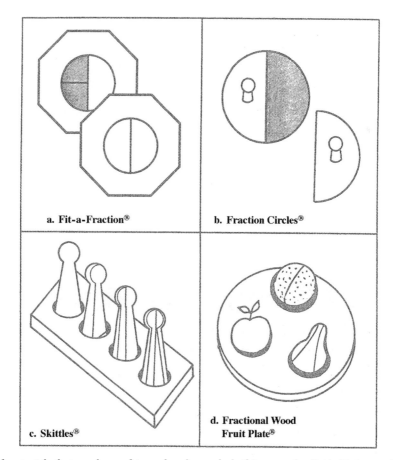

a. **Fit-a-Fraction**®

b. **Fraction Circles**®

c. **Skittles**®

d. **Fractional Wood Fruit Plate**®

**Figure 29–1** Examples of materials that can be used to explore how whole things can be divided into equal parts.

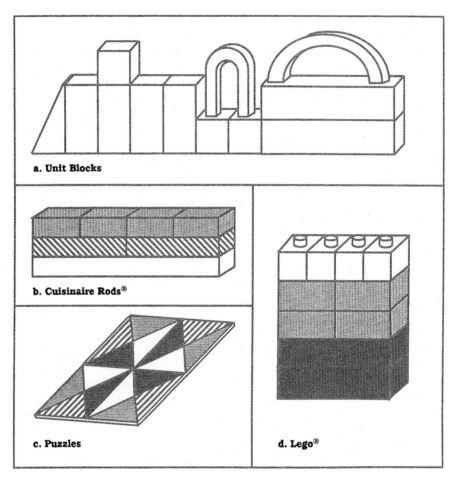

**Figure 29–2** Materials that promote the construction and comparison of parts and wholes.

## ACTIVITIES

### Fractions: Construction Paper Models

**OBJECTIVE:** To conceptualize fractional parts of wholes using construction paper and/or poster board models.

**MATERIALS:** Make your own models out of construction paper and/or poster board. Use a different color for each fractional part—for example, a blue whole circle, a red circle the same size cut into halves, a yellow circle cut into thirds, and a green circle cut into fourths.

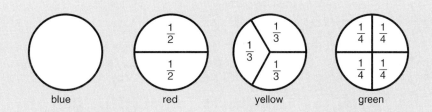

The same colors can be used to make a set of fraction rectangles and a set of fraction squares.

**ACTIVITY:** Let the children explore the sets of fraction models. After they have worked with them several times, ask them some questions.

- What have you learned about these shapes?
- How many red pieces make a circle the same size as the blue circle? How many yellow pieces? How many green pieces?
- Use the same procedure with the rectangles and the squares.

**FOLLOW-UP:** Label the parts as halves, thirds, and fourths of the wholes. Provide the students with matching construction paper shapes, and have them make their own models by folding. Start with rectangles and squares.

## Fractions: Comparing Sizes

**OBJECTIVE:** To compare sizes of halves, thirds, and fourths.

**MATERIALS:** Same as in previous activity.

**ACTIVITY:** Put out the models one set at a time. Ask the children, WHICH IS LARGER—A HALF, A THIRD, OR A FOURTH? HOW MANY FOURTHS MAKE ONE-HALF?

**FOLLOW-UP:** Provide models of other fractions for children who have a good understanding of halves, fourths, and thirds.

## Fractions: Parts of Groups

**OBJECTIVE:** To divide groups of objects into subgroups of halves, thirds, and fourths.

**MATERIALS:** Draw, color, and cut out a mother rabbit, four child rabbits, and twelve carrots (see Figure 29–3 for patterns).

**ACTIVITY:** Place the mother rabbit, two child rabbits, and four carrots in front of the children. MOTHER RABBIT HAS FOUR CARROTS AND WANTS TO GIVE EACH OF HER CHILDREN HALF OF THE CARROTS. HELP HER BY DIVIDING THE CARROTS BETWEEN THE TWO CHILDREN SO EACH HAS HALF. Give the child time to complete the task. NOW SUPPOSE SHE HAS FOUR CARROTS AND FOUR CHILDREN (bring out two more children). SHOW ME HOW THEY CAN SHARE THE CARROTS SO EACH HAS ONE-FOURTH OF THE CARROTS. As long as the children are interested, continue the activity using

*(continued)*

**Figure 29–3** Patterns for the "parts of groups" activity.

different numbers of child rabbits and different amounts of carrots. Emphasize that the carrots must be shared so that it is fair to everyone.

**FOLLOW-UP:** Make other groups of materials (such as children and apples, dogs and bones). Move on to other fractions when the children can do these problems easily.

## Fractions: Liquid Volume

**OBJECTIVE:** To compare fractional parts of liquid volume.

**MATERIALS:** Several sets of color-coded standard measuring cups, if available, and a pitcher of water. If color-coded cups are not available, mark each size with a different color (e.g., 1 cup with blue, ½ cup with red, ⅓ cup with yellow, ¼ cup with green).

**ACTIVITY:** Give each child a set of measuring cups. Let them examine the set and tell you what they notice. After discussion and examination, have everyone pick up their 1-cup size and their ½-cup size. HOW MANY OF THESE SMALL CUPS OF WATER WILL FILL THE LARGE CUP? Let the children predict. FILL YOUR SMALL CUP WITH WATER. POUR THE WATER IN YOUR LARGE CUP. IS THE LARGE CUP FULL? POUR IN ANOTHER SMALL CUP OF WATER. IS THE LARGE CUP FULL NOW? HOW MANY OF

THE SMALLER CUPS WERE NEEDED TO FILL THE LARGER CUP? Follow the same procedure with the ⅓- and ¼-size cups.

**FOLLOW-UP:** Reverse the procedure. Starting with the full 1-cup measure, have the children count how many ½, ⅓, and ¼ cupfuls it takes to empty the full cup. Do the same activity using rice, birdseed, or sand instead of water.

## Fractions: Length

**OBJECTIVE:** To compare fractional parts of lengths.

**MATERIALS:** Cuisinaire Rods.

**ACTIVITY:** Provide the children with a basket full of Cuisinaire Rods. After they have had an opportunity to explore the rods, suggest that they select a long rod and find out which lengths of rods can be placed next to it to show halves, thirds, and fourths.

**FOLLOW-UP:** Follow the same procedure with whole straws and straws cut into halves, fourths, and thirds. Try the activity with other materials such as string, ribbons, and paper strips.

## Fractions: Using Literature

**OBJECTIVE:** To analyze the fractional components of relevant children's literature as an application of the concept of fractions.

**MATERIALS:** Children's trade books that contain fractional concepts, writing and drawing implements, paper, chalk, and chalkboard.

**ACTIVITY:** Read books such as *When the Doorbell Rang* (Hutchins, 1986). Provide problem situations such as making a chart that shows how, as more children come, each gets fewer cookies. Have the children draw pictorial representations of what is happening. For further suggestions and a list of additional books, see Conway and Midkiff (2004), Colker (2005), and Whitin and Whitin (2004) as well as others listed in Unit 15.

**FOLLOW-UP:** Use additional books. Children will become more independent and see more and more ways of looking at fractions.

## Fractions: Story Problems

**OBJECTIVE:** To have the children create and solve fraction story problems.

**MATERIALS:** One or more model problems; paper, pencils, crayons, markers, and scissors; chart paper for model problems.

**ACTIVITY:** Have the students brainstorm real-life situations in which things must be divided into equal parts. Encourage them to write or dictate their own problems, draw a picture of the problem, and write out the solution. If they cannot come up with their own problems, provide one or two

*(continued)*

"Each child has one-half of the pennies."

**Figure 29–4** The teacher can write and illustrate a model story problem that involves the partitioning of a group.

models that they can work through with you. Here are some models (have each problem written on chart paper):

1.  TWO CHILDREN FOUND SIX PENNIES. ONE CHILD TOOK THREE PENNIES. WHAT FRACTIONAL PART OF THE PENNIES WAS LEFT FOR THE OTHER CHILD? Draw two stick figure children. Draw six pennies on another piece of paper. Glue three pennies by one child and three by the other. WHAT PART OF THE PENNIES DOES EACH CHILD HAVE? YES, ONE-HALF. Write: "Each child has one-half of the pennies" (Figure 29–4).

2.  BRENT INVITES THREE FRIENDS OVER FOR PIZZA. IF EACH CHILD GETS A FAIR SHARE, HOW WILL THE PIZZA LOOK WHEN IT IS CUT UP? Give each child a paper pizza. Ask them to fold the pizzas into the right size and number of parts. Cut up one of the pizzas, and glue the parts on the chart. Write: "Each child gets one-fourth."

**FOLLOW-UP:** Encourage the children to create and illustrate their own fraction problems.

## Fractions: Geoboard Shapes

**OBJECTIVE:** To divide geoboard shapes into equal parts.

**MATERIALS:** Geoboards, geoboard shape patterns, and rubber bands.

**ACTIVITY:** Have the children use rubber bands to make rectangles and squares on their geoboards and then divide those shapes into equal parts using additional rubber bands.

**FOLLOW-UP:** Question the children regarding how they know that their shapes are divided into equal parts. Note whether they use the number of geoboard pegs as a clue to making their parts equal.

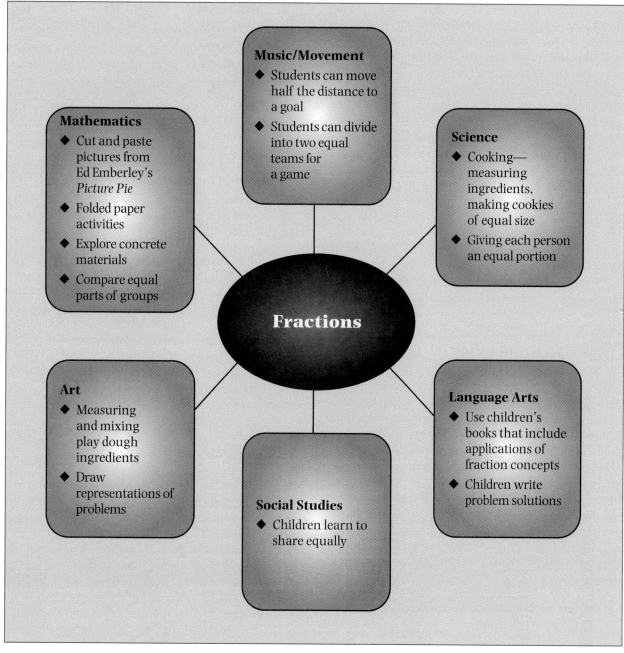

**Figure 29–5** Integrating fraction experiences across the curriculum.

For the more advanced students, notation can be introduced. Show them how one-half can be written as ½, which means one part out of two. Then ask how they think they might write one-third as one part out of three, two-thirds as two parts out of three, and so on. Have them write the numerical fractions that match the parts of some of the materials suggested earlier in the unit.

The connection between fractions and decimals can be made through further concrete activities. Avoid placing any emphasis on decimal points. Work with 10ths and 100ths using models and diagrams in the same manner as you did with the larger fractions. Show through models how 1/10 and 1/100 can also be written as .1 and .01. Students with a strong conceptual foundation can move into operations with fractions and decimals by the fourth grade.

Fraction concepts can be integrated across the curriculum, as depicted in Figure 29–5.

## IDEAS FOR CHILDREN WITH SPECIAL NEEDS

With deaf children, communication is a major consideration (Lewis, 2003). Being able to communicate with sign language provides many advantages for the deaf child. Deaf children who sign have been found to be academically and socially advanced. If the deaf child is in a regular classroom then he will need an interpreter. Bilingual deaf children—those who are proficient in sign and oral language—have an advantage. Deaf children should be introduced to written language at an early age. Allen & Cowdery (2005) make a number of recommendations for teachers of young deaf childen. These include:

■ When speaking, look children directly in the face. Get down to their level.

■ Speak slowly and clearly.

■ Use some gestures but not so many that the child is distracted from lipreading.

■ In a group, seat the child across from the teacher.

■ Get the child's attention by tapping softly on shoulder or hand.

■ Use concrete examples when giving instructions.

■ Read story books with clear, brightly colored illustrations.

■ Keep routines sequenced and on a regular schedule.

The use of concrete materials for math and science is essential for communicating concepts to the deaf child.

## EVALUATION

Continue to note whether the children apply what they have learned about fractions during their everyday activities. Be sure to provide situations in which individual items or groups of items have to be shared equally with others. Note whether the children can use their concept of fractions in these situations. Also note if they apply their concept of fractions during measuring experiences that are a part of food preparation and science investigations. Administer the assessment tasks described in Appendix A.

## SUMMARY

During the primary years, young children expand their informal concept of parts and wholes of objects and groups to the more formal concept of fractions, or equal parts. Primary children learn the vocabulary of fractions and work with fractions at the concrete level. Usually they do not go beyond halves, thirds, and fourths, and most of them are not ready to understand fraction notation until the latter part of the primary period. It is important not to rush young children into the abstract use of fractions until they are ready, because fractions are much more difficult to work with than whole numbers. Teaching children who are deaf requires some special considerations.

## KEY TERMS

| | | |
|---|---|---|
| almost whole | halves | thirds |
| fourths | part(s) | whole(s) |
| fractions | pieces | |

## SUGGESTED ACTIVITIES

1. Visit one or more primary classrooms during math instruction on fractions. Take note of the materials and methods used. Compare what you observe with what is suggested in the text.

2. Assess a primary child's level of development in the concept of fractions. Prepare an instructional plan based on the results. Prepare the materials, and implement the lesson with the child. Evaluate the results. Did the child move ahead as a result of your instruction?

3. Be sure to add fraction activities to your Activity File/Notebook.

4. Try out some of the activities suggested in this unit with primary children of different ages.

5. If the school budget allotted $100 for fraction materials, decide what would be your priority purchases.

6. Using the guidelines from Activity 5, Unit 2, evaluate software designed to reinforce the concept of fractions.

   ■ *Math Express: Fractions* (preschool–grade 6; Eugene, OR: Visions Technology). Fraction skills cover identifying, converting, and comparing fractions; adding, subtracting, multiplying, and dividing fractions; mixed numbers; telling time; adding/subtracting time; and counting money.

   ■ *Richard Scarry's Busytown—Best Math Program Ever* (preschool–grade 1; Hazelton, PA: K–12 Software). Includes fraction activities.

   ■ *Tenth Planet: Fractions Collections Bundle* (grades 2–7; http://store.sunburst.com). Interactive demonstrations and practice activities build skills and understanding of fractions and part-number concepts.

   ■ *Tenth Planet: Representing Fractions* (grades 2–4; http://store.sunburst.com). Students work with one interpretation of a fraction—namely, as a relationship between a whole and its parts. Work with fractions in symbolic and visual representations.

   ■ *Virtual Manipulatives, Number and Operations* (pre-K–2; http://nlvm.usu.edu). Fraction bars, naming fractions, parts and whole, visualizing fractions, pie chart.

## REVIEW

A. Explain why primary children should not be rushed into working with fraction and decimal notation.

B. Identify the statements that are correct.

   1. At the presymbolic level, work with fractions should be limited to halves, thirds, and fourths.

   2. Fraction terminology should be introduced along with fraction notation.

   3. At the presymbolic level, primary children can work with volume, regions, lengths, and groups.

   4. Food experiences are excellent opportunities for working with volume.

5. Begin assessment with the tasks in this unit. It can be assumed that primary-level children can already do the lower-level tasks included in Unit 14.

6. Primary children still need exploratory experiences before being presented with structured fraction activities.

7. Primary children are too young to make the connections between fractions and decimals.

C. Label items 1–4 as being examples of (a) partitioning into groups, (b) a whole object can be divided into equal parts, or (c) a liquid can be divided into equal parts.

1. Liu Pei carefully folds rectangular pieces of paper in half and then in half again and cuts accurately on each line.

2. Ann has six crackers. She wants to be sure that she and both of her friends receive an equal amount. She decides that they should each have two crackers.

3. Jason has a 1-cup measure of milk. Ms. Hebert tells him that they will need one-half cup of milk for their recipe. Jason selects a smaller cup that says ½ on the handle and fills it with milk from the larger cup.

4. Trang Fung is experimenting with the Fit-a-Fraction set.

## REFERENCES

Allen, K. E., & Cowdery, G. E. (2005). *The exceptional child: Inclusion in early childhood education* (5th ed.). Albany, NY: Thomson Delmar Learning.

Colker, L. J. (2005). *The cooking book.* Washington, DC: National Association for the Education of Young Children.

Conaway, B., & Midkiff, R. B. (2004). Connecting literature, language and fractions. In D. Theissen (Ed.), *Exploring mathematics through literature* (pp. 69–78). Reston, VA: National Council of Teachers of Mathematics.

Hutchins, P. (1986). *When the doorbell rang.* New York: Greenwillow.

Lewis, V. (2003). *Development and disability* (2nd ed.). Malden, MA: Blackwell.

National Council of Teachers of Mathematics. (2000). *Principles and standards for school mathematics.* Reston, VA: Author.

National Council of Teachers of Mathematics. (2007). *Curriculum focal points.* Reston. VA: Author.

Payne, J. N., Towsley, A., & Huinker, D. (1990). Fractions and decimals. In J. N. Payne (Ed.), *Mathematics for the young child* (pp. 175–200). Reston, VA: National Council of Teachers of Mathematics.

Whitin, D. J., & Whitin, P. (2004). *New visions for linking literature and mathematics.* Reston, VA: National Council of Teachers of Mathematics.

## FURTHER READING AND RESOURCES

Anderson, C. L., Anderson, K. M., & Wenzel, E. J. (2000). Oil and water don't mix but they do teach fractions. *Teaching Children Mathematics, 7*(3), 174–178.

*Box it or bag it mathematics (K–2).* Portland, OR: Math Learning Center.

*Bridges in mathematics (K–2).* Portland, OR: Math Learning Center.

Burris, A. C. (2005). *Understanding the math you teach.* Upper Saddle River, NJ: Pearson-Merrill/Prentice-Hall.

Chen, J., & McNamee, G. D. (2007). *Bridging: Assessment for teaching and learning in early childhood classrooms, pre-K–3.* Thousand Oaks, CA: Corwin.

Emberley, E. (1984). *Picture pie: A circle drawing book.* Boston: Little, Brown.

Flores, A., Samson, J., & Yanik, H. B. (2006). Quotient and measurement interpretations of rational numbers. *Teaching Children Mathematics, 13*(1), 34–39.

Giles, R. M., Parmer, L., & Byrd, K. (2003). Putting the pieces together: Developing early concepts of fractions. *Dimensions of Early Childhood, 31*(1), 3–8.

Kosbob, S., & Moyer, P. S. (2004). Picnicking with fractions. *Teaching Children Mathematics, 10*(7), 375–378.

Leitze, A. R., & Stump, S. (2007). Sharing cookies. *Teaching Children Mathematics, 13*(7), 378–379.

Moone, G., & de Groot, C. (2007). Fraction action. *Teaching Children Mathematics, 13*(5), 266–271.

Moyer, P. S., & Mailley, E. (2004). *Inchworm and a half*: Developing fraction and measurement concepts using mathematical representations. *Teaching Children Mathematics, 10*(5), 244–252.

National Council of Teachers of Mathematics. (1989). *Curriculum and evaluation standards for school mathematics.* Reston, VA: Author.

Neumer, C. (2007). Mixed numbers made easy: Building and converting mixed numbers and improper fractions. *Teaching Children Mathematics, 13*(9), 488–492.

Ortiz, E. (2000). A game involving fraction squares. *Teaching Children Mathematics, 7*(4), 218–222.

Ortiz, E. (2006). The roll out fractions game: Comparing fractions. *Teaching Children Mathematics, 13*(1), 56–62.

Powell, C. A., & Hunting, R. P. (2003). Fractions in the early years curriculum: More needed, not less. *Teaching Children Mathematics, 10*(1), 6–7.

Riddle, M., & Rodzwell, B. (2000). Fractions: What happened between kindergarten and the army. *Teaching Children Mathematics, 7*(4), 202–206.

Siebert, D., & Gaskin, N. (2006). Creating, naming and justifying fractions. *Teaching Children Mathematics, 12*(8), 394–400.

Stump, S., & Tayeh, C. (2006). Problem solvers: Making brownies and solutions to the better box problem. *Teaching Children Mathematics, 13*(3), 162.

Watanabe, T. (2002). Representations in teaching and learning fractions. *Teaching Children Mathematics, 8*(8), 457–463.

# Unit 30

## Numbers above Ten and Place Value

### OBJECTIVES

After reading this unit, you should be able to:

■ Define place value, renaming, and regrouping.

■ Identify developmentally appropriate instruction for place-value and two-digit whole number operations.

■ Assess children's understanding of numbers above ten and of place value.

■ Provide developmentally appropriate place-value and addition and subtraction instruction with two-digit numbers.

As described in Unit 27, the NCTM (2000, p. 78) standard on number and operations includes expectations for the understanding of operations and how they relate to each other and for fluent computation and making reasonable estimates (discussed in Unit 25). During the primary grades, students should reach an understanding of a variety of means for adding and subtracting and of the relationship between the two operations, should understand the effects of adding and subtracting whole numbers, and should understand the situations where multiplication and division are used. Children should develop skill at whole number computation for addition and subtraction, should be able to use the basic addition and subtraction number combinations, and should use many different computation tools such as "objects, mental computation, estimation, paper and pencil, and calculators" (p. 78). This unit proceeds into working with numbers above

ten and addition and subtraction of double-digit whole numbers.

The focal points (NCTM, 2007) for number and operations for first grade include developing an understanding of whole numbers from 10 to 100 in relation to groups of tens and ones. During grade 2, students develop an understanding of the base-ten numeration system and place-value concepts. They are able to depict equivalent representations of numbers, such as showing 25 to be two tens and one five. In grade 3, students extend their understanding of place value to numbers up to 10,000.

During the latter part of the preoperational period (see Unit 25), children who are adept at manipulating quantities up to ten can move on to working with quantities above ten. Through manipulation of groups of ten and quantities between zero and ten, children move through the teens and up to 20. Some will pick up the pattern of the 20s, 30s, and so on up through the 90s. As children enter concrete operations, they perfect their informal knowledge of numbers above ten and move on to whole number operations with such numbers. To fully understand what they are doing when they use whole number operations involving numbers above ten, they must be able to conceptualize **place value**: the understanding that the same numeral represents different amounts depending on which position it is in. For example, consider the numbers 3, 30, and 300. In the first instance, *3* stands for three 1s and is in the 1s' place. In 30, *3* stands for three 10s and is in the 10s' place. In 300, *3* stands for three 100s and is in the 100s' place. In the latter two numbers, 0 indicates that there is no quantity in the place it holds. In the number 32, *3* is in the 10s' place and *2* is in the 1s' place. An understanding of place value underlies the understanding of certain **trading rules** that govern place value and enable whole number operations to be accomplished. Examples of trading rules include:

- Ten 1s can be traded for one 10.
- One 10 can be traded for ten 1s.
- Ten 10s can be traded for 100.
- One hundred 1s can be traded for 100.

The place-value concept enables us to represent any value using only 10 numerals (0 to 9).

Place value is one of the most difficult concepts for young children to grasp. Being able to rote and rational count above ten is only a beginning step on the way to an understanding of place value. Children need many counting experiences (as described in Unit 9) and many experiences with concrete models in order to develop the place-value concept. All too often, children are rushed into the place-value operations involved in **regrouping** (formerly called borrowing and carrying) as a rote memory activity without the necessary underlying conceptualization. Through an understanding of place value, children will realize that, when they take one from the 10s' column, they are actually taking one group of 10 and that, when they add numbers in the ones' column and arrive at a sum above nine, the

Place-value problems are a challenge for primary grade students.

amount they move to the 10s' column represents one or more groups of 10. Understanding place value will also help them to see that the placement of numerals is critical in determining value. For example, *sixty-eight* can be written as 68 (six 10s and eight 1s) and as 60 + 8 but *not* as 86. The sequence for writing numbers follows fixed rules just like a word sentence. That is, "Ball boy the throws" does not follow the conventions of correctly written English. In the same fashion, *one hundred twenty-one* is not written as 10021. How to guide children to an understanding of this concept is the focus of this unit.

## ASSESSMENT

Understanding place value is a difficult task for young children. They will normally flounder for a while, seeming to understand the concept in some situations and not in others. Teachers should be patient and accepting and give the children time and appropriate experiences. The following are examples of assessment tasks that can be used to discover where the children are on the road to understanding two-digit numbers and the concept of place value.

## SAMPLE ASSESSMENT TASK

**9P**                                             **Concrete Operations Ages 7–8**

### Place Value, Groups of 10: Unit 30

**METHOD:**        Interview.

**SKILL:**         Child is able to count groups of 11 or more objects and tell how many 10s are in the groups.

**MATERIALS:**     A container of 100 counters (e.g., chips, cubes, or sticks).

**PROCEDURE:**     Place the container of counters in front of the child. Say, HERE ARE A BUNCH OF COUNTERS. COUNT OUT AS MANY OF THEM AS YOU CAN. If the child counts out 11 or more ask, HOW MANY 10s DO YOU THINK YOU HAVE? HOW MANY 1s?

**EVALUATION:**    If the child answers correctly, then she probably has the concept of place value for 10s. An incorrect answer indicates that, although she may be able to rational count groups of objects greater than ten, she does not yet understand the meaning of each of the numerals in her response.

**INSTRUCTIONAL RESOURCE:**  Charlesworth, R., and Lind, K. K. (2010). *Math and science for young children* (6th ed.). Clifton Park, NY: Cengage Learning.

## SAMPLE ASSESSMENT TASK

**9Q**                                             **Concrete Operations Ages 7–8**

### Place Value, Grouping to Identify an Amount: Unit 30

**METHOD:**        Interview.

**SKILL:**         The child is able to form two or more subgroups of ten objects, each with some remaining from the original group, and then tell how many he has without counting each individual object.

**MATERIALS:**     A container of 100 counters (e.g., chips, cubes, or sticks).

**PROCEDURE:**     Place a pile of counters (start with about 35) in front of the child. MAKE AS MANY GROUPS OF 10 AS YOU CAN. HOW MANY (counters) DO YOU HAVE ALTOGETHER?

**EVALUATION:**    Note if the child can come up with the answer by counting the number of groups of 10 and adding on the number of 1s or if instead he must count each object to be sure of the total. If the child can determine the answer without counting by ones, this indicates that he is developing the concept of place value.

**INSTRUCTIONAL RESOURCE:**  Charlesworth, R., and Lind, K. K. (2010). *Math and science for young children* (6th ed.). Clifton Park, NY: Cengage Learning.

On average, first graders can learn to read, write, and understand two-digit numbers, second graders three-digit numbers, and third graders four-digit numbers. However, there will be a broad range of normal variation within any particular group. The best rule of thumb in assessment is to be sure children understand one-digit numbers before going on to two-digit, two before three, and so on.

## ACTIVITIES

The following activities are adapted from the selection of resources listed at the end of this unit. Young children need many experiences with place value and in manipulating objects whose number exceeds ten before proceeding to whole number operations with two-digit numbers. Start with counting activities such as those suggested in Unit 9. Then move on to the kinds of activities described in the following pages. The first two activities focus on constructing an understanding of the properties of amounts greater than ten.

### ACTIVITIES

#### Numerals Greater Than 10: Conservation of Large Numbers

**OBJECTIVE:** To understand, when given a group of more than ten objects, that the number of objects remains the same no matter how they are arranged.

**MATERIALS:** Each child will need a container with 50 or more counters (i.e., cubes, chips, or sticks) and a place-value board (cf. Richardson, 1984, p. 212). A place-value board is a piece of paper divided into two sections so that groups can be placed on one side and loose counters on the other side. To make a place-value board, take a 9" × 12" piece of paper or tagboard and then glue or staple a 6" × 9" piece of colored paper on one half. Draw a picture in the upper right-hand corner of the white side so that the child will know how to place the board in the correct position.

Unifix Cubes are excellent for this activity because they can be snapped together. However, cubes or chips that can be stacked or sticks that can be held together with a rubber band may also be used.

**ACTIVITY:** Tell the children to put some amount of counters greater than ten on the white side of their place-value board. Suggest the children work in pairs so they can check each other's counting. When they agree that they have the same amount, say, MAKE A GROUP OF TEN (counters) AND PUT IT ON THE (color) SIDE OF YOUR BOARD. HOW MANY LOOSE (counters) DO YOU HAVE LEFT? HOW MANY (counters) DO YOU HAVE ALTOGETHER? Note how many children realize that they still have the same number of counters. Ask, DO YOU HAVE ENOUGH (counters) TO MAKE ANOTHER TEN? Note if they respond correctly. If they do make another ten, ask again how many loose cubes they have and if the total is still the same. To connect their arrangements to number symbols, write the arrangements on the board: "3 tens and 4 ones" and "2 tens and 14 ones."

*(continued)*

**FOLLOW-UP:** The same activity could be done using containers to put the counters in. Each container could be labeled 10. If small counters such as tiny chips, bottle caps, or beans are used, this would be a more efficient way to keep the groups separated. See Richardson (1984; 1999a; 1999b) for additional variations on this activity.

## Numerals Greater than 10: Measuring

**OBJECTIVE:** To work with large numbers through nonstandard measurement activities (see Unit 18 for background information).

**MATERIALS:** Small objects that can be used as nonstandard units, paper and pencil to record measurements, and measurement cards (as suggested by Richardson, 1984). Each measurement card depicts something in the classroom that can be measured.

**ACTIVITY:** The children measure the items with the objects, group the objects into 10s, then figure out how many they have used. They record the results on their paper.

The chair is 24 paper clips tall.

The table is 36 paper clips wide.

**FOLLOW-UP:** Have the children measure the same items using different nonstandard units and compare the number of units. See Richardson (1984; 1999a; 1999b) for further activities.

Once the children have a good understanding of counting and subdividing groups greater than ten, they are ready for activities that gradually move them into the complexities of place value.

## ACTIVITIES

### Place Value: Constructing Models of Two-Digit Numbers

**OBJECTIVE:** To develop models of two-digit numbers using the place-value board.

**MATERIALS:** Place-value board (described in previous activity) and a supply of cards with individual numerals, 0 to 9, written on each card. Provide the child(ren) with at least two sets of numerals and a supply of counters that can be readily stacked, snapped, or bundled into groups of 10. One child working alone will need 100 counters. If children are working in small groups and sharing the counters, add 50 counters per child.

**ACTIVITY:** Have the children put the place-value boards in front of them. Provide them with an ample supply of numerals in a small container and place the container of counters where it is convenient for everyone to reach. CLOSE YOUR EYES AND PICK TWO NUMERALS. PUT ONE ON YOUR BOARD ON THE (color) SIDE AND ONE ON YOUR BOARD ON THE WHITE SIDE. MAKE A MODEL OF THE NUMERAL YOU HAVE SELECTED.

**FOLLOW-UP:** Have the students repeat this activity with different number combinations. Have them work alone, in pairs, and/or in small groups. Have them do the same activity using base-ten blocks after they have been introduced. (Base-ten blocks will be described later.) The same activity can be adapted to work with 100s and 1,000s when the children are ready. The activity could also be done using spinners, one for each place value.

### Place Value: Estimation with Common Items

**OBJECTIVE:** To estimate amounts and apply knowledge of place value to finding out how close the estimate is.

**MATERIALS:** A container of common items such as a bag of peanuts, dry beans, or cotton balls; a box of paper clips, rubber bands, or cotton swabs; a jar of bottle tops, clothespins, pennies, or other common items; some small cups, bowls, or plastic glasses; flip-chart numerals or paper

*(continued)*

and pencil to write results. (Flip-chart numerals can be made by writing numerals 0 to 9 on cards, punching two holes at the top of each card, and putting the cards on rings.)

**ACTIVITY:** *Estimating* is the math term for guessing or predicting the answer to a math problem. Show the children the container of objects. Let them hold it, examine it, but not open it. LOOK CLOSELY AT THIS (item). HOW MANY (items) DO YOU THINK ARE IN THIS (container)? You record or have the children record each child's guess. Open the container. COUNT OUT GROUPS OF TEN (item) AND PUT THEM IN THE (cups, glasses, and so on). FIND OUT HOW MANY GROUPS OF TEN THERE ARE ALTOGETHER. EACH TIME YOU COUNT OUT TEN, TURN OVER A NUMBER ON YOUR FLIP CHART, or if the children can write, WRITE THE NUMBER THAT TELLS HOW MANY TENS YOU HAVE.

**FOLLOW-UP:** Once the children catch on, put out the estimate of the week. Children can record their guesses on a chart. Then on Friday they can open the container and find out the actual amount. A graph can be made showing the distribution of estimates.

| | | | | | |
|---|---|---|---|---|---|
| 4 | | | | 59 | |
| 3 | | | 39 | 56 | 64 |
| 2 | | 27 | 39 | 45 | 55 | 63 |
| 1 | | 25 | 32 | 40 | 51 | 60 |
| | 10s | 20s | 30s | 40s | 50s | 50s |

For more ideas, see Chapters 11 and 12 of Baratta-Lorton (1976).

Base-ten blocks provide a different kind of model for working with the place-value concept. It is important that children work with a variety of types of materials in model construction so that they do not think there is only one way to view place value with concrete materials. So far we have described making models with discrete items. Base-ten blocks depict each place with a solid model. Units (or 1s) are individual cubes, rods (or 10s) are the equivalent of 10 unit cubes stuck together in a row, flats (or 100s) are the equivalent of 10 rods stuck together, and cubes (or 1,000s) are the equivalent of 10 flats stacked and glued together. See Figure 30–1.

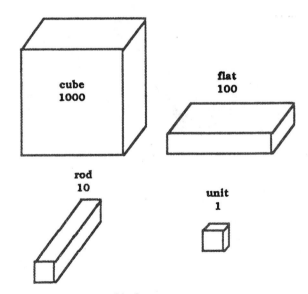

**Figure 30–1** Base-ten blocks.

## ACTIVITIES

### Place Value: Base-Ten Blocks

**OBJECTIVE:** To work with place value using base-ten blocks.

**MATERIALS:** A classroom set of base-ten blocks.

**ACTIVITY:** The base-ten blocks can be used for the activities previously described by adding on another step. Each time the child makes a group of ten, she can record this by selecting a rod. She can then count the rods at the end to find out how many groups of ten she has found.

**FOLLOW-UP:** Many auxiliary materials can be purchased that provide activities with base-ten blocks besides those that come with the Teacher's Guide. Base-ten blocks and teachers' guides can be purchased from suppliers such as Dale Seymour, Creative Publications, ETA, Cuisinaire, and DIDAX Educational Resources (see addresses in Unit 39).

In the computer laboratory, students can experiment with virtual mathematics place-value activities.

Trading is another procedure for working with place value. Primary children need many experiences counting piles of objects, trading for groups of ten, and describing the results. Once they can do these activities with ease, they can move on to regrouping and renaming. Too often they are pushed into regrouping and renaming without an adequate conceptual base built on counting and constructing many groups of ten and relating them (and any 1s remaining) to written numerals. Regrouping happens when one or more items are added or taken away so that an amount moves to the next 10, next 100, next 1,000, and so on. That is, a group might break down into two 10s and six 1s, or 26. Five more units are added so there are now eleven units. Ten units are then moved to the 10s' place, leaving one unit in the 1s' place. There are now three 10s and one unit, or 31. **Renaming** of the group has also occurred. It has now been *renamed* 31.

Reverse trading would take place if units were removed. For example: suppose seven units are to be taken away from the three 10s and one unit; a 10 would be moved over to the units, making eleven units, and seven units could then be removed, leaving two 10s and four 1s, or 24. Primary grade children need to do many trading activities with concrete materials before moving on to paper-and-pencil computations. These trades can be practiced with concrete items, such as cubes and chips, the beads on an abacus, or base-ten blocks. Chip trading materials can be purchased from Dale Seymour.

## ACTIVITIES

### Place Value: Trading Activities

**OBJECTIVE:** To construct the concepts of regrouping and renaming through trading activities.

**MATERIALS:** A supply of paper squares consisting of 100 reds (units) and 30 blues (10s); a place-value board with a 1s' and 10s' place.

**ACTIVITY:** Have the children put their place-value boards in front of them. Place a supply of red and blue paper squares where they can be easily reached. THE BLUE SQUARES ARE 10s AND THE RED SQUARES ARE 1s. Hold up a large 27. SHOW ME HOW YOU CAN MAKE A MODEL OF THIS NUMBER ON YOUR BOARD. Have the children try several examples. When you are sure they understand that the reds are 1s and the blues are 10s, go on to regrouping. Go back to 27. MAKE 27 ON YOUR BOARDS AGAIN. NOW, SUPPOSE SOMEONE GIVES YOU FIVE MORE 1s. TAKE FIVE MORE. WHAT HAPPENS TO YOUR 1s? Encourage them to describe what happens. Remind them that there cannot be more than nine in the 1s' place. Eventually someone will realize that 32 should be modeled with three 10s and two 1s. Have the children discuss what they might do to get a model that has three 10s and two 1s by trading. SUPPOSE YOU TRADE 10 REDS FOR 1 BLUE. WHERE SHOULD THE BLUE BE PLACED? Once everyone has the blue in the 10s' place, ask, SUPPOSE SOMEONE NEEDS FOUR 1s. HOW COULD YOU GIVE THEM FOUR? Encourage them to discuss this problem with each other and ask your questions until someone discovers that another trade will have to be made. Have everyone trade in a blue for ten reds, take four away, and see that they now have two blues and eight reds (28).

**FOLLOW-UP:** Create some story problems and have the children solve them using trading. Then move on to adding and taking away two-digit quantities. Also provide students with pairs of two-digit numbers and have them invent problems using the numbers.

When the children practice trading to regroup and rename on their place-value boards, they are actually adding and subtracting informally. Richardson (1984) explains how to carry this activity over to addition and subtraction of two-digit numbers. Richardson believes that it is confusing to begin two-digit addition and subtraction with numbers that do *not* have to be regrouped, such as

$$
\begin{array}{cccc}
22 & 53 & 46 & 18 \\
+35 & +14 & -34 & -13 \\
\hline
57 & 67 & 12 & 5
\end{array}
$$

This type of addition and subtraction may lead children to believe that adding or subtracting with two digits is exactly the same operation as with one digit. The result may be responses such as this:

$$
\begin{array}{cccc}
25 & 48 & 72 & 37 \\
+16 & +34 & -35 & -28 \\
\hline
311 & 712 & 43 & 11
\end{array}
$$

Note in these examples that the children have added or subtracted each column as though it were an individual one-digit problem. Introduce two-digit addition as follows.

PUT 26 CUBES
ON YOUR BOARD.

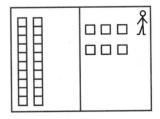

NOW GET 18
CUBES, AND
PUT THEM
NEXT TO YOUR
BOARD.

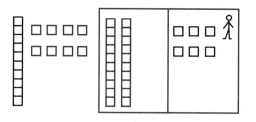

NOW PUT THEM TOGETHER.
HOW MANY 10s? HOW
MANY 1s?
YES, WE HAVE THREE 10s
AND FOURTEEN 1s.
DO WE HAVE ENOUGH TO
MAKE ANOTHER 10?

(Give them time to move
10 cubes.) NOW WE HAVE
FOUR 10s AND FOUR 1s
HOW MANY IS THAT? YES,
THAT IS 44.

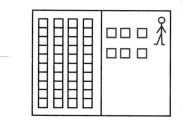

Repeat this process several times with different pairs of
two-digit numbers: Sometimes the sum contains more

than nine units and sometimes it does not. When the
children understand the process without symbols, connect the symbols by writing them on the board as you
go through the process.

Subtraction of two-digit numbers can be introduced in parallel fashion. For example, have the children put out 42 cubes and then tell them they need to
take away 25. They will discover that they have to break
up a 10 to accomplish this task. After doing many examples without written numbers, go through some
problems in which you connect the quantities to numbers at each step, thus gradually introducing the notation. Then have them do mixed sets of problems. Finally,
move on to story problems.

Problems and activities that apply place-value
concepts can be integrated across the curriculum
(Figure 30–2).

## KAMII'S APPROACH

The activities suggested in this unit follow a fairly structured sequence while promoting construction of concepts through exploration. Kamii and colleagues (Kamii,
Lewis, & Livingston, 1993) have been working with
primary children using open-ended activities that provide for more child trial and error and self-sequencing.
Interviewing primary students who had been through
conventional workbook/textbook instruction, they discovered that students were able to do regrouping and
renaming as a rote process without really knowing the
meaning of the numbers they were using. For example,
when asked to do a two-digit problem such as 28 + 45,
they could come up with the correct answer:

$$\begin{array}{r} 1 \\ 28 \\ +45 \\ \hline 73 \end{array}$$

However, when asked what the 1 in 13 means,
they said it meant "one" rather than "ten." Kamii has
had greater success in communicating this concept
to primary children by using games and letting them
discover the relationship of the digits on their own.
No workbooks or worksheets are used, and neither are

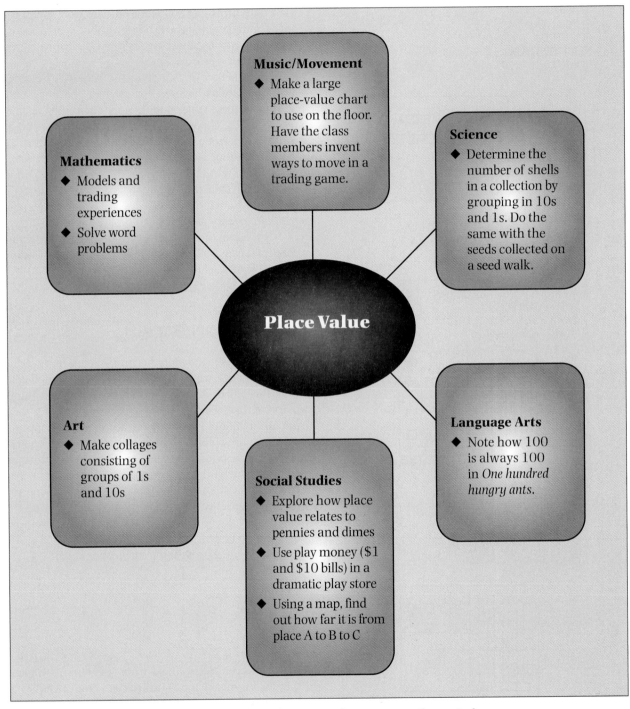

**Figure 30–2** Integrating experiences with place value and quantities above ten across the curriculum.

the kinds of concrete activities described in this unit. Problems are written on the board, children contribute answers, and every answer is listed. Then the children give their rationales for their answers. When working with double-digit addition, their natural inclination is to start on the left. They add the 10s; write the answer; add the 1s; and, if necessary, move any 10s over, erasing the original answer in the 10s' column. Through trial and error and discussion, they develop their own method and construct their own place-value concept. Place value is not taught as a separate skill needed prior to doing double-column addition. This method sounds intriguing and is more fully described in Kamii (2003).

## CALCULATORS

When children explore calculators for counting, they notice that the number on the right changes every time whereas the other numbers change less frequently. Calculators provide a graphic look at place value and the relation of each place to those adjacent. Suggest that the children try 10 and note what happens—that is, which place changes, and by how much each time? This activity will assist children in seeing what the 10s' place means. Concepts constructed using manipulatives can be reinforced with calculator activities. By adding 1 to numbers that end in nine and subtracting 1 from num-

A hand calculator can be a useful tool for working with place value.

bers that end in zero, students can see immediately what happens. Suggest that they guess which number follows 9, 29, and 59. Then have them use their calculators to check their predictions. Use the same procedure, except have them predict what will happen if they subtract 1 from 20, 40, and 70.

## IDEAS FOR CHILDREN WITH SPECIAL NEEDS

Children with motor disabilities such as spina bifida (SB), cerebral palsy (CP), or developmental coordination disorder (DCD) are challenged by any type of motor skills task (Lewis, 2003). They may not be able to interact with objects in any conventional way depending on the degree of their disability. However they can develop cognitive understanding with the right kind of support. Ways have to be found for them to act on their environment. Technology can be designed that allows children with motor disabilities to use whatever movement they have available to assist them in learning and communicating. These children require close attention from adults, who should provide prompting and cueing as they work. In class, teachers need to emphasize the children's strengths.

Children with perceptual problems may have difficulties perceiving the commonalities among numbers above nine. They may need to have the teens lined up vertically so the common element of 1 (in the 10s' place) can be seen. Color coding can be helpful. These children commonly make reversals (e.g., confusing 13 and 31). With numbers of two or more symbols it is important for children to understand spatial terms such as left, right, middle, first, last, and beginning. Some children may need extra help with auditory memory. The teacher may say "fifty-two" but the child may perceive only the "two."

Children may find it interesting to learn how we arrived at base ten for our number system and the systems other cultures use for recording and calculating. Zaslavsky (1996) explains how finger counting is common practice in many cultures. In others, both fingers and toes are used and so the base is 20. Once large amounts become involved, each culture has had to invent a method of recording and calculating. Tally marks on bone or wood have been used for thousands of years. The bar codes used so commonly today are based on groups of tally marks of two heights. Knots on string are another method used to record amounts. The abacus, first developed in China, allows for calculation of large numbers using rows of beads.

## EVALUATION

An evaluation technique suggested by Kamii (2003) shows if children really understand place value in two-digit numbers.

> Show the child a three-by-five-inch card with 16 written on it. Ask, "What does this say?" After the child says 16, count out 16 chips. With the top of a pen circle the 6 of the 16. "What does this *part* (the 6) mean? show me with the chips what this *part* (the 6) means." Circle the 1 of the 16. "What does this *part* (the 1) mean? show me with the chips what this *part* (the 1) means." (p. 161)

Kamii reports that, after conventional instruction with workbooks and possibly some manipulatives, all first and second graders can answer correctly regarding the 6. However, of the primary children Kamii interviewed, none of the late first graders, 33% of late third graders, and only 50% of late fourth graders said that the 1 means 10. Children who learned about place value through constructing it themselves using Kamii's method did considerably better. At the end of the second grade, 66% said that the 1 means 10 and 74% said that the 5 in 54 means 50.

Whichever instructional method you use, be sure to observe carefully the process each child uses. Question children frequently about what they are doing to be sure they really understand the concepts and are not just answering in a rote manner.

## SUMMARY

Learning about place value and working with two-digit whole number operations that require regrouping and renaming are two of the most difficult challenges faced by the primary-level child. Conventionally, they are taught using a workbook approach with few (if any) manipulatives to support the instruction. Also, they are conventionally introduced too early and become rote memory activities for those who have the facility to remember the steps necessary to come up with correct answers. Less capable students flounder in a lack of understanding.

Most mathematics educators believe that children learn the concepts and skills needed to understand place value—as well the processes of regrouping and renaming—through practice in solving problems that use concrete materials. Kamii (2003) takes a different approach, using no concrete materials but guiding children through trial and error and discussion. Children with perceptual and/or motor disabilities will have a need for special assistance.

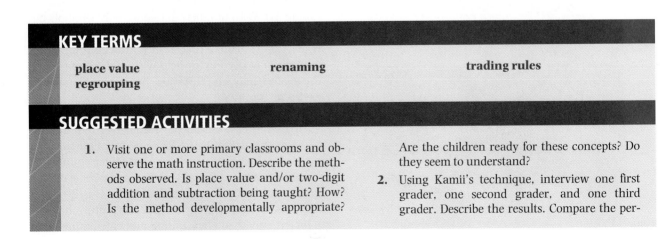

### KEY TERMS

place value
regrouping

renaming

trading rules

### SUGGESTED ACTIVITIES

1.  Visit one or more primary classrooms and observe the math instruction. Describe the methods observed. Is place value and/or two-digit addition and subtraction being taught? How? Is the method developmentally appropriate?

Are the children ready for these concepts? Do they seem to understand?

2.  Using Kamii's technique, interview one first grader, one second grader, and one third grader. Describe the results. Compare the per-

formance of the children you interviewed with those interviewed by Kamii. What did you learn from this experience?

**3.** Review the first-, second-, and third-grade levels of two or more elementary math textbook series. At what level are place value, two-digit addition and subtraction, regrouping, and renaming introduced? What methods of instruction are used? Compare the textbook methods with those described in this unit. What are the similarities and differences? Explain why you would or would not like to use these textbooks.

**4.** Prepare materials for one of the activities suggested in this unit. Try out the activity with a child or small group of children that you believe to be at the right stage for it. Write a report explaining what you did, who you did it with, what happened, and your evaluation of the activity and the children's responses.

**5.** Using the guidelines from Activity 5, Unit 2, evaluate any of the following software designed to reinforce concepts of place value.

■ *Grouping and Place Value* (http://store.sunburst.com). Group and regroup numbers and objects into equal bundles of ones, tens, and hundreds and discover place value.

■ *Numbers Recovered* (http://store.sunburst.com). Helps in the understanding of place value.

■ *Math Essentials: Addition and Subtraction* (http://store.sunburst.com). Includes addition and subtraction with regrouping.

■ *Virtual Manipulatives, Numbers and Operations* (pre-K–2; http://nlvm.usu.edu). Base-ten blocks, chips abacus, color chips.

**6.** Keep your Activity File/Notebook up-to-date.

## REVIEW

**A.** Define the following terms.
1. Place value
2. Regrouping
3. Renaming

**B.** Identify which of the following are descriptions of place value being taught as described in this unit.
1. A kindergarten teacher is drilling her class on 1s', 10s', and 100s' places using a worksheet approach.
2. A second-grade teacher gives one of her students 35 Unifix Cubes and asks him to make as many groups of ten as he can.
3. A primary teacher is beginning instruction on two-digit addition with simple problems such as 12 + 41 so the students will not have to regroup and rename right away.
4. Some primary children are exploring with calculators. Their teacher has suggested they take a list of the numbers 19, 29, 39, and 49 and predict what will happen if 1 is added to each. Then they are to try these operations with their calculators, write

down what happens, and share the results with the other children and the teacher.

**C.** Explain your answers to question B.

**D.** List three kinds of materials that can be used for making place-value models.

**E.** In what ways does Kamii's approach to teaching place value differ from what is conventionally done?

**F.** Check yourself on place value.
1. Identify the number of 100s, 10s, and 1s in each numeral.

| | 100s | 10s | 1s |
|---|---|---|---|
| 37 | | | |
| 4 | | | |
| 276 | | | |

2. In the numeral 3,482, the 4 means ____, the 8 means ____, and the 2 means ____.

3.  
```
  1
 67     The 1 above the 6 means:
+17     _____.
───
 84
```

## REFERENCES

Baratta-Lorton, M. (1976). *Mathematics their way.* Menlo Park, CA: Addison-Wesley.

Kamii, C. (2003). *Young children continue to reinvent arithmetic, 2nd grade* (2nd ed.). New York: Teachers College Press.

Kamii, C., Lewis, B. A., & Livingston, S. J. (1993). Primary arithmetic: Children inventing their own procedures. *Arithmetic Teacher, 41*(4), 200–203.

Lewis, V. (2003). *Development and disability* (2nd ed.). Malden, MA: Blackwell.

National Council of Teachers of Mathematics. (2000). *Principles and standards for school mathematics.* Reston, VA: Author.

National Council of Teachers of Mathematics. (2007). *Curriculum focal points.* Reston, VA: Author.

Richardson, K. (1984). *Developing number concepts using Unifix Cubes.* Menlo Park, CA: Addison-Wesley.

Richardson, K. (1999a). *Developing number concepts: Book 2. Addition and subtraction.* Parsippany, NJ: Seymour.

Richardson, K. (1999b). *Developing number concepts: Book 3. Place value, multiplication, and division.* Parsippany, NJ: Seymour.

Zaslavsky, C. (1996). *The multicultural math classroom.* Portsmouth, NH: Heinmann.

## FURTHER READING AND RESOURCES

Auriemma, S. H. (1999). How huge is a hundred? *Teaching Children Mathematics, 6*(3), 154–159.

Bove, S. P. (1995). Place value: A vertical perspective. *Teaching Children Mathematics, 1*, 542–546.

*Box it or bag it mathematics (K–2).* Portland, OR: Math Learning Center.

*Bridges in mathematics (K–2).* Portland, OR: Math Learning Center.

Burris, A.C. (2005). *Understanding the math you teach: Content and methods for prekindergarten through grade 4.* Upper Saddle River, NJ: Merrill-Pearson/Prentice-Hall.

Huinker, D. (2002). Calculators as learning tools for young children's explorations of number. *Teaching Children Mathematics, 8*(6), 316–321.

Irving, K. J. (2003). The MegaPenny project. *Teaching Children Mathematics, 10*(3), 158–161.

Kari, A. R., & Anderson, C. B. (2003). Opportunities to develop place value through student dialogue. *Teaching Children Mathematics, 10*(2), 78–82.

Perry, J. A., & Atkins, S. L. (2002). It's not just notation: Valuing children's representations. *Teaching Children Mathematics, 9*(4), 196–201.

Princzes, E. J. (1993). *One hundred hungry ants.* New York: Scholastic Books.

Reed, K. M. (2000). How many spots does a cheetah have? *Teaching Children Mathematics, 6*(6), 346–349.

Reys, B. J., & Arbaugh, F. (2001). Clearing up the confusion over calculator use in grades K–5. *Teaching Children Mathematics, 8*(2), 90–94.

Ross, S. R. (2002). Place value: Problem solving and written assessment. *Teaching Children Mathematics, 8*(7), 419–423.

Sheppard, J. (1990). *The right number of elephants.* New York: Harper Collins.

Sisul, J. S. (2002). Fostering flexibility with number in the primary grades. *Teaching Children Mathematics, 9*(1), 202–204.

Sztajn, P. (2002). Celebrating 100 with number sense. *Teaching Children Mathematics, 9*(1), 212–217.

Uy, F. L. (2003). The Chinese numeration system and place value. *Teaching Children Mathematics, 9*(5), 243–247.

Whiteneck, J. W., Knipping, N., Loesing, J., Kim, O., & Beetsma, A. (2002). Starting off the school year with opportunities for all: Supporting first graders' development of number sense. *Teaching Children Mathematics, 9*(1), 26–31.

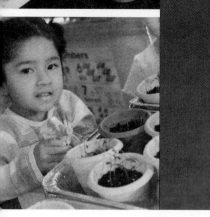

# Unit **31**

## Geometry, Data Collection, and Algebraic Thinking

### OBJECTIVES

After reading this unit, you should be able to:

■ List the basic concepts of geometry that young children learn informally at the primary level.

■ Assess children's readiness for primary-level geometry and data collection experiences.

■ Plan and carry out developmentally appropriate primary-level geometry, data collection, algebraic thinking, estimation, and probability instruction.

■ Be able to construct and interpret graphs and tables.

Standards (NCTM, 2000) for geometry (Units 12, 13), data analysis (Units 10, 20), and algebra (Units 10, 11, 17, 25) were introduced and the topics discussed previously. The initial level of algebraic thinking lies in the understanding of patterns and relationships. These expectations continue into the primary grades, when children are expected to further their capabilities to recognize, name, build, draw, compare, and sort two- and three-dimensional shapes. Further, they should gain some understanding of **symmetry**, be able to create mental images of geometric shapes, recognize shapes from different perspectives, relate ideas in geometry to number and measurement, and locate geometric shapes in the environment. Primary-level children are expected to move further in their understanding of data analysis by being able to describe and explain the meaning of data and make predictions from data. The expectations for understanding probability are at an informal level only.

The focal points (NCTM, 2007) for primary grades include an emphasis on integration of several of the topics in this unit. For first grade, a focal point in geometry is composing and decomposing shapes. Connections include using geometric shapes for informal measurement and on bar graphs in addition to connecting patterns (such as odd and even numbers) as a basis for algebra. A curriculum focal point for second-grade number and operations is learning methods of estimation. Connections are made to geometry as children collect data related to space. More knowledge of number patterns is obtained that lead to later algebraic understanding. A grade-3 focal point in geometry is describing and analyzing two-dimensional shapes so that an understanding of congruence and symmetry is developed. Multiplication and division and their relationship connect with algebra readiness. Whole number operations are applied during data analysis: constructing and analyzing frequency tables, bar graphs, picture graphs, and line plots in order to solve problems.

Weather is the current science topic in Mr. Gonzales's third-grade class in northern Utah. This morning the children are huddled over copies of the past week's weather forecasts that they clipped out of Ogden's local morning paper. They are reading the forecast section to find out what kind of information is included and to discuss how they might organize some of the data presented. They note that the day's forecast is included along with the normal highs and lows for that date. There is a regional forecast for Utah and a forecast map and description of the weather for the entire United States. Selected national and global temperatures along with precipitation and outlook are included in a table. The nation's highs and lows are also reported. The children compile a list of this information and discuss what they can learn and what information might be interesting to record.

Chan's great-great-grandparents came to Utah from Beijing, People's Republic of China. Chan has noticed that Ogden and Beijing are at about the same latitude. He decides to record the high temperatures in Beijing for eight days and compare them with the high temperatures in Ogden for the same time period. First Chan made a chart and then a graph to depict the information from the chart. Then he wrote a description of the information obtained from the graphs. To complete this activity, he applied his mathematical knowledge (measurement, counting, graph making) to an activity that integrates science (the topic of weather), social studies (geography), and reading and language arts (reading and comprehending the article and writing about the information obtained). Figure 31–1 depicts what Chan might have produced.

Groundwork for this type of activity was laid in several previous units: Unit 12 (Early Geometry: Shape), Unit 13 (Early Geometry: Spatial Sense), Unit 20 (Interpreting Data Using Graphs), and Unit 25 (Higher-Level Activities and Concepts). Primary children must have this groundwork before moving on to the activities described in this unit. Children need a basic understanding of shape and space, which they apply to the early graphing and mapping experiences during the preoperational period, before they can move on to higher-level graphing and geometry concepts. Children should know the basic characteristics of shape and be able to identify geometric shapes such as circles, triangles, squares, rectangles, and prisms when they enter the primary level. They should also have the spatial concepts of position, direction, and distance relationships and should be able to use space for making patterns and constructions. Dur-

| Cities | Dates/Temperatures | | | | | | | |
|---|---|---|---|---|---|---|---|---|
| | 22 | 23 | 24 | 25 | 26 | 27 | 28 | 29 |
| Beijing | 28 | 28 | 37 | 37 | 41 | 41 | 45 | 37 |
| Ogden | 36 | 27 | 26 | 26 | 33 | 33 | 42 | 44 |

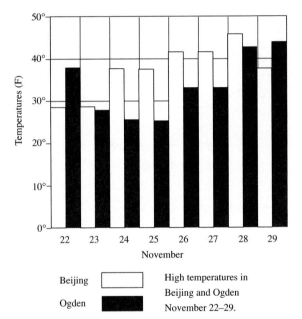

1. Beijing started out colder than Ogden.
2. Beijing gradually got warmer than Ogden.
3. At the end of the eight days, Ogden was warmer than Beijing again.
4. Both cities follow a similar pattern from the high 20s to the low 40s.
5. Both cities are cold in November.
6. Both cities have similar temperatures over time.

**Figure 31–1** Chan's data table and bar graph.

ing the primary years, they should continue with these basic experiences and be guided to more complex levels.

Geometry is studied in a general, informal way during the elementary grades. Spatial concepts are reinforced, and the senses are sharpened. During the primary years, geometric concepts continue to be developed mainly at an intuitive level. However, geometric figures are used to teach other concepts, so children should be familiar with them. For example, multiplication is frequently illustrated in a rectangular grid.

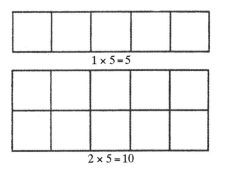

$$1 \times 5 = 5$$

$$2 \times 5 = 10$$

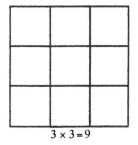

$$3 \times 3 = 9$$

Fractions are commonly illustrated using geometric shapes (see Unit 29), such as the following.

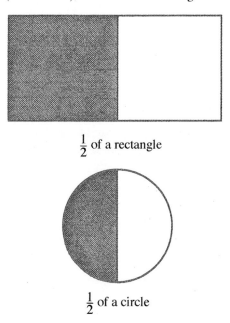

$\frac{1}{2}$ of a rectangle

$\frac{1}{2}$ of a circle

Number lines (which will be described later) are conventionally used to help children visualize greater than, less than, betweenness, and the rules of addition and subtraction. For example, the number line below is used to illustrate that $2 + 3 = 3 + 2$.

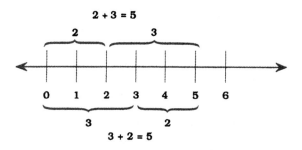

Collecting and organizing data continue to be important applications of mathematics. Graphing is closely related to geometry in that it makes use of geometric concepts such as line and shape. Note that the graphs depicted in this book are based on squares and rectangles. More advanced graphs are based on circles, and others involve the use of line segments to connect points. Tables are the necessary first step in organizing complex data prior to illustrating it on a graph. Charts are closely related to graphs.

In the twenty-first century we look at algebra as "a way of thinking, a method of seeing and expressing relationships" (Moses, 1997). Algebra provides a way to organize and generalize the patterns we observe in everyday activities. Through learning how to develop relationships, we can understand the regularities—not just in mathematics but also in science, history, economics, language, and other areas.

Moses (1997) suggests that algebraic thinking can begin in the early primary grades through the use of geometric concepts such as perimeter and of investigations involving square tiles, string, pipe cleaners, and grid paper. Students can identify geometric and number patterns as they explore these relationships. Technology can also be used to support the development of algebraic thinking. The February 1997 issue of *Teaching Children Mathematics* was devoted to this topic. Algebra was defined in the NCTM (2000) standards and in the "navigation" publications for prekindergarten through grade-2 algebra (Greenes, Cavanagh, Dacey, Findell, & Small, 2001).

Technology involves applications of a broad base of skills. As previously pointed out, design technology is an integration of technology, engineering, mathematics, and science. Another integration is the application of a variety of skills and concepts in the development of robotics projects (Clark, 2002; Murray & Bartelmay, 2005).

In sum: knowledge of geometry, constructing tables and graphs, and algebraic thinking are closely related basic tools for organizing data. The remainder of the unit describes geometry, graphing, the use of charts and tables, and algebraic thinking at the primary level. Also described is LEGO and its relationship with **LOGO** programming, estimation, and probability.

## ASSESSMENT

Readiness for the following primary-level activities should be assessed using the assessment tasks that accompany Units 12 and 13. Readiness is also measured by observing children's capacities to accomplish the graphing activities in Unit 20 and the higher-level graphing and spatial relations (mapping) activities in Unit 25. It is not safe to assume that children have had all the prerequisite experiences before they arrive in your primary classroom. You might have to start with these earlier levels before moving on to the activities suggested in this unit.

## ACTIVITIES

This section begins with geometry and mapping; it then describes LOGO computer applications to mapping and to robotics and design technology. The unit then goes on to the topics of charts and tables, algebraic thinking, estimation, and probability.

## Geometry

Primary children are not ready for the technicalities of geometry, but they can be introduced informally to some of the basic concepts. They can learn about **points** as small dots on paper or on the chalkboard. **Curves** are introduced as smooth but not straight paths that connect two points during a story or a mapping activity. **Lines** appear as number lines, in measurement activities, and as the sides of geometric figures. Children perceive *angles* (space made by the meeting of two straight lines) in geometric figures. *Congruency* or sameness of size and shape is what children deal with when they match and compare the size and shape of various figures, such as when they sort attribute blocks or make collages from paper shapes. Symmetry (correspondence of parts of a figure on opposite sides of a point, line, or plane) is what children are working with when they do the paper folding suggested in the unit on fractions. The terms *point(s)*, *line(s)*, and *curve(s)* may be used with young children without going into the technicalities. The terms *congruency, symmetry,* and *angle* will be introduced beyond the primary level and are not essential to working with the concepts informally. The readings and resources at the end of the unit contain a multitude of ideas for activities that will lay the basis for the formal study of geometry. The following are some examples.

## ACTIVITIES

### Geometry: Geoboard Activities

**OBJECTIVE:** To provide experience exploring the qualities of plane figures.

**MATERIALS:** Geoboards and rubber bands. Geoboards may be purchased or made. A geoboard is a square board with round head screws or smooth, slender cylinders (pegs) made of plastic placed at equal intervals so that it appears to be made up of many squares of equal size. Commercial geoboards have five rows of five pegs each.

Geoboard

**ACTIVITIES:** 1. Put out the geoboards and an ample supply of rubber bands of different sizes and colors (special rubber bands may be purchased with the geoboards). Allow plenty of time for the children to explore the materials informally. Suggest that they see how many different kinds of shapes they can make.

2. Give each child a geoboard and one rubber band. MAKE AS MANY DIFFERENT SHAPES AS YOU CAN WITH ONE RUBBER BAND. Encourage children to count the sides of their shapes and to count the number of pegs in each side. Suggest that they make a drawing of each shape.

3. Give each child a rubber band and an attribute block. MAKE A SHAPE JUST LIKE THE BLOCK'S SHAPE. Start with squares and rectangles, then triangles and hexagons.

4. On graph paper made to match the geoboard, draw patterns that the children can copy with their rubber bands. For example:

5. Have the children draw patterns on graph paper that matches the size of the geoboards. Demonstrate on the chalkboard first to be sure they realize that

(*continued*)

they need to make their lines from corner to corner. Have them try out their capabilities on some laminated blank graphs first. Then have them copy their own patterns on the geoboards. Encourage them to exchange patterns with other children.

**FOLLOW-UP:** Provide more complicated patterns for the children to copy. Encourage those who are capable of doing so to draw and copy more complicated patterns, possibly even some that overlap. Overlapping patterns can be drawn with different colored pencils or crayons and then constructed with rubber bands of matching colors.

## Geometry: Activities with Solids

**OBJECTIVE:** To explore the characteristics of solid geometric figures.

**MATERIALS:** A set of geometric solids (available from ETA, Kaplan, Nienhuis Montessori, DIDAX Educational Resources, Creative Publications, Dale Seymour, Cuisinaire etc.).

Cube          Cylinder          Cone          Pyramid          Sphere

**ACTIVITIES:** Let the children explore the solids, noting the similarities and differences. Once they are familiar with them, try the following activities.

Put out three of the objects. Describe one and see if the children can guess which one it is.

■ IT IS FLAT ALL OVER, AND EACH SIDE IS THE SAME. (cube)

■ IT IS FLAT ON THE BOTTOM. ITS SIDES LOOK LIKE TRIANGLES. (pyramid)

■ IT IS FLAT ON THE BOTTOM, THE TOP IS A POINT, AND THE SIDES ARE SMOOTH. (cone)

■ BOTH ENDS ARE FLAT AND ROUND, AND THE SIDES ARE SMOOTH. (cylinder)

■ IT IS SMOOTH AND ROUND ALL OVER. (sphere)

**FOLLOW-UP:** Have the children take turns being the person who describes the geometric solid. Put up a ramp. Have the students predict which solids will slide, which will roll. Then try them out. See if the children realize that some may roll or slide depending how they are placed.

## Geometry: Symmetry

**OBJECTIVE:** To provide experiences for exploration of symmetry.

**MATERIALS:** Construction paper symmetrical shapes. (See Figure 31–2, on page 449, for some patterns.) The following are some suggested shapes; use your imagination to develop others.

**ACTIVITY:**  Give the children one shape pattern at a time. Have them experiment with folding the shapes until the halves match.

**FOLLOW-UP:**  1.  Have the children use the shapes they have folded to make a three-dimensional collage. PUT GLUE ON JUST ONE HALF OF YOUR FOLDED PAPER.

2.  Give the children paper squares and rectangles. Show them how they can fold them in the middle and then cut the sides so they come out with a figure that is the same on both halves. These can also be used to make three-dimensional collages.

## Geometry: Number Lines

**OBJECTIVE:**  To apply the concept of a line as a visual picture of addition and subtraction and of more than and less than.

**MATERIALS:**  A laminated number line for each child, a large laminated number line that can be used for demonstration (or a permanent number line on the chalkboard), markers (i.e., chips) to mark places on the number lines.

Number Line

**ACTIVITIES:**  1.  *Greater and less than.* PUT A MARKER ON THE 4. FIND A NUMBER THAT IS GREATER THAN 4. PUT A MARKER ON IT. Discuss which numbers were selected. How did they know which numbers were greater than four? Go through the same procedure with the other numbers. Then go through the procedure looking for numbers less than a given number.

(*continued*)

2. *Addition.* HOW CAN WE SHOW TWO PLUS FOUR ON THE NUMBER LINE? Encourage the children to try to figure it out. If they cannot, then demonstrate. FIRST I'LL PUT A MARKER ON 2. NOW I'LL COUNT OVER FOUR SPACES. NOW I'M AT 6. HOW MUCH IS TWO PLUS FOUR? Have the children try several problems with sums of ten or less.

3. *Subtraction.* HOW CAN WE SHOW FIVE MINUS TWO ON THE NUMBER LINE? Encourage the children to try to figure it out. If they cannot, then demonstrate. FIRST I'LL PUT A MARKER ON THE 5. NOW WHICH WAY SHOULD I GO TO FIND FIVE MINUS TWO? Have them try several problems using numbers ten or less.

**FOLLOW-UP:** Have the children illustrate equivalent sums and differences on the number line (e.g., $3 + 4 = 1 + 6, 8 - 4 = 7 - 3$). The children could also make up number line problems for themselves. Suggest that they use the number line to find the answer whenever they need help with a one-digit problem.

## Geometry: Comparing Road and Straight-Line Distances

**OBJECTIVE:** To see the relationship between a direct route and the actual route between points on a map. (This activity is for the more advanced primary students who have learned how to use standard measurement tools.)

**MATERIALS:** Maps of your state for everyone in the class, 1-foot rulers, and marking pens.

**ACTIVITIES:** Have the students explore the maps. See if they can find the legend and if they can tell you what the various symbols mean. Be particularly sure that they know which kinds of lines are roads, how you find out the mileage from one place on the map to another, and how many miles an inch represents on the map. Spend some time finding out how far it is from your town or city to some of the nearby towns and cities. Have the class agree on two places in the state they would like to visit. Using their rulers and marking pens, have them draw a line from your city to the nearest place selected, from that place to the other location selected, and from there back home. They should then have a triangle. Have everyone figure out the mileage by road and then by direct flight by measuring the lines. Add up the three sides of the triangle. Add up the three road routes. Find the difference between the road trip and the direct route. Discuss why the roads are not as direct as the lines.

**FOLLOW-UP:** Encourage interested students to compare road and direct distances to other points in the state.

## Robotics: LEGO and LOGO

LOGO computer language can provide experience with geometry and technology at a number of levels. With just a few simple commands and minimal instruction, children can explore, play, and create an infinite number of geometric shapes and designs. With a little more structured approach, they can learn how to plan out patterns ahead of time and use more complex instructional commands. The cursor, referred to as the **turtle** in LOGO, can be moved about in many directions and at different angles to make straight or curved lines. Problem-solving skills are developed when children work on figuring out how they will make the turtle go just where they want it to in order to come up with a particular design or figure.

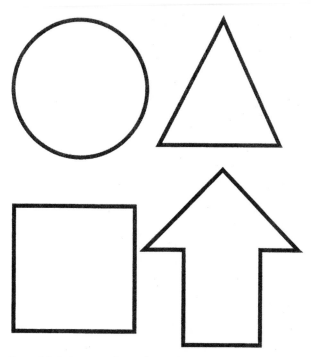

**Figure 31–2** Patterns for exploring symmetry.

Children's building with LEGO building bricks and their exploration of LOGO are combined in connection with math/science/technology via **LEGO/LOGO**, LEGO Mindstorms, and LEGO Dacta robotics, which provide children with the opportunity to explore physics, technology, and mathematics. They have a choice of many tasks that range from assembling a simple traffic light to complex projects such as bridges, playground rides, construction equipment, and vehicles. In the original version the computer was programmed to control operation of the LEGO machines. More recently, National Instruments, LEGO Dacta, and Tufts University have developed a ROBOLAB system that enables students to write computer programs and transfer them into programmable LEGO bricks. Even kindergartners can create their own robot designs. LEGO Mindstorms includes several robotics products with sets for building *Star Wars* robots and many others. With the invention of the programmable bricks, the robots no longer need to be bound to the computer. You may access the Online Companion that accompanies *Math and Science for Young Children* to find a link to their website.

## Design Technology

Design technology was introduced in Units 22 and 25 (see also Dunn & Larson, 1990; Petroski, 2003). Primary grade students can follow more structured directions and work on projects individually or in small cooperative groups. Virginia's Children's Engineering Council, the Virginia *Children's Engineering Journal*, and Children Designing and Engineering provide information and activities that provide problems for design technology; access the Online Companion that accompanies *Math and Science for Young Children* to find a link to their website. Some samples of more complex long-term projects are provided by Children Designing and Engineering (n.d.) and the Virginia Children's Engineering Council (n.d.). An example of a safari park project obtained from Children Designing and Engineering was described in Unit 25. The same site includes several additional projects. The Virginia Children's Engineering Council website also provides projects for students in kindergarten through third grade.

## Collecting and Analyzing Data and Constructing Graphs

Students can collect data, categorize the results, and depict the results in a graphical representation for analysis. Graphing includes constructing graphs, reading information on graphs, and interpreting what the information on a graph means. The data used for making graphs need to be something of interest to the students. Unit 20 presents a list of possible graphing subjects that young children might enjoy working on. Other subjects will grow out of their current interests and activities.

The four most popular types of graphs are picture graphs, bar graphs or histograms, **line graphs**, and circle or pie graphs. The graphs described in previous units fall into the first two categories and are the easiest for young children to construct and interpret. Although pie graphs are beyond the primary level, some primary level children can begin to work with line graphs.

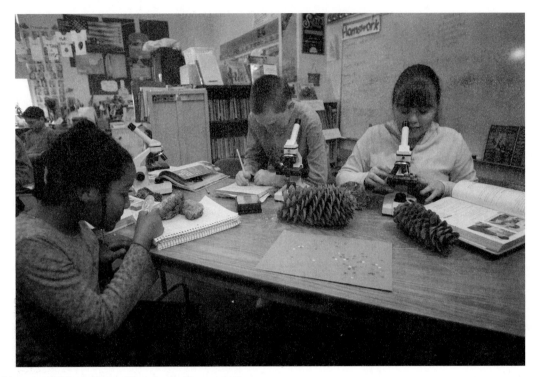

These children record their observations for further analysis.

*Line graphs* demand concrete operational thinking because more than one aspect of the data must be focused on at the same time. Line graphs are made on a squared paper grid and apply the basic skills that children would learn by first doing the squared paper activities with the geoboard. They are especially good for showing variations such as rainfall, temperature, and hours of daylight. In Figure 31–3, Chan's temperature data are translated from the bar graph to the line graph. Note that the left side and the bottom are called the **axes** and that each must be labeled. In this case, the left side is the temperature axis and the bottom is the axis representing days of the week. To find the correct point for each temperature on each day, the child has to find the point where the two meet, mark the point, and connect it to the previous point and the next point with a line. If two or more types of information are included on the same graph, then usually geometric symbols are used to indicate which line goes with which set of data. Jeanne Vissa (1987) suggests some creative ways to introduce the use of coordinate (or line) graphing to young children.

High temperatures in Beijing and Ogden, November 22–29

**Figure 31–3** Chan's data depicted in a line graph.

# ACTIVITIES

## Graphing: Introducing Coordinates

**OBJECTIVE:** To introduce finding coordinates on a graph.

**MATERIALS:** A large supply of stickers of various kinds. On the bulletin board, construct a large 5 × 5 square coordinate graph. The grids can be made using black tape. Place stickers at the intersections of various coordinates (Figure 31–4).

**Figure 31–4** Coordinate graphing can be introduced using a grid with stickers placed at points to be identified.

**ACTIVITIES:** THIS IS THE CITY. DRIVING INTO THE CITY THE CORNER IS HERE AT 0, 0. I WANT TO GO TO (name one of the stickers). TELL ME HOW MANY BLOCKS OVER AND HOW MANY BLOCKS UP I WILL HAVE TO GO. Suppose that the sticker is on 2, 3. YES, I HAVE TO GO OVER TWO BLOCKS AND UP THREE. THIS POINT IS CALLED 2, 3. Draw the children's attention to how the numbers on the bottom and the sides correspond to the point. Go back to 0, 0 and have the children direct you to other points on the graph. Let the children take turns telling you the coordinates of a sticker they would like to have. When they are able to give the correct coordinates, they get a matching sticker to keep.

**FOLLOW-UP:** During center time, encourage children to explore the coordinate map on their own or with a friend. Suggest they trace trips to different "corners" with their fingers. Children who understand the concept of coordinates can use coordinate paper to complete symmetrical shapes (Figure 31–5) and can name the coordinates.

*(continued)*

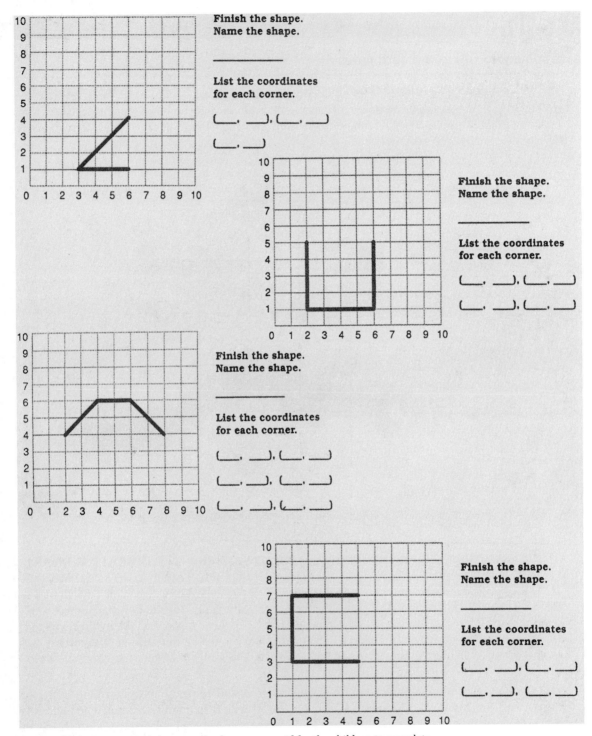

Finish the shape.
Name the shape.

_____

List the coordinates
for each corner.

(__, __), (__, __)

(__, __)

Finish the shape.
Name the shape.

_____

List the coordinates
for each corner.

(__, __), (__, __)

(__, __), (__, __)

Finish the shape.
Name the shape.

_____

List the coordinates
for each corner.

(__, __), (__, __)

(__, __), (__, __)

(__, __), (__, __)

Finish the shape.
Name the shape.

_____

List the coordinates
for each corner.

(__, __), (__, __)

(__, __), (__, __)

**Figure 31–5** Half of a symmetrical shape can be drawn on a grid for the children to complete.

## Charts and Tables

**Charts** and **tables** are constructed to organize data before they are graphed. A simple chart consists of tally marks such as depicted in the chart on floating and sinking objects in Unit 10 (see Figure 10–4). This information could be translated into a single-variable graph showing frequency of floating or sinking for each object or into a double-variable graph (i.e., a double-bar or double-line graph) showing both tendencies. The simple tables shown in Figure 31–1 were used to organize the temperature data prior to constructing the graphs.

## Algebraic Thinking

Michaele Chappell (1997) outlines the roots of algebraic thinking in the primary grades. Primary children are not ready for formal algebraic equations such as $x + 5 = 8$, but they can learn patterns using geometric shapes as variables. For example, in the "guess my rule" game, $\square + \square$ can indicate two $\square$s. When doing missing addend problems (e.g., Tonio has 12¢ and needs 25¢ to buy a candy bar), a triangle can be used to represent the missing addend: $12 + \triangle = 25$. Or counters can be used to set up the problem. Set out and write 12 counters + empty cup = 25. Ask, "How many counters do we need to put in the cup in order to have 25?" A balance could also be used to demonstrate the problem. Chappell believes that the gate to algebra can be opened during the elementary years. The following is a sample activity adapted from those in the NCTM special issue. Additional activities are included in Greenes and colleagues (2001).

## Estimation

Estimation is an important activity at the primary level. As children enter the concrete operations period, they can begin to make rational estimates (Lang, 2001; see

## ACTIVITIES

### Algebraic Thinking: Building Rectangles*

**OBJECTIVE:** To introduce the patterns that determine the area of a rectangle using nonstandard units.

**MATERIALS:** Square tiles from sets such as TexTiles (Creative Publications) or Algebra Tiles (Cuisinaire).

**ACTIVITY:** Provide each child with a group of 20 tiles. USE SOME OF YOUR SQUARE TILES TO MAKE A RECTANGLE WITH A BASE OF TWO TILES. Ask the following kinds of questions.
1. DID YOU ALL MAKE THE SAME RECTANGLE?
2. HOW MANY TILES DID YOU USE IN YOUR RECTANGLE?
3. HOW DID YOU FIGURE OUT HOW MANY TILES YOU USED?
4. WHAT IS THE HEIGHT OF YOUR RECTANGLE?
5. HOW WOULD YOU BUILD A RECTANGLE THAT USES 18 TILES?
6. CAN YOU FIGURE OUT HOW HIGH IT WOULD BE WITHOUT ACTUALLY MAKING IT?
7. IF YOU KNOW HOW HIGH YOU WANT A RECTANGLE TO BE, CAN YOU FIGURE OUT HOW MANY TILES YOU WILL NEED?

**EVALUATION:** Note the different strategies the students use (counting one by one, counting by twos, or others).

**FOLLOW-UP:** Try some of the other activities described in the articles suggested at the end of the unit.

*Adapted from Yackel (1997).

also Unit 25). A jar can be filled with pennies. Students can predict how many they can hold in one hand. Students can compare estimates. Each student can then take a handful, count them, and compare the amounts with their estimates (Olson & Easley, 1996). Finally, using their handfuls as a base, they can estimate how many pennies the jar holds. Show the students a jar filled with interlocking cubes. Have them guess how many there are. Then remove ten cubes and connect them into a train. Now the students have more information. Ask them to make a new estimate. Continue making trains of ten until the jar is empty (Burns, 1997).

## Probability

According to NCTM (2000), the concept of probability is extremely informal at the primary level. It is suggested that children be challenged to answer questions about what is *most likely* and what is *least likely*. For example, in Minnesota in January, is it more likely to snow or rain? Children can tally throws of the dice or the results of tossing a small group of two-sided discs (yellow on one side and red on the other). They will note that some numbers or colors come up more often than others, though they are not yet ready to learn how to calculate probabilities.

## INTEGRATION ACROSS THE CONTENT AREAS

The concepts described in this unit can be applied across the content areas. Many of the articles suggested at the end of the unit provide examples of activities that integrate mathematics with other content areas.

## IDEAS FOR CHILDREN WITH SPECIAL NEEDS

Children with Down's syndrome (DS) also need special attention and accommodations (Lewis, 2003). They tend to be relatively slow in language development as a result of poor short-term memory, especially for auditory material, and poor long-term memory for verbal and spatial material. Such children need lots of repetition of new skills along with review of previously learned skills. Lessons need to be simple and should include a minimum number of materials and instructions. The range of DS abilities is broad, so careful assessment is necessary for appropriate planning. Breaking tasks into small steps is a technique used effectively with DS children (Gargiulo & Kilgo, 2007).

## EVALUATION

Note whether children can follow directions and maintain involvement in the activities. Observing the process in these activities is critical. When children are not able to do an activity, it is important to note where the process breaks down. Does the child have the basic idea but just needs a little more practice and guidance? Does the activity seem to be beyond the child's capabilities at this time? These activities require advanced cognitive and perceptual motor development, so children should not be pushed beyond their developmental level. If children work in pairs or small groups of varied ability, the more advanced can assist the less advanced.

## SUMMARY

Primary experiences with geometry, spatial sense, graphs, tables, charts, algebraic thinking, estimation, and probability build on preprimary experiences with shape, spatial sense, simpler graphs and charts, and patterns. Primary level geometry is an informal, intuitively acquired concept. Children gain familiarity with concepts such as line, angle, point, curve, symmetry, and congruence. Geoboard activities are basic at this level.

Geometric and number concepts can be applied to graphing. Advanced children can develop more complex bar graphs and move on to line graphs. Charts and tables are used to organize data, which can then be visually depicted in a graph. LEGO/LOGO, LEGO Mindstorms, LEGO Dacta robotics, and design technology provide opportunities for more complex experiences combining mathematics, science, and technology. All these activities promote algebraic thinking.

| | | |
|---|---|---|
| axes | line | symmetry |
| charts | line graphs | tables |
| curves | LOGO | turtle |
| LEGO/LOGO | points | |

## SUGGESTED ACTIVITIES

1. Assess some primary children's readiness for the types of geometry and graphing activities discussed in this unit. Describe the results and your evaluation of their degree of readiness.

2. Plan some activities that would be appropriate for the children you assessed. If possible, use these activities with the children. Evaluate the results. Did the children respond as you expected? Was your assessment accurate? What modifications, if any, would you make the next time? Why?

3. Provide the students in this course with some data. Have them develop some charts or tables using the data. Then have them make some line graphs. Do they have any problems in developing graphs?

4. Add geometry, data collection, computer, and algebraic thinking activities to your Activity File.

5. Using the guidelines from Activity 5, Unit 2, evaluate one or more of the following software programs (all are available at http://store.sun burst.com).

   ■ *Easy Sheet* (grades 3–12). An easy-to-use spreadsheet program.

   ■ *Introduction to Patterns*. Students discover many types of patterns.

   ■ *Combining Shapes*. Students manipulate shapes.

■ *Creating Patterns from Shapes*. Explore radiating and tiling patterns.

■ *Mirror Symmetry*. Advances students' understanding of geometric properties and spatial relationships.

■ *Graphers*. Students manipulate a variety of data analysis and graphing activities.

■ *The Graph Club* 2.0. Students can collect data and construct their own graphs.

■ *Lemonade for Sale* (grades 2 and 3).

■ *Shape Up!* (pre-K–6). Supports creativity in two- and three-dimensional shape worlds. Shapes can be put together, change size, change orientation in space, change colors, and so on. This program can write labels, stories, or descriptions and print out pages.

■ *Toy Store* (grades 2–5). Create bar graphs and interpret and collect data.

■ *Zap! Around Town* (K–3). For development of mapping and direction skills.

See also the tools available from Illuminations (http://illuminations.nctm.org) and Virtual Manipulatives (http://nlvm.usu.edu).

## REVIEW

A. List the concepts and experiences that are prerequisite to the geometry and graphing concepts and activities described in this unit.

B. Make three diagrams that illustrate how fractions are visually depicted using geometric shapes.

C. Use a number line to show that $4 + 5 = 3 + 6$.

**D.** Match the terms in Column I with the definitions in Column II.

| Column I | Column II |
|---|---|
| 1. Point | a. Correspondence of parts of a figure on opposite sides of a point, line, or plane |
| 2. Curve | b. The space made by the meeting of two straight lines |
| 3. Line | c. An idea that is represented on paper by a dot |
| 4. Angle | d. Sameness of size and shape |
| 5. Congruency | e. Represented on paper by using a straightedge ruler and pencil |
| 6. Symmetry | f. A smooth but not straight line |

**E.** Make a sketch of a geoboard and explain its purpose.

**F.** Find the following points on an integer-valued $(x, y)$ graph: (0, 0), (3, 2), (3, 4), (0, 3), (4, 1), (1, 2).

**G.** Make a line graph using the following data.

High Temperatures, May 15–20

| City | Sat. | Sun. | Mon. | Tues. | Wed. | Thurs. |
|---|---|---|---|---|---|---|
| New York | 73 | 72 | 74 | 64 | 61 | 60 |
| Cairo | 102 | 111 | 107 | 95 | 93 | 102 |

What conclusions can you make from an examination of the graph?

**H.** Explain how algebraic thinking can be included in the curriculum for elementary grades.

**I.** At what level does probability fit into the K–3 curriculum?

**J.** Explain the value of design technology for primary students.

## REFERENCES

Burns, M. (1997, April). Number sense. *Instructor*, 49–54.

Chappell, M. E. (1997). Preparing students to enter the gate. *Teaching Children Mathematics, 3*, 266–267.

Children Designing and Engineering. (n.d.). What is CD&E? Retrieved November 20, 2004, from http://www.childrendesigning.org

Clark, L. J. (2002). Real world robotics. *Science and Children, 40*(2), 38–42.

Dunn, S., & Larson, R. (1990). *Design technology: Children's engineering.* Bristol, PA: Falmer, Taylor & Francis.

Gargiulo, R., & Kilgo, J. (2007). *Young children with special needs* (2nd ed.). Albany, NY: Thomson Delmar Learning.

Greenes, C., Cavanagh, M., Dacey, L., Findell, C., & Small, M. (2001). *Navigating through algebra in prekindergarten–grade 2.* Reston, VA: National Council of Teachers of Mathematics.

Lewis, V. (2003). *Development and disability* (2nd ed.). Malden, MA: Blackwell.

Lang, F. K. (2001). What is a "good guess" anyway? Estimation in early childhood. *Teaching Children Mathematics, 7*(8), 462–466.

Moses, B. (1997). Algebra for a new century. *Teaching Children Mathematics, 3,* 264–265.

Murray, J., & Bartelmay, K. (2005). Inventors in the making. *Science and Children, 42*(4), 40–44.

National Council of Teachers of Mathematics. (2000). *Principles and standards for school mathematics.* Reston, VA: Author.

National Council of Teachers of Mathematics. (2007). *Curriculum focal points.* Reston, VA: Author.

Olson, M., & Easley, B. (1996). Plentiful penny projects to ponder. *Teaching Children Mathematics, 3,* 184–185.

Petroski, H. (2003, January 24). *Early education.* Presentation at the Children's Engineering Convention (Williamsburg, VA). Retrieved November 20, 2004, from http://www.vtea.org

Virginia Children's Engineering Council. (n.d.). Inspiring the next generation. Retrieved November 20, 2004, from http://www.vtea.org

Vissa, J. (1987). Coordinate graphing: Shaping up a sticky situation. *Arithmetic Teacher, 35*(3), 6–10.

Yackel, E. (1997). A foundation for algebraic reasoning in the early grades. *Teaching Children Mathematics, 3,* 276–280.

## FURTHER READING AND RESOURCES

### General Resources

*Box it or bag it mathematics (K–2).* Portland, OR: Math Learning Center.

*Bridges in mathematics (K–2).* Portland, OR: Math Learning Center.

Burris, A.C. (2005). *Understanding the math you teach.* Upper Saddle River, NJ: Pearson-Merrill/Prentice-Hall.

Chen, J., & McNamee, G. D. (2007). *Bridging: Assessment for teaching and learning in early childhood classrooms, pre-K–3.* Thousand Oaks, CA: Corwin.

Findell, C. R., Cavanagh, M., Dacey, L., Greenes, C. E., Sheffield, L. J., & Small, M. (2004). *Navigating through problem solving and reasoning in grade 1.* Reston, VA: National Council of Teachers of Mathematics.

Findell, C. R., Small, M., Cavanagh, M., Dacey, L., Greenes, C. E., & Sheffield, L. J. (2001). *Navigating through geometry in prekindergarten–grade 2.* Reston, VA: National Council of Teachers of Mathematics.

Greenes, C., Cavanagh, M., Dacey, L., Findell, C., & Small, M. (2001). *Navigating through algebra in prekindergarten–grade 2.* Reston, VA: National Council of Teachers of Mathematics.

Greenes, C. E., & House, P. A. (Eds.). (2003). *Navigating through problem solving and reasoning in prekindergarten–kindergarten.* Reston, VA: National Council of Teachers of Mathematics.

Sheffield, L. J., Cavanagh, M., Dacey, L., Findell, C. R., Greenes, C. E., & Small, M. (2002). *Navigating through data analysis and probability in prekindergarten–grade 2.* Reston, VA: National Council of Teachers of Mathematics.

Small, M., Sheffield, L. J., Cavanagh, M., Dacey, L., Findell, C. R., & Greenes, C. E. (2004). *Navigating through problem solving and reasoning in grade 2.* Reston, VA: National Council of Teachers of Mathematics.

### Geometry/Spatial Sense

Ambrose, R. C., & Falkner, K. (2002). Developing spatial understanding through building polyhedrons. *Teaching Children Mathematics, 8*(8), 442–447.

Brewer, E. J. (1999). Geometry and art. *Teaching Children Mathematics, 6*(4), 220–224, 236.

Dobler, C. P., & Klein, J. M. (2002). First graders, flies, and a Frenchman's fascination: Introducing the Cartesian coordinate system. *Teaching Children Mathematics, 8*(9), 540–545.

Geometry and geometric thinking [Focus issue]. (1999). *Teaching Children Mathematics, 5*(6).

Hale, C. (2003, April). Art workshop: Kids design striking geometric artwork in the style of M. C. Escher. *Instructor,* 31–33.

Lehrer, R., & Curtis, C. L. (2000). Why are some solids perfect? *Teaching Children Mathematics, 6*(5), 324–329.

Linquist, M. M., & Clements, D. H. (2001). Geometry must be vital. *Teaching Children Mathematics, 7*(7), 409–415.

Lord, T. R., & Clausen-May, T. (2002). Giving spatial perception our full attention. *Science and Children, 39*(5), 22–25.

Marsh, J., Loesing, J., & Soucie, M. (2004). Gee-whiz geometry. *Teaching Children Mathematics, 11*(4), 208–209.

Paznokas, L. S. (2003). Teaching mathematics through cultural quilting. *Teaching Children Mathematics, 9*(5), 250–256.

Penner, E., & Lehrer, R. (2000). The shape of fairness. *Teaching Children Mathematics, 7*(4), 210–214.

Senger, E. S., Platte, S. B., & Van Zandt, J. (1997). Mathematical meaning in context. *Teaching Children Mathematics, 3,* 362–366.

### Collecting and Organizing Data

Ashbrook, P. (2006). The early years: Communication about collections. *Science & Children, 44*(3), 18–20.

Baker, A., & Baker, J. (1991). *Counting on a small planet: Activities for environmental mathematics.* Portsmouth, NH: Heinemann.

Barman, C. R., Barman, N. S., Berglund, K., & Goldston, M. J. (1999). Assessing students' ideas about animals. *Science and Children, 37*(1), 44–45.

Berglund, K. (1999). Thought for food. *Science and Children, 36*(4), 38–42.

Braude, S. (2007). The tree of animal life. *Science & Children, 45*(1), 42–51.

Crane, P. (2004). On observing the weather. *Science and Children, 41*(8), 32–36.

Frykholm, J. A. (2001). Eenie, meenie, minie, moe . . . Building on intuitive notions of chance. *Teaching Children Mathematics, 8*(2), 112–118.

Holden, J. C. (1998). Corn dehydration lab. *Science and Children, 36*(1), 26–29.

Hutchison, L., Ironsmith, M., Snow, C. W., & Poteat, G. M. (2000). Third-grade students investigate and represent data. *Early Childhood Education Journal, 27*(4), 213–218.

Keller, J. D., & Brickman, B. (1998). The ball olympics: Up and down, all around. *Science and Children, 36*(2), 26–31, 56.

Manchester, P. (2002). The lunchroom project: A long-term investigative study. *Teaching Children Mathematics, 9*(1), 43–47.

Russell, S. J., & Corwin, R. B. (1990). *Used numbers, sorting: Groups and graphs.* Palo Alto, CA: Seymour.

Stone, A., & Russell, S. J. (1990). Counting: Ourselves and our families. In *Used numbers: Read data in the classroom.* Palo Alto, CA: Seymour.

Whitin, D. J., & Whitin, P. (2003). Talk counts: Discussing graphs with young children. *Teaching Children Mathematics, 10*(3), 142–149.

### Estimation and Probability

Beck, S. A., & Huse, V. E. (2007). A virtual spin on the teaching of probability. *Teaching Children Mathematics, 13*(9), 486.

Guess, graphs, and numbers. (1997, January). *Teaching K–8,* 35.

### Technology

Clements, D. H., & Meredith, J. S. (1993). One point of view: A talk with LOGO turtle. *Arithmetic Teacher, 41*(4), 189–191.

Clements, D. H., & Sarama, J. (1997). Computers support algebraic thinking. *Teaching Children Mathematics, 3,* 320–325.

Clements, D. H., & Sarama, J. (2000). Predicting pattern blocks on and off the computer. *Teaching Children Mathematics, 6*(7), 458–461.

Clements, D. H., & Sarama, J. (2000). Young children's ideas about geometric shapes. *Teaching Children Mathematics, 6*(8), 482–488.

Hadley, K., & Korb, M. (2007). Through the bugscope. *Science & Children, 45*(1), 29–31.

Learning and teaching mathematics with technology [Focus issue]. (2002). *Teaching Children Mathematics, 8*(6).

Lener, C., & Pinou, T. (2007). Learning through loggerheads. *Science & Children, 45*(1), 24–28.

Leveen, L. (2007). Exploring animals, glossopedia style. *Science & Children, 45*(1), 48–51.

Parker, D. L. (2003). Take care of mother earth: Technology and the environment. *Teaching Children Mathematics, 9*(7), 414–419.

Sarow, G. A. (2001). Miniature sleds: Go, go, go! *Science and Children, 39*(3), 16–21.

Woleck, K. R. (2003). Tricky triangles: A tale of one, two, three researchers. *Teaching Children Mathematics, 10*(1), 40–44.

### Algebraic Thinking

Bay-Williams, J. M. (2001). What is algebra in elementary school? *Teaching Children Mathematics, 8*(4), 196–200.

Blanton, M. L., & Kaput, J. J. (2003). Developing elementary teachers' "Algebra eyes and ears." *Teaching Children Mathematics, 10*(2), 70–77.

Burns, M. (2002, October). Algebra in the elementary grades? Absolutely! *Instructor,* 24–28.

Falkner, K. P., Levi, L., & Carpenter, T. P. (1999). Children's understanding of equality: A foundation for algebra. *Teaching Children Mathematics, 6*(4), 232–237.

Femiano, R. B. (2003). Algebraic problem solving in the primary grades. *Teaching Children Mathematics, 9*(8), 444–449.

Ferrini-Mundy, J., Lappan, G., & Phillips, E. (1997). Experiences with patterning. *Teaching Children Mathematics, 3,* 282–288.

Holly, K. A. (1997). Patterns and functions. *Teaching Children Mathematics, 3,* 312–313.

Hynes, M. E., Dixon, J. K., & Adams, T. L. (2002). Rubber-band rockets. *Teaching Children Mathematics, 8*(7), 390–395.

Koester, B. A. (2003). Prisms and pyramids: Constructing three-dimensional models to build understanding. *Teaching Children Mathematics, 9*(8), 436–442.

Lubinski, C. A., & Otto, A. D. (1997). Literature and algebraic reasoning. *Teaching Children Mathematics, 3,* 290–295.

Moyer, P. S. (2001). Patterns and symmetry: Reflections of culture. *Teaching Children Mathematics, 8*(3), 140–144.

Reeves, C. A. (2006). Putting fun into functions. *Teaching Children Mathematics, 12*(5), 250–259.

Rivera, F. D. (2006). Changing the face of arithmetic: Teaching children algebra. *Teaching Children Mathematics, 12*(6), 306–311.

Soares, J., Blanton, M. L., & Kaput, J. J. (2005/2006). Thinking algebraically across the curriculum. *Teaching Children Mathematics, 12*(5), 228–235.

Vsiskin, A. (1997). Doing algebra in grades K–4. *Teaching Children Mathematics, 3,* 346–356.

Willoughby, S. S. (1997). Functions: From kindergarten through sixth grade. *Teaching Children Mathematics, 3,* 314–318.

# Unit 32

## Measurement with Standard Units

### OBJECTIVES

After reading this unit, you should be able to:

- List the reasons that measurement is an essential part of the primary mathematics program.
- Know when to introduce standard units of measurement for length, time, volume, area, temperature, and money.
- Name the two types of standard units of measurement that are used in the United States.
- Plan and carry out developmentally appropriate primary level measurement instruction.

Measurement is an extremely important aspect of mathematics. It is a practical activity that is used in everyday life during experiences such as cooking, shopping, building, and constructing. In the primary curriculum, it is essential to gathering data in science and can also be applied in other areas. Measurement is a major vehicle for integrating mathematics with other content areas. Measuring is also a vehicle for reinforcing other math skills and concepts: The number line is based on length, a popular multiplication model is much like area, and measurement is an area that lends itself naturally to problem-solving activities. Counting, whole number operations, and fractions are used to arrive at measurements and report the results. This unit will build on the basic concepts of measurement described in Units 18, 19, and 22. The focus of this unit is instruction and activities for introducing the concept of standard units and applying that concept to length, volume, area, weight, temperature, time, and money measurement.

The National Council of Teachers of Mathematics (2000) lists several expectations for primary grade

children's accomplishments in measurement. Primary grade children are expected to select an appropriate unit and tool for the attribute being measured, be able to measure objects that require a repeated use of the same tool (e.g., three cups of flour with a cup measure, three-foot table with a foot ruler), use a variety of tools for measuring, and be able to make comparisons and estimates of standard unit measurements.

During the primary grades, measurement is an important connection from number and operations to algebra and geometry. During grade 1, measurement is a means for obtaining data to be analyzed in order to solve problems. During grade 2, linear measurement is a focal point that connects with geometry. In third grade children use their knowledge of fractions as they connect to making finer measurements. Measurement of area is a focal point in fourth grade and of volume in fifth grade.

Unit 18 (see Figure 18–1) described five stages in the development of the measurement concept. During the sensorimotor and preoperational periods, children's measurement activities center on play and imitation and making comparisons (e.g., long–short, heavy–light, full–empty, hot–cold, early–late, rich–poor). During the transition period from ages 5 to 7, children enjoy working with arbitrary units. During concrete operations (which an individual usually enters at age 6 or older), children can begin to see the need for standard units (stage four) and begin to develop skills in using them (stage five). Standard units are not introduced for each concept at the same time. In general, the following guidelines can be observed.

- *Length (linear measure)*. The units of inch/foot and centimeter/meter are introduced in the beginning of primary and for measurement during second grade.

- *Area*. Area is introduced informally with nonstandard units in grade 1 and ties in with multiplication in grade 3.

- *Time*. Time measurement devices and vocabulary were introduced prior to primary, but it is generally the end of primary before conventional time is clearly understood and a nondigital clock can be read with accuracy.

- *Volume (capacity)*. Volume is learned informally during pouring activities, and accuracy is stressed during preprimary cooking. The concept of units of volume is usually introduced in grade 2.

- *Weight*. The standard measurement for weight is usually introduced in third grade.

- *Temperature*. Temperature units are identified in the second grade, by which time children may begin to read thermometers, but it is usually beyond primary before children can measure temperature with accuracy and understanding.

- *Money*. Coins and bills are identified prior to primary and symbols are associated in early primary, but value does not begin to be understood until the end of primary.

The goal in the primary grades is to introduce the meaning of measurement, needed terminology, important units, and most common measurement tools.

Both **English units** (customary in the United States) and **metric units** are introduced during the primary years. Although the metric system is much easier to use because it is based on 10s and is used as the principal system in most countries, it has not been adopted as the official measure in the United States. In the 1970s there was a movement toward U.S. adoption of the system, but it died out and the U.S. Metric Commission was abolished in 1984. However, children must learn the metric system because it is so widely used around the world as well as in industry and science.

## ASSESSMENT

Concrete operational thinking is essential for an understanding of the need for and the use of standard units. Conservation tasks for length (see Figure 18–3), weight (see Figure 18–3), and volume were illustrated earlier in the text. In Unit 18, observational assessment guidelines were suggested for finding out what children at the early stages of understanding of measurement know about volume, weight, length, and temperature. Interview tasks for time can be found in Unit 19. Be sure that children can apply nonstandard measure before moving on to standard measure.

## INSTRUCTION

The concept of measurement develops through measurement experiences. Lecture and demonstration are not adequate for supporting the development of this concept. Also, it is important to take a sequenced approach to the introduction of standard units. Adhere to the following steps.

1.  Do comparisons that do not require numbers (see Unit 11).

2.  Use nonstandard arbitrary units (see Unit 18).
    a.  Find the number of units by counting.
    b.  Report the number of units.

3.  Compare the thing measured to the units used (e.g., a table's width is measured with paper clips or drinking straws).

4. Introduce standard units appropriate for the same type of measurement.
   a. Find the number of units using standardized measuring instruments (i.e., ruler, scale, cup, liter, thermometer).
   b. Report the number of units.

Introduction of new standard measurement techniques and instruments should always be preceded by comparisons and nonstandard measurement with arbitrary units. Naturalistic and informal measurement experiences should be encouraged at all levels.

## The Concept of Unit

Children's ability to measure rests on their understanding of the concept of **unit**. Many children have difficulty perceiving that units can be other than one. That is, one-half foot could be a unit, three centimeters could be a unit, two standard measuring cups could be a unit, one mark on a thermometer equals two degrees, and so on.

By using nonstandard units of measure first, the concept of unit can be developed. Children learn that measurement can be made with an arbitrary unit but that the arbitrary units must be equal to each other when making a specific measurement. For example, when measuring with paper clips, each one must be the same length. Paper clip is not the unit; rather, a paper clip of some specific length is the unit. Through the use of arbitrary but equal units used to measure objects, children construct the concept of a unit. The concept is reinforced by using different arbitrary units (one kind at a time) and then comparing the results in terms of the number of units. For example, the children measure Lai's height using Unifix Cubes, identical drinking straws, and the class math textbook. Soon they realize that measurement with smaller units requires more units than with larger units. When the students move on to standard units, they can compare the number of units needed to measure using teaspoons versus a standard cup measure, inches versus a yardstick, and so on.

Children should be aware that they must be accurate when using units, either arbitrary or standard.

For example, there cannot be gaps or spaces between units when measuring length. That is why it's a good idea to start with Unifix Cubes, Lots-A-Links, or some other units that can be stuck together and easily lined up. Once children are able to measure using as many units as needed to measure the whole length, capacity, and so on, then they can advance to using one or more units that must be moved to make a complete measurement. For example, they could make a 10-Unifix-Cube length measure, place it on the item to be measured, mark where it ends, move the measure to that point, keep going until finished, and then add the 10s and any remaining cubes to arrive at the length in cubes. For capacity, individual measuring cups could be filled and then the number of empties counted after a larger container is filled, or one cup could be used and a record kept of how many cupfuls filled the larger container. As children discover these shortcuts to measurement, they will be able to transfer this knowledge over to standard unit measure and understand the rationale behind foot rulers, meter- and yardsticks, and quart and liter measures.

## Measuring Instruments

With the introduction of standard units comes the introduction of measuring instruments. Rulers, scaled instruments (scales, graduated cylinders, thermometers), and clocks are the tools of standard measurement. Children have problems with these instruments unless they understand what they are measuring and what it means to measure. It is wise to begin with simple versions of the instruments, which are marked only with the unit being used. For example, if the unit is the centimeter, use a ruler that is marked only with centimeters (no millimeters). If the unit is an inch, use a ruler marked only with inches (no ½, ¼, or ⅛ inches). Be sure the children understand how units are marked. For example, on a ruler, the numbers come after the unit, not before. Even most 9-year-olds will say that the ruler illustrated in Figure 32–1 is 5 inches (rather than 6 inches) long. You must be sure children understand that each number tells how many units have been used. Children need many experiences measuring objects shorter than their ruler before they move on to longer

**Figure 32–1** Six-inch ruler.

objects with which they will have to measure, mark, and move the ruler. They also will need to be able to apply their addition skills. For example, if a child is using a 12-inch ruler and measures something that is 12 inches plus 8 inches, can she add 12 + 8? Measuring to the nearest quarter, eighth, or sixteenth of an inch requires that the child understand fractions.

Scaled instruments present a problem because not every individual unit is marked. For example, thermometers are marked every two degrees. A good way to help children understand this concept is to have them make their own instruments. They can make graphs using different scales or make their own graduated cylinders. The latter can be done by taking a large glass and putting a piece of masking tape down the side, as shown in Figure 32–2.

Take a smaller container, fill it with spoonfuls, count how many it holds, and empty it into the glass. Mark the level of the water and the number of spoonfuls. Fill the small container, empty into the glass, and mark again. In the example, the small container holds five teaspoons of water. This measure can be used to find out how much other containers will hold.

Clocks are one of the most difficult instruments for children to understand. Although there are only three measures (hours, minutes, and seconds), the circular movement of the hands makes reading the face difficult. Children vary greatly as to when they are finally able to read a clock face accurately. There is no set age for being able to tell time. Skills needed to tell time must be learned over many years and through practice with clock faces with movable hands. Digital clocks are easier to read but do not provide the child with a visual picture of the relationship between time units.

Money also offers difficulties because the sizes of the coins do not coincide with their value (i.e., the dime is smaller than the penny and the nickel). Bills provide no size cues but do have numerical designations that relate one bill to the other. Relating the coins to the bills is a difficult task for young children.

**Figure 32–2** Items used to illustrate the concept of scaled instruments.

## MEASUREMENT ACTIVITIES

This section includes activities that will help children construct the concepts of measuring length, volume (capacity), area, weight (mass), temperature, time, and money using standard units. Refer to previous units in this text for the comparison and arbitrary (nonstandard) measurement experiences that must occur prior to introducing standard units of measurement. Also, remember to work on the concepts of the units used for each type of measurement as well as actual measurement.

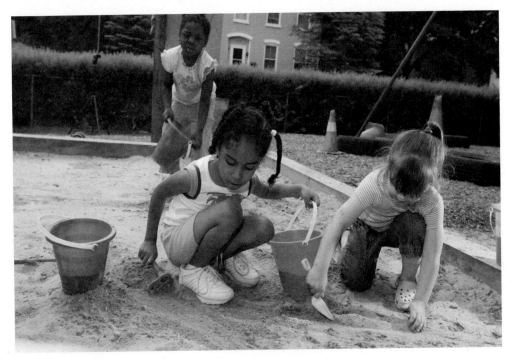

An understanding of volume measurement begins with explorations in the sandbox.

# ACTIVITIES

## Standard Measurement: Linear

**OBJECTIVE:** To be able to use standard units of measure to compare lengths of objects; to discover that the smaller the units, the more will be needed to measure a distance; and to use a ruler for measuring objects.

**MATERIALS:** Rulers (inch/foot, yardstick, centimeter, meterstick); tape measures; paper, pencils, crayons, markers, and poster board; and the book *How Big Is a Foot?*

**ACTIVITIES:** These activities are introduced following many exploratory experiences that involve comparing visually and with arbitrary units. The same objects can be measured using both methods to emphasize the need for standard units. The first activity is designed to develop an understanding of this need.

1. YOU HAVE MEASURED MANY THINGS AROUND THE ROOM, INCLUDING YOURSELVES, AND MADE COMPARISONS. WHAT YOU COMPARE AGAINST IS CALLED YOUR *UNIT OF MEASUREMENT*. WHAT ARE SOME UNITS OF MEASUREMENT YOU HAVE USED? (Children should name items used such as paper clips, Unifix Cubes, books, etc.) WHEN YOU TELL HOW LONG OR HOW TALL SOMETHING IS, YOU HAVE TO TELL WHICH UNIT OF MEASURE YOU USED. WHY? WHAT PROBLEM COULD OCCUR IF YOU ARE TELLING THIS INFORMATION TO SOMEONE WHO CANNOT SEE YOUR UNIT OF MEASURE? Encourage discussion. For example, they might suggest that if measuring with

Unifix Cubes you send the person a cube, or if measuring with a piece of string you send the person a piece of string of the same length. Next, read *How Big Is a Foot?* and discuss the problem encountered by the king. For ideas on how to use this book, see Lubinski and Thiessen (1996).

Now the students should be beginning to understand why standard units of measurement are necessary. Clarify this point by summing up: IF EVERYONE IN THE WORLD KNOWS EXACTLY WHAT THE UNITS OF MEASUREMENT ARE, IT IS MUCH EASIER TO EXPLAIN HOW LONG, WIDE, AND TALL SOMETHING IS. THAT IS WHY WE HAVE *STANDARD* UNITS OF MEASURE. WE USE INCHES, FEET, AND YARDS. (Pass around foot rulers and yardsticks for children to examine and compare.) IN MOST PLACES IN THE WORLD, IN SCIENCE LABORATORIES, AND IN FACTORIES, CENTIMETERS, DECIMETERS, AND METERS ARE USED. Pass around metersticks. Point out that the base-ten blocks they've been using are marked off in centimeters (1s units) and in decimeters (10s units), and that ten 10s placed end to end is a meter. Have them test this with the metersticks and the base-ten blocks. THESE UNITS ARE THE SAME EVERYWHERE AND DO NOT CHANGE. GET INTO PAIRS AND MEASURE EACH OTHER'S BODY PARTS USING YOUR RULERS AND TAPE MEASURES. BEFORE YOU START, MAKE A LIST OF THE PARTS YOU PLAN TO MEASURE. Have the students call out the names of the parts they plan to measure. When they finish have them compare their results.

2. Have the children use their foot rulers and two other units (such as a shoe and a pencil) to measure the same objects. Have them record the results in a table.

| Object | Length | | | |
|---|---|---|---|---|
|  | Feet | Inches | Shoes | Pencils |
| Table |  |  |  |  |
| Windowsill |  |  |  |  |
| Bookshelf |  |  |  |  |

Discuss the results and what they mean.

3. Have the children make their own inch and centimeter rulers. Provide them with strips of cardboard 6 inches long, and have them mark them off in units as shown in the figure.

Ask the children to make comparative measures around the classroom. Then send the rulers home along with a note to the parents.

(*continued*)

Dear Parents,

We are working with different ways of measuring length. Your child is bringing home an inch ruler and a centimeter ruler and is supposed to measure six things at home with each ruler and record the results. Please help your child if necessary. Have your child share the results with you and explain the differences in the number of inches versus the number of centimeters of length found for each object. Thanks for your help with this project.

Sincerely,

*Jon Wang, Second Grade Teacher*

|  | **Length** | |
|---|---|---|
| **Object** | *Inch ruler* | *Centimeter ruler* |
| 1. | | |
| 2. | | |
| 3. | | |
| 4. | | |
| 5. | | |
| 6. | | |

**FOLLOW-UP:** Do many more linear measurement activities using standard units, as suggested in the resources at the end of the unit.

## Standard Measurement: Volume

**OBJECTIVE:** To be able to use standard units of measure to compare volumes of materials; to learn that the smaller the units, the more will be needed to measure the volume; to learn how to use standard measures of volume such as teaspoons, tablespoons, cups, pints, quarts, and liters.

**MATERIALS:** Containers of many different sizes (boxes, baskets, buckets, jars, cups, bowls, pans, bottles, plastic bags, and so on) and standard measures of volume (set of customary and set of metric measuring cups, liter and quart measures, customary and metric measuring spoons).

**ACTIVITIES:** These activities are introduced following many exploratory experiences of comparing visually and with arbitrary units. The same container's capacities can be measured with arbitrary and with standard units to emphasize the need for standard units. The first activity is designed to develop an understanding of this need.

1. Discuss volume following the same format as was used for linear measurement. YOU HAVE EXPLORED THE VOLUME OR SPACE INSIDE OF MANY CONTAINERS BY FILLING AND EMPTYING CONTAINERS OF DIFFERENT SIZES AND SHAPES. WHAT KINDS OF UNITS HAVE YOU USED? Encourage them to name some of the smaller units that they used to fill larger containers. See if they can generalize from

the length discussion that there are problems in communication when standard units are not used. Pass around the standard measurement materials. Encourage the children to talk about the characteristics of these materials. Do they recognize that they have used these types of things many times to measure ingredients for cooking? Do they notice the numbers and scales marked on the materials?

2. Using the standard units, have the children find out the capacities of the containers previously used for exploration. Have them use materials such as water, rice, beans, and/or sand for these explorations. They should record their findings in a table such as the one below:

|  | Number of units to fill | |
| --- | --- | --- |
| **Container** | *Using standard cup measure* | *Using small juice glass* |
| 1. | | |
| 2. | | |
| 3. | | |
| 4. | | |
| 5. | | |
| 6. | | |

**FOLLOW-UP:** Continue to do exploratory measurement of capacity. Also, continue with cooking activities, giving the children more responsibility for selecting the needed measurement materials.

## Standard Measurement: Area

**OBJECTIVE:** To explore area in a concrete manner and its relationship to linear measurement.

**MATERIALS:** Inch and centimeter cubes, two-dimensional patterns (with and without squares), paper grids, and paper squares (or purchase Learning Measurement Inch by Inch from Lakeshore).

**ACTIVITIES:** Area can be explored with squared paper and cubes long before formal instruction. Remember that area-type activities are frequently used as the visual representations of multiplication.

1. On poster board, make some shapes such as those shown below that are in inch or centimeter units. Have the children find out how many inch or centimeter cubes will cover the whole shape.

SHAPES WITH SQUARES MARKED

SHAPES WITHOUT SQUARES MARKED

(continued)

2.  Make a supply of paper grids (inch or centimeter squares, about 5 × 4 squares). Make a supply of construction paper squares. Have the children make up their own areas by pasting individual squares on the grid. Have them record on the grid how many squares are in their area. (Or use Learning Measurement Inch by Inch.)

**FOLLOW-UP:** If rulers have been introduced, ask the children to measure the lines on the grids and patterns with their rulers. Discuss how they might figure out how many square inches or centimeters are on a plane surface using their rulers.

## Standard Measurement: Weight

**OBJECTIVE:** To be able to use standard units of measure to compare the weights of various materials and to use balance and platform scales.

**MATERIALS:** Balance scales with English and metric weights, a set of platform scales, a metric and/or customary kitchen scale, paper and pencil for recording observations, and many objects and materials that can be weighed.

**ACTIVITIES:** The children should have already explored weight using comparisons.

1.  WHEN YOU LOOK AT TWO OBJECTS, YOU CAN GUESS IF THEY ARE HEAVY OR LIGHT, BUT YOU DON'T REALLY KNOW UNTIL YOU LIFT THEM BECAUSE SIZE CAN FOOL YOU. YOU COULD EASILY LIFT A LARGE BALLOON, BUT A ROCK OF THE SAME SIZE WOULD BE TOO HEAVY TO LIFT (have a balloon and a rock available for them to lift, if possible). A MARSHMALLOW WOULD BE EASIER TO LIFT THAN A LUMP OF LEAD OF THE SAME SIZE. THE LEAD AND THE ROCK HAVE MORE STUFF IN THEM THAN THE BALLOON AND THE MARSHMALLOW. THE MORE STUFF THERE IS IN SOMETHING, THE HARDER A FORCE IN THE EARTH CALLED GRAVITY PULLS ON IT. WHEN SOMETHING IS WEIGHED, WE ARE MEASURING HOW HARD GRAVITY IS PULLING ON IT. YOU HAVE COMPARED MANY KINDS OF THINGS BY PUTTING ONE KIND OF THING ON ONE SIDE OF A BALANCE SCALE AND ANOTHER ON THE OTHER SIDE. NOW YOU WILL WORK WITH CUSTOMARY AND METRIC WEIGHTS IN YOUR PAN BALANCE ON ONE SIDE AND THINGS YOU WANT TO WEIGH ON THE OTHER SIDE. Discuss the sets of pan balance weights and have them available for the children to examine. Explain that they are all made of the same material so that size is relative to weight. Have the children weigh various objects and materials (water, rice, beans, and so on). Compare the weights of a cup of water versus a cup of rice or a cup of beans. Which weighs more? How much more? Remind the children that they will have to add the amounts for each weight to get a total. Suggest that they work in pairs so they can check each other's results.

2.  Show the children how to read the dial on the kitchen scale. Provide a variety of things to weigh.

3.  If a platform scale for people is available, have everyone in the class weighed, record the results, and have the children make a graph that depicts the results.

4.  Have the children go through newspaper grocery-store advertisements and cut out pictures of items that have to be weighed at the store to find their cost.

5.  Have the children weigh two objects at the same time. Remove one and weigh the remaining object. Subtract the weight of the single object from the weight of the two. Now weigh the other object. Is the weight the same as when you subtracted the first weight from the total for both objects?

**FOLLOW-UP:** Continue putting out interesting things to weigh. Make something with a metric recipe that specifies amounts by weight rather than volume.

## Standard Measurement: Temperature

**OBJECTIVE:** To be able to use standard units of measure to compare temperatures and to learn how to use a thermometer to measure temperature.

**MATERIALS:** Large demonstration thermometer, small thermometers for student use, outdoor thermometer.

**ACTIVITIES:** These activities assume that children have talked about and have had experiences with hot, warm, and cold things and hot, comfortable, and cold weather.

1. Let the children examine the demonstration thermometer. Have them decide why there are two scales (Fahrenheit and Celsius) and how each is read. Discuss their experiences with thermometers (e.g., when they are ill or go to the doctor for a checkup, for measuring the outdoor and indoor air temperature, for controlling the thermostat on their furnaces and air conditioners).
2. Provide some hot water and ice cubes. Ask the children to measure the temperature of the water and record the result. Have them add an ice cube, let it melt, measure again, and record the result. Keep adding ice cubes and recording the results. Have the children make a line graph to illustrate how the ice affects the temperature. Is any other factor affecting the water temperature? (Answer: the air temperature.) Compare the results with the temperature of tap water.
3. If possible, post an outdoor thermometer outside the classroom window and have the children record the temperature each day in the morning, at noon, and at the end of the day. After a week, have them make some graphs depicting what they found out. Ask interested students to write daily weather reports for posting on the bulletin board.

**FOLLOW-UP:** Have interested children record the daily weather forecasts from the radio, TV, or newspaper. Compare the forecast temperatures with those recorded at school.

## Standard Measurement: Time

**OBJECTIVE:** To be able to use standard units to measure time and to read time accurately from a conventional clock.

**MATERIALS:** Large clock model with movable hands (e.g., the well-known Judy Clock), miniature model clocks that can be used individually during small group activities, a 60-minute timer that can be used to help develop a sense of time duration, a class monthly calendar (teacher made or purchased).

**ACTIVITIES:** 1. Children should have some sense of time sequence and duration by the time they reach the primary level. A timer is still useful to time events such as "Five minutes to finish up" or "Let's see if anyone can finish before the 10-minute timer rings." The major task for the primary child is understanding the clock and what it tells us and

*(continued)*

eventually learning how to work with time in terms of the amount of time from one clock reading to another. Children can work together with the Judy Clock or with their smaller models, moving the hands and identifying the time. Much of clock knowledge comes from everyday activities through naturalistic and informal experiences. You can support these experiences by having a large wall clock in your classroom and having visual models of important times during the day that the children can match to the real clock. For example, the daily schedule might be put on the wall chart with both a conventional clock face and the digital time indicated for each major time block, as shown below.

2. Clock skills may be broken down as follows:
   a. Identify the hour and the minute hands and the direction in which they move.
   b. Be able to say the time on the clock at the hour, and be able to place the hands of the clock for the hour. Know that the short hand is on the hour, and the long hand is on 12.
   c. Identify that it is after a particular hour.
   d. Count by 5s.
   e. Tell the time to the nearest multiple of 5.
   f. Count on from multiples of 5 (10, 11, 12, . . .).
   g. Write time in digital notation (3:15).
   h. Tell time to the nearest minute, and write it in digital notation.
   i. Match the time on a digital clock to a conventional clock's time.
   j. Identify time before a particular hour and count by 5s to tell how many minutes it is before that hour.
3. Each child can make a clock to take home. Use a poster board circle or paper plate. Provide each child with a paper fastener and a long and short hand. Have them mark the short hand with an *H* and the long hand with an *M*. Send a note home to the parents suggesting some clock activities they can do with their child.
4. Provide the children with blank calendars each month that they can fill in with important dates (holidays, birthdays, etc.).

**FOLLOW-UP:** Continue to read children stories that include time concepts and time sequence. For more advanced students who understand how to read clocks and keep track of time, have them keep a diary for a week recording how much time they spend on activities at home (eating, sleeping, doing homework, reading, watching TV, playing outdoors, attending soccer practice, going to dancing lessons, etc.). Ask them to add up the times at the end of the week and rank the activities, in terms of time spent on them, from most to least. They might even go on to figure out how much time per month and year they spend on each activity if they are consistent from week to week.

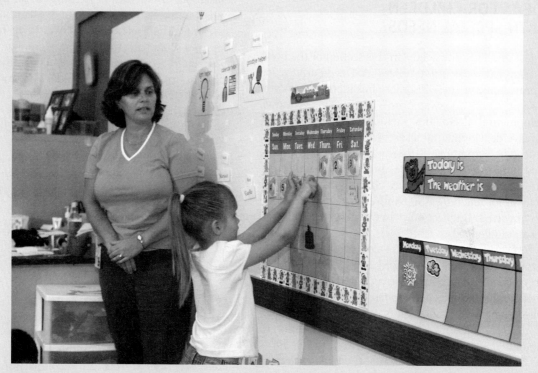

A monthly calendar supports a child's developing understanding of time.

## Standard Measurement: Money

**OBJECTIVE:** To be able to tell the value of money of different denominations, associate the symbol ¢ with coins and $ with dollars, find the value of a particular set of coins, be able to write the value of particular sets of coins and bills.

**MATERIALS:** Paper money and coin sets, pictures of coins, Money Bingo game (Trend Enterprises).

**ACTIVITIES:** Money is always a fascinating subject for young children. Money activities can be used not only to learn about money but also to provide application for whole numbers and later for decimal skills.

1. Dramatic play continues to be an important vehicle of learning for primary children. First graders enjoy dramatic play centers such as those described in Unit 22. Second and third graders begin to be more organized and can design their own dramatic play activities using available props. They enjoy writing plays and acting them out. Play money should always be available in the prop box.

2. Make some price tags (first with amounts less than $1, later with more). Have the children pick tags out of a box one at a time and count out the correct amount of play money.

3. Have the children go through catalogs and select items they would like. Have them list the items and the prices and add up their purchases. Younger children can write just the dollar part of the prices.

**FOLLOW-UP:** Play Money Bingo. The bingo cards have groups of coins in each section. Cards with different amounts of cents are picked, and the children have to add up their coins to find out if they have a match.

## IDEAS FOR CHILDREN WITH SPECIAL NEEDS

The last disability considered in this section of the book is the autism spectrum disorders (ASD). Awareness of the prevalence of these disorders has increased greatly in recent years ("As awareness," 2007). This group of developmental disabilities includes autistic disorder, pervasive developmental disorder, and Asperger's syndrome. The symptoms of these disorders vary, but afflicted children typically have social and communication disorders and may display challenging behaviors. The focus for teaching ASD children is getting them socially involved. Intellectually they range from gifted to severely challenged.

According to Lewis (2003), communication with these children must be clear and simple. Tasks need to be broken down into small steps. The most common instructional methods are applied behavioral analysis, applied verbal analysis, and floortime (Gargiulo & Kilgo, 2007). These methods all require constant attention to the child.

In this text we have looked at the wide variety of disabilities children may display. Some typical children may have difficulties with mathematics that can be identified in the early grades. Mathematics Recovery (MR) (Wright, Martland, Stafford, & Stanger, 2002) is a program for helping first graders (6- or 7-year-olds) who are struggling with mathematics. The one-on-one instruction is individualized and problem based. Wright and colleagues present a detailed plan for working with difficult students.

## EVALUATION

Evaluation of children's progress with measurement should be done using concrete tasks; here are some examples. Give the children a list of three items in the classroom to measure. Arrange a set of measuring cups, material to measure, and a container to measure into; then ask each child to turn in his answer. Set up a scale with three items of known weight, have each child weigh each item individually, and record the amount. Put out three model thermometers with different temperatures and have each child, in turn, tell you the readings and whether they indicate hot, comfortable, or cold. Show the child the time on a model clock and ask him to tell you the time and explain how he knows. Have each child identify coins and then put them together to make various amounts, making the amounts appropriate to the child's level at the time.

## SUMMARY

Measurement skills are essential for successful everyday living. People need to know how to measure length, volume, area, weight, temperature, time, and money. These concepts develop gradually through many concrete experiences from gross comparisons (e.g., long–short, heavy–light, hot–cold, early–late) to measurement with arbitrary units and finally to measurement with standard English (customary) and/or metric units. Measurement activities are valuable opportunities for applying whole number skills and fraction knowledge (and later decimals) as well as for obtaining data that can be graphed for visual interpretation. Measurement concepts are acquired through practice with real measuring tools and real things to measure. Lecture and demonstration alone are not adequate methods of instruction.

## KEY TERMS

| English units | metric units | unit |
|---|---|---|

## SUGGESTED ACTIVITIES

1. On your Activity File cards for this unit, make note of the prerequisite activities in Units 18, 19, and 22.

2. Locate an article on helping preservice teachers to understand metrics, preferably with one or more suggested activities. Try the activities with the other members of your class. Have the students in your class evaluate whether the experience was helpful in providing a better understanding of the metric system and in suggesting some appropriate instructional ideas.

3. Assess one first-grade, one second-grade, and one third-grade student on readiness for using standard units of measure. Write a report that describes your assessment, recording the children's responses and comparing the three children's readiness.

4. Prepare materials for the suggested evaluation tasks. Evaluate one first-grade, one second-grade, and one third-grade student on their understanding of standard units of measure. Write a report describing your evaluation: record the children's responses and compare the three children's levels of understanding.

5. Plan instructional activities based on the results of your interviews with the primary children. If possible, use the activities with the children.

6. Develop a plan for a measurement center that can serve a first-, second-, or third-grade classroom. Include one station for each type of measurement discussed (or five stations for one type of measurement). If possible, procure the materials and set up the center in a classroom for a week. Keep a record of what the children do in the center. At the end of the week, evaluate the center. Was it appropriate? Were the materials set up in such a way that the children could work independently? Did children return again? Did they try the activities at each station? Would you do it the same way next time? Why? What changes would you make?

7. Using the guidelines from Activity 5, Unit 2, evaluate one or more of the following software programs.

   ■ *Numbers Undercover* (K–3; http://store.sunburst.com). Time, measurement, and money mysteries.

   ■ *Math Blaster* (ages 5–7; http://store.sunburst.com). Includes time, money, and measurement.

   ■ *Lemonade for Sale* (http://store.sunburst.com). Work with bar graphs and money.

   ■ *The Penny Pot* (http://store.sunburst.com). Basic money concepts.

   ■ *Key Skills for Math* (http://store.sunburst.com). Shapes, numbers and measurement.

   ■ *Learn about Physical Science: Matter, Measurement, Mixture* (http://store.sunburst.com)

   ■ *Magic School Bus: Whales and Dolphins* (Redmond, WA: Microsoft). Measure and weigh whales and dolphins.

   ■ *Trudy's Time and Place House* (http://www.riverdeep.net). Explores geography and time.

   ■ *LeapFrog Cash Register* (Emeryville, CA: LeapFrog Enterprises). Coin identification, money values, quantities, numbers, and counting.

   ■ *Measures* (http://www.dositey.com). Time measuring activities.

   ■ *Shopping Math* (http://www.dositey.com). Buying toys.

   ■ *MatchTime* (preschool–6; http://www.K12software.com)

   ■ *Light Weights/Heavy Weights* (K–4; www.nasaexplores.com). Weight prediction.

## REVIEW

**A.** List two reasons that measurement is an essential part of the primary mathematics curriculum.

**B.** There are five stages children pass through on their way to understanding and using standard units of measure. Put the steps in the correct developmental order.

1. Understands the need for standard units
2. Works with arbitrary units
3. Applies standard units of measure
4. Makes gross comparisons (e.g., heavy–light, hot–cold)
5. Plays and imitates

**C.** Children are not ready to understand all the different units of standard measure at the same time. Match the measurement concepts on the left with the usual time of readiness on the right.

| Measurement concept | Time when ready for standard units |
|---|---|
| 1. Length | a. In grade 2. |
| 2. Time | b. Introduced in grade 2 but well beyond primary when accuracy is achieved. |
| 3. Volume | c. Introduced gradually starting in preprimary, but not done accurately until the end of primary or later (instrument is difficult to understand). |
| 4. Area | d. Value is not really understood until the end of primary. |
| 5. Weight | e. Units introduced in grade 1; measurement in grade 2. |
| 6. Temperature | f. Introduced in grade 3. |
| 7. Money | g. Mainly informal during primary but important for visual representation of multiplication. |

**D.** Name the two types of units used in the United States. Which is the conventional (customary) standard?

**E.** Why should U.S. students learn the metric system if it is not the standard in the United States?

**F.** Which cognitive developmental stage must children have reached before they are able to understand and apply standard units of measure?

**G.** List the most important factors in understanding the concept of *unit*.

**H.** Provide two or more examples of the difficulties associated with using measuring instruments. Explain how these difficulties can be eased.

**I.** Select a type of measurement. Describe how you would introduce measurement of that type following the sequence of instruction described in this unit.

**J.** Describe three types of disabilities discussed in Section 5 of this book.

## REFERENCES

As awareness and concern grow, autism moves into public spotlight. (2007). *ACD Developments, 21*(2), 1, 9, 10–12.

Gargiulo, R., & Kilgo, J. (2007). *Young children with special needs* (2nd ed.). Albany, NY: Thomson Delmar Learning.

Lewis, V. (2003). *Development and disability* (2nd ed.). Malden, MA: Blackwell.

Lubinski, C. A., & Thiessen, D. (1996). Exploring measurement through literature. *Teaching Children Mathematics, 2,* 260–263.

Myller, R. (1972). *How big is a foot?* New York: Atheneum.

National Council of Teachers of Mathematics. (2000). *Principles and standards for school mathematics.* Reston, VA: Author.

National Council of Teachers of Mathematics. (2007). *Curriculum focal points.* Reston, VA: Author.

Wright, R. J., Martland, J., Stasfford, A. K., & Stanger, G. (2002). *Teaching number.* Thousand Oaks, CA: Chapman.

# FURTHER READING AND RESOURCES

## General References

*Box it or bag it mathematics (K–2)*. Portland, OR: Math Learning Center.

*Bridges in mathematics (K–2)*. Portland, OR: Math Learning Center.

Burris, A. C. (2005). *Understanding the math you teach*. Upper Saddle River, NJ: Pearson-Merrill/Prentice-Hall.

Clements, D. H., Sarama, J., & DiBiase, A. (2004). *Engaging young children in mathematics: Standards for early childhood mathematics education*. Mahwah, NJ: Erlbaum.

Dacey, L., Cavanagh, M., Findell, C. R., Greenes, C. E., Sheffield, L. J., & Small, M. (2003). *Navigating through measurement in prekindergarten–grade 2*. Reston, VA: National Council of Teachers of Mathematics.

Dougherty, B. J., & Venenciano, L. C. H. (2007). Measure up for understanding. *Teaching Children Mathematics, 13*(9), 452–456.

Findell, C. R., Cavanagh, M., Dacey, L., Greenes, C. E., Sheffield, L. J., & Small, M. (2004). *Navigating through problem solving and reasoning in grade 1*. Reston, VA: National Council of Teachers of Mathematics.

Greenes, C. E., Dacey, L., Cavanagh, M., Findell, C. R., Sheffield, L. J., & Small, M. (2003). *Navigating through problem solving and reasoning in prekindergarten–kindergarten*. Reston, VA: National Council of Teachers of Mathematics.

Measurement [Focus issue]. (2006). *Science & Children, 44*(2).

Teaching and learning measurement [Focus issue]. (2006). *Teaching Children Mathematics, 13*(3).

West, S., & Cox, A. (2001). *Sand and water play*. Beltsville, MD: Gryphon House.

## Linear Measurement

Ashbrook, P. (2006). The early years. Learning measurement. *Science & Children, 44*(2), 44–45.

Battista, M. T. (2006). Understanding the development of students' thinking about length. *Teaching Children Mathematics, 13*(3), 140–146.

Clarkson, C. L. M., Robelia, B., Chahine, I., Fleming, M., & Lawrenz, F. (2007). Rulers of different colors:

Inquiry into measurement. *Teaching Children Mathematics, 14*(1), 34–39.

Design a house. (1991). In A. Baker & J. Baker, *Counting on a small planet*. Portsmouth, NH: Heinemann.

Hartweg, K. (2003). Responses to the shopping spree problem. *Teaching Children Mathematics, 10*(3), 154–157.

Hendrix-Martin, E. (1997). Students use their bodies to measure animals. *Teaching Children Mathematics, 3*, 426–430.

Joram, E., Hartman, C., & Trafton, P. R. (2004). "As people get older, they get taller": An integrated unit on measurement, linear relationships, and data analysis. *Teaching Children Mathematics, 10*(7), 344–351.

Kamii, C. (2006). Measurement of length: How can we teach it better? *Teaching Children Mathematics, 13*(3), 154–158.

Kelly, B. (1997). Problem solvers: Animals and fences at a zoo. *Teaching Children Mathematics, 3*, 438.

Levin, B., Berger, D., & Cave, L. (2001). Where did you go this summer? *Teaching Children Mathematics, 8*(1), 18–19.

Moyer, P. S., & Mailley, E. (2004). *Inchworm and a half*: Developing fraction and measurement concepts using mathematical representations. *Teaching Children Mathematics, 10*(5), 244–252.

Richardson, K. (1997). Too easy for kindergarten and just right for first grade. *Teaching Children Mathematics, 3*, 432–437.

Rozanski, K. D., Beckmann, C. E., & Thompson, D. R. (2003). Exploring size with *The Grouchy Ladybug*. *Teaching Children Mathematics, 10*(2), 84–89.

Ruggles, J., & Slenger, B. S. (1998). The "measure me" doll. *Teaching Children Mathematics, 5*(1), 40–44.

Shreero, B., Sullivan, C., & Urbano, A. (2003). World-record math. *Teaching Children Mathematics, 9*(9), 530–531.

Smith, L. A., Sterling, D. R., & Moyer-Packenham, P. S. (2006). Activities that *really* measure up. *Science & Children, 44*(2), 30–33.

Suh, J. M., Moyer, P. S., & Sterling, D. R. (2003). Junior architects: Designing your dream clubhouse using measurement and geometry. *Teaching Children Mathematics, 10*(3), 170–177.

## Volume

Ashbrook, P. (2006). The early years. Learning measurement. *Science & Children, 44*(2), 44–45.

Fitzsimmons, P. F., & Goldhaber, J. (1997). Siphons, pumps, and missile launchers: Inquiry at the water tables. *Science and Children, 34*(4), 16–19, 42.

Poth, J. R. (2006). Bird station investigation. *Teaching Children Mathematics, 13*(3), 174–180.

Water use and abuse. (1991). In A. Baker & J. Baker, *Counting on a small planet*. Portsmouth, NH: Heinemann.

## Time

Forrest, K., Schnabel, D., & Williams, M. E. (2006/2007). Math by the month. Special days. *Teaching Children Mathematics, 13*(5), 264.

Lemme, B. (1998). Putting mathematics into routine classroom tasks. *Teaching Children Mathematics, 4*(5), 250–253.

Lemme, B. (2000). Integrating measurement projects: Sand timers. *Teaching Children Mathematics, 4*(5), 132–135.

Martin, H. (1999). Days of the month: The calendar of mathematics. *Teaching Children Mathematics, 5*(9), 530–531.

Monroe, E. E., Orme, M. P., & Erickson, L. B. (2002). *Working cotton*: Toward an understanding of time. *Teaching Children Mathematics, 8*(8), 475–479.

Pace, R. D. (2004). On time with Arthur. *Teaching Children Mathematics, 10*(8), 416–419.

## Area

Casa, T. M., Spinelli, A. M., & Gavin, M. K. (2006). This about covers it! Strategies for finding area. *Teaching Children Mathematics, 13*(3), 168–173.

Nitabach, E., & Lehrer, R. (1996). Developing spatial sense through area measurement. *Teaching Children Mathematics, 2*, 473–477.

Outhred, L. N., & Mitchelmore, M. C. (2000). Young children's intuitive understanding of rectangular area measurement. *Journal for Research in Mathematics Education, 31*(2), 144–167.

## Money

Green shopping. (1991). In A. Baker & J. Baker, *Counting on a small planet*. Portsmouth, NH: Heinemann.

Kulas, L. L. (1997). May I take your order? *Teaching Children Mathematics, 3*, 230–234.

Lemme, B. (1998). Putting mathematics into routine classroom tasks. *Teaching Children Mathematics, 4*(5), 250–253.

Mailley, E., & Moyer, P. S. (2004). Investigations: The mathematical candy store: Weight matters. *Teaching Children Mathematics, 10*(8), 388–391.

Olson, M., & Olson, J. (2002). Responses to the puzzling prices problem. *Teaching Children Mathematics, 8*(8), 470–474.

Shreero, B., Sullivan, C., & Urbano, A. (2003). Careers that count. *Teaching Children Mathematics, 9*(5), 274–275.

Wiener, C., & Smith, C. (2004). Making sense out of cents. *Teaching Children Mathematics, 11*(4), 188–192.

## Weight

Brahier, D. J., & Bell, J. (2002). Dino-mite explorations. *Teaching Children Mathematics, 8*(9), 532–535.

Lennox, J. (1996). "Weighing" dinosaurs. *Science and Children, 34*(3), 16–19.

McGregor, J. (1996). Do you measure up? *Teaching Children Mathematics, 3*, 84–85.

## Temperature

Baby, it's cold outside. (1991). In A. Baker & J. Baker, *Counting on a small planet*. Portsmouth, NH: Heinemann.

Chia, D. T. (1998). Weather mathematics: Integrated science and math. *Teaching Children Mathematics, 5*(1), 19–22.

Moore, D. A. (1999). Some like it hot: Promoting measurement and graphical thinking by using temperature. *Teaching Children Mathematics, 5*(9), 538–543.

## Emergent Readers' Books

Young, S. L. (1998). *The garage sale*. Columbus, OH: Zaner-Blozer. [Money]

Young, S. L. (1998). *One o'clock is time for one nap*. Columbus, OH: Zaner-Blozer. [Time]

Young, S. L. (1998). *The treasure map*. Columbus, OH: Zaner-Blozer. [Measuring distance]

# SECTION 6

Using Skills,
Concepts, and
Attitudes for
Scientific
Investigations in
the Primary
Grades

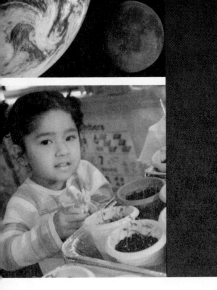

# Unit 33

## Overview of Primary Science

### OBJECTIVES

After reading this unit, you should be able to:

- Develop appropriate science learning experiences for the primary age child.
- Design lessons that guide students in primary science investigations.
- Incorporate process skills into science investigation lessons.
- Guide students in collecting, observing, sorting, and classifying objects.

The teaching standards presented in the *National Science Education Standards* (NRC, 1996) take into account the idea that science teaching is a complex activity that lies at the heart of the National Resource Council's vision of science education. The *Standards* highlight the important role of teachers in the development of science learning and present strategies for teaching science in a way that reflects how science is actually practiced. The standards for science teaching are grounded in five assumptions.

- The vision of science education described by the *Standards* requires changes through the entire system.
- What students learn is greatly influenced by how they are taught.
- The actions of teachers are deeply influenced by their perceptions of science as an enterprise and as a subject to be taught and learned.
- Student understanding is actively constructed through individual and social processes.

- Actions of teachers are deeply influenced by their understanding of and relationships with students.

This unit relates the skills needed for primary science investigations and the fundamental process skills to science lessons. Children in the primary grades continue to be avid explorers. Even though they are beginning to refine their inquiry skills, to identify changes in observed events, and to understand relationships among objects and events, they still require time to interact with and manipulate concrete objects. Students need to have many and varied opportunities for investigating, collecting, sorting and cataloging, observing, note taking and sketching, interviewing, and polling.

As children leave kindergarten and enter the primary level, they are also leaving the preoperational level and entering concrete operations. They begin to be able to use abstract symbols such as numbers and written words with understanding if they are tied to concrete experiences such as science investigations. They are also entering a period of industriousness in which they enjoy

478

long-term projects, building things, making collections, and playing games that require taking turns, learning systems of rules, and making predictions. Peers are becoming increasingly important; thus, working in small groups becomes a basic instructional strategy.

Primary age children may find it difficult to classify by more than one characteristic, transfer abstract ideas to objects and events outside of their direct experience, or draw inferences from data and identify complex patterns in data taken over a long time. Primary age children also have difficulty with experimentation as a process of testing ideas and with the logic of using evidence to formulate explanations. However, they can design investigations to try things to see what happens; they tend to focus on concrete results of tests and will entertain the idea of a "fair" test in which only one variable at a time is changed.

The units in this section contain lesson examples, strategies, and classroom vignettes of how some of the science topics suggested by the 1996 *Standards* might be taught in the primary grades. The Unifying Concepts and Processes Standard discussed in Unit 5 highlights the connections between scientific ideas and is a natural part of any investigation. Children will not fully understand these powerful ideas that characterize science until they are much older, but aspects of the ideas will be integrated in developmentally appropriate ways in this section.

This unit begins with an overview of the *National Science Education Standards*, followed by examples of how the love of collecting and the ability to play games can be applied in the science curriculum. Next, planning for investigations is described, followed by suggestions on how to manage the classroom. Finally, examples of how instructional technology can be used to enhance science investigations are described.

## THE NATIONAL SCIENCE EDUCATION STANDARDS FOR SCIENCE TEACHING

The science teaching standards focus on the qualities that are most closely associated with science teaching and the vision of science education described in the *National Science Education Standards*.

### Teaching Standard A

Teachers of science plan an inquiry-based science program for their students. In doing this, teachers:

- Develop a framework of year-long and short-term goals for students.
- Select science content and adapt and design curricula to meet the interests, knowledge, understanding, abilities, and experiences of students.
- Select teaching and assessment strategies that support the development of student understanding and nurture a community of science learners.
- Work together as colleagues within and across disciplines and grade levels.

### Teaching Standard B

Teachers of science guide and facilitate learning. In doing this, teachers:

- Focus and support inquiries while interacting with students.
- Orchestrate discourse among students and scientific ideas.
- Challenge students to accept and share responsibility for their own learning.
- Recognize and respond to student diversity and encourage all students to participate fully in science learning.
- Encourage and model the skills of scientific inquiry as well as the curiosity, openness to new ideas and data, and skepticism that characterize science.

### Teaching Standard C

Teachers of science engage in ongoing assessment of their teaching and of student learning. In doing this, teachers:

- Use multiple methods and systematically gather data about student understanding and ability.
- Analyze assessment data to guide teaching.
- Guide students in self-assessment.

■ Use student data, observations of teaching, and interactions with colleagues to reflect on and improve teaching practice.

■ Use student data, observations of teaching, and interactions with colleagues to report student achievement and opportunities to learn to students, teachers, parents, policy makers, and the general public.

## Teaching Standard D

Teachers of science design and manage learning environments that provide students with the time, space, and resources needed for learning science. In doing this, teachers:

■ Structure the time available so that students are able to engage in extended investigations.

■ Create a setting for student work that is flexible and supportive of science inquiry.

■ Ensure a safe working environment.

■ Make the available science tools, materials, media, and technological resources accessible to students.

■ Identify and use resources outside the school.

■ Engage students in designing the learning environment.

## Teaching Standard E

Teachers of science develop communities of science learners that reflect the intellectual rigor of scientific inquiry and the attitudes and social values conducive to science learning. In doing this, teachers:

■ Display and demand respect for the diverse ideas, skills, and experiences of all students.

■ Enable students to have a significant voice in decisions about the content and context of their work and require students to take responsibility for the learning of all members of the community.

■ Nurture collaboration among students.

■ Structure and facilitate ongoing formal and informal discussion based on a shared understanding of rules of scientific discourse.

■ Model and emphasize the skills, attitudes, and values of scientific inquiry.

## Teaching Standard F

Teachers of science actively participate in the ongoing planning and development of the school science program. In doing this, teachers:

■ Plan and develop the school science program.

■ Participate in decisions concerning the allocation of time and other resources to the science program.

■ Participate fully in planning and implementing professional growth and development strategies to themselves and their colleagues.

# COLLECTING

Primary children love to collect. They are increasingly aware of details, and their ability to compare and categorize objects is developing. They are apt to begin collecting pocketfuls of small and portable objects that they see around them. Use this natural inclination to encourage children to observe, compare, sort, and classify. Collections can consist of many things such as plants, animals, feathers, fur, rocks, sand, seashells, soils, and anything else that interests children.

However, whatever the composition of the collection, it should be viewed as a means of encouraging inquiry, not as an end in itself. In this way, simple identification of objects does not become the focal point of collecting. Instead, children will learn the basic steps in scientific inquiry.

## Getting Started by Using Magnifiers

A **magnifier** is useful for both collecting and classifying. Handheld plastic magnifiers are perfect for all ages, are inexpensive, and have the advantage of being mobile for outdoor explorations. Magnifying boxes are hollow plastic boxes with a removable magnifier at the top. They are ideal for observing small treasures and animals such as live insects. When using magnifiers, carefully catch the insects, observe them, and then return

**Figure 33–1** Introduce children to magnifiers.

them to their environment without injury. In this way, you will encourage humaneness as well as observation.

Children can also use the jumbo-sized magnifier mounted on a three-legged stand. There is no need to hold objects with this type of magnifier, and objects of different sizes can be examined at the same time. Although some dexterity is required for adjusting most magnifiers, the effort is important because the magnifiers are a bridge to using microscopes. In the following scenario, second graders are introduced to magnifiers before collecting (Figure 33–1).

> Mrs. Han introduces magnifiers by letting the children explore for a period of time on their own. She does not tell them what to look at; rather, she gives them time to "mess around" with the magnifiers. "Wow!" observes Trang Fung. "Look how big the hair on my arm looks." As she continues to look around at objects close to her, Dean motions her over to his table. "Look, Trang. Look at the sleeve of my shirt." "It looks different. Something is in my shirt." "Mrs. Han," asks Sara, "Do things always look bigger with magnifiers? Can we always see more?" "Let's look through them and see," suggests the teacher.
>
> Mrs. Han plans several opportunities to view objects in different ways. She asks the children to describe the object before viewing with a

magnifier, to describe what they see while they are viewing, to compare how objects look under different powers, and to compare and contrast appearances of objects after viewing is completed. She asks, "How does the object appear under the magnifier? Why do you think it looks different?"

The teacher groups the children and has them examine different areas of the room, their clothes, lunch, and a spiderweb. She explains that the magnifying glass itself is called a **lens** and confirms that things look different under a magnifier. She explains that this is because of the way the magnifier is constructed but does not suggest technical explanations. Primary children will enjoy noticing details not seen with the naked eye.

## Focusing the Collecting

Practice collecting on the school grounds or in the neighborhood. Help children focus on their collections by giving them suggestions. After collecting, suggest classification systems, let children come up with their own, or try sorting objects in different ways. At this age, the primary purpose of collecting is not identification. Rather, collecting should be viewed as an opportunity to encourage inquiry and become aware of the variety of similarities and differences in nature. As children collect, they observe, compare, classify, and begin to think as a scientist might think. The following collecting ideas will get the class started.

1. *Leaves.* Collect and sort leaves by color, shape, vein patterns, edges, and so on. Ask, "How many red leaves can you find? Can you find leaves that are smooth? Do some of the leaves feel different? Try putting all of the leaves that smell the same in a pile." Children will want to associate the leaf with its name on a label (Figure 33–2). Suggestions for displaying collections are found in Unit 40.

2. *Shells.* Collect different types of empty shells—for example, nutshells, eggshells, snail shells, or seashells. Ask, "What kind of objects have a shell? How do you think they use their shell?"

3. *Litter.* Collect litter around the school ground. Ask, "What type of litter did you find most often? Where did you find it?"

4. *Seeds.* Seeds can be found on the ground or flying in the air. Walk through a field, and examine the seeds clinging to your trouser legs and socks. Sort the seeds by size, color, and the way they were dispersed. Ask, "What type of seed did you find most often?" Suggestions for setting up a center on seeds are found in Unit 39.

5. *Spiderwebs.* Spiderwebs are all around us, but children will need practice and patience to collect them. Spray powder on the web, then put a piece of dark paper on one side of it. Hold the web in place with hairspray. Ask, "How are the spiderwebs the same? How are they different?" Children might enjoy pulling twine through white craft glue to duplicate the way a spider forms its web. Let dry and hang.

6. *Feathers.* Feathers can be found at home, at school, and on the way to school. Children will enjoy examining the feathers with magnifiers. Point out the zipperlike barbs that open and close the feathers. Ask, "How are the feathers alike? How do they differ?" If children are studying birds, identify the function of the different types of feathers (Figure 33–3).

**Figure 33–2** Leaves, shells, and seeds are fun to collect, sort, and label.

**Figure 33–3** Zipperlike barbs can be seen with the help of a magnifier.

7. *Rocks.* Collect rocks and sort them by color, size, shape, texture, and hardness. Ask, "What size rocks do you have? What color rocks do you have? What shapes are your rocks? How do they feel? How are the rocks alike? How are the rocks different? Do the rocks have the same hardness when you scratch them?"

8. *Rubbings.* Another way to collect is to collect impressions of objects. Rubbings of bark and fossils are made by holding one side of a piece of paper against an object and rubbing the other side with a dark crayon. Mount the resulting patterns on colored construction paper and display. Have the children compare and classify the patterns.

9. *Modeling clay.* Modeling clay can be used to create an impression of fossils, bark, leaves, and seeds. Simply press the clay against the object, remove, and compare impressions.

10. *Plaster molds.* Footprints can be preserved by forming a plaster mold. Mix plaster, build a small cardboard rim around the footprint, and pour plaster into the impression that you have found. Carefully remove the plaster when dry, and return the cast to the room for comparison (Figure 33–4).

**Figure 33–4** Making a plaster mold of raccoon tracks. "What animal made these tracks?"

## Collecting Small Animals without Backbones

Mr. Wang asks his students, "What is your favorite animal?" "That's easy," Derrick says. "I like lions, seals, and cats." "Me, too," Theresa says. "But I really like horses the best." Brent chimes in that his favorite pet is a gerbil, and Liu Pei insists that dogs are the best animals because they guard your house.

A few students mention reptiles as a favorite animal, but most of the children name mammals. To introduce **invertebrates** as animals and clear up a common misconception, the teacher has the children run their hands down their back. He asks, "What do you feel?" "Bones," says Theresa. "I feel my backbone." Mr. Wang asks the children if their favorite animals have backbones. "Yes, of course they do," Brent answers.

Mr. Wang explains that not all animals have backbones; these animals are called invertebrates. He mentions a few such as worms, sponges, mollusks, starfish, crayfish, spiders, and insects and is surprised at the children's interest.

The teacher decided to plan a collecting trip to a nearby pond and field. Each student was to wear old clothes, including long pants, and bring a washed peanut butter-sized jar. Mr. Wang had prepared insect sweepers and a few catch jars (Figure 33–5).

Before leaving on the trip, Mr. Wang gave instructions. "We will need to be quiet and to look high and low." Derrick cut in, "And under rocks, bushes, and fallen branches." "Yes," the teacher said. "Look carefully where you walk."

The class worked in teams during the hunt, and each team tried to capture only one kind of animal. "Remember where you captured your animal," Mr. Wang reminded the children. "We will turn the insects loose in the same habitat that we found them."

After returning to the room, the teams used nature books to find out how to keep their captives alive. Each animal was displayed with an index card giving its name, habitat where it was found, and the collector's name. The animal was on display for two days and then released to its original habitat. Many questions were raised. "Does my worm like to eat raisins?" Derrick wanted to know. Brent was interested in knowing if his worm was able to see, and Liu Pei wondered if her sow bugs would dig in the dirt of their container.

**INSECT NET**

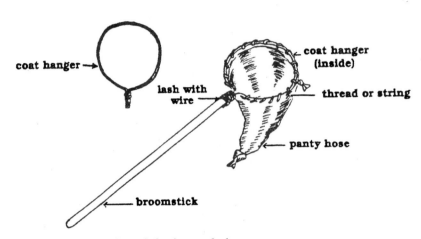

**Figure 33–5** Making an insect sweeper from discarded nylons and a hanger.

Mr. Wang encouraged close observation and investigation with such questions as, "Does the animal like rough or smooth surfaces? Does it spend most of its time in the light or in the dark?"

The next day, Liu Pei brought in animals she had found on her way to school. The display was growing. Children classified the animals by color, number of legs, and where they were found. "Let's group the animals into those found on land and those found on water," Theresa said. "Don't forget the air," Brent suggested. "Some were found in the air."

The invertebrate display was an excellent way to observe animals and their habitats. The students had an opportunity to classify, investigate characteristics, study life cycles, and expand their definition of animals. Some students developed a skit involving metamorphosis, others worked on a wall chart, and all gained an appreciation of the little creatures and their world.

## GAMES

Primary age children enjoy games. "Put the Lobster in the Chest" is a game that offers an opportunity for spatial awareness exploration and verbal communication while reinforcing science content. Refer to Unit 16 for preliminary strategies for using this science board game.

## Put the Lobster in the Chest

To play this game, which is similar to "Battleship," you must first create two identical game boards and sets of playing pieces. Correlate the activity to a science topic of your choice. For instance, if you are doing a unit on farm animals, a pasture or a farmyard would be the obvious choice. For example, imagine that you are off the coast of Maine. For the game pieces, select animals commonly found in this setting. In this case, you might include lobsters, crabs, eels, clams, whales, dolphins, and seals. You will need two of each animal. Or, use three-dimensional game pieces.

It is best to play this game as a class before having the students break into pairs or small groups. When you give the instruction, "Put the lobster into the chest," students can consult with each other and ask you questions to make sure they know which is the lobster. Separate the players with a box or similar barrier so they cannot see each other's board (Figure 33–6). A typical beginning interchange might go as follows.

INITIATOR:  Take the long thing with claws and put it beneath the floating green stuff.

FOLLOWER:  Just on the sand?

INITIATOR:  No. Put it on the sand under the plant.

**Figure 33–6** "Put the lobster under the plant."

FOLLOWER: Under the floating stuff near the brown fish?

INITIATOR: That's right.

The follow-up discussion is crucial to this game. After playing, always have the players compare their boards and talk about any differences between them.

## DEFINING INVESTIGATIONS

Hands-on manipulative activities promote literacy skills and the learning of science concepts. Yet many teachers shy away from allowing children the active participation needed to develop these skills and concepts. Messy science investigations are avoided for several common reasons. One reason is that some teachers do not feel comfortable teaching science. Other teachers find managing children and materials an overwhelming task, and still others believe that investigations should be reserved for older children.

These fears should be put to rest. You do not need an extensive science background to guide children in science investigations. What you do need is instruction in how to do it and some background information that will allow you to answer some simple questions. What is most essential for teaching science is a teacher's sense of security and ability to say, "I don't know. How do you

think we can find the answer to your question?" Explore strategies for teaching investigations to primary age children, and try the suggested strategies for managing children and materials. Early science experiences provide the necessary background for future, more sophisticated skill and concept development.

## Teaching Science Investigations

Science investigations usually begin with a question. For example, ask: "How long can you keep an ice cube from melting?" Children can initiate investigations by asking their own questions, such as, "How long will this ice cube last if I leave it on my plate?"

After the initial question or questions, you usually predict what you think is going to happen. In the ice cube example, a child might predict, "I think the ice cube will last until lunch."

**Determining variables** simply means taking all the factors into account that might affect the outcome of the investigation. Although most third-grade students can handle the term **variable**, it is not advisable to introduce this term to kindergarten through second-grade children. This component of investigation is usually too difficult for primary age children to understand. Instead, ask questions that help children consider variables in the investigation. For example, ask, "What are we trying to find out? What shall we change?" The idea of keeping something constant can be understood by talking about the idea of fairness. It just would not be fair for everything not to be the same.

Keep records of observations, results, procedures, information obtained, and any measurements collected during the investigation. **Conclusions**, of course, are statements that tell if the original prediction, **hypothesis**, was rejected. Ask, "What happened? Is this what you thought would happen? Did anything surprise you?"

This procedure resembles the scientific method for a reason: Children are unconsciously using the scientific method as they observe, predict, and reach conclusions. Encouraging them to investigate capitalizes on their natural interest.

In fact, we could call investigations student research. Basically, children are trying to find the answers to questions for which they do not know the answers. As they investigate, they find answers to their questions in the same way a scientist does. They are thinking like scientists.

Hands-on science means just that: learning from materials and processes of the natural world through direct observation and experimentation. Direct experience, experimentation, and observation are sources of students' learning about science and are essential to learning. This hands-on learning begins in infancy with sensory stimulation that hones infants' observation and discrimination skills and readies them for the more detailed explorations of toddlerhood. However, hands-on instruction alone does not constitute inquiry teaching. There is a substantial difference between an open-ended, inquiry approach to an activity and an approach that is hands-on but does not encourage problem solving and inquiry. For example, one approach to teaching the concept that water expands when it freezes might be as follows.

1. Fill a plastic container with water.
2. Place the container in the freezer and have the children observe the condition of the water after a period of time.
3. Ask the children, "What happened? How would you explain this?"

Compare this lesson to another way of approaching the same concept. Assemble materials and present the following challenge: "Can you prove at least three things that happen or don't happen to water when it freezes? Be prepared to share what you have discovered with others."

Both lessons provide children with a teacher-selected topic and a hands-on experience. The first, however, offers only one strategy (a procedure) that can be used to demonstrate an already given solution (water expands). Although this is a useful strategy, the second approach promotes inquiry because it requires that children first figure out what they observe happening (or not happening) to water when it freezes and then plan a way to convince someone else of their discovery.

Although both activities are hands on, use process skills, and require physical manipulation of objects to gain an understanding of a science concept, only the second activity involves problem solving from which

inquiry is most likely to spring. By listening to students who are actively engaged in conceptual problem solving and investigations, the teacher will uncover many scientific misconceptions that will provide instructional materials for years to come (refer to Unit 6 for additional problem-solving suggestions).

# MANAGING THE CLASS

## Distributing Materials and Working Together

A lack of classroom management can wreck your best plans. In addition to planning your lesson, give a few moments to consider how you will organize your children and the materials they will work with. The following suggestions will start you thinking.

## Organize Children for Learning

Organize the class into teams of no more than four children. It is essential that each child have responsibilities on the team. Designate a team leader, who is responsible for seeing that all materials are correctly obtained, used, and put away. The recorder is responsible for obtaining and putting away, recording, writing books, and reporting results to the class. Appoint a judge, who has the final word in any science activity-related disputes, and an investigator, who is responsible for seeing that the team follows the directions when conducting the science activity. Make sure the children understand their responsibilities. These job roles are easily adaptable for use with most cooperative learning experiences.

## Organize Materials for Learning

Materials can be organized several ways. One possibility is to distribute materials from four distribution centers in your room. Each center should be labeled as 1, 2, 3, or 4 and should contain all the equipment needed for an exploration. Then, number the children in the team 1, 2, 3, 4. The 1s are responsible for acquiring the materials at distribution center 1, the 2s at center number 2, and so on. Locate the distribution sites in separate areas of the room to reduce confusion, give a time limit for collection of materials, and provide a materials list so the team leaders can check to see that everything needed is on their table.

If you are teaching a structured lesson, you may want to make a list that indicates what each individual will do during the exploration. For example, if you want the children to explore concepts of surface tension with soap and pepper, have the 1s pour the water into the cup, the 2s tap the pepper in the cup, the 3s coat the toothpick with liquid detergent, and the 4s plunge the toothpick into the pepper.

Science explorations are fun. To maintain discipline while conducting complex activities with the whole class, an organization system for children and materials is needed. Establish simple and clear rules for classroom operation. Once the children are comfortable with the rules and organization system, you need only periodically review what is expected to keep them on task.

## Pocket Management Strategy

Primary teacher Maureen Awbrey prepares for managing children in learning areas by making a personalized library card pocket for each child in her class. Each pocket has the child's picture on it and a distinguishing symbol such as an orange triangle or a green square. Children learn their classroom jobs and become familiar with symbols as they review their job list each morning.

After the children are comfortable with their personal symbols and pockets, Mrs. Awbrey introduces them to the learning areas of the room. Each area is designated by a pocket and symbols that tell the children how many individuals may work in an area. For example, four circles mean that four children are permitted in the area. If Mrs. Awbrey does not want the children to use certain equipment, she places a "closed" sign in the area.

Colored strips of laminated paper containing the child's name and that of an available learning area are kept in the child's pocket. These strips are called *tickets.* When Scott wants to construct a zoo in the block center, he takes his block ticket to the block area and puts it in the pocket. When he is finished working in the block area, he removes his ticket and puts it in a basket. In this way, children rotate through the room and are exposed to a variety of learning experiences.

## SAMPLE INVESTIGATIONS

The following investigations allow children to develop science processes as they conduct scientific investigations.

---

## ACTIVITIES

### How Long Does it Take for a Paper Towel to Dry?

**CONCEPT:** Water disappears into the air during evaporation.

**OBJECTIVE:** To investigate the length of time it takes for paper towels to dry.

**MATERIALS:** Bowl of water, paper towels, cardboard, pie plates, variety of fabric swatches.

**NATURALISTIC AND INFORMAL ACTIVITIES:** Encourage children to experiment with wetting the different swatches of fabric and hanging them on the clothesline. Say, ARE ALL OF YOUR CLOTHES DRY? ARE SOME DRIER THAN OTHERS? WHY DO YOU THINK THAT HAPPENED?

**STRUCTURED ACTIVITY:** Ask children how their clothes get dry after they are washed. Are they put in a dryer? Are they hung on a line? Say, LET'S PRETEND THESE PAPER TOWELS ARE CLOTHES AND SEE HOW LONG THEY WILL TAKE TO DRY.

1. Soak a paper towel under water.
2. Squeeze out all the water that you can.
3. Open the towel and lay it on a pie plate.

*(continued)*

4. Leave the plate on a table. Have children check and record the time.
5. Feel the towel at 30-minute intervals to see if it is dry. When it is dry, record the time.
6. How long did the towel take to dry? Have the groups share their findings on a class chart.

**EXTENSIONS:** Do you think it will make a difference if you put the towels in the sun or in the shade? Which wet towel do you think will dry first? Do you think wind will make a difference in how fast a paper towel dries? Set up a fan to create wind. Measure the difference in drying time.

## Can Goldfish be Trained?

**CONCEPT:** Animals can be trained to respond to light and other signals.

**OBJECTIVE:** Children should be able to train a goldfish to respond to light.

**MATERIALS:** Goldfish (at least two), tank, flashlight, fish food.

**PROCEDURE:** Ask, HAVE YOU EVER TRAINED A PET TO DO SOMETHING? Children usually have a dog that sits or stays. DO YOU THINK THAT GOLDFISH KNOW WHEN IT IS TIME TO EAT? HOW COULD WE TRAIN THE GOLDFISH TO GO TO A CORNER OF THEIR TANK TO EAT? Discuss possibilities.

Shine the flashlight into a corner of the tank. Ask, DO THE GOLDFISH SWIM TOWARD THE LIGHT? (No.) Each day sprinkle a little food in the water as you shine the flashlight in the corner (Figure 33–7). Ask, WHAT ARE THE FISH DOING? (Swimming toward the light.)

Do this for several days in a row. Then, shine the light without adding food. Ask, WHAT HAPPENS WHEN YOU ONLY SHINE THE LIGHT? (Fish come to the light, but only for a couple of days if food is not offered.)

**EXTENSIONS:** Ask, WILL THE FISH RESPOND TO DIFFERENT SIGNALS? DO BOTH FISH RESPOND IN THE SAME WAY? WILL DIFFERENT TYPES OF FISH RESPOND IN THE SAME WAY? Have children record their attempts and successes. They may want to write stories about their fish, tell others, and invite other classes to see their trained fish.

**Figure 33–7** "Can a goldfish be trained to respond to light?"

## Examples of Topics to Investigate

1. Can we design a container to keep an ice cube from melting?

2. Will mold grow on bread?

3. Can we get a mealworm to change direction?

4. What objects in our classroom will attract a magnet?

5. Can a seed grow without dirt?

6. Which part of a wet spot dries faster: the top, middle, or bottom? Or does it all dry at the same time? (See Figure 33–8.)

**Figure 33–8** Use a chalkboard for investigating the drying time of wet spots.

## COMPUTER ACTIVITIES THAT ENHANCE LOGICAL THINKING

Children like to have fun when they learn. Why not make precomputer activities fun while developing early problem-solving skills? Have students look for patterns, guess the rules that might govern those patterns, and apply the rules to a situation.

### The Floor Turtle

In the following scenario, Mrs. Red Fox is aware that young children learn best by becoming physically involved in activities. The teacher selects *Valiant Turtle* to spark interaction among her students. Commands typed into Terrapin LOGO move the cordless computerized floor turtle forward or backward and turn as far to the right or left as the child desires.

Sara types TFD 10 (turtle forward 10 steps). "Oh, look, the turtle went forward," she says. Sara then types TBK (turtle backward), TRT, and TLT (turtle right or left turn, respectively), and a number of steps. The class is delighted with the floor turtle's response and everyone wants a turn.

Trang Fung gets ready to make a prediction. She asks, "What commands are you going to give the turtle, Sara? Okay, I think the floor turtle will stop right here." Trang Fung places a piece of masking tape with her name on it on the predicted spot. She waits as Sara gives commands. "Wow, I was really close. Let's try it again, Sara."

As the children play with the floor turtle, they observe unit amounts and estimate distances. Steps and direction are predicted. The following are suggested floor turtle activities.

1. Put a sticker on the floor where the floor turtle will start and another where it stops. Measure the distance.

2. Have a child stand with feet apart in the path of the turtle. Ask, "How many steps will the turtle need to take to pass under Dean's legs?"

3. Have the turtle pass over two different types of floor surfaces. Have students investigate: "Will the turtle travel the same distance over carpet as it will over tile?" This activity will also help children begin to understand friction.

4. Send the floor turtle over a certain path. Have students list the way it will have to move. Ask, "Which way will involve the fewest number of steps?" Children can interact with each other, form and test hypotheses, list a sequence of steps that the floor turtle will follow, and become aware that they control the turtle.

### Recognizing Rules for Patterns and Shapes

Elements of a pattern can be recognized and rules developed that apply to those patterns. *Gertrude's Secrets* is an older game but still a favorite with children; it gives them a chance to keep patterns going by offering attribute games. *Electronic Builder* also allows children to make their own patterns. Before introducing the pattern games, show the children the space bar and the up, down, left, and right keys on the computer keyboard. Mrs. Red Fox designs an off-computer activity that prepares the students for the software.

Mrs. Red Fox makes squares, diamonds, and hexagons with three different colors of construction paper. She shows the children three pieces together that would fit a certain rule; for example, all shapes held up are red. She asks, "Can you tell me a rule for this group?" "Yes," says Dean. "Those shapes are all red." "Good," answers Mrs. Red Fox.

She continues to play games with a secret rule. For example, she holds up cutouts that are all diamonds or all yellow, and the children guess what the rule is. Then she asks, "If all of these pieces are yellow, what other pieces will also fit in this group?" When the children master this game, they are ready to play the game "Loop" on *Gertrude's Secrets.*

The cutout shapes can also be used to make an attribute train. A piece is selected at random to make the train's "engine." "Cars" are made by attaching a shape that is different in only one way, either shape or color, to the previous one. The game continues until all the shapes have joined the train. Play a game called "Trains" on *Gertrude's Secrets* when children fully understand the off-computer train game.

## Instructional Technology Enhances Unifying Concept and Processes

Instructional technology, such as computers and digital cameras, provides yet another way for children to document and enhance their science investigations. The focus in the following scenario is on the national science education standard (NRC, 1996) of unifying concepts and processes of *change, constancy,* and *measurement.*

## How My Tree Changes and Stays the Same

Mr. Brown takes the opportunity to encourage his primary students' interest in learning more about the plants and trees that they have observed in the school yard and thereby focus on the unifying concepts of change, constancy, and measurement. At the beginning of the year, he takes his students outside to "adopt" a plant for the year. He takes along a digital camera and lets each team of two or three students take a digital picture of a plant or tree they are interested in observing. He encourages the students to choose a plant that is no taller than they are and to make observations about their plant.

George's team chooses a young sugar maple tree. Mr. Brown asks the team to describe its tree. "It has funny-shaped leaves with pointy tips—and they're green," says Jim. Diana points: "The leaves look almost like my hand, with five 'fingers.'" Mr. Brown asks about the bark of the tree. "Well, it's kind of smooth compared to that tree over there," says George, "and it's kind of gray." Mr. Brown asks the children whether they think their tree will change during the year. Diana says, "It will get bigger." George wonders if trees have flowers like other plants do. Mr. Brown lets the children take pictures of their tree or plant with the digital camera.

Mr. Brown asks, "How can you measure how tall your plant is?" George suggests string, and the children use lengths to measure their plant. Diana takes a picture of George and Jim using a string to measure the height of the small tree. The children also decide to use the string to wrap around the trunk of the tree near the bottom. George suggests that one of them stand by the tree so that they can see how it changes.

The children record their observations, and back in the classroom Mr. Brown downloads the digital images and puts them onto disks for the students to use in their observations. Mr. Brown uses *ClarisWorks*, an integrated software package with word processing and drawing capabilities, in his classroom. Mr. Brown has already created a "stationary" file, which cannot be changed by students. When students open the file, it becomes an "untitled" document that is saved by the students when it is time to save. Mr. Brown's stationary file contains a text box that is already set up with very large text and a simple font at the bottom and room at the top for the digital images. Students open the file, insert the digital image, and type their observations in the text box.

The children took their adopted trees very seriously, and often came running into the room with observations about the changes in their plant. About three weeks after the students made their original observations, Diana came into class very excited about the leaves on her tree: "Our tree is changing color." Mr. Brown took advantage of the excitement and took the students, and the digital camera, outside so everyone could make the next set of observations. "Our leaves are turning orange," exclaimed Jim. George noticed that some of the leaves were starting to fall onto the ground. "Look at this," said George, "the last time it had more leaves on this branch, didn't it?" The team wasn't sure about George's observation. Mr. Brown encouraged the students to take another picture so that they could compare the tree to their last picture.

The observations and measurements continued throughout the year. The students took digital images and made a new page for their tree's "change over time" document. In the spring, some of the plants had flowers. Mr. Brown asked, "How have your plants changed during the year?" He used the *ClarisWorks* documents that the students had done over the year to create a "slide show" of each team's plant changes over time. The slide-show feature of *ClarisWorks* turns any word processing, drawing, painting, or spreadsheet document into a slide show that can run by itself (and continue looping throughout the day) or be shown one slide at a time. *PowerPoint 2000* is another software program that can be used to accomplish these activities.

As students viewed the slide shows, they made comments about how their trees and other plants had changed or stayed the same. "Look at how much bigger our tree got," said Jim. "Yeah, and it changed color during the year. How come Michael's team tree didn't change color?" asked Diane. Michael's team had chosen a young pine tree. Mr. Brown encouraged the students to examine the changes that had occurred during the year as they watched the slide shows and to explore the similarities and differences in how the plants change. Jim wondered what the tree would look like when it

was older, so he went out to find a more mature tree to observe.

The activities that have been described here are especially useful for children living in areas where seasons are not as pronounced as in other areas. For example, using a digital camera to capture the changes in a tree throughout the year in Florida would help children see the subtle changes that they might otherwise miss.

Instructional technology provides a wonderful means by which student observation can be displayed and evaluated. Digital images make comparison of trees over time much easier, and a slide show provides additional opportunities to see the changes flash by in minutes. Additionally, the children's documents can be printed out for inclusion in student portfolios or displayed on bulletin boards.

## SUMMARY

When children investigate, they develop science processes and science concepts. Science concepts are the "big ideas" in science; they explain the way the world is viewed.

Primary age children continue to be avid investigators. At this age, they refine their inquiry skills and begin to understand abstract symbols that are tied to concrete experiences. This unit suggests science learning experiences that enhance the primary child's special fondness for collecting and playing games. Ideas for classroom management as well as simple classroom investigations are also suggested.

### KEY TERMS

| | | |
|---|---|---|
| conclusions | invertebrates | magnifier |
| determining variables | lens | variable |
| hypothesis | | |

### SUGGESTED ACTIVITIES

1. Observe differences in the ability to classify. Design lessons that take advantage of children's abilities to observe detail.

2. Begin a collection of 20 objects from nature. How could you use this collection in your teaching? Use the collection in this

way and share children's responses with others.

3. Select a collecting topic such as leaves. Describe naturalistic, directed, and structured collecting activities that might take place with leaves. Observe children as they collect and identify each of these three types of learning.

4. Identify the process skills and science concepts emphasized in the investigation activities in this unit. Design an investigation and introduce it to primary age children. Record children's responses. What type of questions did children ask? How did they go about conducting the investigation?

5. Children can use word processors and reference programs to write about science topics. Use one of the software packages listed below with children. Ask what they like about the programs and what they would like to see changed.

*Word Processing and Integrated Packages*

- *ClarisWorks* (Santa Clara, CA: K–12 Micromedia)
- *EasyBook* (Pleasantville, NY: Sunburst Communications)
- *Electronic Builder* (KidWare; Redmond, WA: Edmark)
- *Gertrude's Secrets* (Fremont, CA: The Learning Company)

- *KidWorks Deluxe* or *KidWorks 2* (Torrance, CA: Davidson & Associates)
- *Storybook Weaver Deluxe* (Minneapolis, MN: MECC)
- *The Children's Writing and Publishing Center* (Fremont, CA: The Learning Company)
- *Valiant Turtle* (Harvard Associates)

*Reference Packages*

There are a number of reference programs available. Many of them will also read the text for children. Most include text, pictures, sounds, and video clips.

- *Compton's Interactive Encyclopedia* (Carlsbad, CA: Compton's New Media)
- *First Connections: The Golden Book Encyclopedia* (Lansing, MI: Hartley)
- *Random House Kids Encyclopedia* (Glendale, CA: Knowledge Adventure)
- *Ultimate Children's Encyclopedia* (Fremont, CA: The Learning Company)

6. Evaluate one or more of the computer programs listed above.

## REVIEW

A. Give two differences in the way that primary age children learn and the way that kindergarten age children learn.

B. How are primary grade science experiences similar to kindergarten lessons?

C. Why encourage children to collect? What preparations and procedures will you follow before, during, and after collecting?

D. What are invertebrates and why should they be mentioned in the early grades?

## REFERENCE

National Research Council. (1996). *National science education standards.* Washington, DC: National Academies Press.

# FURTHER READING AND RESOURCES

Abruscato, J. (2004). *Teaching children science: A discovery approach* (6th ed.). Boston: Allyn & Bacon.

Abruscato, J. (2004). *Teaching children science: Discovery activities and demonstrations for the elementary and middle grades* (2nd ed.). Boston: Allyn & Bacon.

American Association for the Advancement of Science (AAAS). (2007). *Atlas of science literacy: Project 2061* (Vol. 2). Washington, DC: Author.

Ansberry, K., & Morgan, E. (2007). *More picture perfect science lessons: Using children's books to guide inquiry.* Arlington, VA: NSTA Press.

Campbell, B., & Fulton, L. (2003). *Science notebooks: Writing about inquiry.* Portsmouth, NH: Heinemann.

Campbell, S. (1987). A playful introduction to computers. *Science and Children, 24*(8), 38–40.

Carin, A. A., Bass, J. E., & Contant, T. L. (2005). *Teaching science as inquiry* (10th ed.). Upper Saddle River, NJ: Prentice-Hall.

Fathman, A. K., & Crowther, D. T. (2005) *Science for English Language Learners: K–12 classroom strategies.* Arlington, VA: NSTA Press.

Green, B., & Schlichting, S. (1985). *Explorations and investigations.* Riverview, FL: Idea Factory.

Haughland, S. W., & Wright, J. L. (1997). *Young children and technology: A world of discovery.* Boston: Allyn & Bacon.

Howe, A. C., & Nichols, S. E. (2001). *Case studies in elementary science: Learning from teachers.* Upper Saddle River, NJ: Prentice-Hall.

Kneidel, S. S. (1993). *Creepy crawlies and the scientific method.* Golden, CO: Fulcrum.

Lederman, N. G., Lederman, J. S., & Bell, R. L. (2005). *Constructing science in elementary classrooms.* Boston: Allyn & Bacon.

Lind, K. K. (1993). Collector's choice. *Science and Children, 31*(3), 34–35.

Lind, K. K. (1997). Science in the developmentally appropriate integrated curriculum. In C. H. Hart, D. C. Burts, & R. Charlesworth (Eds.), *Integrated curriculum and developmentally appropriate practice: Birth to age eight.* Albany, NY: SUNY Press.

Lowery, L. F. (1997). *NSTA pathways to the science standards.* Arlington, VA: National Science Teachers Association.

McClurg, P. (1984). Don't squash it! Collect it! *Science and Children, 21*(8), 8–10.

McIntyre, M. (1984). *Early childhood and science* Washington, DC: National Science Teachers Association.

National Research Council. (1999). *Selecting instructional materials: A guide for K–12.* Washington, DC: National Academies Press.

Ohana, C. (2007). Creative integration [Theme issue]. *Science & Children, 44*(6), 6.

Pearce, C. R. (1999). *Nurturing inquiry: Real science for the elementary classroom.* Portsmouth, NH: Heinemann.

Peters, J. M., & Gega, P. C. (2002). *Science in elementary education.* Upper Saddle River, NJ: Merrill.

Prairie, A. P. (2005). *Inquiry into math, science, and technology: For teaching young children.* Clifton Park, NY: Thomson Delmar Learning.

Saul, W., & Jagusch, S. A. (Ed.). (1992). *Vital connections: Children, science, and books.* Portsmouth, NH: Heinemann.

Saul, W., Reardon, J., Pearce, C., Dieckman, D., & Neutze, D. (2002). *Science workshop: Reading, writing, and thinking like a scientist.* Portsmouth, NH: Heinemann.

Smith, E., Blackmer, M., & Schlichting, S. (1987). *Super science sourcebook.* Riverview, FL: Idea Factory.

Their, M. (2002). *The new science literacy: Using language skills to help students learn science.* Portsmouth, NH: Heinemann.

VanDeman, B. (1984). The fall collection. *Science and Children, 27*(1), 20–21.

Wetzel, D. R. (2005). *How to . . . Weave the Web into K–8 science.* Arlington, VA: NSTA Press.

Zeitler, W. R., & Barufaldi, J. P. (1988). *Elementary school science instruction—A perspective for teachers.* White Plains, NY: Longman.

# Unit 34
## Life Science

## OBJECTIVES

After reading this unit, you should be able to:

- Develop an understanding of life science concepts that are appropriate for primary grade children.
- Develop structured and unstructured science learning activities with primary age children.
- Describe appropriate conditions for the care of animals in the classroom.
- Apply unit webbing strategies to life science content.

Whether they live in large cities or small towns, children display an eagerness to learn about the living things around them. The countless opportunities that exist to acquire firsthand knowledge of plants and animals make learning fun for both children and teacher. The *National Science Education Standards* (NSES) emphasize that during the primary grades, children begin to develop an understanding of biological concepts through direct experience with living things, their life cycles, and their habitats. Questions such as "Why did that animal eat the other animal?" and "Do all animals eat plants?" are the first of many such questions that begin all investigations. Primary experiences lay the groundwork for the progressive development in later grades of the major biological concepts.

This unit begins with life science concepts that are basic to primary grade learning; it then presents an example of a seed unit planned with the webbing strategy discussed in Unit 7. Next, guidelines for animal care and a variety of investigations and learning experiences with animals are described. Finally, sources for teach-ing about plants, animals, and the environment are suggested.

## LIFE SCIENCE

The *NSES* (NRC, 1996) recommend that, as a result of activities in the primary grades, all students should develop an understanding of the characteristics of **organisms**, the life cycles of organisms, and organisms and environments.

## The Characteristics of Organisms

Young children's ideas about the characteristics of organisms develop from basic concepts of living and non-living things. Piaget noted that many children associate "life" with any objects that are active in any way. Thus, movement becomes the defining characteristic of life, and **anthropomorphic** explanations are given to organisms. Eventually children's conception of the characteristics of life include other activities such as eating, breathing, and reproduction, but students must have a variety of experiences with organisms to develop this knowledge base.

The science standards point out that primary age children can understand that organisms have basic needs. For example, animals need air, water, and food; plants require air, water, nutrients, and light. Organisms can survive only in environments in which their needs are met. There are many different environments that support the life of different types of organisms.

Children can begin to understand that each plant or animal has different structures that serve different functions in growth, survival, and reproduction. The behavior of individual organisms is influenced by internal cues (such as hunger) and by external cues (such as a change in the environment). Humans and other organisms have senses that help them detect internal and external cues.

## Life Cycles of Organisms

The NSES emphasize that children should begin to understand that plants and animals have life cycles that include being born, developing into adults, reproducing, and eventually dying, and that plants and animals closely resemble their parents.

## Organisms and Their Environments

Upper primary students will begin to develop the understanding that all animals depend on plants. Some animals eat plants for food and other animals eat the animals that eat plants. A plant or animal's behavior patterns are related to the nature of their environment, including the availability of food and resources and the physical characteristics of the environment.

Children will begin to note that all organisms cause changes in the environment in which they live. Some of these changes are detrimental to the organisms and some are beneficial. Humans depend on their natural and constructed environments and also change the environments in beneficial and harmful ways.

## PLANNING FOR LIFE SCIENCE

A knowledge of life science concepts is basic to planning and teaching life science to primary age children. The fundamental life science concepts are the major ideas that we want students to understand. Thus, learning experiences are planned around them. For example, Figure 34–1 shows a unit planning web, as described in Unit 7, that focuses learning activities around three basic concepts involving the topic of seeds. The following concepts can be used in lesson planning and are basic to understanding plants, animals, and all living things.

Figure 34–1 Planning web for a seed unit.

## Living Things

1. Living things can be distinguished from nonliving things.
2. Plants and animals are living things.
3. Animals and plants affect one another.
4. Living things have unique features that help them live in different kinds of places.
5. Most living things need water, food, and air.

## Seeds and Plants

1. Seeds differ in size, shape, color, and texture.
2. Seeds **germinate** and grow into a specific type of plant.
3. Some seeds grow inside fruits.
4. Some seeds grow into flowers, shrubs, and trees.
5. Some seeds grow into food that we eat.
6. Seeds are dispersed in several ways.
7. Seeds need water, light, and warmth to grow.
8. Seeds and plants grow and change.
9. Leaves tend to grow toward light, and roots tend to grow into the soil.
10. Plants grow from seeds, roots, and stems.
11. Some plant forms do not have seeds, roots, or stems.
12. Some plants grow in the light, and some plants grow in the dark.
13. Some plants change in different seasons.

## Animals

1. Animals need food, water, shelter, and a unique temperature.
2. Animals have individual characteristics.
3. Animals have unique adaptations. They move, eat, live, and behave in ways that help them survive.
4. Animals go through a life cycle.
5. Pets are animals that depend on us for special care. We love and take care of our pets.
6. There are many kinds of pets.
7. Different kinds of pets need different types of care to grow and be healthy.
8. Aquariums are places for fish and other living things to grow.

## PLANNING AND TEACHING A SEED UNIT

The learning experiences suggested in this unit follow the format described in Unit 7 and are designed to meet the needs, interests, and developmental levels of primary age children as described in Unit 33. Each lesson states a concept, a teaching objective based on what the child should be able to do, materials needed, and suggestions for teaching the concept. Extensions, integrations, and possible evaluation procedures are indicated in the body of the lesson when appropriate and at the end of the unit.

## ACTIVITIES

### Seeds

**CONCEPT:** Seeds germinate and grow into plants; seeds contain a baby plant.

**OBJECTIVE:** Discover that a seed has three parts. Identify the **embryo** inside of the seed.

**MATERIALS:** Lima beans that have been soaked overnight (if you soak them longer, they may rot), paper towels, a variety of seeds.

**PROCEDURE:** Show children a lima bean seed. Ask, WHAT DO YOU THINK MIGHT BE INSIDE OF THIS SEED? CAN YOU DRAW A PICTURE OF HOW YOU THINK THE INSIDE OF THE SEED LOOKS?

**Figure 34–2** All seeds have three basic parts.

Have children open the lima bean seed with their thumbnails. Ask, WHAT DO YOU NOTICE ABOUT YOUR SEED? HOW DOES THE SEED FEEL? IS THERE A SMELL? DOES THE INSIDE OF THE SEED LOOK LIKE THE PICTURE YOU HAVE DRAWN? Discuss similarities and differences. Have students draw a picture of the bean after it is opened.

Point out that there are three basic parts in all seeds: the seed cover (for protection), food for the baby plant (*cotyledon*), and the baby plant itself (*embryo*) (Figure 34–2). Introduce the term *germinate*. (This is when the seed grows—it sprouts.) Have students paint a picture of the plant as they think it will look when it has grown.

**NATURALISTIC AND INFORMAL ACTIVITIES:** Have a variety of seeds in the science center so the children can soak them and then see if they have the same parts as the lima beans. When you observe children opening the beans ask, "How are the seeds like the lima beans? How are they different?" This could be done in an unstructured way as part of a seed center. In beans and peas, there are two seed halves. In seeds such as corn and rice, there is only one seed half or cotyledon.

## Baby Plants

**CONCEPT:** Seeds germinate and grow into plants.

**OBJECTIVE:** Observe and describe how seeds grow into plants. Describe how the embryo grows into a plant.

**MATERIALS:** Lima beans, paper towels, water, cotton, clear containers or glass tumblers.

**PROCEDURE:** Say, YESTERDAY WE SAW A BABY PLANT INSIDE OF A SEED. DO YOU THINK IT WILL GROW INTO A BIG PLANT? LET'S FIND OUT.

Soak lima beans overnight. Have children line the inside of a drinking glass with a wet, folded paper towel. Then, stuff cotton into the glass. This holds the paper towel in place.

Put soaked seeds between the paper towel and glass. Then, pour water to the edge of the bottom seed in the glass (the paper towel and cotton will absorb most of the liquid). The sprouting seeds will be easy for the children to see through the clear container. Have the children draw the sprouting lima bean and write a story about the investigation.

(*continued*)

Ask, WHAT DO YOU SEE HAPPENING? WHAT COLORS DO YOU SEE? WHICH WAY ARE THE ROOTS GROWING? WHERE IS THE EMBRYO GETTING ITS FOOD? (From the cotyledon.) As the plant gets larger, the seed becomes smaller. In fact, the plant will begin to die when the cotyledon is used up.

When the food provided by the seed is used up, ask, WHAT OTHER TYPE OF FOOD CAN WE GIVE THE PLANT? Discuss the possibility of transplanting the young plants to soil as a continuation of the project.

**EXTENSION:** This concept can be extended throughout the year. It is a good science activity with the advantage of going from simple observation to experimentation. The concept lends itself to a short study of seeds or an extended study of how light, moisture, heat, color, soil, air, and sound affect the growth of plants.

## Glass Garden

**CONCEPT:** Moisture is needed for seeds to sprout.

**OBJECTIVE:** Observe the growth of seeds.

**MATERIALS:** Mung beans, cheesecloth, jar.

**PROCEDURE:** Soak a handful of mung beans in a jar, and cover the jar tightly with cheesecloth. Protect the jar from light by wrapping it in a towel. Then, have children simulate rain by rinsing and draining the seeds three times a day. Have children predict what will happen to the seeds. Ask, DID THE SEEDS SPROUT EVEN THOUGH THEY WERE IN THE DARK? (Yes.) DO YOU THINK THE SEEDS WILL SPROUT IF WE KEEP THEM IN THE DARK BUT DO NOT WATER THEM? (No.) Repeat the activity, and investigate what will happen if the seeds are kept in the dark and not watered.

**NATURALISTIC AND INFORMAL ACTIVITIES:** Have a variety of seeds in the science center so the children can experiment with them to see if they all react in the same way as the mung beans.

**EXTENSION:** You may want to make a salad and top it off with the mung sprouts. Several variables can be tried—one at a time, of course—so that children can investigate variables in sprouting seeds and growing plants.

**TEACHING NOTE:** Lima beans usually work well, but mung beans show the speedy growth that impatient young children may demand. Mung beans will not grow as tall as others, but they will show growth. Corn, on the other hand, takes longer than lima beans to germinate.

## What's Inside?

**CONCEPT:** Seeds come from the fruit of plants.

**OBJECTIVE:** Discover that seeds develop inside of fruit.

**MATERIALS:** A variety of fruits, pinecones, flowers; plastic knives and paper towels.

**PROCEDURE:** Select several fruits, and place them on a table with plastic knives and paper towels. Have children examine the fruits and ask, WHAT DO YOU THINK IS INSIDE OF THE FRUIT?

Invite children to cut the fruits open. Ask, WHAT DID YOU FIND? HOW MANY SEEDS DID YOU FIND? ARE ALL OF THE SEEDS THE SAME COLOR? WHAT DO YOU THINK THE SEEDS ARE DOING INSIDE OF THE FRUIT?

Explain that a fruit is the part of a flowering plant that holds the seeds. Ask, CAN YOU NAME ANY FLOWERS IN YOUR BACKYARD THAT HAVE SEEDS? (Sunflowers, dandelions.) ARE THEY FRUITS? (Yes.) Point out that not all fruits are edible.

**EXTENSION:** Show a picture of a pine tree. Ask, DOES THIS TREE HAVE FLOWERS? (No.) DOES IT HAVE SEEDS? (Yes.) WHERE ARE THE SEEDS? (Cones.) Have children examine pinecones to find out how the seeds are attached. Compare the seeds enclosed in fruits to those attached to cones. Point out that seeds can grow inside of a flower, surrounded by fruit, or in a cone.

## Traveling Seeds

**CONCEPT:** Seeds need to travel to grow.

**OBJECTIVE:** Investigate why seeds travel by simulating growing conditions.

**MATERIALS:** Two containers, soil, seeds.

**PROCEDURE:** Have children bring in seeds from the school grounds or their neighborhood. Examine the seeds, and discuss where they were found. Hold up a seed and ask, DO WE HAVE THIS KIND OF PLANT ON OUR SCHOOL GROUNDS? (No.) HOW DID THE SEED GET HERE? (Wind.) I WONDER WHY IT BLEW AWAY?

After discussing, ask, DO YOU THINK THAT SEEDS WILL GET A CHANCE TO GROW IF THEY ALL FALL AT THE BOTTOM OF THE PARENT PLANT? LET'S SEE WHAT HAPPENS WHEN SEEDS FALL IN ONE PLACE.

Fill two containers with seeds. Have children help plant seeds close together in one container and far apart in the other. Ask, WHICH CONTAINER DO YOU THINK WILL GROW THE MOST PLANTS? Discuss and list suggested reasons. Have children take turns giving all of the seeds water, light, warmth. Watch them for many days. Have children measure the growth of the plants and record what they see. Then ask, IN WHICH CONTAINER DO SEEDS GROW BETTER? (Spaced apart.) In this way, children will see a reason for a seed to travel.

## Scattering Seeds

**CONCEPT:** Seeds are adapted to disperse in several ways.

**OBJECTIVE:** Identify several ways of dispersing seeds.

**MATERIALS:** Seeds, magnifying glasses, mittens.

**PROCEDURE:** Arrange seeds from weeds, grasses, and trees in a science center. Have a magnifying glass and mitten available for students to examine seeds. Give basic directions, and let children "mess around" and explore the seeds. Ask, WHICH SEEDS SEEM TO CATCH IN THE MITTEN? (Hairy ones or ones with burrs.) Have children predict and draw what they think they will see when they observe a burr through a magnifying glass. Say, LET'S LOOK THROUGH THE MAGNIFYING GLASS AND DRAW WHAT WE SEE. Discuss the before and after pictures and describe the tiny hooks and how they are used. Introduce the term *disperse* and use it in sentences and stories about the burr with tiny hooks. Refer to Unit 33 for suggestions for the use of magnifiers.

*(continued)*

**EXTENSION:** Take children outside to explore how different seeds are dispersed by shaking seeds from pods, beating grass seed spikes to release grains, brushing hairy seeds against clothes, and releasing winged seeds. Compare what happens to each seed.

## Invent a Seed

**CONCEPT:** Seeds are modified to travel in a specific way.

**OBJECTIVE:** Modify a seed for travel.

**MATERIALS:** Dried bean or pea seeds, a junk box (colored paper, glue, rubber bands, tape, cotton, ice-cream-bar sticks, balloons, pipe cleaners, paper clips, string), scissors.

**PROCEDURE:** Show children a coconut (the largest seed) and ask, HOW DO YOU THINK THIS COCONUT TRAVELS? (Water.) Display pods such as milkweed to demonstrate a pod that bursts and casts its seeds to the wind. HOW WILL THE BURR TRAVEL? (Catch on things.) Birds and other animals eat fruit such as berries. Then, they digest the fruit and leave the seeds somewhere else. WHY DID THE BIRD WANT TO EAT BERRIES? (They were good to eat.) Children will conclude that seeds have specific modifications to travel in specific ways. To reinforce the term *modify*, have students modify their clothes for different weather or activities.

Ask, IF YOU WERE A SEED, HOW WOULD YOU LIKE TO TRAVEL? Discuss preferences, and then assign one of the following means of travel to each small group of children: attract animal, catch on fur, pops or is shot out, floats on water, or carried by wind. Give each group seeds and junk box materials, and ask them to invent a way for their seed to travel. When the children have completed their creations, have them demonstrate how their seed travels (Figure 34–3).

**EXTENSION:** Make a bulletin board that displays the modified seeds traveling in the way the students intended. Have children examine seeds and think of other objects that work in the same way. (For example, the burr is the inspiration for the development of Velcro.)

**HOW SEEDS TRAVEL**

**Figure 34–3** Seed dispersal methods.

## More Seed Suggestions

1. *Sock walk.* Drag a sock through a field. Then cover with soil and water, and wait for a variety of plants to grow from the seeds caught on the sock. Or put the sock in a plastic bag, shake the seeds out of the sock, and examine them. Ask, "What types of seeds did the sock attract?"

2. *Egghead hair.* Draw a face on half of an eggshell. Place the egg in an egg carton, and fill the eggshell with moist soil. Sprinkle grass seed on top, then water. Grass will grow in five days. Attach construction paper feet with clay to display (plastic eggs also work well). To show the benefit of light on leaves, first grow the grass hair in the dark. Discuss the resulting pale, thin grass and ask, "How can we make the grass green and healthy?" Place the egg person in the light, and be prepared to trim the healthy green hair (Figure 34–4).

3. *Collections.* Seeds make an easy and fun collection. Collect from your kitchen, playground, or neighborhood.

## Investigation Questions for Growing Seeds

1. How deep can you plant a seed and still have it grow?

2. If you crush a seed, will it still grow?

**Figure 34–4** "Can you grow healthy grass hair for your eggshell people?"

3. In what direction will the sprouts in the glass garden grow if the glass is turned upside down?

## SUBJECT INTEGRATIONS

## Science and Math

1. *Seed walk.* Take a seed walk around the school. Ask, "Where shall we look for seeds? What do you think we might see?" Gather seeds, and use as materials to sort, match, count, and weigh in the science center.

2. *How many ways.* Provide a box of seeds for students to classify. Compare size, shape, color, and texture of the seeds. Construct a seed graph.

3. *Greenhouse.* Simulate a greenhouse by placing a plastic bag over a container of germinating seeds. Place seeds in a jar on a moist paper towel. Put the jar inside of a plastic bag, and record the amount of time needed for sprouting. Compare sprouting time with seeds that are not placed in a plastic bag (Figure 34–5).

**Figure 34–5** Make your own greenhouse.

4. *Cooking.* Create a fruit salad with the fruits gathered for seed activities. Or measure ingredients and follow a recipe to make apple pie or other tasty dishes. Nut butter can be made by passing the seeds or nuts through a nut grinder. Store in the refrigerator and use as spreads.

5. *Seed count.* Have the children add to find out how many seeds were planted or count the number of seeds planted by each child and multiply to see how many seeds there are in all. Next, give problems using different numbers of seeds and children.

## Science and Social Studies

1. *Seeds swell.* Years ago, seeds were used to stretch tight leather shoes. To simulate this, fill a small bottle with beans, cover beans with water, close the bottle with plastic wrap, and secure with rubber bands. Beans will swell and lift the plastic.

2. *Neighborhood map.* Have children bring in seeds that they have found. Make a map of where the seeds might be found.

3. *Seeds can be edible.* Try to bridge the gap between the processed food that the children eat and its raw form. Show pictures of wheat, fruit trees, and vegetables growing. Discuss edible seeds such as pumpkin, sunflower, peanuts, and those that are not eaten such as watermelon and apple seeds.

4. *Careers.* Discuss different jobs associated with growing plants. Make hats, and act out these jobs.

5. *Woodworking.* Create boxes and planters for growing seeds.

## Science and Language Arts

1. Have students remove the *s* from *seed* and make new words (weed, feed, need, bleed).

2. Pretend you are a seed. Draw a picture, and write a story about how you will look and where you might travel.

3. Dramatize the growth of an embryo into a plant.

4. Make a seed book (in the shape of a lima bean), and fill it with bean stories and drawings.

5. Read, tell, and dramatize stories about seeds such as "Jack and the Beanstalk," "The Story of Johnny Appleseed," or *The Popcorn Book* by Tomie dePaola.

6. Share the following books aloud: *Growing Vegetable Soup* (Ehlert, 1987), *The Carrot Seed* (Krauss, 1945), and *From Seed to Pear* (Mitgutsch, 1971). Have the children make books using a similar theme and share with younger children.

## Science and Music

1. Sing songs about seeds and plants from your music book.

2. Use seeds to create musical instruments such as maracas and other types of "shaking" instruments in tubes with plastic lids.

3. Some children can make whistles from acorn caps. Hold thumbs in a V shape, with the top of the thumbs forming the V, under the hollow side of the cap. Blow gently at the base of the V to make a sound.

## Science and Art

1. Create landscapes that would be favorable for seed growth.

2. Make faces on moist sponges with birdseed. Trim the green growth into different patterns.

3. Design seed mosaics. Glue seeds to paper or cardboard to make pictures.

4. Jewelry can be made by stringing seeds with thread and needle. You may need to boil seeds and wait for them to soften. Some children might want to paint the seeds and use them to decorate costumes.

5. Stick burrs together to make a basket. What else can you make from burrs? Pinecones and walnut shells can become birds and other creatures by adding glue and construction paper.

# ADDITIONAL PLANT ACTIVITIES BASED ON SCIENCE CONCEPTS

When your unit on seeds is completed, you might want to develop additional concepts about plants. Here are a few suggestions.

## Concept: Plants Grow from Roots and Stems

Growing plants from cuttings can be an exciting experience for primary age children. They will enjoy observing familiar products from a grocery bag doing unfamiliar things. Investigations with cuttings are long term and provide opportunities for record keeping, process skill development, and subject integration. You will need water, light, and common vegetables to reinforce that seeds are not the only way that plants reproduce.

1. *Dish garden.* To make a dish garden, cut off the top inch of carrots, beets, or white turnips. Keep the tops in dishes of water while the children observe the roots growing. Shoots will usually appear in a week to 10 days. Ask, "Can you tell what this plant is by the leaves?"

2. *Hanging around.* Suspend a yam or a fresh sweet potato, tapered end down, in a jar filled with water. Insert toothpicks so that only one-third of the sweet potato is in the water (Figure 34–6). Put the jar in a warm, dark place until buds and roots grow. Then put it in a sunny place, and prepare a string trellis for the upcoming foliage to climb. Children can chart the number of days for root and foliage growth and observe and record changes. Ask, "What happens to the sweet potato as the vine grows?"

3. *Pineapple tops.* Cut a 2½-inch section of pineapple fruit below the leaves. Put the pineapple top in a dish with water. When the roots develop, put the plant in potting soil and make a greenhouse by covering it with a plastic bag. Keep the pineapple greenhouse warm but not in direct sunlight. In about three weeks, take the new plant out of the greenhouse, add water, and place it in the sun. Eventually, tiny pineapples may form (six to 12 months).

Figure 34–6 "Will a sweet potato grow in a glass of water?"

## Concept: Molds Grow in Dark, Moist Conditions

Children have probably seen mold in their own refrigerators or bread baskets but do not realize that mold is an organism called fungi. Observing a mold garden gives children an opportunity to focus on recording observations, keeping records, and writing predictions as they investigate the world of mold.

1. To begin the lesson, show the children a molding orange and ask, "What is on the orange? Is the orange good to eat? Where have you seen mold?" Make a list of the conditions of the places where mold has been found. There should be replies of "moist," "dark," and types of materials such as fruit and bread.

2. To make the mold garden, fill a glass jar about one-third full of sand. Sprinkle water on the sand, and place items that the children bring in on top of the sand. Screw the lid on the jar and

begin observations, discussion, and predictions. "Which objects do you think mold will grow on first? Will any objects not grow mold?" Place the mold garden in a dark place and prepare the children to observe. Changing colors, shapes, and sizes should prove interesting.

3. You might want to mention the important role that fungus plays in breaking down materials and in returning the components to the soil.

## Teaching Notes

1. Most mold of this type is harmless, but do not take any chances. Keep the lid on the jar. In addition, have children wash their hands if any moldy items are touched; do not sniff molds (check for mold allergies among students); and when the activity is completed, throw away all mold gardens without opening them and in a tightly sealed bag.

2. Growing mold in soil is speedy because soil is rich in organic materials, and for that reason it is recommended by some science educators. However, a teacher does not know what else might be in the soil sample, ready to grow. Thus, play it safe and slow—stick to sand.

3. Mold is a type of fungus that lacks chlorophyll. Although warmth, darkness, and moisture are ideal conditions for mold growth, neither warmth nor darkness is necessary for growth. Further investigations of conditions for mold growth may be appropriate in your classroom.

## ANIMALS IN THE CLASSROOM

Caring for and studying living things in the classroom and outdoors can be an excellent way to develop a respect for and knowledge of the daily requirements of all forms of life. As children care for a living thing, they seem to develop a sensitivity and sense of responsibility for the life around them. As they maintain the living organism, they become aware of the conditions under which that animal (or plant) survives as well as the conditions under which it will perish. You hope that these understandings and attitudes will carry over into the child's life and the human condition in general.

Before you think about caring for any living organisms, take the precautions listed in this unit. It is vital that living things do not suffer from too much care, such as overfeeding and handling, and too little care, such as improper diet, water, temperature, and shelter. In other words, before allowing an animal in your classroom, be sure you know how to take care of it.

Care of the animal should begin before the animal arrives. It is recommended that the entire class have an opportunity to help prepare the cage or environment. As preparations are made, discuss why and what you are doing and so develop the children's understanding of the specific needs of a species.

When the animal arrives in class, give the new visitor time to become acclimated to its new surroundings. The expected enthusiasm and interest that an animal visitor is likely to generate may overwhelm the newcomer. Instruct children to quietly observe the animal in pairs for brief periods of time. Then, small groups can watch, always quietly, as everyone (animal and children) adjusts to the environment.

When planning for an animal visitor, ask yourself and your students the following questions.

1. What type of cage or environment does this animal require?

2. What temperature must be maintained?

3. What type of food is needed, and how should that food be presented?

4. Will the animal be able to live in the room over weekends? What will happen to the animal during vacations?

5. Is this an endangered animal? Has this animal been illegally captured or imported? For example, for each parrot of many species that a child encounters, about 10 parrots have perished in capture or transport. Or as in the case of a species such as the ball python, some animals will never eat in captivity. Limit animal use to those bred in captivity.

6. Does the animal need special lights? Many reptiles must have ultraviolet light, a warm and cool area of their cage, and live food.

7. Will this animal make a good classroom visitor? Should it be handled? Avoid impulse purchases that will lead to future problems.

## Tips for Keeping Animals in the Classroom

When animals are in the classroom, care should be taken to ensure that neither the children nor the animals are harmed. Mammals protect themselves and their young by biting, scratching, and kicking. Pets such as cats, dogs, rabbits, and guinea pigs should be handled properly and should not be disturbed when eating. For example, rats, rabbits, hamsters, and mice are best picked up by the scruff of the neck, with a hand placed under the body for support. Observe also the following precautions.

1. Check school district procedures to determine if there are any local regulations to be observed. Personnel at the local humane society or zoo are often very cooperative in assisting teachers to create a wholesome animal environment in the classroom. However, zoos receive numerous requests for adoption and usually do not want classroom animals for their collection or "feeder stock."

2. Caution students never to tease animals or to insert their fingers or objects through wire mesh cages. Report animal bites and scratches immediately to the school's medical authority. Provide basic first aid. Usually children follow the example set by the teacher. If you treat the animals with respect then the children will, too.

3. Purchase fish from tanks in which all fish appear healthy.

4. Discourage students from bringing personal pets to school. If they are brought into the room, they should be handled only by their owners, provided a place for fresh water and a place to rest, and then sent home.

5. Guidelines for collecting invertebrates and caring for them in the classroom are provided in Unit 33.

## Teaching with Animals

Entire teaching units can be designed around observing animals in the classroom. Science concepts and subject integrations occur naturally as children observe, categorize, and communicate their experiences with animals. The benefits of observing animals far outweigh the cautions and are well worth your time and energy. Here are guiding questions and integrations that lead to investigations.

1. Describe how the animal moves. Do you move that way? See if you can figure out why the animal moves in the way that it does. Does anything make it move faster or slower? Add your observations to the observation list (Figure 34–7).

2. How does the animal eat its food? Does it use its feet or any other part of its body to help it eat? Does it prefer a specific type of food? Make a chart or graph showing preferences.

3. What do the animals do all day? Keep a record of the animal's activities, or pinpoint several specific behaviors such as recording the type of food eaten. Are there times when the animal is more or less active? Take pictures of the animal at the same time of the day. Chart the results.

4. What do the animals do at night? Children have many questions about what the classroom animals do at night. One instructional technology tool for finding an answer to the question "What does Harry the Hamster do when we leave the room?" is to set up a digital camera, such as the Quickcam, that will take video and time-lapse pictures. For example, the camera

---

**Michael Parker**                        **Gerbils**

**They play.**
**The gerbils drink water.**
**They are hiding in their house.**
**He's lookin, playin.**
**He jumped back down in the house.**

Figure 34–7 Michael observes and records some of the daily activities of gerbils.

can be set to take a picture every 15 minutes or to take a 5-minute video every 20 minutes. The digital images can provide a way for children to collect data to answer their questions.

5. How do animals react to different objects in their environment? Offer gerbils paper towel tubes, and watch them play. Write a story that sequences the actions of the gerbils.

6. What type of sounds do the animals make? Identify different taped animal sounds, and decide if you can tell the size of an animal by its sound. Have children tape-record different sounds made by the animal such as sleeping, eating, playing, drinking. Play the tape and have children make up stories about what they think is happening.

7. How can we keep earthworms in the classroom? Have children research what is required for keeping earthworms healthy. Earthworms make good pets because they can be handled with less stress to the animal than mammals, birds, reptiles, and **amphibians**.

8. Describe the animal's body covering. Why do you think it has this type of covering? Compare the body coverings of different animals. Design a center that allows children to feel objects that simulate animal coverings (refer to Unit 39). Observe these coverings on a trip to the zoo.

9. How does the animal drink? Can you think of other animals that drink in the same way? Categorize ways that animals drink (a cat laps water, a snake sucks water).

10. Although 7- and 8-year-olds are not yet ready for formal outlining, building a web is a good way to organize what they are learning about animals. This type of organization refreshes memory for what children have seen or studied and relates any information they are collecting. Figure 34–8 presents their ideas in a loosely structured way. The teacher selects the main divisions and writes them on the chalkboard. Then, the children give the main points. If the children are working in committees to research different aspects, this strategy illustrates the relatedness of the entire project.

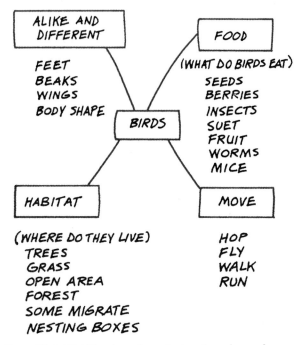

Figure 34–8 Webbing to review what we have learned.

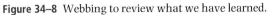

## A TRIP TO THE ZOO

A trip to the zoo is a terrific way to offer children opportunities to explore the world of animals. Observing animals in a zoo setting is a high-interest activity that helps children learn about animals and their needs. The following suggestions are designed to help maximize the unique setting of a zoo.

### Before, During, and After

To make the most of your zoo visit, plan learning experiences that will be taught before going to the zoo, during the zoo visit, and after returning to the classroom. For example, you might want to focus your plans on the similarities and differences between reptiles and amphibians. In the following scenario, Mrs. Red Fox decides to relate class discussions and observations to turtles.

Before going to the zoo, Mrs. Red Fox prepares learning stations for her class. The stations will prepare the children for their zoo visit.

*Station 1.* Mrs. Red Fox prepares items that simulate body covering for the children to feel. To represent the dry, scaly skin of most reptiles, she rolls shelled sunflower seeds in clay. Oiled cellophane represents the moist, glandular skin of most amphibians. As children visit this station, they are invited to touch the simulated coverings and match picture cards of animals that might feel dry or slimy.

*Station 2.* To emphasize the role of **camouflage** in both reptiles and amphibians, the teacher prepares two pieces of black construction paper. A yellow pipe cleaner is taped to one piece of paper and a black pipe cleaner is taped to another. Ask, "Which is harder to see? How do you think this helps the animal survive? Design camouflage for a green pipe cleaner that lives in a desert."

*Station 3.* Some reptiles and amphibians rely on sensing vibrations to "hear" because they do not have outer ears. Mrs. Red Fox has the children tap a tuning fork on a surface and hold it near their ear. She says, "Describe what happens. Tap the fork again and press it against your cheek. What happens this time?" The class discusses how vibrations tell the animal what is happening. Some of the children begin comparing how birds and mammals hear and sense vibrations.

*Station 4.* Mrs. Red Fox has the children draw what they think a turtle will look like and what kind of home it will have.

## At the Zoo

Mrs. Red Fox divides her class into small groups and assigns a chaperone to each small group. Each group has a turtle task card. When the groups come to the turtle exhibit, the chaperone helps the children complete the questions. The children are asked to observe and answer the following questions.

- How many turtles do you see?
- What are they doing?
- Are turtle toes like your toes?

- What are the turtles eating?
- Try walking around the areas as slowly as the turtle is moving. How does it feel?
- How are you and the turtle alike?
- How are you different?
- What other animals are living with the turtle?
- Is it easy to find the turtles in the exhibit?

As the children move to an amphibian exhibit such as frogs, toads, and salamanders, they make comparisons between the turtles and the amphibians. Mrs. Red Fox makes sure that the exhibit signs are read and that questions are asked to gather additional information.

## After the Zoo Visit

Mrs. Red Fox reinforces what the children have learned with a variety of learning experiences. The class makes turtle candy from caramels, nuts, and chocolate bits, and the children create a play about turtles and how they live.

Each child creates a shoe-box diorama of the turtle habitat. The teacher asks, "Did the turtle live in the same way that you thought it would? What was different? What was the same?" She has the children compare what they knew about turtles before the visit to the diorama that they created after the visit. Mrs. Red Fox has storybooks and reference books available for children to find out more about reptiles and amphibians.

## Additional Animal Activities

The following questions and activities can be used before, during, or after a trip to the zoo.

1. "How many toes does a giraffe have? What color is a giraffe's tongue? Can you touch your nose with your tongue?" Explain that giraffes use their tongues the way we use forks and spoons.

2. A snake is covered with scales. Ask, "Are the scales on a snake's stomach the same shape and size as those on its back? Does a snake have feathers? Does a snake have fur?"

3. People have several different types of teeth in their mouth. After looking in a few mouths, have

the children look at a crocodile's teeth. "Are the teeth all the same type? Why do you think so?"

4. "What do we use to protect our feet? How are the feet of the sheep and deer adapted to where they live?" When in front of the hoofed animal display, have students stretch out their arms and then slowly move their arms together while looking directly ahead. "When can you see your hands?" Direct the children's attention to the hoofed animals. "Where are the deer's eyes located?" Discuss the location of the eyes, and name some advantages of having eyes that can see behind you.

5. In front of the aquarium ask, "How do you think fish breathe? Do fish have noses?" And, "Find a fish that feeds from the top of the tank. Find one that feeds from the bottom of the tank. Do any of the fish feed in the middle of the tank?"

6. "Do any of the animals have babies?" Refer to these questions when observing animal babies. "Do the babies look like the adult? How are they different?" And, "Does the baby move around on its own? Is one of the adults taking care of the baby? What is the adult doing for the baby?"

7. Other books that can be read aloud or put in the classroom library are *The Puffins Are Back* (Gibbons, 1991), *The Salamander House* (Mazer, 1991), *Frogs, Toads, and Lizards* (Parker & Wright, 1990), *Tigress* (Cowcher, 1991), and *Look Out for Turtles* (Berger, 1992).

Learning at the zoo can be an exciting experience. For a successful trip, plan activities for before, during, and after a zoo visit. If this is your first trip to the zoo, concentrate on familiar body parts and activities. For example, how does the animal move, eat, hear, see, or protect itself? Use these questions to encourage discussion of the special abilities and adaptations of animals.

## SUMMARY

Teaching life science concepts on a firsthand basis is essential to planning and teaching science to primary age children. Children display an eagerness to learn about the living things around them. This unit provides activities about seeds, plants, and molds; it also contains suggestions for caring for and studying living things (both indoors and outdoors) and keeping animals in the classroom.

Animal observations capitalize on the interest of children. The benefits of these observations far outweigh any cautions. A trip to the zoo can be a meaningful experience if specific plans are made for the visit. Prepare activities to do before, during, and after the trip. An early morning nature walk can also be used to look for local wildlife.

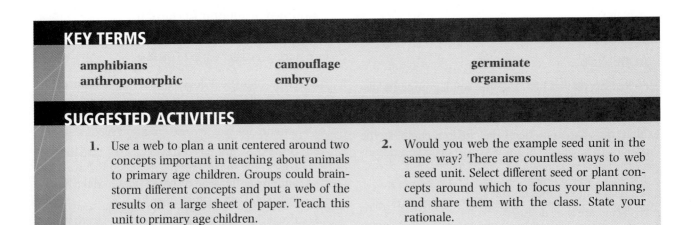

### KEY TERMS

| | | |
|---|---|---|
| amphibians | camouflage | germinate |
| anthropomorphic | embryo | organisms |

### SUGGESTED ACTIVITIES

1. Use a web to plan a unit centered around two concepts important in teaching about animals to primary age children. Groups could brainstorm different concepts and put a web of the results on a large sheet of paper. Teach this unit to primary age children.

2. Would you web the example seed unit in the same way? There are countless ways to web a seed unit. Select different seed or plant concepts around which to focus your planning, and share them with the class. State your rationale.

3. Develop questions and evaluation strategies for the seed unit.

4. Design an activity for teaching with a classroom animal. How many subject integrations will you use in your animal activity?

5. Identify the teaching strategies that were discussed in Units 5, 6, and 7. Compare lists. Which strategies did you use in designing your activity?

6. Visit your school's computer lab. Identify all software that teaches or reinforces life science concepts. Preview several pieces of software that you believe will be helpful in teaching a unit on plants or animals. Choose one piece of software to use as part of a lesson or unit. Develop a lesson and teach it to a small group of children. Write down children's comments and behaviors as they interact with the software. Based on these comments and behaviors, evaluate the effectiveness of the software in helping the students better understand the concept(s) being taught. The following are suggested software programs.

■ *Adventures with Oslo: World of Water* (grades K–6; Lewisville, NC: Science for Kids)

■ *The Animals 2.0* (grades 2–12; Novato, CA: Mindscape)

■ *The Backyard* (pre-K–2; Novato, CA: Broderbund Software)

■ *"Cell" ebration* (grades K–3; Lewisville, NC: Science for Kids)

■ *EcoAdventures in the Rainforest* (grades 3–up; San Diego, CA: Chariot)

■ *Explorapedia: The World of Nature* (grades 2–6; Redmond, WA: Microsoft)

■ *Get Up Close* (ages 6+; Charlotte, VT: Schoolhouse Interactive)

■ *Junior Nature Guides* (ages 7–12; New York: ICE)

■ *Magic Schoolbus: Ocean* (ages 6–10; Redmond, WA: Microsoft)

■ *Microscope Nature Explorer* (ages 8+; Pound Ridge, NY: Orange Cherry)

■ *National Geographic CDs for Educators: A World of Animals, A World of Plants, Animals and How They Grow* (grades pre-K–3; Washington, DC: National Geographic)

■ *One Small Square: Backyard* (ages 8+; Los Angeles: Virgin Sound and Vision)

■ *Sammy's Science House* (pre-K–2; Redmond, WA: Edmark)

■ *The World of Nature* (Fairfield, CT: Queque)

■ *Zoboomafoo Animal Alphabet* (Fremont, CA: The Learning Company)

■ *Zookeeper* (grades 1–5; Torrance, CA: Davidson & Associates)

■ *Zootopia* (ages 8+; Galesburg, MI: Lawrence Productions)

■ *Zurk's Alaskan Trek* (ages 6–10; Palo Alto, CA: Soleil Software)

■ *Zurk's Rainforest Lab* (pre-K–3; Palo Alto, CA: Soleil Software)

## REVIEW

A. List six life science concepts that are appropriate for primary age children.

B. What planning strategy can you use to develop a life science teaching unit?

C. Answer *True* or *False*:

_____ a. Animals can suffer from overfeeding and too much care.

_____ b. Wait until the animal arrives before preparing a home.

_____ c. Children should be encouraged to bring personal pets to the classroom.

_____ d. Most school systems do not have rules about animals in the classroom.

**D.** What are questions you should ask yourself as you prepare for an animal in your classroom?

**E.** What are some appropriate technological resources that can be used with a life science unit? How would they be incorporated?

## REFERENCES

Berger, M. (1992). *Look out for turtles!* New York: Harper Collins.

Cowcher, H. (1991). *Tigress.* New York: Farrar, Straus, & Giroux.

dePaola, T. (1978). *The popcorn book.* New York: Holiday House.

Ehlert, L. (1987). *Growing vegetable soup.* San Diego, CA: Harcourt, Brace, Jovanovich.

Gibbons, G. (1991). *The puffins are back.* New York: Harper Collins.

Krauss, R. (1945). *The carrot seed.* New York: Harper & Row.

Mazer, A. (1991). *The salamander house.* New York: Knopf.

Mitgutsch, A. (1971). *From seed to pear.* Minneapolis, MN: Carolrhoda Books.

National Research Council. (1996). *National science education standards.* Washington, DC: National Academies Press.

Parker, N. W., & Wright, J. R. (1990). *Frogs, toads, and lizards.* New York: Greenwillow.

## FURTHER READING AND RESOURCES

Althouse, R. (1988). *Investigating science experiences for young children.* New York: Teachers College Press.

American Association for the Advancement of Science (AAAS). (2007). *Atlas of science literacy: Project 2061* (Vol. 2). Washington, DC: Author.

Brainard, A. H., & Wrubel, D. H. (Eds.). (1995). *Through the rainbow: Children, science and literature.* Washington, DC: Council for Elementary Science International.

Brummet, D. C., Lind, K. K., Barman, C. R., DiSpezio, M. A., & Ostlund, L. K. (1995). *Destinations in science.* Menlo Park, CA: Addison-Wesley.

Chaille, C., & Britain, L. (2003). *Young child as scientist: A constructivist approach to early childhood science education.* Boston: Allyn & Bacon.

Chalufour, I., & Worth, K. (2004). *Building structure with young children.* St. Paul, MN: Redleaf Press.

Cobb, V. (1984). *Science experiments you can eat.* New York: Lippincott.

Council for Elementary Science International. (1984). *Outdoor learning experiences.* Columbus, OH: SMEAC Information Reference Center.

Dean, R. A., Dean, M. M., & Motz, L. (1987). *Safety in the elementary classroom.* Washington, DC: National Science Teachers Association.

DeVito, A., & Krockover, G. H. (1980). *Creative sciencing: Ideas and activities for teachers and children.* Boston: Little, Brown.

Esler, W. K., & Esler, M. K. (2001). *Teaching elementary science: A full spectrum science instruction approach* (8th ed.). Belmont, CA: Wadsworth.

Grollman, S., & Worth, K. (2003). *Worms, shadows, and whirlpools: Science in the early childhood classroom.* Portsmouth, NH: Heinemann.

Hadley, K., & Korb, M. (2007). Through the bugscope. *Science & Children, 45*(1), 29–31.

Hendrix-Martin, E. (1997). Students use their bodies to measure animals. *Teaching Children Mathematics, 3,* 426–430.

Howe, A. C. (2002). *Engaging children in science* (3rd ed.). Upper Saddle River, NJ: Prentice-Hall.

Kepler, L. (1996). *Windowsill science centers.* New York: Scholastic Books.

Lederman, N. G., Lederman, J. S., & Bell, R. L. (2005). *Constructing science in elementary classrooms.* Boston: Allyn & Bacon.

Lener, C., & Pinou, T. (2007). Learning with loggerheads. *Science & Children, 45*(1), 24–28.

Leveen, L. (2007). Exploring animals, glossopedia style. *Science & Children, 45*(1), 48–51.

Lind, K. K. (1995). A trip to the zoo. *Science and Children, 32*(8), 37–38.

Lind, K. K. (1997). Science in the developmentally appropriate integrated curriculum. In C. H. Hart, D. C. Burts, & R. Charlesworth (Eds.), *Integrated curriculum and developmentally appropriate practice: Birth to age eight.* Albany, NY: SUNY Press.

McIntyre, M. (1984). *Early childhood and science.* Washington, DC: National Science Teachers Association.

Peters, J. M., & Gega, P. C. (2002). *Science in elementary education.* Upper Saddle River, NJ: Merrill.

Raines, S. C. (1994). *450 more story s-t-r-e-t-c-h-e-r-s for the primary grades.* Mt. Rainier, MD: Gryphon House.

Raines, S. C., & Canady, R. J. (1992). *Story s-t-r-e-t-c-h-e-r-s for the primary grades.* Mt. Rainier, MD: Gryphon House.

Ritz, W. C. (2007). *A head start on science: Encouraging a sense of wonder.* Arlington, VA: NSTA Press.

Sheehan, K., & Waidner, M. (2000). *Earth child 2000.* Tulsa, OK: Council Oak Books.

Silverman, E., Coffman, M., & Younker, B. A. (2007). Cheep, chirp, twitter, and whistle. *Science & Children, 44*(6), 20–25.

Tolman, M. N., & Morton, J. O. (1987). *Life science activities for grades 2–8.* West Nyack, NY: Parker.

Victor, E., & Kellough, R. D. (2003). *Science K–8, An integrated approach.* Upper Saddle River, NJ: Prentice-Hall.

# Unit 35

# Physical Science

## OBJECTIVES

After reading this unit, you should be able to:

- Design physical science investigations appropriate for primary age children.
- Develop an understanding of physical topics that are appropriate for primary grade children.
- Develop structured and unstructured physical science learning activities with primary grade children.
- Apply unit webbing strategies to physical science content.
- Integrate science with other subject areas.

Physical science experiences are fun and exciting for primary age children. Even though these experiences can be dramatic and astounding for children, teaching the concepts is more foolproof than you might think. This is true for several reasons.

First, the physical sciences abound with opportunities for using discrepant events (discussed in Unit 6) that put students in disequilibrium and ready them for learning. Thus, they are eager and ready to explore. Second, most experiences are instantly repeatable. In this way, the child can continue exploring without elaborate preparation. And finally, the hands-on nature of physical science explorations makes them ideal for use with primary age children.

The *National Science Education Standards* (NSES) state that, as a result of the activities in the primary grades, all students should develop an understanding of properties of objects and materials; position and motion of objects; and light, heat, electricity, and magnetism. At the primary level, the NSES content standards (NRC, 1996) focus on the properties and motion of objects and

on energy. Children can best understand these topics by acting on objects and observing what happens to them.

This unit begins with the physical science concepts that are basic to primary grade learning and presents an example of ways that the topic of air can be integrated with science concepts of movement and changes in matter, gravity, light, and color. The subject integrations and lessons are part of the webbing scheme depicted in Figure 7–4 of Unit 7. Suggestions for the teaching of sound are also included.

## PHYSICAL SCIENCE CONCEPTS

The following concepts are basic to understanding the physical sciences. Use this list to identify concepts around which you can develop a planning web such as those described in Units 7 and 34.

- Air takes up space.
- Air has weight.

- Air is all around us.
- Things that make sound vibrate.
- Moving air pushes things.
- Air slows moving objects.
- Things near the earth fall to the ground unless something holds them up.
- Everything is made from material called *matter*.
- All matter takes up space.
- Matter can change into a solid, liquid, or gas.
- Matter can be classified according to observable characteristics.
- **Physical changes** and **chemical changes** are two basic ways of changing things.
- In a physical change, appearances change but the substance remains the same (tearing paper, chopping wood).
- In a chemical change, the characteristics change so that a new substance is formed (burning, rusting).
- A mixture consists of two or more substances that retain their separate identities when mixed together.
- Temperature tells how hot or cold an object is.
- There are many types of energy—light, heat, sound, electricity, motion, magnetic.
- Magnets can be used to make some things move without being touched.
- Static electricity is produced when two different materials are rubbed together.

- There are three parts to a simple electric circuit: a source of electricity, a path for electricity to travel, and something that uses the electricity (a light bulb or bell).
- Some materials allow electricity to pass through them.
- To see color, light is needed.
- The way to change how something is moving is to give it a push or a pull.
- Machines make it easier to move things.
- Things move in many ways, such as straight, zigzag, around and around, back and forth, and fast and slow.

## PLANNING AND TEACHING A UNIT ABOUT AIR

The learning experiences suggested in this unit follow the format described in Unit 7 and used in the seed unit (refer to Unit 34). Each lesson states a concept, an objective, materials, and suggestions for teaching the concept. Extensions, integrations, and possible evaluation procedures are indicated in the body of the lesson, when appropriate, and at the end of the unit. The topic of air is explored with bubble and sound lessons.

### Exploring Bubbles

Children love to play with bubbles. They love to create bubbles, chase bubbles, and pop bubbles. Why not take advantage of this interest to teach science concepts with a subject children already know something about?

## ACTIVITIES

### The Bubble Machine

**CONCEPT:** Bubbles have air inside of them.

**OBJECTIVE:** Construct a bubble machine by manipulating materials to produce bubbles.

**MATERIALS:** Mix a bubble solution of eight teaspoons (½ cup) liquid soap and 1 quart water. Punch holes about halfway down the side of enough paper cups for each child. A box of drinking straws will also be needed. Write each child's name over the hole.

*(continued)*

**PROCEDURE:** Assemble a bubble machine by inserting a straw through a hole in a paper cup and filling with detergent solution to just below the hole. Have the children observe the machine as you blow bubbles. Ask, WHAT DO YOU THINK IS HAPPENING? Have the children assemble bubble machines. Each child should insert a straw into the hole in the side of the paper cup and then pour some detergent solution into the cup just below the hole. Give children time to try bubble blowing and ask, WHAT DO YOUR BUBBLES LOOK LIKE? DESCRIBE YOUR BUBBLES. HOW MANY BUBBLES CAN YOU BLOW? WHAT IS INSIDE OF THE BUBBLE?

**EXTENSIONS:** Make bubble books with drawings that depict the bubble machine experiences. Encourage children to write about their pictures. Read the books to the class; then put them in the library center for perusal.

## Inventing Bubble Machines

**CONCEPT:** Many different shapes will create bubbles.

**OBJECTIVE:** Make a shape that will create a bubble. Observe air entering bubbles and taking up space.

**MATERIALS:** Mixed bubble solution; soft, bendable wire; pans for bubble solution.

**PROCEDURE:** YOUR BUBBLE MACHINE WORKS WELL. CAN YOU BEND WIRE INTO SHAPES THAT WILL MAKE BUBBLES? Have children "mess around" with wire to create a variety of shapes for making bubbles (Figure 35–1). Have them test the shapes by blowing air into the bubble film or moving the wire shape through the air. Ask, DID YOU MAKE A BUBBLE? WAS YOUR BUBBLE THE SAME SHAPE AS THE WIRE?

**NATURALISTIC AND INFORMAL ACTIVITIES:** In the science center have other materials available for bubble machine making such as a pierced spatula, turkey baster, berry basket bottom, sieve, and other kitchen items (Figure 35–2). Ask, WHAT SHAPE DO YOU THINK THESE BUBBLES WILL BE? WHAT DO YOU NOTICE ABOUT THE SIZE OF THE BUBBLES? (Different sizes.) Have children record predictions and results for the different bubble blowers.

**Figure 35–1** Wire shapes for blowing bubbles.

**Figure 35–2** Kitchen shapes make interesting bubbles.

## Tabletop Bubbles

**CONCEPT:** Air takes up space.

**OBJECTIVE:** Use air to create bubble sculpture. Predict how the bubbles will act on top of tables.

**MATERIALS:** Bubble solution, straws, cups, flat trays.

**PROCEDURE:** Have children dip out a small amount of bubble solution on a tray and spread it around. Ask, WHAT DO YOU THINK WILL HAPPEN IF YOU BLOW AIR INTO THE BUBBLE SOLUTION? (Bubbles will form.) Instruct children to dip a straw into the soap on the tray and blow gently. Give them time to "mess around" with tray top bubble blowing. Present challenges. CAN YOU BLOW A BUBBLE THE SIZE OF A BOWL? Have several children work together to make a community bubble. One child begins blowing the bubble and others join in by adding air to the inside of the bubble. (The straws must be wet to avoid breaking the bubble.) Bubble cities of the future can be made by adding more solution to the tray and blowing several bubble domes next to one another.

**EXTENSION:** Bubbles inside of bubbles. CAN YOU FIT A BUBBLE INSIDE OF A BUBBLE? Have children blow a bubble. Then insert a wet straw inside of the bubble and start a new bubble. WHAT HAPPENS IF THE SIDES TOUCH? (Figure 35–3). Make bubble chains. Have children blow a bubble with a straw. Then, wiggle the straw and blow another one. Soon, a chain of bubbles will form. Ask, HOW MANY BUBBLES CAN YOU MAKE?

## Investigation Questions for Exploring Air and Bubbles

1. Will other liquids create bubbles?
2. Will adding a liquid called **glycerin** to the bubble solution make the bubbles stronger? (Yes.) Can you think of other things to add to the bubble solution to make the bubbles last longer? Test your formulas.
3. Are bubbles always round? (Yes, unless some of them stick together. Forces acting inside and outside of the soap film are the same all over it.)

Figure 35–3 "Can you fit a bubble inside of a bubble?"

## SUBJECT INTEGRATIONS

### Bubbles and Science

1. *Observe bubbles.* Describe color, movement, size, and shape. How many different colors do you see in the soap bubble? How do the colors move and change? Look at the bubbles through different colors of cellophane or polarized sunglasses. Do the bubbles change?
2. *Classify bubbles.* Classify by color, size, shape (bubble machine bubbles will stick together and take different shapes), location, how the bubble was made.

3. *Changes in matter.* Ask children to describe some changes that they notice in bubbles. Ask, "Did anything change?" (Yes.) "Did you see a physical change in the bubble solution?" (Yes, matter changes form only in a physical change.)

## Bubbles and Art

1. *Bubble painting.* Mix bubble solution with liquid poster paint. Put the mixture in a bowl. As the child blows into the paint with a straw, a paint bubble dome forms. Lay construction paper over the bubble. As the paint bubble bursts, it splatters paint on the paper.

2. *Bulletin board.* Make a background of large construction paper bubbles. Display children's writing and art activities in this way.

## Bubbles and Math

1. *How high?* Measure the height of the bubbles on a tray top. Measure how long a bubble lasts, predict and measure how many bubbles can be blown, and how far they can float. Graph the results.

2. *Lung capacity.* Make a graph of who has the largest lung capacity. Have children discover a way of determining lung capacity by blowing bubbles.

## Bubbles and Language Arts

Science experiences can provide inspiration for important first steps in writing.

1. *Bubble books.* Provide paper for children to record their bubble explorations. These can be illustrated and bubble shaped.

2. *Books about bubbles.* Read storybooks about bubbles (see Appendix B).

3. *Chart story.* Have children write or dictate stories about what they observed when they examined air inside of bubbles (Figure 35–4).

## Bubbles and Food Experiences

Children can observe the tiny air bubbles that go into various whipped mixtures. For example, whipped milk topping can be made for cookies. You will need half a cup of instant dry skim milk and half a cup of cold water.

Beat with an electric mixer at high speed for 4 minutes. Have children watch the mixture change. Then, add 2 tablespoons of sugar and half a teaspoon of vanilla and beat at high speed until the mixture stands in peaks. You may want to add the ingredient "air bubbles" to your recipe. Remind children that air went into what they are eating.

## Concept: Air Can Move Things and Slow Things Down

The following suggestions extend science concepts.

1. *Moving bubbles.* Have children move bubbles in the direction they want them to go by fanning them with paper (Figure 35–5).

2. *Paper fans.* Make paper fans to move air. These can be accordion-pleated sheets of paper or small paper plates stapled to ice-cream-bar sticks.

3. *Glider designs.* Make gliders, and find out how far they can fly.

4. *Straw painting.* Blow paint with plastic straws. Pick up the paint with air pressure (as with the bubble solution), drop it on paper, and blow the puddles of paint into a design.

```
Matthew

To day we were sintest again  it was a lot of fun.  We were seeing
if air took up space.  Some people thoght that it did and some
thoght it didn't.  I blew a very very very very big bubble but it
popped in my face.  There were different colors and shapes.  But
they didn't taste good.
```

Figure 35–4 Matthew has made many observations about bubbles.

**Figure 35–5** "Can you make bubbles move?"

5. *Make pinwheels.* Have children fold squares of paper and then hold them in front of a fan or in the wind. Ask, "What happens to the paper?" (It moves.) Help children make pinwheels from typing paper or wallpaper. A pushpin will hold the pinwheel to a pencil eraser and allow it to turn freely. Ask, "How did we produce motion?"

6. *Air walk.* Take children on a walk to find things that are moved by air. Discuss and write about what you have seen. Local windmills are ideal, but weather socks, flags, trees, seeds, clothes on a clothesline, and other moving things work well.

7. *Exploring parachutes.* Have children make parachutes out of squares of cloth. Tie each corner with string, then thread the four strings through a wooden bead or washer. Drop the parachute from various heights, and predict what will happen. Cut a hole in the top of the parachute, and observe any differences. Make parachutes out of different materials, such as plastic or cupcake liners, and compare their flight.

8. *Baby seeds.* Open milkweed pods in the wind and watch the wind disperse the seeds. Refer to the seed lessons in Unit 34 for further investigations.

9. *Air movers.* Have children experiment with different objects found in the room to see which is most effective in moving bubbles.

## Exploring Sound

Children love to make music, but they probably do not know anything about the nature of sound. Help them understand that sound is caused when something vibrates by using the following lessons to teach children to see, hear, and feel the sound vibrations around them. Then, make musical instruments that reinforce the concepts.

## ACTIVITIES

### Good Vibrations

**CONCEPT:** Sound is caused when something vibrates.

**OBJECTIVE:** Observe objects vibrating and making sounds. Construct musical instruments based on concepts of sound.

**MATERIALS:** Paper plates, rubber bands, bottle tops, hole punch, paper cups, waxed paper, coffee cans, flexible tubing.

**PROCEDURE:**  1. Have children begin vibration observations by gently resting their fingers over their vocal cords and saying "Ahhhh" and "Eeee." Ask, WHAT DO YOU FEEL? (Something moving.) Explain that they are feeling vibrations occurring in their vocal cords, where all sounds they make with their voices come from.

2. Then have them place their fingertips against their lips while they simultaneously blow and hum. Reinforce the connection between vibration and sound by touring your classroom. Ask children to identify things that vibrate—the aquarium pump,

*(continued)*

kitchen timer, air vent, and overhead lights. If possible, let them feel the vibrations in these objects and listen to the sounds each makes.

3. *Drum.* Make a simple drum out of a coffee can that has a plastic top. Place grains of rice on the can lid and tap lightly, while your students watch and listen. Ask, WHAT HAPPENS TO THE RICE WHEN YOU DO THIS? (It bounces up and down to the sound of the drum.)

4. *Drumsticks.* Make drumsticks from tennis balls and dowels (Figure 35–6). Punch a hole in the ball, apply glue to the end and edges of the dowel or stick, and push it into the center of the ball. Or use a butter brush, wadded-up rubber bands, or a plastic lemon.

5. *Humming cup.* Make a humming cup by cutting the bottom out of a small paper cup. Then have the children cover the newly opened ends with waxed paper and secure with rubber bands. Say, PLACE YOUR LIPS LIGHTLY AGAINST THE WAXED PAPER END OF THE CUP AND HUM (Figure 35–7). They will get another feel for sound. Paper towel tubes can be used in a similar way to make horns.

6. *More horns.* A yard of flexible tubing will provide an opportunity for children to whisper back and forth and feel sound traveling to their ears through a talking tube. Then, tape a funnel to one end and make a buglelike horn.

7. *Tambourines.* You can construct this favorite instrument by decorating and shellacking paper plates in which you have already punched holes. Distribute bottle caps that also have holes punched in them, and have children tie two or three caps to each hole in their plates. This is a noisy but fun way to show the relationship between vibrations and sound.

**NATURALISTIC AND INFORMAL ACTIVITIES:** Put a variety of musical instruments in a sound center. Give the children time to explore the instruments and record their observations in their science journals.

**EXTENSIONS:** *Build a Band.* Making musical instruments will give children an opportunity to observe vibrations in other ways. Make a variety of instruments and decorate for a special occasion.

## Wind Instruments

Wind instruments such as flutes, whistles, and panpipes depend on vibrating columns of air for their sound. The longer the column of air, the lower the pitch. (The highness or lowness of a sound is its *pitch.* The more vibrations per second, the higher the tone that is produced; the fewer vibrations, the lower the tone.) The following lesson demonstrates the relationship between the length of an air column and musical pitch.

Figure 35–7 "Can you feel the vibrations of a humming cup?"

**Figure 35–6** George makes drumsticks from tennis balls.

## ACTIVITIES

### Bottles, Water, and Air

**CONCEPT:** Pitch is the highness or lowness of a sound.

**OBJECTIVE:** Recognize differences in sound. Construct wind instruments.

**MATERIALS:** Ten bottles of the same height, water.

**PROCEDURE:** Prepare by filling glass soda bottles to varying levels with water. (Plastic bottles are too easily knocked over.) Hold up an empty bottle and ask, WHAT DO YOU THINK IS IN THE BOTTLE? WHAT DO YOU THINK WILL HAPPEN IF THE AIR IN THE BOTTLE VIBRATES? Demonstrate by blowing across the top of the empty bottle. Teach children to direct air across the mouth of a bottle. This is worth taking the time to do. Instruct children to press the mouth of the bottle lightly against their lower lip and direct air straight across the mouth of the bottle. (Do not blow into the bottle—the secret is blowing straight across.) Give them time to "mess around" with their new skill. Then ask, WHAT DO YOU THINK WILL HAPPEN IF YOU BLOW ACROSS A BOTTLE WITH WATER IN IT? Pour water into bottles, and have children find out what will happen. Children will discover that the bottles make sounds that vary in pitch. They might even play a tune (Figure 35–8).

**NATURALISTIC AND INFORMAL ACTIVITIES:** Invite musicians to the classroom to share their instruments and answer questions.

**EXTENSION:** Emphasize the meaning of pitch by reading a familiar tale in which high- and low-pitched sounds figure. For example, ask children to imitate the three billy goats gruff. Dramatize differences in pitch with voice and body activities.

## Properties of Matter

The *NSES* suggest that young children need to understand that matter can be classified according to observable characteristics such as size, shape, color, weight, temperature, and the ability to react with other substances. Children's experience observing, manipulating, and classifying common objects provides the foundation for much of their later learning.

Children build concepts related to the properties of objects and materials by engaging in a variety of experiences requiring them to observe and describe the properties of objects, comparing objects for their observable similarities and differences, and sorting or grouping objects based on their similarities. The following activities provide early experiences with ordering and classifying according to observable characteristics using the senses.

### BOTTLES AND WATER

Collect eight bottles to make a scale—your job will be easier if they are all the same kind and size. To tune the bottles, you'll need to fill them to varying heights with water.

Start by dividing the volume of water that one of the bottles could accommodate by the number of notes you wish to produce. For example, if you want a one-octave scale, divide the volume by eight. Then, leaving bottle one empty, put $\frac{1}{8}$ of the volume into bottle two, $\frac{1}{4}$ into bottle three, $\frac{3}{8}$ into bottle four, and so on until bottle eight contains $\frac{7}{8}$ of its volume of water. Adjust the amount of water up and down in the bottles until the scale intervals sound (more or less) true. Use masking tape to mark the correct level on each bottle.

**Figure 35–8** Formula for bottle music.

## Shape and Size

Make a "feely sock" for each child that has two objects in it. One object should be the same in all socks, such as a Unifix Cube or other item that is familiar to the children. The second object should be distributed in pairs so that there are two socks that match. Ask, "Describe the objects that are in your feely sock." After each child has described the objects in the socks, invite the children to find the sock that matches their sock. When a child believes that he has the match, ask the children to pull out their objects and to compare the objects to see if their descriptions of the size, shape, and textures of their object provided accurate details.

## Smell

Make "scent jars" from film canisters, pieces of sponge, and food flavorings such as cinnamon oil, peppermint, clove oil, and so on. For each scent, make three canisters. Label the canisters on the bottom with letters or colors so that children can check to make sure they have found the correct matches to their scents. Distribute the canisters and ask the children to smell their canister and describe the scent and anything that smells like the scent. Ask the children to find their matching canisters and discuss the descriptions that helped them find each other.

## Temperature

Laminate six different colors of construction paper and lay them side by side to create a classification mat. Place cups of water of differing temperatures on the mats. Ask the children to use their sense of touch to order the cups from hottest to coolest. Children should place the hottest cup at one end and the coolest at the other end, and then try to figure out which ones go in between. When they have arranged the cups, ask them to check their work by using a thermometer or temperature probe. The activity will need to be completed quickly before the temperatures even out. Children can generate their own ways of comparing, and a table or graph can be produced.

## Weight

Gather a large selection of balls, including some that are very similar in weight. The collection might include tennis balls, Styrofoam balls, Ping-Pong balls, marbles, ball bearings, softballs, golf balls, and so on. Use the colored mat system described in the Temperature section to provide students with a system for organizing the balls. Ask students to order the balls from heaviest to lightest. Once students have made their determinations, have them use a balance to see if their predictions were correct. Children will have to work to determine the best way to use the balance. (Placing the heaviest object in one bucket on the balance and then testing all other objects to see if any are heavier will work well.) Once the heaviest has been confirmed, children can continue with the next objects, comparing them all to each other until the order is established. This ordering activity can become a classification activity when objects are combined and weight is used to determine when sets of objects are to be grouped together.

# ACTIVITIES

## Change

**CONCEPT:** Chemical changes.

**OBJECTIVE:** Explore chemical changes.

**MATERIALS:** 3-oz plastic cups, plastic bowls, 4–8-oz bottles of glue (do not use washable glue), distilled water, borax.

**PROCEDURE:**   1.  Mix equal parts of glue and distilled water into a large container.
2.  In a second container, mix 1 liter of distilled water and 1 tablespoon of borax.

3. Divide the children into pairs and have one member of each pair measure 2 ounces of the glue solution into a plastic cup.
4. Have the second child measure 2 ounces of the borax solution into a second cup.
5. Pour the solutions into the bowl and stir, being careful to keep it in the bowl.
6. Ask, "What happened when you mixed the two solutions? Does the result look like either of the solutions before they were mixed? Is this a new substance?"

**CONCEPT:** Physical changes.

**OBJECTIVE:** Explore physical changes.

**MATERIALS:** Water, sand, bowls, paper.

**PROCEDURE:**
1. Have each child pour water and sand in small bowls.
2. Put the bowls in the sun.
3. Check the bowls before leaving school.
4. Ask, "What happened to the sand and water? Has a new substance been formed? Is this a physical or chemical change?"

# EXPLORING LIGHT

Children need many concrete experiences with light to provide the conceptual background necessary for later understanding. Help children understand the *National Science Education Standard* for light—light travels in a straight line until it strikes an object, and light can be reflected by a mirror, refracted by a lens, or absorbed by objects—with the following learning experiences.

## Light Beam Tag

To encourage children to discover that light travels in a straight line, play light beam tag with mirror tiles that are at least 5" × 5" (rough edges should be covered with duct tape). Focus the beam on one student's mirror. The student must use the mirror to reflect the beam to another student's mirror. The light intensity should be enough to reflect to two or three children at one time. When two or three children are successfully reflecting each other's beams, clap the chalkboard eraser in the areas where the light is traveling. The class will be able to observe the light beams traveling in straight lines between the children with the mirrors. This activity could also be used to reinforce the concept that light can be reflected by a mirror.

## Instructional Technology: The Light Sensor

Young children come up with numerous questions regarding light when they are introduced to instructional technology that measures light levels. The following scenario demonstrates how a light sensor can be introduced to young children.

Early in the year, Mr. Wang had introduced his students to *Sensing Science*, an elementary-level sensor and probeware package that consists of software; probes and sensors that measure temperature, light, sound, motion, and other variables; and the hardware that interfaces the computer and the probes and sensors. The focus of *Sensing Science* is to teach young children simple data collection and graphing in a developmentally appropriate manner. For instance, the first activity with the light probe involves pointing the sensor toward a bright light. The computer screen turns completely white. When the probe is covered, thus allowing no light, the computer screen turns completely black. When pointed toward varying levels of light, the computer screen turns shades of gray. Mr. Wang asked, "What do you think the sensor was sensing?" After several suggestions and trials, the children quickly realized that the amount of light striking the sensor made the changes.

Mr. Wang showed the children other ways the amount of light could be indicated and features in

*Sensing Science* that recorded the highest and lowest reading like an EKG. There were many opportunities to take measurements and ask questions and a lot of interest in the "snapshots" of light levels that the program can display on a simple table. In this way, the children could compare two or more light levels by comparing the numbers.

The children decided to use the technology to help them solve a problem. The children had been working on constructing a classroom planetarium out of cardboard boxes and glowing star stickers. They had reached the point where they needed a curtain that would cover the entrance and block out all light during their "star shows" yet would be easy to move aside the rest of the time to allow light to enter and be absorbed by the glowing stickers (so they would glow brightly during the star shows). Several children brought in materials from home to use for the curtain, including old sheets, blankets, and an old tarp. The children cut the cloth into equal pieces to determine which would block the most light. One piece of cloth was a light color and a medium weave; another was a gray color and a tight weave. The last one was black and of a loose weave. Most of the children predicted that the black cloth would block the most light. Mr. Wang asked, "How could you use the light sensor to help you solve the problem?" Some of the children decided to find out by putting the cloth over a flashlight and then holding the sensor up to it. Another group decided to cover the light sensor with the cloth and hold it up to the light. Mr. Wang allowed the groups of children to try their investigations. When they were finished, several tables were produced.

The children were amazed that the gray cloth blocked out the most light. Mr. Wang asked, "Why do you think the gray cloth worked the best?" Liu Pei said maybe it had something to do with the color. Maybe all gray cloths worked better than white or black. Derrick thought it had to do with how close together the threads were. He held up each piece of cloth and looked through it, pointing out how much more space was between the threads on the white and black cloths. The other children also observed this and started gathering their materials and setting up additional investigations. Liu Pei wanted to test some cloths that were the same except for their color to see if the gray really worked best. Derrick thought it would be a great idea to do the same thing

with some pieces of cloth that were the same color but had different amounts of space between the threads.

Mr. Wang was pleased that the children wanted to do investigations regarding light. He knew that the children would carry out many more investigations throughout the year about concepts regarding how different colors absorb and reflect light. Perhaps the children would want to set up investigations testing the reflective qualities of sheets of construction paper or the amount of light allowed to pass through pieces of colored transparencies. The *Sensing Science* probes were going to be a great tool for facilitating inquiry in his classroom.

## Assessment Strategies

Because many primary children are beginning readers, simple performance assessments designed around process skills and anecdotal records can be used to determine understanding. When recording children's oral explanations of what is happening, it is better to place the emphasis on the child's ability to communicate ideas and not on use of terminology. When children are completing a task, write down snippets of informal conversation relating to the task.

Another assessment strategy might include having the children sort objects into categories, setting out an object that does not fit into a category. Observe how the children either incorporate the object or change the categories, and relate these observations to progress.

## SUMMARY

When children explore physical science concepts, they are learning basic skills that develop future understandings. To be effective, these lessons must emphasize process skills, concrete experiences, and integrations. Thus, students see a relationship between the concepts and their world.

Children are not expected to understand distinctions in all physical science concepts. Many of the concepts are explored to prepare them for future learning. Physical science concepts can be presented in many ways and with a variety of instructional strategies.

## KEY TERMS

| chemical changes | glycerin | physical changes |
| --- | --- | --- |

## SUGGESTED ACTIVITIES

1. Which process skills are used in the bubble unit? Identify each skill and how it is incorporated into the study of air inside of bubbles. Teach the unit to children. Which integrations and activities did you use?

2. Interview teachers of primary age children to find out what types of physical science activities they introduce to children. Do any of these activities include the exploration of materials? Record your observations for discussion.

3. Brainstorm strategies to prepare children to understand physical science topics such as magnets, light, and electricity. Pick a topic, and prepare a learning experience that will aid in future concept development.

4. Select a physical science concept, and prepare a learning cycle to teach that concept. Teach it to children. Record your observations for discussion.

5. Present a lesson about sound for primary age children. What types of learning experiences will you design for your students? Explain how you will apply Piaget's theory of development to this topic.

6. Go to a bookstore or library, and identify books that would enhance the teaching of physical science. Present an evaluation of these materials and how you might use them to reinforce science concepts.

7. Go to a school system computer support unit and ask for software that complements physical science concepts for young children. If there are any sensors and probes available for use with young children, try them for yourself.

Determine which concepts and processes are taught or reinforced by the software. Plan a lesson that uses the software, teach it to a small group of students, and evaluate the lesson's effectiveness. Did the software provide instruction that would be difficult to do in other ways? What are the benefits of using the software or probeware? Share the results with your class. Suggested software includes the following.

- ■ *Adventures with Oslo: Tools and Gadgets* (grades K–up; Lewisville, NC: Science for Kids)

- ■ *Bumptz Science Carnival* (grades 1–5; Emeryville, CA: Theatrix Interactive)

- ■ *Gizmos and Gadgets* (ages 7–12; Fremont, CA: The Learning Company)

- ■ *Graph Club* (grades K–4; Watertown, MA: Tom Snyder Productions)

- ■ *Gryphon Bricks* (Ages 5+; San Diego, CA: Gryphon Software)

- ■ *Invention Studio* (ages 9+; Bethesda, MD: Discovery Communications)

- ■ *Mystery Objects* (grades 2–4; Minneapolis, MN: MECC)

- ■ *Sammy's Science House* (pre-K–2; Redmond, WA: Edmark)

- ■ *Sensing Science* (Grand Island, NY: Data Harvest Educational). Sensor and probeware program.

- ■ *Widget Workshop* (ages 8–12; Walnut Creek, CA: Maxis)

## REVIEW

A. Explain why primary age children should explore physical science activities (give at least two reasons).

B. List the major concept areas in physical science that are appropriate for primary age children. Pick four concepts that are about the same topic, such as states of matter, and develop a planning web for teaching those topics.

C.  Identify a lesson that you plan to use in teaching a physical science concept in a primary classroom. Using your understanding of age-appropriate science teaching and learning, explain your rationale for selecting the content and teaching strategies in the lesson.

## REFERENCE

National Research Council. (1996). *National science education standards.* Washington, DC: National Academies Press.

## FURTHER READING AND RESOURCES

Abruscato, J. (2004). *Teaching children science: A discovery approach* (6th ed.). Boston: Allyn & Bacon.

Abruscato, J. (2004). *Teaching children science: Discovery activities and demonstrations for the elementary and middle grades* (2nd ed.). Boston: Allyn & Bacon.

Allison, L., and Katz, D. 1983. *Gee, wiz!* Boston: Little, Brown.

Althouse, R. (1988). *Investigating science experiences for young children.* New York: Teachers College Press.

American Association for the Advancement of Science (AAAS). (2007). *Atlas of science literacy: Project 2061* (Vol. 2). Washington, DC: Author.

Barrow, L. H. (2007). Bring light onto shadows. *Science & Children, 44*(9), 43–45.

Campbell, B., & Fulton, L. (2003). *Science notebooks: Writing about inquiry.* Portsmouth, NH: Heinemann.

Chalufour, I., & Worth, K. (2003). *Discovering nature with young children.* St. Paul, MN: Redleaf Press.

Froschauer, L. (1993). *Teaching elementary science with toys: CESI sourcebook VII.* Columbus, OH: ERIC Clearinghouse for Science, Mathematics, and Environmental Science.

Harlan, J., & Rivkin, M. (2003). *Science experiences for the early childhood years: An integrated affective approach.* Upper Saddle River, NJ: Pearson-Merrill/Prentice-Hall.

Hawkinson, J., & Faulhaber, M. (1969). *Music and instruments for children to make.* Chicago: Whitman.

Hillen, J., Mercier, S., & Hoover, E. (1994). *Primarily physics.* Fresno, CA: AIMS Education Foundation.

Lederman, N. G., Lederman, J. S., & Bell, R. L. (2005). *Constructing science in elementary classrooms.* Boston: Allyn & Bacon.

Lind, K. K. (1985). The beat of the band. *Science and Children, 23*(3), 32–33.

Lind, K. K. (1986). The beat goes on. *Science and Children, 23*(7), 39–41.

Malone, M. (Ed.). (1996). *Physical science activities for elementary and middle school. CESI sourcebook V.* Columbus, OH: ERIC Clearinghouse for Science, Mathematics, and Environmental Science.

Orii, E., & Orii, M. (1989). *Simple science experiments with light.* Milwaukee, WI: Gareth Stevens Books.

Parker, D. L. (2003). Take care of mother earth: Technology and the environment. *Teaching Children Mathematics, 9*(7), 414–419.

Perez, J. (1988). *Explore and experiment.* Bridgeport, CT: First Teacher Press.

Peters, J. M., & Gega, P. C. (2002). *Science in elementary education.* Upper Saddle River, NJ: Merrill.

Sheehan, T. F. (2006). *City science series: Blocks of rocks.* Vero Beach, FL: Rourke.

Victor, E., & Kellough, R. D. (2003). *Science K–8, An integrated approach.* Upper Saddle River, NJ: Prentice-Hall.

Zubrowski, B. (1979). *Bubbles.* Boston: Little, Brown.

# Unit 36

## Earth and Space Science

### OBJECTIVES

After reading this unit, you should be able to:

- Design earth and space science investigations for primary age children.
- Develop an understanding of earth and space science concepts appropriate for primary age children.
- Develop structured and unstructured earth and space science learning experiences for primary age children.

The *National Science Education Standards* (NSES) emphasize the observational nature of earth and space science. In primary grades, children learn about Earth and space by making observations as they explore, collect, describe, and record information. Children investigate and gain an understanding of the properties of earth materials such as water, soil, rocks, and **minerals**.

A major role of the teacher in primary earth and space science lessons is to guide children in observing natural changes of all kinds. These include cyclical changes, such as the movement of the sun and moon, and variable changes, such as the weather.

Most children in the primary years are able to order and group objects by a single characteristic and to communicate and make comparisons about their observations.

This unit begins with lessons about various earth materials that are used by us in different ways. For example, soil, rocks, and other earth materials are used for building, fuels, and growing plants. Suggestions for introducing children to earth materials, space, and weather are included. Lessons about rocks that can be developed into a unit and integrated into the classroom are suggested.

## EARTH AND SPACE SCIENCE AND THE ENVIRONMENT

- Earth's materials are rocks, soils, fossil fuels, water, and the gases in Earth's atmosphere.
- Earth's materials are nonliving.
- Earth's materials have properties that make them useful to us in different ways.
- Soils have properties of color and texture.
- Soils have the capacity to retain water and help plants survive.
- Rocks are formed in different ways.
- Rocks are nonliving things.

- Sand is made up of tiny pieces of rock.
- Water and wind change the surface of the earth.
- Mountains and land are made of rocks and soil.
- **Evaporation** means a liquid changes into a gas (vapor) in the air.
- **Condensation** means a gas changes to a liquid. Water vapor is an example of condensation.
- The **atmosphere** is the air around us. It has conditions such as wind, moisture, and temperature. **Weather** is what we call the conditions of the atmosphere.
- There are four seasons, and each has unique weather.
- Temperature is how hot or cold something is.
- Clouds and fog are made of droplets of water.
- The earth has a layer of air and water around it.
- Water is a liquid and is called *ice* when it is solid.
- The sun gives off light and heat and warms the land, air, and water.
- A light source at a great distance looks small.
- The sun, moon, stars, and clouds have properties, locations, and movements that can be observed and described.
- The sun, moon, and stars all appear to move slowly across the sky. The moon appears to change in size and shape. Sometimes the moon can be seen at night, and sometimes it can be seen during the day.

- There are many stars in the sky. They do not look the same in brightness and color and are not scattered evenly.
- The patterns of stars stay the same and appear to move across the sky.
- The quality of air, water, and soil is affected by human activity.

## PLANNING AND TEACHING A UNIT ON ROCKS

Children need a variety of concrete experiences that enable them to learn the properties of earth materials. For example, as children begin to observe rocks, they will see that some are made up of a single substance but that most are made up of several substances (minerals). Assessment of children's skills and understanding of concepts takes place as children group a variety of rocks according to one of their properties, such as color, pattern, buoyancy, or layering.

The learning experiences suggested in this unit follow the format described in Unit 7 and used in Units 34 and 35. Each lesson states a concept, an objective, materials, and suggestions for teaching the concepts. Extensions, integrations, and possible evaluation procedures are indicated in the body of the lesson, when appropriate, and at the end of the unit.

The following basic geology lessons introduce fundamental concepts and stimulate children's curiosity about rocks, minerals, and earth processes. The strategies will acquaint primary age children with the nature of rocks in a way that is immediate, exciting, and fun.

## ACTIVITIES

### A Carton of Rocks

**NATURALISTIC ACTIVITY:**  In the science center have a variety of rocks, magnifiers, and books about rocks available for the children to explore and make observations. The books can be used to identify rocks.

**INFORMAL ACTIVITY:**  When the children begin to examine the rocks, ask, "What color, shape, size rocks do you have? Are any of the rocks the same? How are the rocks alike? How are they different?"

**STRUCTURED ACTIVITY:**

**CONCEPT:**  There are many kinds of rocks.

**OBJECTIVES:**  Observe different types of rocks. Classify rocks in different ways.

**MATERIALS:**  An egg carton for each child or group, small labels that can be glued on the box, pencils or pens, a handful of rocks.

**PROCEDURE:**  Show the children the rocks in your hand. Ask the children, WHAT ARE THESE, AND WHERE ARE THEY FOUND? Give each small group of children a few rocks, and encourage them to develop classification schemes for them, such as flat, speckled, animal-shaped. Younger children will notice size and color first, then shape and the way the rock feels. Have the children develop labels for the categories.

Take the children to any place where there are rocks. Set a generous time limit, and have them search for different types of rocks to fill their egg cartons. Then, have the children share and classify what they have found. Use labels to identify rocks in the egg carton collections (speckled, round, and so on).

**EXTENSION:**  1.  Older children are able to compare rock characteristics with pictures in rock identification handbooks.
2.  Use various rocks to create a rock collage.
3.  Read *Sylvester and the Magic Pebble* by William Steig. A round red pebble makes a nice prop.

## Thinking Like a Geologist

**CONCEPT:**  Some rocks are harder than other rocks.

**OBJECTIVE:**  Examine rocks and minerals to determine how hard they are. Classify rocks by characteristics.

**MATERIALS:**  An assortment of rocks (a rock and mineral set, if possible), roofing nails, pennies.

**PROCEDURE:**  Give groups of children an assortment of rocks to observe. After they have had time to observe the rocks, ask, CAN YOU SCRATCH ANY OF THE ROCKS WITH YOUR FINGERNAIL? As they notice a difference in rocks, ask, CAN SOME ROCKS BE SCRATCHED IN THIS WAY? (Yes.) WHAT ELSE COULD YOU USE TO SCRATCH ROCKS?

After children try to scratch rocks with different objects such as the penny and fingernail, explain that finding out if a rock crumbles easily is one of the things a **geologist** does. (Even though children may not remember the term, the labeling is important.)

Tell the children that they are going to think like a geologist and determine how hard a rock is. Make a list of ways that the children will test the rocks. For example:

- can be rubbed off on fingers
- can be scratched with fingernail
- can be scratched with a penny
- hard to scratch

Have the children test the rocks and place them with the statement that best describes the rock. Ask, WHICH ROCKS DO YOU THINK ARE THE HARDEST? (Those that are hard to scratch; Figure 36–1.)

(*continued*)

**Figure 36–1** Labeling rocks by hardness.

Then, take the children outside to see which rocks can be used to draw streaks or lines on the sidewalk. Children might even see distinctive colors. Ask, WHAT COLORS ARE THE STREAKS? Have children compare the colors in the rocks with the colors of the streaks. Ask, CAN WE CLASSIFY ROCKS IN THIS WAY? (Yes.) You may want to review some of the ways that geologists classify rocks (appearance, texture, hardness, color). Graph the findings.

**EXTENSION:** As children wash their hands, compare wet and dry rocks. What differences do they notice? Geologists use hardness and streak tests to identify minerals. Introduce the term *minerals* when children notice bits of color in the rocks. Explain that rocks are made up of many different ingredients (minerals).

## Exploring Cookies

**CONCEPT:**  Rocks are formed in different ways.

**OBJECTIVE:**  Identify similarities between rocks and cookies. Stimulate curiosity about earth processes.

**MATERIALS:**  Oatmeal chocolate chip cookie recipe on chart and on index cards, ingredients for making cookies (two cookies for each child).

**PROCEDURE:**  Pass out recipe cards to the small groups. Show the children what the various ingredients look like as you discuss those used in making oatmeal chocolate chip cookies. Give each small group of children samples of the cookie ingredients. Bake the cookies. Then, give each child two cookies (one to examine and one to eat).

Have the children explore the cookie and compare the ingredients and the information on the recipe card with the final product. Ask, CAN YOU SEE THE INGREDIENTS? (Some of them.) WHICH INGREDIENTS DO YOU SEE? CAN YOU TASTE ANY OF THE INGREDIENTS? (Figure 36–2.) DO THE INGREDIENTS LOOK THE SAME? (No, some have changed.) Once the children recognize that some ingredients are still recognizable after baking and some are no longer in the same state, ask, IN WHAT WAY HAVE THEY CHANGED? (Melted, dissolved, and so on.) WHAT CHANGED THE INGREDIENTS? (Mixing, pressing, heat.) Discuss heat and chemical changes, if appropriate.

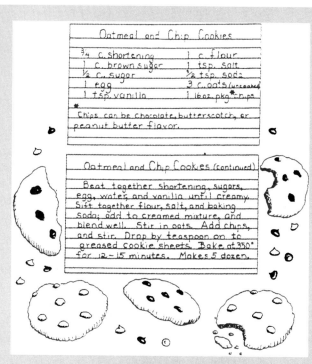

**Figure 36–2** "Compare the ingredients for making cookies with the cookies."

Give children an assortment of rocks, and tell them that rocks have ingredients, too. The earth acts like a baker and turns ingredients into rocks. (Rock ingredients, *minerals*, are turned into rock by pressure, heat, and moving around.) Let children handle mineral samples and try to find evidence of these samples in the rocks.

**EXTENSION:** Take a rock field trip. Have each child find an egg-sized rock. Wrap the rock in cloth and have an adult hit it with a hammer. Use hand lenses to examine the pieces of broken rock. Ask, HOW MANY PIECES OF ROCK ARE THERE NOW? Have the children explore the shape, size, and color of the fragments and describe the inside and outside appearance of the rock. The inside of a dull-looking rock is usually filled with pattern, texture, and color. Use a small light to help compare the shine and luster of various rocks. Have the children draw or color what they see through the hand lens.

## HOW ROCKS ARE FORMED

Primary students commonly believe that the ground is composed mostly of soil and that rocks are only what they can hold and carry in their hands. Through pictures and discussion of mountains, cliffs, and deserts, help students understand the great variety, size, and distribution of rocks on and in the earth. Most of the earth's crust is solid rock, a nonliving material made of different kinds of minerals. The forces that make the major types of rock are too complex for lower-level primary grades to understand. However, you may want to introduce upper-level children to a few examples that simulate the basic ways that rocks are formed.

You can make the study of rocks more meaningful for your students if you know the basic way rocks are formed and a few common examples of each.

## Igneous Rocks

**Igneous rocks** are formed through the cooling of magma or lava. Examples of igneous rocks formed by the rapid cooling of surface lava are pumice, obsidian, and basalt. Granite is the most common example of slow, below-surface cooling of molten rock. Refer to the igneous rock fudge cooking experience (Subject Integrations, later in this unit).

## Sedimentary Rocks

These rocks are formed from eroded rocks, sand, clay, silt, pebbles, and other stones. Compressed skeletons, shells, and dissolved chemicals also form **sedimentary rocks**. These rocks are usually deposited in layers and are compacted and cemented by the pressure of the overlying sediments. Examples of sedimentary rocks are conglomerate, sandstone, shale, and limestone. **Fossils** are frequently found in sedimentary rock. Refer to the "pudding stone" cooking experience (described in Subject Integrations).

## Metamorphic Rocks

The term *metamorphic* means "changed in form." **Metamorphic rocks** are formed when sedimentary and igneous rocks are completely changed in form through pressure and heat. For example, limestone becomes marble, shale becomes slate, and sandstone may become quartzite. These rocks are harder than most rocks.

Show the effect of pressure by pressing a bag of marshmallows or several spongy rubber balls under books on a flat surface. Have the children describe the change in the physical appearance of the objects, and relate the change to the metamorphic process.

To simulate the effect of heat on the rocks, melt several different colored marshmallows together into one interlocking marshmallow. Have children observe and describe the changes.

## SUBJECT INTEGRATIONS

### Rocks and Science

1. *Smooth rocks.* Additional ideas about rocks and their formation can be introduced by walking along a beach or stream and observing the smooth stones at the bottom of the stream or on the shore. Children can collect rocks and begin to draw comparisons about what makes the rocks smooth. Have them watch the action of the waves or stream. Ask, "What is happening?" Compare using sandpaper with the action of sand against the rocks.

2. Many children may not make the connection between rocks and sand as broken pieces of rock (sand also contains bits of broken and worn-down sea shells). Have students use hand lenses to examine and compare grains of sand and rocks.

3. *Sand from rocks.* Have children rub two rocks together to simulate wear on them. Discuss how this wear might take place in nature (water current, waterfalls, wind, and so on).

### Rocks and Art

1. *Rock gardens.* Construct small rock gardens. Use pictures of Japanese gardens as inspiration.

2. *Rock necklaces.* Glue yarn to the back of flat, round rocks to make necklaces.

3. *Vegetable fossils.* Make mold fossils of vegetables.

### Rocks and Language Arts and Reading

1. *Storybooks.* Read *Stone Soup* (Paterson, 1981) and make vegetable soup. See Unit 26 for suggestions.

2. *Rock-shaped book.* Make rock-shaped covers for this bookmaking activity from brown construction paper. Inside pages should also be in the shape of the rock cover. Punch two holes in the top of the book, and fasten with metal rings or yarn. You may want to start the book with phrases like "A rock is a _____" (Figure 36–3).

**Figure 36–3** "Record observations in your rock-shaped book."

3. *My rock.* Have each child select a rock and describe it. The children can record or dictate descriptions. Encourage them by asking, "What does your rock feel like? Does your rock have a smell?" Stimulate thinking with, "My rock is as sparkly as a _____." Then have children write a biography of their rock.

## Rocks and Math

1. *Ordering rocks.* Put rocks in order of size, shape, weight, and color, then from smoothest to roughest. Try doing this activity blindfolded.

2. *Weighing rocks.* Use a small balance to weigh rocks. Predict which rocks are the heaviest.

3. *Flannelboard rocks.* Make flannelboard rock shapes for math problem solving. Different sizes, colors, and shapes can be put in order, organized into patterns, sorted, counted, added, and subtracted.

4. *Rock jar.* Fill a jar with rocks, and have the children estimate how many rocks are in the jar. Verify the number of rocks in the jar by counting by groups of 10.

5. *Dinosaur rocks.* Have children predict the number of rocks needed to build a dinosaur cave. Children can determine the needs of a dinosaur, such as enough rocks to shelter it and keep larger dinosaurs out of the cave.

## Rocks and Cooking Experiences

1. *Igneous rock fudge.* After showing children pictures of volcanoes, find out what children know about them. Have pumice available for the children to examine. Some children might notice that the stone is light and has air bubble spaces. Explain that igneous means fire and that the pumice stone is an igneous rock that was once hot, liquid iron in a volcano that hardened as it cooled.

   To illustrate how lava cools, make fudge in a medium-sized pan. Mix ⅓ cup water, 1 cup sugar, a pinch of salt, 3 tablespoons of cocoa, and 1 teaspoon of vanilla. Boil the mixture for three minutes and then cool in two different ways. To cool the fudge fast and produce a shiny, smooth surface (black glassy obsidian is a good example), pour some of the mixture into a pie plate that is resting in a bowl of ice. For rough and lumpy granite-like fudge, cool at room temperature in another pie pan. Ask, "Which way do you think the piece of granite was cooled?"

2. *Pudding stones.* To illustrate conglomerate rock called pudding stone, have the children mix papier-mâché and add various types of gravel and weathered stones to the mixture (Figure 36–4). Or, make pudding and add raisins and other food bits for a tasty pudding stone snack.

**Figure 36–4** Making a conglomerate rock.

## Rocks and Social Studies

1. *Geologist.* Have a geologist visit the class and discuss his or her job and the tools that are used on the job.

2. *Mapping.* Group the children into pairs and allow them to hunt for rocks on the playground. When they return to the classroom, have each pair draw a map of where their rocks were found. Discuss each map, focusing on prominent land features in each area.

# FOSSILS

Children will not be able to grasp the enormous time spans represented in the lessons about fossils and dinosaurs. It is most important that they understand that the dinosaurs existed long before humans; cartoon depictions of cave dwellers and dinosaurs are inaccurate.

Fossils can be shells and bones, prints of leaves, shells, footprints, trees that have turned to stone, or insects that were trapped in tree sap. Discuss how the fossils might have been formed and whether they came from a plant or an animal. Ask, "What living things from the past can be identified by fossils?"

One way to illustrate this is to have students wear old shoes and go outside to make footprints in mud or damp sand. Have various students walk, jump, and so on and ask other students to figure out from the prints how each person was moving.

Fossils are most likely to be found in sedimentary rock. One way children can recognize this kind of rock is that it crumbles or scratches fairly easily and may have a smell when it gets wet. To make a fossil, give the children a few leaves and have them press them into clay. Remove the leaf and observe the imprint (Figure 36–5). Encourage the children to match the various leaves with the imprint that was made.

# SOIL SAMPLES

Visiting an outdoor study site on a regular basis will encourage children to observe the properties and changes in earth materials and vegetation. As children collect

**Figure 36–5** Making a mold fossil.

rocks and observe the vegetation, they will become aware that soil varies in texture, color, and fertility from place to place. The study site is also a good place to observe erosion and the effect of seasonal changes on the ground.

If the weather permits, take children outside to gather soil samples from different areas of the study site. Using a garden trowel, place the soil samples in separate plastic containers and label the containers. Of course, you want to be sure there is no broken glass or other dangerous materials in the ground.

After initial observations at the study site, cover several of the classroom tables with newspapers and distribute hand lenses for children to gain a close-up look at the small rocks, soils, and grains of sand that may be in the soil. After the children have had time to explore, ask them to describe the soil. Encourage them to smell the soil and look for color and other properties. As the children describe the soil, record their responses on a chart. Encourage further observations by asking, "Is your sample wet or dry? Do you see any plants or bugs?" Children will begin to compare areas of the study sites and generate more questions.

After the students have had time to explore the study site's soil, continue the observations with a lesson on soil composition. Ask, "What do you think is in soil?" Children begin to understand that soil is made of broken and pulverized bits of rock and organic matter, such as decayed leaves and plants and the remains of animals, which provide the nutrients necessary for plant growth.

Half fill a jar with water, then spoon in soil that has a good mixture of humus, clay, sand, and gravel (you may need to add some of these ingredients). Shake the jar well, then set it on a table for children to observe the layers of materials as they settle. As the soil settles, examine the layers with a hand lens. Discuss the color and what might be in each layer, such as bits of gravel, some sand, fine pieces of rock that form, mud and clay, and plant and insect parts. Children will enjoy exploring the soil samples used in the demonstration. Return to the question, "What do you think is in soil?"

Take a second trip to the outdoor study site. Spread the children out around the site. Use plastic hoops (sorting or hula) to create defined observation areas. Give each child a magnifier. Have the children observe the area and draw and/or describe the soil, vegetation, and insects within the space. After returning to the classroom compare and then graph the results.

Revisit the study site before and after a rain shower. Notice how the soil types change when wet. As the children walk along, ask, "How does the hard-packed soil feel as you walk on it? How does the loose soil on the baseball field feel? How do you think the loose soil will feel after a rain?"

All living things depend in some part on soil for their food. People use soil for many purposes, including growing food and building homes. Encourage children to continue their soil explorations and begin to generate a list and picture collage of the uses of soil. As a culminating experience, either visit your local cooperative extension office or invite a staff member to visit the class and discuss soil testing.

## Weather

Lessons on weather and seasons are especially appropriate for primary age children. In addition to discussing and studying the daily weather, take the children on a field trip to observe weather equipment in action. Local trip opportunities might include airports, television and radio stations, or high-school or college weather stations. Visiting a weather station familiarizes children with the instruments and information they will study as they follow and record changes in weather and differences in seasons. Include the construction of weather instruments, graphing, storybooks, subject integrations, and hands-on experiences as you teach children about weather.

Temperature, rain, and snow tend to be high, medium, and low in the same months every year. Have children plot patterns of the freezing of water, melting of ice, and disappearance of water on cold surfaces. The following lessons in temperature and sunlight provide an opportunity for children to begin correlating changes in daily temperature with seasons.

## A Lesson on Temperature

Begin a discussion of temperature by asking children to explain how they know if it is hot or cold outside. After discussing observations, introduce the idea of using a thermometer as a way of measuring temperature. Distribute thermometers to pairs or small groups to examine, and have the children record their observations. Ask, "What happens when you hold the thermometer between your hands for a minute? Is the temperature different when you hold the thermometer at the base of the bulb?" And, "What do you think will happen if you put the thermometer in a glass of cold water? What will happen if you put the thermometer in a glass of hot water?"

Provide the groups with cups of hot and cold water, and let them investigate what will happen when the thermometers are placed in the cups of water. Have the children keep a record of their investigations and share results with other groups. Keeping records helps children to articulate their observations about how the thermometer works.

Pairs or groups of children will enjoy checking and recording temperature readings at different times of the day in a chosen location in the classroom or on the school grounds. Over a period of days, they can compare the pattern that emerges and make predictions. Because the goal of this lesson is for children to be aware that the temperature varies at different times of the day and because thermometers can be difficult to read, temperature need not be measured precisely.

Keep a class temperature chart so that the patterns seen over weeks and months can be related to the changing seasons. Identify clothing, activities, and food that are associated with each season. Include them on the temperature chart. A large paper body figure, such as those described in Unit 38, could be clothed to reflect seasonal changes.

Children may enjoy brainstorming words associated with each season and creating a "Hot and Cold" book following a pattern such as "as hot as _____" or "as cold as _____." Encourage the sensory aspect of the seasons by discussing seasonal smells, sounds, and tastes. One way to do this is by collecting pictures from magazines that represent the sights, sounds, tastes, and activities of the season and displaying them as posters. A touch board made from objects found in the seasons provides an interesting class display. Refer to the temperature activity in Unit 35.

## Extending the Concept

To extend the concept, ask: "Do you think shadows affect temperature? How could you test your idea? Record what happens." To continue the investigation of factors that can affect an object's temperature, such as color, ask, "Do you think there will be a difference between a thermometer placed in a dark-colored envelope and one placed in a light-colored envelope? Why do you think so?" Challenge children to find the hottest and coldest location in the classroom or on the playground, and ask them to give reasons for the varying temperatures. Encourage children to design ways to test different ideas.

In the same way, the amount of sunlight on the same day each month can be recorded. Children can observe and record the daylight or dark when they come to school, eat supper, or go to bed. Discuss how the length of days affects our lives. As the year progresses, children will begin to correlate the changes in daily temperature and sunlight with the seasons.

To extend the concept of seasons, choose a tree from either the playground or an adjacent area and conduct observations periodically throughout the year. Have the children work in pairs using a digital video camera or a camera that utilizes still shots. The observations should include size of the tree, colors of the bark and the leaves, amount of leaves (lots, few, etc.), smell of leaves, and feel of leaves. Play back the video (or show the series of still shots) and have the children discuss the changes in the tree over the year and the seasons associated with the different observation times.

## A Thermometer Table

Construct a thermometer table by having the children collect a variety of thermometers to compare and explore, such as oven thermometers, indoor-outdoor thermometers, and the many kinds of thermometers used to measure body temperature.

## A Party for All Seasons

At the beginning or the end of each season, children may want to have a season party. Planning groups will enjoy designing and creating the many aspects of the season party. The party could include single-portion recipes and samples of seasonal food, aromatic jars, touch boxes, and music and pantomime games of the indoor and outdoor activities typically done in each season. Children will enjoy painting murals and pictures of seasonal activities and constructing props for the activities.

## WATER

*Evaporation* and *condensation* mean disappear and reappear. Years before children begin to understand that evaporating water that seems to disappear is still present in the form of small molecules (water vapor), they can observe the process and should be provided many opportunities to explore the phenomena. The following lesson, "Wet Spots," is an example that allows children to see the effect of the science concept.

The process of evaporating water spots will reinforce the NSES content standard (NRC, 1996) of inquiry as well as the content of changes in matter. Mr. Wang makes a large wet spot on the chalkboard and draws a circle around it every minute. As the water disappears slowly, a series of chalk circles are left on the board. Mr. Wang asks the child, "How could you evaporate the water more quickly?" George says, "Blow on it." Sarah wants to use a blow dryer. Some children want to shine a light on it. Mr. Wang encourages the children to try all of their suggestions, one variable at a time.

The wet spots lesson continues the next day with more questions. Children want to know if the time of day makes a difference and whether cold or hot water would evaporate faster. Some even began to invent ways to evaporate the water spot without touching it. Mr. Wang challenges the children to find a way to preserve a wet spot for a long time. Refer to Unit 33 for more ideas for more investigations.

## Puddle Pictures

Ask, "What happens to puddles on warm sunny days?" Have children use a paintbrush to make a picture on the sidewalk. Carefully trace around the puddle with side-walk chalk to create a picture. Ask, "How did the water in your puddle picture change? Where do you think the water goes when it dries?" And, "What does it change into?" Have the children record the progress of the evaporating puddle on paper and with different colored chalk to mark the progress of the disappearing puddle. Ask, "What caused the water to change into water vapor?"

Relate this experience to observations of the drying process in the home. Have the children predict the fastest way to dry a shirt: lay it flat, hang it on a clothesline, or crumple it up in a bundle? Ask, "How can you be sure the water goes into the air?" Help children design an investigation that reduces a shirt's (or paper towel's) exposure to the air. Develop the idea that when water dries, it evaporates, or changes into a gas called water vapor.

Ask children to look for examples of water changing from water vapor back into a liquid such as dew on the grass, frost on the window, and fog or steam on the mirror.

Once children have observed examples of evaporation and have begun to understand the role of heat, it is time to focus on examples of condensation. Begin the experience by asking the children to predict what they think happens when cold air and hot air collide. After predictions are made, pour very hot water into a large-mouth glass jar. Make a pocket out of tin foil and insert it into the mouth of the jar. Put ice cubes into the pocket. Have the children observe and explain what they think happened.

# SPACE SCIENCE

Space travel, the moon, sun, and stars intrigue young children. They will not be able to comprehend the vastness of space or the enormity of the sun, moon, and earth, yet there are aspects of space science that they can readily observe.

The sun is the most observable object in the sky. (CAUTION: Children should never look directly into the sun.) Ask, "On what side of the building does the sun shine in the morning?" Then, "On what side of the building does the sun shine when we leave for the day?" Take the children for a walk around the building, and note where the sun's rays are shining at different times of the day. Draw these changes on a chart. Ask, "Why do you think that the sun's rays shine in different places?"

Take the children outside of the building in the morning, and have them draw the school building and the location of the sun. Begin a bulletin board mural. Make the school building and surrounding features, and have the children place a construction paper sun where it belongs in the morning sky. Then make paper sun rays shining on the school building.

Shadow play is natural for young children as they learn about the sun. Draw chalk outlines of the shadows cast, and then try casting shadows on a cloudy day. Ask, "Do you have a shadow today? Why not?" Discuss the color of the sun and the moon. Ask, "Is the moon the same color every night? Can you see the moon during the day?" (Yes.) Many children think that the moon goes to bed at night. Help them speculate on why the moon does not look as bright during the day.

If children think that the stars are held up with tape, do not discourage them. They are in good intellectual company. Aristotle, for example, thought that stars were embedded in concentric crystalline spheres. A primary age child cannot understand interstellar concepts. Help the child notice that things in the sky look different at various times of the day and night.

## Moon Patterns

The child's concept and grasp of the universe grows slowly over time. Ideas about light and sight are prerequisites to understanding the night sky. The priority in space-related lessons for young children is on describing what the sky looks like and identifying changes in shape and movement. The moon looks different every day and makes an ideal subject for observing and comparing.

Children can easily observe the pattern that the moon makes as it goes from one full moon to the next. Since moon phases appear at regular intervals, they

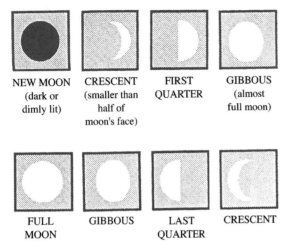

| NEW MOON (dark or dimly lit) | CRESCENT (smaller than half of moon's face) | FIRST QUARTER | GIBBOUS (almost full moon) |

| FULL MOON | GIBBOUS | LAST QUARTER | CRESCENT |

**Figure 36–6** The phases of the moon.

can serve as a natural clock. It is not as important that children remember the names of the phases of the moon as that they see the pattern of change in the sky. As children record the differences that they see, they should describe and compare the various shapes the moon seems to have (Figure 36–6). The observations can be recorded in special moon watch books made of construction paper and writing paper in the shape of the moon.

## The Dos and Don'ts of Using Binoculars

This is an ideal time to introduce the children to binoculars and telescopes. By third grade, children should know that binoculars and telescopes magnify the appearance of objects in the sky. The craters, mountains, and other features on the moon's surface will provide a source of much discussion and imagination. Binoculars work especially well with young children.

The following are some binocular dos and don'ts: Do *not* try to find an object with the binoculars held up to your eyes. *Do* look at the object you want to look at, and *then* bring the binoculars up to your eyes. This will work better if you focus the binoculars first. To do this, look at an object, bring the binoculars up to your eyes, and then focus until the object is clear. Caution children to *never* look at the sun with a pair of binoculars or a telescope—blindness could be the result.

## Craters of the Moon

As children look at the moon more closely and more often, they will begin to notice the many interesting features that can be seen by the naked eye or with binoculars. Take advantage of children's natural interest in the night sky, and let them record and draw their observations in greater detail.

Children will enjoy creating a lunar landscape. This can be done in the sand table by dropping different size balls into very wet sand. If a sand table is not available, a box of sand makes a good substitute. The children can compare the splatter marks extending from the impression made from the ball as it hits the sand to similar marks seen on the moon. Have the children compare the drawing that they have made of their moon observations with the sand craters they have made.

Features of the moon are ideal for simulation with clay and other sculpting materials. Murals, paintings, and other art forms provide reinforcement for the children's observations. If the child does not remember how a feature looks or her drawing is not as clear as she wants it to be, she can easily look at the moon the next night.

Observing the moon cycle will stimulate children's natural curiosity. They will want to know more about the night sky. There are a variety of things in the sky that can be seen at night. Planets, comets, meteors, stars, satellites, and airplanes fill the sky. The familiar patterns of stars called **constellations** will provide much excitement. Keep in mind that it is not important for children to know the names of the constellations. They need to be aware that the pattern of stars stays the same as it appears to move across the sky. This movement is another pattern of movement in the sky that is readily observed.

## SUMMARY

Rocks and minerals are not simply objects lying on the ground; they are part of the continually changing process of the earth. As children study earth science topics such as rocks, minerals, weather, and space, they study the conditions and forces that affect their planet. An early introduction to these difficult concepts exposes children to their world and helps ready them for future understanding.

## KEY TERMS

| | | |
|---|---|---|
| atmosphere | fossils | minerals |
| condensation | geologist | sedimentary rocks |
| constellations | igneous rocks | weather |
| evaporation | metamorphic rocks | |

## SUGGESTED ACTIVITIES

1. Recall your rock collecting experiences in elementary school. Where did you find your rocks? Did you display your rocks? Did you know what your rocks were or how they were formed? What did you learn when you were collecting? What educational value do you attribute to making collections?

2. Create your own teaching web. Select lessons from the rock unit, and design a unit that is appropriate for a group of children you are teaching. You should add ideas to the ones presented. Teach the lesson to children, and record your observations for class discussion.

3. Which process skills are used in the rock unit? Give an example of each skill and when it was used. Can you think of additional ways to integrate process skills into the unit on rocks?

4. Present a lesson on weather to primary age children. What types of learning experiences will you design for your students? How do you plan to apply what you know about Piaget's theory of development to the teaching of weather?

5. Examine a teacher's edition of an elementary school science textbook. Identify a lesson on rocks and one on weather. Do you agree with the way the lesson is presented? Explain why or why not. How would you teach the lesson?

6. Select an earth science topic and concept and prepare a learning cycle lesson to teach that idea. Teach it to children.

7. Imagine that your class has just returned from collecting rocks. What types of questions will you ask to help students generate a list of characteristics that can be used to classify rocks into different groups? Your questions could take a variety of forms. Use your question list with children, and note the interactions for class discussion.

8. Locate software that is available at your school or in your school system that teaches or reinforces earth or space science concepts. Try the software yourself and select a program to present to the class, such as the following. You may also access the Online Companion to find relevant links to websites.

   ■ *EcoAdventures in the Rainforest* (grades 3–up; San Diego, CA: Chariot)

   ■ *Eyewitness References: Encyclopedia of Space and the Universe* (ages 8+; London: Dorling Kindersley)

   ■ *Magic School Bus: Earth* (ages 6–10; Redmond, WA: Microsoft)

   ■ *Magic School Bus: Solar System* (ages 6–10; Redmond, WA: Microsoft)

   ■ *National Geographic CDs for Educators: Earth* (pre-K–3; Washington, DC: National Geographic)

   ■ *National Geographic CDs for Educators: Exploring the Solar System and Beyond* (pre-K–3; Washington, DC: National Geographic)

   ■ *National Geographic CDs for Educators: Seasons* (pre-K–3; Washington, DC: National Geographic)

   ■ *Night Sky Interactive* (ages 8+; Escondido, CA: Beachware)

   ■ *Sammy's Science House* (pre-K–2; Redmond, WA: Edmark)

## REVIEW

**A.** What is the purpose of introducing young children to earth science concepts?

**B.** List three earth and space science concepts appropriate for primary age children and create a planning web for teaching at least one of these concepts.

## REFERENCES

National Research Council. (1996). *National science education standards.* Washington, DC: National Academies Press.

Paterson, D. (1981). *Stone soup.* Mahwah, NJ: Troll Associates.

Steig, W. (1973). *Sylvester and the magic pebble.* New York: Simon & Schuster.

## FURTHER READING AND RESOURCES

American Association for the Advancement of Science (AAAS). (2007). *Atlas of science literacy: Project 2061* (Vol. 2). Washington, DC: Author.

Ashbrook, P. (2006). Roll with it. *Science & Children, 43*(8), 16–18.

Brainard, A. H., & Wrubel, D. H. (1995). *Through the rainbow: Children, science, and literature.* Washington, DC: Council for Elementary Science International.

Brummet, D. C., Lind, K. K., Barman, C. R., DiSpezio, M. A., & Ostlund, K. L. (1995). *Destinations in science.* Menlo Park, CA: Addison-Wesley.

Carin, A. A., Bass, J. E., & Contant, T. L. (2005). *Activities for teaching science as inquiry* (6th ed.). Upper Saddle River, NJ: Prentice-Hall.

Chalufour, I., & Worth, K. (2005). *Exploring water with young children.* St. Paul, MN: Redleaf Press.

Chessin, D. (2007). Simple machine science centers. *Science & Children, 44*(6), 36–41.

Dighe, J. (1993). Children and the earth. *Young Children, 48*(3), 58–63.

Eichinger, J. (2004). *Activities for integrating science and mathematics, K–8* (2nd ed.). Upper Saddle River, NJ: Prentice-Hall.

Harlan, J., & Rivkin, M. (2003). *Science experiences for the early childhood years: An integrated affective approach.* Upper Saddle River, NJ: Pearson-Merrill/Prentice-Hall.

Herman, M. L., Passineau, J. F., Schimpf, A. L., & Treuer, P. (1991). *Teaching kids to love the earth.* Duluth, MN: Pfeifer-Hamilton.

Inventor's toolbox: The elements of machines. Retrieved August 22, 2008, from http://www.mos.org/sln/Leonardo/InventorsToolbox.html

Kepler, L. (1996). *Windowsill science centers.* New York: Scholastic.

Lind, K. K. (1991). *Water, stones, and fossil bones.* Washington, DC: National Science Teachers Association.

Lowery, L. (Ed.). (1997). *Pathways to the science standards.* Arlington, VA: National Teachers Association.

McBiles, J. L. (1985). *Mining, minerals, and me.* Nashua, NH: Delta Education.

McCormack, A. (1979). *Outdoor areas as learning laboratories* (Council for Elementary Science International Sourcebook). Columbus, OH: SMEAC Information Reference Center.

Measurement [Focus issue]. (2006). *Science & Children, 44*(2).

Perez, J. (1988). *Explore and experiment.* Bridgeport, CT: First Teacher Press.

Peters, J. M., & Gega, P. C. (2002). *Science in elementary education.* Upper Saddle River, NJ: Merrill.

Raines, S. C. (1994). *450 More story s-t-r-e-t-c-h-e-r-s for the primary grades.* Mt. Rainier, MD: Gryphon House.

Raines, S. C., & Canady, R. J. (1992). *Story s-t-r-e-t-c-h-e-r-s for the primary grades.* Mt. Rainier, MD: Gryphon House.

Renner, J. W., & Marek, E. A. (1988). *The learning cycle and elementary school science teaching.* Portsmouth, NH: Heinemann.

Sarow, G. A. (2001). Miniature sleds, go, go, go! (2001). *Science & Children, 39*(3), 16–21.

Sheehan, K., & Waidner, M. (2000). *Earth child 2000.* Tulsa, OK: Council Oak Books.

Sheehan, T. F. (2006). *City science series: Playground science.* Vero Beach, FL: Rourke.

Spizman, R. F., & Garber, M. (1991). *What on earth can you do with kids?* Carthage, IL: Good Apple.

Victor, E., & Kellough, R. D. (2003). *Science K–8, An integrated approach.* Upper Saddle River, NJ: Prentice-Hall.

Williams, R. A., Rockwell, R. E., & Sherwood, E. A. (1987). *Mudpies to magnets.* Mt. Rainier, MD: Gryphon House.

# Unit 37

# Environmental Awareness

## OBJECTIVES

After reading this unit, you should be able to:

- Design environmental awareness investigations for primary age children.
- Develop an understanding of environmental concepts appropriate for primary age children.
- Develop structured and unstructured environmental learning experiences for primary age children.

In the past, environmental science topics have been included with other earth and space science topics. The *National Science Education Standards* (NRC, 1996) identified these topics with the standard for science in personal and social perspectives. Under this standard, children are expected to develop an understanding of the characteristics and changes in populations, types of resources, changes in the environment, and science and technology in local settings. A major role of the teacher in the primary grades is to guide children in investigating and gaining an understanding of the characteristics and changes within their local and regional population, resources available in our world, and how our decisions make an impact on the availability of those resources.

## CONCEPTS AND APPROACHES

- **Environments** are the space, conditions, and factors that affect an individual's ability to survive.

- **Resources** include anything that can be used to fill a need. Natural resources include coal, water, and so on.
- **Recycling** is the process of recovering used materials.

Environmental investigations are a natural way for children to enjoy and explore the world around them. When children explore the environment, they will engage in active participation and cooperation as they begin developing their own understanding. Experiences are often free or inexpensive and readily accessible to a variety of audiences and learning styles.

The suggestions and lessons in this section are based on one or more of the three common approaches to environmental education outlined by Dighe (1993):

1. the *awareness* approach focuses on children's feelings and appreciation of the world around them;

2. the *environmental concept* approach introduces ideas that will lead to learning about environmental concerns;

3. the ***conservation*** approach provides opportunities for children to take action and see a result of that action.

The results of these lessons need to be observable and should not be too dramatic or controversial. To be effective, children need to see a direct result of their actions. For example, children can see a direct result of picking up trash or monitoring use of lights in the room.

To introduce the word *environment*, use a brainstorming approach: Write the word on the chalkboard and ask, "What do you think the word *environment* means?" List the ideas named by the children, and keep that list posted. Children may want to modify the list as their awareness of the environment progresses. Periodically, have the children return to modify the list as meaning develops.

## WATER

### Water Changes the Earth

Water is everywhere. It flows in rivers and streams and makes up the oceans that cover the earth's surface. Draw children's attention to the bodies of water around them—rivers, lakes, oceans, and the like. Show pictures of different bodies of water, and discuss experiences.

Water is the single most important force that shapes the surface of the earth. Water from melting glaciers, rain, and snow forms streams and rivers and moves sand, which gradually wears away mountains and carves hills and valleys. To explore the concept of **erosion**, complete the following activity.

Take a class walk, and look for evidence of water changing the surface of the earth. Discuss how these changes can be beneficial or harmful.

## ACTIVITIES

### Water Changes

**CONCEPT:** Water changes the face of the earth.

**OBJECTIVES:** Observe and record changes in the soil as a result of moving water.

**MATERIALS:** Rocks, soil, liter soda bottles filled with water, half-gallon paper milk cartons, trays, scissors or knives.

**PROCEDURE:** Divide children into pairs. Give each pair a milk carton, some soil and rocks, a liter soda bottle, a tray, and a pair of scissors. Have the children cut the panel of the milk carton under the spout (Figure 37–1). Fill the carton three-fourths full with soil and rocks. Put the carton in the tray and place a rock under one end of the carton. Make a small channel for a stream to flow. Ask the children, WHAT WILL HAPPEN WHEN YOU POUR WATER IN THE CHANNEL? One of the pair should slowly pour the water in the higher end of the tray. The other partner should observe and record what happens through writing or drawing. Ask the children, WHAT HAPPENED WHEN YOU POURED WATER INTO THE CHANNEL? After the children have discussed their observations ask, WHAT DO YOU THINK WILL HAPPEN IF WE ADD A SMALL AMOUNT OF ROCKS AND GRAVEL TO THE CHANNEL?

**EXTENSION:** 1. Find a river or stream and have the children take samples of muddy water so they can observe the sediment when it settles.

**Figure 37–1** Water changes the face of the earth.

## Using Water

Living things—people, plants, and animals—consist mainly of water and must have it to live. In fact, water is more important for survival than food. Ask children to name some of the ways they use water. Encourage responses by asking, "What are some other ways people use water? Why is water important to business? To people who fish or raise farm animals?" Begin a chart to record children's responses to the ways living things use water. Add to the chart throughout the lesson as other uses of water are discussed.

After completing the following activity, it will emerge that the school depends on water in many ways. Children may appreciate its availability and how difficult life would be without such access to water. Encourage children to draw or cut out pictures of water uses in their home or school.

Ask children to keep a personal "Water Use Log." They should record their use of water for one day. Begin by recording activities from the time they get up until the time they fall asleep.

## ACTIVITIES

### How Our School Uses Water

**CONCEPT:** People are dependent on water. Water is used in many ways.

**OBJECTIVES:** Investigate and record how water is used.

**MATERIALS:** Investigation journals, pens, pencils, cameras (optional).

**PROCEDURE:** Ask the children, HOW DO YOU THINK WATER IS USED AT OUR SCHOOL? Assign groups of children locations such as the kitchen, bathroom, art room, cleaning closets, and water fountains. Brainstorm with the children a list of questions to be asked to find out where the water comes from, how it is used, and how the water used could be measured. Have each group observe in its designated area and interview people who use or work in the area. After completing their research, groups should return to the classroom and a summary of the collected information should be made and discussed. Discuss questions such as: HOW MANY WATER SOURCES WERE FOUND? HOW MUCH WATER DOES THE SCHOOL USE? IS WATER WASTED? and WHAT WOULD WE DO IF WE DIDN'T HAVE WATER?

**EXTENSION:**   1.   Have children record how their family uses water during one evening.
　　　　　　　　   2.   Visit a local aquarium and see how it uses water. How is its water use similar or different from that of the school?

## Be a Water Saver

Discuss ways that people waste water, and begin a list of suggestions for how we can save water. To further the awareness of water that is sometimes wasted, suggest that children become water inspectors. Each child or team should list everything in the classroom and at home that requires water and investigate possible ways that water is wasted.

When children have completed their survey ask, "Where did you find leaky faucets? Does the toilet tank leak?" To find out if a toilet tank leaks, put food coloring in the tank, and wait 15 minutes. If the water in the bowl turns the color you put in the tank, you have a leak. Ask, "How many leaky toilets can you find? How many leaky toilets are in our school? Whom do you need to tell about your findings?"

Water wasted from leaky faucets can be measured by placing a cup under the faucet and collecting the drips (Figure 37–2). Ask, "How much water drips from the faucet in one hour?" Collect the water, and have the children think of a way to use the water instead of pouring it down the drain.

After investigating and studying water waste, children may then want to explain how they personally plan to conserve water. Children can illustrate one way they use water wisely. Have students pantomime a scene to show a way to conserve water at home or at school.

**Figure 37–2** "How much water is wasted?"

## Water for a Day

Provide each student with a paper cup and a 1-liter bottle of water. Tell them that this is their day's water supply for drinking, washing their hands, and so on. However, tell students they can flush the toilet. Tape faucets shut, and put a tub in the sink to collect water that would have gone down the drain. Have the children predict how much water they will use and record this information on a chart. At the end of the day, have them use a large graduated cylinder to measure any water that remains in their bottles and the water in the tub. Record the data on charts, and water the plants with the remaining water. Ask, "Did you use as much water as you thought you would use?"

## Is This Water Clean?

As more people use water, there has been an increase in water **pollution**. In some areas, raw sewage is pumped into rivers and streams or pesticides and fertilizers are washed from lawns and farmland into the water system, and pollutants such as metals and petroleum products may enter a river or an ocean. It is important to point out that not all pollutants are visible. Some children think that because water looks clear, it is safe to drink. Emphasize to children they should never drink water unless they know it is safe.

## Is It Safe to Drink?

Every day, wastes are being pumped into the world's water supply, but they are not always easy to detect. To develop the idea that you cannot always see pollution in water, cut off the bottom of a piece of celery, and divide the celery in half lengthwise. Fill two glasses halfway with apple juice, and add three drops of red food coloring to one and three drops of blue food coloring to the other. Place one-half of the celery in each glass, and let it stand for several hours. Take the celery out, and cut it into slices. Ask, "What color is the celery at the top of the stalk? Taste the celery. Can you taste the apple juice?" Try this investigation with food coloring and water.

After completing this activity, read the children's book *Magic School Bus: Through the Waterworks* (Cole, 1986). Take a trip to the local water treatment facility or have a representative visit your classroom. If you have the opportunity to visit a local facility, make a class book upon returning to record the children's observations. The software version of *Through the Waterworks* can be used as a center activity. Once the children have had an opportunity to explore the software, discuss how the children's trip in the software is alike or different from that which your class experienced.

## TRASH AND LITTER

### How Much Trash?

It is an understatement to say that each person throws away a lot of garbage and trash in a lifetime. To provide children with an opportunity to see how much garbage they use in one day, suggest that they place the garbage they normally toss out in a day or a week in a large **biodegradable** trash bag. They may be able to take this trash bag with them for a day. That night, sort the garbage from the trash bag into labeled categories of use such as organic, paper, plastics, metal, glass, clothes, and mysterious items that do not seem to fit the other categories. This is an especially appropriate classroom or family experience. The bags can be weighed. Most people create at least four pounds of garbage each day. Ways to recycle trash can be explored. Ask, "Which bag weighs the most? Which weighs the least?" And, "Which bag has the most trash in it? Who created most of this trash? Can any of the items be used again?"

A mathematics connection would be to have the children problem solve how much garbage a family of four produces in a day, week, or month. Have children measure the area that four pounds of trash covers. Next, have the children problem solve the area needed to store trash for a family of four for a day, week, or month.

### Keeping the Earth Clean

Make a class book of all of the things you can do to help keep the earth clean. Then take the class on a scavenger hunt. Put the children in pairs, and give each pair a short list of items to locate (newspaper, soda can, candy wrapper, etc.); see Figure 37–3. Children can draw or plot on a map where they found each item. Have the

**Figure 37–3** "Let's keep the earth clean."

children compare findings and discuss how the items might have ended up where they did.

### Litter Collage

Gather people's litter and nature's litter (fallen leaves, twigs, seed pods, and so on), and make a collage from each. Have the children write descriptions under the human litter and nature's litter. Bury some of the litter made by people and some of the litter made by nature. After a month, dig it up, and see what happened to the litter.

## RECYCLING

One of the best ways to recycle is to reuse materials instead of discarding them. Many of the items that are thrown away can be used again in the everyday classroom environment. Look around the classroom, and list the items being reused such as boxes, Styrofoam chips, sheets of paper, larger pieces of cloth, rope, yarn, string, plastic jugs, wood scraps, old magazines, rug scraps, and many more.

The symbol in Figure 37–4 means *packaged in recycled materials.* How many items in your home come in

**Figure 37–4** Packaged in recycled materials.

recycled packaging? How many items can you find in the classroom or in the school?

## Recycling Survey

Have children brainstorm a list of suggestions for a recycling survey. Ask them what they want to know about the recycling habits of their families. Items might include: "Do you recycle? If so, do you recycle aluminum cans?" Additional suggestions might be grocery bags, newspapers, magazines, plastic bottles, plastic containers, and glass bottles and jars. Ask, "Do you think recycling is important? Why or why not?" After developing the survey, have the children give their survey to their family and friends. Compile the results of the survey on a bulletin board made of a huge brown paper bag and discuss the results with the children. Ask, "Does anything about the results on our chart surprise you?"

## Save a Tree

Making paper is a fun and inexpensive way to emphasize the recycling process. Have the children save old newspapers instead of throwing them away. You will also need the following items: a large plastic pan or wading pool filled with warm water, an eggbeater, wire mesh screens, sponges, cotton cloth, and a rolling pin.

Shred paper into strips, and place them into water. Use the eggbeater, a whip, or an old blender to mash the paper into the consistency of oatmeal. For fancy paper, children can sprinkle bits of thread or flower petals into the pulp. To make the sheets of paper, spread and press the pulp onto a wire mesh screen, first dipping the screen under the pulp in the pan of water. Remove excess water from the sheet and underside of the screen.

Place the sheets of paper onto a cotton cloth, cover it with fabric, and squeeze out remaining moisture with a rolling pin. Let the sheets dry, trim them to a desirable size, and the children will be ready to write.

## Paper Logs

Paper logs can be made for holiday treats by putting 20 or 30 sheets of recycled newspaper together and adding a cup of crushed pine cones or cedar shavings between every few pages. These sections are tightly rolled and tied loosely at the end. Fill the pool with water and enough cones and chips to cover half of the water's surface. Add three cups of salt to the mixture (for extra pretty flames), and put the logs in to soak for a week. Turn them once a day. Dry the logs, and give them as presents (Figure 37–5).

Another activity that can be used to explore biodegradable and nonbiodegradable materials is creating a class **landfill**. This should be done outside in a secure area. Have the children collect a variety of paper, Styrofoam, food products (these can be obtained from the school cafeteria), soil, and water. Divide the children into small groups and give each group a large, black trash bag. They are to choose the materials they feel are most likely to break down. Have the children layer the materials in the trash bag and cover with soil. Add water so that the materials are moist but not flooded. Tape each bag shut, label the bag with the group name, and leave it for two weeks. At the end of the two weeks, open the bags and look to see what degraded and what did not. Were the children's predictions correct? This could be followed by a visit to a local landfill.

**Figure 37–5** Paper logs.

## ACTIVITIES

### Disappearing Peanuts

**CONCEPT:** Biodegradable materials can be used to complete tasks previously completed with nonbiodegradable materials.

**OBJECTIVES:** To explore how biodegradable packing peanuts change form when water is applied.

**MATERIALS:** Biodegradable peanuts in a bag marked 1, nonbiodegradable packing peanuts in a bag marked 2, water, trays.

**PROCEDURE:** Have the children take a small amount of packing peanuts from bag 1 and bag 2 and put each in a bowl. Observe the peanuts carefully in each bowl. Ask, HOW ARE THEY ALIKE AND HOW ARE THEY DIFFERENT? WHAT DO YOU THINK WILL HAPPEN WHEN YOU ADD WATER TO EACH OF THE BOWLS? Add water and observe. Ask, WHAT HAPPENED WHEN YOU ADDED WATER? ONCE YOU FINISHED USING THE PACKING PEANUTS, WHICH WOULD TAKE UP LESS SPACE IN A LANDFILL?

**EXTENSION:**  1.  Experiment with other packing materials to see if they are biodegradable.
2.  Call local moving companies and suppliers of moving materials to see if they use biodegradable materials. How does the information you collect affect your local landfill?

## SUMMARY

Environmental awareness is a growing topic in education. It is important to help children gain an understanding that there is only a finite amount of natural resources and that resources must be conserved. Children will find it empowering to know that their efforts make a difference.

## KEY TERMS

| | | |
|---|---|---|
| biodegradable | erosion | recycling |
| conservation | landfill | resources |
| environment | pollution | |

## SUGGESTED ACTIVITIES

1.  Choose one of the activities discussed in the unit and use it with children. Record your observations for class discussion.

2.  Examine a teacher's edition of an elementary science textbook. Make a list of environmental awareness topics discussed in the text. What types of hands-on activities are suggested?

3.  Select an environmental topic and concept and prepare a learning cycle lesson to teach that idea. Use the lesson with children.

4.  Locate software that is available at your school that reinforces environmental science concepts. Try the software. Record your observations for class discussion. Suggested software includes the following (you may also access

the Online Companion to find relevant links to websites).

- ■ *SimTown* (ages 8–12; Walnut Creek, CA: Maxis)

- ■ *Zurk's Alaskan Trek* (ages 6–10; Palo Alto, CA: Soleil Software)
- ■ *Zurk's Rainforest Lab* (pre-K–3; Palo Alto, CA: Soleil Software)

## REVIEW

**A.** What are the three types of basic approaches used to teach environmental education? Identify one activity in this unit for each of these approaches.

**B.** What are typical topics and concepts included in environmental awareness programs? Why should they be included?

**C.** How would you include technology in your environmental education program?

## REFERENCES

Cole, J. (1986). *Magic school bus: Through the waterworks.* New York: Scholastic Books.

Dighe, J. (1993). Children and the earth. *Young Children, 48*(3), 58–63.

National Research Council. (1996). *National science education standards.* Washington, DC: National Academies Press.

## FURTHER READING AND RESOURCES

Abruscato, J. (2004). *Teaching children science: Discovery activities and demonstrations for the elementary and middle grades* (2nd ed.). Boston: Allyn & Bacon.

American Association for the Advancement of Science (AAAS). (2007). *Atlas of science literacy: Project 2061* (Vol. 2). Washington, DC: Author.

Basile, C., & White, C. (2000). A walk in the park is just the beginning. *Dimensions, 28*(3), 3–7.

Basile, C., & White, C. (2000). Respecting living things: Environmental literacy for young children. *Early Childhood Education Journal, 28*(1), 57–61.

Benenson, G., & Neujahr, J. L. (2002). *Designed environments: Places, practices, and plans.* Portsmouth, NH: Heinemann.

Benenson, G., & Neujahr, J. L. (2002). *Mapping.* Portsmouth, NH: Heinemann.

Benenson, G., & Neujahr, J. L. (2002). *Mechanisms and other systems.* Portsmouth, NH: Heinemann.

Benenson, G., & Neujahr, J. L. (2002). *Packaging and other structures.* Portsmouth, NH: Heinemann.

Benenson, G., & Neujahr, J. L. (2002). *Signs, symbols, and codes.* Portsmouth, NH: Heinemann.

Campbell, B., & Fulton, L. (2003). *Science notebooks: Writing about inquiry.* Portsmouth, NH: Heinemann.

Carin, A. A., Bass, J. E., & Contant, T. L. (2005). *Activities for teaching science as inquiry* (6th ed.). Upper Saddle River, NJ: Prentice-Hall.

Chaille, C., & Britain, L. (2003). *Young child as scientist: A constructivist approach to early childhood science education.* Boston: Allyn & Bacon.

Chalufour, I., & Worth, K. (2003). *Discovering nature with young children.* St. Paul, MN: Redleaf Press.

Chalufour, I., & Worth, K. (2004). *Building structure with young children.* St. Paul, MN: Redleaf Press.

Grollman, S., & Worth, K. (2003). *Worms, shadows, and whirlpools: Science in the early childhood classroom.* Portsmouth, NH: Heinemann.

Haines, S. (2006). Outdoor classrooms—Planning makes perfect. *Science & Children, 43*(8), 44–48.

Harlan, J., & Rivkin, M. (2003). *Science experiences for the early childhood years: An integrated affective approach.* Upper Saddle River, NJ: Pearson-Merrill/Prentice-Hall.

Hurwitz, S. (1999, May/June). The adventure outside your classroom door. *Child Care Information Exchange, 127,* 55–57.

Hyers, K. (1999, May/June). Nurturing environmental awareness in children. *Child Care Information Exchange, 127*, 51–53.

International Technology Education Association. (2000). *Standards for technological literacy: Content for the study of technology.* Reston, VA: Author.

Kelly, A. (1999, May/June). Environmental education as a teaching tool. *Child Care Information Exchange, 127*, 58–60.

Kupetz, B. N., & Twiest, M. M. (2000). Nature, literature, and young children. *Young Children, 55*(1), 59–63.

Levine, S., & Grafton, A. (1992). *Projects for a healthy planet.* New York: Wiley.

Lind, K. K. (1991). *Water, stones, and fossils bones.* Washington, DC: National Science Teachers Association.

McMahon, M. M., O'Hara, S. P., Holliday, W. G., McCormack, B. B., & Gibson, E. M. (2000).

Curriculum with a common thread. *Science and Children, 37*(7), 30–35, 57.

National Environmental Education and Training Foundation (NEETF). (2000). *Environment-based education: Creating high performance schools and students.* Washington, DC: Author.

Saul, W., Reardon, J., Pearce, C., Dieckman, D., & Neutze, D. (2002). *Science workshop: Reading, writing, and thinking like a scientist.* Portsmouth, NH: Heinemann.

Shantal, R. (1998). Age-appropriate ecology: Are you practicing it? *Young Children, 53*(1), 70–71.

Snyder, S. L. (1999, May/June). Summertime science for school-agers. *Child Care Information Exchange, 127.*

Stephens, K. (1999, May/June). Sharing nature with children. *Child Care Information Exchange, 127.*

# Unit 38

# Health and Nutrition

## OBJECTIVES

After reading this unit, you should be able to:

- Design health and nutrition investigations for primary age children.
- Develop an understanding of health and nutrition topics that are appropriate for primary age children.
- Develop structured and unstructured learning experiences in health, nutrition, and the human body.
- Integrate science in the primary grades with other subjects.

Optimum growth and development depend on good nutrition, adequate experience, plenty of rest, and proper cleanliness. Concepts in health and **nutrition** need to be introduced to young children so they learn how to take care of their bodies and develop beneficial lifelong habits at an early age. This unit suggests experiences that help children learn about themselves through exploring the human diet, major food groups, and the human body. Lesson ideas for promoting good health habits are also presented.

The *National Science Education Standards* (NRC, 1996) suggest that children should learn to apply the "science in personal and social perspectives" standard to learning critical thinking and developing the ability to produce useful ideas. The problems that are dealt with in this standard (personal health, populations, environments, resources, and technology) are extremely complex. Reality is not simple, and it is hard for young children to see the underlying ideas. We can begin by building a base for extending children's perceptions in

later years. Appropriate concepts for the early primary years focus on children developing an understanding that cleanliness, nutrition, exercise, and rest are necessary for good health. From an early age, children need to make logical decisions and follow rules, such as looking both ways before crossing the street, for their own safety and health.

Keep in mind that primary grade children tend to think that all microbes are "**germs**" and connect eating certain foods with being healthy. They understand hazards such as pollution only to the extent that they themselves might be affected in a direct way. Primary age children tend to expect adults to remove all dangers and risk from their environment, and they understand cause and effect only to the extent of understanding the consequences. For example, children understand the connection between not wearing a coat on a cold day and the outcome of catching a cold, but they will not consider intervening variables such as lowered resistance.

Primary age children are beginning to develop an interest in how their bodies work. Upper primary grade children can learn about personal health by studying the structures of the human body, the functions of these structures, and nutrition as the source of energy.

The following health, nutrition, and human body concepts are basic to primary grade learning.

- Eating a variety of healthful foods and getting enough exercise and rest help people to stay healthy.

- Some things people take into their bodies from the environment can hurt them.

- A balanced diet consists of **carbohydrates**, **fats**, **proteins**, **vitamins**, **minerals**, and water.

- A diet that is a balance of food groups plus water makes up a healthful regimen for normal people.

- You can help yourself stay healthy.

- The human body can be affected by a variety of diseases.

- Some diseases are caused by germs; some are not. Washing one's hands with soap and water reduces the number of germs that can get into the body or be passed on to other people.

- The human body carries on life processes.

- Food is the fuel and the building material of the body.

- The human body must take in and digest food.

- Humans have a distinct body structure for walking, holding, seeing, and talking.

- The human body consists of a number of groups of organs that work together to perform particular functions.

- Movement of the human body is made possible by the skeleton and muscles.

- The human body takes in oxygen and gives off **carbon dioxide**.

- The **circulatory system** is the transportation system of the body.

- Humans reproduce and give off waste products.

- The brain enables human beings to think; it sends messages to other body parts to help them to work properly.

- Senses can warn individuals about danger; muscles help them fight, hide, or get out of danger.

- Humans observe and learn by seeing, hearing, feeling, tasting, and smelling.

- Men and women have made a variety of contributions to science and technology.

# EXPLORATIONS IN HEALTH AND NUTRITION

The learning experiences suggested in this unit introduce fundamental concepts that acquaint children with their bodies and how to stay healthy. Topics include good health habits; treatment of cuts and scrapes; how the body gains energy; the food pyramid and food activities; and bones, teeth, vitamins, and minerals.

## Health Habits

Good health habits begin early in a child's life. Encourage children to begin an understanding of what healthy living really means by providing a variety of instructional techniques and subject integrations that relate to the child's life. Here are a few to get you started.

## ACTIVITIES

### Are your Hands Dirty?

**CONCEPT:** Hands that look clean can still be dirty.

**OBJECTIVE:** Observe the growth of mold on potatoes. Compare the effect of mold growth resulting from handling potatoes with washed and unwashed hands.

**Figure 38–1** "What is happening in the unwashed hands jar?"

**MATERIALS:** Two small potatoes, potato peeler, two clean jars with lids that seal, labels, marker.

**PROCEDURE:** Have children examine their hands. Ask, ARE YOUR HANDS CLEAN? DO YOU SEE ANY DIRT ON THEM? Discuss how hands look when they are dirty. WHAT IS THE DIRTIEST YOUR HANDS HAVE EVER BEEN? THE CLEANEST?

Peel two potatoes, ask a child to handle one of them, and put it in a jar. (Select a child who has not washed his or her hands for several hours.) Point out that the child's hands appear to be clean.

Label the jar with the name of the child and the words *unwashed hands*. Instruct a child to wash his or her hands, handle the second potato, and put it in the remaining jar. Label the jar with the child's name and the words *washed hands*. Discuss the relative cleanliness of the "washed hands" potato.

Place the two jars in a warm place where the children can observe and record what happens. Compare what is happening to the potatoes after a day or two. (Mold is likely to form on the potato handled by unwashed hands.) Compare the potatoes, and discuss how the mold got on the potato (Figure 38–1). (Refer to Unit 34 for additional mold lessons.)

**EXTENSION:** Have children describe and draw what the unwashed and washed hands looked like. Ask, DID THE UNWASHED HANDS LOOK DIRTY? (No.) This would be a good time to discuss germs and the importance of washing hands before handling food. Have children design posters to encourage hand washing before meals.

*Good health habits chart.* Keep a record of your health habits. Answer questions about yourself for a week. (For example: I brushed my teeth after every meal. I took a bath or shower. I washed my hands before meals today. I exercised today.) At the end of the week, look at all of your answers. What can you do to improve your health habits?

## Apples and Me

**CONCEPT:** Microorganisms (germs) can enter our body through cuts and scrapes in the skin.

**OBJECTIVE:** Compare the healing of injuries on an apple with injuries on our skin. Describe how antiseptic keeps germs out of our body.

*(continued)*

**Figure 38–2** Apples with puncture wounds.

**MATERIALS:** Three apples, soil or other type of dirt, antiseptic, two sewing needles.

**PROCEDURE:** Lead the children in a discussion of current injuries that they have received. Such incidents occur often in the primary grades. Encourage children to tell how the injury happened and how it was treated.

Then hold an apple in your hand. Ask, HOW IS THE COVERING OF AN APPLE SIMILAR TO YOUR SKIN? HOW IS IT DIFFERENT? LET'S SEE WHAT HAPPENS WHEN THE SURFACE OF AN APPLE IS INJURED.

Label one apple the *control apple.* You will not injure this apple. Label the second apple *no antiseptic* and the third apple *antiseptic.* Then, stir one of the needles in dirt and puncture the second apple three times. Stir the other needle in dirt, sterilize the needle with antiseptic, and puncture the third apple (Figure 38–2). Place the three apples in a sunny place, and have the children keep a record of changes in the apples. Ask, WHAT DO YOU THINK THEY WILL LOOK LIKE IN ONE DAY? As children record the progress, discuss possible reasons for differences in the appearance of the apples. (The apple punctured by the unsterilized needle will rot fairly quickly.)

After several days, cut all of the apples in half, including the control apple. Ask, WHAT CHANGES DO YOU SEE IN THE APPLES? WHICH APPLE LOOKS THE WORST? DID STERILIZING THE NEEDLE MAKE ANY DIFFERENCE? WHAT DO YOU THINK WOULD HAPPEN IF THE SURFACE OF YOUR BODY WERE PUNCTURED? Discuss the best possible action to take in case of an injury. (Refer to the mold activities in Unit 34.)

**EXTENSION:** Sterilize the needles in different ways, such as using a candle flame to simulate heat sterilization or applying various commercial antiseptics to compare products.

Children will be interested in trying out this experiment with different types of foods and different types of injuries (scraping, cutting, slicing, and so on). Ask, IS THERE ANY SPECIAL WOUND THAT WILL LET THE MOST MICROORGANISMS FIND THEIR WAY THROUGH YOUR SKIN AND INTO YOUR BODY? (Puncture wounds.)

*Test types of dirt.* Fingernail dirt, shoe dirt, desk dirt—find out if some dirt is "dirtier" than others.

*Germ story.* Write a story about invading germs and what can be done to stop them. Children will enjoy acting out the invasions of germs into the body and their subsequent destruction by antiseptic.

## Foods We Eat: Plant Power

**CONCEPT:**  We get energy from plants.

**OBJECTIVE:**  Identify the parts of plants that store food and the parts we eat.

**MATERIALS:**  A variety of foods, toothpicks.

**PROCEDURE:**  When teaching about foods, it is important to stress that they are necessary for growth and development. One way to do this is to compare children's bodies to the bean seeds in Unit 34. Ask, WHERE DID THE BEANS GET THE ENERGY TO SPROUT? (From the food stored in them.) Remind children that young plants use the food stored in the seed to grow. Ask, CAN YOU GET ENERGY FROM SEEDS? (Yes, when you eat them.)

Show the children different plants, and ask, WHERE DO YOU THINK GREEN PLANTS STORE THEIR FOOD? (Leaves.) Hold up carrots and turnip plants and ask, WHERE DO THESE PLANTS STORE THEIR FOOD? (Roots.) Show a picture of sugarcane plants (or a piece, if available) and ask, WHERE DO YOU THINK THE SUGARCANE STORES ITS FOOD? (Stem, which is between the root and the leaves.) Remember that the white potato is really a stem plant and the sweet potato is a root plant.

After you assess student progress, you may want to continue the lesson by introducing them to food for plants and to fruits and flowers (such as broccoli and cauliflower) that store food. Ask, WHERE DO YOU THINK THESE PLANTS STORE FOOD? (Flowers.)

**EXTENSION:**  Reinforce the idea that energy comes from plants and their stored food with a plant-tasting party. You will need enough food samples for the entire class to taste. (You could ask each child to bring a sample.) Before the tasting party, have the children group plants by the parts that store food, wash the plants, cut them into bite-size parts, and put a toothpick in each piece. Ask, DO WE USE ALL OF THESE PLANT PARTS FOR FOOD? (Yes, taste seeds, leaves, roots, stems, fruits, and flowers and discuss favorite plant parts.)

## Food Pyramid

**CONCEPT:**  Foods from the basic groups provide the nutrients necessary for good health.

**OBJECTIVE:**  Identify the food groups and the number of servings per day that are suggested (Figure 38–3).

**MATERIALS:**  Magazine pictures of food.

*(continued)*

**PROCEDURE:** Have children cut out magazine pictures from each food group. Mount the pictures on construction paper, add identifying food group labels, and pin to a bulletin board. Let the children decide if the pictures are labeled correctly. Move misplaced pictures to the correct categories and create a food pyramid.

**EXTENSION:** *Bag it.* Label lunch bags for each food group. Then, cut out and laminate pictures of food. Have children sort the cutouts into the correct bags. You can use this idea in a center or as an interactive bulletin board.

*Food group biography.* Choose a group, and write your biography. If you were a food group, which one would you be? What would it be like to be this food group? Does your food group have a future?

*Sell your food group.* Make a television or radio commercial that will persuade the class that your food group is worthy of being eaten every day.

**NOTE:** Although the Food Pyramid developed in 1992 by the United States Department of Agriculture (USDA) Center for Nutrition Policy & Promotion, shown in Figure 38–3, has been replaced by a new USDA design (see Figure 38–4), it is still a useful guide for children in the early years. The 2005 MyPyramid food guidance system retains the basic food groups but puts greater emphasis on physical activity, variety, proportionality, moderation, gradual improvement, and finally, personalization. If appropriate, help the children print out a detailed assessment and analysis of their current eating and physical activity habits at MyPyramid Tracker. You may access the Online Companion to find links to their website.

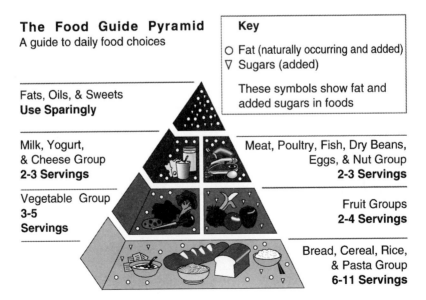

**Figure 38–3** A food pyramid.

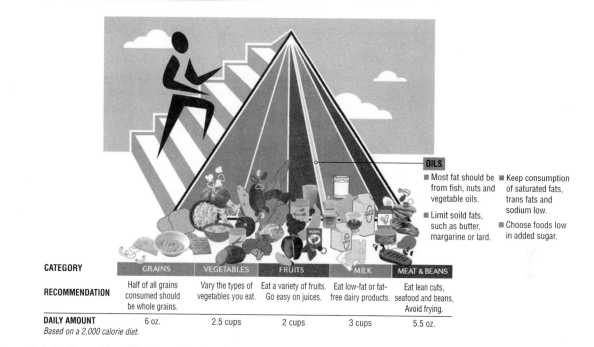

| CATEGORY | GRAINS | VEGETABLES | FRUITS | MILK | MEAT & BEANS |
|---|---|---|---|---|---|
| RECOMMENDATION | Half of all grains consumed should be whole grains. | Vary the types of vegetables you eat. | Eat a variety of fruits. Go easy on juices. | Eat low-fat or fat-free dairy products. | Eat lean cuts, seafood and beans, Avoid frying. |
| DAILY AMOUNT | 6 oz. | 2.5 cups | 2 cups | 3 cups | 5.5 oz. |

*Based on a 2,000 calorie diet.*

**OILS**
■ Most fat should be from fish, nuts and vegetable oils.
■ Limit soild fats, such as butter, margarine or lard.
■ Keep consumption of saturated fats, trans fats and sodium low.
■ Choose foods low in added sugar.

**Figure 38–4** MyPyramid—USDA's new food guidance system.

## ADDITIONAL FOOD ACTIVITIES

1. *Fatty foods.* Ask, "How can you find out if food has fat in it?" Place a drop of liquid fat on a piece of brown paper. Hold the paper up to the light and ask, "Does the light come through where the fat is?" After a few hours ask, "Is the spot dry or does it stay the same?" (Stays the same.) Test the fat in foods such as peanut butter, nuts, olives, and milk by leaving the food on brown paper for a few hours. Then ask, "Is the spot dry, or does it stay the same?" After testing several foods ask, "How do you know there is fat in these foods?" (Fatty oils stay on the paper.)

2. *Sugar time.* Show the children a variety of food containers (jars, boxes, and so on). Have them predict which foods contain sugar. After they write their predictions on a prediction sheet, have them read the ingredients on the food containers to check their predictions. Explain that the ingredients are listed in sequence from greatest amount to smallest. Also note information on vitamin, mineral, and calorie content. Compare results. Then, write the word *sugar* on the chalkboard. Ask, "Does the list on the label say sugar?" (Not always.) Introduce the children to some of the ways sugars are listed: corn syrup, maltose, sucrose, fructose, corn sweetener, syrup, dextrose, glucose, lactose, and molasses. Discuss the amount of sugar in foods, and decide if eating a lot of sugar is a good idea.

3. *Classify foods.* Give children practice in identifying which foods belong in which food group by making charts and food group books. This can be done by using pictures; classifying individual children's diets; and analyzing school lunch menus, the contents of bag lunches, and the evening meal.

4. *Finding out.* Divide the class into small groups, and give each group a list of questions to

**Figure 38–5** Dairy web.

explore about different food groups. Make a web of their findings as they share with the class (Figure 38–5).

5. *Foods I like chart.* Have children write the names of the foods they would like to eat for breakfast, lunch, and dinner on a chart. Then make a chart that lists the foods they actually eat at these meals. Compare the charts and identify foods (like potato chips) that are high in fats, carbohydrates, and/or sugar. Discuss the nutritional value of the foods. Children might want to keep a log of foods that they eat for breakfast over a week's time (or food eaten for lunch or dinner). Compare class eating habits.

6. *Visitors.* Invite a cafeteria worker or restaurant owner to talk about cleanliness and a nutritionist to explain how the lunch menus are created.

7. *Tasting party.* One effective method of evaluating food learning is to have a tasting party in which the children select their meal from a variety of foods. Simply observe which foods the children select to make up the meal.

8. *Recipes.* Integrate social studies by tasting foods from different countries or from different areas of town. Families also cook in different ways. Discuss similarities and differences, and make recipe books of favorite recipes. Have parents or other guests from a variety of ethnic backgrounds make one of their special dishes or share some special food with the class (refer to the many food activities in previous units). This activity is more effective if families share favorite foods throughout the year instead of just at one time, thus precluding a mere "tourist" approach to diversity.

## We Are What We Eat

Study vitamins and minerals as far as the developmental level of your students permits. Here are a few ideas to get you started.

## ACTIVITIES

### Keeping Bones and Teeth Strong

**CONCEPT:**  Food supplies the body with important minerals. Calcium is a mineral that is used to make bones and teeth strong.

**OBJECTIVE:**  Test rocks for the presence of calcium. Observe evidence of calcium.

**MATERIALS:**  Pieces of limestone, chalk, marble, vinegar, hand lenses, medicine droppers.

**CAUTION:**  Hydrochloric acid is usually used for this test. However, when working with young children, use vinegar.

**PROCEDURE:**  Show children the rocks, and ask, WHAT ARE ROCKS MADE OF? (Many answers; one will probably be minerals.) Tell the children that they can test for the presence of a mineral called calcium by dropping acid or vinegar on a rock.

Give children samples of limestone. Ask, WHAT DO YOU THINK WILL HAPPEN IF WE DROP VINEGAR ON A ROCK? Instruct the children to fill the medicine dropper and carefully drop the vinegar on the rocks. Have the children observe and record what happens to the rocks. (Bubbles form.) Generate a list of words that describe children's observations. (Fizz, bubble, smell, and so on.) Explain that the bubbles indicate that calcium is present.

**EXTENSION:** Children enjoy comparing the hard parts of their bodies to rocks. Ask, HOW ARE BONES AND TEETH LIKE ROCKS? (They both contain minerals.) Explain that two minerals, calcium and phosphorus, combine to make bones and teeth hard. Good sources include milk and other dairy foods, fruits, and vegetables. Other foods, such as eggs, leafy green vegetables, meats, grains, and nuts, have some calcium. Bring an end to the lesson by asking, WHERE DO WE GET THE CALCIUM TO MAKE OUR BONES AND TEETH STRONG? (From our foods.)

*Chicken bones.* Testing the brittleness of chicken bones can help children understand that bones are more likely to break if they do not have the necessary minerals. To conduct this test, scrub two large chicken bones thoroughly. Soak one in water and one in vinegar for several days. Have the children compare the bones with handheld lenses and note any differences. Then, predict which of the two bones will break more easily. (Vinegar dissolves calcium and phosphorus.) Compare the chicken bones to human bones.

*Tear or crush?* Have the children examine their teeth with mirrors and identify different sizes and shapes of teeth. How are the front teeth shaped? Ask, WHEN DO YOU USE YOUR FRONT TEETH? HOW DO YOUR FRONT TEETH HELP YOU EAT? WHAT TYPES OF FOOD DO YOU NEED TO CRUSH TO EAT? WHICH TEETH HELP YOU CRUSH FOOD?

This would be a good time to discuss carnivorous and herbivorous animals. Show pictures of animals eating. Ask, WHAT TYPE OF TEETH DO THESE ANIMALS HAVE? After categorizing animals (and dinosaurs) by what they eat and discussing the shape and use of teeth, ask WHICH CATEGORY DO WE BELONG IN? (Both.) WHY? (We have several types of teeth. We eat both plants and animals.)

*How do nutrients get into food?* To show how the roots of vegetables take in minerals from the soil, mix red food coloring and water. Have children observe the small rootlets that grow from the core of a carrot. Then, submerge the carrot in dyed water for 24 hours. Ask, WHAT HAPPENED TO THE RED COLOR? (Passes to the core of the carrot.) HOW DID IT GET THERE? (Through the rootlets.)

You may want to set up this observation with several different vegetables. Children will discover that dissolved minerals come into plants through plant roots. Let them discover that as we eat the plants, we take in the same minerals.

Then ask, IF PLANTS GET MINERALS FROM SOIL WATER, CAN WE GET MINERALS FROM WATER, TOO? (Yes.) Minerals in water are sulfur, chlorine, sodium, calcium, magnesium, potassium, and fluorine. Discuss how we get minerals from water. (Drink, eat, plants, animals.)

## ADDITIONAL MINERAL ACTIVITIES

*Iron.* Iron is a mineral that you need in your blood. The iron combines with protein to form a compound that makes blood red. This compound also carries oxygen to all parts of your body. Meats, beans, peas, grains, and leafy vegetables are good sources of iron. Children will enjoy acting out the oxygen processing function of iron. Ask, "How do we get iron into our bodies?"

Children can "become" blood platelets, oxygen, and food by wearing appropriate labels and drawings.

Make a vein path with red yarn for the children to follow as they trace the journey of a blood platelet. Have children create a script about how iron enters the body and what it does to help them stay healthy.

*Anemia.* You can get sick if you do not get enough iron. Ask, "Do you eat foods that give your body iron?" Discuss foods that contain iron. Explain that when you have had a good night's sleep but still are tired all the time, you may be anemic. People with anemia get tired easily because their blood does not carry enough oxygen. Ask, "What can you do to avoid getting anemia?" (Eat foods that contain iron.)

*Plan a meal.* Have children plan a meal for someone with anemia. If you are studying vitamins, children could plan a meal for someone with beriberi. (People with beriberi lack essential vitamins and minerals and are too weak to use their muscles to do work.)

*Mineral people.* Study the labels of common foods. Categorize cans and boxes of food by the minerals they contain. Then make mineral people such as an Iron Person or a Calcium Person. These figures can be made from the actual foods or boxes or pictures of these foods (Figure 38–6). Then, decide what foods are needed to create Vitamin People.

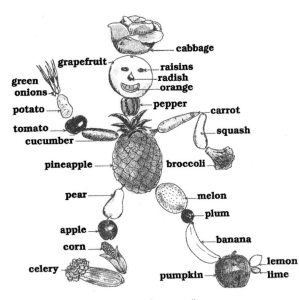

**Figure 38–6** "Create a mineral person."

# STRATEGIES FOR TEACHING THE HUMAN BODY

The internal anatomy of the human body is a hard concept for young children to understand. Concrete experiences on which to base understandings can be difficult to provide. Refer to Unit 26 to review the "garbage bag" strategy for introducing children to the inside of the human body. In addition to the suggestions in Unit 26, the following suggestions will help you provide the children with concrete learning strategies.

## Inside of Me

Although children cannot observe the inside of a human body, they can infer that muscles, bones, and organs are inside of them. For example, bones give the body shape, help the body move, and protect the organs. Preliminary activities should include body awareness activities in which children explore, feel, and identify some of the major bones. Observation of X-ray films can further enhance the children's concept of bones. Then, trace a Halloween skeleton, cut out the bones, and assemble the skeleton using paper fasteners as joints. Try some of the following strategies for teaching about bones with children.

## Our Skeleton Has Joints

Have the children move their arms and legs in a way that explores the way joints work: marching, saluting, swinging arms and legs, and acting like a windmill. Ask, "Do your legs bend when you march? Can you march without bending your legs? Is it easy to do?" Point out and explore the joints that help your body move. Discover the difference between hinge joints, which bend one way, and ball-and-socket joints, which can bend, twist, and rotate (Figure 38–7).

## Find the Joints

Have children work in pairs to make a paper body and locate joints. Have one child lie on a piece of butcher paper and the other child draw the outline of the body. Then, have the children locate joints on the paper body.

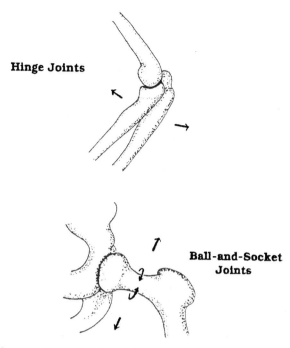

**Hinge Joints**

**Ball-and-Socket Joints**

Figure 38–7 A ball-and-socket joint and a hinge joint.

Discuss why the type of joint used in the body is the most appropriate. Ask, "What would happen if we had a ball-and- socket joint in our knees?"

## Writing about Bones

Explore the advantages and disadvantages of different types of joints by having children write stories about children with joints in different places. For example, if a child had a hinge joint where a shoulder joint is needed, how would the child move? What would a day in the life of that child be like?

## Do Chickens Have Joints?

Find out if the children think that a chicken has joints. Then, make chicken bones available to demonstrate how joints work. After children have had time to explore the chicken bones, ask, "How is your skeleton like a chicken skeleton?" (Both have joints and other similarities.)

## Finger Bones

Have children place their fingers over the light of a flashlight. Ask, "What do you see? How can you tell that you have bones inside of your fingers?" Have a doctor visit your class and discuss the use of X-rays. The children will enjoy seeing X-ray pictures of bones, especially broken bones. This would be a good time to discuss first aid for broken bones.

## Bone Music and Art

Sing "Dry Bones." ("The toe bone's connected to the foot bone, the foot bone's connected to the ankle bone," and so on.) Children can compare skeleton poster bones as they sing, or a model of the backbone can be made with yarn and pieces of macaroni.

## Make a Muscle

Young children enjoy flexing their arm muscles and feeling the muscles they can make, but they might think that arm muscles are the only ones they have. Encourage them to discover other muscles by raising their heels off the ground in a tiptoe position. Ask, "Can you feel your muscles move as they do this?" Have the children lie on mats, stretch out like a cat, then curl up into a ball. Ask, "Which muscles can you feel now?"

Explore facial muscles by wiggling noses and raising eyebrows. Ask, "Does your tongue have muscles?" (Yes.) Give children time to find unexpected muscles in their bodies. Then, apply some of the bone and joint learning experiences to teaching about muscles.

## All about Me

Children like to know that they are the same as others and that they are different, too. Discuss the similarities and differences in people that make them who they are. Give children opportunities to explore their bodies and what makes them an individual.

## Exploring the Body: Using Hands and Feet to Help Us Move

Ask children to find out how many things they can do with their hands such as wave, rub, scratch, or make a

**Figure 38–8** "Make a paper body."

fist. Then, find out how many things can be done with their feet: skip, hop, walk, and tiptoe. Have children write or dictate a list of their findings. Ask, "Can you think of something that you cannot do with your hands or cannot do with your feet? How important is your thumb?" Have the children do an activity without using their thumbs.

## Paper Bodies

Full-sized paper outlines of a child's body can be used as a starting point for many learning experiences. Partners take turns tracing around each other on butcher paper with a crayon (Figure 38–8). Then, each child cuts out his or her body by following along the lines. Examples include:

- *Story character body.* After the paper body is made, have the children study their faces in a mirror and draw their features on one side of the paper body. Children will enjoy creating a fantasy body or storybook character on their own body shape.
- *Math body.* The cutout paper body can be an easy way for children to measure parts of their character's body. They can measure length of body, arms, and so on, and add weight and physical characteristics on a chart.
- *Action body.* After children are familiar with body tracing, let them trace each other in action poses and guess who is doing what and with what. Have magazines available for references of

how a dancer uses muscles, how joints bend as an athlete runs, and how joints are used to sit in a chair.

- *I am curious.* Have children fill the paper body with magazine pictures depicting things they like to do, are curious about, or want to learn about. Ask, "What would you like to learn more about? Find things that you are curious about." Make "I Am Curious" bodies and the like.
- *Body mobile.* Separate this body at the joints and attach the body parts with yarn. These body mobiles can hang from the ceiling.
- *Body parts.* Cut-up paper bodies can be added to a bulletin board or center. The body-part bulletin board features an envelope of body parts that are assembled with thumbtacks. Labels may be added to name the parts, bones, joints, or organs that are being emphasized (Figure 38–9).

## Senses

Studying the senses and how they can be used to gather information is a natural exploration for young children. Refer to Units 16, 24, 26, and 36 for exploration ideas

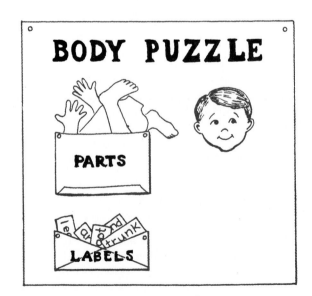

**Figure 38–9** A body-part bulletin board.

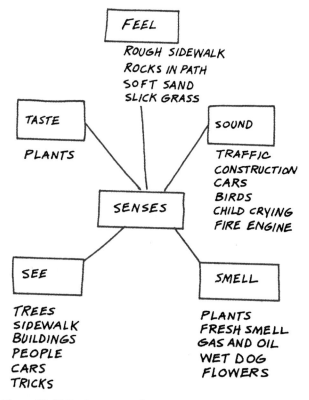

Figure 38–10 Brainstorm with an experience web.

and to the senses learning center in Unit 39 for suggestions. The following sense walk experience is a useful beginning or extension for an ongoing study of the senses.

Ask the children to be absolutely silent as they take a walk around school. Plan to pass the lunchroom; office; custodian's area; gymnasium; other classrooms; and special area rooms, such as art and music. Instruct children to use their senses to notice as many things as they can. When you return to class, make a class chart or web of all the things noticed on the walk, such as different types of noises, smells, textures, sounds, and activity. Ask questions to encourage thinking, such as, "Did the floor of the office feel like the floor of the classroom?" On a different day, take the class on an outside walk and brainstorm an experience web with the children to reinforce observations (Figure 38–10).

## SUMMARY

Good health and nutrition habits begin early in a child's life. For children to begin to understand what it means to be healthy, they need to be exposed to a variety of learning experiences. These experiences should be integrated into the child's life to have meaning and be as concrete as possible for better understanding.

Although children are curious about their bodies and how they work, their knowledge of internal anatomy is limited, and children find the subject especially difficult to understand. Concrete experiences on which to base learning about bones, muscles, and organs must be provided to ensure understanding.

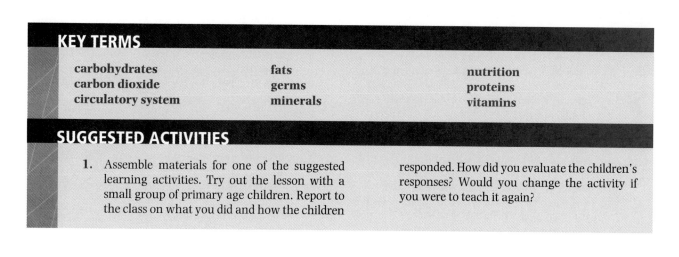

### KEY TERMS

| | | |
|---|---|---|
| carbohydrates | fats | nutrition |
| carbon dioxide | germs | proteins |
| circulatory system | minerals | vitamins |

### SUGGESTED ACTIVITIES

1. Assemble materials for one of the suggested learning activities. Try out the lesson with a small group of primary age children. Report to the class on what you did and how the children responded. How did you evaluate the children's responses? Would you change the activity if you were to teach it again?

2. Design a nutrition learning strategy for your Activity File. Which process skills will you emphasize? How many areas of the curriculum can you integrate into this lesson?

3. Develop your own teaching web. Select lessons from this unit, and design a teaching unit that is appropriate for a group of children you are teaching.

4. Prepare a learning cycle lesson to teach a health, nutrition, or human body concept. Teach it to a group of children, and report to the class. What was the advantage of using the learning cycle? Would another teaching strategy have worked better with this concept or group of children?

5. Locate software in your school's library that teaches or reinforces health and nutrition concepts. Preview the software. Select one piece of software to introduce to a small group of children. As the children interact with the software, record their comments and behaviors. Use these observations to evaluate the software's instructional effectiveness. Write an evaluation in which you address (1) the concept(s) upon which the software focuses, (2) how developmentally appropriate the software's instructional activities are, and (3) how well the students appeared to learn the concepts being taught or reinforced. Present these findings to your class.

## REVIEW

A. List two reasons why health and nutrition education should be an essential part of the science curriculum in the primary grades.

B. Develop a rationale for including health and nutrition concepts in the study of science in the school.

C. Discuss how you would adapt health and nutrition activities for preoperational children and then concrete operational children.

## REFERENCE

National Research Council. (1996). *National science education standards.* Washington, DC: National Academies Press.

## FURTHER READING AND RESOURCES

Abruscato, J. (2000). *Whizbangers and wonderments.* Boston: Allyn & Bacon.

Abruscato, J. (2004). *Teaching children science: A discovery approach* (6th ed.). Boston: Allyn & Bacon.

Abruscato, J. (2004). *Teaching children science: Discovery activities and demonstrations for the elementary and middle grades* (2nd ed.). Boston: Allyn & Bacon.

Allison, L. (1976). *Blood and guts.* Boston: Little, Brown.

American Association for the Advancement of Science (AAAS). (2007). *Atlas of science literacy: Project 2061* (Vol. 2). Washington, DC: Author.

Benenson, G., & Neujahr, J. L. (2002). *Designed environments: Places, practices, and plans.* Portsmouth, NH: Heinemann.

Benenson, G., & Neujahr, J. L. (2002). *Mapping.* Portsmouth, NH: Heinemann.

Benenson, G., & Neujahr, J. L. (2002). *Mechanisms and other systems.* Portsmouth, NH: Heinemann.

Benenson, G., & Neujahr, J. L. (2002). *Packaging and other structures.* Portsmouth, NH: Heinemann.

Benenson, G., & Neujahr, J. L. (2002). *Signs, symbols, and codes.* Portsmouth, NH: Heinemann.

Bershad, C., & Bernick, D. (1979). *Bodyworks: The kids' guide to food and physical fitness.* New York: Random House.

Brummet, D. C., Lind, K. K., Barman, C. R., DiSpezio, M. A., & Ostlund, K. L. (1995). *Destinations in science.* Menlo Park, CA: Addison-Wesley.

Carin, A. A., Bass, J. E., & Contant, T. L. (2005). *Activities for teaching science as inquiry* (6th ed.). Upper Saddle River, NJ: Prentice-Hall.

Carter, C. D., & Phillips, F. K. (1979). *Activities that teach health.* New York: Instructor Publications.

Chaille, C., & Britain, L. (2003). *Young child as scientist: A constructivist approach to early childhood science education.* Boston: Allyn & Bacon.

Harlan, J., & Rivkin, M. (2003). *Science experiences for the early childhood years: An integrated affective approach.* Upper Saddle River, NJ: Pearson-Merrill/Prentice-Hall.

Hendry, L. (1987). *Foodworks.* Menlo Park, CA: Addison-Wesley.

Herbert, D. (1980). *Mr. Wizard's supermarket science.* New York: Random House.

Katz, L. G. (1988). *Early childhood education: What research tells us.* Bloomington, IN: Phi Delta Kappa Educational Foundation.

Kepler, L. (1996). *Windowsill science centers.* New York: Scholastic Books.

King, M. D. (2000). Rev up your veggies! *Science and Children, 38*(1), 20–25.

Lind, K. K. (1983). Apples, oranges, baseballs and me. In D. Stroak (Ed.), *Understanding the healthy body* (pp. 123–125). Columbus, OH: SMEAC Information Reference Center.

Lind, K. K. (1985). The inside story. *Science and Children, 22*(4), 122–123.

Lowery, L. F. (1997). *NSTA pathways to the science standards.* Arlington, VA: National Science Teachers Association.

National Environmental Education and Training Foundation (NEETF). (2000). *Environment-based education: Creating high performance schools and students.* Washington, DC: Author.

*Science and Children.* (1982). Skeleton poster. Washington, DC: National Science Teachers Association.

Sherwood, E. A., Williams, R. A., & Rockwell, R. E. (1990). *Mudpies to magnets.* Mt. Rainier, MD: Gryphon House.

Stronck, D. (1983). *Understanding the human body.* Columbus, OH: SMEAC Information Reference Center.

**Software**

*Betty Crocker Cooking with Kids* (ages 6+; Fairfield, NJ: Allegro New Media)

*Body Park* (pre-K–6; Needham, MA: Virtual Entertainment)

*"Cell"ebration* (K–3; Lewisville, NC: Science for Kids)

*Dr. Health'nstein's Body Fun* (ages 7–14; San Francisco: StarPress Multimedia)

*Incredible Lab* (Pleasantville, NY: Sunburst Communications)

*The Magic Schoolbus: Human Body* (ages 6–10; Redmond, WA: Microsoft)

*Mayo Clinic Family Health Book* (all grades; Rochester, MN: IVI)

*Me, Myself, and I* (K–3; Chicago: Jostens Learning)

*National Geographic CDs for Educators: The Human Body* (pre-K–3; Washington, DC: National Geographic)

*Science #5, House a Fire! Fire Prevention* (grades 3–5; San Ramon, CA: Ellen Nelson Learning Library, Decision Development Corporation)

*The Ultimate 3-D Skeleton* (ages 8+; London: Dorling Kindersley)

*The Ultimate Human Body* (ages 8+; London: Dorling Kindersley)

*Welcome to Bodyland* (pre-K–2; Rochester, MN: IVI)

*What Is a Belly Button* (pre-K–3; Rochester, MN: IVI)

*Note:* You may also access the Online Companion to find relevant links to websites.

# The Math and Science Environment

# Unit 39

# Materials and Resources for Math and Science

## OBJECTIVES

After reading this unit, you should be able to:

- Set up learning centers for math and science.
- Select appropriate materials for teaching math and science.
- List examples of basic materials that can be used to support specific math and science concept development.

Whether learning experiences are presented in an informal, unstructured, or structured approach (a learning cycle, discrepant event, or demonstration) or are used in learning centers or manipulated by an entire class at one time, manipulative science and mathematics require materials for children to explore. Hands-on mathematics and science require that materials be handled, stored, distributed, and replaced whenever they are used. Do not be discouraged. In the long run, once the materials are accumulated and organized, less time is needed for teacher preparation because much of the classroom instruction will be carried out by the interaction of the child and the materials.

There are categories of math and science materials that can be used to guide selections. In Unit 3, six categories of math materials were discussed: real objects, real objects used with pictorial representations, two-dimensional cutouts, pictures, wipe-off folders, and paper and pencil. These categories follow a developmental sequence from the concrete manipulative to the abstract representational. Preoperational children work

with only the first four types of materials. During the transition to concrete operations, the last two categories may be available for those children who can deal with them. All through the concrete operations period, new concepts and skills should be introduced with concrete manipulative and pictorial materials before moving on to the abstract representational.

Many kinds of concrete manipulative materials have been introduced throughout the preceding units. Some are versatile while others serve more specific functions. Pictorial manipulatives and other picture materials have also been suggested. Children's picture books are an especially rich source of pictorial and language information, as was suggested in Unit 15. Stories, poems, and pictures enrich the math curriculum. These materials help teach math vocabulary, illustrate the use of math in a variety of settings, and expand children's ideas of how math can be used. Books should be carefully selected. Be sure the illustrations accurately portray the concepts the book purports to help teach. As noted in Unit 24, special care must be taken when selecting counting books because the illustrations are frequently inaccurate in their depiction of the group symbol relationships. The teacher should ask: "Which concept or concepts are illustrated in this book? How will reading this story or poem help Richard, Liu Pei, or Mary to better understand this concept?" Books should have good artwork and be colorful and well written. The National Council of Teachers of Mathematics publishes a resource catalog (see Figure 39–3 for the NCTM address).

There are several general categories of science materials. The most complete listing of available materials appears each January in *Science and Children*, a journal of the National Science Teachers Association (NSTA). This useful supplement answers the question, "Where do I go for help?" The publication is organized into four main sections: equipment/supplies, media producers, computers/software, and publishers. This unit offers suggestions for the selection of basic science materials and resources and for preparing science learning centers. The guidelines for selecting math materials for young children can also be applied to selecting science materials.

## BASIC MATH AND SCIENCE MATERIALS

There are two basic types of math and science materials: those you purchase, and those you "scrounge." Purchased materials include textbook publishers' kits, general kits, and items purchased at supply houses or local retailers. Materials that are scrounged or contributed by parents and other benevolent individuals are known by many teachers as "good junk" or recycled material. Regardless of how the materials are acquired, they must be organized and managed in a way that promotes learning. (Refer to Unit 33 for additional suggestions for classroom management.)

### The Good Junk Box: Things to Scrounge

Many teachers rely on boxes of miscellaneous materials that have been gathered from many sources. Such a junk box comes in handy. Invite children, friends, businesspeople, and others to add to your junk box. Once people know you collect odds and ends, they will remember you when they are ready to throw something away. Examples include:

- Glass containers and 2-liter bottles make good aquariums, terrariums, and places to display animals.
- Aluminum foil, pie plates, and frozen food containers are useful for numerous activities.
- Film cans make smell and sound containers.
- Hardware supplies are always welcome for the tool center; plastic tubing, garden hoses, and funnels are ideal for water play and making musical instruments.
- Candles, thumbtacks, paper clips, and other "sink or float" items come in handy.
- Refrigerator magnets are useful for magnet experiences; old, leaky aquariums make good housing for small mammals or reptiles.
- Oatmeal containers make drums; shoe boxes are great for dioramas and general organization and storage.
- Toys, clocks, and kitchen tools can be added to the machine center and used for dramatic play.
- Flashlights, batteries, and wire from telephone lines can be used for electricity experiments.
- Pipe cleaners are always useful for art; buttons and other small objects are needed for classifying and comparing.
- Straws, balloons, paper cups, pieces of fabric, and wallpaper are objects for the touch box.
- Some stores invite teachers to collect their old carpet and wallpaper sample books.
- Always keep an eye out for feathers, unusual rocks, shells, seed-growing containers, plastic eggs—the list is endless.
- Items that can be counted, sorted, graphed, and so on, such as plastic lids from bottles, jars, and other containers; thread spools, pinecones, seashells, buttons, and seeds are all useful.
- Egg cartons and frozen food containers can be used for sorting.
- String, ribbon, sticks, and so on can be used for comparing lengths and for informal measuring.
- Small boxes can be used for construction projects.

See Unit 41 for additional suggestions.

Some teachers send home a list of "junk" items at the beginning of the year. Parents are asked to bring or send available items to school. Such a list will be easy to complete when you become familiar with "good junk" and have an idea of some of the items that you will use during the year. In addition, parents are usually responsive to special requests such as vegetables for the vegetable activities like those in Unit 26 or ingredients for the cooking activities in Unit 36.

## Commercial Materials for Science

Your school district might decide to purchase a kit from a publisher when selecting a textbook for teaching science. Publisher kits are available from most major companies and contain materials specifically designed to implement the activities suggested in the textbook. These kits can be helpful in providing the hands-on component of a textbook-based science program.

General kits are available from many sources and range in size from small boxes to large pieces of furniture with built-in equipment such as sinks and cabinets. General kits contain basic materials but may not

be directed to your specific needs. An advantage of the boxes or rolling tables is that they are easy to circulate among teachers.

Specific topic kits such as "Mining, Minerals, and Me" (suggested in Unit 36) are boxed by topic and grade level. The idea is to provide the teacher with the materials necessary to teach a specific science topic. Teachers' manuals and materials allow teachers to use the kit as a supplement to a textbook or as the major means of teaching a science concept.

## Advantages and Disadvantages of Kits

Most kits contain a limited amount of consumable supplies—usually just enough for a class to do all of the activities covered in the teacher manual. Reordering must be continuous for the kit to be used again. However, the kits also contain permanent supplies such as magnifiers, clay, small plastic aquariums, petri dishes, balances, and the like.

The major drawbacks to commercial kits of any type are maintaining the consumables in the kits and finding the money to purchase the kits. Kits are self-

| | | | |
|---|---|---|---|
| Blockbusters | Crystal Climbers | Wonderforms | Block Head |
| Lego® | Rig-A-Jig | Geo-D-Stix | Snap-N-Play Blocks |
| Free Form Posts | Color Cone | Connector | Channel Blocks |
| Sprocketeers | Tectonic | Wood'n Molds | Wee Waffle Blocks |
| Tinkertoys | Structo-Brics | Poki Blocks | Struts |
| Toy Makers | Giant Structo-Cubes | Multi-fit | Duplo® |
| Cloth Cubes | Floresco | Disco Shapes | Gear Circus |
| Snap Wall | Ring-A-Majigs | Snap Blocks | Create It |
| Lock & Stack Blocks | Crystal Octons | Bristle Blocks | LASY Construction Kits |
| Giant Interlockers | Ji-gan-tiks | Bristle Bears | Giant Double Towers |
| Unifix Cubes® | Mobilo | Brio Builder | Gears! Gears! |
| Unit Blocks | Locktagons | Flexo | Frontier Logs 'N Blocks |
| Flexibricks | Connect-A-Cube | Klondikers | Marble Run |
| Play Shapes | Tuff Tuff Blocks | Beam and Boards | Construction Rug |
| Stackobats | Polydron | Hex-A-Links | Sturdiblocks |
| Magnetic Blocks | Play Squares | Pipe Construction | Giant Edu-Blocks |
| Form-A-Tions | 3D Geoshapes | Bendits | Soft Big-Blocks |
| Poly-M | Learning Links | K'Nex | Galaxy Builder |
| Omnifix | Tower-ifics | Habitat | Building Clowns |
| Multilinks® | Edu-Builder | Busy Blocks | Building Shapes |
| Jumbo Cuisinaire Rods | Groovy Parts | Space Wheels | Bolt Builder |
| Mega Blocks | Octagons | Magnastiks | Light Table and Accessories |
| Lincoln Logs | Girders | Keeptacks | Beads |
| Baufix | Play-Panels | Balancing H Blocks | Cuisinaire® Rods |

**Figure 39–1** Construction materials for math.

contained, complete, and ready for use; consequently, they are also expensive.

## Purchased Equipment

There are some items that you might have to purchase to be an effective science teacher. This list includes magnifiers, eyedroppers, plastic tubing, mirrors, a rock and mineral set, magnets, batteries, and bulbs. If you select just one of these items, do not hesitate to choose magnifiers as the most useful piece of science equipment for the early childhood classroom. (Refer to Unit 33 for suggestions on using magnifiers.)

Although they are not interactive in the same way as rollers, ramps, and constructions, magnifiers provide children with their first look at fascinating magnified objects. Piaget was a biologist and probably would have wholeheartedly approved. It is hard to believe that he did not eagerly explore his environment up close at an early age.

There are a multitude of commercially available materials for mathematics. Some materials are versatile and can be used in the development of more than one concept. Basic materials include unit blocks with miniature animals, people, and vehicles; construction materials (Figure 39–1); Unifix Cubes; LEGO; Multilinks; pegboards and pegs; picture lotto games; beads and strings; attribute blocks; geoboards; balance scales; a thermometer; a flannelboard and a magnet board with felt and magnet pieces for concept activities; Montessori Cylinder Blocks (Figure 39–2); a manipulative clock; base-ten blocks; and fraction pies. Hand calculators and

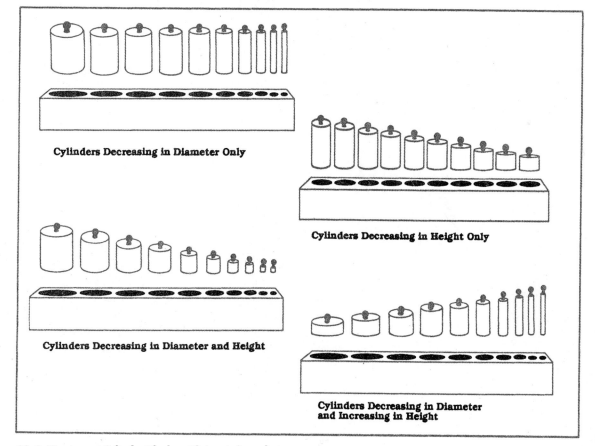

**Figure 39–2** Montessori Cylinder Blocks with insets for ordering.

computers should also be available. Search through the major catalogs (Figure 39–3), and decide what you can afford. Also consider assembling and making materials (see the resource lists at the end of each unit).

## Organizing and Storing Materials

As you collect and develop materials for teaching science and math, storage might become a problem. Most commercial kits have neat, ready-made labeled boxes, but the "junk box" system will need some organizing.

One way to manage a variety of materials is to place them in shoe boxes. The shoe boxes contain the equipment needed to teach a specific concept. If the boxes are clearly marked, they can be very convenient. The trick is to keep everything you need in the box—for example, homemade equipment materials, task cards, materials to duplicate, and bulletin board ideas. To be effective, the box, envelope, or grocery bag should dis-

---

■ AIMS Educational Foundation, P.O. Box 8120, Fresno, CA 93747-8120. Phone: 888-733-2467; Fax: 559-255-6396; Online: www.aimsedu.org.

■ Annenberg Media, 401 9th St., NW, Washington, DC 20004. Phones: 202-879-9654 and 800-LEARNER; Fax: 802-846-1850; E-mail: acpbreso@resolut.com; Online: www.learner.org.

■ Community Playthings, 359 Gibson Hill Road, Chester, NY 10918-2321. Phone: 800-777-4244; Fax: 800-336-5948; Online: www.CommunityPlaythings.com.

■ Constructive Playthings, 13201 Arrington Rd., Grandview, MO 64030-2886. Phone: 800-448-4115; Kansas City area, 800-448-1412; Fax: 816-761-9295; Online: www.cptoys.com; E-mail: ustoy@ustoyco.com.

■ Creative Publications (Wright Group/McGraw Hill), 1221 Avenue of the Americas, New York, NY 10020. Phone: 800-624-0822; Online: www.creativepublications.com.

■ ETA/Cuisinaire, 500 Greenview Court, Vernon Hills, IL 60061-1862. Phone: 800-445-5985; Fax: 800-ETA-9326; Online: www.etacuisenaire.com.

■ Dale Seymour Publications® at Pearson Learning, P.O. Box 2649, Columbus, OH 43216-2649. Phone: 800-321-3106; Online: www.plgcatalog.pearson.com.

■ Delta Education, P.O. Box 3000, Nashua, NH 03061-3000. Phone: 800-442-5444; Fax: 800-282-9560; Online: www.deltaeducation.com.

■ Didax Educational Resources, 395 Main Street, Rowley, MA 01969-0907. Phone: 800-458-0024; Fax: 800-350-2345; Online: www.didax.com.

■ Discount School Supply. Phone: 1-800-627-2829; Online: www.discountschoolsupply.com.

■ Insect Lore, P.O. Box 1535, Shafter, CA 93263-1535. Phone: 800-LIVE BUG (800-548-3284); Fax: 661-746-0334; E-mail: livebug@insectlore.com; Online: www.insectlore.com.

■ Kaplan, P.O. Box 609, 1310 Lewisville-Clemmons Rd., Lewisville, NC 27023-0609. Phone: 800-334-2014; Fax: 800-452-7526; Online: www.kaplanco.com.

■ Lakeshore Learning Materials, 2695 E. Dominguez Street, Carson, CA 90895. Phone: 800-778-4456; Fax: 800-537-5403; Online: www.lakeshorelearning.com.

■ eNasco. Online: www.enco.com.

■ National Council of Teachers of Mathematics, 1906 Association Drive, Reston, VA 22091-1593. Phone: 800-235-7566 or 703-620-9840; Fax: 476-2970; Online: www.nctm.org.

■ National Science Teachers Association, P.O. Box 90214, Washington, DC 20090-0214. Phone: 800-277-5300; Fax: 301-843-0159; Online: www.nsta.org.

■ Nienhuis Montessori U.S.A., 140 E. Dana Street, Mountain View, CA 94041-1508. Phone: 800-942-8697; Fax: 650-964-8162; E-mail: webshop@nienhuis-usa.com; Online: www.nienhuis.com.

■ PCI Educational Publishing, P.O. Box 34270, San Antonio, TX 78265-4270. Phone: 800-594-4263; Fax: 888-259-8284; Online: www.pcicatalog.com.

■ Pearson Learning Group (includes AGS), publishers of Big Math for Little Kids, Pearson Early Learning, 1185 Avenue of the Americas, 17th Floor, New York, NY 10036. Phone: 212-782-3395; Fax: 212-782-3398; Online: www.pearsonlearning.com.

■ Reading Rainbow (literature videos). Phone: 800-228-4630; Online: www.pbskids.org.

■ Rigby Education, 1000 Hart Rd., Barrington, IL 60010 and P.O. Box 797, Crystal Lake, IL 60039-0797. Phone: 800-822-8661; Fax: 800-427-4429; Online: http://rigby.harcourtachievement.com.

■ SRA/McGraw-Hill, 220 East Danieldale Road, Desoto, TX 75115-2490. Phone: 1-888-SRA-4543; Fax: 1-972-228-1982; Online: www.sraonline.com. Have Building Blocks software.

■ Wright Group/McGraw-Hill, 220 East Danieldale Road, Desoto, TX 75115-2490. Phone: 800-648-2970; Fax: 800-593-4418; Online: www.wrightgroup.com.

■ Zaner-Bloser, 1201 Dublin Rd., Columbus, OH 43215-1026. Phone: 800-421-3018; Fax: 800-992-6087; Online: www.zaner-bloser.com.

---

**Figure 39–3** Math and science materials catalogs.

**Figure 39–4** You can store materials needed to teach concepts in a labeled shoe box.

play a materials list on the outside. In this way, you have a self-contained kit for teaching science (Figure 39–4).

Materials relating to a learning center can be stored in boxes under or near the science center. Materials will be handy, and older children will be able to get their own materials. Primary age children can be effective organizers. They will enjoy and benefit from the job of inventorying science materials.

## THE MATH LEARNING CENTER

Materials in the math center should be neatly organized and displayed. Place the materials in containers on low shelves where they are readily accessible to the students. Be sure the procedures for removing, using, and replacing materials are clearly understood by the children. Sometimes a specialized center (i.e., for measurement or classification) can add to the excitement of learning.

Materials can be rotated according to the children's needs and interests and to keep their attention engaged. When new materials are introduced, the teacher should allow opportunities for exploration before the materials are used for structured activities.

Math centers can also focus on specific concepts when they are being introduced. Focused centers can be set up for any of the skills and concepts in the text. Math centers can be set up relative to available space and fur-

nishings. A center might be a set of shelves with an adjacent table and chairs or carpeted area, a small table with a few different materials each day, or a space on the floor where math materials are placed. In one primary classroom in Guilderland, New York, a math bed was installed. A blackboard was at one end and shelves for books and materials at the other end: a comfortable and inviting math center.

The math center should be available to every child, every day. Too frequently, the math center is open only to those children who finish their workbook and other reproducible paper assignments. Unfortunately, it is probably the children who do not finish their paper and pencil work who are most in need of experiences with concrete manipulative materials. If workbooks are required then, after they have been introduced, put them on a special shelf in the math center and let the children who are ready select them from among the other materials available.

Many teachers, especially in the primary grades, feel pressured to follow the textbook and teach group math lessons without using manipulatives to introduce concepts as described throughout this text. It is possible to find a compromise that is beneficial for both students and teacher. For example, one first-grade teacher, feeling discouraged with the progress her students were making in mathematics, decided to try a new approach: She took the objectives for the text assigned to her class and found developmentally appropriate activities that correlated with each one. She selected the activities from *Developing Number Concepts Using Unifix Cubes* (Richardson, 1984), *Mathematics Their Way* (Baratta-Lorton, 1989), *Workjobs* (Baratta-Lorton, 1972), and *Workjobs II* (Baratta-Lorton, 1978). She then assembled the necessary materials. The teacher introduced each concept to the whole class and then divided the class into small groups to work with the concrete materials. The children felt more satisfied, performed their tasks with enthusiasm, and even commented on how much fun it was not to have to write! The teacher had time to circulate and help individual children. A positive side effect emerged from the opportunity to "talk" math: The children's language was extended, and unclear points were clarified. Peer tutoring developed naturally—to the advantage of both the tutors and those who needed help. The games and manipulatives were available for further use during the children's free time. The teacher's enthusiasm and the enthusiasm of the students were picked up by the other first-grade teachers and the principal. The teacher was asked to in-service the other first-grade teachers so that they could adopt the same system.

## THE SCIENCE LEARNING CENTER

You know that the interests of children stem from the kinds of learning materials and experiences available to them. One way to provide stimulating explorations is by setting up learning centers appropriate for an individual child or for a small group of children. As children work in centers, they learn to learn on their own in a planned environment. In this way, instruction is individualized, and children have time to explore science materials.

There are several different types of science learning centers, which are characterized by different purposes and modes of operation. The basic centers can be labeled discovery center, open learning center, inquiry learning center, and science interest center.

### Discovery Center

The word *discovery* implies that some action will be taken on materials and that questions and comments about what is happening take place. All is not quiet in a discovery center. Thus, it should be located away from listening and literacy centers. Discovery centers can be located on large tables, desks against a wall, or any spot that has room. Mobile discovery centers made of trays, shoe boxes, or baskets can simply be picked up and taken to a designated spot on the floor. An area rug makes a good place to work without taking up too much space.

In Figure 39–5, activity trays are used to explore concepts about air. As with any learning center, the size of your center area and ages of the children must be taken into account. For the three activity trays described in Figure 39–5, it is recommended that the teacher use two trays with 5-year-olds and (initially) one tray with younger children.

### Open Learning Center

The science center in an open classroom encourages creativity and contains an abundance of manipulative materials, most of which are homemade. Using minimum directions, the child might be asked to "invent something" with these materials. Guidance is provided in the way of helpful suggestions or questions as the children pursue and tinker with their invention.

An example of an open center is a sink and float center. In this center, reinforcing the concept of sink and float is the central objective. The center contains a plastic tub half full of water and a box of familiar mate-

| Materials | Procedure | Properties to Observe | Extensions |
|---|---|---|---|
| Several varying sizes of paper or plastic bags | Hold the bags open and describe what you see inside. Hold the bag closed and squeeze it. Do you feel anything? Try it again with a different bag. | Air can be felt even when it cannot be seen. | Try this activity with balloons. Ask children what happens to the air when the balloon is flat. |
| Balloons | Blow up a balloon. Hold the mouth of the balloon shut with your fingers. Open your fingers slightly and let some air out. What do you hear? Do your fingers feel anything? | Air can make noise and be felt. | Use flutes, recorders, or whistles to demonstrate how air can make different types of noise. |
| Paper and a stapler | Fold the paper accordion style and staple the end to make a fan. What do you feel when you wave the fan near your face? | Air can be moved and felt. | Use a fan or look outside on a windy day to observe how air moves and how air can move other things. |

Figure 39–5 Using activity trays to observe properties of air.

rials. On the blackboard are the questions, "What will float?" and "What will sink?" With no further direction, the children explore the questions with the materials.

Teacher evaluation is not formal; rather, the teacher visits the center and satisfies any concerns about children's progress. The teacher might find children making piles of things that do and do not float or trying to sink something that they thought would float. Some teachers suggest that the children communicate what happened at the center by drawing or by writing a few sentences.

## Inquiry Learning Center

A more directed discovery approach focuses on a science concept or topic and contains materials to be manipulated by the children, directions for the investigation, and open-ended questions to be asked at the end of the inquiry. The objective is not to reinforce a concept but to engage the child in problem solving beyond what is already known in order to gain new insights.

At an inquiry center, the child might find directions that say "Using the materials in this box, find a way to light the bulb" or "What kinds of materials are attracted to magnets?" Science concepts are turned into questions that are placed on activity cards. There might be a single task or a series of tasks that a primary age child can complete in 15 or 30 minutes.

It would be foolish to send children to an inquiry center without adequate preparation. Discuss directions, procedures, and task cards with the children before beginning center work. The children are expected to achieve a desired learning outcome. So, if things do not go smoothly, ask yourself the following questions: Were the directions clear? Did the children know where to begin and end? Did they know what to do when they were finished? Is the center appropriate for the age group? Did the first group using the center know how to restore the materials for the next group?

## Science Interest Center

Science interest corners, tables, and centers are popular in many schools. This interest center reinforces, enriches, and supplements ongoing programs with materials that stimulate children's interest. The primary goal of the center is to motivate children to want to learn more about the subject at the center.

As general rules, children are not required to visit this center and no formal evaluation of their activities is recorded. Many times the center repeats a lesson exploration. For example, if the class has done the "Thinking Like a Geologist" lesson described in Unit 36, some children might want to try scratching minerals to test hardness or classifying the available rocks. Filmstrips, storybooks, and resource books on rocks and minerals should be available for the children to explore. Children could practice their measuring skills by using string to measure an assortment of objects or become acquainted with a balance scale by comparing the weight of different rocks.

## Plan Your Center

State learning center objectives in such a way that you know what you want the child to learn. Be aware of your children's developmental level. You can avoid inadvertently creating busywork for students by taking steps to carefully plan the concepts to be developed at the center. Start by writing a sentence that communicates what the child is expected to learn at the center. Children must be able to participate in the activities and methods independently. Evaluate the center by asking yourself: Is the center effective in achieving my objectives? How can the center be improved? Figure 39–6 suggests a guide to planning a learning center.

## SELECTING MATH MATERIALS

In a classroom, each child has her individual and age-appropriate needs in mathematics. Every school and classroom includes children who are at various levels of concept development. It is important to provide a wide array of math materials and the time to explore them freely.

In Unit 3, three considerations regarding selection of math and science materials were discussed:

■ The materials should be sturdy and versatile.

■ The materials should fit the outcome objectives selected.

> What is the purpose or objective?
>
> Who will be using this learning center?
>
> What are the concepts children should learn?
>
> What are the skills children should learn?
>
> What activities will take place?
>
> What materials need to be available?
>
> What are the learning objectives?
>
> How will children's progress be evaluated?

**Figure 39–6** Questions to ask when planning a learning center.

- The materials should fit the developmental levels of the children.

In addition, the following should be considered:

- The materials should be safe.
- The materials should be easily supervised.
- The materials should be free of gender, ethnic, age, and socioeconomic bias.
- Book illustrations and content and drawings, photos, and other materials should include depictions of members of diverse cultures in nonstereotyped dress and engaged in authentic activities.

When selecting materials, versatility is important; that is, can the materials be used on a regular basis for teaching a variety of concepts? For example, unit blocks, Unifix Cubes, and Multilinks fit this criterion. No material should be a health hazard. Avoid anything made from a toxic material and anything with sharp edges or small parts or pieces that can lodge in noses or ears or be swallowed.

When taking over a new classroom or at the end of each year in a current classroom, take an inventory of materials. Note their condition: Are parts missing? Do materials need mending or replacement? Are there materials for all concepts in the program and for natu-ralistic, informal, and structured experiences? Are both indoor and outdoor materials and equipment in good condition? With this information, decisions can be made as to what is on hand and what needs to be purchased. In preprimary, when children have shorter attention spans, it is recommended that a variety of small sets of materials (enough for two or three children to share at one time) be purchased. In the primary grades, start with a classroom set of Unifix materials. These materi-als are among the most versatile because they can be used for teaching almost every primary mathematics concept. Many accessories are available and there are numerous resources, already mentioned in this text, from which to select activities. Gradually add base-ten blocks, fraction materials, and other manipulatives.

Another source is materials that can be made by teachers and/or volunteer parents. Waste materials may also be donated: Parents can be asked to save egg cartons, buttons, boxes and other containers, bottle caps, yarn, ribbon, and other materials that can be used in the math program (see the list in Unit 41). Parents might also donate inexpensive items such as toothpicks, golf tees, playing cards, funnels, measuring cups, and so on. Lumber companies might donate scrap lumber. Res-taurant supply companies will often sell teachers trays, various sized containers, and the like at low prices. Try to convince your principal to let you spend your share of supply money on concrete manipulative materials and supplies for making two-dimensional manipula-tives rather than spending on workbooks and copy pa-per. Resources for ideas for teacher-made materials are listed at the end of each unit, and some frequently used catalogs are shown in Figure 39–3.

## SELECTING SCIENCE MATERIALS

Providing materials that encourage children to "mess around" and explore is the responsibility of the teacher. At the center, children use the process skills to observe, investigate, classify, and perhaps hypothesize. Because this learning is not accidental, planning must go into setting up centers and selecting materials. After com-pleting the planning guide suggested in Figure 39–6, consider the following criteria in selecting and arrang-ing materials.

1. *Are the materials open-ended?* Can they be used in more than one way? For example, water play provides the opportunity to explore measuring or floating.

2. *Are the materials designed for action?* In science, children do something to materials to make something else happen. If substances are to be dissolved, which will offer the best comparison: salt, sugar, or pudding mix?

3. *Are the materials arranged to encourage communication among children?* If appropriate, place materials to create cooperation and conversation. Arrange materials in categories such as pitchers of water in one section of the center, substances to be tested in another, and spoons and dishes for mixing in another. Children quickly learn to cooperate and communicate to complete the activity.

4. *Is there a variety of materials?* If the center is to be used over an extended period, some children will visit it many times. A variety of materials will prevent overexposure to the exploration.

5. *Do the materials encourage "What if _____"* *statements?* The sink and float activity described in the open classroom learning center invites children to predict what will happen if they try to float a marble, toothpick, or sponge.

6. *Are the materials appropriate for the maturity of the children?* Consider the maturity level of the class. Select materials that the children can handle safely and effectively.

7. *Do the materials allow for individual differences such as ability, interest, working space, and style?* After considering floating and sinking, some children will begin to consider size and other characteristics of the available objects. Have objects with a variety of textures and features available.

8. *How much direction do the materials require?* In giving directions, consider the age of the children. Although 4- and 5-year-olds might receive directions from a cassette recording, 3-year-olds (and some 4-year-olds) respond best to personal directions. Rebus-type directions are also appropriate.

9. *Do the materials stress process skills?* Process skills are the fundamental skills that are emphasized in science explorations with young children. These skills will come naturally from manipulating materials. However, a variety of appropriate materials is required for this to happen.

10. *Are the materials culturally nonbiased?* Where appropriate, materials should illustrate authentic nonbiased dress and activities.

## Sensory Learning Center

Children have a "sense-able" approach to the world around them. The approach that they use is as basic to science as it is natural to young children. Use the type of center you prefer to give children an opportunity to taste, smell, touch, observe, and hear their environment.

## Thinking Like a Criminologist

Skin prints are a way to take a closer look at the skin children live in. They enjoy examining their fingertips, taking their own fingerprints, and thinking like a criminologist at this center. Because a criminologist investigates crimes by analyzing clues in a systematic way, studying fingerprints is an important part of this job.

You will need one No. 2 pencil, white scratch paper, plain paper, a handheld lens, and a damp paper towel at this station. Show children how to rub soft pencil lead onto a sheet of paper and pick up a good smudge with one finger. Then, they carefully pick up the smudge with a piece of clear tape, pull it away, and press the fingerprint onto a clean paper.

Begin by having students make a set of their own fingerprints on a sheet of clean paper. If someone makes a mistake, simply peel off the tape and start over. Then create a classroom mystery for your students to solve. Ask, "Who was the last person to use the pencil sharpener?" Each group that visits the center can be a group of "suspects." Prepare prints in advance, then show prints that were "found" on the pencil sharpener. Have the children use the handheld lens to compare their prints to the set belonging to the "criminal."

Integrate fingerprinting into art by letting the children use ink pads to make prints from their hands or fingers. Children can bring the prints to life by adding legs, arms, and other features. Fingerprint stories can be developed, and you may even want to include toe prints as a homework assignment. You could go further and classify fingerprints into three basic patterns: whorl, arch, and loop. Refer to the further readings list for resources.

## Do You Hear What I Hear?

Walk in the hallway with a tape recorder and record five interesting sounds. Bring the tape back to the classroom, provide earphones, and have the children draw a picture of the sounds that they hear. Children enjoy using a tape recorder. Let them take turns tape-recording sounds during recess, assemblies, or the lunch period. Challenge them to record unusual sounds and infer what is making the sounds. Add further interest to this center by sending the tape recorder home with a child to tape "home sounds." As children identify the home sounds at the center, have them compare and contrast the sounds in their own homes and write a story about the sounds and how they are created.

The tape recorder also makes a good listening center for a variety of tapes and records. Many of the recordings should be stories. Children will enjoy illustrating the stories. Some will enjoy taping a story of their own for use in the center or as background for plays, puppet shows, or radio programs.

## Red, Yellow, and Blue

The object of this center is to mix the primary colors and observe and record the results. Have the children record the color that results from dropping the correct amounts of color into the correct container.

## Smells, Smells, Smells

Gather small amounts of familiar substances with distinctive odors, such as coffee, popcorn, orange extract, hot chocolate, onions, apples, and peanut butter. Put the items in jars, shoe boxes, plastic sandwich bags, or loosely tied brown paper bags—whichever seems appropriate—and leave small holes in the containers so that the odors can escape. As children take turns smell-ing the containers, ask them to describe the various odors and guess what might be producing these distinctive smells. Make a duplicate set of containers, and ask the children to match the ones that smell alike. Be sure to show children the safe way to smell an unknown substance: They should gently fan the air between their noses and the container with one hand and breathe normally. The scent will come to them.

## Apple or Potato?

Spread vegetable pieces on a plate for children to taste. They will have to work in pairs. One puts on a blindfold, *holds his nose*, and tries to guess what he is tasting. The other child keeps a record by writing down what the vegetable piece really is and what his partner thinks it is. Then, the children trade places, redo the test, and compare their scores.

The children will be surprised that they made a lot of wrong guesses. This is because it is hard to tell one food from another of similar texture. The secret lies inside the nose. Tongues tell only if something is sweet, sour, salty, or bitter; the rest of the information comes from the odor of the food. Lead children to the conclusion that they would have a hard time tasting without their sense of smell.

Tasting liquids that children drink frequently is fun. Pour some milk, orange juice, water, soda, or other popular drinks into paper cups or clean milk cartons and provide clean straws for tasting. Have the children describe the taste and guess what it might be. Some children will enjoy drawing a picture of their favorite flavor. A sip of water or bite of bread in between items helps clear their palates.

## TECHNOLOGY

Computer software suggestions have been inserted throughout the text. Ideally, each classroom should have two or three computers where children can take turns exploring a variety of software. There should also be time for searching the Web for information and using e-mail to communicate with others regarding problems to solve and information to share. Many early childhood and science and mathematics journals have software reviews in every issue as well as frequent reports from teachers describing how their students use technology. Further suggestions are included in Unit 40.

## MATERIALS FOR CHILDREN WITH SPECIAL NEEDS

Gargiulo and Kilgo (2005) provide suggestions for materials that will support the learning of children with disabilities. Self-correcting materials as suggested in previous units can be especially effective for children with disabilities. Many Montessori materials are self-correcting. Computer software may provide immediate feedback. Teacher-made materials can have flaps or windows that reveal the correct answer. Children with physical or multiple disabilities can be provided with battery or electronic materials that operate off switches. Some can be operated by a puff of air or a head movement.

Materials should also provide for cultural diversity. They should reflect the students' cultures, languages, communities, and disabilities. According to de Melendez and Beck (2007), multicultural planning is child-centered, developmentally based, and culturally responsive. Considerations include the children's in-dividual and cultural characteristics, language, social and emotional development, cognitive development, and physical and motor capabilities. Stereotypes should be avoided. Media, pictures, manipulatives, and books should not promote bias toward any group but should promote respect for diversity. For example, languages besides English should be represented in literature, songs, and rhymes and used in the classroom. Ethnic artifacts should be used. Accommodations should be made for children with special needs.

## SUMMARY

Stimulating science and math lessons do not happen by accident. The materials selected to teach science and math—and the format in which they are presented—are essential for successful explorations. Whether materials are purchased or scrounged, they must be flexible and appropriate to the developmental age of the child and the type of science and math learning that is required. Learning centers are designed and used to meet specific teaching objectives and must be evaluated in terms of their effectiveness.

Lists of resource books for teachers and further reading lists are included in this unit. Lists of children's books are located in Appendix B.

## SUGGESTED ACTIVITIES

1. Obtain a copy of the current NSTA Supplement of Science Education Suppliers. Select a science concept and list materials that could be used in teaching that concept.

2. Reflect on the nature of science materials. Then, make a list of materials needed for teaching a science unit that you have developed. Where will you get these materials? How will you organize them for hands-on teaching?

3. Construct a learning center. Use the center with a group of children, and share the effectiveness of the materials with the class.

4. Compile a list of free and inexpensive science teaching materials. Send for some of these materials, and evaluate if they are appropriate for young children. Share this information with the class.

5. Visit a preschool, kindergarten, and primary class. Compare the science teaching materials used in these classes. What are the similarities and differences?

6. Visit a local educational materials store. Make a list of available math materials and their prices. Bring the list to class.

7. Participate in a small group in class, and compare math materials lists. Make cooperative decisions as to what math materials should be purchased if a new prekindergarten, kindergarten, and/or primary classroom is to be furnished. Each group should consider cost as well as purpose.

8. Go to the library. Find and read at least ten children's picture books that contain math concepts (see Appendix B for suggestions). Write a description of each one. Tell how each book could be used with children.

9. Assemble two different homemade math resources that could be used with young children. Select from books, journals, and/or the Internet. Share the materials with the class. Be prepared to show the class how the resources can be made.

10. Visit two preschool, kindergarten, and/or primary classes. Ask to look at the math materials used. Diagram the math learning center or math shelves. Share the information with your class. Describe the strong and weak points of the math setup and list any changes that would make it better.

11. Add a math and science materials list to each of the units in your Activity File/Notebook.

12. Send for free commercial catalogs. Make a list of math materials that are new in each. Write down the descriptions presented in the catalogs. Share this information with your class.

## REVIEW

A. Why are learning centers essential for science and math learning?

B. What are the two main types of science equipment?

C. List some useful items for a science junk box.

D. What are some of the advantages of science kits? What are some of the disadvantages?

E. Match the description with the center.

_____Discovery center

_____Open learning center

_____Inquiry learning center

_____Science interest center

1. Children explore a concept with as little direction as possible; may be initiated by a leading question.

2. Little direction is given. Children "mess around" with materials at small tables or trays.

3. A directed discovery approach focuses on a concept. This center includes directions and is used to encourage children to go beyond what they know about a concept.

4. This center motivates children to want to learn about its materials.

F. Describe each of the following materials.

1. Concrete manipulative math materials

2. Abstract representational math materials

G. Respond to each of the following situations.

1. Mrs. Anderson has four lotto games with some of the cards missing, two geoboards with five rubber bands, and a few unit blocks in her preschool classroom. Mr. Brown has three complete lotto games, a set of Unifix Cubes, a set of unit blocks, a big tub of a variety of jar lids, and three shape puzzles. Give your opinion of the quality of math materials in each classroom. Why do you believe as you do?

2. Miss Collins says she does not believe it is appropriate to teach math to young children. When you observe in her kindergarten, you see children playing at a water table with various containers. Others are weighing toy cars on a balance scale. Is Miss Collins teaching math? If so, explain how.

3. Mr. Dominic teaches first grade. He is going to set up a math center and has been given $500 to purchase basic materials. He asks for your help. What would you suggest?

4. Mrs. Edwards teaches second grade. She has just read this book. She is trying hard to provide a developmentally appropri- ate math environment but cannot decide how to begin. What suggestions would you give her?

## REFERENCES

Baratta-Lorton, M. (1972). *Workjobs.* Menlo Park, CA: Addison-Wesley.

Baratta-Lorton, M. (1978). *Workjobs II.* Menlo Park, CA: Addison-Wesley.

Baratta-Lorton, M. (1989). *Mathematics their way.* Menlo Park, CA: Addison-Wesley.

de Melendez, W. R., & Beck, V. (2007). *Teaching young children in multicultural classrooms* (2nd ed.). Albany, NY: Thomson Delmar Learning.

Gargiulo, R., & Kilgo, J. (2005). *Young children with special needs* (2nd ed.). Albany, NY: Thomson Delmar Learning.

Richardson, K. (1984). *Developing number concepts using Unifix Cubes.* Menlo Park, CA: Addison-Wesley.

## FURTHER READING AND RESOURCES

American Association for the Advancement of Science (AAAS). (2007). *Atlas of science literacy: Project 2061* (Vol. 2). Washington, DC: Author.

Brizuela, B. M. (2004). *Mathematical development in young children: Exploring notations.* New York: Teachers College Press.

Burris, A.C. (2005). *Understanding the math you teach.* Upper Saddle River, NJ: Pearson-Merrill/Prentice-Hall.

Carin, A. A., & Sund, R. B. (1992). *Teaching science through discovery.* New York: Macmillan.

Chen, J. (2007). *Bridging: Assessment for teaching and learning in early childhood classrooms, Pre-K–3.* Thousand Oaks, CA: Corwin.

Cook, H., & Matthew, C. E. (1998). Lessons from a "living fossil." *Science and Children, 36*(3), 16–19.

Copley, J. V. (Ed.). (1999). *Mathematics in the early years.* Washington, DC: National Association for the Education of Young Children.

Copley, J. V. (2000). *The young child and mathematics.* Washington, DC: National Association for the Education of Young Children.

Copley, J. V. (Ed.). (2004). *Showcasing mathematics for the young child.* Reston, VA: National Council of Teachers of Mathematics.

Copley, J. V., Jones, C., & Dighe, J. (2007). *Mathematics. The creative curriculum approach.* Washington, DC: Teaching Strategies.

Dacey, L., & Eston, R. (2002). *Show and tell: Representing and communicating mathematical ideas in K–2 classrooms.* Sausalito, CA: Math Solutions.

Esler, W., & Esler, M. (2001). *Teaching elementary science* (8th ed.). Belmont, CA: Wadsworth.

Gallenstein, N. L. (2003). *Creative construction of mathematics and science concepts in early childhood.* Olney, MD: Association for Childhood Education International.

Glanfield, F., Bush, W. S., & Stenmark, J. K. (Eds.). (2003). *Mathematics assessment: A practical handbook for grades K–2.* Reston, VA: National Council of Teachers of Mathematics.

Green, M. D. (1996). *474 science activities for young children.* Clifton Park, NY: Thomson Delmar Learning.

Haylock, D., & Cockburn, A. (2003). *Understanding mathematics in the lower primary years* (2nd ed.). Thousand Oaks, CA: Chapman.

Hoffman, A. C., & Glannon, A. M. (1993). *Kits, games and manipulatives for the elementary school classroom: A source book.* New York: Garland.

Isbell, R., & Exelby, B. (2001). *Early learning environments that work.* Beltsville, MD: Gryphon House.

Jacobs, V. R., Bennett, T. R., & Bullock, C. (2000). Selecting books in Spanish to teach mathematics. *Teaching Children Mathematics, 6*(9), 582–587.

Jasmine, G. (2000). *Early childhood activities with internet connections.* Westminster, CA: Teacher Created Materials.

Kwan. T., & Texley, J. (2002) *Exploring safely: A guide for elementary teachers.* Arlington, VA: NSTA Press.

MacDonald, S. (2001). *Block book: The complete guide to learning and playing with blocks.* Beltsville, MD: Gryphon House.

Madrazo, G. M., Jr. (1997). Using trade books to teach and learn science. *Science and Children, 34*(6), 20–21.

Managing hands-on materials [Focus issue]. (2004). *Science and children, 11*(9).

McIntyre, M. (1984). *Early childhood and science.* Washington, DC: National Science Teachers Association.

Mix, K. S., Huttenlocher, J., & Levine, S. C. (2002). *Quantitative development in infancy and early childhood.* New York: Oxford University Press.

National Academy of Engineering and National Research Council. (2002). *Technically speaking: Why all Americans need to know more about technology.* Washington, DC: National Academies Press.

National Council of Teachers of Mathematics. (2000). *Principles and standards for school mathematics.* Reston, VA: Author.

National Council of Teachers of Mathematics. (2001–2004). *Navigations Series, pre-K–2.* Reston, VA: Author.

National Research Council. (1996). *National science education standards.* Washington, DC: National Academies Press.

National Research Council. (1999). *Selecting instructional materials: A guide for K–12.* Washington, DC: National Academies Press.

Oppenheim, C. (1993). *Science is fun! For families and classroom groups.* St. Louis, MO: Cracom.

Poppe, C. A., & Van Matre, N. (1985). *Science learning centers for the primary grades.* West Nyack, NY: Center for Applied Research in Education.

Rackow, S. J. (Ed.). (1999). K–8 Science and mathematics education [Special issue]. *ERIC Review, 6*(2).

Radeloff, D. J. (2001). Science discovery centers: Stimulating young children's minds. *Focus on Pre-K and K, 13*(3), 1–3.

Richardson, K. (1999). *Developing number concepts: Planning guide.* Parsippany, NJ: Seymour.

Ritz, W. C. (Ed.). (2007). *A head start on science.* Arlington, VA: NSTA Press.

Rule, A. C., & Barrera, M. T. III. (1999). Science object boxes. *Science and Children, 37*(2), 30–35, 63.

Thiessen, D. (Ed.). (2004). *Exploring mathematics through literature.* Reston, VA: National Council of Teachers of Mathematics.

Wakefield, A. P. (1998). *Early childhood number games.* Boston: Allyn & Bacon.

West, S., & Cox, A. (2001). *Sand and water play.* Beltsville, MD: Gryphon House.

Whitin, D. J., & Whitin, P. (2004). *New visions for linking literature and mathematics.* Urbana, IL: National Council of Teachers of English, and Reston, VA: National Council of Teachers of Mathematics.

Williams, K. C., & Veomett, G. E. (2007). *Launching learners in science, Pre-K–5.* Thousand Oaks, CA: Corwin.

Wright, R. J., Martland, J., Stafford, A. K., & Stanger, G. (2002). *Teaching number: Advancing children's skills and strategies.* Thousand Oaks, CA: Chapman.

*Note:* Resource reviews appear in each issue of *Science and Children* and *Teaching Children Mathematics* as well as in other early childhood periodicals.

# Unit 40

## Math and Science in Action

## OBJECTIVES

After reading this unit, you should be able to:

- Understand the value of children working together cooperatively.
- Plan and use blocks for math and science experiences.
- Describe the benefits of using blocks with primary age children.
- Plan and use woodworking for math and science experiences.
- Plan and use math and science games and activities with young children.
- Plan and use outdoor activities with young children.
- Understand how technology can contribute to active mathematics and science learning.
- Explain the value of culturally relevant mathematics activities.

As reviewed in Units 1 and 3, action in mathematics and science involves hands-on problem solving and inquiry. The National Council of Teachers of Mathematics (NCTM, 2000) describes five process standards: problem solving, reasoning, communicating, connections, and representations. This unit provides an overview of the kinds of activities that should be observed in action in early childhood classrooms.

Math and science go on all the time in the developmentally appropriate classroom for young children. The block builder, like any engineer, builds her building so it will stand up and serve a planned function. The young carpenter measures wood and swings his hammer to get the most power when he hits the nail. Children do finger plays and action songs and explore the outdoors while they apply math and science concepts. As children move into concrete operations, math and

science in action include more complex group games and activities and the introduction of team sports and preplanned building and science projects.

Children continue to be active learners in the primary grades. This is a fact from research based on Piagetian theory. Unfortunately, the active opportunities provided by blocks and outdoor explorations are not always considered in curriculum plans for primary age children. This is a mistake. Remember, primary age children are still concrete operation thinkers who learn to understand the world around them through actively engaging in explorations.

Block play and outdoor explorations give children many opportunities to investigate, test, and change objects. It is from these interactions that children build their own model of the world. (Refer to concept development in Units 1 through 6 to refresh your memory.)

This unit focuses on the interrelationship of blocks, woodworking, songs, action games, problem solving, outdoor activities, technology, and culturally relevant activities that meet the affective, cognitive, and psychomotor learning needs of the young child. The emphasis is on active learning both indoors and outdoors.

A math lesson that meets the NCTM standards should include the following factors (Burrill, 1997): manipulatives, cooperative groups, a teacher who is a facilitator, the use of technology, opportunities to write, and strong connections to the children's world. Activities that meet these criteria can provide a program that will avoid the *Math Curse* (Scieszka and Smith, 1995). As described in Unit 2, math and science in action includes hands-on projects for both individual and group work. Both individuals and groups of two or more can organize their work using the K-W-L-D model (Shaw, Chambless, Chessin, Price, & Beardain, 1997). "K" involves recording what is *known* from studying the problem to be solved. "W" stands for *what* (we) I want to find out; that is, identify the question. The "L" step involves recording what the student or group of students has *learned*. In the final "D" step, the answer is stated and *defended* and the process of problem solving is described—what we (I) did. An important aspect of a problem-solving approach to math and science is allowing plenty of time for students to think through and discuss their solution processes. Even in the midst of lively discussion, a long pause in the conversation may be needed for students to reflect on the problems so that they can create their own unique solutions.

## BLOCKS

Blocks are probably the play material most used by young children. Unfortunately, blocks are seldom seen in classrooms beyond the kindergarten level, even though they have the potential to function as valuable concept-building materials for primary children. Research reported by Wolfgang, Stannard, and Jones (2001) indicates that young children's block play performance during preschool is a predictor of mathematics achievement in middle school and high school.

Children apply basic concepts as they explore the relationships among the various sizes and shapes in a set of unit blocks (Figure 40–1). They note that two of one size may equal one of another, some are longer and some shorter, some are square, some are rectangular, others are triangular, and still others are curved. They are working with fractions and parts and wholes. MacDonald (2001) lists 29 mathematics and 20 science concepts and skills that children can construct and apply when building with unit blocks. Furthermore, block play enhances concepts and skills in art, literacy, physical development, social studies, and socioemotional development (MacDonald, 2001).

The block area needs plenty of space. The blocks and the small vehicles, people dolls, and animals that enhance the accompanying dramatic play activities should be neatly organized on low shelves where they can be easily reached by the children. Shelves should be marked with outlines of each block shape so that the children can return the blocks to the proper place (and practice some one-to-one correspondence). Start the year with a small, easy-to-handle set. As time goes by, more blocks and more shapes can be introduced. The teacher can facilitate exploration by asking questions and making comments. For example, Mrs. Red Fox notes that Trang Fung has used all square blocks in her structure, whereas Sara has developed her structure with larger units. "It looks like each of you have your favorite-sized blocks."

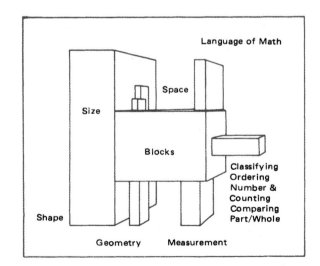

**Figure 40–1** Children can construct many concepts as they work with blocks.

Blocks can be purchased in sets of various sizes. There are a variety of shapes and sizes in each set. The basic unit is a brick-shaped rectangle that is 1⅜" × 2¾" × 5½". The variety of shapes and sizes is listed in Figure 40–2. Unit blocks should be made of good, strong, hard wood with beveled edges so that they will not wear down or splinter. They should be smoothly sanded. The sizes must be precise so that building can be done effectively. Unit block sets are very expensive, but with good care they last for many years. Keep them dry and free of dust. Occasionally they should be oiled or waxed.

At the beginning stage, the child may just handle the blocks and carry them from place to place. At the second stage, the children make rows and lines of blocks. At the third stage, children build bridges. At the fourth stage, children make simple enclosures. At the fifth stage, the children make patterns. These patterns may be balanced and symmetric. At the sixth stage, the children name the structures and use them for dramatic play. At the last stage, the children make structures that represent familiar buildings, such as their own home or even their whole city.

Children enjoy using other types of building materials besides unit blocks. Many preschools have large, hollow, wood blocks. At a lower cost, there are cardboard blocks. Cardboard boxes can enhance the imaginative activity of young children. Large boxes can be the focus of walking *around*, climbing *in*, and climbing *over*. Boxes can be moved about and combined in many different ways, providing experiences with weight, size, shape, and volume. Sheets and blankets can add to the variety of structures. Blocks and boxes provide a rich opportunity for math in action.

## BLOCKS, SCIENCE, AND CHILDREN

Block building and play are not isolated from science. The very nature of building a structure requires that children deal with the processes of science as discussed in Unit 5. As children build, they compare, classify, predict, and interpret problems. Scientific thinking is stimulated as children discover and invent new forms; expand experiences; explore major conceptual ideas in science; measure; and work with space, change, and pattern.

| | Name | Nursery | Kgn. & Primary |
|---|---|---|---|
| | Square | 40 | 80 |
| | Unit | 96 | 192 |
| | Double Unit | 48 | 96 |
| | Quadruple Unit | 16 | 32 |
| | Pillar | 24 | 48 |
| | Half Pillar | 24 | 48 |
| | Small Triangle | 24 | 48 |
| | Large Triangle | 24 | 48 |
| | Small Column | 16 | 32 |
| | Large Column | 8 | 16 |
| | Ramp | 16 | 32 |
| | Ellipse | | 8 |
| | Curve | 8 | 16 |
| | ¼ Circle | | 8 |
| | Large Switch & Gothic Door | | 4 |
| | Small Switch | | 4 |
| | Large Buttress | | 4 |
| | ½ Arch & Small Buttress | | 4 |
| | Arch & ½ Circle | | 4 |
| | Roofboard | | 24 |
| | Number of Shapes | 12 | 23 |
| | Number of Pieces | 344 | 760 |

**Figure 40–2** Childcraft block sets.

## Blocks Encourage Thinking

Blocks force children to distinguish, classify, and sort. This can be seen as a group of second graders learns the different properties of blocks by re-creating a field trip to the zoo. As they plan and build, they deal with the fact that each block has different qualities. Size, shape, weight, thickness, width, and length are considered. As construction progresses, the blocks become fulcrums and levers. Guiding questions such as "Can you make a ramp for unloading the rhinoceros?" and "Where will you put the access road for delivering food to the animals?" will help children focus on an aspect of construction. Some children create zoo animals, workers, and visitors to dramatize a day at the zoo.

Allow time for children to verbalize why they are arranging the zoo in a particular way. This will encourage children to share their problem-solving strategy and will help them clarify their thinking. By observing the children at play, you will also gain insight into their thought processes.

## Balance, Predictions, Interactions, and Movement

One emphasis in science is interactions within systems. In block building, the blocks form a system that is kept in equilibrium through balance. As children build, they work with a cause-and-effect approach to predict stress and to keep the forces of gravity from tumbling their structure. The idea that each part added to the structure contributes to the whole is constantly reinforced as children maintain its stability.

Balancing blocks is an effective way to explore cause and effect. By seeing the reaction of what they do, children begin to learn about causation. The following ideas emphasize action and cause and effect.

1. *Dominoes.* Children develop spatial relationships as they predict what will happen to an arrangement of dominoes (Figure 40–3). Ask, "Can you arrange the dominoes in such a way that they will all be knocked down?"

2. *Construct and roll.* Arrange plastic bottles or blocks in a variety of ways, and have the children try to knock them over with a ball. This bowling-

**Figure 40–3** "Arrange the dominoes so that they all will be knocked down."

like game encourages children to keep score and establish a correspondence between the way blocks are arranged and how the ball is rolled. Ask, "What action caused the blocks to fall down? What action started the ball moving? Did the ball knock down every bottle that fell? If not, what made them fall?"

3. *Pendulum release.* In a pendulum game, a ball moves without being pushed; it is released. Children structure space as they place blocks in a position to be knocked down by the pendulum bob. Have children predict, "If the ball pendulum is pulled back and released, will it knock over the block?"

Pendulums can be made life-sized by securing one end of a length of cotton string to the ceiling and attaching a weighted bob to the other end. Weighted bobs for the pendulum can be made by tying a plastic pill vial filled with sand to the cotton string. However, a smaller model may be more practical. Try this first and then tell the children how to expand to a life-sized model. One end of a length of cotton string or fish line must be attached to a stable support that allows for a swinging motion. A simple effective pendulum can be constructed by placing an eye screw into a board, suspending the board between the backs of two chairs, and attaching the string with the pendulum bob. Children can then sit on the floor and explore the action of the pendulum.

Figure 40–4  "Can you control the speed of the ball?"

4. *Inclines.* In incline activities, the ball moves when released. Exactly where the ball goes is determined by manipulating the incline and the ball. Have children change the incline in different ways to control what happens to the ball. Children will enjoy creating games such as catching the ball with a cup, racing different-sized balls down the incline, and measuring how far the ball travels (Figure 40–4).

5. *Buttons and bobby pins.* The object of this tilt game is to jiggle a button from start to finish without letting it fall off of the board or through a hole. The button or ball is guided by tilting and wiggling the board. To make the game, cut several holes in cardboard, and rub the board with a piece of waxed paper. Position bobby pins with the raised side up on the board, mark a start and finish, and begin the game.

## Pinball Wizards

Children can create pinball machines from scraps of plywood, strips of wood, glue, nails, plastic caps, and marbles. The challenge is for children to invent ways to make a marble fall down a series of ramps and make the trip as long as possible. Have the children glue wooden strips to a backboard at different angles. Then have them adjust their obstacles of nails and blocks as they try out the marble. Ask, "Can you think of a way to slow down the marble?" (You might want to introduce the concept of friction.)

## Blocks and Marbles

Balance and action can be seen as children assemble plastic ramps and chutes with commercial toys such as Marbleworks. Children gain a familiarity with concepts such as gravity, acceleration, and momentum when they design and create a maze of movement by fitting pieces together. To further introduce children to the principle of cause and effect, ask: "What action starts the marble moving?" Then have children predict the way in which the marble will move. Creating different pathways and exploring how the marble moves on them can be exciting.

Complex block and marble sets seem to fascinate primary age children. With these sets, children arrange wooden sections to allow marbles to travel through holes and grooved blocks of different lengths. Children enjoy controlling the movement of the marble down the construction and creating changes that determine direction and speed of the marble. Children can make their own marble runs from decorative molding that is available in paneling supply stores. The track can be nailed onto boards, taped down, or held for observing the movement of marbles (some will move at breakneck speeds). Have your students add a tunnel, try different types of balls, and find ways to use friction to slow down the marbles.

## Another Type of Construction

Constructions introduce children to the conditions and limitations of space. They learn to bridge space with appropriate-sized blocks and objects and to enclose space in different ways. The following ideas involve creating your own construction set with straws.

Use large straws for straw construction, and connect them with string, pipe cleaners, or paper clips. String is the most difficult to use but makes the most permanent construction. Simply stick the string in one end of the straw and then suck on the other end. The string will come through.

You will have to form a triangle with three straws. A triangle is the only shape made with straws that is rigid enough for building. If you are using string as a connector, tie the ends together to form a triangle, or thread three straws on one string to form the triangle.

Pipe cleaners as connectors are another method of building with straws. Push a pipe cleaner halfway into the end of one straw, then slip another straw over the other end of the pipe cleaner. Double up the pipe cleaners for a tighter fit. Children can twist and turn this construction in many ways.

Many teachers recommend paper clips as ideal connectors in straw building. Open a paper clip, bend out the two ends, and slip each end into a straw. Paper clips are rigid and allow for complex building. You might have to add as many as three paper clips to give the structure strength. Paper clips may also be chained for a flexible joint between two straws. Challenge children to think and construct. Ask: "How tall a structure can you make? Why did your structure collapse? Can you make a bridge?"

When the straw frame stands by itself, test it. Ask, "Can you think of a way to test the strength of your structure?" Place a paper clip through a paper cup and hang it somewhere on the straw structure. Ask, "How many paper cups can your structure support? How many paper clips will make the frame work?"

## Block City

Blocks in the classroom provide many opportunities to integrate basic reading and writing, science, math skills and concepts, and social studies into the construction process. Opportunities for integration abound as children explore the busy life of a block city.

Mr. Wang's second grade created a city of blocks. Buildings had to be accurate in the city, and each child builder represented herself in the daily acting out of city life. The block building sessions were preceded by class discussion as the children planned the daily block activities. Accessories (labeled boxes of food, clothing, computers, typewriters, and the like) were constructed from a variety of materials. Children played the roles of shopkeepers, bankers, and other workers. They made decisions such as where the people in the block city would get their money.

When the children had to put out an imaginary fire, they immediately saw a problem. How would they get water to the blaze? This discovery led to an investigation of how water gets into hydrants, utility covers, and water pipes. The children responded to the emergency by adding plastic tubing to the city as well as wire for electricity and telephones.

Not only was the city becoming more realistic, it was becoming less magical. Children no longer thought that water magically appeared when the water faucet was turned on. They knew that a system of pipes carried the water. In fact, the workings of a city in general became less magical. Many common misconceptions were dispelled, and an understanding of how a city functions began to develop.

## The Edible Village

Mrs. Moore's first-grade class integrated the study of their neighborhood with block building. After determining the different sections of the neighborhood and buildings they needed to create, each child was assigned a building. The class created their neighborhood with blocks made of graham crackers. They used flattened caramels for roadways and lollipops for streetlights. Coconut spread over white icing gave the illusion of snow.

The students mixed yellow and green food coloring into icing to create differently colored buildings. Recipes for icing provided opportunities to use measurements and follow directions in sequence. Writing about the creation of the village and what might be happening within graham cracker walls became a springboard for discussion.

Children made decisions about what should and should not be included in the village. They determined the authenticity of buildings and building size. This activity is especially appropriate for primary age children. Children in this age group are able to incorporate more detail and can be exposed to another's viewpoint. For example, the teacher asked, "How will the people know that school is open?" Children began asking each other, "Do we need a hospital? What about a gas station?"

If your city or town is located near a river or lake, be sure to include it in construction. Paper straw bridges could be added and the geography of your area explored. You will find that as the children develop questions, they are motivated to find the answers because they need to know something for construction of the city. Thus, the block experience also becomes a first research experience.

# WOODWORKING

Most young children enjoy working with wood. Woodworking provides hands-on experience with measurement, balance, power, and spatial and size relationships. Children use informal measurement as they check to see if they have a piece of wood that is the one they need and if they have a nail that is the correct length. As children move into the primary level, they can apply standard measurement: "I will need 12 pieces of 12-by-8-inch plywood for my birdhouse." The more advanced primary children can follow simple instructions and use patterns to make projects.

For effective woodworking, the classroom should have a sturdy workbench, good-quality real tools, and assorted pieces of soft wood. The workbench should be large enough for at least two children to work at the same time. Woodworking must always be closely supervised. Workbenches designed for children can be purchased from the major school supply companies, or a large old tree stump can be used.

Two 7 oz.
Claw Hammers

One 12''
Back-type Saw

One 3''
Screwdriver
One 4''
Screwdriver

One Combination
Pliers

**Figure 40–5** Basic woodworking tools for 4- and 5-year-olds: Start with these and add more as children become more proficient.

The basic components of a high-quality tool set for 4- and 5-year-olds are illustrated in Figure 40–5. Older children can use a greater variety of tools. The tools should be easily accessible when in use but kept in a locked closet or on a high shelf when not in use. Beginners do best with short nails with large heads.

Soft wood such as pine is easy to work with. When sawing is introduced, the wood should be put in a vise so it will hold steady and so the child's hands will not be in the line of the saw.

Experienced woodworkers enjoy creating projects using odds and ends with their wood. Wheels can be made from bottle caps and windows from plastic lids. Scraps of cloth or ribbon can be glued on to the wood. Children can apply their math vocabulary as they explain their finished projects.

# MATH GAMES

As described in Unit 24, board games provide opportunities for counting and one-to-one correspondence. They also provide opportunities for developing social skills such as cooperation and following rules.

Young children enjoy playing games. Some 4-year-olds and most 5-year-olds enjoy playing board games. For the preschooler, games should be simple with a minimum of rules.

Board games provide an excellent way to teach math. Candyland, Numberland Counting Game, Chutes and Ladders, Fraction Brothers Circus, Memory, Picture Dominoes, Picture Nines (a domino game), Candyland Bingo, Triominos, Connect Four, Count-a-Color, Farm Lotto, and other bingo and lotto boxed games can be purchased. Board game patterns can be obtained from early childhood publications and **Internet** sites. For more advanced children, basic concepts can be practiced using board games such as Multiplication/Division Quizmo, Addition/Subtraction Mathfacts Game, Multiplication/Division Mathfacts Game, UNO, UNO Dominoes, Yahtzee, and IMMAWhiz Math Games. Two games that help children learn money concepts are Pay the Cashier and Count Your Change.

Lakeshore has wooden board games that provide materials for the youngest game players. Number Bingo can be purchased from Constructive Playthings. Early Childhood Direct carries Color and Shape Bingo, Bingo Bears, a set of readiness math games, and some more advanced games (Number Start, Number Detective, Playcount).

Other basic board games were described in Unit 24. Card games enjoyed by primary children include those suggested by Kamii (see Unit 27) and those that are perennial favorites such as Go Fish, Concentration, Crazy Eights, Old Maid, Flinch, Solitaire, and Fantan. Look through catalogs, and examine games at exhibitors' displays when you attend professional meetings. There is a vast selection available.

Young children enjoy bowling games and games that involve aiming. Dropping clothespins into a container or throwing beanbags through a hole or into a container are appropriate for young children. Once they learn the game, they can keep track of their successes using Unifix Cubes or making tally marks to keep score.

Outdoors or in the gym, children can have races. They can estimate how far they can throw a ball, a beanbag, or a paper plate. Primary children can measure with a yardstick and compare their estimates with their actual throwing distances.

Primary children enjoy jumping rope. They enjoy jumping to jingles such as "Mabel, Mabel." During the primary years, children are in the stage of industry versus inferiority. The struggle between these forces leads them into a natural interest in competitive activities, such as the games listed, and into team sports and races. Adults must find ways for each of the children to achieve so that they do not experience inferiority feelings. Primary children enjoy races that give them practice in time and distance relationships. Hurdle jumping can begin with high and low jumps then move into standard measures of height. Balls, beanbags, or Frisbees can be thrown and the distances compared and measured. Team sports require scorekeeping and an understanding of *more, less,* and *ordinal relations* (i.e., who is up first, second, and so on).

Primary children also enjoy math puzzlers and brainteasers that give them practice in problem solving. Some of these types of problems were introduced in Unit 3. The following are additional examples.

Move one so each set has a sum of 15.

## Magic Triangles

Write the numbers 1 through 6 in the circles of the triangle below in such a way as to have a total of 9 (or 10 or 11 or 12) on each side.

Totals of Nine

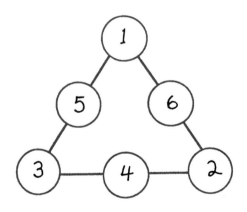

One Solution

## The Lady and the Tiger

How many different squares can you count?

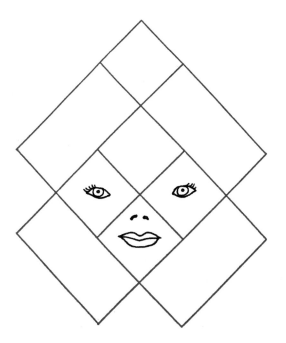

How many different triangles can you count?

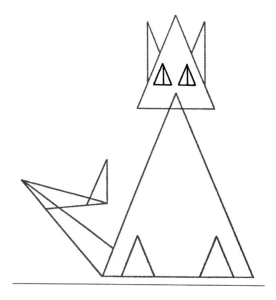

## Your Number

Ask someone to think of a number, but keep it secret. Now tell him to double the number, add eight to the result, divide by two, and subtract the original number. Then have him write down the answer but tell him not to show it to you until you predict the answer. The answer will always be 4.

Young children enjoy games. Board, target, and action games offer them opportunities to apply math concepts. Through observation of children playing games, adults can obtain information regarding a child's development of math skills and concepts. Each issue of *Teaching Children Mathematics* includes a thematic section called Math by the Month that poses problems for elementary students beginning with kindergarten through grade 2. For example, in May 2001 the theme was "summer fun." Four problems were presented: one involved addition and subtraction, another was a geometry walk based in a shape book, a third focused on graphing favorite ice cream flavors, and the fourth used nonstandard and standard foot measurement.

## Finger Plays and Action Songs

Many finger plays and action songs include the application of math concepts. Children may have to hear the song or finger play several times before they join in. If the teacher keeps repeating it, the students will gradually learn and participate. Favorite finger plays are "Five Little Monkeys Jumping on the Bed" and "Five Little Ducks Swimming in a Pond." A longtime favorite song is "Johnny Works with One Hammer." Counting rhymes are particularly enjoyed (Arenson, 1998). Two examples are as follows.

One potato,

Two potato,

Three potato,

Four;

Five potato,

Six potato,

Seven potato,

More.

> Here is the beehive (fist closed),
>
> Where are the bees?
>
> Hidden a way where nobody sees,
>
> Soon they come creeping out of the hive,
>
> (open fingers one at a time)
>
> One! Two! Three! Four! Five!

See the resources listed at the end of the unit. Finger plays and action songs help children learn math concepts through body actions.

## Math in the Environment

The outdoors provides many opportunities for mathematics applications. Children can count the number of windows they can see from the playground. They can do informal measurements of playground equipment and distances across the playground. Shadows can be measured at different times of the day.

Baker and Baker (1991) suggest many outdoor activities in their book *Counting on a Small Planet*. For example, in the activity "All That Rubbish," children examine the rubbish left in their lunch boxes after they have eaten. They chart the results over time and develop conclusions regarding their rubbish. Other investigations include noise pollution, water use and abuse, wind, and other outdoor topics.

A first-grade unit on the rain forest provided many mathematics applications (Thornton, Dee, Damkoehler, Gehrenbeck, & Jones, 1995). The study of the rain forest provided opportunities to advance the students' number sense as they created a sense of the space occupied by the rain forest, built a classroom rain forest, and used related problem-solving experiences. The students kept journals, made graphs, and did some estimating.

## Solving Mathematics Problems

A critical activity in mathematics is problem solving, as detailed in Unit 3. Many examples of children's problem-solving approaches can be found in articles in *Teaching Children Mathematics*. The *Navigation* series on problem solving and reasoning provides examples of problems to be solved (see Findell et al., 2004; Greenes et al., 2003; Small et al., 2004). Prekindergartners and kindergartners can be provided with problems involving number relationships, patterning, nonstandard measurement, and simple data analysis (Greenes et al., 2003). First graders can work with algebraic relationships, geometric relationships, data graphing, and measurement (Findell et al., 2004). Second graders can move on to more complex problems in number, algebraic, geometric, measurement, and reasoning about data relationships (Small et al., 2004). Beginning problem solvers use drawings and/or manipulatives to reach solutions whereas more advanced students gradually invent numerical processes.

## SCIENCE IN ACTION: THE OUTDOORS

Virtually all outdoors is science. This is where children can become a part of the natural world. Whether you use the outdoor environment around you to extend and enhance indoor science lessons or design lessons that focus on available outdoor resources, your students will benefit from the experience.

Children will be enthusiastic about exploring the "real" world. After all, "The real thing is worth a thousand pictures." Although this variation on the old saying—and many of the suggestions for implementing outdoor learning—overlap with field-trip experiences, most of the learning strategies suggested here can also be done in an urban setting. School yards, sidewalks, vacant lots, or any strip of ground can be an area for outdoor learning. The important thing is to get your students outdoors and engage them in challenging learning.

Specific plans for outdoor learning will help ensure a successful experience. The following suggestions include teaching strategies that focus on specific science learnings. Refer to Units 33, 34, 36, and 41 for more outdoor and environmental education ideas.

## Animal Study Activities

Animal homes, habits, and behaviors fascinate children. To begin a successful outdoor experience, assess the previous experiences, skills, and attention spans of your students. Then, review the teacher preparation and control suggestions at the end of this section (Planning for Outdoor Learning) and begin.

## Animal Homes

Involve children in the study of animal homes. First discuss, "Where might an animal live?" Then plan a field trip to look for animal homes. When planning a trip,

keep in mind that most animals make their homes on southern slopes (sunny and warm). When you find a home, examine the area for tracks (Figure 40–6). Make a cast of the tracks and determine if the home is in use. Ask, "How can we tell if an animal lives here?" (One way is to look for signs such as food scraps and activity around the entrance.) Discuss possible reasons for the selection of this particular location for an animal home, and speculate on the possible enemies and living habits of the occupant.

**Figure 40–6** "You can identify an animal by the tracks that you see."

## Finding Insects

Insects can be hard to find, but signs of their presence are common. The paper nest of a hornet or mud nest of a wasp can be found on buildings, rocks, or some tree branches. Be careful—if the nests are occupied, the owners may sting.

The presence of bark beetles can be seen by the "tunnel" left when they strip bark from logs. Most children are familiar with ant nests and know how to find them. Fallen logs are good locations for observing insects in the winter. The insects are usually sluggish, and the stinging types can be more easily observed.

Follow animal home observations with discussion. Ask questions such as, "What have we learned about the kinds of animals that live around our school? What are their needs?" Pick one animal to focus on. Have children write about what one of the animals is thinking as it prepares a home.

## A Different Type of Home

The next time you see a swollen, tumorlike bulge on the stem, flower head, stalk, or root of a plant, you might be looking at a unique insect home known as a *gall*. The gall has a hard outer wall and contains a food supply from the plant tissue. Have your students search for galls growing on flowers, bushes, or trees. Lead the children to discover that certain types of galls are found on specific plants. For example, a gall found on a Canada goldenrod (*Solidago canadensis*) is caused by a small, brown-winged fly. This fly (*Eurosta solidaginis*) forms a gall only on the Canada goldenrod (Figure 40–7).

Children will enjoy dramatizing the life of a gall insect. Say, "Pretend you are tiny and helpless. Find a place where you can be safe." Have the children pull jackets over their heads to simulate how protected the insect feels. Make a large papier-mâché gall for children to crawl into. Furnish it with a battery-powered light, and children will enjoy crawling in to read, write poems, or turn the light off and simply speculate about what it would be like to be a gall insect inside its home.

## Interview a Spider

Children enjoy becoming reporters and interviewing various wildlife. After discussing what a reporter does

**Figure 40–7** A gall is a different type of insect home.

and the techniques of interviewing, teams of children can decide on an animal they want to interview.

## Birds, Birds, Birds

A bird feeder is a good place to begin observing birds. If you do not have a suitable tree near your school, make your own with limbs or cornstalks tied together and propped up to provide perches and shelter. You will be providing birds with much-needed food, and as the birds come to eat, children will have a chance to observe them and their activities at close range.

Children will enjoy making seasonal ornaments and garlands for an outdoor holiday tree. Also, use ground feeders or seed dispensers as added attractions for the birds. To decorate a tree, have students string foods that appeal to a wide range of birds. Give them cubes of cheese, popcorn, raisins, and peanuts (in shells). To attract fruit-eating songbirds, add dried fruits to the strings.

Plain peanuts in their shells appeal to both insect- and seed-eating birds, so hang them on fishing line or skewer them on galvanized wire and attach the line to the tree. Then watch the antics of birds such as blue jays as they break open the shells.

Instruct children to keep a notebook of which foods various birds most like to eat. If you prefer, feed birds in aluminum TV dinner trays. Mount the trays on a board and puncture them so that excess moisture can drain out. Fill the different compartments in the trays with cracked corn, sunflower seeds, commercial bird-seed, and fruit. Then watch as the birds come to feed, and ask questions that help students focus on the differences in the birds' feeding habits. "Which birds prefer to eat on the ground? Do all of the birds eat seeds? Which like fruit the best?"

Have children begin a class (and personal) list of the birds that visit your feeder. With a little practice, children might be beginning a lifelong hobby and interest. You need to be familiar with the birds in your area that will most likely appear at the feeder. Each bird has its own specific habits, food preferences, and actions. Take the children on a field trip and compare birds seen with the birds that visit the schoolyard feeder. (Refer to Unit 41 for additional bird activities.)

## My Wild Plant

Observing a wild plant and learning as much as possible through observation makes a good long-term activity for spring. Visit a vacant lot or school parking lot with the children, and try to find a spot not likely to be mowed, paved, or interfered with during spring months. Or contact your school maintenance personnel, and ask them to leave a small section of the schoolyard untouched for a month.

Have each child select one wild plant as her own for close study. A label with a child's name on it can be taped around the stems of the plant she selects. Encourage children to begin a plant notebook to make entries about their plant (Figure 40–8). For example:

**Figure 40–8** "Describe your plant as it appears today."

1. Describe the plant as it appears today.
2. Measure everything you can with a tape measure.
3. Count all plant parts. Does the plant have an odor?
4. What textures did you find on the plant? (You might be able to record these with crayon rubbings.)
5. Does your plant make any sounds?
6. What other plants are the nearest neighbors of yours?
7. Do any animals live on or visit your plant?

During subsequent visits, determine how the plant has grown and changed. Decide what effect the plant has on other plants and animals living nearby, and determine what is good or bad about this plant. Encourage children to make drawings and take photographs so that they will be able to share the story of their plant with others. Then, predict what the plant and growing site will be like in one year.

## Hugging a Tree

A variation of selecting a special plant is to have children work in pairs to explore a tree. Blindfold one of the partners. Have the other partner lead the blindfolded one to a tree. Give the children time to touch, smell, and hug the tree. Then, bring the children back to a starting point, take the blindfold off, and ask, "Can you find the tree that you hugged?" Children will enjoy finding a special tree to hug; some might even want to whisper a secret to the tree.

## Adopt a Rock

Have children select a favorite rock for their collection and examine it closely. Then, put the rock in a bowl with other rocks. Ask, "Can you find your rock?" Blindfold students and pass the rocks around the group. Ask, "Which rock feels like your rock?" Then, help children trace the rock to the meal eaten last night. For example, rocks break down into soil, plants grow in soil, and animals live in plants.

## What's for Dinner?

After adopting a rock, say to the children, "Go home tonight, and list everything you have for dinner." The next day, have children work in groups to discuss the dinner menu and analyze where their food comes from. Help children trace every food back to a plant; for example, milk to cow to grass. Have reference books available for children to consult. Encourage the children to reach the conclusion that all animals and people need food, and that we all depend upon plants for food. Ask, "Do the plants need people and animals?" After a lively discussion, point out the decay of animal life that nourishes plants. Then, create a food chain for your bulletin board by using yarn to connect pictures of animals, plants, soil, and rocks. Add the sun, and have children create their own food chains to hang from a hanger (Figure 40–9).

## Scavenger Hunts and Other Ten-Minute Activities

Scavenger hunts are an excellent way to challenge children while focusing their attention on the task at hand. Make up a set of file cards they can take out with them. Each card should have a challenge on it; for example,

■ Find a seed.
■ Find three pieces of litter.

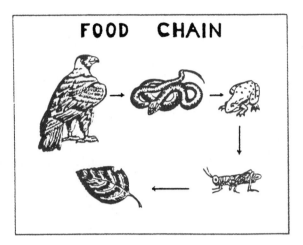

**Figure 40–9** A food chain.

■ Find something a bird uses for nesting material.
■ Find something red.
■ Find something a squirrel would eat.
■ Find something that makes its own food.
■ Find something that shows signs of erosion.
■ Find something that shows change.
■ Find a bird's feather.

Caution the children to collect only small quantities of the item on their card, or not to collect at all if they will damage something. In this case, write a description of the situation. Pass out the cards, and tell the individuals or teams that they have ten minutes to meet the challenge. Discuss the findings back in the classroom.

## Circle Game

If the ground is dry, sit in a circle and pass an object such as a rock, leaf, or twig around the circle. As each child touches the object, he or she must say something that is observed about the object. Say, "You will need to listen and not repeat an observation made by anyone else." Remember, observations are made with the senses. Do not accept inferences or predictions.

While you are still in the circle, move the children apart so that they do not touch each other, and ask them to close their eyes and explore the area around them with just their hands (and bare feet, if the weather is nice). Then ask them to describe or write the textures that they felt.

## Outdoor Learning and Writing Experiences

Writing, drawing, and dictating can be integrated with outdoor learning experiences. Here are a few suggestions.

- Write poems about something that was observed during an outdoor experience.
- Write a story about a living thing in the outdoors that has the power to speak to the humans that come to visit its outdoor area. What might the living thing say? What questions might it ask you?
- Write and draw posters that describe outdoor experiences.
- Keep a written log of outdoor activities.
- Write a short play about the outdoor trip.
- Write letters to someone about one aspect of the outdoor experience.
- Dictate stories about an incident or observation made during the outdoor experience.
- Write how you would feel if you were a plant and it didn't rain for a long time.

A field trip provides an opportunity for a first-hand multisensory nature experience.

## Planning for Outdoor Learning

Taking children outdoors can be a challenge if you are not prepared. To ensure the greatest value from the experience, teachers of all age groups should consider the following.

1. Think about your purpose for including outdoor experiences. How will children benefit? What type of preparation do the children need before they go outdoors?

2. What are the logistics? Will you walk, drive, or ride in cars? What type of clothing is needed? Should you take snacks? Are there people to contact? What are the water and toilet facilities? How much help do you need?

3. Which science concepts will be developed? What do you hope to accomplish?

4. Have you planned what you will be teaching before the experience, during the activity, and after the experience?

5. How much talking do you really need to do?

6. How will you evaluate the experience?

7. What types of follow-up learning will be provided? What subjects can you integrate into the experience?

### Attention Grabbers

Devices for grabbing the attention of a group can be physical, such as pulling out a huge beef thighbone from your bag when you want to discuss animal bones. The bone will be heavy, but this action is guaranteed to grab the attention of your group.

More subtle attention grabbers include:

1. Look intently at an object to focus group attention on the same object.

2. Have children remind you of tasks, carry various items, assist with the activity, and lead in other tasks. This participation helps keep their attention.

3. Lowering your voice when you want to make a point works well in the classroom and outdoors.

4. Change your position. Sit down with the children when they begin to wander, and regroup them.

5. Give the children specific items to look for or match, notes to take, or specific jobs. Children tend to lose interest if they do not have a task.

### Additional Control Strategies

Although you might be proficient at controlling children indoors, the outdoors can be quite a different matter. Here are a few tips.

1. Before the outdoor experience, set up a firm set of rules (as you do indoors). As you know, it is far easier to relax rules than the other way around. However, hurting and frightening animals, crushing plants, and littering should not be tolerated.

2. When children become too active, try an attention grabber or initiate an activity designed to give children a chance to run. For example, "Run to the big pine tree and back to me." Relays with rocks as batons will also expend excess energy.

3. Have a prearranged attention signal for activities that require wandering. A whistle, bell, or hand signals work well.

4. When one child is talking and others desperately want your attention, place your hand on their hand to let them know that you recognize them.

5. Let different children enjoy leading the adventure. Occasionally, remove yourself from the line, take a different place in line, and go in a different direction. In this way, you lead the group in a new direction with different children directly behind you.

6. Play follow the leader with you as the leader as you guide the line where you want it to go. If there is snow on the ground, have the children walk like wolves: Wolves walk along a trail in single file, putting their feet in the footprints of the wolf ahead of them. If you

are at the zoo, try walking to the next exhibit like the animal you have just been observing would walk.

7. Be flexible. If something is not working, just change the activity. Later you can analyze why something was not working the way you had planned.

Exciting outdoor activities do not happen by chance. Begin by planning carefully what you want the children to learn. Then teach the lesson, and evaluate the children's learning and your preparation. You will be off to a good start as an outdoor science educator.

## TECHNOLOGY

Relevant technology has been suggested throughout this text. More software (e.g., *The Magic School Bus Explores the Ocean*) is being put on CD-ROM. Children ages 6 to 10 will enjoy accompanying Ms. Frizzle and her class on a field trip to the sandy beaches and to the ocean's depths. The program also includes games, experiments, and a treasure hunt. In the same series is *Dinosaurs* for children in grades 2–12. This program takes children on a trip to explore the time of the dinosaurs. (See the review of both CD-ROMs in the January 1997 issue of *Science and Children*.)

Exciting adventures await students as they use the Internet. The **World Wide Web** provides opportunities for teachers to share ideas while students can expand their knowledge. For example, a science teacher in Virginia whose students were interested in comparing Atlantic coast shells with shells found in other parts of the world assisted them in connecting with schools in other countries through the Internet (Holden, 1996). The students made contact through e-mail and initiated an exchange of beach materials. Another teacher focused on mathematical thinking by having her students investigate pet ownership around the world through the Internet (Lynes, 1997). The students applied several standards areas: problem solving, communication, reasoning, and connections. The Global Schoolhouse provides access to collaborative projects and communication tools (classroom conferencing, mailing lists, and discussion boards). You may access the Online Companion to find a link to their website.

## Instructional Technology in Action

Instruction technology offers many opportunities for children to learn more about the world around them than would be possible in the confines of the classroom or schoolyard. There are numerous pieces of software available for young children that encourage critical thinking and problem solving. For example, young children can plan towns, roads, parks, and more by using *Stickybear Town Builder* (for grades K–3) or *SimTown* (ages 8–12). The popular children's magazine *Highlights* offers interactive computer software that includes a science corner, hidden pictures, and rebus stories. In using *Thinkin' Things* software, children build higher-level thinking skills as they determine secret rules, make logical comparisons, and determine patterns. *Sammy's Science House* offers pre-K to grade-2 children a gadget builder as well as opportunities to sort and classify plants and animals, to sequence events in a filmlike fashion, and to explore different weather conditions.

The Internet and the World Wide Web (WWW) offer opportunities for students to interact with other students—and even scientists—from across the world, to see images otherwise inaccessible, and to play educational games. Most Web **browsers** (e.g., Internet Explorer, Mozilla Firefox, Netscape, Safari) and Web **search engines** (e.g., Google, Yahoo!, Webcrawler, Lycos) offer some sort of "Just for Kids" option on their home page. You can also find great websites by using a browser to initiate a search. For example, you could enter the phrase "kids and science" in the search field and see what links are listed. Once you locate any site that you want your children to use, be sure to **bookmark** that site; this bookmark (or similar feature; browsers vary) allows you to recall the site later without having to do a search or type an Internet address, or **URL**.

There are many resources available to find out more about using the World Wide Web in your classroom. Wentworth Worldwide Media offers a number of products that can be useful. First, a guide titled *Educator's Internet Companion* has information on how to find websites with lesson plans and how to share ideas with others via the Web; it also provides many

WWW addresses so you can start "surfing the Web" right away. Second, a special newsletter titled *Classroom Connect* offers nine monthly issues jam-packed with ideas, WWW addresses, and lesson-plan ideas.

If your school does not have access to the Web, there are options for you to explore that use WWW sites. For example, *WebWhacker* software allows the user to **download** entire sites for later use on a computer that is not connected to the Internet. However, not all sites will download and the download process can be rather lengthy. Nonetheless, for those that can download, it is wonderful to be able to **surf** websites without even having an Internet connection! Additionally, *Classroom Connect* offers software (the *Educator's Internet CD Club*) that includes entire websites and lesson plans without the need for Internet access.

## CULTURALLY RELEVANT MATHEMATICS AND SCIENCE

Remember that the first NCTM (2000) principle is that of equity. "Excellence in mathematics education requires equity—high expectations and strong support of all students" (p. 12). Respect for and accommodation to differences is essential to instruction in both mathematics and science. As a follow-up to support and elaborate on the equity principle, a special issue of *Teaching Children Mathematics* (Barta, 2001) consists of articles that look at various aspects of mathematics and culture.

In Unit 2, ethnomathematics—the natural mathematics that children learn in their culture—was described. Information regarding ethnomathematics can be obtained from the International Study Group on Ethnomathematics website (Eglash, 2001). You may access the Online Companion to find a link to their website. It is essential to discover and build on the mathematics that children bring to school. It is also necessary to use culturally relevant materials and activities. For example, many of the books suggested throughout this text reflect cultural diversity (see especially Unit 15 and Appendix B). Some books are written in English but focus on other cultures. For example, in the book *Round Is a Mooncake* (Thong, 2000), a young girl seeks out shapes in a Chinese American setting. In *Feast for Ten* (Falwell, 1993), an African American family is followed while shopping for, cooking, serving, and eating a meal. Other books are written in other languages as translations of English-language classics or as stories written originally in other languages. Books in Spanish are increasing in number and are reviewed yearly in *Science and Children* and frequently in *Young Children.* Advice on selecting mathematics-related books in Spanish is the subject of an article by Jacobs, Bennett, and Bullock (2000).

Culturally relevant mathematics and science can be integrated with social studies. Internet activities such as those just described can provide opportunities to learn about other geographic areas and their cultures while obtaining science knowledge and applying mathematics knowledge. Upper grade or younger advanced students can study and compare the mathematical systems of other cultures such as Native American, Roman, and Egyptian. Calendars of various cultures can be compared, such as Chinese, Jewish, and Muslim (Zaslavsky, 2001). White (2001) describes how first graders explored geometry by comparing fabrics from different cultures.

## SUMMARY

Math and science in action mean children exploring the environment. This is done through woodworking, block constructing, game playing, problem solving, and exploring the outdoor areas in their environment. Math and science in action mean children saying, singing, and acting out math and science language and concepts.

When children make block-building decisions, they are thinking like scientists. They focus on a problem and use the thinking skills of math and science to arrive at a solution or conclusions. Block building and other indoor and outdoor explorations give children an opportunity to learn by manipulating and acting on their environment as they build their own model of the world.

The outdoor environment can be used to extend and enhance indoor lessons or as a specific place for engaging children in challenging learning. Suggestions have been given about how to work directly with outdoor learning as well as strategies for focusing children's attention on outdoor learning and encouraging higher-level math and science thinking. Once children learn how to learn outdoors, they will enjoy the fascinating world around them. Technology provides increasing opportunities for learning about science and applying mathematical skills and concepts through software applications and through the broad domain opened up by the Internet. Equity is an essential principle of mathematics and science instruction. Focusing on children's cultural mathematics and science and comparisons with the mathematics and science of other cultures shows respect for diversity.

## KEY TERMS

bookmark
browser
download

Internet
search engine
surf

URL
World Wide Web

## SUGGESTED ACTIVITIES

1. Visit a school supply store or toy store, and examine the types of blocks available for purchase. How do they compare with the blocks described in this unit?

2. Look through some educational supply catalogs (see list in Unit 39), and note the prices of various sets and types of blocks. Which would you select? How much would they cost?

3. Observe some preschool, kindergarten, and/ or primary students playing with blocks. See if you can categorize the developmental stages of their block building. Report on your observations in class.

4. Visit a local hardware store or a local discount store hardware department. Record the types of tools available and the prices. Compare your findings with the prices of similar toys in educational catalogs.

5. Find five math finger plays, songs, and/or rhymes. Teach them to the other members of the class.

6. Try out a math board game or a math action game with a small group of children. Share your experience with the class.

7. Design an outdoor activity, and teach it to a group of primary age children. Share your experience with the class.

8. Secure samples of outdoor education resources. Modify them for primary grades, and include them in your file.

9. Locate a classroom that has access to the Internet. Find out if the students are using the Internet in any math- and/or science-related activities.

10. Prepare a list of positive reinforcement statements that you will use when implementing outdoor education. How do the strategies compare with those used in an indoor setting? Discuss reasons for any differences.

11. Evaluate a software program for young children that emphasizes one of the concepts or skills discussed in this unit. Choose from the following list of software mentioned in this unit and/or from recommended software resources in other units.

   ■ *Magic School Bus: The Ocean* (ages 6–10; Redmond, WA: Microsoft)

   ■ *Magic School Bus: Dinosaurs* (grades 2–12; Redmond, WA: Microsoft)

   ■ *Sammy's Science House* (pre-K–2; San Francisco: Edmark). Order through Broderbund or Riverdeep.

   ■ *SimTown* (ages 8–12; Maxis)

■ *Stickybear Town Builder* (K–3; Norfolk, CT: Optimum Resource). Order from K–12 Software.

■ *Thinkin' Things 1* and *Thinkin' Things 2* (ages 4–13; San Francisco: Edmark). Order through Broderbund or Riverdeep.

Other software selections you might explore:

■ *Learn about Series* (grades K–2; Elgin, IL: Sunburst). A variety of selections such as senses, astronomy, matter, measurement and mixtures, and more.

■ *Memory Fun!* (grades K–3; Elgin, IL: Sunburst). Designed like the memory game Concentration. Provides experience in categorizing and memory.

■ *Thinkin' Things Fripple Town* (grades K–3; San Francisco: Edmark). Promotes thinking skills through art, geography, language arts, mathematics, and science.

■ *WebWhacker* (adults; Houston, TX: Forefront Direct). Utility for downloading websites.

The *Educator's Internet Companion, Classroom Connect*, and the *Educators' Internet CD Club* are available from Wentworth Worldwide Media (address in Appendix B).

## REVIEW

A. Explain the benefits of block play for young children.

B. List several types of block accessory toys.

C. Describe how to set up a woodworking area.

D. At which stage of block building is each of the following examples?
   1. Putting blocks in rows
   2. Carrying blocks around
   3. Building structures for dramatic play
   4. Building simple enclosures

E. List some popular early childhood board games.

F. Explain how finger plays and action songs can support math concept development.

G. Explain the value of the World Wide Web to math and science instruction.

H. What are the benefits of including outdoor activities with primary age children?

I. Describe at least two factors that support cultural equity.

## REFERENCES

Arenson, R. (Illus.). (1998). *One, two, skip a few! First number rhymes.* New York: Barefoot Books.

Baker, A., & Baker, J. (1991). *Counting on a small planet: Activities for environmental mathematics.* Portsmouth, NH: Heinemann.

Barta, J. (Ed.). (2001). Mathematics and culture [Special issue]. *Teaching Children Mathematics, 7*(6).

Burrill, G. (1997, April). Show me the math! *NCTM News Bulletin, 3.*

Eglash, R. (2001). News from the net: The international study group on ethnomathematics. *Teaching Children Mathematics, 7*(6), 336.

Fallwell, C. (1993). *Feast for 10.* New York: Clarion.

Findell, C. R., Cavanagh, M., Dacey, L., Greenes, C. E., Sheffield, L. J., & Small, M. (2004). *Navigating through problem solving and reasoning in grade 1.* Reston, VA: National Council of Teachers of Mathematics.

Greenes, C. E., Dacey, L., Cavanagh, M., Findell, C. R., Sheffield, L. J., & Small, M. (2003). *Navigating through problem solving and reasoning in prekindergarten–kindergarten.* Reston, VA: National Council of Teachers of Mathematics.

Holden, J. C. (1996). The science exchange program. *Science and Children, 34*(3), 20–21.

Jacobs, V. R., Bennett, T. R., & Bullock, C. (2000). Selecting books in Spanish to teach mathematics. *Teaching Children Mathematics, 6*(9), 582–587.

Lynes, K. (1997). Tech time: Mining mathematics through the Internet! *Teaching Children Mathematics, 3*(7), 394–396.

MacDonald, S. (2001). *Block play: The complete guide to learning and playing with blocks.* Beltsville, MD: Gryphon House.

National Council of Teachers of Mathematics. (2000). *Principles and standards for school mathematics.* Reston, VA: Author.

Scieszka, J., & Smith, L. (1995). *Math curse.* New York: Viking.

Shaw, G. M., Chambless, M. S., Chessin, D. R., Price, V., & Beardain, G. (1997). Cooperative problem solving: Using K-W-D-L as an organizational technique. *Teaching Children Mathematics, 3,* 482–486.

Small, M., Sheffield, L. J., Cavanagh, M., Dacey, L., Findell, C. R., & Greenes, C. E. (2004). *Navigating through problem solving and reasoning in grade 2.* Reston, VA: National Council of Teachers of Mathematics.

Thong, R. (2000). *Round is a mooncake.* San Francisco: Chronicle Books.

Thornton, C. A., Dee, D., Damkoehler, D. D., Gehrenbeck, H., & Jones, G. A. (1995). The children's rain forest. *Teaching Children Mathematics, 2*(3), 144–148.

White, D. Y. (2001). Kenta, kilts, and kimonos: Exploring cultures and mathematics through fabrics. *Teaching Children Mathematics, 7*(6), 354–359.

Wolfgang, C. H., Stannard, L. L., & Jones, I. (2001). Block play performance among preschoolers as a predictor of later school achievement in mathematics. *Journal of Research in Childhood Education, 15*(2), 173–180.

Zaslavsky, C. (2001). Developing number sense: What can other cultures tell us? *Teaching Children Mathematics, 7*(6), 312–319.

## FURTHER READING AND RESOURCES

### Planning the Environment and the Curriculum

American Association for the Advancement of Science (AAAS). (2007). *Atlas of science literacy: Project 2061* (Vol. 2). Washington, DC: Author.

Ansberry, K. & Morgan, E. (2007). Science measures up. *Science & Children, 44*(6), 12–14.

Copley, J. V. (Ed.). (1999). *Mathematics in the early years.* Washington, DC: National Association for the Education of Young Children.

Copley, J. V. (2000). *The young child and mathematics.* Washington, DC: National Association for the Education of Young Children.

Douglas, R., Klentschy, M. P., & Worth, K. (Eds.) (with W. Binder). (2006). *Linking science & literacy in the K–8 classroom.* Arlington, VA: NSTA Press.

National Research Council. (1996). *National science education standards.* Washington, DC: National Academies Press.

Richardson, K. (1999). *Developing number concepts: Planning guide.* Parsippany, NJ: Seymour.

### Learning Together

Artzt, A. F., & Newman, C. M. (1990). *How to use cooperative learning in the mathematics class.* Reston, VA: National Council of Teachers of Mathematics.

Barone, M. M., & Taylor, L. (1996). Peer tutoring with mathematics manipulatives: A practical guide. *Teaching Children Mathematics, 3*(1), 8–15.

Gondree, L. L., & Doran, A. (1998). Teach me some science: An elementary/middle school partnership. *Science and Children, 36*(3), 44–48.

Green, D. A. (2002). Last one standing: Creative, cooperative problem solving. *Teaching Children Mathematics, 9*(3), 134–139.

Schulte, P. L. (1999). Lessons in cooperative learning. *Science and Children, 36*(7), 44–47.

Schussheim, J. Y. (2004). Large-scale family math nights: A primer for collaboration. *Teaching Children Mathematics, 10*(5), 254–257.

### Blocks, Construction, and Woodworking

Benenson, G., & Neujahr, J. L. (2002). *Mechanisms and other systems.* Portsmouth, NH: Heinemann.

Benenson, G., & Neujahr, J. L. (2002). *Packaging and other structures.* Portsmouth, NH: Heinemann.

Benenson, G., & Neujahr, J. L. (2002). *Signs, symbols, and codes.* Portsmouth, NH: Heinemann.

Casey, B., & Bobb, B. (2003). The power of block building. *Teaching Children Mathematics, 10*(2), 98–102.

Dunn, S., & Larson, R. (1990). *Design technology.* London: Falmer Press.

Hirsch, E. (Ed.). (1984). *The block book.* Washington, DC: National Association for the Education of Young Children.

Johnson, P. (1992). *Pop-up engineering.* London: Falmer Press.

Kamii, S., & DeVries, R. (1993). *Physical knowledge in preschool education: Implications of Piaget's theory* (Rev. ed.). Englewood Cliffs, NJ: Prentice-Hall.

Lind, K. K., & Milburn, M. J. (1988). The mechanized child. *Elementary School Notes, 3*(5), 32–33.

Lind, K. K., & Milburn, M. J. (1988). More for the mechanized child. *Science and Children, 25*(6), 39–40.

Skeen, P., Garner, A. P., & Cartwright, S. (1984). *Woodworking for young children.* Washington, DC: National Association for the Education of Young Children.

Wellhousen, K., & Kieff, J. (2001). *A constructivist approach to block play in early childhood.* Clifton Park, NY: Thomson Delmar Learning.

Wolfgang, C. H., Stannard, L. L., & Jones, I. (2001). Block play performance among preschoolers as a predictor of later school achievement in mathematics. *Journal of Research in Childhood Education, 15*(2), 173–180.

Zubrowski, B. (1981). *Messing around with drinking straw construction.* Boston: Little, Brown.

**Games**

Church, E. B. (2004). Glorious outdoor games. *Early Childhood Today, 18*(8), 6–12.

Cutler, K. M., Gilkerson, D., Parrott, S., & Bowne, M. T. (2003). Developing games based on children's literature. *Young Children, 58*(1), 22–27.

Feldman, J. R. (1994). *Complete handbook of indoor and outdoor games for young children.* Englewood Cliffs, NJ: Prentice-Hall.

Kamii, C. (1994). *Young children continue to reinvent arithmetic, 3rd grade.* New York: Teachers College Press.

Kamii, C. (1999). *Young children reinvent arithmetic* (2nd ed.). New York: Teachers College Press.

Kamii, C. (2003). *Young children continue to reinvent arithmetic, 2nd grade* (2nd ed.). New York: Teachers College Press.

Kamii, C., & DeVries, R. (1980). *Group games in early education.* Washington, DC: National Association for the Education of Young Children.

Shamrock math game. (2003, March). *Instructor,* 26.

Worstell, E. V. (1961). *Jump the rope jingles.* New York: Collier Books.

**Finger Plays, Songs, and Rhymes**

Aruego, J., & Dewey, A. (Illus.). (1989). *Five little ducks.* New York: Crown.

Christelow, E. (1991). *Five little monkeys sitting in a tree.* New York: Clarion.

Croll, C. (2001). *Fingerplays and songs for the very young.* New York: Random House.

Cromwell, L., & Hibner, D. (1976). *Finger frolics.* Livonia, MI: Partner Press.

Finkel, S., & Seberg, K. (1996). *Circle time math.* Carthage, IL: Teaching and Learning.

Finkel, S., & Seberg, K. (1996). *Circle time science.* Carthage, IL: Teaching and Learning.

Haines, B. J. E., & Gerber, L. L. (2000). *Leading young children to music* (6th ed.). Columbus, OH: Pearson-Merrill/Prentice-Hall.

Kitson, J. (2000). *Fabulous holiday and seasonal fingerplays.* Clifton Park, NY: Thomson Delmar Learning.

Pica, R. (1999). *Moving & learning across the curriculum.* Clifton Park, NY: Thomson Delmar Learning.

Schiller, P., & Moore, T. (1993). *Where is thumbkin?* Beltsville, MD: Gryphon House.

Umansky, K., & Fisher, C. (1999). *Nonsense counting rhymes.* Oxford: Oxford University Press.

Weimer, T. E. (1993). *Space songs for children.* Greenville, SC: Pearce-Evetts.

**Problem Solving**

Buschman, L. (2002). Becoming a problem solver. *Teaching Children Mathematics, 9*(2), 98–103.

Buschman, L. (2003). Children who enjoy problem solving. *Teaching Children Mathematics, 9*(9), 539–544.

Buschman, L. (2004). Teaching problem solving in mathematics. *Teaching Children Mathematics, 10*(6), 302–309.

Hoosain, E., & Chance, R. H. (2004). Problem-solving strategies of first graders. *Teaching Children Mathematics, 10*(9), 474–479.

## Technology

Britton, E., DeLong-Cotty, B., & Levenson, T. (2005). *Bringing technology education into K–8 classrooms: A guide to curricular resources about the designed world.* Thousand Oaks, CA: Corwin Press.

Buckleiter, W. (2004). Teaching with technology: Seeing science with new eyes. *Early Childhood Today, 18*(6), 6–7.

Clements, D. H. (1999). Young children and technology. In *Dialogue on early childhood science, mathematics and technology education* (pp. 92–105). Washington, DC: American Association for the Advancement of Science.

*Computer technology tool kit.* (1997). White Plains, NY: Addison-Wesley Longman Supplementary Division.

Coulter, B. (2000). What's it like where you live? *Science and Children, 37*(4), 46–50.

Craig, D. R. (1999). Science and technology: A great combination. *Science and Children, 36*(4), 28–32.

*The educator's guide to the Internet.* (1997). White Plains, NY: Addison-Wesley Longman Supplementary Division.

Haugland, S. W., & Wright, J. L. (1997). *Young children and technology: A world of discovery.* Boston: Allyn & Bacon.

Haury, D. L., & Milbourne, L. A. (1999). Internet resources. In S. J. Rakow (Ed.), *ERIC Review: K–8 Science and Math Education, 6*(2), 66–67.

*Integrating computers into your classroom: Elementary education, math, and science.* (1997). White Plains, NY: Addison-Wesley Longman Supplementary Division.

O'Brien, G. E., & Lewis, S. P. (1999). Connecting to resources on the Internet. *Science and Children, 36*(8), 42–45. (Includes list of Internet sites.)

Patti, C. A., & Dziubek, P. (1998). MCS sets sail on the Internet. *Science and Children, 36*(2), 32–36.

Perry, L. (2000). Multimedia rocks. *Science and Children, 37*(8), 24–27.

Renwick, L. (2003, March). Science and technology: A perfect match! *Instructor,* 28–29.

Smith, S. W. (2000). Get connected to science. *Science and Children, 37*(7), 22–25. (Includes resource lists.)

Steffe, L. P. (Ed.). (1994). Mathematical learning in computer microworlds [Special issue]. *Journal of Research in Childhood Education, 8*(2).

*Unifix software basic version* (ver. 1). (1996). Rowley, MA: Didax.

Usiskin, Z. (Ed.). (1999, May/June). Groping and hoping for a consensus on calculator use. *Mathematics Education Dialogues.*

## Action Books, Articles, and Videos

Brown, S. (1997). First graders write to discover mathematics' relevancy. *Young Children, 52*(4), 51–53.

Church, E. B. (2004). Tasty no-bake cooking. *Early Childhood Today, 18*(8), 30–36.

Desouza, J. M. S., & Jereb, J. (2000). Gravitating toward Reggio. *Science and Children, 37*(7), 26–29.

Hagerott, S. G. (1997). Physics for first graders. *Phi Delta Kappan, 78*(9), 717–720.

Heuser, D. (2000). Mathematics workshops: Mathematics class becomes learner centered. *Teaching Children Mathematics, 6*(5), 288–295.

Hildebrand, C., Ludeman, C. J., & Mullin, J. (1999). Integrating mathematics with problem solving using the mathematician's chair. *Teaching Children Mathematics, 5*(7), 434–441.

Jones, I. (1999). A workshop approach. *Science and Children, 37*(3), 26–30, 55. (Designs for science learning centers.)

Kroll, L., & Halaby, M. (1997). Writing to learn mathematics in the primary school. *Young Children, 52*(4), 54–60.

Leitze, A. R. (1997). Connecting process problem solving to children's literature. *Teaching Children Mathematics, 3*(7), 398–405.

Martens, M. L. (1999). Productive questions: Tools for supporting constructivist learning. *Science and Children, 36,* 24–27, 53.

Merz, A. H., & Thomason, C. (2002). Sizing up the river. *Teaching Children Mathematics, 9*(3), 149–155.

Murray, A. (2001). Ideas on manipulative math for young children. *Young Children, 56*(4), 28–29.

Overholt, J. L., Dickson, S., & White-Holtz, J. (1999). *Big math activities for young children.* Clifton Park, NY: Thomson Delmar Learning.

Raleigh, J., Rigdon, D., & Goodman, S. (2001). Summer fun. *Teaching Children Mathematics, 7*(9), 528–529.

*Reading Rainbow* (literature videos). Phone: 800-228-4630.

Seefeldt, C. (2004). Science comes alive through music and art! *Early Childhood Today, 18*(6), 28–34.

Shaw, D. G., Cook, C., & Rebelin, T. (2000). Science fairs for all. *Science and Children, 38*(2), 14–19.

Smith, N. L., Babione, C., & Vick, B. J. (1999). Dumpling soup: Exploring kitchens, cultures, and mathematics. *Teaching Children Mathematics, 6*(3), 148–152.

Swindal, D. N. (2000). Learning geometry and a new language. *Teaching Children Mathematics, 7*(4), 246–250.

Warfield, J. (2001). Teaching kindergarten children to solve word problems. *Early Childhood Education Journal, 28*(3), 161–168.

West, S., & Cox, A. (2004). *Literacy play.* Beltsville, MD: Gryphon House.

Wethered, P. A. (1997). An intergalactic voyage: Families, teachers, and students enjoy a week of space projects and activities. *Science and Children, 34*(8), 14–17.

Wickett, M. S. (1997). Links to literature. Serving up number sense and problem solving: *Dinner at the panda palace. Teaching Children Mathematics, 3*(9), 476–480.

Worth, K., & Grollman, S. (2003). *Worms, shadows, and whirlpools: Science in the early childhood classroom.* Portsmouth, NH: Heinemann.

**Studying the Environment**

Aram, R. J., Whitson, S., & Dieckhoff, R. (2001). Habitat sweet habitat. *Science and Children, 38*(4), 23–27.

Church, E. B. (2004). Summertime science. *Early Childhood Today, 18*(8), 38–45, 48.

LeBeau, S. (1997). Mathematics and the environment. *Teaching Children Mathematics, 3*(8), 440–441.

Lingelback, J. (1986). *Hands-on nature.* Woodstock, VT: Vermont Institute of Natural Science.

Mann, R. (2003). Responses to the "A Walk in the Park Problem." *Teaching Children Mathematics, 10*(1), 54–59.

McCormack, A. J. (1979). *Outdoor areas as learning laboratories* (Council for Elementary Science International Sourcebook, I). Columbus, OH: SMEAC Information Reference Center.

Melber, L. W. (2000). Nature in the city. *Science and Children, 37*(7), 18–21, 57.

Millward, R. E. (2000). Photographing wildlife. *Science and Children, 37*(5), 28–31, 53.

Sisson, E. A. (1981). *Nature with children of all ages.* New York: Prentice-Hall.

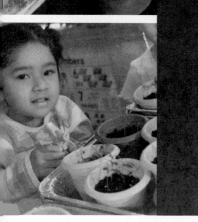

# Unit 41

## Math and Science in the Home

### OBJECTIVES

After reading this unit, you should be able to:

■ Explain the importance of the home as an educational setting.

■ Be knowledgeable about strategies for family involvement in math and science.

■ Provide families with strategies and activities for teaching children at home.

■ Describe a variety of activities that relate math and science to a child's everyday life.

The home is the first educational setting. Learning happens on a daily basis in the home: Children learn as they cook, set the table, sort laundry, observe ants, watch birds, or take a walk in the backyard, neighborhood, or the park. Teachers of young children are in a unique position to help families make good use of these home learning opportunities. This unit provides guidelines for parents and other family members as teachers. It focuses on specific suggestions for emphasizing science and math as vehicles for family learning.

Parents and other family members need to understand that children are eager to learn and can learn if the experiences are developmentally appropriate. As teachers of young children, you can assist parents in recognizing that they do not need to go overboard purchasing expensive materials when there are a multitude of learning opportunities that center on everyday activities using resources naturally present in the environment.

## APPROACHES TO FAMILY INVOLVEMENT IN MATH AND SCIENCE

Encourage family members to find the math and science in their homes. A large part of a child's time is spent in school, but the majority of time is still spent outside of the classroom. Every day at home is filled with opportunities to explore and ask questions that encourage thinking. It should be stressed that family entertainment does not have to be passive, such as watching TV. Activities that incorporate daily routines such as cooking, playing games, doing simple projects, finding materials to bring to school, and exploring the lives of living creatures and plants are suggested as opportunities for discovery, science and math, and family fun.

### Getting the Family Involved

Changes in our economy and lifestyles have resulted in a multitude of family configurations that were rare or nonexistent in the past. A large percentage of mothers of young children work either to boost the family income or because they are the principal breadwinner, so they are not as available as their counterparts were in the past. Fathers work longer hours, sometimes holding down two jobs, and are also less able than in the past to participate in school-based activities. Family involvement in education has changed from the view that parents could be active participants only by coming to school and assisting with classroom activities and attending parent meetings and conferences. These are still important activities, but involvement has been expanded to include all family members and caregivers and to focus on opening lines of communication. Families are now provided with home learning tasks that can be performed as part of everyday living. Further, the use of home visits as a means for developing a good relationship with families is moving up from prekindergarten into the elementary school. The following are suggestions for getting families involved and engaging them in their roles as teachers.

A first step could be the publication of a newsletter that could be sent home each month telling about the past month's events and including information about upcoming activities. (See Figure 41–1 for a sample.) Future activities could be described and/or sent in the form of a monthly calendar. Children can contribute to the newsletter. They can draw pictures and dictate and/or write news stories describing their experiences at school. Two or three children might be asked to contribute to each newsletter. Suggested home activities may be included in the newsletter and/or sent home as a separate booklet. See the NAEYC publication *Family-friendly Communication for Early Childhood Programs* (Diffily & Morrison, 1996).

Getting parents or other family members to school for a meeting can be difficult. However, it is important that they become acquainted with the activities, the environment, their child's teacher, and families of other students. Meetings should provide important information and involve active experiences that will give families an understanding of appropriate educational experiences that can be followed up in the home.

The students should be actively involved in the planning so that their excitement and enthusiasm for the event will spill over to their parents. A program that has shown a great deal of success is Family Math

## Kindergarten News

Published by Mr. Jones's Class *Carver School*
October 1, 2005

### School Gets Off to a Good Start

The day after Labor Day, the children started kindergarten. Eight children came each day to get acquainted with the room and find out what we do in kindergarten. Several children have contributed descriptions of what they liked best about coming to kindergarten.

José: I like being bigger than the 4-year-old classes.
Mimi: I like painting and playing house.
Ronny: My favorite was drawing and writing with markers on big paper and playing with trucks and blocks.
Nina: I liked finding my new friend Marcus.

### Buddy the Bunny Joins Us

Last week, we had a late arrival in our class. Mr. Ortiz, who manages a pet store at the mall, brought us a black-and-white rabbit with a cage and a supply of food. The class discussed a number of names. The majority voted for the name Buddy ("'cause he will be our best friend"). Buddy is very friendly and enjoys fresh vegetables. If your child asks to bring a carrot or a little piece of lettuce, please send it, if possible. The children are taking turns bringing treats for Buddy.

### The Month Ahead

We are looking forward to fall. We are reading the outdoor temperature every morning and recording the data on a graph. We watch each day for the leaves to change. Our observations are written and drawn in our daily class journal. We are planning a walk around the block to collect samples of the leaves that fall from the trees. We will report next month on what we see and what we find.

**Figure 41–1** Sample classroom newsletter.

(Lachance, 2007; Stenmark, Thompson, & Cossey, 1986). Parents come to school and do math activities with their children. They are then provided with instructions for follow-up activities they can do at home. The same procedure could be followed with science (or better yet, math and science could be combined). Another procedure is to hold a Science and/or Math Fun Day (Carey, 1990). For a Fun Day, several activities are set up in a large area, such as a gym or cafeteria. Families can be invited to take part as volunteer helpers and as active participants with their children. By having the Fun Day extend over several hours, busy people can more likely find a time when they can join in. See other resources listed at the end of this unit.

Families can also be asked to send waste materials to school as needed. The items listed in Figure 41–2 as aids to learning math at home are also useful at school. Each child can bring a pack of small brown paper lunch bags to school at the beginning of the year; then, if an item is needed, the children can draw and/or write the name of the item on the bag, take it home, and ask their parents to put the item in the bag to take to school. Do not be concerned if the younger children write symbols that are not conventional pictures or words—they will know what it is and can read the symbol to adults.

Family members who have the time may volunteer to assist in the classroom. Those who are not free during the day or who prefer not to be involved in the classroom are often delighted to make games and other materials at home. There should always be an open invitation for family members to visit school.

Parents or other major caregivers need to meet with their child's teacher in one-to-one conferences to exchange information about children's activities and progress. At these times, teacher and parent or other family member (and even the child) can review the student's portfolio of work and discuss goals for the future. At the same time, family members can describe what they have been doing at home with the child and relate any home events that may be affecting the child's behavior.

Homework becomes an important type of activity in the primary grades. Children can work their way into the more formal homework activities by bringing things requested from home as a part of their prekindergarten and kindergarten experiences. These activities help them to develop responsibility and accustom parents to supporting classroom instruction. Homework should always be an extension of what has been taught at school. It may involve bringing some material to school; doing a simple project; or obtaining some information from a newspaper, magazine, or reference book. Be sure

that all the information needed to guide the child to the completion of the assignment is included in the instructions. Assignments for young children should be something that can be easily completed in 10 to 15 minutes. Even kindergarten teachers are being pressured to provide homework assignments. These assignments should be interactive, requiring a parent or sibling to assist. Figure 41–3 is an example of an activity that works very well with kindergartners. Articles by Kliman (1999) and Kline (1999) provide ideas for home math support and activities. The February 1998 issue of *Teaching Children Mathematics* and the January 2003 issue of *Science and Children* focus on parent and community involvement (Edge, 1998; "Parental Involvement," 2003).

An increasingly popular method for promoting developmentally appropriate home learning activities involves putting together small kits of materials that can be checked out and taken home for two or three days (Czerniak, 1994; Merenda, 1995; Seo & Bruk, 2003). Each kit includes materials and instruction for a home activity and some means for parents and children to return a report on the outcome along with the kit. Many of the activities suggested later in the unit could be made into take-home kits.

Resources are available on the Internet that teachers can download to share with families or that families with Internet connections can download themselves. Government sites such as the U.S. Department of Education (DOE) have many excellent resources that can be downloaded free of charge in both English and Spanish. You may access the Online Companion to find a link to their website. The DOE site booklet *Helping Your Child Learn Science* (March 5, 2004) provides families with children ages 3–10 with information, tools, and activities they can use in the home and community to help their child develop an interest in the sciences and learn about the world around them. This series of publications includes *Helping Your Preschool Child* and many more titles.

## GUIDELINES FOR FAMILIES AS TEACHERS AT HOME

Many families have questions about how they can provide learning experiences at home. They need to be reassured that naturalistic and informal experiences are at

## From the Kitchen

egg cartons
cereal boxes and other empty food boxes
margarine tubs
milk cartons
milk jugs
plastic lids
pumpkin seeds
nuts
nutshells
straws
dry peas, beans, rice
coffee can and lids
other food and juice cans
baby food jars
potato chip cans
frozen food cartons
yogurt, cottage cheese,
    sour cream, or dip containers
milk bottle lids
individual small cereal boxes
soft drink bottle caps
plastic holder (soft drink six-pack carrier)
paper plates
coffee grounds
plastic bottles or jugs (soap, bleach, etc.)
plastic or metal tops or lids
Styrofoam™ meat plates (trays)
plastic bag twists
cardboard rolls (paper towels, foil, etc.)
kitchen scales
plastic forks, spoons
cleaned and dried bones

## From Outside

pebbles
rocks and stones
twigs, sticks, bark
leaves and weeds
pinecones and nuts
seeds
corn kernels and husks
soybeans
flowers
clay, mud, dirt, sand
seashells
bird feathers
acorns
animal teeth
insects
mosses
abandoned nests
nonpoisonous plants

## From All Around the House

sponges
magazines with pictures
catalogs (general, seed, etc.)
old crayons
shoe boxes and other small boxes (i.e., bar soap,
    toothpaste, aspirin, tape, etc.)
other cardboard boxes
    (not corrugated)
corrugated cardboard
cardboard tablet backs
scraps of wallpaper, carpeting
Contac® paper
toothbrushes (for spattering paint)
lumber scraps
gift wrap (used or scraps)
gift wrap ribbon and bows
old greeting cards (pictures)
newspapers
jewelry
wire
clothesline
clocks
watches
small appliances
rubber or plastic hose
plastic tubing
plastic tubs
nails and screws
wood scraps
tools

## From Sewing Scraps

buttons
snaps
fabric
felt
thread
yarn
lace
ribbon
trim
rickrack
spools

**Figure 41–2**  Math and science materials found at home.

## Take Home Activity

**Hello Family!**

We have been working with groups of the amounts 0 to 10. *Ten Black Dots* is one of the books we are using to relate literature and math.

What can you do with ten black dots? This is a question we have worked on. In the book, rhymes suggest answers such as:

1. One dot can make a sun or a moon when day is done.
2. Two dots can make the eyes of a fox or the eyes of keys that open locks.

We have been working with black dots in class. Now it's time to do a job at home.

**Home Job**

1. Talk to your child about how dots can be used to make a picture. Make a list of ideas. Ten black dots are included below.

2. Have your child draw a picture including one or more black dots. Have the child write or dictate for you one or two sentences about the picture. A page is attached for writing and drawing.

**Figure 41–3** Ten Black Dots take-home activity. Based on *Ten Black Dots* (Crews, 1986); created by Rosalind Charlesworth. Note: A page can be attached for writing and drawing at home.

the heart of home learning. All during early childhood, play is the major vehicle for learning, both at school and at home. Exploration and discovery through play allow children to construct concepts. Adults should be encouraged to be positive models for their children. If adults are enthusiastic learners, their children are more likely to be enthusiastic learners, too.

Families can provide a close relationship where exploration is encouraged and where one-to-one conversation can enrich the young child's math and science language development. Adults and older children must be cautioned to be patient and allow children the opportunity to explore, reflect, and construct concepts. They need to understand that children learn through repetition. Children do the same activities over and over before they assimilate what the experience has to offer and feel confident in their understandings. Families also need to realize that children learn through concrete experiences. They need to learn how to use simple household items and waste materials (Figure 41–2) as the focus for learning.

Provide examples of naturalistic, informal, and structured home learning experiences. *Naturalistic experiences* are those in which a concept is applied in an everyday activity, such as sorting laundry, counting out tableware, following an ant trail in the backyard, or watching the clock to get to an appointment on time. *Informal experiences* take place when the alert adult finds a way to involve the child in an activity such as asking the child to set the table, measure out cooking ingredients, learn his telephone number, and count the money in his piggy bank. The adult can also sing a song or chant a rhyme on the spur of the moment and provide materials the child can use on his own (such as blocks, sets of dishes, construction materials, and the like). *Structured activities* usually are not appropriate before age 3. Adults need to take care that, when they introduce structured activities, they do not pressure the child if he seems uninterested or not ready. Suggest that adults pull back and try again in two or three weeks. Emphasize that children need time to explore materials before adults present structured questions or problems to them. Hansen (2005) describes daily learning opportunities with art, food, bath, blocks, chores, games, books, and other home activities.

## MATH AND SCIENCE IN THE HOME, YARD, NEIGHBORHOOD, AND PARK

There are many math and science activities that can be done in the home, backyard, neighborhood, park, or even on a vacation trip. Any of the following activities could be included in a home newsletter and/or activity booklet or monthly calendar. Activities begin with daily home routines and then move into other areas.

### Daily Routines

Families should be encouraged to emphasize the skills of science as they go about their daily routines. Here are some examples.

1. As laundry is sorted and socks are matched, talk about the differences and similarities in the articles. Then fold the clothes, and put them in the correct places. Ask, "Where do the pants go? Where shall we put the T-shirts?" Even small children will begin the process of

classification as they note the differences in characteristics.

2. Children can examine their bodies and compare themselves to animals in a concrete way. They have five toes on each foot, but a horse does not. When a family takes a trip to a farm or a duck pond, the differences and similarities in animal feet can be noted. Ask, "How many toes do you have? How are your toes different from a duck's? Why do you think a duck has a web between its toes?" Activities like this help children be aware of differences in animals and offer opportunities to discuss why an animal is structured in a certain way.

3. When kitchen utensils are returned to drawers after washing or food is put away after a shopping trip, discuss why they go where they do. Say, "Where shall we put the spoons? Should the crackers go in the cupboard or the refrigerator?" Some parents might want to lay items such as spoons, spatulas, or cups on the table and see how many ways children can devise to group items: for example, things you eat with, things you cook with, things you drink with, and so on.

4. Begin a bottle cap collection for classifying, counting, and crafts. Have children sort caps by size, color, and function. Trace around the caps to make designs. Then paste the caps on cardboard, and paint it.

5. Collect scraps of wood, and make things with the wood. Give children a hammer and some nails and say, "Let's make something with this wood." When the wood sculpture is completed, name it and propose a function.

6. As children work with tools (e.g., a hammer, screwdriver, tape measure) and various types of screws, bolts, and nails, ask: "What do we do with this? How is this tool used?" If something needs to be fixed, let the children help fix the item. Children enjoy tightening and loosening screws in a board. Simply begin the screws in a board, and let children practice the type of motion needed to operate a screwdriver.

## Cooking with Children

Cooking provides many opportunities for parents to provide children with practical applications of science and math. When someone is cooking, the child can measure the ingredients, observe them as they change form during cooking (or mixing), and taste the final product.

Children should be given as much responsibility for the food preparation as possible. This might include shopping for the food; washing; possibly cutting (carefully supervised, of course); reading and following the recipe; baking, cooking, or freezing; setting the food on the table; and cleaning up. The more the parent does, the less the child learns.

Try making an easy pizza. You will need muffins, tomato sauce, oregano, mozzarella cheese slices, and meat or mushrooms. Spread half of the muffin with a tablespoon of tomato sauce. Add a pinch of oregano. Put meat or mushroom on the sauce and then add a layer of cheese. Place the little pizza on a cookie sheet and bake for 10 minutes at 425°.

Children enjoy getting creative with food. Create Bugs on a Log by spreading peanut butter on pieces of celery. Top off the "log" with raisin "bugs."

Make Summer Slush. Freeze a favorite fruit juice in ice cube trays. After the cubes are hard, place them in the blender, and blend. Add extra juice if needed for a slushy consistency.

The seeds from a jack-o'-lantern or a Thanksgiving pumpkin pie can be saved. They should be thoroughly cleaned and then dipped in a solution of salt water (1 tablespoon salt in 1½ cups of water). Drain off the water, and spread the seeds on an ungreased cookie sheet. Bake at 350°. Stir every five minutes to be sure that they dry out and toast lightly on all sides. When lightly toasted, remove from oven, cool, crack, and eat.

Curious George's favorite is to spread a banana with peanut butter and roll it in ground nuts or wheat germ. Also fun to make with peanut butter are Kid Feeders. Bird feeders made with peanut butter on pinecones can be made the same day children make Kid Feeders. Quarter an apple and spread peanut butter on the cut sides. Roll the apple slices in one or more of the following: wheat germ, raisins, coconut, ground nuts, or sesame seeds.

## Math and Science Activities Here and There

The following are a selection of home math and science activities. For more ideas, see the resources listed at the end of the unit.

### Find the Numerals

Using a newspaper page of grocery advertisements, find and mark numbers that are alike; for example, "Find all the fours." The child with well-developed motor skills can cut out the numerals and glue those that are alike on separate sheets of paper to make a number book.

### A Monthly Caterpillar

Cut out and number one circle for each day of the month. Make a caterpillar head from one additional circle. Tape the head to the refrigerator or cabinet door. Each day, add the appropriately numbered circle. Point to and count the numbers.

### Traveling Numerals

When driving or walking along highways and streets, have the child watch for numerals to identify.

### Snack Shapes

Cut sandwiches into circles, squares, rectangles, and/or triangles. Buy crackers in a variety of shapes.

### Fraction Food

When the parent or the child is cutting foods (especially bananas or carrots), suggest that the foods be cut in two pieces (halves), three pieces (thirds), and so on. Introduce fraction vocabulary.

### How Many?

Play counting games, such as "How many doorknobs in this room?," "How many legs on the kitchen chairs?," "How many numbers on the microwave?," and so on.

### Measure Things

Encourage the child to describe the size of things using comparison words: *big(-ger, -gest), small(-er, -est), tall (-er, -est), short (-er, -est), wide (-r, -st), narrow (-er, -est)*, and the like. Keep a record of the child's height and weight with a wall measurement poster so the numbers can be checked at any time. Compare the child's measurements with her siblings, friends, and adults. Have the younger child do informal measurements of things in the house and outdoors using paper clips, toothpicks, body parts (such as hands or feet), string, and so on. Have the older (primary level) child use a clearly labeled ruler.

### Learn About Money

Play simple games. For example, play "store" using objects such as empty food containers or the child's toys. Mark each item with a price tag in an amount that is understandable at the child's developmental level: in pennies for younger children and in larger amounts for older children. Work with pennies at first, having the child count out the number of pennies needed to buy an item. When the child is successful with pennies, introduce the nickel as equal to five pennies. Price some items above 5¢, and have the child work with pennies and nickels. Go on to dimes and then quarters when the child is ready.

### Growing Things

Children enjoy caring for and observing their own plants as they grow. Bean seeds usually grow fast and do well under any circumstances. Place three bean seeds in a plastic bag with air holes or in a plastic cup along with a wet paper towel. This will allow the roots and stems to be observed. Keep a record of the plants' growth. Point out the roots, stems, and leaves. Keep the paper towel wet.

### Bathtub Fun

Keep a supply of safe plastic containers and plastic boats in the bathroom. Let the child explore these materials during bath time.

### Freezing and Melting

Put ice or snow in a bowl, and place it in a warm place. Watch it melt. Then take the water in the bowl, and freeze it outside or in the refrigerator. Have the child describe what he observes.

### Eye Spy

Encourage both observational and questioning skills. Take turns describing objects in the room and have the other person(s) guess what it is by asking up to 20 questions.

## MATH AND SCIENCE IN NATURE

The outdoors affords many opportunities for family activities that center on nature. Whether in urban, suburban, or small-town settings, the outdoors affords rich opportunities for observation and interaction.

### Who Invited the Ants?

Encourage families to use their backyard as a resource for teaching science. Many of the activities found in previous units are appropriate for use in the home. Select topics that are relevant to family life, and suggest them to parents. For example, the following suggestions turn uninvited picnic visitors into a family science exploration.

You will need a spoonful of tuna, a spoonful of honey, and a piece of fruit for this activity. Ask, "What would ants eat if you invited them to a family picnic? Let's have a picnic for the ants in our backyard." Then let the fun begin. However, a few cautions should be noted. Ants belong to the same family as bees and wasps (some ants sting). They have strong jaws and their bites can hurt a lot, so be very careful when dealing with ants.

To begin explorations, go on an anthill hunt, usually a small pile of dirt with a hole in the middle of it. Or, if you spot any ants, follow them back to their home. If this does not work, any bare patch of ground will be fine for observing ants.

Arrange the food on the ground (one foot apart). Put the honey on a leaf and place the leaf, tuna, and fruit directly on the ground. Observe closely. Ask, "Which kind of food do the ants go to first? Do you think the ants go to their favorite food or to the food closest to them? Do all of the ants choose the same food?"

Observe ant behavior by asking, "Do the ants carry the food back to the anthill, or eat it on the spot?"

Sometimes ants act like messenger ants. When they find food, they go back to the nest and tell the others. Then everybody comes to your picnic.

This activity extends to the sense of smell. Ask, "How do you think that the ants know where to find the food? Can they see the food? Can they hear the food?" Explain that as the ant runs to tell about the picnic, it leaves a scent trail for the other ants to follow.

### Scent Trails

Which member of the ant family can smell the best? Make a scent trail on your lawn by placing drops of extract on pieces of cut-up sponge. Create trails using several distinctive scents, such as peppermint, cinnamon, or lemon. See if ants can find and follow the trail. Mixing extract with water and spraying it with a spray bottle in a trail pattern on the ground also works well.

Families will enjoy learning more about their picnic visitors. Most of the ants that we see are worker ants. Their job is to build and maintain the nest and find food for the colony. Soldier ants live up to their name by defending the anthill against invaders. There is only one queen ant. She rules the nest and lays the eggs that populate the colony. Some queen ants can live 15 years.

There are a variety of ants with interesting habits and lifestyles to discover. For example, some ants even keep tiny insects called aphids to produce a sweet juice for them. The ants "milk" them for the sweet juice in much the same way that cows are milked. Another kind of ant farmer chews up leaves and spreads them out so that an edible fungus will grow. Some worker honey pot ants use their second stomach to store honeydew. They get so fat with honeydew that they hang in their nest like honey pots. Other ants take the honeydew from them when they are hungry.

## FEED THE BIRDS IN THE BACKYARD OR PARK

To help the children recognize different kinds of birds—and to find differences in birds' sizes, shapes, feeding styles, and food preferences—create your own bird feeding program. In addition to the suggestions for learning about birds found in Unit 40, make beef suet (hard fat from about the kidneys and loins) to help keep up the birds' energy by maintaining their body temperature. Ask a butcher for suet that is short and not stringy (stringy suet is hard for the birds to eat and does not melt down smoothly).

You can offer suet to the birds in many ways. Try putting it in a soap dish attached to a tree limb with chicken wire, or hang it in an onion bag or lobster bait bag. Or make suet ornaments with grapefruit rinds or coconut shells. To do so, chop the suet (or put it through a meat grinder) and then melt it in a double boiler. Pour the liquid suet into the rinds or shells to which you have already attached wire or string hangers, and set the containers aside in a cool place until the suet hardens. Then hang them on your tree.

How about a bottle cap suet log? Simply nail bottle caps to one side of a dead bough. Pour melted suet into the caps and set the bough aside until the suet hardens. Woodpeckers and other medium-sized birds will gather around to eat from the suet log.

Or make attractive suet pinecones. Melt the suet, and spoon it over the pinecones (to which you have already attached string or wire). Sprinkle the cones with millet, push sunflower seeds down into the cone's scales, and spoon more warm suet over the cones to secure the seeds. Place the cones on waxed paper and refrigerate until firm. Later, hang the cones from the tree as a snack for small birds such as chickadees.

Peanut butter mixture makes great food for birds, too, because peanuts have high nutritional content and mixtures made with them can be spread on tree bark, placed in the holes of a log or a bottle cap feeder, or hung from pinecones. But before giving the peanut butter to birds, be sure to mix cornmeal into it (one cup of peanut butter to five cups cornmeal). This will make the peanut butter mixture easier for the birds to swallow. It is possible for birds to choke on peanut butter when it is not mixed with anything.

Try mounting a whole ear of dried corn in a conspicuous place, perhaps by nailing it to a post. Then have the children predict which birds will be able to eat the corn (Figure 41–4). (Only birds with large beaks will be able to crack the whole kernels of corn.)

**Figure 41–4** "What kind of food do you think birds feed their young?"

## A Family Bird Walk

A bird walk will heighten the observational skills of everyone involved. Families can look for birds that:

■ hop when they move on the ground

■ peck at the ground

■ hold their heads to one side and appear to be listening to something in the ground

■ flap their wings a lot when they fly

■ glide and hardly move their wings

■ climb on the side of trees

■ fly alone

■ fly with many other birds

■ make a lot of noise

■ eat alone

■ blend in well with the grass, trees, or sky

Select a favorite bird, and find out as much as you can about it. This can be a family project. Use birdcall audio tapes or videotapes to identify the birds that have been seen and heard on the bird walk. Children will enjoy creating bird stories, art projects, and puzzles as well as reading more about the birds they have observed. For helpful information on identifying birds and creating a backyard habitat, see Burke (1983), Cook (1978), Cosgrove (1976), and Kress (1985).

## Rocks, Seashells, Trees, and Seeds

The following are a selection of activities from a group assembled by teachers Lisa Kirk and Carla Schild for a workshop entitled "Nature's Math Connection."

### Rocks

Rocks always hold a fascination for children. The colors, shapes, and textures afford opportunities for observation and exploration. Rocks can be categorized by size, shape, and color and from smoothest to roughest. With a pan balance, they can be weighed and predictions can be made about which will be heaviest and lightest. Rocks can be washed, and the children can discover that the colors change.

### Seashells

Seashells, sand dollars, and starfish can be compared for similarities and differences. Shells can be sorted, counted, and graphed. They can be sorted by size, shape, color, pattern, or other common features.

### Trees and Seeds

In the backyard, the neighborhood, or the park, children can find leaves, seeds, and cones. A tree walk can prove very interesting. Carry a paper or plastic bag for collecting treasures. First talk about what you might collect, and then begin your hunt. Children can use some of their collection to make a collage; they can glue items onto cardboard. They can sort the items and count and graph the groups. Visit a tree and discuss the parts: trunk, bark, branches, leaves or needles, pods or cones, and roots. Observe the tree in different seasons of the year. Draw pictures of the tree and describe it in each season.

## Exploring Math and Science with Technology

The software listed in most units is available for parental purchase. Hand calculators may be explored at home using the same types of activities suggested in Unit 28. Also, children's television channel websites such as *PBS Kids*, *Noggin*, and *Disney* have many on-line activities using the characters that are familiar to children from their daily television viewing. At the *Sesame Street* site, children can practice counting with the Count's Number of the Day activities or Journey to Ernie for problem solving with matching and pattern recognition. At the *Mr. Rogers' Neighborhood* site there are simple recipes for cooking and projects such as making a bird feeder or a rocket ship. *Bill Nye the Science Guy* includes home science labs in the areas of planets, physical science, and life science. In addition, Animal Planet, Nova, and National Geographic offer informative programs on television. You may access the Online Companion that accompanies *Math and Science for Young Children* at www .earlychilded.delmar.cengage.com for links to these and many more math- and science-related websites.

## SUMMARY

Science and mathematics can provide many opportunities for informal family sharing. Family members can encourage children to explore, ask questions, and think about the world around them. A single guiding question from an adult can turn a daily routine into a learning experience. As children cook, observe, sort, investigate, construct, and explore software and the Internet, they are using the skills needed to learn science and mathematics. Birds, ants, rocks, trees, shells, and other outdoor inhabitants make ideal subjects for observation and exploration.

## SUGGESTED ACTIVITIES

1. Observe a parent–teacher conference. Note how the teacher reports on the child's science and math concepts development and how the parents respond.

2. Write a family newsletter that focuses on science and math in the home. Share the newsletter with the class.

3. Reflect on your own experiences of science and math in the home, either as a child or as a parent. What kinds of opportunities were available to you? Which do you provide?

4. Make a list of guidelines for families to follow when teaching science to their young children at home.

5. Add 15 home science and 15 home math activities to your Activity File/Notebook: five each for prekindergarten, kindergarten, and primary.

6. Plan a workshop for families on science and math in the home. Present the workshop to the class.

7. Interview at least three parents. Ask them what types of science and math activities they do with their children. Find out what problems, concerns, or needs they might have in doing science with their children.

## REVIEW

A. Why is the home a good place to emphasize science and math?

B. List and describe three opportunities for learning science and math in the home.

C. How does cooking relate to science and math?

D. Describe two family nature activities involving math and science.

## REFERENCES

Burke, K. (1983). *How to attract birds.* San Francisco: Ortho Books. (A well-illustrated book with an informative text about providing food, water, and nest sites for both eastern and western birds.)

Carey, J. H. (1990). Science fun: Have a field day in the gym. *Science and Children, 28*(2), 16–19.

Cook, B. C. (1978). *Invite a bird to dinner.* New York: Lathrop. (A children's book about feeding birds with good ideas for making feeders out of everyday materials.)

Cosgrove, I. (1976). *My recipes are for the birds.* New York: Doubleday. (A book full of recipes, featuring treats such as Cardinal Casserole, Finch Fries, and Dove Delight.)

Crews, D. (1986). *Ten black dots.* New York: Mulberry.

Czerniak, C. M. (1994). Backpack science. *Science and Children, 32*(1), 46–47.

Diffily, D., & Morrison, K. (Eds.). (1996). *Family-friendly communication for early childhood programs.* Washington, DC: National Association for the Education of Young Children.

Edge, D. (Ed.). (1998). Beyond the classroom: Linking mathematics learning with parents, communities, and business and industry [Special issue]. *Teaching Children Mathematics, 4*(6).

Hansen, L. E. (2005). ABCs of early math experiences. *Teaching Children Mathematics, 12*(4), 208–212.

Kliman, M. (1999). Parents and children doing mathematics at home. *Teaching Children Mathematics, 6*(3), 140–146.

Kline, K. (1999). Helping at home. *Teaching Children Mathematics, 5*(8), 456–460.

Kress, S. W. (1985). *The Audubon Society guide to attracting birds.* New York: Scribner's.

Lachance, A. (2007). Family math nights: Collaborative celebrations of mathematical learning. *Teaching Children Mathematics, 13*(8), 404–408.

Merenda, R. C. (1995). A book, a bed, a bag: Interactive homework for "10." *Teaching Children Mathematics, 1*(5), 262–266.

Parental involvement: A key factor of science success [Focus issue]. (2003). *Science and Children, 40*(4).

Seo, K., & Bruk, S. J. (2003). Promoting young children's mathematical learning through a new twist on homework. *Teaching Children Mathematics, 10*(1), 26–31.

Stenmark, D. D., Thompson, V., & Cossey, R. (1986). *Family math.* Berkeley, CA: University of California Press.

## FURTHER READING AND RESOURCES

### Teacher Resources

Boling, K. B., & Larson, C. N. (2002). Horizons: A mother-daughter mathematics club. *Teaching Children Mathematics, 8*(5), 284–289.

Clements, D. H., & Sarama, J. (2005). Math play: How young children approach math. *Early Childhood Education Today, 19*(4), 50–57.

Copley, J. V. (Ed.). (1999). *Mathematics in the early years.* Washington, DC: National Association for the Education of Young Children.

Copley, J. V. (2000). *The young child and mathematics.* Washington, DC: National Association for the Education of Young Children.

Families involved in real science together [Special issue]. (1996). *Science and Children, 34*(2).

Hall, J. B., & Acri, R. P. (1995). A fourth-grade family math night. *Teaching Children Mathematics, 2*(1), 8–10.

Kyle, D. W., McIntyre, E., & Moore, G. H. (2001). Connecting mathematics instruction with the families of young children. *Teaching Children Mathematics, 8*(2), 80–86.

Lazerick, B., & Seidel, J. D. (1996). Tech times news from the net. Helping your child learn math. *Teaching Children Mathematics, 3*(3), 141.

Lind, K. K. (1986). The bird's Christmas. *Science and Children, 24*(3), 34–35.

MCCPTA-EPI Hands-on-Science. (1987). *Putting together a family science festival.* Washington, DC: National Science Teachers Association.

National Research Council. (1996). *National science education standards.* Washington, DC: National Academies Press.

Nitzberg, J., & Sparrow, J. (2001). Parent outreach success. *Science and Children, 39*(3), 36–40.

Roberts, D. (1999). The sky's the limit. *Science and Children, 37*(1), 33–37.

Schussheim, J. Y. (2004). Large-scale family math nights: A primer for collaboration. *Teaching Children Mathematics, 10*(5), 254–257.

Smith, L. K., & Tolman, M. N. (1997). Parents share their attitudes and expectations. *Science and Children, 34*(8), 40–43.

Strutchens, M. E. (2002). Multicultural literature as a context for problem solving: Children and parents learning together. *Teaching Children Mathematics, 8*(8), 448–454.

Tally-Foos, K. (2005). Science alive! *Science and Children, 42*(4), 36–39.

Washington, V., Johnson, V., & McCracken, J. B. (1995). *Grassroots success! Preparing families and schools for each other.* Washington, DC: National Association for the Education of Young Children.

Weiss, H. B. (1999). Partnerships among families, early childhood educators, and communities to promote early learning in science, mathematics and technology. In *Dialogue on early childhood science, mathematics, and technology education.* Washington, DC: American Association for the Advancement of Science.

## Family Resources

Allison, L., & Weston, M. (1993). *Eenie meenie miney MATH.* Boston: Little, Brown.

Allison, L., & Weston, M. (1994). *Pint-size SCIENCE.* Boston: Little, Brown.

Baratta-Lorton, M. (1975). *Workjobs for parents.* Menlo Park, CA: Addison-Wesley.

Barber, J., Parizeau, N., & Bergman, L. (2002). *Spark your child's success in math and science: Practical advice for parents.* Berkeley, CA: Lawrence Hall of Science.

Bell, J. L. (1993). *Soap science.* Reading, MA: Addison-Wesley.

Bennett, S., & Bennett, R. (1993). *The official playroom activity book.* New York: Random House.

Carson, M. S. (1989). *The scientific kid.* New York: Harper & Row.

Colker, L. J. (2005). *The cooking book.* Washington, DC: National Association for the Education of Young Children.

Gordon, M. (1995). *Simple science: Float and sink.* New York: Thomson Learning.

Kenschaft, P. C. (1997). *Math power: How to help your child love math, even if you don't.* Reading, MA: Addison-Wesley Longman.

Lewis, J. (1989). *Rub-a-dub-dub, science in the tub.* New York: Meadowbrook.

PBS Parents. Many activities and guidelines. Retrieved August 4, 2008, from http://www.pbs.org

Polonsky, L. (1995). *Math for the very young: A handbook of activities for parents and teachers.* New York: Wiley.

*Science and Children.* (2003/2004). Home connections. (Columns that include at-home science explorations.)

Wanamaker, N., Hearn, K., & Richard, S. (1979). *More than graham crackers.* Washington, DC: National Association for the Education of Young Children.

Wellnitz, W. R. (1992). *Science in your backyard.* Blue Ridge Summit, PA: TAB Books.

The following titles for family activities were retrieved January 23, 2005, from http://www.amazon.com

## Math

Axelrod, A. *Pigs will be pigs: Fun with math and money.*

Bruce, L. *Shapes at home.* (Math all around me)

Brunetto, C. F. *MathART projects and activities.* (grades 3–5)

Churchman, S. *Bringing math home: A parent's guide to elementary school math: Games, activities, projects.*

Coates, G., et al. *Family math for young children: Comparing.* (Equals series)

Egan, L. H. *25 Super cool math board games.* (grades 3–6)

Franco, B. *Counting caterpillars and other math poems.*

Peterson, E. J. *Beginning math at home for children 3–6.*

Schiller, P., & Peterson, L. *Count on math: Activities for small hands and lively minds.*

Schindeler, T. *Marshmallow math; Early math for toddlers, preschoolers, and primary school children.*

Schiro, M., & Walker, A. *Mega-fun math games: 70 quick-and-easy games to build math skills.* (grades 2–5)

Stenmark, J. K. *Family math.* (Equals series)

Taylor-Cox, J. *Family math night: Math standards in action.*

Wickelgren, W. A., & Wickelgren, I. (2001). *Math coach: A parent's guide to helping children succeed in math.*

Williams, A., & Cunningham, D. *Preschool math.*

## Science

Ashbook, P. *Science is simple: Over 250 activities for preschoolers.*

Gennaro, E. D., & Knoll, L. *Take home science kits for grades K–1.*

Lobb, J. *Dig and sow!* (At home with science)

Maynard, C. *Science fun at home.*

Robinson, T. *The everything kids' science experiments book: Boil ice, float water, measure gravity—challenge the world around you.*

School Specialty Publishing. *Life science at home, grades 3–5: It's everyplace you are!*

VanCleave, J. *Janice VanCleave's play and find out about science: Easy experiments for young children.*

Wellnitz, W. R. *Bouncing eggs: Amazing science activities you can do at home.*

**Cooking**

Better Homes and Gardens. *New junior cookbook.*

Cook, D. *Family fun. Cooking with kids.*

Davis, T. *Look and cook: A cookbook for children.*

Ibbs, K. *DK children's cookbook.*

Johnson, E. *A first cookbook for children.*

Nissenberg, S. K. *I made it myself!: Mud cups, pizza puffs, and over 100 other fun and healthy recipes for kids to make.*

Ray, R. *Cooking rocks! Rachael Ray 30-minute meals for kids.*

Wilkes, A. *Children's quick and easy cookbook.*

# APPENDICES

# Appendix A

## Developmental Assessment Tasks*

### CONTENTS

\* Tasks that have been used as samples in the text.

# SENSORIMOTOR: LEVEL 1

---

**1A**

**Sensorimotor**
**Age 2 months**

### General Development

**METHOD:**     Interview.

**SKILLS:**     Perceptual/motor.

**MATERIALS:**     Familiar object/toy such as a rattle.

**PROCEDURES/EVALUATIONS:**
1. Talk to the infant. Notice if he seems to attend and respond (by looking at you, making sounds, and/or changing facial expression).
2. Hold a familiar object within the infant's reach. Note if he reaches out for it.
3. Move the object through the air across the infant's line of vision. He should follow it with his eyes.
4. Hand the small toy to the infant. He should hold it for two to three seconds.

---

**1B**

**Sensorimotor**
**Age 4 months**

### General Development

**METHOD:**     Observation.

**SKILLS:**     Perceptual/motor.

**MATERIALS:**     Assortment of appropriate infant toys.

**PROCEDURES/EVALUATIONS:**
1. Note each time you offer the infant a toy. Does she usually grab hold of it?
2. Place the infant where it is possible for her to observe the surroundings (such as in an infant seat) in a situation where there is a lot of activity. Note if her eyes follow the activity and if she seems to be interested and curious.

---

**1C**

**Sensorimotor**
**Age 6 months**

### General Development

**METHOD:**     Interview and observation.

**SKILLS:**     Perceptual/motor.

**MATERIALS:**     Several nontoxic objects/toys including infant's favorite toy.

**PROCEDURES/EVALUATIONS:**
1. One by one, hand the infant a series of nontoxic objects. Note how many of his senses he uses for exploring the objects. He should be using eyes, mouth, and hands.
2. Place yourself out of the infant's line of vision. Call out to him. Note if he turns his head toward your voice.

3. When the infant drops an object, note whether he picks it up again.
4. When the infant is eating, notice if he can hold his bottle in both hands by himself.
5. Show the infant his favorite toy. Slowly move the toy to a hiding place. Note if the infant follows with his eyes as the toy is hidden.

---

**1D**

**Sensorimotor
Age 12 months**

**General Development**

**METHOD:** Interview and observation.

**SKILLS:** Perceptual/motor and receptive language.

**MATERIALS:** Two bells or rattles; two blocks or other small objects; two clear plastic cups; pillow or empty box; a cookie, if desired.

**PROCEDURES/EVALUATIONS:**

1. Note if the infant will imitate you when you perform the following activities (for each task, provide the infant with a duplicate set of materials).
   a. Shake a bell (or a rattle).
   b. Play peek-a-boo by placing your open palms in front of your eyes.
   c. Put a block (or other small object) into a cup; take it out of the cup, and place it next to the cup.
2. Partially hide a familiar toy or a cookie under a pillow or a box as the child watches. Note whether the infant searches for it.
3. Note whether the infant is creeping, crawling, pulling up to her feet, trying to walk, or is actually walking.
4. Note whether the infant responds to the following verbal commands:
   a. NO, NO.
   b. GIVE ME THE (name of object).

---

## SENSORIMOTOR: LEVEL 2

**2A**

**Sensorimotor
Ages 12–18 months**

**General Development**

**METHOD:** Interview and observation.

**SKILLS:** Perceptual/motor and receptive language.

**MATERIALS:** Several safe containers and a supply of safe, nontoxic objects.

**PROCEDURES/EVALUATIONS:**

1. Give the child several containers and the supply of small objects. Note if he fills the containers with objects and dumps them out repeatedly.
2. Tell the child, POINT TO YOUR NOSE, HEAD, EYES, FOOT, STOMACH.
3. Hide a familiar object completely. Note whether the child searches for it.

---

**2B**

**General Development**

**Sensorimotor**
**Ages 18–24 months**

**METHOD:** Interview and observation.

**SKILLS:** Perceptual/motor and receptive and expressive language.

**MATERIALS:** Child's own toys (or other assortment provided by you, such as a ball, toy dog, toy car, blocks, baby bottle, doll, and the like).

**PROCEDURES/EVALUATIONS:**
1. During playtime observations, note if the child is beginning to organize objects in rows and put similar objects together in groups.
2. Ask the child to point to familiar objects. POINT TO THE BALL (CHAIR, DOLL, CAR).
3. Note whether the child begins to name the parts of her body (usually two parts at 18 months).

---

## PREOPERATIONAL: LEVEL 3

---

**3A***

**One-to-One Correspondence: see Unit 8 for task**

**Preoperational**
**Ages 2–3**

---

**3B**

**Number Sense and Counting: Unit 9**

**Preoperational**
**Ages 2–3**

**METHOD:** Interview.

**SKILL:** Child understands the concept of "twoness" and can rational count at least two objects.

**MATERIALS:** Ten counters (cube blocks, Unifix Cubes, or other objects).

**PROCEDURES:**
1. Ask, HOW OLD ARE YOU?
2. Give the child two objects. HOW MANY (name of objects) ARE THERE? If the child succeeds, try three objects. Go on as far as the child can go.

**EVALUATION:**
1. May hold up appropriate number of fingers or answer "two" or "three."
2. Should be able to rational count two objects (or possibly recognize two without counting).

**3C**

**Logic and Classifying, Informal Sorting: Unit 10**

| | |
|---|---|
| **METHOD:** | Observation and informal interviewing. |
| **SKILL:** | While playing, the child groups toys by various criteria such as color, shape, size, class name, and so on. |
| **MATERIALS:** | Assortment of normal toys for 2- to 3-year-olds. |
| **PROCEDURE:** | As the child plays, note whether toys are grouped by classification criteria (see Unit 10). Ask, SHOW ME THE RED BLOCKS. WHICH CAR IS THE BIGGEST? FIND SOME SQUARE BLOCKS. |
| **EVALUATION:** | The child should naturally group by similarities, should be able to group objects by at least one or two colors, and should be able to find objects from the same class. |

---

**3D**

**Comparing, Informal Measurement: Unit 11**

| | |
|---|---|
| **METHOD:** | Interview. |
| **SKILL:** | Child can respond to comparison terms applied to familiar objects. |
| **MATERIALS:** | Pairs of objects that vary on comparative criteria, such as |

large–small     cold–hot
heavy–light     fat–skinny
long–short      higher–lower

| | |
|---|---|
| **PROCEDURE:** | Show the child the pairs of objects one pair at a time. Ask, POINT TO THE BIG (BALL). POINT TO THE SMALL or LITTLE (BALL). Continue with other pairs of objects and object concept words. |
| **EVALUATION:** | Note how many of the objects the child can identify correctly. |

---

**3E**

**Comparing, Number: Unit 11**

| | |
|---|---|
| **METHOD:** | Interview. |
| **SKILL:** | Shown a set of one and six or more, the child can identify which set has more. |
| **MATERIALS:** | Twenty counters (e.g., pennies, Unifix Cubes, cube blocks). |
| **PROCEDURE:** | Place two groups of objects in front of the child: one group with a set of one object and one group with a set of six or more. Ask, WHICH HAS MORE (object name)? POINT TO THE ONE WITH MORE. |
| **EVALUATION:** | Note if the child identifies the group that contains more. |

**3F**                                                   **Preoperational**
                                                         **Ages 2–3**
**Shape, Matching: Unit 12**

| | |
|---|---|
| **METHOD:** | Interview. |
| **SKILL:** | Child can match an object or cutout shape to another of the same size and shape. |
| **MATERIALS:** | Attribute blocks or shape cutouts; one red circle, square, and triangle; one green circle, square, and triangle. All should be the same relative size. |
| **PROCEDURE:** | Place the three green shapes in front of the child. One at a time, show the child each of the red shapes and tell the child, FIND A GREEN SHAPE THAT IS THE SAME AS THIS RED ONE. |
| **EVALUATION:** | The child should be able to make all three matches. |

**3G***                                                  **Preoperational**
                                                         **Ages 2–3**
**Space, Position: see Unit 13 for task**

**3H***                                                  **Preoperational**
                                                         **Ages 2–3**
**Parts and Wholes, Missing Parts: see Unit 14 for task**

**3I**                                                   **Preoperational**
                                                         **Ages 2–3**
**Ordering, Size: Unit 17**

| | |
|---|---|
| **METHOD:** | Interview. |
| **SKILL:** | Child can order three objects that vary in one size dimension. |
| **MATERIALS:** | Three objects of the same shape that vary in one size dimension, such as diameter. |

Paper towel rolls can be cut into proportional lengths (heights) for this task. More objects can be available in reserve to be used for more difficult seriation tasks.

**PROCEDURE:**    WATCH WHAT I DO. Line up the objects in order from fattest to thinnest (longest to shortest, tallest to shortest). NOW I'LL MIX THEM UP. (Do so.) PUT THEM IN A ROW LIKE I DID. If the child does the task with three objects, try it with five.

**EVALUATION:**    Note whether the objects are placed in a correct sequence.

---

**3J**

**Preoperational
Ages 2–3**

**Measuring, Volume: Unit 18**

**METHOD:**    Observation.

**SKILL:**    Child evidences an understanding that different containers hold different amounts.

**MATERIALS:**    A large container filled with small objects such as small blocks, paper clips, table tennis balls, or teddy-bear counters or with a substance such as water, rice, or legumes; several different size small containers for pouring.

**PROCEDURE:**    Let the children experiment with filling and pouring. Note any behavior that indicates they recognize that different containers hold different amounts.

**EVALUATION:**    Children should experiment, filling containers and pouring back into the large container, pouring into larger small containers, and into smaller containers. Note behaviors such as whether they line up smaller containers and fill each from a larger container or fill a larger container using a smaller one.

---

## PREOPERATIONAL: LEVEL 4

---

**4A**

**Preoperational
Ages 2–3**

**One-to-One Correspondence, Same Things/Related Things: Unit 8**

**METHOD:**    Interview.

**SKILLS:**
1. Child can match, in one-to-one correspondence, pairs of objects that are alike.
2. Child can match, in one-to-one correspondence, pairs of objects that are related but not alike.

**MATERIALS:**
1. Four different pairs of matching objects (such as two toy cars, two small plastic animals, two coins, two blocks).
2. Two groups of four related objects such as four cups and four saucers, four cowboys and four horses, four flowers and four flowerpots, four hats and four heads.

**PROCEDURES:**
1. Matching like pairs. Place the objects in front of the child in a random array. FIND THE THINGS THAT BELONG TOGETHER. If there is no response, pick up one. FIND ONE LIKE THIS. When the match is made, FIND SOME OTHER THINGS THAT BELONG TOGETHER. If there is no spontaneous response, continue to select objects, and ask the child to find the one like each.
2. Matching related pairs. Place two related groups of four in front of the child in a random array. FIND A CUP FOR EACH SAUCER (or A COWBOY FOR EACH HORSE).

**EVALUATIONS:**

1. Note if the child matches spontaneously and if he makes an organized pattern (such as placing the pairs side by side or in a row).
2. Note if the child is organized and uses a pattern for placing the objects (such as placing the objects in two matching rows).

---

**4B**

**Number Sense and Counting, Rote and Rational: Unit 9**

Preoperational
Ages 3–4

| | |
|---|---|
| **METHOD:** | Interview. |
| **SKILL:** | Child can rote and rational count. |
| **MATERIALS:** | Twenty counters (e.g., cube blocks, pennies, Unifix Cubes). |
| **PROCEDURE:** | First have the child rote count. COUNT FOR ME. START WITH ONE AND COUNT. If the child hesitates, ONE, TWO, _____ . WHAT COMES NEXT? Next ask, HOW OLD ARE YOU? Finally, place four counters in front of the child. COUNT THE (objects). HOW MANY (_____ ) ARE THERE? If the child cannot count four items, try two or three. If she counts four easily, put out more counters, and ask her to count as many as she can. |
| **EVALUATION:** | Note if she can rote count more than five and rational count at least five items. When she rational counts more than four, she should keep track of each item by touching each methodically or moving those counted to the side. |

---

**4C**

**Logic and Classifying, Object Sorting: Unit 10**

Preoperational
Ages 3–4

| | |
|---|---|
| **METHOD:** | Interview. |
| **SKILL:** | Child can sort objects into groups using logical criteria. |
| **MATERIALS:** | Twelve objects: two red, two blue, two green, two yellow, two orange, two purple. There should be at least five kinds of objects; for example: |

| Color | Object 1 | Object 2 |
|---|---|---|
| red | block | car |
| blue | ball | cup |
| green | comb | car |
| yellow | block | bead |
| orange | comb | cup |
| purple | bead | ribbon |

In addition, you will need six to ten small containers (bowls or boxes).

| | |
|---|---|
| **PROCEDURE:** | Place the 12 objects in random array in front of the child. Provide him with the containers. PUT THE TOYS THAT BELONG TOGETHER IN A BOWL (BOX). USE AS MANY BOWLS (BOXES) AS YOU NEED. |
| **EVALUATION:** | Note whether the child uses any specific criteria as he makes his groups. |

**4D***                                                             **Preoperational**
                                                                   **Ages 3–4**

Comparing, Number: see Unit 11 for task

---

**4E***                                                             **Preoperational**
                                                                   **Ages 3–4**

Shape, Identification: see Unit 12 for task

---

**4F***                                                             **Preoperational**
                                                                   **Ages 3–4**

Space, Position: see Unit 13 for task

---

**4G***                                                             **Preoperational**
                                                                   **Ages 3–6**

Rote Counting: see Unit 9 for task

---

**4H***                                                             **Preoperational**
                                                                   **Ages 3–6**

Rational Counting: see Unit 9 for task

---

**4I***                                                             **Preoperational**
                                                                   **Ages 3–6**

Time, Identify Clock or Watch: see Unit 19 for task

---

**4J***                                                             **Preoperational**
                                                                   **Ages 3–6**

Symbols, Recognition: see Unit 23 for task

# PREOPERATIONAL: LEVEL 5

---

**5A**

**Preoperational
Ages 4–5**

**One-to-One Correspondence, Same Things/Related Things: Unit 8**
Do tasks in 4A (1 and 2) using more pairs of objects.

---

**5B**

**Preoperational
Ages 4–5**

**Number Sense and Counting, Rote and Rational: Unit 9**
See 4B, 4G, and 4H.

---

**5C**

**Preoperational
Ages 4–5**

**Comparing, Number: Unit 11**

**METHOD:**      Interview.

**SKILL:**        The child can compare the amounts in groups up to five and label the ones that are more, less, and fewer.

**MATERIALS:**   Ten counters (e.g., chips, inch cubes, Unifix Cubes).

**PROCEDURE:**   Present the following groups for comparison in sequence:

  1 versus 5
  4 versus 1
  2 versus 5
  3 versus 2
  5 versus 4

Each time a pair of groups is presented, ask, DOES ONE GROUP HAVE MORE? If the answer is yes, POINT TO THE GROUP THAT HAS MORE. Ask, HOW DO YOU KNOW THAT GROUP HAS MORE? If the child responds correctly to *more*, present the pairs again using LESS and FEWER.

**EVALUATION:**  Note for which comparisons the child responds correctly. Can she give a logical reason for her choices (such as "Four is more than one" or "I counted them")? Does she place them in one-to-one correspondence?

---

**5D***

**Preoperational
Ages 4–5**

**Comparing, Informal Measurement: see Unit 11 for task**

---

**5E***

**Preoperational
Ages 4–5**

**Shape, Geometric Shape Recognition: see Unit 12 for task**

---

**5F***                                                    **Preoperational**
                                                                  **Ages 4–5**

**Parts and Wholes, Parts of a Whole: see Unit 14 for task**

---

**5G***     **Preoperational**
**Ages 4–5**

**Ordering, Sequential/Ordinal Number: see Unit 17 for task**

---

**5H***     **Preoperational**
**Ages 4–5**

**Time, Labeling, and Sequence: see Unit 19 for task**

---

**5I**     **Preoperational**
**Ages 4–5**

**Practical Activities, Money: Unit 22**

**METHOD:** Observation and interview.

**SKILL:** Child understands that money is exchanged for goods and services and can identify nickel, dime, penny, and dollar bill.

**MATERIALS:**
1. Play money and store props for dramatic play.
2. Nickel, dime, penny, and dollar bill.

**PROCEDURE:**
1. Set up play money and props for dramatic play as described in Unit 22. Observe the child, and note if he demonstrates some concept of exchanging money for goods and services and of giving and receiving change.
2. Show the child a nickel, dime, penny, and dollar bill. TELL ME THE NAME OF EACH OF THESE.

**EVALUATION:** Note the child's knowledge of money during dramatic play and note which, if any, of the pieces of money he recognizes.

---

The following tasks can be presented first between ages 4 and 5 and then repeated as the child's concepts and skills grow and expand.

---

**5J***     **Preoperational**
**Ages 4–6**

**Logic and Classifying, Free Sort: see Unit 10 for task**

**5K***

**Preoperational
Ages 4–6**

**Logic and Classifying, Clue Sort: see Unit 10 for task**

---

**5L***

**Preoperational
Ages 4–6**

**Symbols, Sequencing: see Unit 23 for task**

---

**5M**

**Preoperational
Ages 4–5**

**Naturalistic and Informal Activities**

**METHOD:**   Observation.

**SKILL:**   Child can demonstrate a knowledge of math concepts and skills during naturalistic and informal activities.

**MATERIALS:**   Math center (three-dimensional and two-dimensional materials), sand/water/legume pouring table, dramatic play props, unit blocks and accessories, cooking center, math concept books.

**PROCEDURE:**   Develop a recording system and keep a record of behaviors such as the following.

- Chooses to work in the math center.
- Selects math concept books to look at.
- Chooses to work in the cooking center.
- Selects working with sand, water, or legumes.
- Can give each person one napkin, one glass of juice, and so on.
- Spontaneously counts objects or people.
- While playing, spontaneously separates objects or pictures into logical groups.
- Spontaneously uses comparison words (e.g., This one is *bigger*).
- Chooses to build with blocks.
- Knows the parts of people and objects.
- Demonstrates a knowledge of *first, biggest, heaviest,* and other order concepts.
- Does informal measurement such as identifying hot and cold, a bigger container and a smaller container, and so on.
- Evidences a concept of time (What do we do next? Is it time for lunch?).
- Points out number symbols in the environment.
- Uses the language of math (whether he or she understands the concepts or not).

**EVALUATION:**   Child should show an increase in frequency of these behaviors as the year progresses.

## PREOPERATIONAL: LEVEL 6

---

| **6A\*** | **Preoperational**<br>**Ages 5–6** |
|---|---|

**One-to-One Correspondence: see Unit 8 for task**

---

| **6B** | **Preoperational**<br>**Ages 5–6** |
|---|---|

**Number Sense and Counting, Rote and Rational: Unit 9**

**METHOD:**       Interview.

**SKILL:**         Child can rote and rational count.

**MATERIALS:**    Fifty counters (e.g., chips, cube blocks, Unifix Cubes).

**PROCEDURES:**
1.  Rote counting. COUNT FOR ME AS FAR AS YOU CAN. If the child hesitates, say ONE, TWO, _____. WHAT'S NEXT?
2.  Rational counting. Present the child with 20 objects. HOW MANY _____ ARE THERE? COUNT THEM FOR ME.

**EVALUATION:**
1.  *Rote.* By age 5, the child should be able to count to 10 or more; by age 6, to 20 or more. Note if any number names are missed or repeated.
2.  *Rational.* Note the degree of accuracy and organization. Does she place the objects to ensure that no object is counted more than once or that no object is missed? Note how far she goes without making a mistake. Does she repeat any number names? Skip any? By age 6, she should be able to go beyond 10 objects with accuracy.

---

| **6C** | **Preoperational**<br>**Ages 5–6** |
|---|---|

**Shape, Recognition and Reproduction: Unit 12**

**METHOD:**       Interview.

**SKILL #1:**      Identify shapes, Task 4E.

**SKILL #2:**      Child can identify shapes in the environment.

**MATERIALS:**    Natural environment.

**PROCEDURE:**    LOOK AROUND THE ROOM. FIND AS MANY SHAPES AS YOU CAN. WHICH THINGS ARE SQUARE SHAPES? CIRCLES? RECTANGLES? TRIANGLES?

**EVALUATION:**   Note how observant the child is. Does she note the obvious shapes, such as windows, doors, and tables? Does she look beyond the obvious? How many shapes and which shapes is she able to find?

**SKILL #3:**      Child will reproduce shapes by copying.

**MATERIALS:**    Shape cards (as in Task 4E); plain white paper; a choice of pencils, crayons, and markers.

**PROCEDURE:**
1. COPY THE CIRCLE.
2. COPY THE SQUARE.
3. COPY THE TRIANGLE.

**EVALUATION:** Note how closely each reproduction resembles its model. Is the circle complete and round? Does the square have four sides and square corners? Does the triangle have three straight sides and pointed corners?

---

**6D\***  
**Parts and Wholes, Parts of Sets: see Unit 14 for task**

**Preoperational**  
**Ages 5–6**

---

**6E**  
**Ordering, Size and Amount: Unit 17**

**Preoperational**  
**Ages 5–6**

**METHOD:** Interview.

**SKILLS:** Child can order ten objects that vary in one criteria and five sets with amounts from one to five.

**MATERIALS:**
1. *Size.* Ten objects or cutouts that vary in size, length, height, or width. An example for length is shown below.

2. *Amount.* Five sets of objects consisting of one, two, three, four, and five objects each.

**PROCEDURES:**
1. *Size.* Place the ten objects or cutouts in front of the child in a random arrangement. FIND THE (BIGGEST, LONGEST, TALLEST, OR WIDEST). PUT THEM ALL IN A ROW FROM _____ TO _____.
2. Amount. Place the five sets in front of the child in a random arrangement. PUT THESE IN ORDER FROM THE SMALLEST BUNCH (GROUP) TO THE LARGEST BUNCH (GROUP).

**EVALUATIONS:**
1. *Size.* Preoperational children will usually get the two extremes but may mix up the in-between sizes. Putting ten objects in the correct order would be an indication that the child is entering concrete operations.
2. *Amount.* Most 5-year-olds can order the five sets. If they order them easily, try some larger amounts.

---

**6F**  
**Measurement; Length, Weight, and Time: Units 18 and 19**

**Preoperational**  
**Ages 5–6**

**METHOD:** Interview.

**SKILLS:** Child can explain the function of a ruler, discriminate larger from heavier, identify clocks and explain their function.

**MATERIALS:**
1. *Length.* A foot ruler.
2. *Weight.* A plastic golf ball and a marble or other pair of objects where the larger is the lighter.
3. *Time.* A clock (with a conventional face).

**PROCEDURES:**
1. Show the child the rules. WHAT IS THIS? WHAT DO WE DO WITH IT? SHOW ME HOW IT IS USED.
2. Give the child the two objects, one in each hand. Ask, WHICH IS BIGGER? WHICH IS HEAVIER? WHY IS THE SMALL _____ HEAVIER?
3. Show the child the clock. WHAT IS THIS? WHY DO WE HAVE IT? TELL ME HOW IT WORKS.

**EVALUATION:** Note how many details the child can give about each of the measuring instruments. Is she accurate? Can she tell which of the objects is heavier? Can she provide a reason for the lighter being larger and the smaller heavier?

---

6G | **Preoperational Ages 5–6**

**Practical Activities, Money: Unit 22**

**METHOD:** Interview.

**SKILL:** Child can recognize money and tell which pieces of money will buy more.

**MATERIALS:**
1. Pictures of coins, bills, and other similar items.
2. Selection of pennies, nickels, dimes, and quarters.

**PROCEDURES:**
1. Show the child the pictures. FIND THE PICTURES OF MONEY. After he has found the pictures of money, ask, WHAT IS THE NAME OF THIS? as you point to each picture of money.
2. Put the coins in front of the child. Ask, WHICH WILL BUY THE MOST? IF YOU HAVE THESE FIVE PENNIES (put five pennies in one pile) AND I WANT TWO CENTS FOR A PIECE OF CANDY, HOW MANY PENNIES WILL YOU HAVE TO GIVE ME FOR THE CANDY?

**EVALUATION:** Note which picture of money the child can identify. Note if he knows which coins are worth the most. Many young children equate worth and size and thus think a nickel will buy more than a dime.

---

Check back to 5J, 5K, and 5L; then go on to the next tasks. The following tasks can be presented first between ages 5 and 6 and then repeated as the child's concepts and skills grow and expand.

---

6H* | **Preoperational/Concrete Ages 5–7**

**Ordering, Double Seriation: see Unit 17 for task**

---

**6I\***                                                           **Preoperational/Concrete**
**Ages 5–7**

**Ordering, Patterning: see Unit 17 for task**

---

**6J\***                                                               **Preoperational**
**Ages 5 and older**

**Symbols, One More Than: see Unit 23 for task**

---

**6K\***                                                     **Preoperational/Concrete**
**Ages 5–7**

**Sets and Symbols, Write/Reproduce Numerals: see Unit 24 for task**

---

**6L\***                                                     **Preoperational/Concrete**
**Ages 5–7**

**Sets and Symbols, Match Sets to Symbols: see Unit 24 for task**

---

**6M\***                                                    **Preoperational/Concrete**
**Ages 5–7**

**Sets and Symbols, Match Symbols to Sets: see Unit 24 for task**

---

**6N**                                                     **Preoperational/Concrete**
**Ages 5–6**

**Naturalistic and Informal Activities: Units 1–25**

**METHOD:**        Observation.

**SKILL:**           Child demonstrates a knowledge of math concepts and skills during naturalistic and informal activities.

**MATERIALS:**   See Task 5M.

**PROCEDURE:**  See Task 5M. Add the following behaviors to your list.

■ Demonstrates an understanding of *more than, the same amount,* and *less than* by responding appropriately to questions such as, "Do we have the same number of children as we have chairs?"

■ Can match a set to a symbol and a symbol to a set (e.g., if the daily attendance total says 22, he can get 22 napkins for snack).

■ Can do applied concrete whole-number operations (e.g., if four children plan to draw and two more children join them, he knows that there are now six children; or if he has three friends and eight cars to play with, he figures out that each friend can use two cars).

**EVALUATION:**  Child should show an increase in frequency of these behaviors as the year progresses.

## MATH LANGUAGE: LEVEL 7

By the time the child is between 5½ and 6½ years of age, she should be using most of the words listed in Unit 15. The following tasks can be used to find out which words the child uses in an open-ended situation. Show each picture individually. Say, "I have some pictures to show you. Here is the first one. Tell me about it." For each picture, tape-record or write down the child's responses. Later list all the math words. Compare this with the list of math words she uses in class.

# CONCRETE OPERATIONS: LEVEL 8

The following tasks are all indicators of the child's cognitive developmental level. The child who can accomplish all these tasks should be ready for the primary-level instruction described in Section 5.

---

**8A**

**Concrete Operations**
**Ages 6–7**

**Conservation of Number: Unit 1**

**METHOD:**    Interview.

**SKILL:**    Child can solve the number conservation problem.

**MATERIALS:**    Twenty chips, blocks, or coins, all the same size, shape, and color.

**PROCEDURE:**    Set up a row of nine objects. Then proceed through the following four tasks.

1. MAKE A ROW JUST LIKE THIS ONE (point to yours).

   Child    ❑ ❑ ❑ ❑ ❑ ❑ ❑ ❑ ❑

   Adult    ❑ ❑ ❑ ❑ ❑ ❑ ❑ ❑ ❑

   DOES ONE ROW HAVE MORE BLOCKS (CHIPS, COINS), OR DO THEY BOTH HAVE THE SAME AMOUNT? HOW DO YOU KNOW? If child agrees to equality, go on to the next tasks.

2. NOW WATCH WHAT I DO. (Push yours together.)

   Child    ❑ ❑ ❑ ❑ ❑ ❑ ❑ ❑ ❑

   Adult    ❑ ❑ ❑ ❑ ❑ ❑ ❑ ❑ ❑

   DOES ONE ROW HAVE MORE BLOCKS, OR DO THEY BOTH HAVE THE SAME AMOUNT? WHY? (If the child says one row has more, MAKE THEM HAVE THE SAME AMOUNT AGAIN.) (If the child says they have the same amount, tell him, LINE THEM UP LIKE THEY WERE BEFORE I MOVED THEM.) Go on to task 3 and task 4 following the same steps.

3. Task 3

   Child    ❑ ❑ ❑ ❑ ❑ ❑ ❑ ❑ ❑

   Adult    ❑ ❑ ❑ ❑       ❑ ❑ ❑ ❑ ❑

4. Task 4

   Child    ❑ ❑ ❑ ❑ ❑ ❑ ❑ ❑ ❑

   Adult       ❑ ❑ ❑ ❑ ❑ ❑ ❑ ❑ ❑

**EVALUATION:**    If the child is unable to do task 1 (one-to-one correspondence), do not proceed any further. He needs to work further on this concept and needs time for development. If he succeeds with task 1, go on to 2, 3, and 4. Note which of the following categories fit his responses.

**Nonconserver 1.** Indicates longer rows have more but cannot give a logical reason (e.g., the child may say, "I don't know," "My mother says so," or gives no answer).

**Nonconserver 2.** Indicates longer rows have more and gives logical reasons, such as "It's longer," "The long row has more," and the like.

**Transitional.** Says both rows still have the same amount but has to check by counting or placing in one-to-one correspondence.

**Conserver.** Completely sure that both rows still have the same amount. May say, "You just moved them."

---

**8B**

**Concrete Operations**
**Ages 6–7**

**Symbols and Sets, Matching and Writing: Units 23, 24**

**METHOD:**       Interview.

**SKILL:**       Child can match sets to symbols and write symbols.

**MATERIALS:**       Cards with numerals 0 to 20, a supply of counters, paper, and writing implements.

**PROCEDURES:**
1. Present the child with sets of counters. Start with amounts under ten. If the child can do these, go on to the teens. MATCH THE NUMBERS TO THE SETS.
2. Put the numeral cards and counters away. Give the child a piece of paper and a choice of writing instruments. WRITE AS MANY NUMBERS AS YOU CAN. START WITH ZERO.

**EVALUATION:**       Note how high the child can go in matching sets and symbols and in writing numerals.

---

**8C**

**Concrete Operations**
**Ages 6–7**

**Multiple Classification: Unit 25**

**METHOD:**       Interview.

**SKILL:**       Child can group shapes by more than one criterion.

**MATERIALS:**       Make 36 cardboard shapes:
1. Four squares (one each red, yellow, blue, and green).
2. Four triangles (one each red, yellow, blue, and green).
3. Four circles (one each red, yellow, blue, and green).
4. Make three sets of each in three sizes.

**PROCEDURE:**       Place all the shapes in a random array in front of the child. DIVIDE (SORT, PILE) THESE SHAPES INTO GROUPS, ANY WAY YOU WANT TO. After the child has sorted on one attribute (shape, color, or size) say, NOW DIVIDE (SORT, PILE) THEM ANOTHER WAY. The preoperational child will normally refuse to conceptualize another way of grouping.

**EVALUATION:**       The preoperational child will center on the first sort and will not try another criterion. The concrete operations child will sort by color, shape, and size.

---

**8D**

**Concrete Operations**
**Ages 6–7**

**Class Inclusion: Unit 25**

**METHOD:**       Interview.

**SKILL:**       Child can perceive that there are classes within classes.

**MATERIALS:**       Make a set of materials using objects, cutouts, or pictures of objects such as the following.

1.  Twelve wooden beads of the same size and shape that differ only in color (e.g., four red and eight blue).
2.  Twelve pictures of flowers: eight tulips and four daisies.
3.  Twelve pictures of animals: eight dogs and four cats.

**PROCEDURE:**    Place the objects (pictures) in front of the child in random order. PUT THE (object name) TOGETHER THAT ARE THE SAME. Then after they have grouped into two subcategories ask, ARE THERE MORE (WOODEN BEADS, FLOWERS, or ANIMALS) OR MORE (BLUE BEADS, TULIPS, or DOGS)? Have them compare the overall class or category with the larger subclass.

**EVALUATION:**    The preoperational child will have difficulty conceptualizing parts and wholes of sets at the same time.

## CONCRETE OPERATIONS: LEVEL 9

---

**9A***                                                                    **Concrete Operations**
                                                                           **Ages 6–8**

**Addition, Combining Sets up to 10: see Unit 27 for task**

---

**9B***                                                                    **Concrete Operations**
                                                                           **Ages 6–8**

**Subtraction, Sets of 10 and Less: see Unit 27 for task**

---

**9C**                                                                     **Concrete Operations**
                                                                           **Ages 6–8**

**Addition and Subtraction, Understanding Notation: Unit 27**

**METHOD:**    Interview or small group.

**SKILL:**    Child understands the connection between notation and concrete problems.

**MATERIALS:**    Counters (e.g., chips, Unifix Cubes, cube blocks), pencil, and paper.

**PROCEDURE:**    Each child should have a supply of counters, pencils, and paper. TAKE THREE RED (name of counter). NOW PUT TWO GREEN (name of counter) WITH THE THREE RED. WRITE A NUMBER SENTENCE THAT TELLS WHAT YOU DID. When finished, PUT THE RED AND GREEN (counters) BACK. TAKE OUT SIX YELLOW (counters). SEPARATE THREE OF THE YELLOW (counters) FROM THE SIX. WRITE A NUMBER SENTENCE THAT TELLS WHAT YOU DID. Continue with more addition and subtraction problems. Written story problems could be given to children who know how to read.

**EVALUATION:**    Note if the children are able to use the correct notation, that is, $3 + 2 = 5$ and $6 - 3 = 3$.

---

**9D**

**Concrete Operations
Ages 6–8**

**Addition and Subtraction, Create Problems: Unit 27**

**METHOD:** Interview or small group.

**SKILL:** Given a number sentence, the child can create a problem.

**MATERIALS:** Counters (e.g., chips, Unifix Cubes, cube blocks), pencil, and paper.

**PROCEDURE:** Give the children the number sentences below. Tell them to make up a story to go with each sentence using their counters to represent the characters in the story. Nonreaders/nonwriters can dictate their stories; reader/writers can write the stories themselves. Number sentences:

**1.** $3 + 5 = 8$     **2.** $6 - 4 = 2$

**EVALUATION:** Note if the dictated or written problem relates correctly to the number sentence.

---

**9E**

**Concrete Operations
Ages 6–8**

**Addition and Subtraction, Translating Symbols into Concrete Actions: Unit 27**

**METHOD:** Interview or small group.

**SKILL:** The child can translate written problems into concrete actions.

**MATERIALS:** Counters (e.g., chips, Unifix Cubes, cube blocks), pencil, paper, and several addition and subtraction problems.

**PROBLEMS:**

| | | | |
|---|---|---|---|
| **1.** $9 - 4$ | | **6.** $6 - 3$ | |
| **2.** $4 + 5$ | | **7.** $4 - 1$ | |
| **3.** $3 + 2$ | | **8.** $2 + 6$ | |
| **4.** $8 - 6$ | | **9.** $5 + 3$ | |
| **5.** $1 + 7$ | | **10.** $7 - 2$ | |

**PROCEDURE:** Give each child a supply of counters, a pencil, and paper with one or more written problems like those above. It is best to give the problems one at a time the first time. Then give more as the children become more proficient. Point to the first problem, if there is more than one. LOOK AT THIS PROBLEM. SHOW ME THE PROBLEM WITH (counters). NOW WRITE THE ANSWER. READ THE PROBLEM AND THE ANSWER TO ME. If they do this one correctly, have them continue on their own. Ask them to show you if there are any problems they can do without the cubes.

**EVALUATION:** Note whether the children do the problems correctly and especially whether they are accurate in translating the signs. For example, for problem 1, a child might take nine counters and then take four more, ignoring the "minus" sign. Some children might be able to tell you that (say) $2 + 6 = 8$ but not be able to show you with the counters. This behavior indicates the children have learned to use the symbols in a rote fashion but do not understand the concepts that the symbols stand for.

---

**9F\***

**Multiplication, Readiness: see Unit 27 for task**

---

(9G)

**Multiplication, The Process: Unit 27**

**METHOD:**    Interview.

**SKILL:**    Child understands the process of multiplication.

**MATERIALS:**    Counters (e.g., chips, Unifix Cubes, cube blocks), pencil, and paper.
1.   Show the child patterns of counters such as

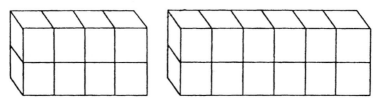

   For each pattern, WRITE AN EQUATION (or NUMBER SENTENCE) THAT TELLS ABOUT THIS PATTERN.
2.   WITH YOUR (counters), SHOW ME TWO TIMES TWO. (Try 3 × 4, 5 × 2, and so on).

**EVALUATION:**
1.   Note if the child writes (a) 2 × 4 = 8 or 4 × 2 = 8 (b) 2 × 6 = 12 or 6 × 2 = 12. It is not uncommon for a child to write 3 × 4 = 12 for the second equation. This response would indicate she has memorized 3 times 4 equals 12 without a basic understanding of the multiplication concept.
2.   For 2 × 2, the child should make two groups of two; for 3 × 4, three groups of four; for 5 × 2, five groups of two. Some children will reverse the numbers, such as two groups of five for the last problem. Other children may just make two groups, such as a group of five and a group of two for 5 × 2.

---

**9H**

**Multiplication, Using Symbols: Unit 27**

**METHOD:**    Interview.

**SKILL:**    Child can solve written multiplication problems.

**MATERIALS:**    Counters (e.g., chips, Unifix Cubes, cube blocks), pencil, and paper.

**PROCEDURE:**    One at a time, give the child written multiplication problems. Tell her, WORK OUT THE PROBLEM WITH COUNTERS AND WRITE DOWN THE ANSWER.

**EVALUATION:**    Note whether the child makes the appropriate number of sets of the right amount. Note whether the child does the correct operation. Sometimes children will forget and add instead of multiply. That is, a child might write 3 × 2 = 5.

**9I***
Concrete Operations
Ages 7–8

**Division, Basic Concept: see Unit 27 for task**

---

**9J**
Concrete Operations
Ages 7–8

**Division, Symbols: Unit 27**

**METHOD:** Interview.

**SKILL:** Child understands the use of symbols in division problems.

**MATERIALS:** Counters (e.g., chips, Unifix Cubes, cube blocks), pencil, and paper.

**PROCEDURE:** Give the child a division story problem. For example: "Chan has eight bean seeds. He wants to plant two in each small pot. How many pots will he need?" READ THE PROBLEM, AND SOLVE IT. WRITE THE NUMBER SENTENCE FOR THE PROBLEM ON YOUR PAPER.

**EVALUATION:** Note if the child can write the correct number sentence. If she can't do the problem from memory, does she figure out that she can use her counters or draw a picture to assist in finding the answer?

---

**9K***
Concrete Operations
Ages 6–8

**Patterns, Extension in Three Dimensions: see Unit 28 for task**

---

**9L**
Concrete Operations
Ages 7–8

**Patterns, Creation: Unit 28**

**METHOD:** Interview.

**SKILL:** Child can create patterns using discrete objects.

**MATERIALS:** Concrete objects such as chips, Unifix Cubes, or cube blocks.

**PROCEDURE:** USING YOUR (counters), MAKE YOUR OWN PATTERN AS YOU HAVE DONE WITH PATTERN STARTERS I HAVE GIVEN YOU. When the child is finished, TELL ME ABOUT YOUR PATTERN.

**EVALUATION:** Note if the child has actually developed a repeated pattern and if she is able to describe the pattern in words.

---

**9M***
Concrete Operations
Ages 7–9

**Patterns, Number Multiples: see Unit 28 for task**

---

**9N***

Fractions, Equivalent Parts: see Unit 29 for task

Concrete Operations
Ages 6–8

---

**9O***

Fractions, One-Half of a Group: see Unit 29 for task

Concrete Operations
Ages 6–8

---

**9P***

Place Value, Groups of 10: see Unit 30 for task

Concrete Operations
Ages 7–8

---

**(9Q*)**

Place Value, Grouping to Identify an Amount: see Unit 30 for task

Concrete Operations
Ages 7–8

---

**(9R)**

Concrete Operations
Ages 7–8

**Place Value, Symbols to Concrete Representations: Unit 30**

| | |
|---|---|
| **METHOD:** | Interview or small group. |
| **SKILL:** | Child can translate from written numerals to concrete representations. |
| **MATERIALS:** | Base-ten blocks or similar material (e.g., Unifix Cubes, sticks, or straws and rubber bands for bundling); eight or ten cards, each with a double-digit number written on it (e.g., 38, 72, 45, 83, 27, 96, 51, 50). |
| **PROCEDURE:** | USING YOUR BASE-TEN BLOCKS, MAKE GROUPS FOR EACH NUMERAL. After each group has been constructed, TELL ME HOW YOU KNOW THAT YOU HAVE (number). |
| **EVALUATION:** | Note if the child constructs the correct amount of 10s and units and can explain accurately how the construction is represented by the numeral. |

---

**9S**

Concrete Operations

**Geometry, Graphs, Charts, and Tables: Unit 31**
    See the prerequisite concepts and skills in Units 12, 13, 20, and 25 and Assessment Tasks 3F, 3G, 4E, 5E, and 6C.

---

**9T**
                                                                              **Concrete Operations**

**Measurement with Standard Units: Unit 32**
   See prerequisite concepts in Units 18 and 19 and Assessment Tasks 3J, 4I, 5H, 5I, level 7, 8A, and 8B.

---

**9U**
                                                                              **Concrete Operations**
                                                                                   **Ages 6, 7, 8**
**Solving Problems: Unit 27**

| | |
|---|---|
| **METHOD:** | Provide the students with problems such as can be found in the resource lists at the end of Unit 3. |
| **SKILL:** | Developing problem solutions. |
| **MATERIALS:** | Pencils and paper, counters (if needed), and problems. |
| **PROCEDURE:** | Provide the students with oral and written problem versions such as the following. *Four little piggies run out to play. Two piggies jump in a mud puddle and get muddy feet. The other two piggies just stick their snouts in the mud.* HOW MANY MUDDY FEET AND MUDDY SNOUTS ARE THERE ALL TOGETHER? |
| **EVALUATION:** | Note the procedures used by the students. Do they draw the pigs and count out the feet and snouts? Do they use counters for the pig parts? Do they use tally marks? Do they write out the numerals and add? |

---

**9V**
                                                                              **Concrete Operations**

**Writing Problems: Unit 15**

| | |
|---|---|
| **METHOD:** | Observation, interview; review of children's written products. |
| **SKILL:** | Children can write and/or draw their own problems and solutions to problems presented to them in their math journals. They can also record their general feelings about mathematics and their descriptions of what they have learned. |
| **MATERIALS:** | Notebook and writing tools (pencils, pens, crayons, felt-tip pens). |
| **PROCEDURE:** | Students should have regular daily opportunities to record their mathematics experiences in their math journals. The journals might contain solutions to problems they have identified and problems derived from class work such as from literature selections. They can also be encouraged to record how they are feeling about mathematics and explain what they are learning. |
| **EVALUATION:** | Have the students read their entries to you and review what they have produced. Look for evidence of their mathematical thinking and their approach to problem solving. Also look for their feelings about math and their view of what they know. Note growth in written expression and organization of illustrated problem solutions. Discuss with the children entries they choose to select for inclusion in their portfolio. |

# REFERENCES AND RESOURCES

## General Resources

Baroody, A. J. (1988). *Children's mathematical thinking.* New York: Teachers College Press. (Includes many examples of children's common mistakes and misconceptions)

Bredekamp, S., & Rosegrant, T. (Eds.). (1995). *Reaching potentials: Transforming early childhood curriculum and assessment* (Vol. 2). Washington, DC: National Association for the Education of Young Children. (Defines appropriate assessment strategies for young children)

Copley, J. V. (1999). Assessing mathematical understanding of the young child. In *Mathematics in the early years* (pp. 182–188). Reston, VA: National Council of Teachers of Mathematics, and Washington, DC: National Association for the Education of Young Children. (Provides an overview of early childhood mathematics assessment)

Evan-Moor. (2006). *Math assessment tasks. Quick check activities.* Monterey, CA: Author. (Paper-and-pencil and pictorial assessments)

Glanfield, F., Bush, W. S., & Stenmark, J. K. (Eds.). (2003). *Mathematics assessment: A practical handbook.* Reston, VA: National Council of Teachers of Mathematics.

Huniker, D. (Ed.). (2006). *Prekindergarten–grade 2 mathematics assessment sampler.* Reston, VA: National Council of Teachers of Mathematics. (Assessment tasks and guidelines for evaluation of student responses)

Mindes, G. (2007). *Assessing young children* (3rd ed.). Clifton Park, NY: Cengage Delmar Learning. (Overview of early childhood assessment)

National Council of Teachers of Mathematics. (2000). *Principles and standards for school mathematics.* Reston, VA: Author.

Richardson, K. (1984). *Developing number concepts using Unifix Cubes.* Menlo Park, CA: Addison-Wesley. (Each chapter ends with a section on analyzing and assessing children's needs)

Webb, N. L. (1993). (Ed.). *Assessment in the mathematics classroom: 1993 yearbook.* Reston, VA: National Council of Teachers of Mathematics. (Contains a series of chapters relevant to assessment in general and relative to grade level and specific skill areas)

## Kathy Richardson Materials

Kathy Richardson's materials always take an assessment approach.

Richardson, K. (1990). *A look at children's thinking: Videos for K–2 mathematics.* Norman, OK: Educational Enrichment.

Richardson, K. (1999). *Developing number concepts: Addition and subtraction.* White Plains, NY: Seymour.

Richardson, K. (1999). *Developing number concepts: Counting, comparing and pattern.* White Plains, NY: Seymour.

Richardson, K. (1999). *Developing number concepts: Place value, multiplication and division.* White Plains, NY: Seymour.

Richardson, K. (1999). *Developing number concepts: Planning guide.* White Plains, NY: Seymour.

# Appendix B
## Children's Books and Software with Math and Science Concepts

## CONTENTS*

*Bold numbers that follow a listing indicate relevant units in this book.

## BIBLIOGRAPHY FOR ADULT REFERENCE

*Note*: See Unit 15.
Burns, M. (1992). *Mathematics and literature (K–3)*. White Plains, NY: Cuisinaire.

Chalufour, I., & Worth, K. (2004). *Building structures with young children*. Washington, DC: National Association for the Education of Young Children.

Ducolon, C. K. (2000). Quality literature as a springboard to problem solving. *Teaching Children Mathematics, 6*(7), 442–446.

Fleege, P. O., & Thompson, D. R. (2000). From habits to legs: Using science-themed counting books to foster connections. *Teaching Children Mathematics, 7*(2), 74–78.

Hellwig, S. J., Monroe, E. E., & Jacobs, J. S. (2000). Making informed choices: Selecting children's trade books for mathematics instruction. *Teaching Children Mathematics, 7*(3), 138–143.

Jacobs, V. R., Bennet, T. R., & Bullock, C. (2000). Selecting books in Spanish to teach mathematics. *Teaching Children Mathematics, 6*(9), 582–587.

Outstanding science trade books for children. *Science and Children*. (Published yearly)

Rice, D. C., Dudley, A. P., & Williams, C. S. (2001). How do you choose science trade books? *Science and Children, 38*(6), 18–22.

Sheffield, S. (1995). *Math and literature (K–3): Book 2*. Sausalito, CA: Math Solutions.

Thiessen, D. (Ed.). (2004). *Exploring mathematics through literature*. Reston, VA: National Council for Teachers of Mathematics.

Thiessen, D., Matthias, M., & Smith, J. (1998). *The wonderful world of mathematics: A critically annotated list of children's books in mathematics* (2nd ed.). Reston, VA: National Council of Teachers of Mathematics.

Welchman-Tischler, R. (1993). *How to use children's literature to teach mathematics*. Reston, VA: National Council of Teachers of Mathematics.

West, S., & Cox, A. (2004). *Literacy play*. Beltsville, MD: Gryphon House.

Whitin, D. J., & Whitin, P. (2004). *New visions for linking literature and mathematics*. Urbana, IL: National Council of Teachers of English, and Reston, VA: National Council of Teachers of Mathematics.

Whitin, D. J., & Wilde, S. (1992). *Read any good math lately? Children's books for mathematical learning, K–6*. Portsmouth, NH: Heinemann.

Whitin, D. J., & Wilde, S. (1995). *It's the story that counts: More children's books for mathematical learning, K–6*. Portsmouth, NH: Heinemann.

See Zaner-Bloser's *Science for Emergent Readers* and *Reading and Math* series. Also see end-of-unit references and monthly reviews in *Teaching Children Mathematics* and *Science and Children*.

# FUNDAMENTAL CONCEPTS

## One-to-One Correspondence

Jocelyn, M. (1999). *Hannah and the seven dresses*. East Rutherford, NJ: Penguin Putnam; **8, 19**.

Marzollo, J. (1994). *Ten cats have hats*. Jefferson City, MO: Scholastic Professional; **8, 9**.

Slobodkina, E. (1968). *Se venden gorras*. New York: Harper; **8, 32**.

Slobodkina, E. (1976). *Caps for sale*. New York: Scholastic Books (Ages 3–6); **8, 15**.

*The three bears*. (1973). New York: Golden Press (Ages 2–5); **8, 9, 17**.

*The three billy goats gruff*. (1968). New York: Grosset & Dunlap (Ages 2–5); **8, 9**.

Wade, L. (1998). *The Cheerios play book*. New York: Simon & Schuster; **8**.

## Number Sense and Counting

Many of the books listed in this section include ordinal numbers. Most also include number symbols.

Aker, S. (1990). *What comes in 2's, 3's, and 4's?* New York: Simon & Schuster (Ages 4–6); **9**.

Anno, M. (1982). *Anno's counting house*. New York: Philomel (Ages 4–7); **9**.

Anno, M. (1986). *Anno's counting book*. New York: Harper-Collins (Ages 4–6); **9**.

Aurego, J., & Dewey, A. (1989). *Five little ducks*. New York: Crown; **9**.

Baker, K. (1994). *Count to ten with big fat hen*. San Diego: Harcourt Brace Voyager; **9**.

Ballart, E. (1992). *Let's count*. Charlottsville, VA: Thomasson-Grant; **9, 30**.

Bang, M. (1983). *Ten, nine, eight*. New York: Greenwillow (Ages 3–5); **9**.

Blumenthal, N. (1989). *Count-a-saurus*. New York: Four Winds Press (Ages 3–6); **9**.

Boynton, S. (1978). *Hippos go berserk*. Chicago: Recycled Paper Press (Ages 3–6); **9, 11, 25, 27**.

Brusca, M. C., & Wilson, T. (1995). *Tres amigos: Un cuento para cantar* [Three friends: A counting book]. New York: Holt, Rinehart, & Winston; **9**.

Carle, E. (1968). *1, 2, 3 to the zoo*. New York: Scholastic Books; **9**.

Carle, E. (1969). *The very hungry caterpillar*. Mountain View, CA: Collins & World (Ages 3–5); **9, 17, 19, v21, 26**.

Carle, E. (2005). *10 little rubber ducks*. New York: HarperCollins; **9**.

Carter, D. A. (1988). *How many bugs in a box?* New York: Simon & Schuster (Ages 3–6); **9**.

Cave, K. (2003). *One child, one seed: A South African counting book*. New York: Henry Holt; **9**.

Christelow, E. (1989). *Five little monkeys jumping on the bed*. New York: Clarion; **9**.

Christelow, E. (1991). *Five little monkeys sitting in a tree*. New York: Clarion; **9**.

Crews, D. (1985). *Ten black dots, revised*. New York: Greenwillow (Ages 4–6); **9**.

Cutler, D. S. (1991). *One hundred monkeys*. New York: Simon & Schuster (Ages 3–6); **9**.

Dunbar, J. (1990). *Ten little mice*. San Diego, CA: Harcourt Brace Jovanovich (Ages 3–6); **9**.

Elkin, B. (1968, 1971). *Six foolish fishermen*. New York: Scholastic Books (Ages 3–6); **9, 33**.

Elkin, B., & Kratky, L. J. (Trans.). (1986). *Seis pescadores disparatados* [Six foolish fishermen]. Chicago: Children's Press; **9**.

Elya, S. M. (2002). *Eight animals on the town*. New York: Penguin (Integrates Spanish vocabulary); **9**

Falwell, C. (1993). *Feast for 10*. New York: Clarion; **9**.

Feelings, M. (1976). *Moja means one: Swahili counting book*. New York: Dial (Ages 3–6); **9**.

Felton, C., & Felton, A. (2003). *Where's Harley?* New York: Kane Press; **9**.

Flemming, D. (1992). *Count*. New York: Holt; **9**.

Friskey, M. (1946). *Chicken little count to ten*. New York: Harcourt, Brace (Ages 3–8); **9, 23, 24**.

Frith, M. (1973). *I'll teach my dog 100 words*. New York: Random House (Ages 3–6); **9**.

Gag, W. (1928, 1956, 1977). *Millions of cats*. New York: Coward-McCann (Ages 3–5); **9, 15, 11**.

Getty Museum. (n.d.). *1 to 10 and back again: A Getty Museum counting book*. Los Angeles: Author; **9, 23, 24**.

Gibson, R. (1998). *I can count*. London: Usborne Playtime; **9, 23, 24**.

Grindley, S. (1996). *Four black puppies*. Cambridge, MA: Candlewick Press; **9**.

Grossman, V. (1991). *Ten little rabbits*. San Francisco: Chronicle Books (Ages 3–6); **9**.

Hamm, D. J. (1991). *How many feet in the bed?* New York: Simon & Schuster (Ages 3–6); **9**.

Heller, N. (1994). *Ten old pails*. New York: Greenwillow; **9**.

Hewavisenti, L. (1991). *Fun with math: Counting*. Chicago: Franklin Watts; **9**.

Hoban, T. (1999). *Let's count*. New York: Greenwillow/Morrow; **9**.

Howe, C. (1983). *Counting penguins*. New York: Harper (Ages 3–5); **9, 21, 26**.

Hudson, C. W. (1987). *Afro-bets 1, 2, 3 book*. Orange, NJ: Just Us Productions; **9, 23, 24**.

Hulme, J. N. (1991). *Sea squares*. Waltham, MA: Little, Brown (Ages 4–6); **9**.

Jenkins, E. (2001). *Five creatures*. New York: Farrar, Straus, & Giroux; **9**.

Jonas, A. (1995). *Splash!* New York: Greenwillow; **9**.

Keats, E. J. (1972). *Over in the meadow*. New York: Scholastic Books (Ages 3–5); **9**.

Kitamura, S. (1986). *When sheep cannot sleep? The counting book*. New York: Farrar, Straus, & Giroux (Ages 2–5); **9**.

Krebs, L. (2003). *We all went on safari. A counting journey through Tanzania*. Cambridge, MA: Barefoot Books (Includes information on Masai, Tansanian wildlife, and Swahili vocabulary); **9, 34**.

Leedy, L. (1985). *A number of dragons*. New York: Holiday House (Ages 1–3); **9**.

Lester, H. (2001). *Score one for the sloths*. New York: Scholastic Books. **9**.

Lewin, B. (1981). *Cat count*. New York: Scholastic Books; **9, 30**.

Lowell, S. (1992). *The three little javelinas*. New York: Scholastic Books; **9**.

MacDonald, S. (2000). *Look whooo's counting*. New York: Scholastic Books; **9**.

Mayer, M., & McDermott, G. (1987). *The Brambleberrys animal book of counting*. Honesdale, PA: Boyds Mill Press (Ages 3–6); **9**.

McGrath, B. B. (1994). *The m&m's counting book*. Watertown, MA: Charlesbridge; **9, 20, 27**.

Michelson, R. (2000). *Ten times better*. Tarrytown, NY: Marshall Cavendish; **9**.

Micklethwait, L. (1993). *I spy two eyes: Numbers in art*. Fairfield, NJ: Greenwillow; **9**.

Moerbeek, K., & Dijs, C. (1988). *Six brave explorers*. Los Angeles: Price Stern Sloan (Ages 4–6); **9**.

Moss, L. (1995). *Zin! Zin! Zin! A violin*. New York: Scholastic Books; **9, 15**.

Parish, S. (1998). *1, 2, 3 of Australian wildlife*. Archerfield BC, Queensland, Australia: Steve Parish; **9, 30, 34**.

Pomerantz, C. (1984). *One duck, another duck*. New York: Greenwillow (Ages 3–7); **9**.

Prodan, J. R. (2000). *Count with me*. Pittsburgh, PA: Darrance; **9**.

Roth, C. (1999). *Ten clean pigs, ten dirty pigs*. New York: North-South Books; **9**.

Ryan, P. M., & Pallotta, J. (1996). *The crayon counting book*. Watertown, MA: Charlesbridge; **9**.

Samton, S. W. (1991). *Moon to sun*. Honesdale, PA: Boyds Mill Press; **9**.

Samton, S. W. (1991). *On the river*. Honesdale, PA: Boyds Mill Press (Ages 4–6); **9**.

Samton, S. W. (1991). *The world from my window*. Honesdale, PA: Boyds Mill Press; **9**.

Sayre, A. P., & Sayre, J. (2003). *One is a snail, ten is a crab*. Cambridge, MA: Candlewick Press; **9**.

Scarry, R. (1975). *Best counting book ever*. New York: Random House (Ages 2–8); **9, 19**.

Sendak, M. (1975). *Seven little monsters*. New York: Scholastic Books; **9**.

Seuss, Dr. (1938). *The 500 hats of Bartholomew Cubbins*. Eau Claire, WI: Hale (Ages 3–7); **9**.

Seuss, Dr. (1960). *One fish, two fish, red fish, blue fish*. New York: Random House (Ages 3–7); **9, 11, 15, 18**.

Sheppard, J. (1990). *The right number of elephants*. New York: Harper-Collins (Ages 4–6); **9**.

Slobodkina, E. (1940, 1947, 1968). *Caps for sale*. New York: Young Scott; **9, 32**.

Slobodkina, E. (1940, 1947, 1968; translation 1995). *Se venden gorras*. New York: Harper Arco Iris; **9, 32**.

Steiner, C. (1960). *Ten in a family*. New York: Knopf (Ages 3–5); **9**.

Stoddart, G., & Baker, M. (1982). *One, two number zoo*. London: Hodder & Stoughton (Ages 5–7); **9, 21, 36, 35**.

Storms, R. (1986). *1, 2, 3: A teaching train book*. Miami, FL: Ottenheimer; **9**.

Tafuri, N. (1986). *Who's counting?* New York: Greenwillow (Ages 2–5); **9**.

Thorne-Thomsen, K., & Rocheleau, P. (1999). *A Shaker's dozen counting book*. San Francisco: Chronicle Books; **9, 32**.

Thornhill, J. (1989). *The wildlife 1-2-3: A nature counting book*. New York: Simon & Schuster (Ages 3–6); **9**.

Tucker, K. (2003). *The seven Chinese sisters*. New York: Scholastic; **9, 17**.

Ungerer, T. (1962). *The three robbers*. New York: Antheum (Ages 3–5); **9**.

Von Noorden, D. (1994). *The lifesize animal counting book*. New York: Dorling Kindersley; **9, 16**.

Walton, R. (1993). *How many How many How many*. Cambridge, MA: Candlewick Press; **9**.

Wildsmith, B. (1965). *Brian Wildsmith's 1, 2, 3's*. New York: Franklin Watts (Ages 3–5); **9**.

Wildsmith, B. (1996). *¿Cuantos animals hay?* New York: Star Bright Books; **9**.

Wilson, K., & Rankin, J. (2003). *A frog in the bog*. New York: Scholastic Books; **9**.

Zaslavsky, C. (1999). *Count on your fingers African style*. New York: Writers & Readers; **9**.

## Classification

Cabrera, J. (1997). *Cat's colors*. New York: Puffin; **10**.

Fiammenghi, G. (1999). *A collection for Kate*. New York: Kane; **9, 10, 11**.

Gordon, M. (1986). *Colors*. Morristown, NJ: Silver-Burdett (Ages 2–6); **10**.

Hill, E. (1982). *What does what?* Los Angeles: Price/Stern/Sloan (Ages 2–4); **10**.

Hoban, T. (1978). *Is it red? Is it yellow? Is it blue?* New York: Greenwillow (Ages 2–5); **10**.

Hughes, S. (1986). *Colors*. New York: Lothrop (Ages 2–4); **10**.

Johnson, J. (1985). *Firefighters A–Z*. New York: Walker (Ages 5–8); **10, 22**.

Wildsmith B. (1967). *Brian Wildsmith's wild animals*. New York: Franklin Watts (Ages 3–8); **10, 21, 26, 35**.

Wildsmith, B. (1968). *Brian Wildsmith's fishes*. New York: Franklin Watts (Ages 3–8); **10, 21, 26, 35**.

Winthrop, E. (1986). *Shoes*. New York: Harper & Row (Ages 3–7); **10, 22**.

## Comparing

Bourgeois, P., & Clark, B. (1987). *Big Sarah's little boots*. New York: Scholastic Books (Ages 3–5); **11**.

Brenner, B. (1966). *Mr. Tall and Mr. Small*. Menlo Park, CA: Addison-Wesley (Ages 4–7); **11, 21, 26, 35**.

Broger, A., & Kalow, G. (1977). *Good morning whale*. New York: Macmillan (Ages 3–6); **11, 21, 26, 35**.

Carle, E. (1977). *The grouchy ladybug*. New York: Crowell (Ages 3–5); **11, 21, 26**.

Eastman, P. D. (1973). *Big dog, little dog*. New York: Random House (Ages 3–4); **11, 21, 26**.

Gordon, M. (1986). *Opposites*. Morristown, NJ: Silver-Burdett (Ages 3–5); **11**.

Graham, A., & Wood, W. (1991). *Angus thought he was big*. Hicksville, NY: Macmillan (Ages 3–5); **11**.

Grender, I. (1975). *Playing with shapes and sizes*. New York: Knopf/Pinwheel Books (Ages 3–6); **11, 12**.

Hoban, T. (1972). *Push pull, empty full*. New York: Macmillan (Ages 3–5); **11**.

Horn, A. (1974). *You can be taller*. Boston: Little, Brown (Ages 3–5); **11**.

Hughes, S. (1985). *Bathwater's hot*. New York: Lothrop (Ages 1–2); **11, 21, 26**.

Hughes, S. (1985). *Noises*. New York: Lothrop (Ages 1–2); **11, 21, 26**.

Lewis, J. (1963). *The tortoise and the hare*. Chicago: Whitman (Ages 4–8); **11, 18**.

Lionni, L. (1968). *The biggest house in the world*. New York: Pantheon (Ages 2–6); **11, 21, 26**.

McMillan, B. (1986). *Becca backward, Becca forward*. New York: Lothrop (Ages 3–6); **11**.

Miller, N. (1990). *Emmett's snowball*. New York: Henry Holt (K–3 and above); **11, 21, 26, 32**.

Most, B. (1989). *The littlest dinosaurs*. New York: Harcourt Brace; **11**.

Novak, M. (2005). *Too many bunnies*. New Milford, CT: Roaring Book Press; **11**.

Presland, J. (1975). *Same and different*. Purton Wilts, England: Child's Play (Ages 4–7); **11**.

Scarry, R. (1976). *Short and tall*. New York: Golden Press (Ages 2–7); **11**.

Scarry, R. (1986). *Big and little: A book of opposites*. Racine, WI: Western (Ages 3–7); **11**.

Shapiro, L. (1978). *Pop-up opposites*. Los Angeles: Price/Stern/Sloan (Ages 3–5); **11**.

## Early Geometry

### Shape

Anno, M. (1991). *Anno's math games III*. New York: Philomel (K–6); **12, 25, 31**.

Budney, B. (1954). *A kiss is round*. New York: Lothrop, Lee, & Shepard (Ages 2–6); **12**.

Carle, E. (1974). *My very first book of shapes*. New York: Crowell (Ages 3–6); **12**.

Dodds, D. A. (1994). *The shape of things*. Cambridge, MA: Candlewick Press; **12**.

Ehlert, L. (1990). *Color farm*. New York: Harper-Collins; **12, 22, 25**.

Emberley, E. (1961). *A wing on a flea: A book about shapes*. Boston: Little, Brown (Ages 5–8); **12**.

Emberley, E. (1970). *Ed Emberley's drawing book of animals*. Boston: Little, Brown (Ages 6–8); **12**.

Emberley, E. (1972). *Ed Emberley's drawing book: Make a world*. Boston: Little, Brown (Ages 6–8); **12**.

Emberley, E. (1995). *El ala de la polilla: Un libro de figuras* [The wing on a flea: A book about shapes]. New York: Scholastic Books; **12**.

Hefter, R. (1976). *The strawberry book of shapes*. New York: Weekly Reader Books (Ages 3–7); **12**.

Hewavisenti, L. (1991). *Shapes and solids*. Chicago: FranklinWatts; **12, 31**.

Hoban, T. (1974). *Circles, triangles, and squares*. New York: Macmillan (Ages 5–8); **12**.

Hoban, T. (1983). *Round and round and round*. New York: Greenwillow (Ages 3–6); **12**.

Hoban, T. (1986). *Shapes, shapes, shapes*. New York: Greenwillow (Ages 3–7); **12**.

Hoban, T. (1997). *Look book*. New York: Morrow Junior Books; **12**.

Hoban, T. (2000). *Cubes, cones, cylinders, and spheres*. New York: HarperCollins; **12**.

MacKinnon, D. (1992). *What shape?* New York: Dial; **12**.

MacKinnon, D., & Sieveking, A. (2000). *Eye spy shapes: A peephole book*. Watertown, MA: Charlesbridge; **12**.

Rau, D. M. (2002). *A star in my orange: Looking for nature's shapes*. Brookfield, CT: Millbrook Press; **12**.

*Shapes: Circle; Square; Triangle* (3 books). (1992). New York: Books for Young Readers (Ages 3–6); **12**.

Sullivan, J. (1963). *Round is a pancake*. New York: Holt, Rinehart, & Winston (Ages 3–5); **12**.

Supraner, R. (1975). *Draw me a square, draw me a triangle, & draw me a circle*. New York: Simon & Schuster/Nutmeg (Ages 3–6); **12**.

Teulade, P. (1999). *El más bonito de todos regalos del mundo* [The most beautiful gift in the world]. Barcelona, Spain: Editorial Corimbo; **12**.

Thong, R. (2000). *Round is a mooncake: A book of shapes*. San Francisco: Chronicle Books; **12**.

### Space

Barton, B. (1981). *Building a house*. New York: Greenwillow (Ages 4–7); **13, 14, 19**.

Berenstain, S., & Berenstain, J. (1968). *Inside, outside, upside down*. New York: Random House (Ages 3–7); **13**.

Brown, M. (1949). *Two little trains*. New York: Scott, Foresman (Ages 2–4); **13, 15**.

Carle, E. (1972). *The secret birthday message*. New York: Crowell (Ages 3–7); **13**.

Dunrea, O. (1985). *Fergus and the bridey*. New York: Holiday (Ages 4–7); **13**.

Hill, E. (1980). *Where's Spot?* New York: Putnam's (Ages 2–4); **13**.

Lionni, L. (1983). *Where?* New York: Pantheon (Ages 2–3); **13**.

Maestro, B., & Maestro, G. (1976). *Where is my friend?* New York: Crown (Ages 2–4); **13**.

Martin, B., Jr. (1971). *Going up, going down*. New York: Holt, Rinehart, & Winston (Ages 6–8); **13, 9**.

Russo, M. (1986). *The line up book*. New York: Greenwillow (Ages 3–5); **13**.

Teulade, P. (1999). *El más bonito de todos regalos del mundo* [The most beautiful gift in the world]. Barcelona, Spain: Editorial Corimbo; **13**.

Weimer, T. E. (1993). *Space songs for children*. Greenville, SC: Pearce-Evetts (Ages 5–7); **13**.

## Parts and Wholes

Axworthy, A. (Illus.). (1998). *Guess what I am*. Cambridge, MA: Candlewick Press; **14**.

Burton, M. R. (1988). *Tail Toes Eyes Ears Nose*. New York: Harper Trophy; **14, 21, 26**.

Carle, E. (1987). *Do you want to be my friend?* New York: Harper Trophy; **14**.

Dubov, C. S. (1986). *Alexsandra, where are your toes?* New York: St. Martin's Press (Ages 1½–3); **14, 21, 26**.

Dubov, C. S. (1986). *Alexsandra, where is your nose?* New York: St. Martin's Press (Ages 1½–3); **14, 21, 26**.

Hutchins, P., & Marcuse, A. (Trans.) (1994). *Llaman a la puerta* [The doorbell rang]. New York: Mulberry; **14, 27**.

Le Tord, B. (1985). *Good wood bear*. New York: Bradbury (Ages 4–7); **14, 32**.

Luciana, B., & Tharlet, E. (2000). *How will we get to the beach?* New York: North-South Books; **14, 31**.

Mathews, L. (1979). *Gator pie*. New York: Scholastic Books (Ages 4–7); **14, 25**.

## Language

Arenson, R. (Illus.). (1989). *One, two, skip a few: First number rhymes*. Brooklyn, NY: Barefoot Poetry Collections; **15**.

Bemelmans, L. (1969). *Madeline*. New York: Viking (Ages 4–7); **8, 9, 15, 19**.

Duvoisin, R. (1974). *Petunia takes a trip*. New York: Knopf/Pinwheel (Ages 4–7); **11, 15, 18, 21, 26, 35**.

Figueredo, D. H. (2000). *Big snowball fight*. New York: Lee & Low Books; **15**.

Hoff, S. (1959). *Julius*. New York: Harper & Row (Ages 4–7); **15, 21, 26, 35**.

*Mathematics in the kitchen, Mathematics at the farm, Mathematics in buildings, Mathematics on the playground, Mathematics in the circus ring*. (1978). Milwaukee: MacDonald–Raintree (Ages 3–7); **15**.

McKellar, S. (1993). *Counting rhymes*. New York: Dorling Kindersley; **15, 27**.

Orozco, J. (1997). *Diez deditos* [Ten little fingers]. New York: Scholastic Books; **15**.

Shelby, A. (1990). *We keep a store*. New York: Orchard Books; **15, 22**.

Umansky, K., & Fisher, C. (1999). *Nonsense counting rhymes*. Oxford: Oxford University Press; **15**.

# APPLICATION OF FUNDAMENTAL CONCEPTS

## Ordering, Seriation, and Patterning

Aker, S. (1990). *What comes in 2's, 3's, & 4's?* New York: Aladdin; **17, 23, 24**.

Asbjörsen, P. C., & Moe, J. E. (1957). *The three billy goats gruff*. New York: Harcourt, Brace, Jovanovich (Ages 2–5); **9, 11, 15, 17**.

Brett, J. (1987). *Goldilocks and the three bears*. New York: Dodd, Mead (Ages 3–5); **17, 21, 26**.

Clements, A. (1992). *Mother Earth's counting book*. New York: Simon & Schuster (Ages 5 and up); **17, 25, 28**.

Hoban, T. (1992). *Look up, look down*. New York: Greenwillow (Ages 5–8); **17**.

Ipcar, C. (1972). *The biggest fish in the sea*. New York: Viking (Ages 3–6); **17, 21, 26, 35**.

Macauly, D. (1987). *Why the chicken crossed the road*. Boston: Houghton-Mifflin (Ages 4–8); **17**.

Maestro, B., & Maestro, G. (1977). *Harriet goes to the circus*. New York: Crown (Ages 5–8); **17, 21, 26, 35**.

Mahy, M. (1987). *17 kings and 42 elephants*. New York: Dial (Ages 2–6); **9, 17, 21, 26, 35**.

Martin, B., Jr. (1963). *One, two, three, four*. New York: Holt, Rinehart, & Winston (Ages 5–7); **9, 17**.

Martin, B., Jr. (1970). *Monday, Monday, I like Monday*. New York: Holt, Rinehart, & Winston (Ages 5–8); **17, 19**.

## Measurement

### Volume, Weight, and Length

Allen, P. (1983). *Who sank the boat?* New York: Coward (Ages 3–5); **18**.

Anderson, L. C. (1983). *The wonderful shrinking shirt*. Niles, IL: Whitman (Ages 3–5); **18**.

Bennett, V. (1975). *My measure it book*. New York: Grosset & Dunlap (Ages 3–5); **18**.

Demi. (1997). *One grain of rice*. New York: Scholastic Books; **18**.

Faulkner, K. (2000). *So big! My first measuring book*. New York: Simon & Schuster; **18, 21, 26**.

Henkes, K. (1995). *The biggest boy*. New York: Greenwillow; **18**.

Lionni, L. (1960). *Inch by inch*. New York: Astor-Honor (Ages 3–5); **17, 21, 26**.

McMillan, B. (1987). *Step by step*. New York: Lothrop (Ages 3–6); **18, 19**.

Myller, R. (1972). *How big is a foot?* New York: Atheneum (Ages 6–8); **18, 32**.

Parkinson, K. (1986). *The enormous turnip*. Niles, IL: Whitman (Ages 4–7); **18, 32, 35**.

Russo, M. (1986). *The lineup book*. New York: Greenwillow (Ages 2–4); **18**.

Schlein, M. (1954). *Heavy is a hippopotamus*. New York: Scott (Ages 3–6); **18, 21, 26**.

Shapp, M., & Shapp, C. (1975). *Let's find out about what's light and what's heavy*. New York: Franklin Watts (Ages 6–8); **18, 32**.

Ward, L. (1952). *The biggest bear*. Boston: Houghton-Mifflin (Ages 3–5); **18, 19**.

Zion, G. (1959). *The plant sitter*. New York: Harper & Row (Ages 3–6); **18, 19**.

## Time

Bancroft, H., & Van Gelde, R. G. (1963). *Animals in winter*. New York: Scholastic Books (Ages 3–6); **19, 32**.

Barrett, J. (1976). *Benjamin's 365 birthdays*. New York: Atheneum (Ages 3–6); **19**.

Berenstain, S., & Berenstain, J. (1973). *The bear's almanac*. New York: Random House (Ages 3–6); **19, 32**.

Bonne, R. (1961). *I know an old lady*. New York: Scholastic Books (Ages 3–5); **19**.

Brown, M. (1984). *Arthur's Christmas*. Boston: Little, Brown (Ages 6–8); **32**.

Brown, M. W. (1947). *Goodnight moon*. New York: Harper & Row (Ages 3–6); **19**.

Carle, E. (1977). *The very hungry caterpillar*. New York: Collins & World (Ages 3–5); **19, 21, 26**.

Carle, E. (1993). *Today is Monday*. New York: Scholastic Books; **19**.

Carle, E., & Marcuse, A. E. (Trans.). (1994). *La oruga muy hambrienta* [The hungry caterpillar]. New York: Philomel; **19, 21, 26**.

Carle, E., & Mlawer, T. (Trans.). (1996). *La mariquita malhumorada* [The grouchy ladybug]. New York: HarperCollins; **19, 21, 26**.

Castle, C. (1985). *The hare and the tortoise*. New York: Dial (Ages 5–8); **19, 32**.

Chalmers, M. (1988). *Easter parade*. New York: Harper (Ages 3–6); **19, 32**.

dePaola, T. (1986). *Merry Christmas, Strega Nona*. San Diego, CA: Harcourt, Brace (Ages 3–6); **19, 32**.

Duvoisin, R. (1956). *The house of four seasons*. New York: Lothrop, Lee, & Shepard (Ages 3–6); **19, 32**.

Flournoy, V. (1985). *Patchwork quilt*. New York: Dial (Ages 4–8); **19, 32**.

Hall, B. (1973). *What ever happens to baby animals?* New York: Golden Press (Ages 2–5); **17, 19**.

Hauge, C., & Hauge, M. (1974). *Gingerbread man*. New York: Golden Press (Ages 2–5); **17, 19**.

Hayes, S. (1986). *Happy Christmas Gemma*. New York: Lothrop (Ages 2–5); **19**.

Hooper, M. (1985). *Seven eggs*. New York: Harper & Row (Ages 3–5); **8, 17, 19**.

Kelleritti, H. (1985). *Henry's Fourth of July*. New York: Greenwillow (Ages 3–6); **19**.

Kraus, R. (1972). *Milton the early riser*. New York: Prentice Hall (Ages 2–5); **19**.

Krementz, J. (1986). *Zachary goes to the zoo*. New York: Random House (Ages 2–8); **19, 21, 26, 32, 35**.

Leslie, S. (1977). *Seasons*. New York: Platt & Munk (Ages 2–5); **19**.

McCully, E. A. (1985). *First snow*. New York: Warner (Ages 3–5); **19, 21, 26**.

Miles, B. (1973). *A day of autumn*. New York: Random House (Ages 3–5); **19**.

Older, J. (2000). *Telling time*. Watertown, MA: Charlesbridge; **19, 32**.

Ormerodi, J. (1981). *Sunshine*. New York: Lothrop, Lee, & Shepard (Ages 2–6); **19**.

Pearson, S. (1988). *My favorite time of year*. New York: Harper & Row (Ages 3–7); **19, 32, 35**.

Porter Productions. (1975). *My tell time book*. New York: Grosset & Dunlap (Ages 5–7); **19, 32**.

Prelutsky, J. (1984). *It's snowing! It's snowing!* New York: Greenwillow (Ages 4–7); **19, 21, 26, 32, 37**.

Provensen, A., & Provensen, M. (1976). *A book of seasons*. New York: Random House (Ages 3–5); **19**.

Richards, K. (2000). *It's about time, Max!* New York: Kane Press; **19**.

Robison, A. (1973). *Pamela Jane's week*. Racine, WI: Whitman Books/Western (Ages 2–5); **19**.

Rockwell, A. (1985). *First comes spring*. New York: Crowell (Ages 2–6); **19, 21, 26, 32, 37**.

Rutland, J. (1976). *Time*. New York: Grosset & Dunlap (Ages 2–7); **19, 32**.

Scarry, R. (1976). *All day long*. New York: Golden Press (Ages 3–6); **19, 32**.

Schlein, M. (1955). *It's about time*. New York: Young Scott (Ages 3–7); **19, 32**.

Schwerin, D. (1984). *The tomorrow book*. New York: Pantheon (Ages 3–6); **19**.

Todd, K. (1982). *Snow*. Reading, MA: Addison-Wesley (Ages 3–8); **19, 21, 26, 32, 37**.

Tudor, T. (1957). *Around the year*. New York: Walck (Ages 3–5); **19**.

Tudor, T. (1977). *A time to keep: The Tasha Tudor book of holidays*. New York: Rand McNally (Ages 3–6); **19**.

Vincent, G. (1984). *Merry Christmas, Ernest & Celestine*. New York: Greenwillow (Ages 4–8); **19, 32**.

Wolff, A. (1984). *A year of birds*. New York: Dodd, Mead (Ages 3–6); **19, 21, 26**.

Zolotow, C. (1984). *I know an old lady*. New York: Greenwillow (Ages 4–8); **19, 21, 26, 32**.

## Graphing

Dussling, J. (2003). *Math matters, fair is fair!* New York: Kane Press; **20, 31**.

Nagda, A. W., & Bickel, C. (2000). *Tiger math: Learning to graph from a baby tiger*. New York: Henry Holt; **20, 31**.

## Practical Activities/Integration

Cohn, J. M., & Elliott, D. L. (1992). *Recycling for math.* Berkeley, CA: Educational Materials Associates (For teachers of kindergarten and up); **22**.

Lesser, C. (1999). *Spots: Counting creatures from sky to sea.* San Diego, CA: Harcourt Brace; **22**.

Shelby, A. (1990). *We keep a store.* New York: Orchard Books; **15, 22**.

Wallace, N. E. (2000). *Paperwhite.* Boston, MA: Houghton-Mifflin; **22**.

## Money

Asch, F. (1976). *Good lemonade.* Ontario, Canada: Nelson, Foster, & Scott (Ages 6–8); **32**.

Brenner, B. (1963). *The five pennies.* New York: Random House (Ages 6–7); **22, 32**.

Brisson, P. (1993). *Benny's pennies.* New York: Bantam Doubleday; **22, 25, 32**.

Credle, E. (1969). *Little pest Pico.* Ontario, Canada: Nelson, Foster, & Scott (Ages 6–8); **32**.

deRubertis, B. (1999). *Deena's lucky penny.* New York: Kane Press; **22, 32**.

Gill, S., & Tobola, D. (2000). *The big buck adventure.* Watertown, MA: Charlesbridge; **22, 32**.

Hoban, L. (1981). *Arthur's funny money.* New York: Harper & Row (Ages 4–7); **22, 32**.

Kirn, A. (1969). *Two pesos for Catalina.* New York: Scholastic Books (Ages 6–8); **22, 32**.

Martin, B., Jr. (1963). *Ten pennies for candy.* New York: Holt, Rinehart, & Winston (Ages 5–7); **22, 32**.

Rockwell, A. (1984). *Our garage sale.* New York: Greenwillow (Ages 3–5); **22**.

Slobodkina, E. (1940, 1947, 1968). *Caps for sale.* New York: Young Scott; **9, 22, 32**.

Slobodkina, E. (1940, 1947, 1968; translation 1995). *Se venden gorras.* New York: Harper Arco Iris; **9, 22, 32**.

Thornburgh, R. (1999). *Count on Pablo.* New York: Kane; **22, 25, 32**.

## Food

*Note:* See also Unit 22.

Brown, M. (1947). *Stone soup.* New York: Scribner's (Ages 3–5); **22, 32, 38**.

Carle, E. (1970). *Pancakes, pancakes.* New York: Knopf (Ages 3–5); **22**.

deRubertis, B. (2006). *La limonada de Lulu.* New York: Kane Press; **22, 32**.

Ehlert, L. (1987). *Growing vegetable soup.* San Diego, CA: Harcourt, Brace, Jovanovich (Ages 3–6); **22, 32, 38**.

Fleming, D. (1992). *Lunch.* New York: Henry Holt; **22, 38**.

Hoban, R. (1964). *Bread and jam for Frances.* New York: Scholastic Books (Ages 3–7); **22, 38**.

McCloskey, R. (1948). *Blueberries for Sal.* New York: Viking (Ages 3–6); **22, 38**.

Norquist, S. (1985). *Pancake pie.* New York: Morrow (Ages 4–8); **22, 32, 38**.

Sendak, M. (1962). *Chicken soup with rice.* New York: Harper & Row (Ages 3–5); **22**.

Sendak, M. (1970). *In the night kitchen.* New York: Harper & Row (Ages 4–6); **22, 32, 38**.

Seymour, P. (1981). *Food.* Los Angeles: Intervisual Communications (Ages 2–5); **22**.

Thayer, J. (1961). *The blueberry pie elf.* Edinburgh, Scotland: Oliver & Boyd (Ages 4–7); **22, 32, 38**.

## Cookbooks

*Note:* See also Unit 22. Can be adapted to all ages.

Ault, R. (1974). *Kids are natural cooks.* Boston: Houghton-Mifflin; **22, 32, 38**.

*Better Homes and Gardens new junior cookbook.* (1979). Des Moines, IA: Meredith; **22, 32, 38**.

Colker, L. J. (2005). *The cooking book.* Washington, DC: National Association for the Education of Young Children.

Kementz, J. (1985). *The fun of cooking.* New York: Knopf; **22, 32, 38**.

Pratt, D. (1998). *Hey kids, you're cookin' now: A global awareness cooking adventure.* Available from http://www.amazon.com

Rothstein, G. L. (1994). *From soup to nuts: Multicultural cooking activities and recipes.* New York: Scholastic Books; **22, 32, 38**.

*Sesame Street cookbook.* (1978). New York: Platt & Munk; **22, 32, 38**.

Shepard, E. H. (1993). *Winnie-the-Pooh's teatime cookbook.* Available from http://www.amazon.com

Walker, B., & Williams, G. (1995). *Little house cookbook.* Available from http://www.amazon.com

*Walt Disney's Mickey Mouse cookbook.* (1975). New York: Golden Press; **22, 32, 38**.

Warner, P. (1999). *Healthy snacks for kids (Nitty Gritty Cookbooks).* Available from http://www.amazon.com

Williamson, S., & Williamson, Z. (1992). *Kids cook! Fabulous food for the whole family.* Charlotte, VT: Williamson; **22, 32, 38**.

## Science

Hall, Z. (1994). *It's pumpkin time!* New York: Scholastic Books; **17, 26, 34**.

Helman, A. (1996). *1 2 3 Moose: A Pacific Northwest counting book*. Seattle, WA: Sasquatch Books; **9, 16, 21, 22, 26**.

Kusugak, M. A. (1996). *My Arctic 1, 2, 3*. Toronto, Ontario, Canada: Annick Press; **9, 16, 21, 22, 26**.

Pallotta, J. (1992). *The icky bug counting book*. Watertown, MA: Charlesbridge; **9, 16, 21, 22, 26**.

Stevens, J., & Crummel, S. S. (1999). *Cook-a-doodle-do*. New York: Harcourt Brace; **22**.

Thornhill, J. (1989). *The wildlife 1-2-3: A nature counting book*. New York: Simon & Schuster; **9, 16, 21, 22, 26**.

Toft, K. M., & Sheather, A. (1998). *One less fish*. Watertown, MA: Charlesbridge; **9**.

Wadsworth, G. (1997). *One on a web*. Watertown, MA: Charlesbridge; **9, 16, 21, 22, 26**.

Wadsworth, G. (1999). *One tiger growls*. Watertown, MA: Charlesbridge; **9, 16, 21, 22, 26**.

Wood, J. *One tortoise, ten wallabies: A wildlife counting book*; **9, 16, 21, 22, 26**.

## SYMBOLS AND HIGHER-LEVEL ACTIVITIES

### Groups and Symbols

Aker, S. (1990). *What comes in 2's, 3's, & 4's?* New York: Aladdin; **17, 23, 24, 25**.

Alain (Bruslein, A.). (1964). *One, two, three going to sea*. New York: Scholastic Books (Ages 5–7); **23, 24, 25, 27**.

Anno, M. (1977). *Anno's counting book*. New York: Crowell (Ages 5–7); **23, 24, 25**.

Balet, J. B. (1959). *The five Rollatinis*. Philadelphia: Lippincott (Ages 4–7); **23, 24, 25**.

Chang, A. (2000). *Grandfather counts*. New York: Lee & Low Books; **23, 24, 25**.

Cuyler, M. (2000). *100th day worries*. New York: Simon & Schuster; **23, 24, 25**.

Duvoisin, R. (1955). *1000 Christmas beards*. New York: Knopf (Ages 3–7); **23, 24, 25**.

Duvoisin, R. (1955). *Two lonely ducks*. New York: Knopf (Ages 4–7); **21, 23, 24, 25, 26, 35**.

Federico, H. (1963). *The golden happy book of numbers*. New York: Golden Press (Ages 3–7); **23, 24, 25**.

Franco, B. (1999). *The tortoise who bragged: A Chinese tale with trigrams*. Sunnyvale, CA: Stokes; **25**.

Francoise (Seignobosc, F.) (1951). *Jean-Marie counts her sheep*. New York: Scribner's (Ages 3–6); **23, 24, 25**.

Friskey, M. (1940). *Seven diving ducks*. New York: McKay (Ages 4–6); **23, 24, 25**.

Garne, S. T. (1992). *One white sail*. New York: Green Tiger Press (Ages 5–8); **25, 26, 27**.

Getty Museum. (n.d.). *1 to 10 and back again: A Getty Museum counting book*. Los Angeles: Author; **9, 23, 24, 25**.

Gibson, R. (1998). *I can count*. London: Usborne Playtime; **9, 23, 24, 25**.

Gollub, M. (2000). *Ten Oni drummers*. New York: Lee & Low; **23, 24, 25**.

Guettier, B. (1999). *The father who had ten children*. East Rutherford, NJ: Dial/Penguin; **23, 24, 25**.

Hoban, T. (1987). *Letters & 99 cents*. New York: Greenwillow (Ages 4–8); **23, 24, 25, 32**.

Hudson, C. W. (1987). *Afro-bets 1, 2, 3 book*. Orange, NJ: Just Us Productions; **9, 23, 24**.

Hulme, J. N. (1993). *Sea squares*. New York: Hyperion; **9, 23, 24, 25**.

Johnson, S. T. (1998). *City by numbers*. New York: Viking/Penguin; **23**.

Keats, E. J. (1971). *Over in the meadow*. New York: Scholastic Books (Ages 3–5); **23, 24**.

Kherdian, D., & Hogrogian, N. (1990). *The cat's midsummer jamboree*. New York: Philomel (Ages 5–8); **25, 26, 27**.

LeSeig, T. (1974). *Whacky Wednesday*. New York: Random House (Ages 5–8); **25**.

McNutt, D. (1979). *There was an old lady who lived in a 1*. Palo Alto, CA: Creative Publications (Ages 4–6); **9, 23, 24**.

Merriam, E. (1993). *12 ways to get to 11*. New York: Aladdin; **24, 25, 27**.

Miller, V. (2002). *Ten red apples: A Bartholomew Bear counting book*. Cambridge, MA: Candlewick; **23, 24, 25**.

*Numbers: Match-up flip book*. (1984). St. Paul, MN: Trend (Ages 4–8); **23, 24**.

Suen, A. (2000). *100 day*. New York: Lee & Low Books; **23, 24, 25**.

Thaler, M. (1991). *Seven little hippos*. Old Tappan, NJ: Simon & Schuster (Ages 5–8); **25, 26, 27**.

Zaslavsky, C. (1999). *Count on your fingers African style*. New York: Writers & Readers; **25**.

## MATHEMATICS CONCEPTS AND ACTIVITIES FOR THE PRIMARY GRADES

As already noted, many of the books listed are appropriate for preprimary and primary children. Many books that are read-along books for the younger children become books for individual reading for older children. A few additional titles are included here.

Aber, & Allen, J. Carrie. *Esta a la altura*. Kane Press (Measuring). **32**.

Anderson, L. (1971). *Two hundred rabbits*. New York: Penguin Books (Ages 7–9); **27**.

Barry, D. (1994). *The Rajah's rice: A mathematical folktale from India*. New York: Freeman; **32**.

Base, G. (2006). *Uno's garden*. Time Warner (K–8); **27, 36**.

Belov, R. (1971). *Money, money, money*. New York: Scholastic Books (Ages 6–8); **32**.

Boynton, S. (1987). *Hippos go berserk*. Chicago: Recycled Paper Press; **30**.

Branco, B., & Salerno, S. (2003). *Mathematickles*. Riverside, NJ: Simon & Schuster; **3**.

Bruce, S., & Billin-Frye, P. (Illus.). *¡Todos ganan!* New York: Kane Press (Division); **27**.

Bruchac, J., & London, J. (1992). *Thirteen moons on turtle's back: A Native American year of moons*. New York: Philomel; **32**.

Calmenson, S., & Cole, J. (1998). *Get well gators!* New York: Morrow Junior Books; **27**.

Cave, K., & Riddel, C. (1992). *Out for the count: A counting adventure*. New York: Simon & Schuster (Ages 6–8); **27, 30**.

Cobb, A. (2000). *The long wait*. New York: Kane Press; **30**.

Dahl, M. (2006). *Know your number series* (6 books). Mankato, MN: Picture Window Books; **25, 30**.

Dahl, R. (1990). *Esio trot*. New York: Viking (Ages 7–8); **32**.

Darwin, S., Grout, B., & McCoy, D. (Eds.). (1992). *How do octopi eat pizza pie?* Alexandria, VA: Time-Life for Children (Ages 6–9); **27, 31, 32**.

Darwin, S., Grout, B., & McCoy, D. (Eds.). (1992). *Look both ways*. Alexandria, VA: Time-Life for Children (Ages 6–9); **27, 31, 32**.

Dennis, J. R. (1971). *Fractions are parts of things*. New York: Crowell (Ages 7–8); **29**.

Driscoll, L. (2003). *The blast off kid*. New York: Kane Press; **27**.

Eboch, C. (2007). *Science measurements: How heavy? How long? How hot?* Mankato, MN: Picture Window Books; **32**.

Friedman, A. (1994). *A cloak for the dreamer*. Jefferson City, MO: Scholastic Professional; **31**.

Friskey, M. (1963). *Mystery of the farmer's three fives*. Chicago: Children's Press (Ages 6–8); **27**.

Gibson, R. (1998). *I can count*. London: Usborne Playtime; **30**.

Gill, S., & Tobolo, D. (2000). *The big buck adventure*. Watertown, MA: Charlesbridge; **3**.

Gordon, J. R. (1991). *Six sleepy sheep*. Honesdale, PA: Boyds Mill Press (Ages 6–8); **27, 28**.

Harper, D. (1998). *Telling time with big mama cat*. San Diego, CA: Harcourt Brace; **32**.

Hawkins, C. (1984). *Take away monsters*. New York: Putnam's (Ages 3–5); **25, 27**.

Heide, F. P. (1994). *The bigness contest*. Boston: Little, Brown; **32**.

Hewavisenti, L. (1991). *Measuring*. Chicago: Franklin Watts; **32**.

Hindley, J. (1994). *The wheeling and whirling-around book*. Cambridge, MA: Candlewick Press; **31**.

Hoban, T. (1998). *More, fewer, less*. New York: Greenwillow; **30**.

Hulme, J. N. (1995). *Counting by kangaroos: A multiplication concept book*. New York: Scientific American Books; **27, 28**.

Jocelyn, M. (2000). *Hannah's collections*. East Rutherford, NJ: Putnam; **28, 31**.

Johnson, J. (1995). *How big is a whale?* Skokie, IL: Rand McNally; **32, 34**.

Johnson, J. (1995). *How fast is a cheetah?* Skokie, IL: Rand McNally; **32, 34**.

Kopp, J. (2000). *Math on the menu: Real-life problem solving for grades 3–5*. Berkeley, CA: Lawrence Hall of Science; **3**.

Krudwig, V. L. (1998). *Cucumber soup*. Golden, CO: Fulcrum; **18, 32**.

Leedy, L. (1994). *Fraction action*. New York: Holiday House; **29**.

Lewis, J. P. (2002). *Arithme-tickle*. Orlando, FL: Harcourt; **3**.

Llewellyn, C. (1992). *My first book of time*. New York: Dorling Kindersley; **32**.

Maestro, B. (1993). *The story of money*. New York: Clarion Books (Ages 6–9); **32**.

Maestro, B. (1999). *The story of clocks and calendars: Marking a millennium*. New York: Lothrop, Lee, & Shepard Books; **32**.

Martin, B., Jr. (1963). *Five is five*. New York: Holt, Rinehart, & Winston (Ages 6–8); **25, 27**.

Martin, B., Jr. (1964). *Delight in number*. New York: Holt, Rinehart, & Winston (Ages 6–8); **9, 27, 32**.

Martin, B., Jr. (1964). *Four threes are twelve*. New York: Holt, Rinehart, & Winston (Ages 6–8); **25, 27**.

Martin, B., Jr. (1964). *If you can count to ten*. New York: Holt, Rinehart, & Winston (Ages 6–8); **25, 27**.

Martin, B., Jr. (1971). *Number patterns make sense*. New York: Holt, Rinehart, & Winston (Ages 8–9); **28, 33**.

McMillan, B. (1991). *Eating fractions*. Jefferson City, MO: Scholastic Book Services (Ages 6–9); **29**.

Merriam, E. (1993). *12 ways to get to 11*. New York: Aladdin; **24, 25, 27**.

Mollel, T. M. (1999). *My rows and piles of coins*. New York: Clarion Books; **32**.

Morgan, R. (1997). *In the next three seconds*. New York: Lodestar; **32**.

Morgan, S. (1994). *The world of shapes, squares, and cubes*. New York: Thomson Learning; **31**.

Morris, A. (1995). *Shoes, shoes, shoes*. New York: Lothrop, Lee & Shepard; **32**.

Murphy, S. J. (1997). *The best vacation ever*. New York: HarperCollins; **27**.

Murphy, S. J. (2005). *Same old horse*. New York: HarperCollins (Ages 6 and up); **31**.

Murphy, S. J., & Remkiewicz, F. (2003). *Less than zero*. New York: HarperCollins; **27**.

Nagda, A. W., & Bickel, C. (2000). *Tiger math: Learning to graph from a baby tiger*. New York: Holt; **31**.

Nagda, A. W., & Bickel, C. (2002). *Chimp math*. New York: Holt; **27**.

Napoli, D. J., & Tchen, R. (2001). *How hungry are you?* New York: Simon & Schuster; **27**.

Nesbit, E. (1989). *Melisande*. San Diego, CA: Harcourt, Brace, Jovanovich (Ages 6–8); **32**.

Neuschwander, C. (1998). *Amanda Bean's amazing dream— a mathematical story*. New York: Scholastic Books; **27**.

O'Donnell, E. L., & Schmidt, K. L. (1991). *The twelve days of summer*. New York: Morrow (Ages 6–8); **27**.

Older, J. (2000). *Telling time*. Watertown, MA: Charlesbridge; **32**.

Pilegad, V. W., & Debon, N. (2003). *The warlord's puppeteers*. Gretna, LA: Pelican; **28**, **31**.

Pinczes, E. J. (1993). *One hundred hungry ants*. New York: Scholastic Books; **30**.

Richards, K. (2006). *¡Ya era hora, Max!* New York: Kane Press; **32**.

Schertle, A. (1987). *Jeremy Bean's St. Patrick's Day*. New York: Morrow (Ages 5–8); **19**, **32**.

Schleim, M. (1972). *Moon months and sun days*. Reading, MA: Young Scott (Ages 6–8); **19**, **32**.

Schwartz, D., & Kellogg, S. (2003). *Millions to measure*. New York: HarperCollins; **30**.

Schwartz, D. M. (1985). *How much is a million*. New York: Scholastic Books; **30**.

Schwartz, D. M. (1989). *If you made a million*. New York: Scholastic Books; **30**.

Scienszka, J., & Smith, L. (1995). *Math curse*. New York: Viking; **27**.

Sharman, L. (1994). *The amazing book of shapes*. New York: Dorling Kindersley; **31**.

Tang, G. (2002). *Mathematics strategies that multiply: The best of times*. New York: Scholastic Books; **27**.

Tompert, A. (1990). *Grandfather Tang's story*. New York: Crown; **31**.

Viorst, J. (1978). *Alexander who used to be rich last Sunday*. New York: Alladin; **27**, **32**.

Viorst, J. (1992). *Sunday morning*. New York: Atheneum (Ages 6–8); **32**.

Weston, M. (1992). *Bea's four bears*. New York: Clarion Books (Ages 6–8); **27**.

Williams, S. (2001). *Dinnertime!* San Diego, CA: Harcourt; **27**.

Yates, P. (2005). *Ten little mummies: An Egyptian counting book*. East Rutherford, NJ: Penguin Putnam; **30**.

Ye, T. (1998). *Weighing the elephant*. Buffalo, NY: Annick Press; **32**.

# BOOKS THAT SUPPORT SCIENCE INVESTIGATIONS

See the reviews and articles in each issue of *Teaching Children Mathematics* and *Science and Children*. Each year's March issue of *Science and Children* includes a section on the year's outstanding trade books in both English and Spanish.

## Series

Cole, J. (1997). *El autobus magico* [The magic school bus]. New York: Scholastic Books (Grades 2–4); **34, 35, 36, 37**.

Delafosse, C., & Jeunesse, G. (1998). *Yo observo: Los animales marinos; Los animales bajo tierra; Las casas de los insectos; Los dinosaurios* [I see: Marine animals; Animals underground; Insects' houses; Dinosaurs]. Madrid, Spain: Ediciones SM (Ages 5–8); **21, 26, 34**.

Falk, J. H., & Rosenberg, K. S. (1999). *Bite-sized science*. Chicago: Chicago Review (Grades K–3; recommended for family activities); **16, 21, 26, 38, 41**.

Glesecke, E. (1999). *Outside my window: Birds, trees, flowers, and mammals*. Portsmouth, NH: Heinemann (Ages 4–8); **21, 26, 34**.

Willis, S. (1999). *How, why and what series in Spanish on floating, weight, moon phases, rain, flight, time, distance, speed for grades 2–4*. New York: Franklin Watts; **34, 35, 36**.

## Reviews

Outstanding science trade books for students K–12. *Science and Children* (Published yearly).

Schon, I. Libros de ciencias en Español. *Science and Children* (Published yearly).

## Life Science

### Animals

Aranega, S., & Portell, J. (1999). *El elefante* [Elephant]. Barcelona, Spain: La Galera (Grades 1–3); **34**.

Arnold, C. (1987). *A Kangaroo's World; A Koala's World*. New York: Morrow (Ages 7–10); **34**.

Arnold, C. (1996). *Bats.* New York: Morrow (Grades 1–3); **26, 34**.

Arnold, C. (1996). *Fox.* New York: Morrow (Grades 2–5); **34**.

Arnosky, J. (1986). *Deer at the brook.* New York: Lothrop (Ages 1–6); **21, 26, 34**.

Arnosky, J. (1987). *Raccoons and ripe corn.* New York: Lothrop (Ages 3–6); **21, 26, 34**.

Arnosky, J. (1994). *All about alligators.* New York: Scholastic Books (Grades K–3); **16, 21, 26, 34**.

Arnosky, J. (1995). *All about owls.* New York: Scholastic Books (Grades K–3); **16, 21, 26, 34**.

Banks, M. (1990). *Animals of the night.* New York: Scribner (Ages 4–6); **21, 26, 34**.

Baredes, C. F., & Lotersztain, I. (2004). *Por que es tan guapo el pavo real? Y otras estrategias de los animales para tener hijos* [Why are peacocks so handsome? And other strategies of animals to have babies]. Argentina: Iamique (Ages 8–11); **16, 21, 26, 34**.

Baredes, C. F., & Lotersztain, I. (2006). *Por que es trompudo el elefante? Y otras curiosidades de los animales a la hora de comer* [Why is the elephant's nose so long? And other animal curiosities at meal time]. Argentina: Iamique (Ages 8–11); **16, 21, 26, 34**.

Baredes, C. F., & Lotersztain, I. (2006). *Por que se rayo la cebra? Y otras armas curiosas que tienen los animales para no ser devorados* [Why do zebras have stripes? And weapons that animals have to defend themselves]. Argentina: Iamique (Ages 8–11); **16, 21, 26, 34**.

Bilgrami, S. (2002). *Incredible animal discovery.* New York: Sterling (Ages 4–8); **16, 21, 26, 34**.

Bilgrami, S. (2003). *Animales increíbles* [Incredible animal discovery]. Mexico City: Planeta (Ages 4–8); **16, 21, 26, 34**.

Bond, F. (1987). *Wake up, Vladimir.* New York: Harper & Row (Ages 3–5); **21, 26**.

Bussolati, E. (1999). *Busca y encuentra* [Search and find]. Madrid, Spain: Editorial Edaf (Grades pre-K–1); **16, 21, 26, 34**.

Bussolati, E. (2000). *Los animales y sus crias* [Animals and their young]. Madrid, Spain: Editorial Edaf (Grades pre-K–1); **16, 21, 26, 34**.

Campbell, R. (2000). *Oscar en la granja* [Oh dear!]. Barcelona, Spain: Ediciones Elfos (Grades pre-K–1); **16, 21, 26, 34**.

Carle, E. (1987). *Have you seen my cat?* New York: Scholastic Books; **16, 21, 34**.

Cole, S. (1985). *When the tide is low.* New York: Lothrop (Ages 3–9); **21, 26, 34**.

Cowcher, H. (1991). *Tigress.* New York: Garrar (Ages 4–8); **21, 26, 34, 36**.

Crow, S. L. (1985). *Penguins and polar bears.* Washington, DC: National Geographic; **21, 26, 34**.

Davis, K. (1999). *Quien salta?* [Who hops?]. Barcelona, Spain: Editorial Juventud (Grades pre-K–3); **16, 21, 26, 34**.

Diehl, J., & Plumb, D. (2000). *What's the difference? 10 animal look-alikes.* New York: Kingfisher (Grades K–4); **26, 34**.

Ehlert, L. (1990). *Feathers for lunch.* San Diego, CA: Harcourt Brace (Ages 4–7); **16, 21, 26, 34**.

Fischer-Nagel, H., & Fischer-Nagel, A. (1986). *Inside the burrow: The life of the golden hamster.* Minneapolis, MN: Carolrhoda (Ages 7–10); **34**.

Flack, M. (1930). *Angus and the ducks.* New York: Doubleday (Ages 3–6); **21, 26, 34**.

Fleming, D. (1993). *In the small, small pond.* New York: Holt (Ages 4–8); **21, 26, 34**.

Fowler, A. (1992). *It's best to leave a snake alone.* Chicago: Children's Press; **21, 26, 34**.

Fredericks, A. D. (2000). *Slugs.* Minneapolis, MN: Lerner (Grades K–6); **26, 34**.

Freeman, D. (1968/1976). *Corduroy.* New York: Viking/Penguin (Ages 3–6); **21, 26, 34**.

Gallagher, K. E. (2001). *The cottontail rabbits.* Minneapolis, MN: Lerner (Grades K–4); **26, 34**.

George, T. C. (2000). *Jellies: The life of jellyfish.* Brookfield, CT: Millbrook Press (Grades K–3); **26, 34**.

Gibbons, G. (1993). *Frogs.* New York: Holiday House (Grades pre-K–3); **16, 21, 26, 34**.

Gill, P. (1990). *Birds.* New York: Eagle Books (Ages 4–8); **21, 26, 34**.

Hickman, P. (1999). *My first look at: A new duck.* Niagara Falls, NY: Kids Can Press (Grades K–3); **26, 34**.

Hirschi, R. (1991). *Loon lake.* New York: Cobblehill (Ages 4–8); **21, 26, 34**.

Horenstein, H. (1999). *A is for . . .? A photographer's alphabet of animals.* New York: Harcourt Brace (Grades K–3); **26, 34**.

Horowitz, R. (2000). *Crab moon.* Cambridge, MA: Candlewick Press (Grades K–6); **34**.

James, S. (1991). *Dear Mr. Blueberry.* New York: McElderry (Ages 3–8); **16, 21, 26, 34, 36**.

Jango-Cohen, J. (2000). *Clinging sea horses.* Minneapolis, MN: Lerner (Grades K–4); **26, 34**.

Jenkins, M. (1999). *The emperor's egg.* Cambridge, MA: Candlewick Press (Grades K–6); **26, 34**.

Johnson, R. L. (2001). *A walk in the desert; A walk in the prairie; A walk in the rain forest.* Minneapolis, MN: Lerner (Grades K–8); **34**.

Johnson, S. A. (1982). *Inside an egg.* Minneapolis, MN: Lerner; **21, 26, 34**.

Johnston, G., & Cutchins, J. (1991). *Slippery babies: Young frogs, toads, and salamanders.* New York: Morrow (Ages 5–8); **21, 26, 34**.

Kalman, B., & Aloian M. (2006). *Muchos tipos de animals* [Many kinds of animals]. New York: Crabtree (Ages 5–9); **16, 21, 26, 34**.

Kalman, B., & Lundblad, K. (2006). *Animales ilamados peces* [Animals called fish]. New York: Crabtree (Ages 5–9); **16, 21, 26, 34**.

Kalman, B., & MacAulay, K. (2004). *Guinea pigs*. New York: Crabtree (Ages 7–8); **16, 21, 26, 34**.

Kalman, B., & MacAulay, K. (2006). *Los cobayos* [Guinea pigs]. New York: Crabtree (Ages 7–8); **16, 21, 26, 34**.

Kalman, B., & MacAulay, K. (2006). *Reptiles de todo tipo* [Reptiles of all kinds]. New York: Crabtree (Ages 5–9); **16, 21, 26, 34**.

Kalman, B., & Sjonger, R. (2004). *Hamsters*. New York: Crabtree (Ages 5–9); **16, 21, 26, 34**.

Kalman, B., & Sjonger, R. (2004). *Puppies*. New York: Crabtree (Ages 5–9); **16, 21, 26, 34**.

Kalman, B., & Sjonger, R. (2006). *Aves de todo tipo* [Birds of all kinds]. New York: Crabtree (Ages 5–9); **16, 21, 26, 34**.

Kalman, B., & Sjonger, R. (2006). *Los cachorros* [Puppies]. New York: Crabtree (Ages 5–9); **16, 21, 26, 34**.

Kalman, B., & Sjonger, R. (2006). *Los hamsters* [Hamsters]. New York: Crabtree (Ages 5–9); **16, 21, 26, 34**.

Kalman, B., & Walker, N. (2004). *Kittens*. New York: Crabtree (Ages 7–8); **16, 21, 26, 34**.

Kalman, B., & Walker, N. (2006). *Los gatitos* [Kittens]. New York: Crabtree (Ages 7–8); **16, 21, 26, 34**.

Koelling, C. (1978). *Whose house is this?* Los Angeles: Price/Stern/Sloan (Ages 3–5); **21, 26**.

Krementz, J. (1986). *Holly's farm animals*. New York: Random House (Ages 3–8); **21, 26, 34**.

Lewin, T., & Lewin, B. (1999). *Gorilla walk*. New York: Lothrop/HarperCollins (Grades K–6); **26, 34**.

Ling, M., & Atkinson, M. (1997). *The snake book*. New York: Dorling Kindersley (Grades 1 and up); **34**.

Lionni, L. (1963). *Swimmy*. New York: Pantheon (Ages 3–6); **21, 26, 34**.

London, J. (1999). *Baby whale's journey*. San Francisco: Chronicle Books (Grades K–3); **26, 34**.

Markle, S. (2004). *Crocodiles*. Minneapolis, MN: Lerner (Ages 7–9); **16, 21, 26, 34**.

Markle, S. (2004). *Great white sharks*. Minneapolis, MN: Lerner (Ages 7–9); **16, 21, 26, 34**.

Markle, S. (2004). *Lions*. Minneapolis, MN: Lerner (Ages 7–9); **16, 21, 26, 34**.

Markle, S. (2004). *Wolves*. Minneapolis, MN: Lerner (Ages 7–9); **16, 21, 26, 34**.

Markle, S. (2006). *Los Cocodrilos* [Crocodiles]. Minneapolis, MN: Lerner (Ages 7–9); **16, 21, 26, 34**.

Markle, S. (2006). *Los liones* [Lions]. Minneapolis, MN: Lerner (Ages 7–9); **16, 21, 26, 34**.

Markle, S. (2006). *Los lobos* [Wolves]. Minneapolis, MN: Lerner (Ages 7–9); **16, 21, 26, 34**.

Markle, S. (2006). *Los tiburones blancos* [Great white sharks]. Minneapolis, MN: Lerner (Ages 7–9); **16, 21, 26, 34**.

Markle, S. (2006). *Slippery, slimy baby frogs*. London: Walker Books for Young Readers (Ages 4–8); **16, 21, 26, 34**.

Mason, A. (2000). *Starting with science series: Living things*. Toronto, Ontario, Canada: Kids Can Press (Grades K–4); **26, 34**.

McCloskey, R. (1941/1976). *Make way for ducklings*. New York: Viking/Penguin (Ages 4–6); **21, 26, 34**.

McFarland, C. (1990). *Cows in the parlor: A visit to a dairy farm*. New York: Atheneum (Ages 5–8); **21, 26, 34**.

Mitsuko and Kamiko (A. Coll-Vinent, trans.). (1999). *El elefante* [Elephant]. Madrid, Spain: El Editorial Carimbo (Grades pre-K–1); **16, 21, 26, 34**.

Mitsuko and Kamiko (A. Coll-Vinent, trans.). (1999). *El gato* [Cat]. Madrid, Spain: El Editorial Carimbo (Grades pre-K–1); **16, 21, 26, 34**.

Murphy, J. (1993). *Backyard bear*. New York: Scholastic Books (Grades 2–4); **34**.

National Geographic Society. (1985). *Books for young explorers* (Set XII). Washington, DC: Author (Ages 3–8); **21, 26, 34**.

Netherton, J. (2000). *Red-eyed tree frogs*. Minneapolis, MN: Lerner (Grades K–4); **26, 34**.

Nicholson, D. (1987). *Wild boars*. Minneapolis, MN: Lerner (Ages 6–10); **34**.

Paladino, C. (1991). *Pomona: The birth of a penguin*. New York: Watts (Ages 5–8); **21, 26, 34**.

Pallotta, J. (1986). *The BIRD alphabet book*. Watertown, MA: Charlesbridge; **16, 21, 34**.

Pallotta, J. (1989). *The yucky reptile alphabet book*. Watertown, MA: Charlesbridge; **16, 21, 34**.

Patent, D. H. (1987). *All about whales*. New York: Holiday House (Ages 6–9); **34**.

Patent, D. H. (1993). *Looking at penguins*. New York: Holiday House (Grades 1–3); **34**.

Patent, D. H. (1994). *Looking at bears*. New York: Holiday House (Grades 1–3); **34**.

Potter, B. (1902). *The tale of Peter Rabbit*. New York: Warne (Ages 4–6); **21, 26, 34**.

Powzyk, J. (1985). *Wallaby creek*. New York: Lothrop (Ages 6–9); **34**.

Robinson, C. (1999). *In the wild: Whales*. Portsmouth, NH: Heinemann (Grades 1–2); **34**.

Roy, R. (1982). *What has ten legs and eats cornflakes? A pet book*. New York: Clarion/ Houghton (Ages 5–8); **34**.

Savage, S. (1992). *Making tracks*. New York: Lodestar (Ages 4–8); **21, 26, 34, 36**.

Savage, S. (2000). *What's the difference?: Birds*. Sydney, NSW, Australia: Steck Vaughn (Grades K–4); **26, 34**.

Sheldon, D. (1991). *The whales' song*. New York: Dial (Ages 4–8); **21, 26, 34**.

Simon, S. (1999). *Crocodiles & alligators*. New York: HarperCollins (Grades K–6); **26, 34**.

Souza, A. (1992). *Slinky snakes*. Minneapolis, MN: Carolrhoda; **34**.

Stanley, C. (1991). *Busy, busy squirrels*. New York: Cobblehill (Ages 4–8); **21, 26, 34, 36**.

Stuart, D. (1994). *Bats: Mysterious flyers of the night*. Minneapolis, MN: Carolrhoda (Grades 2–5); **34**.

Sussman, S., & Sussman, R. J. (1987). *Lies (people believe) about animals*. Niles, IL: Whitman (Ages 7–12); **34**.

Tagholm, S. (2000). *Animal lives: The rabbit*. New York: Kingfisher (Grades K–3); **26, 34**.

Weller, F. (1991). *I wonder if I'll see a whale*. New York: Philomel (Ages 4–8); **21, 26, 34**.

Wells, R. E. (1997). *What's faster than a speeding cheetah?* Morton Grove, IL: Whitman (Ages 7–9); **16, 21, 26, 34**.

Wells, R. E. (2006). *Hay algo mas rapido que un guepardo?* [What's faster than a speeding cheetah?] Barcelona, Spain: Juventud (Ages 7–9); **16, 21, 26, 34**.

Wildsmith, B. (1983). *The owl and the woodpecker*. New York: Oxford University Press (Ages 4–7); **21, 26, 34**.

Yamashita, K. (1993). *Paws, wings, and hooves*. Minneapolis, MN: Lerner (Ages 6–8); **26, 34**.

Yolen, J. (1988). *Owl moon*. New York: Philomel (Grades pre-K–1); **16, 21, 26, 34**.

## Bugs, Spiders, Bees, and Butterflies

Allen, J., & Humphries, T. (2000). *Are you a ladybug?* New York: Kingfisher Books (Grades K–4); **26, 34**.

Arnosky, J. (1996). *Crinkleroot's guide to knowing butterflies and moths*. New York: Simon & Schuster Books for Young Readers (Primary grades); **34**.

Berenstain, S., & Berenstain, J. (1962). *The big honey hunt*. New York: Random House (Ages 3–8); **21, 26, 34**.

Carle, E. (1969). *The very hungry caterpillar*. New York: Philomel (Ages 3–6); **21, 26, 34**.

Carle, E. (1977). *The grouchy ladybug*. New York: Crowell (Ages 3–6); **21, 26, 34**.

Carle, E. (1981). *The honeybee and the robber*. New York: Philomel (Ages 3–6); **21, 26, 34**.

Carle, E. (1984). *The very busy spider*. New York: Philomel (Ages 3–6); **21, 26, 34**.

Clay, P., & Clay, H. (1984). *Ants*. London: A & C Black; **21, 26, 34**.

Dallinger, J. (1981). *Spiders*. Minneapolis, MN: Lerner; **21, 26, 34**.

Facklam, M. (1996). *Creepy, crawly caterpillars*. Boston: Little, Brown (Grades 2–4); **34**.

Fischer-Nagel, H., & Fischer-Nagel, A. (1986). *Life of the ladybug*. Minneapolis, MN: Carolrhoda (Ages 7–10); **34**.

Fleming, D. (1991). *In the tall, tall grass*. New York: Holt (Ages 4–8); **21, 26, 33, 34**.

Guiberson, B. (1991). *Cactus hotel*. New York: Holt (Ages 4–8); **21, 26, 34, 36**.

Hall, M. C. (2006). *Arañas/Spiders* (Pebble Plus Bilingual). Mankato, MN: Capstone Press (Ages 4–7); **16, 21, 26, 34**.

Hall, M. C. (2006). *Grillos/Crickets* (Pebble Plus Bilingual). Mankato, MN: Capstone Press (Ages 4–7); **16, 21, 26, 34**.

Hall, M. C. (2006). *Hormigas/Ants* (Pebble Plus Bilingual). Mankato, MN: Capstone Press (Ages 4–7); **16, 21, 26, 34**.

Hall, M. C. (2006). *Mantis religiosas/Praying mantises* (Pebble Plus Bilingual). Mankato, MN: Capstone Press (Ages 4–7); **16, 21, 26, 34**.

Hall, M. C. (2006). *Mariquitas/Ladybugs* (Pebble Plus Bilingual). Mankato, MN: Capstone Press (Ages 4–7); **16, 21, 26, 34**.

Hall, M. C. (2006). *Saltamontes/Grasshoppers* (Pebble Plus Bilingual). Mankato, MN: Capstone Press (Ages 4–7); **16, 21, 26, 34**.

Hartley, K., Macro, C., & Taylor, P. (1999). *Bug books: Ant, bee, caterpillar, centipede, cockroach, grasshopper, ladybug, mosquito, snail, spider, termite, and worm*. Portsmouth, NH: Heinemann (Grades 2–3); **34**.

Jeunesse, G., & de Hugo, P. (1998). *Los bichos de la casa* [House bugs]. Madrid, Spain: Ediciones SM (Grades 2–4); **34**.

Kneidel, S. S. (1993). *Creepy crawlies and the scientific method*. Washington, DC: National Science Teachers Association (Grades K–6); **26, 34**.

McNulty, F. (1986). *The lady and the spider*. New York: Harper & Row (Ages 5–8); **34**.

Overbeck, C. (1982). *Ants*. Minneapolis, MN: Lerner; **21, 26, 34**.

Pallotta, J. (1986). *The icky bug alphabet book*. Watertown, MA: Charlesbridge; **16, 21, 34**.

Pallotta, J. (1992). *The icky bug counting book*. Watertown, MA: Charlesbridge (Ages 4–8); **16, 21, 26, 33, 34**.

Parker, N. W. (1987). *Bugs*. New York: Greenwillow (Ages 8–10); **34**.

Pinczes, E. J. (1993). *One hundred hungry ants*. New York: Scholastic Books; **16, 21, 34**.

Zemlicka, S. (2003). *From egg to butterfly*. Minneapolis, MN: Lerner (Ages 3–6); **21, 26, 33, 34**.

## Plants

Adler, D. A. (1999). *A picture book of George Washington Carver.* New York: Holiday House (Grades K–6); **26, 34**.

Bash, B. (1990). *Desert giant: The world of the saguaro cactus.* Boston: Little, Brown (Ages 5–8); **21, 26, 34, 36**.

Burns, D. L., & Burns, J. A. (1998). *Plant a garden in your sneaker.* Washington, DC: National Science Teachers Association (Grades 2–6); **34**.

Ehlert, L. (1991). *Red leaf, yellow leaf.* San Diego, CA: Harcourt Brace (Ages 4–8); **21, 26, 34, 36**.

Florian, D. (1991). *Vegetable garden.* New York: Harcourt Brace (Ages 3–5); **16, 21, 26, 34, 37**.

Gibbons, G. (1984). *The seasons of Arnold's apple tree.* San Diego, CA: Harcourt Brace (Ages 3–9); **21, 26, 34**.

Gibbons, G. (1991). *From seed to plant.* New York: Holiday House (Ages 5–8); **21, 26, 34**.

Gibbons, G. (1999). *The pumpkin book.* New York: Holiday House (Grades K–6); **26, 34**.

Hall, Z. (1994). *It's pumpkin time!* New York: Scholastic Books; **16, 21, 34**.

Hindley, J. (1990). *The tree.* New York: Clarkson Potter (Ages 6–12); **26, 34, 36**.

Hirschi, R. (1991). *Fall.* New York: Cobblehill (Ages 4–8); **21, 26, 34, 36**.

Hiscock, B. (1991). *The big tree.* New York: Atheneum (Ages 5–12); **21, 26, 34, 36**.

Johnson, R. L. (2001). *A walk in the desert; A walk in the prairie; A walk in the rain forest.* Minneapolis, MN: Lerner (Grades K–8); **34**.

Krauss, R. (1945). *The carrot seed.* New York: Harper & Row (Ages 3–5); **21, 22, 26, 28**.

Lauber, P. (1988). *Seeds: Pop, stick, glide.* New York: Crown (Ages 6–8); **26, 34**.

Miller, D. (2002). *Are trees alive?* New York: Walker & Company; **21, 26, 34, 36**.

Mitgutsch, A. (1986). *From wood to paper.* Minneapolis, MN: Carolrhoda (Ages 4–7); **21, 26, 34**.

Oechsli, H., & Oechsli, K. (1985). *In my garden: A child's gardening book.* New York: Macmillan (Ages 5–9); **21, 26, 34**.

Ontario Science Centre. *Starting with science series: Plants.* Niagara Falls, NY: Kids Can Press (Grades K–4); **26, 34**.

Posada, M. (2000). *Dandelions: Stars in the grass.* Minneapolis, MN: Carolrhoda/Lerner (Grades K–3); **26, 34**.

Romanova, N. (1985). *Once there was a tree.* New York: Dial (Ages 3–9); **21, 26, 34**.

Schnieper, C. (1987). *An apple tree through the year.* Minneapolis, MN: Carolrhoda (Ages 7–10); **34**.

Silverstein, S. (1964). *The giving tree.* New York: Harper & Row (Ages 3–8); **21, 26, 34**.

Singer, M. (2006). *What stinks?* Plain City, OH: Darby Creek (Ages 9–12); **16, 21, 26, 34**.

Watts, B. (1990). *Tomato.* Morristown, NJ: Silver Burdett & Ginn (Ages 5–8); **21, 26, 34**.

## Physical Science

Adler, D. A. (1999). *How tall, how short, how far away.* New York: Houghton-Mifflin (Grades K–3); **26, 35**.

Ardley, N. (1991). *The science book of air.* New York: Harcourt Brace (Ages 6–8); **21, 26, 35**.

Brandt, K. (1985). *Sound.* Mahwah, NJ: Troll Associates (Ages 3–5); **21, 26**.

Branley, F. (1996). *What makes a magnet?* New York: HarperCollins (Grades K–6); **26, 35**.

Brown, R. (1991). *The world that Jack built.* New York: Dutton (Ages 4–6); **21, 26, 35**.

Burton, V. L. (1939). *Mike Mulligan and his steam shovel.* Boston: Houghton-Mifflin (Ages 3–5); **21, 26**.

Carle, E. (1990). *Pancakes, pancakes!* New York: Scholastic Books; **16, 21, 35**.

Cobb, V. (1983). *Gobs of goo.* Philadelphia: Lippincott (Ages 6–8); **35**.

Crampton, G. (1986). *Scuffy the tugboat.* New York: Western (Ages 3–5); **21, 26**.

dePaola, T. (1978). *The popcorn book.* New York: Scholastic Books; **16, 21, 35**.

Fowler, R. (1986). *Mr. Little's noisy boat.* New York: Grosset & Dunlap (Ages 5–9); **21, 26, 35**.

Graham, J. B. (1999). *Flicker flash.* New York: Houghton-Mifflin; **16, 21, 26, 35**.

Hickman, P., & Stephens, P. (2000). *Animals in motion: How animals swim, jump, slither, and glide.* Niagara Falls, NY: Kids Can Press (Grades K–8); **26, 35**.

Hulme, J. (1991). *Sea squares.* New York: Hyperion (Ages 4–8); **21, 26, 34, 35**.

Isadora, R. (1985). *I touch.* New York: Greenwillow (Ages 0–2); **21, 38**.

Kimiko (A. Coll-Vinent, trans.). (1999). *El avion* [Airplane]. Madrid, Spain: Editorial Corimbo (Grades pre-K–1); **16, 21, 26, 35**.

Koningsburg, E. I. (1991). *Samuel Todd's book of great inventions.* New York: Atheneum (Ages 4–7); **21, 26, 35**.

Murata, Michinori. (1993). *Science is all around you: Water and light.* Minneapolis, MN: Lerner (Ages 6–8); **26, 35, 36**.

Nessmann, P. (2006). *El color* [Color]. Barcelona, Spain: Combel (Ages 8–10); **35**.

O'Leary, J. (2004). *El profesor Topo y sus máquinas* [Professor Mole's machines]. Barcelona, Spain: Combel (Ages 3–6); **35, 36, 40**.

O'Leary, J. (2004). *Professor Mole's machines*. London: Tango Books (Ages 3–6); **35, 36, 40**.

Ontario Science Centre. (2000). *Starting with science: Solids, liquids, and gases*. Niagara Falls, NY: Kids Can Press (Grades K–4); **26, 35**.

Piper, W. (1984). *The little engine that could*. New York: Putnam (Ages 3–5); **21, 26**.

Pluckrose, H. (1986). *Think about hearing*. New York: Franklin Watts (Ages 4–8); **21, 26, 35, 38**.

Robbins, K. (1991). *Bridges*. New York: Dial (Ages 5–12); **21, 26, 35**.

Rockwell, A. (1986). *Things that go*. New York: Dutton (Ages 3–5); **21, 26**.

Scarry, R. (1986). *Splish-Splash sounds*. Racine, WI: Western (Ages 3–7); **21, 26, 35**.

Simon, S. (1985). *Soap bubble magic*. New York: Lothrop (Ages 6–9); **35**.

Taylor, K. (1992). *Flying start science series: Water; light; action; structure*. New York: Wiley (Ages 3–9); **16, 21, 35, 36**.

Wyler, R. (1986). *Science fun with toy boats and planes*. New York: Messner (Ages 5–9); **35**.

# EARTH AND SPACE SCIENCE

Adamson, T. K. (2006). *Júpiter/Jupiter* (Pebble Plus Bilingual). Mankato, MN: Capstone Press (Ages 4–7); **36**.

Adamson, T. K. (2006). *Marte/Mars* (Pebble Plus Bilingual). Mankato, MN: Capstone Press (Ages 4–7); **36**.

Adamson, T. K. (2006). *Mercurio/Mercury* (Pebble Plus Bilingual). Mankato, MN: Capstone Press (Ages 4–7); **36**.

Adamson, T. K. (2006). *Neptuno/Neptune* (Pebble Plus Bilingual). Mankato, MN: Capstone Press (Ages 4–7); **36**.

Adamson, T. K. (2006). *Plutòn/Pluto* (Pebble Plus Bilingual). Mankato, MN: Capstone Press (Ages 4–7); **36**.

Adamson, T. K. (2006). *Saturno/Saturn* (Pebble Plus Bilingual). Mankato, MN: Capstone Press (Ages 4–7); **36**.

Adamson, T. K. (2006). *La Tierra/Earth* (Pebble Plus Bilingual). Mankato, MN: Capstone Press (Ages 4–7); **36**.

Adamson, T. K. (2006). *Urano/Uranus* (Pebble Plus Bilingual). Mankato, MN: Capstone Press (Ages 4–7); **36**.

Adamson, T. K. (2006). *Venus/Venus* (Pebble Plus Bilingual). Mankato, MN: Capstone Press (Ages 4–7); **36**.

Aliki. (1990). *Fossils tell of long ago*. New York: Harper-Collins (Ages 5–8); **21, 26, 36**.

Arnold, C. (1987). *Trapped in tar: Fossils from the Ice Age*. New York: Clarion (Ages 7–10); **36**.

Baird, A. (1996). *The U.S. Space Camp book of astronauts*. New York: Morrow; **36**.

Barrett, J. (1978). *Cloudy with a chance of meatballs*. New York: Macmillan; **16, 21, 36**.

Barton, B. (1990). *Bones, bones, dinosaur bones*. New York: HarperCollins (Ages 5–7); **21, 26, 36**.

Bauer, C. F. (1987). *Midnight snowman*. New York: Atheneum (Ages 4–7); **19, 21, 26, 36**.

Bernhard, E. (2006). *La meteorologia* [Weather]. Barcelona, Spain: Combel (Ages 8–10); **36**.

Bilgrami, S. (2002). *Amazing dinosaur discovery*. New York: Sterling (Ages 4–8); **36**.

Bilgrami, S. (2003). *Dinosaurios increibles* [Amazing dinosaur discovery]. Mexico City: Planeta (Ages 4–8); **36**.

Branley, F. M. (1982). *Water for the world*. New York: Crowell (Ages 7–11); **36**.

Branley, F. M. (1983). *Rain and hail*. New York: Crowell (Ages 5–7); **36**.

Branley, F. M. (1985). *Flash, crash, rumble, and roll*. New York: Crowell (Ages 5–7); **36**.

Branley, F. M. (1985). *Volcanoes*. New York: Crowell (Ages 6–8); **36**.

Branley, F. M. (1986). *Air is all around us*. New York: Crowell (Ages 3–6); **21, 26, 36**.

Branley, F. M. (1986). *Journey into a black hole*. New York: Crowell (Ages 8–10); **36**.

Branley, F. M. (1987). *The moon seems to change; The planets in our solar system; Rockets and satellites*. New York: Crowell (Ages 5–8); **36**.

Branley, F. M. (2000). *The international space station*. New York: Harper Trophy; **36**.

Carrick, C. (1983). *Patrick's dinosaurs*. New York: Clarion (Ages 4–8); **21, 34, 35, 36**.

Caveney, S., & Giesen, R. (1977). *Where am I?* (Rev. ed.). Minneapolis, MN: Lerner (Ages 5–8); **36**.

Cole, J. (1987). *Evolution*. New York: Crowell (Ages 5–8); **34, 36**.

Cole, J. (1987). *The magic school bus inside the earth*. New York: Scholastic Books; **21, 26, 36**.

Cole, J. (1992). *The magic school bus on the ocean floor*. New York: Scholastic Books; **36**.

Dunphy, M. (1999). *Here is the African savanna*. New York: Hyperion (Grades K–6); **26, 36**.

Earle, S. A. (1999). *Hello, fish! Visiting the coral reef*. Washington, DC: National Geographic (Grades K–3); **26, 36**.

Everet, L. (2002). *Rocks, fossils, and arrowheads*. Minnetonka, MN: Northwind Press (Ages 7–11); **36**.

Hoban, T. (1990). *Shadows and reflections*. New York: Greenwillow (Ages 4–8); **26, 36**.

Kandoian, E. (1990). *Under the sun*. New York: Putnam (Ages 4–6); **21, 26, 36**.

Keats, E. J. (1981). *Regards to the man in the moon*. New York: Four Winds (Ages 3–6); **21, 26, 36**.

Krupp, E. C. (2000). *The rainbow and you*. New York: HarperCollins (Grades K–4); **26, 36**.

Langley, A. (2001). *The Oxford first book of space*. New York: Oxford University Press (Grades K–4); **36**.

Lessem, D. (2005). *Sea giants of dinosaur time*. Minneapolis, MN: Lerner (Ages 7–9); **36**.

Lessem, D. (2006). *Gigantes marinos de la epoca de los dinosaurios* [Sea giants of dinosaur time]). Minneapolis, MN: Lerner (Ages 7–9); **36**.

Lewison, W. (1990). *Mud*. New York: Random House (Ages 5–8); **21, 26, 36**.

Lindbergh, R. (1998). *Que es el sol?* [What is the sun?] New York: Lectorum (Ages 5–7); **16, 21, 26, 36**.

Livingston, M. (1992). *Light and shadow*. New York: Holiday House (Ages 4–7); **21, 26, 35, 36**.

Lye, K. (1987). *Deserts*. Morristown, NJ: Silver Burdett (Ages 8–14); **36**.

Maki, C. (1993). *Snowflakes, sugar, and salt*. New York: Lerner (Ages 6–8); **21, 26, 35, 36**.

Malnig, A. (1985). *Where the waves break: Life at the edge of the sea*. Minneapolis, MN: Carolrhoda (Ages 7–10); **36**.

Markle, S. (1987). *Digging deeper*. New York: Lothrop (Ages 8–12); **36**.

McMillan, B. (1990). *One sun: A book of terse verse*. New York: Holiday House (Ages 5–8); **21, 26, 36**.

Most, B. (1991). *A dinosaur named after me*. San Diego, CA: Harcourt Brace (Ages 4–8); **21, 26, 36**.

Otto, C. (1992). *That sky, that rain*. New York: Harper (Ages 4–7); **21, 26, 36**.

Pallotta, J. (1986). *The ocean alphabet book*. Watertown, MA: Charlesbridge; **16, 21, 36**.

Parmall, P. (1991). *The rock*. New York: Macmillan (Ages 5–8); **21, 26, 36**.

Ressmeyer, R. (1992). *Astronaut to zodiac*. New York: Crown (Ages 5–12); **26, 36**.

*Rocks and minerals*. (1988). London: Natural History Museum (Ages 7–12); **36**.

Schlein, M. (1991). *Discovering dinosaur babies*. New York: Four Winds (Ages 6–9); **26, 36**.

Schmid, E. (1990). *The water's journey*. New York: North-South Books (Ages 6–8); **26, 36**.

Seymour, S. (1999). *Tornadoes*. New York: Morrow/HarperCollins (Grades K–6); **26, 36**.

Souza, D. (1992). *Powerful waves*. Minneapolis, MN: Carolrhoda (Ages 6–12); **26, 36**.

Szilagyi, M. (1985). *Thunderstorms*. New York: Bradbury (Ages 3–9); **21, 26, 36**.

Thornhill, J. (1997). *Before & after: A book of nature timescapes*. Washington, DC: National Geographic (Ages 4–6); **16, 21, 26, 33, 35, 36**.

Wade, H. (1977). *Sand*. Milwaukee, WI: Raintree (Ages 4–8); **21, 26, 36**.

Weimer, T. E. (1993). *Space songs for children*. Pittsburgh, PA: Pearce-Evetts (Ages 5–8); **21, 26**.

## Environmental Science: Ecology, Nature, and Conservation

Allen, M. (1991). *Changes*. New York: Macmillan (Ages 4–7); **21, 26, 34, 36**.

Arnosky, A. (1991). *The empty lot*. Boston: Little, Brown (Ages 4–8); **21, 26, 34, 36, 39**.

Bash, B. (1990). *Urban roosts: Where birds nest in the city*. Boston: Little, Brown (Ages 6–12); **26, 34, 36**.

Bruchac, J. (1992). *Native American animal stories*. Golden, CO: Fulcrum (Ages 5–8); **21, 26, 36**.

Cherry, L. (1990). *The great kapok tree: A tale of the Amazon rain forest*. New York: Gulliver (Ages 6–12); **26, 34, 36**.

Fernandes, K. (1991). *Zebo and the dirty planet*. Ontario, Canada: Firefly Books; **16, 21, 36**.

George, W. (1991). *Fishing at Long Pond*. New York: Greenwillow (Ages 4–8); **21, 26, 34, 36**.

Glaser, L. (1997). *Compost! Growing gardens from your garbage*. Brookfield, CT: Millbrook (Ages 5–8); **16, 21, 26, 34, 36, 37**.

Glaser, L. (2000). *Our big home: An earth poem*. Brookfield, CT: Millbrook Press (Grades K–3); **26, 37**.

Greenaway, T. (2001). *The water cycle*. Austin, TX: Steck-Vaughn (Ages 6–9); **16, 21, 26, 36, 37**.

Greene, C. (1991). *Caring for our land*. Waltham, MA: Enslow (Ages 6–8); **16, 21, 26, 34, 37**.

Greene, C. (1991). *The old ladies who liked cats*. New York: HarperCollins (Ages 5–8); **21, 26, 34, 36**.

Grupper, J. (1997). *Destination: Rainforest*. Washington, DC: National Geographic (Ages 6–9); **16, 21, 26, 34, 36, 37**.

Hines, A. (1991). *Remember the butterflies*. New York: Dutton (Ages 4–7); **16, 21, 26, 34, 36**.

Kaner, E. (1999). *Animal defenses: How animals protect themselves*. Niagara Falls, NY: Kids Can Press (Grades K–3); **26, 37**.

Kuhn, D. (1990). *More than just a vegetable garden*. New York: Silver Press (Ages 6–8); **26, 34, 36, 37**.

Leslie, C. (1991). *Nature all year long*. New York: Greenwillow (Ages 6–8); **26, 34, 36, 39**.

Levine, S., & Grafton, A. (1992). *Projects for a healthy planet*. New York: Wiley (Ages 6–12); **26, 34, 36, 39**.

Locker, T. (1991). *The land of the gray wolf*. New York: Dial (Ages 4–8); **21, 26, 34, 36**.

Miller, D. S. (2000). *River of life*. New York: Clarion (Grades K–3); **26, 37**.

Moss, M. (2000). *This is the tree*. La Jolla, CA: Kane/Miller (Grades K–3); **26, 37**.

Norsgaard, E. J. (1990). *Nature's great balancing act: In our own backyard*. New York: Cobblehill (Ages 7–12); **26, 34, 36**.

Parnall, P. (1990). *Woodpile*. New York: Macmillan (Ages 5–8); **21, 26, 34, 36, 39**.

Russell, H. R. (1998). *Ten-minute field trips*. Washington, DC: National Science Teachers Association (Grades K–8); **26, 34**.

Sackett, E. (1991). *Danger on the African grassland*. Boston: Little, Brown (Ages 5–8); **21, 26, 34, 36**.

Sanders, S. R. (1999). *Crawdad creek*. Washington, DC: National Geographic (Grades K–6); **26, 37**.

Schuh, M. C. (2006). *El agua potable* [Drinking water] (Pebble Plus Bilingual). Mankato, MN: Capstone Press (Ages 4–7); **36, 37, 38**.

Seibert, D. (1991). *Sierra*. New York: HarperCollins (Ages 5–8); **21, 26, 34, 36**.

Seibert, P. (1996). *Toad overload: A true tale of nature knocked off balance in Australia*. Danbury, CT: Millbrook Press (Ages 5–8); **16, 21, 26, 34, 37**.

Shetterly, S. H. (1999). *Shelterwood*. Gardiner, ME: Tilbury House (Grades K–6); **26, 37**.

Stock, C. (1991). *When the woods hum*. New York: Morrow (Ages 4–8); **16, 21, 34, 36, 39**.

Taylor, K., & Burton, J. (1993). *Forest life*. New York: Dorling Kindersley (Ages 7–12); **34, 35, 36**.

Tresselt, A. (1992). *The gift of the tree*. New York: Lothrop, Lee & Shepard (Ages 5–8); **21, 26, 34, 36**.

Tweit, S. J. (1997). *City foxes*. Portland, OR: Graphic Arts Center (Ages 4–9); **16, 21, 26, 34, 37**.

## Health Science

Aliki. (1989). *Mis cinco sentidos* [My five senses]. New York: Harper Arco Iris; **16, 21, 36**.

Aliki. (1990). *My feet*. New York: HarperCollins (Ages 4–6); **21, 26, 37**.

Brandenburg, A. (1976). *Corn is maize: The gift of the Indians*. New York: Crowell (Ages 3–5); **21, 22, 26, 37**.

Brown, M. (1947). *Stone soup*. New York: Scribner's (Ages 3–6); **21, 26, 37**.

Carle, E. (1970). *Pancakes, pancakes*. New York: Knopf (Ages 3–5); **21, 22, 26, 37**.

Cole, J. (1989). *The magic school bus: Inside the human body*. New York: Scholastic Books (Ages 6–8); **21, 26, 37**.

de Bourgoing, P., & Hahn, N. (1998) *Visita al medico* [Visit to the doctor]. Madrid, Spain: La Galera (Ages 3–6); **16, 21, 26**.

Farmer, J. (1999). *Bananas!* Watertown, MA: Charlesbridge (Grades K–6); **26, 38**.

Manning, M., & Granstrom, B. (1999). *Mi cuerpo, tu cuerpo* [My body, your body]. Madrid, Spain: Ediciones SM (Grades 1–3); **34**.

Manning, M., & Granstrom, B. (1999). *El mundo está lleno de bebés!* [The world is full of babies!]. Madrid, Spain: Ediciones SM (Grades 1–3); **34**.

McMillan, B. (1994). *Sense suspense: A guessing game for the five senses*. New York: Scholastic Books; **16, 21, 36**.

Nelson, R. (2007). *El oído* [Hearing]. Minneapolis, MN: Lerner (Ages 4–8); **38**.

Nelson, R. (2007). *El olfato* [Smelling]. Minneapolis, MN: Lerner (Ages 4–8); **38**.

Nelson, R. (2007). *El tacto* [Touching]. Minneapolis, MN: Lerner (Ages 4–8); **38**.

Nelson, R. (2007). *La vista* [Seeing]. Minneapolis, MN: Lerner (Ages 4–8); **38**.

Ontario Science Center. (1987). *Foodworks*. Reading, PA: Addison-Wesley (Ages 8–12); **37**.

Pomerantz, C. (1984). *Whiff, whiff, nibble, and chew*. New York: Greenwillow (Ages 4–8); **21, 26, 35**.

Rice, J. (1989). *Those mean nasty downright disgusting but . . . Invisible germs*. Minneapolis, MN: Toys 'n Things Press; **21, 26, 37**.

Roca, N. (2000). *Tu cuerpo, de la cabeza, a los pies* [Your body, from head to toe]. Barcelona, Spain: Editorial Molino (Grades 2–4); **34**.

Schuh, M. C. (2007). *El grupo de la leche/The milk group* (Pebble Plus Bilingual). Mankato, MN: Capstone Press (Ages 4–7); **38**.

Schuh, M. C. (2007). *El grupo de las carnes y los frijoles/The meat and beans group* (Pebble Plus Bilingual). Mankato, MN: Capstone Press (Ages 4–7); **38**.

Schuh, M. C. (2007). *El grupo de las frutas/The fruit group* (Pebble Plus Bilingual). Mankato, MN: Capstone Press (Ages 4–7); **38**.

Schuh, M. C. (2007). *El grupo de las verduras/The vegetable group* (Pebble Plus Bilingual). Mankato, MN: Capstone Press (Ages 4–7); **38**.

Schuh, M. C. (2007). *El grupo de los cereales/The grain group* (Pebble Plus Bilingual). Mankato, MN: Capstone Press (Ages 4–7); **38**.

Schuh, M. C. (2008). *Mantenerse activo/Being active* (Pebble Plus Bilingual). Mankato, MN: Capstone Press (Ages 4–7); **38**.

Schuh, M. C. (2008). *Meriendas saludables/Healthy snacks* (Pebble Plus Bilingual). Mankato, MN: Capstone Press (Ages 4–7); **38**.

Sekido, I. (1993). *Science all around you: Fruits, roots, and fungi*. Minneapolis, MN: Lerner (Ages 6–8); **26, 34, 36, 37**.

Sendak, M. (1962). *Chicken soup with rice*. New York: Harper & Row (Ages 3–5); **21, 22, 26, 28**.

Sendak, M. (1970). *In the night kitchen*. New York: Harper & Row (Ages 3–5); **21, 26, 28**.

Shaw, D. (1983). *Germs!* New York: Holiday House (Ages 8–12); **37**.

*Skeleton*. (1988). London: Natural History Museum (Ages 7–12); **37**.

Suhr, M. (1992). *I'm alive series: How I breathe; I am growing; I can move; When I eat*. Minneapolis, MN: Carolrhoda (Ages 4–6); **21, 26, 37**.

Teilmann, C. (2006). *Conozcamos nuestro cuerpo* [Let's find out about our body]. Barcelona, Spain: Juventud (Ages 7–9); **38**.

Zeitoun, C. (2006). *El cuerpo humano* [The human body]. Barcelona, Spain: Combel (Ages 8–10); **38**.

## CHILDREN'S PERIODICALS THAT EMPHASIZE MATH AND SCIENCE CONCEPTS

*Barney Magazine* and *Barney Family: Ideas for Parents*. P.O. Box 7402, Red Oak, IA 51591. Phone: 515-243-4543.

*Beyond Counting* [Quarterly newsletter]. P.O. Box 218, Barrington, RI 02806.

*Chickadee: The Canadian Magazine for Children*. Young Naturalist Foundation, 56 the Esplanade, Suite 304, Toronto, Ontario, Canada M5E 1A7 (Ages 3–9).

*Child Life*. P.O. Box 10681, Des Moines, IA 50381 (Ages 7–9).

*Children's Playmate Magazine*. Children's Better Health Institute, 1100 Waterway Blvd., P.O. Box 567, Indianapolis, IN 46206 (Ages 4–8).

*Koala Club News*. Zoological Society of San Diego, Inc., P.O. Box 551, San Diego, CA 92212 (Ages 6–15).

*Living Planet*. World Wildlife Fund, 1250 24th St. NW, Washington, DC 20037; http://www.worldwildlife.org

*Math Power* [Monthly magazine (eight issues) with activities for elementary grades]. Scholastic, 2931 East McCarty Street, P.O. Box 3710, Jefferson City, MO 65102-3710. Phone: 800-631-1586; e-mail: mathpower@scholastic.com

*National Geographic News*. P.O. Box 2330, Washington, DC 20009 (Ages 5–12).

*Ranger Rick's Nature Magazine*. National Wildlife Federation, Box 2038, Harlan, IA. Phone: 800-611-1599 (Ages 5–11); http://www.nwf.org

*Scholastic Let's Find Out*. Scholastic Magazines, 1290 Wall Street West, Lyndhurst, NJ 07071 (Age 5).

*Science Weekly*. P.O. Box 70154, Washington, DC 20088 (Ages 4–12).

*Scienceland, Inc*. 501 5th Avenue, Suite 2102, New York, NY 10017 (Ages 3–12).

*Sesame Street*. Children's Television Workshop, P.O. Box 2896, Boulder, CO 80322 (Ages 3–8).

*3 2 1 Contact*. P.O. Box 2933, Boulder, CO 80322 (Ages 6–14).

*Wild Animal Baby* [Monthly magazine (10 issues)]. National Wildlife Federation, Box 2038, Harlan, IA.

*Your Big Back Yard*. National Wildlife Federation, Box 2038, Harlan, IA. Phone: 800- 611-1599 (Ages 3–5); http://www.nwf.org

## INSTRUCTIONAL TECHNOLOGY PUBLISHERS USED IN THIS TEXT

**AIMS Educational Foundation**
P.O. Box 8120
Fresno, CA 93747-8120
888-733-2467
Fax: 559-255-6396

**APTE**
820 Davis Street, Suite 224
Evanston, IL 60201
847-866-1872

**Baby Einstein Company LLC**
1233 Flower Street
Glendale, CA 91201-2417
800-793-1454

**Broderbund at Riverdeep**
100 Pine Street, Suite 1900
San Francisco, CA 94111
415-247-3325

**DLM Early Childhood Express**
at SRA/McGraw-Hill
888-772-4543

**Dositey Corporation**
P.O. Box 49
Arlington, MA 02476
781-210-2324

**Edmark (see Riverdeep)**

**Hulabee Entertainment**
Oberon Media, Inc.
130 West 42nd Street, Suite 850
New York, NY 10036-7804
212-221-9240

**Inspiration Software, Inc.**
K–12 Software
8 West Broad Street, Suite 302
Hazelton, PA 18201
866-K12-SOFT
Fax: 866-539-6077

**LCSI®**
MicroWorlds JR
P.O. Box 162
Highgate Springs, VT 05460
800-321-5646
Fax: 514-331-1380

**LeapFrog Enterprises, Inc.**
Emeryville, CA 94608
800-701-5327

**LEGO® MINDSTORMS™**
800-835-4386

**Lego Systems, Inc.**
555 Taylor Road
P.O. Box 1600
Enfield, CA 06083-1600
Consumer Services 800-422-5346

**Microsoft**
1 Microsoft Way
Redmond, WA 98052
800-426-9400

**Mindscape**
28-32 High Street
Crawley, RH 10 1BW, UK

**NASA**
George C. Marshall Space Flight Center
4890 University Square, Suite 3F
Huntsville, AL 35816
256-544-0340

**Neufeld Learning Systems, Inc.**
7 Conifer Crescent
London, Ontario, Canada NGK 2V3
866-429-6284
Fax: 519-657-3220

**Pearson Learning Group**
Dale Seymour Publications
Customer Service Center
145 South Mt. Zion Road
P.O. Box 2500
Lebanon, IN 46052
800-321-3106
Fax: 800-393-3156

**Riverdeep-Edmark**
**(see Broderbund for address)**
415-659-2000

**ROBOLAB**
National Instruments Corporation
11500 N. Mopac Expressway, Building B
Austin, TX 78730
800-433-3488

**Scholastic, Inc**.
Scholastic Store
557 Broadway
Soho, New York, NY 10012

**School Zone Publishing Company**
P.O. Box 777
Grand Haven, MI 49417

**Sunburst/Tenth Planet**
1550 Executive Drive
Elgin, IL 60123-9979
800-321-7511
Fax: 888-800-3028

**Tivola Publishing**
Viva Media LLC
580 Broadway
New York, NY 10004-1613
212-431-4420

**Tom Snyder Productions**
80 Coolidge Hill Road
Watertown, MA 02172-2817
617-926-6000
800-342-0236

**Visions Technology**
P.O. Box 70479
Eugene, OR 97401

**Wright Group**
McGraw-Hill
19201 120th Avenue, N.E., Suite 100
Bothell, WA 98011-9512
800-648-2970
Fax: 800-543-7323

# Appendix C
## The National Research Council's *National Science Education Standards*

## NATIONAL SCIENCE EDUCATION STANDARDS: AN OVERVIEW

### Toward the Future

Implementing the *National Science Education Standards* is a large and significant process that will extend over many years. However, it can be achieved through the combined and continued support of all Americans. Change will occur locally, and differences in individuals, schools, and communities will produce different pathways to reform, different rates of progress, and different final emphases. Nevertheless, with the common vision of the *Standards*, we can expect deliberate movement over time, leading to reform that is pervasive and permanent.

## INTRODUCTION

The *National Science Education Standards* are designed to guide our nation toward a scientifically literate society. Founded in exemplary practice and research, the *Standards* describe a vision of the scientifically literate person and present criteria for science education that will allow that vision to become reality.

## PRINCIPLES AND DEFINITIONS

The development of the *National Science Education Standards* was guided by certain principles. Those principles are:

- Science is for all students.
- Learning science is an active process.
- School science reflects the intellectual and cultural traditions that characterize the practice of contemporary science.
- Improving science education is part of systemic education reform.

### Perspectives and Terms in the National Science Education Standards

Although terms such as "scientific literacy" and "science content and curriculum" frequently appear in education discussions and in the popular press without definition, those terms have a specific meaning as used in the *National Science Education Standards*.

**Scientific Literacy:** Scientific literacy is the knowledge and understanding of scientific concepts and processes required for personal decision making, participation in civic and cultural affairs, and economic productivity. It also includes specific types of abilities. In the *National Science Education Standards*, the content standards define scientific literacy.

**Content and Curriculum:** The content of school science is broadly defined to include specific capacities, understandings, and abilities in science. The content standards are not a science curriculum. Curriculum is the way content is delivered: It includes the structure, organization, balance, and presentation of the content in the classroom.

**Knowledge and Understanding:** Implementing the *National Science Education Standards* implies the acquisition of scientific knowledge and the development of understanding. Scientific knowledge refers to facts, concepts, principles, laws, theories, and models, and it can be acquired in many ways. Understanding science requires that an individual integrate a complex structure of many types of knowledge, including the ideas of science, relationships between ideas, reasons for these relationships, ways to use the ideas to explain and predict other natural phenomena, and ways to apply them to many events. Understanding encompasses the ability to use knowledge, and it entails the ability to distinguish between what is and what is not a scientific idea. Developing understanding presupposes that students are actively engaged with the ideas of science and have many experiences with the natural world.

**Inquiry:** Scientific inquiry refers to the diverse ways in which scientists study the natural world and propose explanations based on the evidence derived from their work. Inquiry also refers to the activities of students in which they develop knowledge and understanding of scientific ideas, as well as an understanding of how scientists study the natural world.

**Science and Technology:** As used in the *Standards*, the central distinguishing characteristic between science and technology is a difference in goal: The goal of science is to understand the natural world, and the goal of technology is to make modifications in the world to meet human needs. Technology as design is included in the *Standards* as parallel to science as inquiry.

# SCIENCE TEACHING STANDARDS

Science teaching is a complex activity that lies at the heart of the vision of science education presented in the *Standards*. The teaching standards provide criteria for making judgments about progress toward the vision; they describe what teachers of science at all grade levels should understand and be able to do.

The standards for science teaching are grounded in the following five assumptions.

- The vision of science education described by the *Standards* requires changes throughout the entire system.
- What students learn is greatly influenced by how they are taught.
- The actions of teachers are deeply influenced by their perceptions of science as an enterprise and as a subject to be taught and learned.
- Student understanding is actively constructed through individual and social processes.
- Actions of teachers are deeply influenced by their understanding of and relationships with students.

## The Standards

Dividing science teaching into separate components oversimplifies a complex process; nevertheless, some division is required in order to manage the presentation of criteria for good science teaching—accepting that this leaves some overlap. In addition, the teaching standards cannot possibly address all the understanding and abilities that masterful teachers display. Therefore, the teaching standards focus on the qualities that are most closely associated with science teaching and with the vision of science education described in the *Standards*.

**Teaching Standard A:** Teachers of science plan an inquiry-based science program for their students. In doing this, teachers:

- Develop a framework of yearlong and short-term goals for students.
- Select science content and adapt and design curricula to meet the interests, knowledge, understanding, abilities, and experiences of students.
- Select teaching and assessment strategies that support the development of student understanding and nurture a community of science learners.

■ Work together as colleagues within and across disciplines and grade levels.

**Teaching Standard B:** Teachers of science guide and facilitate learning. In doing this, teachers:

■ Focus and support inquiries while interacting with students.

■ Orchestrate discourse among students about scientific ideas.

■ Challenge students to accept and share responsibility for their own learning.

■ Recognize and respond to student diversity and encourage all students to participate fully in science learning.

■ Encourage and model the skills of scientific inquiry as well as the curiosity, openness to new ideas and data, and skepticism that characterize science.

**Teaching Standard C:** Teachers of science engage in ongoing assessment of their teaching and of student learning. In doing this, teachers:

■ Use multiple methods and systematically gather data about student understanding and ability.

■ Analyze assessment data to guide teaching.

■ Guide students in self-assessment.

■ Use student data, observations of teaching, and interactions with colleagues to reflect on and improve teaching practice.

■ Use student data, observations of teaching, and interactions with colleagues to report student achievement and opportunities to learn to students, teachers, parents, policy makers, and the general public.

**Teaching Standard D:** Teachers of science design and manage learning environments that provide students with the time, space, and resources needed for learning science. In doing this, teachers:

■ Structure the time available so that students are able to engage in extended investigations.

■ Create a setting for student work that is flexible and supportive of science inquiry.

■ Ensure a safe working environment.

■ Make the available science tools, materials, media, and technological resources accessible to students.

■ Identify and use resources outside the school.

■ Engage students in designing the learning environment.

**Teaching Standard E:** Teachers of science develop communities of science learners that reflect the intellectual rigor of scientific inquiry and the attitudes and social values conducive to science learning. In doing this, teachers:

■ Display and demand respect for the diverse ideas, skills, and experiences of all students.

■ Enable students to have a significant voice in decisions about the content and context of their work and require students to take responsibility for the learning of all members of the community.

■ Nurture collaboration among students.

■ Structure and facilitate ongoing formal and informal discussion based on a shared understanding of rules of scientific discourse.

■ Model and emphasize the skills, attitudes, and values of scientific inquiry.

**Teaching Standard F:** Teachers of science actively participate in the ongoing planning and development of the school science program. In doing this, teachers:

■ Plan and develop the school science program.

■ Participate in decisions concerning the allocation of time and other resources to the science program.

■ Participate fully in planning and implementing professional growth and development strategies for themselves and their colleagues.

## STANDARDS FOR PROFESSIONAL DEVELOPMENT FOR TEACHERS OF SCIENCE

The *National Science Education Standards* present a vision of learning and teaching science in which all students have the opportunity to become scientifically literate. In this vision, teachers of science are professionals responsible for their own professional development and for the maintenance of the teaching profession. The standards in this chapter provide criteria for making judgments about the quality of the professional development opportunities that teachers of science will need to implement the *National Science Education Standards.* Four assumptions about the nature of professional development experiences, and about the context within which they take place, frame the professional development standards.

- Professional development for a teacher of science is a continuous, lifelong process.

- The traditional distinctions between "targets," "sources," and "supporters" of teacher development activities are artificial.

- The conventional view of professional development for teachers needs to shift from technical training for specific skills to opportunities for intellectual professional growth.

- The process of transforming schools requires that professional development opportunities be clearly and appropriately connected to teachers' work in the context of the school.

## The Standards

The first three professional development standards can be summarized as learning science, learning to teach science, and learning to learn. Each begins with a description of what is to be learned followed by a description of how the opportunities to learn are best designed. The fourth standard addresses the characteristics of quality professional development programs at all levels.

**Professional Development Standard A:** Professional development for teachers of science requires learning essential science content through the perspectives and methods of inquiry. Science learning experiences for teachers must:

- Involve teachers in actively investigating phenomena that can be studied scientifically, interpreting results, and making sense of findings consistent with currently accepted scientific understanding.

- Address issues, events, problems, or topics significant in science and of interest to participants.

- Introduce teachers to scientific literature, media, and technological resources that expand their science knowledge and their ability to access further knowledge.

- Build on the teacher's current science understanding, ability, and attitudes.

- Incorporate ongoing reflection on the process and outcomes of understanding science through inquiry.

- Encourage and support teachers in efforts to collaborate.

**Professional Development Standard B:** Professional development for teachers of science requires integrating knowledge of science, learning, pedagogy, and students; it also requires applying that knowledge to science teaching. Learning experiences for teachers of science must:

- Connect and integrate all pertinent aspects of science and science education.

- Occur in a variety of places where effective science teaching can be illustrated and modeled, permitting teachers to struggle with real situations and expand their knowledge and skills in appropriate contexts.

- Address teachers' needs as learners and build on their current knowledge of science content, teaching, and learning.

- Use inquiry, reflection, interpretation of research, modeling, and guided practice to build understanding and skill in science teaching.

**Professional Development Standard C:** Professional development for teachers of science requires building understanding and ability for lifelong learning. Professional development activities must:

- Provide regular, frequent opportunities for individual and collegial examination and reflection on classroom and institutional practice.

- Provide opportunities for teachers to receive feedback about their teaching and to understand, analyze, and apply that feedback to improve their practice.

- Provide opportunities for teachers to learn and use various tools and techniques for self-reflection and collegial reflection, such as peer coaching, portfolios, and journals.

- Support the sharing of teacher expertise by preparing and using mentors, teacher advisors, coaches, lead teachers, and resource teachers to provide professional development opportunities.

- Provide opportunities to know and have access to existing research and experiential knowledge.

- Provide opportunities to learn and use the skills of research to generate new knowledge about science and the teaching and learning of science.

**Professional Development Standard D:** Professional development programs for teachers of science must be coherent and integrated. Quality pre-service and in-service programs are characterized by:

- Clear, shared goals based on a vision of science learning, teaching, and teacher development congruent with the *National Science Education Standards*.

- Integration and coordination of the program components so that understanding and ability can be built over time, reinforced continuously, and practiced in a variety of situations.

- Options that recognize the developmental nature of teacher professional growth and individual and group interests, as well as the needs of teachers who have varying degrees of experience, professional expertise, and proficiency.

- Collaboration among the people involved in programs, including teachers, teacher educators, teacher unions, scientists, administrators, policy makers, members of professional and scientific organizations, parents, and business people, with clear respect for the perspectives and expertise of each.

- Recognition of the history, culture, and organization of the school environment.

- Continuous program assessment that captures the perspectives of all those involved, uses a

variety of strategies, focuses on the process and effects of the program, and feeds directly into program improvement and evaluation.

# ASSESSMENT IN SCIENCE EDUCATION

The assessment standards provide criteria to judge progress toward the science education vision of scientific literacy for all. The standards describe the quality of assessment practices used by teachers and state and federal agencies to measure student achievement and the opportunity provided students to learn science. By identifying essential characteristics of exemplary assessment practices, the standards serve as guides for developing assessment tasks, practices, and policies. These standards can be applied equally to the assessment of students, teachers, and programs; to summative and formative assessment practices; and to classroom assessments as well as large-scale, external assessments.

## The Standards

The essential characteristic of well-designed assessments is that the processes used to collect and interpret data are consistent with the purpose of the assessment. That match of purpose and process is achieved through thoughtful planning that is available for public review.

**Assessment Standard A:** Assessments must be consistent with the decisions they are designed to inform.

- Assessments are deliberately designed.
- Assessments have explicitly stated purposes.
- The relationship between the decisions and the data is clear.
- Assessment procedures are internally consistent.

**Assessment Standard B:** Achievement and opportunity to learn science must be assessed.

- Achievement data collected focus on the science content that is most important for students to learn.

■ Opportunity-to-learn data collected focus on the most powerful indicators.

■ Equal attention must be given to the assessment of opportunity to learn and to the assessment of student achievement.

**Assessment Standard C:** The technical quality of the data collected is well matched to the decisions and actions taken on the basis of their interpretation.

■ The feature that is claimed to be measured is actually measured.

■ Assessment tasks are authentic.

■ An individual student's performance is similar on two or more tasks that claim to measure the same aspect of student achievement.

■ Students have adequate opportunity to demonstrate their achievements.

■ Assessment tasks and methods of presenting them provide data that are sufficiently stable to lead to the same decisions if used at different times.

**Assessment Standard D:** Assessment practices must be fair.

■ Assessment tasks must be reviewed for the use of stereotypes, for assumptions that reflect the perspectives or experiences of a particular group, for language that might be offensive to a particular group, and for other features that might distract students from the intended task.

■ Large-scale assessments must use statistical techniques to identify potential bias among subgroups.

■ Assessment tasks must be appropriately modified to accommodate the needs of students with physical disabilities, learning disabilities, or limited English proficiency.

■ Assessment tasks must be set in a variety of contexts, must be engaging to students with different interests and experiences, and must not assume the perspective or experience of a particular gender, racial, or ethnic group.

**Assessment Standard E:** The inferences made from assessments about student achievement and opportunity to learn must be sound.

■ When making inferences from assessment data about student achievement and opportunity to learn science, explicit reference needs to be made to the assumptions on which the inferences are based.

## SCIENCE CONTENT STANDARDS

The content standards presented in this chapter outline what students should know, understand, and be able to do in natural science. The content standards are a complete set of outcomes for students; they do not prescribe a curriculum. These standards were designed and developed as one component of the comprehensive vision of science education presented in the *National Science Education Standards* and will be most effective when used in conjunction with all of the standards described in this book. Furthermore, implementation of the content standards cannot be successful if only a subset of the content standards is used (such as implementing only the subject matter standards for physical, life, and earth science).

The eight categories of content standards are:

■ Unifying concepts and processes in science.

■ Science as inquiry.

■ Physical science.

■ Life science.

■ Earth and space science.

■ Science and technology.

■ Science in personal and social perspectives.

■ History and nature of science.

The standard for unifying concepts and processes is presented for grades K–12 because (a) the understanding and abilities associated with major conceptual and procedural schemes need to be developed over an entire education and (b) the unifying concepts and processes transcend disciplinary boundaries.

# CONTENT STANDARD: K–12

## Unifying Concepts and Processes

**Standard:** As a result of activities in grades K–12, all students should develop understanding and abilities aligned with the following concepts and processes:

- Systems, order, and organization.
- Evidence, models, and explanation.
- Constancy, change, and measurement.
- Evolution and equilibrium.
- Form and function.

# CONTENT STANDARDS: K–4

## Science as Inquiry

**Content Standard A:** As a result of activities in grades K–4, all students should develop:

- Abilities necessary to do scientific inquiry.
- Understanding about scientific inquiry.

## Physical Science

**Content Standard B:** As a result of activities in grades K–4, all students should develop an understanding of:

- Properties of objects and materials.
- Position and motion of objects.
- Light, heat, electricity, and magnetism.

## Life Science

**Content Standard C:** As a result of activities in grades K–4, all students should develop an understanding of:

- The characteristics of organisms.
- Life cycles of organisms.
- Organisms and environments.

## Earth and Space Science

**Content Standard D:** As a result of activities in grades K–4, all students should develop an understanding of:

- Properties of earth materials.
- Objects in the sky.
- Changes in earth and sky.

## Science and Technology

**Content Standard E:** As a result of activities in grades K–4, all students should develop:

- Abilities of technological design.
- Understanding about science and technology.
- Abilities to distinguish between natural objects and objects made by humans.

## Science in Personal and Social Perspectives

**Content Standard F:** As a result of activities in grades K–4, all students should develop an understanding of:

- Personal health.
- Characteristics and changes in populations.
- Types of resources.
- Changes in environments.
- Science and technology in local challenges.

## History and Nature of Science

**Content Standard G:** As a result of activities in grades K–4, all students should develop an understanding of:

- Science as a human endeavor.

# CONTENT STANDARDS: 5–8

## Science as Inquiry

**Content Standard A:** As a result of activities in grades 5–8, all students should develop:

- Abilities necessary to perform scientific inquiry.
- Understandings about scientific inquiry.

## Physical Science

**Content Standard B:** As a result of activities in grades 5–8, all students should develop an understanding of:

- Properties and changes of properties in matter.
- Motions and forces.
- Transfer of energy.

## Life Science

**Content Standard C:** As a result of activities in grades 5–8, all students should develop an understanding of:

- Structure and function in living systems.
- Reproduction and heredity.
- Regulation and behavior.
- Populations and ecosystems.
- Diversity and adaptations of organisms.

## Earth and Space Science

**Content Standard D:** As a result of activities in grades 5–8, all students should develop an understanding of:

- Structure of the earth system.
- Earth's history.
- Earth in the solar system.

## Science and Technology

**Content Standard E:** As a result of activities in grades 5–8, all students should develop:

- Abilities of technological design.
- Understandings about science and technology.

## Science in Personal and Social Perspectives

**Content Standard F:** As a result of activities in grades 5–8, all students should develop an understanding of:

- Personal health.
- Populations, resources, and environments.
- Natural hazards.

- Risks and benefits.
- Science and technology in society.

## History and Nature of Science

**Content Standard G:** As a result of activities in grades 5–8, all students should develop an understanding of:

- Science as a human endeavor.
- Nature of science.
- History of science.

# CONTENT STANDARDS: 9–12

## Science as Inquiry

**Content Standard A:** As a result of activities in grades 9–12, all students should develop:

- Abilities necessary to do scientific inquiry.
- Understandings about scientific inquiry.

## Physical Science

**Content Standard B:** As a result of activities in grades 9–12, all students should develop an understanding of:

- Structure of atoms.
- Structure and properties of matter.
- Chemical reactions.
- Motions and forces.
- Conservation of energy and increase in disorder.
- Interactions of energy and matter.

## Life Science

**Content Standard C:** As a result of activities in grades 9–12, all students should develop an understanding of:

- The cell.
- Molecular basis of heredity.
- Biological evolution.
- Interdependence of organisms.

■ Matter, energy, and organization in living systems.

■ Behavior of organisms.

## Earth and Space Science

**Content Standard D:** As a result of activities in grades 9–12, all students should develop an understanding of:

■ Energy in the earth system.

■ Geochemical cycles.

■ Origin and evolution of the earth system.

■ Origin and evolution of the universe.

## Science and Technology

**Content Standard E:** As a result of activities in grades 9–12, all students should develop:

■ Abilities of technological design.

■ Understandings about science and technology.

## Science in Personal and Social Perspectives

**Content Standard F:** As a result of activities in grades 9–12, all students should develop an understanding of:

■ Personal and community health.

■ Population growth.

■ Natural resources.

■ Environmental quality.

■ Natural and human-induced hazards.

■ Science and technology in local, national, and global challenges.

## History and Nature of Science

**Content Standard G:** As a result of activities in grades 9–12, all students should develop an understanding of:

■ Science as a human endeavor.

■ Nature of scientific knowledge.

■ Historical perspectives.

# SCIENCE EDUCATION PROGRAM STANDARDS

The program standards are criteria for the quality of and conditions for school science programs. They focus on issues at the school and district levels that relate to opportunities for students to learn and opportunities for teachers to teach science.

## The Standards

The program standards are rooted in the assumptions that thoughtful design and implementation of science programs at the school and district levels are necessary to provide comprehensive and coordinated experiences for all students across grade levels and that coordinated experiences result in more effective learning. But a balance must be maintained. To the extent that district and school policies and consequent decisions provide guidance, support, and coordination among teachers, they can enhance the science program. However, if policies become restrictive and prescriptive, they make it difficult for teachers to use their professional ability in the service of their students.

**Program Standard A:** All elements of the K–12 science program must be consistent with the other *National Science Education Standards* and with one another and must be developed within and across grade levels to meet a clearly stated set of goals.

■ In an effective science program, a set of clear goals and expectations for students must be used to guide the design, implementation, and assessment of all elements of the science program.

■ Curriculum frameworks should be used to guide the selection and development of units and courses of study.

■ Teaching practices need to be consistent with the goals and curriculum frameworks.

■ Assessment policies and practices should be aligned with the goals, student expectations, and curriculum frameworks.

■ Support systems and formal and informal expectations of teachers must be aligned with the goals, student expectations, and curriculum frameworks.

■ Responsibility needs to be clearly defined for determining, supporting, maintaining, and upgrading all elements of the science program.

**Program Standard B:** The program of study in science for all students should include all the content standards; be embedded in a variety of curriculum patterns that are developmentally appropriate, interesting, and relevant to students' lives; emphasize student understanding through inquiry; and be connected with other school subjects.

**Program Standard C:** The science program should be coordinated with the mathematics program to enhance student use and understanding of mathematics in the study of science and to improve student understanding of mathematics.

**Program Standard D:** The K–12 science program must give students access to appropriate and sufficient resources, including quality teachers, time, materials, and equipment, adequate and safe space, and the community.

■ The most important resource is professional teachers.

■ Time is a major resource in a science program.

■ Conducting scientific inquiry requires that students have easy, equitable, and frequent opportunities to use a wide range of equipment, materials, supplies, and other resources for experimentation and direct investigation of phenomena.

**Program Standard E:** All students in the K–12 science program must have equitable access to opportunities to achieve the *National Science Education Standards.*

**Program Standard F:** Schools must work as communities that encourage, support, and sustain teachers as they implement an effective science program.

■ Schools must explicitly support reform efforts in an atmosphere of openness and trust that encourages collegiality.

■ Regular time needs to be provided and teachers encouraged to discuss, reflect, and conduct research around science education reform.

■ Teachers must be supported in creating and being members of networks of reform.

■ An effective leadership structure that includes teachers must be in place.

# SCIENCE EDUCATION SYSTEM STANDARDS

The science education system standards provide criteria for judging the performance of the components of the science education system responsible for providing schools with necessary financial and intellectual resources.

The overlap in Figure 8–1 illustrates that day-to-day activities of science classrooms are influenced directly and indirectly by many organizations which are themselves systems. Figure 8–2 depicts how individuals and agencies from different systems interact in the preparation, certification, and employment of teachers of science.

## The Standards

**System Standard A:** Policies that influence the practice of science education must be congruent with the program, teaching, professional development, assessment,

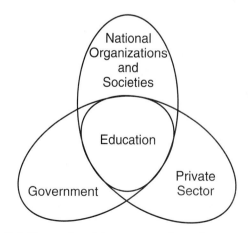

**Figure 8–1** The overlap of three systems that influence science education.

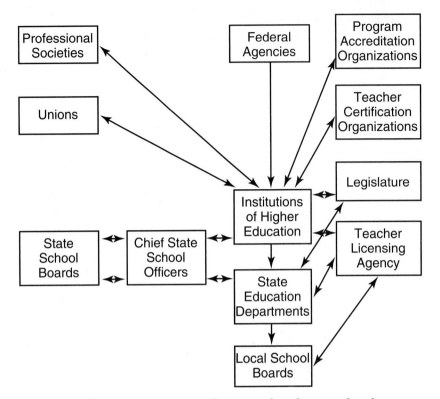

**Figure 8–2** Some organizations that affect the preparation, certification, and employment of teachers.

and content standards while allowing for adaptation to local circumstances.

**System Standard B:** Policies that influence science education should be coordinated within and across agencies, institutions, and organizations.

**System Standard C:** Policies need to be sustained over sufficient time to provide the continuity necessary to bring about the changes required by the *Standards.*

**System Standard D:** Policies must be supported with resources.

**System Standard E:** Science education policies must be equitable.

**System Standard F:** All policy instruments must be reviewed for possible unintended effects on the classroom practice of science education.

**System Standard G:** Responsible individuals must take the opportunity afforded by the standards-based reform movement to achieve the new vision of science education portrayed in the *Standards.*

# Appendix D

## The *NSES* K–4 Science Content Standards and Corresponding Units in *Math and Science for Young Children*

| The National Science Education Standards: Science Content Standards | Unit in *Math and Science for Young Children* | | | | | | | | | |
|---|---|---|---|---|---|---|---|---|---|---|
| | 26 | 33 | 34 | 35 | 36 | 37 | 38 | 39 | 40 | 41 |
| **Content Standard A: Science as Inquiry** | | | | | | | | | | |
| ▪ Abilities necessary to do scientific inquiry | ✓ | ✓ | ✓ | ✓ | ✓ | ✓ | ✓ | ✓ | ✓ | ✓ |
| ▪ Understanding about scientific inquiry | | | | | | | | | | |
| **Content Standard B: Physical Science** | | | | | | | | | | |
| ▪ Properties of objects and materials | | | | | | | | | | |
| ▪ Position and motion of objects | | | | ✓ | | | | | ✓ | ✓ |
| ▪ Light, heat, electricity, and magnetism | | | | | | | | | | |
| **Content Standard C: Life Science** | | | | | | | | | | |
| ▪ The characteristics of organisms | | | | | | | | | | |
| ▪ Life cycles of organisms | ✓ | ✓ | ✓ | | | ✓ | ✓ | | ✓ | ✓ |
| ▪ Organisms and environments | | | | | | | | | | |
| **Content Standard D: Earth and Space Science** | | | | | | | | | | |
| ▪ Properties of earth materials | | | | | | | | | | |
| ▪ Objects in the sky | ✓ | ✓ | | | ✓ | ✓ | | | | ✓ |
| ▪ Changes in earth and sky | | | | | | | | | | |

(continued)

| The National Science Education Standards: Science Content Standards | Unit in *Math and Science for Young Children* | | | | | | | | | |
|---|---|---|---|---|---|---|---|---|---|---|
| | **26** | **33** | **34** | **35** | **36** | **37** | **38** | **39** | **40** | **41** |
| **Content Standard F: Science in Personal and Social Perspectives** | | | | | | | | | | |
| ■ Personal health | | | | | | | | | | |
| ■ Characteristics and changes in populations | | | | | | | | | | |
| ■ Types of resources | ✓ | ✓ | ✓ | ✓ | ✓ | | ✓ | ✓ | ✓ | ✓ |
| ■ Changes in environments | | | | | | | | | | |
| ■ Science and technology in local challenges | | | | | | | | | | |
| **Content Standard G: History and Nature of Science** | | | | | | | | | | |
| ■ Science as a human endeavor | | | | | | | | ✓ | | |

# Glossary

## A

**abstract symbolic activities**—activities that involve the manipulation of groups using number symbols.

**accommodation**—when new information that does not fit into an existing scheme is modified or a new one is made.

**action symbols**—symbols that tell what action to take such as (add) or (multiply).

**add**—to join groups.

**algebra**—at the preoperational level, algebraic thinking involves discovering and creating patterns.

**algorithms**—step-by-step procedures for solving problems.

**almost whole**—when a small part of something is removed, young children will view it as almost whole.

**amphibians**—animals that live both on land and in water.

**anthropomorphic**—giving human shapes or characteristics to animals.

**arbitrary units**—the third stage of measurement where anything can be used as a unit of measure; extends through the latter part of the preoperational period.

**assess**—the first step in instruction; where are the children now in their development?

**assessment**— gathering information and evidence about student knowledge.

**assimilation**—fitting information into an existing scheme.

**association**—one of the criteria that can be used as a common feature to form a group (i.e., things that do a job together, come from the same place, or belong to a special person).

**atmosphere**—gaseous mass surrounding a star or planet; all of Earth's air.

**autonomy**—the aim of education is to achieve independent thinking.

**awareness**—the first stage in the learning cycle as adapted to early childhood education: a broad recognition of objects, people, events, and concepts that develops from experience.

**axes**—the names for the left side and bottom of a line graph.

## B

**balanced reading**—a view that reading instruction should include a balance of phonics and whole language focus.

**basic facts**—number combinations that add up to 1 through 10.

**bilateral symmetry**—a line can be drawn through the middle of the shape or object; if divided, each side or part would be exactly like the other half.

**biodegradable**—capable of being readily decomposed by biological means.

**bookmark**—allows one to mark a website that one may want to visit again without having to conduct another search.

**browser**—enables searches on the World Wide Web.

## C

**camouflage**—the appearance of an animal or insect that allows it to blend with its environment for protection.

**carbohydrates**—organic compound comprised of carbon, hydrogen, and oxygen found in foods such as sugars and starches.

**carbon dioxide**—odorless gas that passes out of the lungs.

**cardinality**—an understanding that the last number named is the amount in a group.

**cardinal meaning**—the last number counted is the amount in the group.

**centration**—the characteristic of preoperational children that causes them to focus on the most obvious aspects of what they perceive.

**charts and tables**—means of visually depicting data.

**checklist**—a list of skills that can be dated as children accomplish them.

**chemical change**—a change where substances mix and form something new.

**choose objectives**—after assessment, decide what the child should learn next.

**chrysalis**—an insect in the developmental stage, between the larval stage and adult stage, when the insect is in a case or cocoon.

**circle**—a continuous curved line.

**circulatory system**—body system relating to the circulation of the blood.

**classification**—putting things into logical groups.

**classifying**—grouping or sorting according to properties such as size, shape, color, use, and so on.

**class inclusion**—one class may be included in another (beagles and poodles are included in the class of dogs).

**class name**—one of the criteria that can be used as a common feature to form a group (e.g., animals, furniture, people).

**cognitive structure**—the grouping of closely related facts and phenomena related to a concept.

**color**—one criterion that can be used to place things in a logical group.

**common features**—one of the criteria that can be used to form a group (e.g., all have doors, handles, points).

**communicating**—recording ideas, directions, and descriptions orally or in written form such as pictures, maps, graphs, or journals so others can understand what you mean; one of the science process skills.

**communications**—oral, written, and pictorial language are used to explain problem-solving and reasoning processes.

**comparing**—finding a relationship between two items or groups of items based on a specific characteristic or attribute; one of the science process skills.

**comparisons**—the second stage of measurement, which extends through the preoperational period; comparisons such as weight, length, and temperature are made.

**computational fluency**—computing with efficiency, accuracy, and flexibility.

**concept application phase**—after completing investigations and problem-solving experiences, taking the knowledge and applying it to a new situation; this phase expands the concept.

**concept introduction phase**—initial investigation and problem-solving experiences designed by the teacher and/or children to acquire knowledge of a topic; this phase provides opportunities to accommodate information.

**concepts**—the building blocks of knowledge; they allow for organizing and categorizing information.

**conceptual subitizing**—seeing number patterns within a group such as a large number of dots (usually more than five).

**conclusions**—statements that tell if the original prediction or hypothesis was rejected.

**concreteness**—the degree to which materials approach reality.

**concrete operations**—the third period identified by Piaget, during which children attain conservation.

**concrete whole number operations**—solving simple addition, subtraction, division, and multiplication problems using concrete materials.

**condensation**—to pass into a denser form, as vapor into a liquid.

**connections**—the bridge between the informal mathematics learned out of school with the formalities of school mathematics; concrete materials can serve this function.

**conservation**—the ability to retain the original picture in the mind when material has been changed in its arrangement in space; also, the care and protection of natural resources.

**constellations**—a number of fixed stars arbitrarily considered a group, usually referred to by a name or number.

**construction**—making a space into which some particular items can fit.

**contrived problems**—problems devised by the teacher for which the teacher models a problem-solving procedure.

**convergent questions and directions**—having only one possible answer or activity.

**cultural time**—the time that is fixed by clocks and calendars.

**curiosity**—a desire to learn or know.

**curves**—curved but not straight paths that connect two points.

**cylinder**—a three-dimensional figure with parallel circular bases.

# D

**data collection**—recording information collected during observations.

**defining and controlling variables**—determining which variables in an investigation should be studied or should be controlled to conduct a controlled experiment; one of the science process skills.

**descriptive lessons**—lessons in which children mainly observe, interact, and describe their observations.

**design technology**—an area of engineering where math, science, and technology become integrated.

**determining variables**—taking all the factors into account that might affect the outcome of an investigation.

**development**—changes that take place as a result of growth and experience.

**direction**—in spatial relations, indicates "which way" (i.e., up, down, across).

**discrepant event**—an event that has an unexpected conclusion.

**disequilibrium**—occurs when children realize that they do not understand something they previously thought they understood.

**distance**—in spatial relations, indicates relative distance (e.g., near or far).

**divergent questions and directions**—provide opportunities for guessing and experimenting.

**divide**—to separate a whole into parts.

**dividend**—the amount to be broken into equal parts in the division operation.

**divisor**—the number of parts that a group is divided into in the division operation.

**download**—loading information onto a personal computer from the Internet.

**dramatic role-playing**—taking on roles in pretend play.

**duration**—how long an event takes (e.g., minutes, days).

**duration (time) words**—clock (minutes, hours) and calendar (days, weeks) words.

# E

**ECE**—Early Childhood Education

**ECSE**—Early Childhood Special Education

**ELL**—English Language Learner(s)

**embryo**—rudimentary plant contained in a seed.

**English units**—units of measure customarily used in the United States (such as inches, feet, and yards).

**environment**—all the conditions, circumstances, and influences surrounding and affecting the development of an organism or group of organisms.

**equality**—when groups have the same amount.

**equals**—an action term represented by the = sign.

**equilibrium**—is established when children have enough information to satisfy their curiosity and to create a new cognitive structure.

**erosion**—the moving away of soil by water or wind.

**estimation**—making a sensible and reasonable guess regarding "how many" or "how much" without counting or measuring.

**ethnomathematics**—mathematics learned outside of school.

**evaluate**—to find out if an objective has been reached through observation or questioning.

**evaporation**—changing into vapor or the removal of moisture from milk, fruit, and so on.

**exploration phase**—the second stage in the learning cycle as adapted to early childhood education: the construction of personal meaning.

# F

**factors**—the numbers operated on in multiplication.

**fats**—an oily, yellow or white substance found in plant and animal matter.

**focal points**—curriculum standards areas broken down by grade levels.

**formal operations**—Piaget's final period, which extends from about age 11 through adulthood.

**fossils**—hardened remains of animal or plant life from a previous geological period.

**fourths**—the parts of a substance or a group when the substance or group is separated or divided into four equal parts.

**fractions**—an area of formal mathematics that grows out of an informal understanding of parts and wholes; during the primary grades, children learn about halves, fourths, and thirds (they also use terms such as *pieces, whole,* and *almost whole*).

**function**—one of the criteria that can be used as a common feature to form a group (i.e., all used for the same thing such as eating or playing music).

# G

**general (time) words**—words such as "time" and "age."

**geoboard**—a square board with headed screws or pegs sticking up at equal intervals; rubber bands are stretched between pegs to make a variety of shapes.

**geologist**—specialist in geology.

**germinate**—to start developing or growing; to begin sprouting.

**germs**—microscopic organisms that cause disease.

**glycerin**—a thick, odorless, colorless liquid prepared from hydrolysis of fats and oils.

**goals**—broad statements that indicate what you want children to know and be able to do after completing a certain unit of curriculum.

**graphs**—visual representations of two or more comparisons.

**grouping**—the process of placing two or more smaller groups into a larger group.

# H

**half**—a fraction term that can be used informally with young children; it indicates the division of a whole into two parts that are the same.

**halves**—the parts of a substance or a group after it is separated or divided into two equal parts.

**heuristics**—questions that children generate when solving problems.

**hierarchical classification**—classes within classes, with a series developing larger and larger classes.

**holistic evaluations**—evaluation in which a rubric is used to place portfolios in groups such as strong, average, and weak.

**hypothesis**—a statement, based on observations, that can be tested by experiment; one of the science process skills.

# I

**IEP**—Individualized Educational Plan

**IFSP**—Individualized Family Service Plan

**igneous rocks**—rocks formed through cooling of magma or lava.

**inferring**—based on observations but suggests more meaning about a situation than can be directly observed; one of the science process skills.

**informal learning**—learning experiences initiated by the adult as children engage in their everyday natural activities.

**informal measurement**—measurement done by comparison or using nonstandard units (e.g., a shoe, a paper clip, a block).

**inquiry**—the third stage in the learning cycle; as adapted to early childhood education, learners compare their findings; a major focus of science process skill.

**integrated curriculum**—curriculum that integrates math, science, social studies, language arts, music and movement, and visual arts, usually through projects and/or thematic units.

**Internet**—the worldwide computer connection.

**invertebrate**—having no backbone or spinal column.

# L

**landfill**—an area of land where garbage is stored, mainly items that cannot be recycled.

**larva**—insect in the earliest stage of development.

**learning cycle**—phases of learning used for curriculum development and as teaching strategies: exploration, concept development, concept application.

**LEGO/LOGO**—a combination of LEGO bricks and LOGO programming that children can use to explore physics, technology, and mathematics.

**length**—in measurement, denotes how long, wide, or deep.

**lens**—a piece of glass, with two curved surfaces, that is used in a magnifier to enlarge images.

**lesson plan**—a planned, sequenced series of steps to be implemented in order to accomplish a goal or objective; also, an educational activity plan.

**less than (<)**—a group or quantity comparison term and symbol.

**line**—a connection between two points.

**line graphs**—graphs made on squared paper grids connecting data points.

**logical grouping**—groups whose members have a logical connection (such as number, color, shape, or class).

**logico-mathematical knowledge**—knowledge that enables us to organize and make sense out of the world, such as classification and number concepts.

**LOGO**—a computer language that can be applied to many geometric experiences.

# M

**machine**—a device that transmits or changes the application of energy; for example, a pulley, lever, or screw.

**magnifier**—lens that enlarges the apparent size of an object.

**mammals**—a group of vertebrates whose females have milk-secreting glands for feeding their young.

**manipulative materials**—materials featuring parts and pieces that can be picked up and moved by the child in the process of problem solving.

**material**—one criterion that can be used to place items in a logical group (e.g., wood, plastic, glass).

**mathematics learning disorder (MLD)**—about 6% of school-age children cannot remember basic facts and/or cannot carry out basic procedures.

**measurement**—assigning a number to things so they can be compared in terms of the same attribute.

**measuring**—quantitative descriptions made by an observer either directly through observation or indirectly with a unit of measure; one of the science process skills.

**metamorphic rocks**—rocks formed when sedimentary and igneous rocks are completely changed in form through pressure and heat.

**metric units**—measurement units based on groups of 10.

**minerals**—inorganic substances that occur naturally in the earth and have a consistent and distinctive set of physical properties.

**more than (>)**—a group or quantity comparison term and symbol.

**multiple classification**—classifying in terms of more than one criterion.

**multiple intelligences**—areas of strength identified by Howard Gardner.

# N

***National Science Education Standards***—national expectations for what children will know and be able to do in the area of science.

**naturalistic learning**—learning that occurs as children go about their daily activities.

**nonroutine problems**—problems that involve more than one step and do not follow a predictable pattern.

**notation**—number and operations symbols.

**number**—one of the criteria that can be used to form a group (e.g., pairs or other groups of the same amount).

**number sense**—the concept or understanding of number.

**number sentences**—sentences that symbolize an operation; for example, $3 + 4 = 7$ and $8 > 6$.

**numerals**—number symbols (i.e., 1, 2, 3, etc.).

**nutrition**—a process by which an organism takes food to promote growth.

# O

**objectives**—statement of how you plan to achieve your goals.

**object permanence**—the realization that objects exist even when they are out of sight.

**object recognition**—the ability to identify objects using previously acquired information such as color, shape, and size.

**observing**—using the senses to gather information about objects and events; one of the science process skills.

**one more than**—a concept basic to sequencing or ordering groups of amounts each of which is one more than the other.

**one-to-one correspondence**—the recognition that one group has as many members as another.

**ordering**—putting items in a logical sequence.

**organism**—any living thing.

**organization and pattern**—arrangement of parts in a space so that they all fit.

# P

**part(s)**—things have parts (e.g., legs, doors, handles) and groups have parts (e.g., each child gets two cookies).

**pattern**—one criterion that can be used to place items in a logical group (e.g., stripes, dots, plaid).

**patterning**—making or discovering auditory, visual, and motor regularities.

**perceptual subitizing**—being able to state how many are in a group without counting or grouping.

**performance-based assessment**—giving one or more students a task to do, which will indicate the student level of understanding of science concepts and thinking skills.

**personal experience**—the view of time held by young children (e.g., "When I was a baby . . .").

**phonics**—an approach to beginning reading that focuses on the elements of printed text such as letters and sounds.

**physical change**—when the physical appearance of a substance changes but is not chemically altered.

**physical knowledge**—knowledge of things in their environment and their characteristics.

**pieces**—a term used by young children to indicate their beginning knowledge of fractional parts.

**place value**—pertains to an understanding that the same numeral represents different amounts, depending on its position.

**plan experiences**—deciding which strategies should be used to enable the child to accomplish instructional objectives.

**play**—the major medium through which children learn.

**play stage**—the first stage of measurement, during which children imitate adults and/or older children using measurement tools such as rulers or measuring cups; this stage extends into the preoperational period.

**points**—introduced as small dots and later applied to making line graphs.

**pollution**—to make unclean or impure as in water, air, or soil.

**portfolio**—a purposeful collection of student work.

**position**—in spatial relations, an indication of "where" (e.g., on, off, under, over).

**preconcepts**—incomplete concepts that develop before true concepts.

**predicting**—making reasonable guesses or estimations based on observations and prior knowledge and experiences; one of the science process skills.

**preoperational period**—the second Piagetian developmental period, which extends from about age 2 to age 7.

**preprimary**—the period before children enter first grade.

**primary**—grades 1–3.

**principles**—basic rules that guide high-quality mathematics education.

**problem solving**—a major mathematics process standard.

**process skills**—label for fundamental mathematics concepts such as classifying, comparing, and measuring when applied to science.

**product**—the result of a multiplication operation.

**proteins**—nitrogenous substances (consisting of amino acids, carbon, hydrogen, oxygen, nitrogen, and sometimes sulfur) that occur in all animal and plant matter.

**pupa**—an insect in the stage of development between the larval and adult forms.

## Q

**quantities above ten**—once children understand the base quantity of ten, they can move on to working with larger quantities.

**quantity comparison**—considering two groups of objects and deciding if they have the same amount or if one group has more.

**quotient**—the result of the division operation.

## R

**rational counting**—attaching a number name to each object counted.

**reasoning**—the ability that enables children to draw logical conclusions, apply logical classification skills, justify problem solutions, and make sense out of mathematics and science.

**record folder**—a collection of anecdotal records and checklists.

**rectangular prism**—a three-dimensional figure with identical rectangular bases and four rectangular sides.

**recycling**—reusing existing materials.

**regrouping**—moving groups from one column of numbers to another.

**relational symbols**—indicate that quantities are related; for example, equal (=), less than (<) and more than (>).

**relational (time) words**—words such as "soon," "yesterday," "early," and so forth.

**remainder**—in division, the result may not come out with equal groups; there may be a remainder.

**renaming**—after a group has been moved using regrouping, the new number is renamed.

**representation**—demonstrating thought and understanding through oral and written language, physical gestures, drawings, and invented and conventional symbols.

**representational thought**—the ability to think through the solution to a problem before acting.

**reptiles**—a group of cold-blooded vertebrates that crawl on their bellies or creep on short, stubby legs.

**resources**—anything that can be used to fill a need; natural resources include coal, water, and so on.

**reversibility**—when the arrangement of material is changed, the mind can reverse the process of change and visualize the original arrangement.

**rote counting**—reciting the names of the numerals in order from memory.

**routine problems**—problems that follow a predictable pattern.

**rubrics**—evaluation guides that show students' criteria for self-assessment.

## S

**scaffolding**—assistance in learning from someone who is more mature.

**search engine**—programs (such as Google) that return a list of websites containing terms that match the user's entry in the program's search field.

**sedimentary rocks**—rocks formed from eroded rocks, sand, clay, silt, pebbles, and other stones.

**select materials**—deciding which materials should be used in order to carry out an instructional plan.

**self-correcting materials**—materials that the child can use independently by trial and error to solve a problem with little or no adult assistance.

**self-regulation**—active mental process of forming concepts (Gallagher & Reid).

**senses**—sight, touch, smell, hearing, and taste.

**sensorimotor period**—first cognitive developmental period identified by Piaget; extends from birth to about age 2.

**sequence**—time as related to the order of events.

**seriation**—putting items in a logical sequence.

**shape**—criterion that can be used to place items in a logical group (e.g., square, circular, triangular) and can be reproduced with geoboards or stencils.

**signs**—the tools of the mind, such as language, that we use for thinking.

**size**—a measurement term referring to volume, height, weight, and/or length.

**skepticism**—attitude whereby a person does not accept things easily on face value.

**skip counting**—counting using quantities and number symbols other than ones such as "2-4-6-8 . . ." or "5-10-15 . . .".

**social activity**—time as viewed from the sequence of routine daily activities.

**social knowledge**—the knowledge created by people, such as rules of conduct.

**sorting**—the process of separating a larger group into two or more smaller groups.

**spatial relations**—a critical element in geometry relating to understanding of relative positions, direction, and distance.

**special days**—time as indicated by holidays and other special days.

**specific (time) words**—words that refer to a specific time, such as "morning" and "night."

**sphere**—a three-dimensional circular figure.

**square**—a shape with four equal sides and four corners.

**stage one, object graphs**—the first stage in graphing, which uses real objects such as cube blocks; usually two items are compared.

**stage two, picture graphs**—the second stage of graphing, where more than two categories may be compared and a more permanent record (such as pictures) may be kept.

**stage three, square paper graphs**—the third stage of graphing, where more than two categories may be compared and a more permanent record (such as using paper squares) may be kept.

**standards**—provide guidance as to what children should know and be able to do at different ages and stages.

**standard units**—units of measurement that are standardized (e.g., inches, centimeters, pounds, liters, miles) that everyone agrees on; children begin to understand the need for standard units during the concrete operational period.

**structured learning**—learning in which the adult chooses the experience for the child and provides some direction to the child's actions.

**subitizing**—knowing instantly how many is in a group without counting.

**subset**—a smaller group within a larger group.

**subtract**—separate a group into two smaller groups.

**sum**—the result of combining groups.

**surf**—to explore the Internet.

**symbolic behaviors**—behaviors that appear during representational play, as when children use materials to represent something else (e.g., sand for food).

**symbolic level**—the stage at which children have connected sets and symbols and can record the solutions to concrete problems using number symbols.

**symmetry**—correspondence of two sides of a figure on each side of a line.

## T

**tables**—means of visually depicting data.

**teach**—do planned experiences with children.

**teachable moment**—a time when adults recognize that a child has chosen an activity that provides a time to insert instruction.

**temperature**—in measurement, denotes how hot or cold.

**terrapins**—North American freshwater or tidewater turtles.

**texture**—one of the criteria that can be used as a common feature to form a group (e.g., rough, smooth, hard, soft).

**thematic units and projects**—instructional methods that provide for the integration of math, science, and other content areas.

**thirds**—the parts of a substance or a group when the substance or group is separated or divided into three equal parts.

**times ($\times$)**—the action term for multiplication.

**tortoises**—turtles that live on land.

**total**—the resulting group amount when groups are combined.

**trading rules**—establish what happens when numbers are regrouped.

**triangle**—a shape with three straight sides and three points.

**triangular prism**—a three-dimensional figure with identical triangular bases and three rectangular sides.

**turtle**—the name for the cursor when using LOGO language to solve geometry problems.

## U

**understanding**—the basic premise of the NCTM principles and standards; stands in opposition to just memorizing.

**unit**—measurements must be made with the same unit to be accurate and comparable.

**URL**—an Internet address.

**utilization**—the fourth stage in the learning cycle as adapted to early childhood education: learners can apply and use their understandings in new settings and situations.

## V

**variable(s)**—anything changeable.

**vitamins**—complex organic substances found in most foods and needed for a normal functioning body.

**volume**—in measurement, denotes how much.

# W

**weather**—the general condition of the atmosphere at a given time in regard to temperature, moisture, cloudiness, and so on.

**webbing**—strategy used to depict a variety of possible concepts and curricular experiences.

**weight**—in measurement, denotes how heavy.

**whole language**—an approach to beginning reading that focuses on developing reading naturally by beginning with good literature.

**whole number operations**—addition, subtraction, multiplication, and division.

**whole(s)**—all of some object or a group of objects.

**World Wide Web (WWW)**—contains Internet sites that enable students and teachers to connect with others around the world and to seek out a multitude of information.

# Z

**zone of proximal development (ZPD)**—the area between where the child is now operating independently and where the child might be able to operate with the assistance of an adult or a more mature peer.

# Index

Note: *Italic* page numbers indicate material in figures, tables, boxes, or charts.